THAYER'S
LIFE OF BEETHOVEN

THAYER'S
LIFE OF
BEETHOVEN

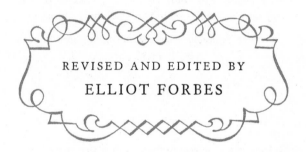

REVISED AND EDITED BY
ELLIOT FORBES

PRINCETON, NEW JERSEY
PRINCETON UNIVERSITY PRESS

PREFACE

IT IS interesting to compare the early biographical histories of Mozart, Haydn, and Beethoven; their patterns have such similarities. First a necrology or hastily assembled biographical book at the time of death: for Mozart, Schlichtegroll's *Nekrolog auf das Jahr Siebzehn Hundert Einundneunzig*; for Haydn, Mayr's *Brevi notizie* in 1809; and Schlösser's inaccurate *Beethoven* in 1827. Then come the worked-out biographical notices by those who knew their subject or one close to him. Mozart's Czech friend Němeček published his *Leben* in 1798; there was also Von Nissen, Constance Mozart's second husband, who did not complete his biography until thirty years later. In the case of Haydn, three biographies appeared written by men each of whom had had talks with Haydn during his last years. In 1810 appeared *Biographische Nachrichten* by the painter Dies and *Biographische Notizen* by the legation officer Griesinger; two years later, the writer Carpani published his *Le Haydine* in Milan.

It was not until eleven years after Beethoven's death that his old Bonn friend Dr. Franz Wegeler and his student Ferdinand Ries got together to publish their joint *Biographische Notizen über Ludwig van Beethoven*. Two years later appeared Anton Schindler's *Biographie*, a work which assumes a central position in considering the origin of Thayer's *Life of Beethoven*.

A parallel in the biographical history of these three composers can be made through one more stage. The definitive biography was written, but the respective author's work was followed in each case by the editorial revision of others, which changed the nature of the original literary work. Jahn had his Deiters and Abert; Pohl his Botstiber; and Thayer his Deiters, Riemann, and Krehbiel. The original biographical works appeared as follows: Jahn, 1856-1859 in four volumes; Thayer translated by Deiters, 1866-1879 in three volumes; and Pohl, 1875-1882 in two volumes. Here the comparison ends. For Jahn had completed the account of Mozart's life and Abert's revision of 1919-1921 turned out to be a new book with new analytical insight into the various approaches to the music, based only in part on the research of Jahn. Pohl, on the other hand, had succeeded in bringing Haydn's life only as far as the year 1790, and Botstiber's third volume in 1927 was a necessary completion of this life, and was based on the material that Pohl had left.

Thayer's *Life of Beethoven* has had a much more complicated history. Like Pohl, he did not live to see his work completed, but succeeded in bringing Beethoven's life up to the year 1817. For the writing of the last ten years of Beethoven's life, he left a rich collection of source material, including transcriptions he had made in Berlin of the surviving Conversation Books. But Thayer, although accomplished in German, did not feel confident as to the manner of presentation for a German-reading public. Therefore he chose his friend, Hermann Deiters—the same who reedited Jahn's great work for its third and fourth editions—to translate his English text into German and use it as he thought best. The first result of this collaboration was an edition of the work actually completed by Thayer in three volumes appearing in 1866, 1872 and 1879—that is, Beethoven's life through 1816. The first volume bears a dedication: "To Mrs. Mehetabel Adams (of Cambridge in Massachusetts) and Lowell Mason, Doctor of Music,(of South Orange in New Jersey) this German edition of a work, the researches for which they so essentially aided, is inscribed by The Author." Increasing ill health, which had been bothering Thayer since 1852, was responsible for the fatal delay of the work to follow; he died in 1897 at the age of eighty with no more of his life's work in print. Deiters was left with the Thayer papers. He decided first to bring out a revision of Volume I, which appeared in 1901. Then he set out to bring Beethoven's life to a conclusion. The advance sheets of Volume IV were in his hands when he died in 1907. This brought the life to the year 1823. Breitkopf and Härtel meanwhile had purchased the copyright from the original publisher, Weber, and then chose Hugo Riemann to complete the job. Volumes IV and V were brought out in 1907-1908, Volumes II and III reedited in 1910-1911, and a new revision of Volume I appeared in 1917.

From the start, Thayer had wanted to bring out his work in English but felt that for two reasons this could not be done right away: first, he was unable to oversee the printing in his native land; and second, at that time it was not customary to publish works of this kind serially in English. But by the time Riemann was at work, a demand for scholarly books on music was growing in America, and Thayer's niece, Mrs. Jabez Fox, persuaded Henry Edward Krehbiel to undertake the job. Krehbiel's aim was to base the English *Life of Beethoven* as much as possible on the original Thayer manuscript from which Deiters had worked. For the last ten years of Beethoven's life he felt as free as his German counterpart to choose his own method of presenting the material. The result was Krehbiel's English version, which was published by the Beethoven Association of New York in 1921.

We must now take up the life of the author and the circumstances which persuaded him to undertake this great task in the first place.

Thanks to the archives in the Beethoven-Haus at Bonn, a short sketch of Thayer's life in his own words has been preserved in the form of a letter written to Deiters on August 1, 1878. This is the year before the appearance of Volume III of the first edition.

I have received several requests to furnish materials for a sketch of *my* biography! I shall give you some particulars and refer the applicants to you. Perhaps you can earn a few marks in this way—

Father. Alexander Thayer, a physician and surgeon of great talents and skill, but he died too young to have attained more than local fame. He lived in South Natick in the state of Massachusetts, where he died in 1824.

Mother. Susanna Bigelow, died 1845.

My Thayer ancestor came from England to Massachusetts as early as 1636, my Bigelow ancestor in 1629—so that I am descended from two of the very oldest Anglo-American families.

I am the eldest of three children—two sons and a daughter—the latter died in 1844—I was born at South Natick, October 17, 1817.

Education. Public schools at Natick.

Academy (quasi *Gymnasium*) Andover.

Harvard University, Cambridge. I graduated from the college in 1843, was there three years as assistant in the University Library, and graduated from the University Law School in 1848. In the summer of 1848 I was employed in the United States Geological Survey of the copper mine district around Lake Superior.

In 1845, while employed in the library, I thought of preparing an American edition [*Umarbeitung*] of the English translation of Schindler's book on Beethoven; and some volumes which I imported from England for this purpose bear my date of receiving them as 1846. In April, 1849 I sailed for Europe.

From May to October I was in Bonn studying German and collecting facts on Beethoven. I supported myself in part by writing letters for American newspapers. In October I went to Berlin where I was most of the time until the spring of 1851. That year I went to Vienna for a short time and afterwards to the great London Exhibition. As I had no more money to remain in Europe, I returned to America in a sailing vessel from Bremen, arriving in New York in November, 1851.

By various kinds of literary labor I paid my debts and supported myself until the summer of 1852, when I took a position on the editorial staff of the great newspaper, the New York Tribune.

My duties were at night, and my health failed, and from that time to this I have lived in almost constant suffering with my head. I overworked my brain on that newspaper and have never recovered.

In the summer of 1854, I returned to Berlin to work out a plan I had now formed of a pretty exhaustive biography of Beethoven for *American* (not for German) readers, with the hope of supporting myself by writing for the Tribune and one or two other papers. I studied the Beethoven Conversation Books and all the materials then in the Royal Library. But the sickness in my head became very bad again, and after several months of incapacity for labor, I went back to America (Spring of 1856), as my Berlin friends believed—to die!

In the autumn of 1856 I had a long and severe illness—fever—I was an invalid from August to December. In 1857 I had earned a small sum of money to bring me back to my Beethoven work in Germany. One day in New York I learned that the man who had had this money in his hands was bankrupt! I was left with about £2 sterling in my possession.

By the aid of the gentleman and lady to whom my Beethoven biography is dedicated, I was enabled to return to Europe in August, 1858.

I remained in Berlin the following winter laboring hard; in the summer of 1859 I went to Vienna—Autumn of 1860, Bonn, thence to Paris, thence to London—I returned in August to Vienna, where I was employed in the American Legation. I remained in that position until the end of 1864 when I moved to Trieste and assumed the function of U.S. Consul on January 1, 1865.

My writings have been almost exclusively for periodicals and most of all, newspapers; especially for Dwight's Journal of Music and the New York Tribune. Several articles—Beethoven, Bach, Handel, Mozart, Haydn, Gluck—in Appleton's American Encyclopedia are by me. A volume (small one) of musical novelettes in English, my *Chron. Verzeichniss* of Beethoven's works, and the two volumes of his biography are my printed volumes.

If you prepare anything about me, please note that I was the *first person ever to use* Beethoven's Sketch Books for chronology, as well as the first to seek out old advertisements and the like.— The fact that the *Chronologisches Verzeichniss* was in part intended as a basis for the researches of others should also be noted. What is surprising is this: that so very much has proved to be correct.

Thayer showed an early inclination for serious writing. At Harvard he won the Boylston Prize for an essay on tendencies in modern philosophy. Later he was to write an anti-slavery story and a scientific study on "The Hebrews and the Red Sea." Meanwhile, Thayer had developed a love of music, first as a singer of hymns and glees in his native Natick, then through his own research, a project compiling a volume of New England Psalmody from 1620 to 1800, which was never published. He read Schindler's Beethoven biography as translated by Moscheles and compared it with Edward Holmes's *Life of Mozart* (New York, 1845) and found the latter a good example of a composer's biography in English. He was to do battle with Schindler's writings and theories until the end of his life, and his point of view may be summed up by a gem from a contribution to Dwight's *Journal* (IV, p. 165): "An ounce of historical accuracy is worth a pound of rhetorical flourish."

During his graduate years at Harvard, Thayer was struck by the discrepancies between the reminiscences of Anton Schindler, on the one hand, and the biographical notices of Ferdinand Ries and Franz Wegeler on the other. Wegeler, through their common friends, the Breunings, had known Beethoven up to the age of 19 in Bonn, and was in close touch with him again during the first two Vienna years, that is, until October, 1794. Ries's family were also from Bonn, and he became Beethoven's pupil in Vienna for a few years until he had to leave in 1805 for service in the army. He returned for two years in 1808. Schindler, on the other hand, while he met

Beethoven in 1814, did not become his close associate until 1822. Schindler's quickly formed ambition to become Beethoven's official secretary, helper and spokesman—a claim to fame that he clung to until his death in 1864— was threatened by the younger Karl Holz, to whom Beethoven was attracted in the last two years of his life—a cheerier, more imaginative companion than the bluff, serious Schindler. Thayer noticed not only the inconsistencies in available sources concerning Beethoven's life but also that Schindler in his preface lashed out against the recently published *Notizen* by Ries and criticized him for representing Beethoven's character in such rough terms ("so schroff"). Beethoven was Schindler's own hero, and nothing deprecatory about him was to be said by others. The historian in Thayer was awakened, and he determined to bring Schindler's biography, the *Notizen* of Wegeler and Ries and other material from English sources into an ordered, connected account. But the more he got into the project the more it fascinated him, and he soon realized that to pursue this aim satisfactorily, he would have to get at original sources in Europe. The trials that he underwent in this labor have already been reviewed in his own words.

Thayer's material came from these different sources: court records (particularly at Düsseldorf), contemporary notices and accounts, Beethoven's own documents—letters, sketches, memoranda, and Conversation Books—and reminiscences from anyone he could visit who had been in any way associated with Beethoven or had personal recollection of him. While he was continuing his research, a body of literature more fanciful than anything written by Schindler had sprung up concerning Beethoven's life. This German prose provided a strange contrast to the careful, methodical first volume of text which, still in English, Thayer handed over to Deiters in 1865 to be translated and edited. In a letter to his collaborator he stated his principle: "I fight for no theories and cherish no prejudices; my sole point of view is the truth. . . . I have resisted the temptation to discuss the character of his (B's) works and to make such a discussion the foundation of historical speculation, preferring to leave such matters to those who have a greater predilection for them. It appears to me that Beethoven the *composer* is amply known through his works and in this assumption the long and wearisome labors of so many years were devoted to Beethoven the *man*."

Unlike Jahn, then, Thayer was concerned only with the facts about Beethoven, the man and his music, not with analytical interpretation of the music, or even the external description of the construction of the music, as in the case of Pohl. Thayer's area of interpretation was with the relative validity of the evidence he was using, which he tried to judge as objectively as possible. Further, he was concerned with factual information in depth. He did not start with the year 1770, but with the history of the Bonn Court for a century before, not with the members of the Breuning family per se, but with a sketch of their past and their position in Bonn society.

Now we may consider why there is need for a new edition of Thayer when other biographies such as Jahn and Pohl are allowed to rest as they are. These other biographies are more nearly period pieces in that they represent a combination of biographical and musical thinking of their period, or periods as in the case of Pohl-Botstiber. But inasmuch as Thayer's work is primarily the orderly organization of documentation, with judgments concerning the trustworthiness of the varying types of evidence, the only element that may be called dated in his writing is its style. Meanwhile, the inaccuracies that Beethoven research of the last thirty years has disclosed in the texts of both Thayer-Deiters and Thayer-Krehbiel call for correction in the very spirit of Thayer's original inquiry.

However, there is a school of thought in this field that maintains: if the text needs to be revised, and if what is left is in the style of the mid-nineteenth century, why not rewrite the whole biography? The answer is, first, that Thayer's literary work is a classic in its field and should be preserved, and, second, that his method in Beethoven biography, so revolutionary in his day, is now not only accepted but is in tune with the spirit of contemporary research in this field.

However, to distinguish between what is real Thayer and what is the work of his editors, is not always easy because of the deplorable fact that after Krehbiel's use of the Thayer papers in the first part of this century they disappeared—whether destroyed or mislaid we do not know. Of their history we know only the following facts. When Thayer died in 1897, his belongings were shipped to America. His niece, Mrs. Fox of Cambridge, asked Mr. Krehbiel, who had been in correspondence with Thayer for the last ten years, to take charge of sifting the material in his papers. What was needed for completion of the German edition of the biography was sent back to Dr. Deiters in 1898. There the bulk of the papers remained until Riemann had first completed the editing of Volumes IV and V in 1907-1908 following Deiters' death, and then the reediting of Volumes II and III for a second edition in 1910-1911. Krehbiel acquired them again, and his work was virtually completed in 1914; but World War I, plus complications with publishers, postponed the printing of his edition until 1921. At this point, the situation becomes unclear. Mrs. Fox's daughter, Gertrude Behr of Tamworth, New Hampshire remembers several boxes and packing cases of her great-uncle's papers in Cambridge. In 1953 the late Miss Helen Krehbiel, daughter of the editor, wrote that since she was not living at home at the time of her father's death, she did not know how her step-mother had disposed of the papers, but "merely signed whatever she asked, as the Thayer Beethoven went from one owner to another. There *were* papers, boxes of them, notes, conversation books etc." Unfortunately, the legal files of the estate of the widow, Mrs. Marie Krehbiel, have all been destroyed. Krehbiel's Beethoven library was left to the Beethoven Association in New York upon his death in 1923. When this society disbanded in 1940, its collection of books was left to the New York Public Library. Neither in the 125th St. Warehouse, nor in the old Beethoven Room (alas, no more in existence), nor in the basement vaults of the Library, have these boxes shown up. All that is left of the papers is a loose-sheet draft of the Thayer-Krehbiel collaboration, consisting of some sheets in Thayer's handwriting, some with Krehbiel's writing pasted over parts or all of them, and the rest in Krehbiel's own characteristic red ink.

Thayer's own ideas as to editorial procedure and Deiters' response to them are represented in the Foreword to Volume I of the first edition, in the form of a letter from author to translator and a reply from translator to author. We have already quoted from the first, in which Thayer makes clear that he is concerned with the facts about Beethoven, the man. In an earlier paragraph, he states that in writing his English text he had an English-speaking public in mind who knew little about Germany and the history of her music, and that he therefore expected Deiters to select from this mass of material what was appropriate for German readers. Deiters in his reply asserts that German readers can also derive benefit from Thayer's historical survey that precedes the life proper. Thayer pleads that, as he called it, "fine writing" in connection with the facts be sacrificed in favor of presentation of their documentation. He asks that a distinction be made between his own words and Deiters' additions and that the former be used literally. The close degree to which Deiters was faithful to Thayer in the presentation of the early years can be checked by comparing the first German edition with those passages that Krehbiel retained in his presentation of an edition based on Thayer's original text. By implication this comparison also shows the extent to which Krehbiel trimmed Thayer's original bulk of documentation. But, when in 1901 Deiters brought out the second edition of Volume I, he could no longer resist the temptation mentioned by Thayer, namely to describe the music or as he put it, "supply a short passage concerning the characteristics of individual works." These passages at any rate can be safely identified as non-Thayer.

Where Riemann expanded this feature of discussions of compositions as he went along, Krehbiel rejected it throughout. In addition, he deleted rather than added historical detail, the opposite of what had been suggested by Thayer as appropriate for American readers—but then this was 1914 and not 1865.

When we consider the last ten years of Beethoven's life, the problem of interpreting what is original Thayer becomes much more complicated. Since Thayer left only a mass of notes, now lost, each editor was on his own. The difference has been summarized by Krehbiel in the Introduction to his edition: "Being as free as the German editors in respect to the portion of the biography which did not come directly from the pen of Thayer, the editor of this English edition chose his own method of presentation touching the story of the last decade of Beethoven's life, keeping in view the greater clearness and rapidity of narrative which, he believes, would result from a grouping of material different from that followed by the German editors in their adherence to the strict chronological method established by Thayer."

This decision results in a certain amount of confusion to the reader and therefore has not been followed by the present editor. Let us cite an outstanding example. In his account of the years 1824-1826, Krehbiel writes about all aspects of the composer's life *except* that concerning his troubled relationship with his nephew. This account includes the period at Gneixendorf in the fall of 1826, which preceded Beethoven's last illness. This trip to his brother Johann's estate in the country was undertaken solely because Karl, the nephew, had a head wound caused by an attempt at suicide; and Beethoven and Breuning (who was now co-guardian) did not think it wise to be in Vienna under these circumstances. But only after Beethoven has reached Gneixendorf is the reader let in on the background of the crisis that made this move necessary. Then he is taken back to late 1823, from which time the growing state of attrition between uncle and nephew is traced up to the dramatic climax of a suicide attempt.

The editorial problem in handling Beethoven's last years may be further illuminated by considering the existing representations of Beethoven's relations with his close associates. Wegeler and Ries have very little to offer concerning this period; Schindler a great deal—plus the Conversation Books that Schindler allowed to survive. Added to this is the interesting little book by Stephen von Breuning's son, Gerhard, who was a young boy at the bedside of Beethoven in his last illness, a book entitled *Aus dem Schwarzspanierhause.*

Schindler, in his effort to be Beethoven's right-hand man, resented anyone who threatened this position: the young Karl Holz, brother Johann, and also nephew Karl, who, by 1824, was included in decision-making councils and often burdened by his uncle with secretarial jobs. One of Thayer's great labors in the writing of the later years was to correct the prejudices and the consequent slantings of Schindler. In an address which Thayer gave to the *Schillerverein* in Trieste, later published in book form (*Ein kritischer Beitrag zur Beethoven-Literatur* [Berlin, 1877]), he disclosed how Schindler and all the pseudo-biographers that followed in his wake have misrepresented Johann's feelings toward his famous brother by painting him as one utterly callous to the needs of Ludwig. The matter of the latter's lodging in rooms next to his brother in the spring of 1822, which Schindler described as "so dark that they are hardly fit for a cobbler," provides a case in point. Both Beethoven's letters to his brother and excerpts from the Conversation Books show clearly that the rooms finally settled upon were of his own choice. The point is that in this and other matters Schindler had evidence that he did not care to investigate or to use. His diatribes against Beethoven's relatives and associates had had a vast effect which Thayer felt he had to answer by extensive dialectic.

Now, the matter of Beethoven's relation to his nephew is not so completely set to rights. What Thayer left in the way of complete notes and a guide to their treatment can only be guessed. Deiters takes a fairly lofty position and sympathizes along the way with the boy's duress, but implies that really he was a pretty shallow wayward person. Krehbiel warms to his subject and gives a rather subjective interpretation of the relationship; the more he writes the angrier he gets as he visualizes Beethoven's sufferings. Thus his presentation lacks the objectivity of a Thayer and ignores evidence that shows that some of the notions concerning Karl's behavior cannot withstand close scrutiny without comment concerning extenuating circumstances. The pitfall, of course, is that in presenting the evidence from the Conversation Books we usually have only one side of the conversations recorded (except in public places, where Beethoven sometimes did resort to writing his part, as he could not judge the volume of his own voice). Thus Krehbiel, let us say, can slant the probable gist of Beethoven's remarks one way to support his convictions, while the Sterbas in their recent controversial book, *Beethoven and His Nephew*, can slant it just the opposite.

The present editor has attempted to sustain Thayer's manner strictly in the treatment of the final years: that is, to guide the reader to the matter at hand by presenting all pertinent evidence in chronological order as objectively as possible so that the reader may make his own value judgment in each case as fairly as possible.

The work for the present revision of the Thayer text has taken the following form. First, a full comparison of all the German texts with the English was made, then the documentary material from all these sources worth including was chosen. Wherever the information to be included was *clearly* the contribution of Deiters, Riemann, or Krehbiel, it has been so indicated. However, the majority of the text used consists of the coordinated treatment of Thayer's notes and manuscript by these three editors, and this material represents the *Urtext* of the present edition. It was found to be impractical to make distinctions in the text between those portions which are to be found only in the German edition and those which are common to both. To have done so would have impaired its readability, interrupted the flow, and needlessly confused the reader. However, it is necessary that the reader know what additions and corrections of the text are the work of the present editor. For this purpose a printer's sign, ---◄{ }►---, has been used to mark off these passages and distinguish them clearly from the *Urtext*.

Before examining the method of presenting new material, a word more must be said on the problem of handling Thayer's material. It has been necessary to delete some portions of his text because recent Beethoven research has proved them inaccurate, but a number of other passages have been deleted because they are now redundant. For Thayer, at the time that he was preparing his work, was trying to set the record straight concern-ing Beethoven's life to counteract not only Schindler, whose revised third edition had appeared in 1860 with further inconsistencies, but Lenz (*Beet-hoven—eine Kunststudie*—Part I concerning the life, in 1855), Oulibischev (*Beethoven, ses Critiques et ses Glossateurs*, 1857), Marx (*Ludwig van Beethovens Leben und Schaffen*, 1859), and finally Nohl (*Beethovens Leben*, Volume I of which came out in 1864). Only Nohl had come up with new material based on work with newspapers, almanacs, court calendars, etc. As a result there is a certain amount of Thayer that is concerned with false arguments followed by his counter-arguments, all of which is of no interest to the present-day reader, since the falsehoods that had been per-petuated until the appearance of his own biography have been refuted re-peatedly since then.

Here seems to be the best place to give an explanation of the so-called Fischoff Manuscript. This manuscript is a collection of some sixty pages of miscellaneous Beethoven notices, which Thayer had summed up in his aforementioned letter to Dr. Deiters (in the Preface to the first German edition) in the following way. Its importance lies first in the copies it contains of a great number of letters and documents that have no longer survived; second, in a great number of notes, remarks, and memoranda and their particular order; and third, some personal reminiscences of Beet-hoven's friend Zmeskall von Domanovecz, which, while they show the un-certainty of the author's memory after thirty-five years, nevertheless make a very interesting and worthwhile supplement to the knowledge of Beet-hoven's first years in Vienna. Furthermore, the manuscript has been as-sembled from the few printed sources existing in the years 1830-1837. The material was left to the composer's nephew Karl, and after his death in 1858 to his widow Caroline. She lent the greater part of the collection to an unknown person who sold it for his own profit! But luckily, Karl's guardian, Jacob Hotschevar, had previously made a copy of the material to which he added some anecdotes and the like. This copy, which is all that has survived, appears to have been given to Joseph Fischoff, Professor in the Vienna Conservatory of Music. After his death in 1857, it passed through the hands of the music dealer, Julius Friedländer, who sold it to the Berlin Library in 1859. As material received second hand, the history of which was imperfectly known, Thayer urged caution in its use for establishing bio-graphical fact.

A comparison of the German and English editions shows a certain amount of difference in the order in which material is presented in the later years. As we have said, this difference becomes marked in the presentation of the last ten years of Beethoven's life. The present editor has rearranged the order of some portions of the text for greater readability. These changes have been necessary both because new material has been woven into the old and because portions of the old text concerned with what is now useless dialectic have been deleted. The basis for this rearrangement is the presentation of the material in the strict chronological order of Thayer's original concept. Thus the genesis of the composition of the *Missa Solemnis* is presented in the chapter of 1819 and not delayed as in the German edition until 1823. Each of the later chapters concludes with a list of the works composed and published in that given year. An indispensable aid in the preparation of these lists as well as the list of posthumous first publications in Appendix D has of course been the *Thematisches Verzeichnis* of Georg Kinsky, completed by Hans Halm.

Unless otherwise indicated, the quotations in the text from the sketch-books are those from past editions. After the path-breaking contribution by Nottebohm to the deciphering and interpretation of the sketchbooks, an ideal editorial standard for their publication was established by Karl Lothar Mikulicz in his edition of the so-called Landsberg Sketchbook. This has been followed by the fine Beethoven-Haus (Bonn) sketchbook editions under the editorship of Joseph Schmidt-Görg and Dagmar Weise, and most recently the so-called Wielhorsky Sketchbook edition by Nathan Fishman. For the chronological implications of these sketchbooks I am in debt to such scholars as Max Unger, and for the continuing discovery of new works and different versions of old ones to a number of others, and in particular, to Willy Hess.

The readings of the Conversation Books have been checked with the partial three volume edition of Georg Schünemann and cross references to this source have been supplied. His indications of separate entries—between which there were presumably replies by Beethoven—have been followed and indicated by the sign ∙〰∙. The work of Theodor von Frimmel in almost all areas of Beethoven biography has been a basic source for the revisions of the text, as has been the research of Donald W. MacArdle.

Three important contributions to our knowledge of Beethoven's correspondence have been Max Unger's *Ludwig van Beethoven und seine Verleger*, Oscar Sonneck's *Beethoven Letters in America* and *New Beethoven Letters* edited by Donald W. MacArdle and Ludwig Misch. A complete understanding of this area has been made possible by the exhaustive research of Emily Anderson, which resulted in her definitive three-volume work, *The Letters of Beethoven*.

It was the privilege of this editor to work with the late Miss Anderson in her home in Hampstead, England, in the spring of 1953, and she most kindly allowed the checking of the letters translated by Krehbiel against her reading of the original German text. These translations have been revised where necessary. Beethoven's characteristic use of dashes and under-linings (indicated by italics) has been observed throughout. Since

Thayer's wish was to represent a document in full wherever possible, a few letters that are given in substantial form in an older edition have been given in their complete form without the addition of the sign ⸺⧊ ⧉⸺ which denotes my own contributions.

The aim in the preparation of this edition has been to present Thayer's *Life of Beethoven* to an English-reading public as I believe he would have wanted it, using all the new research on Beethoven that Thayer would have used himself had it been available. In the text to follow, the word *writer* or *author* refers to Thayer, the word *editor* always the present editor. Inevitably, a fine line has had to be drawn between significant corrections which are indicated as the editor's and insignificant ones, which are not so indicated and which undoubtedly would have been made by the author were he living today. These latter come from misprints, simple inaccuracies due to our present-day knowledge of the available data, the need for more complete source identifications, and the necessity for adjusting the spelling of certain words to correspond with present-day usage. The spelling in documents and letters has been made to correspond with that of the original as nearly as possible. The spelling of proper names and geographical places in the narrative has necessitated a compromise for the sake of uniformity and hence, clarity. For locations, the spelling most commonly used today has been adopted. A proper name like Razumovsky may be found in a number of different forms, and the choice of spelling must be based on that in most common usage in Beethoven's time. A further refinement is made in the case of the name of Beethoven's nephew. Since his uncle usually spelled his name Karl, the name of the boy's father appears consistently as Carl Caspar for the sake of clear distinction.

Footnotes have been limited to source identification wherever possible. Lengthy footnotes in the Krehbiel edition have either been added to the text, to the appendix, or omitted. Footnote material drawn from past editions is followed by the source in parentheses; any other material is the editor's. Since the footnotes in the German editions are more complete than in the English, these have been the basis for citation except in cases where the English edition has supplied new information. In certain cases, the footnote material in the present edition has been drawn from the main text of past editions and is so indicated. In the rare case where a footnote reference has been inaccurate in the German edition, the cross reference has not been made. Occasionally, material from past editions has formed the basis for my additions to the main text. If this addition has been essentially rewritten, it is indicated as my own; such a case is the discussion of the Diabelli Variations in Chapter 36, where in footnotes 64 and 74 the references to the German edition are given.

Finally, I wish to express my gratitude to those who helped prepare this edition: to Professor Oliver Strunk, who invited me to undertake the task and offered encouragement at every phase of the work; to the late Professor

Erich Hertzmann, whom I consulted early and often as to how to proceed; to Donald W. MacArdle, who was generous in offering the assistance of his own wide knowledge and experience in the field and the use of his valuable abstracts of periodical writings; to the late Miss Emily Anderson as already noted; to Professor Joseph Schmidt-Görg and Dr. Dagmar Weise, who gave me cordial assistance in Bonn; to Professor Otto Erich Deutsch, who offered counsel in the undertaking of research in Vienna; to the late Kurt Smolle, who kindly offered a copy of his findings concerning the succession of Beethoven's residences; to Dr. L. Ashby Adams, who evaluated the evidence concerning Beethoven's deafness; to Professor and Mrs. Arthur Mendel, who were kind enough to be readers of early chapters; to Professor Lewis Lockwood, who gave valuable suggestions after reading the entire text; and to Mrs. William Hanle, of the Princeton University Press, who with fine patience, wisdom, and humor has shepherded the text into print.

Lastly, an expression of profound gratitude goes to Kathleen A. Forbes, my wife, who not only typed all the drafts of this edition, but also offered constant editorial assistance through every phase of its preparation.

Elliot Forbes
Cambridge, Mass.
January, 1964.

NOTE TO THE REVISED EDITION

Since the printing of the first edition, there has come to light the welcome news of the discovery of the tomb of Alexander Wheelock Thayer. This editor received a letter dated November 24, 1964, from John P. Sabec, a member of the local staff of the Trieste American Consulate, which describes the event.[1] In the course of studying the history of the American Consulate in Trieste, Mr. Sabec read in a book, *Trieste and America* by Oscar d'Incontrera, that Thayer had been buried in Trieste. With Vice Consul Samuel E. Fry, he set out thereupon to find the grave. A search through the Anglican cemetery and the nearby Evangelical cemetery produced no results. Finally Mr. Sabec persuaded Mr. d'Incontrera, who had seen the grave, to revisit the plot, and the tomb was rediscovered. It was located at the lowest level of the Evangelical cemetery, hidden from view by a thick growth of ivy.

Mr. Sabec's concern did not stop there, for he discovered that the lease on the tomb had expired and that unless funds were forthcoming the tomb-

---

[1] See Kenneth E. Linlithgow and John P. Sabec, "Thayer Centenary" in *Foreign Service Journal* (January, 1966), pp. 34-36.

stone would be removed and reused. The present editor was able to put him in touch with Mrs. Gertrude Behr, the grandniece of Thayer, in Tamworth, New Hampshire, who has generously supplied the money for the back rent and for forty years future lease on the burial plot. Meanwhile the Evangelical community has rebuilt the leaning retaining wall behind the tomb and will undertake the continuing preservation of this historic grave.

On Memorial Day, 1965, there was held a commemoration ceremony at the tomb. To the original inscription, "Alexander Wheelock Thayer—born in Natick, Mass. U S A, October 22, 1817—Died in Trieste, Austria—July 15, 1897" were added the two lines, "Biographer of Ludwig van Beethoven" and "American Consul in Trieste 1865-1882."

A number of corrections have been made in the text of this edition and a few translations improved. Also the index has been thoroughly revised in attempt at greater completion.

The editor would like to thank the following people for helpful suggestions which have come either from letters or from printed reviews of the first edition: Norman C. Brennan, Alfred Frankenstein, Lewis Kandel, the late Donald W. MacArdle, Ludwig Misch, Walter L. Strauss, and Alan Tyson. Most of all, thanks go to my wife, who has done a substantial share of the work.

CONTENTS

CONTENTS

LIST OF ABBREVIATIONS

A Emily Anderson, *Letters of Beethoven*. Three volumes. London, 1961.

AMZ *Allgemeine Musikalische Zeitung*. Leipzig. Also referred to as *Allg. Mus. Zeit.*

Beeth. Gustav Nottebohm, *Beethoveniana*. Leipzig, 1872.

II Beeth. Gustav Nottebohm, *Zweite Beethoveniana*. Leipzig, 1887.

BJ *Beethovenjahrbuch*, Theodor von Frimmel, editor. Two volumes. Leipzig, 1908-1909.
Beethoven-Jahrbuch, Paul Mies and Joseph Schmidt-Görg, editors. Volumes 1953/54, 1955/56, 1957/58, 1959/60.

Biographie Anton Schindler, *Biographie von Ludwig van Beethoven*. Third edition, two volumes in one. Münster, 1860. Anton Schindler, *Biographie von Ludwig van Beethoven,* first edition, Münster, 1840, is occasionally cited and is indicated by *Biographie*, 1840 or first edition.

DM *Die Musik*. Berlin and Leipzig.

FRBH Theodor von Frimmel, *Beethoven-Handbuch*. Two volumes. Leipzig, 1926.

GA *Beethovens Werke. Kritische Gesamtausgabe*. Twenty-five volumes. Breitkopf and Härtel, Leipzig, 1866-1868, 1888. Also referred to as Collected Works Edition.

Kerst Friedrich Kerst, editor, *Die Erinnerungen an Beethoven*. Two volumes. Stuttgart, 1913.

KHV Georg Kinsky, *Das Werk Beethovens. Thematisch-bibliographisches Verzeichnis seiner sämtlichen vollendeten Kompositionen*. Completed and edited by Hans Halm, Munich, 1955.

KK Kastner-Kapp, *Ludwig van Beethovens sämtliche Briefe*, Emerich Kastner, editor. Revised and enlarged by Julius Kapp. Leipzig, 1923.

MQ *The Musical Quarterly*. New York.

NBJ *Neues Beethoven-Jahrbuch*, Adolph Sandberger, editor. Augsburg and Braunschweig.

Notizen Franz Wegeler and Ferdinand Ries, *Biographische Notizen über*
(*Not.*) *Ludwig van Beethoven*. Coblenz, 1838. With a supplement (Nachtrag) by F. Wegeler. Coblenz, 1845.

Schünemann Georg Schünemann, editor, *Ludwig van Beethovens Konversationshefte*. Three volumes. Berlin, 1941-1943.

TDR   Alexander Wheelock Thayer, *Ludwig van Beethovens Leben,* Hermann Deiters, editor. Revised and completed by Hugo Riemann. Five volumes. Leipzig, 1907-1917.

TK   Alexander Wheelock Thayer, *The Life of Ludwig van Beethoven,* Henry Edward Krehbiel, editor. Three volumes. New York, 1921.

Other abbreviations

CM   Convention Money or Coin (Konventions-münze).

VS   Vienna Standard (Wiener Währung).

WoO   Werke ohne Opuszahl (Works without opus number). Cf. KHV.

BIBLIOGRAPHY

ALL periodical references are given in full in the footnotes of the text. A few of the most common, along with certain book sources, have been abbreviated as the preceding list of abbreviations shows. The bibliography that follows is limited to the remaining books, which are primarily concerned with the subject of Beethoven, that have been used in the preparation of this text. A number of them are given full reference in the text as well for the convenience of the reader.

Boettcher, Hans. *Beethoven als Lieder-Komponist.* Augsburg, 1928.

Braunstein, Josef. *Beethovens Leonore-Ouvertüre.* Leipzig, 1927.

von Breuning, Gerhard. *Aus dem Schwarzspanierhause.* Vienna, 1874.

Brümmer, Eugen. *Beethoven im Spiegel der zeitgenössischen rheinischen Presse.* Würzburg, 1932.

Czeke, Marianne. *Brunsvik Teréz Grófnö Naplói és Feljegyzései*; I Kötet. Budapest, 1938.

von Frimmel, Theodor. *Beethoven im zeitgenössischen Bildnis.* Vienna, 1923.

——, *Beethoven Studien.* 2 vols. Munich and Leipzig, 1904-1906.

——, *Neue Beethoveniana.* Vienna, 1888.

Hess, Willy. *Beethoven. Supplemente zur Gesamtausgabe.* 5 vols. Breit-kopf and Härtel: Wiesbaden, 1959-1962.

——, *Beethovens Oper Fidelio.* Zurich, 1953.

——, *Verzeichnis der nicht in der Gesamtausgabe veröffentlichten Werke Ludwig van Beethovens.* Wiesbaden, 1957.

de Hevesy, A. *Petites Amies de Beethoven.* Paris, 1910.

Kalischer, Alfred C. *Beethoven und seine Zeitgenossen.* 4 vols. Berlin, 1908-1910.

——, *Beethovens Sämtliche Briefe.* 5 vols. Berlin, 1907-1908. (Volumes II and III revised by Theodor von Frimmel, 1910-1911.)

Kaznelson, Siegmund. *Beethovens ferne und unsterbliche Geliebte.* Zurich, 1954.

La Mara (Marie Lipsius). *Beethovens unsterbliche Geliebte.* Leipzig, 1909.

——, *Beethoven und die Brunsviks.* Leipzig, 1920.

von Lenz, Wilhelm. *Beethoven. Eine Kunststudie.* 6 vols. 1855-1860. Volumes IV-VI published separately as *Kritischer Katalog der sämtlichen Werke Ludwig van Beethovens mit Analysen derselben.* Hamburg, 1860.

Ley, Stephan. *Aus Beethovens Erdentagen.* Bonn, 1948.

——, *Beethoven als Freund der Familie Wegeler—v. Breuning.* Bonn, 1927.

———, *Wahrheit, Zweifel und Irrtum in der Kunde von Beethovens Leben.* Wiesbaden, 1955.

MacArdle, D. W., and Misch, L. *New Beethoven Letters.* Norman, 1957.

Marx, A. B. *Ludwig van Beethoven, Leben und Schaffen.* 2 vols. Berlin, 1859.

Mikulicz, K. L. *Ein Notierungsbuch von L. van Beethoven.* Leipzig, 1927.

Misch, Ludwig. *Beethoven-Studies.* Norman, 1953.

Nohl, Ludwig. *Beethoven, Liszt, Wagner.* Vienna, 1874.

———, *Beethoven nach den Schilderungen seiner Zeitgenossen.* Stuttgart, 1877.

———, *Beethovens Leben.* 3 vols. (Volume I, *Beethovens Jugend,* Vienna, 1864; Volume II, *Beethovens Mannesalter,* Leipzig, 1867; Volume III, *Beethovens letzte Jahre,* Leipzig, 1877.)

———, *Briefe Beethovens.* (Volume I, Stuttgart, 1865; Volume II, *Neue Briefe Beethovens,* Stuttgart, 1867.)

Nottebohm, Gustav. *Beethovens Studien.* Leipzig and Winterthur, 1873.

———, *Ein Skizzenbuch von Beethoven.* Leipzig, 1865. *Ein Skizzenbuch von Beethoven aus dem Jahre 1803.* Leipzig, 1880. Republished as *Zwei Skizzenbücher von Beethoven aus dem Jahren 1801 bis 1803,* ed. Paul Mies. Leipzig, 1924.

———, *Thematisches Verzeichniss.* Second edition. Leipzig, 1868. (First edition, 1851.)

Orel, Alfred (ed.). *Ein Wiener Beethovenbuch.* Articles by Probst, Böck, Reuther, Biberhofer, Wagner, Orel, Trost, and Englmann. Vienna, 1921.

———, *Grillparzer und Beethoven.* Vienna, 1941.

Pachler, Faust. *Beethoven und Marie Pachler-Koschak.* Berlin, 1866.

Papp, Victor. *Beethoven és a Magyorok.* Budapest, 1927.

Prod'homme, Jacques-Gabriel. *Cahiers de Conversation.* Paris, 1946.

———, *La Jeunesse de Beethoven.* Paris, 1920.

Reinitz, Max. *Beethoven im Kampf mit dem Schicksal.* Vienna, 1924.

Rolland, Romain. *Beethoven—Les grandes époques créatrices: De l'Heroique à l'Appassionata.* Paris, 1928.

———, *Goethe et Beethoven.* Paris, 1930.

Schiedermair, Ludwig. *Der junge Beethoven.* Bonn and Leipzig, 1925.

Schindler, Anton. *The Life of Beethoven.* Translation of *Biographie von Ludwig van Beethoven* by I. Moscheles. 2 vols. London, 1841.

Schmidt-Görg, Joseph. *Beethoven. Dreizehn unbekannte Briefe an Josephine Gräfin Deym, geb. v. Brunsvik.* Beethovenhaus: Bonn, 1957.

———, *Beethoven. Ein Skizzenbuch aus den Jahren 1819-20.* Beethovenhaus: Bonn, 1952.

Schweisheimer, Waldemar. *Beethovens Leiden.* Munich, 1922.

von Seyfried, Ignaz Ritter. *L. v. Beethovens Studien.* Vienna, 1832.

———, *Beethoven: Studies in Thorough-bass, Counterpoint and the Art of*

Scientific Composition. Translation of *L. v. Beethovens Studien* by Henry H. Pierson. Leipzig, 1853.

Smolle, Kurt. *Beethovens unsterbliche Geliebte.* Vienna, New York, and Zurich, 1947.

Sonneck, Oscar (ed.). *Beethoven, Impressions of Contemporaries.* New York, 1927.

———, *Beethoven Letters in America.* New York, 1927.

———, *The Riddle of the Immortal Beloved.* New York, 1927.

Sterba, E., and R. *Beethoven and his Nephew.* New York, 1954.

Thayer, Alexander Wheelock. *Chronologisches Verzeichniss.* Berlin, 1865.

———, *Ein kritischer Beitrag zur Beethoven-Literatur.* Berlin, 1877.

———, *Ludwig van Beethovens Leben.* Translated and edited by Hermann Deiters. First edition in three volumes, Berlin: volume I, 1866; volume II, 1872; volume III, 1879.

Thomas-San-Galli, Wolfgang A. *Beethoven und die unsterbliche Geliebte.* Munich, 1910.

Unger, Max. *Auf Spuren von Beethovens unsterblicher Geliebten.* Langensalza, 1910.

———, *Ein Schweizer Beethovensammlung Katalog.* Zurich, 1929.

———, *Ludwig van Beethoven und seine Verleger S. A. Steiner und Tobias Haslinger in Wien, Adolph Martin Schlesinger in Berlin.* Berlin and Vienna, 1921.

Van Aerde, Raymond. *Les Ancêtres Flamands de Beethoven.* Malines, 1927.

Veröffentlichungen des Beethoven-Hauses in Bonn. 10 vols. Ludwig Schiedermair, editor. Bonn, 1920-1934.

Veröffentlichungen des Beethovenhauses in Bonn. Neue Folge.

Erste Reihe: *Skizzen und Entwürfe.* See individual publications under Schmidt-Görg and Weise.

Zweite Reihe: *Beethoven-Jahrbuch.* See abbreviation list under *BJ.*

Dritte Reihe: *Ausgewählte Handschriften in Faksimile-Ausgabe.* See under Schmidt-Görg and Weise.

Volkmann, Hans. *Beethoven in seinen Beziehungen zu Dresden.* Dresden, 1942.

———, *Neues über Beethoven.* Berlin, 1904.

Weise, Dagmar (ed.). *Beethoven—ein Skizzenbuch zur Chorfantasie Op. 80 und zu anderen Werken.* Beethovenhaus: Bonn, 1957.

———, *Beethoven—Entwurf einer Denkschrift an das Appellationsgericht in Wien vom 18. Februar 1820.* Beethovenhaus: Bonn, 1953.

CHAPTER I

THE ELECTORAL COURT
AT BONN

ONE of the compensations for the horrors of the French Revolution was the sweeping away of many of the petty sovereignties into which Germany was divided, thereby rendering a union of the German People and the rise of a German Nation possible. The first to fall were the numerous ecclesiastical-civil members of the old, loose confederation, some of which had played no ignoble nor unimportant part in the advance of civilization; but their day was past. The people of these states had in divers respects enjoyed a better lot than those who were subjects of hereditary rulers, and the old German saying: "It is good to dwell under the crook," had a basis of fact. At the least, they were not sold as mercenary troops; their blood was not shed on foreign fields to support their princes' ostentatious splendor, to enable mistresses and ill-begotten children to live in luxury and riot. But the antiquated ideas to which the ecclesiastical rulers held with bigoted tenacity had become a barrier to progress, the exceptions being too few to render their farther existence desirable. These members of the empire, greatly differing in extent, population, wealth and political influence, were ruled with few or no exceptions by men who owed their positions to election by chapters or other church corporations, whose numbers were so limited as to give full play to every sort of intrigue; but they could not assume their functions until their titles were confirmed by the Pope as head of the church, and by the Emperor as head of the confederation. Thus the subject had no voice in the matter, and it hardly need be said that his welfare and prosperity were never included among the motives and considerations on which the elections turned.

The sees, by their charters and statutes, we think without exception, were bestowed upon men of noble birth. They were benefices and sinecures for younger sons of princely houses; estates set apart and consecrated to the use, emolument and enjoyment of German John Lacklands. In the long list of their incumbents, a name here and there appears, that calls up historic associations;—a man of letters who aided in the increase or diffusion of the cumbrous learning of his time; a warrior who exchanged his robes for a coat of mail; a politician who played a part more or less honorable or the reverse in the affairs and intrigues of the empire, and, very rarely, one whose daily walk and conversation reflected, in some measure, the life and principles of the founder of Christianity. In general, as they owed their places wholly to political and family influences, so they assumed the vows and garb of churchmen as necessary steps to the enjoyment of lives of affluence and pleasure.

So late as far into the eighteenth century, travelling was slow, laborious and expensive. Hence, save for the few more wealthy and powerful, journeys, at long intervals, to a council, an imperial coronation or a diet of the empire, were the rare interruptions to the monotony of their daily existence. Not having the power to transmit their sees to their children, these ecclesiastics had the less inducement to rule with an eye to the welfare of their subjects: on the other hand, the temptation was very strong to augment their revenues for the benefit of relatives and dependents, and especially for the gratification of their own tastes and inclinations, among which the love of splendor and ostentatious display was a fruitful source of waste and extravagance.

Confined so largely to their own small capitals, with little intercourse except with their immediate neighbors, they were far more dependent upon their own resources for amusement than the hereditary princes: and what so obvious, so easily obtained and so satisfactory as music, the theatre and the dance! Thus every little court became a conservatory of these arts, and for generations most of the great names in them may be found recorded in the court calendars. One is therefore not surprised to learn how many of the more distinguished musical composers began life as singing boys in cathedral choirs of England and Germany. The secular princes, especially those of high rank, had, besides their civil administration, the stirring events of war, questions of public policy, schemes and intrigues for the advancement of family interests and the like, to engage their attention; but the ecclesiastic, leaving the civil administration, as a rule, in the hands of ministers, had little to occupy him officially but a tedious routine of religious forms and ceremonies; to him therefore the theatre, and music for the mass, the opera, the ball-room, and the salon, were matters of great moment—they filled a wide void and were cherished accordingly.

The three German ecclesiastical princes who possessed the greatest power and influence were the Archbishops of Mainz, Trèves and Cologne—Electors of the Empire and rulers of the fairest regions of the Rhine. Peace appears hardly to have been known between the city of Cologne and its earlier archbishops; and, in the thirteenth century, a long-continued and even bloody quarrel resulted in the victory of the city. It remained a free imperial town. The archbishops retained no civil or political power within its walls, not even the right to remain there more than three days at any one time. Thus it happened, that in the year 1257 Archbishop Engelbert selected Bonn for his residence, and formally made it the capital of the electorate, as it remained until elector and court were swept away in 1794.

Of the last four Electors of Cologne, the first was Joseph Clemens, a Bavarian prince, nephew of his predecessor Maximilian Heinrich. The choice of the chapter by a vote of thirteen to nine had been Cardinal Fürstenberg; but his known, or supposed, devotion to the interests of the French king had prevented the ratification of the election by either the Emperor or the Pope. A new one being ordered, resulted in favor of the Bavarian, then a youth of eighteen years. The Pope had ratified his election and appointed a bishop to perform his ecclesiastical functions *ad interim*, and the Emperor invested him with the electoral dignity December 1, 1689. Vehse[1] says of him:

"Like two of his predecessors he was the incumbent of five sees; he was Archbishop of Cologne, Bishop of Hildesheim, Liège, Ratisbon and Freisingen. His love for pomp and splendor was a passion which he gratified in the magnificence of his court. He delighted to draw thither beautiful and intellectual women. Madame de Raysbeck, and Countess Fugger, wife of his chief equerry, were his declared favorites. For seventeen years, that is, until the disastrous year 1706, when Fénelon consecrated him, he delayed assuming his vows. He held the opinion, universal in the courts of those days, that he might with a clear conscience enjoy life after the manner of secular princes. In pleasing the ladies, he was utterly regardless of expense, and for their amusement gave magnificent balls, splendid masquerades, musical and dramatic entertainments, and hunting parties."

St. Simon relates that several years of his exile were passed at Valenciennes, where, though a fugitive, he followed the same round of costly pleasures and amusements. He also records one of the Elector's jests which in effrontery surpasses anything related of his contemporary, Dean Swift. Some time after his consecration, he caused public notice to be given, that on the approaching first of April he would preach. At the appointed time he mounted the pulpit, bowed gravely, made the sign of the cross, shouted "Zum April!" (April fool!), and retired amid a flourish of trumpets and the rolling of drums.[2]

Dr. Ennen[3] labors energetically to prove that Joseph Clemens' fondness in later years for joining in all grand church ceremonies rested upon higher motives than the mere pleasure of displaying himself in his magnificent robes; and affirms that after assuming his priestly vows he led a life devoted to the church and worthy of his order; thenceforth never seeing Madame de Raysbeck, mother of his illegitimate children, except in the presence of a

---

[1] Karl Eduard Vehse, *Geschichte der deutschen Höfe seit der Reformation* (Hamburg, 1857), Vol. 45, pp. 296ff. (TDR, I, 9.)

[2] *Ibid.*

[3] Leonhard Ennen, *Der spanische Erbfolgekrieg und Kurfürst Joseph Clemens von Cöln* (Jena, 1851), pp. 259ff. (TDR, I, 9, n. 1.) .

third person. It seems proper to say this much concerning a prince whose electorship is the point of departure for notices of music and musicians in Bonn during the eighteenth century; a prince whose fondness for the art led him at home and in exile to support both vocal and instrumental bands on a scale generous for that age; and who, moreover, made some pretensions to the title of composer himself, as we learn from a letter which under date of July 28, 1720, he wrote to a court councillor Rauch to accompany eleven of his motets. It is an amusingly frank letter, beginning with a confession that he was an *Ignorant* who knew nothing about notes and had absolutely no knowledge of *musique*, wherefore he admits that his manner of composing is "very odd," being compelled to sing anything that came into his head to a composer whose duty it was to bring the ideas to paper. Nevertheless he is quite satisfied with himself. "At all events I must have a good ear and gusto, for the public that has heard has always approved. But the *methodum* which I have adopted is that of the bees that draw and collect the honey from the sweetest flowers; so, also, I have taken all that I have composed from good masters whose *Musikalien* pleased me. Thus I freely confess my pilfering, which others deny and try to appropriate what they have taken from others. Let no one, therefore, get angry if he hears old arias in it, for, as they are beautiful, the old is not deprived of its praise. . . . I ascribe everything to the grace of God who enlightened me, the unknowing, to do these things." Not all "composers," royal or mean, are as honest as the old Elector!

It is fortunate for the present purpose, that the portion of the electoral archives discovered after a lapse of nearly seventy years and now preserved at Düsseldorf, consists so largely of documents relating to the musical establishment of the court at Bonn during the last century of its existence. They rarely afford information upon the character of the music performed, but are sufficiently complete, when supplemented by the annual Court Calendars, to determine with reasonable correctness the number, character, position and condition of its members. The few petitions and decrees hereafter to be given in full because of their connection with the Beethovens, suffice for specimens of the long series of similar documents, uniform in character and generally of too little interest to be worth transcription.

In 1695 a decree issued at Liège by Joseph Clemens, then in that city as titular bishop, though not consecrated, adds three new names to the "Hoff-Musici," one of which, Van den Eeden, constantly reappears in the documents and calendars down to the year 1782. From a list of payments at Liège in the second quarter of 1696, we find that Henri Vandeneden (Heinrich Van den Eeden) was a bass singer, and that the aggregate of vocalists, instrumentalists, with the organ-blower (*calcant*), was eighteen persons.

Returned to Bonn, Joseph Clemens resumed his plan of improving his music, and for those days of small orchestras and niggardly salaries he set it upon a rather generous foundation. A decree of April 1, 1698, put in force the next month, names 22 persons with salaries aggregating 8,890 florins.

After the death of Maximilian Heinrich the government passed into the hands of Cardinal Fürstenberg, his coadjutor, who owed the position to the intrigues of Louis XIV, and now used it by all possible means to promote French interests. The king's troops under French commanders, he admitted into the principal towns of the electorate, and, for his own protection, a French garrison of 10,000 men into Bonn. War was the consequence; an imperial army successfully invaded the province, and, advancing to the capital, subjected its unfortunate inhabitants to all the horrors of a relentless siege, that ended October 15, 1689, in the expulsion of the garrison, now reduced to some 3,900 men, of whom 1,500 were invalids. Yet in the war of the Spanish Succession which opened in 1701, notwithstanding the terrible lesson taught only eleven years before, the infatuated Joseph Clemens embraced the party of Louis. Emperor Leopold treated him with singular mildness, in vain. The Elector persisted. In 1702 he was therefore excluded from the civil government and fled from Bonn, the ecclesiastical authority in Cologne being empowered by the Emperor to rule in his stead. The next year, the great success of the French armies against the allies was celebrated by Joseph Clemens with all pomp in Namur, where he then was; but his triumph was short. John Churchill, then Earl of Marlborough, took the field as commander-in-chief of the armies of the allies. His foresight, energy and astonishing skill in action justified Addison's simile—whether sublime or only pompous—of the angel riding in the whirlwind and directing the storm. He was soon at Cologne, whence he despatched Cochorn to besiege Bonn. That great general executed his task with such skill and impetuosity, that on May 15 (1703) all was ready for storming the city, when d'Allègre, the French commander, offered to capitulate, and on the 19th was allowed to retire. "Now was Bonn for the third time wrested from the hands of the French and restored to the archbishopric, but alas, in a condition that aroused indignation, grief and compassion on all sides," says Müller.[4]

Leopold was still kindly disposed toward Joseph Clemens, but he died May 5, 1705, and his successor, Joseph I, immediately declared him under the ban of the Empire. This deprived him of the means and opportunities, as Elector, for indulging his passion for pomp and display, while his neglect hitherto, under dispensations from the Pope, to take the vows necessary to the performance of ecclesiastical functions, was likewise fatal to that indulgence as archbishop. But this could be remedied; Fénelon, the famous Archbishop of Cambray, ordained him subdeacon August 15, 1706; the Bishop of Tournay made him deacon December 8, and priest on the 25th; on January 1, 1707, he read his first mass at Lille, and indulged his passion for parade to the full, as a pamphlet describing the incident, and silver and copper medals commemorating it, still evince. "Two years later, May 1, 1709, Joseph Clemens received from Fénelon in Ryssell (Lille) episcopal consecration and the

[4] K. A. Müller, *Geschichte der Stadt Bonn*, 1843, p. 208. (TDR, I, 15.)

pallium."—(Müller.) Upon the victory of Oudenarde by Marlborough, and the fall of Lille, he took refuge in Mons. The treaty of Rastadt, March, 1714, restored him to his electoral dignities and he returned to the Rhine; but Dutch troops continued to hold Bonn until December 11, 1715. On the morning of that day they evacuated the city and in the afternoon the Elector entered in a grand, solemn procession commemorated by an issue of silver medals.

During all these vicissitudes Joseph Clemens, from whatever source he derived the means, did not suffer his music to deteriorate and, returned to Bonn, no sooner was the public business regulated and restored to its former routine than he again turned his attention to its improvement.

Joseph Clemens died November 12, 1723, having previously secured the succession to his nephew Clemens August, last of the five Electors of Cologne of the Bavarian line. The new incumbent, third son of Maximilian Emanuel, Elector of Bavaria and his second wife, a daughter of the celebrated John Sobieski of Poland, was born August 17, 1700, at Brussels, where his father resided at the time as Governor General. From his fourth to his fifteenth year he had been held in captivity by the Austrians at Klagenfurt and Gratz; then, having been destined for the church, he spent several years at study in Rome. As a child in 1715 he had been appointed coadjutor to the Bishop of Regensburg; in 1719 he was elected to the two sees of Paderborn and Münster made vacant by the death of his brother Moritz, was chosen coadjutor to his uncle of Cologne in 1722, made his solemn entry into Bonn as elector May 15, 1724, was the same year also elected Bishop of Hildesheim, in 1725 Provost of the Cathedral at Liège, in 1728 Bishop of Osnabrück, and, finally, in 1732 reached the dignity of Grand Master of the Teutonic Order.

His rule is distinguished in the annals of the electorate for little else than the building, repairing, renewing and embellishing of palaces, hunting-seats, churches, convents, and other edifices. At Bonn he erected the huge building, now the seat of the University, the foundation of which had been laid by his uncle. The handsome City Hall was also his work; the villa at Poppelsdorf was enlarged by him into a small palace, Clemensruhe, now the University Museum of Natural History. In Brühl, the Augustusburg dates from his reign, and Münster, Mergentheim, Arnsberg and other places show similar monuments of his prodigality in the indulgence of his taste for splendor. "Monstrous were the sums," says Dr. Ennen, "squandered by him in the purchase of splendid ornaments, magnificent equipages, furniture costly for its variety, and of rare works of art; upon dazzling court festivities, sleighing-parties, masquerades, operas, dramas and ballets; upon charlatans, swindlers, female vocalists, actors and dancers. His theatre and opera alone cost him 50,000 thalers annually and the magnificence of his masked balls, twice a week in winter, is proof sufficient that no small sums were lavished upon them."

The aggregate of the revenues derived from the several states of which Clemens August was the head nowhere appears; but the civil income of the electorate alone had, in his later years, risen from the million of florins of his predecessor to about the same number of thalers—an increase of some 40 per centum; added to this were large sums derived from the church, and sub- sidies from Austria, France and the sea-coast states amounting to at least 14,000,000 francs; indeed, during the Elector's last ten years the French subsidies alone made an aggregate of at least 7,300,000 francs; in 1728 Hol- land paid on account of the Clemens Canal 76,000 thalers. At the centennial opening of the strong-box of the Teutonic Order he obtained the fat accumu- lations of a hundred years; and 25 years later he opened it again. Yet, though during his rule peace was hardly interrupted in his part of Europe, he plunged ever deeper and more inextricably into debt, leaving one of large proportions as his legacy to his successor. He was a bad ruler, but a kindly, amiable and popular man. How should he know or feel the value of money or the neces- sity of prudence? His childhood had been spent in captivity, his student years in Rome, where, precisely at that period, poetry and music were cultivated, if not in very noble and manly forms, at least with a Medicean splendor. The society of the Arcadians was in full activity. True, both Clemens August and his brother were under the age which enabled them to be enrolled as "Shep- herds," and consequently their names appear neither in Crescimbeni nor in Quadrio; but it is not to be supposed that two young princes, already bishops by election and certain of still higher dignities in the future, were excluded from the palaces of Ruspoli and Ottoboni, from those brilliant literary, artistic and luxurious circles in which, only half a dozen years before, their young countryman, the musician Handel, had found so cordial a welcome. Those were very expensive tastes, as the citation from Ennen shows, which the future elector brought with him from Rome. Italian palaces, Italian villas, churches, gardens, music, songstresses, mistresses, an Italian holy staircase on the Kreuzberg (leading to nothing); Italian pictures, mosaics and, what not? All these things cost money—but must he not have them?

This elector is perhaps the only archbishop on record to whose epitaph may truthfully be added: "He danced out of this world into some other";— which happened in this wise: Having, in the winter of 1760-61, by some unexpected stroke of good fortune, succeeded in obtaining from the usually prudent and careful bankers of Holland a loan of 80,000 thalers, he embraced the opportunity of making a long-desired visit to his family in Munich. Owing to a sudden attack of illness he was once on the point of turning back soon after leaving Bonn. He persevered, however, reached Coblenz and crossed over to the palace of the Elector of Trèves at Ehrenbreitstein, where he arrived at 4 p.m., February 5, 1761. At dinner an hour later he was unable to eat; but at the ball, which followed, he could not resist the fascination of the Baroness von Waldendorf—sister of His Transparency of Trèves—and danced with her "eight or nine turns." Of course he could not refuse a similar compliment to several other ladies. The physical exertion of dancing, joined to the excitement of the occasion and following a dreary winter-day's journey, was too much for the enfeebled constitution of a man of sixty years. He fainted in the ballroom, was carried to his chamber and died next day.

It seems to have been the etiquette, that when an elector breathed his last, the musical chapel expired with him. At all events, no other explanation appears of the fact that so many of the petitions for membership, which are still preserved, should be signed by men who had already been named in the Court Calendars. It is also to be remarked that some of the petitioners receive appointments "without salary." These seem to have been appointments of the kind, which in later years were distinguished in the records and in the calendars by the term "accessist," and which, according to the best lights afforded by the archives, may be considered as having been provisional, until the incumbent had proved his skill and capacity, or until a vacancy occurred through the death or resignation of some old member. There are indications that the "accessists," though without fixed salary, received some small remuneration for their services; but this is by no means certain. It would seem that both vocalists and instrumentalists who received salaries out of the state revenues were limited to a fixed number; that the amount of funds devoted to this object was also strictly limited and the costs incurred by the engagement of superior artists with extra salaries, or by an increase of the number, were defrayed from the Elector's privy purse; that the position of "accessist" was sought by young musicians as a stepping-stone to some future vacancy which, when acquired, insured a gradually increasing income during the years of service and a small pension when superannuated; that the etiquette of the court demanded, even in cases when the Elector expressly called some distinguished artist to Bonn, that the appointment should be apparently only in gracious answer to an humble petition, and that, with few exceptions, both singers and members of the orchestra were employed in the church, the theatre and the concert-room.

Clemens August made his formal entry into Bonn, May 15, 1724. A number of petitions are passed over, but one granted "without salary" on February 18, 1727, from Van den Eeden must be given in its entirety:

Supplique tres humble a S. A. S. E. de Cologne pour Gille Vandeneet.
Prince Serenissime, Monseigneur.   BONN, d. 18 Feb., 1727.
Vandeneet vient avec tout le respect qui luy est possible se mettre aux pieds de V. A. S. E. luy representer qu'ayant eu l'honneur d'avoir estre second organiste de feu S. A. S. E. d'heureuse memoire, elle daigne luy vouloir faire la même grace ne demendant aucun gage si long tems qu'il plaira a V. A. S. E. promettant la servire avec soin et diligence.

Quoi faisant etc. etc.

On the same date Van den Eeden received his appointment as second court organist. June 8, 1728, a decree was issued granting him a salary of 100 florins. To a third petition the next year, signed Van den Enden, the answer was an increase of his salary to 200 thalers, and thus a future instructor of Ludwig van Beethoven became established in Bonn. The records need not concern us now until we reach the following, which forms part of the history of the grandfather of the subject of this biography:

March, 1733.

DECRETUM

For Ludovicum van Beethoven as Electoral Court Musician.

Cl. A. Whereas His Serene Highness Elector of Cologne, Duke Clemens August in Upper and Lower Bavaria, etc. Our Gracious Lord having, on the humble petition of Ludovico van Beethoven, graciously declared and received him as Court Musician, and assigned him an annual salary of 400 florins Rhenish, the present decree under the gracious hand of His Serene Electoral Highness and the seal of the Privy Chancellor, is granted to him, and the Electoral Councillor and Paymaster Risack is herewith commanded to pay the said Beethoven the 400 fl. *quartaliter* from the beginning of this year and to make a proper accounting thereof. B. . . . . March, 1733.

Thirteen years later we find this:

Allowance of an additional 100 Thalers annually to the
Chamber Musician van Beethoven.

Inasmuch as His Serene Highness Elector of Cologne, Duke Clement August of Upper and Lower Bavaria, our most Gracious Lord has increased the salary of his Chamber Musician van Beethoven by the addition of 100 thalers annually which became due through the death of Joseph Kayser, instrument maker, the Court Chamber Councillor and Paymaster Risach is hereby informed and graciously commanded to pay to him the said Beethoven the 100 fl. a year in quarterly installments against voucher from the proper time and to make the proper accounting. Witness, etc. Poppelsdorf, August 22, 1746.

On May 2, 1747, Johann Ries became Court Trumpeter with a salary of 192 thalers. This is the first representative we have met of a name which afterwards rose to great distinction, not only in the orchestra of the Elector but also in the world at large. On March 5, 1754, he was formally appointed Court Musician (violinist) having set forth in his petition that instead of confining himself to the trumpet he had made himself serviceable in the chapel by singing and playing other instruments. Later he took ill and was sent to Cologne. We shall presently meet his two daughters and his son Franz Ries, the last of whom will figure prominently in the life-history of Beethoven. Under date March 27, 1756, occur several papers which have a double interest. They relate to the Beethoven family and are so complete as to exhibit the entire process of appointment to membership in the electoral chapel. The original documents are not calculated to give the reader a very exalted idea of the orthographical knowledge of the petitioner or the Chamber Music Director Gottwaldt; but that fault gives us the clue to the correct pronunciation of the name Beethoven.

To His Electoral Serenity of Cologne, etc. My most Gracious Lord
the humble petition and prayer of
Joan van Biethoffen.

Most Reverend, most Serene Elector,
Most Gracious Lord, Lord, etc.

May it please your Electoral Serenity graciously to hear the humble representations how in the absence of voices in Your Highness's Court Chapel my insignificant self took part in the music for at least four years without the good fortune of having allotted by Your Serene Electoral Highness a small *salario*.

I therefore pray Your Serene Electoral Highness most humbly that it graciously please you (in consideration of my father's faithful service for 23 years) to rejoice me with a decree as court musician, which high grace will infuse me with zeal to serve Your Serene Highness with the greatest fidelity and zealousness.

Your
Serene Electoral Highness's
Most humble-obedient-faithful servant,
Joan van Biethoffen.

—⸙{André M. Pols[5] has reviewed the explanations that have been offered for the derivation of the name Beethoven. The etymological explanation of "Beet" (beetroot) and "Hof" (garden) was challenged by the "van" preceding the name which signifies "from" (a given locality). A place near Tongeren in Belgium was called *Betho*, spelled *Betue* in the thirteenth century; it is written *Betouwe* by the beginning of the fifteenth century. Pols suggests that the "ouwe" signifies "land" and that "bet" is the root of "beter" (besser). Thus the name would mean land that lay fallow until *ver-bet-erd* (verbessert) or improved through cultivation. In 1582 the country-seat is mentioned in the archives as Bethove or Bethoven. At the end of the sixteenth century in the records at Hasselt, there is a teacher whose name is interchangeably Jan Smeets and Jan van Bethoven. This is supported by the following entry in the records of 1608, "Jan Smeets Betgomensis, scoelmeester," that is, Jan Smeets from Bethoven, teacher.}⸙—

To the Music Director Gottwaldt for a report of his humble
judgment. Attestation by the most gracious
sign manual and seal of the privy chancellary.

Bonn, March 19, 1756.

(Signed) Clemens August (L.S.)

Most reverend, most serene Elector,
Most gracious Lord, Lord, etc.

Your Serene Electoral Highness has referred to my humble judgment the petition of Joan van Piethoffen, the supplicant prays Your Electoral Highness for a gracious decree as accessist in the court music, he has indeed served for two

[5] André M. Pols, "Beethovens Flämische Abstammung," *NBJ*, VII (1937), 17-28. See also M. A. Vincent, "Le Nom de Beethoven," in *Isidor Teirlinck Album*, 1931, pp. 133-41, who independently reaches the same conclusion.

years with his voice on the Duc Sall [doxal], hopes in time to deserve the good will of Your Serene Highness by his industry, and his father who enjoys the grace of serving Your Highness as bass singer prays his appointment, I pray most humbly and obediently for instruction concerning your Highness's good will in the matter, submit myself humbly and obediently to Your Serene Highness's grace and remain in greatest humility.

Your Serene and Electoral Highness's
Most Humble and obedient servant
Gottwaldt, Director of the Chamber Music.

A further report was made to the Elector as follows:

Coloniensis gratiosa.   BONN, March 27, 1756.

Chamber Music Director Gottwaldt *ad supplicam* of Joan van Betthoffen has served two years on the docsal and hopes through his industry to serve further to the satisfaction of Your Electoral Highness, to which end his father who through Your Highness's grace serves as bass singer will seek completely to qualify him which may it please Your Serene Highness to allow.

Idem Gottwaldt *ad supplicam* Ernest Haveckas, accessist in the court music, reports that suppliant, though not fully capable as yet hopes by special diligence to make himself worthy of Your Highness's service and would be encouraged and rejoiced in his efforts if Your Serene Highness would graciously deign to grant him a *decreto*, humbly praying to be informed as to Your Highness's wishes in the matter.

DECRETUM
Court Musician's Decree for Johan van Biethofen.

Clm. A. Whereas His Serene Electoral Highness of Cologne, Duke Clement August in Upper and Lower Bavaria etc. Our Gracious Lord on the humble petition of Johan van Biethofen and in consideration of his skill in the art of singing, also the experience in the same already gained, having graciously declared and accepted him as court musician, appoint and accept him by this writing; therefore the said Biethofen receives this decree with the gracious sign manual and seal of the Privy Chancellary, and those who are concerned to recognize him hereafter as an Electoral court musician and to pay him such respect as the position deserves. Bonn, March 25, 1756.

Johann van Beethoven was 16 years old at this time. Why he should appear in the Court Calendar as an accessist four years after the publication of this decree appointing him Court Musician does not appear.

But slender success has rewarded the search for means of determining the character and quality of that opera and music, upon which, according to Ennen, Clemens August lavished such large sums. The period embraced in that elector's rule (1724–1761) was precisely that in which the *old* Italian opera, the oratorio and the sacred cantata reached their extreme limits of development through the genius of Handel and J. S. Bach. It closes at the moment when Gluck, C. P. E. Bach and Joseph Haydn were laying the immovable foundations of a new operatic, orchestral and pianoforte music, and before the perfected sonata-form, that found universal adoption in all non-vocal compositions of the better class. Little music comparatively was issued from the press in those days, and consequently new forms and new styles made their way slowly into vogue. Another consequence was that the offices of composer for the chamber, the church, the comedy, or however they were named, were by no means sinecures—neither at the imperial court of Maria Theresia, nor at the court of any petty prince or noble whose servants formed his orchestra. Composers had to furnish music on demand and as often as was necessary, as the hunter delivered game or the fisherman fish. What a volume of music was produced in this manner can be seen in the case of Joseph Haydn at Esterhaz, whose fruitfulness did not, in all probability, exceed that of many another of his contemporaries. The older Telemann furnished compositions to the courts of Bayreuth and Eisenach as well as the Gray Friars at Frankfurt-am-Main, and also performed his duties as musical director and composer at Hamburg. He wrote music with such ease that, as Handel said, he could write for eight voices as rapidly as an ordinary man could write a letter. Under such conditions did the men write who are mentioned as official composers in our narrative. It is probable that not a note of theirs remains in existence, and equally probable that the loss is not at all deplorable except as it leaves the curiosity of an antiquary unsatisfied. A few text-books to vocal pieces performed on various occasions during this reign have been preserved, their titles being *Componimento per Musica*, music by Giuseppe dall'Abaco, Director of the Chamber Music (1740); *La Morte d'Abel* (no date is given, but "il Signor Biethoven" sang the part of Adamo); *Esther* ("From the Italian of S. F. A. Aubert," the text partly in German, partly in Italian); *Anagilda* (*Drama per Musica*).

After the unlucky ball at Ehrenbreitstein the crook and sceptre of Cologne passed from the Bavarian family which had so long held them into the hands of Maximilian Friedrich of the Suabian line Königsegg- (or Königseck-) Rothenfels. For a century or more this house had enjoyed fat livings in the church at Cologne, in which city the new elector was born on May 13, 1708. He was the fourth of his race who had held the important office of Dean of the Cathedral, from which post he was elevated to the electorship on April 6, 1761, and to the ecclesiastical principality of Münster the next year; with which two sees he was fain to be content. He was by nature an easy, good-tempered, indolent, friendly man, of no great force of character—qualities which in the incumbent of a rich sinecure just completing his fifty-third year, would be too fully confirmed and developed by habit to change with any change of circumstances; and which, says Stramberg,[6] made him unusually popular throughout the land despite the familiar little verse:

[6] Christian von Stramberg, *Denkwürdiger und nützlicher Rheinischer Antiquarius* (Koblenz, 1860), Ser. 3, Vol. 7, p. 352.

Bei Clemens August trug man blau und weiss,
Da lebte man wie im Paradeis;
Bei Max Friedrich trug man sich schwarz und roth,
Da litt man Hunger wie die schwere Noth.

The condition of the finances had become such through the extravagant expenditures of Clemens August that very energetic measures were necessary, and to the effects of these, during the first few years of Max Friedrich's rule, in throwing many persons out of employment, these doggerel lines doubtless owe their origin.

It was fortunate for the Elector's subjects that his indolence was made good by the activity and energy of a prime minister who found his beau ideal of a statesman in Frederick II of Prussia, whom, in his domestic policy, he imitated as far as the character of the two governments allowed. This was equally if not more true in the principality of Münster. While one must have respect for the memory of Belderbusch, the all-powerful minister at Bonn, for his statesmanship, one may add in the case of Fürstenberg, the equally all-powerful minister at Münster, admiration and regard for the man. The former was respected, feared, but not loved in the electorate; the latter was respected and very popular in the principality. To Kaspar Anton von Belderbusch the new Elector owed his elevation; to his care he entrusted the state; to his skill and strength of character he was indebted for release from the pecuniary difficulties which beset him and for the satisfaction, as the years rolled by, of seeing his states numbered among the most prosperous and flourishing in Germany. Belderbusch's first care was to reduce the expenditure. "He put a stop to building," says Ennen,[7] "dismissed a number of the actors, restricted the number of concerts and court balls, dispensed with the costly hunts, reduced the salaries of court officials, officers and domestics, lessened the *état* for the kitchen, cellar and table of the prince, turned the property left by Clemens August into money and comforted the latter's creditors with the hope of better times." But though economy was the rule, still, where the Elector considered it due to his position, he could be lavish. Whatever opinions may be entertained as to the wisdom and expediency of clothing ecclesiastics with civil power, it would be unjust not to give the bright as well as the dark side of the picture. This is well put by Kaspar Riesbeck in relation to the Rhenish states whose princes were churchmen, and his remarks are in place here, since they relate in part to that in which the childhood and youth of Beethoven were spent.[8] "The whole stretch of the country from here to Mainz is one of the richest and most populous in Germany. Within this territory of 18 German miles there are 20 cities lying hard by the shore of the Rhine and dating, for the greater part, from the

---

[7] Leonhard Ennen, *Frankreich und der Niederrhein* II, p. 387. (TDR, I, 43, n. 1.)
[8] Kaspar Riesbeck, *Briefe eines reisenden Franzosen in Deutschland* (1784), II, p. 349ff. (Cf. TDR, I, 43.)

period of the Romans. It is still plainly to be seen that this portion of Germany was the first to be built up. Neither morasses nor heaths interrupt the evidences of cultivation which stretch with equal industry far from the shores of the river over the contiguous country. While many cities and castles built under Charlemagne and his successors, especially Henry I, in other parts of Germany have fallen into decay, all in this section have not only been preserved but many have been added to them. . . . The natural wealth of the soil in comparison with that of other lands, and the easy disposition of its products by means of the Rhine, have no doubt contributed most to these results. Nevertheless, great as is the prejudice in Germany against the ecclesiastical governments, they have beyond doubt aided in the blooming development of these regions. In the three ecclesiastical electorates which make up the greater part of this tract of land nothing is known of those tax burdens under which the subjects of so many secular princes of Germany groan. These princes have exceeded the old assessments but slightly. Little is known in their countries of serfdom. The appanage of many princes and princesses do not force them to extortion. They have no inordinate military institution, and do not sell the sons of their farmers; and they have never taken so active a part in the domestic and foreign wars of Germany as the secular princes. Though they are not adept in encouraging their subjects in art culture, varied agriculture has been developed to a high degree of perfection throughout the region. Nature does of its own accord what laws and regulations seek to compel, as soon as the rocks of offence are removed from the path."

Henry Swinburne, whose letters to his brother were published long after his death under the title of *The Courts of Europe*,[9] writes under date of November 29, 1780:

Bonn is a pretty town, neatly built, and its streets tolerably well paved, all in black lava. It is situated in a flat near the river. The Elector of Cologne's palace faces the South entry. It has no beauty of architecture and is all plain white without any pretensions.

We went to court and were invited to dine with the Elector (Königsegge). He is 73 years old, a little, hale, black man, very merry and affable. His table is none of the best; no dessert wines handed about, nor any foreign wines at all. He is easy and agreeable, having lived all his life in ladies' company, which he is said to have liked better than his breviary. The captains of his guard and a few other people of the court form the company, amongst whom were his two great-nieces, Madame de Hatzfeld and Madame de Taxis. The palace is of immense size, the ball-room particularly large and low. . . . The Elector goes about to all the assemblies and plays at Tric-trac. He asked me to be of his party but I was not acquainted with their way of playing. There is every evening an assembly or play at court. The Elector seems very strong and healthy, and will, I think, hold the Archduke a good tug yet.

[9] London, 1841, Vol. I, pp. 371-72.

This Archduke was Max Franz, youngest son of Maria Theresia, whose acquaintance Swinburne had made in Vienna, and who had just been chosen coadjutor to Max Friedrich. A curious proof of the liberality, not to say laxity, of the Elector's sentiments in one direction is given by Stramberg in his *Rheinischer Antiquarius*,[10] to wit, the possession of a mistress in common by him and his minister Belderbusch—the latter fathering the children—and this mistress was the Countess Caroline von Satzenhofen, Abbess of Vilich!

The reduction which was made by Belderbusch upon the accession of Max Friedrich in the expenses of the theatre and other amusements does not appear, except in the case of the kapellmeister, to have extended to the court music proper, nor to have been long continued in respect to the "operetta and comedy." The first in order of the documents and notices discovered relating to the musical establishment of this Elector are of no common interest, being the petition of a candidate for the vacant office of kapellmeister and the decree appointing him to that position. They are as follows:

Very Reverend Archbishop and Elector
        most gracious Lord Lord!

May it please Your Electoral Grace to permit a representation of my faithfully and dutifully performed services for a considerable space as vocalist as well as, since the death of the kapellmeister, for more than a year his duties *in Dupplo*, that is to say by singing and wielding the baton concerning which my demand still remains *ad referendum* much less have I been assured of the position. Inasmuch as because of particular *recommendation* Dousmoulin was preferred over me, and indeed unjustly, I have been forced hitherto to submit to fate.

But now, gracious Elector and Lord, that because of the reduction in salaries Kapellmeister Dousmoulin has already asked his demission or will soon do so, and I at the command of Baron Belderbusch am to begin *de novo* to fill his office, and the same must surely be replaced,—Therefore

There reaches Your Electoral Grace my humble petition that you may graciously be pleased (: inasmuch as the "Toxal" must be sufficiently supplied with *musique*, and I must at all events take the lead in the occurring church ceremonies *in puncto* the chorales:) to grant me the justice of which I was deprived on the death of Your Highness's *antecessori* of blessed memory, and appoint me kapellmeister with some augmentation of my lessened salary because of my services performed in *Duplo*. For which highest grace I shall pour out my prayers to God for the long continuing health and government of your Electoral Grace, while in deepest submission I throw myself at your feet.

> Your Electoral Grace's most humble servant
> Ludwig van Beethoven
> "Passist."

M.F. Whereas We, Maximilian Friedrich, Elector of Cologne, on the demission of our former kapellmeister Touche Moulin, and the humble petition of our bass singer Ludwig van Beethoven have appointed the latter to be kapellmeister with

[10] *Op.cit.*, p. 576.

the retention of his position as bass singer and have added 97 rthlr. *species* 40 alb. to his former salary of 292 rthlr. *species* 40 alb. per annum divided in *quartalien*, which appointment is hereby made and payment ordered by our grace, our exchequer and all whom it may concern are called on to observe the fact and do what is required under the circumstances.

Attest, etc.   Bonn, July 16, 1761.

Next in order, at an interval of rather more than a year, is the following short paper in reply to a petition, not preserved, of the new kapellmeister's son:

Supplicanten is hereby graciously assured that in the event of a *vacatur* of a court musician's salary he shall have special consideration. Attest our gracious sign manual and the impress of the seal of the Privy Chancellary.

Bonn, November 27, 1762.   Max Fried. Elector.

              v. Belderbusch, (:L. S.:)

About December, 1763, a singer, Madame Lentner, after some four and a half years of service, gave up her appointment, giving occasion, through the vacancy thus caused, for the following petition, report and decrees:

Most Reverend Elector, Most Gracious
     Lord, Lord.

Will Your Electoral Grace deign to receive the representation that by the acceptance of service elsewhere of Court Musician Dauber there has fallen to the disposition of Your Reverend Electoral Grace a salary of 1,050 rth., wherefore I, Joannes van Beethoven, having graciously been permitted for a considerable time to serve as court musician and have been graciously assured by decree of appointment to the first vacancy, and have always faithfully and diligently performed my duties and graciously been permitted to be in good voice, therefore my prayer is made to Your Reverend and Electoral Grace for a grant of the aforesaid 1,050 rth. or a gracious portion thereof, which act of highest grace I shall try to merit by fidelity and zeal in the performance of my duties.

       Your Reverend Electoral Grace's most obedient servant
             Joannes van Beethoven,
               vocalist.

This petition was seconded by the father in the following manner:

Most Reverend Archbishop and Elector,
     Most gracious Lord, Lord.

Your Electoral Grace having graciously been pleased to submit for my humble report the humble petition of Your Highness's court musician Joann Ries that his daughter be appointed to the place in the court music of Your Highness made vacant by the discharged soprano Lentner *sub Litt. A.*

Humbly obeying Your gracious command I submit an impartial report that for about a year the daughter of the court musician Ries has frequented the "Duc sahl" [doxal] and sung the soprano part and that to my satisfaction.

But now that my son Joannes van Beethoven has already for 13 years sung soprano, contralto and tenor in every emergency that has arisen on the "Duc sahl," is also capable on the violin, wherefore Your Reverend Electoral Grace 27 *Novembris 1762* granted the accompanying decree graciously bearing your own high sign manual *sub Litt. B.*

My humble and obedient but not anticipatory opinion is that the court singer Lentner's vacated salary *ad* 300 fl. (:who went away without the gracious permission of Your Highness over a quarter of a year ago and reported to me *in specie* she was going without permission and would not return:) be graciously divided so that my son be decreed to receive 200 florins and the daughter of Court Musician Ries 100 fl.

Zu Ewr. Churfürst. gnaden beständige hulden und gnaden mich unterthänigst erlassendt in tieffester submission ersterbe.

> Your Reverend Electoral Grace's most humble and obedient
> Ludwig van Beethoven,
> Kapellmeister.

Increase of salary of 100 rthr. for Court Musician Beethoven.
M. F.

Whereas We, Maximilian Friedrich, Elector of Cologne, on the humble petition of our court musician Johann van Beethoven, have shown him the grace to allow him 100 rthr. out of the salary vacated by the departure of the singer Lentner to be paid annually in *quartalien* we hereby confirm the allowance; for which this decree is graciously promulgated to be observed by our Electoral exchequer which is to govern itself accordingly.

Attest p.   Bonn, April 24, 1764.

Under the same date a decree was issued appointing Anna Maria Ries, daughter of Johann Ries, Court Singer, with a salary of 100 th. A few days later the following action was taken:

M. F. E.

To the Electoral Exchequer touching the appointment of Court Musician Beethoven and the Singer Ries.

You are hereby graciously informed that our court musician Bethoven junior and the singer Ries will soon lay before you two decrees of appointment. Now inasmuch as with this the salary of the former singer Lentner is disposed of but since she received an advance of 37½ rth. from our Master of Revenues and 18 rth. *spec.* was paid to her creditors we graciously command you herewith so to arrange the payment of the two salaries that the advance from the Revenues and then the payment to the creditors be covered from Lentner's salary; and that until this is done the salaries of the beforementioned Ries and Bethoven do not begin.

We etc.   Bonn, April 27, 1764.

On April 3, 1778, Anna Maria Ries received an additional 100 fl. A few more documents lead us to the family of Johann Peter Salomon:

ad Supplicam Philip Salomon.

To inform our Kapellmeister van Betthoven appointed on his humble petition that we are not minded to grant the letter prayed for to the Prince v. Sulkowsky, but in case his son is not returned by the beginning of the coming month 8bris, we are graciously determined to make disposition of his place and salary.

Attest. Münster, August 8, 1764.

Sent, the 22 *dito*.

In spite of this order on July 1, 1765, the Elector gave a document to the son, Johann Peter Salomon, certifying that he had served him faithfully and diligently and had "so conducted himself as to deserve to be recommended to every one according to his station." This was the beginning of the career of Salomon. He became concertmaster to Prince Henry of Prussia, played in Paris, and in 1781 took up a residence in London where, as violinist and conductor, he became brilliantly active and successful. He made repeated visits to Bonn, once in 1790, when he was on his way to London accompanied by Haydn. As a result of the petition, the father, Philipp Salomon, and his daughter were appointed Court Musicians by decree dated August 11, 1764.

Several papers, dated April 26, 1768, although upon matters of very small importance, have a certain interest as being in part official communications from the pen of Kapellmeister van Beethoven, and illustrating in some measure his position and duties. They show, too, that his path was not always one bordered with roses. Being self-explanatory they require no comment:

I.

Most Reverend Archbishop and Elector,

Most Gracious Lord, Lord.

Will Your Electoral Grace deign to listen to the complaint that when Court Singer Schwachhofer was commanded in obedience to an order of His Excellency Baron von Belderbusch to alternate with Jacobina Salomon in the singing of the solos in the church music as is the custom, the said Schwachhofer in the presence of the entire chapel impertinently and literally answered me as follows: I will not accept your *ordre* and you have no right to command me.

Your Electoral Grace will doubtless recall various *disordre* on the part of the court chapel indicating that all respect and *ordonance* is withheld from me, each member behaving as he sees fit, which is very painful to my sensibilities.

Wherefore my humble prayer reaches Your Electoral Highness that the public affront of Schwachhofer be punished to my deserved *satisfaction* and that a decree issue from Your Highness to the entire chapel that at the cost of Your Gracious displeasure or punishment according to the offence my *ordre* shall not be evaded.

Your Electoral Grace's

Humble and Most Obedient Servant

Ludovicus van Beethoven.

II.

To Kapellmeister van Beethoven

Concerning the Court Musicians.

M. F. E.

Receive the accompanying Command to the end that its contents be conveyed to all of our court musicians or be posted on the "toxal." We remain, etc.

Bonn, April 26, 1768.

III.
Command respecting the Court Musicians.

Having learned with displeasure that several of our court musicians have tried to evade the *ordre* issued by our Kapellmeister or refused to receive them from him, and conduct themselves improperly amongst themselves, all of our court musicians are hereby earnestly commanded without contradiction to obey all the commands given by our Kapellmeister in our name, and bear peaceful relations with each other, since we are determined to proceed with rigor against the guilty to the extent of dismissal in certain cases.

Sig. Bonn, April 26, 1768.

On November 17, 1769, Johann van Beethoven submitted a petition in which he exhibited anew his genius for devising methods for varying the spelling of his own name. That he could no longer live on 100 th. salary is evident when it is remembered that he had now been married two years; but as there were several applicants for a salary which had fallen to the disposal of the Elector, it was divided among the four most needy. Beethoven's petition contains a fact or two in regard to his duties as Court Musician which are new:

To His Electoral Grace

of Cologne, etc., etc.

The Humble Supplication
and Prayer   of

Johann Bethof, Court Musician.

Most Reverend Archbishop and Elector,

Most Gracious Lord, Lord.

May Your Most Reverend Electoral Grace, graciously permit the presentation of this humble *supplicando,* how for many years I have served Your Highness faithfully and industriously on the "Duc saahl" and the theatre, and also have given instruction in various *supjecta* concerning the aforesaid service to the entire satisfaction of Your Electoral Grate, and am engaged now in study to perfect myself to this end.

My father also joins in this *supplic* in his humble capacity of the *theatri* and will participate in the gladness should Your Electoral Grace graciously grant the favor; as it is impossible for me to live on the salary of 100 th. graciously allowed me, I pray Your Electoral Grace to bestow upon me the 100 th. left at Your gracious disposal by the death of Your court musician Philip Haveck; to merit this high grace by faithful and diligent service shall be my greatest striving.

Your Electoral Grace's most humble

Joannes Bethof,

Court Musician.

In answer to this there came the following decree:

Whereas we, Max. Frid. p. on the death of Court Musician Philipp Haveck and the submissive petition of our court musician Philipp Salomon bestowed upon him the grace of adding 50 fl. for his two daughters to the salary which he already enjoys out of the salary of the above mentioned Haveck per year; we confirm the act hereby; wherefore we have graciously issued, this decree, which our Electoral Court Exchequer will humbly observe and make all necessary provisions.

Attest. p. Münster, 17th 9bris 1769.

[On the margin:] "Gracious addition of 50 fl. for the court musician Philipp Salomon" and, besides Brandt and Meuris, also *"in simili* for Court Musician Joann Bethoff 25 fl."

On the evening of December 24th, 1773, Kapellmeister van Beethoven died. Since the Court Calendar for 1774 had already been printed, his name still stood at the head of the court musicians in this edition.

Musique du Cabinet, de la Chapelle
et de la cour
Intendat—vacat.
Maître de la Chapelle—Mons. Louis van Beethoven
Musiciens Respectives.

Voix

Mess. Lucas Charles Noisten
    Jean van Beethoven
    Christophe Herm. Jos. Brandt
    [Joseph] Daumer, accessist
Mad. Anne Marie Ries
    Maximil. Valentine Delombre,
      née Schwachhofer
    Anne Marie Geyers,
      née Salomon
    Anne Jacobine Salomon
    Elisabeth Trewers, accessistin.

Violons

Mess. Jean Ries
    Erneste Riedel
    Erneste Haveck
    Ferdinand Trewer
    Philippe Salomon
    Ignace Willmann
    Louis Toepser, accessiste

Basse de Viole

Jean Joseph Magdefrau
Francois Tussy

Organiste

Mess. Gilles van den Eeden
    Joseph Clement Meuris, adj.

Contre Basse

Math. Ant. Marie Poletnich

Bassons

Jean [Jos.] Antoine Meuris
[Theodor] Zillicken

Braccistes

Jos. Clem Belserosky
Jean Gottlieb Walter

It is noteworthy that except for two bassoons there are no wind-instruments. The company of Life Guards had two trumpeters: Diederich Baumgarten and Ludwig Toepser (violinist above); these two, along with Franz Bayer and Wilhelm Stumpff, also court trumpeters, are listed *bei dem Hof-Fuder-Amt*; besides these there is still Joh. Bap. Reynard (or Renard), court kettledrummer.

There need be no apology for filling a few more pages with extracts from documents found in the Düsseldorf archives; for now a period has been reached in which the child Ludwig van Beethoven is growing up into youth and early manhood, and thrown into constant contact with those whose names will appear. Some of these names will come up many years later in Vienna; others will have their parts to play in the narrative of that child's life. Omitting, for the present, a petition of Johann van Beethoven, we begin them with that of Joseph Demmer, of date January 23, 1773, which first secured him his appointment after a year's service and three months' instruction from "the young Mr. van Beethoven."

Most Reverend Archbishop and Elector,
Most Gracious Lord, etc., etc.

I have been accepted as chorister in the cathedral of this city at a salary of 80 th. per year, and have so practised myself in music that I humbly flatter myself of my ability to perform my task with the highest satisfaction.

It being graciously known that the bass singer van Beethoven is incapacitated and can no longer serve as such, and the contra-bassist Noisten can not adapt his voice: therefore this my submissive to Your Reverend Electoral Grace that you graciously be pleased to accept me as your bass singer with such gracious salary as may seem fit; I offer should it be demanded to attend the operettas also and qualify myself in a short time. It depends upon a mere hint from Your Electoral Grace alone; that it shall not be burdensome to the cantor's office of the cathedral to save the loss of the 80 th. yearly which it has bestowed upon me.

I am in most dutiful reverence

Your Electoral Grace's most obedient
Joseph Demmer.

Pro Memoria.

Cantor Demmer earned at the utmost 106 rth. per year if he neglected none of the greater or little *Horis.*

Pays the Chamber Chancellor Kügelgen
for board, annually,   66 rth.
for *quartier* [lodging] 12 rth.

moreover, he must find himself in clothes and washing since his father, the sub-sacristan in Cologne, is still overburdened with 6 children.

He has paid 6 rth. to young Mr. Beethoven for 3 months.

In response to another petition after the death of L. van Beethoven the following decree was issued:

Decree as Court vocal bass for Joseph Demmer.

Whereas His Electoral Grace of Cologne, M. F. our most gracious Lord, on the humble petition of Joseph Demmer has graciously appointed and accepted him as His Highness's vocal bass on the Electoral Toxal, with a yearly salary of 200 fl. divided in *quartalien* to begin with the current time, the appointment is confirmed hereby and a decree granted to the same Demmer, of which, for purposes of payment, the Electoral Chancellary will take notice and all whom it may concern will respect and obey the same and otherwise do what is necessary in the premises. Attest. p. Bonn, May 29, 1774.

Two years later, leave of absence, but without salary, was granted to Joseph Demmer to visit Amsterdam to complete his education in music. Here follows further notes drawn from documentary sources:

1774. May 26. Andreas Lucchesi was appointed Court Kapellmeister in place of Ludwig van Beethoven, deceased, with a salary of 1,000 fl.

May 29. The salary of Anna Maria Ries was raised from 250 fl. to 300 fl. On May 13, 1775, together with Ferdinand Trewer (Drewer), violinist, she received a leave of absence for four months, to begin in June, with two quarters' pay in advance. In the Court Calendar for 1775, which was printed about seven months in advance, she was already described as Madame Drewers, née Ries. She was considered the best singer in the chapel.

November 23. Franz Anton Ries was granted 25 th. payable quarterly. On April 13, 1778, he received a six months' leave with two quarters paid in advance, in order to visit Vienna. Brother of Anna Maria, he later became the best violinist of the orchestra and from time to time directed at performances.

1775. March 23. Nikolaus Simrock appointed on petition "Court Hornist on the Electoral Toxal, in the cabinet and at table," and was granted a salary of 300 fl. on April 1. This is the first appearance in these records of a name which afterwards rose into prominence.

1777. April 20. B. J. Maürer, violoncellist, "who has served in the court chapel from the beginning of the year till now on a promise of 100 th.," prays for an appointment as court 'cellist at a salary of 400 th. Appointed at a salary of 200 th.; we shall have occasion to recur to him presently in connection with notices touching Beethoven.

Under date May 22, 1778, J. van Beethoven informed the Elector that "the singer Averdonck, who is to be sent to Kapellmeister Sales at Coblenz, is to pay 15 fl. per month for board and lodging but that only a *douceur* is to be asked for her instruction and that to take her thither will cost 20 th." There followed upon this the following document:

To the humble announcement of Court Musician Beethoven
touching the singer Averdonck
Electoral Councillor Forlivesi is to pay to the proper authorities for a year beginning next month, 15 fl. a month and for the traveling expenses 20 rth. once and for all as soon as the journey is begun. Attest. p. Bonn, May 22, 1778.

This pupil of Johann van Beethoven, Johanna Helena Averdonk, born in Bonn on December 11, 1760, and brought forward by her teacher at a concert in Cologne, received 120 th. "as a special grace" on July 2, and was appointed Court Singer on November 18, 1780, with a salary of 200 th. She died nine years later, August 13, 1789.

The petitions sent in to the Elector were rarely dated and were not always immediately attended to; therefore the date of a *decretum* is not to be taken as conclusive in regard to the date of facts mentioned in a petition. An illustration is afforded by a petition of Franz Ries. He returned from a tour to

Vienna and prayed for a salary of 500 fl. "not the half of what he can earn elsewhere." The petition is dated March 2. Two months passing without bringing him an answer, he petitioned again and obtained a decree on May 2 that in addition to his salary of 28 th. 2 alb. 6, he would receive "annoch so viel,"—again as much—i.e., 400 florins.

1780. August. Court Organist Van den Eede prays that in consideration of his service of 54 years he be graciously and charitably given the salary vacated by the death of Court Musician Salomon. Eighteen others make the same prayer. The decision of the privy council is in these words: "To be divided between Huttenus and Esch. A degree as musical vocalist must first be given to the latter."

1781. February 15. The name of C. G. Neefe is now met with for the first time. He had been in Bonn since 1779. He petitions for appointment to the position of organist in succession to Van den Eede, obviously aged and infirm. A decree was issued *"placet et expediatur* on the death of Organist Van den Eede," and a salary of 400 fl. granted.

1782. May 16. Johann van Beethoven petitions for "the three measures (*Malter*) of corn."

The archives of Düsseldorf furnish little more during the time of Max Friedrich save certain papers relating to the Beethoven family, which are reserved for another place.

The search for means to form some correct idea of the character of the musical performances at the Elector's court during this reign has been more successful than for the preceding; but much is left to be desired down to the year 1778, when the theatre was placed upon a different basis and its history is sufficiently recorded. Such notices, however, in relation to the operatic entertainments as have been found scattered, mostly in newspapers of Bonn, in those years, are numerous enough to give an idea of their character; while the remarks upon the festivities of the court, connected with them, afford a pretty lively picture of social amusement in the highest circle. We make room for some of the most significant occurrences, in chronological order:

1764. January 3. Galuppi's opera *Il Filosofo di Campagna*, given in the Electoral Theatre with great applause.

January 8. A grand assembly at the palace in the afternoon, a magnificent supper in the grand gallery at which many spectators were present, and finally a masked ball.

March 23. Second performance of *La buona Figliuola*, music by Piccini.

May 13. Elector's birthday; *Le Nozze*, music by Galuppi, and two ballets.

May 20. *Il Filosofo* again, the notice of which is followed by the remark that the Elector is about to move to Brühl for the summer but will visit Bonn twice a week "on the days when operas are performed."

September 21. *La Pastorella al Soglio* (composer not named, probably Latilla), and two ballets.

December 16. *La Calamità di cuori*, by Galuppi, and two ballets. This was "the first performance by the Mingotti company under the direction of Rizzi and Romanini."

1765. January 6. *Le Aventure di Rodolfo* (Piccini?), given by the same company together with a pantomime, *L'Arlequino fortunato per la Maggia*. After the play there was a grand supper at which the Pope's nuncio was a guest, and finally a masked ball kept up till six in the morning.

1767. May 13. The Archbishop's birthday. Here is the programme condensed from the long description of the festivities in the *Bonnischer Anzeiger*:

1, Early in the morning three rounds from the cannon on the city walls;
2, The court and public graciously permitted to kiss His Transparency's hand;
3, Solemn high mass with salvos of artillery;
4, Grand dinner in public, at which both papal nuncios, the foreign ministers and the nobility were the guests; and the eating was accompanied by "exquisite table-music";
5, After dinner "a numerously attended assembly";
6, "A serenata composed especially for this most joyful day" and a comic opera in the palace theatre;
7, Supper of 130 covers;
8, *Bal masqué* until 5 a.m.

Evidently the finances under Belderbusch's management had improved, or else the Elector had become very reckless in his expenditures. The two dramatic pieces were "Serenata festivale, tra Bacco, Diana ed il Reno," the authors unnamed, and *Schiava finta*, "drama giocoso dal celebre don Francesco Garzia, Spagnuolo," the music probably by Piccini; "Giovanni van Beethoven" sang the part of Dorindo.

1768. May 16. "On the stage of the Court Theatre was performed with much applause a musical poem in German, especially written for the birthday of His Highness and afterwards an Italian intermezzo entitled *La Nobiltà delusa*."

1769. The festivities in honor of the birthday of the Elector took place May 17, when, according to the *Anzeiger*, "an Italian musical drama written expressly for the occasion was performed"—but the title suggests the possibility of a mistake; *Il Riso d'Apolline*, with music by Petz, had been heard in 1701.

1770. A revival of a French oratorio, *Saint Ciprien et Sainte Justine Martirs*, originally presented under Clemens August. The composer is unknown, the revival was with Italian text, and Ludwig, the Kapellmeister, sang the part of "Eusebio Sacerdote Christiano occulto."

1771. For this year a single discovery only has rewarded search, that of a textbook, one of particular interest: *Silvain*, "comédie en une acte, mêlée d'ariettes représentée" etc. Text by Marmontel, music by Grétry. "Dolmon père, Mons. Louis van Beethoven, Maître de Chapelle; Dolmon, fils ainé, Jean van Beethoven." etc.

1772. On February 27, *Le Donne sempre Donne*, music by Andreas Lucchesi. In March, on the occasion of the opening of the Estates, *La Contadine in Corte*, music by Sacchini.

The pieces given on the birthday this year were *Il Natal di Giove*, music by Lucchesi, and *La buona Figliuola*, music by Piccini. On the 17th the latter was repeated on the arrival of the French ambassador.

1773. May 13. The Elector's birthday; *L'Inganno scoperto, overo il Conte Caramella*, music by Lucchesi, in which Ludovico van Beethoven sang the part of "Brunoro, contadino e tamburino."

There are three more operettas which evidently belong to the succeeding winter when the Bonn company had the aid of two singers from the electoral court of Trèves. Their titles are *L'Improvisata, o sia la Galanteria disturbata*, by Lucchesi, *Li tre Amanti ridicoli*, by Galuppi, and *La Moda*, by Boroni. Ludwig van Beethoven did not sing in them. The means are still wanting to fill up the many gaps in the annals of this period or to carry them on during the next three years. Perhaps, however, the loss is not of much importance, for the materials collected are sufficient to warrant certain conclusions in regard to the general character of the court music. The musicians, both vocal and instrumental, were employed in the church, concert-room and theatre; their number remained without material change from the days of Christopher Petz[11] to the close of Kapellmeister van Beethoven's life; places in this service were held to be a sort of heritage, and of right due to the children of old incumbents, when possessed of sufficient musical talent and knowledge; few if any names of distinguished virtuosos are found in the lists of the members, and, in all probability, the performances never rose above the respectable mediocrity of a small band used to playing together in the light and pleasing music of the day.

The dramatic performances appear to have been confined to the operetta; and the vocalists, who sang the Latin of the mass, seem to have been required to be equally at home in German, Italian and French in the theatre. Two visits of the Angelo Mingotti troupe are noted; and one attempt, at least, to place the opera upon a higher basis by the engagement of Italian songstresses, was evidently made in the time of Clemens August; it may be concluded that no great improvement was made—it is certain that no permanent one was; for otherwise the Bonn theatrical revolution of 1778 would not have been needed. This must be noticed in detail.

Chronologically the following sketch belongs to the biography of Ludwig van Beethoven, as it embraces a period which happens in his case to be of special interest, young as he was;—the period from his 8th to his 14th year. But the details given, though of great importance for the light which they throw upon the musical life in which he moved and acted, would hardly be of so much interest to most readers as to justify breaking with them the course of the future narrative.

It was a period of great awakening in theatrical matters. Princes and courts were beginning everywhere in Germany to patronize the drama of their mother tongue and the labors of Lessing, Gotter and other well-known

[11] Johann Christoph Petz was appointed Kapellmeister January 1, 1695. See TDR, I, 12.

names, in the original production of German, or in the translation of the best English, Italian and French plays, were justifying and giving ever new impulse to the change in taste. From the many itinerant troupes of players performing in booths, or, in the larger cities, in the play-houses, the better class of actors were slowly finding their way into permanent companies engaged and supported by the governments. True, many of the newly established court theatres had but a short and not always a very merry life; true, also, that the more common plan was merely to afford aid and protection to some itinerant troupe; still the idea of a permanent national theatre on the footing of the already long-existing court musical establishments had made way, and had already been carried out in various places before it was taken up by the Elector at Bonn. It can hardly be supposed that the example of the imperial court at Vienna, with the immense means at its disposal, could exert any direct influence upon the small court at Bonn at the other extremity of Germany; but what the Duke of Gotha and the Elector at Mannheim had undertaken in this direction, Max Friedrich may well have ventured and determined to imitate. But there was an example nearer home—in fact in his own capital of Münster, where he, the prince primate, usually spent the summer. In 1775, Dobbler's troupe, which had been for some time playing in that city, was broken up.

The Westhus brothers in Münster built up their own out of the ruins; but it endured only a short time. Thereupon, under the care of the minister, H. von Fürstenberg (one of those rare men whom heaven elects and equips with all necessary gifts to cultivate what is good and beautiful in the arts), a meeting of the lovers of the stage was arranged in May and a few gentlemen of the nobility and a few from the parterre formed a council which assumed the direction. The Elector makes a considerable contribution. The money otherwise received is to be applied to the improvement of the wardrobe and the theatre. The actors receive their honoraria every month.[12]

At Easter, 1777, Seyler, a manager famous in German theatrical annals, and then at Dresden, finding himself unable to compete with his rival, Bondini, left that city with his company to try his fortunes in Frankfurt-am-Main, Mainz, and other cities in that quarter. The company was very large— the Theatre Lexicon (Article "Mainz") makes it, including its orchestra, amount to 230 individuals!—much too large, it seems, in spite of the assertion of the Theatre Lexicon, to be profitable. Be that as it may, after an experience of a year or more, two of the leading members, Grossmann and Helmuth, accepted an engagement from Max Friedrich to form and manage a company at Bonn in order that "the German art of acting might be raised to a school of morals and manners for his people." Taking with them a pretty large portion of Seyler's company, including several of the best members, the managers reached Bonn and were ready upon the Elector's return from

---

[12] Reichardt, *Theaterkalender*, *1778*, p. 99 (TDR, I, 73, n. 1.)

Münster to open a season. "The opening of the theatre took place," says the Bonn *Dramaturgische Nachrichten*, "on the 26th of November, 1778, with a prologue spoken by Madame Grossmann, *Wilhelmine Blondheim*, tragedy in three acts by Grossmann, and *Die grosse Batterie*, comedy in one act by Ayrenhofer." The same authority gives a list of all the performances of the season, which extended to the 30th of May, 1779, together with débuts, the dismissals and other matters pertaining to the actors. The number of the evenings on which the theatre was open was 50. A five-act play, as a rule, occupied the whole performance, but of shorter pieces usually two were given; and thus an opening was found occasionally for an operetta. Of musical dramas only seven came upon the stage and these somewhat of the lightest order except the first—the melodrama *Ariadne auf Naxos*, music by Benda. The others were:

1779. February 21. *Julie*, translated from the French by Grossmann, music by Dezède.

February 28. *Die Jäger und das Milchmädchen*, operetta in one act, music by Duni.

March 21. *Der Hufschmied*, in two acts, music by Philidor.

April 9. *Röschen und Colas*, in one act, music by Monsigny.

May 5. *Der Fassbinder*, in one act, music by Audinot.

May 14. A prologue with songs "Dedicated to the Birthday Festivities of His Electoral Grace of Cologne, May 13, 1779, by J. A. Freyherr vom Hagen." Music by Helmuth.

The selection of dramas was, on the whole, very creditable to the taste of the managers. Five of Lessing's works, among them *Minna von Barnhelm* and *Emilia Galotti*, are in the list and some of the best productions of Bock, Gotter, Engel and their contemporaries; of translations there were Colman's *Clandestine Marriage* and *Jealous Wife*, Garrick's *Miss in her Teens*, Cumberland's *West Indian*, Hoadly's *Suspicious Husband*, Voltaire's *Zaire* and *Jeannette*, Beaumarchais's *Eugénie*, two or three of the works of Molière, and Goldoni, etc.;—in short, the list presents much variety and excellence.

Max Friedrich was evidently pleased with the company, for the *Nachrichten* has the following in the catalogue of performances: "On the 8th [of April] His Electoral Grace was pleased to give a splendid breakfast to the entire company in the theatre. . . . The company will occupy itself until the return of His Electoral Grace from Münster, which will be in the middle of November, with learning the newest and best pieces, among which are *Hamlet, King Lear* and *Macbeth*, which are to be given also with much splendor of costume according to the designs of famous artists."

It may be remarked here that the "Bonn Comedy House" (for painting the interior of which Clemens August paid 468 thalers in 1751, a date which seems to fix the time at which that end of the palace was completed), occupied that portion of the University Archaeological Museum room next to the Coblenz Gate.[13] The older building had large doors opening from the stage into the passageway so that this space could be used as an extension of the stage in pieces requiring it for the production of grand scenic effects. Above the theatre was the "Redouten-Saal" of Max Franz's time. The Elector had, of course, an entrance from the passages of the palace into his box. The door for the public, in an angle of the wall now built up, opened out upon the grove of horse-chestnuts. The auditorium was necessarily low, but spacious enough for several hundred spectators. Though much criticized by travellers as being unworthy so elegant a court, not to say shabby, it seems to have been a nice and snug little theatre.

Meanwhile affairs with Seyler were drawing to a crisis. He had returned with his company from Mannheim and reopened at Frankfurt, August 3, 1779. On the evening of the 17th, to escape imprisonment as a bankrupt, whether through his own fault or that of another—the Theatre Lexicon affirms the latter case—he took his wife and fled to Mainz. The company was allowed by the magistrates to play a few weeks with a view of earning at least the means of leaving the city; but on October 4, its members began to separate. Borchers and his wife went to Hamburg, Benda and his wife went to Berlin, etc., but C. G. Neefe, the music director, and Opitz descended the Rhine to Bonn with their families and joined the company there. Neefe assumed the direction of the music in the theatre for awhile.

The season 1779-80 opened on December 3rd, the evening after the Elector's return from Münster, with a prologue "Wir haben Ihn wieder!" The text was by Baron von Hagen and there were airs, recitatives, and choruses by Neefe.

The season was interrupted on March 16 by a trip to Frankfurt made by the Grossmann troupe in order to open the theatre there on March 28th. In early April the company returned to Bonn and continued the season until its close at the end of May. The performances in which music was to be provided were as follows: Benda's *Pygmalion*, February 24th; Monsigny's *Die schöne Arsene* (*La belle Arsène*), March 9th; Hiller's *Jagd*, May 7th; Dezède's *Die drei Pächter* (*Les trois fermiers*), May 21st; Schweitzer's *Die Dorfgala*, May 26th; Monsigny's *Der Deserteur* (*Le Déserteur*), May 28th; Benda's *Walder*, May 31st.

The troupe then went to Cologne where they played from June 4th to August 25th. Grossmann later visited Frankfurt from whence he was called back to Bonn by the arrival there of Maximilian. The season of 1780-81 was longer, lasting from October 4th until April 5th; but performances with music were few. The first was Grétry's *Das Blendwerk* (*La fausse Magie*), November 19th; then Philidor's *Der Hufschmied* (*Blaise le savetier*), December 6th; Benda's *Der Holzhauer*, December 13th; an opera by Paisiello

---

[13] According to Professor Schmidt-Görg, director of the Beethoven Archives in Bonn, this building served as the University Library until it was destroyed by bombing in October, 1944. It is being rebuilt.

(which one is not clear), January 31st; Dezède's *Die drei Pächter*, February 11th; Grétry's *Das Urteil des Midas* (*Le Jugement de Midas*), February 21st.

With the close of the winter season, Grossmann and Helmuth started once again on a spring tour: Frankfurt from April 17th to June 1st, Pyrmont from June 17th to August 5th, Kassel from August 13th to September 29th.[14]

The season of 1781-82 was a busy one; of musical dramas alone 17 are reported as newly rehearsed from September, 1781, to the same time in 1782, viz:

MUSIC BY

Die Liebe unter den Handwerkern (*L'Amore Artigiano*)	Gassmann
Robert und Calliste	Guglielmi
Der Alchymist	Schuster
Das tartarische Gesetz	d'Antoine (of Bonn)
Der eifersüchtige Liebhaber (*L'Amant jaloux*)	Grétry
Der Hausfreund (*L'Ami de la Maison*)	Grétry
Die Freundschaft auf der Probe (*L'Amitié à l'Épreuve*)	Grétry
Heinrich und Lyda	Neefe
Die Apotheke	Neefe
Romeo und Julie	Benda
Sophonisba (Deklamation mit Musik)	Neefe
Lucille	Grétry
Milton und Elmire	Michl
Die Samnitische Vermählungsfeier (*Les Mariages Samnites*)	Grétry
Ernst und Lucinde	Grétry
Günther von Schwarzburg	Holzbauer

It does not follow, however, that all these operas, operettas and plays with music were produced during the season in Bonn. The company followed the Elector to Münster in June 1782, and removed thence to Frankfurt-am-Main for its regular series of performances at Michaelmas. It came back to Bonn in the autumn.

The season 1782-83 was as active as the preceding. Some of the newly rehearsed spoken dramas were *Sir John Falstaff*, from the English, translations of Sheridan's *School for Scandal*, Shakespeare's *Lear*, and *Richard III*, Mrs. Cowley's *Who's the Dupe?* and, of original German plays, Schiller's *Fiesco* and *Die Räuber*, Lessing's *Miss Sara Sampson*, Schroeder's *Testament*, etc., etc. The number of newly rehearsed musical dramas—in which class are

---

[14] The additional information on the Bonn theatre has been supplied by Joseph Wolter, *Gustav Friedrich Wilhelm Grossmann*, Diss. (Cologne, 1901).

included such ballad operas as General Burgoyne's *Maid of the Oaks*—reached twenty, viz:

MUSIC BY

Das Rosenfest	Wolf [of Weimar]
Azalia	Johann Küchler
	[Bassoonist in the Bonn chapel]
Die Sklavin (La Schiava)	Piccini
Zémire et Azor	Grétry
Das Mädchen im Eichthale	
(Maid of the Oaks)	d'Antoine
	[Captain in the army of the Elector of Cologne]
Der Kaufmann von Smyrna	J. A. Juste
	[Court Musician in The Hague]
Die seidenen Schuhe	Alexander Frizer
	[or Fridzeri]
Die Reue vor der That	Dezède
Der Aerndtetanz	J. A. Hiller
Die Olympischen Spiele (Olympiade)	Sacchini
Die Lügnerin aus Liebe	Salieri
Die Italienerin zu London	Cimarosa
Das gute Mädchen (La buona figliuola)	Piccini
Der Antiquitäten-Sammler	André
Die Entführung aus dem Serail	Mozart
Die Eifersucht auf der Probe	
(Il Geloso in Cimento)	Anfossi
Rangstreit und Eifersucht auf dem Lande	
(Le Gelosie villane)	Sarti
Unverhofft kommt oft (Les Évènements	
imprévus)	Grétry
Felix, oder der Findling (Félix ou	
l'Enfant trouvé)	Monsigny
Die Pilgrimme von Mekka	Gluck

But a still farther provision was made for the Elector's amusement during the season of 1783-84, by the engagement of a ballet corps of eighteen persons. The titles of five newly rehearsed ballets are given in the report from which the above particulars were taken, and which may be found in the theatrical calendar for 1784.

With an enlarged company and a more extensive repertory, preparations were made for opening the theatre upon the Elector's return, at the end of October, from Münster to Bonn. But the relations of the company to the court were changed. Let the *Theaterkalender* describe the new position in which the stage at Bonn was placed:

Bonn. His Electoral Grace, by a special condescension, has graciously determined to make the theatrical performances gratuitous and to that end has closed a contract with His Highness's Theatrical Director Grossmann according to which besides the theatre free of rent, the illumination and the orchestra, he is to receive an annual subvention for the maintenance of the company. On His Highness's command there will be two or three performances weekly. By particular grace the director is permitted to spend several summer months in other places. The members are to be drawn from the above-named Grossmann company.

The advantages of this plan for securing a good repertory, a good company and a zealous striving for improvement are obvious; and its practical working during this, its only, season, so far as can now be gathered from scanty records, was a great success. It will hereafter be seen that the boy Ludwig van Beethoven was often employed at the pianoforte at the rehearsals and possibly also at the performances of the company of which Neefe was the musical director. A company consisting almost exclusively of performers who had passed the ordeal of frequent appearance on the stage and had been selected with full knowledge of the capacity of each, and which, moreover, had gained so much success at the Bonn court as to be put upon a permanent footing, must have been one of more than the ordinary, average excellence, at least in light opera. No comments need be made upon the influence which daily intercourse with it, and sharing in its labors, especially in the direction of opera, must have exerted upon the mind of a boy of twelve or thirteen years possessed of real musical genius.

The theatrical season, and with it the company, came to an untimely end. Belderbusch died in January, 1784. Madame Grossmann died in childbed on March 29, and on April 15 the Elector followed them to another world. After the death of the Elector Maximilian Friedrich the Court Theatre was closed for the official mourning and the company dismissed with four weeks' salary.

It is consonant to the plan of this introductory chapter that some space be devoted to sketches of some of the principal men whose names have already occurred and to some notes upon the musical amateurs of Bonn who are known, or may be supposed, to have been friends of the boy Beethoven. These notices make no claim to the credit of being the result of original research; they are, except that of Neefe, little more than extracts from a letter, dated March 2, 1783, written by Neefe and printed in Cramer's *Magazin der Musik* (Vol. I, pp. 337 *et seq.*). At that time the "Capelldirector," as Neefe calls him, was Cajetano Mattioli, born at Venice, August 7, 1750, whose appointments as concertmaster and musical director in Bonn were made on May 26, 1774 and April 24, 1777. Neefe says:

"He studied in Parma with the first violinist Angelo Moriggi, a pupil of Tartini, and in Parma, Mantua and Bologna conducted grand operas like *Orfeo, Alceste*, etc., by the Chevalier Gluck with success. He owed much to the example set by Gluck in the matter of conducting. It must be admitted that he is a man full of fire, of lively temperament and fine feeling. He penetrates quickly into the intentions of a composer and knows how to convey them promptly and clearly to the entire orchestra. He was the first to introduce accentuation, instrumental declamation, careful attention to forte and piano, or all the degrees of light and shade in the orchestra of this place. His bowing has great variety. In none of the qualifications of a leader is he second to the famed Cannabich of Mannheim. He surpasses him in musical enthusiasm, and, like him, insists upon discipline and order. Through his efforts the musical repertory of this court has been provided with a very considerable collection of good and admirable compositions, symphonies, masses and other works, to which he makes daily additions; in the same manner he is continually striving for the betterment of the orchestra. Just now he is engaged in a project for building a new organ for the court chapel. The former organ, a magnificent instrument, became a prey of the flames at the great conflagration in the palace in 1777. His salary is 1,000 fl.

"The kapellmeister [appointed May 26, 1774] was Mr. Andrea Lucchesi, born May 28, 1741, at Motta in Venetian territory. His teachers in composition were, in the theatre style, Mr. Cocchi of Naples; in the church style, Father Paolucci, a pupil of Padre Martini at Bologna, and afterwards Mr. Seratelli, Kapellmeister of the Duke of Venice. He is a good organist and occupied himself profitably with the instrument in Italy. He came here with Mr. Mattioli as conductor of an Italian opera company in 1771. Taken altogether he is a light, pleasing and gay composer whose part-writing is cleaner than that of most of his countrymen. In his church-works he does not confine himself to the strict style affected by many to please amateurs."

Neefe enumerates Lucchesi's compositions as follows: nine works for the theatre, among them the opera *L'Isola della Fortuna* (1765), *Il Marito geloso* (1766), *Le Donne sempre Donne, Il Matrimonio per astuzia* (1771) for Venice, and the two operas composed at Bonn, *Il Natal di Giove* and *L'inganno scoperto*, various intermezzi and cantatas; various masses, vespers and other compositions for the church; six sonatas for the pianoforte and violin; a pianoforte trio, four pianoforte quartets and several pianoforte concertos. His salary was 1,000 florins.

The organist of the Court Chapel was Christian Gottlob Neefe, son of a poor tailor of Chemnitz in Saxony, where he was born February 5, 1748. He is one of the many instances in musical history in which the career of the man is determined by the beauty of his voice in childhood. At a very early age he became a chorister in the principal church, which position gave him the best school and musical instruction that the small city afforded—advantages so wisely improved as to enable him in early youth to gain a living by teaching. At the age of 21, with 20 thalers in his pocket and a stipend of 30 thalers per annum from the magistrates of Chemnitz, he removed to Leipzig to attend the lectures of the university, and at that institution in the course of time he passed his examination in jurisprudence. Upon this occasion he argued the negative of the question: "Has a father the right to disinherit a son for devoting himself to the theatre?" In Chemnitz Neefe's teachers in music had been men of small talents and very limited acquirements, and even in Leipzig he owed more to his persevering study of the theoretical works of Marpurg and C. P. E. Bach than to any regular instructor. But there he had the very great advantage of forming an intimate acquaintance with, and becoming an object of special interest to, Johann Adam Hiller, the celebrated director of the Gewandhaus Concerts, the then popular and famous composer, the introducer of Handel's *Messiah* to the German public, the industrious writer upon music, and finally a successor of Johann Sebastian Bach as Cantor of the Thomas School. Hiller gave him every encouragement in his power in his musical career; opened the columns of his musical *Wöchentliche Nachrichten* to his compositions and writings; called him to his assistance in operatic composition; gave him the results of his long experience in friendly advice; criticized his compositions, and at length, in 1777, gave him his own position as music director of Seyler's theatrical company, then playing at the Linkische Bad in Dresden. Upon the departure of that troupe for Frankfurt-am-Main, Neefe was persuaded to remain with it in the same capacity. He thus became acquainted with Fräulein Zinck, previously court singer at Gotha but now engaged for Seyler's opera. The acquaintance ripened into a mutual affection and ended in marriage not long afterward.

It is no slight testimony to the high reputation which he enjoyed that at the moment of Seyler's flight from Frankfurt (1779) Bondini, whose success had driven that rival from Dresden, was in correspondence with Neefe and making him proposals to resign his position under Seyler for a similar but better one in his service. Pending the result of these negotiations Neefe, taking his wife with him, temporarily joined Grossmann and Helmuth at Bonn in the same capacity. ─From Leux[15] we learn that once Bondini's contract arrived, Grossmann tried to persuade him to stay, first with promises and favors, then with threats. When this was unsuccessful, the director had his effects seized. While Neefe was objecting, time ran out for the securing of the Dresden job.─ Having once got him, Grossmann was determined to keep him—and succeeded.

There were others besides Grossmann and Helmuth who thought Neefe too valuable an acquisition to the musical circles of Bonn not to be secured. Less than a year and a half after his arrival there, the minister Belderbusch and the countess Hatzfeld, niece of the Elector, secured to him, though a Protestant, an appointment to the place of court organist. The salary of 400 florins, together with the 700 florins from Grossmann, made his income equal to that of the court kapellmeister. It is difficult now to conceive of the forgotten name of C. G. Neefe as having once stood high in the list of the first North German composers; yet such was the case. Among Neefe's published compositions, besides the short vocal and clavier pieces in Hiller's

[15] Irmgard Leux, *Christian Gottlob Neefe* (Leipzig, 1925), p. 66.

periodical and other collections, there had already appeared operettas in vocal score, *Die Apotheke* (1772), *Amor's Guckkasten* (1772), *Die Ein-sprüche* (1773), and *Heinrich und Lyda* (1777); also airs composed for Hiller's *Dorf-Barbier* and one from his own unpublished opera *Zemire und Azor*; twelve odes of Klopstock—sharply criticized by Forkel in his *Musikal-isch-Kritische Bibliotek*, much to the benefit of the second edition of them; and a pretty long series of songs.

—**Of** instrumental music he had printed twelve clavier sonatas dedicated to Philipp Emanuel Bach (1773); six clavier sonatas and a set of variations dedicated to Agricola (1774); six clavier sonatas with optional accompani-ment for violin (1776); *Vademecum für Liebhaber des Gesangs und Clavier*; and a clavier concerto in G dedicated to the Elector of Saxony. The following remained in manuscript: Partita in D minor for 2 horns, 2 oboes, 2 flutes, 2 bassoons and string quartet (1772); Partita in E-flat for 2 oboes and string quartet (1774); and a violin sonata (1781). Of these four, only the man-uscript to the partita in E-flat has survived.[16]**

The *Sophonisbe* music was also finished and twenty years later, after Mozart had given a new standard of criticism, it was warmly eulogized in the *Allgemeine Musikzeitung* of Leipzig. At the date of his letter to Cramer (March 2, 1783) he had added to his published works the clavier score of *Sophonisbe*. His manuscripts, he adds (Cramer's *Magazin*, I, p. 382), consist of (a) the scores of the operettas which had appeared in pianoforte arrangements; (b) the score of his opera *Zemire und Azor*; (c) the score of his opera *Adelheit von Veltheim*; (d) the score of a bardic song for the tragedy *The Romans in Germany*; (e) the scores of theatrical between-acts music; (f) the score of a Latin *Pater noster*; (g) various other smaller works. He had in hand the composition of the operetta *Der neue Gutsherr*, the pianoforte score of which, as also that of *Adelheit von Veltheim*, was about to be published by Dyck in Leipzig. A year before at a concert for amateurs at the house of Mr. von Mastiaux he had produced an ode by Klopstock, *Dem Unendlichen*, for four chorus voices and a large orchestra, which was afterwards performed in Holy Week in the Fräuleinstiftskirche. In short, Neefe brought to Bonn a high-sounding reputation, talent, skill and culture both musical and literary, which made him invaluable to the mana-gers when new French and Italian operas were to be prepared for the German stage; great facility in throwing off a new air, song, entr'acte or what not to meet the exigencies of the moment; very great industry, a *cacoethes scribendi* of the very highest value to the student of Bonn's musical history in his time and a new element into the musical life there.

Let us return to Neefe's letter to Cramer again for some notices of music outside the electoral palace:

[16] According to Leux, *op.cit.*, p. 118; in the Bibliothek Schwerin.

Belderbusch, the minister, retained a quintet of wind-instruments, 2 clarinets, 2 horns and a bassoon.

The Countess von Belderbusch, wife of a nephew of the minister, whose name will come up again, "plays skilfully upon the clavier."

The Countess von Hatzfeld, niece of the Elector, was "trained in singing and clavier playing by the best masters of Vienna to whom, indeed, she does very much honor. She declaims recitatives admirably and it is a pleasure to listen to her sing arias *di parlante*. She plays the fortepiano brilliantly and in playing yields herself up completely to her emotions, wherefore one never hears any restlessness or unevenness of time in her *tempo rubato*. She is enthusiastically devoted to music and musicians."[17]

Chancellor and Captain von Schall "plays clavier and violin. Though not adept on either instrument he has very correct musical feeling. He knows how to appreciate the true beauties of a composition, and how to judge them, and has large historical and literary knowledge of music."

Frau Court Councillor von Pelzer "plays the clavier and sings. She has a strong, masculine contralto of wide range, particularly downwards."

Johann Gottfried von Mastiaux, of the Finance Department and incumbent of divers high offices, is a self-taught musician. He plays several instruments himself and has given his four sons and a daughter the best musical instruction possible in Bonn. All are pianists and so many of them performers on other instruments that the production of quintets is a common family enjoyment. He is a devoted admirer of Haydn, with whom he corresponds, and in his large collection of music there are already 80 symphonies, 30 quartets and 40 trios by that master. His rare and valuable instruments are so numerous "that he could almost equip a complete orchestra. Every musician is his friend and welcome to him."

Count Altstädter: "in his house one may at times hear a very good quartet."

Captain Dantoine, "a passionate admirer and knower of music; plays the violin and the clavier a little. He learned composition from the books of Marpurg, Kirnberger and Riepel. Formed his taste in Italy. In both respects the reading of scores by classical masters has been of great service to him." Among his compositions are several operettas, symphonies and quartets "in Haydn's style."

The three Herrn. Facius, "sons of the Russian agent here, are soundly musical; the two elder play the flute and the youngest plays the violoncello." [According to Fischer the members of this family were visitors at the house of the Beethovens.]

There are many more music-lovers here, but the majority of them are too much given to privacy, so far as their musical practice goes, to be mentioned here. Enough has been said to show that a stranger fond of music need never leave Bonn without nourishment. Nevertheless, a large public concert institution under the patronage of His Electoral Grace is still desirable. It would be one more ornament of the capital and a promoter of the good cause of music.

What with the theatre, the court music, the musical productions in the church and such opportunities in private it is plain that young talent in those days in Bonn was in no danger of starvation for want of what Neefe calls "musikalische Nahrung."

[17] To her Beethoven dedicated his variations on "Venni Amore." (TDR, I, 98.)

So much upon the *dramatis personae*, other than the principal figure and his family. Let an attempt follow to describe the little city as it appeared in 1770—in other words, to picture the scene. By an enumeration made in 1789, the population of Bonn was 9,560 souls, a number which probably for a long series of years had rarely varied beyond a few score, more or less—one, therefore, that must very nearly represent the aggregate in 1770. For the town had neither manufactures nor commerce beyond what its own wants supported; it was simply the residence of the Elector—the seat of the court, and the people depended more or less directly upon that court for subsistence—as a wag expressed it, "all Bonn was fed from the Elector's kitchen." The old city walls—(the "gar gute Fortification, dass der Churfürst sicher genug darinnen Hof halten kann" of Johann Hübner's description)—were already partially destroyed. Within them the whole population seems to have lived. Outside the city gates it does not appear that, save by a chapel or two, the eye was impeded in its sweep across gardens and open fields to the surrounding villages which, then as now hidden in clusters of walnut and fruit trees, appeared, when looked upon from the neighboring hills, like islands rising upon the level surface of the plain. The great increase of wealth and population during the last 50 years[18] in all this part of the Rhine valley under the influence of the wise national economy of the Prussian government, has produced corresponding changes in and about the towns and villages; but the grand features of the landscape are unchanged; the ruins upon the Drachenfels and Godesberg looked down, as now, upon the distant roofs and spires of Bonn; the castle of Siegburg rose above the plains away to the East; the chapel crowned the Petersberg, the church with the marble stairs the nearer Kreuzberg.

The fine landing place with its growing trees and seats for idlers, the villas, hotels, coffee-houses and dwellings outside the old walls, are all recent; but the huge ferryboat, the "flying bridge," even then was ever swinging like a pendulum from shore to shore. Steam as a locomotive power was unknown, and the commerce of the Rhine floated by the town, gliding down with the current on rafts or in clumsy but rather picturesque boats, or impelled against the stream by the winds, by horses and even by men and women. The amount of traffic was not, however, too great to be amply provided for in this manner; for population was kept down by war, by the hard and rude life of the peasant class, and by the influences of all the false national-economic principles of that age, which restrained commerce by every device that could be made to yield present profit to the rulers of the Rhine lands. Passengers had, for generations, no longer been plundered by mail-clad robbers dwelling upon a hundred picturesque heights; but each petty state had gained from the Emperor's weakness "vested rights" in all sorts of custom-levies and taxes. Riesbeck (1780) found nine toll-stations between Mainz and Coblenz; and

---

[18] The reader is reminded that Thayer wrote this in the early 1860's.

thence to the boundary of Holland; he declared there were at least sixteen, and that in the average each must have collected 30,000 Rhenish florins per annum.

To the stranger, coming down from Mainz, with its narrow dark lanes, or up from Cologne, whose confined and pestiferously dirty streets, emitting unnamed stenches, were but typical of the bigotry, superstition and moral filth of the population, little Bonn seemed a very picture of neatness and comfort. Even its ecclesiastical life seemed of another order. The men of high rank in the church were of high rank also by birth; they were men of the world and gentlemen; their manners were polished and their minds enlarged by intercourse with the world and with gentlemen; they were tolerant in their opinions and liberal in their views. Ecclesiastics of high and low degree were met at every corner as in other cities of the Rhine region; but absence of military men was a remarkable feature. Johann Hübner gives the reason for this in few and quaint words:—"In times of war much depends upon who is master of Bonn, because traffic on the Rhine can be blockaded at this pass. Therefore the place has its excellent fortification which enables the Elector to hold his court in ample security within its walls. But he need not maintain a garrison there in time of peace, and in time of war troops are garrisoned who have taken the oath to the Emperor and the empire. This was settled by the peace of Ryswick as well as Rastatt."

While the improvement in the appearance of the streets of Bonn has necessarily been great, through the refitting or rebuilding of a large portion of the dwelling-houses, the plan of the town, except in those parts lying near the wall, has undergone no essential change, the principal one being the open spaces, where in 1770 churches stood. On the small triangular Römer-Platz was the principal parish church of Bonn, that of St. Remigius, standing in such a position that its tall tower looked directly down the Acherstrasse. In 1800 this tower was set on fire by lightning and destroyed; six years later the church itself was demolished by the French and its stones removed to become a part of the fortifications at Wesel. On the small, round grass plot as one goes from the Münster church toward the neighboring city gate (Neuthor) stood another parish church—a rotunda in form—that of St. Martin, which fell in 1812 and was removed; and at the opposite end of the minster, separated from it only by a narrow passage, was still a third, the small structure dedicated to St. Gangolph. This, too, was pulled down in 1806. Only the fourth parish church, that of St. Peter in Dietkirchen, is still in existence and was, at a later date, considerably enlarged. After the demolition of these buildings a new division of the town into parishes was made (1806).

This account by Thayer concerning the city of Bonn and the surrounding valley, it must be borne in mind, was written in the middle of the nineteenth century and is naturally out of date in certain respects. The present editor has chosen to let it stand and adds only the fact that the church of St. Peter was torn down in 1881 and a new church in Gothic style was built by the architect Heinrich Wietnase. This is the present Stiftskirche on the Kölnstrasse.

The city front of the electoral palace, now the university, was more imposing than now, and was adorned by a tall, handsome tower containing a carillon, with bells numerous enough to play, for instance, the overture to Monsigny's *Deserter*. This part of the palace, with the tower and chapel, was destroyed by fire in 1777.

The town hall, erected by Clemens August, and the other churches were as now, but the large edifice facing the university library and museum of casts, now occupied by private dwellings and shops, was then the cloister and church of the Franciscan monks.

Let the fancy picture, upon a fine Easter or Pentecost morning in those years, the little city in its holiday attire and bustle. The bells in palace and church tower ringing; the peasants in coarse but picturesque garments, the women abounding in bright colors, come in from the surrounding villages, fill the market-place and crowd the churches at the early masses. The nobles and gentry—in broad-flapped coats, wide waistcoats and knee-breeches, the entire dress often of brilliant colored silks, satins and velvets, huge, white, flowing neckcloths, ruffles over the hands, buckles of silver or even of gold at the knees and upon the shoes, huge wigs becurled and bepowdered on the heads, and surmounted by the cocked hat, when not held under the arm, a sword at the side, and commonly a gold-headed cane in the hand (and if the morning be cold, a scarlet cloak thrown over the shoulders)—are daintily picking their way to the palace to kiss His Transparency's hand or dashing up to the gates in heavy carriages with white wigged and cocked-hatted coachmen and footmen. Their ladies wear long and narrow bodices, but their robes flow with a mighty sweep; their apparent stature is increased by very high-heeled shoes and by piling up their hair on lofty cushions; their sleeves are short, but long silk gloves cover the arms. The ecclesiastics, various in name and costume, dress as now, save in the matter of the flowing wig. The Elector's company of guards is out and at intervals the thunder of the artillery on the walls is heard. On all sides, strong and brilliant contrasts of color meet the eye, velvet and silk, purple and fine linen, gold and silver—such were the fashions of the time—costly, inconvenient in form, but imposing, magnificent and marking the differences of rank and class. Let the imagination picture all this, and it will have a scene familiar to the boy Beethoven, and one in which as he grew up to manhood he had his own small part to play.

CHAPTER II

THE BEETHOVEN FAMILY

T H E results of work by van Aerde, Pols, and a number of other scholars make it possible to trace Beethoven's family to Malines in Belgium and to discard the early researches of de Burbure, followed by Thayer, which carried the origin of the family back three generations to a Henry Adelard van Beethoven of Antwerp. Pols laid the ground for future research on the subject by showing that none of Henry Adelard's sons logically could be the Ludwig van Beethoven who came to Bonn in 1733 to serve as musician in the Elector's court, and became the grandfather of the composer.[1] In Bonn besides Ludwig there were Cornelius and Michael van Beethoven, newly settled in the town on the Rhine, and through these names van Aerde[2] was able to show from whence they had all come, by study of documents in the city archives at Malines.

Michael was born in Malines in 1684, the son of Cornelius van Beethoven and presumably Catherine van Leempoel. We will return to the speculation concerning his forebears in a moment. He took up the baker's trade, and in 1707 married Mary Louise Stuykers. Of their four sons there survived only Cornelius, born in 1708, and Ludwig, born in 1712. Cornelius, a chandler

[1] André M. Pols, "Is Lodewijk van Beethoven van Antwerpse oorsprung," in *De Gulden Passer*, v (1927), p. 51. MacArdle has ably summed up the argument in *The Musical Quarterly*, xxv (1949), p. 529: "Pols based his contention on the fact that Henry Adelard had twelve children, including (3) Ludwig, baptized December 23, 1712, and (12) Ludwig Joseph, baptized December 9, 1728. The history of Ludwig Joseph is known in sufficient detail—the records of his three marriages and his death in 1808 appear in the parish registers of Antwerp—to prove conclusively that he could not have been Ludwig the choir singer of Bonn. . . . No records appear regarding Ludwig (3) except his baptismal record,

but two pieces of negative evidence may be taken as conclusive that he was not the Ludwig who later settled in Bonn. Had Ludwig (3) been alive at the birth of his youngest brother, it is most improbable that the latter would also have been given the name of Ludwig, whereas the practice of using the name of a deceased child for an infant was very general in Flanders during that period. Furthermore, a legal document of 1753 listed five children, not including Ludwig (3), as being the only surviving children of Henry Adelard."

[2] Raymond van Aerde, *Les ancêtres flamands de Beethoven* (Malines, 1928).

and purveyor to the court, was the first to move to Bonn; this took place around the year 1731.

Ludwig, the younger son, was admitted to the choir school of the church of St. Rombaut just before his sixth year. Here he was trained until he was thirteen. Van Aerde[3] has discovered a contract showing that in 1725 Antoine Colfs, organist since 1717 at St. Rombaut, was engaged to teach Ludwig the organ and the art of accompanying and realizing figured bass at the keyboard, until he should be capable of playing for services at St. Rombaut and other churches. His father was to pay for the instruction, and the student was to substitute at the organ at the master's discretion without recompense. Thus it was a trained musician who was appointed first singer then choir director at St. Peter's Church in Louvain in the month of November, 1731. From here Ludwig went to Liège in the summer of 1732 to become a bass in the choir at St. Lambert's Cathedral. But it was not long before the young musician received an invitation from Clemens August, Archbishop of Cologne and Bishop of Liège, to serve at his private court in Bonn. His future employer may well have heard the singer for himself in one of his visits to Liège. So claims Fischer.[4] Ludwig's request for a certificate from the chapter at Liège was turned down on March 2, 1733, perhaps in an effort to hold him in his job; but within days Ludwig was on his way to Cologne, from whence he could proceed to Bonn by boat.

Now let us turn back to the further story of Ludwig's father Michael. As the master baker's estate grew, he took up a side line of trading in luxury items such as lace, pictures and furniture, which soon became his principal business. In a few years his affairs began to slip; he took to traveling while his wife was left to pay the ever-increasing debts by selling off, bit by bit, their estate. By 1739 the rumors of bankruptcy had begun. A document at Cleves[5] shows that on April 10 of this year Michael was made a citizen of that city, where he had been presumably promoting his business in lace. By 1741 he was so far in debt that nothing remained but to leave Malines for good. On the 12th of March, 1741, Michael signed away his remaining possessions to his relative, Henry Willems, one of his many creditors, and fled with his wife to Bonn to join their sons. According to the laws in Malines, the heirs of an insolvent debtor were also liable for the debt, and van Aerde found papers showing that both Cornelius and Ludwig had been so approached; but naturally in another country they were protected from having to pay, since they were outside the jurisdiction of the Flemish courts. The remainder of Michael's life was spent uneventfully in Bonn, where he died in June, 1749. His wife died in December of the same year.

Here seems the appropriate place to mention what is known of Michael's ancestors. While it is certain that he was the son of a Cornelius van Beethoven

---

[3] "A la recherche des ascendants de Beethoven," *Revue belge d'archéologie et d'histoire de l'art,* IX (1939), pp. 156-57.

[4] TDR, I, 443.

[5] Van Aerde, *op.cit.,* p. 155.

of Malines, there is no document to prove the origins of this Cornelius, since there were two bearers of that name.[6] The one that scholars agree was the most likely to have been the father of Michael was the one who was born on October 20, 1641, at Bertem near Louvain. He grew up to be a carpenter and shopkeeper, establishing himself in Malines around 1670. In 1673 he married Catharine van Leempoel and had three children; Johann Baptist (born 1677), Cornelius (born 1680) and Michael, who was baptized at St. Rombaut's Church on March 24, 1685. He died in Malines in 1716. That the parents of this Cornelius were Marc van Beethoven and Sara Haesarts has been virtually proved by van Boxmeer,[7] who discovered a document in the land records at Nederockerzeel showing that Cornelius van Beethoven of Malines and his wife Catharine Leempoel (sic) sold a piece of land on March 17, 1676, which is identified in a document of February 13, 1637, as belonging to the inheritance of Sara Haesarts. The records show that Sara Haesarts was baptized at Nederockerzeel in 1616, but Marc's dates are not exactly known; they were married in Louvain in 1635 and their family consisted of Leonard (born 1636), Maria (born 1637), Cornelius (born 1641)[8] and Anna (born 1644).

Marc's father was presumably named Henry van Beethoven. Le Maire[9] has found land records in the Archives Générales du Royaume at Brussels which show in the same document the following: that Henry van Beethoven and his wife Catharine van Boevenkerke on May 20, 1623 bought a field—"een dachwant beempts, te Haecht over 't Goorbroeck," that the sale was completed on the 29th of the same month to Henry and his wife whose name is now spelled van Boevenbecke, that in 1656 the same land was in the hands of Marc van Beethoven, son of the above mentioned Henry, and that this same property in Haecht belonged in 1672 to Cornelius van Beethoven as the result of the death of his father, Marc. The document further indicates that Cornelius, conjointly with his wife, Catharine van Leempoel, sold this land in 1703. Haecht and Nederockerzeel are but a few miles apart, both in that area between Malines and Louvain; and Le Maire points out that this land is consequently in the same general locality as that inherited by Cornelius from his mother, Sara Haesarts, which was discovered by van Boxmeer.

[6] In his earlier work (*Les ancêtres flamands de Beethoven*, p. 34, n. 1), Van Aerde considered with reservations another Cornelius, born in 1630, who was the son of Arnold van Beethoven and Catharine Verstrecke who lived in Perck. Arnold was the son of Marc van Beethoven (*ca.* 1568–1640) and Adrienne Proost (?-1635) of Nederockerzeel. This village, where lived many members of the van Beethoven family, is some eight miles south of Malines. Thus while probably not in the direct line of the composer's ancestors, this family was surely closely related, as suggested also by the names Arnold and Marc being in both branches. See Jos. Schmidt-Görg, "Stand und Aufgaben der Beethoven-Genealogie," in *Beethoven und die Gegenwart*, ed. Arnold Schmitz (Berlin and Bonn, 1937), pp. 140-41.

[7] Philipp van Boxmeer, "L'atavisme musical du grand van Beethoven et son ascendance brabançonne," *Le Folklore Brabançon*, August–October, 1935.

[8] It remains a mystery why in this one baptismal record the father's name is listed as "Bartholomé" instead of Marc.

[9] Octave Le Maire, "Les origines brabançonnes de Beethoven," *Le Parchemin*, 11 (1937), pp. 135-37.

Le Maire will not follow van Boxmeer, however, back into the next generation and beyond. The latter continues back three more generations to find the origin of the family in Campenhout, another small village in this same area, only two and a half miles away from Nederockerzeel.

There is relatively rich documentation concerning the next ancestor, Arnold van Beethoven. From church and land records, one can place his birth in Campenhout around the year 1535. He first married Josine van Vlesselaer, by whom he had three sons and one daughter: Marc, Henry, Lambert and Anna. From the known fact that Anna's son John was born in 1592, van Aerde[10] estimates that Anna was born about 1570, and Marc, who was the eldest, around 1563. From this he proceeds to challenge van Boxmeer's theory that this Marc, son of Arnold, could be the same Marc who married Sara Haesarts and produced four children between 1635 and 1644. That is, it is unlikely that a man would produce offspring from the age of seventy-two to eighty-one. But just here is where Le Maire's evidence concerning Henry, father of Marc, seems to provide the missing link; for we know that Arnold's second son was named Henry. If this be one and the same Henry, then Arnold would be Marc's grandfather, a relationship that seems likely since Campenhout, Haecht and Nederockerzeel are in the same region and but a few miles from each other.

Arnold's wife Josine van Vlesselaer suffered the fate of being suspected of sorcery. In 1595 she was tried, convicted as a witch or practitioner with evil spirits and ordered to be burned at the stake. Arnold was sixty at the time, unable to work because of paralysis in his left arm; but all his adversity did not prevent him from marrying a second time. The parish records of Haecht show that his marriage to Petronilla Gheerts took place on February 1, 1600, and that a son John was baptized in Campenhout on July 19, 1601.

According to van Boxmeer, Arnold's father was named Marc and his grandfather John. This is based on a document at Campenhout dated May 8, 1571, which mentions a Marc van Beethoven, son of John, who married Anne Smets. From this our authority suggests that the composer's earliest known ancestor (if the line has been correctly traced) was born about 1500.

For the most plausible speculation concerning the origin of the family we turn once again to van Aerde who states:[11]

"Concerning the distant origins, that is the cradle of the family, there are strong factors in favor of the Limbourg-Liège regions. The first thing to advance this thesis is the form of name: Betho, Bethenhove, Bethof, representing a place;[12] second is the fact, demonstrated clearly in the Malines archives, of frequent immigrations of people from the regions to the East towards the central provinces of the country, and vice-versa. This mutual attraction is explained by the industrial riches of the one part and the rich

---

10 "A la recherche des ascendants de Beethoven," pp. 134-38.

11 *Ibid.*, pp. 133-34.
12 See page 12 above.

grazing and farming lands of the other. Also we have noted that the commercial transactions between our Malines regions and those of Cologne-Liège were very important and increased in the periods when the Malines cloth trade was enjoying its expansion (thirteenth and fourteenth centuries). It is not to be doubted that with the exchange of products there was the migration of families between one region and the other. All this naturally is pure conjecture lacking the confirmation of evidence.

"At this point one fact is established: it is the settling of the van Beethovens in Brabant before the sixteenth and probably already in the fifteenth century when they spread to different cities and rural regions of the central provinces. A curious thing to be noted is that a certain Jean van Beethoven had already chosen Campenhout or Boortmeerbeek [about five miles to the north] as a place of residence before 1500; this was the center for the van Beethoven family up to the eighteenth century. From there, the descendants either for economic reasons or through marriage scattered to outlying regions such as Bergh, Perck, Steenockerzeel, Nederockerzeel, Putte; later a group settled in Louvain and its suburbs: Leefdael, Rotselaer, Berthem. Finally branches of the family were being established in Antwerp and Malines."

A detailed analysis of these various branches has been made by Joseph Schmidt-Görg[13] who has established seven different stems. The first is from Campenhout and forms the direct line to the composer; there are two stems from Haecht, and one each from Nederockerzeel, Leefdael, Rotselaer and Antwerp. Let us now return to that branch of the family which made a longer migration, from Malines into another country; the van Beethovens in Bonn.❧—

There Cornelius, on February 20, 1734, married a widow named Helena de la Porte (née Calem), in the church of St. Gangolph, Ludwig van Beethoven, the young court singer, being one of the witnesses. Cornelius became a citizen of Bonn on January 17, 1736, on the ground that he had married the widow of a citizen, and in 1738 he stands alone as representative of the name in the list of Bonn's citizens. He lost his wife, and for a second married Anna Barbara Marx, *virgo*, on July 5, 1755. She bore him two daughters (1756 and 1759), both of whom died young and for both of whom Ludwig van Beethoven was sponsor. Cornelius died in 1764 and his wife in 1765.

Ludwig, meanwhile, had become Court Musician in Bonn with a salary of 400 florins, by a decree of Elector Clemens August, dated March, 1733. The salary was a large one for those days, particularly in the case of a young man who only three months before had completed his twentieth year. The next recorded fact in his history may be seen in the ancient register of the parish of St. Remigius, now preserved in the town hall of Bonn. It is the marriage on September 7, 1733, of Ludwig van Beethoven and Maria

---

[13] *Beethoven und die Gegenwart,* pp. 114-61.

Josepha Poll, the husband not yet 21 years of age, the wife 19. Then follows in the records of baptisms in the parish:

1734, August 28.

Parents:	Baptized:	Sponsors:
Ludwig van Beethoven	Maria Bernardina	Maria Bernardina Mengal
Maria Josepha Poll	Ludovica	Michael van Beethoven;
		in his place Cornelius
		van Beethoven.

The child Bernardina died in infancy, October 17, 1735. Her place was soon filled by a son, Marcus Josephus, baptized April 25, 1736, of whom the parents were doubtless early bereaved, for no other notice whatever has been found of him. After the lapse of some four years the childless pair again became parents, by the birth of a son, whose baptismal record has not been discovered. It is supposed that this child, Johann, was baptized in the Court Chapel, the records of which are not preserved in the archives of the town and seem to be lost; or that, possibly, he was born while the mother was absent from Bonn. An official report upon the condition and characters of the court musicians made in 1784, however, gives Johann van Beethoven *born in Bonn* and aged forty-four—thus fixing the date of his birth towards the end of 1739 or the beginning of 1740.

The gradual improvement of the elder Beethoven's condition in respect of both emolument and social position, is creditable to him alike as a musician and a man. Poorly as the musicians were paid, he was able in his last years to save a small portion of his earnings; his rise in social position is indicated in the public records;—thus, the first child is recorded as that of L. v. Beethoven, "musicus"; as sponsor to the eldest daughter of Cornelius van Beethoven, he appears as "Dominus" van Beethoven;—to the second as "Musicus Aulicis"; in 1761 he becomes "Herr Kapellmeister," and his name appears in the Court Calendar of the same year, third in a list of twenty-eight "Hommes de chambres honoraires." The Elector maintained a benevolence towards him and appointed him his "Kammermusikus"; also the early consideration of his son, Johann, attests to this fact. Of the elder Beethoven's appointment as head of the court music no other particulars have been obtained than those to be found in his petition and the accompanying decree printed in Chapter 1. From these papers it appears that the bass singer had the promise of the place from Clemens August as successor to Zudoli, but that the Elector, when the vacancy occurred, changed his mind and gave it to his favorite young violinist Touchemoulin. He held the position for so short a time, however, that his name never appears as kapellmeister in the Court Calendar. He resigned on account of the reduction of his salary by Belderbusch, prime minister of the new Elector who just at that period succeeded Clemens August. The elevation of a singer to such a place was not a very uncommon event in those days, but that a kapellmeister should still retain his place as singer probably was. Hasse and Graun began their careers as vocalists, but more to the point are the instances of Steffani, Handel's predecessor at the court of Hanover, and of Righini, successively kapellmeister at Mainz and Berlin. In all these cases the incumbents were distinguished and very successful composers. Beethoven was not. Wegeler's words, "the kapellmeister and bass singer had at an earlier date produced operas at the National Theatre established by the Elector," have been rather interpreted than quoted by Schindler and others thus: "it is thought that under the luxury-loving Elector Clemens August, he produced operas of his own composition"—a construction which is clearly forced and incorrect. Strange that so few writers can content themselves with exact citations! Not only is there no proof whatever, certainly none yet made public, that Kapellmeister van Beethoven was an author of operatic works, but the words in his own petition, "inasmuch as the Toxal must be sufficiently supplied with *musique*,"[14] can hardly be otherwise understood than as intended to meet a possible objection to his appointment on the ground of his not being a composer. Wegeler's words, then, would simply mean that he put upon the stage and conducted the operatic works produced, which were neither numerous nor of a very high order during his time. His labors were certainly onerous enough without adding musical composition. The records of the electoral court which have been described and in part reproduced in the preceding chapter, exhibit him conducting the music of chapel, theatre and "Toxal," examining candidates for admission into the electoral musical service, reporting upon questions referred to him by the privy council and the like, and all this in addition to his services as bass singer, a position which gave him the principal bass parts and solos to sing both in chapel and theatre. Wegeler records a tradition that in Gassmann's operetta *L'Amore Artigiano* and Monsigny's *Déserteur* he was "admirable and received the highest applause." If this be true it proves no small degree of enterprise on his part as kapellmeister and of well-conserved powers as a singer; for these two operas were first produced, the one in Vienna, the other in Paris, in 1769, when Beethoven had already entered his fifty-eighth year.

The words of Demmer in his petition of January 23, 1773, "the bass singer van Beethoven is incapacitated and can no longer serve as such," naturally suggest the thought that the old gentleman's appearance as Brunoro in Lucchesi's *L'Inganno scoperto* in May, 1773, was a final compliment to his master, the Elector, upon his birthday. He did not live to celebrate another; the death of "Ludwig van Beethoven, Hofkapellmeister," is recorded at Bonn under date of December 24, 1773.

At home the good man had his cross to bear. His wife, Josepha, who with one exception had buried all her children, and possibly on that very account, became addicted to the indulgence of an appetite for strong drink, and was

[14] See page 17 above.

at the date of her husband's death living evidently as a boarder in a cloister
—⋯✤[on the Kölnstrasse.]✤⋯—[15] How long she had been there does not appear, but
doubtless for a considerable period. The son, too, was married, but though
near was not in his father's house. The separation was brought about by his
marriage, to which the father was not agreed. The house in which the
kapellmeister died was that next north of the so-called Gudenauer Hof,
later the post-office in the neighboring Bonngasse, and bore the number 386.
The kapellmeister appears, upon pretty good evidence, to have removed
hither from the Fischer house in the Rheingasse, where he is said to have
lived many years and even to have carried on a trade in wine. The change
of dwelling may have taken place in 1767.

When one recalls the imposing style of dress of the era, the short, muscular
man, with dark complexion and very bright eyes, as described by Wegeler
and depicted by the court painter Radoux, presents quite an imposing
picture to the imagination.[16]

—⋯✤[It is appropriate here to consider the Fischer family, who for four generations owned the house in the Rheingasse, No. 934 (now No. 7) in which
two generations of the van Beethoven family had quarters, and which was
long considered to be the composer's birthplace. Here Johann was presumably
raised, and he became a friend and companion of Theodor Fischer, who
was a baker. Of Theodor's nine children, the eldest was Cäcilia, born in
1762, and the youngest was Gottfried, born in 1780, ten years after the composer, at which time the van Beethovens were living once again in the
Fischer house. There the brother and sister continued to live until well into
the nineteenth century. After 1838, at which time the Beethoven monument
was unveiled in Bonn, visitors came in increasing numbers to see the birthplace and relics of the composer, and the Fischers naturally were barraged
with questions concerning the early days of the family. Thus Gottfried was
persuaded to put these reminiscences in writing. He kept adding to his
manuscript for almost twenty years during which time he grew senile while
his sister remained mentally alert. She died in 1845, but Gottfried lived on
until 1864. He was uneducated and the Fischer manuscript is written for the
most part in poor German, a strange mixture of notes, often repetitious,
based on tradition, and vivid description of three different generations of the
van Beethoven family which are undoubtedly the recollections of Cäcilia.

From the Fischer manuscript[17] we learn of a visit the family paid to the

[15] According to Fischer (and Thayer)
"Köln," but more likely Kölnstrasse. See
Schiedermair, *Der Junge Beethoven* (Bonn and
Leipzig, 1925), p. 95.

[16] "The grandfather was a man short of
stature, muscular, with extremely animated
eyes, and was greatly respected as an artist."
Wegeler, *Notizen*, p. 8. (TDR, I, 114, n. 2.)
The Radoux portrait has been in the possession
of the Reichert family in Vienna, descendants

of Beethoven's nephew Karl. The copy in the
Beethovenhaus in Bonn was made by Frau
Weidinger, Karl's granddaughter.

[17] Thayer saw the manuscript but refused
to buy it at the exorbitant price set by old
Fischer, who in his time prized it highly.
Although Thayer attached little value to it as
a source because of its inaccuracies, he did
permit Deiters to print it with critical comments in the appendix to Volume I of the

home of the kapellmeister: "everything was so beautiful and proper and well arranged, with valuables, all six rooms were provided with beautiful furniture, many paintings and cupboards, a cupboard of silver service, a cupboard with fine gilded porcelain and glass, an assortment of the most beautiful linen which could be drawn through a ring; everything from the smallest article sparkled like silver."

Of the early life of Johann van Beethoven there are no particulars preserved except such as are directly or indirectly conveyed in the official documents. Such of these papers as came from his own hand, if judged by the standard of our time, show a want of ordinary education; but it must not be forgotten that the orthography of the German language was not then fixed; nor that many a contemporary of his, who boasted a university education, or who belonged to the highest ranks of society, wrote in a style no better than his. This is certain: that after he had received an elementary education he was sent to the Gymnasium, for as a member of the lowest class (*infima*) of that institution he took part in September, 1750, as singer in the annual school play which it was the custom of the *Musæ Bonnenses* to give. It would seem, therefore, that his good voice and musical gifts were appreciated at an early period. Herein, probably, is also to be found the reason why his stay at the Gymnasium was not of long duration. The father had set him apart for service in the court music, and himself, as appears from the statements already printed, undertook his instruction; he taught him singing and clavier playing. Whether or not he also taught him violin playing, in which he was "capable," remains uncertain. In 1752, at the age of 12, as can be seen from his petition of March, 1756, and his father's of 1764, he entered the chapel as soprano. According to Gottwald's report of 1756 he had served "about 2 years"; the contradiction is probably explained by an interruption caused by the mutation of his voice. At the age of 16, he received his *decretum* as "accessist" on the score of his skill in singing and his experience already acquired, including his capability on the violin, which was the basis of the decree of April 24, 1764, granting him a salary of 100 rth. per annum.

So, at the age of 22, the young man received the promise of a salary, and at 24 obtained one of 100 thalers. In 1769, he received an increase of 25 fl., and 50 fl. more by the decree of April 3, 1772.[18] He had, moreover, an opportunity to gain something by teaching. Not only did he give lessons in singing and clavier playing to the children of prominent families of the city, but he

---

biography in 1866. Meanwhile it was bought by the city of Bonn and turned over to the Beethoven Archives in 1889. After further study of the manuscript, Dr. Deiters attached more importance to Fischer's testimony and incorporated such material as could be used into the main body of the text of Volume I when it was revised in 1901. This treatment has been the basis of subsequent editions. (TDR, I, 434ff.)

[18] In June, 1775, Johann received an allowance of 60 thalers for the support of his mother, this allowance to inure to Johann when his mother should die. Schiedermair, *op.cit.*, p. 122.

also frequently was called on to prepare young musicians for service in the chapel.

A few years later, as we have seen, he seems to have been intrusted with the training of Johanna Helene Averdonk, whom he brought forward as his pupil in March, 1778, and the singer Gazzenello was his pupil before she went elsewhere. It was largely his own fault that the musically gifted man was unfortunate in both domestic and official relations. His intemperance in drink, perhaps inherited from his mother but attributed by old Fischer to the wine trade in which his father embarked, made itself apparent at an early date, and by yielding to it more and more as he grew older he undoubtedly impaired his voice and did much to bring about his later condition of poverty. How it finally led to a catastrophe we shall see later.

--∘⊰[Reports by Johann's contemporaries mention not only the dark side of his character but also his competence as a court official and teacher who was often overburdened by these duties. That he must have "performed his duties precisely," as stated by Fischer, is substantiated by the fact that he was offered the job of tenor singer at the cathedral in Liège in the spring of 1770, which he was persuaded to refuse. Thus Schiedermair believes that Johann did not inherit an intemperance for drink but developed the habit only in his later life when the steadying influence of his wife had gone.]⊱∘--[19]

According to the testimony of the widow Karth, he was a tall, handsome man, and wore powdered hair in his later years. Fischer does not wholly agree with her: "of medium height, longish face, broad forehead, round nose, broad shoulders, serious eyes, face somewhat scarred, thin pigtail." Three and a half years after obtaining his salary of 100 th. he ventured to marry. Heinrich Keverich, the father of his wife, was overseer of cooking in that palace at Ehrenbreitstein in which Clemens danced himself out of this world, but he died before that event took place.[20] His wife, as the church records testify, was Anna Clara Westorff. Her daughter Maria Magdalena, born December 19, 1746, married a certain Johann Laym, valet of the Elector of Trèves, on January 30, 1763. She bore him one son who died in infancy. On November 28, 1765, the husband died, and Maria Magdalena was a widow before she had completed her 19th year. In a little less than two years the marriage register of St. Remigius, at Bonn, was enriched by this entry:

12ma 9bris. Praevia Dispensatione super 3bus denuntiationibus copulavi D. Joannem van Beethoven, Dni. Ludovici van Beethoven et Mariae Josephae Poll conjugum filium legitimum, et Mariam Magdalenam Keferich viduam Leym ex Ehrenbreitstein, Henrici Keferich et annae clarae Westorffs filiam legitimam. Coram testibus Josepho clemente Belseroski et philippo Salomon.

[19] (NBJ, III (1927), 32.)
[20] The church records at Ehrenbreitstein say that he died August 2, 1759, in Molzberg, at the age of 58; his funeral took place in Ehrenbreitstein. A Frau Eva Katharina Keverich, who died at Ehrenbreitstein on October 10, 1753, at the age of 89 years, was his mother. (TDR, I, 117, n. 2.)

That is, Johann van Beethoven has married the young widow Laym. How it came that the marriage took place in Bonn instead of the home of the bride we are told by Fischer. Kapellmeister van Beethoven was not at all agreed that his son should marry a woman of a lower station in life than his own. He did not continue his opposition against the fixed determination of his son; but it is to be surmised that he would not have attended a ceremony in Ehrenbreitstein, and hence the matter was disposed of quickly in Bonn. After the wedding the young pair paid a visit of a few days' duration to Ehrenbreitstein. ⸺However, Schiedermair[21] points out that the young bride's family were respected and well-to-do; among the forbears on her mother's side were merchants, councillors and senators.⸺

Fischer describes Madame van Beethoven as a "handsome, slender person" and tells of her "rather tall, longish face, a nose somewhat bent (*gehöffelt*, in the dialect of Bonn), spare, earnest eyes." Cäcilia Fischer could not recall that she had ever seen Madame van Beethoven laugh; "she was always serious." Her life's vicissitudes may have contributed to this disposition:—the early loss of her father, and of her first husband, and the death of her mother scarcely more than a year after her second marriage. It is difficult to form a conception of her character because of the paucity of information about her. Wegeler lays stress upon her piety and gentleness; her amiability and kindliness towards her family appear from all the reports; nevertheless, Fischer betrays the fact that she could be vehement in controversies with the other occupants of the house. "Madame van Beethoven," Fischer continues, "was a clever woman; she could give converse and reply aptly, politely and modestly to high and low, and for this reason she was much liked and respected. She occupied herself with sewing and knitting. They led a righteous and peaceful married life, and paid their house-rent and baker's bills promptly, quarterly, and on the day. She was a good, a domestic woman, she knew how to give and also how to take in a manner that is becoming to all people of honest thoughts." From this it is fair to assume that she strove to conduct her household judiciously and economically; whether or not this was always possible in view of the limited income, old Fischer does not seem to have been informed. She made the best she could of the weaknesses of her husband without having been able to influence him; her care for the children in externals was not wholly sufficient. Young Ludwig clung to her with a tender love, more than to the father, who was "only severe"; but there is no evidence as to how much influence she exerted upon the emotional life and development of her son. Nor must it be forgotten that in all probability she was naturally delicate and that her health was still further weakened by her domestic troubles and frequent accouchements. The "quiet, suffering woman," as Frau Karth called her, died in 1787 of consumption at the age of

[21] *Der Junge Beethoven*, pp. 96ff. See also Schmidt-Görg, *op.cit.*, p. 118.

40 years. Long years after in Vienna Beethoven was wont, when among his intimate friends, to speak of his "excellent" (*vortreffliche*) mother.

At the time when Johann van Beethoven was married, there was quite a colony of musicians, and other persons in the service of the court, in the Bonngasse, as that street is in part named which extends from the lower extremity of the market place to the Cologne gate. Kapellmeister van Beethoven had left the house in the Rheingasse upon his son's marriage and lived at No. 386. In the adjoining house, north, No. 387, lived the musical family Ries. The last house on that side before the street assumes the name Kölnerstrasse was the dwelling of the hornist, afterwards publisher, Simrock. Nearly opposite the kapellmeister's the second story of the house No. 515 was occupied (but not till after 1771) by the Salomons; the parterre and first floor by the owner of the house, a lace-maker or dealer in laces, named Clasen. Of the two adjoining houses the one at No. 515 was the dwelling of Johann Baum, clerk of the Court cellar; in the other lived Courtin, a master locksmith, doubtless the Jean Courtin, "serrurier," of the Court Calendar for 1773. In No. 517 was the family Hertel, twelve or fifteen years later living under the Beethovens in the Wenzelgasse, and not far off a family, Poll, perhaps relations of the elder Frau Beethoven. Conrad Poll's name is found in the Court Calendars of the 1770's as one of the eight Electoral "Heiducken" (footmen). In 1767 in the rear of the Clasen house, north,[22] there was a lodging to let; and there the newly married Beethovens began their humble housekeeping. Their first child was a son, Ludwig Maria, baptized April 2, 1769, whose sponsors were the grandfather Beethoven and Anna Maria Lohe, wife of Jean Courtin, the next-door neighbor. This child lived but six days. In less than two years the loss of the parents was made up by the birth of him who is the subject of this biography.

[22] The house is now owned by the Beethoven-Haus Verein, and maintained as a Beethoven museum. (TK, I, 52, n. 1.)

CHAPTER III

BEETHOVEN'S BIRTH AND CHILDHOOD, 1770 TO 1784

THERE is no authentic record of Beethoven's birthday. Wegeler, on the ground of custom in Bonn, dates it the day preceding the ceremony of baptism—an opinion which Beethoven himself seems to have entertained. It is the official record of this baptism only that has been preserved. In the registry of the parish of St. Remigius the entry appears as follows:

Parentes:	Proles:	Patrini:
D: Joannes van	17ma Xbris.	D: Ludovicus van
Beethoven & Helena	Ludovicus	Beethoven &
Keverichs, conjuges		Gertrudis Müllers
		dicta Baums

The sponsors, therefore, were Beethoven's grandfather, the kapellmeister, and the wife of the next-door neighbor, Johann Baum, clerk of the electoral cellar. Since it was the custom at the time in the Catholic Rhine country not to postpone the baptism beyond 24 hours after the birth of a child, it is in the highest degree probable that Beethoven was born on December 16, 1770. ─••─A note from Albrechtsberger to Beethoven dated December 15th (in the Vienna Beethoven exhibition of 1927, dated in the catalogue 1795), begins "All best wishes to you tomorrow on your name-day."[1]─••─

Of several certificates of baptism the following is copied in full for the sake of a remark written upon it by the master's own hand:

Department de Rhin et Moselle
Mairie de Bonn
Extrait du Registre de Naissances de la Paroisse
de St. Remy à Bonn
Anno millesimo septingentesimo, de decima septima Decembris baptizatus est

---

[1] See Ley, "Zu Beethovens Geburtstag," *NBJ*, VII (1937), p. 29.

Ludovicus. Parentes D: Joannes van Beethoven et Helena[2] Keverichs, conjuges.
Patrini, D: Ludovicus van Beethoven et Gertrudis Müllers dicta Baums.

> Pour extrait conforme
> délivré à la Mairie de Bonn.
> Bonn le 2 Juin, 1810.
> [Signatures and official seals]

On the back of this paper Beethoven wrote:

1772

> The baptismal certificate seems to be incorrect,
> since there was a Ludwig born before me.
> A Baumgarten was my sponsor, I believe.
> Ludwig van Beethoven

The composer, then, even in his fortieth year still believed the correct date to be 1772, which is the one given in all the old biographical notices, and which corresponds to the dates affixed to many of his first works, and indeed to nearly all allusions to his age in his early years. Only by keeping this fact in mind, can the long list of chronological contradictions, which continually meet the student of his history during the first half of his life, be explained or comprehended. Whoever examines the original record of baptism in the registry at Bonn, sees instantly that the certificate, in spite of Beethoven, is correct; but all possible doubt is removed by the words of Wegeler: "Little Louis clung to this grandfather . . . with the greatest affection, and young as he was when he lost him, his early impressions always remained lively. He liked to speak of his grandfather with the friends of his youth, and his pious and gentle mother, whom he loved much more than he did his father, who was only severe, was obliged to tell him much of his grandfather. The picture of him finished by Court Painter Radoux is the only one that he had moved from Bonn to Vienna and which gave him pleasure until his death."

Had 1772 been the correct date the child never could have retained personal recollections of a man who died on December 24, 1773.

⟶⟨Here Thayer concluded that the boy's age was purposely falsified by Johann, who may well have had the recent career of the Mozart children in mind. Thayer cited the official report of 1784[3] in which the age is given correctly as an example of where untruth could not be risked. But one wonders whether the falsification of age could be purposely any the more risked in a dedication to the Elector; yet the boy composer in dedicating three piano sonatas to Maximilian Friedrich in 1783 wrote "by Ludwig van Beethoven, eleven years old." That family records were imperfectly kept at that time is amply illustrated by the discrepancies of birth dates mentioned in contemporary writings.⟩⟶

[2] The mistake in the mother's name is sufficiently explained by the use of Lena as the contraction of both Helena and Magdalena.

(TDR, I, 123, n. 1.)
[3] See page 79 below.

Dr. C. M. Kneisel, who championed the cause of the house in the Bonngasse in a controversy conducted in the *Kölnische Zeitung* in 1845, touching the birthplace of Beethoven, remarks that the mother "was, as is known, a native of the Ehrenbreitstein valley and separated from her relatives; he [Johann van Beethoven] was without relatives and in somewhat straitened circumstances financially. What, then, was more natural than that he should invite his neighbor, Frau Baum, a respected and well-to-do woman, *in whose house the baptismal feast was held*, to be sponsor for his little son?" This last fact indicates clearly the narrowness of the quarters in which the young couple dwelt. Does it not also hint that the grandfather was now a solitary man with no home in which to spread the little feast? Let Johann van Beethoven himself describe the pecuniary condition in which he found himself upon the death of his father:

Most Reverend Archbishop,
Most Gracious Elector and Lord, Lord.

Will Your Electoral Grace be pleased to hear that my father has passed away from this world, to whom it was granted to serve His Electoral Grace Clemens August and Your Electoral Grace and gloriously reigning Lord Lord 42 years, as Kapellmeister with great honor, whose position I have been found capable of filling, but nevertheless I would not venture to offer my capacity to Your Electoral Grace, but since the death of my father has left me in needy circumstances my salary not sufficing and I compelled to draw on the savings of my father, my mother still living and in a cloister at a cost of 60 rth. for board and lodging each year and it is not advisable for me to take her to my home. Your Electoral Grace is therefore humbly implored to make an allowance from the 400 rth. vacated for an increase of my salary so that I may not need to draw upon the little savings and my mother may receive the pension graciously for the few years which she may yet live, to deserve which high grace it shall always be my striving.

Your Electoral Grace's
Most humble and obedient
Servant and musicus jean van Beethoven

There is something bordering on the comic in the coolness of the hint here given that the petitioner would not object to an appointment as his father's successor, especially when it is remembered that Lucchesi and Mattioli were already in Bonn and the former had sufficiently proved his capacity by producing successful operas, both text and music, for the Elector's delectation. The hint was not taken; what provision was granted him, however, may be seen from another petition of January 8, 1774, praying for an addition to his salary from that made vacant by the death of his father, and a pension to his mother who is kept at board in a cloister. A memorandum appears on the margin to the effect that the Elector graciously consents that the widow, so long as she remain in the cloister, shall receive 60 rth. quarterly. Another petition of a year later has been lost, but its contents are indicated in the response, dated June 5, 1775, that Johann van Beethoven on the death of his mother shall have the enjoyment of the 60 rth. which had been granted her. The death of the mother followed a few months later and was thus announced in the *Intelligenzblatt* of Bonn on October 3, 1775: "Died, on September 30, Maria Josepha Pols, widow van Beethoven, aged 61 years." In a list of salaries for 1776 (among the papers at Düsseldorf) for the "Musik Parthie" the salary of Johann van Beethoven is given at 36 rth. 45 alb. payable quarterly. The fact of the great poverty in which he and his family lived is manifest from the official documents (which confirm the many traditions to that effect) and from the more important recollections of the aged people of Bonn brought to light in a controversy concerning the birthplace of the composer.

From the Bonngasse the Beethovens removed, when is uncertain, to a house No. 7 or No. 8 on the left as one enters the Dreieckplatz in passing from the Sternstrasse to the Münsterplatz. They were living there in 1774, for the baptism of another son on the 8th of April of that year is recorded in the register of the parish of St. Gangolph, to which those houses belonged. This child's name was Caspar Anton Carl, the first two names from his sponsor the Minister Belderbusch, the third from Caroline von Satzenhofen, Abbess of Vilich. Was this condescension on the part of the minister and the abbess intended to soothe the father under the failure of his hopes of advancement? From the Dreieckplatz the Beethovens migrated to the Fischer house, No. 934 in the Rheingasse, so long held to be the composer's birthplace and long thereafter distinguished by a false inscription to that effect. Whether the removal took place in Ludwig's fifth or sixth year is not known; but at all events it was previous to the 2nd of October, 1776, for upon that day another son of Johann van Beethoven was baptized in the parish of St. Remigius by the name of Nikolaus Johann. According to Fischer's report the family removed from this house in 1776 for a short time to one in the Neugasse, but returned again to the house in the Rheingasse after the palace fire in 1777. One thought which suggests itself in relation to these removals of Johann van Beethoven may, perhaps, be more than mere fancy: that in expectation of advancement in position upon the death of his father he had exchanged the narrow quarters of the lodging in the rear of the Clasen house for the much better dwelling in the Dreieckplatz; but upon the failure of his hopes had been fain to seek a cheaper place in the lower part of the town down near the river.

There is nothing decisive as to the time when the musical education of Ludwig van Beethoven began, nor any positive evidence that he, like Handel, Haydn or Mozart, showed remarkable genius for the art at a very early age. Schlosser has something on this point, but he gives no authorities, while the particulars which he relates could not possibly have come under his own observation. W. C. Müller[4] had heard from Franz Ries and Nikolaus Simrock

---

[4] *AMZ*, May 23, 1827. (TDR, I, 128, n. 1.)

that Johann van Beethoven gave his son instruction upon the pianoforte and violin "in his earliest childhood. . . . To scarcely anything else did he hold him." In the dedication of the pianoforte sonatas (1783) to the Elector, the boy is made to say: "Music became my first youthful pursuit in my fourth year," which might be supposed decisive on the point if his age were not falsely given on the title-page. This much is certain: that after the removal to the Fischer house the child had his daily task of musical study and practice given him and in spite of his tears was forced to execute it. "Cäcilia Fischer," writes Hennes[5] (1838), "still sees him, a tiny boy, standing on a little footstool in front of the clavier to which the implacable severity of his father had so early condemned him. . . . The patriarch of Bonn, Head Burgomaster Windeck, will pardon me if I appeal to him to say that he, too, saw the little Louis van Beethoven in this house standing in front of the clavier and weeping." To this writes Dr. Wegeler:[6] "I saw the same thing. How? The Fischer house was, perhaps still is, connected by a passage-way in the rear with a house in the Giergasse, which was then occupied by the owner, a high official of the Rhenish revenue service, Mr. Bachen, grandfather of Court Councillor Bachen of this city. The youngest son of the latter, Benedict, was my schoolmate, and on my visits to him the doings and sufferings of Louis were visible from the house."

It must be supposed that the father had seen indications of his son's genius, for it is difficult to imagine such an one remaining unperceived; but the necessities of the family with the failure of the petition for a better salary— sent in just at the time when the Elector was so largely increasing his expenditures for music by the engagement of Lucchesi and Mattioli and in other ways—are sufficient reasons for the inflexible severity with which the boy was kept at his studies. There is but one road to excellence, even for the genius of a Handel or a Mozart—unremitted application. To this young Ludwig was compelled, sometimes, no doubt, through the fear or the actual infliction of punishment for neglect; sometimes, too, the father, whose habits were such as to favor a bad interpretation of his conduct, was no doubt harsh and unjust. And such seems to be the truth. At any rate, the boy at an early date acquired so considerable a facility upon the clavier that his father could have him play at court and when he was seven years old produce him with one of his pupils at a concert in Cologne. Here is the announcement of the concert:

AVERTISSEMENT

Today, March 26, 1778, in the musical concert-room in the Sternengass the Electoral Court Tenorist, B E E T H O V E N, will have the honor to produce two of his scholars; namely, Mdlle. Averdonc, Court Contraltist, and his little son of six years. The former will have the honor to contribute various beautiful arias, the latter various clavier concertos and trios, in which he flatters himself that he

[5] Letter to the *Kölnische Zeitung*, No. 196 (1838). (TDR, I, 453, n. 3.)
[6] *Ibid.*, No. 210. (TDR, I, 129, n. 1.)

will give complete enjoyment to all ladies and gentlemen, the more since both have had the honor of playing to the greatest delight of the entire Court.

Beginning at five o'clock in the evening.

Ladies and gentlemen who have not subscribed will be charged a florin. Tickets may be had at the aforesaid Akademiesaal, also of Hr. Claren auf der Bach in Mühlenstein.

Unfortunately we learn nothing concerning the pieces played by the boy nor of the success of his performance. That the violin as well as the piano-forte was practised by him is implicitly confirmed by the terms in which Schindler records his denial of the truth of the well-known spider story:[7] "The great Ludwig refused to remember any such incident, much as the tale amused him. On the contrary, he said it was more to be expected that every-thing would have fled from his bad scraping, even flies and spiders."

The father's main object being the earliest and greatest development of his son's musical genius so as to make it a "marketable commodity," he gave him no other school education than such as was afforded at one of the public schools. Among the lower grade schools in Bonn was the so-called Tirocinium, a Latin school, which prepared pupils for the gymnasium but was not directly connected with it, but had its own corps of teachers, like the whole educational system of the period, under the supervision of the Academic Council established by Max Friedrich in 1777. The pupils learned, outside of the elementary studies (arithmetic and writing are said to have been ex-cluded), to read and write Latin up to an understanding of Cornelius Nepos. Johann Krengel, a much respected pedagogue, was teacher at the time and was appointed municipal schoolmaster in 1783 by the Academic Council. Here also taught Rubert, undoubtedly the Huppert mentioned in the Fischer manuscript. To this school young Beethoven was sent; when, is uncertain. His contemporary and school-fellow Wurzer, Electoral Councillor and after-wards president of the Landgericht, relates the following in his memoirs: "One of my schoolmates under Krengel was Luis van Beethoven, whose father held an appointment as court singer under the Elector. Apparently his mother was already dead at the time,[8] for Luis v. B. was distinguished by uncleanliness, negligence, etc. Not a sign was to be discovered in him of that spark of genius which glowed so brilliantly in him afterwards. I imagine that he was kept down to his musical studies from an early age."

Wurzer entered the gymnasium in the fall of 1781; Beethoven did not. This, therefore, must have been the time at which all other studies were abandoned in favor of music. As Schiedermair points out,[9] when Johann stopped the boy's education intentionally after the public elementary schools, he was following the pattern set by the majority of parents in Bonn, includ-

[7] *Biographie*, 1st ed., pp. 18-19. (TDR, I, 131, n. 1.)

[8] Error. Beethoven's mother did not die until 1787, long after he had left school. This story,

however, supports the belief, mentioned earlier, that the mother's care in externals was not always of the best. (TDR, I, 132, n. 2.)

[9] *Der Junge Beethoven*, p. 128.

ing the wealthy ones. This had been the pattern of his own life: he started as soon as possible, from the bottom, upon the career of court musician. He was in no position to provide the boy with any other kind of schooling; but since the earliest evidences of his son's talent, it had been clear to him that Ludwig was a born musician.⟩❧

The lack of proper intellectual discipline is painfully obvious in Beethoven's letters throughout his life. In his early manhood he wrote a fair hand, so very different from the shocking scrawl of his later years as to make one almost doubt the genuineness of autographs of that period; but in orthography, the use of capital letters, punctuation and arithmetic he was sadly deficient all his life long. He was still able to use the French tongue at a later period, and of Latin he had learned enough to understand the texts which he composed; but even as a schoolboy his studies appear to have been made second to his musical practice with which his hours out of school were apparently for the most part occupied. He was described by Dr. Müller as "a shy and taciturn boy, the necessary consequence of the life apart which he led, observing more and pondering more than he spoke, and disposed to abandon himself entirely to the feelings awakened by music and (later) by poetry and to the pictures created by fancy." Of those who were his schoolfellows and who in after years recorded their reminiscences of him, not one speaks of him as a playfellow, none has anecdotes to relate of games with him, rambles on the hills or adventures upon the Rhine and its shores in which he bore a part. Yet from the Fischer manuscript[10] we learn of play with his brothers by the river or in the court gardens; and "if the weather was unfavorable, the children played in the Fischer's yard with the Fischer children and others from the neighborhood." Fischer writes specifically of playful boyish pranks that Ludwig carried out with his brother Carl over, which Ludwig could laugh heartily; and he would have us believe that these capers were not always of a harmless character. Further on Fischer states, "Later one could not say that Ludwig cared much for companions or society. And then, when he had to turn his mind to music or set to work by himself, he assumed quite another demeanor and insisted on due respect. His happiest hours were those when he was free of all company, when his parents were all away and he was left alone by himself."

Music and ever music; hence the power of clothing his thoughts in words was not developed by early culture, and the occasional bursts of eloquence in his letters and recorded conversations are held not to be genuine, because so seldom found. As if the strong mind, struggling for adequate expression, should not at times break through all barriers and overcome all obstacles! Urged forward thus by the father's severity, by his tender love for his mother and by the awakening of his own tastes, the development of his skill and talents was rapid; so much so that in his ninth year a teacher more competent than his father was needed.

[10] TDR, I, 450, 458-59, 461.

The first to whom his father turned was the old court organist van den Eeden, who had been in the electoral service about fifty years and had come to Bonn before the arrival there of Ludwig van Beethoven, the grandfather. One can easily imagine his willingness to serve an old and deceased friend by fitting his grandson to become his successor; and this might account for Schlosser's story[11] that at first he taught him gratis, and that he continued his instructions at the command and expense of the Elector. The story may or may not be true, but nothing has been discovered in the archives at Düsseldorf confirming the statement; in fact concerning the time, the subjects and the results of van den Eeden's instruction we are thrown largely upon conjecture.

Mäurer, the violoncellist, in some reminiscences of that period communicated to this work by Professor Jahn, says: "In his eighth year Court Organist van den Eeden took him as a pupil; nothing has been learned of his progress." This, if Mäurer was correct in stating his age, would have been about 1778. It is after this time that Mäurer refers to his study under Pfeiffer.

Schlosser does not say that this instruction was on the organ and it is unlikely that the boy, who was destined for a more systematic instruction in pianoforte playing, was put at the organ at so early an age. It was a deduction, probably, from the fact that van den Eeden was an organist and that later Beethoven displayed a great deal of dexterity upon that instrument. It is noteworthy that Wegeler (p. 11) says nothing definite as to whether or not Beethoven took lessons from van den Eeden; he merely thought it likely, because he knew no one else in Bonn from whom Beethoven could have learned the technical handling of the organ. But there were several such in Bonn irrespective of Neefe. Schindler makes certainty out of Wegeler's conjecture and relates that Beethoven often spoke of the old organist when discoursing upon the proper position and movement of the body and hands in organ and pianoforte playing, he having been taught to hold both calm and steady, to play in the connected style of Handel and Bach. This may have been correct so far as pianoforte playing is concerned; but Schindler had little knowledge of Beethoven's Bonn period, and the possibility of a confusion of names is not excluded even on the part of Beethoven himself, who received hints from several organists. Mäurer, after speaking of Pfeiffer, continues as follows: "Van den Eeden remained his only teacher in thorough-bass. As a man of seventy he sent the boy Louis, between eleven and twelve years old, to accompany the mass and other church music on the organ. His playing was so astonishing that one was forced to believe he had intentionally concealed his gifts. While preluding for the Credo he took a theme from the movement and developed it to the amazement of the orchestra so that he was permitted to improvise longer than is customary. That was the opening of his brilliant career." Mäurer seems to know nothing of Neefe when he says

[11] Johann Aloys Schlosser, *Ludwig van Beethoven* (Prague, 1828), pp. 5ff.

that van den Eeden was Beethoven's only teacher in thorough-bass. What he says, too, about the lad's performance at the organ as substitute obviously rests upon a confounding of van den Eeden with another of Beethoven's organ teachers—most likely Neefe.

It is our conjecture that van den Eeden taught the boy chiefly pianoforte playing, he being a master in that art; but his influence was small. It must be remembered that van den Eeden was a very old man, as whose successor Neefe had been chosen in 1781, and who died in June, 1782. Nowhere does he, like the other teachers of Beethoven, disclose individual traits; he is a totally colorless picture in the history of Beethoven's youth. Nor does it appear that there was any intimacy between him and the Beethoven family, since otherwise he would not have been missing in the notices of Fischer, who does not even know his name. The judgment of the father that his instruction was inefficient was probably correct.

A fitter master, it was thought, was obtained in Tobias Friedrich Pfeiffer, who came to Bonn in the summer of 1779, as tenor singer in Grossmann and Helmuth's theatrical company. Mäurer says that Pfeiffer was a skillful pianist and oboist, and gave the boy lessons, but not at any regular hours. Often when he came with Beethoven, the father, from the wine-house late at night, the boy was roused from sleep and kept at the pianoforte until morning. Fischer also has a story concerning Pfeiffer's erratic habits, so Mäurer's story may have some truth in it.

About this time the young court musician Franz Georg Rovantini lived in the same house with Beethoven. He was the son of a violinist Johann Conrad Rovantini who had been called to Bonn from Ehrenbreitstein and who died in 1766. He was related to the Beethoven family. The young musician was much respected and sought after as teacher. According to the Fischer document the boy Beethoven was among his pupils, taking lessons on the violin and viola. But these lessons, too, came to an early end; Rovantini died on September 9, 1781, aged 24.

A strong predilection for the organ was awakened early in the lad and he eagerly sought opportunities to study the instrument, apparently even before he became Neefe's pupil. In the cloister of the Franciscan monks at Bonn there lived a friar named Willibald Koch, highly respected for his playing and his expert knowledge of organ construction. We have no reason to doubt that young Ludwig sought him out, received instruction from him and made so much progress that Friar Willibald accepted him as assistant. In the same way he made friends with the organist[12] in the cloister of the Minorites and "made an agreement" to play the organ there at 6 o'clock morning mass. It would seem that he felt the need of familiarity with a larger organ than that of the Franciscans. On the inside of the cover of a memorandum book which he carried to Vienna with him is found the note: "Measurements (*Fussmass*)

---

[12] Herr Pater Hanzmann. He is mentioned in the Fischer manuscript. See TDR, I, 455.

of the Minorite pedals in Bonn." Plainly he had kept an interest in the organ. Still another tradition is preserved in a letter to the author from Miss Auguste Grimm, dated September, 1872, to the effect that Heinrich Theisen, born in 1759, organist at Rheinbreitbach near Honnef on the Rhine, studied the organ in company with Beethoven under Zenser, organist of the Münster-kirche at Bonn, and that the lad of ten years surpassed his fellow student of twenty. The tradition says that already at that time Ludwig composed pieces which were too difficult for his little hands. "Why, you can't play that, Ludwig," his teacher is said to have remarked, and the boy to have replied: "I will when I am bigger."

When Beethoven's studies with van den Eeden began and ended, whether they were confined to the organ or pianoforte, or partook of both—these are undecided points. It does not appear that any instruction in composition was given him until he became the pupil of Neefe. In the facsimile which follows the part devoted to thorough-bass in the so-called "Studien,"[13] the composer says: "Dear Friends: I took the pains to learn this only that I might write the figures readily and later instruct others; for myself I never had to learn how to avoid errors, for from my childhood I had so keen a sensibility that I wrote correctly without knowing it had to be so, or could be otherwise."

During Ludwig's period of training his horizon was not limited entirely to his family and the immediate neighborhood; many of his father's colleagues—singers, actors and instrumentalists—must have been visiting constantly, often to participate in music-making at his parents' home. This contact with musicians, in which he took an increasingly active part, was a way for the boy to absorb the activity, the manners and the prevailing thought of his native city. Naturally his impressions of the world about him were also made by his own wanderings.

The feeling for nature which manifests itself later with Beethoven and forms a stimulation for his compositions was already being cultivated at Bonn. Ludwig derived great pleasure, according to Fischer, from the beautiful view of the Rhine and the *Siebengebirge*[14] to be seen from the back of his house; "for Beethoven loved the Rhine." It can be safely assumed that Beethoven tramped around the lovely outskirts of Bonn at an early age, and there are stories handed down to confirm it. Fischer relates that during the Elector's absences, at which time the musicians were free, father Johann van Beethoven would travel into the country with his son Ludwig and the young Rovantini at the invitation of various music-lovers. One of their trips, for instance, was to the region of Rheinbach. One place that was visited during this trip was Flamersheim, where Baron Friedrich Wilhelm of Dalwigk, Chamberlain of the District of Utrecht, had his castle. They passed through different localities in this region and came to Ahrweiler where they visited Burgomaster Schopp.

[13] Ignaz Ritter von Seyfried, *L. v. Beethovens Studien* (Vienna, 1832).
[14] The mountain range with seven peaks on the other side of the Rhine.

Since Rovantini took part in this trip it could not be later than the summer of 1781, one of the times when the Elector Max Friedrich was absent. Regions on the right side of the Rhine were also visited; Hennef, Siegburg, Bensberg and Oberkassel were named. In Siegburg, where it was customary to visit "Herr Prelate," a tradition has been preserved of a later time when the young Beethoven played the organ in the abbey there. In Oberkassel there was the estate of a Herr von Meinertzhagen who is known to have been a patron of the young Beethoven. Since several of the persons called on were noted as friends of music, it is to be supposed that the father visited there with the special purpose of exhibiting his youthful prodigy.[15]

Mother and son undertook a voyage to Holland in the beginning of the winter of 1781. The widow Karth, one of the Hertel family, born in 1780 and still living in Bonn in 1861, passed her childhood in the house No. 462 Wenzelgasse, in the upper story of which the Beethovens then lived. She distinctly remembered sitting, when a child, upon her own mother's knee, and hearing Madame van Beethoven—"a quiet, suffering woman"—relate that when she went with her little boy Ludwig to Holland it was so cold on the boat that she had to hold his feet in her lap to prevent them from being frostbitten; and also that, while absent, Ludwig played a great deal in great houses, astonished people by his skill and received valuable presents. The circumstance of the cold feet warmed in the mother's lap is precisely one to fasten itself in the memory of a child, and form a point around which other facts might cluster.

--⚜{Krehbiel has added the following: There seems to have been no knowledge on the part of Beethoven's biographers of this visit to Holland until Thayer brought the incident to notice. It is, therefore, highly significant that the Fischer family also recalled the circumstance and, besides, knew what brought it about. The sister of young Rovantini, who died in September, 1781, was employed as governess in Rotterdam, and on receiving intelligence of the death of her brother came to Bonn, together with her mistress (whose name has not been preserved), to visit his grave. For a month she was an inmate of the Beethoven house; there was a good deal of music-making and some excursions to neighboring places of interest, including Coblenz. The visitors invited the Beethoven family to make a trip to Holland. Inasmuch as Johann van Beethoven could not get away, the mother went with the lad, and as a party of five, they embarked upon the voyage. This must have been in October or November, 1781, which agrees with the story of the extreme cold encountered on the voyage. They remained a considerable time, but whether or not Ludwig gave a concert as he had intended, is not known. Despite the attentions showered on him by the wealthy lady from Rotterdam and the many honors, the pecuniary results were disappointing. To Fischer's question how he had fared Beethoven is reported to have answered: "The

---

[15] This paragraph, based on the Fischer manuscript, was undoubtedly written by Deiters. See TDR, I, 144-45.

Dutch are skinflints (*Pfennigfuchser*); I'll never go to Holland again."⊱–

Christian Gottlob Neefe succeeded the persons mentioned as Beethoven's master in music. When this tutorship began and ended, and whether or not it be true that the Elector engaged and paid him for his services in this capacity, as affirmed by divers writers—here again positive evidence is wanting. Neefe came to Bonn in October, 1779; received the decree of succession to the position of Court Organist on February 15, 1781, and was thus permanently engaged in the Elector's service. The unsatisfactory nature of the earlier instruction, as well as the high reputation of Neefe, placed in the strongest light before the Bonn public by those proceedings which had compelled him to remain there, would render it highly desirable to Johann van Beethoven to transfer his son to the latter's care. It would create no surprise should proof hereafter come to light that this change was made even before the issue of the decree of February 15, 1781;—that even then the pupil was profiting by the lessons of the zealous Bachist. Whether this was so or not, it was more than ever necessary that the boy's talents should be put to profitable use, for the father found his family still increasing. The baptism of a daughter named Anna Maria Franziska after her sponsors Anna Maria Klemmers, *dicta* Kochs, and Franz Rovantini, court musician, is recorded in the St. Remigius register February 23, 1779, and her death on the 27th of the same month. The baptism of August Franciscus Georgius van Beethoven—Franz Rovantini, *Musicus Aulicus* and Helene Averdonk, *patrini*, follows nearly two years later—January 17, 1781. There is no minister of State now to lend his name to a child of Johann van Beethoven, nor any lady abbess. Rovantini, one of the youngest members of the orchestra (relative and friend of the family), a Frau Kochs, and the young contralto whose musical education the father had superintended, take their places—another indication that the head of the family is gradually sinking in social position.

It is Schlosser who states that "the Elector urged Neefe to make it his particular care to look after the training of the young Beethoven." How much weight is to be attached to this assertion of a man who hastily threw a few pages together soon after the death of the composer, and who begins by adopting the old error of 1772 as the date of his birth, and naming his father "Anton," may safely be left to the reader. That the story may possibly have some foundation in truth is not denied; but the probabilities are all against it. Just in these years Max Friedrich is busy with his tric-trac, his balls, his new operettas and comedies, and with his notion of making the theatre a school of morals. The truth seems to be (and it is the only hypothesis that suggests itself, corresponding to the established facts), that Johann van Beethoven had now determined to make an organist of his son as the surest method of making his talents productive. The appointment of Neefe necessarily destroyed Ludwig's hope of being van den Eeden's successor; but Neefe's other numerous employments would make an assistant indispensable, and to this place the boy might well aspire. It will be seen in the course of the narrative that Beethoven never had a warmer, kinder and more valuable friend than Neefe proved throughout the remainder of his Bonn life; that, in fact, his first appointment was obtained for him through Neefe, although this is the first hint yet published that the credit does not belong to a very different personage. What, then, so natural, so self-evident as that Neefe, foreseeing the approaching necessity of some one to take charge of the little organ in the chapel at times when his duties to the Grossmann company would prevent him from officiating in person, should gladly undertake the training of the remarkable talents of van den Eeden's pupil with no wish for any other remuneration than the occasional services which the youth could render him?

Dr. Wegeler remarks: "Neefe had little influence upon the instruction of our Ludwig, who frequently complained of the too severe criticisms made on his first efforts in composition." The first of these assertions is evidently an utter mistake. In 1793 Beethoven himself, at all events, thought differently: "I thank you for the counsel which you gave me so often in my progress in my divine art. If I ever become a great man yours shall be a share of the credit. This will give you the greater joy since you may rest assured," etc. Thus he wrote to his old teacher. As to the complaint of harsh criticism it may be remarked that Neefe, reared in the strict Leipzig school, must have been greatly dissatisfied with the direction which the young genius was taking under the influences which surrounded him, and that he should labor to change its course. He was still a young man, and in his zeal for his pupil's progress may well have criticized his childish compositions with a severity which, though no more than just and reasonable, may have so contrasted with injudicious praise from other quarters as to wound the boy's self-esteem and leave a sting behind; especially if Neefe indulged in a tone at all contemptuous, a common fault of young men in like cases. Probably, in some conversation upon this point Beethoven may have remarked to Wegeler that Neefe had criticized him in his childhood rather too severely.

But to return from the broad field of hypothesis to the narrow path of facts. "On this day, June 20, 1782," Neefe writes of himself and the Grossmann company, "we entered upon our journey to Münster, whither the Elector also went. The day before my predecessor, Court Organist van den Eeden, was buried; I received permission, however, to leave my duties in the hands of a vicar and go along to Westphalia and thence to the Michaelmas fair at Frankfurt." The Düsseldorf documents prove that this vicar was Ludwig van Beethoven, now just eleven and a half years of age. In the course of the succeeding winter, Neefe prepared that very valuable and interesting communication to Cramer's *Magazin der Musik* which has been so largely quoted. In this occurs the first printed notice of Beethoven, one which is honorable to head and heart of its author. He writes, under date of March

2, 1783:[16] "Louis van Betthoven, son of the tenor singer mentioned, a boy of eleven years and of most promising talent. He plays the clavier very skilfully and with power, reads at sight very well, and—to put it in a nutshell—he plays chiefly *The Well-Tempered Clavichord* of Sebastian Bach, which Herr Neefe put into his hands. Whoever knows this collection of preludes and fugues in all the keys—which might almost be called the *non plus ultra* of our art—will know what this means. So far as his duties permitted, Herr Neefe has also given him instruction in thorough-bass. He is now training him in composition and for his encouragement has had nine variations for the pianoforte, written by him on a march—by Ernst Christoph Dressler—engraved at Mannheim. This youthful genius is deserving of help to enable him to travel. He would surely become a second Wolfgang Amadeus Mozart were he to continue as he has begun."

This allusion to Mozart, who had not then produced those immortal works upon which his fame now principally rests, speaks well for the insight of Neefe and renders his high appreciation of his pupil's genius the more striking.

The title of the original publication of the Variations by Goetz of Mannheim ran as follows: "Variations pour le clavecin sur une Marche de Mr. Dressler, composeès et dediès à son Excellence Madame la Comtesse de Wolfmetternich, nèe Baronne d'Assebourg, par un jeune amateur Louis van Betthoven, agè de dix ans." Georg Kinsky establishes the publication date as 1782 or at the latest, the beginning of 1783.[17] The Countess Wolff-Metternich was the wife of Count Ignaz von Metternich, "Konferenzmeister" and president of the High Court of Appeals, who died in Bonn, March 15, 1790. Ernst Christoph Dressler, composer of the theme varied by Beethoven, was an opera singer in Cassel.

There were many examples of the sonata and variations forms to serve as models for the boy. The three-movement sonata in its short compact form was particularly developed by Carl Philipp Emanuel Bach, and there is no doubt that the young Beethoven was acquainted with these works. Whether this experience was gained primarily through Neefe, who himself writes that he studied Emanuel Bach intensively, is not certain; presumably Beethoven already knew his work in his own home. The only reference to his (Beethoven's) father made by Beethoven in all the manuscripts examined for this work, an official document or two excepted, is written in Beethoven's hand upon an unfinished copy of one of Emanuel Bach's cantatas, *Morgengesang am Schöpfungstage*, "Written down by my dear father." One of the works most used by him in compiling his *Materialen für Contrapunkt* in 1809 was Emanuel Bach's *Versuch über die wahre Art das Clavier zu Spielen*.

It is particularly to Neefe's credit that he brought Sebastian Bach's *Well-*

---

[16] Vol. I, p. 394. (TDR, I, 150, n. 1.)

[17] "Beethoven-Erstdrucke bis zum Jahre 1800," *Philobiblon*, Jhrg. II, Heft 8 (1930), pp. 329ff. See also KHV, WoO 63.

Tempered Clavichord to his pupil's attention, because with it he provided the young genius with material to offset the shallowness of many of the compositions of the day with which Beethoven, because of his professional duties, could not escape contact. From Bach's preludes and fugues, which he was also to play a great deal later in life, he not only derived considerable instruction, but he found, as is evidenced in many of his later works (e.g., the prelude in F minor), a pattern for imitation. In general, however, his model was not Bach but Mozart. That Beethoven early became familiar with Mozart's music in his own home may be regarded as certain. From 1784 on, he was in a position to become acquainted almost at once with Mozart's latest major works and the latter's influence upon his own music can be traced almost everywhere. That Neefe encouraged him in this may be assumed, although definite proof is lacking. In any case, however, the musical life of Bonn and his own participation in it offered him ample opportunity to become acquainted with the most significant compositions by contemporary masters of operatic, orchestral, and church music, and it is not necessary to assume that he was influenced by Neefe in every instance.

However that may be, it must be assumed that Neefe, his character being what it was, proceeded conscientiously, carefully, and "as best he could" methodically with his instruction of the young genius. If nevertheless there were gaps in his instruction it was due to limitations in his own knowledge and ability. He himself, it must be remembered, had by his own admission never had a complete course in composition, although he had gained much from his association with J. A. Hiller. Being in the theatre, and having the kind of mind that he did, what he valued most was the achievement of simplicity and intelligibility in music. He himself was not quite secure in the more difficult polyphonic forms and so could not teach them. For this lack Beethoven had to make up later with Albrechtsberger in Vienna. On the other hand, Neefe brought to the young artist another element which was extremely valuable in the development of his particular talent. Having studied philosophy, he liked to relate musical forms to the spiritual life of man, and in this direction exercised a decisive influence on Beethoven's artistic philosophy. Perhaps also by his suggesting graceful melodic and harmonic touches and by counseling variety in the repetition of an idea, etc., he may have awakened in Beethoven that critical sense which later we find developed to so high a degree. Whether we should go farther and assume with Nottebohm that he exerted a moral influence upon Beethoven's character is, in view of the complete lack of details concerning their personal relationship, questionable. It is not inconceivable that, from the human standpoint, the constant association with an admirable man who was also enthusiastic about his art, may have been important to Beethoven, particularly in view of the less pleasant experiences of his home. In Fischer's memoirs, it may be added, Neefe and his wife are mentioned among those who frequent the Beethoven house.

A second work belonging to this period was a two-part fugue in D for the organ, which according to Nottebohm was probably played at his trial for the post of second court organist.

The place of assistant organist to Neefe was no sinecure; although not involving much labor, it brought with it much confinement. The old organ had been destroyed by the fire of 1777, and a small chamber instrument still supplied its place. It was the constantly recurring necessity of being present at the religious services which made the position onerous. According to the Court Calendar:

On all Sundays and regular festivals high mass at 11 a.m. and vespers at 3 (sometimes 4) p.m. The vespers will be sung throughout in *Capellis solemnibus* by the musicians of the electoral court, the middle vespers will be sung by the court clergy and musicians in plain chant with the exception of the *Magnificat*, which will be performed in concerted music. On all Wednesdays in Lent the *Miserere* will be sung by the chapel at 5 p.m. and on all Fridays the *Stabat Mater*. Every Saturday at 3 p.m. the Litanies at the altar of Our Lady of Loretto. Every day throughout the year two masses will be read, the one at 9, the other at 11—on Sundays the latter at 10.

Such a programme gave the organist something at least to do, and when Neefe left Bonn for Münster, June 20, 1782, he left his pupil no easy task. Before the close of the theatrical season of the next winter (1782-83) the master was obliged to call upon the boy for still further assistance. "In the winter of 1784," writes the widow Neefe, "my husband of blessed memory was temporarily entrusted with the direction of the church music as well as all other music at the court while the Electoral Kapellmeister L[ucchesi] was absent on a journey of several months." The date is wrong, for Lucchesi's petition for leave of absence was granted April 26, 1783. Thus overwhelmed with business, Neefe could no longer conduct at the pianoforte the rehearsals for the stage, and Ludwig van Beethoven, now 12 years old, became also "cembalist in the orchestra." In those days, every orchestra was provided with a harpsichord or pianoforte, seated at which the director guided the performance, playing from the score. Here, then, was in part the origin of that marvellous power, with which in later years Beethoven astonished his contemporaries, of reading and playing the most difficult and involved scores at first sight. The position of cembalist was one of equal honor and responsibility. Handel and Mattheson's duel grew out of the fact that the former would not leave the harpsichord on a certain occasion before the close of the performance. Gassmann placed the young Salieri at the harpsichord of the Imperial Opera House as the best possible means of training him to become the great conductor that he was. This was the high place of honor given to Haydn when in London. In Ludwig van Beethoven's case it was the place in which he, as Mosel says of Salieri, "could make practical use of what he learned from books and scores at home." Moreover, it was a place in which he could, even in boyhood, hear to satiety the popular Italian, French and German operas of the day and learn to feel that something higher and nobler was necessary to touch the deeper feelings of the heart; a place which, had the Elector lived ten years longer, might have given the world another not merely great but prolific, nay inexhaustible, operatic composer.

The cembalist's duties doubtless came to an end with the departure of the Elector for Münster in May or June, and he then had time for other pursuits, of which composition was one. A song, "Schilderung eines Mädchens," by him was printed this year in Bossler's *Blumenlese für Liebhaber,* and a Rondo in C for pianoforte, anonymous, which immediately follows, was also of his composition. A more important work, which on October 14, 1783, was announced as published by Bossler with a magniloquent dedication to Max Friedrich, was the already mentioned three sonatas for pianoforte, according to the title "composed by Ludwig van Beethoven, aged 11 years." The title of the original publication: "Drei Sonaten für Klavier, dem Hochwürdigsten Erzbischofe und Kurfürsten zu Köln, Maximilian Friedrich meinem gnädigsten Herrn gewidmet und verfertiget von Ludwig van Beethoven, alt eilf Jahr." Beethoven wrote on a copy of the first sonatas: "These Sonatas and the Variations of Dressler are my first works."[18] He probably meant his first published works.

To turn again to the Beethoven family matters. This summer (1783) had brought them sorrow again. The child Franz George, now just two and a half years old, died August 16th. This was another stroke of bad fortune which wounded the heart of the father at a time when his pecuniary difficulties were increasing; he was now losing his voice, and his character is described in an official report made the next summer by the words "of tolerable conduct."

If the duties of Neefe during the last season had been laborious, in the coming one, 1783-84, they were still more arduous. It was the first under the new contract by which the Elector assumed all the costs of the theatre, and a woman, Mme. Grossmann, had the direction. It was all-important to singers, actors and whoever was concerned that the result of the experiment should be satisfactory to their employer; and as the opera was more to his taste than the spoken drama, so much the more difficult was Neefe's task. Besides his acting as kapellmeister in the place of Lucchesi, still absent, there was "every forenoon rehearsal of opera," as Mme. Grossmann wrote to Councillor Tabor, at which, of course, Neefe had to be present. There was ever new music to be examined, arranged, copied, composed—what not?—

[18] See WoO 47. Nottebohm (*Thematisches Verzeichniss,* pp. 148, 198) notes that in this copy, which belonged to Otto Jahn, there was added a pencil notation in Beethoven's hand: "Before these works, however, songs and a set of variations in C minor appeared in an issue of Bossler's Journal." Moreover, the date "1781" was added in pencil on the title page. A lapse of the composer's memory concerning the variations; they were published not by Bossler but by Goetz.

all which he must attend to; in short, he had everything to do which could be imposed upon a theatrical music director with a salary of 1,000 florins. It therefore became a busy time for his young assistant, who still had no recognition as member of the court chapel, not even as "accessist"—the last "accessist" organist was Meuris (appointed 1767)—and consequently no salary from the court. But he had now more than completed the usual year of probation to which candidates were subjected, and his talents and skill were well enough known to warrant his petition for an appointment. The petition has not been discovered; but the report made upon it to the privy council has been preserved, together with the endorsement. The report upon the petition is as follows:

Most Reverend Archbishop and Elector,
Most Gracious Lord, Lord.

Your Electoral Grace has graciously been pleased to demand a dutiful report from me on the petition of Ludwig van Beethoven to Your Grace under date the 15th inst.

Obediently and without delay [I report] that suppliant's father was for 29 years, his grandfather for 46, in the service of Your Most Reverend Electoral Grace and Your Electoral Grace's predecessors; that the suppliant has been amply proved and found capable to play the court organ as he has done in the absence of Organist Neefe, also at rehearsals of the plays and elsewhere and will continue to do so in the future; that Your Grace has graciously provided for his care and subsistence (his father no longer being able to do so). It is therefore my humble judgment that for these reasons the suppliant well deserves to have graciously bestowed upon him the position of assistant at the court organ and an increase of remuneration. Commending myself to the good will of Your Most Reverend Electoral Grace I am Your Most Reverend Grace's

most humble and obedient servant
Bonn, February 23, 1784.   Sigismund Altergraff zu
Salm und Reifferscheid.

The action taken is thus indicated:

High Lord Steward Count v. Salm, referring to the petition of *Ludwig van Betthofen* to become assistant to court organist Neefe, is of the humble opinion that the grace ought to be bestowed upon him, also that a small increase to his present support be granted.

Ad. sup.
Ludwig van Betthoven
On the obedient report the suppliant's
submissive prayer, rests.
Bonn, February 29, 1784.

The necessity of the case, the warm recommendation of Salm-Reifferscheid, very probably, too, the Elector's own knowledge of the fitness of the candidate, and perhaps the flattery in the dedication of the sonatas—for these were the days when dedications were but half disguised petitions for favor—were sufficient inducements to His Transparency at length to confirm the young organist in the position which Neefe's kindness had now for nearly two years given him.

The appointment was made,[19] but the salary had not been determined upon when an event occurred which wrought an entire change in the position of theatrical affairs at Bonn:—the Elector died on April 15, and the theatrical company was dismissed with four weeks' wages. Lucchesi returned to Bonn; Neefe had nothing to do but play his organ, cultivate his garden outside the town and give music lessons.

In February, 1784 the great inundation of the Rhine took place, and the terror of this event remained for a long time in the minds of the citizens of Bonn. At this time the Beethoven family still lived in the Rheingasse. The Fischer manuscript relates expressly and this time clearly from distinct family memories that Frau van Beethoven sought to stay the alarm of the residents with encouraging words, but at the last had to make her escape with the others into the Giergasse over boards and down ladders.[20] Around 1785 they moved to a better part of the town, i.e. in the pleasant house No. 462 Wenzelgasse. The house is very near the Minorite Church, which contained a good organ, concerning the pedal measurements of which, as we have seen, Beethoven made a memorandum in a note-book which he carried with him to Vienna.

--◆{Frimmel[21] asserts that soon the family was once again in the Fischer house in the Rheingasse. But the constant music-making was irksome to the landlord and his neighbors, and the third and last move of the Beethoven family out of the Fischer house occurred around 1787. The house in the Wenzelgasse, to which the family had moved back, was where Beethoven's mother was to end her life. Then, five years later, after the composer had already moved to Vienna, his father died in this house also.}◆--

In the *Neue Blumenlese für Klavierliebhaber* of this year, Part I, pp. 18 and 19, appeared a Rondo for Pianoforte, in A major, "dal Sig^{re} van Beethoven";[22] and Part II, p. 44, the Arioso "An einen Säugling, von Hrn. Beethoven."[23] "Un Concert pour le Clavecin ou Fortepiano composé par Louis van Beethoven âgé de douze ans," in E-flat, 32 pp. manuscript written in a boy's hand, may also belong to this year.[24]

[19] Schiedermair, on the other hand, interprets the last words of the report (*auszuwerfen sey*) to mean "be thrown out," thus refused, rather than granted, and adds that there is no explanation of the Elector's decision available (see *Der Junge Beethoven*, pp. 165-66). Thayer's interpretation, however, seems the more likely.

[20] Here Thayer gave no credence to the Fischer manuscript. The present editor has chosen to follow TDR. Cf. TK, I, 75 and

TDR, I, 167.

[21] Theodor Frimmel, *Beethoven Handbuch* (Leipzig, 1926), II, 441.

[22] *GA*, Serie 18, No. 196. (TDR, I, 168, n. 3.)

[23] *Ibid.*, Serie 23, No. 229. (TDR, I, 168, n. 3.)

[24] The manuscript contains the solo part complete with the orchestral preludes and interludes in transcription for pianoforte. There are indications that it was scored for

The widow Karth perfectly remembered Johann van Beethoven as a tall, handsome man with powdered head. Ries and Simrock described Ludwig to Dr. Müller "as a boy powerfully, almost clumsily built." In the Fischer manuscript he is described as "short of stature, broad shoulders, short neck, large head, round nose, dark brown complexion; he always bent forward slightly when he walked. In the house he was called *der Spagnol* (the Spaniard)." How easily fancy pictures them—the tall man walking to chapel or rehearsal with the little boy trotting by his side, through the streets of Bonn, and the gratified expression of the father as the child takes the place and performs the duties of a man!

The following works were composed between 1782 and 1785:

1782. Variations for Pianoforte on a March by E. Chr. Dressler, WoO 63.
1782-3. Three Sonatas for Pianoforte, WoO 47.
1783. Fugue in D major for Organ, WoO 31.
Rondo in C major for Pianoforte, WoO 48.
Rondo in A major for Pianoforte, WoO 49.
Song. "Schilderung eines Mädchens," WoO 107.
Song. "An einen Säugling," WoO 108.
1784. Concerto for Pianoforte and Orchestra in E-flat major, WoO 4.
1785. Three Quartets for Piano and Strings, WoO 36.
1785. Song. "Urians Reise um die Welt," Op. 52, No. 1.
1785? Minuet for Pianoforte in E-flat major, WoO 82.
In his *Thematisches Verzeichniss* Nottebohm[25] states that on an old copy of this last work is written in another hand, "dans l'âge de 13 ans." The copy has disappeared; Kinsky questions the trustworthiness of Nottebohm's evidence and believes at any rate that the work was revised before its publication in Vienna in 1805.

---

small orchestra—strings, flutes, and horns only. The composition has been published in the supplement to the collected works of Beethoven, Serie 25, No. 310. (TK, I, 75, n. 4. Cf. TDR, I, 168-69.)
[25] Leipzig, 1868, p. 149.

CHAPTER IV

ELECTOR MAX FRANZ AND
HIS COURT—
THE VON BREUNING FAMILY—
THE YEARS 1784 TO 1786

"MARIA THERESIA was a tender mother, much concerned to see all her children well provided for in her lifetime and as independent as possible of her eldest son, the heir to the throne. This wish had already been fulfilled in the case of several of them. . . . The youngest son, Maximilian (born in Vienna, December 8, 1756), was already chosen coadjutor to his paternal uncle, Duke Karl of Lorraine, Grand Master of the Teutonic Order. But to provide a more bountiful and significant support, Prince Kaunitz formulated a plan which pleased the maternal heart of the monarch, and whose execution was calculated to extend the influence of the Court of Vienna in the German Empire. It was to bestow more ecclesiastical principalities upon the Archduke Maximilian. His eyes fell first upon the Archbishopric and Electorate of Cologne and the Archbishopric and Principality of Münster. These two countries had one and the same Regent, Maximilian Friedrich, descended from the Suabian family of Königseck-Rothenfels, Counts of the Empire. In view of the advanced age of this ruler his death did not seem far distant; but it was thought best not to wait for that contingency, but to secure the right of succession at once by having the Archduke elected Coadjutor in Cologne and Münster. Their possession was looked upon as a provision worthy of the son of an Empress-Queen. As Elector and Lord of the Rhenish shore, simultaneously co-director of the Westphalian Circuit (a dignity associated with the archbishopric of Münster), he could be useful to his house, and oppose the Prussian influence in the very part of Germany where it was largest."

Thus Dohm[1] begins the seventh chapter of his *Denkwürdigkeiten* where, in a calm and passionless style, he relates the history of the intrigues and negotiations which ended in the election of Maria Theresia's youngest son on August 7, 1780, as coadjutor to the Elector of Cologne and, on the 16th of the same month, to that of Münster, and secured him the peaceful and immediate succession when Max Friedrich's functions should cease. The news of the election at Cologne reached Bonn on the same day about 1 o'clock p.m. The Elector proceeded at once to the Church of the Franciscans (used as the chapel since the conflagration of 1777), where a "musical 'Te Deum'" was sung, while all the city bells were ringing. Von Kleist's regiment fired a triple salvo, which the cannon on the city walls answered. At noon a public dinner was spread in the palace, one table setting 54, another 24 covers. In the evening at 8:30 followed the finest illumination ever seen in Bonn, which the Elector enjoyed riding about in his carriage. After this came a grand supper of 82 covers, then a masked ball "to which every decently clad subject as well as any stranger was admitted, and which did not come to an end till nearly 7 o'clock."

Max Franz was in his twenty-eighth year when he came to Bonn. He was of middle stature, strongly built and already inclining to that corpulence which in his last years made him a prodigy of obesity. If all the absurdities of his eulogists be taken for truth, the last Elector of Cologne was endowed with every grace of mind and character that ever adorned human nature. In fact, however, he was a good-looking, kindly, indolent, somewhat choleric man; fond of a joke; affable; a hater of stiff ceremony; easy of access; an honest, amiable, conscientious ruler, who had the wisdom and will to supply his own deficiencies with enlightened and skilful ministers, and the good sense to rule, through their political foresight and sagacity, with an eye as much to the interests of his subjects as his own.

In his boyhood he was rather stupid. Swinburne dismisses him in two lines: "Maximilian is a good-natured, neither here-nor-there kind of youth." The brilliant, witty, shrewdly observant Mozart wrote to his father (November 17, 1781): "To whom God gives an office he also gives an understanding. This is really the case with the Archduke. Before he became a priest he was much wittier and more intellectual and talked less, but more sensibly. You ought to see him now! Stupidity looks out of his eyes; he talks eternally, always in falsetto; he has a swollen neck—in a word, the man is completely transformed." His mother had supplied him with the best instructors that Vienna afforded, and had sent him travelling pretty extensively for an archduke in those days. One of his journeys was to visit his sister Marie Antoinette in Paris, where his awkwardness and breaches of etiquette caused as much amusement to the anti-Austrian party as they did annoyance to the Queen, and afterwards to his brother Joseph, when they came to his ears.

[1] Christian Wilhelm von Dohm, *Denkwürdigkeiten meiner Zeit* (Lemgo and Hannover, 1814), I, 295ff.

In 1778 he was with Joseph in the campaign in Bavaria. An injury to his knee, caused by a fall of his horse, is the reason alleged for his abandonment of a military career; upon which he was prevailed upon, so the *Historisches Taschenbuch* (II, Vienna, 1806) expresses it, to become a candidate for the Coadjutorship of Cologne. If he had to be "prevailed upon" to enter the church, the more to his credit was the course he pursued when once his calling and election were sure.

The rigid economy which he introduced at court immediately after his accession in 1784 gave rise to the impression that he was penurious. It may be said in his defence that the condition of the finances required retrenchment and reform; that he was simple in his tastes and cared nothing for show and magnificence, except upon occasions when, in his opinion, the electoral dignity required them. Then, like his predecessors, he was lavish. His personal expenses were not great, and he waited until his revenues justified it before he indulged to any great extent his passion for the theatre, music and dancing (stout as he was, he was a passionate dancer), and his table. He was, through the nature of his physical constitution, an enormous eater, though his drink was only water.

The influence of a ruler upon the tone and character of society in a small capital is very great. A change for the better had begun during the time of Max Friedrich, but under his successor a new life entered Bonn. New objects of ambition were offered to the young men. The church and cloister ceased to be all in all. One can well understand how Wegeler in his old age, as he looked back half a century to the years when he was student and professor— and *such* a half-century, with its revolutionary and Napoleonic wars, its political, religious and social changes!—should write (*Notizen*, p. 59): "In fact, it was a beautiful and in many ways active period in Bonn, so long as the genial Elector, Max Franz, Maria Theresia's youngest son and favorite, reigned there." How strongly the improved tone of society impressed itself upon the characters of the young is discernible in the many of them who, in after years, were known as men of large and liberal ideas and became distinguished as jurists, theologians and artists, or in science and letters. These were the years of Beethoven's youth and early manhood; and though his great mental powers were in the main exercised upon his art, there is still to be observed through all his life a certain breadth and grandeur in his intellectual character, owing in part, no doubt, to the social influences under which it was developed.

It is highly honorable to the young Max Franz that he refused to avail himself of a privilege granted him in a Papal bull obtained for him by his mother—that of deferring the assumption of priestly vows for a period of ten years—but chose rather, as soon as he had leisure for the step, to enter the seminary in Cologne to fit himself for consecration. He entered November 29, rigidly submitted himself to all the discipline of the institution for the period of eight days, when, on December 8, the nuntius, Bellisoni, ordained him sub-deacon; after another eight days, on the 16th, deacon; and on the 21st, priest; thus showing that if there be no royal road to mathematics, there is a railway with express train for royal personages in pursuit of ecclesiastical science. Returning to Bonn, he read his first mass on Christmas eve in the Florian Chapel.

The cause of science and education the Elector had really at heart. In 1785 he had established a botanic garden; now he opened a public reading room in the palace library and sent a message to the theological school in Cologne, that if the improved course of instruction adopted in Austria was not introduced, he should found other seminaries. On the 26th of June he was present at the opening of a normal school; and on August 9th came the decree raising the Bonn *Hochschule* to the rank of a university by authority of an Imperial diploma.

Upon the suppression of the Jesuits in 1774, Max Friedrich devoted their possessions and revenues to the cause of education. New professorships were established in the gymnasium and in 1777 an "Academy" was formed. This was the first step; the second was to found an independent institution called the Lyceum; and at his death an application was before the Emperor for a university charter. This was granted in April, and Monday, the 20th of November, 1786, was the day appointed for the solemn inauguration of the new institution. The Court Calendar for the next year names six professors of theology, six of jurisprudence, civil and ecclesiastical, four of medicine, four of philosophy and seven of philology. In later editions new names are added; in that of 1790, Wegeler is professor of midwifery.

Though economical, Max Franz drew many a man of superior abilities— men of letters and artists—to Bonn; and but for the bursting of the storm which was even then gathering over the French border, his little capital might well have had a place in German literary history not inferior to that of Weimar. Nor are instances wanting in which he gave generous aid to young talent struggling with poverty; though that he did so much for Beethoven as is usually thought is, at least, doubtful.

This man, not a genius, not overwhelmingly great mentally, nor, on the other hand, so stupid as the stories told of his boyhood seem to indicate, yet very fond of music and a patron of letters and science,—this man, to whom in that period of vast intellectual fermentation the *Index Expurgatorius* was a dead letter, gave the tone to Bonn society.

That solid musical education that she had received from her father, Maria Theresia bestowed upon her children, and their attainments in the art seem to have justified the time and labor spent. In 1749, at the ages of seven and six, Christina and Maria Elisabeth took part in one of the festive musical pieces; Marie Antoinette was able to appreciate Gluck and lead the party in his favor in later years in Paris. Joseph II is as much known in musical as in civil and political history. When Emperor he had his daily hour of music in his private apartments, playing one of several instruments or singing, according to the whim of the moment; and Maximilian, the youngest, acquired a good degree of skill both in singing and in the treatment of his favorite instrument, the viola. Beethoven once told Schindler that the Elector thought very highly of Mattheson. In his reminiscences of a visit to Vienna in 1783, J. F. Reichardt[2] gives high praise to the musical interest, skill and zeal of Emperor Joseph and his brother Archduke Maximilian, and a writer in Cramer's *Magazin*,[3] probably Neefe, tells of a "remarkable concert" which took place at court in Bonn on April 5, 1786, at which the Elector played the viola, Duke Albrecht the violin, "and the fascinating Countess Belderbusch the clavier most charmingly."

Maximilian had become personally acquainted with Mozart in Salzburg in 1775, where the young composer had set Metastasio's *Il Re pastore* to music to be performed in his honor (April 23rd); from which time, to his credit be it said, he ever held the composer and his music in kindest remembrance. When in 1781 Mozart determined to leave his brutal Archbishop of Salzburg and remain in Vienna, the Archduke showed at all events a desire to aid him.

On November 17, 1781, the composer writes: "Yesterday the Archduke Maximilian summoned me to him at 3 o'clock in the afternoon. When I entered he was standing before a stove in the first room awaiting me. He came towards me and asked if I had anything to do to-day. 'Nothing, Your Royal Highness, and if I had it would always be a grace to wait upon Your Royal Highness.' 'No, I do not wish to constrain anyone.' Then he said that he was minded to give a concert in the evening for the Court of Wurtemburg. Would I play something and accompany the aria? I was to come to him again at 6 o'clock. So I played there yesterday."[4]

Jahn, in his biography of Mozart, continues in the same vein: "Mozart was everything to him; he signalized him at every opportunity and said, if he were Elector of Cologne, Mozart would surely be his Kapellmeister. He had also suggested to the Princess [of Wurtemburg] that she appoint Mozart her music teacher, but received the reply that if it had rested with her she would have chosen him; but the Emperor (—'for him there is nobody but Salieri!' cried out Mozart peevishly—) had recommended Salieri because of the singing, and she had to take him, for which she was sorry."[5]

Jahn gives no reason why Mozart was not engaged for Bonn at the time of Maximilian's succession. Perhaps he would have been if Lucchesi had resigned in consequence of the reduction of his salary; but he kept his office of kapellmeister and could not very well be dismissed without cause. Mattioli's resignation was followed by the call of Joseph Reicha to the place of concertmaster; but for Mozart no vacancy occurred at that time. Maximilian was in Vienna during most of the month of October, 1785, and

---

[2] *AMZ*, October 13, 1813. (TDR, I, 185.)
[3] *Magazin der Musik*, ed. C. F. Cramer (Hamburg, 1786), II3, 959. (TDR, I, 187, n. 1.)

[4] Otto Jahn, *Wolfgang Amadeus Mozart* (Leipzig, 1889), I, 718. (TDR, I, 187, n. 2.)
[5] *Ibid.*

may have desired to secure Mozart in some way, but just at that time the latter was, as his father wrote, "over head and ears busy with the opera *Le Nozze di Figaro*." Old Kapellmeister Bonno could not live much longer; which gave him hope, should the opera succeed, of obtaining a permanent appointment in Vienna. In short, his prospects seemed just then so good that we need not be surprised at his determination—if he really should receive an offer from the Elector—to remain in the great capital rather than to take his young wife so far away from home and friends as the Rhine then was, and, in a manner, bury himself in a small town where so few opportunities would probably be given him for the exercise of the vast powers which he was conscious of possessing.

Was it the good or ill fortune of the boy Beethoven that Mozart came not to Bonn? His marvellous original talents were thus left to be developed without the fostering care of one of the very greatest of musical geniuses, and one of the profoundest of musical scholars; but on the other hand it was not oppressed, perhaps crushed, by daily intercourse with that genius and scholarship.

Maximilian, immediately after reaching Bonn as Elector, ordered full and minute reports to be made out concerning all branches of the administration, of the public and court service and of the cost of their maintenance. Upon these reports were based his arrangements for the future. Those relating to the court music are too important and interesting to be overlooked, for they give us details which carry us instantly into the circle which young Beethoven had just entered and in which, through his father's connection with it, he must from earliest childhood have moved. They are three in number, the first being a list of all the individuals constituting the court chapel; the second a detailed description of the singers and players, together with an estimate of their capabilities; the third consists of recommendations touching a reduction in salaries. A few paragraphs may be presented here as most intimately connected with significant personages in our history; they are combined and given in abstract from the first two documents. Among the tenors we find:

J. van Beethoven, age 44, born in Bonn, married; his wife is 32 years old, has three sons living in the electorate, age 13, 10 and 8 years, who are studying music, has served 28 years, salary 315 fl.

Johann Beethoven has a very stale voice, has been long in the service, very poor, of fair deportment and married.

Among the organists:

Christ. Gottlob Neefe, age 36, born at Chemnitz; married, his wife is 32, born at Gotha, has two daughters in the electorate, aged 5 and 2, has served three years, was formerly Kapellmeister with Seiler; salary 400 fl.

Christian Neffe, the organist, in my humble opinion might well be dismissed, inasmuch as he is not particularly versed on the organ, moreover is a foreigner, having no *Meritten* whatever and of the Calvinist religion.

Ludwig van Beethoven, age 13, born at Bonn, has served two years, no salary.

Ludwig Betthoven, a son of the Betthoven sub No. 8, has no salary, but during the absence of the Kapellmeister Luchesy he played the organ, is of good capability, still young, of good and quiet deportment and poor.

One of the items of the third report, proposing reductions of salaries and removals, has a very special interest as proving that an effort was made to supplant Neefe and give the post of court organist to young Beethoven. It reads:

Item. If Neffe were to be dismissed another organist would have to be appointed, who, if he were to be used only in the chapel could be had for 150 florins, the same is small, young, and a son of one of the court *musici*, and in case of need has filled the place for nearly a year very well.

Schiedermair[6] brings to light the ticklish situation Beethoven was in when the opposition to Neefe joined forces with the promoters of Beethoven, as is demonstrated by the wording of the item from the third report quoted above. The student was obviously caught between gratitude for his teacher's help and his own self interest.

The temporary resolution of this conflict is indicated by the list of "annual salaries of the Court Chapel and Music," dated June 27, 1784, which includes Neefe, organist, 200 florins in salary, and directly afterwards, Beethoven, organist, 150 florins in salary. This appears to be a compromise decision in which the salary for the boy had clearly been taken out of the salary of his teacher.

Thus the attempt to have Neefe dismissed from the service failed, but the reduction of his salary to the pittance of 200 florins had already led him to look about him to find an engagement for himself and his wife in some theatre, when Maximilian, having become acquainted with his merits (notwithstanding his Calvinism), restored his former allowance by a decree dated February 8, 1785.

When Joseph Reicha came to Bonn in Mattioli's place is still undetermined with exactness; but a decree raising him from the position of concertmaster to that of concert director, and increasing his salary to 1,000 florins, bears the date June 28, 1785. In the general payroll of this year Reicha's salary is stated to be 666 thalers 52 alb., that of "tenorist Beethoven" 200 thalers, and of "Beethoven jun." 100 thalers.

Schindler records—and on such points his testimony is good—that he heard Beethoven attribute the marvellous developments of Mozart's genius in great measure to the "consistent instruction of his father," thus implying his sense of the disadvantages under which he himself labored from the want of regular and systematic musical training through the period of his childhood and youth. Czerny also related that Beethoven had spoken to him of the harsh treatment and insufficient instruction received from his father.

---

[6] *Der Junge Beethoven*, p. 166.

"But," he added, "I had talent for music."[7] It is, however, by no means certain that had Ludwig van Beethoven been the son of Leopold Mozart, he would ever have acquired that facility of expression which enabled Wolfgang Mozart to fill up the richest and most varied scores almost as rapidly as his pen could move, and so as hardly to need correction—as if the development of musical idea was to him a work of mere routine, or perhaps, better to say, of instinct. *Poeta nascitur, non fit,* not only in respect to his thoughts but to his power of clothing them in language. Many a man of profoundest ideas can never by any amount of study and practice acquire the art of conveying them in a lucid and elegant manner. On the other hand there are those whose thoughts never rise above the ordinary level, but whose essays are very models of style. Handel said of the elder Telemann, that he could compose in eight parts as easily as he (Handel) could write a letter; and Handel's own facility in composition was something astonishing. Beethoven, on the contrary, as his original scores prove, earned his bread by the sweat of his brow. But no amount of native genius can compensate for the want of thorough training. If, therefore, it be true that nature had in some degree limited his powers of expressing his musical as well as his intellectual ideas, so much greater was the need that, at the age which he had now reached, he should have opportunity to prosecute uninterruptedly a more profound and systematic course of study. Hence, the death of Maximilian Friedrich, which must have seemed to the Beethovens at first a sad calamity, proved in the end a blessing in disguise; for while it did not deprive the boy of the pecuniary benefits of the position to which he had just been appointed, it gave him two or three years of comparative leisure, uninterrupted save by his share of the organist's duties, for his studies, which there is every reason to suppose he continued under the guidance of his firm friend Neefe.

These three years were a period of theatrical inactivity in Bonn. For the carnival season of 1785, the Elector engaged Böhm and his company, then playing alternately at Cologne, Aix-la-Chapelle and Düsseldorf. This troupe during its short season may have furnished the young organist with valuable matter for reflection, for in the list of newly studied pieces, from October 1783 to the same month 1785—thus including the engagement in Bonn—are Gluck's *Alceste* and *Orpheus,* four operas of Salieri (the *Armida* among them), Sarti's *Fra due Litiganti* and *L'Incognito* in German translation, Holzbauer's *Günther von Schwarzburg* and five of Paisiello's operas. These were, says the report in the *Theaterkalender* (1786), "in addition to the old and familiar French operettas, *Zémire et Azor, Sylvain, Lucile, Der Prächtige, Der Hausfreund,* etc., etc." The three serious Vienna operas, *Alceste, Orpheus* and *Armida,* in such broad contrast to the general character of the stock pieces of the Rhenish companies, point directly to Maximilian and the Bonn season. The elector of Hesse-Cassel, being then in funds by the sale of

[7] From a note by Otto Jahn. (TDR, I, 203, n. 1.)

his subjects to George III for the American Revolutionary War just closed, supported a large French theatrical company, complete in the three branches of spoken and musical drama and ballet. Max Franz, upon his return from Vienna in November, 1785, spent a few days in Cassel, and, upon the death of the Elector and the dismissal of the actors, a part of this company was engaged to play in Bonn during January and February, 1786. The performances were thrice a week, Monday, Wednesday and Saturday, and, with but two or three exceptions, consisted of a comedy, followed by a light opera or operetta. The list contains eight of Grétry's compositions, three by Dezède, two by Philidor, and one each by Sacchini, Champein, Pergolesi, Gossec, Fridzeri, Monsigny and Schwarzendorf (called Martini)—all of light and pleasing character, and enjoying then a wide popularity not only in France but throughout the Continent.

Meantime Grossmann had left Frankfurt and with Klos, previously a manager in Hamburg, had formed a new company for the Cologne, Bonn and Düsseldorf stages. This troupe gave the Carnival performances in 1787, confining them, so far as appears, to the old round of familiar pieces.

Each of these companies had its own music director. With Böhm was Mayer, composer of the *Irrlicht* and several ballets; with the French company Jean Baptiste Rochefort was "music-master"; and Grossmann had recently engaged Burgmüller, of the Bellomo company, composer of incidental music for *Macbeth*. Hence, during these years, Neefe's public duties extended no farther than his service as organist, for Lucchesi and Reicha relieved him from all the responsibilities of the church and concert-room.

That the organ service was at this time in part performed by the assistant organist is a matter of course; there is also an anecdote, related by Wegeler on the authority of Franz Ries, which proves it. On Tuesday, Friday and Saturday of Holy Week, portions of the Lamentations of Jeremiah† were included in the chapel service, recited by a single voice, accompanied on the pianoforte (the organ being interdicted) to the familiar Gregorian chant tune.

On one occasion, in the week ending March 27, 1785, the vocalist was Ferdinand Heller, too good a musician to be easily disconcerted, the accompanist Ludwig van Beethoven, now in his fifteenth year. While the singer delivered the long passages of the Latin text to the reciting note the accompanist might indulge his fancy, restricted only by the solemnity fitted to the service. Wegeler relates that Beethoven "asked the singer, who sat with unusual firmness in the tonal saddle, if he would permit him to throw him out, and utilized the somewhat too readily granted permission to introduce so wide an excursion in the accompaniment while persistently striking the reciting note with his little finger, that the singer got so bewildered that he could not find the closing cadence. Father Ries, the first violinist, then Music

† Joseph Schmidt-Görg has discovered a sketch by Beethoven in the Kafka sketchbook for a setting of the *Lamentations*. See "Ein neuer Fund in den Skizzenbüchern: die Lamentationen des Propheten Jeremias," *BJ*, 1957/58, pp. 107-110.

Director of the Electoral Chapel, still living, tells with details how Kapell-meister Lucchesi, who was present, was astonished by Beethoven's playing. In his first access of rage Heller entered a complaint against Beethoven with the Elector, who commanded a simpler accompaniment, although the spirited and occasionally waggish young prince was amused at the occurrence."

Schindler adds that Beethoven in his last years remembered the circum-stance, and said that the Elector had "reprimanded him very graciously and forbidden such clever tricks in the future." The date is easily determined: In Holy Week, 1784, neither Maximilian nor Lucchesi was in Bonn; in 1786 Beethoven's skill would no longer have astonished the kapellmeister. Of the other characteristic anecdotes related of Beethoven's youth there is not one which belongs to this period (May, 1784–April, 1787), although some have been attributed to it by previous writers.

Nothing is to be added to the record already made except that, on the authority of Stephan von Breuning, the youth was once a pupil of Franz Ries on the violin, which must have been at this time; that, according to Wegeler, his composition of the song "Wenn jemand eine Reise thut"[8] fell in this period, and that he wrote three pianoforte quartets, the original manu-script of which bore the following title: "Trois Quatuors pour le Clavecin, Violino, Viola e Basso. 1785. Composé par (de L.) Luis van Beethoven, agé 13 ans."[9] The reader will remark and understand the discrepancy here be-tween the date and the author's age. Were these quartets intended for publication and for dedication to Max Franz, as the sonatas had been for Max Friedrich? During their author's life they never saw the light, but Beethoven used motives from them later (in Opus 2). They were published in 1832 by Artaria and appear as Nos. 75 to 77, Series 10, in the Complete Works.

It should be mentioned here that Beethoven now or soon afterwards began to give lessons. That this happened before the death of his mother and that the purpose was to increase the slender family income we learn from Beethoven himself and from Wegeler.[10]

One family event is recorded in the parish of St. Remigius—the bap-tism of Maria Margaretha Josepha, daughter of Johann van Beethoven, on May 5, 1786.

In 1527, the year in which the administration of the office of *Hochmeister* of the Teutonic Order was united with that of the *Deutschmeister*, whose residence had already been fixed at Mergentheim in 1525, this city became the principal seat of the order. From 1732 to 1761 Clemens Augustus was *Hoch-und Deutschmeister* of the order; according to the French edition of the Court Calendar of 1761, Christoph von Breuning was *Conseiller d'État*

---

[8] "Urians Reise um die Welt," Op. 52, No. 1, published in 1805. (TK, I, 88, n. 1.)

[9] The figure indicating the composer's age

was first written "14" and then changed. (TDR, I, 208, n. 2.)

[10] *Notizen*, pp. 18-19. (TDR, I, 211, n. 1.)

et Référendaire, having succeeded his father-in-law von Mayerhofen in the office.

Christoph von Breuning had five sons: Georg Joseph, Johann Lorenz, Johann Philipp, Emanuel Joseph and Christoph. Lorenz became chancellor of the archdeanery of Bonn, and the *Freiadliges Stift* at Neuss; after the death of his brother Emanuel he lived in Bonn so that, as head of the family, he might care for the education of the latter's children. He died there in 1796. Johann Philipp, born 1742 at Mergentheim, became canon and priest at Kerpen, a place on the old highway from Cologne to Aix-la-Chapelle, where he died June 12, 1832. Christoph was court councillor at Dillingen.

Emanuel Joseph continued in the electoral service at Bonn; at the early age of 20 years he was already court councillor (*Conseiller actuel*). He married Hélène von Kerich, born January 3, 1750, daughter of Stephan von Kerich, physician to the elector. Her brother, Abraham von Kerich, canon and scholaster of the archdeanery of Bonn, died in Coblenz in 1821. A high opinion of the intellect and character of Madame von Breuning is enforced upon us by what we learn of her influence upon the youthful Beethoven. Court Councillor von Breuning perished in a fire in the electoral palace on January 15, 1777. The young widow (she had barely attained her 28th year), continued to live in the house of her brother, Abraham von Kerich, with her three children, to whom was added a fourth in the summer of 1777. Immediately after the death of the father, his brother, the canon Lorenz von Breuning, changed his residence from Neuss to Bonn and remained in the same house as guardian and tutor of the orphaned children. These were:

1. Eleonore Brigitte, born April 23, 1771. On March 28, 1802, she was married to Franz Gerhard Wegeler of Beul-an-der-Ahr, and died on June 13, 1841, at Coblenz.

2. Christoph, born May 13, 1773, a student of jurisprudence at Bonn, Göttingen and Jena, municipal councillor in Bonn, notary, president of the city council, professor at the law school in Coblenz, member of the Court of Review in Cologne, and, finally, *Geheimer Ober-Revisionsrath* in Berlin. He died in 1841.

3. Stephan, born August 17, 1774. He studied law at Bonn and Göttingen, and shortly before the end of the electorship of Max Franz was appointed to an office in the Teutonic Order at Mergentheim. In the spring of 1801 he went to Vienna, where he renewed his acquaintance with Beethoven. They had simultaneously been pupils of Ries in violin playing. The Teutonic Order offering no chance of advancement to a young man, he was given employment with the War Council and became Court Councillor in 1818. He died on June 4, 1827. His first wife was Julie von Vering, daughter of Ritter von Vering, a military physician; she died in the eleventh month of her wedded life. He then married Constanze Ruschowitz, who became the mother of Dr. Gerhard von Breuning, born August 28, 1813, author of *Aus dem Schwarzspanierhause.*

4. Lorenz (called Lenz, the posthumous child), born in the summer of 1777, studied medicine and was in Vienna in 1794-97 simultaneously with Wegeler and Beethoven. He died on April 10, 1798 in Bonn.

Madame von Breuning, who died on December 9, 1838, after a widowhood of 61 years, lived in Bonn until 1815, then in Kerpen, Beul-an-der-Ahr, Cologne and finally with her son-in-law, Wegeler, in Coblenz.

From the Wegeler *Notizen*[11] we learn of Beethoven's early friendship with the von Breuning family: "Ludwig received his first acquaintance with German literature, especially poetry, as well as his first training in social behaviour in the midst of the von Breuning family in Bonn. . . . In this house reigned an unconstrained tone of culture in spite of youthful wilfulness. Christoph von Breuning made early essays in poetry, as was the case (and not without success) with Stephan von Breuning much later. The friends of the family were distinguished by indulgence in social entertainments which combined the useful and the agreeable. When we add that the family possessed considerable wealth, especially before the war, it will be easy to understand that the first joyous emotions of Beethoven found vent here. Soon he was treated as one of the children in the family, spending in the house not only the greater part of his days, but also many nights. Here he felt that he was free, here he moved about without constraint, everything conspired to make him cheerful and develop his mind. Being five years older than Beethoven I was able to observe and form a judgement on these things."

In the preface to the *Notizen* Franz Wegeler affirms, "I was born in Bonn in 1765 and became acquainted with the 12 year old youth who was already a composer, and maintained the closest relationship with him uninterruptedly until September, 1787 when, at the end of my medical studies, I visited the Viennese schools and institutes." Wegeler did not return to Bonn until October, 1789.

Stephan's son, Gerhard von Breuning, has given us a description of how the Breuning family circle enlarged.[12]

"Children attract playmates, school children bring home friends after school. So must have grown the little family circle in the house of my grandmother through the years from the outside; the cultivated influence of this virtuous woman extended not only to her children but also to other young people. . . . A poor student of amiable and industrious character soon became daily a member of this household. This was Franz Gerhard Wegeler, the son of an Alsatian burgher, who sensed early a craving for knowledge, for expanding the limitations of his poor origin in order to develop himself for the career by which he was to be known by those around him. [Rector of the University at Bonn; later privy councillor and a distinguished doctor.]

"After he had already become attached to this house, he made the

[11] Pages 9-10.
[12] *Aus dem Schwarzspanierhause* (Vienna, 1874), p. 6.

acquaintance in 1782 of the son of a musician of the Electoral Court Chapel who, although still more a boy than a young man, already was burning with enthusiasm for the muse of music, just as the other was for science and art, and already he was playing the piano admirably.

"Eleonore and Lenz needed a piano teacher and Wegeler's young friend needed to give lessons for the support of himself and his parents. Thus it was that the young Ludwig van Beethoven became introduced into the hospitable home of my grandmother."

Riemann[18] has suggested that the year of the meeting between Beethoven and both Wegeler and Stephan von Breuning may well have been not 1782 but 1784, since at that time he would have been "already a composer," and since Wegeler refers to the fact (*Notizen*, p. 14) that Stephan "lived in the closest relation with him from his tenth year to his death." Stephan was born in 1774. Then, too, there was the confusion concerning the year of Ludwig's birth which may well have caused Wegeler to retain the impression of a boy that he thought was twelve who was in reality close to fourteen years of age. Although Wegeler later saw the baptismal register in the Bonn parochial record before writing the *Notizen*, he wouldn't necessarily have remembered to apply this discrepancy to the long-held memory of their first meeting. In turn Gerhard von Breuning arrived at the date 1782 by taking Wegeler's "12 year old youth" literally without perhaps taking into account that only in the last month of 1782 did Beethoven reach the age of twelve.

Thayer rejected this early a date for the meeting between Beethoven and the von Breuning family and adopted the date of late 1787. This was based on the later recollections of the widow Karth (who was not born until about 1780) and on the fact that there is no mention that the von Breuning family gave assistance to the composer in the tragic summer of 1787 after his mother's death. Thayer further implies that Wegeler's own intimacy with the von Breunings was not until after his return from Vienna in 1789. Every editor of the Thayer biography from Deiters on has questioned this stand in view of the general trustworthiness of Wegeler's *Notizen* and particularly in view of Wegeler's family tie with the von Breunings. Surely a man of sound mind, as Wegeler was when he wrote the *Notizen* in 1838, would not be mistaken as to the time that he first met his wife's family.

Beethoven's own words on this matter are to be found in a letter to Wegeler written in the early Vienna years: "Ah Wegeler, my only comfort lies in this, that you have known me almost from my childhood." We may conclude that the association between Beethoven and the Wegeler–von Breuning circle started in all likelihood around 1784.

[18] TDR, I, 222, n. 1.

CHAPTER V

THE YEARS 1787 TO 1788 — THE OPERATIC SEASONS FROM 1789 TO 1792

THERE is a letter from Bonn, written by Neefe, dated April 8, 1787, in Cramer's *Magazin* (II, 1385), which contains a passing allusion to Beethoven, and it affords another glimpse of the musical life there. It is given here in part: "Our residence city is becoming more and more attractive for music-lovers through the gracious patronage of our beloved Elector. He has a large collection of the most beautiful music and is expending much every day to augment it. It is to him, too, that we owe the privilege of hearing often good virtuosi on various instruments. Good singers come seldom. The love of music is increasing greatly among the inhabitants. The pianoforte is especially liked; there are here several *Hammerclaviere* by Stein of Augsburg, and other correspondingly good instruments. Among the amateurs who occupy their beautiful hands with these instruments, I shall name the Countesses Hatzfield, Belderbusch, Felise Metternich, Frau von Waldenfels, Fräulein v. Weichs, Frau v. Cramer, Frau Belzer, wife of the Privy Councillor, Fräulein v. Gruben, Fräulein v. Mastiaux etc. The youthful Baron v. Gudenau plays the pianoforte right bravely, and besides young Beethoven, the children of the kapellmeister deserve to be mentioned because of their admirable and precociously developed talent. All of the sons of Herr v. Mastiaux play the clavier well, as you already know from earlier letters of mine."

"This young genius deserves support to enable him to travel," wrote Neefe in 1783. In the springtime of 1787 the young "genius" was at length enabled to travel. Whence or how he obtained the means to defray the expenses of his journey, whether aided by the Elector or some other Maecenas, or dependent upon the small savings from his salary and—hardly possible—from the savings from his music lessons painfully and carefully hoarded for the purpose, does not appear.[1] The series of papers at Düsseldorf is at this point broken; so that not even the petition for leave of absence has been discovered.

⸺The approximate dates of the journey have been established by Panzerbieter[2] from the midweek reports of visitors in the *Münchener Zeitung* in the spring of 1787. On April 1st is listed the arrival of "Herr Peethofen, Musikus von Bonn bei Kölln," again on April 25th staying at the tavern "zum schwarzen Adler" is "Herr Peethoven, Kurköllnischer Kammervirtuos von Bonn." Panzerbieter estimates that to reach Munich on April 1st, Beethoven must have started his trip about March 20th and reached Vienna on April 7th. But clearly he spent another night in Munich on April 25th, which suggests his having left Vienna about April 20th. Thus he was in Vienna less than two weeks.⸺

Schindler[3] was told by some old acquaintances of Beethoven that "on that visit two persons only were deeply impressed upon the lifelong memory of the youth of sixteen years: the Emperor Joseph and Mozart." Beethoven could have seen the former only before April 11th, for on that day the Emperor set out for Kiev to join the Russian Empress Catherine for his tour of the Crimea.

Meanwhile Mozart, recently returned from Prague, was already deeply engrossed in the composing of *Don Giovanni*. On April 4th he was writing to his father, having just received news of his poor health. (Leopold Mozart died within two months.) It was not an auspicious time for the start of lessons with the master.

The oft-repeated anecdote of Beethoven's introduction to Mozart is stripped by Professor Jahn of Seyfried's superlatives and related in these terms:[4] "Beethoven, who as a youth of great promise came to Vienna in the spring of 1787, but was obliged to return to Bonn after a brief sojourn, was taken to Mozart and at that musician's request played something for him which he, taking it for granted that it was a show-piece prepared for the occasion, praised in a rather cool manner. Beethoven observing this, begged Mozart to give him a theme for improvisation. He always played admirably when excited and now he was inspired, too, by the presence of the master whom he reverenced greatly; he played in such a style that Mozart, whose attention and interest grew more and more, finally went silently to some friends who were sitting in an adjoining room, and said, vivaciously, 'Keep your eyes on him; some day he will give the world something to talk about.'"

The lessons given were few—a fact which accounts for the circumstance

---

[1] Wegeler's assertion (*Notizen*, p. 13) that the financing of Beethoven's trip to Vienna was made possible through Count Waldstein's influence will be seen to be erroneous, if it applies to 1787. (TDR, I, 212, n. 1)

[2] Eduard Panzerbieter, "Beethovens erste Reise nach Wien im Jahre 1787," *Zeitschrift für Musikwissenschaft*, x (1927), 153-61.

[3] *Biographie von Ludwig van Beethoven* (3rd ed., Munster, 1860), I, 14-15.

[4] W. A. Mozart (3rd ed.), II, 40. (TDR, I, 214, n. 2.)

that no member of Mozart's family in after years, when Beethoven had become world-renowned, has spoken of them.

⟶Ries (*Notizen*, p. 86) says: "During his visit to Vienna he received some instruction from Mozart, but the latter, as Beethoven lamented, never played for him." That is, during the lessons which must have been confined consequently to theory. But according to a communication from Czerny to Otto Jahn, Beethoven had explained to him that he had heard Mozart play: "he had a fine but choppy (*zerhacktes*) way of playing, no *ligato*." Czerny adds that Beethoven played this way at first, treating the pianoforte like an organ.[5] From these notices it is presumed that there was some occasion, public or private, attended by Beethoven at which Mozart performed on the piano. It is an open question whether Beethoven played before an assembled company; the newspapers of this period report only performances by such "wonder-children" as Johann Nepomuk Hummel (born 1778) and the ten-year-old Cesarius Scheidl who played a pianoforte concerto between the parts of an oratorio in the grand concert of the "Society of Musicians" on December 22nd of the preceding year.

As has been made clear, Beethoven must have left Vienna around April 20th since he spent the night of the 25th in Munich.⟶

That the youth in passing through Augsburg must have become acquainted with the pianoforte-maker Stein and his family is self-evident. There is something in a Conversation Book which seems to prove this, and also to add evidence to the falsification of his age. It is this: in the spring of 1824 Andreas Streicher and his wife—the same Stein's "Mädl"—whose appearance at the pianoforte when a child of eight and a half years is so piquantly described by Mozart, called upon Beethoven on their way from Vienna into the country. A few sentences of the conversation, written in the hand of the composer's nephew, are preserved. The topic for a time is the packing of movables and Beethoven's removal into country lodgings for the summer; and at length they come upon the instruments manufactured by Streicher; after which Karl writes: "Frau von Streicher says that she is delighted that at 14 years of age you saw the instruments made by her father and now see those of her son." True, it may be said that this refers to Beethoven's knowledge of the Stein "Hammerclaviere" then in Bonn; but to any one thoroughly conversant with the subject these words are, like Iago's "trifles light as air," confirmation strong of the other view. His introduction to the family of the advocate Dr. Schaden in Augsburg, is certain. Reichardt was in that city in 1790 and wrote of Frau Nanette von Schaden as being of all the women he knew, those of Paris not excepted, far and away the greatest pianoforte player, not excelled perhaps, by any virtuoso in skill and certainty; also a singer with much expression and excellent declamation—"in every respect an amiable and interesting woman." The earliest discovered letter of Beet-

[5] See TDR, I, 215.

hoven to Schaden, and dated Bonn, September 15, 1787, proves the friendship of the Schadens for him and fully explains the causes of his sudden departure from Vienna and the abrupt termination of his studies with Mozart.

Well born, especially worthy friend!

I can easily imagine what you must think of me, and I cannot deny that you have good grounds for not thinking favorably of me. I shall not, however, attempt to justify myself, until I have explained to you the reasons why I hope my apologies will be accepted. I must tell you that from the time I left Augsburg my cheerfulness as well as my health began to decline. The nearer I came to my native city the more frequent were the letters from my father urging me to travel with all possible speed, as my mother was not in a favorable state of health. I therefore hurried forward as fast as I could, although myself far from well. My longing once more to see my dying mother overcame every obstacle and assisted me in surmounting the greatest difficulties. I found my mother still alive but in the most deplorable state; her disease was consumption, and about seven weeks ago, after much pain and suffering, she died. She was such a kind, loving mother to me, and my best friend. Ah, who was happier than I when I could still utter the sweet name, mother, and it was heard? And to whom can I say it now? Only to the silent images of her evoked by the power of the imagination. I have passed very few pleasant hours since my arrival here, having during the whole time been suffering from asthma, which may, I fear, eventually develop into consumption. To this is added melancholy, almost as great an evil as my malady itself. Imagine yourself in my place, and then I shall hope to receive your forgiveness for my long silence. You showed me extreme kindness and friendship by lending me three carolins in Augsburg, but I must entreat your indulgence for a time. My journey cost me a great deal, and I have not the smallest hopes of earning anything here. Fate is not propitious to me here in Bonn.

Pardon my detaining you so long with my chatter; it was necessary for my justification.

I do entreat you not to deprive me of your valuable friendship; nothing do I wish so much as in some degree to become worthy of your regard.

I am, with the greatest respect

Your most obedient servant and friend,
L. v. Beethoven,
Court Organist to the Elector of Cologne.[6]

The Bonn *Intelligenzblatt* supplies a pendant to this sad letter:—"1787, July 17. Died, Maria Magdalena Koverich [*sic*], named van Beethoven, aged 49 years."[7] When Ferdinand Ries, some thirteen years later, presented his father's letter of introduction to Beethoven in Vienna, the latter "read the letter through" and said: "I cannot answer your father just now; but do you write to him that I have not forgotten how my mother died. He will be satisfied with that." "Later," adds Ries, "I learned that, the family being greatly in need, my father had been helpful to him on this occasion in every way."

[6] Lady Wallace's translation, amended. The letter is preserved in the Beethoven-Haus Museum in Bonn. (TK, I, 93, n. 1.)

[7] The age of Beethoven's mother at the time of her death is here incorrectly given. It should be 40. (TDR, I, 218, n. 1.)

A petition of Johann van Beethoven, offered before the death of his wife, describing his pitiable condition and asking aid from the Elector, has not been discovered; but the substance of it is found in a volume of *Geheime Staats-Protocolle* for 1787 in form following:

July 24, 1787

Your Elec. Court Musician makes obedient representation that he has got
Highness   into a very unfortunate state because of the long-continued sick-
has taken   ness of his wife and has already been compelled to sell a portion
possession of his effects and pawn others and that he no longer knows what
of this   to do for his sick wife and many children. He prays for the bene-
petition.   faction of an advance of 100 rthlr. on his salary.

No record is found in the Düsseldorf archives of any grant of aid to the distressed family; hence, so far as now appears, the only successful appeal for assistance was made to Franz Ries, then a young man of 32 years, who generously aided in "every way" his unfortunate colleague.

At this point Thayer's question, "Where then was the Breuning family? Where Count Waldstein?" must be answered. First of all, it was six months before Count Waldstein arrived in Bonn, as we shall see later. But it is probable that Beethoven had known the von Breuning family for some three years, and the absence of any evidence that they came to the boy's help can only be explained in one of two ways. Either they were at their summer home in Kerpen at the time, or else the sensitive Beethoven held back from revealing his feelings concerning a relationship so intimate to people outside the family. The von Breuning family may have been compelled to offer help indirectly to avoid hurting the feelings or wounding the pride of their friend.[8]

"My journey cost me a great deal, and I have not the smallest hope of earning anything here. Fate is not propitious to me here in Bonn." In poverty, ill, melancholy, despondent, motherless, ashamed of and depressed by his father's ever increasing moral infirmity, the boy, prematurely old from the circumstances in which he had been placed since his eleventh year, had yet to bear another "sling and arrow of outrageous fortune." The little sister, now a year and a half old—but here is the notice from the *Intelligenzblatt*:— "Died, November 25, Margareth, daughter of the Court Musician Johann van Beethoven, aged one year." And so faded the last hope that the passionate tenderness of Beethoven's nature might find scope in the purest of all relations between the sexes—that of brother and sister.

Thus, in sadness and gloom, Beethoven's seventeenth year ended.

Emanuel Philipp, Count Waldstein and Wartemberg von Dux, and his wife, a daughter of Emanuel Prince Lichtenstein, were parents of eleven children. The fourth son was Ferdinand Ernst Gabriel, born March 24, 1762. Uniting in his veins the blood of many of the houses of the Austrian Empire,

[8] See Schiedermair, *op.cit.*, p. 291.

there was no career, no line of preferment open to younger sons of titled families, which was not open to him, or to which he might not aspire. It was determined that he should seek activity in the Teutonic Order, of which Max Franz was Grand Master.

--⚜{From the research of Josef Heer[9] it is possible to fill in some details concerning Count Waldstein's relation to the Electoral Court at Bonn. Although by 1782 Max Franz at least knew Waldstein by name, it was not until six years later that the Count came to stay in Bonn. In the spring of 1784 he was in Venice and Malta hoping in vain to be sent on the Tunisian Campaign. A letter from his mother proves that he was again in Malta in the spring of 1785. After another year of travels he returned to Austria in the spring of 1786, at which time there was still a year before he was to enter the order. At Easter time in 1787 he was to begin his novitiate but asked for a two months' delay in order to handle the management of some family property. The Count did not begin his year's novitiate in Bonn but in Ellingen, on June 8, 1787, where he was to serve uninterruptedly under the commander of that region for a period of six months. Thereupon Max Franz called him to Bonn, where he arrived between January 29 and February 1, 1788, to serve out the remaining months. From the tone of Waldstein's letter to Ellingen, on February 5, 1788, after he had arrived, Heer suggests that this was his first visit to Bonn.[10]}⚜--

A Bonn correspondent for the *Wiener Zeitung* of July 2, 1788, reporting on the final ceremony says that the presence of high rulers at the time made the small capital very lively. The Governor of the Austrian Lowlands, Prince Anton of Saxony (the brother-in-law of the Elector), the Elector of Trèves, his sister Princess Kunigunde (great-aunt of King John of Saxony), the Elector of Mainz and Baron Dalberg, the Saxon Ambassador, were assembled there; and "on the day before yesterday [that is, June 17th] our gracious sovereign, as *Hoch-und Deutschmeister*, gave the accolade with the customary ceremonies to the Count von Waldstein, who had been accepted in the Teutonic Order."

Frau Karth remembered distinctly the 17th of June upon which Waldstein entered the order, the fact being impressed upon her mind by a not very gentle reminder from the stock of a sentinel's musket that the palace chapel was no place for children on such an occasion.

Against these facts we can weigh Wegeler's summary of Count Waldstein (*Notizen*, p. 13).

"The first, and in every respect the most important, of the Maecenases of Beethoven was Count Waldstein, Knight of the Teutonic Order, and (what is of greater moment here) the favorite and constant companion of the young Elector, afterwards Commander of the Order at Virnsberg and Chancellor of

[9] *Der Graf von Waldstein und sein Verhältnis zu Beethoven* (Leipzig, 1933), in *Veröffentlichungen des Beethovenhauses in* Bonn, IX, 9-15.
[10] *Ibid.*, p. 11.

the Emperor of Austria. He was not only a connoisseur but also a practitioner of music. He it was who gave all manner of support to our Beethoven, whose gifts he was the first to recognize worthily. Through him the young genius developed the talent to improvise variations on a given theme. From him he received much pecuniary assistance bestowed in such a way as to spare his sensibilities, it being generally looked upon as a small gratuity from the Elector. Beethoven's appointment as organist, his being sent to Vienna by the Elector, were the doings of the Count. When Beethoven at a later date dedicated the great and important Sonata in C major, Op. 53, to him, it was only a proof of the gratitude which lived on in the mature man. It is to Count Waldstein that Beethoven owed the circumstance that the first sproutings of his genius were not nipped; therefore we owe this Mæcenas Beethoven's later fame."

Wegeler's testimony concerning the warm relationship between the Count and the Elector is borne out by their correspondence. On the other hand, Wegeler is not reliable concerning the extent that the Count helped the young composer. When Beethoven received his appointment as second organist in 1784, the Count was in Malta; and during the first trip to Vienna (1787), the Count was presumably attending to the affairs of family property. One looks rather to Neefe and the Elector for support of the young artist's travels. But as Heer points out, with a memory as accurate as Wegeler's one seeks an explanation of the contradiction. Thus, it is conceivable that Beethoven and Waldstein met before the latter's arrival in Bonn. In Augsburg, for instance, there lived at the time Johann Friedrich von Waldstein, canon and brother to the Count. Connected also to the cathedral chapter at this time was Caspar Anton von Mastiaux, a good pianoforte player and friend of Beethoven's. Heer points out further that Mozart's visit of a month to Prague, starting January 11, 1787, was at the estate of Count Johann Joseph Thun, whose wife Wilhelmine was Waldstein's aunt. Since the Count was mostly in Bohemia, in February, 1787, he may well have met Mozart at his aunt's and have been in a position to supply Max Franz with information concerning the plans of the master with whom the Elector's young genius was being sent to study. If Waldstein knew of Beethoven's arrival in Vienna, he may have been glad to meet a representative of the court to which he knew he was soon to go.

It is likely, however, that if the Count, in the name of the Elector, helped Beethoven to reach Vienna it was for his second trip—and what turned out to be his final move there—in 1792.

It was in the cultivated circle of the von Breuning family that the friendship between Beethoven and the Count was allowed to develop. By this time Ludwig was seventeen, and the role of this family in his life was constantly increasing in value to him both morally and intellectually. It must not be forgotten that besides Madame von Breuning and her children the scholastic Abraham von Kerich and the canon Lorenz von Breuning were members of the household. The latter especially seems to have been a fine specimen of the enlightened clergy of Bonn who, according to Riesbeck, formed so striking a contrast to the priests and monks of Cologne; and it is easy to trace Beethoven's life-long love for the ancient classics—Homer and Plutarch at the head—to the time when the young Breunings would be occupied with them in the original under the guidance of their accomplished tutor and guardian. The uncle, Philipp von Breuning, may also have been influential in the intellectual progress of the young musician, for to him at Kerpen "the family von Breuning and their friends were annually for a vacation of five or six weeks. There, too, Beethoven several times spent a few weeks right merrily, and was frequently urged to play the organ," as Wegeler tells us in the *Notizen*.

The recent loss of his mother had left a void in his heart which so excellent a woman as Madame von Breuning could alone in some measure fill. He was at an age when the evil example of his father needed a counterbalance; when the extraordinary honors so recently paid to science and letters at the inauguration of the university would make the strongest impression; when the sense of his deficiencies in everything but his art would begin to be oppressive; when his mental powers, so strong and healthy, would demand some change, some recreation, from that constant strain in the one direction of music to which almost from infancy they had been subjected; when not only the reaction upon his mind of the fresh and new intellectual life now pervading Bonn society, but his daily contact with so many of his own age, friends and companions now enjoying advantages for improvement denied to him, must have cost him many a pang; when a lofty and noble ambition might be aroused to lead him ever onward; when, the victim of a despondent melancholy, he might sink into the mere routine musician, with no lofty aims, no higher object than to draw from his talents means to supply his necessities and gratify his appetites.

The distinction between persons of noble birth and the ordinary citizens of Bonn, who could not afford to own a house, was not sharp enough to prevent a mixture of the two in the salon life of such families as the von Mastiaux, von Breuning, von Belderbusch and Hatzfeld. Here there was talk of art, science and the politics of the day or performance of chamber music. Burghers and aristocrats also met together in reading societies, and the *Lesegesellschaft* at Bonn admitted Count Waldstein as a member as early as February 16, 1788. He became director of the society in 1794. The list of members or visitors to the meetings included many of the musicians of the *Hofkapelle*. Beethoven himself might have become a member except for the statute forbidding university students to join. Despite his lack of training at the Gymnasium, Beethoven attended some university lectures, a practice not uncommon at the time. Ernst Bücken has found a university register of philosophy "candidates" in 1789 which includes Karl Kügelgen, Anton Reicha and Beethoven.[11]

The association between Waldstein and the von Breunings during the spring of 1788 grew rapidly into friendship, as is confirmed by the fact that already in June the Count knew the family well enough to borrow from them a sum of money to help defray the expenses of the ceremony of his induction into the Teutonic Order. Furthermore, the von Breunings for generations had held positions in the order. One can imagine much music-making at that lively house on the city side of the Münsterplatz in which both Beethoven and Count Waldstein could participate, for this nobleman had had the best of musical education in Vienna during his childhood.

We have seen that relations between Waldstein and the Elector became close; both were great admirers of Mozart, and the Elector must have welcomed someone with whom he could talk about the Austrian Court. While his influence was felt on artistic matters, the Count never held a high court appointment. Occasionally acting as ambassador, he seemed to excel in arranging ceremonies of state such as at the Imperial Enthronement of Frankfurt in October, 1790, when he supervised the participation of the Elector and his retinue.

While all that Wegeler says of this man's kindness to Beethoven cannot be accepted, there is no reason whatever to doubt that those qualities which made the youth a favorite with the Breunings, added to his manifest genius, made their way to the young count's heart and gained for Beethoven a zealous, influential and active friend. Frau Karth remembered Waldstein's visits to the composer in the years following in his rooms on the Wenzelgasse and was confident that he made the young musician a present of a pianoforte. Still, in June, 1788, Waldstein possessed no such influence as to render a petition for increase in salary, offered by his protégé, successful. That document has disappeared, but a paper remains among the Düsseldorf archives, dated June 5, concerning the petition, which is endorsed "Beruhet." Whatever this word may here mean it is certain that Ludwig's salary as organist remained at the old point of 100 thalers, which, with the 200 received by his father, the three measures of grain and the small sum that he might earn by teaching, was all that Johann van Beethoven and three sons, now respectively in their eighteenth, fifteenth and twelfth years, had to live upon; and therefore so much the more necessity for the exercise of Waldstein's generosity.

After the death of the mother, says Frau Karth, a housekeeper was employed and the father and sons remained together in the lodgings in the Wenzelgasse. Carl was intended for the musical profession; Johann was put apprentice to the court apothecary, Johann Peter Hittorf. Two years, however, had hardly elapsed when the father's infirmity compelled the eldest son, not yet nineteen years of age, to take the extraordinary step of placing himself at the head of the family. One of Stephan von Breuning's reminis-

[11] Schiedermair, op.cit., pp. 195-96.

cences shows how low Johann van Beethoven had sunk: viz., that of having seen Ludwig furiously interposing to rescue his intoxicated father from an officer of police.

Here again the petition has disappeared, but its contents are sufficiently made known by the terms of the decree dated November 20, 1789:

His Electoral Highness having graciously granted the prayer of the petitioner and dispensed henceforth wholly with the services of his father, who is to withdraw to a village in the electorate, it is graciously commanded that he be paid in accordance with his wish only 100 rthr. of the annual salary which he has had heretofore, beginning with the approaching new year, and that the other 100 thlr. be paid to the suppliant's son besides the salary which he now draws and the three measures of grain for the support of his brothers.

It is probable that there was no intention to enforce this decree in respect of the withdrawal of the father from Bonn, and that this clause was inserted *in terrorem* in case he misbehaved himself; for he continued, according to Frau Karth, to dwell with his children, and his first receipt, still preserved, for the reduced salary is dated at Bonn—a circumstance, however, which alone would prove little or nothing.

Early in the year 1788, the mind of the Elector, Max Franz, was occupied with the project for forming a company of *Hofschauspieler*; in short, with the founding of a National Theatre upon the plan adopted by his predecessor in Bonn and by his brother Joseph in Vienna. His finances were now in order, the administration of public affairs in able hands and working smoothly, and there was nothing to hinder him from placing both music and theatre upon a better and permanent footing; which he now proceeded to do. The Klos troupe, which had left Cologne in March, played for a space in Bonn, and on its dispersal in the summer several of its better actors were engaged and added to others who had already settled in Bonn. The only names which it is necessary to mention here are those of significance in the history of Beethoven. Joseph Reicha was director; Neefe, pianist and stage-manager for opera; in the orchestra were Franz Ries and Andreas Romberg (violin), Ludwig van Beethoven (viola), Bernard Romberg (violoncello), Nikolaus Simrock (horn) and Anton Reicha (flute). A comparison of the lists of the theatrical establishment with that of the court chapel as printed in the Court Calendars for 1778 and the following years, shows that some of the singers in the chapel played in the theatrical orchestra, while certain of the players in the chapel sang upon the stage. Other names appear in but one of the lists.[12]

As organist the name of Beethoven appears still in the Court Calendar, but as viola player he had a place in both the orchestras. Thus, for a period

[12] In a letter to Grossmann in April, 1791, Neefe makes the statement ". . . everyone (with the exception of Steiger) has been appointed to serve together for life in the theatre, the church, and the concert." See Irmgard Leux, "Neue Neefeiana," *NBJ*, I (1924), 95.

of full four years, he had the opportunity of studying practically orchestral compositions in the best of all schools—the orchestra itself. This body of thirty-one members, under the energetic leadership of Reicha, many of them young and ambitious, some already known as virtuosi and still keeping their places in musical history as such, was a school for instrumental music such as Handel, Bach, Mozart and Haydn had not enjoyed in their youth; that its advantages were improved both by Beethoven and others of the younger men, all the world knows.

One fact worthy of note in relation to this company is the youth of most of the new members engaged. Maximilian seems to have sought out young talent, and when it proved to be of true metal, gave it a permanent place in his service, adopted wise measures for its cultivation, and thus laid a foundation upon which, but for the outbreak of the French Revolution, and the consequent dispersion of his court, would in time have risen a musical establishment, one of the very first in Germany.

This is equally true of the new members of his orchestra. Reicha himself was still a relatively young man, born in 1746. He was a virtuoso on the violoncello and a composer of some note; but his usefulness was sadly impaired by his sufferings from gout. The cousins Andreas and Bernhard Romberg, Maximilian had found at Münster and brought to Bonn. They had in their boyhood, as virtuosi upon their instruments—Andreas violin, Bernhard 'cello—made a tour as far as Paris, and their concerts were crowned with success. Andreas was born near Münster in 1767, and Ledebur (*Tonkünstler Berlins*) adopts the same year as the date also of Bernhard's birth. They were, therefore, three years older than Beethoven and now just past 21. Both were already industrious and well-known composers and must have been a valuable addition to the circle of young men in which Beethoven moved. The decree appointing them respectively Court Violinist and Court Violoncellist is dated November 19, 1790.

Anton Reicha, a fatherless nephew of the concertmaster, born at Prague, February 27, 1770, was brought by his uncle to Bonn in 1785. He had been already for some years in that uncle's care and under his instruction had become a good player of the flute, violin and pianoforte. In Bonn, Reicha became acquainted with Beethoven, who was then organist at court. "We spent fourteen years together," says Reicha, "united in a bond like that of Orestes and Pylades, and were continually side by side in our youth. After a separation of eight years we saw each other again in Vienna, and exchanged confidences concerning our experiences."[13] At the age of 17 composing orchestral and vocal music for the Electoral Chapel, a year later flautist in the theatre, at nineteen (1790) both flautist and violinist in the chapel and so intimate a friend of Beethoven, who was less than a year his junior—were Reicha's laurels no spur to the ambition of the other?

[13] From 1785 to 1792 in Bonn, and from approximately 1802 to 1808 in Vienna; thus, more nearly a ten-year separation. See *FRBH*, II, 57.

The names of several of the performers upon wind-instruments were new names in Bonn, and the thought suggests itself that the Elector brought with him from Vienna some members of the *Harmoniemusik* which had won high praise from Reichardt, and it will hereafter appear that such a band formed part of the musical establishment in Bonn—a fact of importance in its bearing upon the questions of the origin and date of various known works both of Beethoven and of Reicha, and of no less weight in deciding where and how these men obtained their marvellous knowledge of the powers and effects of this class of instruments.

The arrangements were all made in 1788, but not early enough to admit of the opening of the theatre until after the Christmas holidays, namely, on the evening of January 3, 1789. The theatre had been altered and improved. An incendiary fire threatened its destruction the day before, but did not postpone the opening. The opening piece was *Der Baum der Diana* by Vincenzo Martin. It may be thought not very complimentary to the taste of Maximilian that the first season of his National Theatre was opened thus, instead of with one of Gluck's or Mozart's masterpieces. It suffices to say that he, in his capacity of Grand Master of the Teutonic Order, had spent a good part of the autumn at Mergentheim and only reached Bonn on his return on the last day of January. Hence he was not responsible for that selection.

The season which opened on January 3, 1789, closed on May 23. Within this period the following operas were performed, Beethoven taking part in the performances as a member of the orchestra: *Der Baum der Diana* (*L'Arbore di Diana*), Martin; *Romeo und Julie*, Georg Benda; *Ariadne* (duo-drama by Georg Benda); *Das Mädchen von Frascati* (*La Frascatana*), Paisiello; *Julie*, Dezède; *Die drei Pächter* (*Les trois Fermiers*), Dezède; *Die Entführung aus dem Serail*, Mozart; *Nina*, Dalayrac; *Trofonio's Zauberhöhle* (*La grotta di Trofonio*), Salieri; *Der eifersüchtige Liebhaber* (*L'Amant jaloux*), Grétry; *Der Schmaus* (*Il Convito*), Cimarosa; *Der Alchymist*, Schuster; *Das Blendwerk* (*La fausse Magie*), Grétry.

The second season began October 13, 1789, and continued until February 23, 1790. On the 24th of February news reached Bonn of the death of Maximilian's brother, the Emperor Joseph II, and the theatre was closed. The repertory for the season comprised *Don Giovanni*, Mozart (which was given three times); *Die Colonie* (*L'Isola d'Amore*), Sacchini; *Der Barbier von Sevilla* (*Il Barbiere di Siviglia*), Paisiello; *Romeo und Julie*, Georg Benda; *Die Hochzeit des Figaro* (*Le Nozze di Figaro*), Mozart (given four times); *Nina*, Dalayrac; *Die schöne Schusterin*, Umlauf; *Ariadne*, Georg Benda; *Die Pilgrimme von Mecca*, Gluck; *Der König von Venedig* (*Il Re Teodoro*), Paisiello; *Der Alchymist*, Schuster; *Das listige Bauernmädchen* (*La finta Giardiniera*), Paisiello; *Der Doktor und Apotheker*, Dittersdorf. A letter to the *Berliner Annalen des Theaters* mentions three operas which are not in the list of the theatrical calendar and indicates that the theatre, although closed after receipt of the intelligence of the death of Joseph, was soon reopened and several pieces performed, among them *Il Marchese Tulipano* by Paisiello. The writer also mentions performances of Anfossi's (or Sarti's) *Avaro inamorato*, Pergolese's *Serva padrona* and *La Villanella di spirito*, composer unmentioned, by an Italian company headed by Madame Bianchi.

The third season began October 23, 1790, and closed on March 8, 1791. Between the opening and November 27, performances of the following musical-dramatic works are recorded: *König Theodor in Venedig* (*Il Re Teodoro*), Paisiello; *Die Wilden* (*Azemia*), Dalayrac; *Der Alchymist*, Schuster; *Kein Dienst bleibt unbelohnt*, (?); *Der Barbier von Sevilla*, Paisiello; *Die schöne Schusterin*, Umlauf. At Christmas time the theatre was closed. From December 27, 1790, to March 7, 1791, were given: *Lilla*, Martin; *Die Geitzigen in der Falle*, Schuster; *Nina*, Dalayrac; *Dr. Murner*, Schuster. On March 8, the season closed with a ballet by Horschelt, *Pyramus und Thisbe*.

The reporter in the *Theaterkalender* says: "On Quinquagesima Sunday (March 6) the local nobility performed in the Ridotto Room a characteristic ballet in old German costume. The author, His Excellency Count Waldstein, to whom the composition and music do honor, had shown in it consideration for the chief proclivities of our ancestors for war, the chase, love and drinking. On March 8, all the nobility attended the theatre in their old German dress and the parade made a great, splendid and respectable picture. It was also noticeable that the ladies would lose none of their charms were they to return to the costumes of antiquity."

Before proceeding with this history a correction must be made in this report: the music to the *Ritterballet*, which was the characteristic ballet referred to, was not composed by Count Waldstein but by Ludwig van Beethoven. We shall recur to it presently. Owing to a long-continued absence of the Elector, the principal singers and the greater part of the orchestra, the fourth season did not begin till the 28th of December, 1791. Between that date and February 20, 1792, the following musical works were performed: *Doktor und Apotheker*, Dittersdorf; *Robert und Caliste*, Guglielmi; *Félix*, Monsigny; *Die Dorfdeputirten*, Schubaur; *Im Trüben ist gut Fischen* (*Fra due Litiganti, il Terzo gode*), Sarti; *Das rote Käppchen*, Dittersdorf; *Lilla*, Martin; *Der Barbier von Sevilla*, Paisiello; *Ende gut, Alles gut*, music by the Electoral Captain d'Antoine; *Die Entführung aus dem Serail*, Mozart; *Die beiden Savoyarden* (*Les deux petits Savoyards*), Dalayrac.

The fifth season began in October, 1792. Of the nine operas given before the departure of Maximilian and the company to Münster in December, *Die Müllerin* by de La Borde, *König Axur in Ormus* by Salieri, and *Hieronymus Knicker* by Dittersdorf, were the only ones new to Bonn; and in only the first two of these could Beethoven have taken part, unless at rehearsals; for at the beginning of November he left Bonn—and, as it proved, forever. Probably Salieri's masterpiece was his last opera within the familiar walls of the Court Theatre of the Elector of Cologne.

Beethoven's eighteenth birthday came around during the rehearsals for the first season, of this theatre; his twenty-second just after the beginning of the fifth. During four years (1788-92) he was adding to his musical knowledge and experience in a direction wherein he has usually been represented as deficient—as active member of an operatic orchestra; and the catalogue of works performed shows that the best schools of the day, save that of Berlin, must have been thoroughly mastered by him in all their strength and weakness. Beethoven's titanic power and grandeur would have marked his compositions under any circumstances; but it is very doubtful if, without the training of those years in the Electoral "Toxal, Kammer und Theater" as member of the orchestra, his works would have so abounded in melodies of such profound depths of expression, of such heavenly serenity and repose and of such divine beauty as they do, and which give him rank with the two greatest of melodists, Handel and Mozart.

CHAPTER VI

THE YEARS 1789 TO 1792—THE MOVE
TO VIENNA

AS A PENDANT to the preceding sketches of Bonn's musical history a variety of notices belonging to the last three years of Beethoven's life in his native place are here brought together in chronological order. Most of them relate to him personally, and some of them, through errors of date, have been looked upon hitherto as adding proofs of the precocity of his genius.

Prof. Dr. Wurzer communicated to the *Kölnische Zeitung* of August 30, 1838, the following pleasant anecdote: "In the summer of the year 1790 or 1791 I was one day on business in Godesberger Brunnen. After dinner Beethoven and another young man came up. I related to him that the church at Marienforst (a cloister in the woods behind Godesberg) had been repaired and renovated, and that this was also true of the organ, which was either wholly new or at least greatly improved. The company begged him to give them the pleasure of letting them hear him play on the instrument. His great good nature led him to grant our wish. The church was locked, but the prior was very obliging and had it unlocked for us. B. now began to play variations on themes given him by the party in a manner that moved us profoundly; but what was much more significant, poor laboring folk who were cleaning out the débris left by the work of repair, were so greatly affected by the music that they put down their implements and listened with amazement and obvious pleasure. *Sit ei terra levis!*"

The greatest musical event of the year (1790) in Bonn occurred just at its close—the visit of Joseph Haydn, on his way to London with Johann Peter Salomon, whose name so often occurs in the preliminary chapters of this work. Of this visit, Dies has recorded Haydn's own account:[1] "In the capital, Bonn, he was surprised in more ways than one. He reached the city on Saturday [Christmas, December 25] and set apart the next day for rest. On

---

[1] A. C. Dies, *Biographische Nachrichten von Joseph Haydn* (Vienna, 1810), pp. 78-79.

Sunday, Salomon accompanied Haydn to the court chapel to listen to mass. Scarcely had the two entered the church and found suitable seats when high mass began. The first chords announced a product of Haydn's muse. Our Haydn looked upon it as an accidental occurrence which had happened only to flatter him; nevertheless it was decidedly agreeable to him to listen to his own composition. Toward the close of the mass a person approached and asked him to repair to the oratory, where he was expected. Haydn obeyed and was not a little surprised when he found that the Elector, Maximilian, had had him summoned, took him at once by the hand and presented him to the virtuosi with the words: 'Here I make you acquainted with the Haydn whom you all revere so highly.' The Elector gave both parties time to become acquainted with each other, and, to give Haydn a convincing proof of his respect, invited him to dinner. This unexpected invitation put Haydn into an embarrassing position, for he and Salomon had ordered a modest little dinner in their lodgings, and it was too late to make a change. Haydn was therefore fain to take refuge in excuses which the Elector accepted as genuine and sufficient. Haydn took his leave and returned to his lodgings, where he was made aware in a special manner of the good will of the Elector, at whose secret command the little dinner had been metamorphosed into a banquet for twelve persons to which the most capable musicians had been invited."

Was the young musician one of these "most capable musicians"? Sunday evening, March 6th, came the performance of Beethoven's music to the *Ritterballet* before noticed; but without his name being known. Bossler's *Musikalische Correspondenz* of July 13, 1791, contains a list of the "Cabinet, Chapel and Court Musicians of the Elector of Cologne." Names designated by an asterisk were "solo players who may justly be ranked with virtuosi"; two asterisks indicated composers. Four names only—those of Joseph Reicha, Perner and the two Rombergs—had the two stars; Beethoven had none. "Hr. Ludwig van Beethoven plays pianoforte concertos; Hr. Neefe plays accompaniments at court and in the theatre and at concerts. . . . Concertante violas are played by virtuoso violinists"—that is all, except that we learn that the Elector was losing interest in the instrument on which Beethoven played in the orchestra: "His Electoral Highness of Cologne seldom plays the viola nowadays, but finds amusement at the pianoforte with operas, etc., etc."

At Mergentheim, the capital of the Teutonic Order, a grand meeting of commanders and knights took place in the autumn of 1791, the Grand Master Maximilian Franz presiding, and the sessions continuing from September 18 to October 20, as appears from the records at Vienna. The Elector's stay there seems to have been protracted to a period of at least three months. During his visit there of equal length two years before, time probably dragged heavily, so this time ample provision was made for theatrical and musical amusement. Among the visiting theatrical troupes was one called the "Häusslersche Gesellschaft," which played in summer at Nuremberg, in winter in Münster and

Eichstädt. The entrepreneur was Baron von Bailaux, the kapellmeister Weber, the elder; and among the personnel were Herr Weber, the younger, and Madame Weber. From Max Weber's biography of his father it appears that these Webers were the brother and sister-in-law of Carl Maria von Weber, then a child of some five years. "The troupe," says the reporter of the *Theaterkalender*, "performs the choicest pieces and the grandest operas." So the father, Franz Anton von Weber, must have found himself at length in his own proper element, and still more so a year later, when he himself became the manager.

This company for a time migrated to Mergentheim and resumed the title of "Kurfürstliches Hoftheater." Beethoven soon came thither also. Did he, when in after years he met Carl Maria von Weber, remember him as a feeble child at Mergentheim? Had his intercourse there with Fridolin von Weber, pupil of Joseph Haydn, any influence upon his determination soon after to become also that great master's pupil?

Simonetti, Maximilian's favorite and very fine tenor concert-singer, and some twenty-five members of the electoral orchestra, with Franz Ries as conductor—Reicha was too ill—including Beethoven, the two Rombergs and the fine octet of wind-instruments, formed an equally ample provision for the strictly musical entertainments. Actors, singers, musicians—Simonetti and the women-singers excepted—most of them still young, all in their best years and at the age for its full enjoyment, made the journey in two large boats up the Rhine and Main. The departure took place between August 28 and September 1, the return apparently in the last days of October, 1791, judging by the roll call at meetings of the Bonn Literary Society which Simrock attended regularly as treasurer. Before leaving Bonn the company assembled and elected the bass singer, Lux, king of the expedition, who in distributing the high offices of his court conferred upon Bernhard Romberg and Ludwig van Beethoven the dignity of, and placed them in his service as, kitchen-boys—scullions. It was the pleasantest season of the year for such a journey, the summer heats being tempered by the coolness of the Rhine and the currents of air passing up and down the deep gorge of the river. Vegetation was at its best and brightest, and the romantic beauty of its old towns and villages had not yet suffered either by the desolations of the wars soon to break upon them or by the resistless and romance-destroying march of "modern improvement." Coblenz and Mainz were still capitals of states, and the huge fortress Rheinfels was not yet a ruin. When Riesbeck passed down the Rhine ten years before, his boat "had a mast and sail, a flat deck with a railing, comfortable cabins with windows and some furniture, and in a general way in style was built like a Dutch yacht."[2] In boats like this, no doubt, the jolly company made the slow and, under the circumstances, perhaps, tedious journey against the current of the "arrowy Rhine." But a glorious time and a merry they had of it. Want of speed was no misfortune

[2] *Op.cit.*, II, pp. 342-43.

to them, and in Beethoven's memory the little voyage lived bright and beautiful and was to him "a fruitful source of loveliest visions."

The Bingerloch was then held to be a dangerous, as it certainly was a difficult pass for boats ascending; for here the river, suddenly contracted to half its previous width, plunged amid long lines of rugged rocks into the gorge. So, leaving the boats to their conductors, the party ascended to the Niederwald; and there King Lux raised Beethoven to a higher dignity in his court—Wegeler does not state what it was—and confirmed his appointment by a diploma, or letters patent, dated on the heights above Rüdesheim. To this important document was attached by thread ravelled from a sail, a huge seal of pitch, pressed into the cover of a small box, which gave to the instrument a right imposing look—like the Golden Bull at Frankfurt. This diploma from the hand of his comic majesty was among the articles taken by the possessor to Vienna where Wegeler saw it, still carefully preserved, in 1796.

At Aschaffenburg-am-Main was the large summer palace of the Electors of Mainz; and here dwelt Abbé Sterkel, now a man of 40 years; a musician from his infancy, one of the first pianists of all Germany and without a rival in this part of it, except perhaps Vogler of Mannheim. His style both as composer and pianist had been refined and cultivated to the utmost, both in Germany and Italy, and his playing was in the highest degree light, graceful, pleasing—as Ries described it to Wegeler, "somewhat ladylike." Ries and Simrock took the two young Rombergs and Beethoven to pay their respects to the master, "who, complying with the general request, sat himself down to play. Beethoven, who up to this time," says Wegeler, "had not heard a great or celebrated pianoforte player, knew nothing of the finer nuances in the handling of the instrument; his playing was rude and hard. Now he stood with attention all on a strain by the side of Sterkel"; for this grace and delicacy, if not power of execution, which he now heard were a new revelation to him. After Sterkel had finished, the young Bonn concertplayer was invited to take his place at the instrument; but he naturally hesitated to exhibit himself after such a display. The shrewd Abbé, however, brought him to it by a pretence of doubting his ability.

A year or two before, Kapellmeister Vincenzo Righini, a colleague of Sterkel in the service of the Elector of Mainz, had published *Dodeci Ariette*, one of which, "Vieni (Venni) Amore," was a melody with five vocal variations, to the same accompaniment. Beethoven, taking this melody as his theme, had composed, dedicated to the Countess of Hatzfeld and published twenty-four variations for the pianoforte upon it. Some of these were very difficult, and Sterkel now expressed his doubts if their author could himself play them. His honor thus touched, "Beethoven played not only these variations so far as he could remember them (Sterkel could not find them), but went on with a number of others no less difficult, all to the great surprise of the listeners, perfectly, and in the ingratiating manner that had struck him in Sterkel's playing."[3]

Once in Mergentheim the merry monarch and his jolly subjects had other things to think of and seem to have made a noise in the world in more senses than one. At all events Carl Ludwig Junker, Chaplain at Kirchberg, the residence of Prince Hohenlohe, heard of them and then went over to hear them. Junker was a dilettante composer and the author of some half-dozen small works upon music—musical almanacs published anonymously, and the like, all now forgotten save by collectors, as are his pianoforte concertos— but at that time he was a man of no small mark in the musical world of Western Germany. He came over to Mergentheim, was treated with great attention by the Elector's musicians, and showed his gratitude in a long letter to Bossler's *Musikal. Correspondenz* (Speyer, November 23, 1791), in which superlatives somewhat abound, but which is an exquisite piece of gossip and gives the liveliest picture that exists of the "Kapelle." We have room for only a portion of it:

". . . Here I was also an eye-witness to the esteem and respect in which this chapel stands with the Elector. Just as the rehearsal was to begin Ries was sent for by the Prince, and upon his return brought a bag of gold. 'Gentlemen,' said he, 'this being the Elector's name-day he sends you a present of a thousand thalers.' And again, I was eye-witness of this orchestra's surpassing excellence. Herr Winneberger, Kapellmeister at Wallenstein, laid before it a symphony of his own composition, which was by no means easy of execution, especially for the wind-instruments, which had several solos *concertante*. It went finely, however, at the first trial, to the great surprise of the composer. An hour after the dinner-music the concert began. It was opened with a symphony of Mozart; then followed a recitative and air sung by Simonetti; next, a violoncello concerto played by Herr Romberger [Bernhard Romberg]; fourth, a symphony by Pleyel; fifth, an air by Righini, sung by Simonetti; sixth, a double concerto for violin and violoncello played by the two Rombergs; and the closing piece was the symphony of Winneberger, which had very many brilliant passages. The opinion already expressed as to the performance of this orchestra was confirmed. It was not possible to attain a higher degree of exactness. Such perfection in the *pianos, fortes, rinforzandos*—such a swelling and gradual increase of tone and then such an almost imperceptible dying away, from the most powerful to the lightest accents— all this was formerly to be heard only in Mannheim. It would be difficult to find another orchestra in which the violins and basses are throughout in such excellent hands. . . . The members of the chapel, almost without exception, are in their best years, glowing with health, men of culture and fine

[3] Wegeler's story (*Notizen*, p. 17) of the meeting between Beethoven and Sterkel is confirmed in every detail by a letter from N. Simrock to Schindler, a copy of which was found among the posthumous papers of Thayer. (TDR, I, 266, n. 1; TK, I, 114, n. 1)

personal appearance. They form truly a fine sight, when one adds the splendid uniform in which the Elector has clothed them—red, and richly trimmed with gold.

"I heard also one of the greatest of pianists—the dear, good Bethofen, some compositions by whom appeared in the Speier *Blumenlese* in 1783, written in his eleventh year. True, he did not perform in public, probably the instrument here was not to his mind. It is one of Spath's make, and at Bonn he plays upon one by Steiner. But, what was infinitely preferable to me, I heard him extemporize in private; yes, I was even invited to propose a theme for him to vary. The greatness of this amiable, light-hearted man, as a virtuoso, may in my opinion be safely estimated from his almost inexhaustible wealth of ideas, the altogether characteristic style of expression in his playing, and the great execution which he displays. I know, therefore, no one thing which he lacks, that conduces to the greatness of an artist. I have heard Vogler upon the pianoforte—of his organ playing I say nothing, not having heard him upon that instrument—have often heard him, heard him by the hour together, and never failed to wonder at his astonishing execution; but Bethofen, in addition to the execution, has greater clearness and weight of idea, and more expression—in short, he is more for the heart—equally great, therefore, as an *adagio* or *allegro* player. Even the members of this remarkable orchestra are, without exception, his admirers, and all ears when he plays. Yet he is exceedingly modest and free from all pretension. He, however, acknowledged to me, that, upon the journeys which the Elector had enabled him to make, he had seldom found in the playing of the most distinguished virtuosi that excellence which he supposed he had a right to expect. His style of treating his instrument is so different from that usually adopted, that it impresses one with the idea, that by a path of his own discovery he has attained that height of excellence whereon he now stands.

"Had I acceded to the pressing entreaties of my friend Bethofen, to which Herr Winneberger added his own, and remained another day in Mergentheim, I have no doubt he would have played to me hours; and the day, thus spent in the society of these two great artists, would have been transformed into a day of the highest bliss."

The following passage in Wegeler's *Notizen* (pp. 15-16) opens up a controversial point concerning the first meeting between Beethoven and Haydn: "When Haydn first came back from England, a breakfast was given him by the Electoral Orchestra at Godesberg, a resort near Bonn. At this occasion Beethoven laid before him a cantata which was noticed especially by Haydn and which made him urge Beethoven to continue his studies. *Later* this cantata was supposed to be performed in Mergentheim, but several places were so difficult for the wind players that some musicians explained that they couldn't be played and the performance was cancelled." The italics are ours—the cantata was probably the funeral cantata, written in the spring of 1790 in memory of the death of Emperor Joseph II; or it could have been a cantata written later in the same year in honor of the elevation of Emperor Leopold II. The rehearsal clearly took place during the Mergentheim trip in the early autumn of 1791. But there is a confusion in Wegeler's testimony since Haydn was on his way to England at the end of 1790 and was returning from England in the late spring of 1792. Wegeler implies that this is the return trip of 1792 and yet refers to the Mergentheim incident as occurring later. In the Pohl-Botstiber biography of Haydn, Wegeler's evidence and Thayer's interpretation of it to mean that the meeting took place in 1792 is all that is given as proof that the meeting did occur in 1792 rather than 1790.

"In Mergentheim," wrote Simrock to Schindler at a later time, "I only remember that he wrote a cantata there which we did rehearse several times but did not perform in court. We had all manner of protests over the difficult places before us, and he asserted that each player must be able to perform his part correctly; we proved we couldn't, simply because all the figures were completely unusual, therein lay the difficulty. Father Ries, who was the leader in Mergentheim declared earnestly that this was also his opinion, and so it was not performed at court, and we have never seen anything more of it since."[4]

Schiedermair[5] has suggested that it would have been more natural for Beethoven to be revising a work in 1791 if it had been first shown to a master composer; then Simrock's reminiscences would not necessarily be dismissed as erroneous (Thayer's opinion), but rather accepted as evidence that when the horn player saw the composer making alterations in his score, he assumed that the cantata was newly composed. Schiedermair asks further whether Wegeler might not have confused the Christmas 1790 dinner in honor of Haydn, as reported by Dies, with a Godesberg breakfast, which may have been given for another artist, such as the one given for the Portuguese singer, Madame Todi. That Beethoven showed a cantata to Haydn and received encouragement to continue composing can be accepted as certain, but whether this happened in 1790 or in 1792 must remain in doubt. Assuming that Hadyn did stop at Bonn again at the end of his second trip to England, it may well have been for the second time that he was meeting the promising young composer of the Electoral orchestra. Lack of earlier mention of Beethoven's making a trip to Vienna to study with the master leads one to believe that the idea took shape at the later time.—

Many a eulogy has been written upon Max Franz for his supposed protection of, and favors granted to, the young Beethoven. It has, however, already been made clear that except the gracious reprimand at the time when the singer Heller was made the subject of the boy's joke, all the facts and anecdotes upon which those eulogies are based belong to a much later than the supposed period. The appointment of Beethoven as Chamber Musician (1789) was no distinguishing mark of favor. Half a dozen other youths of

[4] TDR, I, 273.   [5] Op.cit., p. 212.

his age shared it with him. His being made Court Pianist was a matter of course; for whom had he as a rival? Had he been in any great degree a favorite of the Elector, what need had there been of his receiving from Waldstein, as Wegeler states, "much pecuniary assistance bestowed in such a way as to spare his sensibilities, it being generally looked upon as a small gratuity from the Elector?" One general remark may be made here which has a bearing upon this point, namely: that Beethoven's dedications of important works throughout his life were, as a rule, made to persons from whom he had received, or from whom he had hopes of receiving, pecuniary benefits. Indeed, in one notable case where such a dedication produced him nothing, he never forgot nor forgave the omission. Had he felt that Maximilian was in any single instance really generous toward him, why did he never dedicate any work to him?[6] Why in all the correspondence, private memoranda and recorded conversations, which have been examined for this work, has Beethoven never mentioned him either in terms of gratitude, or in any manner whatever? All idea that his relations to the Elector were different from those of Bernhard Romberg, Franz Ries or Anton Reicha, must be given up. He was organist, pianist, member of the orchestra; and for these services received his pay like others. There is no proof of more, no indication of less.

But with Waldstein, the case was otherwise. The young count, eight years older than Beethoven, coming direct from Vienna, where his family connections gave him access to the salons of the very highest rank of the nobility, was thoroughly acquainted with the noblest and best that the imperial capital could show in the art of music. Himself more than an ordinary dilettante, he could judge of the youth's powers and became his friend. We have seen that he used occasionally to go to the modest room in the Wenzelgasse, that he even employed Beethoven to compose his *Ritterballet* music, and we shall see that he foretold the future eminence of the composer and that the name, Beethoven, would stand next those of Mozart and Haydn on the roll of fame. Waldstein's name, too, is in Beethoven's roll of fame; it stands in the list of those to whom important works are dedicated. The dedication of the twenty-four variations on "Venni Amore" to the Countess Hatzfeld indicates, if it does not prove, that Beethoven's deserts were neither unknown nor unacknowledged at her house.

During the last years in Bonn when he could find little joy or satisfaction at home, it became his habit to spend evenings at the tavern. At that time the favorite place of resort for the professors of the new university and for young men whose education and position at court or in society were such as to make them welcome guests, was the house on the Market-place later known as the Zehrgarten; and there, says Frau Karth, Beethoven was accustomed also to go. Its mistress was the Widow Koch who spread also a table for a select

---

[6] In a letter to the publisher Hoffmeister in June, 1801, Beethoven indicated that the First Symphony was to be dedicated to Max Franz. His death in the following month caused the dedication to be changed to Baron von Swieten.

company of boarders. Her name, too, often appears in the *Intelligenzblatt* of Bonn in advertisements of books and music. Of her three children, a son and two daughters, the beautiful Barbara—the Babette Koch mentioned in a letter of Beethoven's—was the belle of Bonn. Wegeler's eulogy of her (*Notizen*, p. 58) contains the names of several members of that circle whom, doubtless, the young composer so often met at the house. "She was a confidential friend of Eleonore von Breuning, a lady who of all the representatives of the female sex that I met in a rather active and long life came nearest the ideal of a perfect woman—an opinion which is confirmed by all who had the good fortune to know her well. She was surrounded not only by young artists like Beethoven, the two Rombergs, Reicha, the twin brothers Kügelgen and others, but also by the intellectual men of all classes and ages, such as D. Crevelt, Prof. Velten, who died early, Fischenich, who afterward became Municipal Councillor, Prof. Thaddäus Dereser, afterward capitular of the cathedral, Wrede, who became a bishop, Heckel and Floret, secretaries of the Elector, Malchus, private secretary of the Austrian minister von Keverberg, later Government Councillor of Holland, Court Councillor von Bourscheidt, Christian von Breuning and many others."

About the time Beethoven left Bonn for Vienna, the wife of Count Anton von Belderbusch, nephew of the deceased minister of that name, had deserted her husband for the embraces of a certain Baron von Lichtenstein, and Babette Koch was engaged as governess and instructress of the motherless children. In process of time Belderbusch obtained a divorce (under the French law) from his adulterous wife and married the governess, August 9, 1802.

But it was in the Breuning house that Beethoven enjoyed and profited most. The mother's kindness towards him gave her both the right and the power to urge and compel him to the performance of his duties; and this power over him in his obstinate and passionate moods she possessed in a higher degree than any other person. Wegeler (*Notizen*, pp. 18ff.) gives an anecdote in point: Baron Westphal von Fürstenberg, until now in the service of the Elector, was appointed minister to the Dutch and Westphalian Circuit and to the courts of Cologne and Trèves, his headquarters being at Bonn. He resided in the large house which is now occupied by the post-office, directly behind the statue of him who was engaged as music teacher in the count's family. The Breuning house was but a few steps distant diagonally across a corner of the square. Here Madame von Breuning was sometimes compelled to use her authority and force the young man to go to his lessons. Knowing that she was watching him he would go, *ut iniquae mentis asellus*, but sometimes at the very door would turn back and excuse himself on the plea that to-day it was impossible to give a lesson—to-morrow he would give two; to which, as upon other occasions when reasoning with him was of no avail, the good lady would shrug her shoulders with the remark: "He has his *raptus* again," an expression which the rapt Beethoven never forgot. Most happy was it for him that in Madame von Breuning he had a friend who understood his character thoroughly, who cherished affection for him, who could and did so effectually act as peace-maker when the harmony between him and her children was disturbed. Schindler is a witness that just for this phase of her motherly care Beethoven, down to the close of life, was very grateful.[7] "In his later days he still called the members of this family his guardian angels of that time and remembered with pleasure the many reprimands which he had received from the lady of the house. 'She understood,' said he, 'how to keep insects off the flowers.' By insects he meant certain friendships which had already begun to threaten danger to the natural development of his talent and a proper measure of artistic consciousness by awakening vanity in him by their flatteries. He was already near to considering himself a famous artist, and therefore more inclined to give heed to those who encouraged him in his illusions than such as set before him the fact that he had still to learn everything that makes a master out of a disciple." This is well said, is very probable in itself, and belongs in the category of facts as to which Schindler is a trustworthy witness.

Stephan von Breuning became so good a violinist as to play occasionally in the electoral orchestra. As he grew older, and the comparative difference in age between him and Beethoven lessened, the acquaintance between them became one of great intimacy. Frau Karth says he was a frequent visitor in the Wenzelgasse, and she had a lively recollection of "the noise they used to make with their music" in the room overhead. Lenz, the youngest of the Breunings, was but fifteen when his teacher left Bonn, but a few years after he became a pupil of Beethoven again in Vienna and became a good pianist. For him the composer seems to have cherished a warm affection, one to which the seven years' difference in their ages gave a peculiar tenderness.

Beethoven's remarkable powers of improvising were often exhibited at the Breuning house. Wegeler has an anecdote here (*Notizen*, p. 20): "Once when Beethoven was improvising at the house of the Breunings (on which occasions he used frequently to be asked to characterize in the music some well-known person) Father Ries was urged to accompany him upon the violin. After some hesitation he consented, and this may have been the first time that two artists improvised a duo."

Beethoven had in common with all men of original and creative genius a strong repugnance to the drudgery of forcing the elements of his art into dull brains and awkward fingers; but that this repugnance was "extraordinary," as Wegeler says, does not appear. A "Frau von Bevervörde," one of his Bonn pupils, assured Schindler that she never had any complaint to make of her teacher in respect to either the regularity of his lessons or his general course of instruction. Nor is there anything now to be gathered from the traditions at Vienna which justifies the epithet. Ries's experience is not here in point, for his relations to Beethoven were like those of little Hummel to

[7] *Biographie*, I, pp. 17-18.

Mozart. He received such instruction gratis as the master in leisure moments felt disposed to give. There was no pretence of systematic teaching at stated hours. The occasional neglect of a lesson at Baron Westphal's, as detailed in the anecdote above given, may be explained on other ground than that of extraordinary repugnance to teaching. Beethoven was, in 1791–92, just at the age when the desire for distinction was fresh and strong; he was conscious of powers still not fully developed; his path was diverse from that of the other young men with whom he associated and who, from all that can be gathered now on the subject, had little faith in that which he had chosen. He must have felt the necessity of other instruction, or, at all events, of better opportunities to compare his powers with those of others, to measure himself by a higher standard, to try the effect of his compositions in another sphere, to satisfy himself that his instincts as a composer were true and that his deviations from the beaten track were not wild and capricious. Waldstein, we know from Wegeler (and this is confirmed by his own words), had faith in him and his works, and it will be seen that another, Fischenich, had also. But what would be said of him and his compositions in the city of Mozart, Haydn, Gluck? To this add the restlessness of an ambitious youth to whom the routine of duties, which must long since in great measure have lost the charm of novelty, had become tedious, and the natural longing of young men for the great world, for a wider field of action, had grown almost insupportable.

Or Beethoven's *raptus* may just then have had a very different origin; Jeannette d'Honrath, or Fräulein Westerholt, was perhaps the innocent cause—two young ladies whose names are preserved by Wegeler of the many for whom he says his friend at various times indulged transient, but not the less ardent, passions. The former was from Cologne, whence she occasionally came to Bonn to pass a few weeks with Eleonore von Breuning. Wegeler says of her (*Notizen*, p. 42): "She was a beautiful, vivacious blond, of good education, and amiable disposition, who enjoyed music greatly and possessed an agreeable voice; wherefore she several times teased our friend by singing a song, familiar at the time, beginning:

> 'Mich heute noch von dir zu trennen
> Und dieses nicht verhindern können,
> Ist zu empfindlich für mein Herz!'

for the favored rival was the Austrian recruiting officer in Cologne, Carl Greth, who married the young lady and died on October 15, 1827, as Field Marshal General, Commander of the 23rd Regiment of Infantry and Commandant at Temesvar."[8]

The passion for Miss d'Honrath was eclipsed by a subsequent fancy for a Fräulein von Westerholt. The Court Calendars of these years name "Hochfürstlich Münsterischer Obrist-Stallmeister, Sr. Excellenz der Hochwohlge-

---

[8] In one of Beethoven's conversation books, *anno* 1823, may be read in Schindler's handwriting: "Captain v. Greth's address, Commandant in Temesvar." (TK, I, 121, n. 1.)

borene Herr Friedrich Rudolph Anton, Freyherr von Westerholt-Giesenberg, kurkölnischer und Hochstift-Münsterischer Geheimrath." This much betitled man, according to Neefe (Spazier's *Berlin. Mus. Zeitung*, 19 October 1793), "played the bassoon himself and maintained a fair band among his servants, particularly players of wind-instruments." He had two sons, one of whom was a master of the flute, and two daughters. The elder daughter—the younger was still a child—Maria Anna Wilhelmine, was born on July 24, 1774, married Baron Friedrich Clemens von Elverfeldt, called von Beverföde-Werries, on April 24, 1792, and died on November 3, 1852. She was an excellent pianist. In Münster, Neefe heard "the fiery Mad. von Elverfeldt" play "a difficult sonata by Sardi [Giuseppe Sarti] with a rapidity and accuracy that were marvelous."

It is not surprising that Beethoven's talent should have met with recognition and appreciation in this musical family. He became the young woman's teacher. Count Westerholt as the chief equerry had to accompany the Elector on his visits to Münster, where, moreover, he owned a house. There is a tradition in the family that young Beethoven went with them before the young lady's marriage thus probably around 1790. He had the disease violently, nor did he "let concealment, like a worm i' the bud," feed upon his cheek. Forty years afterward Bernhard Romberg had anecdotes to relate of this "Werther love." And as we now know, she was that "Frau von Beververde" with whom Schindler became acquainted through the mediation of Romberg in her later years (see above).

To the point of Beethoven's susceptibility to the tender passion let Wegeler again be cited:[9] "The truth as I learned to know it, and also my brother-in-law Stephan von Breuning, Ferdinand Ries, and Bernhard Romberg, is that there was never a time when Beethoven was not in love, and that in the highest degree. These passions, for the Misses d'Honrath and Westerholt, fell in his transition period from youth to manhood, and left impressions as little deep as were those made upon the beauties who had caused them. In Vienna, at all events so long as I lived there, Beethoven was always in love and occasionally made a conquest which would have been very difficult if not impossible for many an Adonis."

A relationship that was deeper and more enduring was Beethoven's feeling for Eleonore von Breuning. Upon the exact nature of it Wegeler was silent. However, in December of 1826 Beethoven wrote in a letter to Wegeler: "I still have the silhouette of your Lorchen, so you see how precious even now are all the dear, good memories of my youth." Of this Wegeler (*Notizen*, p. 52) says: "In two evenings the silhouettes of all the members of the von Breuning family and more intimate friends of the house were made by the printer Neesen of Bonn. In this way I came into the possession of that of Beethoven which is here printed. Beethoven was probably in his sixteenth year at the time."

[9] *Notizen*, pp. 42, 43. (TDR, I, 286.)

Another souvenir of youthful friendship which the composer preserved
was the following compliment to him on his twentieth birthday, surrounded
by a wreath of flowers:

ZU B'S GEBURTSTAG VON SEINER SCHÜLERIN

Gluck und langes Leben
Wünsch ich heute dir;
Aber auch daneben
Wünsch ich etwas mir!

Mir in Rücksicht deiner
Wünsch ich deine Huld,
Dir in Rücksicht meiner
Nachsicht und Geduld.

Von Ihrer Freundin u. Schülerin
Lorchen von Breuning

1790

The verbal play can scarcely be given in English rhymed couplets. The
sentiment is: "Happiness and long life I wish you today, but something do I
crave for myself from you—your regard, your forbearance and your patience."

Two letters from Beethoven to Eleonore von Breuning—one dated November 2, 1793, the other undated but written in 1794—show that a quarrel
or rift had occurred between them at some time before his departure from
Bonn. The cause of it is not known, but these letters, to which we shall
return, sought to reestablish and affirm their close friendship.

A review of some of the last pages shows that for the most part after 1789
the life of Beethoven was a busy one, but that the frequent absences of the
Elector, as recorded in the newspapers of the day, left many a period of
considerable duration during which, except for the meetings of the orchestra
for rehearsal and study, he had full command of his time. Thus he had
plenty of leisure hours and weeks to devote to composition, to instruction in
music, for social intercourse, for visits to Kerpen and other neighboring
places, for the indulgence of his strong propensity to ramble in the fields and
among the mountains, for the cultivation in that beautiful Rhine region of
his warm passion for nature.

The new relations to his father and brothers, as virtual head of the family,
were such as to relieve his mind from anxiety on their account. His position
in society, too, had become one of which he might justly be proud, owing,
as it was, to no adventitious circumstances, but simply to his genius and high
personal character. Of illness in those years we hear nothing, except Wegeler's
remark (Notizen, p. 11): "When the famous organist Abbé Vogler played
in Bonn (1790 or 1791) I sat beside Beethoven's sickbed"; a mere passing
attack, or Wegeler would have vouchsafed it a more extended notice in his
subsequent remarks upon his friend's health. Thus these were evidently

happy years, in spite of certain characteristic and gloomy expressions of Beethoven in letters hereafter to be given, and years of active intellectual, artistic and moral development.

The probability that in July, 1792, it had been proposed to Haydn to take Beethoven as a pupil has been mentioned; but it is pretty certain that the suggestion did not come from the Elector, who, there is little doubt, was in Frankfurt at the coronation of his nephew Emperor Franz (July 14) at the time of Haydn's visit. Whatever arrangements may have been made between the pupil and master, they were subject to the will of the Elector, and here Waldstein may well have exerted himself to his protégé's advantage. At all events, the result was favorable and the journey determined upon. Perhaps, had Haydn found Maximilian in Bonn, he might have taken the young man with him; as it was, some months elapsed before his pupil could follow.

Some little space must be devoted to the question, whence the pecuniary resources for so expensive a journey to and sojourn in Vienna were derived. The good-hearted Neefe did not forget to record the event in very flattering terms when he wrote next year in Spazier's *Berliner Musik-Zeitung*: "In November of last year Ludwig van Beethoven, assistant court organist and unquestionably now one of the foremost pianoforte players, went to Vienna *at the expense of our Elector* to Haydn in order to perfect himself under his direction more fully in the art of composition."

In a note he adds: "Inasmuch as this L. v. B. according to several reports is said to be making great progress in art and owes a part of his education to Herr Neefe in Bonn, to whom he has expressed his gratitude in writing, it may be well, (may Herr N's modesty permit it) to append a few words here, since, moreover, they redound to the credit of Herr B.: 'I thank you for your counsel very often given me in the course of my progress in my divine art. If ever I become a great man, yours will be some of the credit. This will give you the greater pleasure, since you can remain convinced, etc.'"

"At the expense of our Elector"—so says Neefe; so, too, Fischenich says of Beethoven "whom the Elector has sent to Haydn in Vienna." Maximilian, then, had determined to show a favor to the young musician similar to the one received not long before by the artists Kügelgen. This idea is confirmed by Beethoven's noting, in the small memorandum book previously referred to, the reception soon after reaching Vienna of 25 ducats and his disappointment that the sum had not been a hundred. (A receipt for his salary, 25 th. for the last quarter of this year, still in the Düsseldorf archives, is dated October 22, and seems at first sight to prove an advance per favor; but many others in the same collection show that payments were usually made about the beginning of the second month of each quarter.) There is also a paper in the Düsseldorf collection, undated, but clearly only a year or two after Beethoven's departure, by which important changes are made in the salaries of the Elector's musicians. In this list Beethoven does not appear among those paid from the *Landrentmeisterei* (i.e., the revenues of the state), but is to receive from the *Chatouille* (privy purse) 600 florins—a sum equivalent to the hundred ducats which he had expected in vain. It is true these changes were never carried out, but the paper shows the Elector's intentions.

With such facts before us, how is Beethoven to be relieved of the odium of ingratitude to his benefactor? By the circumstance that, for anything that appears, the good intentions of the Elector—excepting in an increase of salary hereafter to be noted, and the transmission of the 25 ducats—were never carried out; and the young musician, after receiving his quarterly payment two or three times,[10] was left entirely dependent upon his own resources. Maximilian's justification lies in the sea of troubles by which he was so soon to be overwhelmed.

The Elector, although Archduke of Austria, was also head of a neighboring state to France. Thus, while criticising France's intentions, he behaved more as a neutral than did Austria or Prussia. But when in October, 1792, Mainz fell and the whole left bank of the Rhine appeared to have surrendered defenceless to the enemy, the archives and valuables at Bonn were packed ready if necessary to be removed by ship. The Elector left his residence on October 22 but soon returned since danger for the upper Rhine had disappeared with the timely intervention of the Prussians at Coblenz. But with the French occupation of the Netherlands by the middle of December, combined with the inconvenient behavior of the Austrians in his own province, the Elector felt compelled to move to Münster on December 21, where he spent the winter. By March the Netherlands were again in Austrian hands, and the Elector returned to Bonn April 21, 1793. But the French victories in the summer of 1794 filled Bonn with those in flight, and Maximilian Franz was forced to leave Bonn for the last time on October 2, 1794, from whence he went to Münster, then Frankfurt, and finally Mergentheim by the first half of December.[11]

The fact that by the fall of 1792 towns were being deserted by the upper classes may explain why Beethoven was able to obtain permission to leave Bonn for Vienna just before the start of the theatrical and musical season. He was given only enough money with which to travel and the promise that more would be forwarded thither.

Beethoven's departure from Bonn called forth lively interest on the part of his friends. The plan did not contemplate a long sojourn in the Austrian capital; it was his purpose, after completing his studies there, to return to Bonn and thence to go forth on artistic tours. This is proved by an autograph album dating from his last days in Bonn, which some of his intimate friends, obviously those with whom he was wont to associate at the Zehrgarten, sent with him on his way. The majority of the names are familiar to us, but many which one might have expected to find, notably those of the

---

[10] Actually up to March, 1794.
[11] *Allgemeine Deutsche Biographie* (Leip- zig, 1884), Vol. 21, article on Maximilian Franz.

musicians of Bonn, are missing. Eleonore von Breuning's contribution was a quotation from Herder:

Freundschaft, mit dem Guten, [Friendship, with that which is good,
Wächset wie der Abendschatten, Grows like the evening shadow
Bis des Lebens Sonne sinkt. Till the setting sun of life.]

Bonn, den 1. November Ihre wahre Freundin Eleonore Breuning
    1792

Most interesting of all the inscriptions in the album, however, is that of Count Waldstein, which was first published by Schindler (Vol. I, p. 18) from a copy procured for him by Aloys Fuchs. It proves how great were the writer's hopes, how strong his faith in Beethoven:

Dear Beethoven! You are going to Vienna in fulfillment of your long frustrated wishes. The Genius of Mozart is mourning and weeping over the death of her pupil. She found a refuge but no occupation with the inexhaustible Haydn; through him she wishes to form a union with another. With the help of assiduous labor you shall receive *Mozart's spirit from Haydn's hands.*
                                        Your true friend
Bonn, October 29, 1792.   Waldstein.

The dates in the album prove that Beethoven was still in Bonn on November 1, 1792, and indicate that it was the last day of his sojourn there. In Duten's *Journal of Travels*, as translated and augmented by John Highmore, Gent. (London, 1782)—a Baedeker's or Murray's handbook of that time—the post-road from Bonn to Frankfurt-am-Main is laid down as passing along the Rhine via Andernach to Coblenz, and thence, crossing the river at Ehrenbreitstein, via Montabaur, Limburg, Würges and Königstein;—corresponding to the route advertised in the *Intelligenzblatt* a few years later—time 25 hours, 43 minutes.

This was the route taken by Beethoven and some unknown companion. Starting from Bonn at 6 a.m. they would, according to Dutens and Highmore, dine at Coblenz about 3 p.m. and be in Frankfurt about 7 next morning.

The first three pages of the memorandum book above cited contain a record of the expenses of this journey as far as Würges. One of the items is this: "Trinkgeld at Coblenz because the fellow drove us at the risk of a cudgelling right through the Hessian army going like the devil, one small thaler." This army marched from Coblenz on November 5; but on the same day a French corps, having advanced from Mainz beyond Limburg, took possession of Weilburg. The travellers could not, therefore, have journeyed through Limburg later than the night of the 3rd. We conclude, then, that it was between November 1st and 3rd that Beethoven bade farewell to Bonn, and at Ehrenbreitstein saw Father Rhine for the last time.

The temptation is too strong to be resisted to add here the contents of the three pages of the memorandum book devoted to this journey, and the reasonings—fancies, if the reader prefers the term—drawn from them, upon which is founded the assertion that Beethoven had a travelling companion. This is probable in itself, and is confirmed by, first, two handwritings; second, the price paid for post-horses (thus, the first entry is for a station and a quarter at 50 *Stüber*, the regular price being one florin, or 20 *Stüber* per horse for a single passenger; there were, therefore, two horses and 10 *Stüber* extra per post for the second passenger); third, the word "us" in the record of the *Trinkgeld* at Coblenz; fourth, the accounts cease at Würges, but they would naturally have been continued to Vienna had they been noted down by Beethoven from motives of economy; fifth, the payment of 2 fl. for dinner and supper is certainly more than a young man, not overburdened with money, would in those days have spent at the post-house.

We may suppose, then, that the companions have reached the end of their journey in common, and sit down to compute and divide the expenses. Beethoven hands his blank-book to his friend, who writes thus:

[Page 1] From Bonn to Remagen, 1 1-4 Stat. at 50 Stbr........ 3 fl.
          From Remag. to Andernach, 1 1-2 St. 3.45
              Tip 45
              Tolls 45
          From Andernach to Coblenz, 1 St. .... 3.
              Tips to Andernach 50
              "   to Coblenz ....
          Tolls to Andernach 42
          Tolls to Coblenz ....

These last three items are not carried out, and Beethoven now takes the book and adds the items of the "Tolls to Andernach" thus:

Sinzig ......   7 St(über)   Reinecke   5   St.
Preissig ....   10 St.   Norich ....   4 1-2 St.

These 26½ Stüber, changed into Kreutzers, make up the 42 in the column above. On the next page he continues:

[Page 2] Coblenz, tolls .... 30 x
          Rothehahnen (Red Cocks) .... 24 x
          Coblenz to Montebaur .... 2 rthlr. and 1-2 d
              Tolls for Coblenz .... 48 x
          Tip because the fellow drove us at the risk
          of a cudgelling right through the Hessian
          army going like the devil .... one small thaler
              Ate dinner .... 2 fl.
          Post from Montebaur to Limburg .... 3 fl. 57 x
          10 x road money
          15 x   "   "

[Page 3]   Supper .... 2 fl.
           in Limburg .... 12 Batzen
               Tips .... 14 x
           Grease money .... 14 x
           Tip for postillion .... 1 fl.

The other hand now writes:

> The same money for meals and tips, besides 12 x
> road money to Wirges.

The entries of the second and third pages are now changed into florin currency and brought together, making 22 fl. and 14 x; add the expenses on the first page to this sum and we have a total of about 35 fl. from Bonn to Würges for two young men travelling day and night, and no doubt as economically as was possible. The next entries are by Beethoven's hand in Vienna, and give evidence that he was in that city on or before November 10th. We are left to imagine his arrival in Frankfurt and his departure thence via Nuremberg, Regensburg, Passau and Linz in the public post-coach for Vienna.

CHAPTER VII

THE COMPOSITIONS WRITTEN AT BONN, 1786-1792

BUT for the outbreak of the French Revolution, Bonn seems to have been destined to become a brilliant centre of learning and art. Owing to the Elector's taste and love for music, that art became—what under the influence of Goethe poetry and drama were in Weimar—the artistic expression and embodiment of the intellectual character of the time. In this art, among musicians and composers, Beethoven, endowed with a genius whose originality has rarely if ever been surpassed, "lived, moved and had his being." His official superiors, Lucchesi, Reicha, Neefe, were indefatigable in their labors for the church, the stage and the concert-room; his companions, Andreas Perner, Anton Reicha, the Rombergs, were prolific in all the forms of composition from the set of variations to even the opera and oratorios; and in the performance of their productions, as organist, pianist and viola player, he, of course, assisted. The trophies of Miltiades allowed no rest to Themistocles. Did the applause bestowed upon the scenes, duos, trios, quartets, symphonies, operas of his friends awaken no spirit of emulation in him? Was he contented to be the mere performer, leaving composition to others? And yet what a "beggarly account" is the list of compositions known to belong to this period of his life! Calling to mind the activity of others, particularly Mozart, developed in their boyhood, and reflecting on the incentives which were offered to Beethoven in Bonn, one may well marvel at the small number and the small significance of the compositions which preceded the Trios Op. 1, with which, at the age of 24 years, he first presented himself to the world as a finished artist. But a change has come over the picture in the progress of time. Not only are the beginnings of many works which he presented to the world at a late day as the ripe products of his genius to be traced back to the Bonn period; fate has also made known to us compositions of his youth which, for a long time, were lost in whole or in part, and which, in connection with the three great pianoforte quartets of 1785, not only disclose a steady progress, but also discover the self-developed individual artist at a much earlier date than has heretofore been accepted. Now that we are again in possession of the cantatas and other fruits of the Bonn period, or have learned to know them better as such, we are able to free ourselves from the old notion which presented Beethoven as a slowly and tardily developed master.

The most interesting of Beethoven's compositions in the Bonn period are unquestionably the cantatas on the death of Joseph II and the elevation of Leopold II. Beethoven did not bring them either to performance or publication; they were dead to the world. Nottebohm called attention to the fact that manuscript copies of their scores were announced in the auction catalogue of the library of Baron de Beine in April, 1813. It seems probable that Hummel purchased them at that time; at any rate, after his death they found their way from his estate into the second-hand bookshop of List and Francke in Leipzig, where they were bought in 1884 by Armin Friedmann of Vienna. Dr. Eduard Hanslick acquainted the world with the rediscovered treasures in a feuilleton published in the *Neue Freie Presse* newspaper of Vienna on May 13, 1884, and the funeral cantata was performed for the first time at Vienna in November, 1884, and at Bonn on June 29, 1885. Both cantatas were then included in the Complete Works of Beethoven published by Breitkopf and Härtel.

The "Cantata on the Death of Joseph the Second, composed by L. van Beethoven," was written between March and June, 1790. The Emperor died on February 20th, and the news of his death reached Bonn on February 24th. The *Lesegesellschaft* at once planned a memorial celebration, which took place on March 19th. At a meeting held to make preparations for the function on February 28, Prof. Eulogius Schneider (who delivered the memorial address) expressed the wish that a musical feature be incorporated in the programme and said that a young poet had that day placed a poem in his hands which only needed a setting from one of the excellent musicians who were members of the society or a composer from elsewhere. Beethoven's most influential friends, at the head of them Count Waldstein, were members of the society. Here, therefore, we have beyond doubt the story of how Beethoven's composition originated. The minutes of the last meeting for preparation, held on March 17, state that "for various reasons the proposed cantata cannot be performed." Among the various reasons may have been the excessive difficulty of the parts for the wind-instruments which, as we have seen, frustrated a projected performance at Mergentheim; although it is also possible that Beethoven, who was notoriously a slow worker, was unable to complete the music in the short time which was at his disposal. —⸺ The reason for assuming that it was this cantata which was both shown to Haydn and rehearsed at Mergentheim is that Beethoven clearly valued this work. He borrowed the material of the first soprano aria (with chorus) for a part of the second finale of *Fidelio: sostenuto assai*, "O Gott! O Gott! welch' ein Augenblick!"

After looking at the score sent to him by Hanslick, Brahms wrote to his friend: "Even if there were no name on the title page none other could be conjectured—it is Beethoven through and through! The beautiful and noble pathos, sublime in its feeling and imagination, the intensity, perhaps violent in its expression, moreover the voice leading and declamation, and in the two outside sections all the characteristics which we may observe and associate with his later works."[1]— The text of the cantata was written by Severin Anton Averdonk, son of an employee of the electoral Bureau of Accounts, and brother of the court singer Johanna Helene Averdonk, who, in her youth, was for a space a pupil of Johann van Beethoven. Beethoven set the young poet's ode for solo voice, chorus and orchestra without trumpets and drums.

Leopold's election as Roman Emperor took place on September 30, 1790, his coronation on October 9, when Elector Max Franz was present at Frankfurt. This gives us a hint as to the date of the "Cantata on the Elevation of Leopold II to the Imperial Dignity." Whether or not the Elector commissioned it cannot be said. Presumably Averdonk was again the poet. The two cantatas, though especially the former, mark the culmination of Beethoven's creative labors in Bonn; they show his artistic individuality ripened and a sovereign command of all the elements which Bonn was able to teach him from a technical point of view.

Two airs for bass voice[2] with orchestral accompaniment are, to judge by the handwriting, also to be ascribed to about 1790. The first is entitled "Prüfung des Küssens [The Test of Kissing], v. L. v. Beethowen." The use of the "w" instead of the "v" in the spelling of the name points to an early period for the composition. The text of the second bears the title, "Mit Mädeln sich vertragen," and was taken by Beethoven from the original version of Goethe's "Claudine von Villa Bella." Paper, handwriting and the spelling of the name of the composer indicate the same period as the first air.

To these airs must be added a considerable number of songs as fruits of Beethoven's creative labors in Bonn. The first of these, "Ich, der mit flatterndem Sinn," was made known by publication in the Complete Works. A sketch found among sketches for the variations on Mozart's "Se vuol ballare," led Nottebohm to set down 1792 as the year of its origin.[3] Of the songs grouped and published as Op. 52 the second, "Feuerfarbe," belongs to the period of transition from Bonn to Vienna. On January 26, 1793, Fischenich wrote Charlotte von Schiller: "I am enclosing with this a setting of the 'Feuerfarbe' on which I would like to have your opinion. It is by a young

---

[1] This letter was written in May, 1884 and first published in the Feuilleton of the *Neue Freie Presse* (Vienna), June 27, 1897, pp. 1-3.

[2] The bass was presumably the Electoral singer, Joseph Lux. (TDR, I, 302.) He was described by Junker in Bossler's *Musikal Correspondenz* (November 23, 1791) as a good bass singer and superlative comic actor.

[3] *II Beeth.*, p. 573. (TDR, I, 303.)

man of this place whose musical talents are universally praised and whom the Elector has sent to Haydn in Vienna. He proposes also to compose Schiller's 'Freude,' and indeed strophe by strophe. I expect something perfect for as far as I know him he is wholly devoted to the great and the sublime. Haydn has written here that he would put him at grand operas and soon be obliged to quit composing. Ordinarily he does not trouble himself with such trifles as the enclosed, which he wrote at the request of a lady." From this it is fair to conclude that the song was finished before Beethoven's departure from Bonn. Later he wrote a new postlude, which is found among the *motivi* for the Octet and the Trio in C minor. Of the other songs in Op. 52 the origin of several may be set down as falling in the Bonn period. That of the first, "Urians Reise um die Welt," we have already seen. Whether or not these songs, which met with severe criticism in comparison with other greater works of Beethoven, were published without Beethoven's knowledge, is doubtful. Probability places the following songs in the period of transition, or just before it:

1. "An Minna," sketched on a page with "Feuerfarbe," and other works written out in the early days of the Vienna period.
2. A drinking-song, "to be sung at parting,"—"Erhebt das Glas mit froher Hand." To judge by the handwriting, an early work, presumably circa 1787.
3. "Elegie auf den Tod eines Pudels,"—the same.
4. "Klage," to be placed in 1790, inasmuch as the original manuscript form appears simultaneously with sketches of the funeral cantata.
5. "Wer ist ein freier Mann?" whose original autograph in the British Museum bears the inscription "ipse fecit L. v. Beethoven," and must be placed between 1791 and 1792.[4] A revised form is probably a product of 1795, and to a third, Wegeler appended a different text, "Was ist des Maurers Ziel?" published in 1806.
6. The "Punschlied" may be a trifle older.
7. The autograph of "Man strebt die Flamme zu verhehlen," in the possession of the Gesellschaft der Musifreunde, which has been placed between 1792–95,[5] bears in Beethoven's handwriting the words "pour Madame weissenthurn par louis van Beethoven."

Madame Weissenthurn was a writer and actress, and from 1789 a member of the Burgtheater in Vienna, and it is more than likely that Beethoven did not get acquainted with her until he went to Vienna, although she was born on the Rhine.

Turn we now to the instrumental works which date back to the Bonn period. The beginning is made with the work which, in a manner, first brought Beethoven into close relationship with the stage—the *Ritterballet*,

[4] *Ibid.*, pp. 561-62.
[5] See Mandycsewski's *Revisionsbericht* to

GA. Ser. 25, p. iv. (TDR, I, 305.) See KHV, p. 582.

produced by the nobility on Carnival Sunday, March 6, 1791, and which, consequently, cannot have been composed long before, say in 1790 or 1791. ⸺⊰According to Wegeler (*Notizen*, p. 16), this work was considered for a long time to be by Count Waldstein, since Beethoven was not listed as the composer, the more so since the Count had organized the ballet in connection with Habich, a dancing master from Aix-la-Chapelle. Schiedermair[6] suggests that this mistake in authorship may have originated from an error in reporting for the theatre calendar.⊱⸺ Of the contents of the piece we know nothing more than is contained in the report from Bonn, namely, that it illustrated the predilection of the ancient Germans for war, the chase, love and drinking; the music, being without words, can give us no further help. It consists of eight short numbers, designed to accompany the pantomime: 1) March; 2) German Song; 3) Hunting Song; 4) Romance (entitled "Minnelied" in the autograph); 5) War Song; 6) Drinking Song; 7) German Dance; 8) Coda.

It seems as if the last year of Beethoven's sojourn in Bonn was especially influential in the development of his artistic character and ability. Of the works of 1792, besides trifles, there were two of larger dimensions which, if we were not better advised, would unhesitatingly be placed in the riper Vienna period. The autograph of the Octet for wind-instruments, published after the composer's death and designated at a later date as Op. 103, bears the inscription "Parthia in Es" (above this, "dans un Concert"), "Due Oboe, Due Clarinetti, Due Corni, Due Fagotti di L. v. Beethoven." From a sketch which precedes suggestions for the song "Feuerfarbe," Nottebohm[7] concludes that the Octet was composed in 1792, or, at the very latest in 1793. ⸺⊰A letter from Max Franz to Haydn in 1793[8] in which the Elector refers to the work as having been performed in Bonn makes it clear that the Octet was composed before the fall of 1792.⊱⸺ Moreover it is improbable that Beethoven would have found either incentive or occasion soon after reaching Vienna to write pieces of this character, and it is significant that in his later years he never returned to a combination of eight instruments. But there was an incentive in Bonn in the form of the excellent dinner-music of the Elector described by Chaplain Junker, which was performed by two oboes, two clarinets, two horns and two bassoons. For the same combination of instruments, Beethoven also composed a Rondino in E-flat, published in 1829 by Diabelli, probably from the posthumous manuscript. From the autograph Nottebohm argued that it was written in Bonn, and what has been said about the Octet applies also to the Rondino. The autograph of a little duet in G for two flutes bears the inscription: "For Friend Degenharth by L. v. Beethoven. August 23rd, 1792, midnight."

[6] *Op.cit.*, p. 389. Facing this page is a facsimile of the composer's piano transcription of Nos. 4-7. The autograph of the piano transcription of the whole ballet is in the Beethoven Archives (Catalogue No. 74) at Bonn.
[7] *Il Beeth.*, p. 518. (TDR, I, 309.)
[8] See page 145 below.

There is a fragment of a Concerto for Violin in C major, of which the autograph is in the archives of the Gesellschaft der Musikfreunde in Vienna. The handwriting indicates that it belongs to the early Vienna if not the Bonn period. That it is a first transcription is indicated by the fact that there are many erasures and corrections. The fragment contains 259 measures, embracing the orchestral introduction, the first solo passage, the second *tutti* and the beginning of the free fantasia for the solo instrument; it ends with the introduction of a new transition *motif* which leads to the conjecture that the movement was finished and that the missing portion has been lost. Schiedermair has printed a facsimile of the ten-page fragment as a supplement to *Der junge Beethoven*. He places it in the Bonn period: 1790-92.

Mr. Shedlock's extracts from the Kafka sketchbook[9] in the British Museum show that Beethoven tried his youthful hand at a symphony. Among the earliest sketches there is one in C minor marked "Sinfonia," which begins as follows:

Presto

Bass: C

Instead, Beethoven put this theme to use in the second movement (in E-flat minor) of the First Pianoforte Quartet, which was composed in 1785.[10]

A Trio in E-flat for Pianoforte, Violin and Violoncello, found among Beethoven's posthumous papers, was published in 1830 by Dunst in Frankfurt-am-Main. On the original publication its authenticity was certified to by Diabelli, Czerny and Ferdinand Ries, and it was stated that the original manuscript was in the possession of Schindler; Wegeler verified the handwriting as that of Beethoven. There is a remark in Gräffer's written catalogue of Beethoven's works: "Composed *anno* 1791, and originally intended for the three trios, Op. 1, but omitted as too weak by Beethoven." Whether or not this observation rests on an authentic source is not stated.

Dr. Deiters points out as characteristics of this Trio the freedom in invention and development, the large dimensions of the free fantasia portion, its almost imperceptible return to the principal theme, and the introduction of a coda in the first movement. These indicate that it was not written by Beethoven at the age of fifteen as Schindler states but long after the pianoforte quartets. Thematic motives from this movement recur in later works, for instance, the Sonata in F minor, Op. 2, and the Pianoforte Concerto in C major. Beethoven seems to have used the designation "Scherzo" in it for the first time.[11]

[9] *Musical Times*, Vol. 33 (1892), p. 333. (Cf. TDR, II, 59.)

[10] See *II Beeth.*, p. 567, and Fritz Stein, "Ein unbekannte Jugendsymphonie Beet-

hovens?" in *Sammelbände der Internationalen Musikgesellschaft*, Vol. 13 (1911-12), pp. 130ff. In the latter the sketch is quoted in full.

[11] See TDR, I, pp. 318-19.

Whether or not the Pianoforte Trios, Op. 1, were composed in Bonn may be left without discussion here, since we shall be obliged to recur to the subject later. The facts about them that have been determined beyond controversy are, that they were published in 1795; were not ready in their final shape in 1794; and were already played in the presence of Haydn in 1793.

The Variations in E-flat for Pianoforte, Violin and Violoncello, which were published in 1804 by Hoffmeister in Leipzig as Op. 44, may belong to the last year of Beethoven's life in Bonn. Nottebohm[12] found a sketch of the work alongside one of the song "Feuerfarbe," which fact points to the year 1792; Beethoven in a letter to the publisher appears not to have laid particular store by it, a circumstance easily understood in view of the great works which had followed the youthful effort.

Besides these compositions there is a Trio for Pianoforte, Flute and Bassoon. On the autograph, preserved in Berlin, the title, placed at the end, is "Trio concertant ą clavicembalo, flauto, fagotto, composto da Ludovici van Beethoven organista di S. S. Electeur de cologne." The designation of the composer as organist, etc., fixes the place of its origin, and the handwriting indicates an early date. The combination of instruments in the piece leads one to conjecture that it may have been composed for the family von Westerholt. Count von Westerholt played the bassoon, his son the flute, and his daughter the pianoforte. Moreover, their descendants have affirmed that the trio was written for their family.

---◦₰{Three Duos for Clarinet and Bassoon may belong to the Bonn period. Thayer without evidence considered that they might have been written around 1800 for the clarinettist Beer and the bassoonist Mattauschek. Players of these instruments were also among the wind ensemble used for dinner-music at the Bonn court described above.[13]}₰◦---

It is more than likely that the variations for Pianoforte and Violin on Mozart's "Se vuol ballare" ought to be assigned to the latter part of the Bonn period. They were published in July, 1793, by Artaria with a dedication to Eleonore von Breuning, to whom Beethoven sent the composition with a letter in 1794. The dedication leads to the presumption that the work was carried to Vienna in a finished state and there subjected only to the final polish. The postscript of the letter to Fräulein von Breuning betrays the reason for the hurried publication: Beethoven wanted to checkmate certain Viennese pianists whom he had detected copying peculiarities of his playing in improvisation which he suspected they would publish as their own devices.[14]

---

[12] *Beeth.*, p. 7. In the first edition of the Thayer biography (I, 115) mention is made of a sketchbook, originally owned by Aloys Fuchs, containing sketches for these variations, for the Quartet, Op. 18, No. 3, the fourth movement of the Septet, Op. 20, and the variations on "Ich denke dein." This would date the work in 1799. Unfortunately, Thayer's evidence was based only on a memorandum from Jahn, for the pages in question had since been removed from the sketchbook. See KHV, pp. 105-106.

[13] See TDR, II, 39-40.

[14] See pages 163-64 below.

Besides the pieces already mentioned, Beethoven wrote the following works for pianoforte in Bonn:

1. A Prelude in F minor.[15] According to a remark in another hand on a printed copy, Beethoven wrote it when he was 15 years old, that is, in 1786 or, the question of his age not being determined at the time, 1787. The prelude is, as a matter of fact, a fruit of his studies in the art of imitation; and the initiative, probably, came from Bach's preludes. ---*{Schiedermair has shown a connection between this prelude and Bach's Prelude XII from Part I of *The Well-Tempered Clavichord*.[16]}*---

2. Two Preludes through the Twelve Major Keys for Pianoforte or Organ; published by Hoffmeister in 1803 as Op. 39. ---*{Beethoven noted on a corrected copy: "1789 von Ludwig van Beethoven."[17]}*--- These were obviously exercises written for Neefe while he was Beethoven's teacher in composition.

3. Variations on the arietta "Venni Amore," by Righini, in D major. The arietta begins: "Venni Amore nel tuo regno, ma compagno del Timor." Righini gave his melody five variations. Beethoven composed 24 variations for pianoforte in 1790. They were published in Mannheim in 1791. Then they were revised in Vienna in 1801 for publication through Traeg. In the first version they were inscribed to Countess Hatzfeld (née Countess de Girodin), who has been praised in this book as an eminent pianist. The story of the encounter between Beethoven and Sterkel in which these variations figure has also been told. Beethoven had a good opinion of them; Czerny told Otto Jahn that he had brought them with him to Vienna and used them to "introduce" himself.

Two books of variations are to be adjudged to the Bonn period because of their place of publication and other biographical considerations. They are the Variations in A major on a theme from Dittersdorf's opera *Das rote Käppchen* ("Es war einmal ein alter Mann")[18] and the Variations for four hands on a theme by Count Waldstein. Beethoven's intimate association with Waldstein in Bonn is a familiar story, but we hear little of it in the early Viennese days. The variations on a theme of his own seem likely to have been the product of a wish expressed by the Count. That Beethoven seldom wrote for four hands, and certainly not without a special reason, is an accepted fact.

Another Bonnian product, which has come down to us as only a fragment, is the Sonata in C major for Pianoforte, published by Dunst in Frankfurt, with a dedication to Eleonore von Breuning. In a letter to her in 1794 he writes: "I have a great deal to do or I would have transcribed the sonata I promised you long ago; it is a mere sketch in manuscript. . . ."[19] Eleonore

---

[15] It was published in 1805 by the Kunst- und Industrie-Comptoir of Vienna, and Kinsky believes that it was completely revised for this publication (KHV, p. 501). Cf. Nottebohm's *Beethovens Studien*, p. 12. (TDR, I, 323, n. 1.)

[16] *Op.cit.*, p. 354. For further speculation concerning Bach's influence on specific works of Beethoven, see *FRBH*, 1, pp. 12ff. See also Schmid, "Beethovens Bachkenntnis," *NBJ*, v (1933), 64.

[17] See KHV, p. 96.

[18] *Das rote Käppchen* was first performed in February, 1792. See *A* [Letter no.] 2.

[19] For full letter see page 163 below.

von Breuning received it from him in 1796. In the copy sent to the publisher eleven measures at the end of the Adagio were lacking. These were supplied by Ferdinand Ries in the manner of Beethoven. There can scarcely be a doubt that Beethoven finished the Adagio, and it can be assumed that he also composed a last movement, which has been lost.

That Beethoven also tried his powers in a wider field we know from the two cantatas; the two airs for bass and orchestra and the *Ritterballet*; and it is not by any means a wild suggestion that he had tried his strength in other concertos for pianoforte and full orchestra than that of 1784.

—•◦{In the Beethoven Archives at Bonn (Catalogue No. 135) there is a sheet on which is written out the opening themes of the three movements of an oboe concerto as follows:[20]

[20] With the kind permission of Dr. Joseph Schmidt-Görg, director of the Beethoven Archives at Bonn.

This tantalizing indication that such a concerto was started adds evidence to the theory that a number of works for individual players may well have been sketched and perhaps completed that have not survived. In this case there is direct evidence, from a letter written in 1793 from Haydn to the Elector, that Beethoven completed an oboe concerto, most likely a realization of the sketch given above. That it was composed at Bonn was affirmed by the Elector's reply.[21]

It is a striking fact to anyone who has had occasion to examine carefully the chronology of publication of Beethoven's works, that up to nearly the close of 1802 whatever appeared under his name was worthy of that name; but that then, in the period of his second, third and fourth symphonies, of the Sonatas, Op. 47, 53, 57 and of *Leonore*, to the wonder of the critics of that time serial advertisements of the Kunst- und Industrie-Comptoir in Vienna announced the Violin Sonatas, Op. 30 and the seven Bagatelles, Op. 33; in another the "Grand Sinfonie," Op. 36, and the Variations on "God Save the King"; on May 15, 1805, the Waldstein Sonata and the Romance, Op. 50; and on June 16 the songs, Op. 52, which the *Allgemeine Mus. Zeitung* describes as "commonplace, poor, weak, in part ridiculous stuff."

One must remember Ries's personal bias against the brothers of his teacher as one reads his explanation (*Notizen*, p. 124) of this enigma: "All trifles and many things which he did not want to publish because he thought them unworthy of his name, were secretly given to publicity by his brother. Thus songs which he had composed years before his departure for Vienna, became known only after he had reached a high degree of fame. Thus, too, little compositions which he had written in autograph albums were filched and published." But the publishing of his minor works was facilitated by the composer's habit of preserving his manuscripts which he carried with him to each of the many houses into which he moved. And yet, as Ries writes in his *Notizen* (p. 113): "Beethoven attached absolutely no value to his autographs; after they had once been engraved they generally were piled on the floor in his living room or an anteroom among other pieces of music. I often brought order into his music, but when Beethoven hunted for anything, everything was sent flying in disorder. At that time I might have carried away the autograph manuscripts of all the pieces which had been printed, or had I asked him for them he would unquestionably have given them to me without a thought."

These words of Ries are confirmed by the small number of autographs of printed works in the auction catalogue of Beethoven's posthumous papers—most of them having remained in the hands of the publishers or having been lost, destroyed or stolen.

If a list be drawn up of Beethoven's published compositions between 1795 and December, 1802, with the addition of other works known to have been

---

[21] See page 144 below.

composed in those years, the result will be nearly as follows (omitting single songs and other minor pieces): symphonies, 2; ballet (*Prometheus*), 1; sonatas (solo and duo), 32; romances (violin and orchestra), 2; serenades, 2; duos (clarinet and bassoon), 3; sets of variations, 16; sets of dances, 9; "Ah! perfido" and "Adelaide," 2; pianoforte concertos, 3; trios, 11; quartets, 6; quintets, 3; sextets, 2; septet, 1; pianoforte rondos, 3; rondo for pianoforte and orchestra, 1; marches (for four hands), 3; an aggregate of 103 compositions in eight years or ninety-six months. And most of them *such* compositions! That Beethoven was a remarkable man all the world knows; but that he could produce at this rate, study operatic composition with Salieri, sustain, nay, increase his reputation as a pianoforte virtuoso, journey to Prague, Berlin and other places, correct proof-sheets for his publishers, give lessons and yet find time to write long letters to friends, to sleep, to eat, drink and be merry with companions of his own age—this is, to say the least, "a morsel difficult of digestion." The more so from the fact that at the very time when he began to devote himself more exclusively to composition such marvellous fertility suddenly ceased. The inference is obvious. Many of the works published by Beethoven during the first dozen years of his Vienna life were taken thither from Bonn. They doubtless were more or less altered, amended, improved, corrected, but nevertheless belong as compositions to those years when "Beethoven played pianoforte concertos, and Herr Neefe accompanied at Court in the theatre and in concerts." While the other young men were trying their strength upon works for the orchestra and stage, the performance of which would necessarily give them notoriety, the Court Pianist would naturally confine himself mostly to his own instrument and to chamber music—to works whose production before a small circle in the salons of the Elector, Countess Hatzfeld and others would excite little if any public notice. But here he struck out so new, and at that time so strange a path that no small degree of praise is due to the sagacity of Count Waldstein, who comprehended his aims, felt his greatness and encouraged him to trust to and be guided by his own instincts and genius.

When Neefe, in 1793, calls Beethoven "beyond controversy one of the foremost pianoforte players," it excites no surprise. Ten years before he had played most of Bach's *Well-Tempered Clavichord*, and had now long held the offices of Second Court Organist and Court Pianist; but what sufficient reason could Waldstein have had for his faith that this pianist, by study and perseverance, would yet be able to seize and hold the sceptre of Mozart? And upon what grounds, too, could Fischenich, on January 26, 1793, write, as he did in the aforementioned letter to Charlotte von Schiller, that he expected from him something perfect, and that Haydn had written that he would "put him at grand operas and soon be obliged to quit composing."

Note the date of this—January 26, 1793. Haydn must have written some time before this, when Beethoven could not have been with him more than six or eight weeks. Did the master found his remark upon what he had seen in his pupil or upon the compositions which his pupil had placed before him? ⸻Deiters cannot forbear the suspicion that Haydn's words were not completely in earnest, which idea might well be borne out in the light of Haydn's and Beethoven's relationship, as we shall see.⸻

Finally, the closing lines of a short article in the *Jahrbuch der Tonkunst für Wien und Prag*, 1796—which notice was not written later than the spring of 1795, nine or ten months before the publication of the Sonatas Op. 2—are pregnantly suggestive: "We have a number of beautiful sonatas by him, amongst which the last ones particularly distinguish themselves." These works were, therefore, well-known in manuscript even at the time when he was busy with his studies under Haydn and Albrechtsberger.

⸻Schiedermair has summed up the state of our knowledge of Beethoven's creative efforts in Bonn as follows:[22] "If we reckon along with the compositions that have been preserved and are genuine, that portion, probably not inconsiderable, which today is irreparably lost, although perhaps a piece or two might still come to light amongst the papers in the archives of some European or American library; if we further imagine that many an idea, first conceived in Bonn, is scarcely recognizable for us today as it is reshaped for a later work in Vienna in which it becomes gloriously transformed, then we are faced with the fact that a productivity has started around 1785, bursting forth with ever increasing strength, which must be considered unusually rich despite the fact that the actual number of works that have survived is lower than that found in the similar period of life of other great musicians. It goes without saying that neither the activity within a limited period of a man's life nor the quantity of work constitute the significance of an artist. Besides, as we consider Beethoven's official duties, his family cares, the rewarding intercourse with friends in which his sense of companionship was not always carefree, we are perceiving the life of a youth filled with indefatigable work and constant effort."

There are a number of compositions, the origin of which remains in doubt between the late Bonn and the early Vienna period. Such a work is the String Trio Op. 3, which will be discussed in a later chapter. Riemann would attribute the origin of certain chamber works, for instance, to the last years in Bonn because of a stylistic affinity with the music that was being performed at court.[23] One may add that some of the results of these influences may have been delayed in realization to the first years in Beethoven's new home.

From Schiedermair's list of compositions and fragments that were composed in Bonn,[24] we find that the following have not been included so far in our text:

1. A sonata movement and a sketch of an Allegretto in F which (along

---

[22] *Op.cit.*, p. 227.
[23] See "Beethoven und die Mannheimer," *DM*, VII₁₃ (1908), pp. 3-19.

[24] *Op.cit.*, pp. 216ff. Also on the list is a piano concerto in D which has been proved to be by Johann Josef Rösler. See KHV, p. 721.

with a copy of Schubart's "Auf, auf! ihr Brüder!" in E-flat) was written out for Wegeler. From the autograph in the Wegeler collection at Coblenz, a facsimile has been published in Leopold Schmidt's *Beethoven Briefe* (1908).

2. "An Laura" (text by Matthisson). The autograph is in W. Heyer's *Musikhistorisches Museum* in Cologne.[25]

3. A fragment of a Romance in E minor for Pianoforte (Klavier), Flute, Bassoon *concertant* with the accompaniment of strings and 2 oboes. The autograph is in the British Museum.

4. A sketch of "Liedschen von der Ruhe: Im Arm der Liebe" (W. Ueltzen's poem was first published in 1788), which is the first version of Op. 52, No. 3.

5. Sketches for Goethe's "Flohlied" (text from *Faust*, published in 1790) which in its final version is printed as Op. 75, No. 3.

Unger dates the Six Easy Variations on a Swiss Air for the harp or pianoforte around 1790 on the basis of an autograph, which he believes is in Beethoven's own hand, to be found in the Bodmer collection at the Beethovenhaus in Bonn.[26]

Now to consider certain doubtful and spurious compositions. — Among the papers found in Beethoven's apartments after his death was the manuscript of a Sonata in B-flat for Pianoforte and Flute, which passed into the hands of Artaria. It is not in Beethoven's handwriting; thus there is little evidence of its authenticity. — Yet Hess points out that the very fact that this piece is in many ways awkward and unrewarding makes it unlikely that Beethoven would have preserved the manuscript unless it were his own.[27]

The autographs of three pieces for four hands, a Gavotte, an Allegro and a fragment of a *Marcia lugubre*, form part of a collection in the British Museum (BM, No. 31,748), which was listed as "Mozart Autographs" in the "Catalogue of Additions to the Manuscripts in the British Museum," published in 1882 to cover the period 1876-81. In 1910/1911 they were considered to be not Mozart but early Beethoven by St. Foix and Wyzewa, and they were published by St. Foix in his "Oeuvres inédites de Beethoven" as Tome II of *Publications de la Societé Française de Musicologie* (1926). In 1944 it was discovered accidentally that all three pieces were from Koželuch's ballet *La Ritrovata Figlia di Ottone II* (produced at Vienna on February 24, 1794).[28] Unknown is the arranger of these pieces for four hands.

BM, No. 31,748 further includes two genuine Mozart pieces (K.93 and K.406, now 516b) and two other works, namely, a Trio in D, for Pianoforte,

[25] By omitting the recitative section, Diabelli was able to convert the song into a piano piece, which he added to the eleven Bagatelles, Op. 119, as No. 12, in a publication of 1828: "L. v. B. Nouvelles Bagatelles pour le Piano Op. 112 [*sic*!] Vienne chez A. Diabelli & Co."

[26] See Max Unger, "Eine Schweizer Beethoven-Sammlung," *NBJ*, v, 40, no. 2.

[27] Willy Hess, "Der Erstdruck von Beethovens Flötensonate," *NBJ*, vi (1935), 141. A correct edition edited by Hess has been published by Peters (1951).

[28] Otto E. Deutsch, "Koželuch Ritrovata," *Music and Letters*, Vol. 26 (1945), p. 47. See also *Music and Letters* Correspondence, Vol. 33 (1952), Nos. 1, 2, 3; also *Schweizerische Musikzeitung*, Vol. 92 (1952), p. 14.

Violin and Violoncello in two movements (two pages of the first Allegro are missing) and a Rondo in B-flat for piano. These last two works were also published by St. Foix in the volume referred to above, thus contesting their earlier assignment to Mozart.[29] The recent attempts to resolve their authorship, which has included the further investigation of all the available works of Koželuch, has been unsuccessful, and in both cases it remains in doubt.

Mention should be made here of the so-called "Jena Symphony." In 1909 Prof. Fritz Stein, Musical Director of the University of Jena, announced that he had discovered among the music of the Academic Concerts (founded in 1780) the complete parts of a symphony in C. On the second violin part was written "par Louis van Beethoven"; on the 'cello part "Symphonie von Bethoven," both by an unknown hand. Stein prepared a score from these parts, which was published by Breitkopf and Härtel as "Symphonie in C Dur mit Ludwig van Beethovens Namen überliefert." The authorship of the symphony remained in doubt until H. C. Robbins Landon[30] discovered another set of parts to this symphony in the monastery at Göttweig. These parts reveal that the symphony was written by the Würzberg Hofkapell-meister, Friedrich Witt (1770–1837). Landon reasons that the Jena parts were acquired as being by Witt; then the title page was lost and Beethoven's name was subsequently added to the two parts.

Two sonatinas, in G major and F major, are published in the Complete Works Edition (Ser. 16, Nos. 37 and 38). Thayer lists them in his *Chronologisches Verzeichniss*[31] and questions whether they correspond to Item No. 157 listed in the public sale of Beethoven's effects after his death: "Two complete small pieces for P. F. From his early period." Riemann believes they are by Beethoven, but Kinsky[32] questions this for two reasons. First, Item No. 157 was bought by Artaria; if these were one and the same and by Beethoven, Artaria would have published them. Second, they were published instead by Cranz and then by Böhme in Hamburg, both of whom describe them as "arranged." Nottebohm also doubts their authenticity.

The compositions of the later Bonn years should be listed together as a unit: 1786–92.

1786-7. Prelude for Pianoforte in F minor, WoO 55.
1787-8. Song. "Erhebt das Glas mit froher Hand," WoO 109.
          Song. "Elegie auf den Tod eines Pudels," WoO 110.
1787-90. Song. "Punschlied," WoO 111.
1789.   Two Preludes for Pianoforte or Organ, Op. 39.
1789-90. Sonatina for Pianoforte in F major, WoO 50.
1788-91. Song. "An Laura" (text by Fr. v. Matthisson), WoO 112.

[29] See second edition of Köchel's *Thematic Catalogue of Mozart's Works* (Waldersee), nos. 412, 52a, 511a.
[30] "The Jena Symphony," *Music Review,* Vol. 18 (1957), pp. 109-13.
[31] Berlin, 1865, p. 11.
[32] KHV, pp. 719-20. Cf. Nottebohm, *Verzeichniss,* p. 148.

Trio for Pianoforte, Flute and Bassoon, WoO 37.

Two Airs for Bass and Orchestra, WoO 89 and 90.

1790.   Cantata on the Death of Joseph II, for Voices and Orchestra (text by S. A. Averdonk), WoO 87.

Song. "Klage" (text by L. Hölty), WoO 113.

Cantata on the Elevation of Leopold II, for Voices and Orchestra (text by S. A. Averdonk), WoO 88.

Twenty-four Variations for Pianoforte on a theme from Righini's "Venni Amore," WoO 65. 1st version.

1790-91. Music for a *Ritterballet*, WoO 1.

1791.   Trio for Pianoforte, Violin and Violoncello in E-flat major, WoO 38.

1790-92. Fragment of a Concerto for Violin and Orchestra in C major, WoO 5.

Six Easy Variations on a Swiss Air for harp or pianoforte, WoO 64.

Sonata for Pianoforte in C major, WoO 51.

Song. "Wer ist ein freie Mann?" (text by G. C. Pfeffel), WoO 117.

Variations for Pianoforte Four Hands on a Theme by Count Waldstein, WoO 67.

?   Three Duets for Clarinet and Bassoon, WoO 27.

1792.   Duet for Two Flutes, WoO 26.

Octet for Two Oboes, Clarinets, Horns and Bassoons, Op. 103.

Rondino for Two Oboes, Clarinets, Horns and Bassoons, WoO 25.

Song. "Ich, der mit flatterndem Sinn" (text by J. W. L. Gleim), WoO 114.

Thirteen Variations for Pianoforte on a Theme from Dittersdorf's opera, *Das rote Käppchen*, WoO 66.

?   Fourteen Variations for Piano, Violin and Violoncello, Op. 44.

Transitional. Song ."An Minna," WoO 115.

Song. "Man strebt die Flamme zu verhehlen," WoO 120.

Song. "Que le temps me dure" (text by J. J. Rousseau), WoO 116. The song was sketched in two different versions; both autographs are in the Berlin State Library.[33]

Variations for Pianoforte and Violin on "Se vuol ballare," from Mozart's *Nozze di Figaro*, WoO 40.

Eight Songs, Op. 52:

"Urians Reise um die Welt" (text by M. Claudius). Early according to Wegeler.

"Feuerfarbe" (text by S. Moreau). Composed before Fischenich's letter to Charlotte von Schiller of January 26, 1793.

"Das Liedchen von der Ruhe" (text by H. W. F. Ueltzen).

"Mailied" (text by J. W. Goethe).

"Mollys Abschied" (text by G. A. Bürger).

"Die Liebe" (text by G. E. Lessing).

---

[33] This song and the later song "Plaisir d'aimer" were discussed and described by Jean Chantanvoine (*DM*, I₁₂, 1902, pp. 1078ff.), who prints the first version. In *Zeitschrift für Musik*, Vol. 102 (1935), pp. 1200-1203, Max Unger has established the date and published both versions of the song.

"Marmotte" (text by J. W. Goethe).

"Das Blümchen Wunderhold" (text by G. A. Bürger).

And what works of this growing talent were available thus far in other than manuscript form? The list of publications is small:

1782. By Götz in Mannheim:

Variations for Pianoforte on a March by Dressler, dedicated to Countess Felice von Wolf-Metternich, WoO 63.

1783. By Bossler in Speyer:

Three Sonatas for Pianoforte, dedicated to Elector Max Friedrich, WoO 47.

In Bossler's *Blumenlese für Klavierliebhaber*:

Rondo in C for Pianoforte, WoO 48.

Song. "Schilderung eines Mädchens," WoO 107.

1784. In Bossler's *Neue Blumenlese für Klavierliebhaber*:

Rondo in A for Pianoforte, WoO 49.

Song. "An einen Säugling" (text by J. V. Döhring), WoO 108.

1791. By Götz in Mannheim:

Variations for Pianoforte on Righini's "Venni Amore," dedicated to Countess Maria Anna Hortensia von Hatzfeld, WoO 65.

CHAPTER VIII

BEETHOVEN'S TEACHERS
IN VIENNA—

VIENNESE COMPOSERS AND SOCIETY

IT WOULD be pleasant to announce the arrival of Ludwig van Beethoven in Vienna with, so to speak, a grand flourish of trumpets, and to indulge the fancy in a highly-colored and poetic account of his advent there; but, unluckily, there is none of that lack of data which is favorable to that kind of composition; none of that obscurity which exalts one to write history as he would have it and not as it really was. The facts are too patent. Like the multitude of studious youths and young men who came thither annually to find schools and teachers, this small, thin, dark-complexioned, pockmarked, dark-eyed, bewigged young musician of 22 years had quietly journeyed to the capital to pursue the study of his art with a small, thin, dark-complexioned, pockmarked, black-eyed and bewigged veteran composer. In the well-known anecdote related by Carpani of Haydn's introduction to him, Anton Esterhazy, the prince, is made to call the composer "a Moor." Beethoven had even more of the Moor in his looks than his master. His front teeth, owing to the singular flatness of the roof of his mouth, protruded, and, of course, thrust out his lips; the nose, too, was rather broad and decidedly flattened, while the forehead was remarkably full and round—in the words of Court Secretary Mähler, who twice painted his portrait, a "bullet."

"Beethoven," wrote Junker, "confessed that in his journeys he had seldom found in the playing of the most distinguished virtuosi that excellence which he supposed he had a right to expect." He now had an opportunity to make his observations upon the pianists and composers at the very headquarters, then, of German music, to improve himself by study under the best of them and, by and by, to measure his strength with theirs. He found very soon that the words of the poet were here also applicable: "'Tis distance lends enchantment to the view," and did not find—now Mozart was gone—"what he supposed he had a right to expect." For the present, however, we have to do but with the young stranger in a large city, seeking lodgings, and making such arrangements for the future as shall not be out of due proportion to the limited pecuniary means at his command. If the minute details which here follow should seem to be too insignificant in themselves, the bearing they have upon some other future questions must justify their introduction.

Turning again to the memorandum book, the first entries which follow the notes of the journey from Bonn to Würges are merely of necessities to be supplied—"wood, wig-maker, coffee, overcoat, boots, shoes, pianoforte-desk, seal, writing-desk, pianoforte-money" and something illegible followed by the remark: "All beginning with next month." The next page gives a hint as to the day of his arrival. It contains the substance of two advertisements in the *Wiener Zeitung* of pianofortes for sale, one near the Hohen Markt and two "im Kramerschen Breihaus No. 257 im Schlossergassel, am Graben." The latter appears *for the last time* on the 10th of November; Beethoven was, therefore, then in Vienna.

But he intended to cultivate the Graces as well as the Muses. The next page begins with this: "Andreas Lindner, dancing-master, lives in the Stoss am Himmel, No. 415," to which succeeds a note, evidently of money received from the Elector, possibly in Bonn but more likely in Vienna: "25 ducats received of which, expended on November (?) half a sovereign for the pianoforte, or 6 florins, 40 kreutzer—2 florins were of my own money." The same page also shows him in the matter of his toilet preparing even then for entrance into society: "Black silk stockings, 1 ducat; 1 pair of winter silk stockings, 1 florin, 40 kreutzers; boots, 6 florins; shoes, 1 florin, 30 kreutzers." But these expenses in addition to his daily necessities are making a large inroad upon his "25 ducats received"; and on page 7 we read: "On Wednesday the 12th of December, I had 15 ducats." (The 12th of December fell upon Wednesday in the year 1792.) Omitting for the present what else stands upon page 7, here are the interesting contents of page 8—and how suggestive and pregnant they are: "In Bonn I counted on receiving 100 ducats here; but in vain. I have got to equip myself completely anew."

Several pages which follow contain what, upon inspection, proves evidently to be his monthly payments from the time when "all was to begin next month," of which the first may be given as a specimen: "House-rent, 14 florins; pianoforte, 6 florins, 40 kreutzers; eating, each time 12 kreutzers; meals with wine, 16½ florins; 3 kreutzers for B. and H.; it is not necessary to give the housekeeper more than 7 florins, the rooms are so close to the ground." Beethoven's first lodgings were in an attic-room which he soon exchanged for a room on the ground floor of a house No. 45 Alserstrasse occupied by one Strauss, a printer. The house now on the site is No. 30. Another occupant of the house was Prince Lichnowsky, who soon after took him into his lodgings. He remained in this house until May, 1795.

Beethoven was hardly well settled in his lodgings, the novelty of his position had scarcely begun to wear off under the effect of habit, when startling tidings reached him from Bonn of an event to cloud his Christmas holidays, to weaken his ties to his native place, to increase his cares for his brothers and make an important change in his pecuniary condition. His father had suddenly died—"1792, Dec. 18, *obiit* Johannes Beethoff," says the death-roll of St. Remigius parish. The Elector-Archbishop, still in Münster, heard this news also and consecrated a joke to the dead man's memory. On the 1st of January, 1793, he wrote a letter to Court Marshal von Schall in which these words occur: "The revenues from the liquor excise have suffered a loss in the deaths of Beethoven and Eichhoff. For the widow of the latter, provision will be made if circumstances allow in view of his 40 years of service . . ." [in the electoral kitchen.]

Franz Ries was again to befriend Beethoven and act for him in his absence, and the receipt for his first quarter's salary (25th.) is signed "F. Ries, in the name of Ludwig Beethoven," at the usual time, namely the beginning of the second month of the quarter, February 4. But the lapse of Johann van Beethoven's pension of 200 thalers, was a serious misfortune to his son, particularly since the 100 ducats were not forthcoming. The correspondence between Beethoven and Ries not being preserved it can only be conjectured that the latter took the proper steps to obtain that portion of the pension set apart by the electoral decree for the support of the two younger sons; but in vain, owing to the disappearance of the original document; and that, receiving information of this fact, Beethoven immediately sent from Vienna the petition which follows, but which, as is mostly the case with that class of papers in the Bonn archives, is without date:[1]

Most Worthy and Illustrious Elector!
Most Gracious Lord!

Several years ago Your Serene Electoral Highness was pleased to retire my father, the tenor singer van Beethoven, from service, and by a most gracious decree to set aside 100 thalers of his salary to me that I might clothe, nourish and educate my two younger brothers and also to discharge our father's debts.

I was about to present this decree to Your Highness's Revenue Exchequer when my father urgently begged me not to do so inasmuch as it would have the appearance in the eyes of the public that he was incapable of caring for his family, adding that he himself would pay me the 25 thalers quarterly, which he always did promptly.

However, upon the death of my father in December of last year, when I wished to make use of Your Highness's grace by presenting the above-mentioned gracious decree I learned to my horror that my father had made away with the same.

With most obedient veneration I therefore pray Your Electoral Highness for the gracious renewal of this decree and that Your Highness's Revenue Exchequer be directed to pay over to me the sum graciously allowed to me due for the last quarter at the beginning of last February.

Your Electoral and Serene Highness's
    Most obedient and faithful
        Lud. v. Beethowen, Court Organist.

[1] Presumably at the beginning of May, 1793, in view of the date of the answer.

The petition was duly considered by the Privy Council and with the result indicated by the endorsement:

ad. sup.
of the
Court Organist
L. van Beethoven

... "The 100 reichsthaler which he is now receiving annually is increased by a further 100 reichsthaler in quarterly payments beginning with January 1st, from the 200 rth. salary vacated by the death of his father; he is further to receive the three measures of grain graciously bestowed upon him for the education of his brothers." The Electoral Court Chancellery will make the necessary provisions. Attest p.

Bonn, May 3, 1793."

The order to the exchequer followed on May 24th, and on June 15th, Franz Ries had the satisfaction of signing two receipts—one for 25 thalers for January, February and March, and one for 50 thalers for the second quarter of the year. According to the accounts of the office of revenues that still exist at Düsseldorf, Beethoven received the salary of 50 thalers in quarterly payments until March, 1794. From this time onward no hint has been discovered that Beethoven ever received anything from the Elector or had any resources but his own earnings and the generosity of newly-found friends in Vienna. These resources were soon needed. The remark that two florins of the payment towards the pianoforte were out of his own money proves that he possessed a small sum saved up by degrees from lesson-giving, from presents received and the like; but it could not have been a large amount, while the 25 ducats and the above recorded receipts of salary were all too small to have carried him through the summer of 1793. Here is the second of his monthly records of necessary and regular expenses in further proof of this: "14 florins house-rent; 6 fl. 40 x, pianoforte; meals with wine, 15 fl. and a half;—(?), 3 florins; maid, 1," the sum total being as added by himself "11 ducats and one-half florin." And yet at the end of the year there are entries that show that he was not distressed for money. For instance: "the 24th October, i.e., reckoning from November 1st, 112 florins and 30 kreutzer"; "2 ducats for a seal; 1 florin, 25 kreutzers, copyist"; "Tuesday and Saturday from 7 to 8. Sunday from 11 to 12, 3 florins"; and the final entry not later in date than 1794 is: "3 carolins in gold, 4 carolins in crown thalers and 4 ducats make 7 carolins and 4 ducats and a lot of small change."

In what manner Beethoven was already in 1794 able to remain "in Vienna without salary until recalled," to quote the Elector's words, will hereafter appear with some degree of certainty; but just now he claims attention as pupil of Haydn and Albrechtsberger. The citations made in a previous chapter from the letters of Neefe and Fischenich prove how strong an impression Beethoven's powers, both as virtuoso and composer, had made upon Joseph Haydn immediately after his reaching Vienna; and no man then living was better able to judge on such points. But whether the famous kapellmeister, just returned from his English triumphs, himself a daring and successful innovator and now very busy with compositions in preparation for his second visit to London, was the man to guide the studies of a headstrong, self-willed and still more daring musical revolutionist was, *a priori*, a very doubtful question. The result proved that he was not.

The memorandum book has a few entries which relate to Haydn. On page 7, which contains the entry of 15 ducats on the 12th of December, 1792, there is a column of numerals (mostly 2 groschen), the first of which reads, "Haidn 8 groschen"; and on the two pages which happen to have the dates of October 24 and 29, 1793, are these two entries: "22 x, chocolate for Haidn and me"; "Coffee, 6 x for Haidn and me." These notes simply confirm what was known from other sources, namely, that Beethoven began to study with Haydn very soon after reaching Vienna and continued to be his pupil until the end of the year 1793, or the beginning of 1794, since Haydn left Vienna on January 19th of that year. They indicate, also, that the scholar, whatever feelings he may have indulged towards the master in secret, kept on good terms with him, and that their private intercourse was not confined to the hours devoted to lessons in Haydn's room in the Hamberger house, No. 1275 (later 992) on the (no longer existing) Wasserkunstbastei.

We turn again to Nottebohm concerning the course of Beethoven's studies with Haydn. He has made a most thorough examination of all the known manuscripts and authorities which bear upon this question.[2] The substance of the instruction was strict counterpoint. Haydn had made an abstract of Fux's *Gradus ad Parnassum*, a book which he valued highly, and this was used also by Beethoven. The exercises were undertaken in the different species of counterpoint upon six plain chants (from the six old modes). Two hundred and forty-five such exercises are extant, but there can well be more, since the manuscript is not complete. Forty-two of these exercises have changes or indications of mistakes by Haydn. The mistakes indicated refer to parallel fifths and octaves, the handling of parts which accompany a suspension, crossing of voices and treatment of the leading tone, and others which strict counterpoint does not allow. But Haydn has not consistently found all the mistakes in the great majority of the exercises in which corresponding errors are to be found. They lack his corrections. It is apparent that on account of the claims of his own works he was not exacting or systematic as a teacher nor did he devote the necessary time to the continuous training of his student.

Since all the exercises that were made during this instruction have not survived, it must be assumed that many more contrapuntal exercises preceded these since Beethoven shows in the exercises that do exist that he was already well acquainted with many of the principles of strict writing.

The fact seems to be that Beethoven, conscious of the disadvantages attending the want of thorough systematic instruction, distrustful of himself and desirous of bringing to the test many of his novel and cherished ideas,

[2] Nottebohm, *Beeth.*, pp. 168-77; *Beethovens Studien*, pp. 21-43. (TDR, I, 350, n. 2.)

had determined to accomplish a complete course of contrapuntal study, and thus renew, revise and reduce to order and system the great mass of his previous theoretical knowledge. He would, at all events, thoroughly know and understand the *regular* that he might with confidence judge for himself how far to indulge in the *irregular*. To this view, long since adopted, the results of Nottebohm's researches add credibility. It explains, also, how a young man, too confident in the soundness of his views to be willing to alter his productions because they contained passages and effects censured by those about him for being other than those of Mozart and Haydn, was yet willing, with the modesty of true genius, to shut them up in his writing-desk until, through study and observation, he could feel himself standing upon the firm basis of sound knowledge and then retain or exclude, according to the dictates of an enlightened judgment.

Beethoven, however, very soon discovered that also in Haydn, as a teacher, he had "not found that excellence which he supposed he had a right to expect." Ries remembered a remark made by him on this point (*Notizen*, p. 86): "Haydn had wished that Beethoven might put the word, 'Pupil of Haydn,' on the title of his first works. Beethoven was unwilling to do so because, as he said, though he had had some instruction from Haydn he had never learned anything from him."

Still more in point is the oft-repeated story of Johann Schenk's kindness to Beethoven, related by Seyfried in Gräfer's and Schilling's lexica and confirmed by Schindler, which, when divested of its errors in dates, may be related thus: Among Beethoven's earliest acquaintances in Vienna was the Abbé Joseph Gelinek, one of the first virtuosos then in that city and an amazingly fruitful and popular composer of variations. It was upon him that Carl Maria von Weber, some years afterwards, wrote the epigram:

> Kein Thema auf der Welt verschonte dein Genie,
> Das simpelste allein—Dich selbst—variirst du nie!

> "No theme on earth escaped your genius airy,—
> The simplest one of all—yourself—you never vary."

Czerny told Otto Jahn that his father once met Gelinek tricked out in all his finery. "Whither?" he inquired. "I am asked to measure myself with a young pianist who is just arrived; I'll work him over." A few days later he met him again. "Well, how was it?" "Ah, he is no man; he's a devil. He will play me and all of us to death. And how he improvises!"

It was in Gelinek's lodgings that Schenk heard Beethoven improvise for the first time, ". . . a treat which recalled lively recollections of Mozart. With many manifestations of displeasure, Beethoven, always eager to learn, complained to Gelinek that he was never able to make any progress in his contrapuntal studies under Haydn, since the master, too variously occupied, was unable to pay the amount of attention which he wanted to the exercises he had given him to work out. Gelinek spoke on the subject with Schenk and asked him if he did not feel disposed to give Beethoven a course in composition. Schenk declared himself willing, with ready courtesy, but only under two conditions: that it should be without compensation of any kind and under the strict seal of secrecy. The mutual agreement was made and kept with conscientious fidelity."

--◆{This excerpt would seem to bear out Nottebohm's researches as to the amount of time Haydn was able or willing to put on Beethoven's exercises. Johann Schenk was born in Vienna in 1753. He was a pupil of Wagenseil, gained his livelihood from his compositions and private teaching, and died in 1836 in straitened circumstances. He composed operas, religious and instrumental music; his opera, *Der Dorfbarbier* (1796), was his most successful work and long remained popular in the operatic repertoire. The following excerpt from Schenk's autobiography,[3] communicated to Thayer by Otto Jahn, was written in the summer of 1830 by a man in his seventies. This would account for the great confusion and inaccuracy as regards dates; moreover, it is conceivable that after this length of time there is some exaggeration and confusion in the narration of events.}◆--
We shall now permit Schenk to tell his own story:

"In 1792, His Royal Highness Archduke Maximilian, Elector of Cologne, was pleased to send his charge Louis van Beethoven to Vienna to study musical composition with Haydn. Towards the end of July, Abbé Gelinek informed me that he had made the acquaintance of a young man who displayed extraordinary virtuosity on the pianoforte, such, indeed, as he had not observed since Mozart. In passing he said that Beethoven had been studying counterpoint with Haydn for more than six months and was still at work on the first exercise; also that His Excellency Baron van Swieten had earnestly recommended the study of counterpoint and frequently inquired of him how far he had advanced in his studies. As a result of these frequent incitations and the fact that he was still in the first stages of his instruction, Beethoven, eager to learn, became discontented and often gave expression to his dissatisfaction to his friend. Gelinek took the matter much to heart and came to me with the question whether I felt disposed to assist his friend in the study of counterpoint. I now desired to become better acquainted with Beethoven as soon as possible, and a day was fixed for me to meet him in Gelinek's lodgings and hear him play on the pianoforte.

"Thus I saw the composer, now so famous, for the first time and heard him play. After the customary courtesies he offered to improvise on the pianoforte. He asked me to sit beside him. Having struck a few chords and tossed off a few figures as if they were of no significance, the creative genius gradually unveiled his profound psychological pictures. My ear was con-

[3] The autograph, according to Emily Anderson, is now in the Benedictine Abbey, Göttweig. See *A*, I, p. 17, n. 3.

tinually charmed by the beauty of the many and varied motives which he wove with wonderful clarity and loveliness into each other, and I surrendered my heart to the impressions made upon it while he gave himself wholly up to his creative imagination, and anon, leaving the field of mere tonal charm, boldly stormed the most distant keys in order to give expression to violent passions. . . .

"The first thing that I did the next day was to visit the still unknown artist who had so brilliantly disclosed his mastership. On his writing desk I found a few passages from his first lesson in counterpoint. A cursory glance disclosed the fact that, brief as it was, there were mistakes in every mode. Gelinek's utterances were thus verified. Feeling sure that my pupil was unfamiliar with the preliminary rules of counterpoint, I gave him the familiar textbook of Joseph Fux, *Gradus ad Parnassum*, and asked him to look at the exercises that followed. Joseph Haydn, who had returned to Vienna towards the end of the preceding year,[4] was intent on utilizing his muse in the composition of large masterworks, and thus laudably occupied could not well devote himself to the rules of grammar. I was now eagerly desirous to become the helper of the zealous student. But before beginning the instruction I made him understand that our coöperation would have to be kept secret. In view of this I recommended that he copy every exercise which I corrected in order that Haydn should not recognize the handwriting of a stranger when the exercise was submitted to him. After a year, Beethoven and Gelinek had a falling out for a reason that has escaped me; both, it seemed to me, were at fault. As a result Gelinek got angry and betrayed my secret. Beethoven and his brothers made no secret of it longer.

"I began my honorable office with my good Louis in the beginning of August, 1792, and filled it uninterruptedly until May, 1793, by which time he finished double counterpoint in the octave and went to Eisenstadt. If His Royal Highness had sent his charge at once to Albrechtsberger his studies would never have been interrupted and he would have completed them."

Here follows a passage, afterwards stricken out by Schenk, in which he resents the statement that Beethoven had finished his studies with Albrechtsberger. This would have been advisable, but if it were true, Gelinek as well as Beethoven would have told him of the fact. "On the contrary, he admitted to me that he had gone to Herr Salieri, Royal Imperial Kapellmeister, for lessons in the free style of composition." Then Schenk continues:

About the middle of May he told me that he would soon go with Haydn to Eisenstadt and stay there till the beginning of winter; he did not yet know the date of his departure. I went to him at the usual hour in the beginning of June but my good Louis was no longer to be seen. He left for me the following little billet which I copy word for word:

4 Haydn, according to Wurzbach, returned to Vienna on July 24, 1792. (TDR, I, 355, n. 1.)

"Dear Schenk!

It was not my desire to set off to-day for Eisenstadt. I should like to have spoken with you again. Meanwhile rest assured of my gratitude for the favors shown me. I shall endeavor with all my might to requite them. I hope soon to see you again, and once more to enjoy the pleasure of your society. Farewell and

do not entirely forget
your
Beethoven."

It was my intention only briefly to touch upon my relations with Beethoven; but the circumstances under which, and the manner in which I became his guide in musical composition constrained me to be somewhat more explicit. For my efforts (if they can be called efforts) I was rewarded by my good Louis with a precious gift, viz.: a firm bond of friendship which lasted without fading till the day of his death.

Schenk's date of August, 1792, for the start of Beethoven's instruction with him is obviously in error since the student did not arrive in Vienna until November of that year. Nor is it easy to accept the statement that "Beethoven had been studying counterpoint with Haydn for more than six months" before Gelinek broached the subject to Schenk of assisting the composer in his study. There are two possible ways to explain the confusion. Either one accepts Thayer's thesis that Schenk erred in the year but not in the month, thus that the study dates were August, 1793, to May, 1794, or one accepts only Schenk's termination date of May, 1793. In this case the term of study with Haydn before the advent of Schenk's teaching would be a matter of weeks instead of months.

The former thesis would imply that the instruction with Schenk began in August, 1793, and that indeed Beethoven had already been Haydn's pupil more than six months. This would render unlikely Schenk's account of finding Beethoven on his *first* exercises in counterpoint, "unfamiliar with the preliminary rules óf counterpoint." This then would date Beethoven's note to Schenk as 1794 and would mean that he went to Eisenstadt, but without Haydn, for the latter had left for England in January of that year. According to Nottebohm,[5] it was in 1794 that Beethoven was studying "double counterpoint at the octave," but this was with his new teacher Albrechtsberger, after Haydn's departure, and at this time there was no longer the need for Schenk's services.

On the other hand, if one can trust Schenk's memory to the extent that it was *with Haydn* that Beethoven went to Eisenstadt in 1793, then it is possible that Beethoven's work with Schenk began after some *weeks* with Haydn, rather than months, suggested by the fact that in this case it would be more likely that Beethoven was still on his first lesson in counterpoint and still making mistakes in basic rules. In that case, then, Beethoven continued his composition exercises for both masters until early June, when he departed

---

[5] *Beeth.*, p. 198.

for Eisenstadt, presumably with Haydn. That Haydn was in Eisenstadt in June, 1793, is verified by a letter he wrote from there to Madame Loise Polzelli in Bologna, dated June 20, 1793.[6] However in this letter he says: "At present I am alone with your son [Pietro, a pupil of Haydn], and I shall stay here for a little while to get some fresh air and have a little rest."

Thus, both theses are full of contradictions. What is important about the Schenk story, however, is the proof it offers that Beethoven was dissatisfied with the instruction he received from Haydn—so dissatisfied that he did accept Schenk's help but agreed to keep it secret, and that a friendship remained in after years between the two men. We know also that during a great part of 1793 Beethoven was doing exercises for Haydn, and that this relationship was broken off when Haydn went to England on January 19, 1794.

The relations between Haydn and his pupil did not long continue truly cordial; yet Beethoven concealed his dissatisfaction and no break occurred. Thoughtless and reckless of consequences, as he often in later years unfortunately exhibited himself when indulging his wilfulness, he was at this time responsible to the Elector for his conduct, and Haydn, moreover, was too valuable and influential a friend to be wantonly alienated. So, whatever feelings he cherished in secret, he kept them to himself, went regularly to his lessons and, as noted above, occasionally treated his master to chocolate or coffee. As Neefe tells us, Haydn wished to take him to England. Why was that plan not carried out? Did Maximilian forbid it? Would Beethoven's pride not allow him to go thither as Haydn's pupil? Did zeal for his contrapuntal studies prevent it? Or had his relations to the Austrian nobility already become such as offered him higher hopes of success in Vienna than Haydn could propose in London? Or, finally, was it his ambition rather to make himself known as Beethoven the composer than as Beethoven the pianoforte virtuoso? Pecuniary reasons are insufficient to account for the failure of the plan; for Haydn, who now knew the London public, could easily have removed all difficulty on that score. Neefe's letter was written near the end of September, 1793, when already "a number of reports" had reached Bonn "that Beethoven had made great progress in his art." These "reports," we know from Fischenich, came in part from Haydn himself. Add to that the wish to take his pupil with him to England—which was certainly the highest compliment he could possibly have paid him—and the utter groundlessness of Beethoven's suspicions that Haydn "was not well-minded towards him," as Ries says in his *Notizen* (p. 85), is apparent. Yet these suspicions, added to the reasons above suggested, sufficiently explain the departure of the master for London without the company of his pupil, who now (January, 1794) was transferred to Albrechtsberger.

[6] C. F. Pohl and H. Botstiber, *Joseph Haydn* (Leipzig, 1927), III, 70. See also H. C. R. Landon, *The Collected Correspondence of*   *Joseph Haydn* (Fairlawn, N.J.), 1959, pp. 139-40.

--☙⟨The questions raised by Thayer may be further considered in connection with three letters recently discovered by Fritz von Reinöhl[7] which add to our knowledge of the relation of Haydn's student at this time to his past employer, the Elector at Bonn. The first letter, from Haydn to the Elector, gives evidence of the high regard that Haydn had for his pupil and his great desire to help him. Only the signature is in Haydn's handwriting:

Most Reverend Archbishop and Elector,

I am taking the liberty of sending to your Reverence in all humility a few pieces of music, a quintet, an eight-voice "Parthie," an oboe concerto, a set of variations for the piano and a fugue composed by my dear pupil Beethoven who was so graciously entrusted to me. They will, I flatter myself, be graciously accepted by your Reverence as evidence of his diligence beyond the scope of his own studies. On the basis of these pieces, expert and amateur alike cannot but admit that Beethoven will in time become one of the greatest musical artists in Europe, and I shall be proud to call myself his teacher. I only wish that he might remain with me for some time yet.

While I am on the subject of Beethoven, may your Reverence permit me to say a few words concerning his financial affairs. For the past year he was allotted 100# [ducats]. That this sum was insufficient even for mere living expenses your Reverence will, I am sure, be well aware. Your Reverence, however, may have had good reasons for sending him out into the great world with so small a sum. On this assumption and in order to prevent him from falling into the hands of usurers, I have on the one hand vouched for him and on the other advanced him cash, so that he owes me 500 fl., of which not a kreutzer has been spent unnecessarily. I now request that this sum be paid him. And since to work on borrowed money increases the interest, and what is more is very burdensome for an artist like Beethoven, I thought that if your Reverence would allot him 1000 fl. for the coming year, your Reverence would be showing him the highest favor, and at the same time would free him of all anxiety. For the teachers which are absolutely indispensable to him and the expenses which are unavoidable if he is to be admitted to some of the houses here, take so much that the barest minimum that he needs comes close to 1000 fl. As to the extravagance that is to be feared in a young man going out into the great world, I think I can reassure your Reverence. For in hundreds of situations I have always found that he is prepared, of his own accord, to sacrifice everything for his art. This is particularly admirable in view of the many tempting opportunities and should give your Reverence the assurance that your gracious kindness to Beethoven will not fall into the hands of usurers. In the hopes that your Reverence will graciously accept this request of mine in behalf of my dear pupil, I am, with deepest respect, your Reverence's most humble and obedient servant

Joseph Haydn
Kapellmeister of Prince Nicholas Esterhazy

Vienna, November 23, 1793.

[7] "Neues zu Beethoven Lehrjahr bei Haydn," *NBJ*, VI (1935), 36-37. See also Landon, *op.cit.*, pp. 141-42.

On the same day Beethoven also wrote to the Elector as follows:

Most Reverend, most high and gracious Elector and Master!

To be worthy of the highest favor of Your Electoral Highness is my single concern. For this I have used all my mental powers in the common purpose of music this year in order to be able to send to your Electoral Highness in the coming year something which more nearly approaches your kindness to me and your nobility than that which was sent to Your Electoral Highness by Herr Heiden. In the confidence that your Electoral Highness will not deprive me of the kindness once granted I am in deepest respect Your Electoral Highness' most humble and most obedient

Ludwig van Beethoven

Vienna, November 23, 1793.

Only the Elector's reply to Haydn has survived, and the embarrassing position into which it put the composer would indicate a less than complete understanding between Haydn and Beethoven at the time that the compositions were sent. This is a rough draft in an official hand, corrected by the Elector himself, and dated December 23, 1793.

The music of young Beethoven which you sent me I received with your letter. Since, however, this music, with the exception of the fugue, was composed and performed here in Bonn before he departed on his second journey to Vienna, I cannot regard it as progress made in Vienna.

As far as the allotment which he has had for his subsistence in Vienna is concerned, it does indeed amount to only 500 fl. But in addition to this 500 fl. his salary here of 400 fl. has been continuously paid to him, he received 900 fl. for the year. I cannot, therefore, very well see why he is as much in arrears in his finances as you say.

I am wondering therefore whether he had not better come back here in order to resume his work. For I very much doubt that he has made any important progress in composition and in the development of his musical taste during his present stay, and I fear that, as in the case of his first journey to Vienna, he will bring back nothing but debts.

Of the works listed the Quintet is presumably lost. The Quintet for piano and winds, Op. 16, can hardly be in question since this work was first performed in the spring of 1797. The string quintet, Op. 4, is equally doubtful since it is a revision of the eight-voice "Parthie" which was also sent, a fact which would have undoubtedly provoked more scornful comment from the Elector had two versions of the same material been sent. The Parthie is undoubtedly the wind octet later to be published as Op. 103. The oboe concerto also appears to be lost, but Thayer in his *Chronologisches Verzeichniss*[8] lists the work as formerly in the possession of Diabelli and Co. (See the sketches for the concerto previously shown on page 126.) To discover which "variations for piano" were sent would add to our knowledge of just which keyboard works of this type were composed before Beethoven left for

[8] Page 168.

Vienna. The one original piece that was sent, of which there is no trace, reveals that Beethoven had written a fugue at some time before his instruction with Haydn ended.

The fact that of all of the works sent to the Elector only one may have been written in Vienna suggests that in his first year of study in Vienna Beethoven concerned himself almost solely with theory, laying the foundation for his future technique as a composer; and although he was revising works written in Bonn, he probably did not compose any works of importance during this time.[9] Undoubtedly Haydn could not have realized that these were Bonn works, but since Beethoven mentioned in his letter what "was sent to Your Electoral Highness by Herr Heiden" one wonders whether Beethoven knew which works were sent or not. The stiffness of the Elector's reply could not have pleased Haydn and perhaps the awkwardness of this situation contributed to Haydn's leaving for England without Beethoven.

In the pretty extensive notes copied from the memorandum book already so much cited, there are but two which can with any degree of certainty be referred to a date later than 1793. One of them is this:

Schuppanzigh, 3 times a W.
Albrechtsberger, 3 times a W.

The necessary inference from this is that Beethoven began the year 1794 with three lessons a week in violin-playing from Schuppanzigh (unless the youth of the latter should forbid such an inference)[10] and three in counterpoint from the most famous teacher of that science. Seyfried[11] affirms that the studies with the latter continued "two complete years with tireless persistency." The coming narrative will show that other things took up much of Beethoven's attention in 1795, and that before the close of that year, if not already at its beginning, his course with Albrechtsberger ended.

Johann Georg Albrechtsberger was born in 1736 at Klosterneuburg and died in Vienna in 1809. In 1772 he was appointed Court Organist and in 1792 Kapellmeister at St. Stephen's in Vienna. He was not only a celebrated teacher of music theory, about which he wrote a number of books and pamphlets, but also a very prolific composer of masses, symphonies, quartets and many other chamber combinations.

Concerning the nature of the instruction which Beethoven received from Albrechtsberger (which was based chiefly on the master's *Anweisung zur*

[9] See Max Unger, "Kleine Beethoven-Studien," *NBJ*, viii (1938), 80.

[10] Ignaz Schuppanzigh (1776–1830) was an outstanding violinist of his day and was first violinist of the quartet playing for Prince Lichnowsky.

[11] Ignaz Xaver, Ritter von Seyfried (1776–1841) was Kapellmeister in Schikaneder's Theatre from 1797 to 1828 and became a great admirer of Beethoven's music. In 1832 he wrote a book, *Beethovens Studien im General-bass* (Haslinger, Vienna) which, as Nottebohm showed in his *Studien* forty years later, is a disorganized presentation of all that Seyfried could find in the way of exercises among Beethoven's posthumous papers. In presenting them he overlooked the fact that many of them were written many years later, often for the benefit of Beethoven's pupils.

Komposition) we turn to Nottebohm.[12] It began again with simple counterpoint, in which Beethoven now received more detailed directions than had
been given him by Haydn. Albrechtsberger wrote down rules for him,
Beethoven did the same and worked out a large number of exercises on two
cantus firmi which Albrechtsberger then corrected according to the rules of
strict writing. There followed contrapuntal exercises in free writing, in imitation, in two-, three- and four-part fugue, choral fugue, double counterpoint
in the different intervals, double fugue, triple counterpoint and canon. The
last was short, as here the instruction ceased. Beethoven worked frequently
in the immediate presence and with the direct cooperation of Albrechtsberger.
The latter labored with obvious conscientiousness and care, and was ever
ready to aid his pupil. If he appears at times to have been given over to
minute detail and conventional method, it must be borne in mind that rigid
schooling in fixed rules is essential to the development of an independent
artist, even if he makes no use of them, and that it is only in this manner
that freedom in workmanship can be achieved. Of this the youthful Beethoven was aware and every line of his exercises bears witness that he entered
into his studies with complete interest and zeal. (Once Beethoven writes an
unprepared seventh-chord with a suspension on the margin of an exercise
and adds the query: "Is it allowed?")[13] This was particularly the case in his
exercises in counterpoint and imitation, where he strove to avoid errors, and
their beneficial results are plainly noticeable in his compositions. Several
of the compositions written after the lessons, disclose how "he was led from
a predominantly figurative to a more contrapuntal manner of writing." There
is less of this observable in the case of fugue, in which the instruction itself
was not free from deficiencies; and the pupil worked more carelessly. The
restrictive rules occasionally put him out of conceit with his work; "he was
at the age in which, as a rule, suggestion and incitation are preferred to instruction," and his stubborn nature played an important rôle in the premises.
However, it ought to be added that he was also at an age when his genial
aptness in invention and construction had already found exercise in other
directions. Even though he did not receive thorough education in fugue
from Albrechtsberger, he nevertheless learned the constituent elements of
the form and how to apply them.[14] Moreover, in his later years he made
all these things the subjects of earnest and devoted study independent of
others; and in the compositions of his later years he returned with special and

[12] Deiters used the investigations of Nottebohm, in *Beethovens Studien*, pp. 47ff. and
Beethoveniana, pp. 173ff., in the compilation
of the story of the study under Albrechtsberger.
This took the place of the original narrative
by Thayer. (TK, I, 153, n. 1.)

[13] *Beethovens Studien*, p. 196. (TDR, I,
360, n. 2.)

[14] A collection of sketches in the British
Museum (Add. 29,801), which was purchased

from J. Kafga in 1875, includes certain studies
on fugue subjects, which date undoubtedly
from this period. See J. S. Shedlock "Beethoven's Sketchbooks," *The Musical Times*,
London, Vol. 33 (1892), p. 396. One completed fugue in C is among these sketches and
has been reprinted in A. E. F. Dickinson's
"Beethoven's Early Fugal Style," *The Musical
Times*, Vol. 96 (1955), pp. 78-79.

manifest predilection to the fugued style. Nothing could be more incorrect than to emphasize Beethoven's lack of theoretical education. If, while studying with Albrechtsberger, but more particularly in his independent compositions, Beethoven ignored many of the strict rules, it was not because he was not able to apply them, but because he purposely set them aside. Places can be found in his exercises in which the rules are violated; but the testimony of the ear acquits the pupil. Rules are not the objects of themselves, they do not exist for their own sake, and in despite of all artistic systems; it is the reserved privilege of the evolution of art-means and prescient, forward genius to point out what in them is of permanent value, and what must be looked upon as antiquated. Nature designed that Beethoven should employ music in the depiction of soul-states, to emancipate melody and express his impulses in the free forms developed by Ph. Em. Bach, Mozart, Haydn and their contemporaries. In this direction he had already disclosed himself as a doughty warrior before the instruction in Vienna had its beginning, and it is very explicable that to be hemmed in by rigid rules was frequently disagreeable to him. He gradually wearied of "creating musical skeletons." But all the more worthy of recognition, yea, of admiration, is the fact that the young composer who had already mounted so high, should by abnegation of his creative powers surrender himself to the tyranny of the rules and find satisfaction in conscientious practice of them.

Referring to the number of pages (160) of exercises and the three lessons a week, Nottebohm calculates the period of instruction to have been about fifteen months. Inasmuch as among the exercises in double counterpoint in the tenth there is found a sketch belonging to the second movement of the Trio, Op. 1, No. 2, which Trio was advertised as finished on May 9, 1795, it follows that the study was at or near its end at that date. The conclusion of his instruction from Albrechtsberger may therefore be set down at between March and May, 1795. Nottebohm summed up his conclusions from the investigations which he made of Beethoven's posthumous papers thus: prefacing that, after 1785, Beethoven more and more made the manner of Mozart his own, he continues:[15] "The instruction which he received from Haydn and Albrechtsberger enriched him with new forms and media of expression and these effected a change in his mode of writing. The voices acquired greater melodic flow and independence. A certain opacity took the place of the former transparency in the musical fabric. Out of a homophonic polyphony of two or more voices, there grew a polyphony that was real. The earlier obbligato accompaniment gave way to an obbligato style of writing which rested to a greater extent on counterpoint. Beethoven has accepted the principle of polyphony; his part-writing has become purer and it is noteworthy that the compositions written immediately after the lessons are among the purest that Beethoven ever composed. True, the Mozart model still shines through the fabric, but we seek it less in the art of figura-

15 *Beethovens Studien*, p. 201.

tion than in the form and other things which are only indirectly associated with the obbligato style. Similarly, we can speak of other influences—that of Joseph Haydn, for instance. This influence is not contrapuntal. Beethoven built upon his acquired and inherited possessions. He assimilated the traditional forms and means of expression, gradually eliminated foreign influences and, following the pressure of his subjective nature with its inclination towards the ideal, he created his own individual style."

The third of Beethoven's teachers in Vienna was the Imperial Kapellmeister Anton Salieri; but this instruction was neither systematic nor confined to regular hours. Beethoven took advantage of Salieri's willingness "to give gratuitous instruction to musicians of small means."[16] He wanted advice in vocal composition, and submitted to Salieri some settings of Italian songs which the latter corrected in respect of verbal accent and expression, rhythm, metrical articulation, subdivision of thought, mood, singableness, and the conduct of the melody which comprehended all these things. Having himself taken the initiative in this, Beethoven devoted himself earnestly and industriously to these exercises, and they were notably profitable in his creative work. "Thereafter [also in his German songs] he treated the text with much greater care than before in respect of its prosodic structure, as also of its contents and the prescribed situation," and acquired a good method of declamation. That Salieri's influence extended beyond the period in which Beethoven's style developed itself independently cannot be asserted, since many other and varied influences made themselves felt later.

This instruction began soon after Beethoven's arrival in Vienna and lasted in an unconstrained manner at least until 1802; at even a later date he asked counsel of Salieri in the composition of songs, particularly Italian songs. According to an anecdote related by Czerny, at one of these meetings for instruction Salieri found fault with a melody as not being appropriate for an air. The next day he said to Beethoven: "I can't get your melody out of my head." "Then, Herr von Salieri," replied Beethoven, "it cannot have been so utterly bad." The story may be placed in the early period; but it appears from a statement by Moscheles that Beethoven still maintained a friendly association with Salieri in 1809. Moscheles, who was in Vienna at this time, found a note on Salieri's table which read: "The pupil Beethoven was here!"

Ries, speaking of the relations between Haydn, Albrechtsberger and Salieri as teachers and Beethoven as pupil, says (Notizen, p. 86): "I knew them all well; all three valued Beethoven highly, but were also of one mind touching his habits of study. All of them said Beethoven was so headstrong and self-sufficient (selbstwollend) that he had to learn much through harsh experience which he had refused to accept when it was presented to him as a subject of study. Particularly Albrechtsberger and Salieri were of this opinion; the dry rules of the former and the comparatively unimportant

[16] Ibid., pp. 207ff. (TDR, I, 365, n. 1.)

ones of the latter concerning dramatic composition (according to the Italian school of the period) could not appeal to Beethoven." It is now known that the "dry rules" of Albrechtsberger could make a strong appeal to Beethoven as appertaining to theoretical study, and that the old method of composition to which he remained true all his life always had a singular charm for him as a subject of study and investigation.

Here, as in many other cases, the simple statement of the difficulties suggests their explanation. Beethoven the pupil may have honestly and conscientiously followed the precepts of his instructors in whatever he wrote in that character; but Beethoven the composer stood upon his own territory, followed his own tastes and impulses, wrote and wrought subject to no other control. He paid Albrechtsberger to teach him counterpoint—not to be the censor and critic of his compositions. And Ries's memory may well have deceived him as to the actual scope of the strictures made by the old master, and have transferred to the pupil what, fully thirty years before, had been spoken of the composer. As has been mentioned, Beethoven's relations with Salieri at a later date were still pleasant; the composer dedicated to the kapellmeister the three violin sonatas, Op. 12, which appeared in 1799. Nothing is known of a dedication to Albrechtsberger. According to an anecdote related by Albrechtsberger's grandson Hirsch, Beethoven called him a "musical pedant"; yet we may see a remnant of gratitude toward his old teacher in Beethoven's readiness to take an interest in his young grandson.

We have now to turn our attention to Beethoven's relations to Viennese society outside of his study.

The musical drama naturally took the first place in the musical life of Vienna at this period. The enthusiasm of Joseph II for a national German opera, to which the world owed Mozart's exquisite *Entführung*, proved to be but short-lived, and the Italian *opera buffa* resumed its old place in his affections. The new company engaged was, however, equal to the performance of *Don Giovanni* and *Figaro* and Salieri's magnificent *Axur*. Leopold II reached Vienna on the evening of March 13, 1790, to assume the crown of his deceased brother, but no change was, for the present, made in the court theatre. Indeed, as late as July 5 he had not entered a theatre, and his first appearance at the opera was at the performance of *Axur*, September 21, in the company of his visitor King Ferdinand of Naples. But as soon as the Emperor was firmly settled on the imperial throne and had successfully annulled Joseph's numerous reforms, brought the Turkish war to a close and ended his diverse coronations, he gave his thoughts to the theatre. Salieri,[17] though now but forty-one years of age, and rich with the observation and experience of more than twenty years in the direction of the opera, was,

---

[17] Antonio Salieri was born in Legnano in 1750. He came to Vienna in 1766 and in 1770 wrote the first of his forty some operas. He also wrote a great many religious works, some ballet music and a number of purely instrumental works. He died in 1825.

according to Mosel, graciously allowed, but according to other and better authorities, compelled, to withdraw from the operatic orchestra and confine himself to his duties as director of the sacred music in the court chapel and to the composition of one operatic work annually, if required. The *Wiener Zeitung* of January 28, 1792, records the appointment of Joseph Weigl, Salieri's pupil and assistant, now twenty-five years old, "as Kapellmeister and Composer to the Royal Imperial National Court Theatre with a salary of 1,000 florins." The title Composer was rather an empty one. Though already favorably known to the public, he was forbidden to compose new operas for the court stage. To this end famous masters were to be invited to Vienna. A first fruit of this new order of things was the production of Cimarosa's *Il Matrimonio segreto*, February 7, 1792, which with good reason so delighted Leopold that he gave the performers a supper and ordered them back into the theatre and heard the opera again *da capo*. It was among the last of the Emperor's theatrical pleasures; he died March 1st, and his wife on the 15th of May following. Thus for the greater part of the time from March 1 to May 24, the court theatres were shut; and yet during the thirteen months ending December 15, 1792, Italian opera had been given 180 times—134 times in the Burg and 46 times in the Kärnthnerthor-Theater—and ballet 163 times; so that, as no change for the present was made, there was abundance in these branches of the art for a young composer, like Beethoven, to hear and see. All accounts agree that the company then performing was one of uncommon excellence and its performances, with those of the superb orchestra, proved the value of the long experience, exquisite taste, unflagging zeal and profound knowledge of their recent head, Salieri. Such as Beethoven found the opera in the first week of November, 1792, such it continued for the next two years—exclusively Italian, but of the first order.

A single stroke of extraordinary good fortune—a happy accident is perhaps a better term—had just now given such prosperity to a minor theatrical enterprise that in ten years it was to erect and occupy the best playhouse in Vienna and, for a time, to surpass the Court Theatre in the excellence and splendor of its operatic performances. We mean Schikaneder's Theater auf der Wieden; but in 1793 its company was mean, its house small, its performances bad enough.

Schikaneder's kapellmeister and composer was John Baptist Henneberg; the kapellmeister of Marinelli, head of another German company in the Leopoldstadt, was Wenzel Müller, who had already begun his long list of 227 light and popular compositions to texts magical or farcical. Some two weeks after Beethoven's arrival in Vienna, on November 23rd, Schikaneder announced, falsely, the one-hundredth performance of *Die Zauberflöte*, an opera the success of which placed his theatre a few years later upon a totally different footing, and brought Beethoven into other relations to it than those of an ordinary visitor indulging his taste for the comical and, according to Seyfried, listening to and heartily enjoying very bad music.

The leading dramatic composers of Vienna, not yet named, must receive a passing notice. Besides Cimarosa, who left Vienna a few months later, Beethoven found Peter Dutillieu, a Frenchman by birth but an Italian musician by education and profession, engaged as composer for the Court Theatre. His *Il Trionfo d'Amore* had been produced there November 14, 1791, and his *Nanerina e Padolfino* had lately come upon the stage. Ignaz Umlauf, composer of *Die schöne Schusterin* and other not unpopular works, had the title of Kapellmeister and Composer to the German Court Opera, and was Salieri's substitute as kapellmeister in the sacred music of the Court Chapel. Franz Xavier Süssmayr, so well known from his connection with Mozart, was just now writing for Schikaneder's stage; Schenk for Marinelli's and for the private stages of the nobility; and Paul Wranitzky, first violinist and so-called Musikdirektor in the Court Theatre, author of the then popular *Oberon* composed for the Wieden stage, was employing his very respectable talents for both Marinelli and Schikaneder.

The church music of Vienna seems to have been at a very low point in 1792 and 1793. Two composers, however, whose names are still of importance in musical history, were then in that city devoting themselves almost exclusively to this branch of the art; Albrechtsberger, Court Organist, but in a few months (through the death of Leopold Hoffmann, March 17, 1793) to become musical director at St. Stephen's; and Joseph Eybler (some five years older than Beethoven), who had just become *Regens chori* in the Carmelite church, whence he was called to a similar and better position in the Schottische Kirche two years later.

Public concerts, as the term is now understood, may be said not to have existed, and regular subscription concerts were few. Mozart gave a few series of them, but after his death there appears to have been no one of sufficient note in the musical world to make such a speculation remunerative. Single subscription concerts given by virtuosos, and annual ones by some of the leading resident musicians, of course, took place then as before and since. The only real and regular concerts were the four annual performances in the Burgtheater, two at Christmas and two at Easter, for the benefit of the musicians' widows and orphans. These concerts, established mainly by Gassmann and Salieri, were never exclusive in their programmes—oratorio, symphony, cantata, concerto, whatever would add to their attraction, found place. The stage was filled with the best musicians and vocalists of the capital and the superb orchestra was equally ready to accompany the playing of a Mozart or of an ephemeral *Wunderkind*. Riesbeck was told ten years before that the number taking part in orchestra and chorus had even then on some occasions reached 400—a statement, however, which looks much like exaggeration.

Very uncommon semi-private concerts were still kept up in 1793. The reader of Mozart's biography will remember that in 1782 this great composer joined a certain Martin in giving a series of concerts during the morning hours in the Augarten Hall, most of the performers being dilettanti and the music being furnished from the library of von Kees. These concerts found such favor that they were renewed for several years and generally were twelve in number. According to the *Allg. Mus. Zeitung*: "Ladies of even the highest nobility permitted themselves to be heard. The auditorium was extremely brilliant and everything was conducted in so orderly and decent a fashion that everybody was glad to support the institute to the best of his energies. The receipts from the chief subscription were expended entirely on the cost of the concerts. Later Herr Rudolph assumed the direction."

This man, still young, and a fine violin player, was the director when Beethoven came to Vienna, and the extraordinary spectacle was still to be seen of princes and nobles following his lead in the performance of orchestral music to an audience of their own class at the strange hours of from 6 to 8 in the morning!

From the above it appears that Vienna presented to the young musician no preëminent advantages either in opera, church music or its public concerts. Other cities equalled the Austrian capital in the first two, and London was then far in advance of all in the number, variety and magnificence of the last. It was in another field that Vienna surpassed every competitor. As Gluck twenty years before had begun the great revolution in operatic music completed by Mozart, so Haydn, building on the foundation of the Bachs and aided by Mozart, was effecting a new development of purely instrumental music which was yet to reach its highest stage through the genius and daring of the youth now his pupil. The example set by the Austrian family through so many generations had produced its natural effect, and a knowledge of and taste for music were universal among the princes and nobles of the empire. Some of the more wealthy princes, like Esterhazy, maintained musical establishments complete even to the Italian opera; others were contented with hearing the mass sung in their house-chapel to an orchestral accompaniment; where this was impossible, a small orchestra only was kept up, often composed of the officials and servants, who were selected with regard to their musical abilities; and so down to the band of wind-instruments, the string quartet, and even to a single organ-player, pianist or violinist. What has been said in a former chapter of music as a quasi-necessity at the courts of the ecclesiastical princes, applies in great measure to the secular nobility. At their castles and country-seats in the summer, amusement was to be provided for many an otherwise tedious hour; and in their city residences during the winter they and their guests could not always feast, dance or play at cards; and here, too, music became a common and favored recreation. At all events, it was the fashion. Outside the ranks of the noble-born, such as by talents, high culture or wealth occupied high social positions, followed the example and opened their salons to musicians and lovers of music, moved thereto for the most part by a real, rarely by a pretended, taste for the art—in either case aiding and encouraging its progress. Hence, an enormous demand for chamber music, both vocal and instrumental, especially the latter. The demand created the supply by encouraging genius and talent to labor in that direction; and thus the Austrian school of instrumental music soon led the world.

During certain months of the year, Vienna was filled with the greatest nobles, not only of the Austrian states, but of other portions of the German Empire. Those who spent their time mostly in their own small courts came up to the capital but for a short season; others reversed this, making the city their usual residence and visiting their estates only in summer. By the former class many a once (if not still) famous composer in their service was thus occasionally for short periods brought to the metropolis—as Mozart by the Archbishop of Salzburg, and Haydn by Prince Esterhazy. By the latter class many of the distinguished composers and virtuosi resident in the city were taken into the country during the summer to be treated as equals, to live like gentlemen among gentlemen. Thus Salieri was a guest of Prince Schwarzenberg, Schenk of Auersperg. Mozart traveled with Lichnowsky to Berlin, Dittersdorf with Count Lemberg to Troppau etc. Another mode of encouraging the art was the ordering or purchasing of compositions; and this not only from composers of established reputation, as Haydn, Mozart, C. P. E. Bach, but also from young and as yet unknown men; thus affording a twofold benefit—pecuniary aid and an opportunity of exhibiting their powers. Thus Prince Kraczalkowitz and Count Batthyany bought six symphonies from the young Gyrowetz; Esterhazy ordered from him three masses, a vesper, and a *Te Deum*; Auersperg employed Schenk's talent for his private theatre; and as regards chamber music, the catalogues of private collections show long rows of manuscripts, ordered or bought from composers now completely forgotten.

The instrumental virtuosi, when not permanently engaged in the service of some prince or theatre, looked in the main for the reward of their studies and labors to the private concerts of the nobility. If at the same time they were composers, it was in such concerts that they brought their productions to a hearing. The reader of Jahn's biography of Mozart will remember how much even he depended upon this resource to gain the means of support for himself and family. Out of London, even so late as 1793, there can hardly be said to have existed a "musical public," as the term is now understood, and in Vienna at least, with its 200,000 inhabitants, a virtuoso rarely ventured to announce a concert to which he had not already a subscription, sufficient to ensure him against loss, from those at whose residences he had successfully exhibited his skill. Beethoven, remaining "in Vienna without salary until recalled," found in these resources and his pupils an ample income.

But this topic requires something more than the above general remarks. Some twelve years previous to Beethoven's coming to Vienna, Riesbeck,[18] speaking of the art in that capital, had written: "Musicians are the only ones

---

[18] *Op.cit.*, I, pp. 275-76. (Cf. TDR, I, 376.)

[artists] concerning whom the nobility exhibit taste. Many houses maintain private bands for their own delectation, and all the public concerts prove that this field of art stands in high respect. It is possible to enlist four or five large orchestras here, all of them incomparable. The number of real virtuosi is small, but as regards the orchestral musicians scarcely anything more beautiful is to be heard in the world."

How many such orchestras were still kept up in 1792-93 it is, probably, now impossible to determine. Those of Princes Lobkowitz, Schwarzenberg and Auersperg may safely be named. Count Heinrich von Haugwitz and doubtless Count Batthyany brought their musicians with them when they came to the capital for "the season." The Esterhazy band, dismissed after the death of Haydn's old master, seems not yet to have been renewed. Prince Kraczalkowitz had reduced his to a band of eight wind-instruments—oboes, clarinets, bassoons, horns—a kind of organization then much in vogue. Baron Braun had one to play at dinner as at the supper in *Don Giovanni*—an accessory to the scene which Mozart introduced out of his own frequent experience. Prince Karl Lichnowsky and others retained their own players of string quartets.

The grandees of the Bohemian and Moravian capitals—Kinsky, Clamm, Nostiz, Thun, Buquoi, Hartig, Salm-Pachta, Sporck, Fünfkirchen, etc.— emulated the Austrian and Hungarian nobles. As many of them had palaces also in Vienna, and most, if not all, spent part of the year there, bringing with them a few of the more skilful members of their orchestras to execute chamber music and to form the nucleus of a band when symphonies, concertos and grand vocal works were to be executed, they also added their contingent to the musical as well as to the political and fashionable life of the metropolis. The astonishingly fruitful last eight years of Mozart's life falling within the period now under contemplation, contributed to musical literature compositions wonderfully manifold in character, thus setting an example that forced other composers to leave the beaten track. Haydn had just returned from his first stay in London, enriched with the pregnant experience acquired during that visit. Van Swieten had gained during his residence in Berlin appreciation of and love for the works of Handel, Bach and their schools, and since his return to Vienna, about 1778, had exerted, and was still exerting, a very powerful and marked influence upon Vienna's musical taste.

Thus all the conditions precedent for the elevation of the art were just at this time fulfilled at Vienna, and in one department—that of instrumental music—they existed in a degree unknown in any other city. The extraordinary results as to the quantity produced in those years may be judged from the sale-catalogue (1779) of a single music-dealer, Johann Traeg, which gives of symphonies, symphonies-concertantes and overtures (the last being in a small minority) the extraordinary number of 512. The music produced at private concerts given by the nobility ranged from the grand oratorios, operas, symphonies, down to variations for the pianoforte and to simple songs. Leading musicians and composers, whose circumstances admitted of it, also gave private concerts at which they made themselves and their works known, and to which their colleagues were invited.

Prince Lobkowitz, at the time Beethoven reached Vienna, was a young man of twenty years. He was born on December 7, 1772, and had just married, on August 2, a daughter of Prince Schwarzenberg. He was a violinist of considerable powers and so devoted a lover of music and the drama, so profuse a squanderer of his income upon them, as in twenty years to reduce himself to bankruptcy. Precisely Beethoven's supposed age, the aristocrat of wealth and power and the aristocrat of talent and genius became exceedingly intimate, occasionally quarrelling and making up their differences as if belonging by birth to the same sphere.

The reigning Prince Esterhazy was that Paul Anton who, after the death of his father in 1790, broke up the musical establishment at Esterhaz and gave Haydn relief from his thirty years of service. He died in 1794, and was succeeded by his son Nikolaus, a young man just five years older than Beethoven. Prince Nikolaus inherited his grandfather's taste for music, re-engaged an orchestra, and soon became known as one of the most zealous promoters of Roman Catholic church music. The best composers of Vienna, including Beethoven, wrote masses for the chapel at Esterhaz, where they were performed with great splendor.

Count Johann Nepomuk Esterhazy, "of the middle line zu Frakno," was a man of forty-five years, a good performer upon the oboe, and (which is much to his credit) had been a firm friend and patron of Mozart.

Of Count Franz Esterhazy, a man of thirty-five years, Schönfeld, in his *Jahrbuch der Tonkunst*, thus speaks: "This great friend of music at certain times of the year gives large and splendid concerts at which, for the greater part, large and elevated compositions are performed—particularly the choruses of Handel, the 'Sanctus' of Emanuel Bach, the 'Stabat Mater' of Pergolese, and the like. At these concerts there are always a number of the best virtuosi."[19]

It was not the present Prince Joseph Kinsky (who died in 1798 in his forty-eighth year) but his son Ferdinand Johann Nepomuk who at a later period became a distinguished patron of Beethoven. At this time he was a bright boy of eleven years, upon whose youthful taste the strength, beauty and novelty of that composer's works made a deep impression.

Prince Karl Lichnowsky, the pupil and friend of Mozart, had a quartet concert at his dwelling every Friday morning. The regularly engaged musicians were Ignaz Schuppanzigh, son of a professor in the Real-Schule, and a youth at this time of sixteen years, first violin; Louis Sina, pupil of Förster, also a very young man, second violin; Franz Weiss, who completed his fifteenth year on January 18, 1793, viola; and Anton Kraft, or his son

[19] Schönfeld, *Jahrbuch der Tonkunst für Wien und Prag* (Prague, 1796), p. 70.

Nikolaus, a boy of fourteen years (born December 18, 1778), violoncello. It was, in fact, a quartet of boy virtuosi, of whom Beethoven, several years older, could make what he would. The Prince's wife was Maria Christiane, twenty years of age, one of those "Three Graces," as Georg Förster called them, daughters of that Countess Thun in whose house Mozart had found such warm friendship and appreciation, and whose noble qualities are so celebrated by Burney, Reichardt and Förster. The Princess, as well as her husband, belonged to the better class of amateur performers upon the pianoforte.

Court Councillor von Kees, Vice-President of the Court of Appeals of Lower Austria, was still living. He was, says Gyrowetz, speaking of a period a few years earlier, "recognized as the foremost music-lover and dilettante in Vienna; and twice a week he gave in his house society concerts at which were gathered together the foremost virtuosi of Vienna, and the first composers, such as Joseph Haydn, Mozart, Dittersdorf, Hoffmeister, Albrechtsberger, Giarnovichi and so on. Haydn's symphonies were played there." In Haydn's letters to Madame Genzinger the name of von Kees often occurs— the last time in a note of August 4, 1792, which mentions that the writer is that day to dine with the Court Councillor. This distinguished man left on his death (January 5, 1795) a very extensive collection of music.

Gottfried, Freiherr van Swieten, son of Maria Theresia's famous Dutch physician, says Schönfeld,[20] is, "as it were, looked upon as a patriarch of music. He has taste only for the great and exalted. He himself many years ago composed twelve beautiful symphonies ['stiff as himself,' said Haydn]. When he attends a concert our semi-connoisseurs never take their eyes off him, seeking to read in his features, not always intelligible to every one, what ought to be their opinion of the music. Every year he gives a few large and brilliant concerts at which only music by the old masters is performed. His preference is for the Handelian manner, and he generally has some of Handel's great choruses performed. As late as last Christmas [1794] he gave such a concert at Prince von Paar's, at which an oratorio by this master was performed."

Neukomm told Prof. Jahn that in concerts, "if it chanced that a whispered conversation began, His Excellency, who was in the habit of sitting in the first row of seats, would rise solemnly, draw himself up to his full height, turn to the culprits, fix a long and solemn gaze upon them, and slowly resume his chair. It was effective, always." He had some peculiar notions of composition; he was, for instance, fond of imitations of natural sounds in music and forced upon Haydn the imitation of frogs in *The Seasons*. Haydn himself says:[21] "This entire passage in imitation of a frog did not flow from

---

[20] *Ibid.*, pp. 72-73.
[21] Haydn wrote this note as an N.B. to a musical correction enclosed in a letter of December 11, 1801, to August Eberhard Müller

of Leipzig, the arranger of the pianoforte reduction of *The Seasons*. See Landon, *op.cit.*, p. 197.

my pen. I was constrained to write down the French croak. At an orchestral performance this wretched conceit soon disappears, but it cannot be justified in a pianoforte score."

But to van Swieten, surely, is due the credit of having founded in Vienna a taste for Handel's oratorios and Bach's organ and pianoforte music, thus adding a new element to the music there. —From a study of van Swieten's literary remains, Schmid[22] concludes that Bach's larger choral works as well as the motets, mentioned by Schindler,[23] were performed at his musical gatherings, and thus came to Beethoven's acquaintance.— The costs of the oratorio performances were not, however, defrayed by him, as Schönfeld seems to intimate. They were met by the association called by him into being, and of which he was perpetual secretary, whose members were the Princes Liechtenstein, Esterhazy, Schwarzenberg, Auersperg, Kinsky, Trautmannsdorf, Sinsendorf, and the Counts Czernin, Harrach, Erdödy and Fries; at whose palaces as well as in van Swieten's house and sometimes in the great hall of the Imperial Royal Library the performances were given at midday to an audience of invited guests. Fräulein Martinez, who holds so distinguished a place in Burney's account of his visit to Vienna—that pupil of Porpora at whose music-lessons the young Joseph Haydn forty years before had been employed as accompanist—still flourished in the Michael's House and gave a musical party every Saturday evening during the season. "Court Councillor and Chamber Paymaster von Meyer is so excellent a lover of music that his entire personnel in the chancellary is musical, among them being such artists as a Raphael and a Hauschka. It will readily be understood, therefore, that here in the city as well as at his country-seat there are many concerts. His Majesty the Emperor himself has attended some of these concerts."[24]

These details are sufficient to illustrate and confirm the remarks made above upon Vienna as the central point of instrumental music. Of the great number of composers in that branch of the art whom Beethoven found there, a few of the more eminent must be named.

Of course, Haydn stood at the head. The next in rank—*longo intervallo*—was Mozart's successor in the office of Imperial Chamber Composer, Leopold Koželuch, a Bohemian, now just forty years of age. Though now forgotten and, according to Beethoven, "miserabilis," he was renowned throughout Europe for his quartets and other chamber music. A man of less popular repute but of a solid genius and acquirements far beyond those of Koželuch, whom Beethoven greatly respected and twenty-five years later called his "old master," was Emanuel Aloys Förster, a Silesian, now forty-five years of age. His quintets, quartets and the like ranked very high, but at that time were known for the most part only in manuscript. Anton Eberl, five years the senior of Beethoven, a Viennese by birth, had composed

[22] E. F. Schmid, "Beethovens Bachkenntnis," NBJ, v (1933), p. 76.

[23] *Biographie*, I, 45n.

[24] Schönfeld, *op.cit.*, pp. 71-72.

two operettas in the sixteenth year of his age which were produced at the Kärnthnerthor-Theater, one of which gained the young author the favor of Gluck. He seems to have been a favorite of Mozart and caught so much of the spirit and style of that master as to produce compositions which were printed by dishonest publishers under Mozart's name, and as his were sold throughout Europe. In 1796 he accompanied the Widow Mozart and her sister, Madame Lange, the vocalist, in the tour through Germany, gaining that reputation in other cities which he enjoyed at home, both as pianist and composer. His force was in instrumental composition, and we shall hereafter see him for a moment as a symphonist tearing away the palm from Beethoven!

Johann Vanhall, whose name was so well known in Paris and London that Burney, twenty years before, sought him out in his garret in a suburb of Vienna, was as indefatigable as ever in production. Gerber says in his first Lexicon (1792) that Breitkopf and Härtel had then fifty of his symphonies in manuscript. His fecundity was equal to that of Haydn; his genius such that all his works are now forgotten. It is needless to continue this list.

One other fact illustrating the musical tastes and accomplishments of the higher classes of the capital may be added. There were, during the winter 1792-93, ten private theatres with amateur companies in activity, of which the more important were in the residences of the nobles Stockhammer, Kinsky, Sinsendorf and Strassaldo, and of the bookseller Schrambl. Most of these companies produced operas and operettas.

CHAPTER IX

THE YEARS 1793 TO 1795

HOWEVER quiet and "without observation" Beethoven's advent in Vienna may have been at that time when men's minds were occupied by movements of armies and ideas of revolution, he could hardly have gone thither under better auspices. He was Court Organist and Pianist to the Emperor's uncle; his talents in that field were well known to the many Austrians of rank who had heard him in Bonn when visiting there or when paying their respects to the Elector in passing to and from the Austrian Netherlands; he was a pupil of Joseph Haydn—a circumstance in itself sufficient to secure him a hearing; and he was protected by Count Waldstein, whose family connections were such that he could introduce his favorite into the highest circles, the imperial house only excepted. Waldstein's mother was a Liechtenstein; his grandmother a Trautmannsdorf; three of his sisters had married respectively into the families Dietrichstein, Crugenburg and Wallis; and by the marriages of uncles and aunts he was connected with the great houses Oettingen-Spielberg, Khevenhüller-Melisch, Kinsky, Palfy von Erdöd and Ulfeld—not to mention others less known. If the circle be extended by a degree or two it embraces the names Kaunitz, Lobkowitz, Kohary, Fünfkirchen, Keglevics and Colloredo-Mansfeld.

Dr. Burney, in closing his *Present State of Music in Germany*, notes the distinction in the styles of composition and performance in some of the principal cities of that country, "Vienna being most remarkable for fire and animation; Mannheim for neat and brilliant execution; Berlin for counterpoint and Brunswick for taste." Since Burney's tour (1772) Vienna had the highest example of all these qualities united in Mozart. But he had passed away, and no great pianist of the first rank remained; there were extraordinary dilettanti and professional pianists "of very neat and brilliant execution," but none who possessed great "fire, animation and invention," qualities still most valued in Vienna and in which the young Beethoven, with all the hardness and heaviness of manipulation caused by his devotion to the organ, was wholly unrivalled. With all the salons in the metropolis open to him, his success as a virtuoso was, therefore, certain. All the contemporary authorities, and all the traditions of those years agree in the fact of that success, and that his playing of Bach's preludes and fugues especially, his reading of the most difficult scores at sight and his extemporaneous performances excited ever new wonder and delight. Schindler records that van Swieten, after musical performances at his house, "detained Beethoven and persuaded him to add a few fugues by Sebastian Bach as an evening blessing," and he preserves a note without date, though evidently belonging to Beethoven's first years in Vienna, which proves how high a place the young man had then won in the old gentleman's favor:

To Hr. Beethoven in Alstergasse, No. 45, with the Prince Lichnowsky: If there is nothing to hinder next Wednesday I should be glad to see you at my home at half past 8 with your nightcap in your bag. Give me an immediate answer.

Swieten

Let the reader now recall to mind some of the points previously dwelt upon: the Fischenich letter of January and Neefe's letter of October, 1793, which record the favorable reports sent to Bonn of Beethoven's musical progress; his studies with Haydn and Schenk; the cares and perplexities caused him temporarily by the death of his father and the unpleasant circumstances attending that event; his steady success as a virtuoso; his visit in the summer to Prince Esterhazy; and it is obvious with what industry and energy he engaged in his new career, with what zeal and unfaltering activity he labored to make the most of his opportunities. In one year after leaving Bonn he felt his success secure, and no longer feared Hamlet's "slings and arrows of outrageous fortune."

At this time he wrote to his old friend, Eleonore von Breuning in Bonn. Though often reprinted from the *Notizen*, this letter is too important and characteristic to be here omitted:

Vienna, November 2, 93.

Most estimable Leonore!

My most precious friend!

Not until I have lived almost a year in the capital do you receive a letter from me, and yet you were most assuredly perpetually in my liveliest memory. Often in thought I have conversed with you and your dear family, though not with that peace of mind which I could have desired. It was then that the wretched quarrel hovered before me and my conduct presented itself as most despicable, but it was too late; oh what would I not give could I obliterate from my life those actions so degrading to myself and so contrary to my character. True, there were many circumstances which tended to estrange us, and I suspect that tales whispered in our ears of remarks made one about the other were chiefly that which prevented us from coming to an understanding. We both believed that we were speaking from conviction; whereas it was only in anger, and we were both deceived. Your good and noble character my dear friend is sufficient assurance to me that you forgave me long ago, but we are told that the sincerest contrition consists in acknowledgement of our faults; and to do this has been my desire.—And now let us drop a curtain on this whole affair, only drawing from it this lesson, that when friends quarrel it is much better to have it out face to face than to turn to a go-between.

With this you will receive a dedication from me to you concerning which I only wish that the work were a larger one and more worthy of you.[1] I was plagued here to publish the little work, and I took advantage of the opportunity, my estimable E., to show my respect and friendship for you and my enduring memory of your family. Take this trifle and remember that it comes from a friend who respects you greatly. Oh if it but gives you pleasure, my wishes will be completely fulfilled. Let it be a reminder of the time when I spent so many and such blessed hours at your home. Perhaps it will keep me in your recollection, until I eventually return to you, which, it is true, is not likely to be soon, but oh how we shall rejoice then, my dear friend. You will then find in your friend a happier man, from whose visage time and a kindlier fate shall have smoothed out all the furrows of a hateful past.

If you should chance to see B. Koch, please say to her that it is not nice of her never once to have written to me. I wrote to her twice and three times to Malchus,[2] but no answer. Say to her that if she doesn't want to write she might at least urge Malchus to do so. In conclusion I venture a request; it is this: I should like once again to own a waistcoat knit of hare's wool by your hands, my dear friend. Pardon the immodest request, my dear friend, but it proceeds from a great predilection for everything that comes from your hands. Privately I may acknowledge that a little vanity is also involved in the request; I want to be able to say that I have something that was given me by the best and most estimable girl in Bonn. I still have the waistcoat that you were good enough to give me in Bonn, but it has grown so out of fashion that I can only treasure it in my wardrobe as something very precious because it came from you. You would give me much pleasure if you were soon to rejoice me with a dear letter from yourself. If my letters should in any way please you I promise in this to be at your command so far as lies in my power, as everything is welcome to me which enables me to show how truly I am

Your admiring true friend
L. v. Beethoven

Next we come to the fragment of another letter to Eleonore von Breuning also contained in Wegeler's *Notizen* (p. 60). It, like the one quoted above, shows how bitterly Beethoven's conscience could be troubled by his own impulsiveness or acts of temper, which were always to threaten his relationships with his friends. This letter is particularly interesting because of the postscript, which Wegeler had appended to the 1793 letter above. This order was followed by subsequent editors, including Deiters and Krehbiel, until it was proved by Leopold Schmidt,[3] upon comparison of the ink, the paper and

---

[1] "Se vuol ballare" variations, WoO 40. These were sent to Eleonore with a later letter.

[2] Wegeler (*Notizen*, p. 59) identifies Malchus as the subsequent Graf von Marienrode,

Minister of Finance in Westphalia and later Würstemburg, a "classical writer."

[3] *Beethoven-Briefe* (Berlin, 1909), p. 95. See also Schiedermair, pp. 204ff. In Thayer's

the script of the three passages, that the undated letter and the postscript belong together. The letter was probably written in May or June, 1794.⟩⟩

How surprised I was by the beautiful cravat made by your own hand. The thing itself was so pleasant, at the same time it awoke in me a feeling of sadness. Its effect was to bring back the former times of the past, and, moreover, a sense of shame because of your generous behaviour towards me. In truth, I did not think that you still thought me worthy of your remembrance. Oh, if you could have been witness to the way I reacted yesterday to this incident, you would certainly not find that I am exaggerating when I tell you that your remembrance made me weep and feel very sad.—However little I may deserve consideration in your eyes, I beg of you, *my friend*, (let me ever call you so) to think of me as one who has suffered very much and continues to suffer through the loss of your friendship. I shall never forget you and your dear mother, you were so good to me that this loss to me cannot and will not easily be restored. I know what I have lost and what you were to me, but I would have to recall scenes, were I to fill in these gaps, which are unpleasant both for you to hear and for me to describe to you.

As a slight return for your kind remembrance of me I take the liberty of sending these variations and the rondo for violin.[4] I have a great deal to do or I would have transcribed the sonata I promised you long ago,[5] it is a mere sketch in manuscript, and to copy it would be difficult even for one as skilled as Paraquin.[6] You could have the rondo copied and then send the score back to me. This is all that I can send to you now which would be at all useful to you; since you are now traveling to Kerpen,[7] I thought that these trifles might perhaps give you some pleasure.

Farewell, my friend it is impossible for me to call you otherwise. However little you may think of me, please realize that I revere you and your mother just as much as formerly, and if I could contribute in any other way to your pleasure, I beg of you not to forget me. This is still the only means which is left for me to express my gratitude for the friendship which I have received from you. A happy journey, and bring your dear mother back again in sound health. Think occasionally of one who continues to venerate you,

your true friend, Beethoven

PS. The V. [variations] you will find a little difficult to play, especially the trills in the coda; but don't let this alarm you. It is so contrived that you need play only the trill, leaving out the other notes because they are also in the violin part. I never would have composed it so, had I not often observed that here and there in V. there was somebody who, after I had improvised of an evening, noted down many of the peculiarities, and made parade of them the next day as his own.

---

personal copy of the *Notizen*, in the Harvard University Library, there is an indication that the postscript belongs with the undated letter.

[4] WoO 40 and WoO 41.

[5] WoO 51.

[6] A singer and double bass player in the Electoral Orchestra, who, according to Wegeler (*Notizen*, p. 62) was highly regarded as man and artist.

[7] Madame von Breuning frequently visited her brother-in-law, Johann Philipp von Breuning, at his house in Kerpen, a village between Cologne and Aix-la-Chapelle. Sometimes Beethoven had joined the family on these trips in the past, and, according to Gerhard von Breuning (*Aus dem Schwarzspanierhause*, p. 7) had often played the church organ there.

Foreseeing that some of these things would soon appear in print, I resolved to anticipate them. Another reason that I had was to embarrass the local pianoforte masters. Many of them are my deadly enemies, and I wanted to revenge myself on them, knowing that once in awhile somebody would ask them to play the variations and they would make a sorry show of them.

The instant and striking success of Beethoven as virtuoso by no means filled up the measure of his ambition. He aspired to the higher position of composer, and to obtain this more was needed than the performance of variations, however excellent. To this end he selected the three Trios afterwards published as Opus 1, and brought them to performance at the house of Prince Lichnowsky, to whom they were dedicated. Happily for us, Beethoven related some particulars concerning this first performance of these compositions in Vienna to his pupil Ries, who gives us the substance of the story thus (*Notizen*, p. 84): "It was planned to introduce the first three Trios of Beethoven, which were about to be published as Op. 1, to the artistic world at a soirée at Prince Lichnowsky's. Most of the artists and music-lovers were invited, especially Haydn, for whose opinion all were eager. The Trios were played and at once commanded extraordinary attention. Haydn also said many pretty things about them, but advised Beethoven not to publish the third, in C minor. This astonished Beethoven, inasmuch as he considered the third the best of the Trios, as it is still the one which gives the greatest pleasure and makes the greatest effect. Consequently, Haydn's remark left a bad impression on Beethoven and led him to think that Haydn was envious, jealous and ill-disposed toward him. I confess that when Beethoven told me of this I gave it little credence. I therefore took occasion to ask Haydn himself about it. His answer, however, confirmed Beethoven's statement; he said he had not believed that this Trio would be so quickly and easily understood and so favorably received by the public."

The Fischoff manuscript[8] says: "The three Trios for pianoforte, violin and violoncello, Op. 1 (the pearls of all sonatas), which are in fact his sixth work, justly excited admiration, though they were performed in only a few circles. Wherever this was done, however, connoisseurs and music-lovers bestowed upon them undivided applause, which grew with the succeeding works as the hearers not only accustomed themselves to the striking and original qualities of the master but grasped his spirit and strove for the high privilege of understanding him."

More than two years passed by, however, before the composer thought fit to send these Trios to the press; perhaps restrained by a feeling of modesty, since he was still a student, perhaps by a doubt as to the success of compositions so new in style, or by prudence, choosing to delay their publication until they had been so often performed from the manuscript as to secure their comprehension and appreciation, and thus an adequate number of subscribers. In the meantime he prepared the way for them by publishing a few

[8] See Preface, page xiv.

sets of variations. Those on "Se vuol ballare," revised and improved with a new coda, came out in July, 1793, with a dedication to Eleonore von Breuning. Then the thirteen variations upon the theme "Es war einmal ein alter Mann," from Dittersdorf's *Das rote Käppchen*, appeared, and these were followed by those for four hands on the Waldstein theme. In fact, Beethoven evidently was in no haste to publish his compositions. It will be remembered from the postscript to the 1794 letter to Eleonore von Breuning that he sent the "Se vuol ballare" variations to press partly at the request of others and partly to entrap the rival pianists of Vienna. A few years later we shall find him dashing off and immediately publishing variations on popular theatrical melodies; but works of greater scope, and especially his pianoforte concertos, were for the most part long retained in his exclusive possession.

We must tarry a moment longer with the Trios. That the author is disposed to place their origin in the Bonn period has already appeared. Argument in favor of this view can be found in the fact of their early performance in Vienna, for there can be no reasonable question of the correctness of Ries's story, for which Beethoven himself was authority, that they were played at the house of Prince Lichnowsky in the presence of Haydn. This performance must have taken place before January 19, 1794, because on that day Haydn started for England. Now, Beethoven's sketches show that he was still working on at least the second and third of the Trios after 1794, and that they were not ready for the printer before the end of that year. Further explanation is offered by the following little circumstances: since Haydn was present, the performance at Prince Lichnowsky's must have been from manuscript. In the morning meeting which probably took place before the soirée, Beethoven's attention was called to the desirability of changing in the last movement of the second Trio, the time-signature from 4/4 to 2/4. Beethoven made the change. From these facts it may be concluded that after a first there was a final revision of these Trios, and that the former version disappeared or was destroyed after the latter was made. It has been intimated that the author believes that the rewriting of compositions completed in Beethoven's early period is more far-reaching than is generally assumed. The case therefore seems to present itself as follows: Haydn heard the Trios at Lichnowsky's in their first state; Beethoven then took them up for revision and in the course of 1794 and the beginning of 1795 brought them to the state in which we know them.

Beethoven was stimulated without question by performances of other artists. In these years he wrote two works for two oboes and English horn. Nottebohm surmises that they were instigated by a terzetto for the same combination composed by a musician named Wendt and performed at a concert of the Tonkünstler-Gesellschaft by three brothers, Johann, Franz and Philipp Teimer, on December 23, 1793. ⸱⸱⸲⸳The first of the two is the Trio in C, Op. 87, which was written, according to Nottebohm, in 1794. It became widely known in the next few years through the many arrangements of it that were published, evidently with the composer's permission. The second, the variations on "Là ci darem," belongs to the year 1796 and is discussed later.}⟫

The Sextet for four stringed instruments and two horns, Op. 81b, also belongs to this early period as does the double song "Seufzer eines Unge-liebten"—"Gegenliebe." Sketches for the first two movements of the Sextet are upon a sheet in the Berlin State Library alongside sketches for "Seufzer eines Ungeliebten"; on a sheet in the archives of the Gesellschaft der Musik-freunde in Vienna there is a sketch for the ending of "Gegenliebe" alongside early sketches for "Adelaide."[9] The double song is based on two independent, but related poems by Gottfried August Bürger. Particular interest attaches to the second part, "Gegenliebe," from the fact that its melody was used afterwards by Beethoven for the variations in the Choral Fantasia, Op. 80. --⟫Kinsky-Halm has modified Nottebohm's date of 1795 for the song to 1794 or beginning of 1795.}⟫-- It was first published as late as 1837 by Diabelli along with the song, "Turteltaube, du klagest," which was composed much later. The Sextet is therefore credited to the same period. It was published in 1810 by Simrock in Bonn. In a letter which Beethoven sent to Simrock with the manuscript, he wrote to the publisher, who was an admira-ble horn player, that "the pupil had given his master many a hard nut to crack."[10]

--⟫This is an appropriate time to review the history of the String Trio, Op. 3. It was published in 1797; and Thayer believed it was a Bonn product on the basis of a passage written by the English music enthusiast, William Gardiner, in his three-volumed work, *Music and Friends*. That it was this particular trio that Gardiner describes is confirmed by a passage written by the same author in his *Sights in Italy*, published in 1847.[11] "Presently we arrived at Bonn, the birthplace of Beethoven. About the year 1786, my friend the Abbé Dobler, Chaplain to the Elector of Cologne, first noticed this curly black-headed boy, the son of a tenor singer in the cathedral. Through the Abbé I became acquainted with the first production of this wonderful com-poser. How great was my surprise, on playing the viola part to his trio in E-flat, so unlike anything I had ever heard. It was a new sense to me, an intellectual pleasure which I had never received from sounds."

In 1923 the Library of Congress acquired a holograph of the last move-ment of the trio, which differed only slightly from the final version. This acquisition led the head of the music division, Carl Engel, to re-examine the premise upon which Thayer established that the work was composed in 1792. The following is based upon his findings.[12] Gardiner was sixty-eight when he published the first two volumes of *Music and Friends* in 1838, and

[9] See *II Beeth.*, pp. 535-36. (TDR, II, 24.)
[10] See Thayer, *Verzeichniss*, p. 81.
[11] Page 400.
[12] "Beethoven's Opus 3, an 'Envoi de Vienne'?", *MQ*, Vol. 13 (1927), pp. 261ff.

eighty-three when he published the third volume, which alone is cited by Thayer. However, within the three volumes Gardiner refers to his first hearing of the trio in England in four separate passages, each with a different year, ranging from 1793 to 1796.[13] An important clue in this conflict of dates is to be found in Gardiner's introductory sentences preceding the passage quoted by Thayer, which are here included:[14] "*1793*—The honourable Mrs. Bowater, daughter of the Earl of Feversham, was on a visit to the Elector Palatine, when Pichegru invaded the Low Countries. The progress of the French armies was so rapid, that she was obliged to leave Bonn with the utmost speed. The Elector sent his chaplain, the Abbé Dobler, to see her safe to Hamburgh. While there, he was declared an emigrant, and his property seized. Luckily, he had placed some money in our government funds, and his only alternative was to proceed to England. . . . Mrs. Bowater, having lived much in Germany, had acquired a fine taste in music; and as the Abbé was a very fine performer on the violin, music was essential to fill up this irksome period. My company was sought, with that of two of my friends, to make up, occasionally an instrumental quartet. . . . Our music consisted of the quartettos of Haydn, Boccherini, and Wranisky. The Abbé, who never traveled without his violin, had actually put into his fiddle-case a trio composed by Beethoven, just before he set off, which thus, in the year 1793, found its way to Leicester. This composition, so different from anything I had ever heard, awakened in me a new sense, a new delight, in the science of sounds. . . . It was a language that so powerfully excited my imagination, that all other music appeared tame and spiritless."

There was no general flight from Bonn in 1792, as Thayer supposed, nor was Gardiner correct in this version of his first hearing. The general flight did not occur until 1794. In 1792 the Elector, who at this point was antagonizing the Austrians by remaining neutral, left Bonn himself on October 22; his return was a matter of weeks, as the intervention by the Prussians at Coblenz seemed to remove the danger of invasion of the upper Rhine. The antagonistic behavior of the Austrians was his chief concern and was probably the cause of his moving his court to Münster on December 21, where he remained until April 21, 1793. Still no general flight. But by 1794 the Elector was forced to abandon his neutral position and supply troops for the armies of the Coalition; now he was one of France's enemies. Then in the summer of 1794 the French advances threatened the populace all along the Rhine, and the people did flee to the East in the early fall. According to Herman Hüffer in his article on Max Franz,[15] it was on October 2nd that the Elector saw Bonn for the last time; and at this time Pichegru was pressing his army northwards into Belgium and Holland.

---

[13] In Vol. iii, 377, quoting a letter written *ca.* 1820 from the author to Beethoven "in 1796"; in Vol. ii, 793, "so far back as 1795"; in Vol. i, 113, "in the year 1794"; and in Vol. iii, 143, "in the year 1793."

[14] Vol. iii, 142-43. (TDR, I, 312.)

[15] *Allgemeine Deutsche Biographie* (Leipzig, 1884), Vol. 21, pp. 56ff.

The fact that the Abbé Dobbeler was declared an *émigré* and had his property seized shows further that Gardiner's story could have taken place only after the French had entered Bonn in October, 1794. Gardiner implies that the trio was finished soon before Dobbeler's departure from Bonn, and this is supported by a passage from *Glimpses of Ancient Leicester*, by Mrs. T. Fielding Johnson.[16] "Mr. Gardiner claimed with justice to be the first to introduce the name and genius of Beethoven into England. In the year 1794, the Abbé Dobler, an accomplished musician who was chaplain to the Elector of Cologne, being forced from political reasons to leave Germany, was offered a shelter in this country by a Roman Catholic lady of property who had formed his acquaintance abroad—the Hon. Mrs. Bowater of Little Dalby Hall. Here he at once sought the friendship of the well-known dilettante in music, William Gardiner, and subsequently showed him a violin trio in E flat lately written by a young musician—Louis van Beethoven—the son of an innkeeper and chorister in the Elector's Chapel at Bonn. The latter having recognized in the youth an original genius for music, had placed him under the tuition of the great Joseph Haydn at Vienna; and on leaving Germany the Abbé had hastily put the Trio into his trunk with other instrumental music. On looking over the composition, Mr. Gardiner's interest was at once aroused, and inviting Mr. Valentine and other local violinists to try it, the Trio was played over with surprise and delight in a room in the town, in 1794, several years before the works of Beethoven were introduced in London."

Here the year is given correctly and there is still no reason to doubt that this was the first Beethoven work to be introduced in England. If it was composed in 1793 or the first half of 1794, as implied above, then both Wegeler and Schindler were right when they referred to it as a Vienna work. In its length comprising six movements it is a bigger chamber work than any known to have been composed at Bonn.

But if it was a Vienna work how could Dobbeler have acquired the manuscript of the work in Bonn? In manuscript it must have been, since the announcement of publication was in February, 1797. It is probable that Beethoven saw the Elector concerning his status when Max Franz visited Vienna in January, 1794. Would it not be natural for the composer to give his former employer this newly composed trio to take back to Bonn? He was still receiving quarterly payments from the Elector, and this offering would help remove the sting of the set of works sent to Bonn by Haydn only two months before, which the Elector had pointed out were all works composed at Bonn save one. Although no more payments were forthcoming after March, the Elector still retained an interest in Beethoven. In a list of his musicians which he drew up in the autumn of 1794 when he had fled to Münster occurs "Beethoven, without salary in Vienna, until recalled."

16 Leicester, 1806, 2nd edition, pp. 352-53.

Count Waldstein was also in Vienna during the winter and spring of 1794, and returned to Bonn in June. During that time he was in touch with Beethoven, as is shown by a letter from the composer to Simrock dated June 18, in which he offered to send through Count Waldstein the manuscript of the Variations for pianoforte four hands on Waldstein's theme. The Trio, Op. 3, might also have reached Bonn by the same means—via Count Waldstein.

With his old colleague in the Court Orchestra in Bonn, Nikolaus Simrock, though he was a much older man, Beethoven remained in touch after his removal to Vienna. Simrock, who was highly esteemed as man and musician, had embarked in business as a music publisher in Bonn. The "Das rote Käppchen" Variations were published by him in 1793, and the Waldstein Variations the following year. Beethoven's correspondence with Simrock in the summer of 1794 marks the beginning of a long struggle with publishers over revisions and corrections of his works that was to continue until the final year of his life. On June 18[17] he wrote that he was surprised to hear that Simrock was about to print, or had begun to print the Waldstein Variations without consulting him. He continues: "The one thing which I must insist upon is that you now stop the printing and simply write to me whether you had really begun them already. This is so that I may send you the manuscript of them by way of my friend, Count Waldstein, from which you can make the printing, because various things in them have been revised; and I wish to see my works appear in print at least in as perfect shape as possible. Aside from this I have not been willing to have my variations published now since I wanted first to wait until some important works of mine,[18] which will soon be brought out, come into the world."

The letter ends with a correction for the "Das rote Käppchen" Variations and a complaint that only one copy had been sent him, whereas Artaria had given him a fee and twelve copies of the variations he had published.[19] The next letter is of August 2nd and is given in full:—

Dear Simrock:

I deserve a little scolding from you for holding back your variations so long, but, indeed, I do not lie when I say that I was hindered from correcting them sooner by an overwhelming amount of business. You will note the shortcomings yourself, but I must congratulate you on the appearance of your engraving, which is beautiful, clear and legible. Verily, if you keep on thus you will become chief among cutters, that is, note-cutters—[20]

In my previous letter I promised to send you something of mine, and you interpreted the remark as being in the language of the cavaliers. How have I deserved such a title?—Faugh, who would indulge in such language in these democratic times of ours? Well, in order to free myself from this declaration

[17] See KK, No. 9; A, 10.
[18] Undoubtedly the Trios, Op. 1.
[19] To "Se vuol ballare."
[20] An early example of Beethoven's fondness

for punning. *Stechen* means many things in German—among them to sting, stab, tilt in a tournament, take a trick at cards—as well as to engrave or to cut in metal. (TK, I, 183, n. 1.)

that you have made against me, as soon as I have finished the grand revision of my compositions, which will be soon, you shall have something which you will surely engrave—

I have also been looking about me for an agent and have found a right capable young fellow for the place. His name is *Traeg*. You have only to write to him or to me about what terms you wish to make. He asks of you one-third discount. The devil take all such bargaining—It is very hot here, the Viennese are afraid that soon they will be unable to get *ice-cream*, for since the winter was so mild, ice is scarce. Many persons of *importance* have come here, it was said that a revolution was imminent—But it is my belief that so long as the Austrian has his dark *beer* and *sausage* he will not revolt. It is said that the suburban gates are to be closed at ten o'clock at night. The soldiers' guns are loaded with bullets. No one dares speak aloud, for fear of arrest by the police.

If your daughters are already grown up, bring one up to be my wife, for if I am to remain single in Bonn I shall not stay long, of a surety;—You must also be living in fear!—

How is good *Ries?* I shall write to him soon for he can only have an unfavorable opinion of me, but this cursed writing, I cannot get over my antipathy towards it.—*Have you performed my Parthie yet?* Write to me occasionally.

Your Beethoven

Please send also a few copies of the first Variations.

These "first Variations" obviously are those on the theme from *Das rote Käppchen*; the Parthie whose performance he inquires about is the Octet, Op. 103. The letter, like that written to Eleonore von Breuning, shows that Beethoven was still thinking of the possibility or probability of a return to Bonn. Its cheerful tone discloses a comfortable, satisfied frame of mind.

The reminiscences of Wegeler for the period of his stay in Vienna, excepting those which may be better introduced chronologically in other connections, may well find place here. They are interesting and characteristic in themselves, and indicate, also, the great change for the better in Beethoven's pecuniary condition; for a man who keeps a servant and a horse cannot, if honest, be a sufferer from poverty. ——Wegeler was another fugitive from the French occupation of Bonn. Though only twenty-nine years of age, he had become Rector of the University. Then he fled to Vienna, where he remained nearly two years, and where he naturally renewed his friendship with Beethoven.—— He reached that capital in October and found Beethoven not in the "room on the ground floor" where "it was not necessary to pay the housekeeper more than 7 florins," but living as a guest in the family of Prince Karl Lichnowsky; and this explains sufficiently the cessation of those records of monthly payments before noticed.

Wegeler says (*Notizen*, p. 28):

"Carl, Prince of Lichnowsky, Count Werdenberg, Dynast Granson, was a very great patron, yes, a friend of Beethoven's, who took him into his house as a guest, where he remained at least a few years. I found him there toward the end of the year 1794, and left him there in the middle of 1796. Meanwhile, however, Beethoven had almost always a home in the country.

"The Prince was a great lover and connoisseur of music. He played the pianoforte, and by studying Beethoven's pieces and playing them more or less well, sought to convince him that there was no need of changing anything in his style of composition, though the composer's attention was often called to the difficulties of his works. There were performances at his house every Friday morning, participated in by four hired musicians—Schuppanzigh, Weiss, Kraft and another (Link?), besides our friend; generally also an amateur, Zmeskall. Beethoven always listened with pleasure to the observations of these gentlemen. Thus, to cite a single instance, the famous violoncellist Kraft in my presence called his attention to a passage in the finale of the Trio, Op. 1, No. 3, to the fact that it ought to be marked sulla corda G,[21] and the indication 4/4 time which Beethoven had marked in the finale of the second Trio, changed to 2/4. Here the new compositions of Beethoven, so far as was feasible, were first performed. Here there were generally present several great musicians and music-lovers. I, too, as long as I lived in Vienna, was present, if not every time, at least most of the time.

"Here a Hungarian count once placed a difficult composition by Bach in manuscript before him which he played a vista exactly as Bach would have played it, according to the testimony of the owner. Here the Viennese author Förster once brought him a quartet of which he had made a clean copy only that morning. In the second portion of the first movement the violoncello got out. Beethoven stood up, and still playing his own part sang the bass accompaniment. When I spoke about it to him as a proof of extraordinary acquirements, he replied with a smile: 'The bass part had to be so, else the author would have known nothing about composition.' To the remark that he had played a presto which he had never seen before so rapidly that it must have been impossible to see the individual notes, he answered: 'Nor is that necessary; if you read rapidly there may be a multitude of typographical errors, but you neither see nor give heed to them, so long as the language is a familiar one.'

"After the concert, the musicians generally stayed to dine. Here there gathered, in addition, artists and savants without regard to social position. The Princess Christiane was the highly cultivated daughter of Count Joseph von Thun, who, a very philanthropic and respectable gentleman, was disposed to extravagant enthusiasm by his intercourse with Lavater, and believed himself capable of healing diseases through the power of his right hand."

On page 33 of the *Notizen* Wegeler describes the outward conditions of the composer. He says:

"Beethoven, brought up under extremely restricted circumstances, and as it were, under guardianship, though that of his friends, did not know the

[21] Should be "sulla corda C": see score, 31 measures from the end. (TDR, I, 393, n. 1.)

value of money and was anything but economical. Thus, to cite a single instance, the Prince's dinner hour was fixed at 4 o'clock. 'Now,' said Beethoven, 'it is desired that every day I shall be home at half-past 3, put on better clothes, care for my beard, etc.—I can't stand that!' So it happened that he frequently went to the taverns, since, as has been said, in this as in all other matters of economy, he knew nothing about the value of money.

"The prince, who had a loud metallic voice, once directed his serving-man that if ever he and Beethoven should ring at the same time the latter was to be first served. Beethoven heard this, and the same day engaged a servant for himself. In the same manner, once when he took a whim to learn to ride, which speedily left him, the stable of the Prince being offered him, he bought a horse."

Concerning his friend's affairs of the heart, Wegeler had opportunity to make observations in Vienna. He relates on page 43 that while he was in the capital Beethoven "was always in love and made many conquests which would have been difficult if not impossible for many an Adonis." Beethoven's antipathy to teaching before he left Bonn has already been noticed. In Vienna he developed a still stronger repugnance to playing in society when requested to do so. He often complained to Wegeler how grievously this put him out of sorts, whereupon the latter sought to entertain him and quiet him by conversation. "When this purpose was reached," he continues (*Notizen*, p. 19): "I dropped the conversation, seated myself at the writing table, and Beethoven, if he wanted to continue the discourse, had to sit down on the chair before the pianoforte. Soon, still turned away from the instrument, he aimlessly struck a few chords out of which gradually grew the most beautiful melodies. Oh, why did I not understand more of music! Several times I put ruled paper upon the desk as if without intention, in order to get a manuscript of his; he wrote upon it but then folded it up and put it in his pocket! Concerning his playing I was permitted to say but little, and that only in passing. He would then go away entirely changed in mood and always come back again gladly. The antipathy remained, however, and was frequently the cause of differences between Beethoven and his friends and well-wishers."

The following undated letter also belongs to the years of Beethoven's intimate association with Wegeler in Vienna (1794-96). It is significant of Beethoven's character. Though easily offended and prone to anger, no sooner was the first ebullition of temper past than he was so reconciliatory and so open to explanation that usually his contrition was out of all proportion to his fault. For this reason, and because it presents the friend in a light which provoked a protest from his modesty, Wegeler was unwilling to publish the entire letter,[22] which follows:

[22] This was done by Wegeler's grandson, Karl Wegeler, in an essay published in the *Coblenz Zeitung* on May 20, 1890. (TDR, I, 395, n. 1.)

Dearest and best one!

What a detestable image of me you have presented for myself! Oh I acknowledge it, I do not deserve your friendship. You are so noble, so considerate, and this is the first time that I am not allowed to be on an equal footing with you; I have fallen far below you. Ah, for eight weeks I have displeased my best and noblest friend. You think that I have lost some of my goodness of heart, but thank Heaven, no; it was not intentional or deliberate malice which induced me to act as I did towards you, it was my inexcusable thoughtlessness which did not permit me to see the matter in its true light.—Oh how ashamed I am, not only for your sake but also for my own—I scarcely dare to ask for your friendship any more— Ah Wegeler my only comfort lies in this, that you have known me almost from my childhood, and yet, oh let me say this for myself, I was always good, and always strove to be upright and true in my actions. Otherwise how could you have loved me? Could I have changed so fearfully for the worse in such a short time?—Impossible. Could these feelings of goodness and love of righteousness have died forever in me in a moment? No, dear, best Wegeler. Oh venture again to throw yourself entirely into the arms of your B.—trust in the good qualities you used to find in him. I will guarantee that the pure temple of sacred friend- ship which you erect shall remain firm forever, no accident, no storm shall ever shake its foundations—firm—eternal—our friendship—forgiveness—oblivion—a new revival of the dying, sinking friendship—Oh Wegeler, do not reject this hand of reconciliation, place yours in mine—Ah God.—But no more—I am coming to see you and shall throw myself in your arms and entreat you to restore to me my lost friend; and you will be reconciled to me, to your penitent, loving, never- forgetting

Beethoven again,

It was only now that I received your letter, because I have just returned home.

We return to the chronological record of events. The first of these in the year 1795, was Beethoven's first appearance in public as virtuoso and composer. The annual concerts in the Burgtheater established by Gassmann for the benefit of the widows of the Tonkünstlergesellschaft were announced for the evenings of March 29 and 30. The vocal work selected for performance was an oratorio in two parts, *Gioas, Re di Giuda*, by Antonio Cartellieri; the instrumental, a Concerto for Pianoforte and Orchestra, composed and played by Ludwig van Beethoven. Cartellieri was a young man of twenty-three years (born in Danzig, September 27, 1772) who, a year or two since, had come from Berlin to study operatic composition with the then greatest living composer in that field, Salieri. As the direction of these Widow and Orphan concerts was almost exclusively in the hands of Salieri, one is almost tempted to think that he may on this occasion have indulged a pardonable vanity in bringing forward two of his pupils, if we did not know how strong an attraction the name of Ludwig van Beethoven must have been for the public which, as yet, had had no opportunity to learn his great powers except by report. The day of the performance drew near but the Concerto was not yet written out. "Not until the afternoon of the second day before the concert did he write the rondo, and then while suffering from a pretty severe colic which frequently afflicted him. I [Wegeler] relieved him with simple remedies so far as I could. In the anteroom sat four copyists to whom he handed sheet after sheet as soon as it was finished. . . . At the first rehearsal, which took place the next day in Beethoven's room, the pianoforte was found to be half a tone lower than the wind-instruments. Without a moment's delay Beethoven had the wind-instruments and the others tune to B-flat instead of A and played his part in C-sharp." Thus Wegeler in his *Notizen* (p. 36). But he has confounded two compositions. The concerto which Beethoven played on March 29, 1795, was not that in C (Op. 15) which was not yet finished, but, in all probability, that in B-flat (Op. 19).[23] For the fact that the Concerto in B-flat was composed before that in C we have the testimony of Beethoven himself, who wrote to Breitkopf and Härtel on April 22, 1801: "In this connection I wish to add that one *of my first concertos,* and therefore *not one of the best of my compositions,* is to be published by *Hofmeister,* and that Mollo is to publish *a concerto which*, indeed *was written later . . ."* etc. The Concerto in B-flat was published in 1801 by Hoffmeister and that in C in the same year by Mollo and Co. in Vienna, the latter a little in advance of the former, wherefore there need be no surprise at the earlier opus number.

To these concertos must be added the Rondo in B-flat for Pianoforte and Orchestra found unfinished among Beethoven's compositions and published by Diabelli and Co. in 1829. Sonnleithner, on the authority of Diabelli, says it was completed by Czerny, who also filled out the accompaniment. There is no authentic record of the time of its composition. Jahn surmised that it may have been designed for the Concerto in B-flat. Its contents indicate an earlier period. A sketch printed by Nottebohm,[24] judged by the handwriting, is not of later date than 1795. It is associated with a Romanza for Pianoforte, Flute and Bassoon. Mandyczewski[25] compared the original manuscript, now in the library of the Gesellschaft der Musikfreunde, with the printed form and decided that the work was completed in plan and *motivi* by Beethoven, who, however, did not carry out the cadenzas and only indicated the passages. The share which Czerny had in it is thus indicated; he added the cadenzas and extended the pianoforte passages which Beethoven had only indicated, making them more effective and brilliant. The use of the high registers of the pianoforte, which Czerny employs somewhat too freely in view of the simple character of the piece, was not contemplated by Beethoven, who once remarked of Czerny: "He uses the piccolo too much for me." In Mandyczewski's opinion the handwriting points to a time before

[23] Nottebohm shows further (*II Beeth.*, pp. 67, n. 1) that in Beethoven's room, a rehearsal of the B-flat Concerto would be more feasible, since it is not scored for trumpets and kettledrums as is the Concerto in C. (TDR, I, 400, n. 2.)

[24] *II Beeth.*, p. 70. (TDR, II, 89.)

[25] See E. Mandyczewski in his article "Beethovens Rondo in B für Pianoforte und Orchester," in *Sammelbände der IMG,* 1 (1900), 295-306. (TDR, II, 89, n. 2.)

1800, and the contents indicate the early Vienna if not the Bonn period. Mandyczewski also thinks that the inserted romanza-like Andante is probably a very early composition and that the correspondence in key and time signature with the last movement of the B-flat Concerto might indicate that the rondo was originally designed as part of that work, a supposition which is strengthened by the fact that the original manuscript is neither dated nor signed. This internal evidence has much in its favor, the more since it is not at all obvious what might have prompted Beethoven to write an independent rondo for concert use. There is no external evidence; if there were, the conception of the B-flat Concerto would have to be set at a much earlier date than has yet been done. The first Vienna sketches for the Concerto, as Nottebohm shows, prove that the present three movements belonged together from the beginning. They were, therefore, surely played at the first performance in 1795. Attention may here be called to Wegeler's statement (*Notizen*, p. 56) that the rondo of the first Concerto (he says, of course, the Concerto in C) was not composed until the second afternoon before the performance. There may possibly have been another. This is not necessarily disproved by the fact that sketches for the present one were in existence. The question is not settled by the evidence now before us, but the probabilities are all with Mandyczewski.

Beethoven also took part in the second concert on March 30, the minutes of the Tonkünstlerschaft recording that he "improvised on the pianoforte"; and though busily engaged he also embraced an opportunity to testify to his devotion to the manes of Mozart. On March 31, 1795, Mozart's widow arranged a performance of *La Clemenza di Tito* in the Burgtheater. "After the first part," says the advertisement, "Hr. Ludwig van Beethoven will play a Concerto of Mozart's composition on the Pianoforte." We opine that this concerto was Mozart's in D minor, which Beethoven loved especially, and for which he wrote cadenzas.

The Trios, Op. 1, had now become so well known and appreciated in musical circles as to justify their publication, and accordingly, an advertisement inviting subscriptions for Ludwig van Beethoven's "three Grand Trios" appeared in the *Wiener Zeitung* on May 9, 13 and 16, 1795. Three days later a contract was signed by the author and Artaria and Company. The printed list of subscribers gives 123 names, mostly belonging to the higher circles, with subscriptions amounting to 241 copies. As Beethoven paid the publisher but one florin per copy, and the subscription price was one ducat, he made a handsome profit out of the transaction.

Some other incidents recorded by Wegeler belong to this year. Haydn reached Vienna upon his return from his second trip to England on August 20, 1795. Beethoven had now ready the three Sonatas, Op. 2, and at one of the Friday morning concerts at Prince Lichnowsky's he played them for Haydn, to whom they were dedicated. These sonatas were, therefore, the second group of compositions which Beethoven considered illustrative of his artistic ideals and worthy of publication.[26] Nothing can be said with positiveness touching the time of their origin. Schönfeld's words in his *Jahrbuch der Tonkunst von Wien un Prag*:[27] "We already have several of his Sonatas, among which his last are particularly noteworthy," which were written at least eight months before the Sonatas appeared in print, lead to the conclusion that they were known in Vienna in manuscript in the spring of 1795. Their appearance in print was announced in the *Weiner Zeitung* of March 9, 1796.

Still another anecdote recorded by Wegeler[28] refers to another composition of this period: "Beethoven was seated in a box at the opera with a lady of whom he thought much at a performance of *La Molinara*. When the familiar 'Nel cor più non mi sento' was reached the lady remarked that she had possessed some variations on the theme but had lost them. In the same night Beethoven wrote the six variations on the melody and the next morning sent them to the lady with the inscription: 'Variazioni, etc. Perdute par la—ritrovata par Luigi van Beethoven.' They are so easy that it is likely that Beethoven wished that she should be able to play them at sight." Paisiello's *La Molinara*, composed in 1788 for Naples, was performed on March 8, 1794 in the Court Opera, and again on June 24 and 27, 1795 in the Kärnthnerthor-Theater in Vienna. Considering the time of the publication of these unpretentious but genial little variations, their composition may be set down after the latter performances. At the same period, Beethoven wrote variations on another theme, "Quant' è più bello," from the same opera, which were published before the former and dedicated to Prince Karl Lichnowsky. It is likely that a few more sets of variations, a form of composition for which Beethoven had a strong predilection at the time, had their origin in these early years of Beethoven's life in Vienna. The Variations in C on the "Menuet à la Viganò" from the ballet *Le nozze disturbate*, may confidently be assigned to the year 1795. The ballet was performed for the first time on May 18, 1795, at Schikaneder's theatre; the Variations are advertised as published on February 27, 1796.

In 1828 Diabelli and Co. published a *Rondo a Capriccio* in G which had been purchased at the auction sale of Beethoven's effects after his death. It bore on the title page the inscription: "Die Wuth über den verloren Groschen, ausgetobt in einer Caprice" (Rage over the lost penny, stormed out in a Caprice). Later it received the opus number 129. The autograph of this work was recently discovered by Otto Albrecht in the possession of Mrs. E. A. Noble of Providence. Beethoven's original title was "Alla ingharese quasi un capriccio," and its more familiar title was added by Schindler. A study of the autograph was made by Eric Hertzmann, who concluded from the handwriting and from a comparison with the sketches of the

26 The first movement of Op. 2, No. 3 contains three themes borrowed from the same movement of the Piano Quartet in C (1785), WoO 36, III. (TDR, I, 408.)
27 Page 8.
28 *Notizen*, p. 80. (TDR, I, 408.)

period that it was written between 1795 and 1798. The published version by Diabelli obscured the fact that the composition was unfinished and that this was an arrangement containing discrepancies and omissions which was prepared after the composer's death.[29]⸳—

The Gesellschaft der bildenen Künstler had, in the year 1792, established an annual ball in the Redoutensaal in the month of November; and Haydn, just then returned covered with glory from England, composed a set of twelve minuets and twelve German dances for the occasion. In 1793, the Royal Imperial Composer Koželuch followed Haydn's example. In 1794, Dittersdorf wrote the same number of like dances for the large hall, and Eybler for the small. In view of this array of great names, and considering that as yet the Trios, Op. 1, were the only works of a higher order than the variations which Beethoven had sent to press, the advertisements for the annual ball to be given upon the 22nd of November, 1795, give a vivid proof of the high reputation which the young man had gained as a composer now at the end of his third year in Vienna. These advertisements conclude thus: "The music for the Minuets and German dances for this ball is an entirely new arrangement. For the larger room they were written by the Royal Imperial Kapellmeister Süssmayr; for the smaller room by the master hand of Hr. Ludwig van Beethoven out of love for the artistic fraternity." These dances, arranged for pianoforte by Beethoven himself, came from the press of Artaria a few weeks later, as did also Süssmayr's; Beethoven's name in the advertisement being in large and conspicuous type.

—⸳Besides the Twelve Minuets and Twelve German Dances for Orchestra, written for the Redoutensaal, Beethoven also wrote two sets of Six Minuets, which Kinsky-Halm assigns to this year.[30] The first set for two violins and bass was edited by Kinsky and published by Schott in Mainz (1933) from parts copied from the Artaria Collection by Erich Prieger. The second set has survived only in a piano transcription made by Beethoven for publication the following year. Thayer has recorded a notation by Dr. Sonnleithner in his *Verzeichniss* (p. 170): "These 6 minuets were indeed published by Artaria and Comp (?) but for the P-F; considering the content and the indication, 2nd part, it is most likely that they were composed for orchestra."

Thayer also lists three Canons which were published by both Seyfried and Nottebohm.[31] They were a part of the exercises for Albrechtsberger.⸳—

As the year began with the first, so it closed with Beethoven's second appearance in public as composer and virtuoso; and here is the advertisement of the performance from the *Wiener Zeitung* of December 16:

[29] See Otto Albrecht, "Adventures and Discoveries of a Manuscript Hunter," *MQ*, Vol. 31 (1945), p. 495; Erich Hertzmann, "The Newly Discovered Autograph of Beethoven's *Rondo à Capriccio*, Op. 129," *MQ*, Vol. 32 (1946), pp. 171-95. A new edition of the work from the original manuscript has been prepared by Hertzmann and was published in 1949 by G. Schirmer.

[30] See KHV, pp. 441-43.

[31] Thayer, *Verzeichniss*, p. 159; Seyfried, *Beethovens Studien*, pp. 327, 329, 331; Nottebohm, *Beethovens Studien*, pp. 191-93.

Next Friday, the 18th instant, Herr Kapellmeister Haydn will give a grand musical concert in the small Redoutensaal, at which Mad. Tomeni and Hr. Mombelli will sing. Hr. van Beethoven will play a Concerto of his composing on the Pianoforte, and three grand symphonies, not yet heard here, which the Kapellmeister composed during his last sojourn in London, will be performed.

One would gladly know what concerto was played.[32] But there was little public criticism then outside of London and very rarely any in Vienna. The mere fact of the appearance of Beethoven at his old master's concert is, however, another proof that too much stress has been laid upon a hasty word spoken by him to Ries. Haydn wanted Beethoven to put "Pupil of Haydn" on the title page of his first works. Beethoven was unwilling to do so because, as he said, "though he had taken some lessons from Haydn he had never learned anything from him." Nothing could be more natural than for Haydn, knowing nothing of the studies of his pupil with Schenk, to express such a wish in relation to the Sonatas dedicated to him, and equally natural that the author should refuse; but to add to the attractions of the concert was a very different matter—a graceful and delicate compliment which he could with pleasure make.

The compositions of the years 1793 to 1795 were:

1793-4. Rondo for Pianoforte and Violin, WoO 41.
  Trio for Strings, Op. 3.
  Three Trios for Pianoforte, Violin and Violoncello, Op. 1.
1794. Trio for Two Oboes and English Horn, Op. 87.
1794-5. Concerto No. 2 for Pianoforte and Orchestra in B-flat major, Op. 19 (1st version).
  Rondo a Capriccio for Pianoforte, Op. 129.
  Rondo for Pianoforte and Orchestra, WoO 6.
  Sextet for Strings and Horns, Op. 81b.
  Song. "Seufzer eines Ungeliebten" and "Gegenliebe" (text by G. A. Bürger), WoO 118.
  Three Sonatas for Pianoforte, Op. 2.
1795. Six Minuets for Orchestra, WoO 10.
  Six Minuets for Two Violins and Bass, WoO 9.
  Song. "Wer ist ein freier Mann?" (text by Pfeffel), WoO 117 (2nd version).
  Three Canons: WoO 159 and 160.
  Twelve German Dances for Orchestra, WoO 8.
  Twelve Minuets for Orchestra, WoO 7.
  Variations for Pianoforte on the "Minuet à la Viganò" from Haibel's *Le nozze disturbate*, WoO 68.
  Variations for Pianoforte on "Nel cor più non mi sento," from Paisiello's *La Molinara*, WoO 70.
  Variations for Pianoforte on "Quant' è più bello," from Paisiello's *La Molinara*, WoO 69.

[32] It was probably that in B-flat. See *II Beeth.*, p. 72. (TDR, I, 413, n. 1.)

There are also a number of Italian songs on texts by Metastasio which must be listed here, although the subject is not taken up until the next chapter. They are:

1792-4. Duet for Soprano and Tenor, "Bei labbri, che Amore" (text: *La gelosia*), WoO 99, No. 1.

Trio for Soprano, Alto and Bass, "Guira il nocchier" (text: *La gelosia*), WoO 99, No. 5b.

Trio for Soprano, Alto and Tenor, "Ma tu tremi" (text: *La tempesta*), WoO 99, No. 6.

1792-5. Duet for Soprano and Tenor, "Sei mio ben" (text: *Cantata 24*).[33]

Quartet for Soprano, Alto, Tenor and Bass, "Guira il nocchier" (text: *La gelosia*), version in C major.

Tenor Melody, "E pur fra le tempeste" (text: *La tempesta*).

1795. Song with Unison Chorus, "O care selve" (text: *Olimpiade*), WoO 119.

The following works were published between 1793 and 1795:

1793. By Artaria:

Variations for Pianoforte and Violin on "Se vuol ballare" from Mozart's *Le Nozze di Figaro*, dedicated to Eleonore von Breuning, WoO 40.

By Simrock in Bonn:

Variations for Pianoforte on "Es war einmal ein alter Mann," from Dittersdorf's *Das rote Käppchen*, WoO 66.

1794. By Simrock in Bonn:

Variations for Pianoforte, Four Hands, on a Theme by Count Waldstein, WoO 67.

1795. By Artaria:

Three Trios for Pianoforte, Violin and Violoncello, Op. 1, dedicated to Prince Karl von Lichnowsky.

Twelve German Dances for Orchestra, transcribed for Pianoforte, WoO 8.

Twelve Minuets for Orchestra, transcribed for Pianoforte, WoO 7.

By Traeg:

Variations for Pianoforte on "Quant' è più bello," from Paisiello's *La Molinara*, dedicated to Prince Karl Lichnowsky, WoO 69.

[33] See Hess, *Verzeichnis*, p. 60.

CHAPTER X

THE YEARS 1796 AND 1797

THE narrative resumes its course with the year 1796, the twenty-sixth of Beethoven's life and his fourth in Vienna. If not yet officially, he was *de facto* discharged from his obligations to the Elector Maximilian and all his relations with Bonn and its people were broken off. Vienna had become his home, and there is no reason to suppose that he ever afterwards cherished any real and settled purpose to exchange it for another—not even in 1809 when, for the moment, he had some thought of accepting Jerome Bonaparte's invitation to Cassel.

He had now finished his course of contrapuntal study with Albrechtsberger; he was first of the pianoforte players of the capital and his name added attraction even to the concert which Haydn, returning again from his London triumphs, had given to introduce some of his new works to the Viennese; his "masterhand" was already publicly recognized in the field of musical composition; he counted many nobles of the higher ranks in his list of personal friends and had been, perhaps even now was, a member of Prince Karl Lichnowsky's family. The change in his pecuniary condition might have thrown a more equitable temperament than his off its balance. Three years ago he anxiously noted down the few kreutzers occasionally spent for coffee or chocolate "für Haidn und mich"; now he was keeping his own servant and a horse.

Moreover, by this time the three Beethoven brothers had become reunited, for Vienna had become the new home of Caspar Anton Carl and Nikolaus Johann. Beethoven's first letter to Simrock of June 18, 1794 began: "Dear Simrock! My brother told me here that you had already printed my variations for four hands or surely would print them." By this time therefore Caspar Anton Carl had moved to Vienna, and it is prophetic that the first reference to him in correspondence should be in connection with the publication of one of Ludwig's compositions. Nikolaus Johann, the younger brother, made the move eighteen months later. An entry in the Regensburg record of arrivals and departures shows that there arrived on December 13, 1795 "2 Herren Gebrüder Breuning, Kaufleute von Bonn," and the next day "Herr Bathofen Mediziner aus Göttingen [sic]." Having met at Regensburg these three departed for Vienna on December 15th.[1] But according to police records they were held up in Linz from December 18th (the date that Ludwig was performing in Haydn's concert) to December 23rd because they lacked passes and had to be cleared by the police.[2] Due to this complication with the authorities, papers recording their arrival have been found in the Ministry of Justice in Vienna. The late Minister Kurt Smolle of Vienna[3] discovered two half-burned papers from which he was able to decipher: "concerning the brothers Joseph and [burnt] Breuning who left Bonn two years ago and Johann van B[burnt] who is coming direct from Bonn." This makes it clear that it was Johann and not Ludwig, as supposed by both Wegeler and Thayer, who was traveling with the Breuning brothers. In a letter to his mother in January, 1796, Stephan von Breuning wrote of his participation in this trip. But for the older brother to be referred to as "Joseph," instead of Christoph, as assumed by Wegeler, must remain a puzzle.[4] Dr. Smolle has established the day of their arrival in Vienna as December 26th.

The composer's brothers, if at all a burden, were no longer a heavy one. Carl Caspar, according to the best information now obtainable, soon gained moderate success in the musical profession and, with probably some occasional aid from Ludwig both pecuniary and in obtaining pupils, earned sufficient for his comfortable support; while Johann had secured a situation in that apothecary shop "Zum Heiligen Geist" which, in 1860, was still to be seen in the Kärnthnerstrasse near the former site of the gate of that name. His wages were, of course, small and we shall soon see that Ludwig offered him assistance if needed, though not to Carl; but Johann's position gradually improved and he was able in a few years to save enough to enable him, unaided by his brother, to purchase and establish himself in a business of his own.[5]

"Fate had become propitious to Beethoven"; and a final citation from the memorandum book will show in what spirit he was determined to merit the continuance of Fortune's favor. If we make allowance for the old error as to his real age, this citation may belong to a period a year or two later; but may it not be one of those extracts from books and periodical publications which all his life long he was so fond of making? This seems to be the more

<hr />

[1] See Eduard Panzerbieter, "Beethoven in Regensburg, 1795," *NBJ*, VI (1935), 48.

[2] This is mentioned by Wegeler in the *Notizen* supplement, 1906 edition, p. 216.

[3] To whom I am indebted for the information concerning both Linz and Vienna.

[4] Stephan's only other brother was, of course, Lorenz. However, Joseph was a middle name used more than once in the Breuning family in the preceding generation.

[5] Czerny described Beethoven's brothers to Otto Jahn as follows: "Carl: small of stature, red-haired, ugly; Johann: large, dark, a handsome man and complete dandy." (TDR, II, 6, n. 1.)

probable supposition. The words are these: "Courage! In spite of all bodily weaknesses my spirit shall rule. You have lived 25 years. This year must determine the complete man. Nothing must remain undone."

And now let the chronological narrative of events be resumed. As the year 1795 had ended with a public appearance of Beethoven as pianoforte player and composer, so also began the year 1796; and, as on a former occasion in a concert by Haydn, so this time he played at a concert given by a singer, Signora Bolla, who afterward became famous, in the Redoutensaal. Again he played a pianoforte concerto.

Also at this time he was doubtless occupied with the last corrections of the Sonatas, Op. 2, dedicated to Haydn, the six Minuets (second part), the Variations on the theme from *Le nozze disturbate* and those on "Nel cor più non mi sento," all of which works are advertised in the *Wiener Zeitung* in the course of the next two months.

---❧Meanwhile Beethoven had undertaken what turned out to be a concert tour lasting from February to July. Here follows the first record of this trip.❧---

To my brother Nikolaus Beethoven
to be delivered at the apothecary shop near the Kärthner Gate.
Hr. von Z. will please hand this letter to the wig-maker who will care for its delivery.

Prague, February 19 [1796]

Dear Brother!

So that you may now at least know where I am and what I am doing I must needs write you. In the first place I am getting on well—very well. My art wins for me friends and respect; what more do I want? This time, too, I shall earn considerable money. I shall remain here a few weeks more and then go to *Dresden, Leipzig and Berlin*. It will probably be six weeks more before I shall return—I hope that you will be more and more pleased with your sojourn in Vienna; but beware of the whole guild of wicked women. Have you yet called on *Cousin Elss*? You might write to me at this place if you have inclination and time.

P. Linowski will probably soon return to Vienna; he has already gone from here. If you need money you may go to him boldly, for he still owes me some. For the rest I hope that your life will grow continually in happiness and to that end I hope to contribute something. Farewell dear brother and think occasionally of

Your true faithful brother L. Beethoven

Greetings to Brother Caspar. My address is the Golden Unicorn on the Kleinseite.[6]

A debt of gratitude is certainly due Johann van Beethoven for having carefully preserved this letter for full half a century and leaving it to his heirs,

[6] The words "Greetings to Brother Caspar" were crossed out and Thayer believed this to have been done at the time of writing. "Hr. von Z" is doubtless Zmeskall, who is thus shown to have been a trusted friend in 1796. "P. Linowski" is Prince Lichnowsky. (TDR, II, 9, n. 2; cf. TK, I, 192, n. 1.) Kalischer (*Sämt. Briefe*, I, 22-23) suggests that the Prince was in debt to Beethoven through having subscribed for twenty copies of Op. 1.

notwithstanding all the troubles which afterwards arose between the brothers, since it is hardly more valuable and interesting for the facts which it states directly than for what it indicates and suggests more or less clearly.

It, with other considerations, render it well nigh certain that Beethoven had now come to Prague with Prince Lichnowsky as Mozart had done, seven years before, and that upon leaving Vienna he had had no intention of pursuing his journey farther; but encouraged by the success thus reported to his brother, he suddenly determined to seek instruction and experience, pleasure, profit and fame in an extended tour.

The musical public of Prague was the same that had so recently honored itself by its instant and noble appreciation of Mozart, and had given so glorious a welcome to *Figaro, Don Giovanni* and *Titus*. There being no royal or imperial court there, and the public amusements being less numerous than in Vienna, the nobility were thrown more on their own resources for recreation; and hence, besides the traditional taste of the Bohemians for instrumental music, their capital was, perhaps, a better field for the virtuoso than Vienna. "The considerable money" to be earned would be the presents of the nobility for his performances in their salons, and, perhaps, for composition.

The conception of the aria "Ah, perfido! spergiuro" is generally associated with Beethoven's sojourn in Prague. The belief rests upon the fact that upon the cover of a copy which he revised Beethoven wrote the words "Une grande Scène mise en musique par L. v. Beethoven à Prague, 1796." On the first page is written: "Recitativo e Aria composta e dedicata alla Signora Contessa di Clari da L. v. Beethoven." Now, on November 21st, 1796, Madame Duschek, the well known friend of Mozart, at a concert in Leipzig sang "An Italian Scena composed for Madame Duschek by Beethoven," and it was easy to conclude that the aria was really written by Beethoven for Madame Duschek. On a page of sketches preserved in Berlin among others there are sketches belonging to "Ah, perfido!" which do not agree with the printed page. On the lower margin of the first page is the remark: "pour Mademoiselle la Comtesse de Clari." Nottebohm (*II Beeth.*, p. 222) was led by these things to surmise that the aria was written in Vienna in 1795, before the visit to Prague. In any case, we are permitted to associate the date 1796 only with the completion of the work in Prague; and the purpose may well have been to have it sung by Madame Duschek, who is thus proved to have belonged to the circle of Beethoven's friends in Prague. Nevertheless, the aria was originally intended for the Countess Josephine Clary, a well known amateur singer who married Count Christian Clam-Gallas in 1797. The scena first appeared in print in the fall of 1805, when it was published in a collection made by Hoffmeister and Kühnel. Beethoven placed it upon the programme of his concert in 1808.

Another family in which Beethoven was received on the footing of a friend was that of Appellate Councillor Kanka. Both father and son were dilettante composers and instrumental players—the father on the violoncello, the son on the pianoforte. Gerber gives them a place in his Lexicon. "Miss Jeanette" (the daughter), says the eulogistic Schönfeld, "played the pianoforte with great expression and skill." The son adopted his father's profession, and became a distinguished writer on Bohemian law, and in later years did Beethoven good service as legal adviser.

That Beethoven carried out his intention of stopping at Dresden is shown by two letters, discovered by Braubach,[7] from the music dilettante Chamberlain von Schall to the Elector Max Franz. From the first, dated April 24, 1796: "The young Beethoven arrived here [Dresden] yesterday. He had letters from Vienna for Count Elz; he will play for the court and then go from here to Leipzig-Berlin. He is said to have improved immensely and to compose well. . . ." From the second, dated May 6th: "Beethoven has delayed here almost eight days, everyone who heard him play was enchanted. Beethoven was granted by the Elector of Saxony, a man who knows music, the favor to play in the evening all alone without accompaniment for an hour and a half.[8] H.R.H. was exceedingly well satisfied and presented him with a golden *tabatière*. Beethoven went from here to Leipzig and Berlin. . . ." In his answer Maximilian Franz hopes that "Beethoven will profit more from his trip than Simonetti who was applauded everywhere but never presented with a gift."

While there is no record of Beethoven's arrival in Leipzig, it can be assumed from von Schall's letter that he left Dresden approximately eight days after his arrival on April 23rd and reached his next stop about May 1st or 2nd. In a letter to Breitkopf and Härtel of July 5, 1806, Beethoven refers to his acquaintance with the Leipzig musician, August Eberhard Müller, which presumably was made at this time. One assumes along with Schindler that the master's memory was faulty in his conversation in 1822 with Rochlitz, summarized by the latter:[9] "He began by praising Leipzig and its music. . . . Otherwise he knew nothing of Leipzig and had only passed through the city when a *youth* on his way to Vienna." If the stop was not until 1796, which seems likely, it was clearly of short duration.

His next appearance was in Berlin. In after years he was fond of talking about his sojourn there, and some particulars have thus been preserved. "He played," says Ries (*Notizen*, p. 109), "several times at the court (that of King Frederick William II), where he played the two grand sonatas with obbligato violoncello, Op. 5, written for Duport, first violoncellist of the King, and himself. On his departure he received a gold snuff-box filled with Louis d'ors. Beethoven declared with pride that it was not an ordinary

---

[7] See Schiedermair, *op.cit.*, pp. 320-21.

[8] From court records Volkmann has discovered that the date of this audience was April 29. See Hans Volkmann, *Beethoven . . . Bezieh-*

ungen zu Dresden (Dresden, 1942), p. 24.

[9] Friedrich Johann Rochlitz, *Für Freunde der Tonkunst* (Leipzig and Cnobloch, 1832), IV, pp. 339ff.

snuff-box, but such a one as it might have been customary to give to an ambassador."

This king shared the love for music of his uncle, Frederick the Great, while his taste was better and more cultivated. His instrument was the violoncello, and he often took part in quartets and sometimes in the rehearsals of Italian operas. He exerted a powerful and enduring influence for good upon the musical taste of Berlin. It was he who caused the operas of Gluck and Mozart to be performed there and introduced oratorios of Handel into the court concerts. His appreciations of Mozart's genius, and his wish to attach that great master to his court, are well known; and these facts render credible a statement with which Carl Czerny closes a description of Beethoven's extemporaneous playing, contributed to Cocks's *London Musical Miscellany* (August 2, 1852): "His improvisation was most brilliant and striking. In whatever company he might chance to be, he knew how to produce such an effect upon every hearer that frequently not an eye remained dry, while many would break out into loud sobs; for there was something wonderful in his expression in addition to the beauty and originality of his ideas and his spirited style of rendering them. After ending an improvisation of this kind he would burst into loud laughter and banter his hearers on the emotion he had caused in them. 'You are fools!' he would say. Sometimes he would feel himself insulted by these indications of sympathy. 'Who can live among such spoiled children?' he would cry, and only on that account (as he told me) he declined to accept an invitation which the King of Prussia gave him after one of the extemporary performances above described."

Kapellmeister Reichardt had withdrawn himself from Berlin two years before, having fallen into disfavor because of his sympathy with the French Revolution. Neither Himmel nor Righini, his successors, ever showed a genius for chamber music of a high order, and, indeed, there was no composer of reputation in this sphere then living in that quarter. The young Beethoven by his two sonatas had proved his powers and the King may have seen in him precisely the right man to fill the vacancy—no small proof of superior taste and judgment. What the German expression was which the translator of Czerny's letter has rendered "accept an invitation which the King gave him" there is no means of knowing; but as it stands it suggests an invitation to enter permanently into his service. The death of the King the next year, of course, prevented its being ever renewed.

Friedrich Heinrich Himmel, five years older than Beethoven, whom the King had withdrawn from the study of theology and caused to be thoroughly educated as a musician, first under Naumann in Dresden and afterwards in Italy, had returned the year before and had assumed his duties as Royal Pianist and Composer. As a virtuoso on his instrument his only rival in Berlin was Prince Louis Ferdinand, son of Prince August and nephew of Frederick II, two years younger than Beethoven and endowed by nature with talents and genius which would have made him conspicuous had fortune not given him royal descent. He and Beethoven became well known to each other and each felt and did full justice to the other's musical genius and attainments. Now let Ries speak again (*Notizen*, p. 110): "In Berlin he [Beethoven] associated much with Himmel, of whom he said that he had a pretty talent, but no more; his pianoforte playing, he said, was elegant and pleasing, but he was not to be compared with Prince Louis Ferdinand. In his opinion he paid the latter a high compliment when once he said to him that his playing was not that of a king or prince but more like that of a thoroughly good pianoforte player. He fell out with Himmel in the following manner: One day when they were together Himmel begged Beethoven to improvise; which Beethoven did. Afterwards Beethoven insisted that Himmel do the same. The latter was weak enough to agree; but after he had played for quite a time Beethoven remarked: 'Well, when are you going fairly to begin?' Himmel had flattered himself that he had already performed wonders; he jumped up and the men behaved ill towards each other. Beethoven said to me: 'I thought that Himmel had been only preluding a bit.'[10] Afterwards they were reconciled, indeed, but Himmel could never forgive or forget. They also exchanged letters until Himmel played Beethoven a shabby trick. The latter always wanted to know the news from Berlin. This bored Himmel, who at last wrote that the greatest news from Berlin was that a lamp for the blind had been invented. Beethoven ran about with the news and all the world wanted to know how this was possible. Thereupon he wrote to Himmel that he had blundered in not giving more explicit information. The answer which he received, but which does not permit of communication, not only put an end to the correspondence but brought ridicule upon Beethoven, who was so inconsiderate as to show it then and there."

With Carl Fredrich Christian Fasch and Carl Friedrich Zelter he also made a friendly acquaintance, and twice at least attended meetings of the Singakademie, which then numbered about 90 voices. The first time, June 21st, says the *Geschichte der Singakademie* (Berlin, 1843), "A chorale, the first three numbers of a mass [by Fasch] and the first six of the 119th Psalm were sung for him. Hereupon he seated himself at the pianoforte and played an improvisation on the theme of the final fugue: 'Meine Zunge rühmt im Wettgesang dein Lob.' The last numbers of 'Davidiana' [a collection of versets by Fasch] formed the conclusion. No biographer has mentioned this visit or even his sojourn in Berlin. Nor does Fasch pay special attention to it; but the performance must have pleased, for Beethoven repeated it at the next meeting on June 28th."

[10] Beethoven told the story to Mme. von Arnim with the additional particular that they were walking in *Unter den Linden* and went thence to a private room of the principal coffee-house where there was a pianoforte, for the exhibition of their skill. (TDR, II, 16.)

The performance of the Society must also have pleased Beethoven, and with good reason; for Fasch's mass was in sixteen parts and the psalm and "Davidiana," in part, in eight; and no such music was then to be heard elsewhere north of the Alps.

In 1810, Beethoven, speaking of his playing on that occasion, told Mme. von Arnim (then Elizabeth Brentano) that at the close his hearers did not applaud but came crowding around him weeping; and added (ironically?), "that is not what we artists wish—we want applause!" Fasch's simple record of Beethoven's visit is this:

June 21, 1796. Hr. van Beethoven extemporized on the "Davidiana," taking the fugue theme from Ps. 119, No. 16. . . . Hr. Beethoven, pianist from Vienna, was so accommodating as to permit us to hear an improvisation. . . . June 28, Hr. van Beethoven was again so obliging as to play an improvisation for us.

Early in July, the king left Berlin for the baths of Pyrmont, the nobility dispersed to their estates or to watering places, and the city "was empty and silent." Beethoven, therefore, could have had no inducement to prolong his stay; but the precise time of his departure is unknown.

Notwithstanding Wegeler's statement (*Notizen*, p. 28) that he left Beethoven a member of the family of Prince Lichnowsky "in the middle of 1796," it is as certain as circumstantial evidence can well make it that the Doctor and Christoph von Breuning had returned to Bonn before Beethoven reached Vienna again; but Stephan and Lenz were still there. The former obtained at this time an appointment in the Teutonic Order, which so many of his ancestors had served, and his name appears in the published "Calendars of the order" from 1797 to 1803, both inclusive, as "Hofrathsassessor." He then soon departed from Vienna to Mergentheim, whence he wrote (November 23rd) with other matters the following upon Beethoven to Wegeler and Christoph:[11] "I do not know whether or not Lenz has written you anything about Beethoven; but take notice that I saw him in Vienna and that according to my mind, which Lenz has confirmed, he has become somewhat staider, or, perhaps I should say, has acquired more knowledge of humanity through travels (or was it because of the new ebullition of friendship upon his arrival?) and a greater conviction of the scarceness and value of good friends. A hundred times, dear Wegeler, he wishes you here again, and regrets nothing so much as that he did not follow much of your advice."

Except this notice of his bearing and demeanor, there is a complete hiatus in Beethoven's history from his appearance in the Singakademie until the following November. The so-called Fischoff manuscript has a story of a "dangerous illness," which was caused by his own imprudence this summer. "In the year 1796, Beethoven, on a hot summer day, came greatly overheated to his home, threw open doors and windows, disrobed down to his trousers and cooled himself in a draft at the open window. The consequence was a

[11] *Notizen*, Nachtrag, pp. 19-20. (TDR, II, 19.)

dangerous illness, which, on his convalescence, settled in his organs of hearing, and from this time on his deafness steadily increased."

--⁕{A sickness of the gravity here described seems somewhat improbable in this year in view of the further travels which Beethoven made in the following autumn. We reconsider this notice in connection with the summer of 1797.}⁕-- The most plausible suggestion is that coming back, flushed with victory with the success of his tour, and delighted with the novelty of traveling at his ease, Beethoven made an excursion to Pressburg and Pesth, of which afterwards Ries was informed and made record (*Notizen*, p. 109): "Beethoven hardly traveled at all. In his younger years, near the end of the century, he was once in Pressburg and Pesth [Budapest] and once in Berlin." --⁕{That the trip to Pressburg and Budapest took place about four months after his return from Berlin has come to light from a letter written by Beethoven while in Pressburg to Andreas Streicher, dated November 19, 1796, which refers to a concert to be given there by Beethoven on the 23rd. Meanwhile, Frimmel had discovered a reference to "Beethoven's stay with Heinrich Klein at Pressburg" in an article by Johann Batka, director of the city archives at Pressburg, which undoubtedly refers to this visit.[12] Having investigated the source of this fact, Frimmel points out that Beethoven's friend, the pianist Johann Nepomuk Hummel, was from Pressburg, was a member of the Klein circle, and consequently may have been instrumental in bringing Klein and the composer together. He was highly respected as a musician in Pressburg; and a continuation of his friendship with Beethoven is shown by the fact that in the Conversation Books of 1819 reference is made to two visits from "Professor Klein of Pressburg."

To return to the letter to Andreas Streicher, it was first published with a facsimile by Oscar Sonneck.[13] It is here given in full because of its interest concerning the composer's attitude towards the piano, and his relation with the Streichers:

Dear Streicher!

The day before yesterday I received your fortepiano which has turned out to be really excellent. Everyone else is anxious to own one, and I—you can laugh all right, I would be lying were I not to tell you that it is too good for me, and why?—because it takes away my freedom to create the tone for myself. Nevertheless it will not keep you from making all your fortepianos in this way, there will probably be fewer people who have such whims.

My Academy takes place on Wednesday, the 23rd of this m[onth]. If *Stein* would care to come I will be very glad to see him, he can count on spending

---

[12] *Beethoven Studien* (Munich and Leipzig, 1906), II, pp. 33ff. Frimmel wrote to Batka to verify the source of the statement and learned that "an old double-bass player, Sebastiani, who had once played the C minor Symphony under Beethoven and then had come to the Pressburg Theatre Orchestra, had spoken of this visit by Beethoven."

[13] From *Beethoven's Letters in America* by Oscar Sonneck, copyright, 1927, by G. Schirmer, Inc.

the night at my house.—Concerning the sale of the fortepiano, this idea had already occurred to me before it had to you and I shall certainly strive to bring it about.—I thank you heartily dear St. for your readiness to serve me so well. I only wish that I were able in some way to return your kindness, and that you, without my having to say it to you, were convinced how much I want the worth of your instruments to become recognized both here and everywhere, and how much I value your friendship and want you to regard me as your loving and warm friend

Beethoven

Pressburg November 19th anno 96 post Christum Natum

Everything lovely to your wife and to the *bride and bridegroom*.

The reader will not have forgotten Marie Anna Stein of Augsburg—pianoforte-maker Stein's "Mädl," as Mozart called her. After the death of her father (February 29, 1792), she, being then just 23 years of age, assisted by her brother, Matthäus Andreas, a youth of sixteen years, took charge of and continued his business. The great reputation of the Stein instruments led to the removal of the Steins to Vienna. It is known that Beethoven, immediately upon their arrival, renewed his intercourse with them. An imperial patent, issued January 17, 1794, empowered Nanette and Andreas Stein to establish their business "in the Landstrasse 301, zur Rothen Rose," and in the following July they arrived, accompanied by Johann Andreas Streicher, an "admirable pianist and teacher" of Munich, to whom Nanette was engaged. The business flourished nobly under the firm-name "Geschwister Stein" until 1802, "when they separated and each carried on an independent business."

To Thayer's account may be added a few details concerning Andreas Streicher. Frimmel has established that he arrived in Augsburg in 1793 and married Nanette on January 7, 1794, before their move to Vienna in July.[14] The mention of the "bride and bridegroom" does not refer to the Streichers but to Nanette's brother, Matthäus Stein and his wife, Maria Josefa Dischler. They were married just a week before this letter was written. That Streicher was involved in the pianoforte business before the separation of the Steins is shown by his having sent a pianoforte to Hungary, the sale of which he hoped would be furthered by Beethoven's performance upon it.

From another letter to Streicher, undated, and also published for the first time by Sonneck,[15] a further insight is gained of Beethoven's attitude towards the pianoforte. This much can appropriately be included here: "It is certain that the manner of playing the *pianoforte* is still the most uncultivated of all instruments. Often one believes to hear only a harp, and I am glad, my dear, that you are one of the few who comprehend and feel that one may sing on the pianoforte too, if one is but capable of feeling. I hope

[14] See *FRBH* (Leipzig, 1926), II, 263. See also Otto E. Deutsch, "Neue Beethoven-Briefens Amerika," *Neues Wiener Journal*, May 15, 1927, pp. 6ff.

[15] *Op.cit.*, 184-85.

that the time will come when the harp and the pianoforte will be two totally different instruments."

November, 1796, also marked the publication of a minor work of the composer. — This was the year of that astounding series of victories ending at Arcole, gained by the young French general Napoleon Bonaparte. The Austrian government and people alike saw and feared the danger of invasion, a general uprising took place and volunteer corps were formed in all quarters. For the Vienna corps, Friedelburg wrote his "Abschiedsgesang an Wiens Bürger beim Auszug der Fahnen-Division der Wiener Freiwilliger," and Beethoven set it to music. The original printed edition bears date "November 15, 1796." It does not appear to have gained any great popularity, and a drinking-song ("Lasst das Herz uns froh erheben") was afterwards substituted for Friedelberg's text, and published by Schott in Mainz.

The rapid progress of the French army had caused the Germans in Italy to become distrustful of the future and to hasten homeward. Among them were Beethoven's old companions in the Bonn orchestra, the cousins Andreas and Bernhard Romberg, who in the spring of this year (May 26th), had kissed the hand of the Queen of Naples, daughter of the Empress Maria Theresia, and then departed to Rome to join another friend of the Bonn period, Karl Kügelgen. The three coming north arrived at Vienna in the autumn; the Rombergs remained there for a space with Beethoven, while Kügelgen proceeded to Berlin. Baron von Braun—not to be mistaken for Beethoven's "first Maecenas" the Russian Count Browne—had heard the cousins the year before in Munich and invited them "to give Vienna an opportunity to hear them." There is no notice of their concert in the Vienna newspapers of the period, and the date is unknown. From Lenz von Breuning is gleaned an additional fact which alone gives interest to the concert for us. He writes to Wegeler in January, 1797:[16] "Beethoven is here again; he played in the Romberg concert. He is the same as of old and I am glad that he and the Rombergs still get along with each other. Once he was near a break with them; I interceded and achieved my end to a fair extent. Moreover, he thinks a great deal of me just now."

It is clear that the Rombergs, under the circumstances, must have largely owed their limited success to Beethoven's name and influence. In February, 1797, they were again in their old positions in Schroeder's orchestra in Hamburg.

Beethoven during this winter must be imagined busily engaged with pupils and private concerts, perhaps also with his operatic studies with Salieri, certainly with composition and with preparation for and the oversight of various works then passing through the press; for in February and April (1797) Artaria advertised the two Violoncello Sonatas, Op. 5, the

[16] Not 1796, as erroneously printed in the Appendix to the *Notizen*, p. 20. (TDR, II, 20, n. 1.)

Pianoforte Sonata for four hands, Op. 6 and the Twelve Variations on a Danse Russe;[17] these last are the variations which he dedicated to the Countess Browne and which gave occasion for the anecdote related by Ries illustrating Beethoven's forgetfulness; for this dedication he had "received a handsome riding-horse from Count Browne as a gift. He rode the animal a few times, soon after forgot all about it and, worse than that, its food also. His servant, who soon noticed this, began to hire out the horse for his own benefit and, in order not to attract the attention of Beethoven to the fact, for a long time withheld from him all bills for fodder. At length, however, to Beethoven's great amazement he handed in a very large one, which recalled to him at once his horse and his neglectfulness." (*Notizen*, p. 120.)

On Thursday, April 6, 1797, Schuppanzigh gave a concert, on the programme of which Beethoven's name figured twice. Number 2 was an "Aria by Hr. van Beethoven, sung by Mad. Willmann"; No. 5 was a "Quintet for Pianoforte and 4 wind-instruments, played and composed by Hr. L. v. Beethoven." This was the beautiful Quintet, Op. 16, the time of whose origin is thus indicated.

But the war was renewed and the thoughts of the Viennese were occupied with matters more serious than the indulgence of their musical taste. On the 16th of March, Bonaparte forced the passage of the Tagliamento and Isonzo. During the two weeks following he had conquered the greater part of Carniola, Carinthia and the Tyrol and was now rapidly approaching Vienna. On the 11th of February, Lorenz Leopold Hauschka's "Gott erhalte unsern Kaiser" with Haydn's music had been sung for the first time in the theatre and now, when on April 7th the Landsturm was called out, Friedelberg produced his war-song "Ein grosses, deutsches Volk sind wir," to which Beethoven also gave music. The printed copy bears the date April 14th, suggesting the probability that it was sung on the occasion of the grand consecration of the banners, which took place on the Glacis on the 17th. Beethoven's music was, however, far from being so fortunate as Haydn's, and seems to have gained as little popularity as his previous attempt; but as the preliminaries to a treaty of peace were signed at Leoben on the 18th, and the armies, so hastily improvised, were dismissed three weeks afterwards, the taste for war-songs vanished.

The little that is known of Beethoven's position as a teacher at this period is very vague and unsatisfactory; enough, however, to render it sufficiently certain that he had plenty of pupils, many of them young ladies of high rank who paid him generously. In the triple capacity of teacher, composer and pianist his gains were large and he was able to write in May to Wegeler that he was doing well and steadily better.

It is very possible that the illness mentioned by the Fischoff manuscript may have occurred during this summer. There can be little doubt that the

[17] Artaria also advertised the Trio, Op. 3 and the Quintet, Op. 4 as "completely new"; however, they had already appeared in the spring of 1796. See KHV, pp. 10-12.

original authority for the statement is Zmeskall, and therefore the fact of such an attack may be accepted as certain. But the date, as well as the inference that in it lay the original cause of the composer's subsequent loss of hearing, must be left mainly to conjecture.

From May to October, 1797, Beethoven's history is still a blank and nothing but the utter silence of Lenz von Breuning in his correspondence with his family at Bonn on a topic so likely to engage his sympathies as the dangerous illness of his friend, appears to prevent the filling of this blank in part by throwing him upon a bed of sickness. True, Lenz may have written and the letter have been lost or destroyed; or he may have neglected to write because of his approaching departure from Vienna, which took place in the autumn. His album, still preserved, has among its contributors Ludwig and Johann van Beethoven and Zmeskall. Ludwig wrote as follows:

> Truth exists for the wise,
> Beauty for a feeling heart.
> They belong to each other.[18]

Dear, good Breuning,
Never shall I forget the time which I spent with you *in Bonn* as well as here. Hold fast your friendship for me, you will always find me the same.

Your true friend L. v. Beethoven

Vienna 1797
the 1st of October.

They never met again. Lenz died on April 10th of the following year.

In November, Beethoven enjoyed a singular compliment paid him by the association of the Bildende Künstler—a repetition of his dances composed two years before for the artists' ball; and on the 23rd of December, he again contributed to the attractions of the Widows and Orphans Concert by producing the Variations for two Oboes and English Horn on "Là ci darem la mano," played by Czerwenka, Reuter and Teimer.

We come to a consideration of the facts touching the compositions of the years 1796 and 1797.

Among the most widely known of these is "Adelaide." The composition of this song must have been begun in the first half of 1795, if not earlier, for sketches of it are found among the exercises in double counterpoint written for Albrechtsberger. Other sheets containing sketches for "Adelaide" and the setting of Bürger's "Seufzer eines Ungeliebten" are preserved in the library of the Gesellschaft der Musikfreunde in Vienna and the British Museum in London.[19] The song was published by Artaria in 1797, under the title "Adelaide von Matthisson. Eine Kantate für eine Singstimme mit Begleitung des Klaviers. In Musik gesetzt und dem Verfasser gewidmet von Ludwig van

---

[18] From Schiller's *Don Carlo*, Act IV, Scene 21, Marquis of Posa to the Queen. (*Sämtliche*   *Werke, Säkular-Ausgabe*, IV, 230.)
[19] See *II Beeth.*, pp. 535-39. (TDR, II, 24.)

Beethoven." The opus number 46 was given to it later. In 1800 Beethoven sent a copy of the song to the poet and accompanied it with the following letter:

Most honored Sir!

You are herewith receiving from me a composition which has been in print for several years, but concerning which you probably, to my shame, know nothing. Perhaps I can excuse myself and explain how it came about that I dedicated something to you which came so warmly from my heart yet did not inform you of the fact, by saying that at first I was unaware of your place of residence, and partly also I was diffident, not knowing but that I had been over-hasty in dedicating a work to you without knowing whether or not it met with your approval. Even now I send you Adelaide with some timidity. You know what changes are wrought by a few years in an artist who is continually going forward; the greater the progress one makes in art the less one is satisfied with one's older works.—My most ardent wish will be fulfilled if my musical setting of your heavenly Adelaide does not wholly displease you, and if it should move you soon to write another poem of its kind, and you, not finding my request too immodest, should send it to me at once, I will put forth all my powers to do your beautiful poetry justice. Look upon the dedication as partly a token of the delight which the composition of your A. gave me, partly as an evidence of my gratitude and respect for the blessed pleasure which your poetry has always given *and always will give* me.

Vienna, August 4th, 1800.

When playing A[delaide] sometimes recall
   your sincere admirer   Beethoven

Whether or not Matthisson answered this letter is not known; but when he republished "Adelaide" in the first volume of his collected poems in 1815, he appended to it a note to this effect: "Several composers have vitalized this little lyric fantasy with music; but according to my strong conviction none of them so threw the text into the shade with his melody as the highly gifted Ludwig van Beethoven in Vienna."

The "Opferlied," the words of which were also written by Matthisson, is one of the poems to which Beethoven repeatedly recurred. "It seems always to have presented itself to him as a prayer," says Nottebohm. Its last words, "The beautiful to the good," were written in autograph albums even in his later years.

 Herbst[20] believes that his preoccupation with this text could have started in the Bonn period since the poem was published in 1790, and proceeds to show the existence of four distinct musical versions. The two later versions with orchestral accompaniment will concern us hereafter. The first setting for voice and piano is an unpublished autograph in Berlin (Grasnick 8), a single page with unidentified sketches on the other side, which were added later when the song was no longer of use. Since the

---

[20] Kurt Herbst, "Beethovens Opferliedkompositionen," *NBJ*, v (1933), pp. 137ff.

sketches are in the style of Beethoven's early piano sonatas and trios, it is to be dated at the latest in the first Vienna years. This must have been the version for which Wegeler substituted a Masonic text in 1797 (*Notizen,* p. 67).

Sketches for the second version (Grasnick 1 sketchbook) are easily distinguished from those for the first and fourth version by the opening figure:

They appear close to sketches for the arietta "Der Kuss" in the Grasnick 1 sketchbook, which has been generally dated 1798-99.[21] This version was not published until 1808 along with two other songs by Simrock.

Here mention must also be made of two arias which Beethoven wrote for introduction in Umlauf's comic opera *Die schöne Schusterin.* The two songs composed by Beethoven are an arietta, or rather strophic song, "O welch' ein Leben," for tenor, and an aria, "Soll ein Schuh nicht drücken?" for soprano. The words of the latter are in the original libretto. The words of the tenor song, though not part of the original text, were obviously written for the opera. The melody was also used by Beethoven as a setting for Goethe's "Mailied," one of eight songs which were published in 1805, as Op. 52. Both songs, as written for the opera, were published for the first time in the Complete Edition of Beethoven's works from the copies preserved in the Berlin Library. Sketches found by Nottebohm prove that these two contributions to the opera were composed in Vienna. A sketch of the first aria is found among the sketches for the sonata Op. 10, no. 1, the variations on "Une fièvre brûlante" and the two variations on "Là ci darem." Nottebohm dates these sketches from the middle of 1796 to the end of 1797. Considering the date of the revival of the opera (April, 1795), one may date the origin of both songs in the year 1796.[22]

In his *Beethovens Studien,* Nottebohm has analysed in detail the study in setting Italian texts which Beethoven received from Salieri. The autographs of these songs have been restudied by Willy Hess, and the following is based on the findings of these two men.[23] Beethoven's Italian songs can be divided into those that are *a cappella,* written mostly between 1793 and 1797, and those with accompaniment, most of which were written from the

[21] *II Beeth.,* p. 478.

[22] *Ibid.,* pp. 29-31. (TDR, II, 30, n. 2)

[23] *Beethovens Studien* (Lpz. 1873), pp. 207-32. See also Hess, "24 unbekannte italienische A-cappella-Gesänge Beethovens," *DM,* Vol. 33 (1941), pp. 240ff; and "Welche Werke Beethovens fehlen in der Breitkopf und Härtelschen Gesamtausgabe?" in *NBJ,* VII, pp. 122-25.

middle 1790's to 1802.[24] Here we will list only those composed before 1798.

Beethoven wrote two arias for soprano and orchestra. One is "Ah perfido!", Op. 65, which has already been mentioned. The other is "Primo amore," which is to be found as No. 8 in Series 25 of the Collected Works. Nothing is known about the work beyond the fact that a copy of the song was found in the Artaria Collection[25] marked "dal L. v. B." Presumably it was written during the period in which Beethoven was studying with Salieri. The similarity in concept to "Ah perfido!" makes it also a possible candidate for "An Italian Scena composed for Madame Duschek by Beethoven."

For voice with piano accompaniment there are two songs set to texts by Metastasio, "O care selve" and "La partenza." The first,[26] which Thayer believed was begun in Bonn, is dated by Nottebohm at the same time as the second version of "Der freie Mann," 1794-95. "La partenza" was written later at the same time as "Zärtliche Liebe," with which it was published in 1803. (See GA, Serie 23, No. 38.)

Nottebohm has established the following chronological order for the numerous *a cappella* settings on Metastasio texts of this period. There are three songs written before Beethoven first shows in "O care selve" that he is familiar with elision in Italian. They are the duet "Bei labbri che Amore"; the terzett "Guira il nocchier"; and the terzett "Ma tu tremi," which can thus all be dated 1793-94. From the improved text treatment the following can be dated 1795 or after: the terzett "Per te d'amico aprile," the two quartet settings of "Nei campi e nelle selve" and the duet "Scrivo in te" (text unknown). Nottebohm dates the next group 1797 at the latest because sketches have been found along with those for the Serenade, Op. 25:[27] the three versions of "Fra tutte le pene" for duet, terzett and quartet; the duet "Salvo tu vuoi lo sposo";[28] and the terzett and quartet settings of "Quella cetra ah pur tu sei."

In a supplement to the collected works, Hess has published Beethoven's unaccompanied Italian songs for more than one voice.[29] This source reveals three more songs written before 1798 from autographs in the Artaria Collection and the Gesellschaft der Musikfreunde: another setting for quartet (in

[24] Of the 32 Italian songs listed in Thayer's *Verzeichniss*, 264, numbers 7-15 are not by Beethoven but by Cornet and Doblof, and numbers 1-19 and 22 are listed with accompaniments which, however, were supplied by Randhartinger.

[25] According to Kinsky, KHV, p. 548, two other copies served also as sources: one owned privately in Vienna and the other by the *Steiermärk-Musikverein* in Graz.

[26] See GA, Serie 25, No. 16. It is not clear where Thayer got a four-part version of this song (*Verzeichniss*, p. 164). His musical quote is similar to the solo version and the "Coro, Solo" idea is there represented but by a chorus

in unison. A three-part canon without text on a similar melody is quoted by Nottebohm from a page of Beethoven's exercises with Albrechtsberger (pp. 192-93).

[27] Nottebohm argues 1797 as a likely date for this serenade since it is known that Beethoven's other serenade, Op. 8, was published and therefore probably composed in this year. KHV dates Op. 25 as 1795-96.

[28] Hess points out that the only available autograph of this duet (in the Berlin Library) exists as a sketch.

[29] *Beethoven Supplemente zur Gesamtausgabe I*, Willy Hess, ed. (Wiesbaden, 1959).

C major) of "Guira il nocchier," the duet "Sei mio ben," and a tenor melody "E pur fra le tempesta" (which Hess has supplied with a pianoforte accompaniment). From sketches and a fair copy of all these, they may be dated among the earlier songs.

Most important of the instrumental compositions of this period is the Quintet for Strings, Op. 4, which is frequently set down as an arrangement (or revised transcription) of the Octet, Op. 103. The Quintet, however, though it employs the same *motivi* as the Octet, is an entirely new work, made so by the radical changes of structure—changes of register to adapt the themes to the stringed instruments and changes in the themes themselves.[30] The origin of the Quintet can be placed in the early Vienna years, most probably just before the spring of 1796, when it was published. It was advertised along with Opus 3, 5 and 46 as "wholly new" by Artaria in the *Wiener Zeitung* of February 6, 1797.

The two Sonatas for Pianoforte and Violoncello, Op. 5, belong to the year 1796, and are the fruits of the visit to Berlin. There is no reason to question Ries's story that Beethoven composed them for Pierre Duport and played them with him. The dedication to Friedrich Wilhelm II and the character of the works lend credibility to Ries's account of their origin. Beethoven played them with Bernhard Romberg in Vienna at the close of 1796 or beginning of 1797, and they were published soon afterward, being advertised by Artaria in the *Wiener Zeitung* of February 8, 1797. The Twelve Variations on a theme from Handel's *Judas Maccabaeus*, were published by Artaria in 1797, dedicated to the Princess Lichnowsky, née Countess Thun. There were no performances of Handel's oratorios in Vienna at this time, but it is not improbable that the suggestion for the Variations came from Baron van Swieten.

Here seems to be the place to refer to the Allegro movement in sonata form for viola and violoncello which Beethoven gave the title, "Duett mit zwei Augengläsern obligato von L. v. Beethoven" (Duet with two Eyeglasses obbligato, by L. v. Beethoven), to be found in the volume of sketches from this period (1784-1800) which the British Museum bought from J. N. Kafka in 1875.[31] The two players "with two eyeglasses obbligato" were probably Beethoven and Zmeskall.[32]

The Sextet for Wind-Instruments (2 clarinets, 2 bassoons, 2 horns), published by Breitkopf and Härtel in 1810 (it received the opus number 71 later), belongs to this period. Sketches for the last movement, which differ from

[30] See Alfred Orel, "Beethovens Oktett Op. 103 und seine Bearbeitung als Quintett Op. 4," *Zeitschrift für Musikwissenschaft*, Vol. 3 (1920), pp. 159-79.

[31] See the articles by J. S. Shedlock in *The Musical Times*, June to December, 1892. Mr. Shedlock made a copy of the duet for Dr. Deiters. (TDR, II, 38-39.) Edited by F. Stein,

it has been published by Peters (1912).

[32] In 1798 Beethoven wrote to Zmeskall (see *A*, 30): "Je vous suis bien obligé pour votre faiblesse de vos yeux." Beethoven the violist and Zmeskall the 'cellist both wore them, according to Prodhomme, *La Jeunesse de Beethoven*, p. 326.

the ultimate form, however, are found amongst the sketches for the Piano-forte Sonata, Op. 10, No. 3. The inception of the Sonata must fall sometime between the middle of 1796 and the middle of 1798, since the subscription for it was opened in the beginning of July, 1798, and other works of a similar character were already completed in 1797. It is, therefore, possible to place the origin of the earlier movements of the Sextet in an earlier period, a proceeding which is confirmed by the circumstance that the beginning is found before sketches for "Ah perfido!" (which was composed in 1796 at the latest), on a sheet of sketches in the Artaria collection. The Kafka volume of sketches in the British Museum contains sketches for the minuet and trio of the Sextet, "Ah, perfido!" and the Pianoforte Sonata, Op. 49, No. 2. This fact also indicates the year 1796. Beethoven let the work lie a long time. It had its first hearing at a chamber concert for the benefit of Schuppanzigh in April, 1805; but it was not until 1809 that he gave it out for publication. On August 3rd of that year he wrote to Breitkopf and Härtel: "By the next mailcoach you will receive a song, *or perhaps two*, and a sextet for wind-instruments," and on August 8th: "The sextet is one of my earlier things and, moreover, was written in a single night—nothing can really be said of it beyond that it was written by an author who at least has produced a few better works; yet for many people such works are the best." The statement that the work was written in a single night must be taken in a Pickwickian sense, for sketches of it have been found.

It is plain that at this time Beethoven had a particular predilection for wind-instruments. Erich Prieger owned a fragment of a Quintet in E-flat for Oboe, three Horns and Bassoon, formerly in the possession of Artaria. The beginning of the first movement is lacking, but can be supplied from the repetitions in the second part. The Adagio is intact, but there are only a few measures of the Minuet. Influenced, no doubt, by the performances of such compositions, Beethoven composed at this time a second work for two oboes and English horn, the Variations on "Là ci darem" from Mozart's *Don Giovanni*. They were performed on December 23, 1797, as already mentioned, at the concert for the benefit of the Widows and Orphans in the National Court Theatre. From the sketches, Nottebohm surmises that the work was written in 1796 or 1797.[33]

The beautiful Quintet in E-flat, Op. 16, for Pianoforte and Wind-Instruments, was played at a concert given by Schuppanzigh on April 6, 1797, as already mentioned. It had probably been completed not long before. Sketches are found in connection with a remark concerning the Sonata in C minor, Op. 10, No. 1. In the minutes of a meeting of the Tonkünstlergesellschaft under date May 10, occurs this entry: "On the second day Hr. van Beethoven produced a Quintet and distinguished himself in the Quintet and incidentally by an improvisation." The word "dabey" (incidentally) seems to indicate that he introduced an improvisation in the Quintet as he did on a later

[33] *II Beeth.*, p. 31.

occasion to the embarrassment of the other players, but to the delight of the listeners.[34] The Quintet was published by Mollo in Vienna in 1801, and was dedicated to Prince Schwarzenberg. It appeared simultaneously in one arrangement made by Beethoven himself as a Quartet for Pianoforte and Strings, as Ries expressly declares. Beethoven had nothing to do with the arrangement as a String Quartet published by Artaria as Op. 75.

Touching the history of the Serenade for Violin, Viola and Violoncello, Op. 8, little else is known beyond the fact that its publication was announced in the *Wiener Zeitung* on October 7, 1797, by Artaria. Mr. Shedlock called attention in the *Musical Times* of 1892 (p. 525) to sketches which appeared along with others of the Pianoforte Concerto in B-flat, and the Trio, Op. 1, No. 2. That Beethoven valued the work highly is a fair deduction from the fact that he published it soon after its composition and authorized the publication of an arrangement for Pianoforte and Viola which he had revised. This arrangement received the opus number 42, though probably not from Beethoven. Hoffmeister in Leipzig, who published it in 1804 under the title "Notturno pour Fortepiano et Alto, par Louis van Beethoven, d'un Notturno pour Violon, Alto et Violoncelle et arrangé par l'auteur—Oeuvre 42," advertised it in the *Intelligenzblatt der Zeitschrift für die elegante Welt* on December 17, 1803. It is this arrangement, no doubt, to which Beethoven referred in a letter to Hoffmeister, dated September 22, 1803, in which he said: "These transcriptions are not mine, though they were much improved by me in places. Therefore, I am not willing to have you state that I made them, for that would be a lie and I could find neither time nor patience for such work."

The Serenade, Op. 25, for Flute, Violin and Viola also belongs here. It was probably composed before Op. 8. Beethoven entrusted its publication in the beginning of 1802 to Cappi, who had just begun business. Then, like Op. 8, it was published by Hoffmeister (as Op. 41) in an arrangement for Pianoforte and Flute (or Violin), which, no doubt, was included in Beethoven's protest against being set down as the transcriber.

Prominent among the compositions of this time is the Sonata in E-flat for Pianoforte, Op. 7. The only evidence of the date of its composition is the announcement of its publication by Artaria in the *Wiener Zeitung* of October 7, 1797. There are sketches for the third movement in the Kafka volume, but they afford no help in fixing a date. The Sonata is inscribed to the Countess Babette Keglevich, one of Beethoven's pupils, who afterwards married Prince Innocenz Odescalchi in Pressburg. Nottebohm quotes the following from a letter written by a nephew of the Countess: "The Sonata was composed for her when she was still a maiden. It was one of the whims, of which he [Beethoven] had many, that, living as he did *vis-à-vis*, he came in morning gown, slippers and tasseled cap (*Zipfelmütze*) to give her lessons." Inasmuch as the sketches mentioned belong only to the third movement and the sheet contains the remark: "diverse 4 bagatelles de B. inglese

---

[34] Ries tells the story in his *Notizen*, p. 79. (TDR, II, 47.) See page 350 below.

Ländler, etc.," Nottebohm supposes that the movement was originally intended for one of the Bagatelles and was later incorporated in the Sonata.

It is very probable that the two little Sonatas, Op. 49, belong to this period. Everybody knows that the second movement of the second Sonata (the minuet) is based on the same motive as the third movement of the Septet. That the motive is older in the Sonata than in the Septet is proved by the fact that sketches for it are found along with some to "Ah, perfido!" (1795-96) and the Sextet for Wind-Instruments, Op. 71. This circumstance establishes its early origin, say in 1795 or, at latest, 1796. Nottebohm considers it likely that the first Sonata was finished at the latest in 1798, certainly before the Sonata "Pathétique" and the Trio for strings, Op. 9, No. 3. The Sonatas were ready for publication as early as 1802, in which year brother Carl offered them to André in Offenbach. They were not published until 1805, when they appeared with the imprint of the Bureau d'Arts et d'Industrie, as appears from an advertisement in the *Wiener Zeitung* of January 19, 1805. Here, too, belongs the little Sonata in D for four hands, Op. 6, published by Artaria in October, 1797, as Nottebohm surmises. It was probably composed for purposes of instruction. Except a few trifles (marches, and two sets of variations) Beethoven wrote nothing more for four hands, though Diabelli offered him 40 ducats for a four-hand sonata in 1824.

In the pianoforte compositions of these two years are to be included the Variations in A on a Russian dance from the ballet *Das Waldmädchen*, published in April, 1797, and dedicated to the Countess Browne, née Bietinghoff. *Das Waldmädchen*, by Traffieri, music by Paul Wranitsky, was first performed at the Kärthnerthor Theater on September 28, 1796, and was repeated sixteen times the same year. This fixes the time of the composition of the Variations approximately. They were probably written before the end of 1796.

Sketches for the Variations for Pianoforte on a theme from Grétry's *Richard, Coeur de Lion* ("Une fièvre brûlante") are found by the side of sketches for the first movement of the Sonata in C minor, Op. 10, No. 1, which circumstance indicates that 1796 was the year of their origin. According to Sonnleithner, *Richard, Coeur de Lion* was first performed at the Hoftheater, Vienna, on January 7, 1788; then again on June 13, 1799 in the Theater auf den Wieden; but a ballet, *Richard Löwenherz*, by Vigano, music by Weigl, in which Grétry's romance ("Une fièvre brûlante") was interpolated, was brought forward on July 2, 1795, in the Hof-und National-theater and repeated often in that year, and it was thence, no doubt, that the suggestion for the Variations came to Beethoven.

A few single piano pieces belong in these years. The Rondo in C, Op. 51, No. 1, was published by Artaria in 1797. The following, brought to light by Nottebohm and Mandyczewski, were first published in the B & H Complete Works, Series 25 (Supplement): No. 299 is an Allegretto in C minor, 3/4 time; No. 297 contains two bagatelles: a Presto in C minor and an Allegretto in C major. Sketches for the first bagatelle are associated with those for the C minor Sonata, Op. 10, No. 1. From the remark: "Very short minuets to the new sonatas. The Presto remains for that in C minor," written about this time, Nottebohm[35] concludes that the first bagatelle was conceived as an intermezzo in the C minor sonata, and that, possibly, the Allegretto in C minor had a similar origin.

--*{Among Beethoven's early works there are two pieces for mandolin with pianoforte accompaniment which are published in the Complete Edition: Sonatina in C minor and Adagio in E-flat major. The name of Wenzel Krumpholz comes to mind in connection with the performance of these pieces; Krumpholz was a violinist and mandolin virtuoso. According to Arthur Chitz, who spent some time in research in the Clam-Gallas Archives, the Adagio as published in the Complete Edition is an early draft, the final version being still in the library of Count Clam-Gallas in Prague. Upon the autograph is written "Pour la belle J. par L. v. B." This is the Countess Josephine Clary. To these should be added a Sonatina in C major and Variations in D major for the same combination of instruments; they were also written for the Countess, who in 1797 married Count Christian v. Clam-Gallas.[36]}*--

Of Beethoven's dances up to the year 1803 only a portion have been included in the Complete Edition of Breitkopf and Härtel. Thus in Series 2 there are twelve minuets and twelve German dances for orchestra (written for the Redoutensaal in 1795) and twelve contradances for orchestra (1802); in Series 18 (Small Pieces for Pianoforte) there are six minuets (1795), a set of six "Ländlerische Tänze" (1802), and a set of seven "Ländlerische Tänze"[37] (before 1799), and a minuet in E-flat (?); in Series 25 (Supplement) there are six "Ländlerische Tänze" for two violins and bass (1802), six German dances for pianoforte and violin (1795-6) and an Allemande in A major for pianoforte (ca. 1800).

--*{From Willy Hess's list,[38] we can make the following additions. The orchestral parts for twelve minuets for orchestra (1799) were discovered by A. von Perger in the Vienna City Library. They were published by Heugel in Paris in a piano transcription (1903) and in a score (1906) edited by

---

[35] *II Beeth.*, p. 31. Later Beethoven wanted to give the Sonata an Intermezzo in C major (*ibid.*, p. 479), but did not carry out the intention. (TDR, II, 57, n. 2.)

[36] See the article "Une oeuvre inconnue de Beethoven pour mandoline et piano," by Arthur Chitz, *S.I.M. Revue Musicale*, Vol. 8, No. 12 (1912), pp. 24-31, at the end of which is printed the Sonatina in C major. The Variations have been printed by K. M. Komma in *Sudentendeutsches Musikarchiv* No. 1 (1940), and the final version of the Adagio in *Sudentendeutsches Musikarchiv* No. 2. The Theme and Variations in D major were published by R. Haas in the *Sudentendeutsches Musikarchiv*, Reichenberg, 1940.

[37] Willy Hess, *Schweitzerische Musikzeitung und Sängerblatt*, Vol. 70 (1930), p. 866, believes that the seven "Ländlerische Tänze" were originally written for two violins and bass, but the score is lost and only the pianoforte arrangement is extant. This is supported by the fact that the six "Ländlerische Tänze" for pianoforte (Series 18, No. 197) are transcriptions by the composer (according to the title page of the first edition) of the six "Ländlerische Tänze" for two violins and bass (Series 25, No. 291) except that the order of dances Nos. 1 and 2 has been reversed.

[38] "Welche Werke fehlen in der Breitkopf und Härtelschen Gesamtausgabe," *NBJ*, VII (1937), p. 104.

J. Chantavoine, who added a viola part to the original. Twelve German dances for orchestra (ca. 1796-7), preserved only in a piano transcription revised by Beethoven, have been edited by O. E. Deutsch and published by Strache in Vienna (1929). The six minuets for two violins and bass (1795) have been mentioned earlier. In the Paris Conservatory[39] are the autographs of a minuet in A-flat arranged both for string quartet and for piano alone. The later dances will be mentioned as the years of their origin are reached.⟩⟩⦿—

A list of the compositions of 1796-1797 follows:

1795-6.   Scene and Aria, "Ah perfido!", for Soprano and Orchestra, Op. 65
    (text of first part by Metastasio).
   Serenade for Flute, Violin and Viola, Op. 25.
   Six German Dances for Violin and Piano, WoO 42.
   Sonata for Pianoforte, Op. 49, No. 2.
   Song. "Adelaide" (text by Matthisson), Op. 46.
   Song. "Opferlied" (text by Matthisson), 1st version.[40]
1796.   Pieces for Mandoline and Pianoforte Accompaniment:
    Adagio in E-flat, WoO 43.
    Sonatina in C minor, WoO 43.
    Sonatina in C major, WoO 44.
    Variations in D, WoO 44.
   Quintet for Strings, Op. 4. [Revision of the Wind Octet, Op. 103.]
   Rondo for Pianoforte, Op. 51, No. 1.
   Sextet for Two Clarinets, Horns and Bassoons, Op. 71.
   Song. "Abschiedsgesang an Wiens Bürger" (text by von Friedelberg),
    WoO 121.
   Two Sonatas for Pianoforte and Violoncello, Op. 5.
   Variations for Pianoforte on a Russian Dance from Wranitzky's *Das*
    Waldmädchen, WoO 71.
   Variations for Pianoforte on "Une fièvre brûlante" from Grétry's
    Richard, Coeur de Lion, WoO 72.
   Variations for Pianoforte and Violin on a Theme from Handel's *Judas*
    Maccabaeus, WoO 45.
179(?).   "Lustig-traurig" for Pianoforte, WoO 54.
1795-7.   Duet for Viola and Violoncello ("Duett mit zwei obligaten Augen-
    gläsern"), WoO 32.
   Songs set to texts by Metastasio:
    Duet for Soprano and Tenor, "Scrivo in te" (*Il nome*), WoO 99,
     No. 11.
    Quartet for Soprano, Alto, Tenor and Bass, "Nei campi e nelle selve"
     (Cantata 27), WoO 99, No. 7. Two versions.
    Trio for Soprano, Alto and Bass, "Per te d'amico aprile" (*Il nome*),
     WoO 99, No. 9.
1796-7.   Allegretto for Pianoforte in C minor, WoO 53.
   Presto for Pianoforte in C minor, WoO 52.
   Quintet for Pianoforte, Oboe, Clarinet, Bassoon and Horn, Op. 16.

[39] See Max Unger, "Die Beethovenhand- tek," *NBJ*, vi (1935), pp. 106-107.
schriften der Pariser Konservatoriumsbiblio- [40] See KHV, p. 588.

Serenade for Violin, Viola and Violoncello, Op. 8.

Sonata for Pianoforte, Op. 7.

Sonata for Pianoforte Four Hands, Op. 6.

Two Arias from Umlauf's *Die schöne Schusterin*, WoO 91. (1) for Tenor and Orchestra; (2) for Soprano and Orchestra.

Variations on "Là ci darem la mano" from Mozart's *Don Giovanni* for Two Oboes and English Horn, WoO 28.

1797. Songs set to texts by Metastasio:

Duet for Tenor and Bass, "Fra tutte le pene" (*Zenobia*), WoO 99, No. 3.

Duet for Soprano and Tenor, "Salvo tu vuoi la sposo?" (*Zenobia*).

Quartet for Soprano, Alto, Tenor and Bass, "Fra tutte le pene" (*Zenobia*), WoO 99, No. 3. Two versions.

Quartet for Soprano, Alto, Tenor and Bass, "Quella cetra ah pur tu sei" (*Pel giorno natalizio di Maria Teresa*) WoO 99, No. 10. Two versions.

Trio for Soprano, Alto and Tenor, "Fra tutte le pene" (*Zenobia*), WoO 99, No. 3.

Trio for Soprano, Tenor and Bass, "Quella cetra ah pur tu sei" (*Pel giorno natalizio di Maria Teresa*), WoO 99, No. 10.

Song. "Kriegslied der Österreicher" (text by von Friedelberg), WoO 122.

The publications for the years 1796-97 were:

1796.   By Artaria:

"Abschiedsgesang an Wiens Bürger," dedicated to Major v. Kövesdy, WoO 121.

Quintet for Two Violins, Violas and Violoncello, Op. 4 [revision of the Wind Octet, Op. 103].

Six Minuets for the Pianoforte (Transcription), WoO 10.

Three Sonatas for the Pianoforte, Op. 2, dedicated to Joseph Haydn.

Trio for Violin, Viola and Violoncello, Op. 3.

Variations for Pianoforte on a Minuet from Haibel's *Le nozze disturbate*, WoO 68.

By Traeg:

Variations for the Pianoforte on a Duet "Nel cor più non mi sento" from Paisiello's *La Molinara*, WoO 70.

1797.   By Artaria:

"Adelaide," Op. 46, dedicated to the author of the text, Friedrich v. Matthisson.

"Kriegslied der Österreicher" (text by von Friedelberg), WoO 122.

Rondo for Pianoforte, Op. 51, No. 1.

Serenade for Violin, Viola and Violoncello, Op. 8.

Sonata for Pianoforte, Four Hands, Op. 6.

Sonata for Pianoforte, Op. 7, dedicated to Countess Babette v. Keglevics.

Two Sonatas for Pianoforte and Violoncello, Op. 5, dedicated to King Friedrich Wilhelm II of Prussia.

Variations for Pianoforte and Violoncello on a Theme from Handel's *Judas Maccabaeus*, dedicated to Princess Christiane v. Lichnowsky, WoO 45.

Variations for Pianoforte on the Russian Dance from Wranitzky's *Das Waldmädchen*, dedicated to Countess Margarete v. Browne, WoO 71.

CHAPTER XI

THE YEARS 1798 AND 1799

EARLY in the year 1798, a political event occurred which demands notice here from its connection with one of Beethoven's noblest and most original works—the *Sinfonia Eroica*.

The extraordinary demands made by the French Directory upon the Austrian government as preliminary to the renewal of diplomatic intercourse, after the peace of Campo Formio—such as a national palace and French theatre for the minister and the right of jurisdiction over all Frenchmen in the Austrian dominions—all of which were rejected by the Imperial government, had aroused to a high pitch the public curiosity both as to the man who might be selected for the appointment and as to the course he might adopt. This curiosity was by no means diminished by the intelligence that the new minister was Jean Baptiste Bernadotte, the young general who had borne so important a part in the recent invasion of Istria. He arrived in Vienna on February 5, 1798. The state of the Empress's health, who was delivered of the Archduchess Maria Clementine on the 1st of March, delayed the private audience of Bernadotte for the presentation of his credentials to the Emperor until the second of that month, and his public audience until the 8th of April. During the festivities of the court, which then took place, Bernadotte was always present, and a reporter of that day says both the Emperor and Empress held more conversation with him than with any other of the "cercle." This familiar intercourse, however, came speedily to an end; for on the 13th Bernadotte had the rashness to display the hated tricolor from his balcony and to threaten to defend it by force. A riot occurred, and it was thought that in the extreme excitement of popular feeling nothing but the strong detachments of cavalry and infantry detailed for his protection saved his life—saved it to ascend the throne of Sweden on the twentieth anniversary of his arrival in Vienna!

Since etiquette allowed a foreign minister neither to make nor receive visits in his public capacity until after his formal reception at court, the

General, during the two months of his stay, except the last five days, "lived very quietly." Those who saw him praised him as "well behaved, sedate and modest." In his train was Rodolphe Kreutzer, the great violinist.

Bernadotte had now just entered his 34th year; Kreutzer was in his 32nd; both of them, therefore, in age, as in tastes and acquirements, fitted to appreciate the splendor of Beethoven's genius and to enjoy his society. Moreover, as the Ambassador was the son of a provincial advocate, there was no difference of rank by birth, which could prevent them from meeting upon equal terms. Under such circumstances, and remembering that just at that epoch the young General Bonaparte was the topic of universal wonder and admiration, one is fully prepared for the statement of Schindler upon the origin of the "Heroic" Symphony:[1] "The first idea for the symphony is said to have gone out from General Bernadotte, then French Ambassador in Vienna, who esteemed Beethoven very highly. This I heard from several of Beethoven's friends. I was also told so by Count Moritz Lichnowsky (brother of Prince Lichnowsky), who was often in the society of Bernadotte with Beethoven. . . ."

Again Schindler adds[2] that in 1823 "Beethoven had a lively recollection that Bernadotte had really first inspired him with the idea of the 'Eroica' Symphony."

On March 29, 1798, Beethoven and Schuppanzigh participated in a benefit concert for the singer Josefa Duschek.[3] It is significant that their contribution was a violin sonata (probably one of the three from Op. 12), since a sonata up to this time was written with a small salon rather than a concert-hall in mind. And to play chamber music at a public concert remained an unusual event until after the composer's lifetime.

Salieri again engaged him for the Widows and Orphans concerts of April 1st and 2nd in the Court Theatre. The vocal work was Haydn's *Seven Last Words*; the instrumental compositions: on the first evening a symphony by von Eybler; on the second Beethoven's Quintet Op. 16. The event was heightened by the presence of Kaiser Franz and the imperial family.

It was now no longer the case that Beethoven was without a rival as pianoforte virtuoso. He had a competitor fully worthy of his powers; one who divided about equally with him the suffrages of the leaders in the Vienna musical circles. In fact the excellencies peculiar to the two were such and so different, that it depended upon the taste of the auditor to which he accorded the praise of superiority. Joseph Wölffl of Salzburg, two years younger than Beethoven, a "wonder-child," who had played a violin concerto in public at the age of seven years, was a pupil of Leopold Mozart and

[1] *Biographie*, 1st ed., p. 55. (TDR, II, 64.)
[2] *Ibid.*, p. 124. (TDR, II, 64.)
[3] The program, which has been preserved in the archives of the Gesellschaft der Musikfreunde, announces that a sonata with accompaniment is to be played by Beethoven. The accompanying (obbligato) instrument is not mentioned. (TDR, II, 65, n. 1, 101.) It is safe to assume that it was the violin, played by Schuppanzigh.

Michael Haydn. Being in Vienna, when but eighteen years old, he was engaged, on the recommendation of Mozart, by the Polish Count Oginsky, who took him to Warsaw. His success there, as pianoforte virtuoso, teacher and composer, was almost unexampled.[4] But it is only in his character as pianist that we have to do with him; and a reference may be made to the general principle, that a worthy competition is the best spur to genius. When we read in one of his letters Beethoven's words "I have also greatly perfected my pianoforte playing," they will cause no surprise; for only by severe industry and consequent improvement could he retain his high position, in the presence of such rivals as Wölffl and, a year or two later, J. B. Cramer. A lively picture of Wölffl by Tomaschek, who heard him in 1799, in his autobiography sufficiently proves that Wölffl's party in Vienna was composed of those to whom extraordinary execution was the main thing; while Beethoven's admirers were of those who had hearts to be touched. A parallel between Beethoven and Wölffl in a letter to the *Allgemeine Musikalische Zeitung* dated April 22, 1799, just at the time when the performances of both were topics of general conversation in musical circles, and still fresh in the memory of all who had heard them, is in the highest degree apposite to the subject of this chapter. The writer says: "Opinion is divided here touching the merits of the two; yet it would seem as if the majority were on the side of the latter [Wölffl]. I shall try to set forth the peculiarities of each without taking part in the controversy. Beethoven's playing is extremely brilliant but has less delicacy and occasionally he is guilty of indistinctness. He shows himself to the greatest advantage in improvisation, and here, indeed, it is most extraordinary with what lightness and yet firmness in the succession of ideas Beethoven not only varies a theme given him on the spur of the moment by figuration (with which many a virtuoso makes his fortune and—wind) but really develops it. Since the death of Mozart, who in this respect is for me still the *non plus ultra*, I have never enjoyed this kind of pleasure in the degree in which it is provided by Beethoven. In this Wölffl fails to reach him. But W. has advantages in that he, sound in musical learning and dignified in his compositions, plays passages which seem impossible with an ease, precision and clearness which cause amazement (of course he is helped here by the large structure of his hands) and that his interpretation is always, especially in Adagios, so pleasing and insinuating that one can not only admire it but also enjoy. . . . That Wölffl likewise enjoys an advantage because of his amiable bearing, contrasted with the somewhat haughty pose of Beethoven, is very natural."

No biography of Beethoven which makes any pretense to completeness, can omit the somewhat inflated and bombastic account which Seyfried gives of the emulation between Beethoven and Wölffl. Ignaz von Seyfried at the period in question was one of Schikaneder's conductors, to which position

[4] He returned to Vienna in 1795. (TDR, II, 66.)

he had been called when not quite twenty-one years of age, and had assumed its duties March 1, 1797. He was among the most promising of the young composers of the capital, belonged to a highly respectable family, had been educated at the University, and his personal character was unblemished. He would, therefore, naturally have access to the musical salons and his reminiscences of music and musicians in those years may be accepted as the records of observation. The unfavorable light which the researches of Notte-bohm have thrown upon him as editor of the so-called *Beethovens Studien* does not extend to such statements of fact as might easily have come under his own cognizance; and the passage now cited from the appendix of the *Studien*, though written thirty years after the events it describes, bears all the marks of being a faithful transcript of the writer's own memories:

"Beethoven had already attracted attention to himself by several composi-tions and was rated a first-class pianist in Vienna when he was confronted by a rival in the closing years of the last century. Thereupon there was, in a way, a revival of the old Parisian feud of the Gluckists and Piccinists, and the many friends of art in the Imperial City arrayed themselves in two parties. At the head of Beethoven's admirers stood the amiable Prince Lichnowsky; among the most zealous patrons of Wölffl was the broadly cultured Baron Raymond von Wetzlar, whose delightful villa (on the Grünberg near the Emperor's recreation-castle) offered to all artists, native and foreign, an asylum in the summer months, as pleasing as it was desirable, with true British loyalty. There the interesting combats of the two athletes not infrequently offered an indescribable artistic treat to the numerous and thoroughly select gathering. Each brought forward the latest product of his mind. Now one and anon the other gave free rein to his glowing fancy; sometimes they would seat themselves at two pianofortes and improvise alternately on themes which they gave each other, and thus created many a four-hand Capriccio which if it could have been put upon paper at the moment would surely have bidden defiance to time. It would have been difficult, perhaps impossible, to award the palm of victory to either one of the gladiators in respect of technical skill. Nature had been a particularly kind mother to Wölffl in bestowing upon him a gigantic hand which could span a tenth as easily as other hands compass an octave, and permitted him to play passages of double notes in these intervals with the rapidity of lightning. In his improvisations even then Beethoven did not deny his tendency toward the mysterious and gloomy. When once he began to revel in the infinite world of tones, he was transported also above all earthly things;—his spirit had burst all restricting bonds, shaken off the yoke of servitude, and soared triumphantly and jubilantly into the luminous spaces of the higher æther. Now his playing tore along like a wildly foaming cataract, and the conjurer constrained his instrument to an utterance so forceful that the stou est structure was scarcely able to withstand it; and anon he sank down, exhausted, exhaling gentle plaints, dissolving in melancholy. Again the spirit would soar aloft, triumphing over transitory terrestrial sufferings, turn its glance upward in reverent sounds and find rest and comfort on the innocent bosom of holy nature. But who shall sound the depths of the sea? It was the mystical Sanscrit language whose hieroglyphs can be read only by the initiated. Wölffl, on the contrary, trained in the school of Mozart, was always equable; never superficial but always clear and thus more accessible to the multitude. He used art only as a means to an end, never to exhibit his acquirements. He always enlisted the interest of his hearers and inevitably compelled them to follow the progression of his well-ordered ideas. Whoever has heard Hummel will know what is meant by this. . . .

"But for this [the attitude of their patrons] the *protégés* cared very little. They respected each other because they knew best how to appreciate each other, and as straightforward honest Germans followed the principle that the roadway of art is broad enough for many, and that it is not necessary to lose one's self in envy in pushing forward for the goal of fame!"

Wölffl proved his respect for his rival by dedicating to "M. L. van Beethoven" the pianoforte sonatas, Op. 7, which were highly commended in the *Allg. Mus. Zeit.* of Leipzig of January, 1799. Another interesting and valuable discussion of Beethoven's powers and characteristics as a pianoforte virtuoso at this period is contained in the autobiography of Tomaschek, who heard him both in public and in private during a visit which Beethoven made again this year to Prague. Tomaschek was then both in age (he was born on April 17, 1774) and in musical culture competent to form an independent judgment on such a subject: "In the year 1798, in which I continued my juridical studies, Beethoven, the giant among pianoforte players, came to Prague. He gave a largely attended concert in the Konviktssaal, at which he played his Concerto in C major, Op. 15, and the Adagio and graceful Rondo in A major from Op. 2, and concluded with an improvisation on a theme given him by Countess Sch . . . [Schick?], 'Ah tu fosti il primo oggetto,' from Mozart's *Titus* (duet No. 7). Beethoven's magnificent playing and particularly the daring flights in his improvisation stirred me strangely to the depths of my soul; indeed I found myself so profoundly bowed down that I did not touch my pianoforte for several days. . . . I heard Beethoven at his second concert, which neither in performance nor in composition renewed again the first powerful impression. This time he played the Concerto in B-flat which he had just composed in Prague.[5] Then I heard him a third time at the home of Count C.,[6] where he played, besides the graceful Rondo from the A major Sonata, an improvisation on the theme: 'Ah! vous dirai-je, Maman.' This time I listened to Beethoven's artistic work with more com-

[5] It will be remembered that this concerto was in fact composed before that in C major; but it is not improbable that the revision of the B-flat Concerto was completed for the Prague performance. See Nottebohm, *Il Beeth.*, pp. 479-81. (Cf. TDR, II, 73, n. 1.)

[6] Clam-Gallas.

posure. I admired his powerful and brilliant playing, but his frequent daring deviations from one motive to another, whereby the organic connection, the gradual development of idea was broken up, did not escape me. Evils of this nature frequently weaken his greatest compositions, those which sprang from a too exuberant conception. It is not seldom that the unbiased listener is rudely awakened from his transport. The singular and original seemed to be his chief aim in composition, as is confirmed by the answer which he made to a lady who asked him if he often attended Mozart's operas. 'I do not know them,' he replied, 'and do not care to hear the music of others lest I forfeit some of my originality.'"

The veteran Tomaschek when he wrote thus had heard all the greatest virtuosi of the pianoforte, who, from the days of Mozart to 1840, had made themselves famous; and yet Beethoven remained for him still "the lord of pianoforte players" and "the giant among pianoforte players." Still, great as he was now when Tomaschek heard him, Beethoven could write three years later that he had greatly perfected his playing.

The years 1798 and 1799 offer but scanty materials to the biographers of Beethoven—standing in broad contrast to the next and, indeed all succeeding years, in which their quantity and variety become a source of embarrassment.

Two new and valuable, though but passing acquaintances, were made by Beethoven this year, however—with Domenico Dragonetti, the greatest contrabassist known to history, and Johann Baptist Cramer, one of the greatest pianists. Dragonetti was not more remarkable for his astounding execution than for the deep, genuine musical feeling which elevated and ennobled it. He was now—in the spring of 1799, so far as the means are at hand of determining the time—returning to London from a visit to his native city, Venice, and his route took him to Vienna, where he remained several weeks. Beethoven and he soon met and they were mutually pleased with each other. Many years afterwards Dragonetti related the following anecdote to Samuel Appleby, Esq., of Brighton, England: "Beethoven had been told that his new friend could execute violoncello music upon his huge instrument, and one morning, when Dragonetti called at his room, he expressed his desire to hear a sonata. The contrabass was sent for, and the Sonata, No. 2, of Op. 5, was selected. Beethoven played his part, with his eyes immovably fixed upon his companion, and, in the finale, where the arpeggios occur, was so delighted and excited that at the close he sprang up and threw his arms around both player and instrument." The unlucky contrabassists of orchestras had frequent occasion during the next few years to know that this new revelation of the powers and possibilities of their instrument to Beethoven, was not forgotten.

Cramer, born at Mannheim, 1771, but from early infancy reared and educated in England, was successively the pupil of the noted Bensor, Schroeter and Clementi; but, like Beethoven, was in no small degree self-taught. He was so rarely and at such long intervals on the Continent that his extraordinary merits have never been fully understood and appreciated there. Yet for a period of many years in the first part of the nineteenth century he was undoubtedly, upon the whole, the first pianist of Europe. The object of his tour in 1799 was not to display his own talents and acquirements, but to add to his general musical culture and to profit by his observations upon the styles and peculiar characteristics of the great pianists of the Continent. In Vienna he renewed his intercourse with Haydn, whose prime favorite he had been in England, and at once became extremely intimate with Beethoven.

Cramer surpassed Beethoven in the perfect neatness, correctness and finish of his execution; Beethoven assured him that he preferred his touch to that of any other player; his brilliancy was astonishing; but yet taste, feeling, expression, were the qualities which more eminently distinguished him. Beethoven stood far above Cramer in power and energy, especially when extemporizing. Each was supreme in his own sphere; each found much to learn in the perfections of the other; each, in later years, did full justice to the other's powers. Thus Ries says: "Amongst the pianoforte players he [Beethoven] had praise for but one as being distinguished—John Cramer. All others were but little to him." On the other hand, Mr. Appleby, who knew Cramer well, was long afterwards told by him, "No man in these days has heard extempore playing, unless he has heard Beethoven."

Making a visit one morning to him, Cramer, as he entered the anteroom, heard Beethoven extemporizing by himself, and remained there more than half an hour "completely entranced," never in his life having heard such exquisite effects, such beautiful combinations. Knowing Beethoven's extreme dislike to being listened to on such occasions, Cramer retired and never let him know that he had so heard him.

Cramer's widow communicates a pleasant anecdote. At an Augarten Concert the two pianists were walking together and hearing a performance of Mozart's pianoforte Concerto in C minor (K. 491); Beethoven suddenly stood still and, directing his companion's attention to the exceedingly simple, but equally beautiful motive which is first introduced towards the end of the piece, exclaimed: "Cramer, Cramer! we shall never be able to do anything like that!" As the theme was repeated and wrought up to the climax, Beethoven, swaying his body to and fro, marked the time and in every possible manner manifested a delight rising to enthusiasm.

Schindler's record of his conversations upon Beethoven with Cramer and Cherubini in 1841 is interesting and valuable. He has, however, left one important consideration unnoticed, namely, that the visits of those masters to Vienna were five years apart—five years of great change in Beethoven—a period during which his deafness, too slight to attract Cramer's attention, had increased to a degree beyond concealment, and which, joined to his increased devotion to composition and compulsory abandonment of all ambition as a virtuoso, with consequent neglect of practice, had affected his execution unfavorably. Hence the difference in the opinions of such competent judges as Cramer, describing him as he was in 1799-1800, Cherubini in 1805-6, and two years later Clementi, afford a doubtless just and fair indication of the decline of Beethoven's powers as a mere pianist—not extending, however, at least for some years yet, to his extemporaneous performances. We shall find from Ries and others ample confirmation of the fact.

And now let Schindler speak:[7] "Cherubini, disposed to be curt, characterized Beethoven's pianoforte playing in a single word: 'rough.' The gentleman Cramer, however, desired that less offence be taken at the rudeness of his performance than at the unreliable reading of one and the same composition—one day intellectually brilliant and full of characteristic expression, the next freakish to the verge of unclearness; often confused. Because of this a few friends expressed a wish to hear Cramer play several works publicly from the manuscript. This touched a sensitive spot in Beethoven; his jealousy was aroused and, according to Cramer, their relations became strained."

This strain, however, left no such sting behind it as to diminish Cramer's good opinion of Beethoven both as man and artist, or hinder his free expression of it. To this fact the concurrent testimony of his widow and son, and those enthusiasts for Beethoven Charles Neate, Cipriani Potter and others who knew Cramer well, bear witness. It was the conversation of Cramer about Beethoven which induced Potter, after the fall of Napoleon, to journey to Vienna, to make the acquaintance of the great master and, if possible, become his pupil.

Cramer's musical gods were Handel and Mozart, notwithstanding his life-long love for Bach's clavier compositions; hence the abrupt transitions, the strange modulations, and the, until then, unheard passages, which Beethoven introduced ever more freely into his works were to him, as to Tomaschek and so many other of his contemporaries, imperfections and distortions of compositions, which but for them were models of beauty and harmonious proportion. He once gave this feeling utterance with comic exaggeration, when Potter, then a youth, was extolling some abstruse combinations, by saying: "If Beethoven emptied his inkstand upon a piece of music paper you would admire it!"

Upon Beethoven's demeanor in society, Schindler proceeds thus:[8] "The communications of both [Cramer and Madame Cherubini] agreed in saying that in mixed society his conduct was reserved, stiff and marked by artist's pride; whereas among his intimates he was droll, lively, indeed, voluble at times, and fond of giving play to all the arts of wit and sarcasm, not always wisely especially in respect of political and social prejudices. To this the two were able to add much concerning his awkwardness in taking hold of such objects as glasses, coffee cups, etc., to which Master Cherubini added

[7] *Biographie*, II, 232. (TDR, II, 79.)   [8] *Ibid.*, I, 115. (TDR, II, 80.)

the comment: 'Toujours brusque.' These statements confirmed what I had heard from his older friends touching the social demeanor of Beethoven in general."

Cramer reached Vienna early in September, 1799, and remained there, according to Schindler, through the following winter; but he does not appear to have given any public concerts, although, during the first month of his stay, we learn from a newspaper, he "earned general and deserved applause by his playing." It is needless to dwell upon the advantages to Beethoven of constant intercourse for several months with a master like Cramer, whose noblest characteristics as pianist were the same as Mozart's, and precisely those in which Beethoven was deficient.

Let us pass in review the compositions which had their origin in the years 1798 and 1799. First of all come the three Trios for stringed instruments, Op. 9. The exact date of their conception has not yet been determined, all that is positive being that Beethoven sold them to Traeg on March 16, 1798, and that the publisher's announcement of them appeared on July 21st of the same year. The only sketches for the Trios quoted by Nottebohm show them in connection with a sketch for the last movement of the "Sonate pathétique," which was published in 1799; but this proves nothing. It may be easily imagined that Beethoven desired to make more extended use of the experience gained in writing the Trio, Op. 3, and that he therefore began sketching Op. 9 in 1796 or 1797.

The works were dedicated to Count Browne, who, it will be remembered, was the patron to present Beethoven with a horse in return for the dedication to his wife of the Twelve Variations on a Danse Russe. But the wording of the dedication of the trios, which follows, shows that there was more cause for gratitude than the mere gift of a horse:

> L'auteur, vivement pénétré de Votre Muni
> ficence aussi délicate que libérale, se réjouit, de
> pouvoir le dire au monde, en Vous dédiant cette
> oeuvre. Si les productions de l'art, que Vous
> honores de Votre protection en Connoisseur, dé
> pendaient moins de l'inspiration du génie, que de
> la bonne volonté de faire de son mieux; l'auteur aurait
>   la satisfaction tant désirée, de présenter
> au premier Mécene de sa Muse, la meilleure
> de ses oeuvres.[9]

Count Johann Georg v. Browne-Camus (1767-1827) was from an old Irish family, and was employed by Empress Catherine II in the Russian Imperial Service. The little that is known about him has been supplied mainly by the Ries *Notizen* and more recently by a biography of the Count's

[9] See KHV, p. 22.

tutor, Johannes Büel,[10] who was also to become a friend of Beethoven's, as we shall see. Like Prince Lobkowitz, Count Browne was adversely affected by wealth. The large income that he received from his properties in Livonia resulted in squander and dissipation. Büel writes of his employer, "I live with one of the strangest men, full of excellent talents and beautiful qualities of heart and spirit on the one hand, and on the other full of weakness and depravity." Then he proceeds to describe the count's breakdown which forced him to remain for some months in 1805 in an institution. At any rate, the fact that between 1798 and 1803 the composer dedicated four works to the count and three to the countess indicates the prominence of this family during these years in Beethoven's life. How much longer the relationship lasted is not known.

The first two concertos for pianoforte call for consideration here, for it was not until 1798 that they acquired the form in which they are now known. In the Malherbe Collection in the Library of the Paris Conservatory there is a manuscript which contains, according to Unger,[11] a fragment of the first movement of the B-flat Pianoforte Concerto in score along with the unused sketches for an instrumental piece in C, a "contrapunto all' ottavo" (an exercise for Albrechtsberger), an unpublished minuet for Pianoforte in A-flat and a setting of the same for string quartet. Unger gives as the date "presumably 1794." The passage from the Concerto is, in an obviously early form, from the development section of the first movement. This agrees with the statement that on March 29, 1795, Beethoven played a new concerto, the key of which is not indicated. It is most likely that it was this in B-flat, since the one in C did not exist at the time. Beethoven, it appears, played it a few times afterward in Vienna, and then rewrote it. According to Tomaschek's account he played the B-flat Concerto (expressly distinguished from that in C) in 1798, again in Prague. Tomaschek added, "which he had composed in Prague." This is confounding the original version with the revision, concerning which Nottebohm gives information in his *Zweite Beethoveniana* (pp. 478ff.) on the basis of sketches which point to 1798. The fact of the revision is proved by Beethoven's memoranda, such as "To remain as it was," "From here on everything to remain as it was." The revision of the first movement was radical, and the entire work was apparently undertaken in view of an imminent performance, most likely that of Prague in 1798. It was published by Hoffmeister and Kühnel and dedicated to "Carl Nikl Edlen von Nikelsberg."

That the Concerto in C was composed later than that in B-flat has been proved by Beethoven's testimony as well as other external evidences and is confirmed by the few remaining sketches analyzed by Nottebohm. They appear in connection with a sketch for the cadenza for the B-flat Concerto

[10] Hans Nohl, *Hofrat Johannes Büel 1761-1830* (Frauenfeld, Huber, 1930). See also Stephan Ley, "Kleine Beethoveniana," in *NBJ*, vi (1935), pp. 26-27.

[11] "Die Beethovenhandschriften der Pariser Konservatoriums," *NBJ*, vi (1935), p. 106.

which, therefore, must have been finished when its companion was begun. A sketch for a cadenza for the C major Concerto comes after sketches for the Sonata in D, Op. 10, No. 3, which was published in 1798. This new concerto must, therefore, have been finished. According to the testimony of Tomaschek, he played it in 1798 in the Konviktssaal in Prague. Dedicated to the Princess Odescalchi, née Keglevics, it was published by Mollo in Vienna in 1801. There are three cadenzas for the first movement of the Concerto, which call for an extended compass of the pianoforte and are thus shown to be of later date than the original Concerto.[12]

Now begins the glorious series of sonatas. The first were the three (Op. 10) which, though begun in part at an earlier date, were definitively finished and published in 1798. Eder, the publisher, opened a subscription for them by an advertisement in the *Wiener Zeitung*, July 5, 1798; therefore they were finished at that time. The sketching for them had begun in 1796, as appears from Nottebohm's statement,[13] and Beethoven worked on the three simultaneously. Sketches for the first movement of the first Sonata are mixed with sketches for the soprano air for Umlauf's *Schusterin* which have been attributed to 1796, and the Variations for three Wind-Instruments which were played in 1797. Sketches for the third Sonata are found among notes for the Sextet for Wind-Instruments (composed about 1796) and also for the Concerto in C minor, which, therefore, was begun thus early, and for one of the seven country dances which appeared in 1799, or perhaps earlier. The sketches for the last movement of No. 3 are associated alone with sketches for a cadenza for the C major Concerto which Beethoven played in Prague in 1798, and may therefore be placed in this year. It follows that the three sonatas were developed gradually in 1796-98, and completed in 1798. From the sketches and the accompanying memoranda[14] we learn, furthermore, that for the first Sonata, which now has three movements, a fourth, an Intermezzo, was planned on which Beethoven several times made a beginning but permitted to fall. Two of these movements became known afterwards as "Bagatelles."[15] We learn also that the last movement of the first Sonata, and the second movement of the second, were originally laid out on a larger scale.

The "Sonate pathétique," Op. 13, was published by Eder, in Vienna, in 1799, and afterwards by Hoffmeister, who announced it on December 18 of the same year. Sketches for the rondo are found among those for the Trio, Op. 9, and after the beginning of a fair copy of the Sonata, Op. 49, No. 1. From this there is no larger deduction than that the Sonata probably had its

---

12 The customary range of the piano in the last decade of the 18th century was five octaves: F to F^3. The Concerto itself stays within this range; the first cadenza goes to A-flat^3, the second to A^3, and the third cadenza to C^4.

13 *II Beeth.*, pp. 29ff. (TDR, II, 41.)

14 Among the sketches for the second move-

ment of the Quintet, Op. 16, Beethoven wrote: "For the new sonatas very short minuets. The Presto remains for that in C minor." And in another sketch he writes: "Intermezzo for the sonata in C minor."—Nottebohm, *II Beeth.*, 32, 479. (TDR, II, 91, n. 1.)

15 WoO 52 and 53.

origin about 1798. One of the sketches, however, indicates that the last movement was originally conceived for more than one instrument, probably for a sonata for pianoforte and violin. Beethoven published the two Sonatas, Op. 14, which he dedicated to the Baroness Braun, immediately after the "Sonate pathétique." They came from the press of Mollo and were announced on December 21, 1799. The exact time of their composition cannot be determined definitely. Up to the present time no sketches for the second are known to exist; copious ones for the first, however, are published by Nottebohm in his *Zweite Beethoveniana* (p. 45 *et seq.*), some of which appear before sketches for the Sonata, Op. 12, No. 3, then approaching completion, and some after sketches for the Concerto in B-flat. Because of this juxtaposition, Nottebohm places the conception of the Sonata in 1795.[16]

Touching the history of the Trio, Op. 11, for Pianoforte, Clarinet and Violoncello, little is known. It was advertised as wholly new by Mollo and Co. on October 3, 1798, and is inscribed to the Countess Thun. Sketches for the first and second movements associated with other works that are unknown or were never completed are in the British Museum and set forth by Nottebohm in his *Zweite Beethoveniana* (p. 515). The sketch for the Adagio resembles the beginning of the minuet in the Sonata, Op. 49, No. 2, and is changed later; this points approximately to 1798. The last movement consists of a series of variations on the theme of a trio from Weigl's opera *L'Amor marinaro*, beginning "Pria ch'io l'impegno." Weigl's opera was performed for the first time on October 15, 1797. Czerny told Otto Jahn that Beethoven took the theme at the request of a clarinet player (Beer?) for whom he wrote the Trio. The elder Artaria told Cipriani Potter in 1797, that he had given the theme to Beethoven and requested him to introduce variations on it into a trio, and added that Beethoven did not know that the melody was Weigl's until after the Trio was finished, whereupon he grew very angry on finding it out. Czerny says in the supplement to his "Pianoforte School": "It was at the wish of the clarinet player for whom Beethoven wrote this Trio that he employed the above theme by Weigl (which was then very popular) as the finale. At a later period he frequently contemplated writing another concluding movement for this Trio, and letting the variations stand as a separate work."

If Czerny is correct in his statement, obvious deductions from it are these, which are scarcely consistent with Artaria's story: if the theme was "very popular" at the time the opera must have had several performances, and it is not likely that the melody was unfamiliar to Beethoven, who also, it may be assumed, wrote the title of Weigl's trio, which is printed at the beginning of the last movement of Beethoven's composition. The three Sonatas for Pianoforte and Violin, Op. 12, dedicated to Salieri, were advertised in the

[16] Beethoven transcribed it for string quartet changing the key to F. This version was published in 1802. The two versions may be compared in the Eulenberg score No. 297. (Cf. TDR, II, 98.)

Wiener Zeitung of January 12, 1799, as published by Artaria, which would seem to place their origin around 1798. ⸺It will be recalled that one of these sonatas was presumably played at the concert for Madame Duschek on March 29, 1798.[17]⸺ Nottebohm discusses the juxtaposition of sketches for the second Sonata with sketches for the Pianoforte Concerto in B-flat and the Sonata in E, Op. 14, No. 1, and is inclined to fix 1795 as the year of the sonata's origin. But we are in the dark as to whether the sketches for the Pianoforte Concerto were for its original or its revised form. The character of the sonatas favors the later date.

Among the instrumental compositions of this year belong the Variations for Pianoforte and Violoncello on "Ein Mädchen oder Weibchen" from Mozart's *Die Zauberflöte*, announced by Traeg on September 22, 1798. They were afterwards taken over by Artaria. The ten Variations on "La stessa, la stessissima" from Salieri's *Falstaff, ossia: le tre Burle*, were announced as just published in the *Wiener Zeitung* of March 2, 1799. Salieri's opera was performed on January 3, 1799, in the Hoftheater; Beethoven's, therefore, was an occasional composition conceived and produced in a very short time. Sketches were found among some for the first Quartet, Op. 18, and others. The Variations are dedicated to the Countess Babette Keglevics. Twice more in the same year operatic productions induced similar works. The publication of the Variations on "Kind, willst du ruhig schlafen?" from Winter's *Das Unterbrochenes Opferfest*, was announced in the *Wiener Zeitung* of December 21, 1799, by Mollo and Co.; the opera had its first performance in Vienna on June 15, 1796, and was repeated frequently within the years immediately following—six times in 1799. In this case also it may be assumed that publication followed hard on the heels of composition. Sketches are found in companionship with others belonging to the Quartet, Op. 18, No. 5, and the Septet. The Variations on "Tändeln und Scherzen," from Süssmayr's opera *Soliman II, oder die drei Sultaninnen*, belong to the same time. The opera was performed on October 1, 1799, in the Hoftheater; the publication of the variations by Hoffmeister was announced in the *Wiener Zeitung* on December 18, 1799. They were also printed by Eder. They were dedicated to Countess Browne, née von Bietinghoff. It is interesting to learn from Czerny that these variations were the first of Beethoven's compositions which the master gave him to study when he became his pupil in 1801. Before them he had pieces by C. P. E. Bach and after them the "Sonate pathétique."

⸺Mention may here be made of three songs. The first, "La Tiranna," has survived only in the form of an English publication, copies of which have been found by J. H. Blaxland in the British Museum and the Bodleian Library at Oxford.[18] This publication is entitled "A Favourite Canzonetta

[17] See page 204 above.
[18] See "Eine unbekannte Canzonetta Beet-
hovens," in *Zeitschrift für Musikwissenschaft*, Vol. 14 (1931), pp. 29-34.

for the Pianoforte composed by L. von Beethoven, of Vienna, the poetry by Wm. Wennington. Published in Vienna by the Principal Music Shops and in London by Messrs. Broderip and Wilkinson." Inscribed on the wrapper are the words "Canzonetta La Tiranna." Blaxland discovered that Wennington in 1799 published a translation of La Fontaine's *Der Naturmensch* with a foreword dated Vienna, 1798; further that one of the subscribers was a "Pr. Linhouski." If this was Prince Karl Lichnowsky, this might well have been the means whereby Wennington met Beethoven and received a copy of his "La Tiranna" which he then took back to England, translated and had published. The name of the publisher limits the date of printing to the period 1799 to 1808, and Wennington may well have been responsible for introducing to England the first of Beethoven's music in print. The second is the French song, "Plaisir d'aimer," which was sketched in 1799 (Grasnick 1) along with sketches for the String Quartets, Op. 18. It was first printed by Jean Chantavoine.[19] In the same Grasnick sketchbook are sketches for Beethoven's first setting of Goethe's "Neue Liebe, neues Leben," which was published in 1808 by Simrock along with two other songs ("Opferlied" and "Der freie Mann").[20] A later setting of this text was published as Op. 75, No. 2.

As evidence pointing to the period in which the First Symphony was written we have, first of all, the report of the first performance on April 2, 1800; but inasmuch as the copying of the parts and the rehearsals must have consumed a considerable time, the period would be much too short (especially in view of Beethoven's method of working) if we were also to assume that the Symphony originated in 1800. It is very likely that, with the Quartets, it was sketched at an earlier period and worked out in the main by 1799 at the latest. It was published toward the end of 1801 by Hoffmeister and Kühnel as Op. 21, dedicated to Baron van Swieten and advertised in the *Wiener Zeitung* of January 16, 1802. Beethoven had already planned a symphony while studying with Albrechtsberger. Nottebohm reports on his purposes after a study of some sketches and from him we learn that the theme of the present last movement was originally intended for a first movement.[21] Beethoven must have worked on this composition in 1794-95, perhaps at the suggestion of van Swieten—a conclusion suggested by the fact that the dedication finally went to him.[22]

On the last page of the autograph of the Rondo à Capriccio there are nine staves of sketches which have been transcribed and analysed by Erich Hertzmann.[23] Like the Nottebohm sketches, they include the early version

[19] In *DM*, I₁₂ (1902), 1079-1082. (Cf. TDR, II, 111.)

[20] See O. F. Deutsch, "Beethovens Goethe-Kompositionen," in *Jahrbuch der Sammlung Kippenberg*, Vol. 8 (1930), pp. 112-13.

[21] *II Beeth.*, pp. 228-29. (TDR, II, 107.) There are further sketches on this material in the Kafka *Notirungsbuch*. See J. S. Shedlock, "Beethoven's Sketch Books," *The Musical Times*, Vol. 33 (1892), pp. 591-92.

[22] Max Franz's death cut short Beethoven's intention of dedicating to him his first symphony.

[23] *MQ*, Vol. 32 (1946), pp. 176-78.

of the theme which became the finale of the First Symphony. But there also appears a second theme in G and on the next staff the suggestion of an introduction in triple time which give further support to Nottebohm's theory of an incompleted symphony in C of which this was to be the first movement. In planning here a whole movement which uses a theme that is worked out in the Nottebohm sketches, we are probably seeing the next stage in Beethoven's thinking. Hertzmann points out further the relationship of these musical ideas to other works of this period: the piano variations to "Une fièvre brûlante," the coda of the variations of the Quartet Op. 18, No. 5, and most prominently to the first movement of the Piano Concerto in C major. Since this last work was finished in 1798, it is clear that at some point before this time, Beethoven abandoned his early plan of a symphony and turned to the ideas that led to the new symphony.

The compositions of the years 1798-99 were:

1796-8. Three Sonatas for Pianoforte, Op. 10.
Three Trios for Strings, Op. 9.

1797-8. Song. "La partenza" (text by Metastasio), WoO 124.
Song. "Zärtiche Liebe" (text by Herrosee), WoO 123.
Three Sonatas for Pianoforte and Violin, Op. 12.

1798. Concerto No. 1 in C major for Pianoforte and Orchestra, Op. 15.
[Revision of Concerto No. 2 in B-flat major for Pianoforte and Orchestra, Op. 19.]
Seven "Ländlerische Tänze," presumably for two violins and violoncello or bass, WoO 11. They survive only in piano transcription by the composer.
Sonata for Pianoforte, Op. 49, No. 1.
Song. "La Tiranna," WoO 125.
Trio for Pianoforte, Clarinet and Violoncello, Op. 11.
Variations for Pianoforte and Violoncello on "Ein Mädchen oder Weibchen," from Mozart's *Die Zauberflöte*, Op. 66.

1798-9. Sonata for Pianoforte, Op. 13.
Two Sonatas for Pianoforte, Op. 14.
Song. "Neue Liebe, neues Leben" (text by Goethe), WoO 127.
Song. "Plaisir d'aimer," WoO 128.

1799. Five Pieces for Mechanical Instrument, WoO 33. Written for Count Josef Deym.[24]
Twelve German Dances for Orchestra, WoO 13.
Twelve Minuets for Orchestra, WoO 12.
Trio for Soprano, Tenor and Bass, "Chi mai di questo core" (text by Metastasio from "Il Ritorno"), WoO 99, No. 2.[25]
Variations for Pianoforte on "Kind, willst du ruhig schlafen," from Winter's *Das unterbrochene Opferfest*, WoO 75.
Variations for Pianoforte on "La stessa, la stessissima," from Salieri's *Falstaff*, WoO 73.

[24] See p. 237 below.   [25] See Nottebohm, *Beethovens Studien*, p. 227.

Variations for Pianoforte on "Tändeln und scherzen," from Süssmayr's *Soliman II*, WoO 76.

The publications in the years 1798-99 were:

By Eder:

1798. Three Sonatas for Pianoforte, Op. 10, dedicated to Countess Anna Margarete von Browne.

By Mollo:

Trio for Pianoforte, Clarinet and Violoncello, Op. 11, dedicated to Countess Maria Wilhemine von Thun.

By Traeg:

Three Trios for Strings, Op. 9, dedicated to Count Johann Georg von Browne.

Variations for Pianoforte and Violoncello on "Ein Mädchen oder Weibchen," from Mozart's *Die Zauberflöte* [Op. 66].

Variations for Pianoforte on "Une fièvre brûlante," from Grétry's *Richard Coeur de Lion*, WoO 72.

By Artaria:

1799. Seven "Ländlerische Tänze" for Pianoforte (Transcription), WoO 11.

Three Sonatas for Pianoforte and Violin, Op. 12, dedicated to Antonio Salieri.

Variations for Pianoforte on "La stessa, la stessissima," from Salieri's *Falstaff*, dedicated to Countess Barbara von Keglevics, WoO 73.

By Hoffmeister:

"Grande Sonate pathétique pour le Clavecin ou Pianoforte," Op. 13, dedicated to Prince Karl von Lichnowsky.

Variations for Pianoforte on "Tändeln und scherzen," from Süssmayr's *Soliman II*, dedicated to Countess Anna Margarete von Browne, WoO 76.

By Mollo:

Two Sonatas for Pianoforte, Op. 14, dedicated to Baroness Josefine von Braun.

Variations for Pianoforte on "Kind, willst du ruhig schlafen," from Winter's *Das unterbrochene Opferfest*, WoO 75.

By Broderip, Wilkinson, Hodsoll & Astor, London:

The Canzonetta "La Tiranna," WoO 125.[26]

---

[26] See Alan Tyson, *The Authentic English Editions of Beethoven* (London, 1963), p. 41.

CHAPTER XII

BEETHOVEN'S FRIENDS AND
FELLOW MUSICIANS—
THE BRUNSVIK FAMILY—CHARACTER TRAITS—
SKETCHBOOKS—POSSIBLE ORIGIN OF DEAFNESS

THE chronological progress of the narrative must again be interrupted, since no picture of a man's life can be complete without the lights or shades arising from his social relations—without some degree of knowledge respecting those with whom he is on terms of equality and intimacy and whose company he most affects. The attempt to draw such a picture in the case of Beethoven, that is, during his first years in Vienna, leaves much to be desired, for, although the search for materials has not been unsuccessful, many of the data are but vague and scattered notices. In a Conversation Book, bearing Beethoven's own date "on the 20th of March, 1820," some person unknown writes:[1]

Would you like to know where I first had the honor and good fortune to see you?

More than 25 years ago I lived with Frank of Prague in the Drachengässel in the old Meat Market.
Several noblemen used to meet there, for instance S. E. van B, Cristen, Heimerle, Vogl (now a singer), Kisswetter, basso, now Court Councillor
Graynstein, who has long been living in France, etc.
There was often music-making, supping and punch-drinking—and at the conclusion Your Excellency often gave us joy at my P. F. I was then War Court-Councillor.

War Court-Councillor Schaller
I have pursued at least 15 thousand professions

---

[1] The reading of this passage is from Schünemann, I, 366-67, and has slight variations of spelling from Thayer's transcription.

Did we then meet in Prague?

In what year?

1796, 3 days.

There is nothing in the portions of this Conversation Book to show who this man of "fifteen thousand professions" was, now sitting with Beethoven in an eating-house, and recalling to his memory the frolics of the first year and a quarter in Vienna; nor is there a Frank of Prague sufficiently known to fame as to be now identified. ⸺ Schünemann[2] suggests that "Cristen" was Baron Christ of Ehrenblut (1774-1841); identifies "Heimerle" as Joseph v. Haymerle, clerk at the Appellate Court; and offers the name of Court Councillor Eberhard Perin v. Gradenstein of the Foreign Office as a possible identification of "Graynstein." ⸺ Johann Michael Vogl, less than two years older than Beethoven, was afterwards a very celebrated tenor of the opera. In 1793-94 he was still pursuing the study of jurisprudence, which he abandoned in 1795 for the stage. Thayer suggests that he was consulted upon the merits of "Adelaide" by Beethoven, approved it, and first sang it and made it known, as he was the first, years afterward, to sing in public the "Erlkönig" and other fine productions of Franz Schubert. May not this early friendship for Beethoven have been among the causes of the resuscitation of *Fidelio* in 1814, for the benefit performance of Vogl, Saal and Weinmüller?

The "Kisswetter, basso" was Raphael Georg Kiesewetter, who lived to be renowned as a writer upon topics of musical history, and to play a part in the revival of ancient music in Vienna, not less noteworthy than that of Thibaut in Heidelberg. At the period of the "music-making, supping and punch drinking" by the "noblemen" in the apartments of Frank of Prague, Kiesewetter was a young man of twenty, engaged, like Vogl, in the study of the law. In the spring of 1794—and thus the date of these meetings is determined—he received an appointment in the military chancellery, and went at once to the headquarters at Schwetzingen on the Rhine.

More important and valuable during these years, as subsequently, was the warm, sincere friendship of Nikolaus Zmeskall von Domanovecz (1759-1833), an official in the Royal Hungarian Court Chancellery. "You belong to my earliest friends in Vienna," writes Beethoven in 1816. Zmeskall, to quote the words of Sonnleithner, "was an expert violoncellist, a sound and tasteful composer. Too modest to publish his compositions, he willed them to the archives of the Gesellschaft der Musikfreunde. After personal examination I can only give the assurance that his three string quartets would entitle him to an honorable place among masters of the second rank, and are more deserving to be heard than many new things which, for all manner of reasons, we are compelled to hear."

That Zmeskall was a very constant attendant at the musical parties of

[2] *Ibid.*

Prince Karl Lichnowsky and frequently took part in them, may be seen from Wegeler's record. He was eleven years older than Beethoven, had been long enough in Vienna to know the best society there, into which he was admitted not more because of his musical attainments than because of the respectability of his position and character; and was, therefore, what the young student-pianist needed most, a friend, who at the same time could be to a certain degree an authoritative advisor, and at all times was a judicious one. On the part of Zmeskall there was an instant and hearty appreciation of the extraordinary powers of the young stranger from the Rhine and a clear anticipation of his splendid artistic future. A singular proof of this is the care with which he preserved the most insignificant scraps of paper, if Beethoven had written a few words upon them; for, certainly, no other motive could have induced him to save many notes of this kind and of no importance for ten, fifteen, twenty years, as may be seen in the published letters of the composer. On the part of Beethoven, there was sincere respect for the dignity and gravity of Zmeskall's character, which usually restrained him within proper limits in their personal intercourse; but he delighted, especially in the earlier period, to give, in his notes and letters, full play to his queer fancies and sometimes extravagant humor.

Here are a few examples in point:

Will His Highly Wellborn, His Herrn von Zmeskall's Zmeskality have the kindness to say where one might speak with him tomorrow.

We are your most damnably

devoted Beethoven

[Address] To His Highly Well-Well-Bestborn, the Herr von Zmeskall, Imperial and Royal and also Royal-Imperial Court Secretary.

Also the following:

My dearest Baron Muckcart-driver,

Je vous suis bien obligé pour votre faiblesse de vos yeux.—Moreover I forbid you henceforth to rob me of the good humor into which I occasionally fall, for yesterday your Zmeskall-Domanoveczian chatter made me melancholy. The devil take you, I want none of your moral principles. *Power* is the morality of men who loom above the others, and it is also mine; and if you begin again today I'll torment you until you agree that everything that I do is good and praiseworthy. (For I am coming to the Swan—the Ox would indeed be preferable, but this rests with your Zmeskallian Domanoveczian decision) (Response) Adieu Baron ba . . . . ron ron/nor/orn/rno/onr/ (voilà quelque chose from the old pawnshop)

The relation of the phrase "Je vous suis bien obligé pour votre faiblesse de vos yeux" to the "Duett mit zwei obligaten Augengläsern" has already been mentioned. At the end of this letter occurs an early example not only of Beethoven's playfulness with letters, but his love of puns in his use of the word "Versatzamt" (pawnshop). "Versetzen" also means to transpose (notes, words or letters). Was not the "quelque chose" from the pawnshop the duet for viola and violoncello? —

Mechanical skill was never so developed in Beethoven that he could make good pens from goose quills—and the days of other pens were not yet. When, therefore, he had no one with him to aid him in this, he usually sent to Zmeskall for a supply. Of the large number of such applications preserved by his friend and now scattered among civilized lands as autographs, here are two specimens:

Best of Music Counts! I beg of you to send me one or a few pens of which I am really in great need.

As soon as I learn where really good and admirable pens are to be found I will buy some of them. I hope to see you at the *Swan* today.

Adieu, most precious Music Count

His Highness von Z. is commanded to hasten a bit with the plucking of a few of his quills (among them, no doubt, some not his own). It is hoped that they may not be too tightly grown in. As soon as you have done all that we shall ask we shall be, with excellent esteem your

F———

Beethoven

Had Zmeskall not carefully treasured these notes, they would never have met any eye but his own; it is evident, therefore, that he entered fully into their humor, and that it was the same to him, whether he found himself addressed as "Baron," "Count," "Cheapest Baron," "Music Count," or simply "Dear Z."—which last is the more usual. He knew his man, and loved him; and these "quips and quiddities" were received in the spirit which begat them. The whole tenor of the correspondence between the two shows that Zmeskall had more influence for good upon Beethoven than any other of his friends; he could reprove him for faults, and check him when in the wrong, without producing a quarrel more serious than the one indicated in the protest, above given, against interrupting his "good humor."

As a musician, as well as man and friend, Zmeskall stood high in Beethoven's esteem. His apartments, No. 1166, in that huge conglomeration of buildings known as the Bürgerspital, were for a long series of years the scene of a private morning concert, to which only the first performers of chamber music and a very few guests were admitted. Here, after the rupture with Prince Lichnowsky, Beethoven's productions of this class were usually first tried over. Not until Beethoven's death did their correspondence cease.

Another young man who gained an extraordinary place in Beethoven's esteem and affection, and who departed from Vienna before anything occurred to cause a breach between them, was a certain Karl Amenda, from the shore of the Baltic, who died some forty years later as Provost in Courland. He was a good violinist, belonged to the circle of dilettanti which Beethoven so much affected, and, on parting, received from the composer one of his first attempts at quartet composition. His name most naturally suggests itself to fill the blank in a letter to Ries, July, 1804, wherein some living person, not named, is mentioned as one with whom he (Beethoven) "never had a misunderstanding." Their correspondence shows that their friendship was of the romantic character once so much the fashion; and a letter of Amenda is filled with incense which in our day would bear the name of almost too gross flattery. But times change and tastes with them.

His name appears once in the Zmeskall correspondence, namely, in a mutilated note now in the National Library in Vienna, beginning: "My cheapest Baron! Tell the guitarist to come to me today. *Amenda* is to make an *Amende* [part torn away] which he deserves for his bad pauses [torn] provide the guitarist."[3] ---{The guitarist was Gottfried Mylich, mentioned below.}---

Karl Amenda was born on October 4, 1771, at Lippaiken in Courland. He studied music with his father and Kapellmeister Beichtmer, was so good a violinist that he was able to give a concert at 14 years of age, and continued his musical studies after he was matriculated as a student of theology at the University of Jena. After a three year's course there, he set out on a tour and reached Vienna in the spring of 1798. There he first became precentor for Prince Lobkowitz and afterward music-teacher in the family of Mozart's widow. How, thereupon, he became acquainted with Beethoven we are able to report from a document still in the possession of the family, which bears the superscription "Brief Account of the Friendly Relations between L. v. Beethoven and Karl Friedrich Amenda, afterwards Provost at Talsen in Courland, written down from oral tradition":

After the completion of his theological studies K. F. Amenda goes to Vienna, where he several times meets Beethoven at the table d'hôte, attempts to enter into conversation with him, but without success, since Beeth. remains very *réservé*. After some time Amenda, who meanwhile had become music-teacher at the home of Mozart's widow, receives an invitation from a friendly family and there plays first violin in a quartet. While he was playing somebody turned the pages for him, and when he turned about at the finish he was frightened to see Beethoven, who had taken the trouble to do this and now withdrew with a bow. The next day the extremely amiable host at the evening party appeared and cried out: "What have you done? You have captured Beethoven's heart! B. requests that you rejoice him with your company." A., much pleased, hurries to B., who at once asks him to play with him. This is done and when, after several hours, A. takes his leave, B. accompanies him to his quarters, where there was music again. As B. finally prepared to go he said to A.: "I suppose you can accompany me." This is done, and B. kept A. till evening and went with him to his home late at night. From that time the mutual visits became more and more numerous

---

[3] Miss Anderson supplies an effective interpretation of the second sentence with the missing words in brackets: "*Amenda* instead of paying an *amende* [which he ought to do occasionally] for his failure to observe rests, must let me have this [admirable] guitarist." See *A*, 29.

and the two took walks together, so that the people in the streets when they saw only one of them in the street at once called out: "Where is the other one?" A. also introduced Mylich, with whom he had come to Vienna, to B., and Mylich often played trios with B. and A. His instrument was the second violin or viola. Once when B. heard that Mylich had a sister in Courland who played the piano-forte prettily, he handed him a sonata in manuscript with the inscription: "To the sister of my good friend Mylich." The manuscript was rolled up and tied with a little silk ribbon. B. complained that he could not get along on the violin. Asked by A. to try it, nevertheless, he played so fearfully that A. had to call out: "Have mercy—quit!" B. quit playing and the two laughed till they had to hold their sides. One evening B. improvised marvellously on the pianoforte and at the close A. said: "It is a great pity that such glorious music is born and lost in a moment." Whereupon B.: "There you are mistaken; I can repeat every extempo-rization"; whereupon he sat himself down and played it again without a change. B. was frequently embarrassed for money. Once he complained to A.; he had to pay rent and had no idea how he could do it. "That's easily remedied," said A. and gave him a theme ("Freudvoll und Leidvoll") and locked him in his room with the remark that he must make a beginning on the variations within three hours. When A. returns he finds B. on the spot but ill-tempered. To the question whether or not he had begun B. handed over a paper with the remark: "There's your stuff!" (*Da ist der Wisch!*) A. takes the notes joyfully to B.'s landlord and tells him to take it to a publisher, who would pay him handsomely for it. The landlord hesitated at first but finally decided to do the errand and, returning joyfully, asks if other bits of paper like that were to be had. But in order definitely to relieve such financial needs A. advised B. to make a trip to Italy. B. says he is willing but only on condition that A. go with him. A. agrees gladly and the trip is practically planned. Unfortunately news of a death calls A. back to his home. His brother has been killed in an accident and the duty of caring for the family devolves on him. With doubly oppressed heart A. takes leave of B. to return to his home in Courland. There he receives a letter from B. saying: "Since you cannot go along, I shall not go to Italy." Later the friends frequently exchanged thoughts by correspondence.

Though, as we have learned, it was music which brought Beethoven into contact with Amenda, it was the latter's amiability and nobility of character that endeared him to the composer, who cherished him as one of his dearest friends and confided things to him which he concealed from his other intimates—his deafness, for instance. A striking proof of Beethoven's affec-tion is offered by the fact that he gave Amenda a copy of his Quartet in F (Op. 18, No. 1), writing on the first violin part:

Dear Amenda: Take this quartet as a small memorial of our friendship, and whenever you play it recall the days which we passed together and the sincere affection felt for you then and which will always be felt by

Your warm and true friend
Ludwig van Beethoven

Vienna, 1799, June 25.

In a letter written nearly two years later Beethoven asks his friend not to lend the quartet, as he had revised it.

--◦◦{Before Amenda's return to his home in Courland in the fall of 1799, Beethoven wrote him the following letter:

Today I received an invitation to go to Mödling in the country; I have accepted it and leave for there this evening for a few days. It was all the more welcome since my heart already lacerated would have suffered all the more; although the main storm has been repulsed again, still I am not yet completely certain how my plan against it will be worked out. Yesterday I was offered a trip to Poland in the month of September, whereby the trip as well as the stay costs me nothing, and I can have a good time in Poland and also earn some money; I have accepted it.—Goodbye, dear A., and give me news soon of your stops on the way, and also how and when you arrive in your native land—Pleasant journey and do not forget

Your Bthvn[4]

Nothing came of the invitation to Poland, but presumably this is Beethoven's first contact with Mödling.[5] Kalischer suggests[6] that the "laceration" is connected with Beethoven's unsuccessful proposal of marriage to Magdalena Willmann, which will be discussed presently.}◦◦--

Count Moritz Lichnowsky, brother of Prince Karl, of whom we shall not lose sight entirely until the closing scene, was another of the friends of those years. He had been a pupil of Mozart, played the pianoforte with much skill and was an influential member of the party which defended the novelty and felt the grandeur of his friend's compositions. Schindler saw much of him during Beethoven's last years, and eulogizes the "noble Count" in very strong terms.

Another of that circle of young dilettanti, and one of the first players of Beethoven's compositions, was a young Jewish violinist, Heinrich Eppinger. He played at a charity concert in Vienna, making his first appearance there in 1789. "He became, in after years," says a correspondent of the time, "a dilettante of the most excellent reputation, lived modestly on a small fortune and devoted himself entirely to music." At the period before us Eppinger was one of Beethoven's first violins at the private concerts of the nobility. Häring, who became a distinguished merchant and banker, belonged now to this circle of young amateur musicians, and in 1794 had the reputation of being at the head of the amateur violinists. The youthful friendship between him and the composer was not interrupted as they advanced into life, and twenty years later was of great advantage to Beethoven.

But a more interesting person for us is the instructor under whom

---

[4] The friends continued to correspond with each other for awhile. Amenda was first a private teacher, became a preacher in Talsen in 1802, provost of the diocese of Kadau in 1820, consistorial councillor in 1830, and died on March 8, 1836. A portrait painted in 1808 is preserved in the Beethoven Museum in Bonn. (TDR, II, 121.)

[5] See Frimmel, "Beethoven in Mödling," Heft VIII of *Beethoven-Forschung* (October, 1918), p. 118.

[6] *Sämtliche Briefe*, I, No. 31.

Beethoven in Vienna resumed his study of the violin (a fact happily pre-served by Ries)—Wenzel Krumpholz. He came to Vienna in 1795 to join the operatic orchestra, and at once became noted as a performer of Haydn's quartets. He was (says Eugene Eiserle in Glöggl's *Neue Wiener Musik-Zeitung* of August 13, 1857), "a highly sensitive art-enthusiast, and one of the first who foresaw and recognized Beethoven's greatness."

Krumpholz was a virtuoso on the mandolin, and for that reason, apparently, Beethoven wrote a few pieces for pianoforte and mandolin in these years.[7] ⸺⸻Krumpholz concerns us also as the friend through whom the Czerny family became acquainted with Beethoven. Carl Czerny (1791-1857) was shortly to become one of the composer's real students. The following extracts from Carl Czerny's memoirs (1842) show how this introduction led to his long association with the master. The original manuscript is in the archives of the Gesellschaft der Musikfreunde, and the translation used here is from *Beethoven, Impressions of Contemporaries*, New York, 1926 (pp. 24ff.).

"At that time an old man named Krumpholz (brother of the inventor of the pedal harp) visited us nearly every evening. He was a violinist and as such had a position in the orchestra of the Court Theatre; yet at the same time he was a musical enthusiast whose passion for music was carried to the most extravagant lengths. Nature has endowed him with a just and delicate feeling for the beautiful in tonal art, and though he possessed no great fund of technical knowledge, he was able to criticize every composition with much acumen, and, so to say, anticipate the judgments of the musical world.

"As soon as young Beethoven appeared for the first time, Krumpholz attached himself to him with a persistence and devotion which soon made him a familiar figure in his home, so that he practically spent nearly the whole day with him, and Beethoven, who ordinarily was most reticent with every-one regarding his musical projects, told Krumpholz about all his ideas, played every new composition for him time and again, and improvised for him every day. Although Beethoven often poked fun at the unfeigned ecstasies into which Krumpholz invariably fell, and never called him any-thing but his jester; yet he was touched by his attachment, which led him to affront the bitterest enmities in order to defend his cause against his adversaries, so numerous in those days. For at that time Beethoven's composi-tions were totally misunderstood by the general public, and all the followers of the old Mozart-Haydn school opposed them with the most intense animosity.

"This was the man for whom, day by day, I had to play Beethoven's works, and although he knew nothing of piano playing, he was, quite naturally, able to tell me a great deal about their tempo, interpretation, effects, characteristics, etc., since he often heard them played by Beethoven

[7] See KHV, WoO 43.

himself, and in most cases had been present when they came into being. His enthusiasm soon infected me and before long I, in turn, was a Beethoven worshipper like himself, learned all that Beethoven had written by heart, and, considering my years, played it with skill and enthusiasm. Krumpholz also invariably told me about the new things Beethoven had "under pen," and would sing or play on his violin the themes he had heard in Beethoven's home during the forenoon. Owing to this circumstance I was always informed at a much earlier date than others with regard to what Beethoven had under way. Later this made it possible for me to realize how long, often for years at a time, Beethoven polished his compositions before they were published, and how in new works he used motives which had occurred to him many years before, because our friendly relations with Krumpholz were maintained over a long period of years up to his death, which took place in 1817.

"I was about ten years old when Krumpholz took me to see Beethoven. With what joy and terror I greeted the day on which I was to meet the admired master! Even now this moment is vividly present in my memory. It was a winter's day when my father, Krumpholz, and I took our way from Leopoldstadt (where we were still living) to Vienna proper, to a street called *der tiefe Graben* (the Deep Ditch), and climbed endless flights to the fifth and sixth story, where a rather untidy looking servant announced us to Beethoven and then admitted us. The room presented a most disorderly appearance; papers and articles of clothing were scattered about everywhere, some trunks, bare walls, hardly a chair, save the wobbly one at the Walter fortepiano (then the best), and in this room was gathered a company of from six to eight persons, among them the two Wranitsky brothers, Süssmayr, Schuppanzigh and one of Beethoven's brothers.

"Beethoven himself wore a morning coat of some longhaired, dark grey material, and trousers to match, so that he at once recalled to me the picture in Campe's 'Robinson Crusoe,' which I was reading at the time. His coal black hair, cut *à la Titus*, bristled shaggily about his head. His beard—he had not been shaved for several days—made the lower part of his already brown face still darker. I also noticed with that visual quickness peculiar to children that he had cotton which seemed to have been steeped in a yellowish liquid, in his ears.

"At that time, however, he did not give the least evidence of deafness. I was at once told to play something, and since I did not dare begin with one of his own compositions, played Mozart's great C major Concerto, the one beginning with chords. Beethoven soon gave me his attention, drew near my chair, and in those passages where I had only accompanying passages played the orchestral melody with me, using his left hand. His hands were overgrown with hair and his fingers, especially at the ends, were very broad. The satisfaction he expressed gave me the courage to play his *Sonata pathétique*, which had just appeared, and finally his 'Adelaide,' which my father sang in his very passable tenor. When he had ended Beethoven turned to him and said: 'The boy has talent. I will teach him myself and accept him as my pupil. Send him to me several times a week. First of all, however, get him a copy of Emanuel Bach's book on the true art of piano playing, for he must bring it with him the next time he comes.' Then all those present congratulated my father on this favorable verdict, Krumpholz in particular being quite delighted, and my father at once hurried off to hunt up Bach's book."

The very common mistake of forgetting that there is a time in the lives of distinguished men when they are but aspirants to fame, when they have their reputations still to make, often, in fact, attracting less notice and raising feebler hopes of future distinction in those who know them, than many a more precocious contemporary—this mistake has thrown the figures of Schuppanzigh and his associates in the quartet concerts at Prince Karl Lichnowsky's into a very false prominence in the picture of these first seven years of Beethoven's Vienna life. The composer himself was not the Beethoven whom *we* know. Had he died in 1800, his place in musical history would have been that of a great pianoforte player and of a very promising young composer, whose decease thus in his prime had disappointed well-founded hopes of great future eminence.

This is doubly true of the members of the quartet. Had they passed away in early manhood, not one of them, except perhaps young Kraft, the only one who ever distinguished himself as a virtuoso upon his instrument, would have been remembered in the annals of music. They were during these years but laying the foundation for future excellence and celebrity as performers of Mozart's, Haydn's, Förster's and Beethoven's quartets. Schuppanzigh, first violin, and Weiss, viola, alone appear to have been constantly associated in their quartet-playing. Kraft, violoncellist, was often absent, when his father, or Zmeskall, or some other, supplied his place; and as the second violin was often taken by the master of the house, when they were engaged for private concerts, Sina was, naturally, absent. Still, from 1794 to 1799, the four appear to have practised much and very regularly together. They enjoyed an advantage known to no other quartet—that of playing the compositions of Haydn and Förster under the eyes of the composers, and being taught by them every effect that the music was intended to produce. Each of the performers, therefore, knowing precisely the intentions of the composer, acquired the difficult art of being independent and at the same time of being subordinate to the general effect. When Beethoven began to compose quartets he had, therefore, a set of performers schooled to perfection by his great predecessors, and who already had experience in his own music through his trios and sonatas.

Ignaz Schuppanzigh, the leader, born 1776, died March 2, 1830 in Vienna, originally studied music as a dilettante and became a capital player of the viola; but, about the time when Beethoven came to Vienna, he exchanged that instrument for the violin and made music his profession. He was fond of directing orchestral performances and seems to have gained a considerable degree of local reputation and to have been somewhat of a favorite in that capacity before reaching his 21st year. In 1798-99, he took charge of those concerts in the Augarten established by Mozart and Martin, and afterwards led by Rudolph. Seyfried, writing after his death, calls Schuppanzigh a "natural born and really energetic leader of the orchestra." The difference in age, character and social position between him and Beethoven was such as not to admit between them that higher and nobler friendship which united the latter and Zmeskall; but they could be, and were, of great use to each other, and there was a strong personal liking, if not affection, which was mutual. Schuppanzigh's person early assumed very much of the form and proportions of Sterne's Dr. Slop, and after his return from Russia he is one of the "Milord Falstaffs" of Beethoven's correspondence and Conversation Books. His obesity was, however, already the subject of the composer's jests, and he must have been an exceedingly good-tempered young man, to bear with and forgive the coarse and even abusive text of the short vocal piece (1801) headed "Lob auf den Dicken" ("Praise of the Fat One").[8] But it is evidently a mere jest, and was taken as such. It is worthy of note that Beethoven and Schuppanzigh in addressing each other used neither the familiar "du" nor the respectful "Sie," but "er"—a fact which has been supposed to prove Beethoven's great contempt for the violinist; but as it would prove equal contempt on the other side, it proves too much. Of Sina and Weiss, both Silesians by birth, there is little that need be added here. Weiss became the first viola player of Vienna, and a not unsuccessful composer of ballet and other music.

Anton Kraft (the father) came from Bohemia to pursue his legal studies in Vienna, but abandoned them to enter the Imperial Court Orchestra as violoncellist. In 1778, he accepted an invitation from Haydn to join the orchestra in Esterhaz; where, on the 14th of December of the same year, his son Nikolaus Anton was born. The child, endowed by nature with great musical talents, enjoyed the advantages of his father's instructions and example and of growing up under the eye of Haydn and in the constant study of that great musician's works. Upon the death of Esterhazy and the dispersion of his orchestra, Kraft came with his son, now in his fourteenth year, to Vienna. On April 15, 1792, Nikolaus played a concerto composed by his father at the Widows and Orphans concert, and on the 21st again appeared in a concert given by the father. Notwithstanding a very remarkable success, the son was originally destined for another profession than music; and from this time until his eighteenth year, he played his instrument only as an amateur, and as such Beethoven first knew the youth. But when the young Prince Lobkowitz formed his orchestra in 1796, both the

---

[8] This ditty may be found in the earlier editions (1st to 4th) of Grove's *Dictionary* under "Schuppanzigh."

Krafts were engaged, and Nikolaus Anton thenceforth made music his profession. In the maturity of his years and powers, his only rival among all the German violoncellists was Bernhard Romberg.

Johann Nepomuk Hummel, the pupil of Mozart, was another of the youths whom Beethoven drew into his circle. In 1795, the elder Hummel brought back his son to Vienna (from that very successful concert tour which had occupied the last six years and had made the boy known even to the cities of distant Scotland) and put him to the studies of counterpoint and composition with Albrechtsberger and Salieri. He seems to have been quietly at his studies, playing only in private, until April 28, 1799, when he again appeared in public both as pianist and composer, in a concert in the Augartensaal, directed by Schuppanzigh. "He performed a symphony besides a melodrama composed for the occasion and between them played prettily *composed* improvisations on the pianoforte." That the talented and promising boy of seventeen years should, upon arriving home again, seek the acquaintance and favor of one who during his absence had made so profound an impression upon the Vienna public as Beethoven, and that the latter should have rejoiced to show kindness to Mozart's favorite pupil, hardly needs to be mentioned. A chapter of description would not illustrate the nature of their intercourse so vividly, as two short but exceedingly characteristic notes of Beethoven's which Hummel preserved and which found their way into print after his death:

I

He is not to come to me again. He is a treacherous dog and may the flayer get all such treacherous dogs!

II

Herzens Nazerl:

You are an honest fellow and I now see you were right. Come, then, to me this afternoon. You'll find Schuppanzigh here also and we two will bump, thump and pump you to your heart's delight. A kiss from

Your   Beethoven
also called Mehlschöberl.[9]

In a letter to Eleonore von Breuning, Beethoven described many of the Vienna pianists as his "deadly enemies." Schindler's observations upon the composer's relations with the Viennese musicians, though written in his peculiar style, seem to be very judicious and correct. He writes:[10] "Nobody is likely to expect that an artist who made his way upwards as our Beethoven, although almost confining his activities exclusively to aristocratic circles that

---

[9] "Herzens Nazerl" is to be understood as "Dear little Ignacius of my heart." Unger (*Neue Musik-Zeitung*, Vol. 45 [1924], p. 9) points out that these two notes are now lost, and that it is unclear whether they were addressed to Hummel. Kalischer (*Briefe*, I, 37) assumes that "Nazerl" is a nickname for Hummel's middle name Nepomuk. "Mehlschöberl" is a sort of soup dumpling. (TK, I, 240, n. 1.)

[10] *Biographie*, I, pp. 23-24. (TDR, II, 129.)

upheld him in extraordinary fashion, would remain free from the attacks of his colleagues; on the contrary, the reader will be prepared to see a host of enemies advance against him because of the shining qualities and evidences of genius of our hero, in contrast with the heavy burden of social idiosyncrasies and uncouthness. More than anything else, what seemed least tolerable to his opponents was the notion that his appearance, the excitability which he controlled too little in his intercourse with his colleagues and his lack of consideration in passing judgment were natural accompaniments of genius. His too small toleration of many eccentricities and weaknesses of high society, and on the other hand his severe demand on his colleagues for higher culture, even his Bonn dialect, afforded his enemies more than enough material to revenge themselves on him by evil gossip and slander. . . . The musicians in Vienna at that time, with a very few exceptions, were lacking, not only in artistic, but also in the most necessary degree of general, education and were as full of the envy of handicraftsmen as the members of the guilds themselves. There was a particular antipathy to all foreigners as soon as they manifested a purpose to make their homes in the imperial city."

In a description of musical activity in Vienna in the third year of the *Allgemeine Musikalische Zeitung* (October, 1800, p. 67) is to be found the following: "Should he [the foreign artist] intend to stay here, the whole *corpus musicum* is his enemy." Not until the course of the third decade does the situation change.

Schindler might have added that the change had been in no small degree produced through the instructions and example of Beethoven as they acted upon the Czernys, Moscheles and other young admirers of his genius. In short, Beethoven's instant achievement of a position as artist only paralleled by Mozart and of a social rank which Gluck, Salieri, Haydn had gained only after making their names famous throughout Europe, together with the general impression that the mantle of Mozart had fallen upon him— all this begat bitter envy in those whom his talents and genius overshadowed; they revenged themselves by deriding him for his personal peculiarities and by condemning and ridiculing the novelties in his compositions; while he met their envy with disdain, their criticisms with contempt; and, when he did not treat their compositions with indifference, he too often only noticed them with sarcasm. This picture, certainly, is not an agreeable one, but all the evidence proves it, unfortunately, faithful.

Such men as Salieri, Gyrowetz, Weigl, are not to be understood as included in the term "pianist" as used by Beethoven in his letter to Eleonore von Breuning. For these men "stood high in Beethoven's respect," says Schindler, and his words are confirmed to the fullest extent by the Conversation Books and other authorities; which also show that Eybler's name might have been added to the list. They were all more or less older than Beethoven, and for their contrapuntal learning, particularly in the case of Weigl and Eybler, he esteemed them very highly. No indications, however, have been found, that he was upon terms of close private friendship and intimacy with either.

Beethoven was no exception to the general rule, that men of genius delight in warm and lasting friendships with women of superior minds and culture—not meaning those "conquests" which, according to Wegeler, even during his first three years in Vienna, "he occasionally made, which if not impossible for many an Adonis would still have been difficult." Let such matters, even if detail concerning them were now attainable, be forgotten. His celibacy was by no means owing to a deliberate choice at first of a single life. What is necessary and proper of the little that is known on *this* point will, in due time, be imparted simply and free from gloss or superfluous comment. As to his friendships with the other sex, it would be throwing the view of them into very false perspective to employ those of later years in giving piquancy to a chapter here. Let them also come in due order and thus, while they lose nothing of interest, they may, perchance afford relief and give brightness to canvas which otherwise might sometimes become too sombre. Happily during these prosperous years now before us, the picture has been for the most part bright and sunny and the paucity of the information upon the topic in question of less consequence.

In the present connection one of our old Bonn friends again comes upon the scene. The beautiful, talented and accomplished Magdalena Willmann was invited to sing at Venice during the carnival of 1794.[11] She left Bonn the preceding summer with her brother Max and his wife (Fräulein Tribolet) to fulfill the engagement. After leaving Venice, they gave a concert in Graz, and journeyed on to Vienna. Here Max and his wife remained, having accepted engagements from Schikaneder, while Magdalena went on to Berlin. Not suiting the operatic public there she returned to Vienna, and was soon engaged to sing both German and Italian parts in the Court Opera. Beethoven renewed his intercourse with the Willmanns and soon became so captivated with the charms of the beautiful Magdalena as to offer her his hand. This fact was communicated to the author by a daughter of Max Willmann, still living in 1860, who had often heard her father speak of it. To the question, why Magdalena did not accept the offer of Beethoven, Madame S. hesitated a moment, and then, laughing, replied: "Because he was so ugly, and half crazy!" In 1799, Magdalena married a certain Galvani, but her happiness was short; she died toward the end of 1801.

Two letters of Beethoven[12] have been preserved from the period before us, addressed to Christine Gerhardi, a young woman of high distinction in society at the time for the splendor of her talents and her high culture. Dr. Sonnleithner wrote of her: "She was the daughter of an official at the court of the Emperor Leopold II . . . an excellent singer, but remained a

[11] Beethoven knew her as a member of the Bonn Theatre, and the Willmann family participated in the trip to Mergentheim. (Cf. TDR, II, 132, n. 2.)

[12] *A*, 23 and 24. A third letter (*A*, 45) addressed to Frau Frank-Gerhardi, was obviously written after her marriage.

dilettante and sang chiefly in concerts for charitable purposes (which she herself arranged), or for the benefit of eminent artists. Old Professor Peter Frank was director of the general hospital of Vienna in the neighborhood of which (No. 20 Alserstrasse) she lived. He was a great lover of music, but his son, Dr. Joseph Frank, was a greater; he made essays in composition and arranged musical soirées at the home of his father at which Beethoven and Fräulein Gerhardi took part, playing and singing. The son frequently composed cantatas, which Beethoven corrected, for the namedays and birthdays of his father, and in which Fräulein Gerhardi sang the soprano solos. . . . She was at the time the most famous amateur singer in Vienna, and inasmuch as Haydn knew her well there is no doubt but that he had her in mind when he composed *The Creation*; indeed, she sang the soprano part with great applause not only at Schwarzenberg but also at the first performance in the Burgtheater. All reports agree that she met Beethoven often at Frank's and that he frequently accompanied her singing on the pianoforte. He did not give her lessons."

Dr. Joseph von Frank and Christine Gerhardi were married on August 20, 1798; they moved away from Vienna in 1804.

A few notes upon certain young women to whom Beethoven dedicated compositions at this period of his life may be appropriate here. It was much the custom then for teachers of music to dedicate their works to pupils, especially to those who belonged to the higher social ranks—such dedications being at the same time compliments to the pupils and advertisements for the instructors, with the further advantage often of being sources of pecuniary profit. When, therefore, we read the name of Baroness Albini on the title-page of certain sonatas by Sterkel, of Julia Countess Guicciardi on one by Kleinheinz, of Anna Countess Mailath on songs by Teyber, we assume at once the probability in these and like instances that the relation of master and pupil existed. Beethoven also followed the custom; and the young ladies, subjects of the following notices, are all known or supposed to have taken lessons of him.

Anna Louisa Barbara ("La Comtesse Babette") was the daughter of Karl Count Keglevics de Busin, of Hungarian Croatian lineage, and Barbara Countess Zichy. She was soon married to Prince Innocenzo d'Erba-Odescalchi. Beethoven's dedications to her are the Sonata, Op. 7 (published in 1797), the Variations "La stessa, la stessissima" (1799), the Pianoforte Concerto, Op. 15, 1801 and the Pianoforte Variations in F, Op. 34—the last two to her as Princess Odescalchi. A note by the composer to Zmeskall—which, judging both from its contents and the handwriting, could not have been written later than 1801-1802—shows that the Odescalchi palace was one of those at which he took part in musical soirées.[13]

"Countess Henriette Lichnowsky," writes Count Amade, "was the sister of the ruling Prince Karl, and was doubtless married to the Marquis of

[13] See *A*, 56.

Carneville after the dedication to her of the Rondo (G major, Op. 51, No. 2, published in September, 1802); she lived in Paris after her marriage and died about 1830." The Rondo was first dedicated to Countess Julia Guicciardi, but Beethoven asked for it back in exchange for the C-sharp minor Sonata; to which fact we shall recur presently. Countess Thun, to whom Beethoven dedicated the Clarinet Trio, Op. 11, in 1798, was the mother-in-law of Prince Karl Lichnowsky. She died May 18, 1800.

The Sonata in E-flat, Op. 27, No. 1, was dedicated to Josepha Sophia, wife of Prince Johann Joseph von Liechtenstein, daughter of Joachim Egon, Landgrave of Fürstenberg-Weitra. Whether her father was related at all, and if so, how, to the Fürstenberg in whose house Beethoven gave lessons in Bonn, is not known. Her husband, however, was first cousin to Count Ferdinand von Waldstein. The Baroness Braun to whom Beethoven dedicated the two Pianoforte Sonatas, Op. 14 and the Sonata for Horn in 1801, was the wife of Baron Peter von Braun, a successful businessman, and lessee of the National-Theater and afterwards of the Theater-an-der-Wien. The dedications disclose an early association which eventually led to Beethoven's being asked to compose an opera. It is not known that Beethoven was a social visitor in the house of Baron Braun, but he was a highly respected guest in the house of Count Browne, to whom he dedicated the String Trios, Op. 9. The Countess received dedications to the "Waldmädchen" and "Tandeln und scherzen" Variations as well as the three Pianoforte Sonatas, Op. 10.

To this list should be added the names of the Countesses Therese and Josephine Brunsvik who, with the rest of their family, became such good friends of the composer. Beethoven's relationship with each of the sisters was different, as we shall see, and his friendship also with the brother, Count Franz, was a deep and enduring one.[14] In 1846, Therese started writing her memoirs, which she entitled "My Half Century," based on a journal which she had kept over the years. Published by La Mara,[15] both of these form important sources for the understanding of Beethoven's relationships to the members of this family. The Brunsviks lived in Martonvásár, Hungary, from whence the widowed mother brought Josephine and Therese to Vienna for a brief visit in 1799. Both daughters were well educated and trained sufficiently in music so that the mother wanted them, while in Vienna, to have lessons from none other than Beethoven himself. Therese describes these first meetings:[16]

[14] Beethoven's friendship with the Count was sufficiently intimate so that they addressed each other as "Du" in their correspondence, as Miss Anderson points out (p. 168, n. 1.)

[15] La Mara (Marie Lipsius) brought out two important publications about the Brunsvik family, using Therese's memoirs, parts of the family correspondence, and excerpts from Therese's journal. The first, in which she names Therese as the Immortal Beloved, was published in Leipzig in 1909 and entitled *Beethovens unsterbliche Geliebte*. The second, *Beethoven und die Brunsviks*, was published in Leipzig in 1920. In this she favors Josephine. For convenience in footnotes these works will be referred to by their dates of publication.

[16] From Therese's memoirs, in La Mara, 1909, pp. 63ff. This narrative, and any descrip-

"During the extraordinary sojourn of 18 days in Vienna my mother desired that her two daughters, Therese and Josephine, receive Beethoven's invaluable instruction in music. Adalbert Rosti, a schoolmate of my brother's, assured us that Beethoven would not be persuaded to accept a mere invitation; but that if Her Excellency were willing to climb the three flights of stairs of the house in St. Peter's Place, and make him a visit, he would vouch for a successful outcome of the mission. It was done. Like a schoolgirl, with Beethoven's Sonatas for Violin and Violoncello and Pianoforte under my arm, we entered. The immortal, dear Louis van Beethoven was very friendly and as polite as he could be. After a few phrases de part et d'autre, he sat me down at his pianoforte, which was out of tune, and I began at once to sing the violin and the 'cello parts and played right well. This delighted him so much that he promised to come every day to the Hotel zum Erzherzog Carl—then zum Goldenen Greifen. It was May in the last year of the last century. He came regularly, but instead of an hour frequently stayed from twelve to four or five o'clock, and never grew weary of holding down and bending my fingers, which I had been taught to lift high and hold straight. The noble man must have been satisfied; for he never missed a single day in the 16. We felt no hunger until five o'clock. My good mother bore her hunger—the inn-people, however, were indignant, for it had not yet become the custom to eat dinner at five o'clock in the evening.

"It was then that the most intimate and cordial friendship was established with Beethoven, a friendship which lasted to the end of his life. He came to Ofen, he came to Martonvásár; he was initiated into our social republic of chosen people. A round spot was planted with high, noble lindens; each tree had the name of a member, and even in their sorrowful absence we conversed with their symbols, and were entertained and instructed by them."

On May 23, 1799, Beethoven wrote in an album for his two young pupils a song in D on Goethe's text, "Ich denke dein," and four variations upon it for four hands.[17] Four years later he added two more variations; and the third sister, Charlotte, wrote to Josephine on September 9, 1803:[18] "Apropos de Musique, savez vous deja que Bt. a composé encore deux variations dans notre Stambuch; n'est il pas bien aimable, et adorable . . . ." In the published version these later two variations became the third and the fourth.

Returning to 1799, while in Vienna the ladies also made the acquaintance of Count Joseph Deym, also known as Herr Müller,[19] who was the pro-

---

tions by Therese, unless otherwise noted, are drawn from this source. The section covering this period is pp. 63-69.

[17] Beethoven's original intention had been to give each stanza of Goethe's poem "Nähe des Geliebten" a separate setting, and to this end he made two sketches which are associated with the Quartet sketches and belong to the

year 1799. (See *II Beeth.*, p. 486.)

[18] See J. Schmidt-Görg, "Neue Briefe und Schriftstücke aus der Familie Brunsvik," *BJ* (1955-56), pp. 19-20.

[19] Count Deym had changed his name to Müller because of a duel (then unlawful) which he had fought before he attained his majority. (TK, I, 345.)

prietor of the famed Müller Art Museum in Vienna. The mother thought that this would be a suitable match for Josephine, and unfortunately did not take the time to investigate carefully Deym's financial and social status. "You, dear Josephine, can make me and your sisters happy," Therese quotes her mother as saying when urging the marriage upon her daughter. But Josephine herself was far from happy. The hastily arranged marriage took place, and on June 29, 1799, Josephine moved from Martonvásár into quarters in one wing of the eighty-room museum house in Vienna, married to a man thirty years her senior. She wrote to her sisters: "Separated from you and your love, I shall never be able to be happy, although my husband is very nice, but his education, his outlook, his age are all so different from mine. I want you to choose more successfully than I have, at least to be freer and able to live more according to your own inclination."[20]

By 1800 the Count had gotten badly into debt, partially because he had counted upon, but had never received, a large dowry from the Brunsvik family. Legal wrangles threatened, and the mother, who was in Vienna for the birth of Josephine's first child, pressed for a separation, realising too late that the marriage she had forced upon her daughter offered neither social nor financial advantages. Josephine, on the other hand, was a truly honorable woman; amid stormy scenes with her mother she steadfastly refused to dishonor her marriage vows.

Beethoven proved to be a loyal friend to the young countess in her unhappy circumstances. Therese writes: "The aristocracy turned its back upon him [Deym] because he had gone into business. He could not hunt up his former rich acquaintances. Beethoven was the faithful visitor at the house of the young countess—he gave her lessons gratis and to be tolerated one had to be a Beethoven. The numerous relatives, the sisters of her father and their children, frequently visited their amiable niece. Tableaux were occasionally given; Deym, being himself an artist, was at home in such matters, they gave him pleasure . . . . There were musical soirées. My brother came in vacation-time and made the acquaintance of Beethoven. The two musical geniuses became intimately associated with each other, and my brother never deserted his friend in his frequent financial troubles until his, alas! too early death."

From this it can be seen that Josephine must have derived real comfort from her friendship with the composer, and also that gradually her circle was widening. The following two excerpts from letters written to Therese in the latter part of 1800 confirm this further. On October 28th she writes: "Beethoven is charming. He has promised that he will come every third day to give me a lesson if I am diligent. And that I really am . . . . Beethoven's sonatas are not yet out; as soon as I get them, I will send them to you. I have just learned the first two of the three with violin." On December 10: "We

[20] La Mara, 1920, p. 8.

had music in honor of the archduchess. I had to play and at the same time I was responsible for all arrangements and above all the concern that everything went well. Our rooms were so beautiful that you would have been enchanted. All the doors were opened and everything lit up. I assure you it was a splendid sight! Beethoven played the sonata with violoncello, I played the last of the three sonatas [Op. 12, No. 3] with Schuppanzigh's accompaniment, who played divinely like everybody else. Then Beethoven like a true angel let us hear his new still unpublished quartets [Op. 18] which are the most excellent of their kind. The renowned Kraft undertook the 'cello part, Schuppanzigh the first violin. Imagine what a pleasure it was! The archduchess was enchanted and everything came off wonderfully."[21]

One more excerpt, from a letter Josephine wrote in January, 1801, deserves insertion here: "He [Deym] is rather well disposed, is also tolerably well. Yesterday he was at Beethoven's, in order to look around for what he could give him as a present and finally decided on the silver candlestick that you know well and an inkstand; at the same time he told him so many nice things that Beethoven showed the greatest pleasure and in the afternoon sent Zmeskall especially to thank my husband again. He maintained that nothing else—otherwise he valued silver plate so little—could have been arranged to give him a greater joy. Therefore I am very glad, for the thought oppressed me that the candlestick would not please him very much."

In the Berlin Public Library is the autograph of the first version of the "Ich denke dein" variations which Beethoven wrote for the Countesses Brunsvik.[22] The same autograph contains an Adagio in F major noted on four staves (three with treble, one with bass clef), a Scherzo in G major, 3/4 time, and an Allegro in G major, 2/4. Albert Kopfermann, who published the Adagio for the first time in Vol. I, No. 12, of Die Musik, considers, no doubt correctly, that these last three compositions were written for an automatic musical instrument. They were ordered, undoubtedly, as in the case of Mozart's Andante in F major (K. 616), by Count Deym, in whose museum there was a collection of mechanical instruments.

We return to the subject of Beethoven's friendship with the Countess Deym in 1804; on January 27 of that year the Count died, and the widow's friendship with the composer developed into an affair of the heart.

The year 1800 is an important era in Beethoven's history. It is the year in which, cutting loose from the pianoforte, he asserted his claims to a position with Mozart and the still living and productive Haydn in the

[21] La Mara, 1920, pp. 10ff. Archduchess Julia von Giovane was a cultivated friend of the Deyms.

[22] This first version was published in Prague in 1820, of which copies exist in both the van Hoboken Collection and the Library of Congress. See O. E. Deutsch, "Beethovens Goethe Kompositionen," in the Jahrbuch der Sammlung Kippenberg, Vol. 8 (1930), pp. 107-108, and Vol. 10 (1935), pp. 319-21.

higher forms of chamber and orchestral composition—the quartet and the symphony. It is the year, too, in which the bitter consciousness of an increasing derangement of his organs of hearing was forced upon him and the terrible anticipation of its incurable nature and of its final result in almost total deafness began to harass and distress him. The course of his life was afterwards so modified, on the one hand, by the prosperous issue of these new appeals to the taste and judgment of the public, and, on the other, by the unhappy progress of his malady, each acting and reacting upon a nature singularly exceptional, that some points in his personal character and habits, and a few general remarks upon another topic or two must be made before resuming the narrative of events.

A true and exhaustive picture of Beethoven as a man would present an almost ludicrous contrast to that which is generally entertained as correct. Sculptor and painter in turn has idealized the work of his predecessor, until the composer stands before us like a Homeric god—until those who knew him personally, could they return to earth, would never suspect that the grand form and noble features of the more pretentious portraits are intended to represent the short muscular figure and pock-pitted face of their old friend. In literature evoked by the composer a similar process has gone on, with a corresponding suppression of whatever is deemed common and trivial, until he is made a being living in his own peculiar realm of gigantic ideas, above and apart from the rest of mankind—a sort of intellectual Thor, dwelling in "darkness and clouds of awful state," and making in his music mysterious revelations of things unutterable! But it is really some generations too soon for a conscientious investigator of his history to view him as a semi-mythological personage, or to discover that his notes to friends asking for pens, making appointments to dinner at taverns, or complaining of servants, are "cyclopean blocks of granite," which, like the "chops and tomato sauce" of Mr. Pickwick, contain depths unfathomable of profound meaning. The present age must be content to find in Beethoven, with all his greatness, a very human nature, one which, if it showed extraordinary strength, exhibited also extraordinary weaknesses.

It was the great misfortune of Beethoven's youth—his impulses good and bad being by nature exceedingly quick and violent—that he did not grow up under the influence of a wise and strict parental control, which would have given him those habits of self-restraint that, once fixed, are a second and better nature, and through which the passions, curbed and moderated, remain only as sources of noble energy and power. His very early admission into the orchestra of the theatre as cembalist, was more to the advantage of his musical than of his moral development. It was another misfortune that, in those years, when the strict regulations of a school would have compensated in some measure for the unwise, unsteady, often harsh discipline of his father, he was thus thrown into close connection with actors and actresses, who, in those days, were not very distinguished for the propriety of their manners and morals. Before he became known to the Breuning family and Count Waldstein, he could hardly have learned the importance of cultivating those high principles of life and conduct on which in later years he laid so much stress. And, at that period of life, the character even under ordinary circumstances is so far developed, the habits have become so far formed and fixed, and the natural tendencies have acquired so much strength, that it is, as a rule, too late to conquer the power of a perfect self-command. At all events, the consequences of a deficient early moral education followed Beethoven through life and are visible in the frequent contests between his worse and his better nature and in his constant tendency to extremes. To-day, upon some perhaps trivial matter, he bursts into ungovernable wrath; to-morrow, his penitence exceeds the measure of his fault. To-day he is proud, unbending, offensively careless of those claims which society grants to people of high rank; to-morrow his humility is more than adequate to the occasion. The poverty in which he grew up was not without its effect upon his character. He never learned to estimate money at its real value; though often profuse and generous to a fault, even wasteful, yet at times he would fall into the other extreme. With all his sense of nobility of independence, he early formed the habit of leaning upon others; and this the more, as his malady increased, which certainly was a partial justification; but he thus became prone to follow unwise counsels, or, when his pride was touched, to assert an equally unwise independence. At other times, in the multitude of counsellors he became the victim of utter irresolution, when decision and firmness were indispensable and essential to his welfare. Thus, both by following the impulse of the moment, and by hesitation when a prompt determination was demanded, he took many a false step, which could no longer be retrieved when reflection brought with it bitter regret.

A romantically sentimental admiration of the heroes of ancient classic literature, having its origin in Paris, had become widely the fashion in Beethoven's youth. The democratic theories of the French sentimentalists had received a new impulse from the dignified simplicity of the foreign representatives of the young American Republic, Franklin, Adams, Jay— from the retirement to private life on their plantations and farms of the great military leaders in the contest, Washington, Greene, Schuyler, Knox and others, after the war with England was over; from the pride taken by the French officers, who had served in America, in their insignia of the order of the Cincinnati; and even from the letters and journals of German officers, who, in captivity, had formed friendships with many of the better class of the republican leaders, and seen with their own eyes in what simplicity they lived while guiding the destinies of the new-born nation. Thus through the greater part of Central Europe the idea became current of a pure and sublime humanity, above and beyond the influence of the passions, of which Cincinnatus, Scipio, Cato, Washington, Franklin, were the supposed representatives. Zschokke makes his Heuwen say: "Virtue and the heroes of antiquity had inspired me with enthusiasm for virtue and heroism"; and so, also, Beethoven. He exalted his imagination and fancy by the perusal of the German poets and translations of the ancient and English classics, especially Homer, Plutarch and Shakespeare; dwelt fondly upon the great characters as models for the conduct of life; but between the sentiment which one feels and the active principle on which he acts, there is often a wide cleft. That Beethoven proved to be no Stoic, that he never succeeded in governing his passions with absolute sway, was not because the spirit was unwilling; the flesh was weak. Adequate firmness of character had not been acquired in early years. He who is morbidly sensitive, and compelled to keep constant ward and watch over his passions, can best appreciate and sympathize with the man, Beethoven.

Truth and candor compel the confession, that in those days of prosperity he bore his honors with less of meekness than we could wish; that he had lost something of that modesty and ingenuousness eulogized by Junker ten years before, in his Mergentheim letter. His "somewhat lofty bearing" had even been reported by the correspondent of the *Allgemeine Musikalische Zeitung*. Traces of self-sufficiency and even arrogance—faults almost universal among young and successful geniuses, often in a far higher degree than was true of Beethoven, and with not a tithe of his reason—are unquestionably visible. No one can read without regret his remarks upon certain persons, with whom at this very time he was upon terms of apparently intimate friendship. "I value them," he writes to Amenda in 1801, "only by what they do for me." He speaks of using them "only as instruments upon which I can play when I please." His "somewhat lofty bearing" was matter for jest to the venerable Haydn, who, according to a trustworthy tradition, when Beethoven's visits to him had become few and far between would inquire of other visitors: "How goes it with our Great Mogul?" Nor would the young nobles, whose society he frequented, take offence; but it certainly made him enemies among those whom he "valued according to their service and looked upon as mere instruments"—and no wonder!

Pierson, in his edition of the so-called *Beethovens Studien*, has added to Seyfried's personal sketches a few reminiscences of that Griesinger, who was so long Saxon Minister in Vienna, and to whom we owe the valuable *Biographische Notizen über Joseph Haydn*. One of his anecdotes is to the purpose here and may be taken as substantially historical.[23]

When he was still only an attaché, and Beethoven was little known except as a celebrated pianoforte player, both being still young, they happened to meet at the house of Prince Lobkowitz. In conversation with a gentleman present, Beethoven said in substance, that he wished to be relieved from all bargain and sale of his works, and would gladly find some one willing to pay him a certain income for life, for which he should possess the exclusive

[23] *Beethoven: Studies* by Seyfried, translated by Henry Hugh Pierson (Leipzig, 1853), Appendix, p. 20.

right of publishing all he wrote; adding, "and I would not be idle in composition. I believe Goethe does this with Cotta, and, if I mistake not, Handel's
London publisher held similar terms with him."

"My dear young man," returned the other, "You must not complain; for
you are neither a Goethe nor a Handel, and it is not to be expected that you
ever will be; for such masters will not be born again." Beethoven bit his
lips, gave a most contemptuous glance at the speaker, and said no more.
Lobkowitz endeavored to appease him, and in a subsequent conversation said:

"My dear Beethoven, the gentleman did not intend to wound you. It is an
established maxim, to which most men adhere, that the present generation
cannot possibly produce such mighty spirits as the dead, who have already
earned their fame."

"So much the worse, Your Highness," retorted Beethoven; "but with men
who will not believe and trust in me because I am as yet unknown to universal fame, I cannot hold intercourse!"

It is easy for this generation, which has the productions of the composer's
whole life as the basis of its judgment of his powers, to speak disparagingly
of his contemporaries for not being able to discover in his first twelve or
fifteen works good reason for classing him with Goethe and Handel; but
he who stands upon a mountain cannot justly ridicule him on the plain for
the narrow extent of his view. It was as difficult then to conceive the possibility of instrumental music being elevated to heights greater than those
reached by Haydn and Mozart, as it is for us to conceive of Beethoven
being hereafter surpassed.

In the short personal sketches of Beethoven's friends which have been
introduced, the dates of their births have been noted so far as known, that
the reader may observe how very large a proportion of them were of the
same age as the composer, or still younger—some indeed but boys—when
he came to Vienna. And so it continued. As the years pass by in our narrative
and names familiar to us disappear, the new ones which take their places,
with rare exceptions, are still of men much younger than himself. The older
generation of musical amateurs at Vienna, van Swieten and his class, had
accepted the young Bonn organist and patronized him, as a pianist. But
when Beethoven began to press his claims as a composer, and, somewhat
later, as his deafness increased, to neglect his playing, some of the elder
friends had passed away, others had withdrawn from society, and the number was few of those who, like Lichnowsky, could comprehend that departures from the forms and styles of Mozart and Haydn were not necessarily
faults. With the greater number, as perfection necessarily admits of no
improvement and both quartet and symphony in *form* had been carried to
that point by Haydn and Mozart, it was a perfectly logical conclusion that
further progress was impossible. They could not perceive that there was still
room for the invention or discovery of new elements of interest, beauty,

power; for such perceptions are the offspring of genius. With Beethoven they were instinctive.

One more remark: Towards the decline of life, the masterpieces of literature and art, on which the taste was formed, are apt to become invested in the mind with a sort of nimbus of sanctity; hence, the productions of a young and daring innovator, even when the genius and talent displayed in them are felt and receive just acknowledgement, have the aspect, not only of an extravagant and erring waste of misapplied powers, but of a kind of profane audacity. For these and similar reasons Beethoven's novelties found little favor with the veterans of the concert-room.

The criticism of the day was naturally ruled and stimulated by the same spirit. Beethoven's own confession how it at first wounded him, will come in its order; but after he felt that his victory over it was sure—was in fact gained with a younger generation—he only laughed at the critics; to answer them, except by new works, was beneath him. Seyfried says of him (during the years of the "Eroica," *Fidelio*, etc.): "When he came across criticisms in which he was accused of grammatical errors he rubbed his hands in glee and cried out with a loud laugh: 'Yes, yes! they marvel and put their heads together' because they do not find it in any school of thoroughbass!'" But for the young of both sexes, Beethoven's music had an extraordinary charm. And this not upon technical grounds, nor solely for its novelties, always an attractive feature to the young, but because it appealed to the sensibilities, excited emotions and touched the heart as no other purely instrumental compositions had ever done.

A good example is provided in the account of the trustworthy Moscheles which is given in the introduction to the English translation of Schindler's biography:[24] "I had been placed under the guidance and tuition of Dionysius Weber, the founder and present director of the Prague Musical Conservatory; and he, fearing that, in my eagerness to read new music, I might injure the systematic development of my pianoforte playing, prohibited the library; and, in a plan for my musical education which he laid before my parents, made it an express condition, that for three years I should study no other authors but Mozart, Clementi, and S. Bach. I must confess, however, that, in spite of such prohibitions, I visited the library, gaining access to it through my pocket-money. It was about this time that I learnt from some school-fellows that a young composer had appeared at Vienna, who wrote the oddest stuff possible—such as no one could either play or understand; crazy music, in opposition to all rule; and that this composer's name was *Beethoven*. On repairing to the library to satisfy my curiosity as to this so-called eccentric genius, I found there Beethoven's Sonata pathétique. This was in the year 1804. My pocket-money would not suffice for the purchase of it, so I secretly copied it. The novelty of its style was so attractive to me, and

---

[24] *The Life of Beethoven*, ed. I. Moscheles (London, 1841), I, vii-ix. (TDR, II, 146.)

I became so enthusiastic in my admiration of it, that I forgot myself so far as to mention my new acquisition to my master, who reminded me of his injunction, and warned me not to play or study any eccentric productions until I had based my style upon more solid models. Without, however, minding his injunctions, I seized upon the pianoforte works of Beethoven as they successively appeared, and in them found a solace and a delight such as no other composer afforded me."

And so it was that Beethoven also in his quality of composer soon gathered about him a circle of young disciples, enthusiastic admirers. Their homage may well have been grateful to him—as such is to every artist and scholar of genius, who, striking out and steadfastly pursuing a new path, subjects himself to the sharp animadversions of critics who, in all honesty, really can see little or nothing of good in that which is not to be measured and judged by old standards. The voice of praise under such circumstances is doubly pleasing. It is known that, when Beethoven's works began to find a just appreciation from a new generation of critics, who had indeed been schooled by them, he collected and preserved a considerable number of laudatory articles, whose fate cannot now be traced. When, however, the natural and just satisfaction which is afforded by the homage of honest admirers and deservedly eulogistic criticism, degenerates into a love of indiscriminate praise and flattery, it becomes a weakness, a fault. Of this error in Beethoven there are traces easily discernible, and especially in his later years; there are pages of fulsome eulogy addressed to him in the Conversation Books, which would make the reader blush for him, did not the mere fact that such books existed remind him of the bitterness of the composer's lot. The failing was also sometimes his misfortune; for those who were most profuse in their flatteries, and thus gained his ear, were by no means the best of his counsellors. But aside from the attractive force of his genius, Beethoven possessed a personal magnetism, which attached his young worshippers to him and, all things considered, to his solid and lasting benefit in his private affairs. Just at this time, and for some years to come, his brothers usually rendered him the aid he needed; but thenceforth to the close of his life, the names of a constant succession of young men will appear in and vanish from our narrative, who were ever necessary to him and ever ready at his call with their voluntary services.

The friends that Beethoven drew around him were of two kinds: those whom he loved and to whom he was able to pour out his heart, like Amenda and Wegeler, and those who were merely useful to him either as contacts, like Prince Lichnowsky, or as helpers in everyday matters like Zmeskall and later Schindler and Holz. And it is significant that the first kind of friendship was able to exist only with those from whom he was separated. He could write to them as though they existed apart from what he considered the tawdry world around him. The correspondence with Wegeler and Amenda in a later chapter shows the intensity of this kind of friendship; and these two are almost the only close friends that can be named with whom Beethoven did not have a quarrel. One other friend of this type was Stephan von Breuning, and the very fact that he was in Vienna in the years to come made it inevitable that a point would come when he would either have to submit to Beethoven's will or retain his own integrity; in choosing the latter course he forfeited a friendship with Beethoven, which was to be revived only in the last years of his life. Beethoven's inability to enter into a relationship of the heart with any man who was near him was equally true with his friends of the opposite sex. Earlier biographies have stressed the individual woman's reluctance to enter into a close friendship with him, but as time went on, the reluctance was probably equally his own towards establishing a permanent relationship with a woman from whom he could want only that she give herself in service to him with little if anything in return.}⊱⋯

Art has been so often disgraced by the bad morals and shameless lives of its votaries, that it is doubly gratifying to be able to affirm of Beethoven that, like Handel, Bach and Mozart, he did honor to his profession by his personal character and habits. Although irregular, still he was as simple and temperate in eating and drinking as was possible in the state of society in which he lived. No allusion is remembered in any of his letters, notes, memoranda, nor in the Conversation Books, which indicates a liking for any game of chance or skill. He does not appear to have known one playing-card from another. Music, books, conversation with men and women of taste and intelligence, dancing (according to Ries who adds that he could never learn to dance in time—but Beethoven's dancing days were soon over), and, above all, his long walks, were his amusements and recreations. His whim for riding was of short duration—at all events, the last allusion to any horse owned by him is in the anecdote on a previous page.

One rather delicate point demands a word: and surely, what Franklin in his autobiography could confess of himself, and Lockhart mention without scruple of Walter Scott, his father-in-law, need not be here suppressed. Nor can it well be, since a false assumption on the point has been made the basis already of a considerable quantity of fine writing, and employed to explain certain facts relative to Beethoven's compositions. Spending his whole life in a state of society in which the vow of celibacy was by no means a vow of chastity; in which the parentage of a cardinal's or archbishop's children was neither a secret nor a disgrace; in which the illegitimate offspring of princes and magnates were proud of their descent and formed upon it well-grounded hopes of advancement and success in life; in which the moderate gratification of the sexual was no more discountenanced than the satisfying of any other natural appetite—it is nonsense to suppose, that, under such circumstances, Beethoven could have puritanic scruples on that point. Those who have had occasion and opportunity to ascertain the facts, know that he had not, and are also aware that he did not always escape the common penalties of transgressing the laws of strict purity. But he had too much dignity of character ever to take part in scenes of low debauchery, or even when still young to descend to the familiar jesting once so common between tavern girls and the guests. Thus, as the elder Simrock related, upon the journey to Mergentheim recorded in the earlier pages of this work, it happened at some place where the company dined, that some of the young men prompted the waiting-girl to play off her charms upon Beethoven. He received her advances and familiarities with repellent coldness; and as she, encouraged by the others, still persevered, he lost his patience, and put an end to her importunities by a smart box on the ear.

The practice, not uncommon in his time, of living with an unmarried woman as a wife, was always abhorrent to him—how much so, a sad story will hereafter illustrate; to a still greater degree an intrigue with the wife of another man. In his later years he so broke off his once familiar intercourse with a distinguished composer and conductor of Vienna, as hardly to return his greetings with common politeness. Schindler affirmed that the only reason for this was that the man in question had taken to his bed and board the wife of another.

The names of two married women might here be given, to whom at a later period Beethoven was warmly attached; names which have hitherto escaped the eyes of literary scavengers, and are therefore here suppressed. Certain of his friends used to joke him about these ladies, and it is certain that he rather enjoyed their jests even when the insinuations, that his affection was beyond the limit of the Platonic, were somewhat broad; but careful enquiry has failed to elicit any evidence that even in these cases he proved unfaithful to his principles. A story related by Jahn is also to the point, namely, that Beethoven only by the urgent solicitations of the Czerny family was after much refusal persuaded to extemporize in the presence of a certain Madame Hofdamel. She was the widow of a man who had attempted her life and then committed suicide; and the refusal of Beethoven to play before her arose from his having the general belief at the time, that a too great intimacy had existed between her and Mozart. Jahn, it may be observed, had the great satisfaction of being able to prove the innocence of Mozart in this matter and of rescuing his memory from the only dark shadow which rested upon it.[25]

Beethoven's love of nature was already a marked trait of his character. This was indulged and strengthened by long rambles upon the lofty hills and in the exquisitely beautiful valleys which render the environs of Vienna to the north and west so charming. Hence, when he left the city to spend the hot summer months in the country, with but an exception or two in a long series of years, his residence was selected with a view to the indulgence of this noble passion. Hence, too, his great delight in the once celebrated work of Christian Sturm: *Beobachtungen über die Werke Gottes*, which, how-

[25] O. Jahn, *Gesammelte Aufsätze über Musik* (Lpz., 1866), pp. 230ff. (TDR, II, 151, n. 1.)

ever absurd much of its natural philosophy (in the old editions) appears now in the light of advanced knowledge, was then by far the best manual of popular scientific truth, and was unsurpassed in fitness to awaken and foster a taste for, and the understanding of, the beauties of nature. Schindler has recorded the master's life-long study and admiration of this book. It was one which cherished his veneration for the Creator and Preserver of the universe, and yet left his contempt for procrustean religious systems and ecclesiastical dogmas its free course. "To him, who, in the love of Nature, holds communion with her visible forms, she speaks a various language," says Bryant. Her language was thoroughly well understood by Beethoven; and when, in sorrow and affliction, his art, his Plutarch, his *Odyssey*, proved to be resources too feeble for his comfort, he went to Nature for solace, and rarely failed to find it.

Beethoven's fine sense for the lyric element in poetry was already conspicuous in the fine tact with which the texts of his songs, belonging in date to his last years in Bonn, were selected from the annual publications in which most of them appeared. Another fine proof of this is afforded by a glance through the older editions of Matthisson's poems. In the fourth (1797), there are but two which are really well adapted to composition in the song form—the "Adelaide" and "Das Opferlied." A third Beethoven left unfinished. He had doubtless been led to attempt its composition through the force of its appeal to his personal feelings and sympathies, but soon discovering its non-lyrical character abandoned it. It is the "Wunsch."

Rochlitz in his letters from Vienna (1822) reports Beethoven's humorous account of his enthusiasm for Klopstock in his early life: "Since that summer in Karlsbad I read Goethe every day, that is, when I read at all. He (Goethe) has killed Klopstock for me. You are surprised? And now you laugh? Ah ha! It is because I have read Klopstock. I carried him about with me for years while walking and also at other times. Well, I did not always understand him, of course. He leaps about so much and he begins at too lofty an elevation. Always *Maestoso*, D-flat major! Isn't it so? But he is great and uplifts the soul nevertheless. When I could not understand him I could sort of guess. If only he did not always want to die! That will come quickly enough. "Well, at any rate, what he writes always sounds well."

Thus, whatever scattered hints bearing upon the point come under our notice combine to impart a noble idea of Beethoven's poetic taste and culture, and to show that the allusions to the ancient classic authors in his letters and conversation were not made for display, but were the natural consequence of a love for and a hearty appreciation of them derived from their frequent perusal in translations.

Beethoven's correspondence forms so important a portion of his biography that something must be said here upon his character as a letter-writer. A few of his autograph letters bear marks of previous study and careful elaboration; but, in general, whatever he wrote in the way of private correspondence was dashed off on the spur of the moment, and with no thought that it would ever come under any eye but that for which it was intended. It is therefore easy to imagine how energetically he would have protested could he have known that his most insignificant notes were preserved in such numbers, and that the time would come when they would all be made public; or, still worse, that some which were but the offspring of momentary pique against those with whom he lived in closest relations would be used after his death to their injury; and that outbursts of sudden passion—when the wrong was perhaps as often on his side as on the other—after all the parties concerned had passed away, would have an almost judicial authority accorded to them.

In studying collections of his letters and notes, originals and copies in print or manuscript, the most striking fact is the insignificance of by far the greater number—that so few bear marks of any care in their preparation, or contain matter of any intrinsic value. In fact, perhaps the greater part of the short notes to Zmeskall and others owe their origin to Beethoven's dislike of entrusting oral messages to his servants. For the most part it is in vain to seek in his correspondence anything bearing upon the theory or art of music; very seldom is any opinion expressed upon the productions of any contemporary composer; no vivid sketches of men and manners flow from his pen, like those which render the letters of Mozart and Mendelssohn so charming. The proportion of their correspondence which possesses more than a merely biographical value was large; of Beethoven's very small.

His letters, of course, exhibit the usual imperfections of a hasty and confidential correspondence; sometimes, indeed, of an aggravated character. Some of them contain loose statements of fact, such as all men are liable to make through haste or imperfect knowledge; others contain passages of which the only conceivable explanation is Schindler's statement that Beethoven sometimes amused himself with the harmless mystification of others; but, taken together, the more important letters—while they usually evince his difficulty in finding the best expressions of his thoughts and his constant struggle with the rules of his mother tongue—place his truth and candor in a very favorable light and sometimes rise into a rude eloquence. The reader feels that when the writer is unjust he is under the influence of a mistake or passion—and, as a rule, it is not too late to detect such injustice; that his errors of fact are simply mistakes, honestly made and easily corrected; that if, in the mass, a few paragraphs occur which can be neither fully justified nor excused, it is not to be forgotten that they were not intended for our eyes and that they were written under the constant pressure of a great calamity, which made him doubly sensitive and irritable; and so it will be easy, like Sterne's Recording Angel, to blot such passages with a tear.

Another striking fact of Beethoven's correspondence, when viewed as a whole, is the proof it affords that, except in his hours of profound depression, he was far from being the melancholy and gloomy character of popular belief. He shows himself here—as he was by nature—of a gay and lively temperament, fond of a jest, an inveterate though not always a very happy punster, a great lover of wit and humor. It is a cause for profound gratitude that it was so; since he thus preserved an elasticity of spirits that enabled him to escape the consequences of brooding in solitude over his great misfortune; to rise superior to his fate and concentrate his great powers upon his self-imposed tasks; and to meet with hope and courage the cruel fortune which put an end to so many well-founded expectations and ambitious projects, and confined him to a single road to fame and honor—that of composition. It happens that several of the more valuable and interesting of his letters belong to the period immediately following that now before us, and in them we are able to trace, with reasonable accuracy, the effect which his incipient and increasing deafness produced upon him—first, the anxiety caused by earliest symptoms; then the profound grief bordering upon despair when the final result had become certain; and at last his submission to and acceptance of his fate. There is in truth something nobly heroic in the manner in which Beethoven at length rose superior to his great affliction. The magnificent series of works produced in the ten years from 1798 to 1808 are no greater monuments to his genius than to the godlike resolution with which he wrought out the inspirations of that genius under circumstances most fitted to weaken its efforts and restrain its energies.

Beethoven was seldom without a folded sheet or two of music paper in his pocket upon which he wrote with pencil in two or three measures of music hints of any musical thought which might occur to him wherever he chanced to be. Towards the end of his life his Conversation Books often answered the same purpose; and there are traditions of bills-of-fare at dining-rooms having been honored with ideas afterwards made immortal. This habit gave Abbé Gelinek a foundation for the following amusing nonsense as related by Tomaschek: "He [Gelinek] declared," says Tomaschek,[26] "as if it were an aphorism, that all of Beethoven's compositions were lacking in internal coherency and that not infrequently they were overloaded. These things he looked upon as grave faults of composition and sought to explain them from the manner in which Beethoven went about his work, saying that he had always been in the habit of noting every musical idea that occurred to him upon a bit of paper which he threw into a corner of his room, and that after a while there was a considerable pile of the memoranda which the maid was not permitted to touch when cleaning the room. Now when Beethoven got into a mood for work he would hunt a few musical *motivi* out of his treasure-heap which he thought might serve as principal and secondary themes for the composition in contemplation, and often his selection was not a lucky one. I [Tomaschek] did not interrupt the flow of his passionate, yet awkward speech, but briefly answered that I was unfamiliar with Beethoven's method of composing but was inclined to think that the aberra-

[26] *Libussa*, 1847, p. 436. (TDR, II, 155, n. 1.)

tions occasionally to be found in his compositions were to be ascribed to his individuality, and that only an unprejudiced and keen psychologist, who had had an opportunity to observe Beethoven from the beginning of his artistic development to its maturity in order gradually to familiarize himself with his views on art, could fit himself to give the musical world an explanation of the intellectual cross-relationships in Beethoven's glorious works, a thing just as impossible to his blind enthusiasts as to his virulent opponents. Gelinek may have applied these last words to himself, and not incorrectly."

This conversation took place in 1814, the day after a rehearsal of Beethoven's Symphony in A—the Seventh! Gelinek's pile of little bits of paper in the corner of the room, when touched by the wand of truth, resolves itself into blank music books, to which his new ideas were transferred from the original slight pencil sketches, and frequently with two or three words to indicate the kind of composition to which they were suited. Divers anecdotes are current which pretend to give the origin of some of the themes thus recorded and afterwards wrought out, but few judicious readers will attach much weight to most of them. For although conceptions can sometimes be traced directly to their exciting causes, the musical composer can seldom say more than that they occurred to him at such a time and place—and often not even that.

To return to the sketchbooks—which performed a twofold office; being not alone the registers of new conceptions, but containing the preliminary studies of the instrumental works into which they were wrought out. The introduction to the excellent pamphlet, "Ein Skizzenbuch von Beethoven, beschrieben und in Auszügen dargestellt von Gustav Nottebohm," though properly confined by him to the single book which he was describing, is equally true of so many that have been examined with care as to warrant its general application. The following extracts may be taken as true of the greater part of the sketchbooks.[27] He says: "Before us lies a volume in oblong folio (*Teatro*) of 192 pages and bearing 16 staves on each page, and, save a few empty places, containing throughout notes and sketches in Beethoven's handwriting for compositions of various sorts. The volume is not made up, the way many others were, of pages sewn together, but is bound in craftsman's style, trimmed, and has a stout pasteboard cover. It was bound thus before it was used or received the notes. The sketches are for the greater part only one-part; that is, they occupy but a single staff, only exceptionally are they on two or more staves. It is permissible to assume in advance that they were written originally and in the order in which they follow each other in the sketchbook. When a cursory glance over the whole does not seem to contradict this assumption, a careful study nevertheless compels a modification at times. It is to be observed that generally Beethoven began a new page with a new composition; and, moreover, that he worked alternately or simul-

[27] Leipzig, 1865. See *Zwei Skizzenbücher von Beethoven* (Leipzig, 1824), pp. 3-6. (TDR, II, 157-58.)

taneously at different movements. As a result, different groups of sketches are crowded so closely together that in order to find room he was obliged to make use of spaces which had been left open, and thus eventually sketches for the most different compositions had to be mixed together and brought into companionship."

In some of the books "vi-" not infrequently meets the eye. It was one of Beethoven's modes of keeping the clues in the labyrinth of sketches, being part of the word *vide*. The second syllable, "-de," can always be found on the same or a neighboring page. "N.B.," "No. 100," "No. 500," "No. 1000," etc., and in later sketches "meilleur," are common, all of which signs are explained by Schindler as being a whimsical mode of estimating the comparative value of different musical ideas, or of forms of the same. Again Nottebohm continues: "In spite of this confused working it is plain that Beethoven, as a rule, was conscious from the beginning of the goal for which he was striving, that he was true to his first concept and carried out the projected form to the end. The contrary is also true at times, and the sketchbook disclosed a few instances in which Beethoven in the course was led from the form originally conceived into another, so that eventually something different appeared from what was planned in the first instance. . . . In general, it may be observed that Beethoven in all his work begun in the sketchbook proceeded in the most varied manner, and at times reached his goal in a direction opposite to that upon which he first set out. In one group of sketches the thematic style dominates; the first sketch breaks off abruptly with the principal subject and the work that follows is confined to transforming and reshaping the thematic kernel at first thrown on the paper until it appears to be fitted for development; then the same process is undertaken with intermediary sections; everywhere we find beginnings, never a whole; a whole comes before us only outside of the sketchbook, in the printed composition where sections which were scattered in the sketchbook are brought together. In another group of sketches the thematic and mosaic manner is excluded; every sketch is aimed at a unity and is complete in itself; the very first one gives the complete outline for a section of a movement; those that follow are then complete reshapings of the first, as other readings directed towards a change in the summary character, or a reformation of the whole, an extension of the middle sections, etc. . . . Naturally, the majority of the sketches do not belong exclusively to either of the two tendencies, but hover between them, now leaning towards one, now towards the other."

One readily sees that, when the general plan of a work is clear and distinct before the mind, it is quite indifferent in what order the various parts are studied; and that Beethoven simply adopted the method of many a dramatic and other author, who sketches his scenes or chapters not in course but as mood, fancy or opportunity dictates. It is equally evident that the composer could have half a dozen works upon his hands at the same time, not merely without disadvantage to any one of them, but to the gain of all, since he could turn to one or another as the spirit of compositions impelled; like the author of a profound literary work, who relieves and recreates his mind by varying his labors, and executes his grand task all the more satisfactorily, because he, from time to time, refreshes himself by turning his attention to other and lighter topics. Beethoven writes to Wegeler: "I live only in my notes, and one thing is seldom done before another is begun. As I am writing now I often work on three or four pieces at once." Sometimes works were laid aside incomplete after he had begun the task of writing them out in full; and finished when occasion demanded; but as a rule his practice was quite different, viz.: All the parts of a work having been thus studied until he had determined upon the form, character and style of every important division and subdivision, and recorded the results in his sketchbook by a few of the first measures, followed by "etc." or "and so on," the labor of composition may be said to have been finished, and there remained only the task of writing out the clean copy of what now existed full and complete in his mind, and of making such minor corrections and improvements as might occur to him on revision. The manuscripts show that these were sometimes very numerous, though they rarely extend to any change in the form or to any alteration in the grand effect except to heighten it, or render it more unexpected or exciting. When upon reflection he was dissatisfied with a movement as a whole he seems rarely to have attempted its improvement by mere correction, choosing rather to discard it at once and compose a new one based either upon the same themes or upon entirely new motives. The several overtures to *Fidelio* are illustrations of both procedures.

The sketches of the greater part of Beethoven's songs, after the Bonn period, are preserved, and prove with what extreme care he wrought out his melodies. The sketchbook analyzed by Nottebohm affords a curious illustration in Matthisson's "Opferlied," the melody being written out in full not less than six times, the theme in substance remaining unchanged. Absolute correctness of accent, emphasis, rhythm—of prosody, in short—was with him a leading object; and various papers, as well as the Conversation Books, attest his familiarity with metrical signs and his scrupulous obedience to metrical laws.

From the sketchbooks one can get an idea of the vast fertility of Beethoven's genius. They are in music, like Hawthorne's "Notebooks" in literature, the record of a never ceasing flow of new thoughts and ideas, until death sealed the fountain forever. There are themes and hints, never used, for all kinds of instrumental compositions, from the trifles, which he called "Bagatelles," to symphonies, evidently intended to be as different from those we know as they are from each other; and these hints are in such numbers, that those which can be traced in the published works are perhaps much the smaller proportion of the whole. Whoever has the will and opportunity to devote an hour or two to an examination of a few of these monuments of

Beethoven's inventive genius, will easily comprehend the remark which he made near the close of his life: "It seems to me that I have just begun to compose!"

One topic more demands notice before closing this chapter. In the "Merry-making of the Countryfolk" of Beethoven's "Pastoral" Symphony, at the point where the fun grows most fast and furious and the excitement rises to its height, an ominous sound, as of distant thunder, gives the first faint warning of the coming storm. So in the life of the composer at the moment of that highest success and prosperity, which we have labored to place vividly before the mind of the reader, just when he could first look forward with well-grounded confidence to the noblest gratification of a musician's honorable ambition, a new and discordant element thrust itself into the harmony of his life. This was the symptoms of approaching deafness. His own account fixes their appearance in the year 1799; then they were still so feeble and intermittent, as to have caused him at first no serious anxiety; but in another year they had assumed so much the appearance of a chronic and increasing evil, as to compel him to abandon plans for travel which he had formed, and for which he was preparing himself, with great industry and perseverance, to appear in the twofold capacity of virtuoso and composer. Instead, therefore, in 1801, of having "before now traveled over half the world,"[28] he, for two years, had been confined to Vienna or its immediate vicinity, vainly seeking relief from surgeons and physicians.

The cause of Beethoven's deafness has never been definitively established, although it is clear from Beethoven's own descriptions of his symptoms to Wegeler[29] and from the autopsy report (see Appendix B) that the composer's loss of hearing was due to nerve- or perceptive-type deafness rather than to a conductive or bone type of hearing loss such as otosclerosis. The nerve-type of deafness can result from some sort of severe infection which causes damage to the auditory nerve.[30]

There is no definite proof of such an illness in Beethoven's case, but only scattered, inconclusive evidence. The "dangerous illness" referred to in Chapter X, which the Fischoff manuscript dates 1796, but which might be 1797, is one mention of a bad infection. The other reference is from a more reliable source: Dr. Aloys Weissenbach (1766-1821), a surgeon from Salzburg (and also a writer and poet) made Beethoven's acquaintance in 1814, and wrote at length on the subject in his *Meine Reise zum Kongress* (Vienna, 1816). Himself deaf, he was interested in the composer's infirmity, and discussed it with Beethoven. His description of the origin of the deafness follows: "He once endured a frightful attack of typhus. From this time dates the decay of his nervous system and probably also the great misfortune, to

---

[28] In Beethoven's letter to Wegeler of November 16, 1801, in which he discusses his deafness. See Chapter XIV.

[29] *Ibid.*, and also the letter of June 29, 1801. See Chapter XIV.

[30] I am indebted to Dr. L. Ashby Adams, otolarynxologist of Princeton, N.J. for the medical information contained in this summary.

him, of the loss of his hearing. Often and long have I spoken to him on this subject; it is a greater misfortune for him than for the world. It is significant that before that illness his hearing was unsurpassingly keen and delicate. . . ."

An infection such as typhus could very well have been the origin of the damage to his auditory nerve with consequent degeneration and atrophy, which eventually caused almost complete lack of function. Typhus is also known to cause involvement of the central nervous system. While there is no record of such an illness, beyond the Fischoff allusion, this does not prove anything since, as Thayer remarks, neither is there any record that Beethoven passed through an attack of smallpox beyond that which the disease left upon his face. To date the onslaught of such an infection as Weissenbach described is difficult. It could possibly have taken place before he came to Vienna, and could have been the cause of his melancholy state of health about the time of his mother's death. However, if there is any connection between the infection and the "dangerous illness," which seems likely, it is more probable that it was in the summer of 1796 or 1797. This would also render more credible the fact that the first symptoms of his deafness were noticeable to Beethoven in 1799.}

CHAPTER XIII

THE YEAR 1800

IN the *Hof- und Staats-Schematismus* for the year 1800, at the end of the list of persons employed in the "K.K. Universal-Staatschuldenkasse" are the names of two *Praktikanten*; the first is "Mr. Carl v. Beethoven lives in the Sterngasse, 484." In the list of the same publication in 1801 appears a new department or bureau of the above-named office called the "K.K.n.öst. Klassen-Stever-Kasse" and the second of the three bureau officers is "Mr. Carl v. Beethoven lives unterm Tuchladen, 605."

It is not improbable that, while simply *Praktikant*, he may have needed occasional pecuniary aid, but his preferment to the place of *Kassa-Officier* rendered him independent. This appointment is dated March 24, 1800, and gave him a salary of 250 florins. Small as the sum now appears, it was amply sufficient, with what he could earn by teaching music (and the brother of the great Beethoven could have no lack of pupils), to enable him to live comfortably. In fact, he was better off than many a colleague in the public service, who still with care and economy managed to live respectably. It may therefore be confidently asserted that Beethoven was henceforth relieved of all care on account of Carl, as of Johann, until the bankruptcy of the government and Carl's broken health many years later, made fraternal assistance indispensable. At the beginning of this year Carl had tried his fortune as a composer—but probably with slender profit, since no second venture has been discovered. Six minuets, six "Deutsche" and six contradances by him are advertised in the *Wiener Zeitung* of January 11, in double editions, one for clavier and one for two violins and violoncello.

A grand concert for which Beethoven had been preparing during the winter took place on the 2nd of April. It was his first public appearance for his own benefit in Vienna, and, so far as is known, anywhere except in Prague. All that is now to be ascertained in relation to it is contained in the advertisement,[1] in the programme, and in a single notice, sent to the *Allge-*

---

[1] *Wiener Zeitung*, March 26, 1800. (TDR, II, 171.)

meine Musikalische Zeitung. The programme, which was in the possession of Frau van Beethoven (widow of the composer's nephew) is as follows:

To-day, Wednesday, April 2nd, 1800, Herr *Ludwig van Beethoven* will have the honor to give a grand concert for his benefit in the Royal Imperial Court Theatre beside the Burg. The pieces which will be performed are the following:

1. A grand symphony by the late Kapellmeister Mozart.
2. An aria from "The Creation" by the Princely Kapellmeister Herr Haydn, sung by Mlle. Saal.
3. A grand Concerto for the pianoforte, played and composed by Herr *Ludwig van Beethoven.*
4. A Septet, most humbly and obediently dedicated to Her Majesty the Empress, and composed by Herr *Ludwig van Beethoven* for four stringed and three wind-instruments, played by Herren Schuppanzigh, Schreiber, Schindlecker, Bär, Nickel, Matauschek and Dietzel.
5. A Duet from Haydn's "Creation," sung by Herr and Mlle. Saal.
6. Herr *Ludwig van Beethoven* will improvise on the pianoforte.
7. A new grand symphony with complete orchestra, composed by Herr *Ludwig van Beethoven.*

Tickets for boxes and stalls are to be had of Herr van Beethoven at his lodgings in the Tiefen Graben, No. 241, third story, and of the box-keeper.

Prices of admission are as usual.

The beginning is at half-past 6 o'clock.

The correspondent of the *Allgemeine Musikalische Zeitung* described the concert as follows: "Finally on one occasion Herr Beethoven took over the theatre and this was truly the most interesting concert in a long time. He played a new concerto of his own composition, much of which was written with a great deal of taste and feeling. After this he improvised in a masterly fashion, and at the end one of his symphonies was performed in which there is considerable art, novelty and a wealth of ideas. The only flaw was that the wind-instruments were used too much, so that there was more harmony than orchestral music as a whole. Perhaps we might do well to note the following about this concert. The orchestra of the Italian opera made a very poor showing. First, quarrels about who was to conduct. Beethoven thought quite rightly that he could entrust the conducting not to Herr Conti but to Herr Wranitzky. The gentlemen refused to play under him. The faults of this orchestra, already criticized above, then became all the more evident since B's compositions are difficult to execute. When they were accompanying, the players did not bother to pay any attention to the soloist. As a result there was no delicacy at all in the accompaniments and no response to the musical feeling of the solo player. In the second part of the symphony they became so lax that despite all efforts on the part of the conductor no fire whatsoever could be gotten out of them, particularly from the wind-instruments. With such behavior what good is all the proficiency—which most of the members of this organization undeniably possess? How, under such circumstances, is even the most excellent composition to be effective?"

Which of the pianoforte concertos Beethoven played on this occasion is not clear. The Symphony in C soon became known throughout Germany; while the Septet achieved a sudden popularity so widely extended and enduring as at length to become an annoyance to the composer.[2]

Before the month was out Beethoven again played in public, in a concert given by Johann Wenzel Stich, known as Punto. This Bohemian virtuoso, after several years of wandering, had lately come to Vienna from Paris, via Munich. As a performer upon the horn he was unrivalled by any predecessor or contemporary; but as a composer he was beneath criticism. Beethoven's delight in anyone whose skill afforded him a new experience of the powers and possible effects of any orchestral instrument is known to the reader. Nothing more natural, therefore, than his readiness to compose a sonata for himself and Punto to be played at the latter's concert on April 18th. Ries informs us (*Notizen*, p. 82) that "though the concert was announced with the Sonata the latter was not yet begun. Beethoven began his work the day before the performance and it was ready for the concert." His habit of merely sketching his own part and of trusting to his memory and the inspiration of the moment, even when producing his grand concertos in public, probably rendered him good service on this occasion. The *Allgemeine Musikalische Zeitung* of July 2, 1800, preserves also the interesting fact that owing to the enthusiastic applause the Sonata was immediately repeated.

—*[These two artists performed together again in Budapest on May 7th. Eichner[3] concludes from the notes of the Brunsvik family that Beethoven was in Budapest from the end of April to the beginning of July, during which time he was a frequent visitor to the Brunsvik's country estate. From an issue of the *Ofener und Pester Theatertaschenbuch* we quote, "on this day (May 7) an Akademie of Herr Bethover and Herr Punto. . . . Who is this Bethover? The history of German music is not acquainted with such a name. Punto of course is very well known. Punto is his name as an artist, his real name is Wenzel Stich. . . . Three weeks before his concert in Ofen-Pest Punto appeared in a concert in Vienna, indeed in the company of a certain Beethoven." From the *Ungarrischer Kurrier* we learn that their appearance on May 7th was the last event in a four-day festival celebrating the birthday of the Archduchess Maria Pawlowna. The notice for this day reads, "Carousel, after which a concert was given in the *Theatrum* where a famous *Musikus* named Beethoven drew the attention of all present to himself from his artistic performance." According to the personal chronicle of the aristo-

---

[2] "He could not endure his Septet and grew angry because of the universal applause with which it was received." (Czerny to Jahn.) (TDR, II, 173.)

[3] S. Eichner, "Beethoven in Budapest," *Deutsche Musiker-Zeitung*, No. 38, September 17, 1927, pp. 840-41.

cratic family Vegh at Vereb, who as keen music-lovers expected both Punto and Beethoven to come to Vereb to perform, "Punto alone came because there had been a quarrel between him and Herr von Beethoven in Pest, as a result of which Beethoven remained behind." Eichner concludes that nothing further is known of Beethoven's activities during this stay in Hungary.

April 27th was the anniversary of the day on which Maximilian Franz entered Bonn to assume the duties of Elector and Archbishop. Sixteen years had passed and on this day he, with a small retinue, again entered Vienna. He took refuge "in an Esterhazy villa in a suburb," while the small chateau near which now stands the railway station at Hetzendorf, behind Schönbrunn Garden, was preparing for his residence; whither he soon removed, and where for the present we leave him.

At the end of February or early in March, the charlatan Daniel Steibelt[4] gave a concert in Prague which brought him in 1800 florins, and in April or May, "having finished his speculation, he went to Vienna, his purse filled with ducats, where he was knocked in the head by the pianist Beethoven," says Tomaschek. Ries relates how (p. 81): "When Steibelt came to Vienna with his great name, some of Beethoven's friends grew alarmed lest he do injury to the latter's reputation. Steibelt did not visit him; they met first time one evening at the house of Count Fries, where Beethoven produced his new Trio in B-flat major for Pianoforte, Clarinet and Violoncello (Op. 11), for the first time.[5] There is no opportunity for particular display on the part of the pianist in this Trio. Steibelt listened to it with a sort of condescension, uttered a few compliments to Beethoven and felt sure of his victory. He played a Quintet of his own composition, improvised, and made a good deal of effect with his tremolos, which were then something entirely new. Beethoven could not be induced to play again. Eight days later there was again a concert at Count Fries's; Steibelt again played a quintet which had a good deal of success. He also played an improvisation (which had, obviously, been carefully prepared) and chose the same theme on which Beethoven had written variations in his Trio.[6] This incensed the admirers of Beethoven and him; he had to go to the pianoforte and improvise. He went in his usual (I might say, ill-bred) manner to the instrument as if half-pushed, picked up the violoncello part of Steibelt's quintet in passing, placed it (intentionally?) upon the stand upside down and with one finger drummed a theme out of the first few measures. Insulted and angered he improvised in such a manner that Steibelt left the room before he finished, would never again meet him and, indeed, made it a condition that Beethoven should not be invited before accepting an offer."

[4] Daniel Steibelt (1765-1823) was born in Berlin. Around 1790 he was already active as a touring piano virtuoso, but he soon got into debt, and the manner in which he handled his business affairs gained him the reputation of a swindler. See *FRBH*, II, pp. 251-52.

[5] This is, of course, an error, as the Trio had been before the public since October 3, 1798. (TDR, II, 175.)

[6] From Weigl's "L'amor marinaro." (Cf. TDR, II, 175, n. 2, which gives the German title.)

It was the custom at Vienna for all those whose vocations and pecuniary circumstances rendered it possible, to spend all or some portion of the summer months in the country. The aristocracies of birth and wealth retired to their country seats, lived in villas for the season or joined the throngs at the great watering-places. Other classes found refuge in the villages and hamlets which abounded in the lovely environs of the city, where many a neat cottage was built for their use and where the peasants generally had a spare room or two, cleanly kept and neatly furnished. Beethoven's habit of escaping from town during the hot months was, therefore, nothing peculiar to him. We have reached the point whence, with little if any interruption, Beethoven can be followed from house to house, in city and country, through the rest of his life; a matter of great value in fixing the true dates of important letters and determining the chronology of his life and works—but for the first seven years the record is very incomplete.

Karl Holz told Jahn: "He [Beethoven] lived at first in a little attic-room in the house of the book-binder Strauss in the Alservorstadt, where he had a miserable time." This is one of the facts which an inquisitive young man like Holz would naturally learn of the master during the short period when he was his factotum. This attic-room must have been soon changed for the room "on the ground floor" mentioned in a previous chapter. An undated note of van Swieten is directed to Beethoven at "No. 45 Alsergasse, at Prince Lichnowsky's"; but in the Vienna directory for 1804 is listed an Alserstrasse, and the only number 45 in the "Alsergrund" is in the Lämmelgasse, property of Georg Musial; but Prince Josef [!] Lichnowsky is named as owner of No. 125 in the Hauptstrasse of that suburb. This was the same house; it had merely changed numbers. The site is now occupied by the house No. 30 Alserstrasse. Thence Beethoven went as a guest to the house occupied by Prince Lichnowsky. In May, 1795, Beethoven, in advertising the Trios, Op. 1, gives "the residence of the author" as the "Ogylisches Haus in the Kreuzgasse behind the Minorite church, No. 35 in the first story"; but that is no reason to think that Prince Lichnowsky then lived there. ---From the memoirs of Countess Therese Brunsvik we learn that by the spring of 1799 Beethoven lived in rooms at St. Petersplatz to which one had to climb up three flights on a winding staircase.--- As has been seen by the concert bill on a preceding page, he was during the winter of 1799-1800 in the Tiefen Graben[7] "in a very high and narrow house," as Czerny wrote to F. Luib. For the

---

[7] According to Frimmel, "Beethovens Wohnungen," *Vienna Neue Freie Presse*, August 11, 1899, this house was that of Court Councillor Greiner, then No. 241. On the strength of Czerny's statement that one had to look up to the fifth or sixth story to see Beethoven, and the old report that Beethoven lived "in the Kleine Weintraube," Frimmel was led to think that possibly he lived in one of the houses on the higher ground behind the Greiner house to which there was access from the open place "Am Hof" as well as from the houses in the Tiefen Graben and the Greiner house. The houses which bore the sign "Zur Weintraube" were situated "am Hofe." (TK, I, 269, n. 1.)

summer of 1800, he took quarters for himself and servant in a house in Unter-Döbling, an hour's walk, perhaps, from town.

An authentic and characteristic anecdote can belong only to this summer. There lived in a house hard by a peasant of no very good reputation, who had a daughter remarkably beautiful, but also not of the best fame. Beethoven was greatly captivated by her and was in the habit of stopping to gaze at her when he passed by where she was at work in farmyard or field. She, however, made no return of his evident liking and only laughed at his admiration. On one occasion the father was arrested for engaging in a brawl and imprisoned. Beethoven took the man's part and went to the magistrates to obtain his release. Not succeeding, he became angry and abusive, and in the end would have been arrested for his impertinence but for the strong representations made by some, who knew him, of his position in society and of the high rank, influence and power of his friends.

Throughout this period of Beethoven's life, each summer is distinguished by some noble composition, completed, or nearly so, so that on his return to the city it was ready for revision and his copyist. Free from the demands of society, his time was his own; his fancy was quickened, his inspiration strengthened, in field and forest labor was a delight. The most important work of the master bears in his own hand the date, 1800, and may reasonably be supposed to have been the labor of this summer. It is the Concerto in C minor for Pianoforte and Orchestra, Op. 37.

At the approach of autumn Beethoven returned to his old quarters in the Tiefen Graben. In this year Krumpholz introduced to him Johann Nepomuk Emanuel Dole* žalek, a young man of 20 years, born in Chotieborz in Bohemia, who had come to Vienna to take lessons from Albrechtsberger. He played the pianoforte and violoncello, was a capable musician, in his youth a rather popular composer of Bohemian songs and then, for half a century, one of the best teachers in the capital. Toward the close of his life he was frequently occupied with the arrangement of private concerts, chiefly quartet parties, for Prince Czartoryski and other prominent persons. As long as he lived he was an enthusiastic admirer of Beethoven, and enjoyed the friendship of the composer till his death. Among his observations are the statements concerning the hatred of Beethoven felt by the Vienna musicians already noted. Koželuch, he relates, threw the C minor trio at his (Doležalek's) feet when the later played it to him. Speaking of Beethoven, Koželuch said to Haydn: "We would have done that differently, wouldn't we, Papa?" and Haydn answered, smilingly, "Yes, we would have done that differently." Haydn, says Doležalek, could not quite reconcile himself with Beethoven's music. It was Doležalek who witnessed the oft-told scene in the Swan tavern when Beethoven insisted on paying without having eaten.

One of the most prolific and popular composers whom Beethoven found in Vienna was Franz Anton Hoffmeister, "Kapellmeister and R. I. licensed Music, Art and Book Seller." He was an immigrant from the Neckar valley and (born 1754) much older than Beethoven, to whom he had extended a warm sympathy and friendship, doubly valuable from his somewhat similar experience as a young student in Vienna. This is evident from the whole tone of their correspondence. In 1800, Hoffmeister left Vienna and in Leipzig formed a copartnership with Ambrosius Kühnel, organist of the Electoral Saxon Court Chapel, and established a publishing house there, still retaining his business in Vienna. As late as December 5, 1800, his signature is as above given; but on the 1st of January, 1801, the advertisements in the public press announce the firm of "Hoffmeister and Kühnel, Bureau de Musique in Leipzig." Since 1814 the firm name has been C. F. Peters. Knowing Beethoven personally and so intimately, it is alike creditable to the talents of the one and the taste and appreciation of the other that Hoffmeister, immediately upon organizing his new publishing house, should have asked him for manuscripts. To his letter he received an answer dated December 15, 1800, in which Beethoven says:

Dearest Hr. Brother!

I have been on the point of replying to your inquiry several times, but I am so fearfully lazy about my correspondence and I am loath to write dry letters [of the alphabet] instead of musical notes. Now at last I have prevailed upon myself to comply with your request—

Pro primo you must know that I am very sorry that you, my dear brother in music, did not let me know something of this earlier so that I might have marketed my quartets with you, as well as many other pieces which I have sold. But if Hr. Brother is as conscientious as many other honest engravers who stab[8] us poor composers to death, you will know how to derive profit from them when they appear— I will now set forth in brief what Hr. B[rother] can have from me. 1. A Septet per il violino, viola, violoncello, contra basso, clarinet, corno, fagotto—tutti obbligati (I cannot write anything non-obbligato for I came into this world with an obbligato accompaniment.) This Septet has been very popular. For its more frequent use the three wind-instruments, namely: fagotto, clarinetto and corno might be transcribed for another violin, viola and violoncello.— 2. A grand Symphony for full orchestra— 3. A Concerto for pianoforte[9] which I do not claim to be one of my best, as well as another one which will be published here by Mollo (this for the information of the Leipzig critics) because I am for the present *keeping the better ones for myself until I make a tour.* However, it would not disgrace you to publish it— 4. A grand solo Sonata.[10] That is all I can give you at this moment, a little later you may have a Quintet for stringed instruments as well as, probably, quartets and other things which I have not now with me.—In your reply you might set the prices, and as you are neither *a Jew nor an Italian,*

[8] Another example of Beethoven's fondness for punning on the word *stechen*, to engrave, which can also mean to goad, to prick, to stab.

[9] The Pianoforte Concerto offered to Hoffmeister was that in B-flat, Op. 19. It was published by Hoffmeister and Kühnel towards the end of 1801 and advertised on January 16,

1802. The Concerto published by Mollo in March, 1801, was that in C major, Op. 15. (TK, I, 272, n. 2.)

[10] In B-flat, Op. 22, published by Hoffmeister and Kühnel in March, 1802. (TDR, II, 181, n. 1.)

nor I either one or the other, we shall no doubt come to an understanding.
Dearest Brother, take care of yourself and be assured of the regard
of your brother

L.v.Beethoven

The reference to the Quartets, Op. 18, in this letter, taken in connection
with the apologies for long delay in writing, indicates conclusively enough
that at least the first set, the first three, had been placed in the hands of Mollo
and Co. early in the autumn. The following anecdote in Wiedemann's
Musikalische Effectmittel und Tonmalerei was told by Beethoven's friend
Karl Amenda:[11] "After Beethoven had composed his well-known String
Quartet in F major he played for his friend [Amenda] [on the pianoforte?]
the glorious Adagio [D minor, 9/8 time] and asked him what thought had
been awakened by it. "It pictured for me the parting of two lovers," was the
answer. "Good!" remarked Beethoven, "I thought of the scene in the burial
vault in *Romeo and Juliet*."

Amenda left Vienna in the fall of 1799; Beethoven's dedication on the
copy which he gave his friend was dated June 25, 1799; thus at this time the
1st Quartet was ready in its original form. Czerny says in his notes for Jahn:
"Of the first six Violin Quartets that in D major, No. 3 in print, was the
very first composed by Beethoven. On the advice of Schuppanzigh he called
that in F major No. 1, although it was composed later." Ries confirms this
(*Notizen*, p. 103): "Of his Violin Quartets, Op. 18, he composed that in D
major first of all. That in F major, which now precedes it, was originally the
third." It was, however, in reality the second, as the parts to Amenda show.
To be sure, neither Czerny nor Ries spoke from personal observation at the
time of composition; they must both have learned the facts from Beethoven
himself, or, more probably, from dates on the original manuscripts.

A criticism of three quartets which appeared in the *Allg. Mus. Zeitung*
in 1799, which failed to give the name of the composer, had been applied
erroneously by some writers to Beethoven's Op. 18. These were actually the
works of Emanuel Aloys Förster (born January 26, 1748, in Neurath, Upper
Silesia, died November 12, 1823, in Vienna), a musician who was so highly
esteemed by Beethoven that, on one occasion at least, he called him his "old
master." The phrase can easily be interpreted to mean that Beethoven found
instruction in Förster's chamber music which he heard at the soirées of
Prince Lichnowsky and other art-patrons. Förster's compositions, not many
of which have been preserved in print,[12] are decidedly Beethovenish in character. His eldest son, who in 1870 was still living in Trieste, remembered
Beethoven perfectly well from 1803 to 1813, and communicated to the author
of this biography some reminiscences well worth preserving. It is known

[11] Reprinted by Lenz in *Beethoven. Eine
Kunststudie* (Hamburg, 1860), Part 4, p. 17.
(TDR, II, 186.)
[12] In the *Denkmäler der Tonkunst in Öster-*
reich, xxxv, No. 67 are printed five of
Förster's chamber works: two quartets (Op.
16, Nos. 4 and 5) and three quintets (Op. 19,
20, and 26).

from other sources that Beethoven, after the retirement of Albrechtsberger, considered Förster to be the first of all the Vienna teachers of counterpoint and composition, and this is confirmed by the son's statement that it was on Beethoven's advice that he sent to press the compendious *Anleitung zum Generalbass* which Breitkopf and Härtel published in 1805. A year or two later, Count Razumovsky applied to Beethoven for instruction in musical theory and especially in quartet composition. Beethoven absolutely refused, but so strongly recommended his friend Förster that the latter was engaged. Förster's dwelling in all those years was a favorite resort of the principal composers and dilettanti. Thither came Beethoven; Zmeskall, "a very precise gentleman with abundant white hair"; Schuppanzigh, "a short plump man with a huge belly"; Weiss, tall and thin; Linke, the lame violoncellist, Heinrich Eppinger, the Jewish violin dilettante, the youthful Mayseder, J. N. Hummel, and others. The regular periods of these quartet meetings were Sunday at noon, and the evening of Thursday; but Beethoven in those years often spent other evenings with Förster, "when the conversation usually turned upon musical theory and composition." Notwithstanding the wide difference in their ages (22 years), their friendship was cordial and sincere. The elder not only appreciated and admired the genius of the younger, but honored him as a man; and spoke of him as being not only a great musical composer, but, however at times rough in manner and harsh, even rude, in speech, of a most honorable and noble nature. Add to all this the fact, that Beethoven in later years recommended Förster to pupils as his "old master," and it is no forced and unnatural inference, that he (Beethoven) had studied quartet composition with him, as he had counterpoint with Albrechtsberger, and operatic writing with Salieri. Nor is this inference weakened—it is rather strengthened—by some points in what now follows.

The earliest mention of a string quartet in connection with Beethoven is a proposal recorded by Wegeler in the *Notizen* (p. 29): "Here [at Prince Lichnowsky's] in 1795 Count Apponyi asked Beethoven to compose a quartet for him for a given compensation, Beethoven not yet having written a piece in this genre," which led to no instant result. Then comes the passage from a letter to Amenda (July 1, 1801): "Do not lend your Quartet to anybody, because I have greatly changed it, having just learned how to write quartets properly." Had he learned from study under Förster?

The original manuscripts being lost, further chronological notices concerning the quartets must be sought for in the sketchbooks. Here Nottebohm comes to our assistance. In the Petter Collection at Vienna there are sketches for the last movement of the G major Quartet, the last movement of the B-flat Quartet (among them one which was discarded), both deviating from the printed form more or less, and one for the third and last movements of the F major Quartet. These latter approach pretty closely the ultimate form; thus this quartet was further advanced than the others. Associated with this sketch are sketches for the Sonata in B-flat, Op. 22, and for the easy Variations in G major which were begun while work was in progress on the last movement of the Quartet in G. Beethoven worked simultaneously on the first movement of Op. 22 and the scherzo of the first Quartet; while working on the last movement of the Quartet in B-flat, the rondo of the Sonata was begun. The sketches date from 1799 and 1800. Inasmuch as they occur before those for the Horn Sonata, which was composed very hurriedly and performed on April 18, 1800, the sketches were doubtless written earlier. One of the variations of the Quartet in A major was sketched much earlier— in 1794 or 1795. A little sketch for the first movement of the F major Quartet found beside sketches for the Violin Sonata, Op. 24, no doubt belongs to the revised form of the Quartet. In a sketchbook formerly in the possession of Grasnick in Berlin, there are sketches for the Quartet in D major which are near the ultimate form, except that there is a different theme for the last movement. Then comes a beginning in G major inscribed "Quart 2," the germ of the theme of a second Quartet.[13] There was, therefore, at the time no second Quartet, and that in D is the first. There follows "Der Kuss," sketches for the "Opferlied," for the Rondo in G major, Op. 51, No. 2, for a passage from Schiller's "Ode to Joy," for Gellert's "Meine Lebenzeit verstreicht" in G minor, for an intermezzo for pianoforte, for the revised form of the B-flat Concerto (which he played in Prague in 1798), and for various songs. The indications are, therefore, that the sketches were written in 1798. Then come sketches for the variations on "La stessa, la stessissima," which originated and were published in the beginning of 1799, and after them extended sketches for the first two movements of the F major Quartet, of which those belonging to the first movement are in an advanced stage, those for the second movement less so. A few sketches for a "third" quartet (thus specified) which were not used show that there was no third at the time; therefore, the Quartet in F is the second and was planned in 1799. Another sketchbook contains the continuation of the sketches for the F major Quartet, and, indeed, for all the movements; then an unused sketch for a "third" quartet (still not yet in existence), then to two songs by Goethe (one "Ich denke dein"), then to the movements of the G major Quartet, which is thus indicated to have been the third (the intermezzo in the second movement was conceived later), further sketches for the A major Quartet, which, it follows, was the fourth. Among these sketches are others for the Septet and the Variations on "Kind, willst du ruhig schlafen?" which appeared in December in 1799, and was therefore not composed earlier. All these sketches date from 1798 and 1799; but the Quartets were not finished. In an unused sketch for the Adagio of the Quartet in F occur the words: "les derniers soupirs," which confirm the story told by Amenda. The continuation of the G major Quartet dates to 1800. Up to now no sketches for the Quartet in C minor have been found.[14]

[13] Nottebohm (*II Beeth.*, p. 477) points out that the material was never used.

[14] Riemann (TDR, II, 188, n. 1) suggests an influence upon the material for the C minor

The results of this chronological investigation may be summed up as follows: the composition of the Quartets was begun in 1798, that in D, the third, being first undertaken. This was followed by that in F and soon after, or simultaneously, work was begun on that in G, which was originally designed as the second; but, as that in F was completed earlier, this was designated as the second by Beethoven, and that in G became in point of time the third. The Quartet in F was finished in its original shape by June 25, 1799, on which day he gave it to Amenda; he revised it later.[15] Whether or not this was also done with the others cannot be said; there is no evidence. The remark made in 1801, that he had just learned to write quartets, need not be read as meaning that he had formal instruction from Förster, but is amply explained by his practice on the six Quartets; yet Förster may have influenced him strongly. He then wrote the one in A (now No. 5), intending it to be the fourth; in this he seems to have made use of a *motif* invented at an earlier period. The Quartets in B-flat and C minor followed, the latter being, perhaps, the last. The definitive elaboration of the Quartets lasted certainly until 1800, possibly until 1801. The Quartets then appeared in two sets from the press of Mollo. It is likely that the first three, at least, were in the hands of the publisher before the end of 1800, as is proved by the letter to Hoffmeister. The first three appeared in the summer of 1801 and were advertised as on sale by Nägeli in Zurich already in July; they were mentioned in the *Allg. Musik. Zeitung* on August 26, and in Spazier's *Zeitung für die Elegante Welt.* In October of the same year the last three appeared and Mollo advertised them in the *Wiener Zeitung* of October 28. The Quartets are dedicated to Prince Lobkowitz.

Notice of a valuable present to Beethoven from his lenient and generous patron, Prince Karl Lichnowsky, naturally connects itself with the story of the Quartets—a gift thus described by Alois Fuchs, formerly violinist in the Imperial Court Orchestra, under date of December 2, 1846:

Ludwig van Beethoven owned a complete quartet of excellent Italian instruments given to him by his princely patron and friend Lichnowsky at the suggestion of the famous quartet-player Schuppanzigh. I am in a position to describe each of the instruments in detail.

1. A violin made by Joseph Guarnerius in Cremona in the year 1718 is now in the possession of Mr. Karl Holz, director of the *Concerts spirituels* in Vienna.

2. The second violin (which was offered for sale) was made by Nicholas Amati in the year 1667, and was in the possession of Dr. Ohmeyer, who died recently in Hütteldorf; it has been purchased by Mr. Huber.

3. The viola, made by Vincenzo Ruger in 1690, is also the property of Mr. Karl Holz.

Quartet from the "Duett für zwei obligate Augengläser."

[15] For the original version, see H. J. Wedig, "Beethovens Streichquartett, Op. 18, Nr. 1 und seine erste Fassung," *Veröffentlichungen des Beethovenhauses in Bonn*, Heft 2, Bonn, 1922.

4. The violoncello, an Andreas Guarnerius of the year 1712, is in the possession of Mr. P. Wertheimber of Vienna.

The seal of Beethoven has been impressed under the neck of each instrument and on the back of each Beethoven scratched a big B, probably for the purpose of protecting himself against an exchange. The instruments are all well preserved and in good condition. The most valuable one, without question, is the violin by Joseph Guarnerius, which is distinguished by extraordinary power of tone, for which, indeed, Mr. Holz has refused an offer of 1000 florins.

Beethoven received them from Lichnowsky certainly before 1812, but in what year is unknown. The four instruments were bought by Peter Th. Jokits in 1861, who gave them to the Berlin Library. ––•§(They are now on display at the Beethoven Museum in Bonn. The catalogue of this collection dates the Amati violin 1690 and the Guarnerius violoncello 1675.}§•––

Another proof of the Prince's regard and generosity, however, belongs to this, namely, an annuity of 600 florins to be continued until the composer should find some suitable permanent position.

As for the compositions of the year, it is safe to assume that Beethoven put the finishing touches to the First Symphony, the Septet, Op. 20, and the Quartets, Op. 18. Furthermore, there can be little doubt but that the Sonata for Horn, Op. 17, the Pianoforte Sonata, Op. 22, and the Concerto in C minor belong to this year. The "Variations très faciles" on an original theme in G were sketched and probably completed. The only chronological clues to the Horn Sonata are the date of its first performance, April 18, 1800, and the anecdote by Ries concerning the rapid completion of the work. Nothing is known of the autograph; but according to Nottebohm the beginning of a clean copy of the Adagio is to be found among the sketches for the Sonatas Op. 22 and 23. Punto was still in Munich in 1800, and since the work seems assuredly to have been designed for him, there is equal certainty that it was composed in that year.

The Septet, for four strings and three wind-instruments, dedicated to the Empress Maria Theresia, was played at the concert at which the Symphony in C major was brought forward, April 2, 1800; but it had been heard previously in the house of Prince Schwarzenberg. Inasmuch as sketches for it are found among those for the Quartets, especially the one in A major, which belong to the year 1799, its inception may be placed in that year, though it was probably finished in 1800 shortly before its performance. There is no date on the autograph. It was offered to Hoffmeister in the letter of December 15, 1800, and was published by him in 1802. The Septet speedily won great popularity and was frequently transcribed. Hoffmeister had an arrangement for string quintet which he advertised on August 18, 1802. Ries thought that Beethoven had made it, but he was in error; nevertheless, in the letter mentioned above, Beethoven gave Hoffmeister permission to publish an arrangement in which strings were substituted for the wind-instruments. Later Beethoven did transcribe it as a pianoforte trio with violin or clarinet *ad lib* (Op. 38) as a tribute of gratitude from the composer to his new physician, Dr. Johann Schmidt. The doctor played the violin and his daughter the pianoforte, both fairly well, and Beethoven arranged his popular piece for family use and, as was customary at the time, gave Dr. Schmidt the exclusive possession of the music for one year.

The theme of the minuet in the Septet was borrowed from the Pianoforte Sonata, Op. 49, No. 2, but its treatment is original. There has been considerable controversy without absolutely definitive result touching the melody which is varied in the Andante. Kretschmer-Zuccalmaglio, in *Deutsche Volkslieder*, prints the melody in connection with a Rhenish folksong ("Ach Schiffer, lieber Schiffer"),[16] and there is a tradition that Czerny said that it was taken by Beethoven from that source.

The Pianoforte Sonata in B-flat, Op. 22, also belongs to this year, as appears from the fact that it was offered to Hoffmeister in the letter of December 15. It was still in an unfinished state on the completion of the Sonata for Horn, as is shown by the circumstance that sketches of it are mingled with a fair transcript of a passage from the latter work. There are also sketches for Op. 22 among those for the Quartet in B-flat, Op. 18, No. 6, and the later movements of the Quartet in F—no doubt the revision. The sketches therefore belong to the year 1800, but may date back to 1799, from which it would appear that Beethoven worked an unusually long time on the Sonata. The principal labor was performed most likely in the summer of 1800, which Beethoven spent at Unterdöbling. It was published in 1802 by Hoffmeister and Kühnel. Sketches from the "Six Easy Variations" are found amongst some for the last movement of the Quartet in G, which seem to be nearly finished. Again we can fix the years as 1799 or 1800. Of special importance is the fact that the theme of the Variations is the same as the first episode of the rondo of the Sonata in B-flat, and the circumstance that the sketches are of almost the same date indicates that the identity was not accidental. The Variations were advertised as new by Traeg on December 16, 1800.

---⋯⋟The date of the Variations in E-flat for Pianoforte, Violin and Violoncello, Op. 44, is uncertain. Nottebohm dated the composition 1792-93 on the basis of a sketch (*Beeth.* p. 7); Thayer attributed it to the period of the Septet from a memorandum by Jahn that there were sketches for it on missing pages of the Grasnick sketchbook; and Riemann placed it for musical reasons a year later in the period of *Prometheus* (1800-1801).[17]

Kinsky-Halm date the following two works as having been written by 1800: an Allemande in A for Pianoforte, WoO 81, and the Aria, "Primo amore" for Soprano and Orchestra, WoO 72. Both were published for the first time in Series 25 of the Collected Works Edition.⋟⋯---

---

[16] Berlin, 1838, Vol. 1, No. 102, p. 181. Zuccalmaglio gives for his source "according to a widely known street singer, Frau Lützen-kirchen."

[17] See TDR, II, 410.

Though the number of new compositions produced in 1800 was small, attention must be directed to the fact that the revision and completion of works for publication, together with the planning of new works, gave a good deal of occupation to Beethoven. The big work of the year was the Concerto in C minor, the autograph of which distinctly bears the date of 1800. Amongst the compositions made ready for the printer were the Quartets, which were not ready till near the end of the year. It is certain, moreover, that Beethoven began working on *Prometheus* and the Sonata in E-flat, Op. 27, No. 1, in this year, and the summer must have been a busy one for him.

--◦◦The compositions written in or by 1800 follow:

By 1800. Allemande for Pianoforte, WoO 81.
"Primo amore" for Soprano and Orchestra, WoO 92.
Variations for Pianoforte, Violin and Violoncello, Op. 44 (sketched in 1791-92).

1798-1800. Six String Quartets, Op. 18.

1799-1800. Symphony No. 1 in C major, Op. 21, completed in the beginning of 1800.
Septet for Clarinet, French Horn, Bassoon, Violin, Viola, Violoncello and Contrabass, Op. 20. Completed before April, 1800.
Sonata for Pianoforte, Op. 22, completed in the second half of 1800.

1800. Concerto No. 3 for Pianoforte and Orchestra in C minor, Op. 37.
Six Easy Variations for Pianoforte, WoO 77.
Sonata for Pianoforte and French Horn, Op. 17.
Rondo for Pianoforte, Op. 51, No. 2.

The only work to be published in this year was:

By Traeg:
"VI Variations très faciles pour le Forte-piano," WoO 77.◦◦--

CHAPTER XIV

THE YEAR 1801

CORRESPONDENCE WITH PUBLISHERS—
EARLY CRITICISMS OF BEETHOVEN'S
MUSIC—LETTERS TO AMENDA AND WEGELER
CONCERNING DEAFNESS—FERDINAND RIES

THE tone of Beethoven's correspondence and the many proofs of his untiring industry during the winter 1800-1801 and the early part of the succeeding spring, suggest a mind at ease, rejoicing in the exercise of its powers, and a body glowing with vigorous health. But for his own words to Wegeler: "I have been really miserable this winter," the passing allusions to ill health in his replies to Hoffmeister's letters would merely impress the reader as being half-groundless apologies for lack of punctuality in writing. This chapter will exhibit the young master both as he appeared to the public and as he showed himself in confidential intercourse to the few in whose presence he put aside the mask and laid open his heart; and will, therefore, it is believed, be found fully to justify what has been said of his heroic energy, courage and endurance under a trouble of no ordinary nature.

In the beginning of the year he wrote to Hoffmeister as follows under date "January 15 (or thereabouts), 1801":

. . . Your enterprises delight me also and I wish that if works of art ever bring profit that it might go to real artists instead of mere shopkeepers—Your purpose to publish the *works of Sebastian Bach* is something which does good to my heart which beats only for the lofty and magnificent art of this patriarch of harmony, and I hope soon to see them in vigorous sale. I hope as soon as golden peace has been declared to be helpful in many ways, especially if you offer the works for subscription.—As regards our real business, since you ask it I can meet your wishes by offering the following items: Septet (concerning which I have already written you, and which can be profitably arranged for piano for greater circulation) 20 ducats—a symphony 20 ducats—a concerto 10 ducats—a grand solo sonata (Allegro, Adagio, Minuetto, Rondo) 20 ducats. (This sonata is a first-class piece, my dearest Herr Brother!) Now for an explanation: you will wonder, perhaps, that I have made no distinction here between sonata, septet and symphony; this is because I find that a septet or symphony has a smaller sale than a sonata, though a symphony ought unquestionably to be worth more. (N.B. The septet consists of a short introductory Adagio, then Allegro, Adagio, Minuetto, Andante with variations, Minuetto, again a short Adagio introduction and then Presto.—I put the price of the concerto at only 10 ducats because, as I have already written, I do not consider it one of my best—I do not think the amount excessive for the whole. I have tried, at least, to make the price as moderate as possible for you.—As regards the money order you may, since you leave the matter to me, issue it to Geimüller or Schuller.—The whole sum would thus be 70 ducats; how many thalers in gold that amounts to does not concern me, because I am a really poor businessman and arithmetician.—

This disposes of the troublesome business, I call it so because I wish things were different in the world. There ought to be only one *art-market* in the world where an artist would need only to carry his art-works and take away with him as much as he needed. As it is one must be half tradesman, and how we must adapt ourselves—good God—that is what I again call *troublesome.*—As regards the Leipzig c[ritics],[1] let them talk, they will certainly never make anyone immortal by their twaddle, nor will they rob anybody of immortality to whom Apollo has decreed it.—

Now may heaven preserve you and *your associate.* I have not been well for some time now and at present it is difficult for me to write notes, still more so letters of the alphabet. I hope we will have the occasion often to confirm how much you are my friend and I am

your brother and friend

L.v.Beethoven

For a speedy answer—goodby.

The next letter requires a word of introduction. That military campaign which included the disastrous field of Hohenlinden (December 3, 1800), had filled the hospitals in Vienna, and among the various means of raising funds for the benefit of the wounded was a series of public concerts. The two in which they reached their climax took place in the large Ridotto room (*Redouten-Saal*) of the imperial palace. The one arranged by Baron von Braun as Director of the Court Opera was a performance of Haydn's *Creation* conducted by the composer, on January 16th; the other was arranged by Mme. Frank (Christine Gerhardi) for January 30th. That lady, Mme. Galvani (Magdalena Willmann) and Herr Simoni were the singers, Beethoven and Punto the instrumental solo performers; Haydn directed two of his own symphonies, Paër and Conti directed the orchestra in the accompaniments to the vocal music. From J. H. F. Müller's *Abschied von der K. K. Hof-National Schaubühne* comes the program of this interesting concert.

[1] The German, according to Unger, reads "Leipziger R"[ezensenten]—which refers to the critics of the Leipzig *Allgemeine Musikal-* *ische Zeitung.* See *DM*, Vol. 15 (1923), p. 338 and, Vol. 17 (1925), p. 432.

First part

Symphony by Herr Joseph Haydn, Doctor of Music, conducted by himself.
Scena and Aria with chorus from the opera *Merope* by Herr Nasolini.
  Sung by Madame von Frank.
A Sonata on the piano-forte, composed and played by Herr van Beethoven and
  accompanied on the French horn by Herr Punto.
Scena and Duetto from the opera *Merope* by Herr Nasolini.
  Sung by Madame von Frank and Herr Simoni, singers at the R. I. Court
  Chapel.

Second part

Symphony by Herr Joseph Haydn, Doctor of Music, conducted by himself.
Terzetto with chorus from the opera *Orazi und Curiazi* [*Gli Orazi e Curiazi*] by
  Cimarosa, sung by Madame Galvani, Madame von Frank and Herr Simoni.
Aria with horn obbligato by Rispoli, sung by Herr Simoni and accompanied by
  Herr Punto.
Scena and Finale from the opera *Orazi und Curiazi* by Cimarosa.
  Sung by Madame Galvani, Madame von Frank and Herr Simoni, with ac-
  companiment by the chorus.

In the first public announcement printed in the *Wiener Zeitung* the only
artist mentioned was "the famous amateur singer Frau von Frank, née Gerhardi," as the giver of the concert. This called out from Beethoven the following letter:

Pour Madame de Frank.

I think it my duty, dear lady, to remind you that in the second announcement
of our concert you do not allow your husband to forget again that those who contribute their talents to the same should also be made known to the public.—This
is the custom, and I do not see, if this is not done, how the attendance is to be
increased, which after all is the chief aim of this c[oncert]—Punto is not a little
wrought up about the matter, and he is right, and it was my intention even before
I saw him to remind you of what must have been the result of grave haste or
great forgetfulness. Look after this, dear lady, since if it is not done you will be
faced with *real ill humor.*—Because I have been convinced by others as well as
myself that I am not a useless factor in this concert, I know that not only I but
Punto, Simoni, and Galvani will ask that the public be informed also of our zeal
for the philanthropic purposes of this concert; otherwise we must all conclude
that we are useless.—

Wholly yours,
L.v.Bthvn

Whether this sharp remonstrance produced any effect cannot now be ascertained, but the original advertisement was repeated in the newspaper on the
24th and 28th *verbatim.*

In the state of affairs then existing it was no time to give public concerts
for private emolument; moreover a quarrel with the orchestra a year before
might have prevented Beethoven from obtaining the Burgtheater again, and

the new Theater-an-der-Wien was not yet ready for occupation; but there is still another adequate reason for his giving no *Akademie* (concert) this spring. He had been engaged to compose an important work for the court stage.

Salvatore Vigano, dancer and composer of ballets, both action and music, the son of a Milanese of the same profession, was born at Naples, March 29, 1769. He began his career at Rome, taking female parts because women were not allowed there to appear upon the stage. He then had engagements successively at Madrid—where he married Maria Medina, a celebrated Spanish danseuse—Bordeaux, London and Venice, in which last city, in 1791, he composed his *Raoul, Sire de Croqui*. Thence he came to Vienna, where he and his wife first appeared in May, 1793. His *Raoul* was produced on June 25th at the Kärnthnerthor-Theater. After two years of service here he accepted engagements in five continental cities and returned to Vienna again in 1799. The second wife of Emperor Franz, Maria Theresia, was a woman of much and true musical taste and culture, and Vigano determined to compliment her in a ballet composed expressly for that purpose. Haydn's gloriously successful *Creation* may, perhaps, have had an influence in the choice of a subject, *The Men of Prometheus*, and the dedication of Beethoven's Septet to the Empress may have had its effect in the choice of a composer. At all events, the work was entrusted to Beethoven.

If the manner in which this work has been neglected by Beethoven's biographers and critics may be taken as a criterion, an opinion prevails that it was not worthy of him in subject, execution or success. It seems to be forgotten that as an orchestral composer he was then known only by two or three pianoforte concertos and his first Symphony, and that for the stage he was not known to have written anything. There is a misconception, too, as to the position which the ballet just then held in the Court Theatre. As a matter of fact it stood higher than ever before and, perhaps, than it has ever stood since. Vigano was a man of real genius and had wrought a reform which is clearly, vigorously and compendiously described in a memoir of Heinrich von Collin, from which we quote:[2] "In the reign of Leopold II the ballet, which had become a well-attended entertainment in Vienna through the efforts of Noverre, was restored to the stage. Popular interest turned at once to them again, and this was intensified in a great degree when, besides the ballet-master Muzarelli, a second ballet-master, Mr. Salvatore Vigano, whose wife disclosed to the eyes of the spectators a thitherto unsuspected art, also gave entertainments. The most important affairs of state are scarcely able to create a greater war of feeling than was brought about at the time by the rivalry of the two ballet-masters. Theatre-lovers without exception divided themselves into two parties who looked upon each other with hatred and contempt because of a difference of conviction. . . . The new ballet-

[2] Heinrich Joseph von Collin, *Sämtliche Werke* (Vienna, 1814), VI, 305-307. (TDR, II, 217, n. 1.)

master owed his extraordinary triumph over his older rival to his restoration of his art back from the exaggerated, inexpressive artificialities of the old Italian ballet to the simple forms of nature. Of course, there was something startling in seeing a form of drama with which thitherto there had been associated only leaps, contortions, constrained positions, and complicated dances which left behind them no feeling of unity, suddenly succeeded by dramatic action, depth of feeling, and plastic beauty of representation as they were so magnificently developed in the earlier ballets of Mr. Salvatore Vigano, opening, as they did, a new realm of beauty. And though it may be true that it was especially the natural, joyous, unconstrained dancing of Madame Vigano and her play of features, as expressive as it was fascinating, which provoked the applause of the many, it is nevertheless true that the very subject-matter of the ballets, which differentiate themselves very favorably from his later conceits, and his then wholly classical, skilful and manly dancing, were well calculated to inspire admiration and respect for the master and his creations."

Two or three pages might be compiled of spicy matter upon the beautiful Mme. Vigano's lavish display of the Venus-like graces and charms of her exquisite form; but her name, long before the *Prometheus* ballet, had disappeared from the roll of the theatre and Fräulein Casentini reigned in her stead. There was nothing derogatory to Beethoven in his acceptance of the commission to compose the music to a ballet by Vigano; but by whom commissioned, upon what terms, and when—concerning these and similar particulars, we know nothing. We only know, that at the close of the season before Easter, on the 28th of March, *Die Geschöpfe des Prometheus* was performed for the first time for the benefit of the prima ballerina of the ballet corps, Fräulein Casentini, and that the whole number of its performances this year was fourteen, and in 1802 nine.[3] The pecuniary result to Beethoven must therefore have been satisfactory. True, the full score did not appear in print in Beethoven's lifetime or for a long time thereafter; it was not published, indeed, until the appearance of the critical Complete Edition, in which it figures as No. 11 of Series 2; nothing is known of the original manuscript.[4] A copy revised except as to two numbers, is in the National Library at Vienna. A pianoforte arrangement of the score was published in June, 1801, by Artaria with the opus number 24 and a dedication to Princess Lichnowsky. Hoffmeister printed the overture with the orchestral parts in 1804 as Op. 43.

Alois Fuchs has preserved a characteristic anecdote which came to him "from the worthy hand of a contemporary": "When Beethoven had composed the music to the ballet *Die Geschöpfe des Prometheus* in 1801, he was

[3] See Robert Haas, "Zur Wiener Balletpanto-mime um den Prometheus," in *NBJ*, II, 84-103. For a review of the ballet in the *Zeitung für die elegante Welt* on May 19, 1801, see

TDR, II, 236.

[4] For the sketches see *Ein Notierungsbuch von L. van Beethoven*, ed. Mikulicz (Leipzig, 1927).

one day met by his former teacher, the great Joseph Haydn, who stopped him at once and said: 'Well, I heard your ballet yesterday and it pleased me very much!' Beethoven replied: 'O, dear Papa, you are very kind; but it is far from being a *Creation*!' Haydn, surprised at the answer and almost offended, said after a short pause: 'That is true; it is not yet a *Creation* and I can scarcely believe that it will ever become one.' Whereupon the men said their adieus, both somewhat embarrassed."

From the period immediately following we have another letter from Beethoven to Hoffmeister, dated April 22, 1801, in which he says:

You have good ground for complaint against me and that not a little. My excuse is that I was ill and moreover had a great deal to do besides, so that it was hardly possible for me to think of what I had to send you. Perhaps too, it is the only sign of genius about me that my things are not always in the best of order, and nobody can mend the matter except myself. Thus, for instance, as is usual with me, the pianoforte part in the concerto was not written out in the score, and only now have I done so, hence because of the haste you will receive that part in my own illegible manuscript.

So that the works may appear so far as possible in their proper sequence I point out to you that there should be placed

on the solo sonata	opus 22
on the symphony	opus 21
on the septet	opus 20
on the concerto	opus 19

—I shall send you the *titles* soon.— Set me down as a subscriber for the works of *Johann Sebastian Bach*, also *Prince Lichnowsky*. The transcription of the Mozart sonatas as quartets will do you honor and certainly prove profitable. I should like to be of greater service *on such occasions* but I am a disorderly individual and with the best of intentions am continually forgetting everything. However I have spoken about the matter here and there, and everywhere have found enthusiasm about it— It would be a fine thing if my good brother besides publishing the Septet were also to arrange it for flute, perhaps as a Quintet. This would help the *amateur flautists*, who have already approached me on the subject, and they would swarm around and feed on it like hungry insects.—To say something of myself, I have just written a ballet in which the ballet-master did not do as well as he might have done.— *Baron von Lichtenstein* has presented us with a product not measuring up to the ideas which the newspapers have spread touching his genius; again another bit of evidence against the newspapers. The Baron seems to have taken for his ideal *Hr. Müller at the Kasperle*, without reaching even *him*.— These are the beautiful conditions under which we poor fellows in Vienna are expected to flourish.— My dear brother make haste to give the world a sight of these works and write to me soon so that I may know whether or not I have forfeited your further confidence by my dilatoriness. To your associate Kühnel all kind wishes. In the future all things will go to you promptly and in order.— The quartets may be published in a few weeks—and with this keep well and continue to love your friend

and brother
Beethoven

The names mentioned in this letter are easily identified. Baron Carl August von Lichtenstein (1767-1845) had been so extravagantly praised as head of the Princely Music at Dessau that he was called to assume the kapellmeistership of the Imperial Opera in Vienna near the end of 1800. The contemporary reports of his efficiency as conductor are highly favorable. He deserves the credit of determining to add to the repertory of the Imperial Opera Mozart's *Die Zauberflöte* which, till then, had been heard by the Viennese only in the little theatre Auf-den-Wieden. In the first new work produced (April 16th) upon the imperial stage after Beethoven's *Prometheus* music, Lichtenstein introduced himself to the Vienna public in the character of a composer. It was in his opera *Bathmendi*, completely revised. The result was a wretched failure. Hoffmeister's long and familiar acquaintance with Vienna, its musicians and its theatres, would cause him readily to appreciate the fun and wit of Beethoven's remark that the newly engaged kapellmeister and composer of the Imperial Opera "seems to have taken for his ideal Hr. Müller"—the Offenbach of that time—but without reaching "even him." Considering that the Baron was yet a young man, at the most but three years older than Beethoven, the somewhat bitter remark which follows the jest seems natural enough. ⸻{Wenzel Müller was a conductor and composer who owed his success to light operas which he wrote for Marinelli's theatre in the Leopold-stadt suburb, nicknamed Kasperle.}⸻

One of the earliest projects of the new firm of Hoffmeister and Kühnel was the publication of *J. Sebastian Bach's Theoretical and Practical Clavier and Organ Works*. The first number contained: Toccata in D-flat, fifteen inventions, and *The Well-Tempered Clavichord* in part; the second number: fifteen symphonies in three voices, and a continuation of *The Well-Tempered Clavichord*. Now compare what Schindler says:[5] "Of the archfather Johann Sebastian Bach the stock was a very small one except for a few motets which had been sung at the house of van Swieten; besides these the majority of pieces were those familiarly known, namely, *The Well-Tempered Clavichord*, which showed signs of diligent study, three volumes of exercises, fifteen inventions, fifteen symphonies and a toccata in D minor. This collection of pieces *in a single volume* is to be found in my possession. Attached to these was a sheet of paper on which, in a strange handwriting, was to be read the following passage from J. N. Forkel's book *On the Life and Artwork of Johann Sebastian Bach*: 'The pretence that the musical art is an art for *all* cannot be substantiated by Bach, but is disproved by the mere existence and uniqueness of his works, which seem to be destined only for connoisseurs. Only the connoisseur who can surmise the inner organization and feel it and penetrate to the intention of the artist, which does nothing needlessly, is privileged to judge here; indeed the judgement of a musical connoisseur can scarcely be better tested than by seeing how rightly he has learned the works of Bach.' On both sides of this passage there were inter-

[5] *Biographie*, II, 184-85. (TDR, II, 176.)

rogation points from the thickest note-pen of Beethoven as a gloss on the learned historian and most eminent of all Bachians. No Hogarth could have put a grimmer look, or a more crushing expression, into an interrogation point."

Nägeli,[6] who professed long to have entertained the design to publish Bach's "most admirable works," issued his proposals in February, written with some degree of asperity against "the double competition" which, he had already learned, "was confronting" him. Of his edition of *The Well-Tempered Clavichord* Beethoven also possessed a part.

Under the same date (April 22, 1801) Beethoven wrote to Breitkopf and Härtel:

P.P.

Pardon the tardy answer to your letter to me. I was for a time continually indisposed and also overwhelmed with work, and besides since I am not the most industrious of letter writers, this may serve to excuse me also.— As regards your request for compositions by me I regret that at this time I am unable to oblige you. But please be so kind as to tell me what kinds of compositions you would like to have of mine, namely, symphonies, quartets, sonatas, etc., so that I may act accordingly, and should I have what you need or want, be able to place it at your service.— With my permission, 7 or 8 works of mine are about to appear *at Mollo's* in this place; four pieces *at Hofmeister's* in Leipzig.— In this connection I wish to add that one *of my first concertos*[7] and therefore *not one of the best of my compositions*, is to be published by *Hofmeister*, and that Mollo is to publish *a concerto which*, indeed *was written later*,[8] but which also does *not* rank among *the best of my works in this form*. This is only a hint for your Musikalische Zeitung with regard to criticism of these works, although if one might hear them, that is, well played, one would be best able to judge them.— Musical policy requires that one should keep possession of the best concertos for a time.— You should recommend to your Hrn. critics great care and wisdom especially in the products of younger composers. Many a one may have been frightened off who otherwise might have composed more. As far as I am concerned, I am far from thinking that I am so perfect as to be beyond criticism, yet the howls of your critics against me were at first so humiliating that when I compared myself with others I could not get aroused, but remained perfectly quiet, and reasoned that they do not understand their business. It was easier to remain quiet since I saw praise lavished on people who were held of little account here by the better sort, and who have disappeared from sight no matter how worthy they may otherwise have been.— But pax vobiscum—peace with you and me— I would not have mentioned a syllable about the matter if you had not yourself done so.—

When recently I visited a good friend of mine who showed me the *amount which had been collected for the daughter of the immortal god of harmony*, I marveled at the smallness of the sum which Germany, especially *your Germany*, has contributed in recognition of the person who seems to me worthy of respect for her father's sake. This brings me to the thought, how would it be if I were to

[6] Hans Georg Nägeli of Zürich was a poet and composer as well as publisher.

[7] The Concerto in B-flat, Op. 19. (TDR, II, 240, n. 1.)

[8] The Concerto in C major, Op. 15. (TDR, II, 240, n. 2.)

publish something by subscription for the benefit of this person, acquaint the public each year with the amount and its proceeds in order to protect myself from possible attack.— You could accomplish the most in this matter. Write me quickly how this might best be managed so that something is done before *this Bach* dies, before this brook[9] dries up and we be no longer able to supply it with water.— That you would publish the work is of course self-evident.

Upon the last topic of this letter something remains to be said. It was in the *Intelligenzblatt* of the *All. Mus. Zeit.* for May, 1800, that Rochlitz made a touching appeal for the last survivor of Sebastian Bach's children. "This family," he says, "has now dwindled down to the single daughter of the great Sebastian Bach, and this daughter is now very old. . . . This daughter is starving. . . . The publishers of the *Musik Zeitung* and I offer to obligate if anybody shall entrust us with money to forward it in the most expeditious and careful manner, and to give account of it in the 'Intelligenzblätter.' " The first account was in the paper for December. Regina Susanna Bach published her "thanks" for 96 thalers and 5 silbergroschens contributed, as the "careful account" which was appended showed, by sixteen persons, four of whom, in Vienna, sent more than 80 florins, leaving certainly but a small sum as the offering of her native Germany. One other—and only one—account appeared in June, 1801. It was an acknowledgment by Rochlitz, Breitkopf and Härtel and Fräulein Bach of having received on May 10th the considerable sum of 307 florins Viennese (the equal of 200 thalers) "through the Viennese musician Andreas Streicher, collected by Streicher and Count Fries. At the same time the famous Viennese composer and virtuoso Herr van Beethoven declares he will publish one of his newest works solely for the benefit of the daughter of Bach . . . so that the good old lady may derive the benefit of it from time to time. Therefore he nobly urges that the publication be hastened as much as possible lest the daughter of Bach die before his object be attained." Whether or not any such work was published is not known.

Beethoven had just cause for indignation in the treatment which he had received at the hands of the writers for the *Allgemeine Musikalische Zeitung* mentioned in his letter of January 18, 1801. Hoffmeister had evidently written him on the subject, and his reticence in confining himself in reply to a single contemptuous sentence, though writing in the confidence of private correspondence, is something unexpected; not less so is the manly, dignified and ingenuous style of his answer to Breitkopf and Härtel upon the same topic in the letter of April 22nd. The first number of that famous musical journal (take it all in all, the noblest ever published) appeared October 3, 1798, edited by Rochlitz, published by Breitkopf and Härtel. In the second number, "Z. ." eulogizes the Six Fughettas of the lad, C. M. von Weber; in the tenth, young Hummel's sonatas, Op. 3, are reviewed; in the fifteenth (January 19,

---

[9] *Bach* is the German equivalent of brook. (TK, I, 287, n. 3.)

1799), the name of Beethoven first appears, viz.: in the title of three sonatas dedicated to him by Wölffl. At length, in No. 23, that of March 6, 1799, he is introduced to the readers of the journal as a composer—not of one or more of the eight Trios, ten Sonatas, the Quintet and Serenade, which make up the *opera* 1 to 11 then published—but as the writer of the Twelve Variations on "Ein Mädchen oder Weibchen," and eight on "Une fièvre brûlante."

The criticisms are a perfect reflex of the conventional musical thought of the period and can be read now with amused interest, at least. There is no room here for their production in full. The writer "M. ." recognizes the clever pianoforte player in the Variations but cannot see evidences in them of equal capacity as a composer. He likes some of them and "willingly admits" that those on "Une fièvre brûlante" are "more successful than those of Mozart, who in his early youth also treated the same subject." But Mozart did not write the variations referred to, and when Grétry's *Richard, Coeur de Lion*, from which the theme was borrowed, was first performed in Paris, Mozart was not in his "early youth" but twenty-eight years old. The critic descants with disapproval on "certain harshnesses in the modulations," illustrating them; holds up Haydn as a model chooser of themes; and commends the comments of Vogler on a set of variations by Forkel on "God Save the King," printed in a little book on the subject. Thus Beethoven found, in the first recognition of himself as a composer in that journal, two compositions which he did not think worthy of opus numbers, to the neglect of all his better works, made the subject of censure and ridicule for the purpose of puffing and advertising a pamphlet by Vogler. Were his own subsequent Variations on "God Save the King" an effect of this article?

No. 33 (May 15th) of the *Allgemeine Musikalische Zeitung* contains nearly two pages from the pen of Spazier on Lichtenstein's opera, *Die steinerne Braut*, and a parallel between Beethoven and Wölffl as pianists. Then in the next number the beautiful Trio, Op. 11, finds a reviewer. Here is the whole of his article: "This Trio, which in part is not easier but more flowing than many other pieces by the same author, makes an excellent ensemble on the pianoforte with accompaniment. The composer with his unusual harmonic knowledge and love for serious composition would provide us many things which would leave many hand-organ things far in the rear, even those composed by famous men, if he would but try to write more naturally."

Could one say less?

The critics are now ruminating upon the noble Sonatas for Pianoforte and Violin, Op. 12, and No. 36 (June, 1799), contains the result:

"The critic, who heretofore has been unfamiliar with the pianoforte pieces of the author, must admit, after having looked through these strange sonatas, overladen with difficulties, that after diligent and strenuous labor he felt like a man who had hoped to make a promenade with a genial friend through a tempting forest and found himself barred every minute by inimical barriers, returning at last exhausted and without having had any pleasure. It is undeniable that Hr. Beethoven goes his own gait; but what a bizarre and singular gait it is! Learned, learned and always learned—and nothing natural, no song. Yes, to be accurate, there is *only a mass of learning here, without good method*; obstinacy, but for which we feel but little interest; a striving for strange modulations, an objection to customary associations, a heaping up of difficulties on difficulties till one loses all patience and enjoyment. Another critic (*M.Z.*, No. 24) has said almost the same thing, and the present writer must agree with him completely.

"Nevertheless, the present work must not be rejected wholly. It has its value and may be of excellent use for already practised pianoforte players. There are always many who love difficulties in invention and composition, what we might call perversities, and if they play these Sonatas with great precision they may derive delight in the music as well as an agreeable feeling of satisfaction. If Hr. v. B. wished to deny himself a bit more and follow the course of nature he might, with his talent and industry, do a great deal for an instrument which he seems to have so wonderfully under his control."

Let us pass on to No. 38 of the journal (June 19, 1799), where we find half a dozen notices to arrest our attention. Variations by Schuppanzigh for two violins are "written in good taste and conveniently for the instrument"; variations for the pianoforte by Philip Freund are very satisfactory and "some among them belong to the best of their kind"; variations by Heinrich Eppinger for violin and violoncello "deserve honorable mention"; but "X Variations pour le clavecin sur le Duo 'La stessa, la stessissima' par L. v. Beethoven" the critic "cannot at all be satisfied with, because they are stiff and strained; and what awkward passages are in them, where harsh tirades in continuous semitones create an ugly relationship and the reverse! No, it is true; Hr. van Beethoven may be able to improvise, but he does not know how to write variations."

Now, however, the tide begins to turn. After an interval of nearly four months, in No. 2 of Vol. II (October 9, 1799), the Pianoforte Sonatas, Op. 10, have a page allotted to them. A few sentences to show the tone of the articles will suffice; for the praise of Beethoven needs no repetition: "It is not to be denied that Hr. v. B. is a man of genius, possessed of originality and who goes his own way. In this he is assured by his extraordinary thoroughness in the higher style of writing and his unusual command of the instrument for which he writes, he being unquestionably one of the best pianoforte composers and players of our time. His abundance of ideas, of which a striving genius never seems to be able to let go so soon as it has got possession of a subject worthy of his fancy, only too frequently leads him to pile up ideas, etc. Fancy, in the extraordinary degree which Beethoven possesses, supported, too, by extraordinary knowledge, is a valuable possession, and, indeed, an indispensable one for a composer, etc. The critic, who, after he has tried to accustom himself more and more to Hr. Beethoven's manner, has learned to admire him more than he did at first, can scarcely suppress the wish that . . . it might occur to this fanciful composer to practise a certain economy in his labors. . . . This tenth collection, as the critic has said, seems deserving of high praise. Good invention, an earnest, manly style . . . well-ordered thoughts in every part, difficulties not carried to an excess, an entertaining treatment of the harmony—lift these Sonatas above the many."

In No. 21 (February 19, 1800) justice is done to the "Sonate pathétique." Except a passing notice of the publication of the Quartets, Op. 18, made by a correspondent, Vol. III of the *Allg. Mus. Zeitung* contains *nothing* on the works of Beethoven. So that more than a year passed between the favorable review of the "Sonate pathétique" and the letter to Breitkopf and Härtel of April 22nd. The mild tone of that missive is, therefore, easily explained. The tone of the journal had completely changed; this fact, and time, had assuaged Beethoven's wrath, and finally the publishers in applying to him for manuscripts had made the *amende honorable*.

In the number of May 26, 1802, Vol. IV, along with a notice of the two Sonatas for Pianoforte and Violin, Op. 23 and Op. 24, begins that long series of fair, candid and generously eulogistic articles on Beethoven's works which culminated in July, 1810, in the magnificent review of the C minor Symphony by E. T. A. Hoffmann—a labor of love that laid the foundation of a new school of musical criticism.

In June, 1801, Beethoven wrote again to the publisher Hoffmeister to this effect:

I am a little bit amazed at what you have communicated to me through the local representative of your firm; I am almost vexed to think that you consider me capable of such a trick. It would be a different matter if I had sold my wares only to avaricious tradesmen hoping that they would make a good speculation on the sly, but as *artist towards artist* it is a bit harsh to think such things of me. It looks to me as if the whole matter had been thoroughly planned to test me or that it was a mere surmise. In either case I inform you that before you received *the Septet* from me I sent it to London to Hr. Salomon (for performance at his concerts, out of mere *friendship*), but with the understanding that he should have a care that it should not fall into the hands of strangers, because I intended that it should be published in Germany. If you think it necessary, you may make inquiry of him, but in order to prove my honesty *I give you herewith the assurance that I have not sold the Septet, Concerto, the Symphony and the Sonata to anybody but you, Hoffmeister and Kühnel, and that you may consider them as your exclusive property, and to this I pledge my honor.* You may make as much of this assurance as you please—As for the rest I believe as little that Salomon is capable of being guilty of having the Septet printed as I am of having sold it to him—I am so conscientious that I have denied the applications of *various publishers* to print the pianoforte arrangement of the Septet, and yet I do not know whether or not you intend to make use of it.

---⊶⊰{The long-promised titles, including dedications, of the four above mentioned works follow, and the letter ends with another paragraph of assurance in the same vein as above. Of interest is the title of the First Symphony, with a dedication to the Elector Maximilian Franz. This was crossed out by an unknown hand, presumably after the Elector's death on July 26, 1801. The dedication in the published score is to Baron van Swieten.}⊱⊷---

When the health of poor Maximilian Franz became precarious, the welfare of the Teutonic Order in those revolutionary times demanded that a wise and energetic successor to him as Grand Master should be secured in the person of an efficient coadjutor. The thoughts of all parties concerned fixed upon a man who was then not even a member of the order, in case he would join it and accept the position, namely, the famous Archduke Karl. A Grand Chapter was therefore called at Vienna, which opened June 1st, and which unanimously admitted him to membership, he having received a dispensation from taking the oaths for the time being. On June 3rd he was elected coadjutor and on the 11th he received the accolade. The circular which called the meeting brought to the Austrian capital the whole body of officials employed at Mergentheim, and thus it happened that Stephan von Breuning, whose name appears in the Calendar of the order from 1797 to 1803, inclusive, as Hofrathsassessor, came again to Vienna and renewed intimate personal intercourse with Beethoven.

In the spring of this year Beethoven removed from the Tiefer Graben into rooms overlooking one of the bastions—there is little, if any doubt, the Wasserkunstbastei—and in one of those houses the main entrances to which are in the Sailerstätte. At a later period of his life he came thither again, and with good reason; for those houses not only afforded a beautiful view over the Glacis and the Landstrasse suburb, but plenty of sun and fresh air.

This year he chose Hetzendorf for his summer retreat. Those who know well the environs of Vienna, are aware that this village offers less attraction to the lover of nature than a hundred others within easy distance of the city. There is nothing to invite one, who is fond of the solitude of the forest, but the thick groves in the garden of Schönbrunn some ten minutes' walk distant. It is certainly possible that Beethoven's state of health may have forbidden him to indulge his taste for long rambles, and that the cool shades of Schönbrunn, so easily and at all times accessible, may have determined his choice. It would be pleasant to believe, though there is no evidence to support such a belief, that some feeling of regard for his former patron Maximilian, who had sought retirement at Hetzendorf, was one of the causes which induced the composer to spend this summer there.

Let us now turn to the important letters written in the summer of 1801, beginning with two written to his friend Amenda, which were first published in the *Signale* of 1852, No. 5. The first, without date or record of place, is as follows:

How can Amenda think that I could ever forget him—because I do not write or have not written to him?—as if the remembrance of people could be preserved only in that manner!

A thousand times there comes to my mind the best of all men that I ever knew —yes, along with the two men who had my entire love, of which one lives, you are the third—the memory of you can never be extinguished. You will soon receive a long letter from me concerning my present condition and everything about me that might interest you.

Farewell, dear, good, noble friend, keep me always in your love, your friendship, as I shall forever remain

Your faithful Beethoven

The longer letter which he promised to send to his friend is dated July 1 [1801].[10]

My dear, my good Amenda, my true friend!

I received and read your last letter with mixed pain and pleasure—To what shall I compare your fidelity, your attachment to me? Oh, it is so wonderful that you have always been true to me; and yes, I know you as one who is trustworthy and above all others. You are no *Viennese friend*, no, you are one of those who spring from the ground of my native land. How often do I wish you were with me, for your B is living an unhappy life, quarreling with nature and its creator, often cursing the latter for surrendering his creatures to the merest accident which often breaks or destroys the most beautiful blossoms. Know that my noblest faculty, *my hearing*, has greatly deteriorated. When you were still with me I felt the symptoms but kept silent; now it is continually growing worse, and whether or not a cure is possible has become a question. It is said to be due to the condition of my belly, and so far as that is concerned I am nearly restored to health. I hope, indeed, that my hearing also will improve, but I am doubtful because such diseases are the most incurable. How sad is my lot, I must avoid all things that are dear to me and what is more must live among such miserable and egotistical men as Zmeskall, Schuppanzigh, etc. I must say that amongst them all Lichnowsky is the most satisfactory; in the last year he has settled an income of 600 florins on me. This and the good sale of my works enables me to live without care. I could sell everything that I compose five times over and at a good price—I have composed considerably of late. As I hear that you have ordered a pianoforte from S,[11] I will send you various things in the box of the instrument so that it need not cost you much. Now a man has recently returned here to my great comfort,[12] with whom I can share the pleasures of a close relationship and an unselfish friendship. He is one of the friends of my youth; I have often spoken of you to him and told him that since I left my fatherland you have been the one person close to my heart. Z. does not appeal to him either, he is and always will be too weak for friendship; and I use him and S[13] only as instruments on which I can play when I please. But they can never become real witnesses of my internal and external actions any more

10 For the corrected reading of the date and content of this letter, I am gratefully indebted to Miss Emily Anderson.

11 Probably Streicher.

12 Probably Stephan von Breuning. (TDR,

II, 285, n. 1. Deiters substitutes Breuning for Thayer's guess of Anton Reicha as the "man" in question.)

13 Z. and S. refer obviously to Zmeskall and Schuppanzigh.

than they can be real participants in my life; I value them only by what they do for me. Oh, how happy I should be if my hearing were completely restored, then I would hurry to you. However, as it is I must stay away from everything and the most beautiful years of my life must pass by without my accomplishing all that my talent and powers bid me to do— A sad resignation must be my refuge, although, indeed, I am resolved to rise above every obstacle. But how will it be possible? Yes, Amenda, if my infirmity shows itself to be incurable in half a year, I shall appeal to you, you must abandon everything and come to me. Then I shall travel (my affliction causes me the least trouble in playing and composing, the most in association with others) and you must be my companion. I am sure my good fortune will not desert me. What is there that I might not accomplish? Since you left I have composed everything except opera and church music. Surely you will not deny me, you will help your friend bear his troubles and his affliction. I have also greatly improved my pianoforte playing, and I hope that this tour will, perhaps make your fortune too; afterwards you must remain with me forever.— I have received all of your letters, and despite the fact that I have answered so few, you were always with me, and my heart still beats as tenderly for you as it ever did.— *I beg of you to keep the matter of my deafness a profound secret to be confided to nobody no matter whom.*— Write to me very often; your letters, no matter how short, comfort me, do me good, and I shall expect another from you soon, my dear fellow.— Do not lend your quartet to anybody because I have greatly changed it, having just learned how to write quartets properly, as you will observe when you receive them.— Now, farewell my dear, good fellow; if you ever think of anything I can do for you here, you have only to tell

> Your faithful and truly affectionate
> L.v.Beethoven

It is not difficult to imagine calamities greater than that which now threatened Beethoven—as, the loss of sight to a Raphael or Rubens at the height of his fame and powers; a partial paralysis or other incurable disease of the brain cutting short the career of a Shakespeare or Goethe, a Bacon or Kant, a Newton or Humboldt. Better the untimely fate of a Buckle, than to live long years of unavailing regret over the blasted hopes and promise of early manhood. In such cases there remains no resource; hope itself is dead. But to Beethoven, even if his worst fears should prove prophetic and his infirmity at length close all prospects of a career as virtuoso and conductor, the field of composition still remained open. This he knew, and it saved him from utter despair. Who can say that the world has not been a gainer by the misfortune which stirred the profoundest depths of his being and compelled the concentration of all his powers into one direction?

As the disease made progress and the prospect of relief became less, notwithstanding a grief and anxiety which caused him such mental agony as even to induce the thought of suicide, he so well succeeded in keeping it concealed from all but a few intimate and faithful friends, that no notice whatever is to be found of it until 1802 except in papers from his own hand. They form a very touching contrast to his letters to other correspondents. Neither the head nor the heart is to be envied of the man who can read them without emotion. The two most important are the letters to Wegeler giving full details of his case; doubly valuable because they are not merely letters to a friend, but an elaborate account of the symptoms and medical treatment of his disease, made to a physician of high standing who thoroughly understood the constitution of the patient. They are therefore equally significant for what they contain and for what they omit.

On June 29, he sent the following letter to Wegeler, who published it in his *Notizen* (p. 20):

Vienna, June 29

My good, dear Wegeler,

How greatly I thank you for thinking of me; I have so little deserved it or tried to deserve anything from you. Yet you are so very good and refuse to be offended by anything, not even by my unpardonable negligence, and remain always my true, faithful and honorable friend.— Do not ever think that I could forget you and all of you who were always so true and dear to me. There are moments when I long for you myself, yes, and would like to spend some time with you.— My fatherland, the beautiful country in which I first saw the light of day, is still as clear and beautiful before my eyes as when I left you. In short, I shall look upon that time when I see you again and greet Father Rhine as one of the happiest moments in my life.— When this shall be I cannot yet tell you, but I want to say this much, that when you see me again it will be only as a great man, not only a greater artist but a better and more accomplished man. If conditions are improved in our fatherland, my art will be used only in the service of the poor. Oh happy moment, how happy I am that I myself can create you, can invoke you— You want to know something about my situation, it is not so bad. In the last year, unbelievable as it may sound when I tell you, Lichnowski, who has always remained my warmest friend, (there were little quarrels between us, but haven't they served to strengthen our friendship?) has set aside a fixed sum of 600 florins for me to draw upon so long as I remain without a post suitable for me. My compositions bring me a fair sum, and I may say that I have more commissions than it is possible for me to fill. Besides, I have 6 or 7 publishers after each piece and might have more if I chose; people no longer bargain with me, I ask and they pay. You see how very convenient it is. For instance, I see a friend in need and my purse does not permit me to help him at once; so I have only to get to work and in a short time, help is at hand— Moreover, I am more economical than formerly; if I stay here for good I shall arrange to reserve one day a year for my Akademie, of which I have given several. That evil demon, my bad health, however, has put a spoke in my wheel, namely: my hearing has grown steadily worse during the last three years, which was said to be caused by the condition of my belly, which as you know has always been wretched and has been getting worse, since I am always troubled with diarrhoea, which causes extraordinary weakness. Frank[14] wanted to *tone up* my body by tonic medicines and restore my hearing with almond oil, but prosit, nothing happened, my hearing grew worse and worse, and my bowels remained as they had been. This lasted until the autumn

[14] Peter Frank, director of the general hospital in Vienna. (TDR, II, 272, n. 1.)

of last year, and I was often in despair. Then came a medical ass who advised me to take cold baths for my health; a more sensible one advised the usual lukewarm Danube bath. That worked wonders, my belly improved, but my deafness remained and even became worse. This last winter I was really miserable, since I had frightful attacks of colic and again fell back into my previous condition. Thus I remained until about four weeks ago, when I went to Vering,[15] thinking that my condition demanded a surgeon, and besides I had great confidence in him. He succeeded almost wholly in stopping the awful diarrhoea. He prescribed the lukewarm Danube bath, into which each time I had to pour a little bottle of strengthening stuff. He gave me no medicine of any kind until about four days ago, when he prescribed pills for my stomach and a kind of herb for my ear. Since then I can say I am feeling stronger and better, except that my ears sing and buzz continually, day and night. I can truly say that I am living a wretched life. For two years I have avoided almost all social gatherings because it is impossible for me to say to people "I am deaf." If I belonged to any other profession it would be easier, but in my profession it is a frightful state. Then there are my enemies, who are numerous, what would they say about this?— In order to give you an idea of this singular deafness of mine, I must tell you that in the theatre I must get very close to the orchestra in order to understand the actor, and if I am a little distant I do not hear the high tones of the instruments or singers. It is curious that in conversation there are people who do not notice my condition at all; since I have generally been absent-minded, they account for it in that way. Often I can scarcely hear someone speaking softly, the tones, yes, but not the words. However, as soon as anyone shouts it is intolerable. Heaven knows what will happen to me, *Vering says that there will be an improvement but not a complete cure*— Already I have often cursed my Creator and my existence; *Plutarch* has taught me *resignation*. If possible I will bid defiance to my fate, although there will be moments in my life when I shall be the unhappiest of God's creatures.— I beg of you to say nothing of my condition to anybody, not even to *Lorchen*.[16] I entrust the secret only to you, but I would be glad if you were to correspond with *Vering* on the subject. If my condition continues like this I shall come to you next spring. You can hire a house for me in some pretty place in the country, and for a half a year I shall become a peasant. This might bring about a change. Resignation, what a wretched refuge, and yet the only one remaining open to me.—

You will forgive me for burdening you with a friend's troubles when you yourself have sorrow.— Stephan Breuning is here now and we are together almost daily. It does me so much good to revive the old emotions. He has really become a good, splendid young fellow, who knows a thing or two, and like all of us more or less has his heart in the right place. I have very good lodgings now which look on to the Bastei, and are doubly valuable because of my health. I believe I can arrange it for B[reuning] to come live with me.— You shall have your Antioch[17] and also many of my musical compositions if you do not think they will

[15] Gerhard von Vering, Army surgeon, and from 1797 to 1809 supervising director of the big health institutions and hospitals in Vienna. His daughter, Julie, married Stephan von Breuning in 1808, but died a year later. (Cf. TDR, II, 272, n. 2.)

[16] Eleonore von Breuning, who became the wife of Wegeler in March, 1802. (TDR, II, 273, n. 1.)

[17] A well-known picture by Füger, Director of the Academy of Painting in Vienna. (TDR, II, 273, n. 2.)

cost you too much. Honestly, your love for art still gives me much happiness. If you will write to me how to manage it, I will send you all my compositions, already a goodly number and increasing daily— In return for the portrait of my grandfather which I beg you to send me by mail-coach as soon as possible, I am sending you that *of his grandson*, your good and affectionate Beethoven. It is to be published here by Artaria who has often asked me for one, as have others, including foreign art-dealers. I shall soon write to Stoffel[18] and give him a piece of my mind concerning his stubborn frame of mind. I will make his ears ring with the old friendship, he shall promise me by all that is holy not to annoy you further in your present troubled circumstances— I shall also write to good Lorchen. I have never forgotten one of you good people even though I have not written you, but writing, as you know, was never my forte, even my best friends have not had letters from me in years. I live only in my notes and one composition is scarcely done before another is begun. As I am writing now, I often work on three or four pieces at once.— Write to me often and hereafter I will try to find time to write to you occasionally. Give warmest greetings to all including the good Madame Councillor,[19] and tell her "that I still occasionally have a raptus." As regards Koch, I do not at all wonder over the change. Fortune is round like a ball, and therefore does not always fall on the noblest and best— Concerning Ries, to whom I send hearty greetings, I will write you more in detail about his son, although I think that he would have better luck in *Paris* than in *Vienna*. Vienna is overcrowded and even the most able find it extremely difficult to maintain themselves— In the autumn or winter I shall see what I can do for him, for at that time the public hurries back to the city— Farewell, good, faithful Wegeler; be assured of the love and friendship of

Your

Beethoven

—⋙This letter is important for its descriptions of Beethoven's symptoms of deafness, which strengthen the conclusion that his was a nerve-type deafness. The buzzing in his ears, known as "tinnitus," is symptomatic of nerve damage. Beethoven stated that he could not hear the *high* tones of the instruments or singers. Nerve degeneration usually starts and is most severe in the high pitches, progressing later to the lower ones. He could hear the tones, but not the words, of conversations, because consonant sounds, so necessary for word identification, are generally high pitched. His mention of the "intolerable" distress caused when anyone shouted is a phenomenon of nerve-type deafness: up to a certain noise level the person can hear little or nothing, but beyond that level his hearing is as acute as formerly; hence shouting would indeed be intolerable and might cause true pain.⋘—

On Nov. 16 he wrote in greater detail to Wegeler (*Notizen*, p. 38):

My good Wegeler!

I thank you for the new evidence of your concern on my behalf, all the more since I deserve so little at your hands— You want to know how it goes with me,

---

[18] Christoph von Breuning. (TDR, II, 273, n. 3.) [19] Madame von Breuning. (TDR, II, 274, n. 1.)

what I am using. As little as I like to discuss such matters I prefer to do it with you rather than anyone else.— For several months Vering has had *vesicatories* placed on both my arms, which consist, as you know, of a certain bark.[20] This is a very unpleasant remedy, inasmuch as I am robbed of the free use of my arms for a few days (until the bark has had its effect) to say nothing of the pain. It is true I cannot deny that the buzzing and singing in my ears is somewhat less than formerly, especially in the left ear, where my deafness began. But so far my hearing has not improved in the least, and I am not sure but what it has grown rather weaker— My belly is in a better condition; especially when I have had the lukewarm baths for a few days I feel quite well for 8 or 10 days. I seldom take a tonic for my stomach; I am beginning to use the *herbs on the belly* as you suggested.— Vering will not hear of shower-baths, and I am thoroughly dissatisfied with him. He shows so little care and consideration for such an illness; if I did not go to him, which causes me a great deal of trouble, I should not see him at all.— What do you think of Schmidt?[21] I do not like to change, but it seems to me V is much too much of a practitioner to acquire many new ideas from reading— S seems to me a very different sort of man and, perhaps, would not be so negligent.— People speak wonders of *galvanism*, what do you say to that?—A doctor told me that *in Berlin* he had seen a deaf and dumb child recover his hearing, and a man who had been deaf for seven years get well— I hear even that *your Schmidt* experiments with it.— I am living more pleasantly now, since I mingle more with people. You will scarcely believe how lonely and sad my life has been for the last two years. My bad hearing haunted me everywhere like a ghost and I fled—from mankind. I seemed like a misanthrope, and yet am far from being one. This change has been wrought by a dear fascinating girl who loves me and whom I love. There have been a few blessed moments within the last two years, and it is the first time that I feel that—marriage might bring me happiness. Unfortunately she is not of my station—and now—it would be impossible for me to marry.— I must still hustle about most actively. If it were not for my deafness, I should before now have traveled over half the world, and that I must do.— There is no greater delight for me than to practise and show my art.— Do not believe that I could be happy with you. What is there that would make me happier? Even your solicitude would pain me. I should see pity on your faces every moment and be even more unhappy.— What did those beautiful native regions give me, nothing except the hope of a better situation. This would have been mine now—but for this misfortune— Oh, if I were rid of this affliction I would embrace the world. Really, I feel that my youth is just beginning, for have I not always been in poor health? My physical strength has for some time past been steadily gaining and also my mental powers. Each day I move towards the goal which I sense but cannot describe, only in this way can your B live.— Do not speak of rest—I know of none but sleep, and woe is me that I must give up more time to it than formerly. Grant me but half freedom from my affliction, and then—as a complete and ripened man I shall return to you and renew the old feelings of friendship. You will see me as happy as it is possible to be here below, not unhappy— No, I cannot endure

---

[20] The bark of *Daphne Mezereum*. See *Notizen*, p. 42. (TDR, II, 274, n. 2.)

[21] Johann Adam Schmidt, since 1784 a professor of anatomy at the Josefakademie for army doctors. In 1796 he became an army medical officer. Dr. Schmidt was also the author of a number of scholarly works. (TDR, II, 274, n. 3.)

that—I will take fate by the throat, it shall not wholly overcome me— Oh, it would be so beautiful to live life a thousandfold— A quiet life— No, I feel I am no longer made for that.— Write to me as soon as you can— Help *Steffen* to make up his mind to secure an appointment of some kind in the *Teutonic Order*. There is too much wear and tear in the life here for his health, besides, he lives such an isolated existence that I cannot see how he is to get along. You know what it is like here, I will not say that social life might lessen *his fatigue*, but it is impossible to persuade him to go anywhere. A short time ago I had a musicale at my home with a select group, yet our friend—St.—did not turn up.— Advise him to take more rest and seek more composure, I have done my best in this direction. Without these he will never again be either happy or well.— Tell me in your next letter whether or not it matters if I send you a great deal of my music, you can sell what you do not need and so get back the post-money—my portrait—also— All possible lovely greetings to L[orchen]—also Mama—also Christoph— You love me a little, do you not. Be as well assured of this as of the friendship of

Your Bthvn

In view of the relation in which Wegeler stood to the Breuning family, Beethoven might have well said more about "Steffen" but not easily less. Even in the first letter something of patronizing condescension in the tone makes itself felt, which becomes far too pronounced when he speaks of him in the second letter—that of November. One feels that Breuning had been made sensible, to a painful degree, how great his friend had grown. Wegeler himself is struck by Breuning's non-appearance at Beethoven's private concert, and remarks (*Notizen*, p. 44): "He must have felt his disappointment with this old friend all the more, since Breuning had been developed by Father Ries from an amateur to a most admirable violinist, and had several times played in electoral concerts."

When Beethoven met Stephan von Breuning again in 1801, it was impossible that it be on such terms as those on which they had parted in 1796. Breuning had passed this interval of five years in a small provincial town, Mergentheim, in the monotonous routine of a petty office, in the service of a semi-military, semi-religious institution which had so sunk in grandeur and power as to be little more than a venerable name—a relic of the past. In the same service he had now returned to Vienna. How Beethoven had been employed, and how he had risen, we have seen. Thus, their relative positions in society had completely changed. Beethoven now moved familiarly in circles to which Breuning could have access only by his or some other friend's protection.

When Wegeler says of Stephan von Breuning (*Notizen*, p. 45), "but he had, with short interruptions, spent his life in closest association with Beethoven from his tenth year to his death," he says too much; and too little when he writes (p. 32) that Beethoven "had once broken for a considerable space with Breuning (and with what friend did he not?)." For besides the quarrel, which Ries describes, there came at last so decided a separation that

Breuning's name disappears from our history for a period of eight to ten years—and that, too, not from *his* fault.

The more thoroughly the character of Breuning is examined, not only in his subsequent relations to Beethoven but also in the light of all that is known of him as a public official, as a husband, father and friend, the higher he stands as a man. Under circumstances, in his office, fitted to try his patience beyond the ordinary limits of endurance, he never failed to bear himself nobly, as a man of high principle, ever ready to sacrifice private and personal considerations to the call of duty. In private life he was invariably just, generous, tenacious of the right. Whatever causes he may have had on divers occasions to complain of Beethoven, we learn nothing of them from his correspondence so far as it has been made public, unless a single passage[22] cited by Wegeler be thought an exception; yet this is but the expression of heartfelt sorrow and compassion—not one word of anger. And we know that Beethoven, when in distress, never turned to him in vain for sympathy nor for such aid as was in his power to give. In the miserable years to come the reader will learn enough of Breuning, though by no means a prominent figure, to feel respect and consideration for his character, and to see for himself how unjust to him were those letters—written by Beethoven under the influence of short-lived choler, which Ries has contributed to the *Notizen*.

Comment should now be made concerning the "dear fascinating girl who loves me and whom I love." This was most probably the Countess Giulietta (or Julia) Guicciardi, for reasons which will appear. She was born on November 23, 1784. Her father was an Austrian Court Councillor who was transferred from Trieste to Vienna in 1800; her mother was born Susanne Brunsvik, an aunt of the two sisters Therese and Josephine Brunsvik, whom Beethoven had met in May, 1799. In the letter to Wegeler of November 16, 1801, he continues "there have been a few blessed moments within the last two years," which, if taken literally, means that his first meeting with Julia took place late in 1799 before the family had moved to Vienna, at which time, the reader will note, Julia had just turned fifteen. At any rate when they did meet it was probably at one of the Brunsvik houses; either at Korompa, Hungary, where Beethoven frequently visited, or at Josephine Deym's home in Vienna. It will be remembered that Josephine was enlarging her circle of friends at this time, and that "the numerous relatives, the sisters of her father and their children, frequently visited their amiable niece."

Judging from the two letters to Wegeler just cited, one sees that after withdrawing from society two years before, because of his oncoming deafness, Beethoven experienced fleeting moments of happiness with this girl and was brought back to the company of men by its effect. After the Guicciardi family had taken up residence in Vienna, the meetings were doubtless much more frequent. Meanwhile with the passing reference to a marriage which

---

[22] See *Notizen*, Nachtrag, p. 10.

gives way to concern over his work, we find an example of the composer's decision to plunge into work when faced with the possibility of a permanent attachment with a woman. Now, let us turn to Thayer's account of this girl who so revived his spirits, and who upon her arrival in Vienna became his pupil.

The Countess Guicciardi is traditionally described as having had a good share of personal attractions, and is known to have been a fine looking woman even in advanced years. She appears to have possessed a mind of fair powers, cultivated and accomplished to the degree then common to persons of her rank; but it is not known that she was in any way eminently distinguished, unless for musical taste and skill as a pianist, which may perhaps be indicated in the dedication to her of a sonata by Kleinheinz as well as by Beethoven. To come to the capital from a small, distant provincial town when hardly of an age to enter society and to find herself so soon distinguished by the particular attentions and evident admiration of a man of Beethoven's social position and fame might well dazzle the imagination of a girl of sixteen. It might dispose her, especially if she possessed more than common musical taste and talents, to return in a certain degree the affection proffered to her by the distinguished author of the Symphony, the Quartet, the Septet, the *Prometheus* music, and so many wonderful sonatas, by the unrivalled pianist, the generous, impulsive, enthusiastic artist, although unprepossessing in person and unable to offer either wealth or a title. There was romance in the affair. Besides these considerations there are traditions and reminiscences of old friends of the composer all tending to confirm the opinion of Schindler that the "fascinating girl" was indeed the young Countess Guicciardi.

That writer, however, knew nothing of the matter until twenty years afterwards; but what he learned came from Beethoven himself. It happened, when the topic came up between them, "that, being in a public place where he did not trust himself to speak," says Schindler, Beethoven also wrote his share in the conversation, so far as it related to this subject; hence his words may still be read in a Conversation Book of February, 1823, preserved in the Berlin Public Library. His statements have certainly gained nothing in clearness from his whim of writing them in part in bad French.

It is proper to state, before introducing the citation from this book, that the young lady married Count Wenzel Robert Gallenberg, a prolific composer of ballet and occasional music, on the 3rd of November, 1803. The young pair soon left Vienna for Italy and were in Naples in the spring of 1806; for Gallenberg was one of the composers of the music for the fêtes, on the occasion of Joseph Bonaparte's assumption of the crown of the two Sicilies. When the Neapolitan Barbaja took charge of the Royal Imperial Opera at Vienna, towards the close of 1821, he made the Count an associate in the administration, and thus it happened that Schindler had occasion to call upon him with a message from Beethoven.

Beethoven asked Schindler if he had seen Gallenberg's wife, and then proceeds:[23]

> j'etois bien aimé d'elle et plus que jamais son epoux.
> il' etoit pourtant
> plutôt son amant que moi, mais elle j'en m'apprit nois de son Misere
> et je trouvais un home de bien, qui me donnoit la some de
> 500 fl pour le soulager.
> il' etoit toujours mon ennemi, et c'etoit justement la raison,
> que je fusse tout le bien
> que possible

Schindler: It was for this reason that he added "He is an intolerable fellow."—
Probably because of pure gratitude. But forgive them, Lord, they know not
what they do!!—
mad: la Comtesse?

etait-elle riche?

elle a une belle figure, jusqu'ici!

Mons. G.

est ce qu'il ya long temps, qu'elle est mariée avec Mons.
de Gallenberg?
Beethoven: elle est née guicciardi
ell' etoit encor l'Epouse de lui à avant [son voyage] de l'Italie,—
[arrivé a Vienne] et elle cherchait moi pleureant, mais
je la meprisois.—

Schindler: Hercules at the crossways!—

Beethoven: And if I had wished to give my vital powers with that life, what
would have remained for the nobler, the better?

Schindler's additions, bracketed above, were made probably well after
Beethoven's death, when he was using the Conversation Books as a source
for the writing of his biography of the composer. In this work, unfortunately,
he made the assumption, now proved erroneous, that it was to Julia that
Beethoven wrote the letters known as the "Immortal Beloved" letters, and
dated them 1801. Can Schindler be any better trusted that it was upon the
return to Vienna that Julia sought him out? Indeed it makes better sense
without Schindler's "arrivé a Vienne." That is, when she was yet engaged
to Gallenberg (before the trip to Italy), she went to Beethoven crying, and
he rejected her. This is the logical time to be called "Hercules at the crossways!" and to consider "if I had wished to give my vital powers with that

---

[23] See Schünemann, II, 363-65. The words
in brackets are additions by Schindler. Schünemann's indications of separate entries are
shown by the small ornament.

life, what would have remained for the nobler, the better?" Beethoven, however, did keep a medallion picture of the Countess, which doubtless she gave him, as it was found among his effects at the time of his death.❦

In November, 1852, Jahn had an interview with the Countess Gallenberg. On so delicate a topic as Beethoven's passion for her fifty years before reticence was natural; but had the affair in truth been of the importance that others have given it, some hint must have confessed it. Yet there is nothing of the kind in his notes of the conversation. Here they are: "Beethoven was her teacher.—He had his music sent to her and was extremely severe until the correct interpretation was reached down to the smallest detail.—He laid stress upon a light manner of playing.—He easily became angry, threw down his music and tore it.—He would accept no pay, though he was very poor, except linen under the pretext that the Countess had sewed it."

❦It is hard to believe that this was Beethoven's ordinary attitude towards remuneration for lessons, since in most cases his reason for submitting to the drudgery of teaching was for the money he earned. Therefore, if the Countess's memory is correct, some consideration of his pupil must have dictated this stand. Perhaps it was her relationship to the Countess Deym, to whom he also gave lessons gratis.❦

"He also taught Princess Odescalchi and Baroness Ertmann; they came to him or he went to them. He did not like to play his own compositions but would only improvise. At the slightest disturbance he would get up and go away.

"Count Brunsvik, who played the violoncello, adored him as did his sisters, Therese and Countess Deym.

"Beethoven had given the Countess [Guicciardi] the Rondo in G [Op. 51, No. 2] but begged its return when he had to dedicate something to the Countess Lichnowsky, and then dedicated the Sonata [Op. 27, No. 2] to her.

"Beethoven was very ugly, but noble, refined in feeling and cultured. As a rule, Beethoven was shabbily dressed."

In this simple record the lady's memory evidently errs by overrating the poverty of Beethoven at the time she was his pupil and in making him so negligent in dress. "In his earlier years Beethoven dressed carefully, even elegantly; only later did he grow negligent, which he carried to the verge of uncleanliness," says Grillparzer; and Czerny: "About the year 1813-14, when Beethoven looked well and strong, he also cared for his outward appearance."

❦An undated letter from Josephine Deym to her sisters gives a picture of musical gatherings at the Guicciardi's and the surprising news that Julia had changed teachers: ". . . Yesterday we had a charming musicale at the Guicciardi's. Julie played Beethoven's clarinet trio very beautifully. Then the septet and a new quintet of his were performed. The whole world asks me why Therese doesn't ever come. I can only answer with a sigh. The most ardent of your admirers is Kleinheinz. He speaks of you with enthusiasm. Now when he hears your name, he is happy. He has visited me sometimes, but on account of his many lessons has not often had time to come. Also Miss Guicciardi has taken him for a teacher."[24]

Kleinheinz (1772–1832) was a student of Albrechtsberger who held a position in the house of Count Brunsvik.[25] Beethoven had recommended him himself and later in this letter Josephine is also advising him as a teacher for her sisters "since he is better than Beethoven." It will be remembered that Beethoven never was fond of teaching and later gave it up almost entirely. Thus the change of teachers appears to have been a natural one and was not the cause of any break in Beethoven's relationship with either family, as is shown in the following summary by Thayer.⟩⊱—

There is but one well-authenticated fact to be added, namely, that Beethoven kept up his intercourse with the family Guicciardi certainly as late as May or June, 1803, that is, to within six months of the young lady's marriage. A careful survey and comparison both of the published data and of the private traditions and hints gleaned during a residence of several years in Vienna, result in the opinion (an opinion, note, not a statement resting on competent evidence) that Beethoven at length decided to offer Countess Julia his hand; that she was not indisposed to accept it; and that one of her parents consented to the match, but the other, probably the father, refused to entrust the happiness of his daughter to a man without rank, fortune or permanent engagement; a man, too, of character and temperament so peculiar, and afflicted with the incipient stages of an infirmity which, if not arrested and cured, must deprive him of all hope of obtaining any high and remunerative official appointment and at length compel him to abandon his career as the great pianoforte virtuoso. As the Guicciardis themselves were not wealthy, prudence forbade such a marriage. Be all this as it may, this much is certain: Beethoven did not marry the Countess Julia Guicciardi; Count Wenzel Robert Gallenberg did.

Once again an affair was ended. The testimony of Wegeler, Breuning, Romberg, Ries, has ben cited to the point that Beethoven "was never without a love, and generally deeply engrossed in it." Wegeler adds (*Notizen*, p. 44) "that, so far as I know, every one of his sweethearts belonged to the higher social stations." So, also, friends of Beethoven with whom Jahn conversed in 1852. Thus according to Carl Czerny, he was supposed to have been in love with the Countess Keglevics, and the Sonata in E-flat, Op. 7 (dedicated to her) was called "Die Verliebte" ("The Maiden, or Woman, in Love"). Dr. Bertolini, friend and physician of Beethoven from 1806 to 1816, said: "Beethoven generally had a flame; the Countess Guicciardi, Mme. von Frank, Bettina Brentano and others." He was not insensible to ladies fair

[24] La Mara, 1920, p. 21.
[25] See Adolf Sandberger, "Franz Xavier Kleinheinz," in *Ausgewählte Aufsätze zur Musikgeschichte* (Munich, 1924), II, 226-48.

and frail. Doležalek adds the particular that "he never showed that he was in love."

In short, Beethoven's experience was precisely that of many an impulsive man of genius, who for one cause or another never married and therefore never knew the calm and quiet, but unchanging affection of happy conjugal life. One all-absorbing but temporary passion, lasting until its object is married to a more favored lover, is forgotten in another destined to end in like manner, until, at length, all faith in the possibility of a permanent, constant attachment to one person is lost. Such men after reaching middle age may marry for a hundred various motives of convenience, but rarely for love.

In his first letter to Wegeler, Beethoven writes: "Concerning Ries, to whom I send hearty greetings, I will write you more in detail about his son . . . in the autumn or winter I shall see what I can do for him. . . ." The young Ries has also already been represented in our narrative, along with Wegeler as the author of the valuable *Biographische Notizen über Ludwig van Beethoven* (Coblenz, 1838). It is time to consider his own biography.

The *Intelligenzblatt* of Bonn, under date of November 30, 1784, announces the baptism, on the preceding day, of Ferdinand, son of Franz Ries. "Like many others who have become eminent musicians, his taste and capabilities manifested themselves very early; as, at five years old, he began his musical education under his father, and afterwards under Bernhard Romberg, the celebrated violoncello player."

The French invasion, the departure of Romberg in consequence (1794) from Bonn, and the pecuniary straits to which Franz Ries was reduced, "prevented much attention being, for some time, paid to the instruction of his son. . . . At last, when he was about thirteen, a friend of his father took him to Arnsberg in Westphalia, for the purpose of learning thoroughbass and composition from an organ-player in that neighborhood. . . . The pupil proved so much the more able to teach of the two, that the organist was obliged to give the matter up at once and proposed to young Ries to teach him the violin instead. As a *pis-aller*, this was accepted; and Ries remained at Arnsberg about nine months, after which he returned home. Here he remained upwards of two years, improving himself in his art with great industry. . . . At length, in the year 1801, he went to Munich with the same friend who had formerly taken him to Arnsberg. Here he was thrown upon his own resources; and throughout the trying and dispiriting circumstances which, with slight exception, attended the next years of his life, he appears to have displayed a firmness, an energy, and an independence of mind, the more honorable, perhaps, from the very early age at which they were called into action. At Munich, Mr. Ries was left by his friend, with little money and but very slender prospects. He tried for some time to procure pupils, but was at last reduced to copy music at three-pence per sheet. With this scanty pittance, he not only continued to keep himself free from embarrassments, but saved a few ducats to take him to Vienna, where he had hopes of patronage and advancement from Beethoven. . . . He set out from Munich with only seven ducats and reached Vienna before they were exhausted!"

The citations are from that noble musical journal, the London *Harmonicon,* and belong to an article on Ries published in March, 1824. They correspond to a sketch of Ries's life in the *Rheinischer Antiquarius,*[26] although there are sufficient differences to show that the materials of the two articles were drawn from independent sources. The *Harmonicon* proceeds: "Ries' hopes from his father's early friend, were not disappointed; Beethoven received him with a cordial kindness, too rare, alas! from men who have risen to eminence and distinction towards those whose claim upon them is founded on the reminiscences of their humble state. He at once took the young man under his immediate care and tuition; advanced him pecuniary loans, which his subsequent conduct converted to gifts; and allowed him to be the first to take the title of pupil and appear in public as such." So also the *Notizen* (pp. 116-17): "In the letter of recommendation from my father there had been opened a small credit account to be used in case of need. I never made use of it but, when a few times Beethoven discovered that I was short of funds, he sent me money without being asked and never wanted to take it back. He was really very fond of me, of which fact he once in his absent-mindedness gave me a very comical proof. Once when I returned from Silesia, where I had spent some time at the country-seat of Prince Lichnowsky as pianist on the recommendation of Beethoven, and entered his room he was about to shave himself and had lathered his face up to his eyes—for so far his fearfully stiff beard reached. He jumped up, embraced me cordially and thereby transferred so much of the lather from his left cheek to my right that he had none left. Did we laugh? Beethoven must also have learned privately how matters had gone with me; for he was acquainted with many of my youthful escapades, with which he only teased me."

"But with all his kindness," continues the *Harmonicon,* "Beethoven would not give Ries instruction in thoroughbass or composition. He said it required a particular gift to explain them with clearness and precision, and, besides that, Albrechtsberger was the acknowledged master of all composers. This latter had almost given up teaching, being very old, and was persuaded to take a new pupil only by the strong recommendation of Beethoven and by the temptation of a ducat a lesson. Poor Ries' ducats ran only to the number of 28; after this he was driven to his books again."

So it appears that he was Beethoven's pupil only upon the pianoforte. The manner in which he was taught is also described in the *Notizen* (p. 94): "When Beethoven gave me a lesson I must say that contrary to his nature he was particularly patient. I was compelled to attribute this and his friendly

[26] Part III, Vol. II, p. 62. (TDR, II, 290, n. 1.)

disposition, which was seldom interrupted, chiefly to his great affection and love for my father. Thus, sometimes, he would permit me to repeat a thing ten times, or even oftener. In the Variations dedicated to the Princess Odescalchi (Op. 34), I was obliged to repeat the last *Adagio* variations almost entirely seventeen times; yet he was still dissatisfied with the expression of the little cadenza, although I thought I played it as well as he. On this day I had a lesson which lasted nearly two hours. If I made a mistake in passages or missed notes and leaps which he frequently wanted emphasized he seldom said anything; but if I was faulty in expression, in *crescendos*, etc., or in the character of the music, he grew angry because, as he said, the former was accidental while the latter disclosed lack of knowledge, feeling, or attentiveness. The former slips very frequently happened to him even when he was playing in public."

"I often played on two fortepianos with Ries," says Czerny, "among other things the Sonata, Op. 47, which had been arranged for two pianofortes. Ries played very fluently, clear but cold."[27]

Here we have a key to the identity of so many of Ries's and Czerny's facts and anecdotes of those years, written out by them independently; the latter, as he assures us, having first become acquainted with the *Notizen* through the quotations of Court Councillor Lenz. The two brilliant boys, thrown so much together, would never weary of talking of their famous master. The stories of his oddities and eccentricities, minute facts relating to his compositions, were, therefore, common property; and it is clear that some which in this manner became known to Ries at last assumed in his memory the aspect of personal experience and, as such, are related in the *Notizen*. The author of this work once introduced an incident into something that he was writing, under the full conviction of having been an actor in it, which he now knows was only related to him by his brother. Yet only some six or seven years had elapsed, whereas Ries wrote of a period which ended thirty-five years before.

—Just when the young man arrived in Vienna is not clear; the evidence shows that at some point Ries's memory was playing him tricks. The editor of the *Harmonicon* (who must have gotten his dates from Ries himself) has him arrive in Munich in 1801[28] and after "some time" travel on to Vienna. In the *Notizen*, however, Ries writes (pp. 75-76):

"I had a letter of introduction. When I presented this to Beethoven upon my arrival in Vienna, 1800, he was very busy with the completion of his oratorio *Christus am Oelberge*, since this was to be given for the first time in a big Akademie (concert) at the Vienna theatre for his benefit. He read the letter through and said: 'I cannot answer your father now, but write to him, I could not have forgotten how my mother died; thus he will be satis-

[27] From O. Jahn's posthumous papers. (TDR, II, 295 n.1.)

[28] The *Antiquarius* dates Ries's arrival in Munich 1800. (TDR, II, 290.)

fied.' Later I learned that my father had supported him in every way during this event since the family was very poor.

"Already during the first days Beethoven found that he could use me, and I was often called as early as five o'clock, which also happened on the day of the oratorio."

The oratorio was performed on April 5, 1803, and was written within a short period, presumably just before it was rehearsed. In a letter to Breitkopf and Härtel in 1804 Beethoven refers to it as the labor of "a few weeks"; in later correspondence as the work of "14 days."[29]

But Ries was in close touch with Beethoven well before this time, for he writes (*Notizen*, p. 117): "On many occasions he showed a truly paternal interest in me. From this originated the order (1802), which was written in an ill humor because of an unpleasant predicament into which Carl van Beethoven had gotten me: 'You do not need to come to Heiligenstadt; I have no time to spare.' At the time Count Browne was indulging himself with pleasures, in which, since he was kindly disposed towards me, I was taking part, and was consequently neglecting my lessons."

There are other references in the *Notizen* to the summer of 1802, when Beethoven was in Heiligenstadt, which suggests that at this time a relationship between master and pupil had already been well established. Thus, Beethoven's promise to Ries's father via Wegeler, that "in the autumn [1801] or winter [1801-1802] I shall see what I can do for him," appears to have been carried out.◈––

Among the compositions completed in 1801 were the Sonatas for Pianoforte and Violin, Op. 23 and 24; the Pianoforte Sonatas in A-flat, Op. 26; E-flat, Op. 27, No. 1; and C-sharp minor, Op. 27, No. 2; and D major, Op. 28; and the Quintet in C major, Op. 29. "The Andante in D minor of the Sonata, Op. 28," says Czerny, "was long his favorite and he played it often for his own pleasure."

The Pianoforte Sonata, Op. 26, had its origin, according to Nottebohm, in the year 1800. Of that sonata, completed this year, Czerny says: "When Cramer was in Vienna and was creating a great sensation not only by his playing but also by the three sonatas which he dedicated to Haydn (of which the first in A-flat, 3/4 time, awakened great amazement), Beethoven, who had been pitted against Cramer, wrote the A-flat Sonata, Op. 26, in which there is purposely a reminder of the Clementi-Cramer passage work in the Finale."

Of the two Pianoforte Sonatas, Op. 27, the first (in E-flat) was dedicated to the Princess Johanna von Liechtenstein, née the Landgravine Fürstenberg, the second (in C-sharp minor), to Countess Giulietta Guicciardi. It is apparent, therefore, that they appeared separately at first. Sketches of the first show that they originated in 1801 (*II Beeth.*, 249). Both are designated

[29] See *A*, 96, 325, and 1260.

"quasi fantasia," which plainly indicates a departure from the customary structure. As Beethoven's relationship to the Countess was exaggerated, so also more significance was attached to this sonata than is justified from a sober point of view. ---•§["Everybody is always talking about the C-sharp minor Sonata! Surely I have written better things. There is the Sonata in F-sharp minor—that is something very different,"[30] he once said to Czerny.]§•-- Its popularity was subsequently heightened by the designations "Arbor Sonata" and "Moonlight Sonata" and its creation into a sort of love-song without words. ---•§[The notes of Jahn's conversations with the Countess in 1852 make it clear that Beethoven did not have her in mind at the time of composition. Later an unsuccessful attempt was made to induce the composer to set the first movement of the sonata to words. Georg Heinrichs[31] has shown that Beethoven's friend, Dr. G. C. Grosheim of Cassel, looked through the music of Haydn, Mozart and Beethoven for a proper musical setting for Seume's poem "Die Beterin." He found it in the Adagio of Op. 27, No. 2, and wrote to Beethoven concerning his wish. It was probably his own respect for Seume's work that prompted Beethoven to answer that he would make the setting—presumably an arrangement for voice and piano. Despite his favorable answer (which Heinrichs estimates was made in late 1816 or early 1817) and further appeals by Grosheim thereafter, Beethoven did nothing about it.]§•--

The autograph of the Sonata in D, Op. 28, bears the inscription "Gran Sonata, Op. 28, 1801, da L. van Beethoven." It appeared in print in 1802, having been advertised in the *Wiener Zeitung* of August 14, from the *Industriekontor*, with the dedication, "À Monsieur Joseph Noble de Sonnenfels, Conseiller aulique et Sécrétaire perpétuel de l'Academie des Beaux Arts." Touching the personality of Joseph Noble de Sonnenfels something may be learned from W. Nagel's book *Beethoven und seine Klaviersonaten* and also from Willibald Müller's biography of him. At the time, Sonnenfels was nearly 70 years old and, so far as is known, was not an intimate friend of Beethoven's; the dedication was probably nothing more than a mark of respect for the man of brains with whose ideas Beethoven was in sympathy. The single clue as to the origin of the work is the date (1801) on the autograph; sketches seem to be lacking. The sunny disposition of the music is the only evidence, and this is internal. The work early acquired the sobriquet "Sonata pastorale" (it was first so printed by A. Cranz), and the designation is not inept.

The twelve Contradances are sketched in part on the first staves of the Kessler sketchbook.[32] If we are justified in assuming that they were composed for the balls of the succeeding winter and were played from manuscript, it

---

[30] From Czerny's memoranda to O. Jahn. See Kerst, I, 48.

[31] See *Beethovens Beziehungen zu Kassel und zu G. Chr. Grosheim in Kassel* (Kassel, 1920). Reviewed by Max Unger in *Neue Musik-Zeitung*, Vol. 44 (1923).

[32] See Nottebohm, *Ein Skizzenbuch von Beethoven*, Leipzig (1865), p. 12.

would follow that they are to be counted among the compositions completed in this year.—⸙ Beethoven also used two of these dances, Nos. 7 and 11, in his ballet *Die Geschöpfe des Prometheus*, which was completed early in 1801,[33] in time for its first performance on March 28th.

In his *Verzeichniss*, Thayer lists as Item 81 the 7 Variations for Pianoforte and Violoncello on the theme "Bei Männern, welche Liebe Fühlen" (from Mozart's *Die Zauberflöte*), and dates it 1801 (?). He notes (p. 42): "The performance of *Die Zauberflöte* in the Court Theatre (beginning of 1801), produced by Schickaneder in the new Theater-an-der-Wien, which was repeated for a few months thereafter (to great effect) made this opera the subject of common gossip and was the apparent cause for the above variations."

The compositions for the year were:

1800-1801. Ballet, *Die Geschöpfe des Prometheus*, Op. 43.
Sonata for Pianoforte and Violin, Op. 23.
Sonata for Pianoforte and Violin, Op. 24.
Sonata for Pianoforte, Op. 26.
Sonata for Pianoforte, Op. 27, No. 1.
Twelve Contradances for Orchestra, WoO 14.

1801. "Lob auf den Dicken" for Three Voices and Chorus, WoO 100.
Quintet for Strings, Op. 29.
Sonata for Pianoforte, Op. 27, No. 2.
Sonata for Pianoforte, Op. 28.
Variations for Pianoforte and Violoncello on "Bei Männern, welche Liebe Fühlen" from Mozart's *Die Zauberflöte*, WoO 46.

The publications for the year were:

By Artaria:

Ballet, *Die Geschöpfe des Prometheus*, arranged for Pianoforte (according to Czerny by the composer), [as Op. 24; later to be renumbered Op. 43], dedicated "À sua Altezza la Signora Principessa Lichnowsky, nata Contessa Thun."

By Hoffmeister and Kühnel (in Lpz. Bureau de Musique):

Concerto No. 2 for Pianoforte and Orchestra in B-flat, Op. 19, dedicated "À Monsieur Charles Nikl, noble de Nikelsberg."
Symphony No. 1 in C major, Op. 21, dedicated "À son Excellence Monsieur le Baron van Swieten."

By Mollo:

Concerto No. 1 for Pianoforte and Orchestra in C major, Op. 15, dedicated "À son Altesse Madame la Princesse Odescalchi, née Keglevics."
Quintet for Pianoforte, Oboe, Clarinet, Horn and Bassoon, Op. 16, dedicated "À son Altesse Monseigneur le Prince Regnant de Schwarzenberg."

[33] For the sketches to Op. 43 see the Landsberg sketchbook published by Karl Lothar Mikulicz, *Ein Notierungsbuch von L. van Beethoven* (Leipzig, 1927).

Six String Quartets, Op. 18, 1st Series (Nos. 1-3), dedicated "À son Altesse Monseigneur le Prince Regnant de Lobkowitz."

Six String Quartets, Op. 18, 2nd Series (Nos. 4-5), dedicated "À son Altesse Monseigneur le Prince Regnant de Lobkowitz."

Sonata for Pianoforte and Horn, Op. 17, dedicated "À Madame la Baronne de Braun."

Two Sonatas for Pianoforte and Violin, Op. 23 and 24,[34] dedicated "À Monsieur le Comte Maurice de Fries."

[34] The two sonatas were first announced under a single opus number, 23. Sketches for these two sonatas in the Landsberg sketchbook are evidence of their simultaneous origin. Nottebohm suggests (*II Beeth.*, p. 236) that the reason for changing to separate opus numbers was "that the enclosed violin parts were printed in different sizes and the publisher wanted to avoid the cost of having one of the parts re-engraved." (Cf. TDR, II, 246.)

CHAPTER XV

THE YEAR 1802

THE HEILIGENSTADT TESTAMENT—BEETHOVEN'S BROTHERS—CORRESPONDENCE WITH PUBLISHERS

THE impatient Beethoven, vexed at the tardy improvement of his health under the treatment of Vering, made that change of physicians contemplated in his letter to Wegeler. This was done some time in the winter of 1801-1802, and is all the foundation there is for Schindler's story of "a serious illness in the first months of this year for which he was treated by the highly esteemed physician Dr. Schmidt."[1] The remarkable list of compositions and publications belonging to this year is proof sufficient that he suffered no physical disability of such a nature as seriously to interrupt his ordinary vocations; as is also the utter silence of Ries, Breuning, Czerny, Doležalek and Beethoven himself.

Concerning the failure of his project to follow the example set in 1800 and give a concert towards the close of the winter in the theatre, we learn all we know from a letter written by his brother Carl to Breitkopf and Härtel dated April 22, 1802. Therein we read: "My brother would have written to you himself, but he is ill-disposed towards everything because the Director of the Theatre, Baron von Braun, who, as is known, is a stupid and rude fellow, refused him the use of the Theatre for his concert and gave it to other really mediocre artists. I believe it must vex him greatly to see himself so shabbily treated, particularly as the Baron has no cause and my brother has dedicated several works to his wife."

–••§[Enclosed in the letter is the following message from Beethoven to the firm: "I reserve the privilege of writing soon to you high-born gentlemen myself—many business matters—and also many vexations—render me utterly useless for some things for a time—meanwhile you may trust my brother *implicitly*, who in fact manages all my affairs."[2]

[1] *Biographie*, I, 85.   [2] See *BJ*, I, 88.

In 1802 Beethoven's old friend, Anton Reicha, arrived in Vienna.}•— They were alike in age—Reicha being but a few months the elder—and alike in tastes and pursuits. Reicha was superior in the culture of schools and in what is called musical learning; Beethoven in genius and originality as a composer and in skill as a pianist. The talents of each commanded the respect of the other. Both were aspiring, ambitious, yet diverged sufficiently in their views of art to prevent all invidious rivalry. Reicha gained a reputation which, in process of time, secured him the high position which he held during the last twenty years of his life—that of Méhul's successor in the Paris Conservatoire.

To Beethoven, who was still digesting plans for musical tours, the experience of his friend must have been of great value; not less to Reicha the experience of Beethoven in Vienna. But he was by no means dependent on Beethoven for an introduction into the highest musical circles of the capital. It has been shown in a previous chapter how freely the salons were opened to every talented young musician, but beyond this he bore a well-known name, and the veteran Haydn kindly remembered him as one of the promising young men who had paid him their respects in Bonn. His opera *Ubaldi* was performed in Prince Lobkowitz's palace, and this probably led to his introduction to the Empress Maria Theresia, who gave him an Italian libretto, *Argene Regina di Granata*, for composition, in which the Empress herself sang a part at the private performance in the palace.

Part of a letter written on July 13 to Breitkopf and Härtel affords another illustration of Beethoven's excellent common sense and discrimination in all that pertained to his art.

. . . Concerning the arrangements of the pieces, I am heartily glad that you rejected them. The *unnatural rage* now prevalent to transplant even *pianoforte pieces* to stringed instruments, instruments so utterly opposite to each other in all respects, ought to come to an end. I insist stoutly that only *Mozart* could arrange his pianoforte pieces for other instruments, and also *Haydn*—and, without wishing to put myself in the class of these great men, I assert the same touching *my pianoforte sonatas also*, since not only would whole passages have to be omitted and changed, but also—things would have to be added, and here lies the obstacle, to *overcome which one must either be the master himself* or at least have the same *skill and inventive power*.— I have transcribed only one of my sonatas for string quartet,[3] yielding to great persuasion, and I certainly know that it would not be an easy matter for another to do as well.

The difficulties here mentioned, it will be noticed, are those of transcribing pianoforte music for other instruments; the contrary operation is so comparatively easy that Beethoven rarely performed it himself, but left it for the

[3] The Sonata in E, Op. 14, No. 1, transposed to F major, was published in 1802. See W. Altmann, "Ein vergessenes Streichquartett Beethovens," *DM*, 1905. (TDR, II, 328, n. 1.)

most part to young musicians, whose work he revised and corrected. Ries writes (*Notizen*, pp. 93-94): "There are a great many pieces by Beethoven published with the designation: 'Arrangé par l'Auteur même,' but only four of these are genuine, namely: from his famous Septet he arranged first a Violin Quintet, and then a Pianoforte Trio; out of his Pianoforte Quintet with four wind-instruments he made a Pianoforte Quartet with three string-instruments; finally, he arranged the Violin Concerto which is dedicated to Stephan von Breuning (Op. 61) as a Pianoforte Concerto. Many other pieces were arranged by me, revised by Beethoven, and then sold as Beethoven's by his brother Caspar."

Ries's statement is neither exhaustive nor altogether exact touching the arrangements of the Septet. If Beethoven ever arranged it as a Quintet, the work remained in manuscript, for the one published was arranged by Hoffmeister. But the Trio was begun, and it was probably finished in 1803. Its history has been told.[4] The appearance in print of both Hoffmeister's arrangement and an arrangement of the First Symphony as a Quintet by Mollo caused Beethoven to publish the following protest in the *Wiener Zeitung* of October 20, 1802:

I believe that I owe it to the public and to myself to announce publicly that the two Quintets in C major and E-flat major, of which the first (taken from a symphony of mine) has been published by Hr. Mollo in Vienna, and the second (taken from my familiar Septet, Op. 20) by Hr. Hoffmeister in Leipzig, are not original quintets but transcriptions prepared by the publishers. The making of transcription at the best is a matter against which (in this prolific day of such things) an author must protest in vain; but it is possible at least to demand of the publishers that they indicate the fact on the title page, so that the honor of the author may not be lessened and the public be not deceived. This much to hinder such things in the future. At the same time I announce that a new Quintet of mine in C major, Op. 29, will shortly be published by Breitkopf and Härtel in Leipzig.

As for Beethoven's own transcription of his works, Ries should have added: the String Quartet in F from the Piano Sonata in E, Op. 14, No. 1 (1802); the Piano Trio from the Second Symphony, Op. 36 (1806); the Funeral March for Orchestra from *Leonore Prohaska* from the third movement of the Piano Sonata Op. 26 (1814); the String Quintet, Op. 104 from the Piano Trio, Op. 1, No. 3 (1817); and the four-hand piano transcription, Op. 134, of the Great Fugue for String Quartet, Op. 133 (1827).[5]

When one looked down from the Kahlenberg towards Vienna in the bright, sweet springtime, the interesting country was almost worthy of Tennyson's description:

---

[4] Trio for Pianoforte, Clarinet or Violin and Violoncello, Op. 38, dedicated to Dr. Johann Adam Schmidt. (TDR, II, 207.)

[5] See Friedrich Munter, "Beethovens Bearbeitungen eigener Werke," *NBJ*, VI (1935), 159ff.

It lies
Deep-meadowed, happy, fair with orchard-lawns
And bowery hollows, crown'd with summer sea.

Conspicuous were the villages, Döbling, hard by the Nussdorf bounds of the city, and Heiligenstadt, divided from Döbling by a ridge of higher land in a deep gorge.

Dr. Schmidt having enjoined Beethoven to spare his hearing as much as possible, he removed for the summer to the place last named. There is much and good reason to believe that his rooms were in a large peasant house still standing, on the elevated plain beyond the village on the road to Nussdorf, then probably quite solitary. In those years, there was from his windows an unbroken view across fields, the Danube and the Marchfeld, to the Carpathian mountains that line the horizon. A few minutes' walk citywards brought him to the baths of Heiligenstadt; or, in the opposite direction, to the secluded valley in which at another period he composed the "Pastoral" Symphony. The vast increase of Vienna and its environs in population has caused corresponding changes, but in 1802, that peasant house seems to have offered him everything he could desire; fresh air, sun, green fields, delightful walks, bathing, easy access to his physician, and yet a degree of solitude which is now not easy to conceive as having been attainable so near the capital.

The seclusion of Heiligenstadt was of itself so seductive to Beethoven that the prudence of Dr. Schmidt in advising him to withdraw so much from society may be doubted; the more, because the benefit to his hearing proved to be small or none. It gave him too many lonely hours in which to brood over his calamity; it enabled him still to flatter himself that his secret was yet safe; it led him to defer, too long for his peace of mind, the bitter moment of his confession; and consequently to deprive himself needlessly of the tender compassion and ready sympathy of friends, whose lips were sealed so long as he withheld his confidence. But, in truth, the secret so jealously guarded was already known, but who could inform him of it?

It was well for Beethoven, when the time came for him to return to the city, and to resume the duties and obligations of his profession. To what depths of despondency he sometimes sank in those solitary hours at Heiligenstadt is shown by a remarkable and most touching paper, written there just before his return to town, but never seen by other eyes until after his death. Although addressed to and intended for both his brothers, it is, as Schindler has remarked, "surprising and singular," that the name "Johann" is left utterly blank throughout—not even being indicated by the usual. . . . It is couched in terms of energetic expression, rising occasionally to eloquence—somewhat rude and unpolished indeed, but, perhaps, for that reason the more striking. The manuscript is so carefully written, and disfigured by so few erasures and corrections, as to prove the great pains taken with it before the copy was made.

Ries's paragraph upon Beethoven's deafness, in which he relates a circumstance alluded to in the document, is its most fitting introduction (*Notizen*, pp. 78-79): "The beginning of his hard hearing was a matter upon which he was so sensitive that one had to be careful not to make him feel his deficiency by loud speech. When he failed to understand a thing he generally attributed it to his absent-mindedness, to which, indeed, he was subject in a great degree. He lived much in the country, whither I went often to take a lesson from him. At times, at 8 o'clock in the morning after breakfast he would say: 'Let us first take a short walk.' We went, and frequently did not return till 3 or 4 o'clock, after having made a meal in some village. On one of these wanderings Beethoven gave me the first striking proof of his loss of hearing, concerning which Stephan von Breuning had already spoken to me. I called his attention to a shepherd who was piping very agreeably in the woods on a flute made of a twig of elder. For half an hour Beethoven could hear nothing, and though I assured him that it was the same with me (which was not the case), he became extremely quiet and morose. When occasionally he seemed to be merry, it was generally to the extreme of boisterousness; but this happened seldom."

Following is the text of the document:

For my brothers Carl and   Beethoven

Oh you men who think or say that I am malevolent, stubborn or misanthropic, how greatly do you wrong me. You do not know the secret cause which makes me seem that way to you. From childhood on my heart and soul have been full of the tender feeling of goodwill, and I was ever inclined to accomplish great things. But, think that for 6 years now I have been hopelessly afflicted, made worse by senseless physicians, from year to year deceived with hopes of improvement, finally compelled to face the prospect of *a lasting malady* (whose cure will take years or, perhaps be impossible). Though born with a fiery, active temperament, even susceptible to the diversions of society, I was soon compelled to withdraw myself, to live life alone. If at times I tried to forget all this, oh how harshly was I flung back by the doubly sad experience of my bad hearing. Yet it was impossible for me to say to people, "Speak louder, shout, for I am deaf." Ah, how could I possibly admit an infirmity in the *one sense* which ought to be more perfect in me than in others, a sense which I once possessed in the highest perfection, a perfection such as few in my profession enjoy or ever have enjoyed.— Oh I cannot do it, therefore forgive me when you see me draw back when I would have gladly mingled with you. My misfortune is doubly painful to me because I am bound to be misunderstood; for me there can be no relaxation with my fellow-men, no refined conversations, no mutual exchange of ideas. I must live almost alone like one who has been banished, I can mix with society only as much as true necessity demands. If I approach near to people a hot terror seizes upon me and I fear being exposed to the danger that my condition might be noticed. Thus it has been during the last six months which I have spent in the country. By ordering me to spare my hearing as much as possible, my intelligent doctor almost fell in with my own present frame of mind, though sometimes I ran counter to it by yielding to my desire for companionship. But what a humiliation for me when someone standing next to me heard a flute in the distance and *I heard nothing*, or someone heard a *shepherd singing* and again I heard nothing. Such incidents drove me almost to despair, a little more of that and I would have ended my life—it was only *my art* that held me back. Ah, it seemed to me impossible to leave the world until I had brought forth all that I felt was within me. So I endured this wretched existence— truly wretched for so susceptible a body which can be thrown by a sudden change from the best condition to the very worst.— *Patience*, they say, is what I must now choose for my guide, and I have done so— I hope my determination will remain firm to endure until it pleases the inexorable Parcae to break the thread. Perhaps I shall get better, perhaps not, I am ready.— Forced to become a philosopher already in my 28th year, oh it is not easy, and for the artist much more difficult than for anyone else.— Divine One, thou seest my inmost soul, thou knowest that therein dwells the love of mankind and the desire to do good.— Oh fellow men, when at some point you read this, consider then that you have done me an injustice; someone who has had misfortune may console himself to find a similar case to his, who despite all the limitations of Nature nevertheless did everything within his powers to become accepted among worthy artists and men.— You my brothers Carl and   as soon as I am dead if Dr. Schmid is still alive ask him in my name to describe my malady, and attach this written document to his account of my illness so that so far as is possible at least the world may become reconciled to me after my death.— At the same time I declare you two to be the heirs to my small fortune (if so it can be called); divide it fairly; bear with and help each other. What injury you have done me you know was long ago forgiven. To you, brother Carl I give special thanks for the attachment you have shown me of late. It is my wish that you may have a better and freer life than I have had. Recommend *virtue* to your children; it alone, not money, can make them happy. I speak from experience; this was what upheld me in time of misery. Thanks to it and to my art I did not end my life by suicide—Farewell and love each other— I thank all my friends, particularly *Prince Lichnowsky* and *Professor Schmidt*— I would like the instruments from Prince L to be preserved by one of you, but not to be the cause of strife between you, and as soon as they can serve you a better purpose, then sell them. How happy I shall be if I can still be helpful to you in my grave—so be it— With joy I hasten to meet death— If it comes before I have had the chance to develop all my artistic capacities, it will still be coming too soon despite my harsh fate and I should probably wish it later— yet even so I should be happy, for would it not free me from a state of endless suffering?— Come *when* thou wilt, I shall meet thee bravely— Farewell and do not wholly forget me when I am dead, I deserve this from you, for during my lifetime I was thinking of you often and of ways to make you happy—please be so—

Ludwig van Beethoven
(seal)

Heiglnstadt,
October 6th.
1802

For my brothers Carl and
to be read and executed after my death.

Heiglnstadt, October 10th, 1802, thus I bid you farewell—and indeed sadly—yes, that fond hope—which I brought here with me, to be cured to a degree at least—this I must now wholly abandon. As the leaves of autumn fall and are withered—so likewise has my hope been blighted—I leave here—almost as I came—even the high courage—which often inspired me in the beautiful days of summer—has disappeared—Oh Providence—grant me at last but one day *of pure joy*—it is so long since real joy echoed in my heart— Oh when—Oh when, Oh Divine One—shall I feel it again in the temple of nature and of mankind—Never?—No—Oh that would be too hard.

De profundis clamavit! And yet in that retirement whence came a paper of such profound sadness was wrought out the Symphony in D; a work whose grand and imposing introduction—brilliant Allegro, a Larghetto "so lovely, so pure and amiably conceived," written in the scenes which gave inspiration to the divine "Pastorale" of which its serene tranquility seems the precursor; a Scherzo "as merry, wayward, skipping and charming as anything possible," as even Oulibichef[6] admits; and a Finale, the very intoxication of a spirit "intoxicated with fire"—made it, like the Quartets, an era both in the life of its author and in the history of instrumental music. In life, as in music, the more profoundly the depths of feeling are sounded in the Adagio, the more "merry to the verge of boisterousness" the Scherzo which follows. But who, reading that in October hope had been abandoned and the high courage which had often inspired him in the beautiful days of summer had disappeared, could anticipate that in November, through the wonderful elasticity of his nature, his mind would have so recovered its tone as to leave no trace visible of the so recent depression and gloom? Perhaps the mere act of giving his feelings vent in that extraordinary *promemoria* may have brought on the crisis, and from that moment the reaction may have begun.

After Stephan von Breuning's death on June 4, 1827, his widow turned over to Schindler all of Beethoven's personal papers and documents which had been left in the hands of her husband. The testament was discovered by Schindler probably in later summer since Rochlitz, in a letter to Schindler on October 3, 1827, thanked him for sending a copy of the manuscript. Rochlitz, who had been chosen by the composer to write his biography, was much moved by the document and had it published in the Leipzig

---

[6] Alexander Dimitrievitch Oulibishev (1794-1858), Russian music-lover and admirer of Mozart, author of *Nouvelle Biographie de Mozart* (1843) and *Beethoven, ses critiques et ses glossateurs* (1857).

Allegemeine Musikalische Zeitung.[7] The autograph passed through many hands including those of Franz Liszt and Jenny Lind before it was offered by the latter's husband, Otto Goldschmidt, to the Hamburg *Staats-und Universistätsbibliothek* in 1890.[8]

An engagement which Beethoven had obtained from Count Browne for Ries was one that gave the student leisure to pursue his studies, and he often came to Vienna and Heiligenstadt for that purpose. Two interesting anecdotes from Ries's *Notizen* (pp. 90-92) may be introduced here:

"Count Browne made a rather long sojourn about this time in Baden near Vienna, where I was called upon frequently to play Beethoven's music in the evening in the presence of enthusiastic Beethovenians, sometimes from notes, sometimes by heart. Here I had an opportunity to learn how in the majority of cases a *name* alone is sufficient to characterize everything in a composition as beautiful and excellent, or mediocre and bad. One day, weary of playing without notes, I improvised a march without a thought as to its merit or any ulterior purpose. An old countess who actually tormented Beethoven with her devotion, went into ecstasies over it, thinking it was a new composition of his, which I, in order to make sport of her and the other enthusiasts, affirmed only too quickly. Unhappily Beethoven came to Baden the next day. He had scarcely entered Count Browne's room in the evening when the old countess began to speak of his most admirable and glorious march. Imagine my embarrassment! Knowing well that Beethoven could not tolerate the old countess, I hurriedly drew him aside and whispered to him that I had merely meant to make sport of her foolishness. To my good fortune he accepted the explanation in good part, but my embarrassment grew when I was called upon to repeat the march, which turned out worse since Beethoven stood at my side. He was overwhelmed with praise on all sides and his genius lauded, he listening in a perturbed manner and with growing rage until he found relief in a roar of laughter. Later he remarked to me: 'You see, my dear Ries, those are the great cognoscenti, who wish to judge every composition so correctly and severely. Only give them the name of their favorite; they will need nothing more.'

"This march, however, led to one good result: Count Browne immediately commissioned Beethoven to compose three Marches for Pianoforte, four hands, which were dedicated to Princess Esterhazy (Op. 45).

"Beethoven composed part of the second march while giving me a lesson on a sonata—a thing which still seems incomprehensible to me—which I had to play that evening in a little concert at the house of the count mentioned above. I was also to play the marches with him on the same occasion.

"While the latter was taking place, young Count P. . . . , sitting in the doorway leading to the next room, spoke so loud and so continuously to a

---

[7] Vol. 29, 1827, pp. 705ff.

[8] See Georg Kinsky, "Zu Beethovens Heiligenstädter Testament," *Schweizerische Musikzeitung und Sängerblatt*, Vols. 14/15 (1934), 520. (Cf. TDR, II, 332, n. 1.)

pretty woman, that Beethoven, after several efforts had been made to secure quiet, suddenly took my hands from the keys in the middle of the music, jumped up and said very loudly, 'I will not play for such swine!'

"All efforts to get him to return to the pianoforte were in vain; he would not even allow me to play the sonata. So the music came to an end in the midst of a general ill humor."

According to Jahn's papers the following came from Czerny: "In composing, Beethoven tested his pieces at the pianoforte until he found them to his liking, and sang the while. His voice in singing was hideous. It was thus that Czerny heard him at work on one of the four-hand marches while waiting in a side-room."

---◦◦{In an unaddressed letter, presumably to Ries,[9] Beethoven asked if "Count Browne has already given the two marches to be engraved." The first two were written together at this time, and Kinsky-Halm dates the third as completed in 1803. They were published all together as Op. 45 in 1804.}◦◦---

The following letter to Zmeskall (to which the recipient appended the date, November, 1802) is whimsically written on both sides of a strip of very ordinary coarse writing paper fourteen and a half inches long by four and three-quarters wide:

You may, my dear Z., talk bluntly to Walter about my affair, first because he deserves it and then because since the belief has gone forth that I am no longer on good terms with Walter I am pestered by the whole swarm of pianoforte makers wishing to serve me—and gratis. Each one wants to build a pianoforte for me just to my liking. Thus Reicha was urgently begged by the man who made a pianoforte for him to persuade me to let him make me one, and he is one of the better people at whose place I have seen good instruments— Give him to understand therefore that I will pay him 30 florins, whereas I might have had one from all the others for nothing. But I will pay 30 florins only on condition that it be of mahogany and I also want the one string [*una corde*] pedal. If he does not agree to this, make it plain to him that I shall choose one of the others from whom I shall order, and I shall also introduce him to *Haydn* so that he may see his instrument. A Frenchman, who is a stranger, is coming to me at about 12 o'clock today. Herr R[eicha] and I will have the pleasure of having to *display my art on a piano by Jakesch*—Ad notam—if you would like also to come we should have a good time, for afterwards we, Reicha, our miserable Imperial Baron and the Frenchman, will dine together— You do not need to don a *black coat* as we shall be *a party of men only.*

Another letter to Zmeskall (who noted on it the date November 13, 1802) runs as follows:[10]

Dear Z.— Cancel definitely your *music-making* at Förster's, *nothing else can be done*—

---

[9] See *A*, 61.

[10] The editor is indebted to Miss Emily Anderson (*Notes*, September, 1952) for the corrected reading and translations of the first sentence.

We shall rehearse at *your house tomorrow morning* at half past 8 and the production will be at my house at eleven—

Addio excellent plenipotentiarius regni Beethovenensis.

The rascals have been jailed as they deserved *in their own handwriting.*

This second letter makes reference to two separate matters that deserve attention. "At my house" was no longer in the Hamberger House on the Bastion, but in the one pointed out by Czerny: "Beethoven lived a little later (about 1802) on the Petersplatz, the corner house beside the Guard-house, *vis à vis* of my present lodgings, in the fourth [?] story, where I visited him as often as I did [in the Tiefer Graben]. If you will give me the pleasure of a visit (No. 576 beside Daum, second story) I will show you the windows. There I visited several times every week."[11]

What whim could have induced Beethoven to remove to this house with the bells of St. Peter's on one side and those of St. Stephen's sounding down upon him on the other, and he so suffering with his ears? Perhaps because friends were in the house. Young Förster's[12] earliest recollections of Beethoven date from this winter and this house; for his father's dwelling was in the third story above him. He remembers that Beethoven volunteered to instruct him in pianoforte playing, and that he was forced to rise at six in the morning and descend the cold stairs, child as he was, hardly six years of age, to take his lessons; and on one occasion going up again crying because his master had whipped his little fingers with one of the iron or steel needles used in knitting the coarse yarn jackets worn by women in service.

In his note to Zmeskall, Beethoven referred to "the production." Production of what? The new String Quintet, Op. 29, no doubt. ⸻The letter ends: "The rascals have been jailed as they deserved *in their own handwriting.*" The "rascals" were Artaria and Co., who had unexpectedly made a printing of the Quintet and who were forced to nullify, temporarily, this edition by affixing their signature to a declaration, dated November 12, 1802. The Quintet was dedicated to Count Moritz von Fries who, it will be seen, was implicated along with the publishers in the unpleasantness that developed.⸻

According to Ries (*Notizen*, p. 120): "Beethoven's Violin Quintet (Opus 29) in C major had been sold to a publisher in Leipzig, but was stolen in Vienna and published suddenly by A.[Artaria] and Co. Having been copied in a single night, it was full of errors; whole measures even were missing. Beethoven's conduct in the matter is without parallel. He asked A. to send the fifty copies which had been printed to me for correction, but at the same time instructed me to use ink on the wretched paper and as coarsely as possible; also to cross out several lines so that it would be impossible to make use of a single copy or sell it. The scratching out was particularly in the

[11] Letter to Ferdinand Luib, May 28, 1852.   [12] Son of the composer.
(TDR, II, 338.)

Scherzo. I obeyed his instructions implicitly, and A. was compelled to melt the plates in order to avoid a lawsuit."

A long letter to Breitkopf and Härtel, dated November 13, 1802, gives a lively picture of the excitement which the incident aroused in Beethoven:

I write hurriedly to inform you of only the most important things—know then, that while I was in the country for my health, the *archscoundrel Artaria* borrowed the *Quintet* from *Count Fries on the pretence that it was already published and in existence here* and that they wanted it for the purpose of *reëngraving because their copy was faulty*—as a matter of fact they intended to rejoice *the public* with it a few days ago— Good Count Fr., deceived and not reflecting that a piece of rascality might be in it, gave it to them. He could not ask me, I was not here—but fortunately I learned of the matter in time; it was on *Tuesday of this week*. In my zeal to save my honor and to *prevent* as quickly as possible *your suffering any loss*, I offered two new works to these contemptible persons if they would suppress the entire edition, but a cooler-headed friend who was with me asked, *Do you want to reward these rascals?* The case was finally closed under certain conditions; they assuring me that *whatever you print they would reprint*. These *generous scoundrels* decided therefore to wait three weeks, during which time your copies would have appeared here, before issuing their own (insisting that Count F. had made them a present of the copy). *At the end of this period the contract was to have ended*, and *in return I was to give them a work* which I value at 40 ducats at least. Before this contract was closed, there comes my good brother as if sent by heaven, he hurries *to C*[ount] *F*.; the whole thing is the *biggest swindle* in the world, the *details*, how neatly they kept me out of C[ount] F's way and all the rest in the next letter.—Now I am going to F. too, and the *enclosed Revers* may prove to you that I did all in my power to protect you from injury—and my statement of the case may serve to show you that *no sacrifice was too great* for me to save my honor and *to save you from loss*.

From the Revers you will see what measures must be adopted, and I think you should make all possible haste to send copies here and if possible at the same price *as that of the rascals*.— Sonnleithner and I will take all further measures which *seem to us good, so that their entire edition may be destroyed*.— Please take good notice that *Mollo and Artaria* are really combined in *one firm*, that is, a whole *family of scoundrels*.— The dedication *to Fries* I hope was not forgotten inasmuch as my brother wrote it on the first sheet.— *I have written the Revers for you myself* since my *poor brother* is so very busy, and yet he *did all he could* to save you and me. In the confusion he lost a faithful dog, which he called his favorite; he deserves to be thanked by you personally as I have done on my own account.— Just remember that from Tuesday to *late last night* I devoted myself almost wholly to this matter; and the mere thought of this rascally stroke may serve to make you realize how unpleasant it is for me to have anything to do with such wretched people—

L.v.Beethoven

Revers

The undersigned pledges himself under no circumstances to send out or to sell here or elsewhere the Quintet received from *Herr Graf Fries* composed by Lud.

v. Beethoven until the original edition shall have been in circulation *in Vienna* fourteen days.

Vienna, 12 November, 1802   Artaria Comp.

This Revers is signed by the Comp. in its own hand.

Use the following: to be had à Vienne chez Artaria Comp., à Münich chez Firma Halm, à Frankfort chez Gayl et Hädler, perhaps also in Leipzig chez Meysel—the price is 2 florins, *two gulden Vienna standard.*—

I got ahold of twelve copies, the only ones which they promised me from the beginning, and made corrections from them—*the engraving is abominable.* Make use of all this, you see that on every side we have them in our hands and can proceed against them in the courts—

N.B. Any measures, even personal, taken against A. will have my approval—

Under date of December 5, 1802, Beethoven's brother Carl wrote to Breitkopf and Härtel on the same subject:

Finally I shall inform you touching the manner in which my brother sells his works. We already have in print 34 works and about 18 numbers. These pieces were mostly commissioned by amateurs under the following agreement: he who wants a piece pays a fixed sum for its exclusive possession for a half or a whole year, or longer, and binds himself not to give the manuscript to *anybody*; at the conclusion of the period it is the privilege of the composer to do what he pleases with the work. This was the understanding with Count Fries. Now, the Count has a certain Conti as violin teacher, and to him Artaria turned, and probably for a consideration of 8 or 10 florins he said that the quartet [*sic*] had already been printed and was to be had everywhere. This made Count Fries think that there was nothing more to be lost in the matter and he gave it up without a word to us about it. . . .

The composer sought to strengthen his position by the following in the *Wiener Zeitung*, January 22, 1803:

TO THE LOVERS OF MUSIC

In informing the public that the original Quintet in C long ago advertised by me has been published by Breitkopf and Härtel in Leipzig, I declare at the same time that I have no interest in the edition published simultaneously by Herrn. Artaria and Mollo in Vienna. I am the more compelled to make this declaration since this edition is very faulty, incorrect, and utterly useless to players, whereas Herren Breitkopf and Härtel, the legal owners of the Quintet, have done all in their power to produce the work as handsomely as possible.

As MacArdle points out,[13] Ries's story has little basis. Rather, Artaria felt compelled to defend the integrity of his house by filing a petition in the High Police Court on February 14, 1803, demanding a retraction by Beethoven of his false charges.[14] He made his position clearer in a statement to the court

---

[13] Donald W. MacArdle, "Beethoven, Artaria and the C major Quintet," *MQ*, Vol. 34 (October, 1948), pp. 567ff.

[14] All the documents referred to in this matter may be found in TDR, II, 589ff.

dated February 28, 1803 when he established the following points: after Count Fries had bought the Quintet, he agreed to hand over a copy to Artaria for publication; soon thereafter the Count asked that the issue be delayed "until the edition by Breitkopf and Härtel should have been on sale here in Vienna for fourteen days"; an accompanying declaration by Count Fries[15] states that the firm carried out their promise to the full; Beethoven himself corrected two copies of the edition and was consequently responsible for any mistakes therein; Mollo had nothing to do with the edition.

Two excerpts from Beethoven's reply to Artaria of September 1, 1803, make Count Fries's role in this matter appear very inconsistent. After reviewing his agreement with the Count of half a year's possession of the music, followed by its purchase for publication by Breitkopf and Härtel, the composer continues, "Since Herr Graf v. Friess was not authorized according to our verbal agreement to bring out an edition of this Quintet, I inquired of him concerning Artaria and Mollo, and he indicated to me that they reminded him that an edition of this Quintet had already appeared in Leipzig and that they only wished to publish it as a reprint, and in view of this Hr. Gf. von Fries did not hesitate to give this Quintet to Artaria and Mollo." Further on he states: "As regards Artaria's assertion that he obtained the Quintet for publication from Herr Graf v. Friess by just means, I must reply that when I complained to him concerning the edition prepared by Artaria, Hr. Graf told me in person that Artaria had obtained the Quintet from him by trickery, using the plea mentioned above, therefore I cannot understand at all how the Hr. Graf v. Friess can say in the certificate shown to me that Artaria and Company asked him for permission to publish the Quintet that was bought from me, which request he granted willingly; as I see it, from the showing of this evidence Graf von Fries cannot have remembered any longer what he had said to me." Etc.

Count Fries was conveniently traveling at the time and therefore unavailable for questioning at the hearings.

At the same time, Beethoven admits that he did correct the two copies for Artaria but out of anger did not do a thorough job; he concludes: "However I have not done wrongly by Artaria in reporting in the declaration that his edition is full of mistakes, incorrect, and of no use at all for the performer."

Artaria's reply on September 5th points out that his request for the Quintet from Count Fries could not have involved trickery since he did not know of the Leipzig edition at the time, that the mistakes in his edition are the fault of Beethoven, who should have told him that the copy was unusable.

An impartial musician, appointed by the court to study the edition, found that all of Beethoven's corrections had been observed by the publishers. At

---

[15] "Herren Artaria and Co. requested of me that I allow them to publish the Quintet bought by me from Herr van Beethoven, which request I granted willingly, but I made the condition, however, that they hold back with the sale until the Leipzig edition had appeared locally. That they fulfilled this faithfully is shown by my own signature."

the same time Mollo made it clear that he had nothing to do with any of the negotiations.

It is not surprising to find that the court ruled on September 26 against Beethoven and in favor of the publishers. They ordered the composer to retract his announcement of January 22 in a written statement to be submitted to the court prior to its publication. The court added in a statement on October 12th that should Beethoven fail to comply with this decision, he must realize that it would give full assistance to the plaintiffs to secure their rights through process of law. A report dated December 4, 1803, shows that Beethoven was summoned to court, was told in the clearest way possible to proceed with the disavowal of the announcement so injurious to Artaria and Mollo, yet he remained unwilling to write out the retraction.

On March 31, 1804, however, the following appeared in the *Wiener Zeitung*:

ANNOUNCEMENT TO THE PUBLIC

After having inserted a statement in the *Wiener Zeitung* of January 22, 1803, in which I publicly declared that the edition of my Quintet published by Mollo did not appear under my supervision, was faulty in the extreme and useless to players, the undersigned hereby revokes the statement to the extent of saying that Herren Mollo and Co. have no interest in this edition, feeling that I owe such a declaration to do justice to Herren Mollo and Co. before a public entitled to respect.

Ludwig van Beethoven

Beethoven never did write the retraction of his charges against Artaria despite a further judgment by the Magistrate of Vienna of March 8, 1805, which reiterated the composer's obligation and established the right of the plaintiff to publish himself such a retraction at the expense of the defendant, a right which Artaria never used. Instead, an agreement was signed by the lawyers of the two parties on September 9, 1805 concerning future editions of the work.

Nottebohm (*Beeth.* pp. 3-5) has shown that Ries was further mistaken about the melting of the plates. They were used for four different editions. The first edition was bad and "of no use at all for the performer" because no consideration was made for the turning of pages. This was improved in the second edition in certain places for all parts with the revealing words under the composer's name, "Revû et corigé par lui même." The fourth edition differed from the third only by the fact that the plates were now being used by the firm, T. Mollo.

It is necessary to turn to the annoying and thankless task of examining a broad tissue of mingled fact and misrepresentation and severing the truth from the error; this time the subject is the relations which existed between Beethoven and his brothers in these years. A letter written by Caspar is the occasion of taking it up here. Johann André, a music publisher at Offenbach-am-Main, following the example of Hoffmeister, Nägeli, Breitkopf and Härtel and others, now applied to Beethoven for manuscripts. Caspar wrote the reply:

Vienna, November 23, 1802

High and Wellborn:

You have recently honored us with a letter and expressed the wish to have some of my brother's compositions, for which we thank you very much. At present we have nothing but a Symphony and a grand Concerto for Pianoforte, the first at 300 florins and the second at the same price. If you should want three pianoforte sonatas,[16] I could furnish them for no less than 900 florins, all according to Vienna standard, and these you could not have all at once, but one every five or six weeks, because my brother does not trouble himself with such trifles any longer and composes only oratorios, operas, etc.

Also you are to send us eight copies of *every* piece which you may possibly engrave. I beg of you to let us know whether or not the pieces please you, otherwise I might be prevented from selling them to someone else.

We have also two Adagios for the Violin with complete instrumental accompaniment,[17] which will cost 135 florins, and two little easy Sonatas, each with two movements, which are at your service for 280 florins.[18] In addition I beg you to present our compliments to our friend Koch.

Your obedient
C.v.Beethoven
R. I. Treasury official

This ludicrous display of the young man's self-importance as "Royal Imperial Treasury Official" and Ludwig van Beethoven's factotum is certainly very absurd; but hardly affords adequate grounds for the exceeding scorn of Schindler's remarks upon it. It is in itself sufficiently provocative of prejudice against the writer. But a display of vanity and self-esteem is ridiculous, not criminal.

The general charge brought by Ries against Caspar and Johann van Beethoven is this (*Notizen*, p. 97): "His brothers sought in particular to keep all his intimate friends away from him, and no matter what wrongs they did him, of which he was convinced, they cost him only a few tears and all was immediately forgotten. On such occasions he was in the habit of saying: 'But they are my brothers nevertheless,' and the friend received a rebuke for his good-nature and frankness. The brothers attained their purpose in causing the withdrawal from him of many friends, especially when, because of his hard hearing, it became difficult to converse with him."

Two years after the *Notizen* left the press Schindler published his *Biographie*. In it, although he first knew Beethoven in 1814, Johann some years later and Caspar probably never, and therefore personally could know nothing of the facts of this period, yet he made the picture still darker. The special charge against Caspar is that "about this time [in 1800] he began

[16] Kinsky-Halm (KHV, p. 81) believes this refers to new projected sonatas and not to the three sonatas, Op. 31, the last of which was completed in the spring of 1802.
[17] Op. 40 and 50.
[18] Op. 49.

to rule Beethoven and made him suspicious of his most sincere friends and devotees by means of false representations and even jealousy."[19]

Now, what is really known of Carl Caspar and Johann, though it sufficiently confutes much of the calumnious nonsense which has been printed about them, is not fitted to convey any very exalted idea of their characters. The same Frau Karth, who remembered Ludwig in his youth as always "gentle and lovable," related that Caspar was less kindly in his disposition, "proud and presumptuous," and that Johann "was a bit stupid, yet very good natured."[20] Caspar, like Ludwig, was very passionate, but more violent in his sudden wrath; Johann, slow to wrath and placable. Notwithstanding the poverty of his youth and early manhood, it is not known that Caspar was avaricious; but Johann had felt too bitterly the misery of want and dependence, and became penurious. After he had accumulated a moderate fortune, the contests between his avarice and the desire to display his wealth led to very ludicrous exhibitions. In a word, Beethoven was not a phenomenon of goodness, nor were his brothers monsters of iniquity. That both Ries and Schindler wrote honestly has not been doubted; but common justice demands the reminder that they wrote under the bias of strong personal dislike to one or both brothers. Ries wrote impressions received at a very early time of life, and records opinions formed upon incomplete data. Schindler wrote entirely upon hearsay. Ries had not completed his twenty-first year when he departed from Vienna (1805). Howsoever strong were Beethoven's gratitude to Franz Ries and affection for Ferdinand, fourteen years was too great a disparity in age to allow that trustful and familiar intercourse between master and pupil which could enable the latter to speak with full knowledge; nor does a man of Beethoven's age and position turn from old and valued friends, like the Lichnowskys, Breuning, Zmeskall and others of whatever names, to make a youth of from 18 to 20 years, a new-comer and previously a stranger, even though a favorite pupil, his confidential adviser. Schindler may be passed by as but repeating the *Notizen*. Now, the onus of Ries's charges is this:

First: that Caspar thrust himself impertinently into his brother's business; second: that both brothers intrigued to isolate Beethoven from his intimate friends and that their machinations were in many cases successful.

To the first point it is to be remarked: Besides Beethoven's often expressed disinclination to engage personally in negotiations for the sale of his works—although when he did he showed no lack of a keen eye to profits—his physical and mental condition at this period of his life often rendered the assistance of an agent indispensable. Accounts were to be kept with half a dozen publishers; letters received upon business were numerous and often demanded

[19] *Biographie* (1st ed., 1840), pp. 48-49.

[20] Various letters written by Johann at a later time (1825-39) have been studied by Heinnek Rietsch ("Aus Briefen Johanns van Beethoven," *NBJ*, 1 [1924], 115ff), who points out that, in contrast to Frau Karth's verdict, he appears to have been a precise man of business, who through his own industry achieved a position of wealth.

prompt replies; proof-sheets were constantly arriving for revision and correction; copyists required supervision; an abundance of minor matters continually coming up and needing attention when Beethoven might be on his long rambles over hill and dale, the last man to be found in an emergency. One asks with astonishment, how could so obvious a necessity for a confidential agent have escaped notice? Who should or could this agent be but his brother Caspar? He held an honorable place in a public office, the duties of which necessarily implied the possession of those talents for, and habits of, prompt and skillful performance of business which his early receipt of salary and his regular advancement in position show that he really did possess; his duties detained him in the city at all times, occasional short vacations excepted, and yet left him ample leisure to attend to his brother's affairs; he was a musician by education and fully competent to render valuable service in that "fearful period of arrangements"—as it is well known he did. What would have justly been said of Beethoven if he had passed by one so eminently qualified for the task—one on whom the paternal relation and his own long continued care and protection had given him so many claims—and had transferred the burden from his own shoulders to those of other friends? But if, after adequate trial, the agent proved unsatisfactory, the case would be changed and the principal might with propriety seek needed assistance in other quarters. And precisely this appears to have occurred; for after a few years Caspar disappears almost entirely from our history in connection with his brother's pecuniary affairs. This fact is stronger evidence than anything in Ries's statements, that Beethoven became dissatisfied with his brother's management, and would have still more weight had he been less fickle, inconstant and undecided in matters of business.

In the paragraph upon the efforts of Beethoven's brothers to keep all the composer's friends away from him it is easy to read between the lines that it was Ries himself who oft was "rebuked for his good-nature and frankness," which of itself to some extent lessens the force of the charge. But it is best met by the first half of the Heiligenstadt Will, or Testament, which, along with the confessions to Wegeler and Amenda, open to our knowledge an inner life of the writer studiously concealed from his protégé. In this solemn document, written as he supposed upon the brink of the grave, Beethoven touches upon this very question. We learn from his own affecting words, that the cause of his separation from friends lay, *not* in the machinations of his brothers, but from his own sensitiveness. He records for future use, what he cannot now explain without disclosing his jealously guarded secret. That record now serves a double purpose; it relieves Caspar and Johann from a portion of the odium so long cast upon their memories, and proves Ries to be, in part at least, in error, without impugning his veracity. It is very probable Ries never saw the Will. Had he known and carefully read it, the prejudices of his youth must have been weakened, the opinions founded upon partial knowledge modified. He was of too noble a nature not to have gladly seen the memories of the dead vindicated—not to have been struck with and affected by the words of his deceased master: "To you, brother Carl, I give special thanks for the attachment you have shown me of late."

Thayer's evaluation of Ludwig's feelings towards his brother Carl are further supported by a passage in one of the newly discovered letters from Beethoven to Countess Josephine Deym written in 1804, in which he asks her to give Carl a recommendation. He adds: "Although *wicked people* have spread a rumor that he does not treat me honorably, yet I can assure you that all that is not true, but that he has always looked after my interests with sincere integrity."[21]

The evident care taken by the composer at this period to make the opus numbers really correspond to the chronological order of his works, is a strong reason for concluding that the Violin Sonatas, Op. 30, were completed or nearly so before he removed to Heiligenstadt. Even in that case, what wonderful genius and capacity for labor does it show, that, before the close of the year, in spite of ill health and periods of the deepest despondency, and of all the interruptions caused by his ordinary vocations after his return to town, he had also completed the Sonatas, Op. 31, the two extensive and novel sets of Variations, Op. 34 and Op. 35, and the noble Second Symphony!—all of them witnesses that he had really "entered upon a new path," neither of them more so than the Symphony so amazingly superior to its predecessor in grandeur and originality. This was, in fact, the grand labor of this summer.

For nearly all the works completed in 1802, studies are to be found in the Kessler sketchbook, described in full by Nottebohm,[22] which covers the period from the fall of 1801 to the spring of 1802. The sketches for the Second Symphony are happily plentiful. In the Kessler sketchbook there occurs first a sketch for an "Andante sinfonia" for "Corni soli,"[23] out of which eventually grew the Trio in the Scherzo. Further on there are eleven pages of uninterrupted work on the last movement.[24] Immediately following this come sketches for five of the six "Ländlerische Tänze" (1, 2, 3, 4, 6), another work completed in this year. Meanwhile detailed sketches for the first movement of the Symphony are to be found in the Grasnick sketchbook.[25]

The three Sonatas for Pianoforte and Violin are dedicated to Czar Alexander of Russia, who is said to have given command that a valuable diamond ring be sent to the composer. Lenz could find no record of such an incident in the imperial archives. The sketches show that the movement which now concludes the "Kreutzer" Sonata (Op. 47) was originally designed for the first of the three, the one in A major; and that the Adagio of the second, in

[21] See *A*, 103.
[22] *Ein Skizzenbuch von Beethoven.* (TDR, II, 349, n. 1.)
[23] *Ibid.*, p. 11.
[24] *Ibid.*, pp. 13-19.
[25] Mikulicz, *op.cit.*, pp. 38-53.

C minor, was first contemplated in the key of G. It is an open question whether the theme from the start was intended for this work.

Of the three Piano Sonatas, Op. 31 (G major, D minor, E-flat major), there are sketches for the first two in the Kessler sketchbook, which establishes their dates of origin as 1801-1802.[26] ——The third is sketched in the opening pages of the Wielhorsky sketchbook, and may be dated early 1802. It is noteworthy that none of the three bears a dedication.— The *Notizen* contribute to the later history of the Sonatas. Ries writes (pp. 87-88): "Beethoven had promised the three solo sonatas (Op. 31) to Nägeli in Zurich, while his brother Carl (Caspar) who, unfortunately, was always meddling with his affairs, wanted to sell them to a Leipzig publisher. There were frequent exchanges of words between the brothers on this account because Beethoven, having given his word, wanted to keep it. When the sonatas (the first two) were about to be sent away Beethoven was living in Heiligenstadt. During a walk new quarrels arose between the brothers, and finally they came to blows. The next day he gave me the sonatas to send straight to Zurich, and a letter to his brother enclosed in another to Stephan von Breuning, who was to read it. A prettier lesson could scarcely have been read by anybody with a good heart than Beethoven read his brother on the subject of his conduct the day before. He first pointed it out in its true and contemptible character, then he forgave him everything, but predicted a bad future for him unless he mended his ways. The letter which he wrote to Breuning was also very beautiful."

The first two Sonatas (G major and D minor) appeared in the spring of 1803 in Nägeli's *Répertoire des Clavecinistes* as *Cahier* 5; the third followed a year later, together with the "Sonate pathétique" as *Cahier* 11. Of *Cahier* 5 Nägeli sent copies. Ries reports on the subject as follows (*Notizen*, pp. 88-90):

"When the proof-sheets[27] came I found Beethoven writing. 'Play the Sonata through,' he said to me, remaining seated at his writing-desk. There was an unusual number of errors in the proofs, which fact already made Beethoven impatient. At the end of the first Allegro in the Sonata in G major, however, Nägeli had introduced four measures—after the fourth measure of the last hold:

---

[26] Sketches for the first movement of the first sonata start on four staves as though for a quartet. See *Ein Skizzenbuch, op.cit.*, p. 33.

[27] Kinsky-Halm points out (KHV, p. 79)

that Ries was in error in calling these copies "proof-sheets" as shown by a letter from Carl Caspar to Breitkopf and Härtel dated May 21, 1803: ". . . Please do me the favor in the

"When I played this Beethoven jumped up in a rage, came running to me, half pushed me away from the pianoforte, shouting: 'Where the devil do you find that?' One can scarcely imagine his amazement and rage when he saw the printed notes. I received the commission to make a record of all the errors and at once to send the sonatas to Simrock in Bonn, who was to make a reprint and call it *Edition très correcte*. This indication may still be found on the title page. These extra four measures have been added in some other subsequent editions. Here belong the following notes from Beethoven to me:

1. 'Be good enough to make a note of the errors and send a record of them at once to Simrock, with the request that he publish it soon—the day after tomorrow I will send him the sonata and the concerto.'

2. 'I must ask you again to do the disagreeable work of making a clear copy of the errors in the Zurich sonatas and sending it to Simrock; you will find the list of the errors at my house in the Wieden.'

3. 'Dear Ries!

Not only are the expression marks poorly indicated but there are also false notes in several places—therefore be careful!—or the work will again be in vain. Ch'à detto l'amato bene?' "

The closing words of the second note show that the matter was not brought to an end until late in the spring of 1803, after Beethoven had removed into the theatre buildings An-der-Wien.[28]

After the sonatas became known in Vienna, Doležalek asked Beethoven if a certain passage in the D minor Sonata was correct. "Certainly it is correct," replied the composer, "but you are a countryman of Krumpholz—nothing will go into that hard Bohemian head of yours."

The history of the Seven Bagatelles, Op. 33, has been well summarised by Dr. Riemann:[29] "That some of them, at least the first, stem from the Bonn period would seem to be proved by Beethoven's own inscription on the autograph: 'par Louis van Beethoven 1782,' which caused Thayer to date all of them that early. Yet Nottebohm has shown (in *Ein Skizzenbuch von Beethoven*, p. 12) that the sixth Bagatelle originated in 1802 at the time Beethoven was working on the D major Symphony. Since in these sketches the second part of this bagatelle has not reached its final form, the earlier date here is out of the question. Besides, Beethoven had apparently written '1802' originally on the autograph and subsequently the 8 was changed to a 7 and the 0 to an 8 by him or somebody else." Dr. Riemann's thesis can easily be studied by a look at the facsimile of the autograph of the first Bagatelle, printed by Frimmel in the Beethoven *Jahrbuch* supplement.

---

meanwhile of announcing in your newspaper that the Sonatas by Beethoven, which have just been published in Zurich, have been sent out by mistake without correction and thus there are still many errors therein. . . ." See TDR, II, 619.

[28] Although Schikaneder had moved from the Theater-an-der-Wieden to the Theater-an-der-Wien in 1801, the old name seems to have been still used through force of habit.

[29] TDR, II, 368.

The six Variations in F on an Original Theme, Op. 34, dedicated to the Princess Odescalchi, were probably composed immediately after the Variations in E-flat, Op. 35. In the midst of the sketches for the latter (in the Kessler sketchbook) two measures of the theme of the former are noted and the remark appended: "Each variation in a different time signature [*Takt-art*]—but alternately passages now in the left hand and then almost the same or different ones in the right." Each variation is likewise in a different key. The two sets of Variations were sold to Breitkopf and Härtel in October, 1802. In a letter to the publishers which was enclosed with one from his brother Carl dated October 18, Beethoven writes:

While my brother has written to you, still I have the following to add— I have made two sets of Variations, the first of which can be said to number 8, and the second thirty. Both are written in quite a *new style* and each in an entirely *different way*. I should very much like to have them published by you, *but under the one condition that the honorarium be 50 florins for the two sets*—Do not let me make this offer in vain, for I assure you that you will never regret the two works. *Each theme in them is treated independently and in a wholly different manner.* As a rule I only hear of it from others when I have new ideas, since I never know it myself; but this time— I myself can assure you that in both works *the style is completely new for me.* . . .

A more interesting letter received by Breitkopf and Härtel on December 26, 1802, relates to the same subject. It demands insertion in full:

Instead of making a fuss about a new method of v[ariations] such as would be made by our neighbors the Gallo-Franks, such as, for instance, when a certain French composer presented fugues to me *après une nouvelle Méthode*, which resulted in this, that the *fugue is no longer a fugue*, etc.— I nevertheless want to bring to the attention of the non-connoisseur the fact that these V. are at any rate different from any others. This I thought I could do in the most natural and least conspicuous way by means of a little prefatory note which I beg of you to print *in the small as well as the large variations. I am leaving it for you to say in what language or in how many languages*, since we poor Germans are compelled to speak all tongues.—
Here is the prefatory note:
"Inasmuch as these V. differ noticeably from my earlier ones, instead of designating them like the *former ones* merely by number (Viz.—No. 1, 2, 3 etc.), I have included them in the numerical list *of my greater musical works*, and this all the more because the themes are original.

The Composer"

N.B. If you find it necessary to change or improve anything you have my entire permission.

That by the "large variations," whose number (30) Breitkopf and Härtel seem to have called in question, Beethoven meant his Op. 35, is made plain by a third letter running as follows:

Vienna, April 8, 1803

I have wanted to write you for a long time, but my business affairs are so many that they permit but little correspondence. You seem to be mistaken in your opinion that there are not as many variations as I stated. They could not be exactly indicated; for example when in the large set the variations run into one another in the Adagio, and the Fugue can certainly not be called a variation, nor the Introduction to the big variations, which, as you yourself have seen already, begins with the bass of the theme, then expands to 2, 3, and finally 4 parts; and then the theme at last appears, which again cannot be called a variation, etc.— But if this is not clear to you, send me a proof, as soon as a copy is printed, along with the manuscript, so that I may be spared confusion.— Above all you would do me a great favor if you would omit from the large variations the *dedication to Abbé Stadler* and print the following instead, viz.: *dédiées etc. À Monsieur le Comte Maurice Lichnowsky*; he is a brother of *Prince Lichnowsky* and only recently did me an unexpected favor, and otherwise I have no other opportunity to return the kindness. If you have already engraved the dedication to Abbé Stadler, I will gladly pay the cost of changing the title page. Do not hesitate; write what the expense will be and I shall be glad to pay it. I earnestly beg you to do this if you have not sent out any copies.—

In the case of the *small variations* the dedication to Princess Odescalchi remains.—

I thank you very much for the beautiful things of *Sebastian Bach's*; I will *preserve and study* them—

Should there be a continuation of the pieces send them to me also—

If you have a good text for a cantata or other vocal piece, send it to me.—

In spite of Beethoven's warning, Op. 34 was printed without the proof having been read by him; this provoked another letter calling attention to the large number of errors in the publication, of which Beethoven promised to send a list. He also expressed a fear that the "large variations" would also be faulty, the more since his own manuscript had been put into the hands of the engraver, and asked that the fact that the theme was from his ballet *Prometheus* be indicated on the title page, if there were still time, offering, as in the case of the dedication, to pay the cost of the change. Again he begged to be permitted to correct a proof copy—a request which was ignored in this instance, as it was in the first. The result was a somewhat gentle protest in another letter (September, 1803), in which Beethoven offered the firm the Variations on "God save the King" and "Rule Britannia," the song "Wachtelschlag" and three Marches for the Pianoforte, four hands. The conclusion of the letter, with its postscript, has a double value—as an exhibition of Beethoven's attitude towards the criticism of his day and as a contribution to the debated question touching the illicit printing of some of his early compositions. We quote:

... Please thank the editor of the M.Z. [*Musikalische Zeitung*] for his kindness in inserting the *flattering report* of my oratorio, in which there is so much *downright lying about the prices I charged* and in which I am so infamously treated.

This is I suppose an evidence of impartiality—for aught I care—so long as it makes for the fortune of the M.Z.— What magnanimity is not asked of the true artist, and not wholly without impropriety, but on the other hand, what detestable and vulgar attacks upon us are permitted—

Answer immediately and next time another subject— As always

your devoted

L. v. Beethoven

N.B. All the pieces which I have offered you are entirely new—since unfortunately so many unlucky old things of mine have been sold and printed.[30]

It was through the printing of the letters to Breitkopf and Härtel that the fact became known that Beethoven originally intended to dedicate the Variations in E-flat to Abbé Stadler.

To complete the list of *a cappella* songs set to Italian texts there is still to be included the following—all of which may be dated "by 1802." In the Supplement I to the Collected Works, *Mehrstimmige italienische Gesänge ohne Begleitung* (1959), Hess has published the trio and quartet setting of "Già la notte s'avvicina," which he dates for musical reasons among the latest of the Metastasio text settings. Here is also a second version of the quartet "Guira il nocchier" in B-flat major, estimated by Nottebohm as a late setting. To be published by Hess is the duet "Languisco e moro per te" from the Wielhorsky sketchbook. The music to the quartet "Silvio, amante disperato," cited by Thayer in his *Verzeichniss* (p. 165) is apparently lost.

Sketches for two accompanied settings of Italian texts appear in the Kessler sketchbook, and both works were completed in this year: the aria, "No, non turbati . . . , ma tu tremi, o mio tesoro!" for Soprano and Orchestra, and the trio, "Tremate, empi tremate," for Soprano, Tenor, Bass and Orchestra. Immediately preceding the sketches for the trio are some for a version of "Opferlied" with instrumental accompaniment which was not completed until 1822.[31]

The compositions of the year were:

By 1802.   Quartet for Soprano, Alto, Tenor and Bass, "Silvio amante disperato" (Cantata 27 by Metastasio),[32] WoO 99, No. 12.

            Romance for Violin and Orchestra, Op. 40.

            Romance for Violin and Orchestra, Op. 50.

1800-1802.   Quartet for Soprano, Alto, Tenor and Bass, "Già la notte s'avvicina" (*La Pesca* by Metastasio), WoO 99, No. 4a.

            Quartet for Soprano, Alto, Tenor and Bass, "Guirra il nocchier" (*La gelosia* by Metastasio), 2nd version, WoO 99, No. 5a.

            Trio for Alto, Tenor and Bass, "Già la notte s'avvicina," WoO 99, No. 4b.

1801-1802.   "No, non turbati," for Soprano and String Orchestra (Metastasio), WoO 92a.

[30] I am grateful to Miss Emily Anderson for pointing out that this word may be *gestohlen* (stolen) or *gestochen* (engraved or printed). The latter certainly seems to make more sense.

[31] See Kurt Herbst, *NBJ*, v, 147-48.

[32] See Willy Hess, *Verzeichnis* (Wiesbaden, 1957), p. 59.

String Quartet in F major, transcription of the Sonata for Pianoforte, Op. 14, No. 1.

Symphony No. 2 in D major, Op. 36.

Three Sonatas for Pianoforte, Op. 31.

"Tremate, empi, tremate," for Soprano, Tenor and Bass with Orchestra (Bettoni),[33] Op. 116.

1802.   Bagatelles for Pianoforte, Op. 33.

Duet, "Languisco e moro per te," Hess No. 229.[34]

"Graf, Graf, liebster Graf," WoO 101, musical joke in a letter to Zmeskall.

Three Sonatas for Pianoforte and Violin, Op. 30.

Six Variations for Pianoforte, Op. 34.

Variations for Pianoforte, Op. 35 (on a theme used in Contradance No. 7, WoO 8 and *Prometheus*, Op. 43).

The publications of the year were:

By Artaria:

Six "Ländlerische Tänze" for two Violins and Violoncello/Double Bass, WoO 15; also transcription for Pianoforte.

By Breitkopf and Härtel in Leipzig:

Quintet for two Violins, two Violas and Violoncello, Op. 29, dedicated to Count Moritz von Fries.

By Kunst- und Industrie-Comptoir:

Sonata for Pianoforte, Op. 28, dedicated "À Joseph Noble de Sonnenfels."

String Quartet in F major, transcription of the Sonata for Pianoforte Op. 14, No. 1, dedicated to Baroness Josefine von Braun.

By Cappi in Vienna:

Serenade for Flute, Violin and Viola, Op. 25.

Sonata for Pianoforte, Op. 26, dedicated to Prince Karl von Lichnowsky.

Sonata for Pianoforte, Op. 27, No. 1, dedicated to Princess Josephine von Liechtenstein.

Sonata for Pianoforte, Op. 27, No. 2, dedicated to Countess Giulietta Giucciardi.

By Hoffmeister and Co. and Hoffmeister and Kühnel in Leipzig:

Septet for Violin, Viola, Clarinet, Horn, Bassoon, Violoncello and Double Bass, Op. 20, dedicated to Empress Maria Theresia.

Sonata for Pianoforte, Op. 22, dedicated to Count Johann Georg von Browne.

By Mollo:

Twelve German Dances for two Violins and Violoncello/Double Bass, transcription of Twelve German Dances for Orchestra, WoO 8.

Twelve Contradances for Orchestra, WoO 14; also transcription for Pianoforte of Six Contradances (Nos. 8, 7, 4, 10, 9 and 1).

Twelve Minuets for two Violins and Violoncello/Double Bass, transcriptions of Twelve Minuets for Orchestra, WoO 7.

Variations for Pianoforte and Violoncello on the theme "Bei Männern, welche Liebe fühlen," from Mozart's *Die Zauberflöte*, dedicated to Count Johann Georg von Browne, WoO 46.

By Traeg:

Variations for Pianoforte on Righini's "Venni Amore," WoO 65, revised version.

[33] See KHV, p. 334.   [34] See Hess, *op.cit.*

CHAPTER XVI

THE YEAR 1803

THE COURT THEATRE—WORK ON THE "EROICA" SYMPHONY

IN 1802 August von Kotzebue[1] along with Garlieb Merkel began the publication of a polemical literary journal in Berlin called the *Freymüthige*, Goethe, the Schlegels and their party being the objects of their polemics. Spazier's *Zeitung für die Elegante Welt* (Leipzig) was its leading opponent, until the establishment of a new literary journal at Jena. At the beginning of 1803, Kotzebue was in Vienna on his way to Italy. Some citations from the *Freymüthige* of this time have an especial value, as coming, beyond a doubt, from his pen. His position in society, his knowledge from experience of theatrical affairs in Vienna, his personal acquaintance with Beethoven and the other persons mentioned, all combine to enable him to speak with authority. An article in No. 58 (April 12) on the "Amusements of the Viennese after Carnival," gives a peep into the salon-life of the capital, and introduces to us divers matters of so much interest, as to excuse the want of novelty in certain parts. ". . . Amateur concerts at which unconstrained pleasure prevails are frequent. The beginning is usually made with a quartet by Haydn or Mozart; then follows, let us say, an air by Salieri or Paër, then a pianoforte piece with or without another instrument *obbligato*, and the concert closes as a rule with a chorus or something of the kind from a favorite opera. The most excellent pianoforte pieces that won admiration during the last carnival were a new quintet[2] by Beethoven, clever, serious,

---

[1] Kotzebue was a well-known playwright and director of the Burg Theatre under the banker Baron von Braun. In 1798 trouble between him and members of the company forced his resignation and the next year he had left Vienna for a year's stay in Siberia. Before establishing himself in Berlin, he had a short stay in Jena, where his antagonism to Goethe broke out into an open quarrel. (TDR, II, 379; TK, II, 1.)

[2] Probably the Quintet for Pianoforte and Wind-Instruments, Op. 16, published in March, 1801. (TDR, II, 380, n. 1.)

full of deep significance and character, but occasionally a little too glaring, here and there *Odensprünge* in the manner of this master; then a quartet by Anton Eberl, dedicated to the Empress, lighter in character, full of fine yet profound invention, originality, fire and strength, brilliant and imposing. Of all the musical compositions which have appeared of late these are certainly two of the best. Beethoven has for a short time past been engaged, at a considerable salary, by the Theater-an-der-Wien, and will soon produce at that playhouse an oratorio of his composition entitled *Christus am Ölberg*. Amongst the artists on the violin the most notable are Clement, Schuppanzigh (who gives the concerts in the Augarten in the summer) and Luigi Tomasini. Clement (Director of the orchestra an-der-Wien) is an admirable concert player; Schuppanzigh performs quartets very agreeably. Good dilettanti are Eppinger, Molitor and others. Great artists on the pianoforte are Beethofen, Hummel, Madame Auernhammer and others. The famous Abbé Vogler is also here at present, and plays fugues in particular with great precision, although his rather heavy touch betrays the organist. Among the amateurs Baroness Ertmann plays with amazing precision, clearness and delicacy, and Fräulein Kurzbeck touches the keys with high intelligence and deep feeling. Mesdames von Frank and Natorp, formerly Gerardi and Sessi, are excellent singers."

A few words may be added to this picture from other sources. Salieri's duties being now confined to the sacred music of the Imperial Chapel, Süssmayr being far gone in the consumption of which he died on September 16 (of this year—1803), Conti retaining but the name of orchestral director (he too died the next year), Lichtenstein and Weigl were now the conductors of the Imperial Opera; Henneberg and Seyfried held the same positions under Schikaneder, as in the old house, so now in the new.

Schuppanzigh's summer concerts in the Augarten, and Salieri's Widows and Orphans concerts at Christmas and in Holy Week, were still the only regular public ones. Vogler had come from Prague in December, and Paër, who had removed to Dresden at Easter, 1802, was again in Vienna to produce his cantata *Das Heilige Grab*, at the Widows and Orphans Concert. It was a period of dearth at Vienna in operatic composition. At the Court Theatre Lichtenstein had failed disastrously; Weigl had not been able to follow up the success of his *Corsär*, and several years more elapsed before he obtained a permanent name in musical annals by his *Schweizerfamilie*. Salieri's style had become too familiar to all Vienna longer to possess the charms of freshness and novelty. In the Theater-an-der-Wien, Teyber, Henneberg, Seyfried and others composed to order and executed their work satisfactorily enough—indeed, sometimes with decided, though fleeting, success. But no new work, for some time past, composed to the order of either of these theatres, had possessed such qualities as to secure a brilliant and prolonged existence. From another source, however, a new, fresh and powerful musical sensation had been experienced during the past year at both: and in this wise:

Schikaneder produced, on the 23rd of March, a new opera which had been very favorably received at Paris, called *Lodoiska*, the music composed "by a certain Cherubini." The applause gained by this opera induced the Court Theatre to send for the score of another opera by the same composer, and prepare it for production on the 14th of August, under the title *Die Tage der Gefahr (Der Wasserträger)*. Schikaneder, with his usual shrewdness, meantime was secretly rehearsing the same work, after Seyfried in the beginning of July had made the then long journey to Munich to obtain a copy. On the 13th—one day in advance of the rival stage—the musical public was surprised and amused to see "announced on the billboard of the Wiener Theater the new opera *Graf Armand, oder Die zwei unvergessliche Tage*." In the adaption and performance of the work, each house had its points of superiority and of inferiority; on the whole, there was little to choose between them; the result in both was splendid. The rivalry between the two stages became very spirited. The Court Theatre selected from the new composer's other works the *Medea*, and brought it out November 6. Schikaneder followed, December 18, with *Der Bernardsberg (Elise)*, "sadly mutilated." Twenty years later Beethoven attested the ineffaceable impression which Cherubini's music had made upon him. While the music of the new master was thus attracting and delighting crowded audiences at both theatres, the wealthy and enterprising Baron Braun went to Paris and entered into negotiations with Cherubini, which resulted in his engagement to compose one or more operas for the Vienna stage. Besides this "a large number of new theatrical representations from Paris" were expected (in August, 1802) upon the Court stage. "Baron Braun, who is expected to return from Paris, is bringing the most excellent ballets and operas with him, all of which will be performed here most carefully according to the taste of the French." Thus the *Allg. Mus. Zeitung*.

These facts bring us to the most valuable and interesting notice contained in the article from the *Freymüthige*—the earliest record of Beethoven's engagement as composer for the Theater-an-der-Wien.

Zitterbarth, the merchant with whose money the new edifice had been built and put in successful operation, "who had no knowledge of theatrical matters outside of the spoken drama," left the stage direction entirely in the hands of Schikaneder. In the department of opera that director had a most valuable assistant in Sebastian Mayer—the second husband of Mozart's sister-in-law, Mme. Hofer, the original Queen of Night—a man described by Castelli as a moderately gifted bass singer, but a very good actor, and of the noblest and most refined taste in vocal music, opera as well as oratorio; to whom the praise is due of having induced Schikaneder to bring out so many of the finest new French works, those of Cherubini included. It is probable, therefore, that, just now, when Baron von Braun was reported to have secured Cherubini for his theatre, and it became necessary to discover some new means of keeping up a successful competition, Mayer's advice may have had no small weight with Schikaneder. Defeat was certain unless the operas, attractive mainly from their scenery and grotesque humor, founded upon the "Thousand and One Nights" and their thousand and one imitations, and set to trivial and commonplace tunes, should give place to others of a higher order, quickened by music more serious, dignified and significant.

Whether Abbé Georg Joseph Vogler was really a great and profound musician, as C. M. von Weber, Gänsbacher and Meyerbeer held him to be, or a charlatan, was a matter much disputed in those days, as the same question in relation to certain living composers is in ours. Whatever the truth was, by his polemical writings, his extraordinary self-laudation, his high tone at the courts whither he had been called, his monster concerts, and his almost unperformable works, he had made himself an object of profound curiosity, to say the least. Moreover, his music for the drama *Hermann von Staufen, oder das Vehmgericht*, performed October 3, 1801, at the Theater-an-der-Wien (if the same as in *Hermann von Unna*, as it doubtless was), was well fitted to awaken confidence in his talents. His appearance in Vienna just now was, therefore, a piece of good fortune for Schikaneder, who immediately engaged him for his theatre.

Whether Beethoven had talents for operatic composition, no one could yet know; but his works had already spread to Paris, London, Edinburgh, and had gained him the fame of being the greatest living instrumental composer—Father Haydn of course excepted—and this much might be accepted as certain: viz., that his name alone, like Vogler's, would secure the theatre from pecuniary loss in the production of *one* work; and, perhaps—who could foretell?—he might develop powers in this new field which would raise him to the level of even Cherubini! He was personally known to Schikaneder, having played in the old theatre, and his *Prometheus* music was a success at the Court Theatre. So he, too, was engaged. Thus Schikaneder—that strange compound of wit and absurdity; of poetic instinct and grotesque humor; of shrewd and profitable enterprise and lavish prodigality; who lived like a prince and died like a pauper—has connected his name honorably with both Mozart and Beethoven.

The first mention of this appointment is in a letter from brother Johann to Breitkopf and Härtel, dated February 12, 1803: "You have heard by now that my brother has been engaged by the Wiedener Theater, he is to write an opera, is in charge of the orchestra, can conduct, when necessary, because there is a director already available there every day." The first public report appeared in the Berlin *Freymüthige* of April 12th as already cited. This was followed by a notice in the August 2 issue of the Leipzig *Zeitung für die Elegante Welt* written by a correspondent under date of June 29th: "Abbé Vogler is now writing an opera by H[uber], and Beethoven one by Schikaneder." But in truth Beethoven was still preoccupied with the task of finishing the "Eroica" and was not able to put his mind on opera until late fall, as one can learn from a letter that he wrote to Alexander Macco on November 2, 1803: ". . . only it is impossible for me at this moment to write this oratorio [Meissner's *Der Weg des Leben*] because I am just now beginning my opera."

An immediate result of Beethoven's engagement at the theatre was an opportunity to give a concert, for which he composed his oratorio, *Christus am Ölberg*. Sketches for this work appear in the Wielhorsky sketchbook, now in Russia, first mentioned by von Lenz and described in detail by Ludwig Nohl.[3] The second half of this sketchbook is taken up with work on the introduction and first five numbers of the oratorio, which is followed by sketches for the "Kreutzer" Sonata.

The author of the oratorio text was Franz Huber. Beethoven referred to their collaboration in a letter written to the Gesellschaft der Musikfreunde on January 23, 1824: "Christus am Ölberg was written by me and the poet in a period of 14 days, but the poet was musical and had already written many things for music. I was able to consult with him at any moment." In a letter written nearer the time of composition (to Breitkopf and Härtel in the next year) he speaks of it as the labor of "a few weeks." Therefore, despite contrary evidence from Schindler,[4] it seems clear from Beethoven's own references that the oratorio must have been written in a short time, all at once, and probably just before it was to be rehearsed.

The *Wiener Zeitung* of Saturday, March 26 and Wednesday, March 30, 1803, contained the following:

NOTICE

On the 5th (not the 4th) of April, Herr Ludwig van Beethoven will produce a new oratorio set to music by him, *Christus am Ölberg*, in the R.I. privil. Theater-an-der-Wien. The other pieces to be performed will be announced on the large bill-board.

The final general rehearsal was held in the theatre in the morning of the day of performance, Tuesday, April 5th. On that morning, as was often the case when Beethoven needed assistance in his labors, young Ries was called to him early—about 5 o'clock. In the *Notizen* he gives the following description (pp. 75-76):

"I found him in bed, writing on *separate* sheets of paper. To my question what it was he answered, '*Trombones.*' The trombones also played from *these* sheets at the performance.

"Had someone forgotten to copy these parts? Were they an afterthought?

---

[3] *Beethoven, Liszt, Wagner* (Vienna, 1874), pp. 95ff. See also Boris Schwarz, "Beethoveniana in Soviet Russia," *MQ* (1961), pp. 4-9.

[4] *Biographie*, I, 90. "There were sketches made for this work as early as 1801, during the summer stay in nearby Hetzendorf. He himself [Beethoven] showed the author in 1823 the place, hidden in a thicket in the upper part of the Schönbrunn palace gardens, where the preliminary studies were made." (Cf. TDR, II, 244.)

I was too young at the time to note the artistic interest of the incident; but probably the trombones were an afterthought,[5] as Beethoven might as easily have had the *uncopied parts* as the copied ones. The rehearsal began at eight o'clock in the morning. . . . It was a terrible rehearsal, and at half past two everybody was exhausted and more or less dissatisfied.

"Prince Karl Lichnowsky, who attended the rehearsal from the beginning, had sent for bread and butter, cold meat and wine, in large baskets. He pleasantly asked all to help themselves, and this was done with both hands, the result being that good nature was restored again. Then the Prince requested that the oratorio be rehearsed once more from the beginning, so that it might go well in the evening and Beethoven's first work in this genre be worthily presented. And so the rehearsal began again. The concert began at six o'clock, but was so long that a few pieces were not performed."

The works actually performed were the first and second Symphonies, the Pianoforte Concerto in C minor and *Christus am Ölberg*. As no copy of the printed programme has been discovered, there is no means of deciding what else had been originally planned; but pieces like the "Adelaide," "Ah, perfido!" or the trio "Tremate, empi, tremate" suggest themselves as vocal pieces well fitted to break the monotony of such a mass of orchestral music. It seems strange—knowing as we do Beethoven's vast talent for improvisation—that no extempore performance is reported.

Beethoven must have felt no small confidence in the power of his name to awaken the curiosity and interest of the musical public, for according to the *Allgemeine Musikalische Zeitung*, he doubled the prices of the first chairs, tripled those of the reserved and demanded 12 ducats (instead of 4 florins) for each box.[6] But it was his first public appearance as a dramatic vocal composer, and on his posters he had several days before announced that all the pieces performed would be of his composition. The result, however, answered his expectations, for the concert yielded him 1800 florins.

Seyfried gives a reminiscence of this concert:[7] "In the playing of the concerto movements he asked me to turn the pages for him; but—heaven help me!—that was easier said than done. I saw almost nothing but empty leaves; at the most on one page or the other a few Egyptian hieroglyphs wholly unintelligible to me scribbled down to serve as clues for him; for he played nearly all of the solo part from memory, since, as was so often the case, he had not had time to put it all down on paper.[8] He gave me a secret

[5] To show that Beethoven did have such afterthoughts, Krehbiel cites the example of trombone parts for the Trio in the Scherzo of the Ninth Symphony which he found among Thayer's papers. These parts contained also Beethoven's instructions to the copyist as to where to introduce them in the score, thus proving that they were afterthoughts. (TK, II, 7, n. 1.)

[6] Beethoven responded in a letter to Breitkopf and Härtel in September referring sarcastically to this report "in which there is so much *downright lying about the prices* I charged and in which I am so infamously treated." *A*, 81.

[7] *Cäcilia*, IX, 219-20. (TDR, II, 370.)

[8] The manuscript of the Concerto bears in the composer's hand the date "1800." (TDR,

glance whenever he was at the end of one of the invisible passages and my scarcely concealable anxiety not to miss the decisive moment amused him greatly and he laughed heartily at the jovial supper which we ate afterwards."

The impression made upon reading the few contemporary notices of this concert is that the new works produced were, on the whole, coldly received. The short report (by Kotzebue?) in the *Freymüthige* said: "Even our doughty Beethofen, whose oratorio *Christus am Ölberg* was performed for the first time at suburban Theater-an-der-Wien, was not altogether fortunate, and despite the efforts of his many admirers was unable to achieve really marked approbation. True, the two symphonies and single passages in the oratorio were voted very beautiful, but the work in its entirety was too long, too artificial in structure and lacking expressiveness, especially in the vocal parts. The text, by F. X. Huber, seemed to have been as superficially written as the music. But the concert brought 1800 florins to Beethofen and he, as well as Abbé Vogler, has been engaged for the theatre. He is to write one opera, Vogler three; for this they are to receive 10 per cent of the receipts at the first ten performances, besides free lodgings."

The report of the *Zeitung für die Elegante Welt* was of the opinion "that the first symphony is better than the later one [in D] because it is developed with a lightness and is less forced, while in the second the striving for the new and surprising is already more apparent. However, it is obvious that both are not lacking in surprising and brilliant passages of beauty. Less successful was the following Concerto in C minor which Hr. v. B., who is otherwise known as an excellent pianist, performed also not completely to the public's satisfaction." He found the music to the *Christus* on the whole good; "there are a few admirable passages; an air of the Seraph with trombone accompaniment in particular makes an excellent effect." This may well have been the trombone passage, referred to in Ries's account, which Beethoven composed in bed the morning of the performance.

The writer in the *Allgemeine Musikalische Zeitung* alone spoke of the *Christus* as having been received with "extraordinary approval." He added, "It confirms my long-held opinion that Beethoven in time can effect a revolution in music like Mozart's. He is hastening towards this goal with great strides." Three months afterwards another correspondent flatly contradicted the account of the reception: "In the interest of truth," he writes, "I am obliged to contradict a report in the *Musikalische Zeitung*; Beethoven's cantata did not please." To this Schindler remarks: "Even the composer agreed with this to this extent—that in later years he unhesitatingly declared that it had been a mistake to treat the part of Christ in the modern vocal style. The abandonment of the work after the first performance as well as its tardy appearance in print [1811] permit us to conclude that the author was not

---

II, 370.) According to Kinsky-Halm (KHV,   1802 for this forthcoming performance.
p. 92) the Concerto was revised at the end of

particularly satisfied with the manner in which he had solved the problem, and that he probably made material changes in the music." The *Wiener Zeitung* of July 30, 1803, gives all the comment necessary on the "abandonment" by announcing that the "favorable reception" of the oratorio had induced the Society of Amateur Concerts to resolve to repeat it on August 4. Moreover, Sebastian Mayer's concert of March 27, 1804, opened with the second Symphony of Beethoven and closed with *Christus am Ölberg*, being its fourth performance in one year.[9] Beethoven did revise the work to some extent,[10] for he refers to it in a letter to Breitkopf and Härtel of August 26, 1804: "The oratorio has not yet been published because I have added a whole new chorus to it and have changed some things; for I wrote the whole oratorio in only a few weeks and several things since then have not completely suited me."

A few days after this public appearance we have a sight of Beethoven again in private life. Dr. Joh. Th. Held, the famous physician and professor in Prague, then a young man of just the composer's age (he was born December 11, 1770), accompanied Count Prichowsky on a visit to Vienna. On the morning of the 16th of April these two gentlemen met Beethoven in the street. He, knowing the Count, invited them to Schuppanzigh's, "where some of his pianoforte sonatas which Kleinhals[11] had transcribed as string quartets were to be rehearsed." In his manuscript autobiography (the citations were communicated to this work by Dr. Edmund Schebek of Prague) Held writes: "We met a number of the best musicians gathered together, such as the violinists Krumbholz, Möser (of Berlin), the mulatto Bridgethauer, who in London had been in the service of the then Prince of Wales, also a Herr Schreiber and the 12-year-old Kraft[12] who played second. Even then Beethoven's muse transported me into higher regions, and the desire of all these artists to have our musical director Wenzel Praupner in Vienna confirmed me in my opinion of the excellence of his conducting. Since then I have often met Beethoven at concerts. His piquant conceits modified the gloominess, I might say the lugubriousness, of his countenance. His criticisms were very keen, as I learned most clearly at concerts of the harpist Nadermann of Saxony, and Mara, who was already getting on in years."

The "Bridgethauer" mentioned by Held—whose incorrect writing of the name conveys to the German its correct pronunciation—was the "American ship captain who associated much with Beethoven" mentioned by Schindler and his copyists.

[9] In a Conversation Book from the year 1825, Holz writes that till then *Christus am Ölberg* had always drawn full houses, but that the court official in charge of musical affairs (*Hofmusikgraf*) had not allowed further performances to be given. (TDR, II, 388, n. 1.)

[10] For sketches of this revision see Nottebohm, *Ein Skizzenbuch von Beethoven aus dem Jahre 1803* (Leipzig, 1880), pp. 72-73.

[11] Probably Franz Xavier Kleinheinz is meant. See page 292 above. (TDR, II, 388, n. 3.)

[12] This appears to be a mistake: Nikolaus Kraft (born 1778) was a cellist, almost 25 years old at the time.

George Augustus Polgreen Bridgetower[13]—a bright mulatto then 24 years old, son of an African father and a German or Polish mother, an applauded public violinist in London at the age of ten years, and long in the service, as musician, of the Prince of Wales, afterwards George IV—was never in America and knew as much probably of a ship and the science of navigation as ordinary shipmasters do of the violin and the mysteries of musical counterpoint. In 1802 he obtained leave of absence to visit his mother in Dresden and to use the waters of Teplitz and Carlsbad, which leave was prolonged that he might spend a few months in Vienna. His playing in public and private at Dresden had secured him such favorable letters of introduction as gained him a most brilliant reception in the highest musical circles of the Austrian capital, where he arrived a few days before Held met him at Schuppanzigh's. Beethoven, to whom he was introduced by Prince Lichnowsky, readily gave him aid in a public concert. ⸻The date was to be May 22nd, but the performance had to be postponed for two days and took place on May 24th in the Augartensaal.[14]⸻ It has an interest on account of Beethoven's connection with it; for the day of the concert was the date of the completion and performance of the "Kreutzer" Sonata. Ries writes (*Notizen*, p. 82): "The famous Sonata in A minor, Op. 47, with concertante violin, dedicated to Rudolph Kreutzer in Paris, was originally composed by Beethoven for Bridgetower, an English artist. Here things did not go much better [Ries had referred to the tardiness of the composition of the horn sonata which Beethoven wrote for Punto], although a large part of the first Allegro was ready at an early date. Bridgetower pressed him greatly because the date of his concert had been set and he wanted to study his part. One morning Beethoven summoned me at half after 4 o'clock and said: 'Copy the violin part of the first Allegro quickly.' (His ordinary copyist was otherwise engaged.) The pianoforte part was noted down only here and there in parts. Bridgetower had to play the marvellously beautiful theme and variations in F from Beethoven's manuscript at the concert because there was no time to copy it. The final Allegro, however, was beautifully written, since it originally belonged to the Sonata in A major (Op. 30), which is dedicated to Czar Alexander. In its place Beethoven, thinking it too brilliant for the A major Sonata, put the variations which now form the finale."

⸻Thus, the last movement was composed first and in the preceding year. Sketches for the first and perhaps the second movement[15] appear in the

---

[13] For further details of Bridgetower's life see *The Musical Times* [May, 1908] pp. 302-308. (TK, II, 11, n. 1). Also Hans Volkmann, *Beethoven in seinen Beziehungen zu Dresden* (Dresden, 1942), pp. 149-54.

[14] See Hermann Reuther, "Beethovens Konzerte," *Ein Wiener Beethoven Buch*, ed., A. Orel (Vienna, 1921), p. 91.

[15] Nohl (*op.cit.*, pp. 95-101) could find no trace in the sketches of the second movement, to which N. Fischman, as reported by Boris Schwarz (*op.cit.*, p. 8) disagrees in his commentary on the facsimiles published in *Sovietskaya Muzyka*, 1952, p. 3. See *Voprosy Muzykoznania*, Vol. 2, Yearbook 1955, Moscow, 1956.

last pages of the Wielhorsky sketchbook, which thereby dates the initial work on the first part of the sonata as early 1803. Consequently, at the start of its composition Beethoven did not have Bridgetower in mind, as Ries states, having first met him later in the spring.❧

Bridgetower was thoughtful enough to leave in his copy of the Sonata a note upon that first performance of it, as follows:

Relative to Beethoven's Op. 47.

When I accompanied him in this Sonata-Concertante at Wien, at the repetition of the first part of the Presto, I imitated the flight, at the 18th bar, of the piano-forte of this movement thus:

He jumped up, embraced me, saying: "Noch einmal, mein lieber Bursch!" ["Once again, my dear boy!"] Then he held the open pedal during this flight, the chord of C as at the ninth bar.

Beethoven's expression in the Andante was so chaste, which always characterized the performance of all his *slow movements*, that it was unanimously hailed to be repeated twice.

George Polgreen Bridgetower.

Bridgetower was mentioned in a letter from Beethoven to Baron von Wetzlar, in this language, under date May 18:

Although we have never addressed each other, I do not hesitate to recommend to you the bearer, Hr. Brishdower, a very capable virtuoso who has a complete command of his instrument.—Besides his concertos he plays quartets admirably. I hope very much that you will make him known to others. He has commended himself favorably to *Lobkowitz and Fries* and all other eminent lovers [of music].

I think it would be not at all a bad idea if you were to take him for an evening to *Therese Schönfeld*, where I know many friends assemble, and have him at your house.—I know that you will thank me for having made you acquainted with him.—

Bridgetower, when advanced in years, talking with Mr. Thirwall about Beethoven, told him that at the time the Sonata, Op. 47, was composed, he and the composer were constant companions, and that the first copy bore a dedication to him; but before he departed from Vienna they had a quarrel about a girl, and Beethoven then dedicated the work to Rudolph Kreutzer.

When Beethoven removed from the house "am Peter" to the theatre building, he took his brother Carl Caspar to live with him,[16] as twenty years later he gave a room to his factotum Schindler. This change of lodgings took place, according to Seyfried, before the concert of April 5—which is confirmed by the brother's new address being contained in the *Staats-Schematismus* for 1803—that annual publication being usually ready for distribution in April. A business letter[17] written by Carl to Simrock from the new lodging shows his activity at this time as agent for his brother.

Vienna, May 25, 1803

Highly esteemed Sir;

I have not been able until now to provide you with three sonatas and something else because your answer to my letter of September of last year arrived here so late. At the moment you can have a grand violin *sonata* under the following conditions; it is to appear simultaneously in London, Leipzig, Vienna and Bonn. A copy of a work of this kind to print costs 30# [florins]. Then you can have a big *symphony* alone for 400 fl. If you wish to publish the *Sonatas* which appeared in Zurich, write us and we will send you a list of some 80 mistakes in them.

Now most of the keyboard music and also the Instrumental pieces by my brother have been arranged with care by a skilful composer, thus already several instrumental pieces have been arranged very usefully for the piano with and without accompanying instruments and others for string quartet. You can have these for about 14# apiece. I believe that the offer is very favorable because you could gain great sums of money with little expense.

Please write to me soon concerning this.

Yours sincerely,
C. v. Beethoven

Address
    A ∼ Beethoven
      in Vienna to be delivered
in the Theater-an-der-Wien, 2nd story

When the "Kreuzer" Sonata was published (it was announced by Traeg on May 18, 1805) Carl acknowledged the receipt of a copy in a letter to Simrock, adding that since all the other publishers sent six copies of the works printed by them, he would like five more. Simrock took him to task rather sharply for what he considered a piece of presumption, in a letter which he enclosed to Ferdinand Ries with the statement that he might read it if he wanted to. "I bought the Sonata of Louis van Beethoven," says the indignant publisher, "and in his letter concerning it there is not a word about giving him six copies in addition to the fees—a matter important enough to have been mentioned; I was under the impression that Louis

[16] "Hr. Carl v. Beethoven lives auf-der-Wien 26.," *Staats-Schematismus*, 1803, p. 150; and *ibid.*, 1804, p. 154. "Hr. Ludwig van Beethoven, auf-der-Wien 26."—See *Auskunftsbuch*, 1804, p. 204. "An-der-Wien no. 26, Bartolomau Zitterbarth, K. K. Priv. Schau-spielhaus."—See *Vollständiges Verzeichnis aller . . . der numerirten Häuser, deren Eigenthümer*, etc., etc. (Wien, 1804), p. 133. (TDR, II, 398, n. 1.)

[17] Published by Leopold Schmidt, *Beethoven Briefe* (Berlin, 1909). (TDR, II, 398.)

van Beethoven composed his own works; what I am certain of is that I have fully complied with all the conditions of the contract and am indebted to nobody." In the note to Ries he calls Carl's conduct "impertinent and deserving of a harsher treatment, for Herr Carl seems to me incorrigible."

At the beginning of the warm season Beethoven, as was his annual custom, appears to have spent some weeks in Baden to refresh himself and revive his energies after the irregular, exciting and fatiguing city life of the winter, before retiring to the summer lodgings, whose location he describes in a note to Ries (*Notizen*, p. 128) as "in Oberdöbling No. 4, the street to the left where you go down the mountain to Heiligenstadt."

Beethoven's quarters consisted of an anteroom (which he used as a kitchen) and three rooms, two of which were on the street side. It was a simple wine-grower's house on level ground which at the time was the property of the vinegar-maker, Franz Nusser. For this information regarding the so-called "Eroica house," the editor is grateful to the late Dr. Kurt Smolle of Vienna, who had this to add: The house—Vienna XIX, Döblinger Hauptstrasse No. 92—still stands, though somewhat changed since in the course of time a story has been added. It was also less wide than the present street front; in the place of the present front there was a small path through making a narrow connection between the Hofzeile and the Nussdorferstrasse (now Heiligenstädterstrasse). The street in front of the house was much higher, so that the windows were close to street level. The house is known as "Biederhof" after a later owner, and also as "Eroicahaus." In 1803 it had gardens, vineyards or green fields in both front and rear. True, it was half an hour's walk farther than from Heiligenstadt to the scenes in which he had composed the second Symphony the preceding summer; but to compensate for this, it was so much nearer the city—was in the more immediate vicinity of that arm of the Danube called the "Canal"—and almost under its windows was the gorge of the Krottenbach, which separates Döbling from Heiligenstadt, and which, as it extends inland from the river, spreads into a fine vale, then very solitary and still very beautiful. This was the house, this the summer, and these the scenes, in which the composer wrought out the conceptions that during the past five years had been assuming form and consistency in his mind, to which Bernadotte may have given the original impulse, and which we know as the "Eroica" Symphony. The history of this symphony will be taken up in the next chapter.

As a proof of the growing appreciation of Beethoven in foreign lands, it may be remarked here that in the summer of 1803 he received an Erard pianoforte as a gift from the celebrated Parisian maker. The archives of the Erard firm show that on the 18th of Thermidor, in the XIth year of the Republic (1803), Sébastien Erard made a present of "un piano forme clavecin" to Ludwig van Beethoven in Vienna. The instrument belongs to the museum at Linz.

Let us turn to Stephan von Breuning and a new friend or two. Archduke

Karl, by a commission dated January 9, 1801, had been made Chief of the "Staats- und Konferenzial-Departement für das Kriegs- und Marine-Wesen," and retained the position still, notwithstanding his assumption of the functions of *Hoch- und Deutsch-Meister*. He undertook to introduce wide-reaching reform at the War Department, which demanded an increase in the number of Secretaries and scriveners. Stephan von Breuning is the second in the list of five appointed in 1804, Ignaz von Gleichenstein the fifth. It is believed that the Archduke had discovered the fine business talents, the zeal in the discharge of duty and the perfect trustworthiness of Breuning at the Teutonic House, and that at his special invitation the young man this year exchanged the service of the Order for that of the State. There is abundant evidence that the young Rhinelanders then in Vienna were bound to each other by more than the usual ties; most of them were fugitives from French tyranny, and liable to conscription if found in the places of their birth, though this was not the case with Breuning. There was, in addition to the ordinary feeling of nationality, a common sense of exile to unite them. Between Breuning and Gleichenstein therefore—two amiable and talented young men thus thrown into daily intercourse—an immediate and warm friendship would naturally spring up.

The first evidence of Beethoven's acquaintance with the latter is to be found in a letter, written by Albrechtsberger to Beethoven on February 20, 1797: "The old Baron Joseph Gleichenstein sent his servant to me today to have me request that you, dear Beethoven, accept the invitation to his piano concert tomorrow evening. Also I was to ask if you had already decided whether to give instruction to his son Ignaz. I am supposed to give an answer in case you cannot come tomorrow."[18] And now through their common friend, von Breuning, they were undoubtedly drawn together at this time and established that close friendship which was to last until Gleichenstein left Vienna in 1813. A friend of noble birth like Count Franz Brunsvik, he was one of the very few with whom Beethoven had a "Du" relationship in correspondence.

Another young Rhinelander, to whom Beethoven became much attached, and who returned the kindness with warm affection for him personally and a boundless admiration for his genius, became known to the composer also just at this time. Willibrord Joseph Mähler, born at Ehrenbreitstein—who died in 1860, at the age of 82 years, as pensioned Court Secretary—was a man of remarkably varied artistic talents, by which, however, since he cultivated them only as a dilettante and without confining himself to any one art, he achieved no great distinction. He wrote respectable poetry and set it to correct and not unpleasing music; sang well enough to be recorded in Boeckh's *Merkwürdigkeiten der Haupt- und Residenz-Stadt Wien* (1823) as "amateur singer," and painted sufficiently well to be named, on another page of Boeckh, "amateur portrait painter."

[18] *FRBH*, I, 170.

Soon after Beethoven returned from his summer lodgings to his apartment in the theatre building, Mähler, who had then recently arrived in Vienna, was taken by Breuning thither to be introduced. They found him busily at work finishing the "Eroica" Symphony. After some conversation, at the desire of Mähler to hear him play, Beethoven, instead of beginning an extempore performance, gave his visitors the finale of the new Symphony; but at its close, without a pause, he continued in free fantasia for *two hours*, "during all which time," said Mr. Mähler to the present writer, "there was not a measure which was faulty, or which did not sound original." He added, that one circumstance attracted his particular notice; viz.: "that Beethoven played with his hands so very still; wonderful as his execution was, there was no tossing of them to and fro, up and down; they seemed to glide right and left over the keys, the fingers alone doing the work." To Mr. Mähler, as to most others who have recorded their impressions of Beethoven's improvisations, they were the *non plus ultra* of the art.

He painted a portrait of the composer about 1804-1805, and a second around 1814-15.[19] An undated note of Beethoven to Mähler may be inserted here, as an introduction to Mr. Mähler's remarks upon the portrait to which it refers: "I beg of you to return my portrait to me as soon as you have made sufficient use of it—if you need it longer I beg of you at least to make haste— I have promised the portrait to a stranger, a lady who saw it here, that she may hang it in her room during her stay of several weeks. Who can withstand such *charming importunities*, as a matter of course a portion of the lovely favors *which I shall thus garner* will also fall to *you*."

To the question what picture is here referred to, Mr. Mähler replied to the author [Thayer] in substance: "It was a portrait, which I painted soon after coming to Vienna, in which Beethoven is represented, at nearly full length, sitting; the left hand rests upon a lyre, the right is extended, as if, in a moment of musical enthusiasm, he was beating time; in the background is a temple of Apollo. Oh! If I could but know what became of the picture!"

"What!" was the author's answer, to the great satisfaction of the old gentleman, "the picture is hanging at this moment in the home of Madame van Beethoven, widow, in the Josephstadt, and I have a copy of it."[20]

The extended right hand—though, like the rest of the picture, not very artistically executed—was evidently painted with care. It is rather broad for the length, is muscular and nervous, as the hand of a great pianist necessarily grows through much practice; but, on the whole, is neatly formed and well proportioned. Anatomically, it corresponds so perfectly with all the authentic descriptions of Beethoven's person, that this alone proves it to have

---

[19] See Frimmel, *Beethoven-Studien*, I, 30ff. (TDR, II, 402, n. 1.)

[20] The earlier portrait is in the History Museum in Vienna. Thayer possessed a copy, which is shown in the frontispiece photogravure of this volume. This copy is now owned by the New York Public Library. Frimmel discusses both Beethoven portraits in his *Neue Beethoveniana*, pp. 189ff., *Beethoven-Studien*, II (1905), and *Beethoven-Handbuch*, I, 42 and 44. (Cf. TDR, II, 402, n. 2.)

been copied from nature and not drawn after the painter's fancy. Whoever saw a long delicate hand with fingers exquisitely tapering, like Mendelssohn's, joined to the short stout muscular figure of a Beethoven or a Schubert?

There was, be it noted in passing, a class of good musicians, small in number and exceptional in taste, who, precisely at this time, had discovered a rival to Beethoven, in this his own special field. Thus Gänsbacher writes, as cited by Frölich in his *Biographie Voglers*: "Sonnleithner gave a musical soirée in honor of Vogler and invited Beethoven among others. Vogler improvised at the pianoforte on a theme given to him by Beethoven, 4½ measures long, first an Adagio and then fugued. Vogler then gave Beethoven a theme of three measures (the scale of C major, *alla breve*). Beethoven's excellent pianoforte playing, combined with an abundance of the most beautiful thoughts, surprised me beyond measure, but could not stir up the enthusiasm in me which had been inspired by Vogler's learned playing, which was beyond parallel in respect of its harmonic and contrapuntal treatment."

In this year began the correspondence with Thomson. George Thomson, a Scottish gentleman (born March 4, 1757, at Limekilns, Dunfermline, died at Leith, February 18, 1851), distinguished himself by tastes and acquirements which led to his appointment, when still a young man (1785), as "Secretary to the Board of Trustees for the Encouragement of Arts and Manufactures in Scotland"—a Board established at the time of the Union of Kingdoms (1707) of England and Scotland—an office from which he retired upon a full pension after a service of fifty years. He was, especially, a promoter of all good music and an earnest reviver of ancient Scottish melody. As one means of improving the public taste and at the same time of giving currency to Scottish national airs, he had published sonatas with such melodies for themes, composed for him by Pleyel in Paris, and Koželuch in Vienna—two instrumental composers enjoying then a European reputation now difficult to appreciate. The fame of the new composer at Vienna having now reached Edinburgh, Thomson applied to him for works of a like character. Only the signature of the reply seems to be in Beethoven's hand:

Vienna le 5. 8bre 1803

Monsieur!

J'ai reçu avec bien de plaisir votre lettre du 20 juillet. Entrant volontiers dans vos propositions je dois vous déclarer que je suis prêt de composer pour vous six sonates telles que vous les désirez y introduisant même les airs ecossais d'une manière laquelle la nation ecossaise trouvera la plus favorable et le plus d'accord avec le genie de ses chansons. Quant au honoraire je crois que trois cent ducats pour six sonates ne sera pas trop, vu qu'en Allemagne on me donne autant pour pareil nombre de sonates même sans accompagnement.—

Je vous previens en même tems que vous devez accélérer votre déclaration, par ce qu'on me propose tant d'engagements qu'après quelque temps je ne saurois peutêtre aussitôt satisfaire à vos demandes.—Je vous prie de me pardonner, que cette réponse est si retardée ce qui n'a été causée que par mon sejour à la campagne

et plusieurs occupations très pressantes.—Aimant de préférence les airs ecossais je me plairai particulièrement dans la composition de vos sonates, et j'ose avancer que, si nos intérêts s'accorderont sur l'honoraire, vous serez parfaitement contentés.—
Agrées les assurances de mon Estime distingué.

Louis van Beethoven

Mr. Thomson's endorsement of this letter is this:

5 October 1803. Louis van Beethoven, Vienna, demands 300 ducats for composing six Sonatas for me. Replied 8 Nov. that I wd. give no more than 150, taking 3 of the Sonatas when ready & the other 3 in 6 months after; giving him leave to publish in Germany on his own acct., the day after pubn. in London.

In June, 1804, Beethoven made a second offer of works to Thomson. He was willing to lower the price if a plan were adopted whereby his works would appear simultaneously in Paris, London, Vienna, "or some other towns in Germany."[21] But the sonatas were never composed.

Not long afterwards, on October 22, 1803, Beethoven, enraged at efforts to reprint his works, issued the following characteristic fulmination in large type, filling an entire page of the journal:

WARNING

Herr Carl Zulehner, a reprinter at Mainz, has announced an edition of all my works for pianoforte and string instruments. I hold it to be my duty hereby publicly to inform all friends of music that I have not the slightest part in this edition. I should not have offered to make a collection of my works, a proceeding which I hold to be premature at the best, without first consulting with the publishers and caring for the correctness which is wanting in some of the individual publications. Moreover, I wish to call attention to the fact that the illicit edition in question can never be complete, inasmuch as some new works will soon appear in Paris, which Herr Zulehner, as a French subject, will not be permitted to reprint. I shall soon make full announcement of a collection of my works to be made under my supervision and after a severe revision.

The publication of a complete edition of his compositions was frequently on Beethoven's mind. In 1806 Breitkopf and Härtel tried to get all of Beethoven's works for publication by them; it is likely that similar efforts on the part of Viennese publishers date back as far as 1803. Later the plan played a role in the correspondence with Probst and Simrock. As late as 1824 it was urged by Andreas Streicher. It has already been said that Beethoven at an early date desired to make an arrangement with a publisher by which he might be relieved of anxiety about monetary matters. He wanted to give all his compositions to one publisher, who should pay him a fixed salary.

Alexander Macco, the painter, after executing a portrait of the Queen of Prussia, in 1801, which caused much discussion in the public press but secured to him a pension of 100 thalers, went from Berlin to Dresden and Prague.

[21] See *A*, 89; also MacArdle and Misch, *MQ*, Vol. 41 (1955), pp. 446-48.

In 1803, Macco wrote to Beethoven offering for composition an oratorio text by Prof. A. G. Meissner—a name just then well known in musical circles because of the first volume of the biography of Kapellmeister Naumann. If Meissner had not removed from Prague to Fulda in 1805, and if Europe had remained at peace, perhaps Beethoven might, two or three years later, have availed himself of the offer. Just now he felt bound to decline it, which he did in a letter dated November 2, 1803 for the following reason: ". . . it is impossible for me at this moment to write this oratorio because I am just now *beginning my opera*, which, together with the performance, may occupy me *until Easter.*—If Meissner is not in a hurry to publish his poem I should be glad if he were to leave the composition of it to me. And if the poem is not quite completed, I wish he would not hurry with it, since before or after Easter I would come to Prague and let him hear some of my later compositions, which would make him more familiar with my manner of composition, and would either—inspire him further—or perhaps, make him stop altogether, etc.—"

A letter from Georg August Griesinger to Breitkopf and Härtel, dated November 12, 1803, confirms the fact that Beethoven was working on an opera at last:[22] ". . . would you like me to speak of Beethoven? At present he is composing an opera by Schikaneder, but he told me himself that he is looking for reasonable texts." A second letter written on January 4, 1804, shows how long this labor lasted:[23] "Recently Beethoven has given Schikaneder his opera back because he feels that the text is too ungrateful."

This text was Schikaneder's *Vestas Feuer.*[24] In his *Ein Skizzenbuch von Beethoven aus dem Jahre 1803,*[25] Nottebohm quotes a melodic fragment from one or two pieces which is found to have been sketched for Schikaneder's opera. This is an early form of the main melody of the duet "O namenlose Freude" from *Fidelio.* Thus, some of the work in *Vestas Feuer* was to be reapplied in 1804 to the work on *Fidelio.*[26]

The three[27] great works of the year were the oratorio, the "Kreutzer" Sonata for Violin and the *Sinfonia Eroica.* The title of the second, "Sonata scritta in uno stilo molto concertante quasi come d'un Concerto," is found on the inner side of the last sheet of the sketchbook of 1803 described by Nottebohm.[28] Beethoven wrote the word "brillante" after "stilo" but scratched it out. It is obvious that he wished to emphasize the difference between this

---

[22] Wilhelm Hitzig, "Aus den Briefen Griesingers an Breitkopf und Härtel entnommene Notizen über Beethoven," *Der Bär* (Leipzig, 1927), p. 28.

[23] *Ibid.*, p. 30.

[24] See Raoul Biberhofer, *DM,* Vol. 22 (1930), pp. 409-14; and Willy Hess, *BJ,* 1957-58, pp. 63-106.

[25] Leipzig, 1880, pp. 56-57.

[26] In Rubric II of the sale catalogue of

Beethoven's manuscripts and music, No. 67 is a "Vocal piece with orchestra, complete, but not entirely orchestrated." It is an operatic trio for *Vestas Feuer* using this same melody; the *dramatis personae* are Poros, Volivia and Sartagones. See Appendix C.

[27] Thayer's original text (TK, II, 20) lists "two" great works since he followed Schindler's earlier dating of the oratorio.

[28] *Op.cit.*, p. 74.

Sonata and its predecessors. Simrock's tardiness in publishing the Sonata annoyed Beethoven. He became impatient and wrote to the publisher as follows, under date of October 4, 1804:

Dear, best Herr Simrock:

I have been waiting with longing for the Sonata which I gave you—but in vain—please write what is the state of things concerning it—whether or not you. accepted it from me merely as food for moths—or do you wish to obtain a special Imperial privilegium in connection with it?—Well, it seems to me that might have been accomplished long ago.—

Where in hiding is this slow devil—who is to drive out the sonata?—You are generally the quick devil, are known as Faust once was as being in league with the imp of darkness, and for this reason you are *loved* by your comrades. But again—where in hiding is your devil—or what kind of a devil is it—that sits on my sonata and with whom *you* have not come to an agreement?— Hurry, then, and tell me when I shall see the s[onata] given to the light of day— When you have told me the date I will at once send you a little note to *Kreutzer,* which you will please be kind enough to enclose when you send him a copy (as you in any event will send your copies to Paris or even, perhaps, have them printed there)—This *Kreutzer* is a dear, good fellow who during his stay here[29] gave me much pleasure. I prefer his unassuming manner and unaffectedness to *all the extérieur* without *intérieur* of most virtuosi— As the sonata was written for a thoroughly capable violinist, the dedication to him is all the more appropriate— Although we correspond with each other (i.e., a letter from me once a year)—I hope that he will not have learned anything about it yet— I hear that you are improving your lot more and more; that makes me heartily glad.— Greet every-one in your family and all others whom you think would enjoy a greeting from me.— Please answer soon.

Your Beethoven

Concerning the smaller works of the year, a few details may be noted:

The duet "Nei giorno tuoi felici," for Soprano and Tenor with Orchestra, on a text by Metastasio, was composed around the beginning of the year. The work was first published in 1939 by Willy Hess (Eulenberg) from the auto-graph in the Berlin Public Library.

The Six Songs on poems by Chr. F. Gellert are dedicated to Count Browne, and were very likely occasioned, believes Kinsky-Halm, by the death of Countess Browne on May 13th.[30]

The song "Der Wachtelschlag" on a poem by S. Fr. Sauter has the follow-ing inscription on its autograph: "Der Wachtelschleg komponirt für den Grafen Browne von Ludwig van Beethoven 1803."[31]

The melody of the song "Das Glück der Freundschaft" appears in its final shape in the "Eroica" sketchbook.[32] This draft is to be dated before October since in this month the song was published.

---

[29] Kreutzer came to Vienna with Bernadotte in 1798. (Cf. TK, II, 21.)
[30] See KHV, p. 113.

[31] *Ibid.,* p. 591.
[32] Nottebohm, *op.cit.,* p. 56.

The third March for Pianoforte, Four Hands was completed probably in the early summer and all three were offered to Breitkopf and Härtel in September.

The Seven Variations on "God Save the King" and Five Variations on "Rule Britannia" were offered to Breitkopf and Härtel in September.

The arrangement of the Septet, Op. 20, as a trio for Pianoforte, Clarinet or Violin, and Violoncello (Op. 38) was completed this year at the latest, since its publication was announced, though prematurely, in the *Zeitung für die Elegante Welt* on November 8.

The works completed in 1803 were:

1799-1803. Song. "Ich denke dein" (Goethe), with Six Variations for Pianoforte Four Hands, WoO 74. (Variations 3 and 4 by September, 1803; the rest in 1799.)

1802-1803. "Nei giorni" for Soprano and Tenor with Orchestra (Metastasio), WoO 93.

Sonata for Pianoforte and Violin, Op. 47.

Three Marches for Pianoforte, Four Hands, Op. 45.

Trio for Pianoforte, Clarinet or Violin, and Violoncello, from the Septet, Op. 20.

1803. "Das Glück der Freundschaft," Op. 88.

"Der Wachtelschlag" (S. F. Sauter), WoO 129.

Oratorio, *Christus am Ölberg* (F. X. Huber), Op. 85.

Six Songs by C. F. Gellert, Op. 48:

"Bitten"

"Die Liebe des Nächsten"

"Vom Tode"

"Die Ehre Gottes aus der Natur"

"Gottes Macht und Vorsehung"

"Busslied"

Symphony No. 3 in E-flat major, Op. 55.

Variations for the Pianoforte on "God Save the King," WoO 78.

Variations for Pianoforte on "Rule Britannia," WoO 79.

The publications for the year were:

By Artaria:

Six Songs by Gellert for Voice and Pianoforte, Op. 48, dedicated to Count Johann Georg von Browne.

By Breitkopf and Härtel in Leipzig:

Six Variations for Pianoforte, Op. 34, dedicated to Princess Barbara Odescalchi.

Variations for Pianoforte, Op. 35, dedicated to Count Moritz Lichnowsky.

By Hoffmeister and Kühnel in Leipzig:

Romance for Violin and Orchestra, Op. 40.

Two Preludes through all the 12 Major Keys, Op. 39.

By Kunst- und Industrie-Comptoir:

Seven Bagatelles for Pianoforte, Op. 33.

Three Sonatas for Violin and Pianoforte, Op. 30, dedicated to Emperor Alexander I of Russia.

By Löschenkohl:

"Das Glück der Freundschaft."[33]

By Nägeli in Zurich:

Two Sonatas for Pianoforte, Op. 31, Nos. 1 and 2; in *Répertoire des Clavecinistes*.

By Traeg:

Two Songs: "Zärtliche Liebe" (Karl Fr. Herrosee), WoO 123, and "La Partenza" (Metastasio), WoO 124.

---

[33] At a later date the song received the opus number 88.

CHAPTER XVII

THE YEAR 1804

BEGINNING OF WORK ON "LEONORE"— THE "EROICA" PRIVATELY PERFORMED—BEETHOVEN AND BREUNING— FRIENDSHIP WITH COUNTESS DEYM

DURING the winter of 1803-1804 negotiations were in progress the result of which was to put an end for the present to Beethoven's operatic aspirations. ⸙As we have seen, before January he had abandoned work on Schikaneder's *Vestas Feuer* because "the text is too ungrateful." Johann Friedrich Rochlitz, editor of the Leipzig *Allgemeine Musikalische Zeitung*, meanwhile, had sent the first act of a libretto, which because of its subject matter, Beethoven had been compelled to return to him. In a letter to Rochlitz dated January 4, 1804, he also announced that he had broken completely with Schikaneder and was now beginning work on "an old French libretto."[1]⸙ For a background to these negotiations let Treitschke, a personal actor in the scenes, explain:[2] "On February 24, 1801, the first performance of *Die Zauberflöte* took place in the Royal Imperial Court Theatre beside the Kärnthnerthor. Orchestra and chorus as well as the representatives of Sarastro (Weinmüller), the Queen of Night (Mme. Rosenbaum), Pamina (Demoiselle Saal) and the Moor (Lippert) were much better than before. It remained throughout the year the only admired German opera. The loss of large receipts and the circumstance that many readings were changed, the dialogue shortened and the name of the author omitted from all mention, angered S. [Schikaneder] greatly. He did not hesitate to give free vent to his gall, and to parody some of the vulnerable passages in the performance. Thus

[1] See *A*, 87a.
[2] *Orpheus*, 1841, p. 248. Georg Friedrich Treitschke (1776-1842) was poet and stage-

manager of the Court Opera (TDR, II, 416, n. 1, 438.)

the change of costume accompanying the metamorphosis of the old woman into Papagena seldom succeeded. Schikaneder, when he repeated the opera at his theatre, sent a couple of tailors on to the stage who slowly accompanied the disrobing, etc. These incidents would be trifles had they not been followed by such significant consequences; for from that time dated the hatred and jealousy which existed between the German operas of the two theatres, which alternately persecuted every novelty and ended in Baron von Braun, then manager of the Court Theatre, purchasing the Theater-an-der-Wien in 1804, by which act everything came under the staff of a single shepherd but never became a single flock."

Zitterbarth had, some months before, purchased of Schikaneder all his rights in the property, paying him 100,000 florins for the privilegium alone; and, therefore, being absolute master, "had permitted a dicker down to the sum of 1,060,000 florins Vienna standard. . . . The contract was signed on February 11th and on the 16th the Theater-an-der-Wien under the new arrangement was opened with Méhul's opera *Ariodante*."[3]

Zitterbarth had retained Schikaneder as director; but now Baron Braun dismissed him, and the Secretary of the Court Theatres, Joseph von Sonnleithner, for the present acted in that capacity. Before proceeding, a word upon Sonnleithner may be permitted. The eldest son, born 1766, of Christoph Sonnleithner, Doctor of Laws and Dean of the Juridical Faculty at Vienna, Joseph Ferdinand by name, was educated to his father's profession, and early rose to the positions of Circuit Commissioner and Royal Imperial Court Scrivener (*Kreis-Kommissär und K. K. Hof-Concipist*). All the Sonnleithners, from Dr. Christoph down to the excellent and beloved representative of the family, Leopold, his grandson who died in 1873, have stood in the front ranks of musical dilettanti, as composers, singers, instrumental performers and writers on topics pertaining to the art. Joseph Ferdinand was no exception. He gave his attention particularly to musical and theatrical literature, edited the Court Theatre Calendars, 1794-95, so highly lauded by Gerber, and prepared himself by appropriate studies to carry out Forkel's plan of a "History of Music in Examples," which was to reach the great extent of 50 volumes, folio. To this end he spent nearly three years, 1798-1802, in an extensive tour through northern Europe making collections of rare, old music. Upon his return to Vienna, resigning this project again into the hands of Forkel, he became one of the earliest partners, if not one of the founders, of the publishing house known as the "Kunst- und Industrie-Comptoir" (Bureau d'Arts et d'Industrie), of which Schreyvogel was the recognized head. The latter had been appointed Secretary of the Court Theatre in 1802, but resigned, and, on February 14, 1804, Sonnleithner "was appointed, and on this account was most honorably retired from his former post as Court Scrivener." On what grounds he has been called an "actor" (*Schauspieler*) is unknown.

[3]*AMZ*, Vol. 24, p. 320, TDR, II, 417, n. 1.

In Paris, at the close of the 18th century, Shakespeare's "being taken by the insolent foe and redemption thence" was by far the most popular subject for the stage. Doubtless so many facts stranger than fiction in recent narratives of escape from dungeon and guillotine, rendered doubly fascinating by beautiful exhibitions of disinterested affection, exalted generosity and heroic self-sacrifice, were not without their effect upon public taste. Certain it is that no other class of subjects is so numerously represented in the French drama of that precise period as this. *Les deux Journées* by J. N. Bouilly stands confessedly at its head. In Beethoven's opinion in 1823, this and *La Vestale* were the two best texts then ever written. Two years before *Les deux Journées*—that is, on February 19, 1798—the same poet had produced another of that class of texts, which, if less abounding in pleasing and exciting scenes, still contained one supreme moment that cannot readily find its like. This was *Léonore, ou l'Amour conjugal*; the seventeenth and best in Fétis' list of Pierre Gaveaux's thirty-five operas and operettas.

Gaveaux was a singer at the Théâtre Feydeau in Paris—a man of no great musical science, but gifted with a natural talent for melody and for pleasing though not always correct instrumentation, which secured the suffrages of the Feydeau audience for nearly all the long list of his productions. These were mostly short pieces in one act, in which he wrote the principal tenor part for himself. His *Le petit Matelot* (1794), as *Der kleine Matrose*, became immediately popular throughout Germany; Rellstab at Berlin published a pianoforte arrangement of it in 1798; and it so endured the fluctuations in public taste as still to be performed at Frankfurt-am-Main in 1846. This was followed by his *L'Amour filial* and others, so that, in short, whatever faults the critics found in his music, he was one of those French composers to whose productions the managers of German opera houses ever had an eye. As the *Léonore* was published in score soon after its production, the names of its authors, Bouilly and Gaveau, as well as its success at the Théâtre Feydeau, ensured its becoming known in Germany. But for the use of its subject first by Paër and then by Beethoven, it might perhaps have been simply translated and performed with the original music.

As it was, the Italian composer, Ferdinando Paër, who became Hofkapellmeister at Dresden in 1802, took up the Leonore plot, rewritten in Italian, and composed his *Leonora, ossia l'amore conjugale*, which was first performed in Dresden on October 3, 1804.[4] Meanwhile, Sonnleithner undertook the translation of the Bouilly text into German, and Beethoven set to work at once to collaborate with the Court Secretary. The start of Beethoven's work on the "Leonore" subject can be dated January, 1804, from the letter written by the composer to Rochlitz. A short time afterwards he wrote a letter to his new collaborator which is interesting enough to be quoted in full:[5]

---

[4] According to Engländer (*NBJ*, IV, 119) the author was probably Paër's close associate, the singer Giacomo Cinti.

[5] Unger, "Zur Entstehungs- und Aufführungsgeschichte von Beethovens Oper Leonore," *Zeitschrift für Musik*, Vol. 105 (1938), p. 133.

Dear Sonnleithner!

Since it is so difficult to talk with you, I prefer to write you about the things which we have to discuss.— Yesterday I again received a letter concerning my trip which makes my decision about it unshakable.[6]— Now I beg you most sincerely to see to it that *the poetical part* of the libretto is ready by the *middle of next April*, so that I can continue to work and the opera can be performed by June at the latest, so that I myself can help you in performance.— My brother has told you of my changing lodgings; I have occupied this one conditionally until a better one can be found. The chance came already some time ago and I wanted to assert my right then with *Zitterbarth*, at which point Baron Braun became owner of the theatre.—The rooms occupied by the *painter* above and which are clearly adequate only for a servant, need only to be vacated, then my apartment could be granted to the painter, and the affair would be settled.— Since in my apartment the servant must sleep in the kitchen, the servant I now have is already my third—and this one will not stay long with me either; without considering its other inconveniences.— I know beforehand that if it depends upon the decision of Hr. *Baron* again, the answer will be *no*. In that case I shall look for something elsewhere immediately. Already I am used to the fact that he has nothing good to say about me—let it be—*I shall never grovel*—my world is elsewhere.— Now I expect *an answer from you* on this—meanwhile I do not want to stay an hour longer in this fatal hole. *My brother* told me that according to your complaint I am supposed to have spoken against you, but don't listen to miserable *gossip* at the *theatre*.— The one thing which I find at fault with you is that you listen too much to what *some people* say which they certainly don't deserve.— Forgive my frankness.—

Faithfully your Beethoven

This letter shows first that Beethoven was ready to set the text, waiting only for it to be sent to him; and second that only the "Poetical part of the libretto" was to be set to music.

However, the sale of the theatre made void the contracts with Vogler and Beethoven, except as to the first of Vogler's three operas, *Samori* (text by Huber), which being ready was put into rehearsal and produced May 7th. It was no time for Baron Braun, with three theatres on his hands, to make new contracts with composers, until the reins were fairly in his grasp, and the affairs of the new purchase brought into order and in condition to work smoothly; nor was there any necessity of haste. The repertoire was so well supplied that the new list of pieces for the year reached the number of forty-three, of which eighteen were operas or *Singspiele*.

Therefore Beethoven, who had already occupied the free lodgings in the theatre building for the year which his contract with Zitterbarth and Schikaneder granted him, was compelled to move. Stephan von Breuning even then lived in the house in which in 1827 he died. It was the large pile of building belonging to the Esterhazy estates, known as "das rothe Haus,"

[6] Unger, *ibid.*, believes that the projected journey was to Paris where Beethoven's friends, the pianist Louis Adam, the violinist Rudolph Kreutzer, and the pianoforte maker Sebastian Erard were. This is the only mention of such a trip.

which stood at a right angle to the Schwarzspanier house and church, and fronted upon the open space where now stands the new Votiv-Kirche. Here also Beethoven now took apartments.

It is worth noting that this was the year—October, 1803 to October, 1804—of C. M. von Weber's first visit to Vienna, and of his studies under Vogler. He was then but eighteen years old and the "delicate little man" made no very favorable impression upon Beethoven. But at a later period, when Weber's noble dramatic talent became developed and known, no former prejudice prevented the great symphonist's due appreciation and hearty acknowledgement of it.

Among the noted strangers who came to Vienna this spring was Clementi. According to Czerny, "He sent word to Beethoven that he would like to see him. 'Clementi will have to wait a long time before Beethoven goes to see him,' was the reply." Ries has this to say (*Notizen*, p. 101): "When Clementi came to Vienna, Beethoven wanted to go to him at once, but his brother put it into his head that Clementi ought to make the first visit. Though much older Clementi would probably have done so had not gossip begun to concern itself with the matter. Thus it came about that Clementi was in Vienna a long time without knowing Beethoven except by sight. Often we dined at the same table in the Swan, Clementi with his pupil Klengel and Beethoven with me; all knew each other but no one spoke to the other, or confined himself to a greeting. The two pupils had to imitate their masters, because they feared they would otherwise lose their lessons. This would surely have been the case with me because there was no possibility of a middle way with Beethoven."

The great accomplishment of the year 1803 had been the writing of the Symphony No. 3, the story of which must now be told. Sketches for all four movements are to be found in the so-called "Eroica" sketchbook described by Nottebohm in *Ein Skizzenbuch von Beethoven aus den Jahre 1803*.[7] They occupy the first part of the sketchbook, after which come sketches for the Schikaneder opera, with which, as we have seen, Beethoven was at work in November. Thus, Max Unger[8] dates the main composition period of the symphony from about May to November, 1803. The final shaping of the work probably extended into the beginning of 1804.

Early in the spring a fair copy of the *Sinfonia Eroica* had been made to be forwarded to Paris through the French embassy, so Moritz Lichnowsky informed Schindler. Ries says (*Notizen*, p. 78): "In this symphony Beethoven had Buonaparte in his mind, but as he was when he was First Consul. Beethoven esteemed him greatly at the time and likened him to the greatest Roman consuls. I as well as several of his more intimate friends saw a copy of the score lying upon his table, with the word 'Buonaparte' at the extreme

[7] Leipzig, 1880. Reprinted by P. Mies in *Zwei Skizzenbücher von Beethoven* (Leipzig, 1924).

[8] See the *AMZ* (Berlin), Vol. 67 (1940), p. 114.

top of the title page, and at the extreme bottom 'Luigi van Beethoven,' but not another word. Whether, and with what the space between was to be filled out, I do not know. I was the first to bring him the intelligence that Buonaparte had proclaimed himself emperor, whereupon he flew into a rage and cried out: 'Is he then, too, nothing more than an ordinary human being? Now he, too, will trample on all the rights of man and indulge only his ambition. He will exalt himself above all others, become a tyrant!' Beethoven went to the table, took hold of the title page by the top, tore it in two and threw it on the floor. The first page was rewritten and only then did the symphony receive the title: 'Sinfonia eroica.'"

There can be no mistake in this; for Count Moritz Lichnowsky, who happened to be with Beethoven when Ries brought the offensive news, described the scene to Schindler years before the publication of the *Notizen*.

The acts of the French Tribunate and Senate, which elevated the First Consul to the dignity of Emperor, are dated May 3, 4 and 17. Napoleon's assumption of the crown occurred on the 18th and the solemn proclamation was issued on the 20th. Even in those days, news of so important an event would not have required ten days to reach Vienna. At the very latest, then, a fair copy of the *Sinfonia Eroica* was complete early in May, 1804. That it was a copy, the two credible witnesses, Ries and Lichnowsky, attest. Beethoven's own score—purchased at the sale in 1827, for 3 fl. 10 kr., Vienna standard (less than 3½ francs), by the Viennese composer Hr. Joseph Dessauer—could not have been the one referred to above. It is, from beginning to end, disfigured by erasures and corrections, and the title page could never have answered to Ries's description. It is this:

[At the top:]   N.B. 1. Cues for the other instruments are
to be written into the first violin part.
SINFONIA GRANDE
[here two words are erased]
$\overline{804}$ im August
de Sigr
Louis van Beethoven
Sinfonie 3   Op. 55
[At the bottom:] N.B. 2. The third horn is so written that it
can be played by by[*sic*] a primario as well
as a secundario.

A note to the funeral march is evidently a direction to the copyist, as are the remarks on the title page: "N.B. The notes in the bass which have stems upwards are for the Violoncellos, those downward for the bass-viol."

One of the two words erased from the title was "Bonaparte"; and just under his own name Beethoven wrote with a lead pencil in large letters, nearly obliterated but still legible, "Composed on Bonaparte." The date "804 im August" is written with a different ink, darker than the rest of the title, and may have been inserted long afterwards, Beethoven's memory playing him false. —•ᶴ{This copy now belongs to the Gesellschaft der Musikfreunde.}ᶳ•—

"Afterwards," continues Ries, "Prince Lobkowitz bought this composition for several years' [?] use, and it was performed several times in his palace." In December the famous Munich oboist Ramm was in Vienna and took part with Beethoven in one of Prince Lobkowitz's concerts.

"Here it happened that Beethoven, who was directing [the Eroica] himself, in the second part of the first Allegro where the music is pursued for so many measures in half-notes against the beat, threw the orchestra off in such a way that a new beginning had to be made.

"In the first Allegro occurs a mischievous whim (*böse Laune*) of Beethoven's for the first horn; in the second part, several measures before the theme recurs in its entirety, Beethoven has the horn suggest it at a place where the two violins are still holding a second chord. To one unfamiliar with the score this must always sound as if the horn player had made a miscount and entered at the wrong place. At the first rehearsal of the symphony, which was horrible, but at which the horn player made his entry correctly, I stood beside Beethoven, and, thinking that a blunder had been made I said: 'Can't the damned hornist count?—it sounds infamously false!' I think I came pretty close to receiving a box on the ear. Beethoven did not forgive the slip for a long time.

"On the same evening he played his Quintet for Pianoforte and Wind-Instruments with Ramm as soloist. In the last Allegro there are several holds before the theme is resumed. At one of these Beethoven suddenly began to improvise, took the Rondo for a theme and entertained himself and the others for a considerable time, but not the other players. They were displeased and Ramm even very angry. It was really very comical to see them, momentarily expecting the performance to be resumed, put their instruments to their mouths, only to put them down again. At length Beethoven was satisfied and dropped into the Rondo. The whole company was transported with delight."[9]

There is an anecdote told by a person who enjoyed Beethoven's society," in Schmidt's *Wiener Musik-Zeitung* (1843, p. 28),[10] according to which, as may readily be believed, this new symphony, then so difficult, new, original, strange in its effects and of such unusual lengths, did not please. "Some time after this humiliating failure Prince Louis Ferdinand of Prussia paid a visit to the same cavalier [Lobkowitz] at his country seat." To give him a surprise, the new, and of course, to him utterly unknown symphony, was

---

[9] Ries, *Notizen*, pp. 79-80. (TDR, II, 47.) To get a better idea of this concert, the present editor visited the room in the Lobkowitz palace in Vienna and found the measurements to be about 54 by 24 feet! At each end doors lead off to smaller rooms where it would seem

that the "Eroica" in particular would have been heard to much greater advantage.

[10] Dr. Schmidt is of the opinion that this anecdote was contributed to his journal by Hieronymous Payer, certainly good authority. (TDR, II, 427, n. 1.)

played to the Prince, who "listened to it with tense attention which grew with every movement." At the close he proved his admiration by requesting the favor of an immediate repetition; and, after an hour's pause, as his stay was too limited to admit of another concert, a second. "The impression made by the music was general and its lofty contents were now recognized."

Two works, composed between the fall of 1803 and 1804, should be mentioned here. The first is the Piano Sonata, Op. 53, which was dedicated to Count Waldstein, and the second is the Concerto for Violin, Violoncello and Piano with orchestra, which was probably written with Beethoven's piano student, the Archduke Rudolph, in mind.

After Beethoven had arrived in Vienna, he saw little of Count Waldstein, who was traveling between the years 1795 and 1809; but through the connections that the Waldstein family had with other nobility in Vienna, Beethoven had been able quickly to establish contacts with aristocratic patrons.

The middle movement of this sonata was originally to have been an Andante, and sketches for this as well as the first and last movements are to be found in the latter part of the so-called "Eroica" sketchbook.[11]

Ries reports (*Notizen*, p. 101) that a friend of Beethoven's said to him that the Sonata was too long, for which he was terribly taken to task by the composer. But after quiet reflection Beethoven was convinced of the correctness of the criticism. The Andante in F major was therefore excluded and its place supplied by the interesting Introduction to the Rondo which it now has. A year after the publication of the Sonata, the Andante also appeared separately. In these particulars Ries is confirmed by Czerny, who adds: "Because of its popularity (for Beethoven played it frequently in society) he gave it the title 'Andante favori.' I am the more sure of this since Beethoven sent me the proof together with the manuscript for revision."

Of the Andante Ries continues: "This Andante has left a painful memory in me. When Beethoven played it for the first time to our friend Krumpholtz and me, it delighted us greatly and we teased him until he repeated it. Passing the door of Prince Lichnowsky's house (by the Schottenthor) on my way home I went in to tell the Prince of the new and glorious composition of Beethoven's, and was persuaded to play it as well as I could remember it. Recalling more and more of it the Prince urged me to repeat it. In this way it happened that the Prince also learned a portion of the piece. To give Beethoven a surprise the Prince went to him the next day and said that he too had composed something which was not at all bad. In spite of Beethoven's remark that he did not want to hear it the Prince sat down and to the amazement of the composer played a goodly portion of the Andante. Beethoven was greatly angered, and this was the reason why I *never again heard Beethoven play*."

Sketches for the first movement of the Triple Concerto, Op. 56 appear on the last three pages of the "Eroica" sketchbook. Further work on all

[11] Nottebohm, *op.cit.*, pp. 61-66.

movements is sandwiched in at different places in the so-called "Leonora" sketchbook, which Nottebohm dates 1804.[12] According to Schindler[13] the work was written for Archduke Rudolph, the violinist Seidler and the cellist Kraft. However, the work was dedicated to Prince Lobkowitz.

The concerto was offered as early as October 14, 1803, to Breitkopf and Härtel by brother Carl, although at this time it is unlikely that Beethoven had more than the form of the work in his mind.[14] As we shall see, the composer himself was offering it to the same firm ten months later.

It was bad economy for two young, single men, each to have and pay for a complete suite of apartments in the same house, especially for two who were connected by so many ties of friendship as Breuning and Beethoven. Either lodging contained ample room for both; and Beethoven therefore very soon gave up his and moved into the other. Breuning had his own housekeeper and cook and they also usually dined together at home. This arrangement had hardly been effected when Beethoven was seized with a severe sickness, which when conquered still left him the victim of an obstinate intermittent fever.

Every language has its proverbs to the effect that he who serves not himself is ill served. So Beethoven discovered, when it was too late, that due notice had not been given to the agent of Esterhazy, and that he was bound for the rent of the apartments previously occupied. The question, who was at fault, came up one day at dinner in the beginning of July, and ended in a sudden quarrel in which Beethoven became so angry as to leave the table and the house and retire to Baden with the determination to sacrifice the rent here and pay for another lodging, rather than remain under the same roof with Breuning. "Breuning," says Ries,[15] "a hot-head like Beethoven, grew so enraged at Beethoven's conduct because the incident occurred in the presence of his brother." It is clear, however, that he soon became cool and instantly did his best to prevent the momentary breach from becoming permanent, by writing—as may be gathered from Beethoven's allusions to it—a manly, sensible and friendly invitation to forgive and forget. But Beethoven, worn with illness, his nerves unstrung, made restless, unhappy, petulant by his increasing deafness, was for a time obstinate. His wrath must run its course. It found vent in the following letters to Ries, and then the paroxysm soon passed. The first of these letters was written in July, 1804.

Dear Riess,

Since Breuning did not scruple by his conduct to present my character to you and the landlord as that of a miserable, beggarly, contemptible fellow, I have picked you out first to give my answer to B. by word of mouth. I answer only to one, to the first point of his letter, just in order to vindicate my character in your eyes— Say to him, then, that it never occurred to me to reproach him because of the tardiness of the notice, and that, if B were really to blame for it, each

---

[12] *II Beeth.*, pp. 418-19. (TDR, II, 448.) [14] See TDR, II, 620-21.
[13] *Biographie*, p. 147. [15] *Notizen*, p. 132. (Cf. TDR, II, 429.)

friendly relationship in the world means too much to me for me to give offense to one of my friends because of a few hundred or even more. You know yourself that, in a jocular way, I accused you of being to blame that the notice did not arrive on time. I am sure that you will remember this. I had forgotten all about the matter.— Then my brother began talking at the table and said that he believed it was B's fault; I denied it at once and said that *you* were to blame. It seems to me that this was clear enough to show that I did not hold B to blame. Thereupon B jumped up like a madman and said he would call up the landlord. This conduct to which I am unaccustomed from any of the persons with whom I associate made me lose my self-control; I also jumped up, upset my chair, went away—and did not return.— This behavior induced B to put me in such a light before you and the caretaker, and to write me *a letter* also which I have answered only with silence— I have nothing more to say to Breuning. His mode of thought and action in regard to me proves that there never ought to have been a friendly relationship between us, and such will certainly not exist in the future.—

I have told you all this because your statements have debased my whole way of thinking and acting. I know that if you had known the facts you certainly would not have made them, and this satisfies me.—

And now, I ask you, dear Ries, immediately on receipt of this letter to go to my brother, the apothecary, and tell him that I shall leave Baden in a few days and that he must engage the lodgings in Döbling the moment you have let him know.— I very nearly came today; I am tired of being here, it revolts me.— Urge him for heaven's sake to rent the lodgings at once because I want to get into them immediately.— Tell B nothing and do not show him any part of what is written on the other page. I want to show him from all points of view that I am not so small-minded as he and have written him only after writing this letter to you, although my resolution to end our friendship is and will remain firm.

Your friend
Beethoven

Not long thereafter there followed a second letter:

Baden, July 14, 1804.

If you, dear Riess, are able to find better quarters I shall be glad. Therefore you must tell my brothers that you are not renting these right away— I should very much like to have them on a large quiet square or on the Bastei.— That my brother hasn't yet attended to the wine is unforgivable, since it is so necessary and beneficial for me. I shall take care to be at the rehearsal on Wednesday. I am not happy over the fact that it is at Schuppanzigh's. He ought to be grateful if the humiliations from me make him thinner.— Farewell, dear Riess. We are having bad weather here and I am not safe from people; I must flee in order to be alone.

Your true friend L. v. Beethoven

From a third letter, dated "Baden, July 24, 1804," Ries prints the following excerpt (*Notizen*, pp. 132-34): ". . . No doubt you were surprised at the Breuning affair, believe me, dear friend, my eruption was only the outburst resulting from many unpleasant encounters with him in the past. I have the talent in many cases of being able to conceal my sensitiveness and to repress it; but if I am irritated at a time when I am more susceptible than usual to anger, I burst out more violently than anyone else. Breuning certainly has excellent qualities, but he thinks he is free from all faults, and his greatest ones are those which he thinks he sees in others. He has a spirit of pettiness which I have despised since childhood. My judgement almost predicted the course which affairs would take with Breuning, since our modes of thinking, acting and feeling are so different. However, I thought these difficulties might also be overcome—experience has refuted me. And now, no more friendship! I have found only two friends in the world with whom I have never had a misunderstanding, but what men! One is dead, the other still lives.[16] Although we have not known anything of each other for nearly six years I know that I occupy the first place in his heart as he does in mine. The foundation of friendship demands the greatest similarity between the hearts and souls of men. I ask only that you read the letter which I wrote to Breuning and his letter to me. No, he shall never again hold the place in my heart which he once occupied. He who can think a friend capable of such base thoughts and be guilty of such base conduct towards him is not worthy of my friendship. . . ."

The reader knows too well the character of Breuning to be prejudiced against him by all these harsh expressions written by Beethoven in a fit of choler of which he heartily repented and "brought forth fruits meet for repentance." But, as Ries says, "these letters together with their consequences are too beautiful a testimony to Beethoven's character to be omitted here," the more so as they introduce, by the allusions in them, certain matters of more or less interest from the *Notizen*. Ries writes (pp. 117-18):

"One evening I came to Baden to continue my lessons. There I found a handsome young woman sitting on the sofa with him. Thinking I might be intruding I wanted to go at once, but Beethoven detained me and said: 'Play for the time being.' He and the lady remained seated behind me. I had already played for a long time when Beethoven suddenly called out: 'Ries, play some love music'; a little later, 'Something melancholy!' then, 'Something passionate!' etc.

"From what I heard I could come to the conclusion that in some manner he must have offended the lady and was trying to make amends by an exhibition of good humor. At last he jumped up and shouted: 'Why, all those things are by me!' I had played nothing but movements from his works, connecting them with short transition phrases, which seemed to please him. The lady soon went away and to my great amazement Beethoven did not know who she was. I learned that she had come in shortly before me in order to make Beethoven's acquaintance. We followed her in order to discover her lodgings and later her station. We saw her from a distance (it was moon-

---

[16] Lorenz von Breuning (1777-1798) and probably Karl Amenda (1771-1836).

light),[17] but suddenly she disappeared. Chatting on all manner of topics we walked for an hour and a half in the beautiful valley adjoining. On going, however, Beethoven said: 'I must find out who she is and you must help me.' A long time afterward I met her in Vienna and discovered that she was the mistress of a foreign prince. I reported the intelligence to Beethoven, but never heard anything more about her either from him or anybody else."

The rehearsal at Schuppanzigh's on "Wednesday" (18th) mentioned in the letter of July 14th, was for the benefit of Ries, who was to play in the first of the second series of the regular Augarten Thursday concerts which took place the next day (19th). Ries says on pages 113-114 of the *Notizen*: "Beethoven had given me his beautiful Concerto in C minor (Op. 37) in manuscript so that I might make my first public appearance *as his pupil* with it; and I am the only one who ever appeared as such while Beethoven was alive. . . . Beethoven himself conducted, but he only turned the pages and never, perhaps, was a concerto more beautifully accompanied. We had two large rehearsals. I had asked Beethoven to write a cadenza for me, but he refused and told me to write one myself and he would correct it. Beethoven was satisfied with my composition and made few changes; but there was an extremely brilliant and very difficult passage in it, which, though he liked it, seemed to him too venturesome, wherefore he told me to write another in its place. A week before the concert he wanted to hear the cadenza again. I played it and floundered in the passage; he again, this time a little ill-naturedly, told me to change it. I did so, but the new passage did not satisfy me; I therefore studied the other, and zealously, but was not quite sure of it. When the cadenza was reached in the public concert Beethoven quietly sat down. I could not persuade myself to choose the easier one. When I boldly began the more difficult one, Beethoven violently jerked his chair; but the cadenza went through all right and Beethoven was so delighted that he shouted 'Bravo!' loudly. This electrified the entire audience and at once gave me a standing among the artists. Afterward, while expressing his satisfaction he added: 'But all the same you are willful! If you had made a slip in the passage I would never have given you another lesson.'"

A little farther on in his book Ries writes (p. 115): "The pianoforte part of the C minor Concerto was *never completely written out* in the score; Beethoven wrote it down on separate sheets of paper expressly for me." This confirms Seyfried, as quoted on a previous page.

"Not on my life would I have believed that I could be so lazy as I am here. If it is followed by an outburst of industry, something worth while may be accomplished," Beethoven wrote at the end of his letter of July 24. He was right. His brother Johann secured for him the lodging at Döbling,[18] where he passed the rest of the summer and worked on the two Sonatas, Op. 54 and 57, certainly "something worth while."

---

[17] "Full moon, July 22," almanac of 1804. (TDR, II, 433, n. 1.)

[18] Presumably the same as the summer before.

→·❧[Sketches for both sonatas interrupt those for the opera in the "Leonore" sketchbook. Amidst work on the first finale there are sketches for the second movement of the first sonata; and sketches in connection with all movements of the second sonata are sandwiched in to plans for the last act.]❧·—

In one of the long walks described by Ries (*Notizen*, p. 99), "in which we went so far astray that we did not get back to Döbling, where Beethoven lived, until nearly 8 o'clock, he had been all the time humming and sometimes howling, always up and down, without singing any definite notes. In answer to my question what it was he said: 'A theme for the last movement of the sonata has occurred to me' (in F Minor, Op. 57). When we entered the room he ran to the pianoforte without taking off his hat. I took a seat in the corner and he soon forgot all about me. Now he stormed for at least an hour with the beautiful finale of the sonata. Finally he got up, was surprised still to see me and said: 'I cannot give you a lesson today, I must do some more work.' "

→·❧[The sonata was included in a group of works about which Beethoven wrote Breitkopf and Härtel on August 26, 1804. He offered the following— *Christus am Ölberg*, Symphony No. 3, the Triple Concerto, and the Piano Sonatas, Op. 53, 54 and 57—for 2000 florins "because I want a speedy edition made of my works." About the oratorio, Beethoven explained that it had not yet been published because of revisions including a new chorus; ". . . therefore I have held it back; these changes were made after the time when my brother wrote to you about it." Caspar had written on November 23, 1803; sketches for the revision appear at the end of the "Eroica" sketchbook. Beethoven continues: "The Symphony is entitled *Bonaparte*; besides the regularly used instruments there are in particular three horns obbligato— I believe this will interest the musical public.— I would like you to publish it *in score* instead of in printed parts."[19]

Breitkopf and Härtel were interested and Caspar wrote on September 24 that there would be a delay because there was only one copyist and his brother was too busy writing an opera to oversee the work. Negotiations dragged on into 1805. In a letter dated April 18, Beethoven wrote that because of the amount of work the copyists had he could not promise either Op. 56 or 57 for four to six weeks, but he hoped that publication would proceed on the Symphony and the two sonatas (Op. 53 and 54) which the firm had already received. As for the oratorio, it would be ready at the end of the month. The publishers, however, grew tired of waiting, sent back the music in June and abandoned the whole plan. It was not until the fall of 1806 that Beethoven finally delivered the manuscript of Op. 57 to its eventual publishers, the Kunst- und Industrie-Comptoir.]❧·—

Ries had in the meantime fulfilled Beethoven's wish for a new lodging on the ramparts, by engaging one for him on the Mölkerbastei, three or four houses only from Prince Lichnowsky, in the Pasqualati house—"from the

[19] See TDR, II, 623.

fourth story of which there was a beautiful view," namely, over the broad Glacis, the northwestern suburb of the city and the mountains in the distance. "He moved out of this several times," says Ries, "but always returned to it, so that, as I afterwards heard, Baron Pasqualati[20] was good-natured enough to say: 'The lodging will not be rented; Beethoven will come back.'" To what extent Ries was correctly informed in this we will not now conjecture.

The lessons of Förster's little boy had been interrupted so long as his teacher dwelt in the distant theatre buildings; they were now renewed. This fact was particularly impressed upon the boy's memory by a severe reproof from Beethoven for ascending the four lofty heights of stairs too rapidly, and entering out of breath: "Youngster, you will ruin your lungs if you are not more careful," said he in substance.

Prince Louis Ferdinand, now on his way into Italy, made a short stay at Vienna, renewing his acquaintance with Beethoven; but of their intercourse few particulars are known. Ries relates (*Notizen*, p. 111) that an old countess gave a little musical entertainment "to which, naturally, Beethoven was invited. When the company sat down to supper, plates for the high nobility only were placed at the Prince's table—none for Beethoven. He flew into a rage, made a few ugly remarks, took his hat and went away. A few days later Prince Louis gave a dinner to which some members of the first company, including the old countess, were invited. When they sat down to table the old countess was placed on one side of the Prince, Beethoven on the other, a mark of distinction which Beethoven always referred to with pleasure." The Pianoforte Concerto in C minor had been in the hands of the engraver; upon its publication in late summer, Prince Louis Ferdinand's name appeared on the title. Concerning the compositions of the Prince, Beethoven remarked: "Now and then there are pretty bits in them."—so said Czerny.

Before this time Beethoven and Breuning "met each other by accident and a complete reconciliation took place and every inimical resolve of Beethoven's, despite their vigorous expression in the two letters, was wholly forgotten."— (Ries, *Notizen*, p. 132.) And not this alone; he "laid his peace offering on the altar of reconciliation." This was the gift of the best picture of himself which exists from those years, a beautiful miniature painted upon ivory by Hornemann, still in the possession of Breuning's heirs. With it he sent the following letter:

Let all that *passed between us* for a time, my dear St., be hidden behind this picture— I know that I broke *your heart*, but the feelings within me, which you must have noticed, have sufficiently punished me for that. It was not *spitefulness* that I felt towards you, no, if that were so I should never again be worthy of your friendship. It was passion on *your part* and *on mine*.— But mistrust of you arose within me—men came between us who are not worthy of *you* and *me*.—

---

[20] The baron was physician to Maria Theresia. See Wolfgang Madjera, "Beethovens Wohnung im Pasqualatihause zu Wien," *Der Merker*, XII (1921), 33.

My portrait was long ago intended for you. You know well that I always intended it for somebody; to whom could I give it with so warm a heart as to you, faithful, good, noble Steffen— Forgive me if I have given you pain, I suffered no less myself. Only when I no longer saw you near me for such a long time did I feel to the full how dear to *my* heart you are and always will be.— Surely you will come to my *arms* again as in the past.—

Nor was the reconciliation on Breuning's part less perfect. On the 13th of November he wrote to Wegeler and, to excuse his long silence, says (Wegeler, *Notizen*, Nachtrag, p. 10): "He who has been my friend from youth is often largely to blame that I am compelled to neglect the absent ones. You cannot conceive, my dear Wegeler, what an indescribable, I might say, fearful effect the gradual loss of his hearing has had upon him. Think of the feeling of being unhappy in one of such violent temperament; in addition reservedness, mistrust, often towards his best friends, in many things want of decision! For the greater part, with only an occasional exception when he gives free vent to his feelings on the spur of the moment, intercourse with him is a real exertion, at which one can scarcely trust to oneself. From May until the beginning of this month we lived in the same house, and at the outset I took him into my rooms. He had scarcely come before he became severely, almost dangerously ill, and this was followed by an intermittent fever. Worry and the care of him used me rather severely. Now he is completely well again. He lives on the Ramparts, I in one of the newly built houses of Prince Esterhazy in front of the Alstercaserne, and as I am keeping house he eats with me every day."

Not a word about the quarrel! Not a word to intimate that Beethoven had not occupied his rooms with him until at the usual time for changing lodgings he had crossed the Glacis to Pasqualati's house; not a word of complaint—nothing but the deepest pity and heartiest sympathy.

It is appropriate here to consider the revival of Beethoven's interest in Josephine, Countess Deym. Count Deym had died of pneumonia on January 27, 1804, shortly before the birth of their fourth child. Soon thereafter the widow's health began to fail, and her sister Charlotte came to take care of her. They spent the summer in the suburb of Hietzing. Charlotte wrote to her other sister, Therese von Brunsvik in June: "We have visited Beethoven, who appears very well and who has promised to come to see us. He will not travel this summer, but live perhaps at Hütteldorf so that we shall be very near one another." This visit must have taken place during Beethoven's convalescence from the illness and fever he had had that spring, for at that time he was at nearby Hetzendorf for a short stay. In July, after the quarrel with Breuning, he was at Baden, and later in the summer he chose to go north to Döbling instead of Hütteldorf to the west.

In September, after Josephine had returned to the city, Charlotte wrote to Therese of Josephine's "dreadful nervous breakdown; sometimes she laughed, sometimes wept, after which came utter fatigue and exhaustion."

By November, however, the sisters' correspondence reveals that she had found a diversion in planning musical evenings. On November 10 Charlotte wrote of Beethoven's taking part in two different occasions. One evening besides participating in his quartet, he was "so amiable that he played a sonata and variations when asked to."

On November 20 it is reported that he came almost every other day to give Pepi (Josephine) lessons. A month later Charlotte gives a hint that their friendship was becoming more than that of student and teacher. On December 19 she writes: "Our small musicales have begun again, finally. Last Wednesday we had the first. Pepi played the clavier excellently, I myself haven't yet found the courage to make myself listen. Beethoven comes quite frequently, he is giving Pepi lessons, it is a bit *dangerous*, I must confess." Charlotte's worries are also expressed in a letter to her brother Franz written two days later: "Beethoven is with us almost daily, gives lessons to Pipschen—vous m'entendez, mon coeur!"[21]

In the H. C. Bodmer Collection, now a part of the Beethovenhaus in Bonn, there are thirteen letters from Beethoven to the Countess Josephine Deym, and a fragmentary copy of a letter made by the Countess that is almost certainly from the composer. All fourteen have been published (with facsimiles of the thirteen autographs) by Joseph Schmidt-Görg[22] with commentary to justify the chronological order he established. This order was subsequently adopted by Emily Anderson. According to these datings, the letters were written between 1804 and 1807. Despite the tone of Charlotte's letters, there is nothing in the first three of Beethoven's letters,[23] which belong to this year, to indicate more than a warm friendship. In the third Beethoven shows that he was encouraging the arrangements at the Countess's house for "musicales every two weeks," and that the services of Schuppanzigh and Zmeskall had been enlisted to help. But, as we shall see, Charlotte's concern is confirmed by a new tone that enters into the letters that follow, to which we return in the next chapter.

Turn we again to the Theater-an-der-Wien, for a new contract was made with Beethoven, by which his operatic aspirations and hopes were again awakened, and with a better prospect of their gratification. At the end of August Sonnleithner retired from the direction of the theatre and Baron Braun took the extraordinary step of reinstating his former rival and enemy, Schikaneder—a remarkable proof of the Baron's high opinion of his tact and skill in the difficult business of management. It is worth noting that now, when Schikaneder found himself in a strait for novelty and new attractions for his stage, the project of appealing to Beethoven's genius was revived. It will be remembered that Beethoven had started, early in the year 1804, to set Sonnleithner's text of the "Leonore" subject. Inasmuch as

---

[21] See La Mara, 1920, pp. 43ff.

[22] *Veröffentlichungen des Beethovenhauses*

in Bonn, Neue Folge III, Bonn, 1957.

[23] See *A*, 97, 102 and 103.

the majority of the work on the opera was to be done in 1805, the story of its composition will be continued in the next chapter.

Meanwhile, on October 3, 1804, Paër's version of the "Leonore" was performed at Dresden. A copy of the Paër score was found among Beethoven's papers. The work was not performed at Vienna until February 8, 1809; but Engländer, in a comparative study of the Italian and German versions,[24] notes some common ideas of dramatic and musical treatment, lacking in the Gaveau version, which he believes indicates an influence of the Paër work on the different versions of *Fidelio*. Since it is not certain when Beethoven met Paër or acquired the score, it is impossible to prove any of these relationships.

At this point, when the first of the solo sonatas written for the enlarged pianoforte (Op. 53) was ready for the press; when the Pianoforte Concerto in C minor had just been published; when the *Sinfonia Eroica* with its daring novelties of ideas and construction was awaiting public performance, and Beethoven had entered the lists to compete with Cherubini in another form of the art—here seems to be the fitting place for a few notes upon the degree of popularity, and the extent of circulation, to which his previous compositions had already attained.

We have not written very lucidly, if it be not sufficiently clear that, at Vienna, the works of no other of the younger generation of composers had so ready and extensive a sale as Beethoven's, even though their qualities, most attractive to many, were repellent to others. That was a question of taste. But in those last weeks of 1804, a proof of their general popularity was in preparation by Schreyvogel and Rizzi, which, so far as the present writer has examined the German periodical press from 1790 to 1830, is without a parallel. It was a complete classified catalogue of the "Works of Herr Ludwig van Beethoven," published as an advertisement, January 30, 1805, in the *Wiener Zeitung*, announcing them as "to be had at the Kunst- und Industrie-Comptoir at Vienna in the Kohlmarkt, No. 269."

At the end of 1796—a few sets of Variations excepted—only the first three of Beethoven's *opera* had appeared. Four years afterwards the first publishing houses of Leipzig were contending with those of Vienna for his manuscripts, notwithstanding the worse than contemptuous treatment of his works by the newly founded musical journal.

In January, 1801, at Breslau "the pianoforte players gladly venture upon Beethoven and spare neither time nor pains to conquer his difficulties." In June, Beethoven had "more commissions, almost, than was possible to fill" from the publishers—as he said, "I ask and they pay." In 1802 Nägeli of Zurich applied to him for sonatas with which to introduce to the public his costly enterprise of the *Répertoire des Clavecinistes*. In 1803, although Simrock, of Bonn, had a branch house at Paris, and printed editions of his

[24] Richard Engländer, "Paërs *Leonora* und Beethovens *Fidelio*," *NBJ*, IV (1930), 118-32.

townsman's more important works for circulation in France, Zulehner of Mainz found the demand for them sufficient to warrant the announcement of a complete and uniform edition of the "Works for Painoforte and String Instruments." In May of the same year, the *Correspondance des Amateurs-Musiciens* informs us that at Paris a part of the pianoforte virtuosi play only Haydn, Mozart and Beethoven, and in spite of the difficulties offered by their works there are "quelquefois des Amateurs qui croient les jouer." Soon after this, an application came to Beethoven from distant Scotland for a half a dozen sonatas, on Scottish themes. Further, one could cite Muzio Clementi, not only a fine musician but also a clever businessman, who ran a business of pianofortes and music publishing in partnership with W. W. Collard. In September, 1804, he made an arrangement with Breitkopf and Härtel by which he secured all the compositions which Beethoven might bring to that firm for England at one half the honorarium paid the composer.

The first two Concertos for Pianoforte and Orchestra, published in 1801, are reported to have been played in public within two years at Berlin and Frankfurt-am-Main; the third, advertised in November, 1804, was performed the next month at Berlin. The first Symphony had hardly left Hoffmeister's press, when it was added to the repertory of the Gewandhaus Concert, at Leipzig, and during the three following years was repeatedly performed at Berlin, Breslau, Frankfurt-am-Main, Dresden, Brunswick and Munich; the second, advertised in March, 1804, was the opening symphony of Schick and Bohrer's (Berlin) concerts in the autumn. The *Prometheus* overture was played in the same concerts, December 2, 1803—ten days earlier than the oldest discovered advertisement of its publication. The instant popularity of the Septet in all its forms is well known.

A public performance of the Horn Sonata, March 20, 1803, at the concert of Dulon, the blind flute player, is worth noting, because the pianist was "young Bär"—Meyerbeer.

In our day and generation, to offer so meagre a list of public productions as a proof of popularity in the case of a new author of orchestral works, would be ridiculous. In the multiplication of musical journals and the greatly extended interest taken in musical news wherever an orchestra exists equal to the performance of a symphony, there is also someone to report its doings. This is as it should be. Then, except in the larger capitals, this was rarely so. Hence a few notes above, compiled from the correspondence of the single musical journal of the time, are more than suggestive—they are proof—of many an unrecorded production of the works they name. But more noteworthy than the statistics given by the various correspondents, is this: that, whatever praises they bestow upon the concertos and symphonies of others, they rank Beethoven alone with Haydn and Mozart; and this they do, even before the publication of the third Concerto and the Second Symphony.

Beethoven, then, though almost unknown personally beyond the limits of a few Austrian cities—unaided by apostles to preach his gospel, owing nothing to journalist or pamphleteer, disdaining, in fact, all the arts by which dazzling but mediocre talent pushes itself into notoriety—had, in the short space of eight years, by simple force of his genius as manifested in his published works, placed himself at the head of all writers for the pianoforte, and in public estimation had risen to the level of the two greatest of orchestral composers. The unknown student that entered Vienna in 1792, was now in 1804 a recognized member of the great triumvirate, Haydn, Mozart and Beethoven.

--*Two small works are to be added to the works composed during 1804 (both published in the Complete Works, Series 25). The first is the Bagatelle in C composed at the beginning of the year, for which there are sketches in both the "Eroica" and "Leonore" sketchbooks. The second is the song "Gedenke mein," which was probably composed at the end of the year, and was enclosed in a letter to Breitkopf and Härtel dated January 16, 1805.

The compositions completed in 1804 were:

1803-1804. Andante in F major for Pianoforte, WoO 57.
    Bagatelle in C major for Pianoforte, WoO 56.
    Concerto for Pianoforte, Violin and Violoncello and Orchestra, Op. 56.
    Sonata for Pianoforte, Op. 53.
    Symphony No. 3 in E-flat major, Op. 55. Final work probably at the beginning of 1804.
1804. Sonata for Pianoforte, Op. 54.
    Song. "Gedenke mein," WoO 130.

The publications were:
[In December, 1803, and January, 1804, appeared respectively Serenade for Pianoforte and Flute, Op. 41 (transcription of the Serenade, Op. 25), and Nocturne for Pianoforte and Viola, Op. 42 (transcription of the Serenade, Op. 8). It will be remembered that in a letter to the publisher Hoffmeister of September 22, 1803, Beethoven protested that these transcriptions were not his own, "though they were improved by me in places."]

By Hoffmeister and Kühnel in Leipzig:
 Overture to the Ballet *Die Geschöpfe des Prometheus*, Op. 43.
 Variations for Pianoforte, Violin and Violoncello, Op. 44.
By Kunst- und Industrie-Comptoir:
 Concerto for Pianoforte and Orchestra, No. 3 in C minor, Op. 37, dedicated to Prince Louis Ferdinand of Prussia.
 "Der Wachtelschlag" (S. F. Sauter), WoO 129.
 Symphony No. 2 in D major, Op. 36, dedicated to Prince Karl von Lichnowsky.
 Three Marches for Pianoforte, Four Hands, Op. 45, dedicated to Princess Maria Esterhazy.
 Variations for Pianoforte on "God Save the King," WoO 78.
 Variations for Pianoforte on "Rule Britannia," WoO 79.
By Nägeli in Zurich:
 Sonata for Pianoforte, Op. 31, No. 3; in *Répertoire des Clavecinistes.*--

CHAPTER XVIII

THE YEAR 1805

PUBLIC PERFORMANCE OF THE "EROICA"— COUNTESS JOSEPHINE DEYM— "LEONORE" COMPLETED AND PERFORMED

HE who dwells with wife and children in a fixed abode, usually finds himself, as age draws on, one of a small circle of old friends; and hoary heads, surrounded by their descendants, the inheritors of parental friendships, sit at the same tables and make merry where they had gathered in the prime of life. The unmarried man, who can call no spot on earth's surface his own, who spends his life in hired lodgings, here to-day and there tomorrow, has, as a rule, few friendships of long standing. By divergency in tastes, opinions, habits, increasing with the years, often by the mere interruption of social intercourse, or by a thousand equally insignificant causes, the old ties are sundered. In the memoranda and correspondence of such a man familiar names disappear, even when not removed by death, and strange ones take their places. The mere passing acquaintance of one period becomes the chosen friend of another; while the former friend sinks into the mere acquaintance, or is forgotten. Frequently no cause for the change can be assigned. One can only say—it happened so.

Thus it was with Beethoven, even to a remarkable degree; in part because of his increasing infirmity, in part owing to peculiarities of his character. It was his misfortune, also, that—having no pecuniary resource but the exercise of his talents for musical composition, and being at the same time too proud and too loyal to his ideas of art to write for popular applause—he was all his life long thrown more or less upon the generosity of patrons. But death, misfortune or other causes deprived him of old patrons, as of old friends, and compelled him to seek, or at least accept, the kindness of new ones. A part of this chapter must be devoted to certain new names in both categories, which become prominent in his history in the years immediately before us.

Archduke Rudolph Johann Joseph Rainer, youngest son of Emperor Leopold II, and half-brother of Emperor Franz, was born January 8, 1788, and
therefore was, at the end of 1805, just closing his seventeenth year. Like his
unfortunate uncle, Elector Maximilian, he was destined to the church, and like
him, too, he had much musical taste and capacity. His private tutors were all
men of fine culture, and one of them, Joseph Edler von Baumeister, Doctor of
Laws, remained in later years in his service and will be met with hereafter. In
music he, with the children of the imperial family, was instructed by the R. I.
Court Composer, Anton Tayber, and made such good progress that, if tradition may be trusted, he, while still but a boy, played to general satisfaction in
the salons of Lobkowitz and others. But an archduke has not much to fear
from hostile criticism; a better proof that he really possessed musical talent
and taste is afforded by the fact that, so soon as he could emancipate himself
from Tayber, and have a voice in the selection of a teacher, he became a
pupil of Beethoven. It is largely possible that the old relation of the composer
to Maximilian may have had some influence upon the determination of his
nephew; and it is very probable that Rudolph's decision was based upon
the great reputation of Beethoven and the respect in which, as he saw, the
artist was held by the Schwarzenbergs, Liechtensteins, Kinskys, and their
compeers. But whatever weight be allowed to these and like considerations,
it must have been something more than a capricious desire to call the great
pianist "master," which made him his pupil, friend and patron until death
parted them. One necessarily thinks better of his musical talents for this, just
as Maximilian's musical taste and insight stand higher in our estimation
because of his early appreciation of Mozart's genius.

The precise date of Beethoven's engagement has eluded the research of
even the accurate and indefatigable Köchel. There is so little doubt, however,
that he was the immediate successor of Tayber, as to render reasonably certain
that it occurred at the end of the young Archduke's fifteenth year—that is,
in the winter of 1803-1804. It is perhaps worth remarking, that the *Staats-
Schematismus* for 1803 first gives, in the R. I. Household, a separate chamber
to the boys, Rainer and Rudolph; three years later "Archduke Rudolph,
coadjutor of the Archbishopric of Olmütz," is given one alone; but before
1806 he certainly was the pupil of Beethoven.

In Fräulein Giannatasio's notices from the years 1816-18,[1] she relates: "At
that time Beethoven gave lessons to Archduke Rudolph, a brother of Emperor
Franz. I once asked him if the Archduke played well. 'When he is feeling
just right,' was the answer, accompanied by a smile. He also laughingly
referred to the fact that he would sometimes hit him on the fingers, and that
when the august gentleman once tried to refer him to his place, he pointed
for justification to a passage from a poet, Goethe, I think."

It must have been a mistake of the young lady's to make Beethoven speak

---

[1] See the *Grenzboten*, Leipzig, April 3, 1857. (TDR, II, 544, n. 1.)

here in the present tense; for it is incredible that he should have taken such a liberty in 1816-17, when Rudolph was a man of some thirty years; or indeed at any time after the first lessons in his boyhood. The anecdote therefore in some degree supports the conjecture above offered. So also does Schindler's statement—a point on which he was likely to be well informed by the master himself—that the pianoforte part of the Triple Concerto, Op. 56, was written for the Archduke; for this work was sketched, at the latest, in the spring of 1804, and surely would not have been undertaken until the composer thoroughly knew his pupil's powers, and that his performance would do the master no discredit. And finally, what Ries relates is in the tone of one who had personal knowledge of the circumstances detailed; and thus determines the date as not later than 1804 (*Notizen*, pp. 111-112): "Etiquette and all that is connected with it was never [?] known to Beethoven, nor was he ever willing to learn it. For this reason he often caused great embarrassment in the household of the Archduke Rudolph when he first went to him. An attempt was made by force to teach him to have regard for certain things. But this was intolerable to him; he would promise, indeed, to mend his ways but—that was the end of it. Finally one day when, as he expressed it, he was being tutored [*als man ihn, wie er es nannte, hofmeisterte*] he angrily forced his way to the Archduke and flatly declared that while he had the greatest reverence for his person, he could not trouble himself to observe all the regulations which were daily forced upon him. The Archduke laughed good-naturedly and commanded that Beethoven be permitted to go his own gait undisturbed—it was his nature and could not be altered."

At all events it may be accepted as certain that Beethoven had now formed those relations with the Archduke, which were strengthened and more advantageous to him with each successive year, until death put an end to them.

Meanwhile, however unpopular the composer may have been with his brother musicians in Vienna, he possessed qualities and tastes that endeared him to the best class of rising young men in the learned professions. An example is Dr. Johann Zizius, of Bohemia (born January 7, 1772). He appears at the early age of 28, in the *Staats-Schematismus* for 1800, as a professor of political science to the R. I. Staff of Guards; three years later he has the same professorship in the Theresianum, which he retained to his death in 1824, filling also in his later years the chair of constitutional law in the University. Dr. Sonnleithner made his acquaintance about 1820. In his very valuable and interesting "Musikalische Skizzen aus alt-Wien" (*Rezensionen*, 1863), he describes Zizius in a way which shows him to have been a man after Beethoven's own heart, and his house a gathering place, until the composer's increasing infirmity excluded him in great measure from mixed society.

The attraction of Beethoven's personal character for young persons of more than ordinary genius and culture has already been noted. Another illustration of this was Julius Franz Borgias Schneller, born (1777) at Strassburg, educated at Freiburg im Breisgau, and just now (1805) professor of history in the Lyceum at Linz. Driven into exile because of his active resistance to the French, he had made his way to Vienna, where his fine qualities of head and heart made him a welcome guest in literary circles and gained him the affection of the young writers of the capital. In 1803, he received his appointment at Linz, whence, three years later, he was advanced to the same position in the new university at Graz. Perhaps the most beloved of his friends was Gleichenstein.

---⁂{Here seems to be the appropriate place to mention a friendship that Beethoven surely made through his close association with Count Browne and his family. Privy Councillor Johannes Büel (1761-1830) was for a long time tutor to the Count's son Moritz. In characterizing his friends in Vienna in 1805, Büel wrote: "Beethoven, full of enthusiasm for his art, original, somewhat of a hypochondriac, who when yesterday Browne read to him a letter from me, freely gave vent to his tears."[2] In his biography of Büel, Hans Noll has printed a facsimile of an entry that Beethoven made for Büel's album:[3]

Freundschaft ist Schatten gegen	Friendship is a shade in
den Sonnenstrahl und	sunlight and a shelter
Schirm wider den Regenguss.	in a downpour of rain.
Trübt etwas mein lieber Büel	Reflect back, my dear Büel,
die Erinnerung an dich, so ist's	and you see—
—dass wir unss zu wenig sahen—	that we saw each other too little—
leb wohl—und vergiss ja nicht	farewell—and forget not
deinen warmen Freund	your warm friend
Ludwig van Beethoven	Ludwig van Beethoven

Wien am 29sten juni 1806.

At the time Beethoven believed his friend was returning to his house in Switzerland, but actually he remained in Vienna until 1817. Büel visited Vienna again in 1821, and at this time wrote, "If Beethoven only were not completely deaf and so difficult to deal with, I would give G. his address, but now nothing can be done with him." These are the sad words of a friend who can only treasure a close friendship of the past.}⁂---

We pass to the notices of Ries, Czerny and others, which record divers characteristic anecdotes and personal traits of the master, not susceptible of exact chronological arrangement but which belong to this period. "Of all composers," says Ries (*Notizen*, p. 84), "Beethoven valued most highly Mozart and Handel, then S. Bach. Whenever I found him with music in his hand or lying on his desk it was surely compositions of these heroes. Haydn seldom escaped without a few sly thrusts." Compare this with what Jahn heard from Czerny: "Once Beethoven saw at my house the scores of six quartets by Mozart. He opened the fifth, in A, and said: 'That's a work! that's where Mozart said to the world: Behold what I might have done for

---

[2] Stephan Ley, "Kleine Beethoveniana" in *NBJ*, VI, 27-28.

[3] *Hofrat Johann Büel, 1761-1830* (Frauenfeld, Huber, 1930), p. 240.

you if the time were right!' "[4] And, touching Handel: "Graun's *Tod Jesu* was unknown to Beethoven. My father brought the score to him, which he played through *a vista* in a masterly manner. When he came to a place where Graun had written a twofold ending to be left to the choice of the performer, he said: 'The man must have had the gripes not to be able to say which ending is the better!' At the end he said that the fugues were passable, the rest ordinary. Then he picked up Handel's *Messiah* with the words: 'Here is a different fellow!' and played the most interesting numbers and called our attention to several resemblances to Haydn's *Creation*, etc."[5] "Once," says Ries (p. 100), "when after a lesson we were talking about fugue themes, I sitting at the pianoforte and he beside me, I played the first fugue theme from Graun's *Tod Jesu*; he began to play it after me with his left hand, then brought in the right and developed it for perhaps half an hour. I am still unable to understand how he could have endured the uncomfortable position so long. His enthusiasm made him insensible to external impressions."

In another place (p. 87) he relates: "During a walk I mentioned to Beethoven two pure fifth progressions which sound striking and beautiful in his C minor Quartet (Op. 18). He did not know them and denied that they were fifths. It being his habit always to carry ruled paper with him, I asked him for a sheet and wrote down the passage in all four voices; seeing that I was right he said: '*Well, and who has forbidden them?*' Not knowing how to take the question, I had him repeat it several times until I finally answered in amazement: 'But they are first principles!' The question was repeated again, whereupon I answered: 'Marpurg, Kirnberger, Fux, etc., etc., all theoreticians!'—'And I allow them *thus!*' was his answer."

We quote again from Ries (pp. 106-107): "I recall only two instances in which Beethoven told me to add a few notes to his composition: once in the theme of the rondo of the 'Sonate Pathétique' (Op. 13), and again in the theme of the rondo of his first Concerto in C major, where he gave me some passages in double notes to make it more brilliant. He played this last rondo, in fact, with an expression peculiar to himself. In general he played his own compositions very freakishly, holding firmly to the measure, however, as a rule and occasionally, but not often, hurrying the tempo. At times he would hold the tempo back in his *crescendo* with *ritardando*, which made a very beautiful and highly striking effect. In playing he would give a passage now in the right hand, now in the left, a lovely and absolutely inimitable expression; but he very seldom added notes or ornaments . . . (p. 100). He played his own compositions very unwillingly. Once he was making serious preparations for a long trip which we were to make together, on which I was to arrange the concerts and play his concertos as well as other compositions. He wanted only to conduct and improvise."

And now something more on the subject of Beethoven's improvisations. Says Ries: "This last was certainly the most extraordinary [performance]

---

[4] See Kerst, I, p. 51.   [5] *Ibid.*, pp. 56-57.

any one was ever privileged to listen to, especially when he was in good humor or excited. Not a single artist of all that I have heard ever reached the plane in this respect which Beethoven occupied. The wealth of ideas which crowded in upon him, the moods to which he surrendered himself, the variety of treatment, the difficulties which offered themselves or were introduced by him, were inexhaustible." And Czerny:

"Beethoven's improvisations (with which he created the greatest sensation in the first years of his sojourn in Vienna and even caused Mozart to wonder) was of the most varied kind, whether he was treating themes chosen by himself or set for him by others.

"1. In the first-movement form or the final rondo of a sonata, when he regularly closed the first section and introduced a second melody in a related key, etc., but in the second section gave himself freely to all manner of treatment of the motivi. In Allegros the work was enlivened by bravura passages which were mostly more difficult than those to be found in his compositions.

"2. In the free-variation form, about like his Choral Fantasia, Op. 80, or the choral finale of his Ninth Symphony, both of which give a faithful illustration of his improvisations in this form.

"3. In the mixed genre, where, in the potpourri style, one thought follows upon another, as in his solo Fantasia, Op. 77. Often a few tones would suffice to enable him to improvise an entire piece (as, for instance, the Finale of the third Sonata, D major, of Op. 10).

"Nobody equalled him in the rapidity of his scales, double trills, skips, etc.—not even Hummel. His bearing while playing was masterfully quiet, noble and beautiful, without the slightest grimace (only bent forward low, as his deafness grew upon him); his fingers were very powerful, not long, and broadened at the tips by much playing, for he told me very often indeed that he generally had to practise until after midnight in his youth.

"In teaching he laid great stress on a correct position of the fingers (after the school of Emanuel Bach, which he used in teaching me); he could scarcely span a tenth. He made frequent use of the pedals, much more frequent than is indicated in his works. His playing of the scores of Handel and Gluck and the fugues of Seb. Bach was unique, in that in the former he introduced a full-voicedness and a spirit which gave these works a new shape.

"He was also the greatest *a vista* player of his time (even in score-reading); he scanned every new and unfamiliar composition like a divination and his judgment was always correct, but (especially in his younger years) very keen, biting, unsparing. Much that the world admired then and still admires he saw from the lofty point of view of his genius in an entirely different light.

"Extraordinary as his playing was when he improvised, it was frequently less successful when he played his printed compositions, for, as he never had patience or time to practise, the result would generally depend on accident or his mood; and as his playing, like his compositions, was far ahead of his time, the pianofortes of the period (until 1810), still extremely weak and imperfect, could not endure his gigantic style of performance. Hence it was that Hummel's purling, brilliant style, well calculated to suit the manner of the time, was much more comprehensible and pleasing to the public. But Beethoven's performance of slow and sustained passages produced an almost magical effect upon every listener and, so far as I know, was never surpassed."[6]

Pass we to certain minor characteristic traits which Ries has recorded of his master:

"Beethoven recalled his youth, and his Bonn friends, with great pleasure, although his memory told of hard times, on the whole. Of his mother, in particular, he spoke with love and feeling, calling her often an honest, good-hearted woman. He spoke but little and unwillingly of his father, who was most to blame for the family misery, but a single hard word against him uttered by another would anger him. On the whole he was a thoroughly good and kind man, on whom his moods and impetuousness played shabby tricks. He would have forgiven anybody, no matter how grievously he had injured him or whatever wrong he had done him, if he had found him in an unfortunate position." [*Notizen*, pp. 122-123.]

"Beethoven was often extremely violent. One day we were eating our noonday meal at the Swan inn; the waiter brought him the wrong dish. Scarcely had Beethoven spoken a few words about the matter, which the waiter answered in a manner not altogether modest, when Beethoven seized the dish (it was a mess of lungs with plenty of gravy) and threw it at the waiter's head. The poor fellow had an armful of other dishes (an adeptness which Viennese waiters possess in a high degree) and could not help himself; the gravy ran down his face. He and Beethoven screamed and vituperated while all the other guests roared with laughter. Finally, Beethoven himself was overcome with the comicalness of the situation, as the waiter who wanted to scold could not, because he was kept busy licking from his chops the gravy that ran down his face, making the most ridiculous grimaces the while. It was a picture worthy of Hogarth." [*Notizen*, pp. 121-122.]

"Beethoven knew scarcely anything about money, because of which he had frequent quarrels; since he was always mistrustful, and frequently thought himself cheated when it was not the case. Easily excited, he called people cheats, for which in the case of waiters he had to make good with tips. At length his peculiarities and absentmindedness became known in the inns which he frequented most often and he was permitted to go his way, even when he went without paying his bill." [*Notizen*, p. 122.]

"Beethoven had taken lessons on the violin even after he reached Vienna from Krumpholz and frequently when I was there we played his Sonatas for

[6] *Ibid.*, pp. 60-61.

Pianoforte and Violin together. But it was really a horrible music; for in his enthusiastic zeal he never heard when he began a passage with bad fingering.

"In his behavior Beethoven was awkward and helpless; his uncouth movements were often destitute of all grace. He seldom took anything into his hands without dropping and breaking it. Thus he frequently knocked his ink-well into the pianoforte which stood near by the side of his writing-table. No piece of furniture was safe from him, least of all a costly piece. Everything was overturned, soiled and destroyed. It is hard to comprehend how he accomplished so much as to be able to shave himself, even leaving out of consideration the number of cuts on his cheeks. He could never learn to dance in time." [*Notizen*, pp. 119-120.]

That Beethoven and Ignaz von Seyfried were brought much together in these years, the reader already knows. Their acquaintance during thirty years—which for at least half of the time, was really the "friendly relationship" which Seyfried names it—it was, he says, "never weakened, never disturbed by even the smallest quarrel—not that we were always of a mind, or could be, but we always spoke freely and frankly to each other, without reserve, according to our convictions, without conceitedly trying to force upon one another our opinions as infallible."

"Besides, Beethoven was much too straightforward, open and tolerant to give offence to another by disapprobation, or contradiction; he was wont to laugh heartily at what did not please him and I confidently believe that I may safely say that in all his life he never, at least not consciously, made an enemy; only those to whom his peculiarities were unknown were unable quite to understand how to get along with him; I am speaking here of an earlier time, before the misfortune of deafness had come upon him; if, on the contrary, Beethoven sometimes carried things to an extreme in his rude honesty in the case of many, mostly those who had imposed themselves upon him as protectors, the fault lay only in this, that the honest German always carried his heart on his tongue and understood everything better than how to flatter; also because, conscious of his own merit, he would never permit himself to be made the plaything of the vain whims of the Maecenases who were eager to boast of their association with the name and fame of the celebrated master. And so he was misunderstood only by those who had not the patience to get acquainted with the apparent eccentric. When he composed 'Fidelio,' the oratorio 'Christus am Ölberg,' the symphonies in E-flat, C minor and F, the Pianoforte Concertos in C minor and G major, and the Violin Concerto in D, we were living in the same house and (since we were each carrying on a bachelor's apartment) we dined at the same restaurant and chatted away many an unforgettable hour in the confidential intimacy of colleagues, for Beethoven was then merry, ready for any jest, happy, full of life, witty and not seldom satirical. No physical ill had then afflicted him [?]; no loss of the sense which is peculiarly indispensable to the musician had darkened his life; only weak eyes had remained with him as the results of the smallpox with which he had been afflicted in his childhood, and these compelled him even in his early youth to resort to concave, very strong (highly magnifying) spectacles.

"He had me play the pieces mentioned, recognized throughout the musical world as masterpieces, and, without giving me time to think, demanded to know my opinion of them; I was permitted to give it without restraint, without fearing that I should offend any artistic conceit—a fault which was utterly foreign to his nature."

The above is from *Cäcilia*, Vol. IX, 218, 219. In the so-called *Studien* (appendix) are other reminiscences, which form an admirable supplement to it. Those which belong to the years 1800-1805 follow:

"Our master could not be presented as a model in respect of conducting, and the orchestra always had to have a care in order not to be led astray by its mentor; for he had ears only for his composition and was ceaselessly occupied by manifold gesticulations to indicate the desired expression. He often made a down beat for an accent in the wrong place. He used to suggest a *diminuendo* by crouching down more and more, and at a *pianissimo* he would almost creep under the desk. When the volume of sound grew he rose up also as if out of a stage-trap, and with the entrance of the power of the band he would stand upon the tips of his toes almost as big as a giant, and waving his arms, seemed about to soar upwards to the skies. Everything about him was active, not a bit of his organism idle, and the man was comparable to a *perpetuum mobile*. He did not belong to those capricious composers whom no orchestra in the world can satisfy. At times, indeed, he was altogether too considerate and did not even repeat passages which went badly at the rehearsal: 'It will go better next time,' he would say. He was very particular about expression, the delicate nuances, the equable distribution of light and shade as well as an effective *tempo rubato*, and without betraying vexation, would discuss them with the individual players. When he then observed that the players would enter into his intentions and play together with increasing ardor, inspired by the magical power of his creations, his face would be transfigured with joy, all his features beamed pleasure and satisfaction, a pleased smile would play around his lips and a thundering 'Bravi tutti!' reward the successful achievement. It was the first and loftiest triumphal moment for the genius, compared with which, as he confessed, the tempestuous applause of a receptive audience was as nothing. When playing at first sight, there were frequent pauses for the purpose of correcting the parts and then the thread would be broken; but he was patient even then; but when things went to pieces, particularly in the scherzos of his symphonies at a sudden and unexpected change of rhythm, he would shout with laughter and say he had expected nothing else, but was reckoning on it from the beginning; he was almost childishly glad that he had been successful in 'unhorsing such excellent riders.'

"Before Beethoven was afflicted with his organic ailment, he attended the opera frequently and with enjoyment, especially the admirable and flourishing Theater-and-der-Wien, perhaps, also, for convenience' sake, since he had scarcely to do more than to step from his room into the parterre. There he was fascinated more especially by the creations of Cherubini and Méhul, which at that time were just beginning to stir up the enthusiasm of all Vienna. There he would plant himself hard against the orchestra rail and, dumb as a dunce, remain till the last stroke of the bows. This was the only sign, however, that the art work had interested him; if, on the contrary, the piece did not please him he would turn on his heel at the first fall of the curtain and take himself away. It was, in fact, difficult, yes, utterly impossible to tell from his features whether or not he was pleased or displeased; he was always the same, apparently cold, and just as reserved in his judgments concerning his companions in art; his mind was at work ceaselessly, but the physical shell was like soulless marble. Strangely enough, on the other hand, hearing wretched music was a treat to him which he proclaimed by a peal of laughter. Everybody who knew him intimately knew that in this art he was a virtuoso, but it was a pity that those who were near him were seldom able to fathom the cause of such explosions, since he often laughed at his most secret thoughts and conceits without giving an accounting of them.

"He was never found on the street without a small note-book in which he was wont to record his passing ideas. Whenever conversation turned on the subject he would parody Joan of Arc's words: *'I dare not come without my banner!'*—and he adhered to his self-given rule with unparalleled tenacity; although otherwise a truly admirable disorder prevailed in his household. Books and music were scattered in every corner; here the remnants of a cold luncheon; here sealed or half-emptied bottles; here upon a stand the hurried sketches of a quartet; here the remains of a déjeuner; there on the pianoforte, on scribbled paper the material for a glorious symphony still slumbering in embryo; here a proof-sheet awaiting salvation; friendly and business letters covering the floor; between the windows a respectable loaf of strachino, *ad latus* a considerable ruin of a genuine Veronese salami—yet despite this varied mess our master had a habit, quite contrary to the reality, of proclaiming his accuracy and love of order on all occasions with Ciceronian eloquence. Only when it became necessary to spend days, hours, sometimes weeks, in finding something necessary and all efforts remained fruitless, did he adopt a different tone, and the innocent were made to bear the blame. 'Yes, yes,' was the complaint, 'that's a misfortune! Nothing is permitted to remain where I put it; everything is moved about; everything is done to vex me; O men, men!' But his servants knew the good-natured grumbler; let him growl to his heart's content, and—in a few minutes all would be forgotten, until another occasion brought with it a renewal of the scene.

"He often made merry over his illegible handwriting and excused himself by saying: 'Life is too short to paint letters or notes; and prettier notes would scarcely help me out of needs.'[7]

"The whole forenoon, from the first ray of light till the meal hour, was devoted to mechanical labor, i.e., to transcribing; the rest of the day was given to thought and the ordering of ideas. Hardly had he put the last bit in his mouth before he began his customary promenade, unless he had some other excursion *in petto*; that is to say, he hurried in double-quick time several times around the city, as if urged on by a goad; and this, let the weather be what it might."

And his hearing—how was it with that?

A question not to be answered to full satisfaction. It is clear that the *Notizen* of Wegeler and Ries, the *Biographie* (first editions) of Schindler, and especially the papers from Beethoven's own hand printed in those volumes, have given currency to a very exaggerated idea of the progress of his infirmity. On the other hand, Seyfried as evidently errs in the other direction; and yet Carl Czerny, both in his published and manuscripts notices, goes even farther. For instance, he writes to Jahn: "Although he had suffered from pains in his ears and the like ever since 1800, he still heard speech and music perfectly well until nearly 1812," and adds in confirmation: "As late as the years 1811-1812 I studied things with him and he corrected with great care, as well as ten years before." This, however, proves nothing, as Beethoven performed feats of this kind still more remarkable down to the last year of his life. Beethoven's Lamentation, the testament of 1802, is one extreme, the statements of Seyfried and Czerny the other; the truth lies somewhere between.

In June, 1801, Beethoven is "obliged to lean down to the orchestral rail to hear a drama." The next summer he cannot hear a flute or pipe to which Ries calls his attention. In 1804, as Doležalek tells Jahn, "in the rehearsals to the 'Eroica' he did not always hear the wind-instruments distinctly and missed them when they were playing." The evil was then making, if slow, still sure progress. "In those years," says Schindler, "there was a priest named Pater Weiss in the Metropolitan Church of St. Stephen who occupied himself with healing the deaf and had accomplished many fortunate cures. He was not a mere empiricist, but was familiar with the physiology of the ear; he effected his cures with simple remedies, and enjoyed a wide fame among the people, and also the respect of medical practitioners. With the consent of his physician our terrified tone-poet had also entrusted his case to the priest." Precisely when this was, is unknown; it could not, however, have been until after Dr. Schmidt's treatment had proved hopeless. The so-called Fischoff Manuscript, evidently on the authority of Zmeskall himself, gives a more particular account than Schindler of Pater Weiss's experience with his new

[7] One of Beethoven's puns, the point of which is lost in translation: "Schönere *Noten* brächten mich schwerlich aus den *Nöthen.*" (TK, II, 95, n. 1.)

patient. "Herr v. Zmeskall with great difficulty persuaded Beethoven to go there with him. At first he followed the advice of the physician; but as he had to go to him every day in order to have a fluid dropped into his ear, this grew unpleasant, the more since, in his impatience, he felt little or no improvement; and he remained away. The physician, questioned by Zmeskall, told him the facts, and Zmeskall begged him to accommodate himself to the self-willed invalid, and consult his convenience. The priest, honestly desirous to help Beethoven, went to his lodgings, but his efforts were in vain, inasmuch as Beethoven in a few days refused him entrance, and thus neglected possible help or at least an amelioration of his condition."

The history of the year 1805 is, in the main, the history of the composition of *Leonore* or *Fidelio*. Ries was away with Lichnowsky in Silesia during all of the warm season, and, very soon after his return, was forced to depart again from Vienna for Bonn. Hence the *Notizen* fail us in perhaps the most interesting part of the young man's four years of pupilage under Beethoven. ⸺In a general paucity of known events aside from those connected with the opera, one detail stands out: the change in Beethoven's relationship with the Countess Deym from a warm friendship to a true love affair. Not to break the thread of the story thereafter, the few events of the first half year unconnected with these two subjects shall first be disposed of.⸺

Schuppanzigh had discovered and taught a boy of great genius for the violin, Joseph Mayseder by name (born October 16, 1789), who was already, in his sixteenth year, the subject of eulogistic notices in the public press. With this youth as second, Schreiber, "in the service of Prince Lobkowitz," for the viola, and the elder Kraft, violoncellist, Schuppanzigh during the winter 1804-1805 gave quartets "in a private house in the Heiligenkreuzerhof, the listeners paying five florins in advance for four performances."[8] Up to the end of April the quartets given were by Mozart, Haydn, Beethoven, Eberl, Romberg, with "occasionally larger pieces. Of the latter great pleasure was given by the beautiful Beethoven Sextet in E-flat, a composition which shines resplendent by reason of its lively melodies, unconstrained harmonies, and a wealth of new and surprising ideas." So it is reported in the *Allgemeine Musikalische Zeitung* of the Sextet for wind instruments, which afterwards received the opus number 71, but was composed around 1796.

It was to the discredit of Vienna, where instrumental performers of rare ability so abounded, that for several years regular public orchestral concerts, save those at the Augarten in the summer, had been abandoned. Sensible of this, the bankers Würth and Fellner during the winter of 1803-1804 "had gathered together on all Sunday mornings a select company [nearly all dilettanti] for concerts restricted for the greater part to pieces for full orchestra, such as symphonies [among them Beethoven's First and Second], overtures, concertos, which they played in really admirable style." There

---

[8] See H. von Perger, "Beethovens Leibquartett," *Der Merker*, VIII (1917), 380.

were also "some overtures by a certain Count Gallenberg" who "imitated, or rather copied, Mozart and Cherubini so slavishly, following them even in the details of keys and modulations so faithfully, that it was easy to tell the titles of the overtures upon which his had been made with the greatest certainty." Thus the correspondent of the *AMZ*. In these concerts Clement of the Theater-an-der-Wien was director.

They were renewed the present winter, and the following report appeared in the *AMZ*, February 13, 1805: "Beethoven's Symphony in C major was performed at Herr von Würth's with precision and ease. A splendid artistic production. All instruments are used excellently, in which an uncommon richness of beautiful ideas are charmingly and splendidly developed, and overall pervades continuity, order and light. An entirely new symphony by Beethoven (to be distinguished from the second which was published some time ago by the local Kunst- und Industrie-Comptoir) is written in a completely different style. This long composition extremely difficult of performance, is in reality a tremendously expanded, daring and wild fantasia. It lacks nothing in the way of startling and beautiful passages, in which the energetic and talented composer must be recognised; but often it loses itself in lawlessness. The symphony begins with an Allegro in E-flat that is vigorously scored; a Funeral March in C minor follows which is later developed fugally. After this comes an Allegro scherzo and a Finale, both in E-flat. The reviewer belongs to Herr van Beethoven's sincerest admirers, but in this composition he must confess that he finds too much that is glaring and bizarre, which hinders greatly one's grasp of the whole, and a sense of unity is almost completely lost.—The Symphony in E-flat by Eberl again was extraordinarily pleasing; and really it has so much that is beautiful and powerful, handled with such genius and art, that its effect could hardly be lacking in any performance in which it were well rehearsed. The last piece is very distinguished in which a simple and lovely idea governs the whole, very beautifully and artistically employed and worked out."

Such is the review of the *Sinfonia Eroica* in its first semi-public production and of the pieces which accompanied it! Its first really public performance was in the Theater-an-der-Wien, on Sunday evening, April 7th, where it began the second part of a concert given for his own benefit by Clement. The programme announces it thus: "A new grand symphony in D-sharp[9] by Herr Ludwig van Beethoven, dedicated to his Serene Highness Prince Lobkowitz. The composer has kindly consented to conduct the work."

Czerny remembered, and told Jahn, that on this occasion "somebody in the gallery cried out: 'I'll give another kreutzer if the thing will but stop!' " This is the key-note to the strain in which the Symphony was criticized in communications to the press, that are now among the curiosities of musical literature. The correspondent of the *Freymüthige* divided the audience into

---

[9] According to German tablature, flat tones (E-flat, A-flat) were customarily called sharp tones (D-sharp, G-sharp) right into the 19th century. (TDR, II, 459, n. 2.)

three parties. "Some," says he, "Beethoven's particular friends, assert that it is just this symphony which is his masterpiece, that this is the true style for high-class music, and that if it does not please now, it is because the public is not cultured enough, artistically, to grasp all these lofty beauties; after a few thousand years have passed it will not fail of its effect. Another faction denies that the work has any artistic value and professes to see in it an untamed striving for singularity which had failed, however, to achieve in any of its parts beauty or true sublimity and power. By means of strange modulations and violent transitions, by combining the most heterogeneous elements, as for instance when a pastoral in the largest style is ripped up by the basses, by three horns, etc., a certain undesirable originality may be achieved without much trouble; but genius proclaims itself not in the unusual and the fantastic, but in the beautiful and the sublime. Beethoven himself proved the correctness of this axiom in his earlier works. The third party, a very small one, stands midway between the others—it admits that the symphony contains many beauties, but concedes that the connection is often disrupted entirely, and that the inordinate length of this longest, and perhaps most difficult of all symphonies, wearies even the cognoscenti, and is unendurable to the mere music-lover; it wishes that H. v. B. would employ his acknowledgedly great talents in giving us works like his symphonies in C and D, his ingratiating Septet in E-flat, the intellectual Quintet in D [C major?] and others of his early compositions which have placed B. forever in the ranks of the foremost instrumental composers. It fears, however, that if Beethoven continues on his present path both he and the public will be the sufferers. His music could soon reach the point where one would derive no pleasure from it, unless well trained in the rules and difficulties of the art, but rather would leave the concert hall with an unpleasant feeling of fatigue from having been crushed by a mass of unconnected and overloaded ideas and a continuing tumult by all the instruments. The public and Herr van Beethoven, who conducted, were not satisfied with each other on this evening; the public thought the symphony too heavy, too long, and himself too discourteous, because he did not nod his head in recognition of the applause which came from a portion of the audience. On the contrary, Beethoven found that the applause was not strong enough."

This clear, compendious and valuable statement of the conflicting opinions of the first auditors of the "Eroica" renders further citations superfluous; but a story—characteristic enough to be true—may be added: that Beethoven, in reply to the complaints of too great length, said, in substance: "If *I* write a symphony an hour long it will be found short enough!" He refused positively to make any change in the work, but deferred to public opinion so far, as, upon its publication, to affix to the title of the Symphony a note to the effect, that on account of its great length it should be played near the beginning of a concert, before the audience was become weary.

Ignaz Pleyel, born in 1757, the twenty-fourth child of a schoolmaster at Ruppersthal, a village a few miles from Vienna, a favorite pupil of Haydn and just now the most widely known and popular living instrumental composer except his master, came from Paris this season to visit, after many years absence, the scenes of his youth. He brought with him his last new quartets, "which," writes Czerny, "were performed before a large and aristocratic society at the house of Prince Lobkowitz. At the close, Beethoven, who was also present, was requested to play something. As usual he let himself be begged for an infinitely long time and at last almost dragged by two ladies to the pianoforte. In an ill humor he grabbed a second violin part of the Pleyel quartet from a music desk, threw it on the rack of the pianoforte and began to improvise. He had never been heard to improvise more brilliantly, with more originality and splendor than on this evening! But through the entire improvisation there ran through the middle voices like a thread or *cantus firmus* the notes, in themselves utterly insignificant, which he had found on the accidentally opened page of the quartet, upon which he built up the most daring melodies and harmonies in the most brilliant concerto style. Old Pleyel could show his amazement only by kissing his hands. After such improvisations Beethoven was wont to break out in a ringing peal of amused laughter."

It will be recalled that at the end of 1804, the frequency with which Beethoven was in the company of Countess Josephine Deym was a source of concern to her sisters. At the beginning of 1805 Charlotte Brunsvik in her letters to Therese continued to mention Beethoven's visits "almost every day," describing him now as "exceedingly kind." "He has composed a song for Pepi [Josephine] that she sent you. But she begged you at the same time to show it to no one nor to say that you have the notes if you sing it for anyone." The song was "An die Hoffnung" from Tiedge's *Urania.* On January 20, 1805, Therese wrote Charlotte: "But tell me, Pepi and Beethoven, what shall become of it? She should be on her guard! I believe you were referring to her when you underlined the specific words: '*Her heart must have the strength to say No,*' a sad duty, if not the saddest of all!! . . . . Often one errs and is misunderstood in love. Only one who *experiences* love can form an opinion concerning it. Love, what an omnipotent feeling, what a new life within life!—May the grace of God aid Pepi so that she is not tormented with care and her health may improve!"[10]

According to Miss Anderson's datings, of Beethoven's known correspondence with the Countess, four letters and the fragment of a fifth are to be ascribed to the year 1805.[11]

The first one begins with an assurance to Josephine that gossip about them was not developing. The roots of Josephine's fears were twofold: first, Prince Lichnowsky had seen in Beethoven's room a copy of the song "An

---

[10] La Mara, 1920, pp. 52-54.   [11] See *A,* 110, 112, 113, 114, 115.

die Hoffnung," which evidently bore some message or inscription to Josephine, for, as Beethoven admits, the Prince concluded that "I must surely have some affection for you"; second, that Zmeskall, a good friend of the Brunsvik family, had been asked by the Prince whether Beethoven and Josephine met very often, a subject which was subsequently "magnified" by Zmeskall and Josephine's aunt, the Countess Susanna Guicciardi. Beethoven made clear that the Prince had not mentioned the song to Zmeskall, that the latter had been non-committal in his answer to the Prince, and that no one else was involved.

Beethoven's letter sheds new light on his friends' concern for him and his creative efforts. He had learned that Zmeskall "was to have a word with Tante Gui[12]—and suggest that she should speak to you so that you might encourage me more earnestly *to finish my opera*, because he believed that this might do a lot of good." Also he assured Josephine that Prince Lichnowsky wished for a more intimate association between Beethoven and the Countess, for "such a friendship could not but be advantageous to me." But the great importance of this letter is the change that it shows in Beethoven's own feelings towards Josephine, whom he now calls "beloved J" and "my adored J." However, it is important to note that in none of these letters is the lady addressed as "Du," a form of address to a woman used only in the "Immortal Beloved" letters of 1812.

As with his close friends of the past, Beethoven refers to a period of "real sorrows and the struggle with myself between death and life, a struggle in which I was engaged for some time," and he longed for the chance, uninterrupted, to unburden to her his private grief—which was of course his deafness.

He wrote that he had been determined not to fall in love but that she had conquered him. The letter ends with the following description of their love: "Long—long—of long duration—may our love become— For it is so noble—so firmly founded upon mutual regard and friendship— Even the great similarity between us in so many respects, in our thoughts and feelings— Oh you, you make me hope that *your heart* will long—beat for me— *Mine beats— Beloved J*, I send you all good wishes— *But I also* hope—that *through me* you will gain a little happiness—otherwise I should certainly be—*selfish*."[13]

Of the remaining four letters for this year, only the fragmentary one continues and indeed exceeds the intensity of the first letter. The others are concerned with such matters as the sending of a gift, the time for next meeting, or the request for the return of some music. Here follows the fragmentary copy made by Josephine Deym of an unsigned letter to her, presumably from Beethoven.[14]

---

[12] Countess Guicciardi.

[13] *A*, 110, Miss Anderson's translation; reprinted with her permission and that of her publishers. According to Miss Anderson, there is no signature on the autograph.

[14] *A*, 112, Miss Anderson's translation; reprinted with her permission and that of her publishers, Macmillan & Co., Ltd.

. . . from her—

the only beloved—why is there no language which can express what is far above all mere regard—far above everything—that we can never describe— Oh, who can name *you*—and not feel that however much he could speak about *you*—that would never attain—to *you*—only in music— Alas, am I not too proud when I believe that music is more at my command than words— *You, you*, my all, my happiness—alas, no—even in *my music* I cannot do so, although in this respect thou, Nature, hast not stinted me with thy gifts. Yet there is too little for *you*. Beat, though in silence, poor heart—that is all you can do, nothing more—for *you*—always for *you*—only *you*—eternally *you*—only *you* until I sink into the grave— My refreshment—my all. Oh, Creator, watch over her—bless her days—rather let all calamities fall upon me—

Only *you*— May you be strengthened, blessed and comforted—in the wretched yet frequently happy existence of us mortals—

Even if you had not fettered me again to life, yet you would have meant everything to me—

Since none of the letters is dated it is unclear whether Beethoven continued to see a great deal of the Countess as the year progressed, or whether the romance became less intense. However, it is known that they were neighbors at Hetzendorf during the summer. Then in the fall the Napoleonic invasion forced the Countess to flee the city with her children. She went to the family home at Martonvasar, wintered in Budapest, and did not return to Vienna to live until later in 1806. The nobility of this lady and the conflict that she experienced in her relationship with Beethoven are revealed in her draft of a letter to the composer, printed by Schmidt-Görg, which he dates after the winter of 1804-1805:[15]

The closer relationship with you, dear *Beethoven* these winter months has left impressions in my heart which neither time—nor circumstances will erase— Are you happy or sad?—can you yourself tell— Also—in regard to your feelings through self-control—or free release—what *you*—could thereby change—

My soul, already *inspired* about you before I knew you personally—has been nourished by your affection. A feeling that lies deep in my soul and is incapable of expression made me love you; even before I knew you your music aroused *inspiration* within me—your kind *nature* and your affection strengthened it— This favor which you have accorded me, the pleasure of your company would have been the finest ornament of my life if you had been able to love me less sensuously—that I cannot satisfy this sensuous love—does this cause you anger— I would have to break holy vows were I to listen to your desire— Believe me— it is I through the fulfillment of my duty who suffer the most—and my actions have been surely dictated by noble motives.—

The new contract with Baron Braun gave the composer again a right to the apartments in the theatre building, which he improved, at the same time retaining the dwelling at the Pasqualati house. The city directory for 1805 gives his address at the theatre, and there he received visitors; at the Pasqua-

[15] *Veröffentlichungen des Beethovenhauses in Bonn*, 1957, III, 25-26.

{ 379 }

lati house he was accustomed to seclude himself for work, forbidding his servant to admit any person whatever. In the summer he retired to Hetzendorf, and wrought out his opera, sitting in the same crotched oak in the Schönbrunn Garden that he had used, according to Schindler, four years before. Thus again he had three lodgings at the same time, as in the preceding summer; with this difference, that now one was no expense to him.

Before his migration to Hetzendorf—say about the middle of June, 1805—Beethoven had completely sketched the music of his opera. This is made sufficiently certain by one of those whimsical remarks that he was in the habit of making on the blank spaces of whatever manuscript he happened to have before him. In this case he writes: "June 2nd Finale always simpler. All pianoforte music also. God knows why my pianoforte music always makes the worst impression, especially when it is badly played." This is in the midst of sketches to the final chorus of the opera, and is written upon the upper outer corner of page 291 of the "Leonore" sketchbook (now in the Berlin State Library). Nottebohm dates this sketchbook "for the most part 1804" and has given it a detailed description,[16] from which we draw: "The sketchbook is filled for the most part with work on the last pieces of the first act and on all pieces of the second act . . . .[17] Originally there were four sketchbooks which, because of their similar content, belonged together; the present sketchbook represents the original second and third sections of which the first and fourth are lost. The first must have contained work on the first third of *Leonore*, while the fourth continued work on the second [last] finale and the overture. . . . Without counting subsequent changes and the like, Beethoven took up the principal numbers of the opera in the order in which they stand in the 1805 libretto."[18]

The studies for Fidelio's recitative "Ach brich noch nicht" and aria "Komm Hoffnung" (No. 11), which are found near the end of the volume, seem to form a marked exception to the rule; but if these are really the first sketches, their appearance after the final scenes is explained by two remarks in Beethoven's hand on page 344: "Duetto with Müller [Marcelline] and Fidelio aside," and "Aria for Fidelio, another text which agrees with her." These notes clearly indicate a change of plan in connection with the duet, and that the beautiful air, "Komm Hoffnung," did not stand in Sonnleithner's original text.[19]

Otto Jahn has summed up the sketch work as follows:[20] "One is amazed

---

[16] See *II Beeth.*, pp. 409-459. (Cf. TDR, II, 463, n. 1.)

[17] Nottebohm writes in the context of the *two*-act framework of the two later versions (1806, 1814) of the opera. The first version of 1805 is cast in three acts and for this version his text should read: "on the last pieces of the *second* act and on all pieces of the third act."

[18] Nottebohm, *op.cit.*, pp. 409-10.

[19] *Ibid.*, pp. 447-52. Nottebohm believes that Leonore's aria in E was written after the 1805 version and that the original aria, now lost, was in F and set to Sonnleithner's original text. See *Lpz. AMZ*, VIII, p. 236, and Willy Hess, *Beethovens Oper Fidelio* (Zurich, 1953), p. 179.

[20] *Gesammelte Aufsätze über Musik* (Leipzig, 1866), p. 244. (TDR, II, 465.)

at this everlasting experimentation and cannot conceive how it will be pos-sible to create an organic whole out of such musical scraps. But if one compares the completed art-work with the chaos of sketches one is over-whelmed with wonder at the creative mind which surveyed its task so clearly, grasped the foundation and the outlines of the execution so firmly and surely that with all the sketches and attempts in details the whole grows naturally from its roots and develops. And though the sketches frequently create the impression of uncertainty and groping, admiration comes again for the marvelously keen self-criticism, which, after everything has been tested with sovereign certainty, retains the best. I have had an opportunity to study many of Beethoven's sketchbooks, but I have found no instance in which one was compelled to recognize that the material chosen was not the best, or in which one could deplore that the material which he rejected had not been used."

He might have added, with truth, that some of the first ideas noted to passages, now among the gems of the opera, are commonplace and trivial to such a degree, that one can hardly attribute them to Beethoven. Yet, there they are in his own hand.

In the notices of the "Leonore" sketchbook, made for use in this work, are copied *eighteen* different beginnings to Florestan's air "In des Lebens Frühlingstagen," and ten to the chorus "Wer ein holdes Weib"; others being omitted, because illegible or more than a little repetitious. The studies for that wondrous outburst of joy, "O namenlose Freude," are numerous; but the first bars of the duet are the same in all of them, having been taken by Beethoven from work that he did on Schikaneder's *Vestas Feuer*, mentioned in a previous chapter.

Inborn genius for musical composition, untiring industry, and the ambition to rival Cherubini in his own field, sufficiently explain the extraordinary merits of this work of Beethoven; want of practice and experience in operatic writing, its defects.

Beethoven's seclusion at Hetzendorf from June to September (probably) and his labor of reducing the chaos of the sketchbook into the order and beauty of the score of *Leonore*—on which, as he told Schindler, he worked in the bright summer days, sitting in the shades of Schönbrunn—are un-broken for us except by his first meeting with Cherubini. Some time in July—for that master arrived in Vienna after the 5th of that month, and Vogler was in Salzburg before the 28th—"Cherubini, Beethoven and Vogler were gathered together at Sonnleithner's; everybody played, Vogler first, and without ceasing, so that the company meanwhile sat down to table. Beethoven was full of attention and respect toward Cherubini." Such is Jahn's note of a communication to him by Grillparzer; but Czerny told him: "B. did not give Cherubini a friendly reception in 1805, as the latter com-plained to Czerny later."

At the end of the summer season Beethoven returned to town with his opera ready to be put in rehearsal. Here Ries found him after the latter's return from Silesia, where he had been the pianoforte player for Prince Lichnowsky on his estate. However, with all of Beethoven's kindness to Ries, Beethoven had neither forgotten nor forgiven the affair of the "Andante favori." Ries writes (*Notizen*, pp. 102-103) : "One day when a small company including Beethoven and me breakfasted with Prince [Lichnowsky] after the concert in the Augarten (8 o'clock in the forenoon), it was proposed that we drive to Beethoven's house and hear his opera *Leonore*, which had not yet been performed. Arrived there Beethoven demanded that I go away, and inasmuch as the most urgent appeals of all present were fruitless, I did so with tears in my eyes. The entire company noticed it, and Prince Lichnowsky, following me, asked me to wait in an anteroom, because, having been the cause of the trouble, he wanted to have it settled. But the feeling of hurt to my honor would not permit this. I heard afterward that Prince Lichnowsky had sharply rebuked Beethoven for his conduct, since only love for his works had been to blame for the incident and consequently for his anger. But the only result of these representations was that Beethoven refused to play any more for the company."

It so happened, that Ries thus lost his only opportunity ever to hear the "Leonore-Fidelio" music in its original form; but this Beethoven could not anticipate, as he could have no suspicion that they were so soon to be parted. Bonn, being now under French rule, Ries was liable to conscription, and notice came that he was among the first drawn. "He was therefore," says the *Harmonicon* (1824, No. 15), "obliged to return home immediately, for his disobedience would have exposed his father and family to the risk of ruin." Before Ries's departure from Vienna, Beethoven, himself unable to afford him pecuniary assistance, again proved his kindly feelings towards his pupil by giving him a letter commending him to the benevolence of Princess Liechtenstein.[21]

"To Beethoven's rage," says Ries, "the letter was not delivered, but I kept the original, written on an unevenly cut quarto sheet, as a proof of Beethoven's friendship and love for me." Three years will elapse before we meet Ries again in Vienna—the greater part of which period he passed at Paris in such discouraging circumstances, that he thought seriously of abandoning his profession.

At the Theater-an-der-Wien none of the new operas produced this season had long kept the stage; although two of them—Schikaneder's *Swetards Zaubergürtel*, music by Fischer, and his *Vestas Feuer*, music by J. Weigl— were brought out "with very extraordinary splendor of decorations and costumes." It was now autumn and the receipts did not cover the expenses of the theatre. "From the distance," says Treitschke, "the storm of war rolled towards Vienna and robbed the spectators of the calm essential to the enjoyment of an art-work. But just for this reason all possible efforts were made

[21] See *A*, 121.

to enliven the sparsely attended spaces of the house. *Fidelio* was relied upon to do its best, and so, under far from happy auspices, the opera was produced on November 20 [1805]. It was possible efficiently to cast only the female parts with Mlles. Milder and Müller; the men left all the more to be desired."

Anna Milder (born December 13, 1785), now just completing her twentieth year, was that pupil of Neukomm to whom Haydn had said half a dozen years before: "My dear child! You have a voice like a house!" Schikaneder gave her her first engagement and she began her theatrical career April 9, 1803, in the part of Juno in Süssmayr's *Spiegel von Arkadien*, with a new grand aria composed for her by him. Beethoven had now written the part of Fidelio for her. In later years it was one of her grand performances; though, judging from the contemporary criticisms, it was now somewhat defective, simply from lack of stage experience. Louise Müller, the Marcelline, "had already (in April, 1805) developed in a few years into a tasteful and honest singer, although she did not have the help of a voice of especial volume." She became, in the opinion of Castelli, "a most amiable actress and good singer, particularly in the comic genre."

Demmer, "trained in Cologne," is reported in 1799, when singing at Frankfurt am-Main, as having "a firm, enduring voice with a high range; he played semi-comic rôles admirably. He was best in airs in which there was little agility and more sustained declamation." Castelli praises him; but all contemporary accounts agree that he was not equal to the part of Florestan, for which he was now selected.

Sebastian Mayer,[22] brother-in-law to Mozart (the musical reformer of this theatre), "was insignificant as a singer, but a valiant actor," says Castelli, who knew him most intimately. Schindler has an anecdote of him as Pizarro, apparently derived from Beethoven, to the effect that he had a high opinion of his own powers; that he used to swear by Mozart and confidently undertake everything. In view of this Beethoven resolved to cure him of his weakness, and to this end wrote the passage in Pizarro's air:

[22] Also spelled Meyer and Meier.

the voice moves over a series of scales, played by all the strings, so that the singer at each note which he has to utter, hears an appoggiatura of a minor second from the orchestra. The Pizarro of 1805 was unable with all his gesticulation and writhing to avoid the difficulty, the more since the mischievous players in the orchestra below maliciously emphasized the minor second by accentuation. Don Pizarro, snorting with rage, was thus at the mercy of the bows of the fiddlers. This aroused laughter. The singer, whose conceit was thus wounded, thereupon flew into a rage and hurled at the composer among other remarks the words: "My brother-in-law would never have written such damned nonsense."[23]

Weinkopf (Don Fernando) had "a pure and expressive bass voice," but his part was too meagre and unimportant to affect the success or failure of the opera.

Caché (Jaquino), according to Castelli, was a good actor, "who was also made serviceable in the opera because Meyer, the stage-manager, knew that good acting, in comic operas, was frequently more effective than a good voice. It was necessary to fiddle his song-parts into his head before we came to rehearsals." Rothe (Rocco) was so inferior both as actor and singer, that his name is not to be found in any of the ordinary sources of Vienna theatrical history.

One can well believe that very considerable difficulties attended the performance, as Treitschke states. His words, in a passage above cited, as well as certain expressions of Beethoven's a few months later, indicate that the opera was hurriedly put upon the stage, and the inadequacy of the singers thus increased by the lack of sufficient rehearsals. Seyfried says, "I directed the study of the parts with all the singers according to his suggestions, also all the orchestral rehearsals, and personally conducted the performance." In 1805 Seyfried was young, talented, ambitious, zealous, and nothing was wanting on his part to insure success.

Speaking of the rehearsals recalls to mind one of those bursts of puerile wrath, which were passed over with a smile by some of Beethoven's friends, but gave serious offense to others. Mähler remembered that at one of the general rehearsals the third bassoon was absent; at which Beethoven fretted and fumed. Lobkowitz, who was present, made light of the matter: two of the bassoons were present, said he, and the absence of the third could make no great difference. This so enraged the composer, that, as he passed the Lobkowitz Place, on his way home, he could not restrain the impulse to turn aside and shout in at the great door of the palace: "Lobkowitzian ass!"

There were various stumbling-blocks in the vocal score of *Leonore*. Schindler on this point has some judicious remarks, and they are borne out by his record of conversations with Cherubini and Anna Milder. During his years of frequent intercourse with Beethoven and subsequently, *Leonore* was

---

[23] *Biographie*, pp. 132-33. (TDR, II, 482.) See *II Beeth.* p. 416 for Beethoven's original draft of this passage.

a work upon whose origin and failure he took much pains to inform himself, and its history as finally drawn up by him is much more satisfactory and correct than others of greater pretensions.[24]

---{This holds true especially in connection with the Leonore Overture No. 1 (Op. 138). Because Schindler was not in direct contact with the composer until 1814, Thayer discounts Schindler's testimony concerning this work and along with Nottebohm dates the composition of the overture as 1807. Since then Schindler's original account in his biography (which establishes the year of composition as 1805) has been supported by the research of Levinsohn[25] and Braunstein.[26] Before proving his point on analytical grounds, Braunstein shows that the sketches for No. 1 are connected with sketches for the Fifth Symphony in its *early* stages, thus prior to 1807 and quite logically in 1805.

In the first edition,[27] Schindler writes: "It was the overture in the first place that put our master in a painful situation. It was finished, but the composer himself was not thoroughly satisfied with it, and therefore agreed that it should be tried by a small orchestra, at Prince Lichnowsky's. There it was unanimously pronounced by a knot of connoisseurs to be too light, and not sufficiently expressive of the nature of the work; consequently it was laid aside and never made its appearance again in Beethoven's lifetime."

Schindler adds in the third edition:[28] "The publishers Steiner and Company claimed it forthwith as their property.[29] Not until the fourth decade [of the century] did it appear in print, numbered in the catalogue as the *very latest* work of our master."

The initial performance of the opera was originally scheduled for October 15. A petition from Sonnleithner to the theatre censor, dated October 2, 1805, sheds much light on the vicissitudes of the production:

Court Secretary Josef Sonnleithner begs that the ban of this September 30th on the opera Fidelio be lifted since this opera from the French original of Boully [*sic*] (entitled Leonore, ou l'amour conjugal) *has been most especially revised because the Empress had found the original very beautiful and affirmed* that no opera subject had ever given her so much pleasure; secondly: this opera which was revised by Kapellmeister Paër in Italian has been given already in Prague and Dresden; thirdly: *Beethoven* has spent over a year and a half with the composition, also since the ban was completely unanticipated, rehearsals have already been held and other arrangements have been made in order to give this opera on the name-day of the Empress [October 15]; fourthly: the plot takes

---

[24] *Ibid.*, p. 118. (TDR, II, 485, n. 1.) See also *Der Bär* (Leipzig, 1927), pp. 113-17 for letters from Schindler to Breitkopf and Härtel (written in 1841-42) concerning the opera, and a discussion of them by Wilhelm Lütge.

[25] Albert Levinsohn, "Die Entstehungszeit der Ouvertüre Leonore Nr. 1, Op. 138 mit anschliessenden kritischen Bemerkungen zu Nottebohms Beethoveniana," *Vierteljahrsschrift*

für Musikwissenschaft, Vol. 9 (1893), pp. 128-65.

[26] Josef Braunstein, *Beethovens Leonore-Ouvertüre* (Leipzig, 1927).

[27] *The Life of Beethoven*, ed. Moscheles (London, 1841), I, 92.

[28] *Biographie*, p. 127.

[29] Braunstein (*op.cit.*, p. 17) believes this was between 1814 and 1816.

place in the 16th century, thus there could be no underlying relationship; finally in the fifth place: there exists such a big lack of opera libretti, this one presents the quietest description of womanly virtue and the evil minded governor is executing only a private revenge like Pedrarias in Balboa.[30]

On October 5th, the ban was lifted after some changes had been made in the most harsh scenes. But the postponement of the performance for another five weeks was due not to censorship problems but to the mechanics of getting the music composed, copied and rehearsed. Let one of the notes from Beethoven to Sebastian Mayer suggest the situation:

Dear Mayer! The third act quartet is now all right; what has been written out with red pencil must be written over in ink by the copyist right away, otherwise it will fade away!— This afternoon I shall send for the 1st and 2nd act again because I want to look through them also myself.— I cannot come, because since yesterday I have had *diarrhoea—my usual sickness*. Don't worry about the overture and the rest; if necessary everything could be ready even by tomorrow. In the present *fatal crisis* I have so many other things to do that I must put off everything which is not completely necessary.

Your Friend Beethoven

This overture could have been none other than the so-called Leonore No. 2 since Leonore No. 1, according to Schindler, had been found to be unsatisfactory in a private hearing at Prince Lichnowsky's. As with Leonore No. 3, the autographs for both these overtures have disappeared.

Outside the narrow circle of the playhouse, weightier matters than a new opera now occupied and agitated the minds of the Viennese. On the 20th of October, Ulm fell. On the 30th Bernadotte entered Salzburg, on his way to and down the Danube, Vienna was defenceless. The nobility, the great bankers and merchants—all those whose wealth enabled and whose vocations permitted it—precisely those classes of society in which Beethoven moved, which knew how to appreciate his music, and of whose suffrages his opera was assured, fled from the capital. On November 9th the Empress departed. On the 10th the French armies had reached and occupied the villages a few miles west of the city. On November 13th, about 11 o'clock in the forenoon, the vanguard of the enemy, Murat and Lannes at the head, 15,000 strong, representing all branches of the service, entered Vienna in order of battle, flags flying and music sounding.

On the 15th, Bonaparte issued his proclamation from Schönbrunn, which he made his headquarters. Murat quartered himself in the palace of Archduke Albert; General Hulin, in that of Prince Lobkowitz. It was just at this most unlucky of all possible periods that Beethoven's opera was produced; on November 20, 21 and 22. Beethoven desired to retain the original title of the opera, *Leonore* and the directors of the theatre have been severely

---

[30] See Karl Glossy, "Beiträgen zur Geschichte der Theater Wiens," *Jahrbuch der Grillparzer-Gesellschaft*, I (1801-1820), 1915, pp. 83ff. Also printed in *Archiv für Musikwissenschaft*, II (1920), 404.

censured from that day to this for persisting in giving and retaining the title *Fidelio*.

Beethoven's friend, Stephan von Breuning, prepared a pretty surprise for him by printing a short complimentary poem and having it distributed in the theatre at the second performance. Concerning the circumstance of the performance, the correspondent for Kotzebue's *Freymüthige* (December 26, 1805) describes first the military occupation of Vienna, the officers quartered in the city proper, and the private soldiery in the suburbs. He continues:

"Also in the beginning the theatres were completely empty; gradually the French began to go to them, and they still form the majority of the audience.

"Recently little new of significance has been given. A new Beethoven opera 'Fidelio or Die eheliche Liebe' has not pleased. It was performed only a few times and after the first performance [the theatre] remained completely empty. Also the music was really way below the expectations of amateur and professional alike. The melodies as well as the general character, much of which is affected, lack that happy, clear, magical impression of emotion which grips us so irresistibly in the works of Mozart and Cherubini. The music has some beautiful passages, but it is very far from being a perfect, yes, even successful work. The text, translated by Sonnleithner concerns a story of rescue which has become in fashion ever since Cherubini's 'Deux Journées.'"

In the issue of January 8, 1806, the correspondent of the *Allg. Mus. Zeitung* says that he had expected something very different, in view of Beethoven's undisputed talent. ". . . Up to now Beethoven has sacrificed beauty so many times for the new and strange; thus this characteristic of newness and a certain originality in creative idea was expected from this first theatrical production of his—and it is exactly these qualities that are the least in evidence. Judged dispassionately and with an open mind, the whole is distinguishable neither by invention nor execution. The overture . . . cannot be compared with his overture to the ballet *Prometheus*. As a rule there are no new ideas in the vocal pieces, they are mostly too long, the text repeats itself endlessly, and finally the characterization fails remarkably—as for example the duet in G from the third act after the scene of recognition. For the continuously running accompaniment in the highest register of the violins more nearly expresses mere wild jubilation rather than the quiet feeling of deep sorrow for the circumstances in which they have been reunited. Much better is a four-part canon from the first act and an effective soprano aria in F major [E major?] in which three horns *obbligato* and a bassoon form a beautiful, if at times somewhat overloaded, accompaniment.[31] The choruses are ineffectual and one, which indicates the joy of prisoners over the sensation of fresh air, miscarries completely. . . ."

[31] See n. 19 above.

To understand the criticism of the duet, it must be realized that at the occurrence of this duet, "O namenlose Freude," in the 1805 version, the dramatic situation is quite different from that of the 1814 version. In both cases the trumpet calls have heralded the start of the dénouement, and after the end of the quartet, Pizarro exits followed by Rocco. But in the earlier version Rocco, instead of giving a sign of assurance to the reunited pair which signifies that all danger is past, grabs Leonore's pistol with a vehemence which causes her to faint. The recitative and duet that follow are concerned not only with the joy of reunion but the uncertainty still of a joint death, which is not resolved until the entrance of Don Fernando himself.

Joseph August Röckel (1783-1870), a young man educated at the University of Munich, had for some time been private secretary to the Bavarian *Chargé des Affaires* at Salzburg. The approach of the French armies after the fall of Ulm made his position and prospects very uncertain. It was just then that an agent of Baron Braun came thither in search of a young, fresh tenor to succeed Demmer, whose powers were fast yielding to time. The engagement was offered him and thus it came about, that Röckel, in the autumn of 1805, became first tenor in the Theater-an-der-Wien. After appearing in divers characters with much success, considering his inexperience, he was offered the part of Florestan in the contemplated revival of *Fidelio*. A conversation with the singer at Bath in April, 1861, is authority for these particulars, and a letter from him dated February 26 of the same year adds more. Röckel wrote:

"It was in December, 1805—the opera house An-der-Wien and both the Court theatres of Vienna having been at that time under the intendance of Baron Braun, the Court Banker—when Mr. Meyer, brother-in-law to Mozart and Regisseur of the opera An-der-Wien, came to fetch me to an evening meeting in the palace of Prince Karl Lichnowsky, the great patron of Beethoven. *Fidelio* had already been performed a month previously An-der-Wien—unhappily just after the entrance of the French, when the city was shut against the suburbs. The whole theatre had been taken up by the French, and only a few friends of Beethoven had ventured to hear the opera. These friends were now at that soirée, to bring Beethoven about, to consent to the changes they wanted to introduce in the opera in order to remove the heaviness of the first act. The necessity of these improvements was already acknowledged and settled among themselves. Meyer had prepared me for the coming storm, when Beethoven should hear of leaving out three whole numbers of the first act.

"At the soirée were present Prince Lichnowsky and the Princess, his lady, Beethoven and his brother Kaspar, [Stephan] von Breuning, [Heinrich] von Collin, the poet, the tragedian Lange (another brother-in-law to Mozart), Treitschke, Clement, leader of the orchestra, Meyer and myself; whether

Kapellmeister von Seyfried was there I am not certain any more, though I should think so.

"I had arrived in Vienna only a short time before, and met Beethoven there for the first time.

"As the whole opera was to be gone through, we went directly to work. Princess L. played on the grand piano the great score of the opera and Clement, sitting in a corner of the room, accompanied with his violin the whole opera by heart, playing all the solos of the different instruments. The extraordinary memory of Clement having been universally known, nobody was astonished by it, except myself. Meyer and I made ourselves useful, by singing as well as we could, he (basso) the lower, I the higher parts of the opera. Though the friends of Beethoven were fully prepared for the impending battle, they had never seen him in *that* excitement before, and without the prayers and entreaties of the very delicate and invalid princess, who was a second mother to Beethoven and acknowledged by himself as such, his united friends were not likely to have succeeded in this, even to themselves, very doubtful enterprise. But when after their united endeavors from seven till after one o'clock, the sacrifice of the three numbers was accomplished, and when we, exhausted, hungry and thirsty, went to restore ourselves by a splendid supper—then, none was happier and gayer than Beethoven. Had I seen him before in his fury, I saw him now in his frolics. When he saw me, opposite to him, so intently occupied with a French dish, and asked me what I was eating, and I answered: 'I don't know!' with his lion-voice he roared out: 'He eats like a wolf—without knowing what! Ha, ha, ha!'

"The condemned three numbers were:

1. A great aria with chorus of Pizarro;
2. A comic duo between Leonore (Fidelio) and Marcelline, with violin and violoncello solo;
3. A comic terzetto between Marcelline, Jacquino and Rocco.

Many years after, Mr. Schindler found the scores of these three pieces amongst the rubbish of Beethoven's music, and got them as a present from him."[32]

A question has been raised as to the accuracy of Röckel's memory in his statement of the numbers cancelled on this occasion; to which it may be remarked, that the particulars of this first and extraordinary meeting with Beethoven would naturally impress themselves very deeply upon the memory of the young singer; that the numbers to be condemned had been previously agreed upon by the parties opposed to the composer in the transaction, and doubtless made known to Röckel; that Röckel's relations to Mayer were such as to render it in the highest degree improbable, that he should con-

---

[32] Another description by Röckel of the same scene in greater detail appeared in Rudolph Bunge's essay "Fidelio," (*Gartenlaube*, Leipzig, 1868, pp. 61off.) which is translated into English in Sonneck's *Beethoven, Impressions of Contemporaries* (New York, 1927), pp. 6off.

found Rocco's gold aria with either of the Pizarro airs with chorus belonging to Mayer's part; that both of these belong to the first and second original acts—i.e., to the first act of the opera as Röckel knew it; that he (Röckel) in his letter to the writer is not reporting upon the pieces actually omitted in the subsequent performance three or four months later, but upon those which, at this meeting, Beethoven was with great difficulty persuaded to omit: that the objections made to them were not to the music, but because they retarded the action; and, therefore, that the decision now reached was by no means final, provided that the desired end could be reached in some other way. It appears that Beethoven, now cunningly giving way, succeeded in winning the game, and retaining all three of the pieces condemned. ⟶Instead only the following were omitted altogether: Rocco's aria "Hat man nicht auch Gold beineben" and the melodrama preceding the duet for Rocco and Leonore "Nur hurtig fort." A detailed comparison of the 1805 and 1806 version can best be found in Willy Hess's book *Beethovens Oper Fidelio*.[33]⟵

Beethoven felt the loss of Ries very sensibly; but it was in part supplied by young Röckel, to whom he took a great liking. Inviting him to call, he told him he would give special orders to his servant to admit him at all times, even in the morning when busy. It was agreed that, when Röckel was admitted, if he found Beethoven very much occupied he should pass through the room into the bed-chamber beyond—both rooms overlooked the Glacis from the fourth story of the Pasqualati house on the Mölker Bastei—and there await him a reasonable time; if the composer came not, Röckel should quietly pass out again. It happened one morning upon his first visit, that Röckel found at the street door a carriage with a lady in it; and, on reaching the fourth story, there, at Beethoven's door, was Prince Lichnowsky in a dispute with the servant about being admitted. The man declared he dared not admit anybody, as his master was busy and had given express orders not to admit any person whatever. Röckel, however, having the entrée, informed Beethoven that Lichnowsky was outside. Though in ill humor, he could no longer refuse to see him. The Prince and his wife had come to take Beethoven out for an airing; and he finally consented, but, as he entered the carriage, Röckel noticed that his face was still cloudy.

Outside theatrical circles we catch also a glimpse or two of Beethoven in these months. Pierre Baillot, the violinist, was in Vienna just before the French invasion on his way to Moscow, and was taken by Anton Reicha to see Beethoven. A correspondent for the Leipzig *Signale für die Musikalische Welt* (June 21, 1866) describes the encounter: "They did not find him in his lodgings but in a by no means elegant inn in the Vorstadt. What first

---

[33] Atlantis; Zurich, 1953. The reader is also referred to two editions of *Leonore*, vocal scores with pianoforte accompaniment published by Breitkopf and Härtel; the 1806 version prepared by Otto Jahn and published in 1852, the 1805 version by Erich Prieger and published in 1905.

attracted the attention of the Frenchman was that Beethoven did not have the bulldog, gloomy expression which he had expected from the majority of his portraits; he even thought he recognized an expression of good-nature in the face of the composer. The conversation had just got well under way when it was interrupted by a terrific snore. It came from a stableman or coachman who was taking his little nap in a corner of the room. Beethoven gazed at the snorer a few moments attentively and then broke out with the words: 'I wish I were as stupid as that fellow.' "

A remark of Czerny's is as follows:[34] "When the French were in Vienna for the first time, in 1805, Beethoven was visited by a number of officers and generals who were musical and for whom he played Gluck's *Iphigenia in Tauris* from the score, to which they sang the choruses and songs not at all ill. I begged the score from him and at home wrote out the pianoforte score as I had heard him play it. I still have this arrangement (November, 1852). From that time I date my style of arranging orchestral works, and he was always wholly satisfied with my arrangements of his symphonies, etc."

A lad who, though not yet fifteen years old, was able to write a pianoforte score of such an opera after a single hearing, certainly deserved the testimonial to his talent which, though written by another hand, was signed at the time by Beethoven and sealed. The testimonial, in the possession of the Gesellschaft der Musikfreunde in Vienna, runs as follows:

We, the undersigned, cannot withhold from the lad Carl Czerny, who has made such extraordinary progress on the pianoforte, far surpassing what might be expected from a boy of fourteen years, that for this reason, and also because of his marvelous memory, he is deserving of all possible support, the more since his parents have expended their fortune in the education of this promising son.
Vienna, December 7, 1805.

Ludwig van Beethoven. (Seal)

The master had early and wisely warned him against a too free use of his extraordinary memory. Czerny writes:[35] "My musical memory enabled me to play the Beethovenian works by heart without exception, and during the years 1804-1805 I was obliged to play these works in this manner at Prince Lichnowsky's once or twice a week, he calling out only the desired opus numbers. Beethoven, who was present a few times, was not pleased. 'Even if he plays correctly on the whole,' he remarked, 'he will forget in this manner the quick survey, the *a vista* playing and, occasionally, the correct expression.' "

Schindler closes his account of these last five years in Beethoven's life with great propriety and elegance by quoting a passage copied by the master from Christian Sturm's *Betrachtungen*. It is made up of scattered sentences which may be found on page 197 of the ninth edition (Reutlingen, 1827): "To the praise of thy goodness I must confess that Thou hast tried all means

---

[34] See Kerst, i, p. 57.   [35] *Ibid.*, p. 50.

to draw me to Thee. Now it hath pleased Thee to let me feel the heavy hand of Thy wrath, and to humiliate my proud heart by manifold chastisements. Sickness and misfortune hast Thou sent to bring me to a contemplation of my digressions. But one thing only do I ask, O God, cease not to labor for my improvement. Only let me, in whatsoever manner pleases Thee, turn to Thee and be fruitful of good works."

The compositions which were completed in this year were the opera *Leonore* (*Fidelio*) in its first form, the song "An die Hoffnung," Opus 32 (from Tiedge's *Urania*) and probably the Pianoforte Sonata in F minor, Op. 57. The works composed within the year comprise the first and second "Leonore" overtures and, according to Kinsky, the transcription of the Second Symphony for pianoforte trio.[36] Also work was started in this year on the Fourth Pianoforte Concerto in G major, Op. 58, and doubtless on the revision of his opera.

The publications for the year were:

By Hoffmeister and Kühnel:
"Ah! perfido, sperguiro," for Soprano and Orchestra, Op. 65.
By Kunst- und Industrie-Comptoir:
"An die Hoffnung" (Tiedge), Op. 32. [It is notewothy that this song, although written for the Countess Josephine Deym, bears no dedication.]
Andante in F major for Pianoforte, WoO 57.
Eight Songs, Op. 52.
"Ich denke dein" (Goethe), with Variations for Pianoforte Four Hands, WoO 74, dedicated to the Countesses Josephine Deym and Therese Brunsvik.
Minuet in E-flat for Pianoforte, WoO 82.
Prelude in F minor for Pianoforte, WoO 55.
Romance for Violin and Orchestra, Op. 50.
Sonata for Pianoforte, Op. 53, dedicated to Count Ferdinand von Waldstein.
Trio for Pianoforte, Clarinet or Violin and Violoncello, Op. 38 (transcription of the Septet, Op. 20), dedicated to Johann Adam Schmidt.
Two Easy Sonatas for Pianoforte, Op. 49.
By Simrock:
Sonata for Pianoforte and Violin, Op. 47, dedicated to Rodolphe Kreutzer.

[36] See KHV, p. 90.

CHAPTER XIX

THE YEAR 1806

THE REVISION OF "LEONORE"
THE RAZUMOVSKY QUARTETS
THE FOURTH SYMPHONY

EXCERPTS from a letter written on June 2, 1806, by Stephan von Breuning to his sister and brother-in-law, make a fair opening for the story of the year 1806. In it he reports on *Fidelio*. The letter, though written in the middle of the year, has reference to the period between the original performance late in 1805 and the repetition in the spring of 1806, a period in which it would seem Beethoven was in no mood, or too much occupied otherwise, for correspondence. Von Breuning writes (Wegeler, *Notizen*, p. 62): ". . . Nothing, perhaps, has caused Beethoven so much vexation as this work, the value of which will be appreciated only in the future. . . . Beethoven, who had also observed a few imperfections in the treatment of the text in the opera, withdrew it after three representations. After order had been restored he and I took it up again. I remodelled the whole book for him, quickening and enlivening the action; he curtailed many pieces, and then it was performed three[1] times with great success. Now, however, his enemies in the theatre arose, and as he had offended several persons, especially at the second representation, they succeeded in preventing further performances. Before this, many obstacles had been placed in his way; to let one instance stand as proof for the others, he could not even get permission to secure an announcement of the opera under the changed title *Fidelio*, as it is called in the French original, and as it was put into print after the changes were made. Contrary to promise the first title *Leonore* appeared on the poster. This is all the more unpleasant for Beethoven since the cessation of the performances on which he was depending for his honorarium, which consists in a percentage of the receipts, has embarrassed him in a financial

---

[1] Twice only. (TDR, II, 501, n. 1.)

way. He will recover from the set-back all the more slowly since the treatment which he has received has robbed him of a great deal of his pleasure in and love for work. . . ."

The words "Fidelio" and "Leonore" are here misplaced, interchanged, whether by Breuning or his copyist is not known. The letter is a reflection of Beethoven's disappointment and indignation at fancied injuries; it was written in ignorance of divers material facts, and contains inaccuracies, which—since its publication by Wegeler in 1838—have colored many attempts to write the early history of the opera.

It is noteworthy that Breuning, instead of Sonnleithner, revised the text and made the new disposition of the scenes. Furthermore, in a letter to Sonnleithner near the end of the period of revision Beethoven withheld from him the knowledge of Breuning's share in the rewriting:[2]

Dear best Sonnleithner!

I hope you will not refuse me when I beg you very sincerely *to give me a small statement in writing that I may again have the libretto printed with your name* [!] *with its present alternations*— When I made the changes, you were thoroughly occupied with your *Faniska*,[3] and so I made them myself. You would not have had the patience to undertake these changes and it would have made for further delays in the performance of our opera.— Therefore I quietly dared to hope for your consent. *The three acts have been made into only two.* In order to effect this and give the opera a livelier course, I have *shortened everything* as much as possible, the chorus of *prisoners* and music of that sort particularly.— All this made it necessary *to revise only the first act*, and therein lies the *change* in the libretto—

I will carry the cost of printing, and beg you once again for a *granting of my request*—

respectfully yours   Beethowen

P.S. The time is so short, otherwise I would have sent you the libretto to convince you—
P.P.S. Send me, best S. this statement right away by my servant, because I must show it to the *censor*.

At the performances in November, the effect of the overture had been ruined by a passage in the Allegro, which was too difficult for the wood-wind instruments. "Instead of simply removing this obstacle (31 measures)," says Schindler,[4] "Beethoven thought it advisable to rewrite the whole, inasmuch as he was already engaged upon a revision of the other parts of the work. He retains the motives of the Introduction as well as the Allegro, has the motive of the latter played by violoncellos and violins simultaneously for the sake of greater sonority, and on the existing foundation rears a new structure, including several new thoughts."

[2] Max Unger, "Zur Entstehungs- und Aufführungsgeschichte von Beethovens Oper *Leonore*," *Zeitschrift für Musik*, Vol. 105 (1939), p. 138.
[3] Opera by Cherubini.
[4] *Biographie*, I, 128.

And thus for Beethoven the winter passed. To compete with successful new works which Schikaneder offered the Vienna audiences of 1806 was no light matter; and it is easy to imagine that Beethoven felt this, and determined, at all events in his own field of instrumental composition, to leave no doubt who was master. Hence, that monumental work, the great overture to *Leonore* in its third form. He was, as usual, dilatory in meeting his engagements. January and February passed and March drew to a close, and the overture was not ready. This was too much for Baron Braun's patience. He, therefore, selected the best night of the season—Saturday, March 29, the last before the closing of the theatre for Holy Week and Easter—and gave Beethoven distinctly to understand, that if the opera were not performed on that evening, it should not be given at all. This was effectual and the new score was sent in; but so late, as Röckel well remembered, as to allow but two or three rehearsals with pianoforte and only one with orchestra; and these were directed by Seyfried—the composer appearing at neither.

Beethoven and Breuning supposed that a change of title from *Fidelio* to *Leonore* had been agreed to by the directors, and indeed the new text-book and Breuning's poem on the occasion were so printed; but it was determined otherwise. By the new arrangement of the scenes, the number of acts was reduced to two. The new play-bill therefore substitutes "Opera in two Acts" for "three"; excepting this, the change of date, and of Röckel's for Demmer's name as Florestan, it is a facsimile of the previous ones, and announces: "Fidelio oder die Eheliche Liebe." For this determination the directors may well have urged, not only a proper regard for the composer of *Sargino* (Paër) and the Italian *Leonore*, but the manifest impropriety of misleading the public by giving a new title to a work which remained essentially unchanged. As on the original production, Breuning wrote a poem: "To Herr Ludwig van Beethoven, on the occasion of the reproduction of the opera composed by him and first performed on November 20, 1805, now given under the new title *Leonore*."

The correspondent of the *Allg. Mus. Zeit.*, under date of April 2, wrote: "Beethoven has again produced his opera *Fidelio* on the stage with many alterations and abbreviations. An entire act has been omitted, but the piece has benefited and pleased better." On Thursday, the 10th, it was given again.

Two notes written to Sebastian Mayer between the two performances show Beethoven's dissatisfaction with the first performance and with the preparation in general:

Dear Mayer;

Baron Braun tells me that *my opera* is supposed to be performed on *Thursday*; I shall ask you please to see to it that the choruses get more rehearsals, for last time they were full of blunders. Also, we must have another rehearsal on *Thursday in the theatre with the whole orchestra*— The *orchestra* for sure was not at fault, but—*on the stage several were*; but that was too much to ask since the time was too short. But I had to bring it off then for B. Braun had threatened me with the fact that if the opera were not given on Saturday it would not be given any more. I am counting on your loyalty and friendship, which you have shown me in the past, to take care of this opera now; after this the opera will no longer need such rehearsals and you can perform it when you want to. Here are two libretti, I ask you to give one to *Röckel*. Farewell, dear Mayer, and give my affair your attention.

Your friend Beethoven

In the second note, Beethoven's dissatisfaction had mounted, and the orchestra was sharply criticized:

Dear Mayer!

Please ask Hr. v. Seyfried to conduct my opera today, I want to look at it and hear it from a distance. Thus at least my patience will not be so greatly tried as if I were to hear my music bungled close at hand!— I cannot help thinking that it has been done on purpose. I will say nothing about the wind-instruments, but— that all *pp*, crescendos, all *decres.* and all fortes, *ff*, have been scratched out of my opera! At any rate they are not all played. All delight in composing departs when one hears one's music played *thus*! Tomorrow or the day after I will fetch you for dinner. Today I am unwell again.

Your friend Beethoven

P.S.—If the opera is to be given the day after tomorrow there must be a rehearsal again *tomorrow* in the room—otherwise it will get worse and worse each day!

Seyfried's autograph record of all performances in the Theater-an-der-Wien, through a long series of years, gives *Sargino* instead of *Fidelio* for Saturday the 12th—and *Agnes Bernauer* for the Sunday and Monday following. That this old, well-known drama was so repeated affords a strong presumption that an opera—we think *Fidelio*—was withdrawn "because obstacles had suddenly appeared" after it was too late to supply its place with another. At all events, the production of *Fidelio* on Thursday, April 10th, was the last; for which fact two explanations are given—that in Breuning's letter, and one by Röckel in his letter to the author. Breuning attributes it to the composer's enemies—to a cabal, to "several persons whom Beethoven had offended, especially at the second representation"; Röckel, to Beethoven's own imprudence and folly.

Breuning, a Secretary in the War Office, could have had little leisure for theatrical matters in those melancholy days during the French occupation and immediately after; it is a cause of surprise that he found time for the revision of the *Fidelio* text; his record, therefore, could hardly have been made except upon the representations of his friend—the last man to admit that he was in fault. But Röckel was behind the scenes in a double sense: he sang the part of Florestan and while Beethoven's "friends were, most of them, married men, not able to walk and dine out with him like myself, another bachelor, to whom he took a fancy—I could call upon him in the morning and in fine weather stroll and dine with him in the country." Breuning and Röckel are alike men of unimpeachable veracity; but the latter speaks from personal knowledge and observation.

Breuning's statement is improbable. Who were Beethoven's enemies? Who formed the cabal? Baron Braun, Schikaneder, Seyfried, the stage-manager Mayer, Director Clement, the solo singers (Mlle. Milder, Wein-kopf, Röckel), were all his friends; and, for anything now known, so were Mlle. Müller, Rothe and Caché. As to orchestra and chorus, they might refuse to play under Beethoven as conductor—nothing more; and, as he had already conducted four if not five times, this would create no great difficulty, as the bâton would necessarily pass into the hands of Seyfried at the first or second subsequent performance. Moreover, now that the opera was fairly upon the stage and making its way, it was for the interest of all parties, from Baron Braun down to the scene-shifters, to continue it so long as it would draw an audience. That it was making its way is proved not only by all the contemporary accounts, but by this: that notwithstanding the necessarily empty houses in November, Beethoven's percentage of the receipts finally amounted to nearly 200 florins.

In the second of the notes to Mayer, Beethoven is guilty of monstrous injustice. A moment's reflection shows this. The orchestra and chorus had duly rehearsed and three times publicly performed *Fidelio* as first written. Since then (see Jahn's edition) most of the numbers, perhaps every one, had been more or less changed. Now every musician knows that it is easier to play a piece of new music correctly at sight, than a well-known composition in which material alterations have been made. And yet, because some forty men—playing on a dozen different instruments, and after a single rehearsal at which the composer was not present to explain his intentions—did not effect the impossibility of reading the music correctly and at the same time note all the marks of expression, Beethoven writes: "I cannot help thinking that it has been done on purpose."

All things considered, there can be no hesitation in preferring the testimony of the singer of Florestan to that of the Court War Councillor. Röckel writes:

"When the opera was produced in the beginning of the following year, it was exceedingly well received by a select public, which became more numerous and enthusiastic with each new representation; and no doubt the opera would have become a favorite if the evil genius of the composer had not prevented it, and as he, Beethoven, was paid for his work by a percentage, instead of a mere honorarium, an advantage which none enjoyed before him, it would have considerably advanced his pecuniary arrangements. Having had no theatrical experience, he was estimating the receipts of the house much higher than they really were; he believed himself cheated in his percentage, and without consulting his real friends on such a delicate point, he hastened to Baron Braun—that high-minded and honorable nobleman—

and submitted his complaint. The Baron, seeing Beethoven excited and conscious of his *one susceptibility* (i.e., suspicious temper), did what he could to cure him of his suspicions against his employees, of whose honesty he was sure. Were there any fraud, the Baron said, his own loss would be beyond comparison more considerable than Beethoven's. He hoped that the receipts would increase with each representation; until now, only the first ranks, stalls and pit were occupied; by and by the upper ranks would likewise contribute their shares.

" 'I don't write for the galleries!' exclaimed Beethoven.

" 'No?' replied the Baron, 'My dear Sir, even Mozart did not disdain to write for the galleries.'

"Now it was at an end. 'I will not give the opera any more,' said Beethoven, 'I want my score back.' Here Baron Braun rang the bell, gave orders for the delivery of the score to the composer, and the opera was buried for a long time. From this encounter between Beethoven and Baron Braun one might conclude that the former's feelings had been injured by the comparison with Mozart; but since he revered Mozart highly, it is probable that he took offence more at the manner in which they were uttered than at the words themselves.—He now realized plainly that he had acted against his own interests, and in all probability the parties would have come to an amicable understanding through the mediation of friends if Baron Braun had not very soon after retired from the management of the united theatres, a circumstance that led to a radical change of conditions."

The orchestral parts of the opera, however, evidently remained at the theatre, and a note to Baron Braun, written by Beethoven only a few weeks later, shows the composer in a more conciliatory mood. He asked the Baron's permission to borrow the following: ". . . *flauto primo*, the three trombones and the four horn parts of my opera.—I need them, but only for a day, in order to have a few *trifles* copied for myself, which *could not be written into the score for want of room*, also because *Prince Lobkowitz is thinking of giving the opera at his house* and has asked me for it.—I am not completely well, otherwise I would have come myself to pay my respects—"

There were other reasons why Beethoven desired to render his score perfect. Whether the opera was performed in the Lobkowitz palace is not recorded; but Breuning ends his letter of June 2nd thus: "I will only write you the news that Prince Lichnowsky has now sent the opera to the Queen of Prussia, and that I hope the performances in Berlin will show the Viennese what they have at home."

Breuning's hope was vain; the opera was not given in Berlin at this time. In truth, Beethoven had overshot the mark. The overture was too novel in form and grand in substance to be immediately understood; and, in 1806, there was not an audience in Europe able to find, in the fire and expression of the principal vocal numbers, an adequate compensation for the superficial graces and melodic beauties of the favorite operas of the time, which seemed to them to be wanting in *Fidelio*. Even Cherubini, who was all this time in Vienna, failed to comprehend fully a work which, though a first and only experiment, was destined to an ever-increasing popularity, when nearly all his own then universally admired operas had disappeared from the stage. Schindler records that he "told the musicians of Paris concerning the overture that because of its confusion of modulations he was unable to recognize the principal key." And farther, that he (Cherubini), in listening to *Fidelio*, had come to the conclusion that till then Beethoven had paid too little heed to the art of singing, for which Salieri was not to blame.

In 1836, Schindler conversed with the Fidelio of 1805-1806, Madame Milder-Hauptmann, on the subject: "She said, among other things, that she, too, had had severe struggles with the master chiefly about the unbeautiful, unsingable passages, unsuited to her voice, in the Adagio of the air in E major—but all in vain, until, in 1814, she declared that she would never sing the air again in its then shape. That worked."

Anselm Hüttenbrenner, who became a pupil of Salieri a dozen years later, wrote in a letter to Ferdinand Luib, under date February 21, 1858: "Speaking of Beethoven Salieri told me the composer had submitted *Fidelio* to him for an opinion: he had taken exception to many things and advised Beethoven to make certain changes; but Beethoven had *Fidelio* performed just as he had written it—and never visited Salieri again." These last words are too strong; Beethoven's pique against his old master was in time forgotten; for Moscheles (also in a letter to Luib) wrote on February 28, 1858: "I cannot recall seeing Schubert at Salieri's, but I do remember the interesting circumstance that once I saw a sheet of paper lying at Salieri's on which in great letters written by Beethoven were the words: '*The pupil Beethoven was here!*' "

The order of time requires a passing notice of a family event which proved in the end a cause of infinite trouble and vexation to Beethoven and all connected to him by the ties of kindred or friendship. On the 25th of May, 1806 "a marriage contract was closed between Carl Caspar v. Beethoven, R. I. Officer of the Revenue, and of this city, and Johanna Reiss, daughter of Anton Reiss, civilian, upholsterer." Their only child, a son, was born—according to the baptismal certificate—on September 4, 1806. Whether Caspar's salary had been increased above 250 florins (before his appointment in 1809 as Liquidators'-Adjunct with 1000 florins and 160 additional for lodging) does not appear, undoubtedly it had been. Reiss was a man of considerable wealth for one in his sphere of life, and able, it is said, to give his daughter a marriage portion of 2000 florins. It appears, too, that the valuable house in the Alservorstadt owned by Carl at the time of his death was an inheritance of his wife's from her father's estate; indeed, half the right to the property was legally secured to her. —It would seem natural that after his marriage, Caspar should gradually cease to manage his brother's business affairs. The break was not immediate, as is shown by a letter of July 5 to Breitkopf and

Härtel in which Beethoven refers to a possible trip of Caspar's to Leipzig "for his office," at which time the firm was to discuss with him an agreement concerning the possible sale of some compositions. However after this date it seems clear that Carl Caspar no longer took an active part in negotiations with publishers.🙵◦—

The notices of Beethoven's own movements during this year are scanty. *Fidelio* and studies to instrumental works employed him during the winter, but not to the exclusion of social intercourse, as one of his characteristic memoranda indicates. It is written with lead pencil on a page of the new quartet sketches: "Just as you are now plunging into the whirlpool of society—just so possible is it to compose works in spite of social obstacles. Let your deafness no longer be a secret—even in art."

Breuning's report (June 2), that Beethoven had lost "a great deal of his pleasure in and love for work," had even then ceased to be true. On the 26th of May, the writing out of the first of the Razumovsky Quartets had been begun—and with this came a series of works which distinguished the year 1806 as one of astonishing productiveness—but more on this point in due time.

Two brothers, differing in age by nineteen years, had owed their rise from the condition of singers at the Russian Court into positions of great wealth and political importance to their gratification of the lascivious lusts of two imperial princesses, afterwards known in history as the Empresses Elizabeth Petrovna and Catherine II. Thus the two Razums, born in 1709 and 1728, of half-Cossack parentage, in the obscure Ukraine village of Lemeschi, became the Counts Razumovsky, nobles of the Russian Empire. They were men of rare ability, and, like Shakespeare's Duncan, "bore their faculties so meek," that none of the monarchs under whom they served, not even those who personally disliked either of them, made him the victim of imperial caprice or ill will. A whimsical proof of the rapidity with which the new name became known throughout Europe is its introduction in 1762 into a farce of the English wit, Samuel Foote.[5] The Empresses provided their paramours with wives from noble families and continued their kindness to the children born of these unions—one of whom came in time to occupy a rather prominent place among the patrons of Beethoven.

Andreas Kyrillovitch (born October 22, 1752), fourth son of the younger Razumovsky, was destined for the navy and received the best education possible in those days for his profession, even to serving in what was then the best of all schools, an English man-of-war. He had been elevated to the rank of captain when, at the age of 25, he was transferred to the diplomatic service. He was Ambassador successively at Venice, Naples, Copenhagen and Stockholm; less famous, perhaps, for his diplomacy than notorious

[5] Young Wilding: "Oh how they [the women] melt at the Gothic names of General Swapinbach, Count Rousoumoffsky, Prince Montecuculi and Marshal Fustinburgh." (*The Liar.*) (TDR, II, 546, n. 1.)

for the profuseness of his expenditures, and for his amours with women of the highest rank, the Queen of Naples not excepted.

Razumovsky was personally widely known at Vienna, where he had married (November 4, 1788) Elizabeth, Countess Thun, elder sister of the Princess Karl Lichnowsky, and whither he was transferred as Ambassador early in 1792, being officially presented to the Emperor on Friday, May 25, as the *Wiener Zeitung* records. Near the end of Czar Paul's reign (in March, 1799) he was superseded by Count Kalichev; but on the accession of Alexander he was restored, his "presentation audience" taking place October 14, 1801. His dwelling and office had formerly been in the Johannes-Gasse, but now (1805-1806) he was in the Wallzeil, but on the point of removing to a new palace built by himself. Schnitzler[6] says: "Razumovsky lived in Vienna like a prince, encouraging art and science, surrounded by a luxurious library and other collections and admired and envied by all; what advantages accrued from all this to Russian affairs is another question."

True to the traditions of his family, the Count was a musician and one of the best connoisseurs and players of Haydn's quartets, in which he was accustomed to play the second violin. It is affirmed, evidently on good authority, that he had studied these works under that master himself. It would seem a matter of course, that this man, so closely connected, too, with Lichnowsky, would be one of the first to appreciate and encourage the genius of the young Beethoven upon his removal from Bonn to Vienna. But the evidence is scanty for the earlier years. In the subscription to the Trios, Op. 1, in 1795, where we find the Countess of Thun, her daughters and the Lichnowskys down (in the aggregate) for 32 copies, "S.E. le Comte Rasoumoffsky, Embassadeur de Russie" is listed for one. His name does not appear in print again in connection with Beethoven until 1803, when he is listed as a subscriber for the tickets to Bridgetower's concert, May 24th, at which the "Kreutzer" Sonata received its first performance. ─Frimmel[7] believes that the relationship between Razumovsky and the composer was a good deal closer in the early years than Thayer thought. From 1796 to 1800 a Fräulein von Kissow (later Frau von Bernhard) was in Vienna and lived at the home of a Secretary of the Russian Embassy named von Klüpfeld (or Klüpfell). In 1864 Frau von Bernhard told Ludwig Nohl that during this period (from her 13th to her 17th year) she saw Beethoven frequently at the house.[8] Frimmel reasons: "Therefore the master was acquainted almost certainly with Count Razumovsky, since Secretary Klüpfeld would have told him about the new star, Beethoven, in the Vienna firmament." The Count may have been providing the opportunity at his home for the rehearsal of pieces freshly composed by Beethoven (as mentioned by Seyfried and Schindler) already for some time. At any rate, at the end of 1805 Beethoven received a commission for three quartets from the Count. Since he had

---

[6] Article in *Raumer's historische Taschenbuch für 1863.* (TDR, II, 546, n. 1.)

[7] *FRBH,* II, 52-53.

[8] *Ibid.,* I, 38.

already returned to the idea of quartet writing, this commission was soon to be fulfilled.⟩⟩⊷—

It is quite certain that Beethoven took no summer lodgings in 1806; but he did leave the city at the end of the summer. In a postscript to a letter to Breitkopf and Härtel dated September 3rd he writes: "My present place of sojourn is here in Silesia so long as autumn lasts—with Prince Lichnowsky—who sends greetings to you.— My address is L. v. Beethoven in Troppau—." In the main part of the letter Beethoven laid down the conditions under which he would be willing to enter into a contract offered him by the Leipzig publishers which would obligate him "not to sell any more of my works in Germany to anyone except you." Breitkopf and Härtel received another letter from Beethoven on November 18 after his return to Vienna, in which he suggested that his word of honor would be preferable to the problem of figuring out the wording of a contract. He writes: "For the present I offer you three quartets and a pianoforte concerto— I cannot give you the promised symphony yet—because a gentleman of quality has taken it from me, but I have the privilege of publishing it in half a year." All of these negotiations were without result, and the compositions mentioned were published by the Industrie-Comptoir. These were the Razumovsky Quartets and the Fourth Piano Concerto. The symphony referred to was doubtless the fourth, in B-flat, and the "gentleman of quality" Count von Oppersdorff, to whom it was dedicated.

Count Oppersdorff's castle was in Upper Silesia right near the city Ober-Glogau. He was an enthusiastic music-lover and maintained an orchestra which he was so anxious to have complete that he demanded that all who were in his service could play a musical instrument. Through ties partly of friendship, partly of kinship, the Oppersdorff family had various connections with many of Austria's noble families, such as Lobkowitz and Lichnowsky. The Lichnowsky seat, Grätz, near Troppau, was scarcely a day's travel from Ober-Glogau. Thus it was that Prince Lichnowsky and Beethoven together made a visit to the Oppersdorff castle, on which occasion the orchestra performed the Second Symphony.[9]

In October Breuning wrote to Wegeler: "Beethoven is at present in Silesia with Prince Lichnowsky and will not return till near the end of this month. His circumstances are none of the best at present, since his opera, owing to the cabals of his opponents, was performed but seldom, and therefore yielded him nothing. His spirits are generally low and, to judge by his letters, the sojourn in the country has not cheered him." This visit to the Prince came to an abrupt termination in a scene which has been a fruitful theme for the silly race of musical novelette writers. The simple truth is related by Seyfried in the appendix to his *Studien* (page 23) and is here copied literally except

[9] This information was given to Deiters by the son of one of Oppersdorff's legal advisers, who as a member of the staff was a member of the orchestra and participated in this particular performance. See TDR, III, 11.

for a few additional words interspersed, derived by the present writer from a conversation with the daughter of Moritz Lichnowsky: "When he [Beethoven] did not feel in the mood it required repeated and varied urgings to get him to sit down to the pianoforte. Before he began playing he was in the habit of hitting the keys with the flat of his hand, or running a single finger up and down the keyboard, in short, doing all manner of things to kill time and laughing heartily, as was his wont, at the folly. Once while spending a summer with a Maecenas at his country-seat, he was so pestered by the guests [French officers], who wished to hear him play, that he grew angry and refused to do what he denounced as menial labor. A threat of arrest, made surely in jest, was taken seriously by him and resulted in Beethoven's walking by night to the nearest city, Troppau, whence he hurried as on the wings of the wind by extra post to Vienna."[10]

Fräulein Giannatasio del Rio related the same scene:[11] "Once (around 1816) Beethoven was in a gay talkative mood and told us of the time which he spent at Prince Lichnowsky's. He spoke of the Prince with much respect. He told how once during the invasion when the Prince had a number of Frenchmen as his guests, he (the Prince) repeatedly tried to coerce him to play for them on the pianoforte and that he had stoutly refused; which led to a scene between him and the Prince, whereupon B. indiscreetly and suddenly left the house.—He once said that it is easy to get along with nobility, but it was necessary to have something to impress them with."

To propitiate him for the humiliation which he had suffered, the bust of his patron had to become a sacrifice; he dashed it into pieces from its place on a cabinet to the floor. Alois Fuchs recorded an anecdote which illustrates the feeling which made Beethoven so unwilling to play before the French officers.[12] After the battle at Jena (October 14, 1806) Beethoven met his friend Krumpholz, to whom he was warmly attached, and, as usual, asked him, "What's the news?" Krumpholz answered that the latest news was the report just received that the great hero Napoleon had won another decisive victory over the Prussians. Greatly angered, Beethoven replied to this: "It's a pity that I do not understand the art of war as well as I do the art of music, I would conquer him!"

A letter by Beethoven, dated Vienna, November 1, returns us to his involvement with a project of George Thomson's—that of making the most extensive collection possible of the music of Scotland. Many compilations, various in

---

[10] Frimmel, in his *Beethoven* (2nd ed., 1903, p. 42), tells the story in essentially the same manner on the authority of a grandson of Dr. Weiser, house physician of Prince Lichnowsky. The story ends with Beethoven's sending a letter to Prince Lichnowsky containing this passage: "Prince, what you are you are by accident of birth; what I am I am through myself. There have been and will still be thousands of princes; there is only one

Beethoven." Authentic or not, the expression may well have come from the lips of Beethoven in a fit of anger. (Dr. Weiser's version had previously been printed by F. X. Bach in the *Wiener Deutsche Zeitung*, August 31, 1873.) (TDR, II, 519, n. 1.)

[11] *Grenzboten*, XVI, Nr. 14 (1857), April 3. (TDR, II, 519, n. 2.)

[12] *Schmidts Wiener Musikzeitung* (1846, No. 39). (TDR, II, 520, n. 1.)

extent and merit, had been published, but all of them, as Thomson justly remarks, "more or less defective and exceptionable." In one of his prefaces he says:

"To furnish a collection of all the fine airs, both of the plaintive and the lively kind, unmixed with trifling and inferior ones—to obtain the most suitable and finished accompaniments, with the addition of characteristic symphonies to introduce and conclude each air—and to substitute congenial and interesting songs, every way worthy of the music, in the room of insipid or exceptionable verses, were the great objects of the present publication. . . .

"For the composition of the symphonies and accompaniments, he [the editor] entered into terms with Mr. Pleyel, who fulfilled part of his engagement satisfactorily; but having then stopped short, the editor found it necessary to turn his eyes elsewhere. He was so fortunate, however, as to engage Mr. Koželuch, and afterwards, Dr. Haydn, to proceed with the work, which they have finished in such a manner as to leave him nothing to regret on Mr. Pleyel's breach of engagement. . . ."

Doubtless Thomson would have applied sooner to Haydn, had he known that the great master would condescend to such a labor. The appearance of William Napier's two volumes of "Original Scots Songs, in three parts, the Harmony by Haydn," removed any doubt on this point. For Napier, Haydn simply added a violin part and a figured bass; for Thomson, a full pianoforte score, parts for violin and violoncello, and an instrumental introduction and coda. A very remarkable feature of the enterprise was, that the composers of the accompaniments had no knowledge of the texts, and the writers of the poetry no knowledge of the accompaniments. The poets, in many cases, had a stanza of the original song as a model for the metre and rhythm; in all others, they and the composers alike received the bare melody, with nothing else to guide them in their work but Italian musical terms: allegro, moderato, andante, etc., etc., affettuoso, espressivo, scherzando, and the like. This is also true of the Welsh and Irish melodies. Beethoven began his labors for Thomson with the last named. In the preface to the first volume, dated "Edinburgh, anno 1814," after describing his work in collecting Irish airs, Thomson says: "They were sent to Haydn to be harmonized along with the Scottish and Welsh airs; but after that celebrated composer had finished the greater part of those two works, his declining health only enabled him to harmonize a few of the Irish Melodies; and upon his death, it became necessary to find another composer to whom the task of harmonizing them should be committed.[13] Of all composers that are now living, it is acknowledged by every intelligent and unprejudiced musician, that the only one, who occupies the same distinguished rank with the late Haydn is BEETHOVEN. Possessing the most original genius and inventive fancy, united to profound science,

[13] Thomson's memory was a little at fault when this preface was written; the proposal was made to Beethoven before Haydn's death. (TDR, II, 522, n. 1.)

refined taste and an enthusiastic love of his art—his compositions, like those of his illustrious predecessor, will bear endless repetition and afford ever new delight. To this composer, therefore, the Editor eagerly applied for symphonies and accompaniments to the Irish Melodies; and to his inexpressible satisfaction, Beethoven undertook the composition. After years of anxious suspense and teazing disappointment, by the miscarriage of letters and manuscripts, owing to the unprecedented difficulty of communication between England and Vienna, the long expected symphonies and accompaniments at last reached the Editor, three other copies having previously been lost upon the road."

Near the close of his preface, Thomson says: "After the volume was printed and some copies of it had been circulated, an opportunity occurred of sending it to Beethoven, who corrected the few inaccuracies that had escaped the notice of the Editor and his friends; and he trusts it will be found without a single error."

Following is a translation of the letter to Thomson referred to, which was written in French:

Vienna, November 1, 1806.[14]

Dear Sir:

A little excursion to Silesia which I have made is the reason why I have postponed till now answering your letter of July 1. On my return to Vienna I hasten to communicate to you what I have to say and what I have decided as to the proposals you were so kind as to make me. I will speak with all candor and exactitude, which I like in business affairs, and which alone can forestall any complaint on either side. Here, then, my dear Sir, are my statements:

1mo. I am not indisposed, on the whole, to accept your propositions.

2do. I will take care to make the compositions easy and pleasing, as far as I can and as far as is consistent with that elevation and originality of style which, as you yourself say, favorably characterize my works and from which I shall never stoop.

3^{tio}. I cannot bring myself to write for the flute, as this instrument is too limited and imperfect.

4to. To give greater variety to the compositions which you will publish, and to give me a freer field in these compositions, in which the task of making them easy would ever thwart me, I can promise you only three trios for violin, viola and violoncello, and three quintets for two violins, two violas and violoncello. Instead of the remaining three trios and three quintets, I shall give you three quartets, and finally two sonatas for pianoforte with accompaniment for two violins and flute, and one quintet.— In a word, I would ask you, in regard to the second series of compositions you ask of me, to rely completely upon my

[14] The original letter in French is in the British Museum. It is dated "Vienne le 1 - - 9bre 1806," that is, November 1. However, on the back of the last sheet is written "1806, Beethoven, Vienne 1 Oct. 1806." Only the signature of the letter is in Beethoven's hand. It is clear from other accounts that Beethoven had not returned to Vienna by October 1st, therefore November 1 is undoubtedly the correct date. (Cf. TDR, II, 523, n. 1.)

taste and good faith, and I assure you that you will be entirely satisfied—
However, if you cannot agree to any of these changes, I do not wish to insist
upon them obstinately.—

5to. I should be glad if the second series of compositions were published six
months after the first.

6to. I must have a clearer explanation of the statement which I find in your
letter that no copy printed under my name shall be introduced into Great Britain;
for if you agree that these compositions are to be published in Germany and also
in France, I do not see how I can prevent copies from being taken into your
country.—

7mo. Finally, as regards the honorarium, I understand that you are offering me
100 pounds sterling, or 200 Vienna ducats *in gold* and not in Vienna bank-notes,
which under the present circumstances entail too great a loss; for if paid in these
notes the sum would be too little for the works which I am sending you in
proportion to the honorarium which I receive for all my other compositions.—
Even the honorarium of two hundred ducats *in gold* is by no means excessive
payment for everything that has to be done in order to satisfy your wishes—

Finally, the best way of making the payment would be for you to send me by
post, at the time when I send you the first and again the second series, a bill of
exchange for 100 ducats *in gold* drawn upon a banking house in Hamburg;
or for you to commission someone in Vienna each time to give me such a bill
of exchange at the time he receives from me the first and the second series.—

At the same time please let me know the date on which you will publish each
series, so that I may oblige the publishers who issue these same compositions in
Germany and France to abide by the same.—

I hope that you will find my declarations reasonable and of such a sort that
we can reach some definite agreement.— In this case it would be well to draw
up a formal contract, which please have the kindness to prepare in duplicate, and
of which I shall return you one copy with my signature.—

I await only your answer before setting to work, and am, with distinguished
esteem, my dear Sir,

Your obedient servant,
Louis van Beethoven

P.S. I will also be glad to fulfill your wish to harmonize the little Scottish airs;
and in this matter I await a more definite proposal, since it is well known to me
that Mr. Haydn was paid one pound sterling for each song.—

Of the various propositions mentioned in this letter, only that of the
Scottish songs led to any results.

Here follows the list of important works sketched from the time
work on the opera began (1804) to the time when its revision was completed
(first half of 1806): Sonata in C, Op. 53; Sonata in F, Op. 54; Triple Concerto, Op. 56; and Sonata in F minor, Op. 57. Furthermore, at least preliminary work had been done by this time in connection with the Fourth
Pianoforte Concerto, Op. 58, the so-called Razumovsky Quartets, Op. 59 and
the Fifth Symphony, Op. 67. Then follow in the second half of 1806 the
Fourth Symphony, Op. 60 and the Violin Concerto, Op. 61.— It affords

a striking example of Beethoven's habit of working on several compositions at the same time, and, moreover, as we believe, of his practice in such cases of giving the works opus numbers in the order of their completion.

It will be remembered that the Sonata in F minor, Op. 57, near completion when offered to Breitkopf and Härtel in August, 1804, was still unpublished in 1806. Beethoven, journeying into Silesia, took the manuscript and had it also with him on his return to Vienna per extra post from Troppau after the explosion at Lichnowsky's. "During his journey," wrote M. Bigot[15] half a century afterwards on a printed copy belonging to the pianist Mortier de Fontaine, "he encountered a storm and pouring rain which penetrated the trunk into which he had put the Sonata in F minor which he had just composed [!]. After reaching Vienna, he came to see us and laughingly showed the work, which was still wet, to my wife, who at once began to look carefully at it. Impelled by the striking beginning she sat down at the pianoforte and began playing it. Beethoven had not expected this and was surprised to note that Madame Bigot did not hesitate at all because of the many erasures and alterations which he had made. It was the original manuscript which he was carrying to his publisher for printing. When Mme. Bigot finished playing she begged him to give it to her; he consented, and faithfully brought it to her after it had been printed."

Czerny says, very justly, of the unauthorized change afterwards[16] made in the title: "In a new edition of the Sonata in F minor, Op. 57, which Beethoven himself considered his greatest, the title 'Appassionata,' for which it is too great, was added to it. This title would be more fitly applied to the E-flat Sonata, Op. 7, which he composed in a very impassioned mood."

The Fourth Pianoforte Concerto was offered to Hoffmeister and Kühnel along with *Christus am Ölberg* for 600 florins on March 27, 1806, by brother Carl. The composer himself wrote to Breitkopf and Härtel on July 5 that his brother, who was traveling to Leipzig, would bring with him "the overture to my opera in pianoforte arrangement, my oratorio and a *new pianoforte concerto*." It is not known whether this projected trip ever took place. New offers were made in the fall, still with no results. Thus the work, composed probably by the spring of this year,[17] may not have received its final touches until the end of the year through lack of a publisher.

A song translated by Breuning from Solie's opera *Le Secret* was probably the first fruits of the newly awakened "desire and love for work," which proved so nobly productive during the summer. It is the one published at different times under the titles "Empfindungen bei Lydiens Untreue," and "Als die Geliebte sich trennen wollte." A slight token of gratitude for the recent zealous kindness of Breuning in the matter of the opera, such as this

---

[15] Bigot, the librarian of Count Razumovsky, will be discussed further in the next chapter.

[16] In 1838, in an arrangement for four hands published by Cranz in Hamburg.

[17] There is a sketch for the opening of the first movement near the end of the "Eroica" sketchbook, thus early 1804. See Nottebohm, *Ein Skizzenbuch* (1880), p. 69.

song, would not long be delayed even by Beethoven. But, whether or not this was the first composition after the withdrawal of *Fidelio*, it is certain that just one week before the date of the Breuning letter (to the Wegelers on June 2, with which this chapter opened), Beethoven had set resolutely to work upon grander themes than Empfindungen bei Lydiens or any other Mädchens Untreue. These are now to be considered. He began to work out the quartets, Op. 59, on May 26.

These quartets were evidently planned as far back as the fall of 1804, judging from a letter written by Carl to Breitkopf and Härtel on November 24th of that year: "I cannot yet say anything definite to you about the quartets, as soon as they are ready, I will write to you immediately." Sketches for the last three movements of Op. 59, No. 1, especially for the second movement, occur in the latter part of the "Leonore" sketchbook.[18] Thus Beethoven's own words on the autograph of the first quartet— "Quartetto I^mo. . . Begun on May 26, 1806" probably refer to the final working out of the work. On July 5, 1806, Beethoven wrote to Breitkopf and Härtel: ". . . you may also negotiate with him [Carl] touching some new violin *quartets* of which I have already completed one and now am intending to devote myself almost wholly to this work. . . ."

Other sketches for all three quartets exist on thirty-four separate sheets which have been preserved in the Archives of the Gesellschaft der Musikfreunde.[19] On September 3, 1806, Beethoven wrote to Breitkopf and Härtel: ". . . you may have at once *3 violin quartets*. . . ." The opus number, the reports of their performance[20] during the next winter, and, especially, the date of their publication (January, 1808), making allowance for Razumovsky's right to them for a year, all point to November or December as the latest possible date for their completion.

The idea of employing popular airs as themes was by no means new to Beethoven. Without referring to the example set by Haydn, Pleyel, Koželuch, it had been proposed to him by Thomson; and as to Russian melodies, he must have read the *Allg. Musik-Zeitung* very carelessly not to have had his curiosity aroused by the articles on Russian music published in that journal in 1802—a curiosity which, in the constant intercourse between Vienna, Moscow and St. Petersburg, there would be no difficulty in gratifying. Czerny writes, however, "He had pledged himself to weave a Russian melody into every quartet." But Lenz, himself a Russian and a musician, says: "The Russian themes are confined to the Finale of No. 1 and the third movement of the Second Quartet." This is a case in which Czerny's authority can scarcely be gainsaid; otherwise, it might be supposed that the composer of his own motion introduced these two themes in compliment to Razumovsky. "The Adagio, E major, in the second Razumovsky Quartet, occurred to

---

[18] See Nottebohm, *II Beeth.*, pp. 79-81. (TDR, II, 531.)

[19] *Ibid.*, pp. 82-90.

[20] *AMZ*, ix (February 27, 1807), 400, (TDR, II, 531.)

him when contemplating the starry sky and thinking of the music of the spheres," writes Czerny in Jahn's notes.

Perhaps no work of Beethoven's met a more discouraging reception from musicians than these now famous Quartets. One friendly contemporary voice alone is heard—that of the *Allg. Mus. Zeit.* (February 27, 1807): "Three new, very long and difficult Beethoven string quartets, dedicated to the Russian Ambassador, Count Razumovsky, are also attracting the attention of all connoisseurs. The conception is profound and the construction excellent, but they are not easily comprehended—with the possible exception of the 3rd in C major which cannot but appeal to intelligent lovers of music because of its originality, melody and harmonic power." An article on May 5th concerning the question of publication speaks in the same tone. "In Vienna Beethoven's most recent, difficult but fine quartets have become more and more popular. Music-lovers hope to see them printed soon."

Czerny told Jahn that "when Schuppanzigh first played the Razumovsky Quartet in F, they laughed and were convinced that Beethoven was playing a joke and that it was not the quartet which had been promised." And, according to Doležalek, when Gyrowetz bought these Quartets he said: "Pity to waste the money!" The Allegretto vivace of the first of these quartets was long a rock of offence. "When at the beginning of the year 1812," says Lenz, "the movement was to be played for the first time in the musical circle of Field Marshal Count Soltikoff in Moscow, Bernhard Romberg trampled under foot as a contemptible mystification the bass part which he was to play. The Quartet was laid aside. When, a few years later, it was played at the house of Privy Councillor Lwoff, father of the famous violinist, in St. Petersburg, the company broke out in laughter when the bass played his solo on *one* note.—The Quartet was again laid aside."

Thomas Appleby, father of Samuel Appleby, collector of valuable papers referring to the violinist Bridgetower, was a leader in the musical world of Manchester, England, and a principal director of concerts there. When these quartets came out in London, Clementi sent a copy of them to him. They were opened and thrown upon the pianoforte. Next day Felix Radicati and his wife, Mme. Bertinotti, called and presented letters, they being upon a concert tour. During the conversation the Italian went to the pianoforte, took up the quartets and seeing what they were, exclaimed (in substance): "Have you got these here! Ha! Beethoven, as the world says, and as I believe, is music-mad;—for these are not music. He submitted them to me in manuscript and, at his request, I fingered them for him. I said to him, that he surely did not consider these works to be music?—to which he replied, 'Oh, they are not for you, but for a later age!'"

Young Appleby believed in them, in spite of Radicati, and after he had studied his part thoroughly, his father invited players of the other instruments to his house and the first in F was tried. The first movement was declared by all except Appleby to be "crazy music." At the end of the violoncello solo on one note, they all burst out laughing; the next four bars all agreed were beautiful. Sudlow, an organist, who played the bass, found so much to admire and so much to condemn in the half of this second movement, which they succeeded in playing, as to call it "patchwork by a madman." They gave up the attempt to play it, and not until 1813, in London, did the young man succeed in hearing the three Quartets entire, and finding them, as he had believed, worthy of their author.

The Symphony in B-flat, Op. 60, was the great work of this summer season. Sketches prove that its successor, the fifth in C minor, had been commenced, and was laid aside to give place to this. Nothing more is known of the history of its composition except what is imparted by the author's inscription on the manuscript: "Sinfonia 4ta, 1806. L. v. Bthvn."

In singular contrast to these grand works and contemporary with their completion, as if written for amusement and recreation after the fatigue of severer studies, are the thirty-two Variations for Pianoforte in C minor. They belong to this autumn, and are among the compositions which their author would gladly have seen pass into oblivion. Jahn's notes contain an anecdote in point. "Beethoven once found Streicher's daughter practising these Variations. After he had listened for awhile he asked her: 'By whom is that?' 'By you.' 'Such nonsense by me? Oh Beethoven, what an ass you were!'"

Although the composer did not succeed in bringing his new Symphony and Concerto to public performance this year, an opportunity offered itself for him to give the general public as fine a taste of his quality as composer for the violin as he had just given to the frequenters of Razumovsky's quartet parties in the Op. 59, namely, the Violin Concerto, Op. 61. The work was superscribed by its author: "Concerto par Clemenza pour Clement, primo Violino e Direttore al Theatro a Vienna, dal L. v. Bthvn., 1806";—or, as it stands on Franz Clement's concert programme of December 23 in the Theater-an-der-Wien: "2. A new Violin Concerto by Hr. Ludwig van Beethoven, played by Hr. Clement." It was preceded by an overture by Méhul, and followed by selections from Mozart, Cherubini and Handel, closing with a fantasia by the concert-giver. The sketches for the Concerto all belong to this year and appear alongside sketches for the Violoncello Sonata, Op. 69, and the Fifth Symphony.[21] When Dr. Bertolini told Jahn that "Beethoven as a rule never finished commissioned works until the last minute," he named this Concerto as an instance in point; and another contemporary notes that Clement played the solo *a vista*, without previous rehearsal.

——Kinsky suggests that 1806 is a likely year to date the Twelve Ecossaises for Orchestra. The only evidence that these pieces were written occurs in the *Wiener Zeitung* of March 21, 1807, where Twelve Ecossaises for 2 violins, bass, 2 flutes and 2 horns in parts, and also in piano score, are advertised by

---

[21] See Nottebohm, *II Beeth.*, p. 533. (TDR, II, 540.)

Johann Traeg. No actual music has survived. As Thayer points out in his *Chronologisches Verzeichniss* (No. 136), Traeg advertised at the same time Twelve Waltzes for 2 violins and bass, which turned out to be scherzos from his symphonies and sonatas! Related to this set may well be the Six Ecossaises for Pianoforte, all in the key of E-flat, which were published in the Collected Works Edition (Series 25, No. 39). These might be transcription of some of the Twelve Ecossaises.[22]

The compositions for the year were:

1805-1806. Three String Quartets, Op. 59.
1805-1806. Concerto No. 4 for Pianoforte and Orchestra in G major, Op. 58.
        Leonore (*Fidelio*), Version No. 2, Op. 72.
1806.   Concerto for Violin and Orchestra, Op. 61.
        Overture to *Leonore*, No. 3.
        Song. "Als die Geliebte" or "Empfindungen bei Lydiens Untreue," WoO 132.
        Symphony No. 4 in B-flat major, Op. 60.
        Thirty-two Variations for Pianoforte, WoO 80.
        Six Ecossaises for Pianoforte, WoO 83.
        Twelve Ecossaises for Orchestra, WoO 16.

The publications for the year were:

By Artaria:
    Trio for Two Oboes and English Horn, Op. 87.
    [Trio for Pianoforte, Violin and Violoncello, Op. 63, transcription of the String Quintet, Op. 4, *but not by Beethoven.*]
By Kunst- und Industrie-Comptoir:
    Sonata for Pianoforte, Op. 54.
    Symphony No. 3 in E-flat major, Op. 55, dedicated to Prince Franz Joseph von Lobkowitz.
By Simrock:
    "Maurerfragen," Masonic text by Wegeler set to "Der freie Mann," WoO 117.

---

[22] See KHV, pp. 452-53; 536-37. In the *Revisionsbericht* for Serie 25, Mandyczewski notes that the Six Ecossaises have survived from a copy made by Nottebohm from one belonging to L. v. Sonnleithner.

CHAPTER XX

THE YEAR 1807

WORK ON THE FIFTH SYMPHONY—
THE MASS IN C

AMONG the group of ardent pro-Beethovenists in Vienna, there were a number of female pianists, some of whom, like the Princess Lichnowsky, we have already encountered. At their head stood the Baroness Dorothea von Ertmann, wife of an Austrian officer who was stationed in those years at or near Vienna. The Baroness studied Beethoven's compositions with the composer, and was, as all contemporary authorities agree, if not the greatest player of these works at least the greatest of her sex. On New Year's Day, 1804, Beethoven sent a print (with two angels, one with a lyre, the other with music paper and stylus) enclosed with a greeting card which read, "To the Baroness Ertmann on New Year's Day 1804 from your friend and admirer Beethoven." The Baroness (née Dorothea Graumann) was born in 1781 at Offenbach-am-Main and in 1798 married Major Peter von Ertmann. This card shows that already by 1804 this lady, who was admired everywhere for her excellent pianoforte playing was acquainted with Beethoven.

Reichardt,[1] a most competent judge, heard her repeatedly in the winter of 1808-1809 and recorded a highly favorable impression of her from which we quote: "A lofty noble manner and a beautiful face full of deep feeling increases my expectation still further at the first sight of the noble lady; and then as she performed a great Beethoven sonata I was surprised as almost never before. I have never seen such power and innermost tenderness combined even in the greatest virtuosi; from the tip of each finger her soul poured forth, and from her hands, both equally skillful and sure, what power and authority were brought to bear over the whole instrument. Everything

---

[1] Johann Friedrich Reichardt (1752-1814), composer and litterateur, formerly in the service of Frederick the Great in Berlin, spent the winter of 1808-1809 in Vienna. His *Vertraute Briefe, geschrieben auf einer Reise nach Wien* (1810) is an important source for this period.

that is great and beautiful in art was turned into song with ease and expression! And it was not one of those fine pianos that one finds so frequently here, but the great artist instilled her sensitive spirit into the instrument and forced it to serve her as perhaps no other hands have been able to do."

Well might the master call her his "Dorothea-Cäcilia!" In one of his most delightful letters the young Felix Mendelssohn describes his visit at Milan (1831) to the Ertmanns, "the most agreeable, cultured people conceivable, both in love as if they were a bridal couple, and yet married 34 years," where he and the lady delighted each other by turns in the performance of Beethoven's compositions and "the old General, who now appeared in his stately gray commander's uniform, wearing many orders, was very happy and wept with joy"; and in the intervals he told "the loveliest anecdotes about Beethoven, how, in the evening when she played for him, he used the candle snuffers as a toothpick, etc." In this letter there is one touching and beautiful reminiscence of the Baroness. "She related," says Mendelssohn, "that when she lost her last child, Beethoven at first did not want to come into the house; at length he invited her to visit him, and when she came he sat himself down at the pianoforte and said simply: 'We will now talk to each other in tones,' and for over an hour played without stopping, and as she remarked: 'he told me everything, and at last brought me comfort.'"

Another member of this group was a young lady, who during her five years' residence in Vienna, became one of the most devoted as well as most highly accomplished players of Beethoven's compositions—Marie Bigot. From 1809 to her death in 1820 she lived in Paris, where her superiority, first as dilettante, then as professional player and teacher, made her the subject of one of the most pleasing sketches in Fétis's *Biographie Universelle des Musiciens*. From this we learn that she was born of a family named Kiene on March 3, 1786, at Colmar in Alsatia and married M. Bigot, who took her to Vienna in 1804. In the Austrian capital she became acquainted with Haydn, and formed a friendship also with Beethoven and Salieri. Such associations naturally fired her ardently musical nature, and at 20 years of age she had already developed great skill and originality. The first time that she played in the presence of Haydn, the old gentleman was so moved that he clasped her in his arms and cried: "O, my dear child, I did not write this music—it is you who have composed it!" And upon the printed sheet from which she had played he wrote: "On February 20, 1805, Joseph Haydn was happy." The melancholy genius of Beethoven found an interpreter in Madame Bigot, whose enthusiasm and depth of feeling added new beauties to those which he had conceived. One day she played a sonata which he had just composed, in such a manner as to draw from him the remark: "That is not exactly the character which I wanted to give this piece; but go right on. If it is not wholly mine it is something better." (*Si ce n'est pas tout à fait moi, c'est mieux que moi.*)

Bigot, according to Reichardt, was "an honest, cultivated Berliner, Librarian of Count Razumovsky." As this was precisely in those years when Beethoven was most patronized by that nobleman, the composer and the lady were thus brought often together, and very warm, friendly relations resulted. A very characteristic letter of Beethoven to the Bigots suggests that his attentions to the young wife had at one time the appearance of being a little too pointed. ---⁂{There are two letters that precede it which set the scene. The first is to Marie[2] and contains an enthusiastic invitation to a midday drive since the weather was so beautiful. Beethoven urged acceptance even though the husband was at work; as for the baby Caroline, she could be wrapped up and brought along. The second letter, to Herr Bigot, is dated Thursday, March 5.[3] It shows that the invitation for the day before had been refused, and that an uncomfortable scene had just occurred in which Beethoven was unable to express himself to the husband, and therefore had to pour out his unsettled feelings in this letter.}⁂— The third letter follows:

Dear Marie, dear Bigot!

It is only with the deepest regret that I am compelled to recognize that the purest and most harmless feelings can often be misunderstood— Considering, dear M, how you greeted me I never thought of interpreting it otherwise than that you were giving me your friendship.— You must deem me very vain and contemptible if you assume that the kindnesses of such an excellent person as yourself could make me believe—that I had at once won your love— Moreover, it is one of my first principles *never to stand in other than friendly relations with the wife of another man. I do not wish by any other such relations to fill my soul with distrust against her who some day may share her fate with me*—and so ruin for myself the loveliest and purest life.— It is possible that I may have jested a few times with Bigot in a way that was not too refined; I told you myself that I am occasionally ill behaved. I am completely natural with all my friends and hate all restraint. I count Bigot amongst them; if something I do displeases him, the friendship with both of you demands that you tell me so—and I will certainly have a care never to offend him again—but how can good Marie put so bad a construction on my actions?— —

With regard to my invitation to take you and Caroline driving, it was but natural that I should believe, Bigot having opposed your going with me alone, that both of you deemed it unbecoming or objectionable—and when I wrote to you I had no other purpose than to make you understand that I saw no harm in it. And when I declared that it was a matter of great importance to me that you should not refuse, it was only to persuade you to enjoy the *gloriously beautiful day*. I had your and Caroline's pleasure in mind more than my own, and I thought I could compel you to accede to my wishes when I said that *mistrust on your part or a refusal would really offend me*.— You ought really to ponder how you will make amends to me—for having spoilt for me—a day that was so bright because of my cheerful mood and the cheerful weather.— If I said that you misunderstood me, your present judgement of me shows that I was right,

[2] *A*, 138.   [3] *A*, 138a.

not to mention *what* you yourself thought *in connection with it*— When I said that *something evil* might come of it if I came to see you, that was more than anything else a *joke* which had only the one purpose of showing how everything about you attracts me, that I have no greater wish than always to live with you, which also is the truth— Even in case there was a hidden meaning in it, even the most sacred friendship can yet have secrets, but to *misinterpret* the secret of a friend—because one cannot at once guess it, that you should *not* do, dear Bigot and dear Marie. *Never, never* will you find me ignoble; from childhood on I learned to love virtue—and all that is beautiful and good— You have hurt me to the quick— It shall only serve to make our friendship the firmer.— I am really not at all well today and it would be difficult to see you. Yesterday after the quartets my feelings and imagination continually called up before me the fact that I had made you suffer. I went to the Redoute last night to seek distraction, but in vain; everywhere I was haunted by visions of all of you, always saying to me, they are so good and probably suffering because of you.— Dejected in spirits I hurried away— Write me a few lines—

Your true and faithful friend Beethoven
embraces you all.

This friendship continued; within the next year Beethoven wrote four more notes to Herr Bigot. After this, however, there is no further evidence of correspondence.

The Hungarian Count Peter Erdödy married, June 6, 1796, the Countess Anna Marie Niczky (born 1779), then just seventeen years of age. There is nothing to show how or when the very great intimacy between the Countess and Beethoven began; but for many years she was prominent among the most useful and valued of his many female friends, and it is not at all improbable that the vicinity of the Erdödy estate at Jederslee am Marchfelde was one reason for his frequent choice of summer lodgings in the villages on the Danube, north of the city. Reichardt describes the Countess, in December, 1808, as a "very beautiful, fine little woman who from her first confinement (1799) was afflicted with an incurable disease which for ten years has kept her in bed for all but two to three months"—in which he greatly exaggerates the evil of her condition—"but nevertheless gave birth to three healthy and dear children who cling to her like burrs; whose sole entertainment was found in music; who plays even Beethoven's pieces right well and limps with still swollen feet from one pianoforte to another, yet is so merry and friendly and good—all this saddens me during an otherwise joyous meal in which six or eight good musical souls participated." The three children were Marie (Mimi), Friederike (Fritzi) and August. A tutor, Joseph Xaver Brauchle (often referred to as Magister) was employed for the children about 1803. With him also Beethoven became friendly.

The manner in which Beethoven received support from the aristocracy is suggested in a report from Vienna, dated February 27 (1807) to the *Allgemeine Musikalische Zeitung*:[4] "Beethoven's big symphony in E-flat, which

[4] Issue of March 18, 1807 (IX, 400).

has been recently reviewed so scrupulously and impartially in these pages, will be performed along with the other two symphonies by this composer (in C and D) and also with a fourth, still unknown symphony by him, in a very select circle that contributed a very considerable sum for the benefit of the composer."⟩⋆— These performances, which took place in March, were described at the beginning of April in the *Journal des Luxus und der Moden*:

Beethoven gave two concerts at the house of Prince L. at which nothing but his own compositions were performed; namely his first four symphonies, an overture to the tragedy *Coriolan*, a pianoforte concerto and some airs from the opera *Fidelio*. Richness of ideas, bold originality and fullness of power, which are the particular merits of Beethoven's muse were very much in evidence to everyone at these concerts; yet many found fault with lack of a noble simplicity and the all too fruitful accumulation of ideas which on account of their number were not always adequately worked out and blended, thereby creating the effect more often of rough diamonds.

Was "Prince L." Lobkowitz or Lichnowsky? The details above given point decisively to the former. It is true that the paroxysms of wrath, in which Beethoven had so unceremoniously parted from Lichnowsky in the autumn before, had so far subsided that he now granted the Prince the use of his new manuscript overture; but the contemporary notice, from which this fact is derived, is in such terms as of itself to preclude the idea that this performance of it was in one of the two subscription concerts. The reader may judge for himself: "Prince Lichnowsky, who along with Prince Lobkowitz distinguished himself favorably among the aristocracy through his love of music, recently gave a musical concert, abundant in beauty of compositions. A new work of Beethoven's, an overture to Collin's *Coriolan*, received favorable applause from the connoisseur." The expressive quality of the overture is then discussed, but no mention is made of any other of the composer's works.[5]

The manuscript of the overture bears the composer's own date, 1807. Collin's tragedy was originally performed November 24, 1802, with "between-acts music" arranged by Abbé Stadler from Mozart's *Idomeneo*. The next year Lange assumed the leading part with a success of which he justly boasts in his autobiography, and played it so often down to March 5, 1805, as to make the work thoroughly familiar to the theatre-going public. From that date to the end of October, 1809 (how much longer we have no means at hand of knowing), it was played but once—namely on April 24, 1807. The overture was assuredly not written for that one exceptional performance; for, if so, it would not have been played in March in two different concerts. But it is very likely that the single performance of the tragedy was arranged so soon after the two concerts in order to bring together the composition and the work for which it was written. Furthermore Lobkowitz had recently

[5] *Morgenblatt* (Cotta) March 8, 1807. (TDR, III, 9.)

become a member of the theatre direction. The fact that the correspondent for the *Allg. Mus. Zeitung* wrote in December, 1807, "A *new* overture by this composer . . . is full of fire and power; according to the inscription, it was intended for Collin's *Coriolan*,"[6] does not prove so much that the performance of Collin's work in April was done without Beethoven's music as it does that the overture was new to the reviewer and that he had missed this performance as well as the concerts in March both at Lobkowitz's and at Lichnowsky's.

Beethoven had at this time written but four overtures—three to *Fidelio*, and that to *Prometheus*, which had long ceased to be a novelty. He needed a new one. Collin's tragedy was thoroughly well known and offered a subject splendidly suited to his genius. An overture to it was a compliment to his influential friend, the author,[7] and, if successful, would be a new proof of his talent for dramatic composition. How nobly the character of Coriolanus is mirrored in Beethoven's music is well enough known; but the admirable adaptation of the overture to the play is duly appreciated by those only who have read Collin's almost forgotten work.

Clementi, called to Rome by the death of his brother, had arrived in Vienna on his way thither, and embraced the opportunity to acquire the exclusive right of publication in England of various works of Beethoven, whose great reputation, the rapidly growing taste for his music, and the great difficulty of obtaining continental publications in those days of "Napoleonic ideas," combined to render such a right in that country one of considerable value. Clementi reported the results of the negotiations with Beethoven in a letter to his partner, F. W. Collard, with whom he had been associated in business for five years, which J. S. Shedlock made public in the *Athenaeum* of London on July 26, 1902. It runs as follows:

> Messrs. Clementi and Co., No. 26 Cheapside, London.
>
> Vienna, April 22d, 1807.
>
> Dear Collard:
>
> By a little management and without committing myself, I have at last made a compleat conquest of that *haughty beauty*, Beethoven, who first began at public places to grin and coquet with me, which of course I took care not to discourage; then slid into familiar chat, till meeting him by chance one day in the street— "Where do you lodge?" says he; "I have not seen you this *long* while!"—upon which I gave him my address. Two days after I found on my table his card brought by himself, from the maid's description of his lovely form. This will do, thought I. Three days after that he calls again, and finds me at home. Conceive then the mutual ecstasy of such a meeting! I took pretty good care to improve it to our *house's* advantage, therefore, as soon as decency would allow, after praising very handsomely some of his compositions: "Are you engaged with any publisher

---

[6] On the autograph at the Beethovenhaus in Bonn, the words "zum Trauerspiel" (for the tragedy) have been ruled out. See *Katalog der Handschriften des Beethoven-Hauses* (Bonn, 1935), p. 23.

[7] Heinrich von Collin was at that time Court Secretary.

in London?"—"No" says he. "Suppose, then, that you prefer *me*?"—"With all my heart." "Done. What have you ready?"—"I'll bring you a list." In short I agreed with him to take in MSS. three quartets, a symphony, an overture and a concerto for the violin, which is beautiful, and which, at my request he will adapt for the pianoforte with and without additional keys; and a concerto for the pianoforte, for *all* which we are to pay him two hundred pounds sterling. The property, however, is only for the British Dominions. To-day sets off a courier for London through Russia, and he will bring over to you two or three of the mentioned articles.

Remember that the violin concerto he will adapt himself and send it as soon as he can.

The quartets, etc., you may get Cramer or some other very clever fellow to adapt for the Piano-forte. The symphony and the overture are wonderfully fine so that I think I have made a very good bargain. What do you think? I have likewise engaged him to compose two sonatas and a fantasia for the Piano-forte which he is to deliver to our house for sixty pounds sterling (mind I have treated for Pounds, not Guineas). In short he has promised to treat with no one but me for the British Dominions.

In proportion as you receive his compositions you are to remit him the money; that is, he considers the whole as consisting of six articles, viz: three *quartets*, symphony, overture, Piano-forte concerto, violin concerto, and the adaptation of the said concerto, for which he is to receive £200.

For three articles you'll remit £100 and so on in proportion. The agreement says also that as soon as you receive the compositions, you are to pay into the hands of Messrs. R. W. and E. Lee, the stated sum, who are to authorize Messrs. J. G. Schuller and Comp. in Vienna to pay to Mr. van Beethoven, the value of the said sum, according to the course of exchange, and the said Messrs. Schuller and Co. are to reimburse themselves on Messrs. R. W. and E. Lee. On account of the impediments by war, etc., I begged Beethoven to allow us 4 months (after the setting of his MSS.) to publish in. He said he would write to your house in French *stating the time*, for of course he sends them likewise to Paris, etc., etc., and they must appear on the same day. You are also by agreement to send Beethoven by a *convenient* opportunity, two sets of each of the new compositions you print of his. . . . Mr. van Beethoven says, you may publish the 3 articles he sends by *this courier* on the 1st of September, next.

Count Gleichenstein witnessed the signing of the contract, which follows:

La convention suivante a été faite entre Monsieur M. Clementi et Monsieur Louis van Beethoven.

1. Monsieur Louis van Beethoven cède à Monsieur M. Clementi les manuscrits de ses oeuvres ci-après ensuivis, avec le droit de les publier dans ses royaumes unis britanniques, en se réservant la liberté de faire publier ou de vendre pour faire publier les mêmes ouvrages hors des dits royaumes:

    a. trois quators,
    b. une symphonie
       N.B. la quatrième qu'il a composée,
    c. une ouverture de Coriolano, tragédie de Mr. Collin,

   d. un concert pour le piano
      N.B. le quatrième qu'il a composé
   e. un concert pour le violon
      N.B. le premier qu'il a composé,
   f. ce dernier concert arrangé pour le piano avec des notes additionelles.

2. Monsieur M. Clementi fera payer pour ces six ouvrages à Mr. L. v. Beethoven la valeur de deux cents Liv. Sterl. au cours de Vienne par Mrss. Schuller et comp. aussitôt qu'on aura à Vienne la nouvelle de l'arrivée de ces ouvrages à Londres.

3. Si Monsieur L. v. Beethoven ne pouvait livrer ensemble ces six ouvrages, il ne serait payé par Mrss. Schuller et comp. qu'à proportion des pièces, p. ex. en livrant la moitié, il recevra la moitié, en livrant le tiers, il recevra le tiers de la somme convenue.

4. Monsieur L. v. Beethoven promet de ne vendre ces ouvrages soit en Allemagne, soit en France, soit ailleurs, qu' avec la condition de ne les publier que quatre mois après leur départ respectif pour l'Angleterre: pour le concert pour le violon et pour la symphonie et pour la symphonie et pour l'ouverture, qui viennent de partir pour l'Angleterre, Mons. L. v. Beethoven promet de les vendres qu'à condition de ne publier avant le 1. Sept. 1807.

5. On est convenu de plus que Mons. L. v. Beethoven compose aux mêmes conditions dans un temps non determiné et à son aise, trois Sonates ou deux Sonates et une Fantaisie pour le piano avec ou sans accompagnement comme il voudra, et que Mons. M. Clementi lui fera payer de la même manière soixante Livres Sterl.

6. Mons. M. Clementi donnera à Mons. L. v. Beethoven deux exemplaires de chacun de ces ouvrages.

   Fait en double et signé à Vienne
        le 20. Avril 1807.
      Muzio Clementi   Louis van Beethoven
                                    Comme témoin J. Gleichenstein

The quartets, in parts, had been lent to Count Franz Brunsvik and were still in Hungary, which gave occasion to one of Beethoven's peculiarly whimsical and humorous epistles:

on May 11, 1806[8] [*sic*]   Vienna on a Mayday
Dear, dear B!

I just want to tell you that I came to a really satisfactory arrangement with *Clementi*—I shall receive 200 Pds. sterling—and besides I am privileged to sell the same works in Germany and France.—He has also offered me other commissions—so that I am enabled to hope through them to achieve the dignity of a true artist while still young.—I need, *dear B.*, the *quartets*. I have already asked your sister to write to you about them.[9] It takes too long to copy them from my score—therefore make haste and send them direct to me by *letter post*—you shall have them back in 4 or 5 days at the latest.—I beg you urgently for them, since

---

[8] The date, May 11, 1806, provides another instance of the composer's irresponsibility in dating his letters; for the references to the contract with Clementi is irrefutable evidence that it was written in 1807. (Cf. TDR, III, 29 n. 2.)

[9] This was undoubtedly Josephine Deym. See *A*, 142. (Cf. TDR, III, 29, n. 2.)

otherwise I might lose a great deal.—If you can arrange for the Hungarians to ask me to come for a few concerts, do it—you may have me for 200 florins in gold—then I will bring my opera along—I shall never get along with the princely rabble in the theatres—[10]

Whenever *we* (several amici) drink your wine, we get drunk on you, that is, we drink your health—Farewell—hurry—hurry—hurry and send me the quartets—otherwise you may embarrass me greatly.—Schuppanzigh has married—it is said to *one very like him.*—What sort of a family????—Kiss your sister Therese, tell her I fear I shall become great without the help of a monument of hers contributing thereto—Send me tomorrow the quartets—quar—tete—t—e—t—s.

Your friend
Beethoven

If an English publisher could afford to pay so high a price for the manuscripts of a German composer, why not a French one? So Beethoven reasoned, and, Bonn being then French, he wrote to Simrock and also to Pleyel in Paris proposing a contract like that made with Clementi. The letters expressed a desire to sell six new works to a publishing house in France, one in England and one in Vienna simultaneously, with the understanding that they were to appear only after a certain date. They were a symphony, the overture for Collin's *Coriolan*, a violin concerto, 3 quartets, 1 concerto for the pianoforte, the violin concerto arranged for pianoforte "avec des notes additionelles." The price, "very cheap," was to be 1200 florins, Augsburg current. In both cases, a specific day of publication was set for each set of three. Pleyel's answer is not known, but Simrock answered that owing to unfavorable circumstances due to the war, all he could offer, in his "lean condition," was 1600 livres. He also proposed that in case Beethoven found his offer fair, he should send the works without delay to Breuning. Simrock would at once pay Breuning 300 livres in cash and give him a bill of exchange for 1300 livres, payable in two years, provided nobody reprinted any of his works in France, he taking all measures to protect his property under the laws.

The only works on this list that were published by Simrock were the Razumovsky Quartets, which appeared in 1808 in Bonn after their first printing in Vienna by the Kunst- und Industrie-Comptoir, Beethoven's principal publisher at this time. A series of letters from Beethoven to Baron Ignaz von Gleichenstein were written during June and July from Baden, where Beethoven had moved. These letters show the extent that Gleichenstein had taken over the handling of Beethoven's affairs at this time and the strain that had developed between him and his brothers—particularly Johann from whom he had borrowed money. On June 23 Beethoven wrote to the Kunst- und Industrie-Comptoir to introduce Gleichenstein as his agent to arrange with the publishers for an advance payment to him for music which he had

---

[10] At the end of this chapter is a discussion of the change that had taken place in the theatre direction from Baron Braun to a group of the aristocracy.

not yet delivered to the firm.[11] Shortly afterwards he wrote the following letter to his friend:}⁜—

Dear good Gleichenstein,

Please be so good as to give this to the copyist tomorrow—it concerns the symphony as you see—in case he is not through with the quartet tomorrow, take it away and deliver it to the Industriecomptoir.—You may say to my brother that I shall certainly not write to him again.—I know the cause, it is this. Because he has lent me money and spent some on my account, he is (*I know my brothers*) already anxious because I cannot yet pay it back to him: and apparently the other one, filled with the spirit of revenge against me, stirs him up too.—It would be best if I were to collect the whole 1500 florins (from the Industriecomptoir) and pay him with it; then the matter will be at an end—Heaven preserve me from having to receive benefactions from my brothers—Farewell—greetings to West—[12]

Your Beethoven

N.B. I sent the symphony from here to the Industriecomptoir. They have probably received it already—When you next come back, bring along some good sealing-wax.

Evidently the following billet to Gleichenstein was sent directly afterwards: "I think—you had better have them pay you 60 florins more than the 1500 or, if you think that it would be consistent with my honesty—the sum of 1600—I leave this wholly to you, however, only honesty and justice must be the *polestar* which is to guide you." The transaction to which the letter and this note refer must have been the sale of the compositions, the British rights to which had been sent to Clementi. The quartet was probably one of the Razumovsky set and the symphony that in B-flat, since the fifth and the sixth were not published by the Viennese Bureau but by Breitkopf and Härtel.

These undated notes can also be connected with a letter to Gleichenstein in which Beethoven made it clear that his apothecary brother could not be involved in these negotiations with the Industrie-Comptoir "for several reasons." The compelling one was that it was just this firm to which Beethoven was turning for financial aid to satisfy Johann's demands.

The case, in few words, was this:—Eleonore Orelley, sole heir of her sister, Theresia Tiller, was, in the autumn of 1807, seeking a purchaser for the house and "registered apothecary shop" which, until 1872, still existed directly between the market-place and the bridge at Linz on the Danube, and was willing to dispose of them on such terms of payment, as to render it possible even for Johann van Beethoven with his slender means to become their owner. "I know my brothers," writes Beethoven. His brothers also knew him; and Johann had every reason to fear that if he did not secure his debt now when his brother's means were abundant, he might at the crisis

[11] *A*, 147.
[12] Thomas West was the assumed name of Joseph Schreyvogel, one of the directors of the Kunst- und Industrie-Comptoir.

of his negotiation find himself penniless. His demand was too just to be re-sisted and Gleichenstein evidently drew the money from the Kunst- und Industrie-Comptoir and paid it; for on the 13th of March, 1808, the contract of sale was signed at Vienna. By the terms of the contract which fixed the price at 25,000 florins, the vendee agreed to assume incumbrances on the property amounting to 12,600 florins, pay 10,400 florins in cash and 5 per cent interest on 2,000 florins to the vendor during her life, and to be in Linz and take possession of the property on or before March 20, i.e., within a week after the signing of the contract.

The expenses incurred in the negotiations, in his journey to Linz, and in taking possession, left the indigent purchaser barely funds sufficient to make his first payment and ratify the contract; in fact, he had only 300 florins left. The profits of his shop and the rents of his house were so small, that Johann was almost at his wit's end how to meet his next engagements. He sold the iron gratings of the windows—but they produced too little to carry him through. It was a comical piece of good luck for him that the jars and pots upon his shelves were of pure, solid English tin—a metal which Napoleon's non-intercourse decrees fulminated against England had just then raised enormously in price. The cunning apothecary sold his tin, furnished his shop with earthenware, and met his payments with the profits of the transaction. But it is an ill wind that blows nobody any good; the reverses of the Austrian arms in April, 1809, opened the road for the French armies to Linz, and gave Apothecary Beethoven an opportunity to make large contracts for the supply of medicines to the enemy's commissariat, which not only relieved him in his present necessities but laid the foundation for his subsequent moderate fortune.

Before the spring of 1807 Beethoven had received an invitation from Prince Nikolaus Esterhazy to write a mass in honor of his wife, to be per-formed in September for her name-day. On July 26 Beethoven wrote to Prince Esterhazy from Baden:

Most Serene and Gracious Prince.

Having been told that you my Prince, have enquired concerning the mass which you commissioned me to write for you, I take the liberty, my Serene Prince, to inform you that you will receive the same at the latest by the 20th of the month of August—This will leave plenty of time to have it performed on the name-day of her Serene Highness, the Princess.—At the time when I was having the mis-fortune of a benefit date falling through at the theatre, I received an extraordinarily favorable offer *from London* which I felt I must gratefully seize upon due to my impoverished condition; and this retarded the composition of the Mass, much as I wished, Serene Prince, to appear with it before you. Also to this was added an illness of the head, which at first did not permit me to work at all, and now but little. Since people are so eager to misrepresent everything about me, I enclose a letter from my physician.—May I add that I shall deliver the Mass to you with timidity since you, Serene Highness, are accustomed to having the inimitable masterpieces of the great Haydn performed for you.—

Most serene, most gracious Prince! With high esteem your most devoted and humble

Ludwig van Beethoven

At the end of July, Beethoven removed from Baden to Heiligenstadt, devoting the time there to the C minor Symphony and the Mass in C. One of Czerny's notes relates to the Mass: "Once when he [Beethoven] was walking in the country with the Countess Erdödy and other ladies, they heard some village musicians and laughed at some false notes which they played, especially the violoncellist, who, fumbling for the C major chord, produced something like the following:

Beethoven used this figure for the *Credo* of his first mass, which he chanced to be composing at the time." Like all such stories, too much weight cannot be attached to it.

The name-day of Princess Esterhazy, née Princess Marie von Liechtenstein, for which Beethoven promised in the letter above to have the Mass ready, was the 8th of September. In the years when this date did not fall upon a Sunday it was the custom at Eisenstadt to celebrate it on the first Sunday following. In 1807 the 8th fell on a Tuesday and the first performance of Beethoven's Mass, therefore, took place on the 13th. Haydn, as Pohl informs us, had written his masses for this day and had gone to Eisenstadt from Vienna to conduct their performance. So Beethoven now, who seems to have had his troubles with the singers here as in Vienna, if one may found such an opinion upon an energetic note of Prince Esterhazy copied and printed by Pohl. In this note, which is dated September 12, 1807, the Prince called upon his Vice-Kapellmeister, Johann Fuchs, to explain why the singers in his employ were not always on hand at his musical affairs. He had heard on that day with displeasure that at the rehearsal of Beethoven's Mass only one of the five contraltos was present, and he stringently commanded all the singers and instrumentalists in his service to be on hand at the performance of the Mass on the following day.

The Mass was produced on the next day—the 13th. "It was the custom at this court," says Schindler (*Biographie*, p. 189), "that after the religious service the local as well as foreign musical notabilities met in the chambers of the Prince for the purpose of conversing with him about the works which had been performed. When Beethoven entered the room, the Prince turned to him with the question: 'But, my dear Beethoven, what is this that you have done again?' The impression made by this singular question, which was probably followed by other critical remarks, was the more painful on our artist because he saw the Kapellmeister standing near the Prince laugh. Thinking that he was being ridiculed, nothing could keep him at the place where his work had been so misunderstood and besides, as he thought, where a brother in art had rejoiced over his discomfiture. He left Eisenstadt the same day."

The composer's annoyance at Eisenstadt must have been further heightened by the quarters to which he was assigned during his stay. Victor Papp[13] has discovered that instead of being given a room in the castle like a social equal, Beethoven was quartered in the apartment of the Court Secretary of Music, Joseph Baranyai, whose principal house was in Vienna. These accommodations were not designed as living quarters and had been refused by a tenor singer two years earlier as being too damp. Papp prints a facsimile of Baranyai's receipt for 20 florins as compensation for quartering Beethoven from September 10th to 16th. Thus presumably he did not leave on the 13th as claimed by Schindler. However, all of these anecdotes point toward a most unhappy and humiliating experience for Beethoven, and the fact that fourteen years later he referred to this performance to Schindler "with great bitterness" is understandable. A further suggestion that annoyance existed on the composer's part is in the fact that the Prince received neither the manuscript nor the dedication of the Mass.

J. N. Hummel was the kapellmeister who had replaced Haydn at the post since 1804, and as Schindler goes on to say, "the unlucky laugh was not directed at Beethoven, but at the singular manner in which the Prince had criticized the Mass." Schindler's statement that Beethoven had a "falling-out with Hummel" at this time and that "there were other things which fed the hate of Beethoven" is unsupported by what is now known concerning their relationship. It is probable that Beethoven disapproved of a superficial tendency in Hummel's piano playing and composition, but his lasting bitterness over the Eisenstadt occurrence does not appear to have been primarily caused by Hummel.

A letter to Countess Josephine Deym in the spring of this year reintroduces the lady to whom Beethoven had expressed his love two years before and starts the last chapter in this affair of the heart. It will be remembered that in his letter of May 11 to her brother Franz, Beethoven mentioned having just written to his sister. Thus, sometime before May Josephine had returned to Vienna from Budapest, where she had been living during the past year. In this first letter, after urging her to write to her brother Franz about the quartets, he complained of poor health which prevented him from coming to see her. For the month of July she moved her family to Baden, where Beethoven was already established. The next letter is written on September 20 from Heiligenstadt, where he had been before and after the performance of the Mass at Eisenstadt. In it he refers to the fact that immediately after his return from Eisenstadt he called on her twice in Vienna "—but I was not so fortunate—as to see you—That hurt me deeply—." He had been trying

[13] Victor Papp, *Beethoven és a Magyorok* (Budapest, 1927), p. 71.

unsuccessfully to keep a promise with himself to control his feelings for her, but his longing continued, and thoughts of her had followed him to Heiligenstadt and Eisenstadt. He longed to have a long, uninterrupted talk with her so that their hearts and souls could be reunited. At the end of the letter he referred to his improving health and, in the postscript, to the fact that he would be coming to town that day but dared not come to her for fear of being disappointed a third time.[14]

The third letter anticipates the parting of the ways. Beethoven, writing from the country, admitted that at the moment it was better for their peace of mind not to see each other.[15] But another letter is an impassioned plea for frankness and explanation: he had tried to see her again but now did not care to put up with further rebuffs from her servants. He had kept away from her for awhile because he thought she desired it; now he would not express himself further until he knew the truth.[16]

Schmidt-Görg believes that a certain amount of time elapsed before the last letter, which he introduces with a draft of a message from Josephine to Beethoven:[17]

For a long time I have wanted to hear news of your state of health, and long ago I would have informed myself about it had not modesty held me back—Now tell me how things are going, what are you doing? How is your health, your state of mind, your behavior?—A deep concern which I have and will continue to have as long as I live about everything to do with you compels me to gain information. Or does my *friend Beethoven*, may I use that term, believe I have changed.—What else would this doubt express to me than that you yourself had not remained the same.

Beethoven's final letter provides a wistful close to the affair:[18]

Please deliver the sonata to your brother, my dear Josephine—I thank you for wishing still to appear as if I were not altogether banished from your memory, even though this came about perhaps more at the instigation of others—You want me to tell you how I am. A more difficult question could not be put to me—and I prefer to leave it unanswered, rather than—to answer it *too truthfully*—All good wishes, dear J[osephine].

As always, your Beethoven
who is eternally devoted to you.

A controversy for the possession of the two Court Theatres and that of An-der-Wien involved certain legal questions which, in September, 1806, were decided by the proper tribunal against the old directors, who were thus at the end of the year compelled to retire. Peter, Baron von Braun, closed his twelve years' administration with a circular letter addressed to his recent subordinates, dated December 28 in which, after bidding them an affec-

---

[14] See *A* 151.
[15] See *A* 153.
[16] See *A* 154.
[17] *Veröffentlichungen des Beethovenhauses*

in Bonn, III, p. 33.
[18] *A* 156. Translation by Miss Anderson, reprinted with her permission and that of her publishers.

tionate adieu, he said: "With imperial consent I have turned over the vice-direction of the Royal Imperial Court Theatre to a company composed of the following cavaliers: the Princes Lobkowitz, Schwarzenberg and Ester-hazy, and the Counts Esterhazy, Lodrin, Ferdinand Palffy, Stephen Zichy and Niklas Esterhazy."

In this change, Beethoven naturally saw a most hopeful prospect of an improvement in his own theatrical fortunes. Acting on a hint from Lobko-witz, he addressed to the new directors a petition:

To the Worshipful R.I. Theatre Direction:

The undersigned flatters himself that during his sojourn in Vienna he has won some favor and approval not only from the high nobility but from the general public as well, and that he has secured an honorable acceptance of his works at home and abroad.

Nevertheless, he has been obliged to struggle with difficulties of all kinds and has not yet been able to establish himself here in a position which would enable him to fulfil his desire to live wholly for art, to develop his talents to a still higher degree of perfection, which must be the goal of every true artist, and to make certain for the future the fortuitous advantages of the present.

Inasmuch as the undersigned has always striven less for a livelihood than for the interests of art, the ennoblement of taste and the uplifting of his genius towards higher ideals and perfection, it necessarily happened that he often was compelled to sacrifice profit and advantage to the Muse. Yet works of this kind have won for him a reputation in foreign lands which assures him a favorable reception in a number of important places, and a destiny commensurate with his talents and abilities.

But in spite of this the undersigned cannot deny that the many years he has spent here, the favor and approval which he has enjoyed from high and low, the wish wholly to fulfil the expectations which he has been fortunate enough to awaken and, let him venture to say, the patriotism of a German have made this very place more estimable and desirable to him than any other.

Therefore, he cannot forbear, before deciding to leave the city so dear to him, to follow the suggestion kindly made to him by His Serene Highness the ruling Prince Lobkowitz, who intimated to him that the *Worshipful Theatre Direction* would not be disinclined to engage the undersigned under proper conditions for the service of the *theatres* under their management and to ensure his further stay here by offering him the *means of a comfortable livelihood* favorable to the exercise of his talents.

Inasmuch as this intimation is in perfect accord with the desires of the under-signed, he takes the liberty to submit an expression of his willingness as well as the following conditions for the favorable consideration of the Worshipful Direction:

1. He promises and contracts to compose every year at least one grand opera, the subject to be selected jointly by the *Worshipful Direction* and the undersigned; in return he asks a fixed remuneration of 2400 florins per annum and the gross receipts of the third performance of each such opera.

2. He agrees to deliver gratis each year a small operetta or a *divertissement,*

choruses or occasional pieces according to the wishes or needs of the *Worshipful Direction*, but hopes that the Worshipful Direction will not hesitate in return for such works to grant him at least one day per year for a benefit concert in the theatre building.

If one reflects what an expenditure of time and effort is required for the making of an opera to the absolute exclusion of every other intellectual occupation, and further, that in other cities where the composer and his family have a share in the receipts of every performance, a single successful work may make the fortune of a composer; and still further how small a compensation, owing to the monetary condition and high prices for necessities which prevail here, is at the command of a local artist to whom foreign lands are open, the above conditions can certainly not be thought to be excessive or unreasonable.

In any case, however, whether the Worshipful Direction confirms and accepts this offer or not, the undersigned adds the request that he be granted a day for a concert in one of the theatre buildings; for should the proposition be accepted, the undersigned would at once require his time and powers for the composition of the opera, and therefore be unable to use them for his profit in another direction. Should this present offer be refused, the undersigned would look upon the fulfilment of last year's promise of a concert, which never took place because of various obstacles which intervened, as the final proof of the great favor heretofore enjoyed by him. He requests that in the first case the day be set on the Feast of the Annunciation, in the second on one of the approaching Christmas holidays.

Ludwig van Beethoven, m.p.

Vienna, 1807.

Neither of these requests was granted directly; one of them only indirectly. Nor is it known whether any formal written reply was conveyed to the petitioner.

The time at which this petition was made has been set convincingly by Unger[19] as the end of the year 1807, in contrast to Thayer who dated it the beginning of this year. Unger's arguments follow. In a notice of the Coriolanus overture in the *Allgemeine Musikalische Zeitung*, December 26, 1807, already cited, the reviewer writes: "A new overture of this composer (*who is supposed to become engaged in very advantageous relations with the theatre*), is full of power and fire." (The italics are ours.) This suggests that the request had not yet been rejected; and it is unthinkable that the directors would have kept him waiting a whole year for their answer.

Beethoven's scornful reference to "the princely rabble" in the letter to Count Brunsvik on May 11th is the result of the rejection not of this petition but of his request for an Akademie. This is borne out by the letter to Prince Esterhazy, July 30th, quoted above, in which he apologizes for the delay in the writing of the mass because of his arrangements with Clementi "when I was having the misfortune of a benefit date falling through at the theatre." Obviously this was the concert to which Beethoven was referring in the

[19] See Max Unger, "Beethoven und das Wiener Hoftheater im Jahre 1807," *NBJ*, II (1925), 76-83.

petition with the words "last year's promise of a concert, which never took place because of various obstacles which intervened. . . ."

Beethoven was not encouraged either to write an opera or to have his own Akademie in the forthcoming Christmas holidays. He had to wait a year to achieve this second end; meanwhile the princes, after a year of losses, turned the direction of the theatre over to Court Councillor and art-lover, Joseph von Hartl, who was clearly in no position to consider such a contract.

Though disappointed in December, as he had been in March, in the hope of obtaining the use of the theatre for a concert, Beethoven was not thereby prevented from coming prominently before the public as composer and director. It came about in this way: The want of better opportunities to hear good symphonic music well performed than were afforded by Schuppanzigh's concerts (which were confined to the summer months) or the occasional hastily arranged Akademies of composers and virtuosi, induced a number of music-lovers early in the winter to form an institute under the modest title "Concert of Music-Lovers" (*Liebhaber-Concert*). Says the *Wiener Vaterländische Blätter* of May 27, 1808: "An orchestra was organized, whose members were chosen from the best of the local music-lovers (dilettanti). A few wind-instruments only—French horns, trumpets, etc., were drafted from the Vienna theatres. . . . The audiences were composed exclusively of the nobility of the town and foreigners of note, and among these classes the preference was given to the cognoscenti and amateurs." The hall "zur Mehlgrube," which was first engaged, proved to be too small, and the concerts were transferred to the hall of the University, where "in twenty meetings symphonies, overtures, concertos and vocal pieces were performed zealously and affectionately and were received with general approval." Banker Häring was the director in the earlier concerts but gave way to Clement "because of disagreements." The works of Beethoven reported as having been performed in these concerts are the Symphony in D (in the first concert), the overture to *Prometheus* in November, the "Eroica" Symphony and the Overture to *Coriolan* in December, and about New Year's the Fourth Symphony in B-flat, which also had been played on the 15th of November in the Burgtheater at a concert for the public charities. Most, if not all of these works were directed by their composer.

A paragraph from the *Journal des Luxus* (November, 1806) gives the only satisfactory notice, known to us, of the origin of one of Beethoven's minor but well-known compositions:

A bit of musical pleasantry recently gave rise to a competition amongst a number of famous composers. Countess Rzewuska[20] improvised an aria at the pianoforte; the poet Carpani at once improvised a text for it. He imagined a lover who had

[20] Née Princess Alexandra Rosalia Luborwirska (1791-1865), she married Count Robert Rzewuski. The count's sister, Maria Isabella, was married in 1812 to Count Waldstein. See KHV, p. 596.

died of grief because of the indifference of his ladylove; she, repenting of her hard-heartedness, bedews the grave; and now the shade calls to her:

> In questa tomba oscura
> Lasciami riposar;
> Quando viveva, ingrata,
> Dovevi a me pensar.
>
> Lascia che l'ombra ignude
> Godansi pace almen,
> E non bagnar mie ceneri
> D'inutile velen.

These words have been set by Paër, Salieri, Weigl, Zingarelli, Cherubini, Asioli and other great masters and amateurs. Zingarelli alone provided ten compositions of them; in all about fifty have been collected and the poet purposes to give them to the public in a volume.

The number of the compositions was increased to sixty-three, and they were published in 1808, the last (No. 63) being by Beethoven. This was by no means considered the best at the time, although it alone now survives.

The works ascertained as belonging to this year are: (1) the transcription of the Violin Concerto for Pianoforte, made (as Clementi's letter to Collard says) at Clementi's request; (2) the overture to *Coriolan*, Op. 62; (3) the Mass in C, Op. 86; (4) the Arietta "In questa tomba," WoO 133. — Kinsky suggests that the little March in B-flat for 2 clarinets, 2 horns, 2 bassoons, WoO 29 (published in the *GA*, Ser. 25, Nr. 29) might have been written as "grenadier musik" for Prince Esterhazy in connection with the trip to Eisenstadt in September, 1807. Haydn wrote a march in E-flat for the same instruments intended no doubt for Esterhazy's military music.[21]

During the year Beethoven was also at work on the Fifth and Sixth Symphonies and the cello sonata, Op. 69. But since these works were not completed until 1808, they will be taken up in the next chapter.

The original publications of the year were few:

By Giovanni Cappi:
  Three Pieces from *Fidelio* (2nd version) in piano score: the Trio "Ein Mann ist bald genommen," the Quartet "Mir ist so wunderbar," and the Duet "Um in der Ehe froh zu leben."
By Kunst- und Industrie-Comptoir:
  Concerto for Pianoforte, Violin and Violoncello, Op. 56, dedicated to Prince Franz Joseph von Lobkowitz.
  Sonata for Pianoforte, Op. 57, dedicated to Count Franz Brunsvik.
  Thirty-two Variations for Pianoforte in C minor, WoO 80.
By Traeg:
  Twelve Ecossaises for two violins and bass with two flutes and two horns ad. lib. (also in pianoforte transcription), WoO 16.

---

[21] See KHV, p. 468.

CHAPTER XXI

THE YEAR 1808

COMPLETION OF THE FIFTH
AND SIXTH SYMPHONIES—THE CONCERT
OF DECEMBER 22ND

THE common notion that there was not an understanding or taste for Beethoven's works in Vienna is erroneous. On the contrary, generally in the concerts of these years, Beethoven's works were as often on the programmes as those of Mozart or even Haydn. Few as his published orchestral compositions then were, none were more likely to fill the house. While no other performances of his works at the Liebhaber Concerts are reported, other than those enumerated in the last chapter, perhaps this was for reasons indicated in a letter from Stephan von Breuning to Wegeler, written in March, 1808: "Beethoven came near losing a finger by a *Panaritium* [felon], but he is again in good health. He escaped a great misfortune, which, added to his deafness, would have completely ruined his good humor, which, as it is, is of rare occurrence." ⸻ This is mentioned in Beethoven's own correspondence of the winter. For example, in March he wrote to Heinrich Collin: "However, yesterday my poor finger had to have a drastic nail operation," and later to Count Oppersdorff: "I am still under treatment for my *poor innocent finger,* and have not been able to go out for the last two weeks." He was present, however at the final concert of the series, on March 27th, ⸻ at which in honor of Haydn, whose 76th birthday fell on the 31st, his *Creation* with Carpani's Italian text was given. It is pleasant to know that Beethoven was one of those who, "with members of the high nobility," stood at the door of the hall of the university to receive the venerable guest on his arrival there in Prince Esterhazy's coach, and who accompanied him as "sitting in an armchair he was carried, lifted high, and on his entrance into the hall was received with the sound of trumpets and drums by the numerous gathering and greeted with joyous shouts of 'Long Live Haydn!' "

Immediately after the close of the Liebhaber Concerts, Sebastian Mayer's annual benefit in the Theater-an-der-Wien opened with the *Sinfonia Eroica*. This was on Monday evening, April 11. Two days after (13th) the Charity Institute's Concert in the Burg Theater offered a program of six numbers; No. 1 was Beethoven's Fourth Symphony in B-flat; No. 5, his C minor Pianoforte Concerto, played by Friedrich Stein;[1] and No. 6, the "Coriolan" Overture—all directed by the composer; and, at a benefit concert in May, in the Augartensaal, occurred the first known public performance of the Triple Concerto, Op. 56.

The name of Count Franz von Oppersdorff is connected with both the Fourth and the Fifth Symphony, and the little correspondence there is between the Count and the composer sheds light on their history.

Early sketches for the Fifth Symphony are to be found alongside some for the Fourth Piano Concerto and the first act of *Leonore*; the themes for the first and second movements are at a primitive stage and a finale idea is unused:[2]

---

[1] Carl Friedrich Stein was Nanette Streicher's brother, who followed his sister to Vienna in 1804.   [2] Nottebohm, *Beeth.*, pp. 10-15.

Further sketches appearing at the end of the "Eroica" sketchbook show an advancement in the conception of the first movement theme and the establishment of both Scherzo themes.[3] Both sets may be dated 1804.

Nottebohm has described a much later set of sketches[4] for all the movements, which are alongside work for the Violin Concerto and the Cello Sonata in A, Op. 69 and thus may be dated 1806.

In this year plans for the C minor Symphony were interrupted in favor of the Symphony in B-flat which was the work of the late summer and fall while Beethoven was in Grätz. A receipt from Count Oppersdorff shows that he commissioned this symphony:

> Receipt for 500 fl.
> which I received from Count Oppersdorff for a symphony which I have written for him—
> > By my own hand and signature
> > > Ludwig van Beethoven[5]
> 1807, February third

The Count may well have been influential in arranging its performance at Prince Lobkowitz's a month later, and presumably he was in possession of the score for the customary six-month period judging by Beethoven's letter to Breitkopf and Härtel of November 18, 1806, in which he says: "I cannot give you the promised symphony yet—because a gentleman of quality has taken it from me, but I have the privilege of publishing it in half a year." The symphony with its dedication to the Count was not published, however, until 1808, by the Kunst- und Industrie-Comptoir.

The next letter from Beethoven to the Count is one which can be dated March, 1808 because of the reference to the infection in his finger from which he suffered at this time.

That you, my *beloved friend*, have fled from me without letting me know anything about your departure has really caused me pain—perhaps you were vexed with me about something, but for *my* part it was certainly not *on purpose*— Today I have little time to write more to you; I only want to inform you that *your symphony* has long been ready, and I will now send it to you by the next post— You may retain 50 florins, for the copying, which I will have done for

[3] Nottebohm, *Ein Skizzenbuch* . . . (1880), pp. 70-1.

[4] Most of these are in the Berlin State Library. See *II Beeth.*, pp. 528-34.

[5] The autograph for this receipt is owned by the New England Conservatory of Music; a facsimile is printed in Sonneck's *Beethoven Letters in America* (New York, 1927), p. 104 opp.

you, will cost that sum at least— In case you do not want the symphony, however, let me know it before the next post— In case you accept it, rejoice me as
soon as possible with the 300 fl. still due me.— *The last movement in the symphony
is with 3 trombones and flautini [piccolo]*—though not with 3 kettledrums, but
will make more noise than 6 kettledrums and better noise at that— I am still
under treatment for my *poor, innocent finger*, and because of it have not been
able to go out for the last two weeks— Farewell— let me hear something from
you soon dearest Count— Things are going badly with me— In haste your
most devoted

Beethoven

The mention of the scoring of the last movement shows that this was the
Fifth Symphony which was finally worked out in 1807 and completed in
the spring of 1808. Not only did the Count expect this symphony too but the
reference to the kettledrums suggests that the Count had discussed the
instrumentation of the work with the composer.

As Sonneck so capably argues,[6] all other financial dealings with the Count
must have concerned the Fifth Symphony only, of which we know only of
this one receipt:

That I received on March 29, 1808 one-hundred and fifty fl: in *Bank* notes
from Count Oppersdorf, I certify by my signature

Ludwig van Beethoven

Vienna, March 29, 1808.

To this the following was added:[7]

200 florins received additional in June 1807 in cash, given account of 5.
Sinphoni not yet delivered, however,

November 25, 1808

The price for the Fifth Symphony was probably again 500 florins of which
200 florins was paid in June, 1807, and of the "300 fl. still due me" 150 was
paid on March 29, 1808. That neither the balance was paid nor the symphony
received by the Count is made fairly certain by the final letter that has
survived between the two men:—

Vienna, November 1, 1088[!]

Best Count!

You will look at me in a false light, but necessity compelled me to sell to
someone else the symphony which was written for you and another as well—but
I assure you that I shall soon send you the one intended for you.— I hope that
you have been well, and also your gracious wife, to whom I ask you to give my
best wishes.— I live right under Prince Lichnowsky at Countess Erdödy's, if you
ever wish to give me the honor of a visit. My circumstances are improving—
without my *needing the help of people* who would subject *their friends to churlish-
ness*— Also, I have been asked to be Kapellmeister to the King of Westphalia,

[6] *Op.cit.*, pp. 113-16.
[7] The autograph of this receipt has been lost.
According to Thayer (See TDR, III, p. 13,

n. 1) the first line of this addition to the
receipt was in Beethoven's hand, and the remainder in Count Oppersdorff's.

and it is quite possible that I shall accept the call— Farewell and from time to time think of your most devoted friend

                                                                    Beethoven

---✏️{The "someone else" was Breitkopf and Härtel, to whom Beethoven sold the work in September, 1808. During the summer he had reopened negotiations with this firm after somewhat of a lull, and on June 8 he offered them two symphonies (the fifth and sixth), the Mass, and the Sonata for Pianoforte and Violoncello, Op. 69, for 900 florins, "although there have been so many breakings off between us that I am almost convinced that this renewal will again prove fruitless." He stated that since the Industrie-Comptoir had taken seven major works of his the year before they would probably be willing to take these works also, but that he still preferred Breitkopf and Härtel "to all others." The reply of the publishers is not on record, but in early July Beethoven repeated his offer, reduced the fee to 700 florins, and added two pianoforte sonatas "or instead of these possibly another symphony." The publishers had evidently demurred at the idea of the Mass,}--- for Beethoven writes:

You see that I give more and take less—but that is the limit—you must take the Mass, or else I cannot give you my other works—for I am considering honor and not profit merely. "There is no demand for church music," you say, and you are right if you are referring to music from mere thoroughbassists, but if you will only have the Mass performed once you will see whether there will not be music-lovers who will want it . . .

---✏️{In midsummer, a third letter offered the above works, only with two trios,[8] "since such trios are now rather scarce," substituted for the pianoforte sonatas, "or instead of these trios, a symphony," for 600 florins, and with the Mass given without a fee. The fact that Beethoven was already thinking of writing a seventh symphony is shown both by these letters to the publishers and by the letter to Count Oppersdorff; at the time of the latter letter, he was apparently intending to write it specifically for the Count. Before concluding the negotiations with Breitkopf and Härtel, there must first be considered the history of the Sixth Symphony, also mentioned in each of these letters.

As in the case of the Fifth, ideas later to be used in two different movements of the "Pastorale" appear in 1803-1804 in the "Eroica" sketchbook. The first is the country-dance theme of the third movement trio. The second is a prophetic indication of the mood, although without the final melody, of the whole second movement:[9]

---

[8] Op. 70.
[9] Nottebohm, *Ein Skizzenbuch* . . . (1880), pp. 55-6.

Murmeln der Bäche

je grösser, der Bach je tiefer der Ton ___

Further sketches for the symphony appear along with some for the Mass in C on loose sheets, a few of which were first intended for the score of the B-flat Symphony and thus indicate the winter 1806-1807. Here the main ideas are established for every movement but the second.[10]

Extended work on all the movements is the work of the Fall of 1807 and spring of 1808. Nottebohm describes a sketchbook, dated by him early 1808, in which sketches for the symphony are intermingled with sketches for the cello sonata, Op. 69 and the trios, Op. 70.[11]

From the letters to Breitkopf and Härtel previously quoted we may conclude that by the summer of 1808 the symphony, if not completed, was very nearly so.

The following two documents make clear the outcome of these negotiations:

Herewith I acknowledge today I have received one hundred ducats in gold as the agreed honorarium for five new works of my composition from Herren Breitkopf and Härtel at Leipzig.

Vienna, September 14th, 1808   Ludwig van Beethoven[12]

I the undersigned agree herewith to deliver five new works of my compositions, namely

    1 Symphony in *C Minor* opus
    1 ditto in *F major* opus
    2 trios for pianoforte etc. op.   the *first in D*
the other in   [blank]
    1 sonata for pianoforte with violoncello Op.   *in A*
to Herren Breitkopf and Härtel at Leipzig as [their] exclusive property (England excepted) and that this agreed honorarium has been received today completely and in order.

Vienna September 14, 1808   Ludwig van Beethoven

Only the words in italics are in Beethoven's hand.

Gottfried Härtel came to Vienna at the time the contract was signed. On September 14th Beethoven wrote him a note[13] in which he apologized for not being home when he called; he reported that one symphony was

---

[10] *Il Beeth.*, pp. 369-78. (Cf. TDR, III, 98.)   hand. (TDR, III, 72.)
[11] *Ibid.*, pp. 252-54.   [13] See *A* 174.
[12] Only the signature is in Beethoven's

being sent with the note, and the other, which was still being corrected by the copyist, would be sent "by eleven or half past." It is to be noted that the Mass was not mentioned in the contract. This was not published by Breitkopf and Härtel until 1812.

The autograph of the Fifth Symphony is in the Berlin State Library,[14] that of the Sixth Symphony in the Beethoven-Haus at Bonn. The first use of the word "pastoral" is in a violin part that was used at the first performance (still preserved in the Gesellschaft der Musikfreunde) which reads:

Sinfonia Pastorella
Pastoral-Sinfonie
oder
Erinnerung an das Landleben
Mehr Ausdruck der Empfindung als Mahlerei.

There follow the individual descriptions at the start of each movement.

Those who think programme music for the orchestra is a recent invention, and they who suppose the "Pastoral" Symphony to be an original attempt to portray nature in music, are alike mistaken. It was never so much the ambition of Beethoven to invent new forms of musical works, as to surpass his contemporaries in the use of those already existing. There were few great battles in those stormy years that were not fought over again by orchestras, military bands, organs and pianofortes; and pages might be filled with a catalogue of programme music, long since dead, buried and forgotten.

A remark of Ries, confirmed by other testimony, as well as by the form and substance of many of his master's works, if already quoted, will bear repetition: "Beethoven in composing his pieces often thought of a particular thing, although he frequently laughed at musical paintings and scolded particularly about trivialities of this sort. Haydn's 'Creation' and 'The Seasons' were frequently ridiculed, though Beethoven never failed to recognize Haydn's high deserts," etc. But Beethoven himself did not disdain occasionally to introduce imitations into his works. The difference between him and others in this regard was this: they undertook to give musical imitations of things essentially unmusical—he never.

In the sketches, he has recorded his own views on the subject:

The hearers should be allowed to discover the situations
Sinfonia caracteristica—or recollection of country life
A recollection of country-life
All painting in instrumental music is lost if it is pushed too far
Sinfonia pastorella. Anyone who has an idea of country-life can make out for himself the intentions of the composer without many titles—
Also without titles the whole will be recognized as a matter more of feeling than of painting in sounds.[15]

[14] A facsimile in a limited edition was made by G. Schünemann and published by Staercke in Berlin in 1942.

[15] See II Beeth., p. 375. (TDR, III, 97-8.)

On a bright, sunny day in April, 1823, Beethoven took Schindler for a long ramble through the scenes in which he had composed his Fifth and Sixth symphonies. Schindler writes (i, pp. 153-154): "After we had looked at the bath-house and its adjacent garden at Heiligenstadt and he had given expression to many agreeable recollections touching his creations, we continued our walk towards the Kahlenberg in the direction past Grinzing [?]. Passing through the pleasant meadow-valley between Heiligenstadt and the latter village,[16] which is traversed by a gently murmuring brook which hurries down from a near-by mountain and is bordered with high elms, Beethoven repeatedly stopped and let his glances roam, full of happiness, over the glorious landscape. Then seating himself on the turf and leaning against an elm, Beethoven asked me if there were any yellowhammers to be heard in the trees around us. But all was still. He then said: 'Here I composed the "Scene by the Brook" and the yellowhammers up there, the quails, nightin-'gales and cuckoos round about, composed with me.' To my question why he had not also put the yellowhammers into the scene, he drew out his sketchbook and wrote:

'That's the composer up there,' he remarked, 'hasn't she a more important role to play than the others? *They* are meant only for a joke.' And really the entrance of this figure in G major gives the tone-picture a new charm. Speaking now of the whole work and its parts, Beethoven said that the melody of this variation from the species of the yellowhammers was pretty plainly imitated in the scale written down in Andante rhythm and the same pitch.[17] As a reason for not having mentioned this fellow-composer he said that had he printed the name it would only have served to increase the number of ill-natured interpretations of the movement which has made the introduction of the work difficult not only in Vienna but also in other places. Not infrequently the symphony, because of its second movement, had been declared to be child's play. In some places it shared the fate of the 'Eroica.'"

[16] Schindler here is mistaken. The "walk toward the Kahlenberg" took them northerly into the valley between Heiligenstadt and Nussdorf, where an excessively idealized bust of the composer now marks the "Scene by the Brook." After thirty years of absence from Vienna, Schindler's memory had lost the exact topography of these scenes; and a friend to whom he wrote for information upon it mistook the Grinzing brook and valley for the true ones. This explanation of his error was made by Schindler to Thayer very soon after the third edition of his (Schindler's) book appeared. (TDR, III, 103, n. 1.)

[17] "But the note of the yellowhammer, both in England and in Austria, is not an *arpeggio*—cannot in any way be twisted into one, or represented by one. It is a quick succession of the same note, ending with a longer one, sometimes rising above the preceding note, but more frequently falling. In fact, Schindler himself tells us that it was the origin of the mighty theme which opened the C minor Symphony!"—Grove, *Beethoven and his Nine Symphonies*, p. 211. (TK, II, 121, n. 1.)

Equally interesting, valuable and grateful is Schindler's account of the origin of Beethoven's "Merrymaking of the Countryfolk" in this symphony. Somewhat curtailed it is this (1, pp. 155-157):

"There are facts to tell us of how particular was the interest which Beethoven took in Austrian dance-music. Until his arrival in Vienna (1792), according to his own statement, he had not become acquainted with any folkmusic except that of the mountains, with its strange and peculiar rhythms. How much attention he afterwards bestowed on dance-music is proved by the catalogue of his works. He even made essays in Austrian dance-music, but the players refused to grant Austrian citizenship to these efforts. The last effort dates from 1819 and, strangely enough, falls in the middle of his work on the 'Missa Solemnis.' In the tavern 'To the Three Ravens' in the *vordern Brühl* near Mödling there had played a band of seven men. This band was one of the first that gave the young musician from the Rhine an opportunity to hear the national tunes of his new home in an unadulterated form. Beethoven made the acquaintance of the musicians and composed several sets of *Ländler* and other dances for them. In the year mentioned (1819), he had again complied with the wishes of the band. I was present when the new opus was handed to the leader of the company. The master in high good humor remarked that he had so arranged the dances that one musician after the other might put down his instrument at intervals and take a rest, or even a nap. After the leader had gone away full of joy because of the present of the famous composer, Beethoven asked me if I had not observed how village musicians often played in their sleep, occasionally letting their instruments fall and remaining entirely quiet, then awakening with a start, throwing in a few vigorous blows or strokes at a venture, but generally in the right key, and then falling asleep again; he had tried to copy these poor people in his 'Pastoral' symphony. Now, reader, take up the score and see the arrangement on pages 106, 107, 108 and 109. Note the stereotyped accompaniment figure of the two violins on page 105 and the following; note the sleep-drunken second bassoon[18] with his repetition of a few tones, while contra-bass, violoncello and viola keep quiet; on page 108 we see the viola wake up and apparently awaken the violoncello—and the second horn also sounds three notes, but at once sinks into silence again. At length contra-bass and the two bassoons gather themselves together for a new effort and the clarinet has time to take a rest. Moreover, the Allegro in 2-4 time on page 110 is based in form and character on the old-time Austrian dances. There were dances in which 3-4 time gave way suddenly to 2-4. As late as the third decade of the nineteenth century I myself saw

[18] Carl Holz related the story to Jahn, which he may very well have heard from Beethoven himself. Jahn's memorandum of it is in the following words: "Scherzo of the pastorale. In Heiligenstadt a drunken bassoonist thrown out of the tavern, who then blows the bass notes." (TDR, III, 105, n. 1.)

such dances executed in forest villages only a few hours distant from the metropolis—Laab, Kaltenleutgeben and Gaden."

The subject of Beethoven's imitations, even in play, are therefore musical, not incongruous; and in *his* "Portrait musical de la Nature" are so suggestive as to aid and intensify the "expression of feelings," which was his professed aim.

The once famous musical wonder-child, Wilhelm Rust, of Dessau, at the time a young man of some twenty-two years, had come to Vienna in 1807, and was now supporting himself by giving "children instructions in reading and elementary natural science." In a letter to his "best sister, Jette," dated Haking (a village near Vienna), July 9, 1808, he wrote of Beethoven.

You want much to hear something about Beethoven; unfortunately I must say first of all that it has not been possible for me to get intimately acquainted with him. What else I know I will tell you now: He is as original and singular as a man as are his compositions; usually serious, at times merry but always satirical and bitter. On the other hand he is also very childlike and certainly very sincere. He is a great lover of truth and in this goes too far very often; for he never flatters and therefore makes many enemies. A good fellow played for him and when he was finished Beethoven said to him: "You will have to play a long time before you will realize that you can do nothing." I do not know whether you heard that I also played for him. He praised my playing, particularly in the Bach fugue, and said; "You play that well," which is much for him. Still he could not omit calling my attention to two mistakes. In a Scherzo I had not played the notes crisply enough and at another time I had struck one note twice instead of binding it. Also I played him an Andante with variations which he even praised. He must be unable to endure the French; for once when Prince Lichnowsky had some French guests, he asked Beethoven, who was also with him, to play for them as they had requested; but he refused and said he would not play for Frenchmen. In consequence he and Lichnowsky had a falling out.

Once I met him at a restaurant where he sat with a few acquaintances. He berated Vienna soundly and the decay of its music. In this he is certainly right, and I was glad to hear his judgment, which confirmed mine. Last winter I frequently attended the Liebhaber Concerts, the first of which under Beethoven's direction were very beautiful; but after he retired they became so poor that there was not one in which something was not bungled. . . .

It is very possible that Beethoven will leave Vienna; at any rate he has frequently spoken of doing so and said: 'They are forcing me to it.' He also asked me once how the orchestras were in the North. You wanted to know if any new sonatas by him have been published. As far as I know, none are forthcoming. His last works were symphonies and he is now writing an opera, which is the reason why I cannot go to him any more. Last year he composed a piece which I have not heard and an overture "Coriolan" which is extraordinarily beautiful. Perhaps you have had an opportunity to hear it in Berlin. The theme and variations in C minor which you refer to I also have; it is very beautiful, etc.

In December Rust, writing to his brother Carl, was obliged to correct what he had said about Beethoven's new opera: "All new products which have appeared here are more or less mediocre except those of Beethoven. I think I have written you that he has not yet begun his new opera. I have not yet heard his first opera; it has not been performed since I have been here." These last sentences of Rust remind us of the once current notion that disgust and disappointment at the (assumed) failure of *Fidelio* prevented Beethoven from ever undertaking the composition of another opera. The error was long since exploded, and, indeed, amply refuted by his proposition to the "princely theatre rabble" for a permanent engagement. It is now universally known how earnestly Beethoven all his life long sought a satisfactory text for an opera or an oratorio; his friends always knew it; and his essays in vocal composition had, in spite of the critics, so favorably impressed them and the dramatic writers of the day, that all were eager to serve him.

Thus Schneller writes to Gleichenstein from Graz, on March 19, 1807: "Speak at once to your friend Beethoven and particularly with the worthy Breuning, and learn if Beethoven has a mind to set a comic opera to music. I have read it, and found it varied in situation, beautiful in diction. Talk to him over a good dinner and a good glass of wine." Nothing came of this, nor is it known what the libretto was.

A somewhat more promising offer came from another quarter, but also without result. The celebrated Orientalist, Hammer-Purgstall, had just returned from the East to Vienna, arriving September 10, 1808. Although but thirty-three years of age, he was already famous, and his translations and other writings were the talk of the day. A note by Beethoven without address or date was evidently written to him:

I am almost put to shame by your courtesy and kindness showing me your still unknown literary treasures in manuscript. I thank you, Sir, most sincerely as I return both opera texts— Since I am overwhelmed by work in my own art, it is impossible for me just now to go into details about the Indian opera particularly. As soon as time permits I shall visit you in order to discuss this subject with you as well as the oratorio "Die Sündfluth"—

Please regard me always as among the true admirers of your great services. With sincere regards to you, Sir,

Most respectfully

Beethoven

The new directors of the theatres began their operatic performances at the Kärnthnerthor January 1 and 2, and at the Burg January 4, 1807, with Gluck's *Iphigenia in Tauris*. It was new to Collin and awakened in his mind new ideas of the ancient tragedy, which he determined to embody in a text for a musical drama in oratorio form. According to his biographer, Laban,[19]

---

[19] F. Laban, *Heinrich Jos. von Collin* (Vienna, 1879). (TDR, III, 66, n. 1.)

he projected one on the Liberation of Jerusalem, to offer to Beethoven for setting; but it was never finished. Another essay in the field of musical drama was a *Macbeth* after Shakespeare, also left unfinished in the middle of the second act, "because it threatened to become too gloomy." Nottebohm (*II Beeth.* pp. 225f.) says that the first act of Collin's *Macbeth* was printed in 1809 and must have been written in 1808 at the latest. He also prints a sketch showing that Beethoven had begun its composition. Collin's opera begins, like Shakespeare, with the witches' scene, and the sketch referred to is preceded by the directions: "Overture Macbeth falls immediately into the chorus of witches." In a letter to Thayer, Röckel wrote: "That Beethoven did not abandon the idea of composing another opera was shown by the impatience with which he could scarcely wait for his friend Collin to make an opera book for him of Shakespeare's 'Macbeth.' At Beethoven's request, I read the first act and found that it followed the great original closely; unfortunately Collin's death prevented the completion of the work."

However, Collin did complete a grand opera libretto, *Bradamante*, for which he had an unusual predilection. It also was offered to Beethoven, but seemed too venturesome to him in respect of its use of the supernatural; there were probably other reasons why it did not appeal to him. "And so it happened," says Laban, "that although at a later period Beethoven wanted to undertake its composition, Collin gave the book to Reichardt, who set it to music during his sojourn in Vienna in the winter of 1808-09."

The consequence of Beethoven's fastidiousness and indecision was that he had no text for a vocal composition when he moved to the country for the summer. ——This time the move was directly from the Pasqualati house to Heiligenstadt, No. 8 Grinzingerweg. Beethoven's room looked out on the street, while the rooms overlooking the garden were occupied by the Grillparzer family.[20] The poet, Franz, was then seventeen, and the friendship that developed between the two artists probably began at this time.

According to Grillparzer in his own writings, "The first time I saw Beethoven was in my boyhood—it may have been 1804 or 1805—and it was at a musical evening in the house of my uncle, Joseph Sonnleithner, partner at that time in an art and music business in Vienna."[21] From this evidence, it can be assumed that the story told to Thayer by Grillparzer in 1861 concerning their living next to Beethoven at Unterdöbling took place in the summer of 1808 and not 1800 as Thayer had supposed. It follows here: Mme Grillparzer, mother of the poet, was a lady of great taste and culture, and was fond of music. She used to stand outside her door in order to enjoy Beethoven's playing, as she did not then know of his aversion to listeners. One day Beethoven, springing from his piano to the door to see if anyone were listening, unfortunately discovered her there. Despite her messages to

[20] This information was made possible through the kindness of the late Dr. Kurt Smolle. The simple house, now Grinzinger-strasse Nr. 64, is still standing almost unchanged, with a memorial tablet on the wall.
[21] Kerst, II, p. 42.

him through his servant that her door into the common passageway would remain locked, and that her family would use another, Beethoven played no more.

After a long summer at Heiligenstadt, which may have ended with a short trip to Baden,[22] Beethoven returned to Vienna in the late fall and moved from the Pasqualati house to an address which we learn from the close of a letter to Collin: "My address is 1074 Krugerstrasse at Countess Erdödy's." The circumstance that the composer's new apartments were in the Erdödy lodging strongly suggests the probability that his great intimacy with the Countess dates from the time when he became her near neighbor upon his moving into the Pasqualati house four years before.

The close of the letter to Oppersdorff contains an early allusion to one of the most singular events in Beethoven's life.[23] In the autumn of 1807, Jerome Bonaparte, the Corsican lawyer's youngest son, who had spent his boyhood and youth mostly at sea, and had not yet completed his 23rd year, found himself at Cassel, bearing the pompous title of "King of Westphalia." What could have induced this half-educated, frivolous, prodigal and effeminate young satrap and sybarite to sanction an invitation to his court of the composer most distinguished since Handel for his masculine vigor and manly independence of his art, is one of those small mysteries which seem impenetrable. The precise time when, and by what agency this call was communicated to Beethoven are alike unknown; we only know that before the first of November, 1808, Beethoven received the same through "the High Chamberlain of his Majesty the King of Westphalia, Count Truchess-Waldburg,"[24] that it was to the office of first Kapellmeister, at a salary of 600 ducats, and that it led to events which will be noticed hereafter.

The lists of "Arrivals in Vienna" during this season contain the names of several old and new friends of Beethoven, the dates of whose arrival avail in some instances to correct certain current errors. The following seem worth copying:

June 1: Joseph Linke, musician from Breslau.
July 23: Count von Brunsvik, comes from Pressburg.
July 2: Dominik Dragonetti, musician from Venice [London] comes from Trieste . . .
July 10: Alexander Macco, painter of Anspach, comes from Munich.
July 11: Count Razumovsky, comes from Carlsbad.
August 27: Herr Ferdinand Ries, musical composer of Bonn . . .
November 24: Joh. Fried. Reichardt, Kapellmeister of Hesse-Cassel.

The coming of Reichardt to Vienna and the recording of his observations on the musical life of the Austrian capital in his book entitled *Vertraute*

---

[22] See Frimmel, "Beethoven im Kurort Baden bei Wien," *NBJ*, IV (1930), p. 56.
[23] See *A* 179 for a letter to Gleichenstein on the same subject.

[24] As stated by Beethoven in a letter of April 5, 1809, to Breitkopf and Härtel. (TDR, III, 73, n. 1.)

Briefe were fortunate incidents for the lovers of Beethoven. Reichardt's was one of the great names in music. He stood in the front rank both as composer and writer on the art. His personal character was unspotted; his intellectual powers great and highly cultivated in other fields than music; nor had his dismissal (1794) from the position of Royal Kapellmeister by Frederick William II been founded upon reasons which injured his reputation abroad. He therefore found all, even the highest, musical salons of Vienna open to him, and he received attention which under the circumstances was doubly grateful. A colossal self-esteem, a vanity almost boundless alone could have sent such pages as his *Briefe* to the press without a more thorough expurgation. But this is nothing to the present generation, which owes him a large debt of gratitude for the most lively and complete picture existing of the musical life of Vienna at that period, and especially for his notices of Beethoven, the date of which (winter of 1808-09) adds doubly to their value. His vivid account of Beethoven's *Akademie* on December 22, 1808, will soon be quoted, and his other notices should be read in connection with this biography.[25]

—*Reichardt was Kapellmeister to Jerome Bonaparte, a position which he did not hold long. Though he was involved somewhat later in discussions about the position with Ries, he did not tender the offer from Cassel to Beethoven, as the composer makes clear in his letter to Breitkopf and Härtel of April 5, 1809: "I was definitely not engaged by Reichardt, on the contrary the First Chamberlain of His Majesty the King of Westphalia, Count Truchsess-Waldburg, made me the offer and it was to be as *first Kapellmeister* to His Majesty of Westphalia. I was offered this long before *Reichardt was in Vienna* and he himself was surprised over the fact, as he said, that he had heard nothing of all this."

The return to Vienna for a brief time of the "musical composer of Bonn," Ferdinand Ries, is also of importance to the biography, for once again the *Notizen* becomes a source of information for the events at hand, as we shall see.*—

In the carefully considered "Übersicht des gegenwärtigen Zustandes der Tonkunst in Wien" of the *Vaterländisches Blätter* for May 27 and 31, 1808, it is noted that the violinists Anton Wranitsky and Herr Volta are "in the service of Prince Lobkowitz; Herr Schlesinger in that of the Graf Erdödy; Herr Schmidgen of Count Amadé; Breimann of Esterhazy; and the like of various performers on other instruments. But no such note follows the name of Schuppanzigh, "who is particularly distinguished among quartet players and probably stands alone as a performer of Beethoven's compositions." Nor do the names of Weiss and Linke appear in the article. This fact

---

[25] See Reichardt's *Vertraute Briefe, geschrieben auf einer Reise nach Wien und den Österreichischen Staaten zu Ende das Jahre 1808 und zu Anfang 1809* (Amsterdam, 1810), under date November 30, December 5, 10, 16, 25, 31, 1808; and January 15, March 6, 27; and No. 37 (without date), 1809. (TDR, III, 184-89; TK, I, 166, n. 1.)

and the date of Linke's arrival in Vienna (shown above, June 1) are important in determining when the famous Razumovsky Quartet was founded.

Razumovsky lived in his new palace on the Donau Canal, into which he had very recently removed from the Wollzeil and in which he had put his domestic establishment on a footing of great splendor. It suited his taste to have the first string quartet of Europe in his service. His own skill rendered him amply competent to play the second violin, which he usually did; but the young Mayseder, or some other of the first violinists of the city, was ever ready to take his part when required. Three permanent engagements only were, therefore, necessary, and these now, in late summer or early autumn, 1808, were made. To Schuppanzigh—then the first of quartet players, but still without any permanent engagement—was given the appointment for life of *violino primo*, and to him was entrusted the selection of others. He recommended Weiss for the viola, whom Razumovsky accepted and to whom, for himself and family, he granted a suitable lodging in one of the houses connected with the palace.

Schuppanzigh had been so favorably impressed with the talents and skill of Linke as to secure him the place of violoncellist. He was a young man of 25 years—slightly deformed in person—an orphan from his childhood.

As before stated, Förster was the Count's instructor in musical theory, the accomplished Bigot was librarian and his talented wife pianist. These were the years (1808-1815) when, says Seyfried, "as is known Beethoven was, as it were, cock of the walk in the princely establishment; everything that he composed was rehearsed hot from the griddle and performed to the nicety of a hair, according to his ideas, just as he wanted it and not otherwise, with affectionate interest, obedience and devotion such as could spring only from such ardent admirers of his lofty genius, and with a penetration into the most secret intentions of the composer and the most perfect comprehension of his intellectual tendencies; so that these quartet players achieved that universal celebrity concerning which there was but one voice in the art-world."

But a new topic demands our attention. Beethoven in his later years, in moments of spleen and ill humor, gave utterance both in conversation and in writing to expressions, which have since served as the basis of bitter diatribes against the Vienna public. Czerny—than whom no man could be better informed on the subject of the master's actual position—takes occasion in his notes for Jahn to remark: "It has repeatedly been said in foreign lands that Beethoven was not respected in Vienna and was suppressed. The truth is that already as a youth he received all manner of support from our high aristocracy and enjoyed as much care and respect as ever fell to the lot of a young artist. . . . Later, too, when he estranged many by his hypochondria, nothing was charged against his often very striking peculiarities; hence his predilection for Vienna, and it is doubtful if he would have been left so undisturbed in any other country. It is true that as an artist he had to fight cabals, but the public was innocent in this. He was always marvelled at and respected as an extraordinary being and his greatness was suspected even by those who did not understand him. Whether or not to be rich rested with him, but he was not made for domestic order."

Upon the correctness of these statements, in so far as they relate to Beethoven's last years, the reader will have ample means of judging hereafter; he knows that Czerny is right up to the present date. For, as in the spring so now in autumn, it was Beethoven's popularity that must insure success to the Grand Concert for the public charities; it was his name that was known to be more attractive to the Vienna public than any other, save that of the venerable Haydn; and as Haydn's oratorios were the staple productions at the great charity concerts of vocal music in the Burg theatre, so the younger master's symphonies, concertos and overtures formed the most alluring programmes for the instrumental *Akademies* in the other theatres—at all events, in 1808, this was the opinion of Court Councillor Joseph Hartl, the new theatre director. It was not so much for his love of art, as for the great reputation which his administrative talents had gained him that Hartl was called to assume the labors of directing the theatres, then sunk "into most embarrassing conditions"—a call which he accepted. For three years he administered them wisely, and with all the success possible in the troubled state of the public business and finances.

A supervisor of the public charities, who at the same time controlled the theatres, he was of course able to secure the highest talent for benevolent concerts on terms advantageous to all parties concerned; and thus it came about, that at the concert for public charities in the Theater-an-der-Wien on the evening of Leopold's day, Tuesday, November 15th, Beethoven conducted one of his symphonies, the "Coriolan" Overture, and a pianoforte concerto—perhaps he played the solo of the last; but the want of any detailed report of the concert leaves the point in doubt. Which of the symphonies and concertos were performed on the occasion is not recorded; it is only known that they were not new. In return for Beethoven's noble contribution of his works and personal services to the charity concerts of November 15, 1807 (4th Symphony), April 13 and November 15, 1808, Hartl finally gave him the use of the Theater-an-der-Wien for an *Akademie* on December 22.

--◦◉{That this was the end of a series of frustrating postponements for Beethoven is made clear by his correspondence with Court Secretary Collin, in whom he confided. In a note written early in the year[26] Beethoven listed the number of letters already in his possession concerning a possible day for his concert in return for past services, and gave vent to his wrath over the procrastination of the Theatre Directors. He suggested that a statement be written for Hartl to sign, with Breuning and Collin as witnesses, and even spoke of having discussed with a lawyer his right to compel the management to give him a day. The letter ends: "Tomorrow I'll go see H[artel] myself.

[26] First published by Holde, "An Unknown   (1942), pp. 465-66, from which the excerpt
Beethoven Letter with Comment," *MQ*, xxviii   is taken. See also *A* 164.

I was there once but he wasn't home— I am so vexed that all I want is to be a bear so that every time I lifted my paw I could knock down one of the so-called great — — asses." The tone became more resigned in a letter of the summer in which he wondered whether this inaction would force him to leave Vienna.[27]

With each letter to Collin, discussion continued upon a possible subject for an operatic collaboration—the subject of *Macbeth* was followed by that of *Bradamante*. Though he assured the poet that he would set the plot to music, despite certain reservations he had about the text,[28] the setting of the date for his *Akademie* caused a delay. In the fall he wrote that he would certainly see Collin after the concert, and begged him to be patient.[29] However, as noted above, the text of *Bradamante* was given to Reichardt to set and was performed the next year. Beethoven was not pleased with this outcome, as shown by a characteristic remark in a note probably written in December: "Great enraged Poet, let go of Reichardt—and make use of my notes for your poetry. I promise you that you will not be in need thereby—As soon as my Akademie is over, which robs me of a good deal of my time but which has the purpose of bringing in money for me, I shall come to you and we shall start work on the opera at once. . . ."

The *Akademie* was advertised in the *Wiener Zeitung* of December 17 as follows:

MUSICAL AKADEMIE

On Thursday, December 22, Ludwig van Beethoven will have the honor to give a musical *Akademie* in the R.I. Priv. Theater-an-der-Wien. All the pieces are of his composition, entirely new, and not yet heard in public. . . . First Part: 1, A Symphony, entitled: "A Recollection of Country Life," in F major (No. 5). 2, Aria. 3, Hymn with Latin text, composed in the church style with chorus and solos. 4, Pianoforte Concerto played by himself.

Second Part. 1, Grand Symphony in C minor (No. 6). 2, Holy, with Latin text composed in the church style with chorus and solos. 3, Fantasia for Pianoforte alone. 4, Fantasia for the Pianoforte which ends with the gradual entrance of the entire orchestra and the introduction of choruses as a finale.

Boxes and reserved seats are to be had in the Krugerstrasse No. 1074, first story. Beginning at half past six o'clock.

The importance of the works produced on this occasion, the whimsical occurrences that are related as having taken place, and the somewhat con-flicting statements of persons present, justify an effort to sift the evidence and get at the truth, even at the risk of being tedious. It is unfortunate that the concert of November 15, 1808, was so completely forgotten by all whose contemporary notices or later reminiscences are now the only sources of information; for it is certain that, either in the rehearsals or at the public performance, something happened which caused a very serious misunder-standing and breach between Beethoven and the orchestra; but even this is

[27] *A* 170.   [28] *A* 175.   [29] *A* 185.

sufficient to remove some difficulties otherwise insuperable. Ries records in the *Notizen* (p. 84) that a scene is said once to have happened in which the orchestra compelled the composer to realize his injustice "and in all serious-ness insisted that he should not conduct. In consequence, at the rehearsal, Beethoven had to remain in an anteroom, and it was a long time before the quarrel was settled." Such a quarrel did arise at the time of the November concert. In Spohr's Autobiography is a story of Beethoven's first sweeping off the candles at the piano and then knocking down a choir boy deputed to hold one of them, by his too energetic motions at this concert, the two incidents setting the audience into a "bacchanalian jubilation" of laughter. It is absolutely certain, however, that nothing of the kind occurred at the concert itself.

Compare now these statements by Ries and Spohr with citations from notes of a conversation with Röckel: "Beethoven had made the orchestra of the Theater-an-der-Wien so angry with him that only the leaders, Seyfried, Clement, etc., would have anything to do with him, and it was only after much persuasion and upon condition that Beethoven should not be in the room during the rehearsals, that the rank and file consented to play. During the rehearsals, in the large room in back of the theatre, Beethoven walked up and down in an anteroom, and often Röckel with him. After a movement Seyfried would come to him for criticisms. Röckel believed the story (i.e., if told of a rehearsal) of Beethoven in his zeal having knocked the candles off the pianoforte, and he himself saw the boys, one on each side, holding candles for him."

But the concert-giver's troubles were not ended even by his yielding to the demands of the orchestra. A solo singer was to be found and vocal pieces to be selected. In a note to Röckel Beethoven wrote: ". . . in the matter of the vocal pieces I think that we ought to have one of the women singers who will be singing with us sing an aria first—then we would make two numbers out of the Mass, but with German text. Find out who could do this well for us. It need not be a masterpiece, provided it suits the music well." And in another note: "Be clever in regard to Milder—say to her only that to-day you are begging her in my name not to sing *anywhere else*, to-morrow I will come in person to kiss the hem of her garment—but do not forget *Marconi*. . . ."

Milder was to sing the aria "Ah, perfido! spergiuro," said Röckel, and accepted the invitation at once. But an unlucky quarrel provoked by Beet-hoven resulted in her refusal. After other attempts, Röckel engaged Fräulein Josephine Killitschgy,[30] Schuppanzigh's sister-in-law. Being a young and inexperienced singer, her friends wrought her up to such a point that when Beethoven led her upon the stage and left her, stage fright overcame her and she made wretched work of the aria. Reichardt in a letter describes the

---

[30] In later years she was Frau Schulze, a well-known singer by then, who was the first Leonore in Berlin. (TDR, III, 82.)

Akademie: "I accepted the kind offer of Prince Lobkowitz to let me sit in his box with hearty thanks. There we continued, in the bitterest cold, too, from half past six to half past ten, and experienced the truth that one can easily have too much of a good thing—and still more of a loud. Nevertheless, I could no more leave the box before the end than could the exceedingly good-natured and delicate Prince, for the box was in the first balcony near the stage, so that the orchestra with Beethoven in the middle conducting it was below us and near at hand; thus many a failure in the performance vexed our patience in the highest degree. Poor Beethoven, who from this, his own concert, was having the first and only scant profit that he could find in a whole year, had found in the rehearsals and performance a lot of opposition and almost no support. Singers and orchestra were composed of heterogeneous elements, and it had been found impossible to get a single full rehearsal for all the pieces to be performed, all filled with the greatest difficulties."

Such a programme, exclusive of the Choral Fantasia, was certainly an ample provision for an evening's entertainment of the most insatiably musical enthusiast; nor could a grander termination of the concert be desired than the Finale of the C minor Symphony; but to defer that work until the close was to incur the risk of endangering its effect by presenting it to an audience too weary for the close attention needful on first hearing to its fair comprehension and appreciation. This Beethoven felt, and so, says Czerny, "there came to him shortly before the idea of writing a brilliant piece for this concert. He chose a song which he had composed many years before,[31] planned the variations, the chorus, etc., and the poet Kuffner was called upon to write the words in a hurry according to Beethoven's hints. Thus originated the Choral Fantasia, Op. 80. It was finished so late that it could scarcely be sufficiently rehearsed. Beethoven related this in my presence in order to explain why, at the concert, he had had it repeated. 'Some of the instruments had counted wrong in the rests,' he said; 'if I had let them play a few measures more the most horrible dissonances would have resulted. I had to make an interruption.'"

The particulars of this scene, in which Reichardt suffered so, are more or less circumstantially related by Ries, Seyfried, Czerny, Moscheles and Doležalek. Their statements when compared are not inconsistent and supplement each other, except as to Ries, whose memory evidently exaggerated what really occurred. Substantially they are as follows:

Seyfried (Appendix to *Beethovens Studien*, p. 15): "When the master brought out his orchestral Fantasia with choruses, he arranged with me at the somewhat hurried rehearsal, with wet voice-parts as usual, that the second variation should be played without the repeat. In the evening, however,

[31] "Gegenliebe" from the double-song "Seufzer eines Ungeliebten" and "Gegenliebe," WoO 118, written in 1794-95.

absorbed in his creation, he forgot all about the instructions which he had given, repeated the first part while the orchestra accompanied the second, which sounded not altogether edifying. A trifle too late, the Concertmaster, Unrath, noticed the mistake, looked in surprise at his lost companions, stopped playing and called out drily: 'Again!' A little displeased, the violinist Anton Wranitsky asked 'With repeats?' 'Yes,' came the answer, and now the thing went straight as a string."

The *Allg. Mus. Zeit.* reported: "The wind-instruments varied the theme which Beethoven had previously played on the pianoforte. The turn came to the oboes. The clarinets, if I am not mistaken, make a mistake in the count and enter at once. A curious mixture of tones results. Beethoven jumps up, tries to silence the clarinets, but does not succeed until he has called out quite loudly and rather ill-temperedly: 'Stop, stop! That will not do! Again—again!'

"Czerny: In the Pianoforte Fantasia with chorus he called out at the mistake: 'Wrong, badly played, wrong, again!' Several musicians wanted to go away.

"Doležalek: He jumped up, ran to the desks and pointed out the place.

"Moscheles: I remember having been present at the performance in question, seated in a corner of the gallery, in the Theater-an-der-Wien. During the last movement of the Fantasia I perceived that, like a run-away carriage going down-hill, an overturn was inevitable. Almost immediately after it was, that I saw Beethoven give the signal for stopping. His voice was not heard; but he had probably given directions where to begin again, and after a moment's respectful silence on the part of the audience, the orchestra recommenced and the performance proceeded without further mistakes or stoppage. To those who are acquainted with the work, it may be interesting to know the precise point at which the mistake occurred. It was in the passage where for several pages every three bars make up a triple rhythm."

Seyfried says further: "At first he could not understand that he had in a manner humiliated the musicians. He thought it was a duty to correct an error that had been made and that the audience was entitled to hear everything properly played, for its money. But he readily and heartily begged the pardon of the orchestra for the humiliation to which he had subjected it, and was honest enough to spread the story himself and assume all responsibility for his own absence of mind."

The pecuniary results of this concert to Beethoven are not known.[32]

One of the two December concerts for the Widows and Orphans Fund was on the 22nd, the same evening as Beethoven's; the other on the next. The vocal work selected was, in compliment to the venerable Haydn, his

---

[32] A directive from Prince Esterhazy to his paying-office, dated January 18, 1809, includes the sum of 100 gulden to be paid to Beethoven in support of his "musical Akademie" (published by C. F. Pohl, Grenzboten, November 13, 1868). (TDR, III, 84, n. 1.)

Ritorno di Tobia, first performed in these concerts thirty-three years before. Being too short to fill out the evening, it was preceded, on the 22nd, by an orchestral fantasia of Neukomm—on the 23rd by a pianoforte concerto of Beethoven. From Ries's *Notizen* (pp. 114-115) we learn that Beethoven asked him to play his fourth Concerto in G, giving him only five days in which to learn it. Thinking the time too short, Ries asked permission to play the C minor Concerto instead. Beethoven in a rage went to young Stein, who was wise enough to accept the offer; but as he could not prepare the Concerto in time, he begged Beethoven, on the day before the concert, as Ries had done, for permission to play the C minor Concerto. Beethoven had to acquiesce. Whether the fault was the theatre's, the orchestra's, or the player's, says Ries, the Concerto made no effect. Beethoven was very angry.

Towards the close of 1808, Clementi again arrived in Vienna and was not a little surprised to learn from Beethoven that he had not yet received from London payment for the compositions which he had sold Clementi in April, 1807. He wrote on December 28, 1808, to his partner asking that the money, £200, due Beethoven, as he had delivered the six compositions contracted for, be sent at once. But in September, 1809, the account had not yet been liquidated, as we shall see.

There is reason to believe that a large number of compositions of greater or less extent was projected and in part sketched during this year, but only the following are known to have been completed: the C Minor Symphony, Op. 67; the "Pastoral" Symphony, Op. 68; the Sonata for Pianoforte and Violoncello, Op. 69; the Trios for Pianoforte, Violin and Violoncello, in D and E-flat, Op. 70; the Fantasia for Pianoforte, Orchestra and Chorus, Op. 80; the Song (with four melodies) "Die Sehnsucht," with text by Goethe, WoO 134.

The Sonata for Pianoforte and 'cello was sketched in 1807, and practically completed in that year, the only sketches appearing among those of 1808 being a couple evidently made while the work was being written out. The earlier sketches appear among those of the C minor Symphony. It was dedicated to Gleichenstein. On June 8 Beethoven offered it, as has been seen, to Breitkopf and Härtel, and it was included in the works for which Härtel signed a contract in person on September 14. On January 7, 1809, Beethoven wrote to Breitkopf and Härtel asking that Gleichenstein's title "K.K. Hofconcipist" be elided from the dedication, because it was distasteful to him. It was published in April, 1809, but with a large number of errors which gave occasion to three different letters from the composer to the publishers between July 26th and August 3rd of that year.

The two Trios were dedicated to Countess Erdödy, in whose house Beethoven lived when they were written. The first sketches for them found by Nottebohm belong to the second in E-flat and occur amongst the sketches for the Finale of the "Pastoral" symphony.[33] The Trios are not mentioned

[33] *II Beeth.*, pp. 253-54. (TDR, III, 105.)

in the Breitkopf and Härtel correspondence of the summer until the third letter, but in the second letter, of July 16, Beethoven speaks of two pianoforte sonatas. Thus the ideas in the sketches may have been intended first for pianoforte sonatas. Beethoven played them at Countess Erdödy's in the Christmastide of 1808, when Reichardt was present; he wrote an enthusiastic account of them under date December 31. On May 26, 1809, Beethoven wrote to Breitkopf and Härtel suggesting changes in the text and also asking that the name of Archduke Rudolph be substituted for that of Countess Erdödy in the dedication. The reason given was that the Archduke had become fond of the works and Beethoven had observed that in such cases his patron felt a gentle regret when the music was dedicated to somebody else. Beethoven, of course, said nothing about his quarrel with the Countess (of which something will be said in the next chapter). There was a reconciliation, and Beethoven's solicitude for the feelings of the Archduke apparently evaporated; at any rate, the original dedication remained.

The Choral Fantasia was obviously finished only a short time before its performance and is plainly one of the few compositions on which Beethoven worked continuously after once beginning it. In the Grasnick sketchbook of 1808 there are sketches for the work consecutively on the first seventy-five pages, which have been analysed by Nottebohm.[34] The sketchbook has been carefully transcribed and edited in a critical edition by Dagmar Weise.[35] The most interesting disclosures of Nottebohm's study are that there is no hint of a pianoforte introduction such as Beethoven improvised at the performance; that Beethoven first thought of beginning with the string quartet of the orchestra; that the work was begun before a text was found; and that, as in the case of the Choral Symphony, of which the Fantasia is so interesting a prototype in miniature, Beethoven thought of paving the way for the introduction of the voices by words calling attention to the newcomers among the harmonious company ("Hört ihr wohl?").[36] Czerny's statement that the text was written by Kuffner is questioned by Nottebohm, who points out that the poem is not included in the collected writings of that author, though all manner of fragments and trifles are. Because of the ingenuity and effectiveness with which the words were adapted to the music, Nottebohm suspects Treitschke of having written them in accordance with Beethoven's suggestions as to form and contents. The introductory pianoforte fantasia which was published to take the place of Beethoven's improvisation at the first performance was composed in 1809.

The publications of the year 1808 were:

By Kunst- und Industrie-Comptoir:
Concerto No. 4 for Pianoforte and Orchestra in G major, Op. 58, dedicated to His Highness Archduke Rudolph of Austria.

---

[34] *II Beeth.*, pp. 495-500. (TDR, III, 109.)
[35] *Beethoven—ein Skizzenbuch zur Chorfantasie Op. 80 und zu anderen Werken* (Beethovenhaus: Bonn, 1957).
[36] See *ibid.*, p. 97.

Concerto for Violin and Orchestra in D major, Op. 61, dedicated to Stephan von Breuning.

Concerto for Pianoforte and Orchestra in D major, and arrangement of the Concerto for Violin and Orchestra, Op. 61, dedicated to Frau Julie von Breuning.

Overture to *Coriolan* (Tragedy by H. J. von Collin), Op. 62.

Symphony No. 4 in B-flat major, Op. 60, dedicated to Count Franz von Oppersdorff.

Three String Quartets, Op. 59, dedicated to Count Andreas Kyrillovitsch Razumovsky.

By Mollo:

"In questa tomba oscura" (Carpani), WoO 133 (the last of 63 settings of the same text, dedicated to Prince Franz Joseph von Lobkowitz).

By the periodical *Prometheus*, as a supplement:

"Sehnsucht" (Goethe), WoO 134, No. 1. (Beethoven's four settings of "Sehnsucht" were published together in 1810).

By Simrock:

III Deutsche Lieder: "Neue Liebe, neues Leben" (Goethe), WoO 127 (1st version); "Opferlied" (Matthisson), WoO 126 (2nd version); "Der freie Mann" (Pfeffel), WoO 117 (2nd version).

[By Cianchettini and Sperati in London:[37]

First orchestral score of Symphony No. 2 in D major, with the title "Beethoven's Symph: I" [*sic*] as part of *A Compleat Collection of Haydn, Mozart and Beethoven's Symphonies in Score*, No. xxv, in November-December.

In January, 1809, appeared No. xxvi, the first orchestral score of Symphony No. 1, designated "Beethoven's Symph. II"; and in March-April No. xxvii, correctly entitled "Beethoven's Symph. III—Sinfonia Eroica composta per celebrare la morte d'un Eroe."]

[37] See KHV, pp. 54, 91, 130-31.

CHAPTER XXII

THE YEAR 1809

THE ANNUITY CONTRACT—THE SIEGE OF VIENNA—
PIANO CONCERTO NO. 5

THE offer of an honorable position in Cassel—permanent, so long as
Napoleon's star might remain in the ascendant and his satellite retain his
nominal kingship of Westphalia—was one no less gratifying to Beethoven,
than surprising and perplexing to his friends. Knowing both the strong and
the weak points of his character, they saw the extreme improbability that,
with his increasing deafness, his removal thither could in the end redound
to his profit, honor, or happiness. On the other hand, they saw him—at the
very moment when he was giving new proofs of those stupendous powers
which elevate him far above all other instrumental composers—forced to
consider the question of seeking in a small provincial capital that permanent
provision for his future necessities which, in the home of his choice at the
end of sixteen years' residence, he saw no hope of obtaining. What an inexcusable, unpardonable disgrace to Vienna would be the departure of Beethoven under such circumstances! It was the first time the question had been
presented; but being presented it was promptly met by a request from
persons of "high and the highest rank that he state the conditions under
which" he would decline the call to Cassel and remain in Vienna.

Here was one of those happy opportunities for conferences, notes, letters
and despatches innumerable, which Beethoven all his life seems to have so
eagerly embraced and enjoyed. Several of his notes to Gleichenstein on the
topic have been preserved, but are not worth mentioning, except those containing instructions for the drafting of the conditions of his remaining in
Vienna. A letter dated January 7, 1809, by Beethoven to Breitkopf and
Härtel, indicates that at the opening of the year 1809, Beethoven was still
firmly resolved to go to Cassel. In it occurs this passage:

. . . At last I am forced by the intrigues and cabals and contemptible actions of all kinds to leave my only surviving German fatherland. On the invitation of His Royal Majesty of Westphalia, I am going thither as Kapellmeister with an annual salary of 600 ducats in gold— Just today I have sent my assurance by post that I will come and am only waiting my decree before making preparations for my journey which will be by way of *Leipzig*— Therefore, in order that my journey may be the more brilliant for me, I beg of you, if not too prejudicial to your interests, not to make anything known of my works *till Easter*— In the case of the sonata which is dedicated to Baron Gleichenstein, please omit the K. K. Concipist, as it is distasteful to him— In all probability abusive letters will again be written from here about my last Akademie to the Musikalische Zeitung; I do not ask that all that is against me be suppressed, yet one should realize that nobody has more personal enemies here than I. This is the more easily to be understood, since the state of music here is steadily growing worse— We have Kapellmeisters who know so little about conducting that they can scarcely read a score— It is worst of all, of course, at the Theater auf der Wieden— I had to give my Akademie there and all kinds of obstacles were put in my way.— The people in charge of the Widows' Concert,[1] out of hatred for me, and Herr Salieri is among the first, played me the nasty trick of threatening to expel every musician who played for me from the company— Notwithstanding the fact that several mistakes were made, which I could not help, the public accepted everything enthusiastically— Nevertheless, scribblers from here will certainly not fail again to send miserable stuff against me to the Musikalische Zeitung— The musicians were particularly angry because, when a blunder was made through carelessness in the simplest, plainest place in the world, I stopped them suddenly and loudly called out *"Once again"*— Such a thing had never happened to them before. The public showed its enjoyment at this—but it is daily growing worse. The day before my concert, in the easy little opera "Milton," at the theatre in the city, the orchestra fell into such disorder that Kapellmeister and leader and orchestra veritably suffered shipwreck—for the Kapellmeister instead of being ahead was behind in his beat and then in came the leader. Give me an answer right away, my friend.

Respectfully your most devoted servant   Beethoven

[On the back of the cover]

I am asking you to say nothing with certainty about my appointment in Westphalia until I write to you that I have received my decree.— Farewell and write to me soon— We shall talk about new compositions in Leipzig— Some hints could always be given in the Musikalische Zeitung of my leaving here— and a few digs since no one here has taken the trouble to give me any help.—

It seems likely that the suggestion that formal stipulations for a contract be drawn up under which Beethoven would decline the offer from Cassel and remain in Vienna came from the Countess Erdödy. At any rate Beethoven wrote to Gleichenstein:

---

[1] The two concerts for the Widows and Orphans took place on December 22 and 23, 1808. Thus, the first of these was on the same evening as Beethoven's *Akademie*. (TDR, III, 85.)

Countess Erdödy is of the opinion that you ought to outline a plan with her according to which she might negotiate in case they approach her as she is convinced they will.

Your friend Lud. Beethoven

If you should have time this afternoon, the Countess would be glad to see you.

The outline of the proposition which was to be submitted to certain noble gentlemen was drawn up by Beethoven for Gleichenstein as follows:

Outline for a Musical Constitution

First the offer of the King of Westphalia is to be set forth— B. cannot be held down to any obligation on account of this salary since the chief object of his art, viz., the invention of new works would suffer thereby— This remuneration must be assured to Beethoven until he voluntarily renounces it—the Imperial title also if possible—to alternate with Salieri and Eybler—the promise of active court service as soon as possible—or adjunction if it be worth while. Contract with the theatres likewise with the title of Member of one of the Committees of Theatrical Direction— A fixed day forever for a concert, even if there be a change in the directorate in the theatre, in return for which Beethoven binds himself to compose a new work every year for one of the charity concerts as may be thought most useful—or to conduct two—a place at a money changer's or such kind where Beethoven would receive the stipulated salary—The salary must be paid also by the heirs.

On some of these points Beethoven changed his mind and wrote again thus:

... Please have everything relate to *the true and for me proper practice of my art,* thus you will write what is in my heart and head— The introduction has what I am to get in Westphalia, 600 ducats in gold, 150 for traveling expenses, for which I have to do nothing except conduct the King's concerts which are short and not numerous— I am not even bound to conduct any opera that I may write— From all this it is clear that I can devote myself wholly to the most important purpose of my art to compose works of magnitude—and also have an orchestra at my disposal.

N.B. The title of Member of one of the Theatrical Committees is to be dropped—it would bring nothing but vexation— In regard to the *Imperial duties* I think the point must be handled delicately—nothing about the demand for the title of Imperial Kapellmeister—but only in regard to the fact that once placed in a position through a court salary, I give up the sum which the gentlemen are now paying me. Thus I think that this might best be expressed as a hope and a highest wish sometime to enter the Imperial service, at which time I could at once accept as much less as the sum received from his Imperial Majesty amounts to.—

[on the top of the last page]:

N.B. We shall need it tomorrow at 12 o'clock, because we must then go to Kinsky. I hope to see you today.

Under these instructions the "Conditions" were drawn up, probably by Gleichenstein, in manner and form following:

It must be the striving and aim of every true artist to achieve a position in which he can devote himself wholly to the elaboration of larger works and not be hindered by other matters or economical considerations. A musical composer can, therefore, have no livelier desire than to be left undisturbedly to the invention of works of magnitude and then to produce them in public. In doing this he must also keep his old age in view and seek to make ample provision for himself against that time.

The King of Westphalia has offered Beethoven a salary of 600 ducats in gold for life and 150 ducats travelling expenses, on the single condition that he occasionally play for him and conduct his chamber concerts, which are to be not numerous and short.

This offer is certainly entirely in the interest of art and the artist.

Beethoven, however, has so great a predilection for life in this city, so much gratitude for the many proofs of good will which he has received here, and so much patriotism for his second fatherland, that he will never cease to count himself among Austrian artists and will never make his domicile elsewhere if the opportunities mentioned above are measurably offered him here.

Persons of high and the highest ranks, having asked him to state under what conditions he would be willing to remain here, he has complied with the request as follows:

1. Beethoven should receive from a great personage assurance of a salary for life; even a number of persons of rank might contribute to the sum. This salary under the existing conditions of high cost of living, could not be less than 4000 florins a year. Beethoven desires that the donors of this salary consider themselves co-authors of his new works in the large forms, because they place him in a position to devote himself to their production and relieve him of the need of attending to other affairs.

2. Beethoven should always have freedom to make artistic tours, because only by such can he make himself very well known and acquire some private income.

3. It would be his greatest desire and most ardent wish sometime to enter into the actual Imperial service and by reason of the salary expected from such a source to be able to waive in whole or in part the compensation set forth above; meanwhile merely the title of an Imperial Kapellmeister would make him very happy; if it could be obtained for him his stay here would be still dearer to him.

Should this desire some day be fulfilled and he receive a salary from His Majesty, Beethoven will forgo his claim on as much of the 4000 florins as the Imperial salary amounts to, and if this is 4000 florins, then he would forgo the entire 4000 florins above specified.

4. As Beethoven desires to perform his larger new works from time to time before a greater public, he desires an assurance from the Court Theatrical Directors, for themselves and their successors, that on Palm Sunday of each year he shall have the use of the Theater-an-der-Wien for a concert for his own benefit.

In return for this assurance, Beethoven would bind himself to arrange and conduct a charity concert every year or, in case of inability to do this, to contribute a new work for such a concert.

The conditions proving acceptable, the business was concluded and Beethoven retained in Vienna by this

AGREEMENT:

The daily proofs which Herr Ludwig van Beethoven is giving of his extraordinary talents and genius as musician and composer, awaken the desire that he surpass the great expectations which are justified by his past achievements.

But as it has been demonstrated that only one who is as free from care as possible can devote himself to a single department of activity and create works of magnitude which are exalted and which ennoble art, the undersigned have decided to place Herr Ludwig van Beethoven in a position where the necessaries of life shall not cause him embarrassment or clog his powerful genius.

To this end they bind themselves to pay him the fixed sum of 4000 (four thousand) florins a year, as follows:

> His Imperial Highness, Archduke Rudolph ....Fl. 1500
> The Highborn Prince Lobkowitz .... " 700
> The Highborn Prince Ferdinand Kinsky .... " 1800
> _____
>
> Total ....Fl. 4000

which Herr van Beethoven is to collect in semi-annual installments, *pro rata,* against voucher, from each of these contributors.

The undersigned are pledged to pay this annual salary until Herr van Beethoven receives an appointment which shall yield him the equivalent of the above sum.

Should such an appointment not be received and Herr Ludwig van Beethoven be prevented from practising his art by an unfortunate accident or old age, the participants herein grant him the salary for life.

In consideration of this Herr Ludwig van Beethoven pledges himself to make his domicile in Vienna, where the makers of this document live, or in a city in one of the other hereditary countries of His Austrian Imperial Majesty, and to depart from this domicile only for such set times as may be called for by his business or the interests of art, touching which, however, the high contributors must be consulted and to which they must give their consent.

Given in Vienna, March 1, 1809.

> (L.S.)   Rudolph,
> Archduke.
> (L.S.)   Prince von Lobkowitz,
> Duke of Raudnitz.
> (L.S.)   Ferdinand Prince Kinsky.

This document bears in Beethoven's hand these words:

Received
On February 26, 1809
from the hands
of Archduke
Rudolph, R.H.[2]

---

[2] The original manuscript is in the Museum der Stadt Wien.

The remarks in a former chapter upon the singular attraction for the young of Beethoven and his works are supported by this contract. Lobkowitz, it is true, was near the master's age, being then 35; but Rudolph and Kinsky were respectively but 21 and 27. Ries, who was then much with Beethoven, asserts that the contract with the King of Westphalia "was all ready; it lacked only the signature" before his Vienna friends moved in the matter and "settled a salary on him for life." He continues (*Notizen*, p. 96): "The first fact I knew; of the second I was in ignorance until suddenly Kapellmeister Reichardt came to me and said: 'Beethoven positively would not accept the post in Cassel; would I as Beethoven's only pupil go there on a smaller salary?' I did not believe the first, went at once to Beethoven to learn the truth about it and to ask his advice. I was turned away for three weeks— even my letters on the subject were unanswered. Finally I found Beethoven at the Ridotto. I went to him and told him the reason of my inquiries, whereupon he said in a cutting tone: *'So—do you think that you can fill a position which was offered to me?'* He remained cold and repellent. The next morning I went to him to get an understanding. His servant said to me gruffly: 'My master is not at home,' although I heard him singing and playing in the next room. Since the servant positively refused to announce me I resolved to go right in; but he sprang to the door and pushed me back. Enraged by this I grabbed him by the throat and hurled him down. Beethoven, hearing the racket, dashed out and found his servant still lying on the floor and me pale as death. Angrily excited, I so deluged him with reproaches that he stood motionless and speechless with surprise. When the matter was finally explained to him he said, 'I did not understand it so; I was told that you were trying to get the appointment behind my back.' On my assuring him that I had not yet even given an answer, he at once went out with me to make the mistake good. But it was too late; I did not get the appointment, though it would have been a piece of great good fortune for me at that time."

It requires no great sagacity to perceive from the text of the "Agreement," that none of its signers had any expectation that Beethoven could ever perform the duties of an Imperial Conductor acceptably; and his hope of obtaining the title must have rested upon the influence, which he supposed Archduke Rudolph might exert upon Emperor Franz. Be this as it may, the composer was justly elated by the favorable change in his pecuniary condition; and his very natural exultation peeps out in the correspondence of the time. While the business was still undecided, Gleichenstein had departed on a visit to his native Freiburg, via Munich, taking with him a letter of introduction to the composer at Munich, Peter von Winter, the contents of which Beethoven himself thus epitomizes:

Here, my dear fellow, is the letter to Winter. First it says that you are my friend—secondly, what you are, namely Imperial and Royal Court Secretary—

thirdly, that you are not a connoisseur of music but nevertheless a friend of all that is *beautiful* and *good*—in view of which I have asked the Kapellmeister in case anything of his is performed to let you participate in it. . . .

On March 18, Gleichenstein received a copy or abstract of the contract enclosed in this:

You can see from the enclosed, my dear, good Gleichenstein, how honorable my remaining here has turned out for me—the title of Imperial Kapellmeister will also come later, etc. Write to me as soon as possible whether you think that I ought to make the journey in the present warlike state of affairs and whether you are still firmly resolved to travel with me. Several people have advised me against it, but in this matter I shall follow you implicitly. Since you already have a carriage it should be arranged that for a stretch you travel towards me and I towards you—Write quickly—Now you can help me hunt for a wife. If you find a beautiful one in F[reiburg], who yields a sigh to my harmonies, but it must be no *Elise Bürger*, make connections with her in advance—But she must be beautiful, for I cannot love what is not beautiful—else I should love myself. Farewell and write soon. Present my compliments to your parents, your brother—I embrace you with all my heart and remain your true friend

Beethoven

The jesting on matrimony in this letter and the allusion to the poet Bürger's unlucky marriage with Christine Elizabeth Hahn, attest the writer's lightness of spirit, but are not to be taken seriously. But we shall find in a year's time, when his finances were more secure, that Beethoven was to be definitely considering marriage.

In this connection the following background may be given. At some point after 1806, when he had returned to Vienna, Gleichenstein introduced Beethoven to a family named Malfatti. The culture, refinement, musical taste and high character of the parents, and the uncommon grace and beauty of their two young girls rendered the house very attractive to the composer. There was less than a year's difference in the age of the children: Therese was born January 1, 1792 and Anna December 7th of the same year. In 1811 Anna became the wife of Gleichenstein, and Therese married Court Councillor Wilhem Baron von Drosdick in 1817. According to Dr. Sonnleithner: "Frau Therese Baroness von Drosdick, *née* Malfatti . . . was a beautiful, lively and intellectual woman, a very good pianoforte player and, besides, the cousin [actually niece] of the famous physician and friend of Beethoven's, Dr. von Malfatti. Herein lies the explanation of an unusually kind relationship with Beethoven which resulted in a less severe regard for conventional forms. Nothing is known of a particular intimacy between her and Beethoven." A relative of the Baroness, who knew her intimately, knew also that she and Beethoven formed a lasting friendship, but as to any warmer feeling on either side he knew nothing, nor anything to the contrary. However he did say: "When conversation turned on Beethoven, she spoke of him reverentially, but with a certain reserve."

Through these Malfattis, then, Beethoven became also known personally to the physician of the same name and "they were great friends for a long time. Malfatti became Beethoven's doctor after the sudden death of Dr. Schmidt on February 19, 1808. However, towards each other they were like two hard millstones, and they separated. Malfatti used to say of Beethoven: 'He is a disorderly (*konfuser*) fellow—but all the same he may be the greatest genius.'"

Under date "Vienna, March 4, 1809," Beethoven wrote to Breitkopf and Härtel:

Most honored Sir:

From the enclosed you see how things have changed, and that I shall stay here—although perhaps I can plan to make a little trip after all if the storm clouds that are now threatening don't develop;—but you will get the news in time enough— Here are the Opus nos. etc. of the three works—Sonata for Piano-forte and Violoncello to Herr Baron von Gleichenstein Op. 59. Both symphonies to both men jointly, namely: dedicated to His Excellency Count Razumovsky and to His Serene Highness Prince Lobkowitz—Symphony in C minor Op. 60, Symphony in F Op. 61— Tomorrow you will receive particulars of some minor corrections I made during the performances of the symphonies—for when I gave them to you, I had not yet heard either of them—and one should not pretend to be so divine as not to correct things here and there in one's works— Hr. Stein has offered to transcribe for you the symphonies for two pianofortes. Write to me whether you want it and if so what are you willing to pay?—I send you my best regards, and am in haste

your most devoted friend

L. v. Beethoven

As a postscript in another hand is a formula for the dedication of the trios (then numbered 62) to Countess Erdödy.

The most important change concerned the Fifth Symphony. After the performance in December Beethoven decided that the sustained D of the main theme at measure 4 should be held an extra measure:

This was to be done also at the four similar statements in the movement (meas. 23, 227, 251, and 481).

The corrections, however, were not sent until March 28th, which explains the fact that in the first edition of these two symphonies, appearing about April, 1809, the changes were not made. Paul Hirsch has pointed out how the situation was remedied quickly by the appearance of the second edition before the end of 1809.[3] About this time came out new compositions and

---

[3] "A Discrepancy in Beethoven," *Music and Letters*, Vol. 19 (1938), pp. 266-67.

new editions or arrangements of old ones which occupied the opus numbers from 59 to 66 and compelled Beethoven to change these proposed numbers, 59-62 to 67-70.

The *Allg. Mus. Zeit.* had printed a notice about the offer from Cassel in which Reichardt was represented as having been the intermediary in the negotiations. This brought out from Beethoven the correction dated April 5, addressed to Breitkopf and Härtel, quoted in the chapter immediately preceding. In the postscript he adds: "Do not forget the *First Kapellmeister*, I laugh at such things, but there are Miserabiles who know how to dish up such things in the manner of the cook."

In one of his *Vertraute Briefe* of this year, dated February 7, Reichardt made reference to Beethoven in a new but characteristic role, that of improver of the pianoforte. He writes: "Streicher has abandoned the soft, yielding, repercussive tone of the other Vienna instruments, and at Beethoven's wish and advice has given his instruments greater resonance and elasticity, so that the virtuoso who plays with strength and significance may have the instrument in better command for sustained and expressive tones. He has thereby given his instruments a larger and more varied character, so that they must give greater satisfaction than the others to all virtuosi who seek something more than mere easy brilliancy in their style of playing."

The allusions to a tour in the letters to Gleichenstein and Breitkopf and Härtel, and the provision made in the "Agreement" for the composer's temporary absence from Austria, acquire a particular significance from one of the notes of Röckel's conversation, namely: "Beethoven in those days was full of the project of traveling, and a plan was marked out of visiting the German cities, then England and finally *Spain*; upon which last Röckel laid great stress. He was to have accompanied Beethoven; but he could not leave Vienna, on account of having so many of his brothers and sisters sent to him to care for."

Relations between Beethoven and his brother Carl Caspar were no longer on the same footing as they had been before the latter's marriage. In March, 1809, Beethoven, forwarding a letter to brother Johann, "to be delivered at the apothecary shop 'Zur goldenen Krone'" in Linz, enclosed in it an envelope, inside of which he wrote the words:

Dear Brother— This letter for you has been lying here for a long time.— Would that God would grant the other brother once instead of his unfeelingness— feeling— I suffer infinitely through him. With my bad hearing I always need somebody, and whom shall I trust?

The breach between Beethoven and his brother Carl was now, in business matters, complete; and he needed someone to perform for him the many little offices which he could not with propriety demand to any extent of Zmeskall, Gleichenstein or Röckel, even had they the leisure and the will. Hence, about this time, was formed his connection with a certain Franz

Oliva, clerk in the employ of Offenheimer and Herz. The relations between them were close up to 1811, afterwards less so, but never broken off entirely until the departure of Oliva in 1820 to St. Petersburg, where he found it to his interest to establish himself as a teacher of languages. In due time the *Wiener Zeitung* published an official notice from the Austrian Government calling upon him immediately to return and justify himself for overstaying his leave of absence under pain otherwise of being proceeded against under the emigration laws of the country. Oliva's reply to this was a very practical one; he took a wife, fixed his Lares and Penates in St. Petersburg and begat a daughter, who, in 1854 answered a letter of Otto Jahn's inquiring about her father's relations and correspondence with Beethoven by saying that a fire and the death of Oliva from cholera in 1848, had caused the loss and dissipation of Beethoven's letters and that she was unable to write the details of the intercourse between her father and Beethoven. Inasmuch as she fixed the beginning of this intercourse in 1814, it is not likely that her contribution to this history would have been valuable.

Beethoven's experiment of lodging with Countess Erdödy, as might have been predicted, was not a successful one; he was too irritable, whimsical, obstinate; too ready to take offense, too lax in asking or giving explanations. We have seen in divers cases how, when he discovered himself to be in the wrong, he gladly made every due acknowledgement; but, as in the case of Ries, this was often too late to remedy the mischief already caused. Before the close of the winter, he was evidently becoming discontented; so much so as to take ill even the singular proof of the Countess's good will spoken of in the following note:

I think, my dear Zmeskall, that even after the war is over, if ever it begins, you will be ready to carry on negotiations for peace. What a glorious office!! I leave it wholly in your hands to settle the affair about my servant, but the Countess *Erdödy* must not have the slightest influence over him. She has, as she says, given him 25 fl. and 5 fl. a month *just to make him remain with me.* Now I *must necessarily* believe in this magnanimity—but do not wish it to be continued. . . .

Another note bears Zmeskall's date: "March 7, 1809":

I might easily have thought it—
About the blows, this is dragged in by the hair of the head—this story is at least three months old—and is by no means—what he now makes of it— The whole miserable affair was brought about by a huckster woman and a few other wretches—but I shall not lose much, because he was really spoiled in the house where I am.

What cause of dissension, beyond the ill-advised gratifications to the servant, had arisen between Beethoven and the Countess is not known; but something had occurred, the blame of which he soon saw was all his own, and for which he thus humbly expressed his contrition and asked forgiveness:

My dear Countess;

I have erred, that is true—forgive me. It was assuredly not intentional malice on my part if I have hurt you— Only since last night have I learned the truth about the matter; and I am very sorry that I acted as I did— Read your note coolly and judge for yourself whether I deserve this and whether you did not pay me back six-fold since I offended you unintentionally. Send my note back to me today, and write me only one word that you are no longer angry. I shall suffer infinitely if you do not do this. I can do nothing if things are to continue thus— I await your forgiveness.

There are sufficient grounds for belief that an immediate reconciliation took place; nevertheless, Beethoven decided to go into another lodging, and for a short time he moved into one in the Walfischgasse looking out over the city wall and glacis. —The date of this can be set as March or April from a remark in a letter to Gleichenstein, in which Beethoven chided him for not letting him know of his return from Freiburg, and referred also to the dedication of the 'cello sonata, which was published in April. Undated, the letter begins: "I am living in the Walfischgasse 1087 on the second floor."—

There is another touching and interesting letter to Gleichenstein whose date is determined by these circumstances. Breuning had, in April, 1808, married Julie, the beautiful and highly accomplished daughter of Staff-Physician von Vering. Less than one year thereafter the young wife, by an imprudent use of cold foot-baths, brought upon herself a hemorrhage of the lungs and died suddenly, only 19 years of age, on March 21, 1809. The letter dates from this period:

Dear, good Gleichenstein!

It is impossible for me to refrain from letting you know of my anxiety for Breuning's convulsive and feverish condition, and to beg of you that you strive to form a closer attachment to him or rather to bind him closer to you. *The condition of my affairs* allows me much too little opportunity to perform the high duties of friendship. I beg of you, I adjure you in the name of the good and noble sentiments which you surely feel to take upon yourself from me this truly tormenting care. It would be particularly beneficial if you could ask him to go here and there with you, and (no matter how much he may seek to goad *you* to diligence) restrain him from his immoderate, and what seems to me unnecessary, labors— You would not believe in what an overwrought state I have occasionally found him— You probably know of his trouble yesterday—all the result of his fearful irritability which, if he does not overcome it, will certainly be his ruin—

I therefore place upon you, my dear Gleichenstein, the care of one of my best and most proved friends, the more since your occupation already creates a sort of bond between you, and this you will strengthen by frequently showing concern for his welfare, which you can easily do inasmuch as he is well disposed towards you— But your noble heart, which I know right well, surely needs no injunctions— Act for me and for your good Breuning. I embrace you with all my heart.

Beethoven

While this letter shows Beethoven's concern over his friend's troubles, it also reveals clearly a basic trouble in their relationship: the one's impatience with the irritability and hotheadedness of the other. In later years there was to be a rift between them which lasted until two years before Beethoven's death: this developed when Beethoven resented Breuning's advice about the guardianship and the future of his nephew Karl. However, at an earlier date, just when is not known, there was another rift which was described by Stephan's son by his second marriage, Dr. Gerhard von Breuning, in his book *Aus dem Schwarzspanierhause*,[4] as a story he had heard from his elders. This quarrel resulted from the same type of friction; in this case, Breuning's understandable resentment over Beethoven's impulsiveness and lack of tact. Jacob Rösgen, an employee in the office of the Minister of War in which Breuning was a secretary, had learned certain facts, or suspicions, in relation to Carl Caspar van Beethoven's integrity, which he thought should be communicated to Ludwig as a warning "not to have anything to do with him in financial matters." To this end he, having obtained Breuning's word of honor not to make known the source of the information, imparted to him the whole matter. Breuning "faithfully performed the task which he had assumed; but Ludwig, in his tireless endeavor to better his brother, hastened to take him to task for his conduct and charge him with the acts which had been reported to him; he went so far, when pressed by his brother for the source of his information, as to mention the name of his friend Steffen. Caspar then appealed directly to my father and asked the name of the author of the 'denunciation'; and, when my father resolutely declined to give the name [Rösgen], Caspar indulged himself in abuse to such an extent that he left insulting letters addressed to him and unsealed with the portier of the Ministry of War. My father, angered and pained at this impertinence and at Ludwig's breach of confidence, read the latter a sharp lecture which ended with the declaration that because of such unreliability it would be impossible longer to hold association with him."

Now the threatening war-clouds became more dense. The same French armies which laid the foundations for Johann van Beethoven's prosperity not only prevented Ludwig's contemplated journey but affected him disastrously both pecuniarily and professionally. On May 4th, the Empress left Vienna with the Imperial family. Archduke Rudolph accompanied her, and Beethoven mourned his departure in the well-known first movement of the Sonata, Op. 81a. Beethoven's manuscript bears these inscriptions in his own hand: "The Farewell, Vienna, May 4, 1809, on the departure of his Imperial Highness the revered Archduke Rudolph"; on the Finale: "The Arrival of His Imperial Highness the revered Archduke Rudolph, January 30, 1810."

---

[4] Vienna, 1874, pp. 46-7. The incident has been variously dated. Dr. von Breuning (1813-92) believed it was connected with the rift of 1804. Thayer's date was 1815, the year of Carl Caspar's illness and death. (See TDR, III, 520.) Frimmel (*FRBH*, I, 66), however, dated it as probably 1809, which seems possible in view of Beethoven's note of complaint about Carl to his brother Johann, in this year.

With a garrison of 16,000 troops, 1000 students and artists, the civil militia and a small number of summoned men, Archduke Maximilian was ordered to defend Vienna. Thus it came about that Beethoven, on the 10th of May, found himself shut up in a beleaguered city.

The French commanders demanded the capitulation of Vienna, but Archduke Maximilian rejected the demands, and the French erected a battery on the Spittelberg to shell the city. Every shot directed by this battery against the Kärnthnerthor and the Wasserkunst Bastei was liable to plunge into Beethoven's windows.

At 9 o'clock at night (on the 11th of May) the battery of 20 howitzers opened fire. Rich and poor, high and low, young and old at once found themselves crowded indiscriminately in cellars and fireproof vaults.

Beethoven took refuge in the Rauhensteingasse and "spent the greater part of the time in a cellar in the house of his brother Caspar, where he covered his head with pillows so as not to hear the cannons," so says Ries.[5] More probably Beethoven took this wise precaution to save his feeble organs of hearing from the effect of the sharp reports of bursting shells, for it does not appear that either the cannons on the bastions or those mounted in the streets were fired. "At half-past 2 (the afternoon of the 12th) the white flag was sent up as notice of capitulation to the outposts of the enemy."

The occupation of the capital by the French and the gathering together of opposing armies for the terrible battles of Aspern, Esslingen, Wagram and Znaim produced the inevitable effects of increased consumption and deficient supply of the necessaries of life. Even before the capitulation "the rate of interest went up fearfully, especially in the sale of food, particularly bread, and because of the disappearance of copper coins." From the capitulation to the armistice of July 12th, two months, "the enemy had drawn from the city nearly 10,000,000 florins and demanded enormous requisitions of supplies." There was one requisition, perhaps more than one, which touched Beethoven directly: "A forced loan on the houses of the city and the suburbs amounting to one-quarter of the rentals from owners or the parties to a contract for rent on from 101 to 1000 florins and one-third on from 1001 to 2000 florins, etc." Perhaps at no other time was Beethoven so well able to meet the extraordinary demands upon his purse as now. He had received from Archduke Rudolph 750 florins and from Prince Lobkowitz 350 florins, his first payment of the annuity; and doubtless Breitkopf and Härtel and his other publishers had remitted money or bills. Still he must have felt the pressure of the time severely before Vienna again became free. To whom could he go for aid? Kinsky departed to Prague on February 26; his wife and Prince Lobkowitz on March 14. The Lichnowskys, Palffys, Waldstein, etc., were all away; some in the war; some in the civil service; some on their estates—the Erdödys, for instance, took refuge in Hungary or Croatia. Of personal friends, Breuning seems to have remained—no other is known to have done so. Bigot and his

[5] *Notizen*, p. 121.

wife went off to Paris, never to return; Zmeskall and the public officials in general had followed the Court and the Ministers to places of safety. The posts were interrupted and for many weeks communication with the country prohibited. It was not until near the end of July that the Prater, the Augarten, Schwarzenberg Garten, and the Schönbrunner Garten were opened to the public. For Beethoven, this confinement during this season of the year when he was accustomed to breathe inspiration in vale and forest, was almost intolerable, and increased if possible his old hatred of Napoleon and the French. Young Rust met him one day in a coffee-house and saw him shake his fist at a passing French officer, with the exclamation: "If I, as general, knew as much about strategy as I the composer know of counterpoint, I'd give you something to do!"

On May 31st Joseph Haydn died. It is not known whether Beethoven was present at any of the funeral services.

During the occupation of Vienna, Beethoven was visited by Baron de Trémont, a French officer and music-lover who in his memoirs left recollections of these meetings.[6] Here are a few excerpts: ". . . I admired his genius and knew his works by heart when, in 1809, as Auditor to the Council of State while Napoleon was making war on Austria, I was the bearer of the Council's dispatches to him. Although my departure was hurried, I made up my mind that in case the army should take Vienna I must not neglect the opportunity to see Beethoven. I asked Cherubini to give me a letter to him. 'I will give you one to Haydn,' he replied, 'and that excellent man will make you welcome, but I will not write to Beethoven; I should have to reproach myself that he refused to see someone recommended by me; he is an unlicked bear!'"

The Baron, however, did get himself admitted to Beethoven's lodging, with a letter from Reicha, despite his misgivings about Beethoven's reception of anyone who had to do with the French. In fact, Beethoven liked the young Baron enough to arrange several meetings with him during his sojourn in Vienna. Trémont continues: "I fancy that to these improvisations of Beethoven's I owe my most vivid musical impressions. I maintain that unless one has heard him improvise well and quite at ease, one can but imperfectly appreciate the vast scope of his genius. Swayed wholly by the impulse of the moment, he sometimes said to me, after striking a few chords: "Nothing comes into my head; let's put it off till—." Then we would talk philosophy, religion, politics, and especially of Shakespeare, his idol, and always in a language that would have provoked the laughter of any hearers. . . .

". . . His mind was much occupied with the greatness of Napoleon, and he often spoke to me about it. Through all his resentment I could see that he admired his rise from such obscure beginnings; his democratic ideas were

[6] Trémont's papers are all in the National Library at Paris. These excerpts are drawn from J. G. Prodhomme's "The Baron de Trémont," *MQ*, VI (1920), pp. 374-78. The article and the excerpts were translated by Theodore Baker.

flattered by it. One day he remarked, 'If I go to Paris, shall I be obligated to salute your emperor?' I assured him that he would not, unless commanded for an audience, 'And do you think he would command me?'—'I do not doubt that he would, if he appreciated your importance; but you have seen in Cherubini's case that he does not know much about music.'—This question made me think that, despite his opinions, he would have felt flattered by any mark of distinction from Napoleon. . . ."

During the tedious weeks of this miserable summer, Beethoven was busy selecting and copying in order extracts from the theoretical works of C. P. E. Bach, Türk, Kirnberger, Fux and Albrechtsberger, for subsequent use in the instruction of Archduke Rudolph—a task which, in our opinion, he had for some time had in mind, and had begun, at the very latest, early in the year. This material is largely the basis of that extraordinary imposition upon the musical public prepared by Seyfried and published by Haslinger in 1832, as Beethoven's studies under Haydn and Albrechtsberger. Seyfried in this book entitled *Ludwig van Beethovens Studien im Generalbasse* gathered together all that was to be found in the way of exercises, excerpts from text-books, etc., in Beethoven's posthumous papers and presented them in so confused and arbitrary a manner that only the keenness and patience of a Nottebohm could point the way through the maze (*Beethoveniana*, pp. 154-203). To Seyfried's claim that this was the work of Beethoven's student days Nottebohm answered: "It will require no waste of words to prove the incompatibility of such a claim with the results of our investigations. As a matter of fact, only the smallest portion of the 'Studies' can be traced back to the instruction which Beethoven received from Albrechtsberger."[7]

On the margin of the *Materialien zum Generalbass*, Beethoven wrote: "from 101 to 1000 florins a quarter—all residents or parties to rent-contracts without distinction." This was, of course, written at the time of the forced contribution of June 28th, but it is no proof that the book was then just begun. It shows merely that it was lying before him and offered him a convenient open space for his memorandum. Again on page 17, on the upper margin, stands "Printer's errors in the sonata for pianoforte with obbligato violoncello." This sonata was the one dedicated to Gleichenstein. It was first performed in public on March 5 of this year by the Baroness von Ertmann and the cellist Nikolaus Kraft in an *Akademie* for the latter's benefit. It was published early in April by Breitkopf and Härtel, and in a letter dated July 26, 1809, Beethoven indicated that he would send a list of the errors.

On August 9th a letter from Amsterdam, which was preserved by the widow of Beethoven's nephew Karl, was received by the composer, notifying him of his appointment as a Correspondent of the Fourth Class of the Royal Institute of Science, Literature and the Fine Arts. It gave occasion shortly after its receipt (September 19) for a letter to Breitkopf and Härtel in which

7 *Beeth.*, p. 198. (TDR, I, 363.)

Beethoven says: "*Do you know that I have become a member of the Society of Fine Arts and Sciences?—after all a title—ha ha, it makes me laugh.*"

Considering the war conditions it is understandable why Beethoven was unable to make his regular move into the country of which he was so fond and which was so important for his health. In his letter to Breitkopf and Härtel of July 26 he writes: "I still cannot enjoy life in the country, which is so indispensable for me." Some time before August 3rd he had moved once again to new lodgings, for on this date he informs the Leipzig publishers of his new address: "in the Klepperstall in the Teinfaltstrasse on the third floor, care of the lawyer Gostischa."[8]

Thayer believed that Beethoven finally did get away from the city and visited in the late summer both in Baden and in Hungary. Neither of these visits can be proved, but there is an undated letter from Beethoven in Baden to Dr. Troxler in Vienna, which if written in this year proves the former.

Dear Doctor! A thousand thanks for your trouble on my behalf; earlier your news could have spared me some annoying days— The Baden post is the most wretched, and similar to the whole state. Only today did I receive your letter.— If it is possible expect me early tomorrow between 9 and 10 o'clock at your house— I am coming to Vienna— I would like very much for you to go with me on Tuesday to Clementi since I can make myself understood with foreigners better by my notes than by speaking. Once again hearty thanks for all your friendship and courtesy towards me.

All good wishes to Malfatti.

Continue to regard kindly   your friend Beethoven

The letter was dated 1807 by Thayer who did not know that for the works sold to Clementi in that year no honorarium was received until the spring of 1810. Because of the reference both to Malfatti, of whom Troxler was a friend, and to Clementi, Riemann dated the letter 1809 and supplied the following background. September came and still no payment from Clementi and Co. for the works bought by them in April, 1807. Clementi was in Rome and thither, it would seem, Beethoven sent several letters asking for payment. Clementi now came to Vienna and sent a letter to his London partner, Collard, which, though dateless as to year and day, was, no doubt, the result of Beethoven's importunities. In it he complained of having written five or six letters to them for money with which to meet Beethoven's demands, the composer having "plagued" him with several letters—but in vain. At last a firm of Viennese bankers informed him that a credit for £400 has been sent him, but no letter. He concluded that of this sum £100 were meant for Beethoven and £300 for himself, and that they had received but half of Beethoven's manuscripts. "A most shabby figure you have made me cut in this affair!—and that with one of the first composers of the day! You certainly might have found means in the course of two years and a

[8] See A 223.

half to have satisfied his demands. Don't lose a moment and send me word *what* you have received from him, that I may settle with him."

—⟨Regarding the trip to Hungary, the unsettled conditions would not seem to favor it; yet for lack of evidence to the contrary, Thayer's opinion may be given:⟩— "He was often in Hungary," said Czerny, and there is no good reason to doubt that he went thither now to pass several weeks with the Brunsviks. It was already his practice to grant manuscript copies of his new works for the collection of Archduke Rudolph, whose catalogue, therefore, is of the highest authority in determining their dates. From this source it is known that the Pianoforte Fantasia, Op. 77, previously sketched, and the great F-sharp Pianoforte Sonata, Op. 78, were completed in October. The dedication of these two works to Count Franz and his sister Therese leads to the inference that they are memorials of happy hours spent in their domestic circle.

It was in the fall that Beethoven seems to have thought of trying the experiment of living independently of hotels and eating houses, and dining at home. It was therefore of importance to him, if possible, to obtain the joint services of some man and wife, and such a couple, by the name of Herzog, now offered themselves as servant and housekeeper. This is sufficient introduction to the following excerpts from the Zmeskall correspondence:

⋅〜⋅

. . . Today Herzog, who wishes to become my servant, will come to see you— you may engage him for 30 fl. with his wife *obbligato*—wood, light, small amount of livery.— I must have someone to cook for me, for as long as the present wretched food continues I shall remain ill— Today I am dining at home, because of the better wine. If you will order what you want, I should be glad to have you come to eat with me also— You will get the wine gratis and indeed a better one than that at the beastly Schwan—

⋅〜⋅

Here comes Herzog with his wife— Just listen to what these people would agree to do—she must cook when I want her to—also mend, etc., for this is a highly important matter— I shall come to you afterward in order to hear the result— Perhaps it would be best to ask how much they are willing to do for me?—

Shakespeare's clowns in *A Midsummer Night's Dream* have enriched theatrical speech with "lamentable comedy" and "very tragical mirth": phrases not inappropriate to the domestic dramas in which Beethoven and his servants were the actors, and which he made the subjects of numberless Jeremiads both in conversation and in letters to his friends—especially to Zmeskall and Mme. Streicher. As one example—and surely one is enough— take the Herzogs. They were engaged. All did not go well, however, and Zmeskall, who had previously helped Beethoven with "peace negotiations" with servants, now had again to officiate in this "glorious office" with the Herzogs. The following note to Zmeskall undoubtedly refers to troubles with the Herzogs:

I do not want to see that woman again and although she is *perhaps* better than he I want to hear as little about her as about him— Therefore I am sending you the desired 24 fl. Please add to this the 30 kr., take a 15 kr. piece of stamped paper, have *the servant* write in his own handwriting that *he has received the 24 fl. 30 kr. as money for boots and livery*— You will hear more from me in person concerning how much she has recently lied *to you*— Meanwhile I want you to remember *the respect due yourself as a friend of mine*. Tell them that *it is only from your inducement that more is being given*; otherwise don't have anything to do with them unnecessarily for they are both unworthy of your intercession.— I didn't want to have her husband again but circumstances partly demanded it. I needed a servant; and housekeeper and servant cost too much. Besides I found her several times with her husband down below at the watchmaker's in my house; she even wanted to go out from there with him when I needed her. Therefore, I let him come back, since I had to keep *her* for my lodgings. If I hadn't taken him back I would have been cheated all the more— So the matter ends; *they are both wretched people*—Farewell. I shall see you soon.

Your friend
Beethoven

The imagination can readily form a lively and correct picture of Beethoven's troubles, partly serious, partly tragi-comic, with people of this kind during that wretched time with all the necessaries of life at famine prices, and they on his hands to be provided for. The situation certainly was not one fitted to sweeten the temper of either party; no doubt both had good cause for complaint. We have, however, only the master's side of the question and not the whole of that. One who invariably has troubles with his servants must sometimes himself be in fault; so, perhaps, the Herzogs were not such "wretched people" after all.

During the French occupation the ordinary performances of both Court Theatres were given in the Kärnthnerthor. At the Burg—the real Court Theatre, forming, indeed, a part of the Imperial residence—after being closed some weeks, a French company opened on the 18th of July, played for a time alternately with a German one, and then held—as if in bitter irony—exclusive possession of the stage. Was not Vienna a French city? The Burg a French palace? Did not Napoleon's eagle head the *Wiener Zeitung*? At Schönbrunn the theatre was devoted almost exclusively to Italian opera and ballet, for the amusement of the French Court.

Meanwhile, Manager Hartl had projected a new charity, a theatrical poor fund, and as usual called upon Beethoven to give attraction to the first public performance for its benefit, by directing one or more of his works. Under these circumstances Hartl might reasonably expect munificent support from the conquerors for at least one charity concert for the benefit of the actors and their families. Hence, as on the 8th of September (the Nativity of the Virgin Mary) the Court Theatres would be closed, he selected that day. The programme has eluded search; but one number was the *Sinfonia Eroica*, conducted by its author. Was this selected, in the expectation that Napoleon would be present, to do him homage? If so, it failed of its aim. The day before, Napoleon journeyed from Schönbrunn to Krems and Mölk. Or was it in bitter sarcasm that Beethoven chose it?

An undated letter to Collin should be cited here. In it he asked the Court Secretary to rewrite a note which he had addressed to Beethoven when Hartl gave him the commission for the concert, and which he had lost. Then he continued in part: ". . . As near as I can recollect the contents were: 'that you wrote to me that you had spoken to H. v. Hartl concerning a *day for a concert* and that then he gave you instructions to write to me that if at this year's concert for the theatrical poor, I gave *important works* for the performance, and would myself conduct, I might at once pick out a day for a concert at the Theater-an-der-Wien and that under these conditions I might have a day *every year*. Vive vale. . . .' "

It is unclear whether this note was written in 1808 or 1809. In 1808 the theatrical poor fund had not been established, but Beethoven participated in another kind of charity concert and received his own concert day; in 1809 he was active in a concert for the theatrical poor people, yet did not get a concert for his own benefit in return. Unger[9] has pointed out that it is possible that Hartl wished to help the theatrical poor already in 1808 and could first accomplish it in 1809. This would date the letter in the earlier year. The fact remains that Beethoven contributed his services to the cause of charity in both years and obtained only one concert for his own benefit in return.

In the lists of "newly performed plays" in the two Vienna Court Theatres from August 1, 1803 to July 31, 1805, and from August 1, 1806 to December 31, 1807, Schiller's name does not once occur; not so in the lists after Hartl's undertaking the direction, January 1, 1808. Here we find: 1808: February 13, *Macbeth*, after Shakespeare; July 23, *Kabale und Liebe*; December 17, *Phaedra*, after Racine; 1809: August 23, *Don Carlos*—all by Schiller.

Thus had Schiller suddenly become a leading topic in the conversation of theatrical circles. One sees how Collin and Beethoven had hit upon the "Macbeth" as a subject for opera; and how the composer's youthful idea of making the "Ode to Joy" the subject of a composition was recalled to mind.

It does not appear from any records at hand, that either of the above named dramas was produced with music composed for it; but Hartl now determined, with his next Schiller drama, to put one by Goethe in rehearsal and to provide both with original music. "When it was decided," writes Czerny, "to perform Schiller's 'Tell' and Goethe's 'Egmont' in the city theatres, the question arose as to who should compose the music. Beethoven and Gyrowitz were chosen. Beethoven wanted very much to have 'Tell.' But a lot of intrigues were at once set on foot to have 'Egmont,' supposed to be less adaptable to music, assigned to him. It turned out, however, that he could make masterly music for this drama also, and he applied the full power of his genius to it."[10]

---

[9] *NBJ*, II (1925), p. 82n.
[10] Both in his letters to Breitkopf and Härtel of August 21, 1810, and to Bettina Brentano of February 10, 1811, Beethoven

Perhaps Beethoven's experience with the "Ode to Joy" earlier and the "Egmont" just at this time was the origin of a fine remark to Czerny. "Once, when the talk was about Schiller, he said to me: 'Schiller's poems are very difficult to set to music. The composer must be able to lift himself far above *the poet*; who can do that in the case of Schiller? In this respect Goethe is much easier.' "

Negotiations had been resumed about this time between George Thomson of Edinburgh and Beethoven, touching the arrangement of national melodies. In a letter dated September 25, 1809, Thomson sent Beethoven 43 Welsh and Irish melodies with the request to provide them as soon as possible with ritornellos and accompaniments for pianoforte or pedal harp, and violin and violoncello, and held out the promise of 100 ducats, Vienna standard, or even more as payment. Besides this, Thomson had requested him to write three quintets, two for violins, viola, flute and violoncello, one without flute but two violas instead (with bassoon or double-bass *ad lib.*), and also three sonatas for pianoforte and violin. For these works he offered him 120 ducats Vienna standard. "I make you this offer," said Thomson, "more to show you my taste and predilection for your music than in the hope to profit by the publication." To this proposition Beethoven replied as follows—in French and his own wretched hand, under date of November 23, 1809:

Monsieur!

I will compose the ritornellos to the 43 little songs, but I ask 10 pounds or 20 ducats V.S. more than you offer, that is instead of 50 pounds Sterling, or 100 ducats V.S. I ask 60 pounds Sterling or 120 ducats V.S.— This work, moreover, is of a kind that gives a composer but little pleasure, but I shall nevertheless always be ready to oblige you since I know that you can do a good business with it.— As regards the quintets and the three sonatas, I find the honorarium too little for me— I ask of you for them the sum of 120, i.e., one hundred and twenty pounds Sterling or two hundred and forty ducats V.S.; you offered me 60 pounds Sterling and it is impossible for me to gratify you for such an honorarium.— We are living here in a time when a frightful price is asked for everything, we are paying almost three times as much as formerly—but if you are agreed with the sums that I ask I will serve you with pleasure.—So far as the publication of the works here in Germany is concerned, I think that I would bind myself not to publish them sooner than after seven or eight months if you think this time long enough for your purposes.— As regards the double-bass or bassoon I wish that you would give me a free hand; I may, perhaps find something that will be even more agreeable to you—also we might use a bassoon or other wind-instruments with the flute and write only the third quintet for two violins, two violas and violoncello, since in this way the style would be purer. In short, rest assured Monsieur, that you are dealing with a true artist who, indeed, likes to be decently paid, but who loves fame and also the fame of art more—and who is never satisfied with himself and is always striving to make greater progress in his art.—

states that he composed the *Egmont* music out of love for Goethe and his poetry. (TDR, III, 154, n. 1.)

As regards the songs I have already begun them and will deliver them in about a week to Fries— Therefore please send me an answer soon, Monsieur, and receive the respectful esteem of your servant

Louis van Beethoven

Next time please send me the words of the songs along with them, as they are very necessary in order to get the correct expression.

Towards the end of the year Beethoven took ill, as he informed Breitkopf and Härtel in a letter which was dated December 4 (but from which the figure was stricken; the letter may have been delayed or Beethoven become doubtful, as usual, about the day of the month). In this he writes: "A fever which shook me up thoroughly, prevented me from sending these tardily found errata [in the two Trios] at once." On January 2, 1810, he wrote another letter, beginning: "Scarcely recovered—my illness threw me back again for two weeks—is it a wonder?—we do not even have eatable bread," and concluding with: "I am too weak today to answer your kind letter more fully, but in a few days I will answer everything else in your letter."

His friend Clement of the Theater-an-der-Wien gave Beethoven a pleasing compliment by reproducing in his annual concert (December 24) the *Christus am Ölberg*. On the same evening, by the way, Dobenz's oratorio *Die Sündfluth*, with music by Kauer, was sung at the Leopoldstadt Theatre, as it would seem, from the sarcastic notice in the *Allg. Mus. Zeit.*, with appropriate scenery! If Beethoven heard it, which is doubtful unless at rehearsal, he found he had little reason to mourn his non-acceptance of the text.

Mention should be made of the so-called Petter sketchbook, now part of the Bodmer collection in Bonn. Unger has resolved the conflict between Thayer and Nottebohm concerning the date of this sketchbook by a closer study of the properties of the paper used. The book consists of two parts which did not originally belong together: a first section of only 9 sheets belonging to the year 1809 and a second section of 65 sheets belonging to the second half of 1811.[11] Thus work on the seventh and eighth symphonies which occurs almost completely in the second section of the sketchbook was not really started at all in this year as Thayer had supposed. At this time there are only the merest hints of the work to come. What follows is Thayer's description of the significant material in the first 18 pages which can be dated, as he suggests, the winter of 1808-1809.

On the first two pages are two measures of music—merely a succession of chords—with this remark: "Such [passages] should produce another effect than the miserable enharmonic evasions which every school Miserabili can write, they ought to disclose the change to every hearer." This, though not fixing the date, does at least suggest the time when the writer's mind was unusually occupied with theoretical studies. On the same page is this: "Cotton in my ears at the pianoforte frees my hearing from the unpleasant

---

[11] See Max Unger, "Eine Schweizer Beethoven-Sammlung," *NBJ*, v (1933), p. 455.

buzzing (*das unangenehme rauschende*)"—which suggests a time when his organs of hearing were still very sensitive, and he had not yet abandoned his pianoforte playing. On page 18 Beethoven has written: "Overture Macbeth, the chorus of witches comes in at once."[12] Now that first act of *Macbeth*, read by Röckel in 1808, together with the first act of the oratorio *Die Befreiung Jerusalems*—both written for Beethoven—lay before the composer in print early in the year 1809. Collin had inserted them in the *Hoftheater-Taschenbuch* of that year. The poet died in 1811, leaving both unfinished. His memorandum is evidently the record of an idea which occurred to his mind on perusing the fragment, and determines the date of the first part of the sketchbook to be the beginning of 1809.

The compositions and publications of this year remain to be discussed and enumerated—a task requiring a preliminary remark or two. The great cost of living and the various extraordinary demands upon his purse this year, deranged Beethoven's pecuniary affairs seriously; from the same cause the Vienna publishers were not in a position to pay him adequately and in advance for his manuscripts. The dilatoriness of the London publishers has been mentioned. Happily his relations with Breitkopf and Härtel were such, that they were ready to remunerate him handsomely for whatever new compositions he might send them; and there seems to have been an arrangement made, under which divers new works of this period were published simultaneously by them in Leipzig and by Artaria in Vienna. Nevertheless, Beethoven was pressed for money, not only from the causes above stated, but from the need of an extra supply, in case a project of marriage, now in his mind, should be effected.[13] Of course he counted with certainty upon the regular payment of his annuity, now that the war was over, and a lasting peace apparently secured by the rumored union between Napoleon and Archduchess Marie Louise. But a semi-annual payment of this annuity was far from sufficient to meet the expenses of establishing himself as a married man. In a letter dated "Wednesday the 2nd, Winter month [November] 1809,"[14] Beethoven wrote to Breitkopf and Härtel: ". . . I worked for several weeks in succession so that it seemed rather *for death* than *immortality. . . .*" These labors were the completion and correction for the press of various more or less important works existing in the sketchbooks, and the composition of divers smaller pieces, such as would meet with a ready sale, and hence be promptly and liberally paid for by publishers. It is not at all surprising to find among them a number of songs the texts of which were apt expressions of his feelings at this juncture.

The compositions of 1809 were:

Concerto No. 5 for Pianoforte and Orchestra in E-flat major, Op. 73.

---

[12] See Nottebohm, *II Beeth.*, pp. 225ff. (TDR, III, 67, n. 2; 152.)

[13] To be discussed in the next chapter.

[14] However, Wednesday fell on the first of November. (TDR, III, 160, n. 1.)

"Quartetto per due Violini, Viola e Violoncello, da Luigi van Beethoven, 1809,"
    Op. 74.

Six Songs, Op. 75:

    "Mignon" (Goethe), 2nd version.

    "Neue Liebe neues Leben" (Goethe), 2nd version.

    "Aus Goethes Faust" (sketched before 1800).

    "Gretels Warnung" (v. Halem) (sketched before 1800).

    "An den fernen Geliebten" (Reissig).

    "Der Zufriedene" (Reissig).

Variations for the Pianoforte, D major, Op. 76.

Fantasia for Pianoforte, Op. 77.

Sonata for Pianoforte, F-sharp major, Op. 78.

Sonatina for Pianoforte, G major, Op. 79.

Sonata for Pianoforte: "Das Lebe Wohl, Wien am 4ten May 1809," etc.; "Die
    Abwesenheit. Die Ankunft des . . . Erzh. Rudolph, den 30 Januar, 1810,"[15]
    Op. 81a, E-flat. We suppose the sonata to have been completed in 1809, and
    ready for presentation to the Archduke upon his return; but as this was
    delayed until January 30th, "Die Ankunft," of course, took this date.

Four Ariettas and a Duet, Op. 82:

    "Dimmi, ben mio."

    "T'intendo, sì, mio cor."

    Arietta buffa "L'amante impatiente."

    Arietta assai seriosa "L'amante impatiente."

    Duet "Odi l'aura, che dolce sospira" for Soprano and Tenor, probably
    sketched in part during study with Salieri. The author of the first arietta is
    unknown; the rest are by Metastasio.

March in F major for Military Band, WoO 18, inscribed by Beethoven: "For
    His Royal Highness, the Archduke Anton,[16] 1809."

Other songs:

    "Die laute Klage" (Herder), WoO 135.

    "Andenken" (Matthisson), WoO 136.

    "Lied aus der Ferne" (Reissig), WoO 137.

    "Der Jüngling in der Fremde" (Reissig), WoO 138.

    "Der Liebende" (Reissig), WoO 139.

In a letter to Breitkopf and Härtel, dated August 8, Beethoven said that
he had sent along a sextet (Op. 71) and two German songs as a "return gift
for all the things *which I have asked as gifts from you.*" He also asked for
the complete works of Goethe and Schiller, his "favorite poets, with Ossian
and Homer." One of the two songs referred to was undoubtedly "Andenken."
The second song was probably the "Lied aus der Ferne," the first of five
settings which Beethoven made of poems by C. L. Reissig and which later

---

[15] From the catalogue of the Archduke
Rudolph Collection in the Gesellschaft der
Musikfreunde, which contains the autograph
of the first movement. That of the second
movement was stolen. See KHV, p. 216. (Cf.
TDR, III, 174.)

[16] Older brother of Archduke Rudolph.

gave rise to much annoyance. In a letter to Breitkopf and Härtel, dated February 4, 1810, he writes:

. . . The Gesang in der Ferne which my brother sent you recently was written by a dilettante, as you no doubt observed for yourselves, who pressed me urgently to set it to music, but who has also taken the liberty of having the a[ria] printed. I therefore thought it well to give you a proof of my friendly feeling by informing you of the fact. I hope you will print it at once on receipt. You can send it here and elsewhere as you please. If you make haste you may have it here before it can be printed here. I know for certain that it will be published by *Artaria*— I wrote the aria only as a *favor* and as a favor give it *to you*—. . . .

In this letter Beethoven offered Breitkopf and Härtel the Fantasia (Op. 77), the Choral Fantasia (Op. 80), three Pianoforte Sonatas (Op. 78, 79 and 81a), the Variations (Op. 76, in D major), the Quartet (Op. 74), the Pianoforte Concerto in E-flat (Op. 73), and "12 songs with pianoforte accompaniment, texts partly in German, partly in Italian, nearly all composed throughout (*durchkomponiert*)." That among these songs were four others to Reissig's words ("An den fernen Geliebten," "Der Zufriedene," "Der Jüngling in der Fremde" and "Der Liebende"), which were not published till some years later, is a natural conclusion from a letter to Breitkopf and Härtel, dated October 11, 1810:

That Cavalry Captain Reissig ever paid me anything for my compositions is an abominable lie. I composed them for him as a friendly favor because he was a cripple at the time and stirred my compassion— In writing this I declare that Herren Breitkopf and Härtel are the sole owners of the songs which I have sent you, of which the words are by Cavalry Captain Reissig.

In a still angrier mood he recurs to the songs again in a letter of October 15: "Another thing: you ought to publish immediately the 'Gesang aus der Ferne' which I once sent you, if you have not already done so. The poetry is by that rascal Reissig. It was not published at the time and it took nearly half a year before this rascal told me that, as he said, he had it 'printed by Artaria only for his friends.' I sent it to you by letter post and received for it instead of thanks, stench (*statt Dank Stank*). . . ."

The first sketches for the Fifth Piano Concerto, E-flat, Op. 73, dedicated to Archduke Rudolph, are found in the so-called Grasnick sketchbook[17] after the sketches for the Choral Fantasia, as it was performed for the first time on December 22, 1808. ——Kinsky argues that the first sketches for the concerto should not be dated 1808 as Nottebohm asserts. These sketches are on the last pages of the sketchbook and could only have been started after the rush of composing the Choral Fantasia for the concert of December 22, 1808 was over. Like the later-composed pianoforte introduction to the Fan-

[17] See D. Weise, *Ein Skizzenbuch* . . . , pp. 137-48.

tasia, these sketches belong to the early part of the year 1809.[18] The bulk of the sketches for the concerto are to be found in the so-called Meinert sketch-book[19] and in a group of 27 sheets in the Berlin State Library which are described by Nottebohm (*II Beeth.*, pp. 255 *et seq.*) and dated by him February to October, 1809. The work was finished by the end of the year; the autograph in the Berlin State Library has the inscription "Klavier Conzert 1809. von LvBthwn."

It is mentioned by Beethoven in the correspondence with his publishers for the first time on February 4, 1810. It was in their hands on August 21 of that year, when Beethoven prescribed the dedication to his distinguished pupil, and was published in February, 1811. The Concerto had then already been played in public by Johann Schneider with brilliant success towards the close of 1810, and, as the *Allg. Mus. Zeit.* reported, put a numerous audience into such "a state of enthusiasm that it could hardly content itself with the ordinary expressions of recognition and enjoyment."

The E-flat Quartet, Op. 74 (the so-called "Harp Quartet"), dedicated to Prince Lobkowitz, was written at the same time as the Concerto and Pianoforte Sonata in the same key. Beethoven was evidently hard at work on it when he wrote to Breitkopf and Härtel on the "19th, Wine month" (September) 1809: "Next time a word about quartets which I am writing— I do not like to occupy myself with solo sonatas for the pianoforte, but I promise you a few." Nottebohm says (*II. Beeth.*, p. 91), that the four movements of the Quartet were begun and finished in the order in which they appeared in print.

According to a note by Archduke Rudolph, the Fantasia, Op. 77, was composed in October[20] as was the Sonata, Op. 78.[21] The three Pianoforte Sonatas, Op. 78, 79 and 81a, are closely connected in time, notwithstanding their diversity of sentiment. Sketches for Op. 78 have not been found, but those for the other two are in the sketchbook of Carl Meinert (*II. Beeth.*, p. 255), which ends with the sketches for the Fantasia, Op. 77, composed for Count Franz Brunsvik. The three sonatas were doubtless in the mind of Beethoven when he promised Breitkopf and Härtel "a few" on September 19. On February 4, 1810, he offered to the publishers "three pianoforte solo sonatas—N.B. of which the third is composed of three movements, Parting, Absence and Return, and would have to be published alone." On August 21, 1810, Beethoven wrote about the dedication: "The sonata in F-sharp major— à Madame la Comtesse Therese Brunswick; the fantasia for pianoforte solo—à mon ami Monsieur le Comte François de Brunswick. . . . As regards the two sonatas publish them separately; or, if you want to publish them together, inscribe the one in G major Sonata facile or sonatina, which you

[18] *Katalog des Musikhistorischen Museums von Wilhelm Hayer in Cöln* (Cologne, 1916), IV, p. 168.

[19] Owned first by Carl Meinert in Dessau

and then acquired in 1903 by Charles Malherbe in Paris. (Cf. TDR, III, 166.)

[20] See *II Beeth.*, p. 274n. (TDR, III, 175.)

[21] See Nottebohm, *Verzeichniss*, p. 76.

might also do in case you [do not] publish them together." Breitkopf and Härtel published the sonatas separately and Op. 79 therefore received no dedication. The notion, once current, that Op. 79 (sometimes called the "Cuckoo Sonata") was an older work, is disproved by the sketches of 1809 (Nottebohm, *II. Beeth.*, p. 269). The E-flat Sonata, Op. 81a, seems to have been completely sketched before October and held in readiness against the return of the Archduke, as has been said. Breitkopf and Härtel published it in 1811, without the dates, much to Beethoven's dissatisfaction. The Variations in D, dedicated "to his friend" Oliva, anticipate by two years the use of the same theme as a Turkish march in the incidental music which Beethoven wrote for Kotzebue's *Ruinen von Athen.*

The Military March in F was designed for Archduke Anton and was one of two chosen for a "carrousel" at the court at Laxenburg in 1810. It is the "horse music" of Beethoven's correspondence with Archduke Rudolph.

The year also saw the beginning of the arrangements of the Irish melodies for Thomson.

By 1809, at the latest, Beethoven had written out a cadenza for the first and third movements of Mozart's Concerto in D minor, K. 466 for Ferdinand Ries. This was a favorite concerto with Beethoven which he played himself, it will be remembered, between the acts of the performance of *La clemenza di Tito* arranged by Mozart's widow at the Court Theatre on March 31, 1795. According to Kinsky[22] the handwriting is clearly of a later date; that it was composed for his student is indicated by the fact that the autograph to the first-movement cadenza was found among Ries's possessions.[23]

Also by 1809, according to Kinsky-Halm,[24] Beethoven had written out the cadenzas for the first four pianoforte concertos as well as a cadenza for his transcription for pianoforte of the Violin Concerto, presumably for the Archduke; Op. 15, three cadenzas for the first movement; Op. 19, one for the first movement; Op. 37, one for the first movement;[25] Op. 58, two for the first movement and one for the third movement; Op. 61, one for the first movement and one for the third.

The publications for the year were all by Breitkopf and Härtel:

"Als die Geliebte sich trennen wollte," WoO 132, in the Supplement No. 11 to the *Allgemeine Musikalische Zeitung*, Nov. 22.

Sonata for Pianoforte and Violoncello, Op. 69, "dédiée à Monsieur le Baron de Gleichenstein."

Symphony No. 5 in C minor, Op. 67, "dédiée à son Altesse Sérénissime Monseigneur le Prince régnant de Lobkowitz, Duc de Raudnitz, et à son Excellence Monsieur le Comte de Rasumoffsky."

---

[22] *Op.cit.*, p. 163.

[23] It is now in the Beethovenhaus collection at Bonn; the cadenza to the third movement is in the British Museum.

[24] See KHV, pp. 36, 47, 94, 138, 149.

[25] There is a sketch for another cadenza for this movement in the Bodmer Collection in the Beethovenhaus at Bonn. See Unger, *Ein Schweizer Beethovensammlung Katalog* (Zurich, 1929), p. 168.

Symphony No. 6 in F major, Op. 68, "dédiée à son Altesse Sérénissime Monseigneur le Prince regnant de Lobkowitz, Duc de Raudnitz, et à son Excellence Monsieur le Comte de Rasumoffsky."

Two Trios for Pianoforte, Violin and Violoncello, Op. 70, "dédiées à Madame la Comtesse Marie d'Erdödy née Comtesse Niszky."⊱⸺

CHAPTER XXIII

THE YEAR 1810

DECREASE IN PRODUCTIVITY—THERESE MALFATTI—BETTINA BRENTANO

BEETHOVEN, during the fifteen years since Wegeler's vain effort to induce him to attend lectures on Kant,[1] had become to some considerable degree a self-taught man; he had read and studied much, and had acquired a knowledge of the ordinary literary topics of the time, which justified that fine passage in the letter to Breitkopf and Härtel of November 2, 1809; "There is scarcely a treatise which would be too learned *for me*. Without making the least claim concerning my own learnedness, I have tried since childhood to grasp the *meaning of the better and the wise* of each age. Shame to any artist who does not hold it to be his duty to have at least that amount of proficiency—." Strikingly in point is the interest which he exhibits during these and following years in the Oriental researches of Hammer and his associates. His notes and excerpts prove a very extensive knowledge of their translations, both published and in manuscript; and, moreover, that this strange literature was perhaps even more attractive to him in its religious, than in its lyric and dramatic aspects. In these excerpts—indeed, generally in extracts from books and in his underscoring of favorite passages in them—Beethoven exhibits a keen perception and taste for the lofty and sublime, far beyond the grasp of any common or uncultivated mind. "The moral law in us and the starry heavens above us. Kant!!!" is one of the brief notes from his hand, which now and then enliven the tedious and thankless task of deciphering the Conversation Books. The following, given here from his own manuscript, is perhaps the finest of his transcriptions from Hindu literature:

God is immaterial; since he is invisible he can have no form, but from what we observe in his works we may conclude that he is eternal, omnipotent, omniscient

---

[1] Recorded in the Appendix, p. 9 of the *Notizen*.

and omnipresent—The mighty one is he who is free from all desire; he alone; there is no greater than he.

Brahma; his spirit is enwrapped in himself. He, the mighty one, is present in every part of space—his omniscience is in spirit by himself and the conception of him comprehends every other one; of all comprehensive attributes that of omniscience is the greatest. For it there is no threefold existence. It is independent of everything. O God, thou art the true, eternal, blessed, immutable light of all times and all spaces. Thy wisdom embraces thousands upon thousands of laws, and yet thou dost always act freely and for thy honor. Thou wert before all that we revere. To thee be praise and adoration. Thou alone art the truly blessed one (Bhagavan); thou, the essence of all laws, the image of all wisdom, present throughout the universe, thou upholdest all things.

Sun, ether, Brahma [these words are crossed out].

Beethoven's enjoyment of Persian literature as revealed to him in the translations and essays of Herder and von Hammer will now readily be conceived by the reader; as also the delight with which he read that collection of exquisite imitations of Persian poetry with its long series of (then) fresh notices of the manners, customs, books and authors of Persia, which some years later Goethe published with the title *West-Östlicher Divan*. Even that long essay, apparently so out of place in the work—*Israel in der Wüste*—in which the character of Moses is handled so unmercifully, was upon a topic already of curious interest to Beethoven. This appears from one of his copied papers—one which, as Schindler avers, "he considered to be the sum of the loftiest and purest religion." The history of this paper is this: The Hebrew chronicler describes the great lawgiver of his nation as being "learned in all the wisdom of the Egyptians." This leads Schiller, in his fine essay on "Die Sendung Moses," into a discussion of the nature and character of this wisdom. The following sentences are from his account:

The epoptæ (Egyptian priests) recognized a single, highest cause of all things, a primeval force, natural force, the essence of all essences, which was the same as the demiurgos of the Greek philosophers. There is nothing more elevated than the simple grandeur with which they spoke of the creator of the universe. In order to distinguish him the more emphatically they gave him no name. A name, said they, is only a need for pointing a difference; he who is only, has no need of a name, for there is no one with whom he could be confounded. Under an ancient monument of Isis were to be read the words: "I AM THAT WHICH IS," and upon a pyramid at Sais the strange primeval inscription: "I AM ALL, WHAT IS, WHAT WAS, WHAT WILL BE; NO MORTAL MAN HAS EVER LIFTED MY VEIL." No one was permitted to enter the temple of Serapis who did not bear upon his breast or forehead the name Iao, or I-ha-ho— a name similar in sound to the Hebrew Jehovah and in all likelihood of the same meaning; and no name was uttered with greater reverence in Egypt than this name Iao. In the hymn which the hierophant, or guardian of the sanctuary, sang to the candidate for initiation, this was the first division in the instruction concerning the nature of the divinity: "HE IS ONLY AND SOLELY OF

HIMSELF, AND TO THIS ONLY ONE ALL THINGS OWE THEIR EXISTENCE."[2]

The sentences here printed in capital letters "Beethoven copied with his own hand and kept (them), framed and under glass, always before him on his writing-table."

Beethoven was now at an age when men of thoughtful and independent minds have settled opinions on such important subjects as have received their attention, among which, to all men, religion stands preeminent. Few change their faith after forty; there is no reason to suppose that Beethoven did; no place, therefore, more fit than this will be found to remark upon a topic to which the preceding pages directly lead—his religious views. Schindler writes in the appendix to his biography of Beethoven:[3] "Beethoven was brought up in the Catholic religion. That he was truly religious is proved by his whole life, and many evidences were brought forward in the biographical part (of this work). It was one of his peculiarities that he never spoke on religious topics or concerning the dogmas of the various Christian churches in order to give his opinion about them. It may be said with considerable certainty, however, that his religious views rested less upon the creed of the church, than that they had their origin in deism. Without having a manufactured theory before him he plainly recognized the existence of God in the world as well as the world in God. This theory he found in the whole of Nature, and his guides seem to have been the oft-mentioned book, Christian Sturm's *Betrachtungen der Werke Gottes in der Natur*, and the philosophical systems of the Greek wise men. It would be difficult for anybody to assert the contrary, who had seen how he applied the contents of those writings in his own internal life."

As an argument against Schindler and to prove Beethoven's orthodoxy in respect to the Roman Catholic tenets, the fervid sentiment and sublime devotion expressed in the music of the *Missa Solemnis* have been urged; but the words of the Mass were simply a text on which he could lavish all the resources of his art in the expression of his religious feelings. It should not be forgotten that the only Mass which could be ranked with Beethoven's in D, was the composition of the sturdy Lutheran, J. S. Bach, and that the great epic poem of trinitarian Christianity was by the Arian, John Milton. Perhaps Schindler would have his readers understand more than is clearly expressed. If he means, that Beethoven rejected the trinitarian dogma; that the Deity of his faith is a personal God, a universal Father, to whom his human children may hopefully appeal for mercy in time of temptation, for aid in time of need, for consolation in time of sorrow—if this be Schindler's "deism," is may be affirmed unhesitatingly, that everything known to the present writer, which bears at all on the subject, confirms his view. Beethoven had the habit in moments of temptation and distress, of writing down short

[2] *Sämtliche Werke* (Munich, 1958-59), IV, pp. 792-93.   [3] Page 161. (TDR, III, 197.)

prayers for divine support and assistance, many of which are preserved; but neither in them, nor in any of his memoranda or conversations, is there the remotest indication that he believed in the necessity of any mediator between the soul of man and the Divine Father, under whatsoever name known— priest, prophet, saint, virgin or Messiah; but an even stronger religious sentiment, a more ardent spirit of devotion, a firmer reliance on the goodness and mercy of God are revealed in them, than Schindler seems to have apprehended.

The topics under last notice have carried us far onward, even to the last years of Beethoven. We now return to the end of 1809—to the master in the full vigor and maturity of his powers. The princes, whose generosity had just placed him, for the present at least, beyond the reach of pecuniary anxieties, may well have expected the immediate fulfillment of "the desire that he surpass the great expectations which are justified by his past achievements." They were bitterly disappointed. Kinsky did not live to hear any new orchestral work from that recently so prolific pen; Lobkowitz, whose dissatisfaction is upon record, heard but three; while the Archduke saw the years pass away comparatively fruitless, hardly more being accomplished in ten, than formerly in two—the marvelous year 1814 excepted. The close of 1809 terminated a decade (1800-1809) during which—if quality be considered, as well as number, variety, extent and originality—Beethoven's works offer a more splendid exhibition of intellectual power than those of any other composer produced within a like term of years; and New Year, 1810, began another (1810-19), which, compared with the preceding, exhibits an astonishing decrease in the composer's productiveness.

Schindler's division of Beethoven's life into three distinctly marked periods appears forced—rather fanciful than real; but whoever makes himself even moderately conversant with the subject, soon perceives that a change in the man did take place too great and sudden to be attributed to the ordinary effect of advancing years; but when? The abrupt pause in his triumphant career as composer just mentioned, would seem to determine the time; and, if so, the natural inference is, that both were effects of the same cause. There was a point in the life of Handel when his indefatigable pen dropped from his hand and many weary months passed before he could resume it. The failure of his operas, his disastrous theatrical speculation, consequent bankruptcy, and the culmination of his distresses in a partial paralysis of his physical powers, were the causes. The cessation of Beethoven's labors, although less absolute than in Handel's case, is even more remarkable, as it continued longer and was not produced by any such natural and obvious causes.

Thayer's conception of the barrenness of the decade 1810-19 would have been modified had he known that not only the main work but the origin of most of the important melodic ideas of the Seventh and Eighth Symphonies occurred in 1811 and 1812, and not in 1809 as he had supposed.

Add to this the *Egmont* music, the String Quartet, Op. 95, the Violin Sonata, Op. 96 and the Pianoforte Trio, Op. 97, all the work of the years 1810-12,[4] and it becomes clear that the pace of significant composition work slowed down gradually. A comparative standstill was not reached until 1813; this lasted for about two years before the pace of serious composition started once again to quicken. This slack period is midway between the time, about to be discussed, when Beethoven made his great yet unsuccessful effort to establish a companionship with another and the time when he was able to transfer his need for love and companionship to his nephew, after he had been made his guardian. In between these two points in his life he was adjusting to the fact that the more he needed the companionship and natural communication with others the harder it was to attain. The year 1814 was indeed an exception with its unusual set of circumstances that tended to break down this barrier.

Beethoven's studies were now, for the third time, diverted from other works in hand to an order from the directors of the theatres—the *Egmont* music. The persevering diligence of the last months, of which he speaks in his letters, was evidently for the purpose of clearing his desk of a mass of manuscript compositions sold to Breitkopf and Härtel, before attacking Goethe's tragedy—as decks are cleared for action before a naval battle. The overture bears the composer's own date "1810"; the first performance with Beethoven's music was on the evening of June 15th. Clärchen was played by Antonie Adamberger—a young actress alike distinguished for her beauty, her genius and her virtues—whose marriage in 1817 to the distinguished archaeologist von Arneth was a distinct loss to the Vienna stage. The two songs which Clärchen has to sing necessarily brought Fräulein Adamberger for the moment into personal relations with Beethoven, concerning which she wrote to the present author the following simple and pleasing account under date January 5, 1867:

. . . I approached him [Beethoven] without embarrassment when my aunt of blessed memory, my teacher and benefactress, called me to her room and presented me to him. To his question: "Can you sing?" I replied without embarrassment with a decided "No!" Beethoven regarded me with amazement and said laughingly: "No? But I am to compose the songs in 'Egmont' for you." I answered very simply that I had sung only four months and had then ceased because of hoarseness and the fear that continued exertion in the practice of declamation might injure my voice. Then he said jovially with an adoption of the Viennese dialect: "That will be a pretty how do you do!"—but on his part it turned out to be something glorious.

We went to the pianoforte and rummaging around in my music . . . he found on top of the pile the well-known rondo with recitative from Zingarelli's *Romeo and Juliet*. "Do you sing *that*?" he asked with a laugh which shook him as he sat down hesitatingly to play the accompaniment. Just as innocently and unsuspi-

---

[4] The works listed here represent only the important compositions of this period.

ciously as I had chatted with him and laughed, I now reeled off the air. Then a kind look came into his eye, he stroked my forehead with his hand and said: "Very well, now I know"—he came back in three days and sang the songs for me a few times. After I had memorized them in a few days he left me with the words: "There, that's right. So, so that's the way, now sing thus, don't let anybody persuade you to do differently and see that you do not put a *mortant* in it." He went; I never saw him again in my room. Only at the rehearsal when conducting he frequently nodded to me pleasantly and benevolently. One of the old gentlemen expressed the opinion that the songs which the master, counting on certain effects, had set for orchestra, ought to be accompanied on a guitar. Then he turned his head most comically and, with his eyes flaming, said, "He knows!". . . .

Long afterwards, in a Conversation Book, an unknown hand writes: "I remember still the torment you had with the kettledrum at the rehearsal of *Egmont*."

Beethoven's name appears on both this year's concerts for the Theatrical Poor Fund—March 25, with the first movement of the Fourth Symphony; April 17, with the "Coriolan" Overture; but it does not appear that he conducted on either occasion; it is, however, probable that he did conduct the rehearsals and performances of a symphony in Schuppanzigh's first Augarten concert in May. Add to the above the subsequent notices of the Quartet, Op. 95, and a few minor instrumental pieces and songs, and the meagre history of Beethoven as *composer* for 1810 is exhausted; what remains is of purely private and personal nature.

Kinsky's active service in the campaign of 1809 and his subsequent duties in Bohemia had prevented him hitherto from discharging his obligations under the annuity contract; but the Archduke, perhaps Lobkowitz also, was promptly meeting his; and these payments, together with the honorable remuneration granted by Breitkopf and Härtel for manuscripts, supplied Beethoven, despite the high cost of living, with ample means for comfort, even for luxury. He had at this time no grounds for complaint upon that score.

It was in 1810 that Beethoven received from Clementi and Co. the long-deferred honorarium for the British copyrights bought in April, 1807. Exactly when this money was received by Beethoven cannot be determined from the existing evidence, but it must have been in the early part of the year. On February 4, Beethoven wrote to Breitkopf and Härtel offering them the compositions from Op. 73 to 82, remarking that he was about to send the same works to London. He would probably not have had such a purpose in mind unless he had had a settlement with his London publishers.[5] Additional evidence, though of little weight, is provided by the circumstance

[5] Dr. Riemann is responsible for the clarification that the payment from Clementi did not occur until 1810, and that consequently the letters to Gleichenstein referring to these money matters, to be cited presently, could no longer be dated 1807 as Thayer had done, but must belong to the year 1810. (TK, II, 103, n. 1; 173, n. 1; TDR, III, 25ff.)

that at the same time he was contemplating a change of lodgings, as a letter to Peter von Leber,[6] written on February 8 shows. It was to his old home in the house of Baron Pasqualati which he had occupied two years before, and which he now took again at an annual rental of 500 florins, on April 24th, the start of the spring renting season.

A number of letters to Gleichenstein and Zmeskall to which attention must now be called seem to show us Beethoven in the character of a man so deeply smitten with the charms of a newly acquired lady friend that he turned his attention seriously to his wardrobe and personal appearance and thought unusually long and frequently of the social pleasures at the home of his charmer. ⟶⟨This home was the Malfatti household to which Gleichenstein was a frequent visitor in this year. Beethoven's "charmer" was Therese Malfatti; the object of Gleichenstein's interest was her younger sister Anna, whom he married in 1811. A letter to Wegeler dated May 2, 1810, to be introduced later, shows that Beethoven was considering marriage at this time. By assigning the undated notes to Gleichenstein to the year 1810, Riemann linked the name of Therese Malfatti to Beethoven's marriage project.[7]⟩⟶

In one letter to Gleichenstein, Beethoven writes: "I beg of you to let me know when the M[alfattis] remain home of an evening. You surely had a pleasant sleep—I slept little, to be sure, but I prefer such being awakened to all sleep."

Another letter reads:

Dear good Gleichenstein!

I am sending you 300 fl.— Just let me know if you need more and how much? I'll send it right away—and since I understand so little about these things as it is all so against my nature, please buy for me linen or Bengal for shirts and at least half a dozen neckties.— Use your good judgement but don't delay, you know how I need them—Today I forwarded 300 fl. to Lind and thereby have followed your advice.

Today *Joseph Henickstein* paid me twenty-seven and a half florins for a pound sterling and *invited you and me along with Clementi to lunch tomorrow. Don't refuse, you know how I like being with you.* However send me word whether I may tell Henickstein that you can surely be counted upon— You won't refuse, will you— Greet everyone who is dear to you and me. How gladly would I like to add and *to whom we are dear????* This question mark applies at least to me—

Today and tomorrow I have so much to do that I cannot come to you as I would like to do. Goodbye, be happy—I am not.

Your

Beethoven

---

[6] According to Orel the addressee was not "Professor von Loëb," as read by Nohl, but Peter von Leber, brother-in-law of Baron Pasqualati. In 1808 the Baron sold his share in the house to the von Lebens. See A. Orel, *Ein Wiener Beethoven Buch* (Vienna, 1921), pp. 210-11.

[7] On incomplete evidence, Thayer dated these letters 1817. See Max Unger, "Beethoven and Therese von Malfatti," in *MQ*, XI (1925), pp. 63-72.

Lind was a tailor, Henickstein the son of a banker. Again he wrote to say that he wished "Madame M." would give him permission to pick out a pianoforte for her which she wished to buy "at Schanz's." Though it was his rule never to accept commissions on such sales, he wanted to save money for the lady on this purchase.

On another day he writes:

Here is the s[onata][8] I promised Therese. Since I cannot see her today, give it to her—remember me to all of them. I feel so happy with them all and as though they might heal the wounds inflicted upon my soul by wicked people. Thank you, kind G., for having taken me there— Here are 50 fl. for the neckerchiefs. If you need more, let me know. You are wrong if you think that you are the only one that Gigons follows. I too have had the pleasure of having him not leave my side. He has eaten beside me in the evening, and he even accompanied me home.— In short, he provided me with very good entertainment. At least I could never look up, but quite far down—farewell, love me

Your Beethoven

Gigons was the Malfatti's little dog, and it is evident that Beethoven was pleased by the attention paid him. This is the first of only two allusions which Beethoven makes in all his papers, printed or written relating to him, of a domestic pet animal.

Now we reach the notes to Zmeskall, the first of which is endorsed by the recipient as having been received on April 18, 1810. Beethoven could and did avail himself of Zmeskall's readiness to oblige him to an extent which at length excited misgivings in his own mind that he was really going too far and abusing his friend's kindness. This time Beethoven's want was of a very peculiar nature, namely a looking glass; that it was not for shaving purposes but for a more general control of his toilet is indicated by the second note:

Dear Zmeskall,

Do send me for a few hours your looking-glass which hangs beside your window, mine is broken. If you would be so kind as to buy me one like it today it would be a great favor. I'll recoup you for your expenditure at once— Forgive my importunity dear Z. I hope to see you soon.

Your Bthvn

Dear Z, Do not get angry at my little note—don't you recall the situation I am in, like Hercules once at Queen Omphale's??? I asked you to buy me a looking-glass like yours, and beg you as soon as you are not using yours which I am returning to send it back to me for mine is broken— Farewell and don't write again about me as the great man—for I have never felt the strength of human nature as I feel it just now—

Remain fond of me—

[8] Op. 78? (TDR, III, 206, n. 1.)

Do not get vexed, dear Z. because of my continued demands upon you—but let me know how much you paid for the looking-glass?

Farewell, we shall see each other soon at the Schwan as the food is daily growing worse at the [illegible]— I have had another violent attack of colic since the day before yesterday, but it is better today.

Your friend

Beethoven

--*{There remain the following letters to Gleichenstein and one to Therese herself, all undated. The letter to Wegeler dated May 2nd helps to determine the time when the idea of marriage was utmost in Beethoven's mind. The April 18 date of the Zmeskall note shows that the Malfattis probably had not yet gone to the country, and shows also that the 8th, mentioned in the letter to Therese quoted below, was not April but May or June. Since these letters are undated it is difficult to know exactly in what order to place them. However, the first of these letters suggests some kind of a rebuff, probably from the Malfattis, which touched off Beethoven's sensitivity as to his social position—"am I then nothing more than your musician or musician to the others?" Also the impropriety to which it refers might easily be connected with the mention of the punch in the letter to Therese. But first the letter to Gleichenstein:}*--

Your report plunged me again from the regions of highest rapture into the depths. Why the addition, You would let me know when there would be another musicale? Am I then nothing more than your musician or musician to the others?— That at least is how it can be understood. I can therefore seek support only in my own heart; there is none for me outside of it. No, nothing but wounds have come to me from friendship and such kindred feelings— So be it then, for you, poor B, there is no happiness in the outer world, you must create it in yourself. Only in the ideal world will you find friends. I beg of you to set my mind at rest as to whether yesterday I was guilty of any impropriety, or if you cannot do that then tell me the truth. I hear it as willingly as I speak it— There is still time; the truth may yet help me. Farewell—don't let your friend Dorner[9] know anything of this.

In the late spring the Malfatti family moved to their country home, at which time Beethoven wrote the following letter to Therese:

With this you are receiving, honored Therese, what I promised, and if there had not been the weightiest difficulties, you would have received more in order to show that I always *do more for my friends than I promise*— I hope and have no doubt that you keep yourself as well occupied as pleasantly entertained—but not so much that you cannot also think of us— It would perhaps be presuming upon your kindness or placing too high a value upon myself if I were to write you: "Persons are together not only when they are in each other's company, even the

[9] According to Frimmel, Dorner was the physician to Count J. Ph. Cobenzl. (*FRBH*, I, 114.)

distant one, the absent one, is with us."[10] Who would dare to write such a sentiment to the volatile T. who handles everything in this world so lightly?— In
laying out your plans, do not forget the pianoforte, or music generally; you have
so beautiful a talent for it, why not cultivate it exclusively? You who have so much
feeling for everything that is beautiful and good, why will you not make use of it
in order to learn the more perfect things in so beautiful an art, which always
reflects its light upon us?— I live very solitarily and quietly. Although now and
then lights try to arouse me, there is still for me a void which cannot be filled
since you are all gone and which defies even my art which has always been so
faithful to me— Your pianoforte is ordered and you will have it soon— What
difference will you have found between the treatment of a theme which I invented
one evening and the manner in which I finally wrote it down for you. Figure it
out for yourself, but don't get the punch *to help you—*

How lucky you are to be able to go to the country so soon, I shall not have the
pleasure until the 8th, but I rejoice in the prospect like a child. How joyous I am
when I walk among bushes and trees, herbs, rocks. Nobody can love the country
as I do—since woods, trees, rocks, return the answer which man wants to hear—

[Four lines concerning a song for Nanette are stricken out]

You will soon receive some other of my compositions in which you should not
have to complain too much about the difficulties— *Have you read Goethe's
Wilhelm Meister, and Shakespeare translated by Schlegel?* One has so much
leisure in the country that it might be agreeable were I to send you these works—

By chance I have an acquaintance in your neighborhood; perhaps you will see
me at your home early some morning for half an hour and then I'll be off. You
see I wish to be as little tedious as possible to you. Commend me to the good will
of your father, your mother, although I have no right as yet to ask it of them,
also to your cousin M. Farewell, honored T, I wish you all that is good and
beautiful in life. When you think of me, think of me cheerfully—forget the
wild goings-on— Be convinced that no one can wish that your life may be more
joyous and more happy than I, even if you have no sympathy for

Your devoted servant and friend

Beethoven

N.B. It would really be very nice of you if you were to write a few lines to say
what I can do for you here—

This does not sound like the letter of a man about to propose marriage,
as he does not sound at all sure what his reception may be. Perhaps he *had*
committed some indiscretion, implied in the letter to Gleichenstein above,
and thus felt that as regarded the goodwill of the parents "I have no right
as yet to ask it of them." However, Beethoven wrote the famous letter
of May 2, 1810 to Wegeler in Coblenz, asking him to procure a copy of his
baptismal certificate for him. In this letter he says:

. . . A couple of years ago my quiet, retired mode of life came to an end, and I
was forcibly drawn into activities of the world. I have not as yet formed a

---

[10] From Goethe's *Egmont*, Act V, Egmont to Ferdinand. [*Werke*, ed. Petsch (Lpz.) 11,
p. 271.]

favorable opinion of it but rather one against it—but who is not affected by the storms of the outside world? Yet I should be happy, perhaps one of the happiest of men, if the demon had not taken possession of my ears.— If I had not read somewhere that a man may not voluntarily part with his life as long as a good deed remains for him to perform, I should have long ago been no more—and indeed by my own hand— Oh, life is so beautiful, but to me it is forever poisoned.— You will not refuse my friendly request if I beg of you to secure my *baptismal certificate* for me— Whatever expense may attach to the matter, since you have an account with Steffen Breuning, you can recoup yourself at once from that source and I will make it good at once to Steffen here.— If you should yourself think it worth while to investigate the matter and make the trip from Coblenz to Bonn, charge everything to me.— But one thing must be borne in mind, namely, that there was a brother *born before me*, who was also named Ludwig with the addition Maria, but who died. To fix my age beyond doubt, this brother must first be found, inasmuch as I already know that in this respect a mistake has been made by others, and I have been said to be older than I am.— Unfortunately I myself lived for a time without knowing my age— I had a family register but it has been lost, heaven knows how.— Therefore do not be offended if I urge you to attend to this matter, to find Ludwig Maria and the present Ludwig who was born after him— The sooner you send me the baptismal certificate the greater will be my obligation—. . . .

To the *Notizen* (1838) Wegeler published a few pages of appendix on the occasion of the Beethoven festival at Bonn (1845), giving therein a most valuable paragraph explanatory of this most important letter (*Nachtrag*, p. 14): "It seems that Beethoven, once in his life, entertained the idea of marriage, after having been in love many times, as is related in the *Notizen* [pp. 40, 42ff and 117ff]. Many persons as well as myself were impressed by the urgency with which in his letter of May 10 [*sic*] he besought me to secure his baptismal certificate for him. He wanted to pay all the expenditures, even a journey from Coblenz to Bonn. And then he added explicit instructions which I was to observe in looking up the certificate in order to get the right one. I found the solution of the riddle in a letter written to me three months later by my brother-in-law St. v. Breuning. In this he says: 'Beethoven tells me at least once a week that he intends to write to you; but I believe *his marriage project has fallen through*, and for this reason he no longer feels the lively desire to thank you for your trouble in getting him the baptismal certificate.' In the thirty-ninth year of his life Beethoven had not given up thoughts of marriage."

A short letter to Gleichenstein instructs us slightly touching the conclusion of this psychological drama which, no doubt, tore the heart of Beethoven. It would seem as if at first Beethoven wanted to visit the Malfattis at their country home, but at the last preferred to send a formal proposal of marriage by the hands of Gleichenstein. Here is the letter:

You are living on a calm and peaceful sea or, possibly, are already in a safe harbor— You do not feel the distress of the friend who is still in the storm—or you dare not feel it— What will they think of me in the star Venus Urania, how will they judge without seeing me— My pride is so humbled, I would go there with you uninvited— Let me see you at my lodging tomorrow morning; I shall expect you about 9 o'clock at breakfast— Dorner can come with you at another time— If you were but franker with me; you are certainly concealing something from me, you want to spare me; and this uncertainty is more painful than the most fatal certainty— Farewell. If you cannot come let me know in advance— Think and act for me— I cannot entrust to paper more of what is going on within me—

We have no testimony concerning the refusal beyond the cessation of all correspondence on the subject, and also an utterance of Therese's niece: "It is true that Beethoven loved my aunt and wished to marry her, and also that her parents would never have given their consent." His weakness was not in seeking a wife, for this was wise and prudent, but in the selection of the person; in imagining that the young girl's admiration for the artist—her respect and regard for the friend of her parents and of Gleichenstein—had with increasing years grown into a warmer feeling; and in misconceiving the attention, civilities and courtesies extended to him by all the members of the family as encouragement to a suit, the possibility of which had, probably, never entered the mind of any one of them. It placed Gleichenstein in a dilemma of singular difficulty. How he escaped from it, there are no means of knowing; the affair was, however, so managed, that the rejection of Beethoven's proposal caused no interruption—or at most a temporary one— in the friendly relations of all the parties immediately concerned.

Beethoven's relations with another fair friend, Bettina Brentano, now demand attention. In the Vienna suburban road Erdbeergasse stood the lofty house then numbered 98, its rear windows overlooking Razumovsky's gardens, the Donau canal and the Prater, whence Elizabeth Brentano (Bettina) wrote to Goethe: "Here I live in the house of the deceased Birkenstock, surrounded by two thousand copperplate engravings, as many hand-drawings, as many hundred old ash urns and Etruscan lamps, marble vases, antique fragments of hands and feet, paintings, Chinese garments, coins, geological collections, sea insects, telescopes and numberless maps, plans of ancient empires and cities sunk in ruin, artistically carved walking-sticks, precious documents, and finally the sword of Emperor Carolus."

Joseph Melchior von Birkenstock (born in 1738), the honored, trusted and valued servant of Maria Theresia and Kaiser Joseph, the friend and brother-in-law of the celebrated Sonnenfels—the esteemed correspondent of so many of the noblest men of his time, including the American philosopher Franklin and the Scotch historian Robertson, the reformer of the Austrian school system, the promoter of all liberal ideas so long as in those days progress was allowed— was pensioned in 1803, and thenceforth lived for science, art and literature until his death, October 30, 1809. His house, filled almost to repletion with the artistic, archaeological, scientific collections of which Bettina spoke, was one of those truly noble seats of learning, high culture and refinement, where Beethoven, to his manifest intellectual gain, was a welcome guest.

Sophie Brentano was older than Bettina, very beautiful notwithstanding the loss of one eye, and, like all the members of that remarkable family, very highly talented and accomplished. As Count Heberstein's future bride, she had made a long visit to Vienna, but their marriage was prevented by her untimely death. "She brought about the marriage of her brother Franz[11] with Antonie von Birkenstock," says Jahn. The young wife, who did not feel at home in Frankfurt—and also because of the precarious health of her father, we may add—persuaded Franz Brentano to remove to Vienna, where for several years they made their home in the Birkenstock house which Bettina described so beautifully. In this house, where music was cultivated, Beethoven came and went in a friendly fashion. His "little friend," for whose "encouragement in pianoforte" playing he wrote the little trio in a single movement in 1812, was their daughter Maximiliane Brentano, later Madame Plittersdorf, to whom ten years later he dedicated the Sonata in E major (Op. 109). After Birkenstock's death in 1809 he tried to give a practical turn to his friendship by seeking to persuade Archduke Rudolph to buy a part of his collection. More effective, evidently was the help which Brentano extended to him, who, when he came into financial straits and needed a loan, always found an open purse. Madame Antonie Brentano was frequently ill for weeks at a time during her sojourn in Vienna, so that she had to remain in her room inaccessible to all visitors. At such times Beethoven used to come regularly, seat himself at a pianoforte in her anteroom without a word and improvise; after he had finished "telling her everything and bringing comfort," in his language, he would go as he had come without taking notice of another person.

Before presenting the account of Bettina's relationship with Beethoven and Goethe it is well to remind the reader of her lively imagination and emotional feeling; her love for her two heroes was matched by her sense of the opportunity for literary expansion that presented itself in the chronicling in letter form all that she could about these two artists. On the one hand, she was sensitive enough to recognize that these two geniuses towered above those around them and she was faithful to this concept until her death. On the other hand, she could not resist weaving herself into all that she described so that in her inexhaustible love for them and their art she made it seem that in their lives she played a much greater role than was actually the case. The impression was furthered to the extent that she edited and revised the correspondence before its publication. The extent of this rewriting had been a matter of dispute since 1835, when Bettina, who was then Madame von

[11] Franz Brentano (1765-1844) was born from his father's *first* marriage in 1756; in 1774 Peter Anton Brentano married Maximiliane la Roche, who was Bettina's mother. Thus Franz was Bettina's half-brother. See Arthur Helps and Elizabeth Jane Howard, *Bettina* (New York, 1957), p. 216.

Arnim, had published her correspondence with Goethe under the title *Goethes Briefwechsel mit einem Kinde*. This was greatly clarified when in 1921 this correspondence in its original form became public. Letters had been rewritten and condensed, sometimes many combined into one so that a new approximate date would have to be supplied. Her "letter" of May 28th which follows, for instance, represents a piecing together of notes that she had written at the time. In point of fact, her next letter to Goethe was not written in May but on July 6th when she was in the country. Rolland, who took a charitable view towards this literary endeavor, has said: "The value to the historian [of the *Briefwechsel*] is in effect the value of Bettina's admitted powers of seeing, hearing, and understanding, powers which include a wise estimate as to how far it may be in her interest—she is quite unconscious of this—to speak the naked truth or to embellish it. This must be borne in mind as each letter is read."[12] The additional material used to describe the first meeting of Bettina and Beethoven is compiled from her letter to Pückler-Muskau[13] (1832) and notes from conversations which Thayer had with Madame von Arnim in 1849-50.—

One day in May, Beethoven, sitting at the pianoforte with a song just composed before him, was surprised by a pair of hands being placed upon his shoulders. He looked up "gloomily" but his face brightened as he saw a beautiful young woman who, putting her mouth to his ear said: "My name is Brentano." She needed no further introduction. He smiled, gave her his hand without rising and said: "I have just made a beautiful song for you; do you want to hear it?" Thereupon he sang—raspingly, incisively, not gently or sweetly (the voice was hard), but transcending training and agreeableness by reason of the cry of passion which reacted on the hearer—"Kennst du das Land?" He asked: "Well, how do you like it?" She nodded. "It is beautiful, isn't it?" he said enthusiastically, "marvellously beautiful; I'll sing it again." He sang it again, looked at her with a triumphant expression, and seeing her cheeks and eyes glow, rejoiced over her happy approval. "Aha!" said he, "most people are touched by a good thing; but they are not artist-natures. Artists are fiery; they do not weep." He then sang another song of Goethe's, "Trocknet nicht Thränen der ewigen Liebe."

There was a large dinner party that day at Franz Brentano's in the Birkenstock house and Bettina—for it was she—told Beethoven he must change his old coat for a better, and accompany her thither. "Oh," said he jokingly, "I have several good coats," and took her to the wardrobe to see them. Changing his coat he went down with her to the street, but stopped there and said he must return for a moment. He came down again laughing with the old coat on. She remonstrated; he went up again, dressed himself properly and went with her. But, notwithstanding his rather clumsy drollery, she soon discovered a greatness in the man for which she was wholly unpre-

---

[12] *Goethe et Beethoven* (Paris, 1930), p. 38.
[13] Fürst von Pückler-Muskau (1785-1871) was a German writer of books of travel.

pared. His genius burst upon her with a splendor of which she had formed no previous conception, and the sudden revelation astonished, dazzled, enraptured her. It is just this, which gives the tone to her letter upon Beethoven addressed to Goethe. In fact, the Beethoven of *our* conceptions was not then known; the first attempt to describe or convey in words, what the finer appreciative spirits had begun to feel in his music, was E. T. A. Hoffmann's article on the C minor Symphony, in the *Allg. Mus. Zeit.* of July 21st—five weeks later.

The essential parts of Bettina's long communication to Goethe are these:

Vienna, May 28.

When I saw him of whom I shall now speak to you, I forgot the whole world—as the world still vanishes when memory recalls the scene—yes, it vanishes. . . . It is Beethoven of whom I now wish to tell you, and who made me forget the world and you; I am still not of age, it is true, but I am not mistaken when I say—what no one, perhaps, now understands and believes—he stalks far ahead of the culture of mankind. Shall we ever overtake him?—I doubt it, but grant that he may live until the mighty and exalted enigma lying in his soul is fully developed, may reach its loftiest goal, then surely he will place the key to his heavenly knowledge in our hands so that we may be advanced another step towards true happiness.

To you, I am sure, I may confess I believe in a divine magic which is the essence of intellectual life. This magic Beethoven practises in his art. Everything that he can tell you about is pure magic, every posture is the organization of a higher existence, and therefore Beethoven feels himself to be the founder of a new sensuous basis in the intellectual life; you will understand what I am trying to say and how much of it is true. Who could replace this mind for us? From whom could we expect so much? All human activities toss around him like mechanism, he alone begets independently in himself the unsuspected, uncreated. What to him is intercourse with the world—to him who is at his sacred daily task before sunrise and who after sunset scarcely looks about him, who forgets sustenance for his body and who is carried in a trice, by the stream of his enthusiasm, past the shores of work-a-day things?

He himself said: "When I open my eyes I must sigh, for what I see is contrary to my religion, and I must despise the world which does not know that music is a higher revelation than all wisdom and philosophy, the wine which inspires one to new generative processes, and I am the Bacchus who presses out this glorious wine for mankind and makes them spiritually drunken. When they are again become sober they have drawn from the sea all that they brought with them, all that they can bring with them to dry land. I have not a single friend; I must live alone. But well I know that God is nearer to me than to other artists; I associate with him without fear; I have always recognized and understood him and have no fear for my music—it can meet no evil fate. Those who understand it must be freed by it from all the miseries which the others drag about with themselves."

All this Beethoven said to me the first time I saw him; a feeling of reverential awe came over me when he expressed himself to me with such friendly frankness, seeing that I must have appeared so utterly insignificant to him. I was surprised, too, for I had been told that he was unsociable and would converse with nobody. They were afraid to take me to him; I had to hunt him up alone. He has three lodgings in which he conceals himself alternately—one in the country, one in the city and the third on the bastion. It was in the last that I found him in the third story, walked in unannounced. He was seated at the pianoforte.

He accompanied me home and on the way he said the many beautiful things about art, speaking so loud and stopping in the street that it took courage to listen to him. He spoke with great earnestness and much too surprisingly not to make me forget the street. They were greatly surprised to see him enter a large dinner party at home with me. After dinner, without being asked, he sat down to the instrument and played long and marvellously; there was a simultaneous fermentation of his pride and his genius. When he is in such a state of exaltation his spirit begets the incomprehensible and his fingers accomplish the impossible.

In the letter to Pückler-Muskau in which Mme. von Arnim dwelt more upon the incidents of this meeting, she writes thus:

There was surprise when I entered a gathering of more than 40 people who sat at table, hand in hand with Beethoven. Without ado he seated himself, said little (doubtless because he was deaf). Twice he took his writing-tablet out of his pocket and made a few marks in it. After dinner the entire company went up to the tower of the house to look at the view; when they were gone down again and he and I alone, he drew forth his tablet, looked at it, wrote and elided, then said: "My song is finished." He leaned against the window-frame and sang it out upon the air. Then he said: "That sounds, doesn't it? It belongs to you if you like it, I made it for you, you inspired it, I read it in your eyes just as it was written."

In the Goethe letter she continues:

Since then he comes to me every day, or I go to him. For this I neglect social meetings, galleries, the theatre, and even the tower of St. Stephen's. Beethoven says "Ah! What do you want to see there? I will call for you towards evening; we will walk through the alleys of Schönbrunn." Yesterday I went with him to a glorious garden in full bloom, all the hot-beds open—the perfume was bewildering; Beethoven stopped in the oppressive sunshine and said: "Not only because of their contents, but also because of their rhythm, Goethe's poems have great power over me, I am tuned up and stimulated to composition by this language which builds itself into higher orders as if through the work of spirits and already bears in itself the mystery of the harmonies.

"Then from the focus of enthusiasm I must discharge melody in all directions; I pursue it, capture it again passionately; I see it flying away and disappearing in the mass of varied agitations; now I seize upon it again with renewed passion; I cannot tear myself from it; I am impelled with hurried modulations to multiply it, and, at length I conquer it:—behold, a symphony! Music, verily, is the mediator between the life of the mind and the senses. I should like to talk with Goethe about this—would he understand me? Melody is the sensuous life of poetry. Isn't the intellectual content of a poem transformed into sensuous feeling by the melody? Isn't it through melody that one experiences to the full the sensuous quality of Mignon's Song, and doesn't this emotion in turn stimulate one to fresh creation? The mind wants to expand into the limitless and universal where everything flows into a stream of feelings which spring from simple musical thoughts and which otherwise would die away unheeded. This is harmony, this is what speaks from my symphonies, the sweet blend of manifold forms flows along in a stream to its destination. There indeed one feels that something eternal, infinite, something never wholly comprehensible is in all that is of the mind, and although in my works I always feel that I have succeeded, yet at the last kettle-drum with which I have driven home to my audience my pleasure, my musical conviction, like a child I feel starting once again in me an eternal hunger that but a moment before seemed to have been assuaged. Speak to Goethe about me," he said; "tell him to hear my symphonies and he will say that I am right in saying that music is the one incorporeal entrance into the higher world of knowledge which comprehends mankind but which mankind cannot comprehend. . . . We do not know what knowledge brings us. The encased seed needs the moist, electrically warm soil to sprout, to think, to express itself. Music is the electrical soil in which the mind thinks, lives, feels. Philosophy is a precipitate of the mind's electrical essence; its needs which seek a basis in a primeval principle are elevated by it, and although the mind is not supreme over what it generates through it, it is yet happy in the process. Thus every real creation of art is independent, more powerful than the artist himself and returns to the divine through its manifestation. It is one with man only in this, that it bears testimony of the mediation of the divine in him— Music gives to the mind the relationship to harmony. An isolated thought still has the feeling of the whole, of relatedness in the mind. And thus every thought in music is most intimately and inseparably related to the whole of harmony which is unity.

"Everything electrical stimulates the mind to musical, fluent, out-streaming generation.

"I am electrical in my nature. I must interrupt the flow of my undemonstrable wisdom or I might neglect my rehearsal. Write to Goethe if you understand what I have said, but I cannot be answerable for anything and will gladly be instructed by him." I promised to write you everything to the best of my understanding. . . . Last night I wrote down all that he had said; this morning I read it over to him. He remarked: *"Did I say that? Well, then I had a raptus!"* He read it again attentively and struck out the above and wrote between the lines, for he is greatly desirous that you shall understand him. Rejoice me now with a speedy answer, which shall show Beethoven that you appreciate him. It has always been our purpose to discuss music; it was also my desire, but through Beethoven I feel for the first time that I am not fit for the task.

To this letter Goethe answered:

Your letter, heartily beloved child, reached me at a happy time. You have been at great pains to picture for me a great and beautiful nature in its achievements and its strivings, its needs and the superabundance of its gifts. It has given me great pleasure to accept this picture of a truly great spirit. Without desiring at all to classify it, it yet requires a psychological feat to extract the sum of agreement; but I feel no desire to contradict what I can grasp of your hurried explosion; on the contrary, I should prefer for the present to admit an agreement between my nature and that which is recognizable in these manifold utterances. The ordinary human mind might, perhaps, find contradictions in it; but before that which is uttered by one possessed of such a dæmon, an ordinary layman must stand in reverence, and it is immaterial whether he speaks from feeling or knowledge, for here the gods are at work strewing seeds for future discernment and we can only wish that they may proceed undisturbedly to development. But before they can become general, the clouds which veil the human mind must be dispersed. Give Beethoven my heartiest greetings and tell him that I would willingly make sacrifices to have his acquaintance, when an exchange of thoughts and feelings would surely be beautifully profitable; mayhap you may be able to persuade him to make a journey to Karlsbad whither I go nearly every year and would have the greatest leisure to listen to him and learn from him. To think of teaching him would be an insolence even in one with greater insight than mine, since he has the guiding light of his genius which frequently illumines his mind like a stroke of lightning while we sit in darkness and scarcely suspect the direction from which daylight will break upon us.

It would give me great joy if Beethoven were to make me a present of the two songs of mine which he has composed, but neatly and plainly written. I am very eager to hear them. It is one of my greatest enjoyments, for which I am very grateful, to have the old moods of such a poem (as Beethoven very correctly says) newly aroused in me. . . .

June 6, 1810.

Bettina replied with the following:

Dearest friend!

I communicated your beautiful letter to Beethoven so far as it concerned him. He was full of joy and cried: "If there is anyone who can make him understand music, I am that man!" The idea of hunting you up at Karlsbad filled him with enthusiasm. He struck his forehead a blow and said: "Might I not have done that earlier?—but, in truth I did think of it but omitted to do it because of timidity which often torments me as if I were not a real man: but I am no longer afraid of Goethe."— You may count, therefore, on seeing him next year. . . .

I am enclosing both songs by Beethoven;[14] the other two are by me. Beethoven has seen them and said many pretty things about them, such as that if I had devoted myself to this lovely art I might cherish great hopes; but I merely graze it in flight, for my art is only to laugh and sigh in a little pocket—more than that there is none for me.

Bettina

By the middle of June she was in Bohemia.

--◦◦The three letters from Beethoven to Bettina, written in 1810, 1811 and 1812 were first published in the *Athenaeum für Wissenschaft, Kunst und Leben*.[15] Only the letter of 1811 may be called genuine, the autograph of

---

[14] "Kennst du das Land" and "Trocknet nicht." (TDR, III, 223, n. 1.)

[15] Nürnberg, January, 1839.

which has been found. Riemann believes that "Beethoven's original letters were tricked out by her for literary effect, which would help to explain the disappearance of the autographs of the letters of 1810 and 1812." Judging by the extent that Bettina rewrote the Goethe correspondence, it is possible that Beethoven never put these communications to paper at all.[16] The "letter" of 1810 is included here, however, for it is probably based partly on observations made by Beethoven to Bettina, and partly on a letter as well, which she put in the following letter form:

Vienna, August 11, 1810

Dearest Bettine:

No lovelier spring than this, that say I and feel it, too, because I have made your acquaintance. You must have seen for yourself that in society I am like a frog on the sand which flounders about and cannot get away until some benevolent Galatea puts him into the mighty sea again. I was really high and dry, dearest Bettine; I was surprised by you at a moment when ill-humor had complete control of me, but in truth it vanished at sight of you, and I quickly threw it off. I knew at once that you belonged to another world than this absurd one to which with the best of wills one cannot open his ears. I am a miserable man, and here I am complaining about others!!— Surely you will pardon this with your good heart which looks out of your eyes, and your sense which lies in your ears—at least your ears know how to flatter when they give heed. My ears, unfortunately, are a barrier through which I cannot easily have friendly intercourse with mankind— otherwise!—Perhaps!—I should have had more confidence in you. As it is I could only understand the big, wise look of your eyes, which did something for me which I shall never forget. Dear Bettine, dearest girl! Art!—who understands it, with whom can one converse about this great goddess!— How dear to me are the few days in which we chatted, or rather corresponded with each other. I have preserved all the little bits of paper on which your bright, dearest answers are written. And so I owe it to my bad ears that the best portion of these fleeting conversations is written down. Since you have been gone I have had vexatious hours, hours of shadow, in which nothing could be accomplished. I walked about in the Schönbrunn Alley for fully three hours after you were gone, and on the bastion; but no angel was there to meet me who might fascinate me as you do, Angel. Pardon, dearest Bettine, this departure from the key. I must have such intervals in which to unburden my heart. You have written to Goethe, haven't you?— Would that I might put my head in a bag so that I could see and hear nothing of what is going on in the world, since you, dearest angel, cannot meet me. But I shall get a letter from you, shall I not?— Hope sustains me, it sustains half the world, and I have had her as neighbor all my life. If I had not what would have become of me?— I am sending you herewith, written with my own hand, "Kennst du das Land," as a souvenir of the hour in which I learned to know you. I am sending also the other which I have composed since I parted with you dear, dearest heart!

---

[16] For a comparative study of the other two letters with Bettina's other writings see R. Gottschalk, "Die drei Beethovenbriefe Bet- tinas," *Zeitschrift für Musik*, Vol. 94₃ (1927), pp. 154-59.

Herz, mein Herz, was soll das geben,
Was bedränget Dich so sehr?
Welch ein fremdes, neues Leben!
Ich erkenne Dich nicht mehr.

Yes, dearest Bettine, answer this, write me what is going to happen to me since my heart has become such a rebel. Write to your most faithful friend—

Beethoven

There are a few letters from this period to which attention may be paid. On July 9, 1810, Beethoven wrote to Zmeskall telling him of his distracted state of mind: he ought to go away from Vienna for the sake of his health, but Archduke Rudolph wanted him to remain near him; so he was one day in Schönbrunn, the next in Vienna. "Every day there come new inquiries from strangers, new acquaintances, new conditions even as regards art. Sometimes I feel as if I should go mad because of my undeserved fame; fortune is seeking me and on that account I almost apprehend a new misfortune."

On July 17th he sent to Thomson the Scottish songs which he had arranged, accompanied by a letter (in French) in which he discussed business matters, gave some instructions touching the repetitions in the songs, repeated his offer to compose three quintets and three sonatas and offered to send him such arrangements for quartet and quintet as have been made of his symphonies.

The cessation in Beethoven's productiveness in this period is partly explained by the vast amounts of labor entailed by the preparation of manuscripts for publication, the correction of proofs, etc. Of this there is evidence in a number of letters to Breitkopf and Härtel. On July 2 he wrote demanding an honorarium of 250 ducats for works that he had specified, and sending the first installment: String Quartet in E-flat, Fantasy for pianoforte, two Sonatas for pianoforte, five Variations for pianoforte and six Ariettas (Op. 75) to appear on September 1st. The second installment, he said, should be a Concerto in E-flat, the Choral Fantasia and three Ariettas (Op. 83) to appear on November 1st. The Sonata "Farewell, Absence and Return," five Italian Ariettas (Op. 82) and the score of *Egmont* would make up the third installment.[17]

On August 21, 1810, he wrote to the firm at great length. He sent a draft of a plan for a complete edition of his works, in which Breitkopf and Härtel were to figure as the principal publishers. He reiterated the sum of 250 ducats for the works mentioned previously in the letter of July 2, and said it was a small fee. He continues:

. . . At the time when bank-notes were worth only a little less than silver or gold I received a hundred ducats for three sonatas.— N.B. you yourselves have given me 50 ducats for a quintet— Am I supposed to go backwards instead of forwards,

[17] Beethoven, however, was not able to keep completely to this schedule. See *A* 276.

for I certainly hope that I will not receive this reproach in my art—Also no matter what the worth of a ducat in guldens may be for us, there isn't any profit. Now we pay 30 fl. for a pair of boots, 160 or 170 fl. for a coat, etc. The devil with economy in music— Last year before the French came my 4000 fl. were worth something, this year they're not worth 1000 fl. in convention coin— I am not out to be a musical usurer as you think, who writes only to become rich, by no means! Yet I love an independent life, and this I cannot have without a small income. Also the honorarium must bring some honor to the artist, as indeed to everything that he undertakes. I would not want to tell anyone that Breitkopf and Härtel had given me 200 ducats for these works— You as a more humane and far more educated man than all the other music publishers ought also to have your main purpose not to pay the artist barely enough but rather to lead him on his way so that he, undisturbed, can undertake all the work which is in him and which is expected from him by others— It is not bragging when I tell you that I prefer you to all the others. Often enough I have been approached from *Leipzig*, and here too from others acting as authorized agents from there, and recently in person by someone who was willing to give me what I asked. But I have refused all offers in order to show you that I prefer to do business with you because of your brains (I don't know anything about your heart), and even am willing to take a loss in order to preserve this connection— But I cannot go lower than 250 ducats, I would lose too much, which you cannot expect, consequently here the matter rests. . . .

He then gave directions as to the dedications, and of the *Egmont* he says:

. . . As soon as you have received the score of this you will best know what use to make of it and how to direct the attention of the public to it— I wrote it purely out of love for the poet, and to show this I accepted nothing from the theatre directors who in turn accepted it, and as a reward, as usual and always, treated my work with *great indifference.* There is nothing *smaller than our great folk,* but I make an exception in favor of Archdukes— Give me your opinion as to a complete edition of my works. One of the chief obstacles seems to be in the case of new works which I shall continue to bring into the world I shall have to suffer in the matter of publication. . . .

The postscript contains the following little note containing an important correction in the Scherzo of the Fifth Symphony:

. . . I have found another error in the Symphony in C minor, namely, in the third movement in ¾ time where, after the ♮ ♮ ♮ the minor returns again, it reads (I just take the bass part) thus:

The two measures marked by a X are redundant and must be stricken out, of course also in all the parts that are pausing.

The long, bright summer days, that in other years had awakened his powers to new and joyous activity and added annually one at least to the list of his grandest works, came and departed, leaving no memorial but a few songs and minor instrumental works—the latter apparently to order. True, he wrote to Zmeskall and talked of his art as if great things were in prospect; but he had no heart for such labors, and not until October did he take up and finish the "Quartetto Serioso" (Op. 95) for his friend. He took no country lodgings this summer—alternating between Baden and Vienna, and indulging in lonely rambles among the hills and forests. We think it must have been in this period of song composition and oriental studies that, on such an excursion, he had with him the undated paper containing a selection from the songs in Herder's *Morgenländische Blumenlese* and wrote upon it in pencil: "My decree [meaning the annuity contract] says only 'to remain in the country'—perhaps this would be complied with by any spot. My unhappy ears do not torment me here.— It seems as if in the country every tree said to me 'Holy! Holy!'— Who can give complete expression to the ecstasy of the woods? If everything else fails the country remains even in winter—such as Gaden, untere Brühl, etc.—easy to hire a lodging from a peasant, certainly cheap at this time."

Another half-sheet in the Library of the Musikfreunde in Vienna, mostly covered with rude musical sketches, is a suitable pendant to the above, as it contains these words: "Without the society of some loved person it would not be possible to live even in the country."

It is well known that Beethoven's duties to Archduke Rudolph soon became irksome and at last almost insupportable. It was, however, for his good that he was compelled to perform them and be master of himself to that extent; it was also fortunate that Bettina Brentano came just at this time with beauty, grace and genius to turn his thoughts into other channels. Nor was it without benefit to him that Thomson's melodies, which required no severe study, gave some desultory but profitable employment to his mind. Just at the close of the year it was rumored that he contemplated a journey into Italy "next spring, in order to seek restoration of his health, which had suffered greatly for several years, under southern skies." There was some foundation for this, for some years later Beethoven himself states in one of his letters: "I declined a call to Naples."

There are a series of letters during the year to Beethoven's old friend, Johann Andreas Streicher, that were first published in the *Beethoven Jahrbuch*, 1953/54. The correspondence naturally was concerned primarily with pianofortes. In July, Beethoven noted the address of a Baron Schall whom he was probably assisting in the choice of a pianoforte from Streicher's shop; and there is more than one letter in the latter part of the year concerning a new pianoforte for himself to replace his old Erard which he had had since 1803.

The compositions of the year 1810 are:

The incidental music to Goethe's *Egmont*. It was composed between October, 1809, and June, 1810, and the first performance with Beethoven's music took place on June 15. In a sketchbook dated by Nottebohm 1810 (*II. Beeth.*, pp. 276ff), on the first twenty-nine pages there are sketches for seven numbers in the following order, viz: 7, 1, 8, 9, 2, 3, 6. Sketches for the overture are not to be found in the book, but in other places in connection with sketches for the Pianoforte Trio in B-flat, Op. 97. Beethoven's admiration for Goethe (stimulated, it is fair to assume, by his intercourse with Bettina Brentano) is shown by the fact that, besides the *Egmont* lyrics, others of Goethe's poems were sketched or completed in the year which saw the production of the tragedy. Though Beethoven contemplated dedicating it to Archduke Rudolph, it eventually appeared without a dedication. Beethoven first offered the music to Breitkopf and Härtel in a letter dated June 6, 1810.

Piano piece in A minor, WoO 59. According to Nohl, the discoverer of the manuscript, the inscription read: "For Elise on April 27th as a remembrance from L.v.Bthvn." But inasmuch as the manuscript was found among the possessions of Therese von Malfatti, Unger[18] believes that the inscription should read "For Therese" which in German characters would resemble "Elise." Nohl's copy was used for its publication in the collected works (Ser. 25, No. 35).

Three Songs: "Wonne der Wehmuth," "Sehnsucht," and "Mit einem gemalten Band," Op. 83. The manuscript bears the following inscription in Beethoven's hand: "3 Gesänge—1810—Poesie von Göthe in Musick gesetzt von Ludwig van Beethoven."[19]

Twenty-four Welsh songs with accompaniment for pianoforte, violin and violoncello, WoO 155.[20]

Ecossaise for military band, WoO 22.

Polonaise for military band, WoO 21.

March in C major for military band, WoO 20.

March in F major for military band composed "for His Royal Highness Archduke Anton by Ludwig van Beethoven, 1810, Baden, on the 3rd Summer-month. This March (WoO 19) and the March in F of 1809, which was rewritten for the occasion, were performed at the tournament at Laxenburg held in honor of the birthday of Empress Maria Ludovica on August 25, 1810.[21] With his unsuccessful offer of the three marches to the publisher Peters in 1822, Beethoven wrote on September 13: ". . . however there are some of these marches for which I already have new trios." According to Hess, this cannot refer to the trio of the first march which was added and then struck out before the performance of August 25; but the trios for the other two marches may have been composed at the later date.[22] In 1823 Beethoven wrote to Peters that he would prefer to rename these three marches—which he calls "this Turkish music"—"Zapfen-streiche" [tattoos].

String Quartet, F minor, Op. 95. The autograph manuscript preserved in the

[18] *Op. cit.*, p. 70. See also *DM*, xv₅ (1923), pp. 334-40.

[19] In the Paris Conservatory of Music. See KHV, p. 223.

[20] According to KHV, p. 650, all but two of the twenty-six Welsh melodies were set for Thomson in this year. No. 15 belongs to 1812 and No. 25 to 1814.

[21] For a full description of the different versions of the two marches in F, see Hess, *BJ*, 1953/54, pp. 103-07; *BJ*, 1955/56, pp. 120-21.

[22] The authorities disagree. Hess and Nottebohm argue that Beethoven most likely wrote all the music for these three marches in 1809-10. Kinsky-Halm, KHV, pp. 459-60, believes that the trios to the Marches and maybe the March in C were composed around 1822.

National Library at Vienna bears the inscription: "Quartett serioso—1810—in the month of October. Dedicated to Herr von Zmeskall and written in the month of October by his friend L.v.Bthvn."

—There is a canon "Ewig dein," WoO 161, which exists in two versions: the first version on a single stave has been published in the complete works, Ser. 23; the autograph of the second version, in 3 staves, is in the Bodmer Collection in Bonn, and is dated by Unger "about 1810?"[23]

? Ecossaise for Military Band, WoO 23.

The publications of the year were:

By Artaria:

    Five Songs: "An den fernen Geliebten" (Reissig) (Op. 75, No. 5).

    "Der Jüngling in der Fremde" (Reissig), WoO 138.

    "Der Liebende" (Reissig), WoO 139.

    "Der Zufriedene" (Reissig) (Op. 75, No. 6).

    "Lied aus der Ferne" (Reissig), WoO 137.

These were published in "Achtzehn deutsche Gedichte mit Begleitung des Pianoforte von verschiedenen Meistern . . . dem . . . Erzherzog Rudolph . . . gewidmet von C. L. Reissig" in July.

By Breitkopf and Härtel:

"Andenken" (Matthisson), WoO 136.

Fantasy for the Pianoforte, Op. 77, dedicated to Count Franz von Brunsvik.

Leonore, Op. 72, 1806 version without overture and finales, arranged for piano anonymously by Czerny.

"Lied aus der Ferne" (Reissig), WoO 137, in March.

Overture to *Egmont*, Op. 84.

Overture to *Leonore* [No. 3].

Sextet for 2 clarinets, 2 horns, 2 bassoons, Op. 71.

Six Songs with Pianoforte Accompaniment, Op. 75, dedicated to Princess Caroline von Kinsky, in October:

    "Mignon" (Goethe).

    "Neue Liebe, neue Leben" (Goethe).

    "Aus Goethes Faust."

    "Gretels Warnung" (v. Halem).

    "An den fernen Geliebten (Reissig).

    "Der Zufriedene" (Reissig).

Sonata for the Pianoforte, Op. 78, dedicated to Countess Therese von Brunsvik.

Sonatina for the Pianoforte, Op. 79.

String Quartet, Op. 74, dedicated to Prince Franz Joseph von Lobkowitz.

Variations for the Pianoforte, Op. 76, dedicated to Franz Oliva.

By Kunst- und Industrie-Comptoir:

"Die Sehnsucht von Göthe mit vier Melodien nebst Clavierbegleitung," WoO 134.[24]

By Simrock:

Sextet for String Quartet and 2 Horns, Op. 81b.

---

[23] *Eine Schweizer Beethovensammlung Katalog*, p. 138.

[24] See O. E. Deutsch, "Beethovens Goethe-Kompositionen," in *Jahrbuch der Sammlung Kippenberg*, VIII (1930), p. 111, and x (1935), p. 319.

CHAPTER XXIV

THE YEAR 1811

BETTINA, BEETHOVEN AND GOETHE—A SOJOURN IN TEPLITZ—SKETCHES FOR NEW SYMPHONIES

LET the year start with a letter from Beethoven to Therese Brunsvik of which we learn from a transcript in a letter written by Therese to her sister Josephine, dated February 2, 1811, as follows:

Through Franz I have also received a souvenir of our noble Beethoven which gave me much joy; I do not mean his sonatas, which are very beautiful, but a little writing which I will immediately copy literally:

"Even without prompting, people of the better kind think of each other; this is the case with you and me, dear and honored Therese. I still owe you grateful thanks for your beautiful picture and while naming myself your debtor I must at the same time appear before you in the character of a beggar by asking you if perchance you feel the genius of painting stirring within you to duplicate the little hand drawing which I was unlucky enough to lose. *It was an eagle looking into the sun*; I cannot forget it. But do not think that I am thinking of myself in such a connection, although this idea has been ascribed to me. Many look upon a heroic play without being in the least like it. Farewell, dear Therese, and think occasionally of your truly revering friend

Beethoven"

Therese tried to comply with Beethoven's request. On February 23 she wrote to her sister: "My request to you, dear Josephine, is to reproduce that picture which you are able to do; it would not be possible for me to do anything of the kind." And later she repeated in French: "You have told me nothing about Beethoven's eagle. May I answer that he shall receive it?"[1]

--⟨On February 13, 1810, Josephine had married the Estonian, Baron von Stackleberg, who had been tutor to the two Deym boys. In the following

[1] Published first by Marie Lipsius (La Mara) in Breitkopf and Härtel's *Mittheilungen,* March, 1910, p. 410. (TDR, III, 270, n. 1.)

month the Stacklebergs alternately lived at Witschap in Moravia and at the Müller Gallery in Vienna. Since August, 1810, Therese had been in Witschap as governess for the four Deym children and the first Stackleberg child, born November 30, 1810. From Therese's letters to her sister it is clear that at this time the Stacklebergs were in Vienna.}⚜--

Beethoven's intercourse with the Brentanos kept his interest in Bettina alive. --⚜{She, meanwhile, had become engaged on December 4, 1810, to the poet Ludwig Joachim von Achim and was secretly married to him in 1811.[2] Here follows the one letter to Bettina which may be accepted as genuine.}⚜--

Vienna, February 10, 1811

Beloved, dear Bettine!

I have already received two letters from you and see from your letters to Toni[3] that you still think of me, and much too favorably.— I carried your first letter around with me all summer and it has often made me overjoyed. Even if I do not write to you often and you never see me, yet I write you a thousand times a thousand letters in my thoughts— I could have imagined how you feel amidst the cosmopolitan rabble in Berlin even if you had not written about it; a lot of chatter about art without deeds!!!!! The best description of it is in Schiller's poem "Die Flüsse," where the Spree speaks[4]— You are to be married, dear Bettine, or have already been, and I have not been able to see you once more before then. May all the happiness with which marriage blesses the married, flow upon you and your husband.— What shall I tell you about myself? "Pity my fate," I cry with Johanna.[5] If I can save a few years for myself for that and all other weal and woe I shall thank Him the all-comprehending and Exalted.— If you write to Goethe about me, pick out all the words which express my deepest reverence and admiration for him. I am about to write to him myself concerning *Egmont* for which I have composed music and, indeed, purely out of love for his poems which make me happy. But who can sufficiently thank a great poet, the most precious jewel of a nation?— And now no more, dear good B. It was 4 o'clock before I got home this morning from a bacchanalian feast at which I had to laugh so much that I shall have to weep correspondingly to-day; boisterous joy often forces me powerfully back in upon myself again.— As to Clemens,[6] many thanks for his kind offer. As to the cantata, the subject is not sufficiently important for us here; it is a different matter in Berlin. As concerns my affection, the sister has monopolized it so much that little will be left for the brother; does that suffice him?— Now farewell dear, dear B, I kiss you sadly upon your forehead and thus impress upon you as with a seal all my thoughts of you.— Write soon, soon, often to your friend

Beethoven

Beethoven lives on the Mölker
Bastei in the Pascolati House.

[2] See Helps and Howard, *op.cit.*, p. 127.
[3] Antonie Brentano.
[4] See *Werke, op.cit.*, I, p. 268.
[5] *Ibid.*, II, p. 808 (*Die Jungfrau von Orleans*, Act V, scene 11).

[6] Clemens Brentano, Bettina's brother, who had written the text of a cantata on the death of Queen Louise of Prussia. (TDR, III, 253, n. *.)

In the Goethe archives in Weimar there is a letter which Beethoven wrote to the poet. It runs as follows:

Vienna, April 12, 1811

Your Excellency!

A friend of mine, who is a great admirer of yours (like myself), is making a hasty departure from here, and this urgent opportunity permits me but a moment of time to thank you for the long time that I have known you (for I have known you since my childhood)— That is so little for so much— Bettine Brentano has assured me that you would receive me in a gracious, even a friendly way. But how could I think of such a reception when I can approach you only with the greatest reverence and with an unutterably deep feeling for your glorious creations!— You will soon receive the music to Egmont through Breitkopf and Härtel; this glorious Egmont which through you I have thought over with the same warmth as when I first read it, and experienced it again by setting it to music.— I would very much like to have your judgement on it; also your criticism would be beneficial to me and my art, and would be accepted as gladly as the highest praise.—

Your Excellency's
Great admirer
Ludwig van Beethoven

Goethe's answer to this letter is worth producing here:

Karlsbad, June 25, 1811

Your friendly letter, very esteemed Sir, was received through Herr von Oliva much to my pleasure. For the kindly feelings which it expresses towards me I am heartily grateful and I can assure you that I honestly reciprocate them, for I have never heard any of your works performed by expert artists or amateurs without wishing that I might sometime have the opportunity to admire you at the pianoforte and find delight in your extraordinary talents. Good Bettina Brentano surely deserves the friendly sympathy which you have extended to her. She speaks rapturously and most affectionately of you and counts the hours spent with you among the happiest of her life.

I shall probably find the music which you have designed for Egmont when I return home and am thankful in advance—for I have heard it praised by several, and plan to perform it in connection with the play mentioned on our stage this winter, when I hope thereby to give myself as well as your numerous admirers in our neighborhood a great treat. But I hope most of all correctly to have understood Herr von Oliva, who has made us hope that in the journey which you are contemplating you will visit Weimar. I hope it will be at a time when the court as well as the entire musical public will be gathered together. I am sure that you would find worthy acceptance of your service and aims. But in this nobody can be more interested than I, who with the wish that all may go well with you, commend myself to your kind thought and thank you most sincerely for all the goodness which you have created in us.

The music to *Egmont* was not published till January, 1812, and Goethe had to wait a long time before he was able to form an opinion concerning it.

This was not Beethoven's fault, however. On October 9, 1811, we find him writing to Breitkopf and Härtel: ". . . Do send the whole score, copied at my expense for aught I care (the score that is), to Goethe. How can a German publisher be so discourteous, so rude to the first of German poets? Therefore, quick with the score to Weimar. . . ." This injunction was not obeyed, and on January 28, 1812, Beethoven made another urgent request:

. . . I therefore beg of you humbly to take care of these letters—and with the letter to Goethe[7] send the Egmont (score) but not in the customary way with here and there a piece wanting, etc., but with everything in perfect order. This cannot be postponed any longer. I have pledged my word and am the more particular to have the pledge redeemed when I can compel somebody else, like you, to do it—ha, ha, ha! You deserve it that I employ such language towards you, towards such a sinner who if I had my way would walk in a hairy shirt of penance for all the wickedness perpetrated upon my works.

Beethoven had had the intention of sending the score of the *Egmont* music to Goethe from the moment he began on it, as appears from a memorandum on the autograph manuscript of the Quartet in E-flat, Op. 74, written in 1809: "Score of Egmont to Goethe at once."

On the 28th of February, 1811, Beethoven sent his friend Mähler an invitation to a concert. Mähler accepted the invitation and received a ticket "extraordinaire," signed "B[r]. de Neuwirth," admitting him free to three midday concerts on Thursdays, February 28, March 14 and 28. Beethoven's elasticity of temperament therefore was doing him good service in enabling him to recover from the disappointment of the preceding year; he was now able not only to find diversion and amusement in society, the theatre and the concertroom, but the spirit of composition was again awakened. In three weeks—March 3rd to the 26th—he produced the glorious B-flat Trio, Op. 97, which had been sketched in 1810.

There were now, or soon to be, in the hands of Breitkopf and Härtel's engravers the Pianoforte Concerto, Op. 73, the Fantasia, Op. 80, the Sonate "Les Adieux," Op. 81a, the Ariettes and Songs, Op. 82 and 83, and the *Christus am Ölberg*. The revision of these works for the press, with the correction of the proofs and his duties to the Archduke, are all the professional labors of Beethoven in these months of which we find any trace. Hence, that high appreciation of his greatness, which induced his admirers and friends even then to attach such value to the most trivial written communications from him as to secure their preservation, now does us excellent service; for—the dates of the Trio excepted—his correspondence furnishes the only materials for the history of the first half of this year. To this we turn.

There is a note, which may be dated about the end of March, apologizing to the Archduke for his absence, on the ground of having been for two weeks

[7] This second letter does not seem to have been preserved. (TDR, III, 255, n. 2.)

again with his "tormenting headache." "During the festivities for the Princess of Baden (March 5-12), and because of the sore finger of Your Imp. Highness," he adds, "I began to work somewhat industriously, of which, among other things, a new Trio for the piano is a fruit." Soon after he writes:

Your Imperial Highness! Since despite all my exertions I could find no copyist who would work at my house, I am sending you my manuscript. You would be most kind just to send to *Schlemmer* for a capable copyist who must however copy the trio only in your palace, as otherwise one is never safe from *theft*. I am improving and in a few days I shall again have the honor to wait upon you for the purpose of making up for lost time—I am always anxiously concerned when I cannot be as zealously and as often as I should wish with Your Imperial Highness. It is surely true when I say that it causes me much suffering, but I am not likely to have so bad an attack again soon— Keep me graciously in your memory. Times will come when I shall show you two and threefold that I am worthy of it.

These professions may well excite a smile; for "it is surely true" when *we* say, that his duties to the Archduke had already become extremely irksome; and that the necessity of sacrificing his previous independence in some small degree to them grew daily more annoying and vexatious; so much so that, in fact, he availed himself of any and every excuse to avoid them. The Archduke made a point of adding a complete collection of Beethoven's music to his library; and the master lent his aid in this both by presenting all his new productions in manuscript and in giving titles of older printed works—gaining thereby a secure depository for his compositions, where they were ever at his service. Thus (May 18) he sends[8] for the Sonata "Das Lebewohl, etc.," "as I haven't it myself and must send the corrections"; some time after for the Scottish songs, "as two numbers, one in my handwriting, have been lost and they must be copied again so that they may be sent away."

Here is the place for a letter to Breitkopf and Härtel:

Vienna, May 6th.

Errors—errors—you yourselves are one large error— I must send my copyist there or else go myself if I do not want my works to appear—as mere errors— It appears as if the musical tribunal at L. is unable to produce a single decent proof reader, besides which you send out the works before you receive the corrections— At least in the case of larger works with various parts you might count the measures— But the Fantasia shows what can happen— You will see that a whole measure is missing in the piano transcription of the overture to Egmont.— Here is the list of errors.[9]

My warmest thanks for setting in motion a matter of such interest to me.— Farewell, I hope for improvement— The fantasy has already gone; the sonata also leaves tomorrow.— Make as many errors as you please, permit as many errors

---

[8] To the Archduke's librarian, Baumeister.

[9] Miss Anderson notes, Vol. I, p. 320, n. 8, that the corrections are on both sides of a separate sheet and include errata for Op. 82, Op. 83 and the *Egmont* Overture.

as you please—you are still highly esteemed by me. This is of course the custom of men, that we esteem them because they have not made still greater errors—

Your most humble servant

Beethoven

A postscript follows concerning a correction in the score of the concerto, Op. 73.

About this time Gottfried Chr. Härtel's wife died, and on May 20th Beethoven wrote him a letter of condolence in which he says: "It appears to me that in view of such a separation which confronts nearly every spouse, one might well be dissuaded from entering this state." The letter ends: "What you say about an opera would surely be desirable; the directors, too, would pay *well* for one; but just now the conditions are really unfavorable. However, if you will write me what the poet demands, I will make inquiry concerning the matter. I have written to Paris for libretti, successful melodramas, comedies, etc. (for I distrust writing an original opera with any of our local poets), which I shall then have adapted— O, poverty of intellect— and pocket!"

In 1808 Emperor Franz had sanctioned the building at Pesth of "an entirely new grand theatre with Ridotto room, casino, restaurant and coffee-house," an enterprise which, notwithstanding the catastrophe of 1809, it was then thought would be completed in 1810.[10] It was time, therefore to consider the programme for its opening performances, and as no living musician could give the occasion so much splendor as Beethoven, it was of high importance that his consent to compose the music should be secured as early as possible. This, through Brunsvik and other Hungarian friends, was no difficult task. Although not completed in 1810, the enterprise was so far advanced that the authorities began their preliminary arrangements for its formal opening on the Emperor's name-day, October 4, 1811, by applying to Heinrich von Collin to write an appropriate drama on some subject drawn from Hungarian history, for the occasion. "The piece was to be associated with a lyrical prologue and a musical epilogue." "The fear that he could not complete the work within the prescribed time and that his labors would be disturbed, compelled Collin to decline the commission with thanks."[11] The order was then given to Kotzebue, who accepted it, and, with characteristic rapidity, responded with the prologue *Ungarns erster Wohltäter* (Hungary's first Benefactor), the drama *Belas Flucht* (Bela's Flight), and the epilogue *Die Ruinen von Athen* (The Ruins of Athens). As Emperor Franz had twice fled from his capital within five years, it is not surprising that "*Bela's Flight* for various reasons cannot be given" and gave place to a local piece, *The Elevation of Pesth into a Royal Free City*. Kotzebue's other two pieces

---

[10] In their efforts in later years to sustain this theatre in brilliant style, the Counts Raday and Brunsvik were ruined. (TDR, III, 157,

n. 1.)

[11] Collin died on June 8, 1811. (TDR, III, 264, n. 5.)

were accepted and sent to Beethoven at the end of July, 1811. In a letter to Breitkopf and Härtel on October 9, 1811 Beethoven reported that the package was delivered during the journey to Teplitz, that he started work three weeks later—about August 20th—and that he sent the music off to Pesth on September 13th. Beethoven's correspondence, then, implies that all this incidental music was completed in less than a month. ---⋙But other ideas, such as the "Marcia alla Turca" which was already used in the Piano Variations, Op. 76, may have originated earlier.[12]⋘---

Hartl had now retired from the direction of the Court Theatres, and Lobkowitz and Palffy were again at the helms respectively of the theatre next to the Kärnthnerthor and that An-der-Wien. Beethoven was busy with dramatic compositions and so, very naturally, the project of another operatic work was revived. He had also obtained a subject that pleased him—a French melodrama *Les Ruines de Babylon*—probably from the Prussian Baron Friedr. Joh. Drieberg. This composer, much more favorably known for his researches into ancient Greek music than for his operas, had been five years in Paris, "where he studied composition under Spontini and probably for a short time also under Cherubini," and now for two years in Vienna.

A series of notes from Beethoven to Drieberg, Treitschke and Count Palffy, written in June and July, 1811, show how the operatic project was shaping itself in his mind. On June 6, he was anxious to know if Treitschke had read the book, and wished to re-read it himself before Treitschke began work on it. He expressed dismay to Palffy on June 11, because he had heard that a performance of the melodrama *Les Ruines de Babilone* was projected for the benefit of an actor, Scholz. He set forth how much more desirable it would be to have this work given as an opera, a "work of lasting value." "It is so difficult to find a good libretto for an opera; I have rejected no less than twelve or more in the last several weeks." Beethoven said that he had told the Archduke about the subject and had even written to foreign newspapers of his intention to set it to music. He hoped the Count would forbid the intended performance. Palffy evidently co-operated, for on July 3rd the composer again wrote to Treitschke that he had received a translation "along with Palffy's instructions to arrange everything that is necessary with you. There is nothing now to prevent your keeping your promise to me. But I am again asking you if you really are going to keep it, so that I may know where I stand in the matter—" There the matter seems to have rested, though as will be seen Beethoven was still thinking about an opera text at Teplitz in September.

"It is said," writes the correspondent of the *Allg. Mus. Zeit.*, under date January 8, "that Beethoven may next Spring undertake a journey to southern skies for the purpose of restoring his health, which has suffered severely during the last few years." One effect of his maladies was to produce long-

---

[12] See Nottebohm, *II Beeth.*, pp. 138-45.

continued pains in the head, and it was finally thought best by his physician, Malfatti, to abandon the journey and try the waters of Teplitz. This Beethoven decided to do and to take with him as friend and companion young Oliva. Evidently he had also made plans with Count Brunsvik, as on June 18 he thanked him for agreeing to make the journey with him, and told him that on the advice of his physician he must spend two whole months at Teplitz, wherefore he would not be able to accompany the Count further. He adds: "I pray you so to arrange your affairs as to be here [i.e., Vienna] at the latest by July 1 or 2, as otherwise it will be too late for me; and my doctor is already grumbling that I am waiting so long, although he himself says that the companionship of such a dear good friend would benefit me."

In another letter to the Count he says:

Dear Friend, I cannot accept your refusal; I have let Oliva go away alone and indeed on your account. I must have someone I can trust with me if everyday life is not to become burdensome. I shall expect you by the 12th of this month or it could be the 15th, but then without fail. This is a command from the Most High. This may not be scoffed at without heavy punishment and revenge, rather it is to be obeyed unconditionally— Therefore farewell, dear trusted friend to whom we ask God to give his gracious care. Given in the morning just after rising from the coffee table.

Beethoven

Vienna, July 4th

As I do not know how you came to have the *portrait*,[13] it would be best if you were to bring it with you; no doubt a sympathetic artist will be found who will copy it for friendship's sake.

The remaining details concerning the return trip will be settled soon.

We expect with the speed of lightning six times over only one answer to our command from the Most High Yes, Yes, Yes! quick ÷ otherwise my anger will come all the way to Ofen.

Brunsvik, however, was unable to make the trip with him, although Beethoven remained in Vienna until the end of July. His letter to Breitkopf and Härtel of August 23rd was written three weeks after his arrival in Teplitz; thus he didn't reach the watering place until August 2nd. He used the time up to the end of July to work for Thomson.

In a letter of July 20 to Thomson he announced completion of the Scottish songs (Beethoven used "Scottish" to describe Irish, Scottish and Welsh songs) and complained that because the three copies of the 53 songs which he had previously sent to Thomson had not been received, he had been obliged practically to rewrite them from his sketches—which may have been a somewhat exaggerated statement of the facts.[14] In it, furthermore, he

---

[13] According to Frimmel, this may refer either to an engraving which was made of Beethoven's portrait around 1800, or the oil-painting made for the Brunsvik family. See

Beethoven, Sämtliche Briefe (Kalischer-Frimmel, 1910), II, p. 27.
[14] See KHV, p. 634.

says: "Your offer of 100 ducats in gold for the three sonatas is accepted for your sake and I am also willing to compose three quintets for 100 gold ducats; but for the dozen songs with the text in English my price is 60 ducats in gold (for four songs the price is 25 ducats). For the cantata on 'The Battle of the Baltic Sea'[15] I ask 50 ducats; but on condition that the original text contains no invectives against the Danes, otherwise I cannot undertake it. . . . I will not fail to send you the arrangements of my symphonies in a very short time, and will gladly undertake the composition of an oratorio if the words be noble and distinguished and the honorarium of 600 ducats in gold be agreeable to you."[16]

---≈{Beethoven arrived in Teplitz at the beginning of August and stayed at the "Harfe" in the Badgasse.[17]}≈--- For the first three weeks he was concerned with his cure, plus the correction of proofs, as appears from a letter, dated August 23, to Breitkopf and Härtel:

. . . I have undertaken the revision of the oratorio and the songs and in a few days you will receive both— Here and there the text must remain as in the original. I know that the text is extremely bad, but after one has conceived a complete work even from a bad text, it is difficult to avoid spoiling it by individual changes. And if now there is a single word upon which great stress is laid many times over, it must remain so. And he is a bad composer who does not try or know how to make the best possible thing out of a bad text; and if this is the case a few changes will certainly not improve the whole.— I have left some, since they are really changes for the better—

Farewell and let me hear something from you soon. Oliva is here—and should be writing to you. The favorable reception of Mozart's "Don Juan" rejoices me as much as if it were my own work. Although I know plenty of unprejudiced Italians who render justice to the Germans, the backwardness and the easy-going disposition of the Italian musicians are no doubt responsible for the same deficiencies concerning this in the nation as a whole. But I have become acquainted with many Italian amateurs who preferred our music to their Paisello (I have been more just to him than his own countrymen) etc.

Varnhagen von Ense, then a young man of 25 years and lieutenant in the Austrian service, came from Prague to Teplitz this summer to pass a few weeks with "the goddess of his heart's most dear delight," Rahel Levin. Varnhagen's memoirs offer a series of lively descriptions of the society of that time, especially of the activities in the circle which he, as a young man wanting to make his way in the world, naturally sought out, and which Beethoven with equal zeal avoided. In his *Denkwürdigkeiten*[18] we meet first Beethoven as a solitary rambler in the Schlossgarten at Teplitz, whither, as

---

[15] A poem by Thomas Campbell on the destruction of the Danish fleet on April 2, 1801. (TDR, III, 596, n. 1.)

[16] This letter in French with Beethoven's autograph signature is preserved in the British Museum.

[17] See Frimmel, "Beethovens Aufenhalt in böhmischen Bädern," *Beethoven-Forschung*, x (1925), pp. 37ff.

[18] 1837, ii, p. 345. (TDR, III, 273, n. 1.) In a later edition by J. Kühn (Berlin, 1925), ii, p. 117.

Brunsvik could or would not accompany him, he had journeyed alone.

Let Varnhagen speak for himself: "Kapellmeister Himmel, that dissolute eccentric, whose life was almost completely spent alternating between comfortable champagne drinks and comfortless periods of abstinence, let us hear him play the pianoforte in the Goltz house and at Clary's,[19] also later in a concert and in such a way that even today would still not be eclipsed according to the judgement of connoisseurs, despite the great recent progress in this artistic skill. . . . Yet at the same time I became acquainted with a musician who in my opinion put this one completely in the shade. It was Beethoven, whose presence we had long known about, but no one had yet seen. His deafness made him shy and his peculiarities, which had become more marked through separation from other people, limited the little circulating that he did, and aggravated the difficulty that one had of running into him. However, on some of his lonely rambles in the castle park he had seen Rahel, and her facial expression, which reminded him of another's whom he esteemed, gave him pleasure. A kind young man, named Oliva, who accompanied him as a true friend, arranged the acquaintance easily. The thing that Beethoven stubbornly resisted despite the most urgent pleas, which in one terrible case took the form of a Prince in Vienna wishing to use force to make him play for his guests, by which he would not be bullied; this very thing he was now willing to do and in abundance; he sat down at the piano and he played his newest, still unknown things or indulged in free fantasy. I found the man in him even more appealing than the artist. And when a close friendship between Oliva and me developed soon thereafter, I was also together with Beethoven daily and gained a still closer relationship with him through the prospect, to which he clung eagerly, that I could supply or revise texts for him for dramatic composition. It is known that Beethoven was violently anti-French and pro-German, and this is another thing that we had in common."

This report is amplified by a letter from Varnhagen to his regiment commander Count Bentheim[20] on September 4, 1811 from Teplitz: "I have made Beethoven's acquaintance. The unruly man was very friendly and gentle towards me, said many excellent things and will gladly play for Robert [Rahel Levin] some afternoon, only it is supposed to be kept secret. The strange man lives completely in his art, is very industrious, and is unconcerned about other people. You can be all the more assured by the fact that he greets you with true friendliness and wishes keenly to be excused for his forgetfulness of the moment, but such things probably happen more often with him [than with other people]. He is composing an opera for the Buda

---

[19] Varnhagen's friends; Count August Friedrich Ferdinand Goltz, Prussian minister, and Prince Karl Joseph Clary, who had literary inclinations.

[20] Count Friedrich Wilhelm Bentheim

(1782-1834). Through the bravery he exhibited and the wounds he sustained at the battles of Aspern and Wagram he was awarded the Order of Maria Theresa and in 1818 was made a Prince.

theatre for which Kotzebue has written the text. Because of Robert I am twice as well acquainted with him and cherish it three times as much."

In another passage from the *Denkwürdigkeiten*, Varnhagen speaks warmly of two other Francophobes, Fichte and Friedr. Aug. Wolf, then adds: "The poet Tiedge, who came with the Countess von der Recke was in political agreement with our zealous associates, as was the Countess herself, while we did not approve of both's aesthetic views." And further on he tells that one day Tiedge made "a powerful statement about Napoleon to Beethoven and me: 'You cannot see the man at all on account of the success that stands in front of him!'" Beethoven also had friendly relations with Tiedge and the Countess von der Recke.

Another visitor at Teplitz was Prince Kinsky; and this gave the composer an opportunity to obtain the arrears of his annuity. On the still existing envelope of the contract of 1809 is written: "Money drawn from Kinsky last August."

Also visiting Teplitz was Amalie Sebald, who had come with Countess von der Recke from Berlin, a member of a family who for years had furnished members to Fasch's Singakademie, where she had appeared as a solo singer. She was said to have a "fascinatingly lovely singing voice." Among the friends of Carl Maria von Weber when he was in Berlin in 1812, were Amalie and her sister Auguste, also "highly musical" and a singer. For the former, Weber conceived a warm and deep affection; and now Beethoven was taken an unresisting captive by her charms. An album once owned by Amalie Sebald contains this inscription:

> Ludwig van Beethoven
> Den Sie, wenn Sie auch wollten,
> Doch nicht vergessen sollten.
>
> Teplitz, August 8, 1811.

The couplet might be rudely translated:

> Whom, even if you would
> Forget, you never should.

According to Frimmel,[21] who had seen the autograph, the year 1811 was written in Beethoven's hand, but changed to 1812 in Amalie's hand. He suggests that most likely Amalie had forgotten the right year in the course of time. It is certain that on August 8, 1812 Beethoven was not in Teplitz but in Franzensbad. She is mentioned, the reader will note how familiarly—in this letter to Tiedge, dated Teplitz, September 6, 1811:

Every day the following letter to you, you, you has floated in my mind; I wanted only two words at parting, but not a single word did I receive. The Countess sends a feminine handgrasp; that at least is something to talk about and for it I kiss her hands in my thoughts; but the poet is dumb. Concerning *Amalie*, I know at least that she is alive. Every day I give myself a drubbing for

[21] *FRBH*, II, p. 172.

not having made your acquaintance earlier in Teplitz. It is abominable to know the good for a short time and at once to lose it again. Nothing is more insufferable than to be obliged to reproach one's self with one's own mistakes. I tell you that I shall probably be obliged to stay here until the end of this month. Write me how long you will stay in Dresden. I may feel disposed to take a jump to the Saxon capital. On the day that you went away from here I received a letter from my gracious musically inclined Archduke, that he will not remain long in Moravia and has left it for me to say whether or not I will come. This I interpreted to the best of my wishes and desires and so you see me still within these walls where I sinned so deeply against you and myself. But I comfort myself with the thought that if you call it a sin I am at least a downright sinner and not a poor one. . . . Now fare as well as poor humanity may; to the Countess a right tender yet reverential handgrasp, to Amalie an ardent kiss when no one sees us. And we two embrace each other like men who are permitted to love and honor each other. I expect at least one word without reserve, and I am man enough for this.

The desire here expressed to visit his new friends in Dresden could not be gratified, owing to the necessity of completing and forwarding the music composed for the opening of the Pesth theatre.

"Near the middle of September," continues Varnhagen,[22] "Rahel traveled to Dresden where Marwitz[23] was expecting her and thereupon back to Berlin. I accompanied her as far as Mariaschein. The parting broke my heart, only the confident hope that this was all leading to a lasting reunion gave me the courage to endure the separation. The sympathy of good Oliva and the honest Beethoven helped me over the next days, then my time was also up and I returned to my regiment in Prague." Varnhagen records that he received a letter from Rahel on September 16th which ended, "Greet Beethoven of course and our beloved Oliva! God preserve him!" On September 18th, Varnhagen wrote to Rahel from Prague: "Only Oliva could I endure about me for any length of time; he was sympathetic, but deeply depressed because of violent altercations which he had had with Beethoven."

From the source of these communications we also learn that Varnhagen was expected to adapt an opera text for Beethoven and to revise and improve another. In the same letter of September 18, Varnhagen wrote to Rahel as follows on the subject: "I may translate a French piece as an opera for Beethoven; the other text might be written later, but this contains the entire scenic arrangement. It is entitled 'Giafar' and might bring me from 8 to 10 ducats. Oliva leaves in a few days for Vienna—he greets you heartily. Beethoven still attaches himself very much to me. . . ." But all too soon the plan for the opera faltered. On October 24th Varnhagen writes: "Of Beethoven and Oliva I hear and see nothing; the latter must have been unable to make anything out of the opera which I was to make from a French melodrama and which, unfortunately, another had begun."

[22] *Denkwürdigkeiten*, II², p. 350; 1925 edition, II, p. 121.

[23] Alexander von der Marwitz was a young and close friend of Rahel's.

A remark made by Beethoven to his friend, Kajetan Giannatasio del Rio on September 12, 1816, refers to this period and should be here considered. Kajetan's daughter Fanny records in her diary: "My father thought that B. could rescue himself from his unfortunate domestic conditions only by marriage, did he know anybody etc. Now our long foreboding was confirmed: 'He was unhappy in love! Five years ago he had made the acquaintance of a person, a union with whom he would have considered the greatest happiness of his life. It was not to be thought of, almost an impossibility, a chimera—nevertheless it is now as on the first day.'"

Thayer believed this reference was to Amalie Sebald. The evidence for her is obvious: the note written for her on August 8th and the open allusion "to Amalie an ardent kiss" in Beethoven's letter to Tiedge on September 6th. Yet this same letter by its very content and tone also offers negative evidence. It is in the form of an apology for not having seen more of Tiedge, Countess von der Recke and Amalie Sebald during the last part of their stay. In a double letter to Tiedge and the Countess in October, Beethoven complains of "having missed the best meetings with you on account of the mustachioed Hungarians," referring of course to the music for the opening of the Pesth theatre.

Was composing the only distraction that kept him from seeing his new friends? From a study of Rahel Levin, who became Varnhagen's wife in 1814, Kaznelson[24] has advanced the theory that she was the lady to whom Beethoven was referring in 1816, that it was just at this time that Beethoven was preoccupied with this affair, and that therefore it was more than just composing that kept him from seeing these other new friends before they left. This thesis, which is impossible of proof, is ingeniously developed, against the background of the strained relations that summer between Rahel and Varnhagen, by interpreting what was said and what was left unsaid in the communications both then and later of all who were connected with this circle of friends in such a way as to support this argument.

Judged as a chimerical affair, it should be noted that with Rahel's departure from Teplitz in 1811, all known communication with the composer was at an end, whereas Beethoven saw Amalie again at Teplitz in the summer of 1812. The reader will be able to judge from the tone of the short letters written by Beethoven to the latter at this later time whether this was a growing friendship or the continuation of a deep love.

From the Teplitz guest list, Kaznelson has established that Beethoven did not leave Teplitz for Prague until September 18th, two days after Oliva and Varnhagen had left.[25] From Varnhagen's correspondence with Rahel[26]

[24] Siegmund Kaznelson, *Beethovens ferne und unsterbliche Geliebte* (Zurich, 1954), p. 111.

[25] *Op.cit.*, p. 80. Varnhagen in his *Denkwürdigkeiten* must have had a lapse of memory when he states that Beethoven and Oliva left together.

[26] *Briefwechsel zwischen Varnhagen und Rahel* (Leipzig, 1874), II, p. 154. (TDR, III, 283.)

we learn that Oliva went on to Vienna on September 23, without Beethoven, who made a rather wide detour to visit Lichnowsky. Of this visit we learn in one of Jahn's notices, namely: "In the year 1811. B. was at Prince Lichnowsky's on his estate Grätz near Troppau. The Mass in C was performed at Troppau, for which everything possible was drummed up. The master of athletics was put at the tympani; in the Sanctus Beethoven himself had to show him how to play the solo. The rehearsals lasted three days. After the performance Beethoven improvised on the organ for half an hour to the astonishment of everyone. Fuchs was the soprano soloist."

Beethoven returned to Vienna refreshed and invigorated both in body and mind. A letter written from Vienna to Breitkopf and Härtel on October 9, 1811, has so large an interest on many accounts as to merit inclusion:

From here a thousand excuses and a thousand thanks for your pleasant invitation to Leipzig; I was very sorry not to be able to follow my inclination to go there and to surrounding places. But this time there has been work in every direction. The Hungarian Diet is in session; there is already talk that the Archduke is to become Primate of Hungary and abandon the Bishopric of Olmütz. I have offered to His Imperial Highness, who as Primate of Hungary would have an income of not less than three million, to go through a clean million on my own account (and on account, it is understood, of all the good musical spirits that I would therewith set into action on my behalf). In Teplitz I received no further news, as nothing was known of my purpose to leave the place. I thought concerning the journey which I was contemplating that in view of my attachment for him I must yield (though not willingly), the more since I might be needed at the festivities. Therefore, having chosen the pro, quick to Vienna, where the first thunderous proclamation that I heard was that my gracious lord had given up all thoughts of priesthood and priestly activities and nothing is to come of the whole business.—

It is said that soon he is to become a general (an easy thing to understand, you know) and I am to be Quartermaster-General in the battle which I do not intend to lose—what do you say to that? The Hungarians provided me with another incident; in stepping into my carriage to go to Teplitz, I received a parcel from Ofen [Buda] with the request to compose something for the opening of the new theatre at Pesth. Feeling fairly well after spending three weeks in Teplitz, I sat down, in defiance of my doctor's orders, to help the Mustachios, who are heartily well disposed towards me; and sent my packet thither on September 13, under the impression that the performance was to come off on October 1st, whereas the matter is put off for a whole month. Through a misunderstanding I did not receive the letter in which this was told me until after my arrival here, and yet this theatrical incident also decided me to return to Vienna.— Meanwhile, postponed is not abandoned. I have tasted of travel, it has done me great good, and now already I should like to go away again— I have just received the Lebewohl, etc. I see that after all you have given French titles to other copies. Why? "Lebewohl" is surely something very different from "Les Adieux." The former we say heartily to a single person, the latter to whole gatherings, whole cities— Since you permit me to be criticized so shamefully you must submit to the same treatment. You would also have needed fewer plates, and the turning of pages, which has now been made very difficult, would have been easier. With this, basta— But how in the name of heaven did you come to dedicate my Fantasia with Orchestra to the King of Bavaria? Do answer me that at once. If you are thereby going to procure me an honorable gift, I will thank you, otherwise this is not at all agreeable to me. Did you, possibly, dedicate it yourself? What is the connection? One is not permitted to dedicate things to kings without requesting it.— Besides, there was no dedication of the Lebewohl to the Archduke; and why were not the year, day and date printed as I wrote them? In the future you must agree in writing to retain all superscriptions unchanged as I have written them. Let whomsoever you please review the oratorio and everything else. I am sorry that I ever said a word about those miserable r[eviews]. Who can mind what such r[eviewers] say when he sees how the most wretched scribblers are elevated by them and how they treat most insultingly works of art to which they cannot at once apply their standard as the shoemaker does his last, as indeed they must do because of their unfitness— If there is anything to be considered in connection with the oratorio it is that it was my first work in this form, and an early work, and was composed in fourteen days amidst all possible tumult and other unpleasant, alarming circumstances (my brother was mortally ill).

Rochlitz, if I am not mistaken, spoke unfavorably concerning the chorus of disciples "Wir haben ihn gesehen" in C major even before it had been given to you for publication; he called it comic, an impression which here at least was not experienced by the local public, and amongst my friends there are also critics. That I should write a very different oratorio now, than then, is certain— And now criticize as long as you please, I wish you much pleasure; and if it should hurt a little like the sting of a gnat it will soon be over; and when the engraving is over, then it becomes a complete joke. Cri-cri-cri-cri-cri-ti-ti-si-si-si-si-size-size-size—*you cannot keep this up forever.* Therefore, God be with you. . . .

--»§{This is a play on the word "stich" which can mean "engraving" or "sting."}§«--

Something of his old frolicsome humor again enlivened his notes to Zmeskall: He expected him to dine with him at the Schwan; he begged for more quills, and promised shortly a whole parcel of them, so that Zmeskall "will not have to pull out his own"; he might receive "the great decoration of the Order of the 'Cello"; and so on. Beethoven's notes to Zmeskall are a barometer that indicates very correctly the rising and sinking of his spirits; they were now high—at composition point—and, as the Archduke did not return from Pressburg until the 7th November, he had at least one month for continuing without hindrance the studies that followed the completion of the music for Pesth.

--»§{According to Unger,[27] the last 130 pages of the Petter sketchbook are to be dated from the middle of 1811 to well into the following year. Thayer believed that most of them were to be dated 1809. The importance in the redating of these sketches is in the establishment of 1811 as the year in

[27] *NBJ*, v (1933), p. 45.

which work started on the seventh and eighth symphonies, and even early attempts at what was to become the choral section of the Ninth Symphony. Thayer's summary of these pages follows:

Passing to the middle of page 22, one comes upon this:

With few interruptions, such as a theme for a "symphony without drums," "good triplets of another sort," the Allegretto and Finale of the Seventh Symphony are the subject of the studies for more than forty pages. That modest gem—the theme of the Allegretto—is still the same throughout; but how astonishing the number and variety of forms for its setting, that were tested, before the majestic, the sublime simplicity was attained, which satisfied the exquisite taste of its creator!

On page 71 begin the sketches for the first, on page 83, for the last movement of the Eighth Symphony. Scattered along this part of the sketchbook are divers subjects for pianoforte works; as if Beethoven had in mind a companion piece to the E-flat Concerto for the further display of his powers. In our notes we find, "Overture Concerto," p. 73; p. 83 "Concerto in G"— "Concerto in G or E minor"—"Adagio in E-flat"—"Polonaise for Pianoforte alone." Immediately following the "Polonaise" we read: "Freude schöner Götter Funken Tochter. Work out the overture." Again on leaf 43: "Freude schöner Götter Funken Tochter aus Elysium. Detached fragments, like princes are beggars, etc., not the whole." On the same page again: "Detached fragments from Schiller's Freude brought together in a whole." One of the sketches (according to our copy) begins thus:

Freu - - de, schö - - ner Göt - - ter fun - - ken, Toch - - ter

At one point in the sketches Beethoven notes: "Sinfonia in D moll 3te sinf." (Nottebohm, *II Beeth.*, p. 111); thus it is not out of the question that at this time Beethoven had a work in mind somewhat similar to the later Ninth Symphony, but of only one movement to which the choral idea was attached. In a letter received by Breitkopf and Härtel on June 1, 1812, Beethoven writes: "I am writing three [!] new symphonies of which one is already completed."

Since the "Egmont" Overture and the "Pastoral Symphony," produced by Schuppanzigh in May, and the "Coriolan" Overture at a charity concert on July 14, there is but one notice of the performance of any one of Beethoven's greater compositions, and even this (November 15) is very doubtful. In truth, this was no season for grand musical entertainments with a view to private emolument. The *Finanz-Patent* of February shed its baleful influence on the just and the unjust and compelled all classes alike to study and practice economy. Even the old favorite of the Vienna public, Franz Clement, returning from a musical tour in Russia "had few hearers"; and so it was with Sebastian Mayer, "although Handel's *Acis and Galatea* was performed" in his annual *Akademie*. Two or three virtuosi were able to fill small halls; but no performances on a grand scale were ventured, except for charities; at these the wealthy appeared in force, it being a pleasant and fashionable method of doing something to alleviate the general distress.

⟶⟩⟨In two notes to the Archduke and one to Zmeskall, all written in the fall,[28] Beethoven referred to the rehearsing of symphonies and overtures which were clearly for a concert for His Imperial Highness. The only clue as to what was performed is negative and comes from reference to the need of four horns for the overtures, which eliminates only the overture to *Prometheus*, and but two horns for the symphonies, which eliminates only the "Eroica."⟩⟨⟵

There were other visitors at Teplitz, not mentioned by Varnhagen, with whom Beethoven formed relations more or less cordial. One was the Royal Imperial Gubernialrath and Steyermärkischer Kammerprokurator Ritter von Varena of Graz. Along with Professor Julius Schneller, he was in charge of the arrangements in Graz to bring determined support to the charitable institutions for the poor which were in dire need and distress from the Finance Patent. Beethoven's "Pastoral" Symphony had been performed already on July 25, 1811, as the main number in an *Akademie* in honor of Schneller, and the effect that it made caused its repetition in Schneller's concert for charitable institutions on September 8. The latter concert made over 1630 florins for the benefit of the hostels and hospitals of the Elizabethan nuns.

Varena's acquaintance with Beethoven gained significance in connection with the next concert for charitable institutions of December 22, 1811, since Beethoven presented to him the scores of several short works that had been recently published. Among these was the Choral Fantasy for which Beethoven recommended as pianist, Marie Koschak, a young lady of whom he had heard from Professor Schneller.[29] She scored a great triumph, which was almost frustrated by a malicious trick, namely the removal of the hammers which sound the chord of C major from the piano, presumably after the last rehearsal.[30] The concert made over 5000 florins. A very interesting series of letters to Varena concerning works to be performed at these and other charity concerts at Graz began at this point before the Graz benefit concert of December 22 and continued during the next two years.

[28] See *A* 330, 331 and 332.

[29] Marie Leopoldine Koschak (1794-1855) was born in Graz and in 1816 married Dr. Karl Pachler. The following year she met Beethoven for the first time.

[30] F. Pachler, *Beethoven und M. Pachler-Koschak* (Berlin, 1866), p. 10. (TDR, III, 278.)

The completed compositions of this year were:

Trio in B-flat major, Op. 97.

Music to the *Ruinen von Athen*, Epilogue by A. von Kotzebue, Op. 113.

Music to *König Stephan, Ungarns erster Wohlthäter*, a Prologue by A. von Kotzebue, Op. 117.

Song by Stoll, "An die Geliebte," WoO 140. Two versions both dated December.

The list of publications is as follows:

By Breitkopf and Härtel:

Christus am Ölberg (F. X. Huber), Op. 85, in score.

Concerto No. 5 for Pianoforte in E-flat major, Op. 73,[31] dedicated to Archduke Rudolph.

Fantasia for Pianoforte, Orchestra and Chorus, Op. 80,[32] dedicated to Maximilian Joseph, King of Bavaria.

Four Ariettas and a Duet (Metastasio, text for the first arietta unknown), Op. 82.

Sonata for Pianoforte, Op. 81a, dedicated to Archduke Rudolph, a) with German titles: "Lebewohl, Abwesenheit und Widersehn ... 81sts Werk"; and with French titles: "Les Adieux, l'Absence et le Retour . . . Oeuv. 81."[33]

Three Songs (Goethe), Op. 83, dedicated to Princess Caroline Kinsky:

"Wonne der Wehmut" ("Trocknet nicht").

"Sehnsucht" ("Was zient mir das Herz so?").

"Mit einem gemalten Band" ("Kleine Blumen, kleine Blätter").

---

[31] Published first in 1810 by Clementi as Op. 64.

[32] Published first in 1810 by Clementi as Op. 65.

[33] Simrock published the sextet in 1810 as Op. 81, and the distinction of 81a for the sonata and 81b for the sextet was apparently first established by Breitkopf and Härtel in their thematic catalogue of 1851.

CHAPTER XXV

THE YEAR 1812

THE AUSTRIAN FINANZ-PATENT—SECOND
SOJOURN AT TEPLITZ—LETTERS
TO THE IMMORTAL BELOVED

AS A RESULT of the war, the Austrian economy was severely strained, and the value of the currency steadily decreased. The depreciation of a national currency to null and its subsequent repudiation by the Government that emitted it is, in effect, a domestic forced loan equal in amount to the sum issued; and the more gradual its depreciation, so much more likely is the public burden to be general and in some degree equalized. Such a forced loan was the "Continental Currency" issued by the American Congress to sustain the war against England in 1775-1783; and such were the French "Assignats" a few years later; and such now, to the amount of 80 *per centum* of all the paper in circulation, was the substitution of notes of redemption for the bank-notes at the rate of one for five. This was done by the Austrian *Finanz-Patent*, promulgated February 20th, and put in force March 15, 1811.

The Government assumed that every contract of pecuniary obligation between Austrian subjects, wherein special payment or its equivalent was not stipulated, was payable in bank-notes; and that the real indebtedness under any such contract was in justice and equity to be determined and measured by the value in silver of the bank-notes at the date of the instrument. This second proposition is fallacious and deceptive, because such contracts rested upon the necessary presumptions that the faith and honor of the supreme authority were pledged to the future redemption of its paper at par and that the pledge would be redeemed. But this was not seen or was not regarded. Consequently, there was annexed to the *Finanz-Patent* a table showing decimally the average equivalent of the silver florin (*Convention Münze*) in bank-notes, month by month, from January, 1799 to March, 1811. This table was made a "Scala über den Cours der Bancozettel nach welchem die Zahlungen zufolge des Paragraphs 13 und 14 des Patents vom 20 Hornung, 1811, zu leister sind." ("Scale of the rate of exchange according to which payments are to be made in accordance with paragraphs 13 and 14 of the Patent of February 20, 1811.") We copy two of the months as examples:

	1799	1800	1801	1802	1803	1804	1805	1806	1807	1808	1809	1810	1811
Jan.	1.03	1.13	1.16	1.19	1.30	1.34	1.33	1.47	1.90	2.04	2.21	4.69	5.00
Feb.	1.05	1.14	1.14	1.18	1.27	1.34	1.29	1.49	2.06	2.10	2.48	3.31	5.00

Beethoven's annuity contract bore date March 1, 1809, when one florin in silver was equal to two and forty-eight hundredths in bank-notes. Hence his 4000 shrank to 1617%0 in the new paper money (*Wiener Währung*); but *this* paper money was intended to be, and for some time was, equal to silver. More than this he could not *legally* demand; but the original reasons for the contract, the intentions of the donors and the mutual understanding of the parties gave him a perfect claim *in equity* for the full amount of 4000 florins in notes of redemption. Nor did the princes hesitate to admit its justice. They were men of honor and this was a debt of honor. Archduke Rudolph immediately gave the necessary order and instructions in writing; and Beethoven's anxiety because the others had not yet given him the same security was justified, although he might have expressed it rather more delicately.

Lobkowitz's payments were suspended in September, 1811, for nearly four years, his assumption of the management of the theatres having thrown his financial affairs into disorder and caused the sequestration of his estates.

After the payment for a year and a quarter which Beethoven received from Kinsky on July 31, 1810, the Prince continued to pay 450 florins regularly every quarter, but on July 26, 1811 (from March to May) with the memorandum: "450 bank-notes, or 90 florins of redemption," and again the same on August 30, 1811 (for June-August);—i.e. one fifth of the stipulated sum. Thus Kinsky's annual share of 1800 florins would have been reduced to 360 florins of redemption. It was not until the Court Decree of September 13, 1811, that the more favorable rate of the above table was established. It is to be assumed that the payments thereafter were made in accordance with the scale, thus the 1800 florins would equal 726 florins in the new currency; but the receipts have not been preserved. On June 3, 1812, Oliva asked Varnhagen on behalf of Beethoven to deliver a letter to Prince Kinsky and seek to persuade the prince to come to a decision in the matter of paying the *full* amount of the annuity contract in notes of redemption. The results of this visit are given in Varnhagen's letter to Oliva:

Yesterday I had an exhaustive talk with Prince v. Kinsky. Accompanied by expressions of highest praise for Beethoven, he complied at once with his request and from now on he will send him notes of redemption and will pay the arrears and the future sums in this currency. The cashier here will receive the necessary instructions and Beethoven can collect everything here when he passes through, or if he prefers in Vienna as soon as the prince shall have returned.

Prague, June 9, 1812

But unfortunately this was not carried out. On the 2nd or 3rd of November, Kinsky, while riding at Weldus near Prague, was—by the breaking of his saddle-girth—thrown from his horse with such force as to crack his skull, and survived but ten hours. Beethoven's attempts to "collect everything" after the Prince's death must await discussion until the next chapter.

The opening of the new theatre in Pesth not having taken place in October as proposed, was deferred to Sunday, February 9th, that it might bear the character of a festivity in honor of the Emperor's birthday (February 12th). The performances were repeated on the 10th and 11th to crowded audiences which received Beethoven's music to *König Stephan* and *Die Ruinen von Athen* (reported to be "very original, excellent and worthy of its master") with clamorous applause. Beethoven had been so favorably impressed with Kotzebue's texts that in January, 1812, he applied to him for an opera text:

Vienna, January 28, 1812

Highly respected, highly honored Sir:

While writing music for the Hungarians to your prologue and epilogue, I could not refrain from the lively wish to possess an opera from your unique talent, romantic, serious, heroico-comic or sentimental, as you please; in short, anything to your liking I would accept with pleasure. True, I should prefer a big subject from history and particularly one from the darker periods, Attila, etc., for instance; but I should accept with thanks anything and any subject coming from you, from your poetical spirit, which I could translate into my musical spirit.

Prince Lobkowitz, who sends his greetings, and who now has the sole direction of the opera, will certainly grant you an honorarium commensurate with your deserts. Do not refuse my request; you will find that I shall always be deeply grateful for your compliance. Awaiting your favorable and speedy answer, I subscribe myself

Your admirer

Ludwig van Beethoven

This letter was sent to Breitkopf and Härtel together with one to Goethe (unfortunately lost) with the following request that the two be forwarded to their destinations:

Vienna, January 28, 1812

P.P.

As a punishment for your absolute silence I charge you with the immediate delivery of these two letters. A windbag of a Livonian promised to look after the letter to K for me, but probably, the Livonians like the Russians being windbags and braggarts, he did nothing of the sort, although he made himself out to be a great friend of his— So I ask this, although I could rightly inflict it as a punishment for all the faulty editions, false titles, negligence and so forth. . . . If the three songs by Goethe[1] are not yet printed hurry with them; I should like soon to present them to Princess Kinsky, one of the handsomest and stoutest women in Vienna— And the songs from Egmont, why are they not yet out, really, why is not the whole of E out, out, out?— Do you perhaps want a close tacked on here and there to the entreactes, this I can do too. Or let it be done by a Leipzig proof reader of the Musik-Zeitung, who cannot make head nor tail out of it— Please charge the postage to me— It seems to me, I hear a whisper, that you are looking out for a new wife. To this I ascribe all the confusion mentioned above. I wish you a Xanthippe like the wife of the holy Greek Socrates, so that I might see a German publisher embarrassed, which is saying a great deal, yes, in real embarrassment.[2] I hope soon to be honored with a few lines from you.

Your friend

Beethoven

Walter Scott somewhere remarks: "It is seldom that the same circle of personages, who have surrounded an individual at his first outset in life, continue to have an interest in his career till his fate comes to a crisis. On the contrary, and more especially if the events of his life be of a varied character and worth communicating to others, or to the world, the hero's later connections are usually totally separated from those with whom he began the voyage, but whom the individual has outsailed, or who have drifted astray, or foundered on the passage."

A few years more and this will begin to be very true of Beethoven. The old familiar names will rapidly disappear and new ones take their places; some half a dozen perhaps will remain to the end. But this is not yet. The old friends, Lichnowsky, Razumovsky, Erdödy and that class, Streicher, Zizius, Breuning and their class, are his friends still. We see less of them, because Beethoven is no longer the great pianist performing in the salons of the nobles, or playing his new compositions in the lodgings of his untitled admirers. His astonishing playing in the concert of December, 1808—which completed full thirty years since his appearance in Cologne as a prodigy— proved to be, as it happened, the splendid close of his career as a piano virtuoso.

There are certainly instances of Beethoven's having performed in public in a somewhat minor way after 1808; a record of his performing privately is found in the reminiscences of Friedrich Starke,[3] a musician who, according to Schilling's *Encyclopedia*, learned "to play professionally all string and wind instruments." He had traveled extensively and had heard Mozart play; he studied theory with Albrechtsberger, and for a while was Imperial Regimental Kapellmeister. Later he taught Beethoven's nephew piano and through his association with the composer gained the post of horn-player in the court opera. The following account was written by Ludwig Nohl.[4]

[1] Op. 83. (TDR, III, 300, n. 1.) They were in fact published in October, 1811.

[2] One of Beethoven's frequent puns: *Verleger* (publisher) and *Verlegenheit* (embarrassment).

[3] Born in 1774 in Saxony, died in Vienna in 1835. See *FRBH*, II, pp. 248ff.

[4] *Beethoven, nach den Schilderungen seiner Zeitgenossen* (Stuttgart, 1877), pp. 114-15.

A musical breakfast in the year 1812

. . . Starke was often invited to a meal and after it often had the soul-satisfying experience of hearing Beethoven improvise. The most remarkable and pleasant time was an invitation to a breakfast which for Starke was a real spiritual breakfast. . . . After breakfast which consisted of very good coffee (and which Beethoven made himself in a glass machine), Starke requested a breakfast for his heart and mind, and Beethoven improvised in three different styles, first restrained, second fugal, where a heavenly theme in sixteenth notes was developed in the most wonderful way, and third in chamber style in which Beethoven knew how to combine the greatest intricacies in projecting his special mood.

Starke brought along his horn and offered to play Beethoven's horn sonata in F (Op. 17) with him, which Beethoven accepted with pleasure. When it was discovered that the piano was a half-step too low, Starke offered to play the horn down a half-step; but Beethoven said that the effect would be spoiled and that he would rather play it up a half-step (F-sharp major). "It was begun and Beethoven played it in a wondrously beautiful way; the passages rolled along so clear and fine that one couldn't believe at all that he was transposing. Beethoven also had praise for Starke because he had never heard the sonata performed with shading; he found the *pp* especially fine. The whole thing was a heavenly breakfast."}<

Beethoven had surely earned the right to retire and leave the virtuoso field to his pupils, of whom Baroness Ertmann and Carl Czerny were preeminent as performers of his music. In the more private concerts he had already long given place to the Baroness; and now Czerny began to take it before the public, even to the extent of introducing his last new composition for pianoforte and orchestra, Op. 73. Theodor Körner, lately arrived in Vienna, writes home under date February 15, 1812: "On Wednesday the 11th, for the benefit of the Society of Noble Ladies for Charity, a concert and tableaux, representing three pictures by Raphael, Poussin and Troyes as described by Goethe in his 'Elective Affinities,' were given. The pictures offered a glorious treat; a new pianoforte concerto by Beethoven failed."

Castelli's *Thalia* gives the reason why this noble work on this, its first public performance in Vienna, was so coldly received: "If this composition . . . failed to receive the applause which it deserved, the reason is to be sought partly in the subjective character of the work, partly in the objective nature of the listeners. Beethoven, full of proud confidence in himself, never writes for the multitude; he demands understanding and feeling, and because of the intentional difficulties, he can receive these only at the hands of the knowing, a majority of whom is not to be found on such occasions."[5] That was precisely the truth. The work was out of place. The warblings of Fräulein Sessi and Herr Siboni, and Mayseder's variations on the march in *Aline*,

---

[5] Ignaz Franz Castelli (1781-1862), a well-known poet in his day, made the revision of *Les Ruines de Babylon*, which absorbed Beethoven's attention in 1811. His memoirs (1861) show that he was on friendly terms with the composer during this period.

were suited to the occasion and the audience. Instead of Beethoven's majestic work, Kapellmeister Himmel, who had recently been in Vienna, should have been engaged to remain and exhibit his brilliant finger gymnastics.

The new symphony, to which there are allusions in the correspondence of this year,[6] was the Seventh, which he took up and completed this spring (May 13), with the hope of producing it in a concert about the time of Pentecost—but the project fell through. Under date of London, 14th February, 1876, Mr. E. Speyer writes: "My father . . . on a visit to Vienna in 1832, made the acquaintance of the Abbé Stadler, who communicated to him the following curious fact in relation to Beethoven's Seventh Symphony, viz: That the theme of the Trio

was nothing more or less than a Lower-Austrian Pilgrimage Hymn (*Wallfahrtgesang*), which the Abbé himself had frequently heard sung."[7]

Among the sufferers by the *Finanz-Patent* were the Ursuline nuns at Graz, whose institution, since 1802, had at no time less than 50 wards and always more than 350 pupils. At this juncture they were excessively poor and in debt. In the hope of gaining them some substantial aid, Beethoven's new friend, Varena, now wrote to him offering to pay him properly for the use of some of his compositions in a concert for their benefit to be given on Easter Sunday, March 29. Beethoven at once presented two of his new compositions to the Art Society of Graz for gratuitous use at charity concerts. At the concert on Easter Sunday there were eight numbers, Beethoven being represented by the overture to *König Stephan*, the march with chorus from *Die Ruinen von Athen*, the overture to *Egmont*, and the Septet. The nuns gained on the occasion the handsome sum of 1836 fl. 24k. Vienna Standard (*Wiener Währung*).

The works of Beethoven publicly performed in Vienna during this half year, so far as has been learned, were the Pianoforte Concerto as above stated; on March 22nd, march with chorus from *Die Ruinen von Athen*, in Clement's concert; on April 16th, the *Coriolan* Overture in Streicher's Pianoforte Warerooms, conducted by Schuppanzigh—the first piece in the concert, which opened the way for the great performance of Handel's *Timotheus* in November, which in turn led to the foundation of the Society of the Friends of Music; on April 24th, the *Egmont* Overture in the Concert for the Theatrical Poor Fund; and on May 5th, the overture to *Prometheus* and the C minor Symphony in Schuppanzigh's first Augarten Morning Concert of the season. His (Schuppanzigh's) quartet productions were on Thursdays, at noon;

[6] Beethoven's letters to Varena on May 8th and July 19th, *A* 369 and 378.

[7] This correspondent's father was W. Speyer, or Speier, whose name so often appears in old volumes of the *AMZ*. (TDR, III, 302, n. 1.)

"As it is nearly 12 o'clock and I am going to Schuppanzigh's," says Beethoven in a note to Zmeskall, on Thursday, February 20—unfortunately only as an auditor. No record of the programmes during the season has been discovered.

In explanation of the Zmeskall correspondence which follows, it is to be noted that the "greatest thanks" of one of the notes is merely for keeping his pens in order, and that Zmeskall had been making experiments to determine whether the oscillations of a simple weight and string (without lever) might not answer as a practicable and convenient metrometer.

[January 19]

I am coming to the Schwan today, dear Z. Unfortunately I am always so *free* and you *never*.

•~•

[February 2nd]

Not extraordinary but very ordinary, commonplace quill cutter, whose virtuosity assuredly shows a falling off with this specimen. These quills need a few repairs— When will you throw off your chains, when?— You think fine things about me; but accursed be for me the life in this Austrian Barbary— I shall now go mostly to the Schwan, as I cannot escape too much attention in the other inns.

Fare thee well, that is, as well as I wish you to be without me.

Your friend
Beethoven

Most extraordinary one, we beg that your servant find someone to clean out the rooms. As he knows the quarters, he can at once fix the price— But soon— carnival ragamuffin!!!!!!!!!!

•~•

[February 8]

Most extraordinary, foremost Oscillator of the world, and that without lever!!!!

We owe you the greatest thanks for having endowed us with a portion of your oscillatory power. We wish to thank you for the same in person, and therefore invite you to come *to the Schwan* tomorrow, an inn whose name bears evidence that it was made for the occasion when the talk is about such things.

Wholly your B.

•~•

[February 19]

Dear Z,

Only yesterday did I receive a written notice that the Archduke will pay his share in notes of redemption— I beg of you now to note down for me approximately what you said on Sunday so that I may send it to the other two— It is felt that I should be given a certificate that the Archduke pays in redemption bonds, but I think this unnecessary, the more since these courtiers in spite of their apparent friendship for me say that my demands are not *just*!!!!! Oh heaven help me to bear this; I am no Hercules who can help Atlas bear up the world or do it in his stead.— It was only yesterday that I heard in detail how beautifully Herr Baron Kruft had spoken about me at Zizius's, had judged me— Never mind, dear Z, it will not be for much longer that I shall continue the shameful manner in which I am living here. Art, the persecuted one, finds everywhere an asylum. Did not Daedalus, shut up in the labyrinth, invent the wings which carried him *upwards* into the air; and I, too, will find them, these wings—

Always your
Beethoven

If you have time, send me the desired form this very morning— For nothing, apparently for nothing have I been kept in suspense with polite words; so the time has already been lost.—

The correspondence with the Archduke, of course including the notes to his "spiritual adviser," Baumeister, and his "chamberlain," Schweiger, in the very profuseness of its expressions of devotion, awakens some mistrust of the writer's sincerity. There is too much of profession. True zeal in and a hearty performance of one's duty need few verbal attestations.

[To Baumeister]
March 22, 1812 [in another hand][8]
P.P.

Please send me the overture to the prologue Ungarn's Wohlthäter. It must be hurriedly copied in order to be sent *to Graz* for use there in a concert for the poor.

I count myself altogether too happy when my art is enlisted for such charitable purposes.— You need, therefore, only tell H. I. Highness, our gracious lord, about it and he will certainly be glad to have it delivered to you, the more gladly since you know that all the property of my small intellectual facilities is the sole property of H. I. Highness— As soon as the overture is copied I will return it immediately to His Imperial Highness.

Your faithful servant Ludwig van Beethoven

In a series of notes to the Archduke during the year, he excused his absences from the lessons for varying reasons: for the two previous days because he was "unexpectedly ill at just the time" when he was about to go to him; he had "oftener than usual" waited upon him "in the evening hour, but no one was to be found"; "certain unexpected circumstances prevent" his attendance today, "but I shall make use of the gracious privilege of waiting upon you tomorrow evening." In another letter he writes:

Your Imperial Highness!

I was truly upset not to have received the message from Y. I. H. to come until very late yesterday evening, in fact not until eleven o'clock. I did not return home in the afternoon contrary to my habit. The beautiful weather had lured me into spending the whole afternoon walking, and in the evening I was seeing *Wanda* at the Wieden, and so it happened that not until I came home again could I know of your wish— Should Y. I. H. find it necessary I am at your disposal any moment any hour— I await therefore your gracious command.

Your Imperial Highness's most humble
Ludwig van Beethoven

[8] The present editor is indebted to Miss Anderson for the correct details of this date. See *A*, p. 364.

Wanda, Königen der Sarmaten, a romantic tragedy with songs in five acts by Zacharias Werner with music by Riotte, was performed at the Theatre-ander-Wien on March 16 and repeated on the 17th, 19th and 30th of March and on the 2nd and 20th of April.

The following letter was written perhaps at the end of April:

Your Imperial Highness!

Now for the first time, since I have left my bed, am I able to answer your gracious letter of today. Tomorrow it will still not be possible for me to wait upon you, but perhaps the day after tomorrow— I have suffered much during the last few days, twofold I may say because I could not follow my sincerest desire to devote a great deal of time to you. I hope I shall be through with it, though (I mean my illness) this spring and summer.

The last of these selections affords another illustration of the usefulness of the Archduke's library to the composer, and is to Baumeister:

Sunday, June 28, 1812.
P.P.

I beg of you most politely that you lend me for today the two trios for pianoforte, violin and violoncello which I have composed. The first is in D major, the 2nd in E-flat. If I am not mistaken, His Imperial Highness has *copies of them* in his library— Also the sonata in A major with pianoforte and violoncello— separately printed—also the sonata in A minor with pianoforte and violin, also printed separately. You will receive everything back again tomorrow morning.

Your faithful servant Ludwig van Beethoven

The arrangements of the Irish and Scottish songs for Thomson were continued in this year. A French letter to Thomson under date February 29, 1812, is chiefly devoted to business matters, yet contains some expressions which are characteristic of Beethoven's views and predilections. He writes: "Haydn himself assured me, that he also got 4 ducats in gold for each song, yet he wrote only for violin and pianoforte without ritornellos or violoncello.[9] As regards Herr Koželuch, who delivers each song to you for 2 ducats, I congratulate you and the English and Scottish publishers on a taste which approves him. In this field I esteem myself a little higher than Herr Koželuch (*Miserabilis*), and I hope and believe that you have sufficient discrimination to do me justice." He repeated his request that the texts be sent with the Scottish songs, asked if violin and violoncello are to be treated *obbligato* or if the pianoforte might compose an ensemble in itself, and closed, after having again demanded 9 ducats in gold, with: "We need the gold here, for our country is at present only a paper fountain, and I in particular, for I shall probably leave this country and go to England and then to Edinburgh in Scotland, and rejoice in the prospect of there making your personal acquaintance."

[9] Here Beethoven was mistaken. Haydn composed accompaniments for a volume of Scottish songs for Napier, a London publisher, without ritornellos or violoncello; he wrote as Beethoven wrote for Thomson—with violoncello part as well as ritornellos. In a later letter (February 19, 1813) the same error is repeated. (TDR, III, 310, n. 1.)

There is a little Trio in one movement, which bears the superscription in Beethoven's hand: "Vienna, June 26, 1812. For my little friend Max. Brentano to encourage her in pianoforte playing." On one of his visits to the Brentanos, soon after, "the little maiden, whom he occasionally teased, in a fit of childish petulance unexpectedly poured a bottle of ice-cold water over his head when he was overheated."[10]

As Varnhagen last year, so Theodor Körner this and the next informs us that Beethoven's desire again to try his fortune on the operatic stage was in no wise abated. On June 6th the youthful poet writes: "If Weinlig does not intend soon to compose my Alfred, let him send it back to me; I would then, having bettered my knowledge of the theatre and especially of opera texts, strike out several things, inasmuch as it is too long, and give it to the Kärthner Theatre, as I am everlastingly plagued for opera texts by Beethoven, Weigl, Gyrowitz, etc." On February 10, 1813, he writes: "Beethoven has asked me for 'The Return of Ulysses.' If Gluck were alive, that would be a subject for his Muse."

This was the year in which Beethoven allowed a mask to be taken, at the desire of Streicher, who wished to add his bust to those which already adorned his pianoforte warerooms. The bust was executed by Professor Klein, a pupil of the famous sculptor Fischer. ⸺According to Frimmel,[11] the gypsum mask passed from the hands of the Streicher family to the sculptor Dietrich who was thus aided in the modeling of his Beethoven busts. After Dietrich's death it was acquired by the Viennese Sculptor Society, and from there the sculptor Zumbusch made use of it in erecting his Beethoven monument. This mask is the most reliable source for Beethoven's likeness in this period.⸺

The cause of an estrangement between Beethoven and Oliva is hinted at in two letters from Oliva to Varnhagen. On March 23 Oliva writes: "I should like to write you a good deal about the things that sadden me, about Stoll,[12] and Beethoven still more, but I must postpone it— I was ill lately and it moves me greatly to write about things which are so painful." In a letter of June 3 he says: "Concerning my unfortunate affairs I can only say that Of.[13] has treated me very shabbily and I am compelled to seek another engagement; perhaps I shall accept Beethoven's renewed offer and

---

[10] Related by Court Councillor Wittescheck and confirmed by Schindler, who had "this fact" from Maximiliane—then Frau von Blittersdorf. (TDR, III, 325, n. 2.)

[11] FRBH, I, p. 277, and for further information, *Beethoven Studien* (Munich and Leipzig, 1905), I, pp. 42-50.

[12] Johann Ludwig Stoll (1778-1815) was a poet whose "An die Geliebte" received two settings by Beethoven in December, 1811. That

he was a friend of the composer is clear from the reminiscences of Grillparzer, who recalls their occasional meetings at coffee-houses and rumors of their collaboration in an opera plan which never developed. See Beethoven's letter to Joseph Hammer with a request for help for Stoll, *A* 227.

[13] Offenheimer, the Vienna banker, Oliva's employer, is meant. (TDR, III, 313, n. 1.)

go with him to England. Stoll cheated me in a very miserable manner and even sought to bring about a rupture with Beethoven, in which he was almost successful; I am completely separated from him."

In May, the son of the Corsican advocate Bonaparte held court at Dresden and received his father-in-law, Emperor Franz, Frederick William of Prussia, the princes of the Rheinbund, etc. etc. Before the end of June, he had crossed the Niemen with his half million men on his fatal march to Moscow. As if from a presentiment and in the hope of a disastrous failure of the foolhardy invasion of Russia, Teplitz (that neutral ground, but central point of plot and agitation against the parvenu Emperor) became the scene of a virtual congress of imperial personages, or their representatives, accompanied by families, ministers and retinues. Ostensibly they met for health, recreation, social diversion; but views and opinions were exchanged and arrangements made for such concerted action as the result in Russia might render politic. Herr Aug. Rob. Hiekel, Magisterial Adjunct in Teplitz, has kindly communicated copious excerpts from the lists of arrivals that summer, from which these are selected, through the friendly mediation of Dr. Schebek of Prague, which is gratefully acknowledged:

May 29. Emperor Franz, with a large retinue—Wrbna, Althaer, Kinsky, Zichy, etc., etc.

June 4. Marie Louise, Empress of France and retinue; the Grand Duke of Würzburg and retinue.

July 2. The Empress of Austria and household; the Duke Anton of Saxony, with wife and household.

July 7. The Duke of Saxe-Weimar.

July 14. The King of Saxony with wife and royal household.

July 25. Prince Maximilian of Saxony with wife and royal household.

August 11, 15. Prince Wittgenstein, Baron von Humboldt, and the Prince of Curland, in Prussian service, etc., etc.

Passing from the royal and diplomatic circles, we note:

April 19. Baroness von der Recke, with Demoiselle Meissner and Herr Tiedge.

July 7. Herr Ludwig van Beethoven, Composer, of Vienna, lives in the Eiche, No. 62.

July 8. Herr Carl, Prince von Lichnowsky.

July 15. Hr. Johann Wolfgang von Goethe, Grand Ducal Privy Councillor of Weimar, etc., etc., in the Gold. Schiff, No. 116.

July 24. Herr Ludwig Baron von Arnim, landowner, with wife, then his sister-in-law, Frau v. Savigny, of Berlin.

August 5. Hr. Joachim, Baron v. Muench-Bellinghausen.

August 7. Hr. Clemens Brentano, *Partikulier* of Prague.

August 9. Frau Wilhelmine Sebald, wife of the Royal Prussian Commissioner of Justice, with sister Madame Sommer, of Berlin.

August 18. Hr. Fried. Karl von Savigny, Professor, etc., of Berlin.

August 19. Hr. Varnhagen von Ense, R. I. Lieutenant v. Vogelsang, of Prague.

Beethoven left Vienna for Teplitz, going by way of Prague, where he arrived on July 2 in company with Oliva's friend Willisen. Varnhagen writes to Rahel on July 2: "I am writing after the arrival of Beethoven and Willisen." As appears from a letter from Beethoven to Princess Kinsky (dated December 20, 1812) Beethoven called upon the Prince, discussed financial matters, and received 60 ducats on account, but unfortunately the definitive settlement of the annuity matter was delayed.

Beethoven's biographers have devoted more thought, research and writing to the next five days in Beethoven's life than to any other period, let alone specific days. The reason for this is that Beethoven wrote a three-part letter of such intensity to an unknown lady that ever since its discovery among the composer's possessions after his death, there has been speculation as to when it was written and to whom. While the study of the evidence has now established the year of its writing as 1812, no such success can be claimed for the question of the identity of the intended recipient of this letter. There is voluminous material on this subject, but no proof. Since a summary of this material would interfere with the flow of the narrative, a separate article on the subject has been included in the appendix, and we will limit ourselves in the text to the letter itself and the important findings concerning it.

Early on the morning of July 5th, Beethoven arrived in Teplitz and the next day started the letter referred to above:

July 6, in the morning.

My angel, my all, my very self— Only a few words today and at that with pencil (with yours)— Not till tomorrow will my lodgings be definitely determined upon—what a useless waste of time— Why this deep sorrow when necessity speaks—can our love endure except through sacrifices, through not demanding everything from one another; can you change the fact that you are not wholly mine, I not wholly thine— Oh God, look out into the beauties of nature and comfort yourself with that which must be— Love demands everything and that very justly—*thus it is to me with you, and to you with me*. If only you do not forget that I must live *for me and for you*; if we were wholly united you would feel the pain of it as little as I—My journey was a fearful one; I did not reach here until 4 o'clock yesterday morning. Lacking horses the post-coach chose another route, but what an awful one; at the stage before the last I was warned not to travel at night; I was made fearful of a forest, but that only made me the more eager—and I was wrong. The coach must needs break down on the wretched road, a bottomless mud road. Without such postilions as I had with me I should have remained stuck in the road. Esterhazy, traveling the usual road here, had the same fate with eight horses that I had with four— Yet I got some pleasure out of it, as I always do when I successfully overcome difficulties— Now a quick change to things internal from things external. We shall surely see each other soon; moreover, today I cannot share with you the thoughts I have had during the last few days touching my own life— If our hearts were always close together, I would have none of these. My heart is full of so many things to say to you—ah—there are moments when I feel that speech amounts to nothing at all—Cheer up—remain my true, my only love, my all as I am yours. The gods must send us the rest, what for us must and shall be—

Your faithful Ludwig

Evening, Monday, July 6.

You are suffering, my dearest creature—Just now have I learned that letters must be posted very early in the morning on Mondays—or on Thursdays—the only days on which the mail-coach goes from here to K.— You are suffering— Ah, wherever I am, there you are also— I will arrange it with you and me that I can live with you. What a life!!!! thus!!!! without you—pursued by the goodness of mankind hither and thither—which I as little want to deserve as I deserve it— Humility of man towards man—it pains me—and when I consider myself in relation to the universe, what am I and what is he—whom we call the greatest— and yet—herein lies the divine in man— I weep when I reflect that you will probably not receive the first report from me until Saturday— Much as you love me—I love you more— But do not ever conceal yourself from me—good night— As I am taking the baths I must go to bed— Oh God—so near! so far! Is not our love truly a heavenly structure, and also as firm as the vault of Heaven?—

Good morning, on July 7.

Though still in bed, my thoughts go out to you, my Immortal Beloved,[14] now and then joyfully, then sadly, waiting to learn whether or not fate will hear us— I can live only wholly with you or not at all— Yes, I am resolved to wander so long away from you until I can fly to your arms and say that I am really at home with you, and can send my soul enwrapped in you into the land of spirits— Yes, unhappily it must be so— You will be the more contained since you know my fidelity to you. No one else can ever possess my heart—never—never— Oh God, why must one be parted from one whom one so loves. And yet my life in V[ienna] is now a wretched life— Your love makes me at once the happiest and the unhappiest of men— At my age I need a steady, quiet life—can that be so in our connection? My angel, I have just been told that the mail-coach goes every day—and I must close at once so that you may receive the letter at once.— Be calm, only by a calm consideration of our existence can we achieve our purpose to live together— Be calm—love me—today—yesterday—what tearful longings for you—you—you— my life—my all—farewell.— Oh continue to love me—never misjudge the most faithful heart of your beloved.

ever thine
ever mine   L.
ever ours

——{Unger[15] has established the fact that the "K" undoubtedly refers to Karlsbad; the lady in question had probably seen Beethoven in Prague and had journeyed from there to Karlsbad. In his letter to Varnhagen dated July 14 from Teplitz Beethoven writes: "I was sorry, dear Varnhagen, not to

---

[14] As Miss Anderson points out, the German "unsterbliche Geliebte" should be translated as "eternally beloved." However, since the term "Immortal Beloved" has been used and accepted so frequently in English editions that it has become standard, the present editor has chosen to retain this wording. See *A*, p. 376, n. 1.

[15] "The Immortal Beloved," *MQ*, XIII (1928), pp. 249ff.

be able to spend the last evening in Prague with you. I think myself that it was most improper, only a circumstance which I could not foresee kept me from it. . . ." That Beethoven arrived in Teplitz July 5th, as mentioned in the letter, is verified by his letter of July 17th to Breitkopf and Härtel in which he says: "We say to you only that we have been here since the 5th of July." The fact that he was not registered before July 7th may have been because his place of lodging was not settled until then. ("Not till tomorrow will my lodgings be definitely determined upon.") Using official diplomatic correspondence preserved in Vienna, Kaznelson has discovered that the Esterhazy who was traveling at the same time as Beethoven, but on an alternate route, was Prince Paul Anton II (1786-1866), who was then Austrian ambassador to the Saxon court.[16]

This letter is the only known one in which Beethoven used the "Du" form of address to a woman. Even his love letters to Josephine Deym used the more formal "Sie." Hence, it is possible that the letter was never sent, but was preserved by him from the start, as was the Heiligenstadt Testament. Whoever the lady may have been, the impassioned mood of the writing forms the last and by far the most vehement expression that Beethoven gave to his life-long idealistic concept of union with one of the other sex. And yet, throughout these three outbursts is revealed already the hopelessness of this ideal from the composer's point of view. The tone of the last part of the letter particularly is that of one who is making up his mind and is attempting to convince one fully in love with him of the necessity of this decision. It is not surprising to find a sense of tedium in Beethoven's life as an aftermath to this crisis.

Both the letters to Varnhagen and to Breitkopf and Härtel reflect this. To Varnhagen: "There is not much to be said about Teplitz, few people and among the few nothing extraordinary, wherefore I live alone! alone! alone! alone!" To Breitkopf and Härtel: "How are we?—on that point much cannot yet be said; on the whole there are not such interesting people here as were last year and are few—a multitude of people is less of a bother than are a few." A postscript requests the score of *Christus am Ölberg* and some Goethe songs to be sent to Amalie Sebald in Berlin.

A touching letter was drawn from the composer by a child of eight to ten years, "Emilie M. at H." Emilie was a little pianist with such an enthusiasm for Beethoven that she wrote the composer privately with the help of her governess enclosing a wallet of her own making which she shyly offered.[17] Beethoven's answer is dated Teplitz, July 17, 1812:

My dear good Emilie, my dear friend!

My answer to your letter is late in coming; a mass of business and constant sickness must excuse me. That I am here for the recuperation of my health

[16] S. Kaznelson, *op.cit.*, pp. 46-7.
[17] Thayer received this information from Matthias Sirk in Graz. (TDR, III, 318, n. 2.)

proves the truth of my excuse. Do not tear away the laurel wreaths of Handel, Haydn and Mozart; they possess them, but not I yet.

Your wallet will be preserved along with other things of undeserved respect from many people.

Keep at it, don't just practice art, but penetrate also to its inner laws; it deserves it, for only art and science raise men to the Divine. If you should want something at any time, my dear Emilie, write to me trustingly. A true artist has no pride. Unfortunately he sees that art has no limits; he senses darkly how far he is from the goal; and while he is perhaps admired by others, he mourns that he has not yet arrived to the point where his better genius shines as an example like a distant sun. I would rather come to visit you and your people than many rich persons who betray themselves with the poverty of their inner selves. If I should come sometime to H., I will come to you and your family. I know no other advantages of a man than those which cause him to be counted among better men. Where I find these, there is my home.

If you want to write to me, dear Emilie, address it directly here where I will be for 4 weeks more, or Vienna; it is all the same. Consider me as your friend and as a friend of your family.

Ludwig v. Beethoven

No hint anywhere appears that Beethoven renewed his intercourse with Tiedge and the Countess von der Recke— they may have departed before his arrival. With Varnhagen, too, the meetings during the sojourn at Teplitz this year seem to have been few and fleeting.

On July 19, Goethe enters Beethoven's name for the first time among his "visits"—no doubt those made by him. On the same day he writes to his wife, who had gone on to Karlsbad for a cure: "Say to his Serene Highness Prince Friedrich, that I can never be with Beethoven without wishing that it were in the *goldenen Strauss.* A more self-contained, energetic, sincere artist I never saw. I can understand right well how singular must be his attitude towards the world."

Already on the next day Beethoven made a pleasure trip with Goethe to Bilin, and on the 21st Goethe spent the evening with Beethoven. Hence the note on the 21st, "He played delightfully."

On the 24th of July Baron von Arnim and his wife Bettina arrived in Teplitz. The one who cared the most about the meeting of these two artists was to be denied the sharing of it. In September, 1811, there had occurred a rupture between the Goethes and the von Arnims in Weimar. A remark made by Bettina brought the already strained relations between her and Goethe's wife, Christiane, to the breaking point; Goethe had to side with his wife, and relations between the two families came to an end. Bettina's report to Pückler-Muskau concerning Beethoven and Goethe, which in turn contradicts the spurious third letter from Beethoven to her, is not included here because of its unreliability.[18]

---

[18] For a summary of Bettina's fiction concerning the meeting between Beethoven and Goethe see Emil Ludwig, *Beethoven* (New York, 1943), pp. 222-81.

On the 27th of July, Beethoven went to Karlsbad and on August 8th to Franzensbrunn on the advice of his physician, Dr. Staudenheim. He did not return to Teplitz until the middle of September. Goethe journeyed to Karlsbad on August 11th. That there was no estrangement between them is proved by the letter of Goethe to Christiane advising her to give Beethoven a letter to bring back to Teplitz; he therefore expected Beethoven's return there. Goethe's letter says: "Herr van Beethoven went from here to Karlsbad a few days ago; if you can find him, he would bring me a letter in the shortest time." On August 2nd, Beethoven is still looked upon as the possible courier: "If I receive the consignment through Beethoven I will write again, then nothing more will be necessary" (because Goethe himself went to Karlsbad).

Goethe wrote to Zelter[19] concerning Beethoven as follows: "I made Beethoven's acquaintance in Teplitz. His talent amazed me; unfortunately he is an utterly untamed personality, who is not altogether in the wrong in holding the world to be detestable but surely does not make it any the more enjoyable either for himself or others by his attitude. He is easily excused, on the other hand, and much to be pitied, as his hearing is leaving him, which, perhaps mars the musical part of his nature less than the social. He is of a laconic nature and will become doubly so because of this lack."

A sifting of fact from legend is necessary to complete the story of the relations between Goethe and Beethoven; such, for instance, as the familiar anecdote according to which, when Goethe expressed his vexation at the incessant greetings from passers-by, Beethoven is said to have replied: "Do not let that trouble your Excellency, perhaps the greetings are intended for me." This is variously related to have occurred in a carriage at Karlsbad and in the Prater, and during a walk together on the old walls at Vienna; while the late Joseph Türk, the Vienna jeweler, who was in Teplitz in the summer of 1812, makes that place the scene of the story. It may, therefore, possibly have some foundation in truth.

On July 26th, a large portion of the town of Baden, near Vienna, including the palace of Archduke Anton, the cloister of Augustines, the theatre and casino, the parochial church and the palace of Count Carl Esterhazy, was destroyed by a conflagration which broke out between noon and 1 o'clock. In all, 117 houses were burned. "From Karlsbad under date of August 7, it is reported," writes the *Wiener Zeitung* of August 29th, that "scarcely had the misfortune which recently befell the inhabitants of Baden become known here before the well-known musicians Herr van Beethoven and Herr Polledro[20] formed the benevolent purpose to give a concert for the benefit of the sufferers. As many of the guests of high station were already prepared

---

[19] Carl Friedrich Zelter (1758-1832), an ardent admirer and close friend of Goethe, succeeded Fasch in 1800 as director of the Berlin *Singakademie*.

[20] Giovanni Battista Polledro (1781-1853), violinist, concert-master in Dresden in 1814, Court Kapellmeister in Turin in 1824. (TDR, III, 323, n. 1.)

to depart and it became necessary to seize the favorable moment, and in the conviction that he who helps quickly helps twofold, this purpose was carried out within twelve hours. . . . Universal and rousing applause and receipts amounting to 954 florins, Vienna Standard, rewarded the philanthropic efforts" of the concert-givers. Beethoven himself gives a very different aspect to this concert in a letter to Archduke Rudolph:

Franzenbrunn, August 12, 1812.

Your Imperial Highness!

It has long been my duty to recall myself to your memory, but partly my occupations in behalf of my health and partly my insignificance made me hesitate— In Prague I missed Y.I.H. by just a night; for when I went in the morning to wait upon you, you had departed the night before— In Teplitz I heard Turkish music[21] four times a day, the only musical report which I am able to make. I was together with Goethe a great deal. From T, however, my physician, Staudenheim, commanded me to go to Karlsbad and from there to here— What excursions! and yet but little certainty touching an improvement in my condition! To date I have always had the best of reports concerning the state of Y.I.H.'s health, also your continued favorable disposition and devotion to the musical muse.— Y.I.H. is likely to have heard of a concert which I gave with the help of Herr Polledro for the benefit of the city of Baden destroyed by fire. The receipts were nearly 1000 florins V.S. and if I had not been hindered in the arrangements 2000 florins might easily have been taken in— It was, so to speak, a *poor concert for the poor*. I found only some of my earlier sonatas with violin at the publishers here; as Polledro insisted I had to yield and play an old sonata— The entire concert consisted of a trio played by Polledro, the violin sonata by me, another piece by Polledro and then an improvisation by me— Meanwhile I am glad that the poor Baden people benefited somewhat by the affair— Pray you accept my wish for the best of health and the prayer to be graciously remembered by you.

Your Imperial Highness's most humble
Ludwig van Beethoven

Three days before, Beethoven had written a letter to Breitkopf and Härtel. After referring to the concert, and his various moves to follow the doctor's orders, he adds: "I must refrain from writing more, and instead splash around in the water again. Scarcely have I filled my interior with an ample quantity of it than I must have it dashed around and around over my exterior. I will answer the rest of your letter soon. Goethe is too fond of the atmosphere of the Courts, more so than is becoming to a poet. Why laugh at the absurdities of virtuosi when poets who ought to be the first teachers of a nation, forget all else for the sake of this glitter." The letter ended as it began with reference to the dedication to Kinsky of the Mass in C.

On September 7 Beethoven was on his way back to Karlsbad, where he remained only a few days. Here Goethe and Beethoven may have again

---

[21] By Turkish music is meant military music with drums, cymbals, etc. (TK, II, 225, n. 1.)

met each other, but only between September 8 and 11. On September 12, Goethe departed; but on the 8th he had written in his journal "Beethoven's arrival."

In the middle of September Beethoven returned to Teplitz with no amelioration, but rather an increase of his maladies, and was compelled to remain until near or perhaps quite the end of September. To his great satisfaction, he found there the young lady who had so powerfully attracted him the previous summer. The character of their renewed acquaintance is sufficiently obvious from the series of notes which follow. There are eight in all, but only six are given here. Only the first one bears a date.

Teplitz, September 16, 1812.

For Amalie von Sebald:

Tyrant—I? Your tyrant? Only a misapprehension can lead you to say this even if your judgement of me indicated no agreement of thought with me!— But no blame to you on this account, it is rather a piece of good fortune for you— Yesterday I was not wholly well, and since this morning I have grown worse. Something indigestible was the cause, and the irascible part of me appears to seize upon the bad as well as the good. But do not apply this to my moral nature.— People say nothing, they are only people, they generally see only themselves in others, and that is *nothing*. Away with this; the good, the beautiful needs no people. It is there without help of any kind and that, after all, appears to be the reason for our agreement.— Farewell, dear A. If the moon shines brighter for me this evening than the sun by day, you will see with you the small, smallest of all men.—

Your friend
Beethoven.

I only wish to report that the tyrant is chained to his bed *like a slave*— So it is! I shall be glad if I get by with the loss of the present day only. My promenade yesterday at sun-up in the woods, where it was very misty, has increased my indisposition and probably delayed my improvement— Busy yourself meanwhile with Russians, Lapps, Samoyeds, etc., and do not sing too often the song "Es lebe hoch!"

Your friend
Beethoven

I cannot yet say anything definite about myself; sometimes I feel better and next things appear to be in the old rut, or to be preparing a long sickness for me.— If I could give expression to my thoughts concerning my sickness as definitely as I can express my thoughts in music, I should soon help myself— Today too I must keep to my bed— Farewell, and rejoice in your good health, dear A,

Your friend
Beethoven

[In Amalie Sebald's handwriting]

My tyrant commands an account—here it is:

{ 539 }

A fowl   1 fl. V.S.

The soup   9 kr.

With all my heart I hope that it may agree with you.

[In Beethoven's handwriting]

Tyrants do not pay, but the bill must be receipted, and you can do that best if you come in person, N.B., with the bill to your humbled tyrant.

·~·

I am already better, dear A. If you think it *proper* to come to me alone, you could give me great pleasure; but if you think it *improper* you know how I honor the liberty of all people. And no matter how you act in this and all other cases, according to your principles or caprice, you will always find me kind and

Your friend

Beethoven

·~·

Dear, good A!

After leaving you yesterday my condition grew worse, and from last night till now I have not left my bed. I wanted to send word to you today, but thought it would look as if I wanted to appear important in your eyes, so I refrained— What dream of yours is this that you can be nothing to me? We will talk about that in person, dear A. I have always wished only that my presence might give you rest and peace, and that you would confide in me— I hope to be better tomorrow and then some hours of your stay will still remain for us both to be uplifted and gladdened by Nature—good night, dear A, many thanks for the proofs of your sentiments towards your friend

I will glance through Tiedge.   Beethoven

Hard upon the first letter to Amalie Sebald there followed a letter to Breitkopf and Härtel (September 17) which confirmed the statement concerning his illness and disclosed his desire to leave Vienna, though temporarily, for concert purposes. --◦❧{In the letter, Beethoven mentioned having taken a walk in the woods the day before in the early morning. The same reference is made in one of the notes to Amalie Sebald, which dates it, as Miss Anderson points out, also on September 17 and consequently second in the series.[22]}❧◦--

Beethoven's health must have improved soon after the 16th of September, for Kapellmeister Glöggl's *Linzer Musik-Zeitung* announces his arrival in that place on October 5th. "Now we have had the long wished for pleasure of having within our metropolis for several days the Orpheus and great musical poet of our time, Herr L. van Beethoven; and if Apollo is favorable to us we shall also have an opportunity to admire his art and report upon it to the readers of this journal." He had come thither, probably direct via Prague and Budweis, to pass a few weeks with his brother Johann, who gave him a large room affording him a delightful view of the Danube with its busy landing place and the lovely country road beyond.[23] Franz Glöggl—

[22] See *A*, p. 388, n. 2.   [23] This was the apothecary "zur goldenen

later a music publisher in Vienna, then a youth in Linz—shortly before his death wrote down his reminiscences for use in this work.

"Beethoven was on intimate terms òf friendship with my father, kapellmeister of the cathedral in Linz, and when he was there in 1812, he was at our house every day and several times took meals with us. My father asked him for an Aequale for 6 trombones, as in his collection of old instruments he had a soprano and a *quart* trombone,[24] whereas only alto, tenor and bass trombones were commonly used. Beethoven wanted to hear an Aequale such as was played at funerals in Linz, and one afternoon when Beethoven was expected to dine with us, my father appointed three trombone players and had them play an Aequale as desired, after which Beethoven sat down and composed one for 6[25] trombones, which my father had his trombonists play, etc.

"Among the cavaliers who were in Linz was Count von Dönhoff, a great admirer of Beethoven, who gave several soirées in his honor during the composer's sojourn. I was present at one of these. Pieces were played and some of Beethoven's songs were sung, and he was requested to improvise on the pianoforte, which he did not wish to do. A table had been spread with food in an adjoining room and finally the company gathered about it. I was a young lad and Beethoven interested me so greatly that I remained always near him. Search was made for him in vain and finally the company sat down without him. He was in the next room and now began to improvise; all grew quiet and listened to him. I remained standing beside him at the pianoforte. He played for about an hour and one by one all gathered around him. Then it occurred to him that he had been called to the table long before—he hurried from his chair to the dining-room. At the door stood a table holding porcelain dishes. He stumbled against it and the dishes fell to the floor. Count Dönhoff, a wealthy cavalier, laughed at the mishap and the company again sat down to the table with Beethoven. There was no more thought of playing music, for after Beethoven's fantasia half of the pianoforte strings were broken. I recall this fantasia with pleasure because I was so fortunate as to have heard it so near him."

One of Beethoven's memoranda, copied into the Fischoff manuscript, is this: "In 1812, I was in Linz on account of B." Supposing this B. to stand for Beethoven's brother it confirms certain very unpleasant information obtained in Linz (1860), from perfectly competent authority, namely, that the principal object of the journey thither was to interfere in Johann's domestic affairs.

Krone," bought by Johann in 1808 and known as the water apothecary because of its proximity to the watergate on the Danube. See *Volkes-Zeitung*, Vienna, March 29, 1942, p. 4.

[24] A bass trombone in F, a third lower than the tenor trombone. (TK, II, 230, n. 1.)

[25] Beethoven's three Equale are for four trombones. (TDR, III, 342, n. 2.)

Soon after coming to Linz, the apothecary, being unmarried and having a house much too large for his necessities, leased a part of it to a physician from Vienna, whose wife's sister some time later joined them. She, Therese Obermeyer, was described as possessing a very graceful and finely proportioned figure, and a pleasing, though not beautiful, face. Johann van Beethoven soon became acquainted with her, liked her, and made her his housekeeper and—something more.

When it is considered, that the apothecary was a man of some thirty-five years, that he had gained his present position entirely by his own enterprise, perseverance and good fortune, and that, beyond advice and remonstrance, his brother had no more right to meddle in his private concerns than any stranger, it seems hardly credible that Beethoven, with all his eccentricities of character, could have come to Linz with precisely this purpose in view. But, according to the evidence, this was so. Had the motive of his visit been simply fraternal affection, and had he then and there first discovered his brother's improper connection with Therese, he could justly have employed earnest expostulation and entreaty to the end of breaking it off—but nothing more; if unheeded, he could leave the house. But to come thither for this express object, and employ force to accomplish it, was an indefensible assumption of authority. Such, at all events, was Johann's opinion, and he refused to submit to his brother's dictation. Excited by opposition, Ludwig resorted to any and every means to accomplish his purpose. He saw the Bishop about it. He applied to the civil authorities. He pushed the affair so earnestly, as at last to obtain an order to the police to remove the girl to Vienna if, on a certain day, she should be still found in Linz. The disgrace to the poor girl; the strong liking which Johann had for her; his natural mortification at not being allowed to be master in his own house; these and other similar causes wrought him up almost to desperation. Beethoven, having carried his point, might certainly have borne his brother's anger with equanimity; might have felt pity for him and sought to soothe him in his trouble. But no; when Johann entered his room with reproaches and upbraidings, he, too, became angry and a scene ensued on which—let the curtain be drawn. It was, unhappily, more disgraceful to Ludwig than Johann. The apothecary, to use the language of the card-table, still had the commanding trump. Should he play it? The answer is in the parochial register at Linz. It is the record of marriage, November 8, 1812, of Johann van Beethoven to Therese Obermeyer. There is some slight reason to think that the journey to Linz was suddenly undertaken in consequence of a false report that Johann was about to marry Therese, and with the intention to prevent it. Whether this be true or not he lost the game and immediately hastened away to Vienna, angry and mortified that the measures he had taken had led to the very result which he wished to prevent; had given to the unchaste girl the legal right to call him "brother," and had put it in Johann's power—should he in the future have cause to rue his wedding-day—to reproach him as the author of his misfortune. Indeed, when that unhappy future came, Johann always declared that Ludwig had driven him into this marriage; how the composer then viewed the matter, we shall see when the time comes. One sister-in-law had already been to Beethoven a bitter source of shame and mortification; and now the other?—Time must show. Here we part from the apothecary, and it will be long before we meet him again.

Beethoven's professional occupation in Linz was the completion of the Eighth Symphony, which, on Johann van Beethoven's doubtful authority, was wrought out from sketches during walks to and upon the Pöstlingberg. Beethoven had begun to work industriously on the Eighth Symphony before he went to Teplitz; indeed he seems to have reported to Breitkopf and Härtel in a letter which has not been preserved, but which was sent from Franzensbrunn, that he had finished two symphonies; for the *Allg. Mus. Zeit.* of September 2, 1812, says: "L. van Beethoven, who took the cures first at Teplitz, then in Karlsbad and is now in Eger, has . . . again composed two new symphonies." But the autograph bears the inscription: "Linz in October, 1812." Schindler's account of the origin of the famous Allegretto Scherzando from the Eighth Symphony adds a new name to our *dramatis personae.*

Johann Nepomuk Mälzel (1772–1838) was the son of an organ-builder of Regensburg. He received a thorough musical education, moved to Vienna in 1792, and began life on his own account as a performer upon and a teacher of the pianoforte of no mean ability; but his extraordinary taste for mechanism and talent for invention soon led him to exchange the music-room for the workshop.[26] It is somewhere related, that, having been appointed "Court Mechanician" at Vienna and having a work to execute for the Empress, rooms were assigned him, in 1809, in Schönbrunn. Soon after this, Napoleon took possession of that palace, and while there played a game with Kempelen's chess player (of which Mälzel had become proprietor), Allgaier being (probably) the person concealed in the chest. The truth of the anecdote we cannot warrant. From Schönbrunn, Mälzel removed to rooms in Stein's pianoforte manufactory, and began the construction of a new and improved panharmonicon, having sold his first one in Paris in 1807. This was his principal employment in the year 1812. Carl Stein (from whom the author derived this information) remembered distinctly the frequent visits of Beethoven to Mälzel's workshop, the great intimacy of the two men, and the persevering efforts of the mechanician to construct an ear-trumpet which the deaf composer should find of practical use and benefit. It is well known, that

[26] His brother Leonard (1783-1855) was also a musician and inventor of musical mechanisms. His *Orpheus-Harmonie* was a sensation in 1814 and received testimonials from Salieri, Beethoven, Weigl, Gyrowetz and other prominent musicians. See Frimmel, "Mälzel's Kunst-Kabinett" in *Wiener Zeitung*, Feuilleton, July 26, 1914, pp. 10-12. See also *FRBH*, I, pp. 378-80.

of the four instruments constructed, one was so far satisfactory as to be used occasionally for some eight or ten years. The necessity and practicability of inventing some kind of machine by which composers should be able to indicate exactly the duration of a piece of music—in other words, the rapidity of its execution—had been for several years subjects of wide discussion. An article in the *Wiener Vaterländische Blätter* of October 13, 1813, entitled "Mälzel's musikalischer Chronometer," reads: "On his journeys through Germany, France and Italy, as a consequence of his approved knowledge of mechanics and music, Herr Mälzel had repeatedly been solicited by the most celebrated composers and conservatories to devote his talent to an invention which should be useful to the many, after many efforts by others had proved defective. He undertook the solution of the problem and succeeded in completely satisfying the first composers of Vienna with the model which was recently exhibited, which will be followed soon by the recognition of all others in the countries mentioned. The model has endured the most varied tests which the composers Salieri, Beethoven, Weigl, Gyrowetz and Hummel applied to it. Court Kapellmeister Salieri made the first application of this chronometer to a work of magnitude, Haydn's *Creation*, and noted all the tempos according to the different degrees on the score, etc. Herr Beethoven looks upon this invention as a welcome means with which to secure the performance of his brilliant compositions in all places in the tempos conceived by him, which to his regret have so often been misunderstood."

The *Allgemeine Musikalische Zeitung* of December 1st devotes some two pages to the instrument, from which a few words of description are enough for our purpose: "The external parts of this chronometer . . . consist of a small lever which is set in motion by a toothed wheel, the only one in the whole apparatus, by means of which and the resultant blows on a little wooden anvil, the measures are divided into equal intervals of time."

That "chronometer" was not what is now known as Mälzel's "metronome." The latter instrument with its beat made by pendulum motion was not invented until 1817.

It is now to be seen whether Schindler's account of the Allegretto Scherzando will bear examination. It is this:

"In the Spring of the year 1812, Beethoven, the mechanician Mälzel, Count von Brunsvik, Stephan von Breuning and others, sat together at a farewell meal, the first about to undertake the visit to his brother Johann in Linz, there to work out his Eighth Symphony and afterward to visit the Bohemian baths—Mälzel, however, to journey to England to exploit his famous trumpet-player automaton. The latter project had to be abandoned, however, and indefinitely postponed. The time-machine—metronome—invented by this mechanician, was already in such a state of forwardness that Salieri, Beethoven, Weigl and other musical notabilities had given a public testimonial of its utility. Beethoven, generally merry, witty, satirical, 'unbuttoned,' as he called it, at this farewell meal improvised the following canon, which was at once sung by the participants."[27]

Schindler here prints the now well-known canon[28] and adds: "Out of this canon was developed the Allegretto Scherzando."

The symphony was composed in 1811 and 1812 with the final working-out in the summer of 1812, thus Schindler's statement that the canon preceded the composing of the second movement is not necessarily correct. His date of the meal may be questioned on two counts. First, the lists of "Arrivals in Vienna" do not include Count Brunsvik's name between March, 1810 and February, 1813; and second, Mälzel did not abandon his project of journeying to England until late in the year 1813.

The Conversation Books show, in Schindler's own hand, how he became possessed of the canon. In a Conversation Book (1820) he writes: "The motif of the canon, 2nd movement of the 8th symphony— I cannot find the original—you will, I hope, have the kindness to write it down for me." Again in 1824 he writes: "I am just in the second movement of the 8th symphony—ta, ta, ta—the canon on Mälzel—it was really a very jolly evening when we sang this canon in the 'Kamehl'—Mälzel, the bass. At that time I still sang soprano. I think it was the end of 1817." Correct. Mälzel was then for a few months again in Vienna. On the first of these occasions, therefore, the word "Chronometer" must have been sung, and the "ta, ta, ta" represented the beat of the lever on the anvil. On the second, as Mälzel had returned to Vienna with the "Metronome," that word was substituted, and of course retained in the copy made in 1820.

Pierre Rode,[29] who at his peak had occupied perhaps the first place among living violinists, having been from Russia, made a concert tour in Germany and came in December to Vienna. Spohr, whose judgement of violin playing cannot be impugned, had heard him ten years before with delight and astonishment, and now again in a public concert on January 6. He now thought that he had retrograded; he found his playing "cold and full of mannerisms"; he missed "the former daring in the overcoming of difficulties," and felt himself "particularly unsatisfied by his *cantabile* playing." "The public, too, seemed dissatisfied," he says, "at least he could not warm it into enthusiasm."[30] Still, Rode had a great name; paid to and received from the nobles the customary homage; and exhibited his still great talents in their salons. Beethoven must have still thought well of his powers, for he now took up and completed his Sonata, Op. 96, to be played at one of Lobkowitz's evening concerts by Rode and Archduke Rudolph. The date of the concert was December 29th.

No sketches exist for the first movement but sketches for the other

---

[27] *Biogr.*, I, pp. 195-96.

[28] WoO 162.

[29] Pierre Jacques Joseph Rode (1774-1830), born in Bordeaux, France, was both a com-

poser and violinist.

[30] *Louis Spohr's Selbstbiographie* (Kassel, 1860-1861), I, p. 177.

three movements occur in the last pages of the Petter sketchbook. The autograph, which is in the Pierpont Morgan Library in New York, has the inscription: "Sonate im Februar 1812 oder 13 Sonate von L v Bthvn."[31] From the tone of two notes to the Archduke, the composer seems to have been less satisfied by Rode's performance than he had expected to be. He writes in December, 1812:

Tomorrow very early in the morning the copyist will be able to begin on the last movement. As I meanwhile am writing several other works, I did not make great haste in the last movement for the sake of mere punctuality, the more because I had, in writing it, to consider the playing of Rode. In our finales we like rushing and resounding passages, but this does not please R and—this hindered me somewhat— For the rest all is likely to go well on Tuesday. I take the liberty of doubting if I can appear that evening at Your Imp. Highness's, notwithstanding my zeal in service. But to make it good I shall come tomorrow morning and tomorrow afternoon to meet the wishes of my exalted pupil in all respects.

Ludwig Spohr (1784-1859), born in Brunswick, was violinist, composer and conductor. After a tour as violinist in 1804, he was appointed concertmaster in the ducal orchestra at Gotha. There he met and married the harpist, Dorette Scheidler. By 1807 his reputation was established as a violin virtuoso and he had turned to serious composition. He came to Vienna in 1812 to give concerts and was appointed concertmaster of the orchestra at the Theater-an-der-Wien.

Though it may be slightly in advance of strict chronological order, it would seem well to quote here what Spohr in his Autobiography writes of his personal intercourse with Beethoven. It is interesting and doubly acceptable as the only sketch of the kind belonging to just this period; it is, moreover, trustworthy. In general, what he related of the composer in that work so abounds with unaccountable errors as to necessitate the utmost caution in accepting it; it is pervaded by a harsh and grating tone; and leaves the impression that his memory retained most vividly and unconsciously exaggerated whatever tended to place Beethoven in a ridiculous light. What is here copied is, at least comparatively, free from these objections:[32]

"After my arrival in Vienna (about December 1), I at once hunted up Beethoven, but did not find him and therefore left my card. I now hoped to meet him in one of the musical soirées to which I was frequently invited, but soon learned that since his deafness had so increased that he could no longer hear music distinctly in all its context he had withdrawn from all musical parties and, indeed, become very shy of society. I made another attempt to visit him, but again in vain. At last, most unexpectedly, I met him in the eating-place which I was in the habit of patronizing every

[31] See KHV, pp. 269-70.   [32] Op.cit., I, pp. 197-99.

Wednesday with my wife. I had, by this time, already given a concert (December 17), and twice performed my oratorio (January 21 and 24). The Vienna newspapers had reported favorably upon them. Hence, Beethoven knew of me when I introduced myself to him and greeted me in an extremely friendly manner. We sat down together at a table, and Beethoven became very chatty, which greatly surprised the table company, as he generally looked straight ahead, morose and curt of speech. It was a difficult task to make him understand, as one had to shout so loudly that it could be heard three rooms distant. Afterward, Beethoven came often to this eating-house and visited me at my lodgings, and thus we soon learned to know each other well. Beethoven was frequently somewhat blunt, not to say rude; but an honest eye gleamed from under his bushy eyebrows.

"After my return from Gotha (end of May, 1813), I met him occasionally at the Theater-an-der-Wien, hard behind the orchestra, where Count Palffy had given him a free seat. After the opera he generally accompanied me home and spent the remainder of the evening with me. There he was pleasant toward Dorette and the children. He very seldom spoke about music. When he did so his judgments were very severe and so decided that it seemed as if there could be no contradiction. He did not take the least interest in the works of others; for this reason I did not have the courage to show him mine. His favorite topic of conversation at the time was severe criticism of the two theatrical managements of Prince Lobkowitz and Count Palffy. He was sometimes overloud in his abuse of the latter when we were still inside the theatre, so that not only the public but also the Count in his office might have heard him. This embarrassed me greatly and I continually tried to turn the conversation into something else. The rude, repelling conduct of Beethoven at this time was due partly to his deafness, which he had not yet learned to endure with resignation, partly to the unsettled condition of his financial affairs. He was not a good housekeeper and had the ill-luck to be robbed by those about him. So he often lacked necessities. In the early part of our acquaintance I once asked him, after he had been absent from the eating-house: 'You were not ill, were you?'— 'My boots were, and as I have only one pair I had house-arrest,' was the answer."

Beethoven had other cares, troubles and anxieties in the coming year—to which these reminiscences in strictness belong and serve as a sort of introduction—not known to Spohr. Theirs was not the confidential intercourse which lays bare the heart of friend to friend.

The compositions of the year were:

1811-12. Symphony No. 7 in A major, Op. 92.
  Symphony No. 8 in F major, Op. 93.
1812. Canon, "Ta ta ta," WoO 162.
  Continuation of Irish Airs (WoO 152, 153, 154 and 157).

Continuation of Welsh Airs, WoO 155 —⚜ According to Kinsky, only No. 15, "When mortals all to rest retire."[33]⚜
Sonata for Pianoforte and Violin, Op. 96.
Three Equale for Four Trombones, WoO 30.
Trio for Pianoforte, Violin and Violoncello (for Maximiliane Brentano), WoO 39.

The publications for the year were:

By Breitkopf and Härtel:
Mass in C major, Op. 86, dedicated to Prince Ferdinand Kinsky.
Music to Goethe's *Egmont*, Op. 84, in transcription for the pianoforte. Also the orchestral parts of the songs and entractes.

[33] See KHV, p. 650.

CHAPTER XXVI

THE YEAR 1813

FINANCIAL DIFFICULTIES—SUSPENSION OF PAYMENTS—CONCERTS AT GRAZ—MÄLZEL AND "WELLINGTON'S VICTORY"—CONCERTS OF DECEMBER 8 AND 12

EVER since the establishment of the love letters of July 6-7 as having been written in 1812,[1] the first entries of the so-called journal (*Tagebuch*) of the Fischoff manuscript have taken on new meaning. The first entry has only the year 1812 and probably belongs to the end of the year. The letter in the last sentence of the first entry has been deciphered by many as an A, but it is an unclear sign and identification of the letter is still in doubt.[2] The journal begins thus:

Submission, absolute submission to your fate, only this can give you the sacrifice . . . to the servitude— Oh, hard struggle!— Turn everything which remains to be done to planning the long journey—you must yourself find all that your most blessed wish can offer, you must force it to your will—keep always of the same mind. . . .

Thou mayest no longer be a man, not for thyself, only for others, *for thee there is no longer happiness except* in thyself, *in thy art*— O God, give me strength to conquer myself, nothing must chain me to life. Thus everything connected with A will go to destruction.[3]

The next-following in the manuscript is dated:

May 13, 1813.

To forego a great act which might have been and remains so— O, what a difference compared with an unstudied life which often rose in my fancy— O

---

[1] See Appendix F.

[2] See Kaznelson, *op.cit.*, pp. 123-24.

[3] Between this and the next entry occurs an interesting note on an entirely different subject: "The strict combination of several voices hinders the overall progress of one to the others." This is a reference obviously to a problem in writing music but there is no way of knowing with what work the composer was engaged at the time. (TDR, III, 362, n. 1.)

fearful conditions which do not suppress my feeling for domesticity, but whose execution O God, God, look down upon the unhappy B., do not permit it to last thus much longer—

> Learn to keep silent, O friend! Speech is like silver,
> But to hold one's peace at the right moment is pure gold.[4]

Other causes also joined to render his case now truly pitiable. The result of his interference with his brother Johann, vexatious and mortifying as it was, was of little moment in comparison with the anxiety and distress caused by the condition of his brother Carl Caspar. In 1809, Carl had been advanced to the position of Deputy Liquidator with 1000 fl. salary and 160 fl. rent money; but all salaries being then paid in bank-notes, the minor public officials, especially after the *Finanz-Patent*, were reduced to extreme poverty. Carl van Beethoven was already owner of the house in the Alservorstadt near the Herrnalser Linie, which contained lodgings for some ten or twelve small families, enclosed a court-garden with fruit trees, etc., and was valued (1816) at 16400 fl.: so long as he remained in the Rauhensteingasse, the whole of this house was rented, and, after deducting interest and taxes, gave him a very desirable addition to his miserable salary. When Beethoven writes, that he had wholly to support "an unfortunate sick brother together with his family," it must be therefore understood *cum grano salis*; but that he had for some time been obliged very largely to aid them in obtaining even the necessaries of life is beyond question. Just now, when his own pecuniary prospects were so clouded, his anxieties were increased by his brother's wretched state of health, which partly disabled him for his official duties, and seems to have forced him to pay for occasional assistance. In March, he appeared rapidly to be sinking from consumption, and he became so hopeless of improvement in April as to induce him—in his wellfounded distrust of the virtue and prudence of his unhappy wife—to execute the following

DECLARATION

Inasmuch as I am convinced of the frank and upright disposition of my brother Ludwig van Beethoven, I desire that after my death he undertake the guardianship of my son, Karl Beethoven, a minor. I therefore request the honorable court to appoint my brother mentioned to the guardianship after my death and beg my dear brother to accept the office and to aid my son with word and deed in all cases.[5]

Vienna, April 12, 1813.

Happily for all parties concerned, Spring "brought healing on its wings." Carl's health improved; he was advanced to the position of Cashier of the

---

[4] This couplet is from Saadi's "Rosental," translated in *Zerstreuten Blättern*. Beethoven used the text at the end of 1815 to compose a canon: "Das Schweigen." See KHV, p. 675.

[5] This document is signed and sealed by Carl van Beethoven, R. I. Cashier, Ludwig van Beethoven and Baron Johann von Pasqualati; Peter von Leber and Fr. Oliva as witnesses. (TK, II, 241, n. 1.)

"Universal-Staats-Schulden Kasse," with 40 fl. increase of rent money; and now, at last, the decree was issued for the payment of all salaries (of public officials) in silver. ——Thayer's belief that Carl's need of financial help from his brother at this point was at an end has to be corrected by the discovery of two documents by Reinitz in the records of the St. Stephan's Cathedral.[6] Both are dated October 21, 1814. The first document states that on October 22, 1813, a sum of 1500 florins was lent by the publisher Steiner[7] through the composer to Johanna van Beethoven and that 1000 fl. was to be repaid in six months, the remainder in three months after that. The second document states that if the loan is not repaid after nine months by Carl or Johanna, the ceder (Ludwig v. Beethoven) must pay. However, the latter would be given an extension period of three months, in return for which favor the assignee (Steiner) would receive a new unpublished pianoforte sonata (with or without accompanying instrument) as his property for three months to be used everywhere except England and secure a time advantage over other publishers in the printing of his second or third new pianoforte sonata in return for an equable fee. The two sonatas Op. 90 and Op. 101 were published by Steiner in June, 1815 and February, 1817 respectively. Furthermore, there was at this time a sudden break in Beethoven's on the whole very satisfactory relations with the Leipzig firm, Breitkopf and Härtel. Both of these facts were undoubtedly the result of Beethoven's having had to turn to Steiner for a loan on behalf of his brother.

The nature of Beethoven's relation to his brother is made vivid by a recollection which Karl van Beethoven, Carl Caspar's son, told his wife in later years. At the time when his father was already very sick, the family were seated at table one day having a meal together. Suddenly the door opened and Beethoven burst in demanding, "You thief! Where are my notes?" Then followed a violent quarrel, and Karl's mother Johanna had great difficulty separating the brothers. The music in question was produced from a drawer and thrown in front of Beethoven, who then calmed down and begged his brother's pardon. Carl Caspar, however, was still angry and continued to abuse him, whereupon Beethoven rushed from the room without taking the music with him. Carl continued his abuse and the son remembered his saying that he never wished to have that dragon [*Drachen*] in his house again, etc. "A short time thereafter the uncle [Beethoven] met them on the Ferdinand Bridge[8] and when he noticed the sickly appearance of his brother he fell on his neck and in the public street covered him with kisses so that the people stared in complete bewilderment. Then he put him in a hackney coach and took him home and continued to besiege him almost with kisses in the carriage."[9] ——

In a letter to Archduke Rudolph written in January, Beethoven said

---

[6] Max Reinitz, *Beethoven im Kampf mit dem Schicksal* (Vienna, 1924), pp. 36-9.

[7] Sigmund Anton Steiner, a Viennese publisher whose firm is discussed in Chapter XXVIII.

[8] One of the bridges over what is now called the Danube Canal.

[9] Kerst, *op.cit.*, I, pp. 196-97.

bitterly: "neither word, nor honor, nor written agreement, seems binding."— The words relate to non-payments of the Kinsky and Lobkowitz subscriptions to his annuity.

In settling the affairs of Prince Kinsky, the question arose whether, under the *Finanz-Patent*, Beethoven was entitled to more than the subscription as computed by the scale; or, more correctly, there being *no* question under the law, Beethoven raised one, by claiming the full nominal sum (1800 fl.) in notes of redemption. The curators of the estates—as it was their sworn duty to do—refused to admit the claim until it should be established by the competent judicial authority; and, pending the decision, withheld all payments. As to Lobkowitz, his profuse expenditures had brought him to a suspension of all payments and had deprived him of the control of his vast estates. What has been said of the Kinsky subscription for Beethoven applies, therefore, literally to his. Hence, nothing of the annuity was paid by the Kinsky curators from November 3, 1812, to March 31, 1815; nor by those of Lobkowitz from September 1, 1811, until after April 19, 1815. From the abundant correspondence called out by these differences of opinion, as to whether law or equity should be the rule in the case, three letters to the widowed Princess Kinsky may be selected as explanatory of Beethoven's views.

In the first of these letters, dated at Vienna, December 30, 1812, Beethoven rehearsed the story of the origin of the annuity contract, the disarrangement of the governmental finances, Archduke Rudolph's prompt compliance with the request that payments be made in notes of redemption instead of banknotes, and then mentioned the visit of Varnhagen von Ense to Prince Kinsky at Prague. He told the Princess of his own visit [July, 1812] to Kinsky, who had confirmed the statements in the letter and paid 60 ducats on account— as the equivalent of 600 florins, Vienna Standard. Beethoven continues:

Upon my return to Vienna the arrears were to be brought in order and the instruction given to the treasury to pay my salary in the future in redemption notes. This was His Highness' will. My sickness got worse in Teplitz and I was forced to stay there longer than I had earlier planned. Therefore I sent through my local friend, Herr Oliva to His Highness, who in the month of September of this year was then in Vienna, a very submissive reminder in writing of his promise, and his Highness had the grace to repeat the promise to this gentleman and indeed with the addition that in a few days he intended to have the necessary amount thereby available at the treasury.

Sometime after this he departed.— Upon my arrival in Vienna I enquired of the Prince's Councillor if my salary had been remitted before the Prince's departure and heard to my astonishment that His Highness had arranged nothing in this affair.

The justification of my claim is proved by the testimony of Herr von Varnhagen and Oliva with both of whom His Highness spoke and repeated his promise.— Also I am convinced that the high-born heirs and descendants of this noble prince will continue to act in the spirit of his humanity and generosity and will bring his promises to fulfillment. . . .

In the second letter he repeated the request, having learned first from the Prince's representatives that nothing could be done in the matter until a guardian had been appointed, which office had been assumed by Her Highness. He continues:

You will easily see how painful it is to be deprived so long of money which had been counted on, the more since I am obliged wholly to support an unfortunate sick brother and his family and without self-consideration I have exhausted my resources, hoping by the collection of my salary to care for my own livelihood. The complete righteousness of my claims you may see in the fact that I faithfully reported the receipt of the 60 ducats which the Prince of blessed memory paid me on account in Prague, although the princely councillor told me that I might have concealed the fact, as the Prince had not told him, the councillor, or his cashier anything about it.

Beethoven closed the letter by asking to be excused for bringing the matter to the attention of the Princess.

The third letter, dated February 12, 1813, again urged the duty of the heirs to carry out the intentions of the Prince, stressed once more his own necessities, and formulated his petition as follows:

Namely, I pray Your Serene Highness graciously to command that the salary in arrears from September 1, 1811, be computed in Vienna currency according to the scale of the date of contract, at 1088.42 florins, and paid, and to leave the question whether and to what extent this salary be payable to me in Vienna currency open until the affairs of the estate be brought in order and it becomes necessary to lay the subject before the authorities so that my just demands be realized by their approval and determination. . . .

This represented a compromise on Beethoven's part, an attempt to get *some* money before the affair was finally settled; however this petition was not granted.

Schindler has enlarged upon Beethoven's inexperience and lack of skill in matters of business, and of his propensity to waste his resources in needless changes of lodgings; Wegeler and others inform us of his ignorance of the value of money; Carl Caspar van Beethoven had been a great expense to him; and five-eights of his annuity had for some time remained unpaid. Still, it is impossible to account satisfactorily for the very low state of his finances at this time. He must have been strangely imprudent in non-husbanding his resources. From March 1, 1809, to November 3, 1812, he had received from Kinsky rather more than five semi-annual payments (the "60 ducats" included),[10] from Lobkowitz five and from the Archduke seven— five of them in notes of redemption; in all, 11500 florins. In the Spring of 1810, Collard (Clementi) had paid him £200; from Thomson he had received 150 ducats, if not in July, 1810, at least in July, 1811, and 90 ducats more in

[10] See MacArdle's useful table of the complete Kinsky payments in *New Beethoven Letters* (Norman, 1957), pp. 72-3.

February, 1813, and within the last years Breitkopf and Härtel had certainly paid him several thousand florins for the many works of magnitude purchased by them. Besides all this he had borrowed at least 1100 florins from Brentano, for two or three years only after this he notes: "I owe F. A. B. 2300 fl., once 1100 and 60 ducats"; and we know of no time after the beginning of 1814 when he was under the necessity of applying to that generous friend for any sums like these. But, whatever was the cause, and whoever was in fault, Beethoven was now, up to the time when his brother Carl Caspar received his new appointment, learning by harsh experience a lesson in economy—happily to his profit.

To finish this topic at once, we pass on to the summer, which the composer spent in Baden, meeting there his friends the Streichers. Frau Streicher afterwards related to Schindler, that she found Beethoven in the summer of 1813, in the most desolate state as regards his physical and domestic needs—"not only did he not have a single good coat, but not a whole shirt," and, adds Schindler, "I must hesitate to describe his condition exactly as it was." Frau Streicher, after her return to the city, put his wardrobe and household affairs to rights and, with the help of her husband, saw to the provision of the necessities, and, what was still better, they impressed upon him the necessity of putting money by against the future, and "Beethoven obeyed in every particular." A small sum received from Graz, and the 750 fl. due from the Archduke, September 1st, relieved him for the moment; but before the end of the year, he was again so reduced, probably by the necessary expenditures made on his account by the Streichers, as to obtain a loan of 50 ducats from Mälzel.

There is a rather long letter in French to Thomson, dated February 19, 1813, which informs us touching the progress of the work on the British songs. Beethoven writes:

I have received your three valued letters of August 5, October 30 and December 21, and learned with pleasure that you have at last received the 62 songs which I have set for you and that you are satisfied with all but 9 of them which you specify and in which you would like to have me change the ritournelles and accompaniments. I regret very much that I cannot accommodate you in this. I am not in the habit of rewriting my compositions. I have never done it, being convinced that any partial alteration changes the character of the composition. I regret that you will suffer the loss; but you can scarcely put the blame on me, since it ought to have been your affair to advise me more explicitly of the taste of your country and the small skill of your players. Having now received your instruction on these points I have composed the songs wholly anew and, as I hope, so that they will meet your expectations. You may believe that it was only with great reluctance that I determined to do violence to my ideas and that I never should have been willing to do so had I not realized that since in your collection you wanted to have my compositions exclusively, my refusal would cause you a loss and would negate in consequence all the care and expense you have put into obtaining a complete work. . . . The last two songs in your letter of December 21, pleased me very much. For this reason I composed them con amore, particularly the second one. You noted it in ♮ but as this key seems a little too natural and so little in harmony with the direction Amoroso that it might rather become *Barbaresco*, I have set it in a more appropriate key. If among the airs that you may send me to be arranged in the future there are Andantinos, please tell me whether Andantino is to be understood as meaning faster or slower than Andante, for this term, like so many in music, is of so indefinite a significance that Andantino sometimes approaches as Allegro and sometimes, on the other hand, is played like Adagio. . . .

We come now to correspondence with Varena concerning charity concerts at Graz:

Dear Sir!

No doubt Rode was right in all that he said about me—my health is not of the best—and, without being my fault, my condition otherwise is probably the unhappiest of my life— But neither this nor anything else shall dissuade me from helping the equally innocent sufferers, the Convent ladies, so far as my modest talents will permit.— To this end, two entirely new symphonies are at your services, an aria for bass voice with chorus, several smaller single choruses— If you need the overture to *Ungarns Wohltäter* which you performed last year, it is at your service. *The overture to Die Ruinen von Athen*, although in a smaller style is also at your service.— Amongst the choruses is a chorus of Dervishes, an attractive thing [literally: "a good signboard"] for a mixed public.— In my opinion you would do best to choose a day on which you could give the oratorio "Christus am Ölberg," which has been performed in a number of places. This would then fill half of the concert, for the second half you could play a new symphony, [?] overtures and different choruses, as also the bass aria with chorus mentioned— Thus the evening would not be without variety; but you had better talk this over with the musical councillors in your city and let them decide.— From what you say concerning remuneration for me from a third person, I think I can guess who he is. If I were in my former condition I would flatly say: "Beethoven never takes pay when the benefiting of humanity is concerned"; but now placed in a condition through my great benevolence, the cause of which can bring me no shame, and other circumstances which are to blame, which are caused by men without honesty or honor, I say frankly I would not decline such an offer from a *rich third party*— But there is no thought of a demand, even if *all this about a third party* should prove to be nothing, be convinced that I am just as willing now to be of service to my friends, the reverend ladies as I was last year without the least reward, and as I shall always be to suffering humanity as long as I breathe— And now farewell, write to me soon and I will care for all that is necessary with the greatest zeal— My best wishes for the convent.

> With high esteem your friend
> Ludwig van Beethoven

Beethoven thought that the rich third party referred to in the letter was Louis Bonaparte, ex-King of Holland, then residing in Graz.

Closely connected with this in subject, and no doubt in time, is the following letter to Zmeskall:

Dear Z,

See to the delivery of this letter to Brunsvik at once today, so that it may duly arrive as *soon as possible*. Pardon me the burdens which I place upon you— I have just been asked again to send works to Graz in Steiermark for a concert to be given for the benefit of the Ursulines and their educational convent. Last year such a concert yielded generous receipts. With this concert and that which I gave in Karlsbad for the benefit of the sufferers from the fire in Baden, three concerts have been given in one year for, by and through me—everywhere people are on their feet to hear me.

Your

Beethoven

On April 8 he wrote to Varena again and thanked him for the sum of 100 florins from the nuns. After paying for the copying of parts he planned to send the remainder back to the nuns. And he added:

I thought that the third person to whom you referred was perhaps the *ex-King of Holland* and—yes, from him who probably took from the Hollanders in a less righteous way I would have had no hesitation in accepting something in my present condition. Now, however, I beg kindly that nothing more be said on the subject.— Write me your opinion as to whether if I came to Graz I could give a concert, for it is not likely that Vienna will long remain my place of residence— perhaps it is already too late, but your opinion on the subject would always be welcome.

Meanwhile Beethoven had contributed a "newly composed Triumphal March" to Kuffner's tragedy *Tarpeja* for its first performance in the Burgtheater on March 26. According to Kinsky-Halm[11] there was also a forty-measure "Introduzione de [!] II do Atto," as the inscription reads on an autograph from the Artaria Collection now in the Berlin Library. There is no indication on the autograph of a connection with *Tarpeja* but merely of introductory music for a second act. The fact, however, that the "Triumphal March" was written for the *second* act of *Tarpeja,* as Schünemann has established, makes it that much more likely that this music was also intended for the tragedy.[12]

In April, Beethoven sought permission to give two concerts in the hall of the University. The result is shown in a note to Zmeskall dated April 19:

The hall of the University, my dear Z., is—refused— I received this information day before yesterday, but being ill yesterday I could not come to you to talk it

---

[11] See KHV, pp. 429-30.

[12] Both pieces have been published by Schünemann (Schott, 1938). See Georg

Schünemann, "Ein neuentdecktes Werk von Beethoven," *Neues Musikblatt,* Vol. 18 (1939), No. 44, p. 1.

over, nor is it possible today.— There remains nothing probably except the Kärnthnerthor-theater or the Theater-an-der-Wien, and at that I fancy for only one A[kademie]— If all that does not work out we must resort to the Augarten. There of course we must give two A[kademies]. Think the matter over a bit, my dear, and give me your opinion— It may be that the symphonies will be rehearsed tomorrow at the Archduke's, if I can go out, of which I shall let you know.

Your friend
Beethoven

On April 26th he writes: "Lobkowitz intends to give me the theatre for a day after May 15. It seems to me that this is about as good as none at all— and I am almost of a mind to give up all thoughts of a concert. He above us will surely not let me go utterly to ruin."

We learn from the *Aufmerksame* of Graz that *Christus am Ölberg*, sent there by Beethoven in the preceding year, was sung as the second part of a concert for the poor on Palm Sunday, April 11, with applause which did honor to the good taste of the musical public of the Styrian capital. In Vienna the C minor Symphony opened and the new March from *Tarpeja* closed Schuppanzigh's concert on the 1st of May in the Augarten; but no such enthusiasm was awakened as to induce Beethoven to risk the trouble and expense of producing his new symphonies, and the projected *Akademies* were abandoned.

----In addition to the negotiations with the Kinsky family, Beethoven was concerned about Lobkowitz's non-payment of his part of the annuity. That he enlisted the aid of the Archduke in this respect is apparent from the following notes to Zmeskall.---- On April 23 he writes: "All will go well, the Archduke will take this Prince Fizlypuzly soundly by the ears— . . . . . Moreover, you must not let anything out about the enlistment of the Archduke, for Prince Fizlypuzly will not be coming to the Archduke till Sunday, and if this wicked debtor were to learn anything in advance he would try to get out of it." In May the tone is more optimistic: "I beg of you, dear Z, not to let anything be heard about what I said to you concerning Prince L, as the matter is really going forward and without this step nothing would ever have been certain—" ----Evidently a compromise was offered by the Prince's legal representatives, for in a letter to the Prince dated January 4 [1814][13] Beethoven, after expressing his "profound regard," says that the proposed settlement, whereby he would be paid in future "according to the scale" was unjust, and he appealed to the Prince to amend this in his favor. The matter was not to be settled for some time, and will be taken up again in a later chapter.----

On May 27, Beethoven wrote Varena that he was sending him three choruses, and a bass aria with chorus from the *Ruinen von Athen* as well as a march and two symphonies. These last were the Fourth and Fifth Sym-

---

[13] Printed in *DM*, Vol. 22 (1930), p. 399. For English translation see *A* 457.

phonies. The letter ends: "I do not know but that I may be obliged to leave this place as a fugitive from the country. For this thank the excellent princes who have made it impossible for me to work for the good and useful as is my wont.— Many thanks for the wine and thank also the worthy ladies for the sweetmeats which they sent me."

In a note concerned with the details of the music that was sent, he writes: "For the sake of my health I am hurrying to Baden for a measure of improvement." On the same day he reported his arrival in Baden to the Archduke, who was soon to go there too. From Baden the correspondence with Varena continued, as appears from a letter of July 4, 1813, in which Beethoven says:

Pardon this very belated answer, the reason is still the old one, my troubles, contending for my rights, and all this goes very slowly, since I am dealing with a princely rascal, Prince Lobkowitz. Another noble prince, one of an opposite character, died, but he as little as I was thinking of his death and concerning my affairs he left nothing in writing. This must now be fought out in the law courts at *Prague*. What an occupation for an artist to whom nothing is as dear as his art! And I was brought into all these embarrassments by H.R.H. Archduke Rudolph—

The letter ends with the acknowledgement, with thanks, of 150 florins which Varena had forwarded him from Graz from a local group, and the remark that perhaps he would come to Graz in the fall and give a benefit concert for the nuns or some other worthy institution.

Recalled to Vienna early in July, Beethoven wrote thence to Archduke Rudolph on July 24:

From day to day I thought that I should be able to return to Baden; meanwhile the dissonances which are keeping me here may possibly detain me till next week— It is a torment for me to stay in the city in the summertime, and when I reflect that I am also hindered from attending upon Y. I. H. it torments and repels me the more— Meanwhile it is the Lobkowitz and Kinsky matter which keeps me here. Instead of thinking about a number of measures, I must ponder the number of calls[14] which I must make; without this I should scarcely live to see the end of the matter.— Y. I. H. has doubtless heard of Lobkowitz's misfortunes. It is pitiable, but to be *so* rich is not to be fortunate! It is said that Count Fries alone paid 1900 ducats in gold to Duport[15] and took a mortgage on the old Lobkowitz house. The details are incredible.— I hear that Count Razumovsky will come to Baden and bring his quartet, which would be a very handsome thing, as Y. I. H. would certainly be nicely entertained. I know of no more delightful enjoyment in the country than quartet music.

Graciously accept, Y. I. H., my sincerest wishes for your good health and pity me for being obliged to remain here under such repulsive circumstances. Meanwhile I shall try to make up twofold in Baden all that you are losing thereby—

[14] Beethoven uses the word *Gänge* to have his joke; instead of measures (*Täkte*) he must think about *Gänge*, which in music means passages.

[15] The celebrated dancer and ballet-master. He was later Director of the Kärnthnerthor Theatre. (TDR, III, 382, n. 1.)

Beethoven soon returned to Baden, where for the present he may be left in the enjoyment of nature, taking such pleasure as his deafness still granted in Razumovsky's quartets, and submitting with what patience he could to his servitude with the Archduke.

--⊰⊱The following letter to Franz Brunsvik, dated by Thayer as 1812, should undoubtedly belong to the summer of 1813. It was this summer in which Napoleon was fighting the Allies in the north and which made Beethoven write: "If the billows of war roll nearer here, I shall come to Hungary."⊰⊱--

The letter reads as follows:

Dear friend! Brother!

I ought to have written you earlier; I did so 1000 times in my heart. You ought to have received the T.[rio] and S.[onata][16] much earlier; I cannot understand how M.[17]—could have detained these so long from you. To the best of my recollection I told you that I would send both sonata and trio. Do as you feel inclined, keep the sonata or send it to Forray[18] as you please. The quartet was designed for you long ago, my disorderliness alone is to blame that you receive it only now,—and speaking of disorder I am unfortunately compelled to tell you that it still persecutes me on every hand. Nothing decisive has been done in my affairs. The unhappy war may delay the final settlement still more or make the matter worse.— At one time I resolve upon one thing, at another time upon a different one. Unfortunately I must remain in the neighborhood until the matter is settled.— O unhappy decree, seductive as a siren, against which I should have stopped my ears with wax and had myself bound like Ulysses so that I could not sign. If the billows of war roll nearer here, I shall come to Hungary. Perhaps I shall in any event, since I must needs care only for my miserable self; I shall no doubt fight my way through. Away, nobler, loftier plans— Infinite are our strivings, the commonplace puts an end to all!— Farewell, dear brother, be such to me; I have no one to whom I can give the name. Do as much good around you as the evil times will permit.— In the future put the following directions on the coverings of letters to me: "To J. B. v. Pasqualati." The rascal Oliva (no noble r[as]c[al] however) is going to Hungary; do not have too much to do with him. I am glad that this connection which was brought about by sheer necessity, will by this be entirely broken off.— More by word of mouth.— I am now in Baden, now here;—to be found in Baden through the Sauerhof—Farewell, let me hear from you soon—

Your friend Beethoven.

Mälzel, during the past winter, had opened his *Künstkabinett* as a public exhibition. There were marbles, bronzes and paintings and a variety of contributions, scientific or curious, from various artists—among them a large

---

[16] Trio, Op. 97 and Sonata, Op. 81a.

[17] Almost illegible, this has been read variously as "R" and "M." See *A*, p. 421, n. 2. (Cf. TDR, III, 311, n. 1.)

[18] "Andreas Baron von Forray, husband of

Countess Julie Brunsvik, a cousin of Count Franz Brunsvik, was a good pianoforte player and great music lover," says Köchel. (TDR, III, 311, n. 2.)

electrical machine with apparatus for popular experiments, but the principal attractions were his own Mechanical Trumpeter and the new Panharmonicon. The Trumpeter executed a French cavalry march with signals and melodies which Mälzel himself accompanied on the pianoforte. The Panharmonicon combined the common instruments then employed in military bands, with a powerful bellows—the whole being inclosed in a case. The motive power was automatic and the keys were touched by pins fixed in a revolving cylinder, as in the common hand-organ or music-box. Compositions of considerable extent had each its own cylinder. The first pieces made ready were Cherubini's "Lodoiska" Overture, Haydn's "Military" Symphony, the overture and a chorus from Handel's *Timotheus*; and by the end of January, Mälzel was at work upon an echo piece composed for him some years before by Cherubini. In the course of the summer he added "a few marches" composed by the popular young pianist, Moscheles, who during their preparation much frequented the workshop.

The condition of Carl van Beethoven's health forced his brother to defer the contemplated journey to England; and Mälzel, too, found reason to wait until the end of the year—the idea of his really very beautiful and striking exhibition, the "Conflagration of Moscow," had occurred to him and he willingly remained in Vienna to work it out. The change for the better in Carl Caspar's health and pecuniary condition, and the completion of the "Conflagration," left both Beethoven and Mälzel late in autumn free for their departure. The mechanician was not only a man of unquestionable inventive genius, but he also understood the public; knew as by instinct how to excite and gratify curiosity without disappointing expectation, and had the tact and skill so to arrange his exhibitions as to dismiss his visitors grateful for an amusement for which they had paid. He was personally both respected and popular. He knew by experience the principal cities of the Continent, and London well enough to foresee, that the noble compositions of Handel, Haydn and Cherubini secured the success of his Panharmonicon there; but that if he could add to its repertory some new, striking and popular piece, bearing the now great name of Beethoven, he would increase both its attractiveness and the public interest and curiosity in the composer. Battles and sieges had for many years been favorite subjects for descriptive music, and the grand engagements of the last fifty years were few indeed which had not been fought over again by orchestras, bands and all sorts of instruments. Poor Koczwara—who hanged himself in jest at London in 1792—was the author of a "Grande Battaille" (in D) for orchestra, and the "Battaille de Prague" for pianoforte trio "avec tambour," or pianoforte solo, commemorative of a victory of Frederick II of Prussia. This, for forty years, was a showpiece throughout Europe and even in America. Devenne composed the "Battle of Gemappe"; Neubauer, of Martinestie; Jadin, of Austerlitz; Fuchs, of Jena; and so on, for orchestra. The grand battle piece for two flutes, which is generally supposed to have existed but in a joke, the point of which is its absurdity, was really published—it was an arrangement of Fuchs' "Jena." For the pianoforte solo, or with the accompaniment of two or more instruments, the press teemed with battles. Among them were those of Fleurus, Würzburg, Marengo, Jena (by others than Fuchs), Wagram, the bombardment of Vienna. Steibelt produced two land engagements and a "Combat naval"; Kauer, "Nelson's Battle"; and so on indefinitely.

When, therefore, the news of Wellington's magnificent victory at Vittoria, June 21, 1813, reached Vienna, Mälzel saw instantly that it presented the subject of a composition for his Panharmonicon than which none could be conceived better fitted to strike the popular taste in England. A work which should do homage to the hero, flatter national feeling by the introduction of "Rule Britannia" and "God save the King," gratify the national hatred of the French, celebrate British victory and Gallic defeat, bear the great name of Beethoven and be illuminated by his genius—what more could be desired? He wrought out the plan and explained it to the composer, who, for once, consented to work out the ideas of another. In a sketchbook for this composition, having signals for the battle on its first page, we read: "Wellington's Victory Vittoria, only God save the King, but a great victory overture for Wellington"; and in the so-called *Tagebuch*: "I must show the English a little what a blessing there is in God save the King"; perhaps, also, another remark just after this was occasioned by his experience on this work: "It is certain that one writes most prettily when one writes for the public, also that one writes rapidly." There is nothing in this at all contradictory to Moscheles's positive and unimpeachable testimony on the origin of the work. In a note to his English edition of Schindler's book he writes (I, pp. 153-54): "I witnessed the origin and progress of this work, and remember that not only did Mälzel decidedly induce Beethoven to write it, but even laid before him the whole design of it; himself wrote all the drummarches and the trumpet-flourishes of the French and English armies; gave the composer some hints, how he should herald the English army by the tune of 'Rule Britannia'; how he should introduce 'Malbrook' in a dismal strain; how he should depict the horrors of the battle and arrange 'God save the King' with effects representing the hurrahs of a multitude. Even the unhappy idea of converting the melody of 'God save the King' into a subject of a fugue in quick movement, emanates from Mälzel. All this I saw in sketches and score, brought by Beethoven to Mälzel's workshop, then the only suitable place of reception he was provided with."

The same, in general and in most of its particulars, was related to the author by Carl Stein, who was daily in Mälzel's rooms—they being, as before noted, in his father's pianoforte manufactory—and who was firmly of the opinion, that Mälzel was afterwards very unfairly, not to say unjustly, treated by Beethoven in the matter of this composition. The composer himself says: "I had already before then conceived the idea of a battle which was not practicable on his Panharmonica," thus by implication fully admitting that *this* idea was not his own; moreover, the copy of a part of the Panharmonicon score, in the Artaria Collection, has on the cover, in his own hand: "On Wellington's Victory at Vittoria, 1813, written for Hr. Mälzel by Ludwig van Beethoven." This is all more or less confirmatory of Moscheles, if indeed any confirmation be needed. It is almost too obvious for mention, that Mälzel's share in the work was even more than indicated above, because whoever wrote for the Panharmonicon must be frequently instructed by him as to its capacities and limitations, whether a Beethoven or the young Moscheles. We may reasonably assume, that the general plan of "Wellington's Victory" was fixed during the composer's occasional visits to the city in August and September, and such alterations in the score determined upon as the nature of the instrument demanded; so that early in October the whole was ready for Mälzel to transfer to its cylinder.

On Beethoven's return to his city lodging, between the 15th and 20th of September, his notes to Zmeskall became as usual numerous, the principal topic just now being the engagement of a servant. For such troubles of a domestic nature, it will be remembered, he usually sought Zmeskall's aid, and the circumstances usually provided an opportunity for humor. The preceding winter he had interviewed a man who had formerly worked for Zmeskall— "I did not remember him, but he told me he had been with you and that you were satisfied with everything except the fact that he could not dress your hair properly. . . . For me hair dressing is, as you know, the least of my worries. First of all it would have to be that my finances were dressed and curled." Whatever servant he engaged, however, was evidently not a success, for in September he writes:

Bestborn and Bearer of the Grand Cross of Violoncellicity!

If your servant is honest and knows of an honest servant for me, it would be a great favor to me, if through your *fine fellow* there could be found a fine fellow for me— In any case I should prefer a married man, for though not necessarily more honesty, at least more orderliness can be expected from such— My present beast of a servant is leaving at the end of the month, the new servant could then come at the beginning of next month. . . . As I give no livery except for a cloak, my servant is paid 25 fl. monthly—

Forgive me, dear Zmeskall
Your friend   Beethoven

In another note, possibly of this same time, Beethoven asks: "At the same time let me know whether I am bound to let my servant have *the whole day tomorrow* for his moving?—" At length, with the assistance and under the direction of the excellent Streichers, Beethoven got his lodgings and wardrobe into decent order, and with the aid of Zmeskall he obtained that servant spoken of by Schindler, "who was a tailor and carried on his trade in the anteroom of the composer. With the help of his wife he attended the master with touching care till into the year 1816—and this regulated mode of life did our friend much good. Would that it might have endured a few years longer.

"At this stage of the case there came also evidences of love and admiration from Prince Lichnowsky, which are well worth more detailed notice. The Prince was in the habit of frequently visiting his favorite in his workshop. In accordance with a mutual understanding no notice was to be taken of his presence, so that the master might not be disturbed. After the morning greeting the Prince was in the habit of looking through any piece of music that chanced to be at hand, watching the master at his work for a while and then leaving the room with a friendly 'adieu.' Nevertheless, these visits disturbed Beethoven, who occasionally locked the door. Unvexed, the Prince would walk down the three flights of stairs. As the sartorial servant sat in the anteroom, His Serene Highness would join him and wait until the door opened and he could speak a friendly greeting to the Prince of Music. The need was thus satisfied. This is indeed a beautiful counterpart to what we have already learned of the sentiments of Archduke Rudolph. But it was not given long to the honored Maecenas of Art to rejoice in his favorite and his creations, for already on April 15 of the following year he had departed this life!"[19]

This is touching and trustworthy.

To return to "Wellington's Victory." Schindler, supposing the Panharmonicon to have played it, remarked in the first edition of his book: "The effect of the piece was so unexpected that Mälzel requested our Beethoven to instrumentate it for orchestra."[20] He is mistaken as to the reason; for Mälzel had only, in Beethoven's words, "begun to engrave." In truth, he was musician enough to see from the score, how very effective it would be if instrumentated for grand orchestra, and sagacious enough to perceive, that the composition in that form might prove of far greater advantage to them in London and probably be more attractive afterwards when performed by the Panharmonicon. But there was another consideration far more important.

Before the age of steam a journey from Vienna to London with the many huge cases required for even a part of Mälzel's collection was a very expensive undertaking. The problem now was, how to provide the necessary funds. Beethoven's were exhausted and his own were very limited. To go alone and give exhibitions at the principal cities on the way, involved little or no risk for Mälzel, as the experience of the next year proved; but to make the journey direct, with Beethoven for his companion, was impossible until in some manner a considerable sum of ready money could be provided.

The only resource of the composer, except borrowing, was, of course, the production of the two new Symphonies, one of which had been copied for trial with small orchestra at the Archduke's, thus diminishing somewhat

---

[19] *Biogr.*, I, pp. 187-88. (TDR, III, 388.) [20] *Biographie* (1840), p. 91.

the expenses of a concert. It was five years since he had had a benefit, and therefore one full house might be counted on with reasonable certainty; but no concert of his had ever been repeated, and a single full house would leave but a small margin of profit. Moreover, his fruitless efforts in the Spring to arrange an *Akademie* were discouraging. Unless the new Symphonies could be produced without cost to himself, and the interest and curiosity of the public so aroused as to insure the success of two or three subsequent concerts, no adequate fund for the journey could be gained; but if so great a sensation could in some manner be made as to secure this object, the fame of it would precede and nobly herald them in London.

Beethoven was helpless; but Mälzel's sagacity was equal to the occasion. He knew that for the highly cultivated classes of music-lovers, able and ready to appreciate the best, nothing better could be desired than new Symphonies by Beethoven; but such auditors are always limited in number; the programme must also contain something surprising, sensational, *ad captandum vulgus,* to catch the ear of the multitude, and open their pockets. His Trumpeter was not enough; it had lost its novelty; although with an orchestra instead of pianoforte accompaniment, it would be something. Beethoven alone could, if he would, produce what was indispensable. Time pressed, Mälzel had long since closed his exhibition, and every day of delay was a serious expense. The "Conflagration of Moscow," the model of his Chronometer and the cylinders for his Panharmonicon were all finished, except the "Victory," and this would soon be ready. Before the end of the year, therefore, he could be in Munich, as his interest imperatively demanded, provided Beethoven should not be his companion. There was nothing to detain him in Vienna, after the "Victory" was completed, but his relations to the composer. Him he knew too well to hope from him any work deliberately written with a view to please the multitude, had the time allowed, which it did not.

Preparations were making in October for two grand performances on the 11th and 14th of November, in the R. I. Winter Riding Academy, of Handel's *Timotheus* for the benefit of the widows and orphans of Austrians and Bavarians who had fallen in the late campaign against Napoleon. On this hint Mälzel formed his plan. This was, if Beethoven would consent to instrumentate the "Victory" for orchestra—in doing which, being freed from the limitations of the Panharmonicon, he could give free play to his fancy—he (Mälzel) would return to him the score, risk the sacrifice of it for its original purpose, remain in Vienna, and make it the popular attraction of a grand charity concert for the benefit of the Austrians and Bavarians wounded in the battle at Hanau, trusting that it would open the way for two or more concerts to be given for their own benefit. Under all the circumstances, it is difficult to decide, whether to admire the more Mälzel's good judgment, or his courageous trust in it and in Beethoven's genius. He diclosed his plan and purposes to the composer, they were approved by him, and the score was returned.

While Beethoven wrought zealously on his task, Mälzel busied himself with the preparations for the concert. His personal popularity, the charitable object in view, curiosity to study Beethoven's new productions, especially the battle-piece, secured the services of nearly all the leading musicians, some of whom were there only in passing or temporarily—Dragonetti, Meyerbeer, the bassoon-player Romberg, and others. Tomaschek, who heard the "Victory" next year, writes that he was "very painfully affected to see a Beethoven, whom Providence had probably assigned to the highest throne in the realm of music, among the rudest materialists. I was told, it is true, that he himself had declared the work to be folly, and that he liked it only because with it he had thoroughly thrashed the Viennese." There is no doubt that this was so; nor that they, who engaged in its performance, viewed it as a stupendous musical joke, and engaged in it *con amore* as in a gigantic professional frolic.

—Beethoven wrote to the Archduke to ask that he speak a good word in his behalf through Baron Schweiger to the "Rector Magnificus" of the University, so that he might secure University Hall for his concerts.[21]— This time the use of the Hall was granted and the 8th of December was fixed for his concert. Young Glöggl was in Vienna, visited Beethoven, and was by him granted the privilege of attending the rehearsals. "I remember," he writes, "that in one rehearsal the violin players refused to play a passage in the symphony and rebuked him for writing difficulties which were incapable of performance. But Beethoven begged the gentlemen to take the parts home with them—if they were to practise it at home it would surely go. The next day at the rehearsal the passage went excellently, and the gentlemen themselves seemed to rejoice that they had given Beethoven the pleasure."

Spohr, playing among the violins, for the first time saw Beethoven conduct and was surprised in the highest degree, although he had been told beforehand of what he now saw with his own eyes. He continues: "Beethoven had accustomed himself to indicate expression to the orchestra by all manner of singular bodily movements. So often as a *sforzando* occurred, he tore his arms, which he had previously crossed upon his breast, with great vehemence asunder. At *piano* he crouched down lower and lower as he desired the degree of softness. If a *crescendo* then entered he gradually rose again and at the entrance of the *forte* jumped into the air. Sometimes, too, he unconsciously shouted to strengthen the *forte*. . . . It was obvious that the poor man could no longer hear the *piano* of his music. This was strikingly illustrated in the second portion of the first Allegro of the Symphony.

[21] See *A* 439.

In one place there are two holds, one immediately after the other, of which the second is *pianissimo*. This, Beethoven had probably overlooked, because he began again to beat time before the orchestra had begun to play the second hold. Without knowing it, therefore, he had hurried ten or twelve measures ahead of the orchestra, when it began again and, indeed, *pianissimo*. Beethoven to indicate this had in his wonted manner crouched clean under the desk. At the succeeding *crescendo* he again became visible, straightened himself out more and more and jumped into the air at the point where according to his calculation the *forte* ought to begin. When this did not follow his movement he looked about in a startled way, stared at the orchestra to see it still playing *pianissimo* and found his bearings only when the long-expected *forte* came and was visible to him. Fortunately this comical incident did not take place at the performance."[22]

Mälzel's first placards announcing the concert spoke of the battle-piece as his property; but Beethoven objecting to this, others were substituted in which it was said to have been composed "out of friendship, for his visit to London." No hint was conveyed of Mälzel's share in the composition. The programme was:

I. "An entirely new Symphony," by Beethoven (the Seventh, in A major).

II. Two marches played by Mälzel's Mechanical Trumpeter, with full orchestral accompaniment—the one by Dussek, the other by Pleyel.

III. "Wellington's Victory."

The success of the performances was so unequivocal and splendid as to cause their repetition on Sunday, the 12th, at noon, at the same prices, 10 fl. and 5 fl. "The net receipts of the two performances, after deducting the unavoidable costs, were 4006 florins, which were reverently turned over to the 'hohen Kriegs-Präsidio' for the purposes announced" (*Wiener Zeitung*, December 20). The *Wiener Zeitung, Allg. Mus. Zeit.* of Leipzig, and the *Beobachter*, contained excessively laudatory notices of the music and vivid descriptions of its effect upon the auditors, whose "applause rose to the point of ecstasy." The statements of the contemporary public prints are confirmed by the veteran Spohr, who reports that the Allegretto of the Seventh Symphony "was demanded *da capo* at both concerts."

Schindler[23] calls this rightly "one of the most important moments in the life of the master, at which all the hitherto divergent voices, save those of the professional musicians, united in proclaiming him worthy of the laurel." "A work like the battle-symphony had to come," adds Schindler with good judgment, "in order that divergent opinions might be united and the mouths of all opponents, of whatever kind, be silenced." Schindler also preserved a "Note of Thanks" prepared for the *Wiener Zeitung* and signed by Beethoven, which ends with a just and merited tribute to Mälzel:

[22] Spohr, *op.cit.*, pp. 200-202.   [23] *Biogr.*, I, pp. 191-93.

(For the "Intelligenz-Blatt" of the *Wiener Zeitung*.)

I esteem it to be my duty to thank all the honored participants in the *Akademie* given on December 8, and 12, for the benefit of the sick and wounded Austrian and Bavarian soldiers who fought in the battle at Hanau, for their demonstrated zeal on behalf of such a noble end.

It was an unusual congregation of admirable artists wherein every individual was inspired by the single thought of contributing something by his art for the benefit of the fatherland, and who without consideration of their rank cooperated in subordinate places in the excellent execution of the whole.

While Herr Schuppanzigh at the head of the violins carried the orchestra by his fiery and expressive playing, an Ober-Kapellmeister named Hr. Salieri did not scruple to beat time for the drummers and salvos. Hr. Spohr and Hr. Mayseder, each worthy of leadership because of his art, collaborated in the second and third places and Hr. Siboni and Giuliani also occupied subordinate positions.

To me the direction of the whole was assigned only because the music was of my composition; had it been by another, I should have been as willing as Hr. Hummel[24] to take my place at the big drum, as we were all filled with nothing but the pure love of country and of joyful sacrifice of our powers for those who sacrificed so much for us.

But our greatest thanks are due to H. Mälzel, since it was he who first conceived the idea of this concert and there fell to him afterwards the management, care and arrangement—the most arduous labors of all. I must also thank him in particular, because by the projection of this concert, he gave me the opportunity, long and ardently desired, by means of the composition especially written for this philanthropic purpose and delivered to him without pay, to lay a work of magnitude upon the altar of the fatherland under the existing conditions.

Ludwig van Beethoven[25]

Why was this document not printed? Beethoven had suddenly quarreled with Mälzel. This quarrel will be discussed in the next chapter.

The compositions of the year were:

—⋯❧"An die Hoffnung" from Tiedge's *Urania*, Op. 94, second version.[26] The autograph is in the Harvard University Library.❧⋯—

Canon. "Kurz ist der Schmerz" (first form), WoO 163. "For Herr Naue as a souvenir from L. v. Beethoven, Vienna, November 23, 1813." Johann Fried-

---

[24] In a footnote to Schindler's account of the performance of the battle-piece, Moscheles, the English translator, says (I, p. 147): "I must claim for my friend Meyerbeer the place here assigned to Hummel, who had to act in the cannonade; and this I may the more firmly assert as the cymbals having been intrusted to me, Meyerbeer and I had to play from one and the same part." At the repetitions of the work on January 2 and 24 Hummel directed what may be called the "battery." As there were two large drums, one on one side of the stage and one on the other, Hummel no doubt played one and Meyerbeer the other. Being pianists,

nothing but instruments of percussion could have been assigned to them. (TDR, III, 396, n. 1.)

[25] Schindler omits a final sentence in which Beethoven purposes to issue a list of the musicians and the parts they played. See A 1438.

[26] Thayer believed that the song was only sketched in 1813 and worked out in 1815 for a performance by Franz Wild in the following year. However, Boettcher believes that it was fully composed in 1813, which seems just as likely. See Hans Boettcher, *Beethoven als Lieder-Komponist* (Augsburg, 1928), p. 172 and Table IX.

rich Naue, successor to Türk as Musik-Director, etc. at Halle, born in 1790, appears to have been in Vienna on a visit this autumn.

"Der Bardengeist" (F. R. Hermann), WoO 142.[27]

"Der Gesang der Nachtigall" (Herder), WoO 141.[28]

Introduction to Act II in D and Triumphal March in C for Kuffner's *Tarpeja*, WoO 2.

"Wellington's Victory" for Orchestra, Op. 91.

The publications were:

In the *Hoftheater Musik-Verlag* in Vienna:

Triumphal March from *Tarpeja*, WoO 2a, in pianoforte transcription.[29]

In the *Musenalmanach* of Joh. Erichson for 1814 as a supplement:

"Der Bardengeist" (Hermann), WoO 142. The preface of the almanac is dated November 20, 1813, and the book was doubtless published before New Year's Day, 1814.

---

[27] "On November 3rd, 1813" according to an inscription on the first publication (Cf. TK, II, 259.)

[28] The autograph is dated May 3, 1813. See Boettcher, *op.cit.*, Table x.

[29] See KHV, p. 430.

CHAPTER XXVII

THE YEAR 1814

QUARREL WITH MÄLZEL—THE REVISION OF "FIDELIO"—THE VIENNA CONGRESS

ON THE last day of 1813, the *Wiener Zeitung* contained this public notice:

MUSICAL ACADEMY

The desire of a large number of music-lovers whom I esteem as worthy of honor, to hear again my grand instrumental composition on "Wellington's Victory at Vittoria," makes it my pleasant duty herewith to inform the valued public that on Sunday, the 2d of January, I shall have the honor to perform the afore-mentioned composition with added vocal pieces and choruses and aided by the most admirable musicians of Vienna in the R. I. large Redoutensaal for my benefit.

Tickets of admission are to be had daily in the Kohlmarkt in the house of Baron v. Haggenmüller, to the right of the court on the ground floor, in the comptoir of Baron v. Pasqualati; parterre 2 fl. gallery 3 fl. Vienna standard.

Ludwig van Beethoven.

Mälzel saw, therefore, that the objects for which he had sacrificed the "Battle," for which he had lost so many precious weeks and had spent so much labor and pains, were accomplished in so far as Beethoven's new works were now the subjects of general interest and curiosity, and their repeated performance to large and profitable audiences was secured. To his courage and sagacity this was wholly due. It is thoroughly unjust to deny or ignore the value of his services. What his feelings were now, to find himself deprived of all share in the benefit resulting from them, and therefore left without compensation, may readily be conceived. His Mechanical Trumpeter was necessarily discarded with himself, and Beethoven had to find something to take its place on the programme. The result was the selection of Nos. 6, 7 and 8 of the *Ruinen von Athen* music, viz: the "Solemn March with Chorus" and the concluding Bass aria, sung by Weinmüller, with the choruses. The last was exceedingly appropriate in a concert in the Redoutensaal, it being the number in which (as in the old Bonnian "Blick in die Zukunft") the bust of the monarch is made suddenly to appear.

To ensure the effectiveness of this is the object of a humorous note to Zmeskall, on New Year's Day.

Dear worthy friend!

All would be well if there were but a curtain, without *it the aria will fall through*. Only today have I learned this from S.[1] and it grieves me— Let there be a *curtain* even if it be only a bed-curtain, only a sort of *screen* which can be removed for the moment, a *veil*, etc. There must be something; the aria is too *dramatic, too much written for the theatre*, to be effective in a concert; *without a curtain or something of the sort all of its meaning will be lost!—lost! lost!— To the devil with everything!* The Court will probably come. Baron Schweiger asked me to go there at once; Archduke Karl admitted me to his presence and promised to *come.— The Empress did not accept nor did she decline.*

Hangings!!! or the aria and I will *hang* tomorrow. Farewell in the new year, I press you as warmly to my heart as in the old—*with or without curtain?*

The orchestra was for the most part composed of the same professional and amateur artists as had taken part in the two previous concerts, so that the rehearsals were comparatively inexpensive, the only new music being the selections from *Die Ruinen*; but Salieri, as director of the cannonade, gave place to Hummel. Franz Wild, the singer, was present and records in his *Autobiography*[2] his reminiscences of the occasion thus: "He [Beethoven] mounted the conductor's platform, and the orchestra, knowing his weakness, found itself plunged into an anxious excitement which was justified only too soon; for scarcely had the music begun before its creator offered a bewildering spectacle. At the *piano* passages he sank upon his knee, at the *forte* he leaped up, so that his figure, now shrivelling to that of a dwarf, disappeared under the desk and anon stretched up far above it like a giant, his hands and arms working as if with the beginning of the music a thousand lives had entered every member. At first this happened without disturbance of the effect of the composition, for the disappearance and appearance of his body was synchronous with the dying away and the swelling of the music; but all at once the genius ran ahead of his orchestra and the master disappeared at the *forte* passages and appeared again at the *piano*. Now danger was imminent and at the critical moment Kapellmeister Umlauf took the commander's staff and it was indicated to the orchestra that he alone was to be obeyed. For a long time Beethoven noticed nothing of the change; when he finally observed it, a smile came to his lips which, if ever a one which kind fate permitted me to see could be called so, deserved to be called 'heavenly.'" Note the similarity of this account to Spohr's description of a rehearsal at the close of the preceding chapter.

---

[1] Undoubtedly Schuppanzigh. (TDR, III, 407, n. 1.)

[2] Published in *Rezensionen über Theater und Musik*, Vienna, 1860, No. 4.

The composer had every reason to be satisfied with the result, for not only was it pecuniarily profitable but "the applause was general and reached the highest ecstasy. Many things had to be repeated, and there was a unanimous expression of a desire on the part of all the hearers to hear the compositions again and often, and to have occasion more frequently to laud and admire our native composer for works of his brilliant invention."

So speaks the *Wiener Zeitung* on the 9th, and on the 24th of January it printed this:

NOTE OF THANKS

I had the good fortune on the occasion of a performance of my compositions at the concert given by me on January 2, to have the support and help of a large number of the most admirable and celebrated artists of the city, and to see my works brilliantly made known by the hands of such virtuosi. Though these artists may have felt themselves rewarded by their own zeal for art and the pleasure which they gave the public through their talents, it is yet my duty publicly to express to them my warmest thanks for their mark of friendship for me and ready support.

Ludwig van Beethoven.

"Only in this room" (the large Redoutensaal), says Schindler,[3] "was the opportunity offered to put into execution the manifold intentions of the composer in the Battle Symphony. With the help of the long corridors and the rooms opposite to each other the opposing forces were enabled to approach each other and the desired illusion was strikingly achieved." Schindler was among the listeners on this occasion and gives assurance that the enthusiasm awakened by this performance, "heightened by the patriotic feeling of those memorable days," was overwhelming.

Among the direct consequences of this sudden and boundless popularity of Beethoven's music, to which Mälzel had given the occasion and impulse, was one all the more gratifying, because totally unexpected—the revival of *Fidelio*.

Georg Friedrich Treitschke was born in Leipzig in 1776 and came to the Court Theatre in 1800 as an actor. His talents and fine character raised him in the course of the next two years to the position of poet and stage-manager of the German Court Opera, a post which he continued to hold for many years. During the French invasion in 1809 he was appointed to the management of the Theater-an-der-Wien and in 1811 was reappointed to the Kärthnerthor-Theater. His account of Beethoven and *Fidelio*, from which we draw, was published in *Orpheus, Musikalisches Taschenbuch für das Jahr 1841* (Vienna) edited by Augustus Schmidt (pp. 239ff.).[4] He writes: "The *Inspizienten* of the R. I. Court Opera, Saal, Vogl and Weinmüller, were granted a performance for their benefit, the choice of a work

---

[3] *Biogr.*, I, p. 194. (TDR, III, 409.)
[4] Excerpts were republished by Schindler, *op.cit.*, I, pp. 121ff.

being left to them, without cost." There was no opera, German, French or Italian, likely to draw a remunerative house in the repertory of the theatre which could be produced without expense to the institution. The sensation caused by Beethoven's new music, including the numbers from *Die Ruinen von Athen*, in which Weinmüller had just sung, suggested *Fidelio*. All three had been in Vienna at its production and therefore knew it sufficiently to judge of its fitness for them as singers, and the probability of its now being successful. At all events the name of Beethoven would surely secure for their night a numerous audience. Treitschke continues: "Beethoven was approached for the loan of the opera and very unselfishly declared his willingness, but on the unequivocal condition that many changes be made. At the same time he proposed my humble self as the person to make these changes. I had enjoyed his more intimate friendship for some time, and my twofold position as stage-manager and opera-poet made his wish a pious duty. With Sonnleithner's permission I first took up the dialogue, wrote it almost wholly anew, succinct and clear as possible—an essential thing in the case of *Singspiele*."

The principal changes made by Treitschke were, by his own account, these:

"The scene of the entire first act was laid in an open court; the positions of Nos. 1 and 2 were exchanged; later the guard entered to a newly composed march; Leonora's Air received a new introduction, and only the last movement, 'O du, für den ich alles trug,' was retained.[5] The succeeding scene and duet[6]—according to Seyfried's description 'a charming duettino for soprano voices with concertante parts for violin and violoncello, C major, 9/8 time'—which was on the old book, Beethoven tore out of the score; the former was unnecessary, the latter a concert piece. I was compelled to agree with him; the purpose in view was to save the opera as a whole. A little terzetto for Rocco, Marcelline and Jacquino which followed ('a most melodious terzetto in E-flat' as Seyfried says) fared no better.[7] There had been a want of action and the music did not warm the hearers. A new dialogue was desired to give more occasion for the first finale. My friend was again right in demanding a different ending. I made many plans; at length we came to an agreement: to bring together the return of the prisoners at the command of Pizarro and their lamentation.

"The second act offered a great difficulty at the very outset. Beethoven at first wanted to distinguish poor Florestan with an aria, but I offered the objection that it would not be possible to allow a man nearly dead of hunger to sing bravura. We composed one thing and another; at last, in his opinion,

---

[5] The question of Leonore's aria is a problematical one and is discussed later in the chapter in connection with the performance of July 18, 1814.

[6] This duet, "Um in der Ehe froh zu leben,"

however, *precedes* Leonore's aria.

[7] The Trio, "Ein Mann ist bald genommen," appears much earlier in the opera: as No. 3 in both the 1805 and 1806 versions.

I hit the nail on the head. I wrote words which describe the last blazing up of life before its extinguishment:

'Und spür' ich nicht linde, sanft säuselnde Luft,
Und ist nicht mein Grab mir erhellet?
Ich seh', wie ein Engel, im rosigen Duft,
Sich tröstend zur Seite mir stellet.
Ein Engel, Leonoren, der Gattin so gleich!
Der führt mich zur Freiheit,—ins himmlische Reich!'

"What I am now relating will live forever in my memory. Beethoven came to me about seven o'clock in the evening. After we had discussed other things, he asked how matters stood with the aria? It was just finished, I handed it to him. He read, ran up and down the room, muttered, growled, as was his habit instead of singing—and tore open the pianoforte. My wife had often vainly begged him to play; to-day he placed the text in front of him and began to improvise marvellously—music which no magic could hold fast. Out of it he seemed to conjure the motive of the aria. The hours went by, but Beethoven improvised on. Supper, which he had purposed to eat with us, was served, but—he would not permit himself to be disturbed. It was late when he embraced me, and declining the meal, he hurried home. The next day the admirable composition was finished."

Concerning this air, Röckel writes: "The new Florestan (the Italian Radichi) wanted to be applauded after his air, which was not possible nor fitting to the situation nor desirable after the *pianissimo* conclusion of Florestan's air with the *con sordino* accompaniment of the violins. In order to satisfy him in part, without writing a new air, Beethoven first shortened the Adagio and concluded with an Allegro in the high register of the singer. But as the noise of applause would not have been increased by Rocco and Fidelio, who enter at this moment to dig a grave for the supposedly dead man, the composer decided to end the noisy Allegro with a small coda for the orchestra ending with a new *pianissimo*, by which device the silence essential to the succeeding scene was again restored."

Treitschke continues: "Nearly all the rest in the second act was confined to abbreviations and changes in the poetry. I think that a careful comparison of the two printed texts will justify my reasons. The grandiose quartet: 'Er sterbe,' etc., was interrupted by me with a short pause during which Jaquino and other persons report the arrival of the Minister and make the accomplishment of the murder impossible by summoning Pizarro away. After the next duet Rocco comes and accompanies Florestan and Leonore to the Minister."

At this point, Treitschke avoided what had always appeared to him to be "a great fault"—namely, that the dungeon was the scene of the entire second act—by introducing a change in the scenery so that the conclusion should be "in full daylight upon a bright green courtyard of the palace."

Before the middle of February the alterations to be made were determined by musician and poet, and each began his task; both were hindered by frequent interruptions, and its completion deferred.

Concerning the revision of *Fidelio* there is much information in the so-called Dessauer sketchbook (now in the archives of the Gesellschaft der Musikfreunde in Vienna), which unquestionably belongs in the year 1814. (Cf. Nottebohm, *II Beeth.*, 293ff.). This sketchbook contains first of all two new finales for the opera. On page 72 is the remark: "For Milder, B-flat above," which no doubt refers to the measure before the last in Leonore's aria. Then follow, p. 82, Florestan's aria, p. 90 the melodrama, p. 108 the recitative "Abscheulicher, wo eilst du hin," p. 112 "Un lieto brindisi" (WoO 103), p. 123 sketches for a symphony "2nd movement *Corni*," p. 133 "Sanft wie du lebtest" (Op. 118), p. 141 "Symphony, 2nd movement," p. 142 "Sanft wie du lebtest" again, p. 148 "Ihr weisen Grüner" (WoO 95), p. 160 "Europa steht" (Op. 136, No. 1) with only two or three measures of music, pp. 161-164 again "Ihr weisen Gründer." Besides these, Nottebohm recognized sketches for the Farewell song for Tuscher ("Die Stunde schlägt," WoO 102), for the first movement of the Sonata, Op. 90, and for the overtures to *Fidelio* and the "Namensfeier," Op. 115.

Beethoven's attention was now called away by the concert of which these two notes speak. The first is to Count Brunsvik:

13 Febr. 1814

Dear friend and brother!

You wrote to me recently; now I write to you— You no doubt are rejoicing over all the victories— also over mine— On the 27th of this month I shall give a second concert in the large Redoutensaal— Come up—now that you know of it— Thus I am gradually rescuing myself from my misery, for from my salaries I have not yet received a penny.[8] Schuppanzigh has written to Mihalkovicz[9] asking whether it would be worth our while to come to Ofen; what do you think? Of course such a thing would have to take place in a *theatre*— My opera is going to be performed, but I am writing much of it over.— I hope you are living contentedly, no small accomplishment. So far as I am concerned, good heavens, my kingdom is in the air; like the wind, the tones whirl around me, and often in my soul— I embrace you.—[10]

The second note is to Archduke Rudolph.

Your Imperial Highness!

I hope for pardon for my non-attendance. Your displeasure would punish me

---

[8] Beethoven here, of course, alludes only to the arrears in payment on his annuity of Lobkowitz and Kinsky. (TDR, III, 413, n. 1.)

[9] Johann Alois Mihalkovicz, "Königl. Statthaltereiagent" in Ofen, had been some years before in the same office with Zmeskall in Vienna, and a member of that jovial musical

circle of which young Beethoven was the prominent figure. Like Zmeskall and Brunsvik, he was a fine violoncellist. (TDR, III, 413, n. 2.)

[10] The autograph of this letter is in the Library of Congress.

when I am innocent. In a few days I will make it all up— They intend to perform my opera Fidelio again; this gives me a great deal of work, and despite my healthy appearance I am not well.— For my second concert the arrangements have been made in part, and I must compose something new for *Milder* for it.— Meanwhile I hear, and it is comforting to me, that Your Imperial Highness is in better health,[11] I hope, unless I am flattering myself too much, soon again to contribute to it. In the meantime I have taken the liberty to inform my Lord Falstaff[12] that he will soon graciously be permitted to appear before Y. I. H.— Your Imperial Highness' very obedient servant

Ludwig van Beethoven

The *Wiener Zeitung* of February 24th contains the advertisement of the "Akademie, next Sunday, the 27th inst. in the large Redoutensaal," announcing "a new symphony not yet heard and an entirely new as yet unheard terzetto" as novelties. To Hummel, Beethoven writes:

Best beloved Hummel! I beg of you conduct this time again the drumheads and cannonades with your admirable kapellmeister's and field-marshal's bâton— do it, I beg of you, and if ever I am wanted to cannonade you, I shall be at your service body and soul.—

Your friend Beethoven

The report in the *Allg. Mus. Zeit.* contains the programme in full with a few short and pertinent observations:

1. The new symphony (A major) which was received with so much applause, again. The reception was as animated as at the first time; the Andante (A minor) the crown of modern instrumental music, as at the first performance had to be repeated.

2. An entirely new Italian terzetto (B-flat major) beautifully sung by Mad. Milder-Hauptmann, Hr. Siboni and Hr. Weinmüller, is conceived at the outset wholly in the Italian style, but ends with a fiery Allegro in Beethoven's individual style. It was applauded.

3. An entirely new, hitherto unheard symphony (F major, ¾ time). The greatest interest of the listeners seemed centered on this, the *newest* product of B's muse, and expectation was tense, but this was not sufficiently gratified after the *single* hearing, and the applause which it received was not accompanied by that enthusiasm which distinguishes a work which gives universal delight; in short—as the Italians say—it did not create a furore. This reviewer is of the opinion that the reason does not lie by any means in weaker or less artistic workmanship (for here as in all of B's works of this class there breathes that peculiar spirit by which his originality always asserts itself); but partly in the faulty judgment which permitted this symphony to follow that in A major, partly in the surfeit of beauty and excellence which must necessarily be followed by a reaction. If this symphony should be performed *alone* hereafter, we have no doubt of its success.

[11] The Archduke was so troubled with gout in his hands that he had to abandon pianoforte playing. (TDR, III, 413, n. 4.)

[12] Schuppanzigh. (TDR, III, 413, n. 5.)

4. At the close, "Wellington's Victory in the battle of Vittoria" was given again, the first part, the Battle, having to be repeated. The performance left nothing to be desired; and the attendance was again very large.

The "something new for Milder" resulted in something rather old; for the terzetto in which she sang was the "Tremate, empi, tremate," fully sketched in 1801-1802, but now first written out and completed in its present form.

Schindler discovered among Beethoven's papers, and has communicated substantially in his book, certain accounts of expenses incurred in this concert.[13] Only the Eighth Symphony and the terzetto had to be copied; for these "the specification amounted in total: 452 written pages at 12 kreutzers, makes 90 florins, 24 kr.; the specified cost of the orchestra alone at this concert amounted to 344 florins. Nevertheless, only 7 first violinists and only 6 seconds who were paid some 5 some 7 fl. are mentioned by name, because in each part twice as many dilettanti had played." One of Beethoven's own memoranda gives the exact number of the string instruments: "At my last concert in the large Redoutensaal there were 18 first violins, 18 second, 14 violas, 12 violoncellos, 7 contra-basses, 2 contra-bassoons." Whether the audience numbered 5000, as Schindler reports, or 3000, which is more likely, the clear pecuniary profits of the two concerts were very large. Czerny remembered that on this occasion the Eighth Symphony "by no means pleased" and Beethoven was angry thereat, "because it is much better," he said. Another of his reminiscences is that Beethoven "often related with much pleasure how, when walking on the Kahlenberg after the perform-ance, he got some cherries from a couple of girls and when he asked the price of one of them, she replied: 'I'll take nothing from you. We saw you in the Redoutensaal when we heard your beautiful music.'"

The University Law Students had a composition by Beethoven on the programme of their concert, on February 12; the Medical Students opened their concert, March 6, with the "Egmont" Overture; and the Regiment Deutschmeister, theirs of March 25 with that to *Coriolan*. With these con-certs Beethoven had nothing to do; but in the Annual Spring *Akademie*, March 25, in the Kärnthnerthor-Theater for the Theatre Poor Fund, he conducted the "Egmont" Overture and "Wellington's Victory."

Both poet and composer had now been again delayed in their *Fidelio* studies, in this wise: The French Armies had so often taken possession of the capitals of the various Continental states, that the motives are incon-ceivable, which induced Schwarzenberg to restrain the approach of the allied armies on Paris, until Blücher's persistence, enforced by his victories, at last compelled the Commander-in-Chief to yield the point. When this became known in Vienna, it was determined to celebrate the event, so soon as news of it should arrive, by an appropriate performance in the Court Opera. To this end, Treitschke wrote a *Singspiel* in one act entitled *Gute Nachricht*

[13] *Biogr.*, I, p. 201.

(Good News). Of the nine pieces of music in it, the overture was given to Hummel and the concluding chorus, "Germania, wie stehts du jetzt im Glanze da," to Beethoven.

The following letter to the poet resulted from proposed changes in the scenery of *Fidelio*:

My esteemed T[reitschke]! Following your advice I went to the architects and the affair has already been arranged very much to my advantage. It is better to have to deal with *artists* than with *so-called grandees* (wimmeny-pimmenies)!— You will be able to have your song the very moment you give me the word— For everything connected with my opera my thanks hasten on to you.—If the opportunity arises, you might think of giving *Egmont at the Wieden Theatre* for my benefit. The arrival of the Spaniards, which is only suggested in the play, not visibly presented, might be utilized for the multitude to open the *big hole* of the Wieden Theatre [the stage]—and there might be a good deal of *visual spectacle* besides, and the music would not be wholly lost; and I should willingly add something new if it were asked.—

Esteemed friend! Farewell! Today I spoke with the chief bass-singer of the Austrian Empire, full of enthusiasm for a new opera by—Gyrowetz! In my heart I laughed over the new artistic course which this work will open up.

Wholly your Beethoven

Towards the end of March, Beethoven received the new text to *Fidelio*. To Treitschke he writes: "I have read your amendments to the opera with great pleasure; they determine me the more to rebuild the ruins of an old castle." A letter to the poet refers again to the chorus which he had composed for Treitschke's *Singspiel*:

I beg you, dear T., to send me the score of the song so that the interpolated note may be written into all the instruments— I shall not take it at all amiss if you have it newly composed by Gyrowetz or anybody else—preferably Weinmüller— I make no pretensions in the matter; but I will not suffer that any man—no matter who he may be—change my compositions.

Beethoven's attention was now again called away from the opera by a concert in the hall of the Hotel *zum Römischen Kaiser*, arranged by the landlord and Schuppanzigh for a military charity. Czerny relates that a new grand trio had then for some time been a subject of conversation among Beethoven's friends, though no one had heard it. This work, Op. 97, in B-flat major, was to open the second part of the concert and the composer had consented to play in it. Spohr was by chance in Beethoven's rooms at one of the rehearsals and heard him play—the only time. He writes: "It was not a treat, for, in the first place, the piano was badly out of tune, which Beethoven minded little, since he did not hear it; and secondly, on account of his deafness there was scarcely anything left of the virtuosity of the artist which had formerly been so greatly admired. In *forte* passages the poor deaf man pounded on the keys till the strings jangled, and in *piano* he played so softly that whole groups of tones were omitted, so that the music was unintelligible unless one could look into the pianoforte part. I was deeply saddened at so hard a fate. If it is a great misfortune for any one to be deaf, how shall a musician endure it without giving way to despair? Beethoven's continual melancholy was no longer a riddle to me."[14]

The concert took place at noon on Monday, April 11. Moscheles was present and wrote in his diary: "In the case of how many compositions is the word 'new' misapplied! But never in Beethoven's, and least of all in this, which again is full of originality. His playing, aside from its intellectual element, satisfied me less, being wanting in clarity and precision; but I observed many traces of the *grand* style of playing which I had long recognized in his compositions."

In those days a well-to-do music-lover, named Pettenkofer, gathered a number of young people into his house every Saturday for the performance of instrumental music. One evening a pupil of Schuppanzigh's requested his neighbor at the music-stand, a youth of eighteen years, to take a note from his teacher next day to Beethoven, proposing a rehearsal of the Trio, and requiring no answer but "yes" or "no." "I undertook the commission with joy," he records; "The desire to be able to stand for even a moment beside the man whose works had for several years inspired me with the greatest reverence for their author, was now to be so unexpectedly and strangely realized. The next morning the bearer of the note, with beating heart, climbed the four flights in the Pasqualati house, and was at once led by the sartorial servant to the writing table of the master. After he had read the missive, he turned to me and said 'Yes'; with a few rapidly added questions the audience came to an end; but at the door I permitted myself to tarry a little while to observe closely the man, who had already resumed his writing."

This youth was Anton Schindler. He continues his narrative: "This, almost the most important event in the life-history of the poor student up to that time, was soon followed by the acquaintanceship of Schuppanzigh. He gave me a ticket for the concert of April 11, given by him. . . . On this occasion I approached the great master with more confidence, and greeted him reverently. He answered pleasantly and showed that he remembered the carrier of the note."[15]

And thus ended all personal intercourse between Schindler and Beethoven until the end of the year—*a fact to be noted.*

A few weeks later Beethoven played in the Trio again at a morning concert of Schuppanzigh's in the Prater, and thus—except as accompanist—he took leave of the public as a pianist.

---

[14] Spohr, *op.cit.*, p. 203. At this time Moscheles was a regular listener at the quartet performances at Schuppanzigh's. Concerning one of them, he writes (*Aus Moscheles Leben*, I, p. 18): "I sat beside Spohr, we exchanged opinions about what we heard: Spohr spoke with great heat against Beethoven and his imitators." (TDR, III, 419, n. 1.)

[15] *Biogr.*, I, pp. 229-30. (TDR, III, 420.)

Gute Nachricht was first played also on the evening of Monday, April 11; for the news of the triumphal entry of the allied armies (March 31), as Moscheles records in his diary, reached Vienna the day before. It was repeated on April 12th, 14th, 17th, 24th and May 3rd, in the Kärnthnerthor-Theater, and on June 11th and 14th in the Burg.

Meantime an event had occurred which doubtless made a strong impression on Beethoven but of which unfortunately there is no indication—Prince Karl Lichnowsky, his old friend and protector, died April 15. It is gratifying that the last notice of him in our work is that touching reminiscence by Schindler,[16] which proves that time had neither cooled nor diminished the warm affection that he had conceived twenty years before for the young Bonn pianist.

The following note to Zmeskall was written about this time:

Dear Z., I am not going on the journey, at least I am not going to hurry— the matter must be pondered more carefully— Meanwhile the work[17] has already been sent to the *Prince Regent* [of England]:— *If I am wanted I can be had*, and then *liberty* remains with me to say *yes* or *no*. Liberty!!! What more do I want?

I should like to consult with you about how to settle myself in my lodging.

This new lodging, for which Beethoven now left the Pasqualati house, was in the 1st story of the Bartenstein house, also on the Mölker Bastei (No. 94); so that he still remained in the immediate vicinity of his friends, Princess Christiane Lichnowsky and the Erdödys.

The other matters mentioned in the note call our attention again to Mälzel, who, notwithstanding his bitter disappointment at the turn which his affairs with Beethoven had taken, had still lingered in Vienna several weeks in the hope of making some kind of amicable arrangement with him. As his side of the story was never made public, there is little to add to the information on the subject contained in the papers of Beethoven, preserved by Schindler. From them these facts appear; that Beethoven repaid the fifty ducats of borrowed money; that Mälzel and he had several interviews at the office of the lawyer, Dr. Adlersburg, which had for their subject the "Battle of Vittoria" and the journey to England; that he made various propositions which Beethoven would not accept "to get the work, or at least the right of first performance for himself," and the like; that, incensed by the conduct of the composer and hopeless of benefit from any further consultation, he did not appear at the last one appointed; and that he obtained by stealth so many of the single parts of the "Battle" as to be enabled therefrom to have a pretty correct score of the work written out, with which he departed to Munich and there produced it in two concerts on the 16th and 17th of March. When this became known in Vienna[18] Beethoven's wrath was excited and,

---

16 See Chapter XXVI, page 563.

17 Op. 91.

18 "In April, 1814, Beethoven received from Munich news of the performance of the Battle Symphony in that city by Mälzel, and also a report that the latter had said that he had to recompense himself with this work for a debt of 400 ducats which Beethoven owed him." Schindler, *Biogr.*, I, p. 236. (TDR, III, 422, n. 1.)

instead of treating the matter with contemptuous silence, or at most making an appeal to the public in the newspapers, he committed the absurdity of instituting a lawsuit against a man already far on his way to the other extremity of Europe. At the same time in all haste he prepared a copy of the "Battle" and sent it to the Prince Regent of England, so that at least he might prevent Mälzel from producing it there as a novelty. It was a costly and utterly useless precaution; for, on the one hand, Mälzel found in London no inducement to attempt orchestral concerts, and on the other, the score sent by Beethoven lay buried in the library of the Prince, who neither then nor ever took the slightest notice of it (except to permit its performance, as we shall presently see) or made any acknowledgment to the composer.

Casting aside all extraneous matter contained in Beethoven's documents, the real question at issue is very clear. The two leading facts—one of which is admitted by implication, and the other explicitly stated by Beethoven himself—are already known to the reader: First, that the plan of the work was Mälzel's; second, that the composer wrought it out for the Panharmonicon gratis. In this form, therefore, the composition beyond all doubt was Mälzel's property. There was, therefore, but one point to be decided: Did the arrangement of the work for orchestra at Mälzel's suggestion and request, transfer the proprietorship? If it did, Beethoven had a basis for his suit; if it did not, he had none. This question was never decided; for after the process had lingered through several years, the two men met, made peace, Beethoven withdrew his complaint, and each paid the half of all expenses that had been incurred![19]

Thus had been caused a new interruption of the work of *Fidelio*.

"The beneficiaries," says Treitschke, "urged its completion to take advantage of the favorable season; but Beethoven made slow progress." To one of the poet's notes urging haste, Beethoven wrote, probably in April:

Dear worthy T.! The damned Akademie, which I was compelled to give partly because of my bad circumstances, has set me back so far as the opera is concerned.— The cantata which I wanted to give there robbed me of 4 or 5 days.—

Now, of course, everything must be done at once; and I could write something new more quickly than add new things to old as now. I am accustomed in my composing, even in my instrumental music, to keep the whole in view. But here my whole has—in a certain way—been distributed everywhere and I have got to think myself back into my work ever and anon— It is not likely that it will be possible to give the opera in two weeks' time. I think that it will be in 4 weeks. Meanwhile the first act will be finished in a few days—But there still remains much to do in the second Act, and also a new overture, which will be the easiest because I can compose it entirely new. Before my Akademie a few things only were sketched here and there, in the first as well as the second act. It was not until a few days ago that I could begin to work things out. The score of the

[19] See Appendix G.

opera is as frightfully written as any that I ever saw. I have to look through note after note (it is probably a pilfered one). In short, I assure you, dear T. the opera will secure for me the crown of martyrdom. If you had not given yourself so much pains with it and revised everything so successfully, for which I shall be eternally grateful to you, I would scarcely have been able to bring myself to it—You have thereby saved some good remainders of a ship that was stranded—

If you think that the delay with the opera will be too long, postpone it till some future time. I am going ahead now until everything is finished, and, just like you, I have been changing and improving everything and making it better, which I see more and more clearly every moment. But it cannot go as fast as if I were composing something new—and in 14 days that is impossible— Do as you think best, but as a friend of mine. There is no want of zeal on my part.

> Your Beethoven.

The repetitions of the *Gute Nachricht* came to a conclusion with the performance in the Kärnthnerthor-Theater on May 3, and the beneficiaries became more and more impatient. Hence, Treitschke wrote again to Beethoven, asked him what use was to be made of the chorus "Germania," and urged him to make haste with the work on *Fidelio*. Notwithstanding so much was wanting, the rehearsals had begun in the middle of April, and the performance was now fixed for the 23rd of May. Beethoven's memorandum of his revisal of the opera reads: "The opera Fidelio [?] March to 15th of May, newly written and improved." May 15 was Sunday, the "Tuesday" of his answer to Treitschke was therefore the 17th, and the date of the following letter doubtless about the 14th:

Worthy T! Your satisfaction with the chorus delights me infinitely.— I was of the opinion that you ought to apply all the works to *your profit* and *therefore mine also*. But if you do not want to do this, I should like to have you sell it outright for the *benefit of the poor*.

Your copyists and Wranitsky were here yesterday about the matter, I told them, that *you, worthy Tr.*, were entirely *master in the affair*.— For this reason I await now your frank opinion— Your copyist is—an ass!—but he is completely lacking in the well-known splendid ass's skin [*Eselshaut*][20]— Therefore my copyist has undertaken the work of copying, and *by Tuesday little will remain to be done, and my copyist will bring everything to the rehearsal*— As for the rest, the whole matter of the opera is the most wearisome thing in the world, and I am dissatisfied with most of it—and—there is hardly a piece in it to which in *my present state of dissatisfaction I ought not to have patched for some satisfaction*.— That is the great difference between being able to surrender to free reflection or enthusiasm—

> Wholly your Beethoven.[21]

[20] *Eselshaut*—"Ass's Skin." A fairy play of that name with music by Hummel was performed on March 10, 1814, in the Theater-an-der-Wien. (TK, II, 277, n. 1; TDR, III, 424, n. 2.)

[21] The autograph of this letter is in the Library of Congress.

"The final rehearsal," says Treitschke, "was on May 22nd, but the promised new overture was still in the pen of the creator." It was then, on the 20th or 21st, that Beethoven dined with his friend Bertolini in the *Römischer Kaiser*. After dinner he took a bill of fare, drew lines on the blank side and began to write. "Come, let us go," said Bertolini; "No, wait a little; I have the idea for my overture," replied Beethoven, who remained and finished his sketches then and there. Treitschke continues: "The orchestra was called to rehearsal on the morning of the performance. B. did not come. After waiting a long time we drove to his lodgings to bring him, but—he lay in bed, sleeping soundly, beside him stood a goblet with wine and a biscuit in it, the sheets of the overture were scattered on the bed and floor. A burnt-out candle showed that he had worked far into the night. The impossibility of completing the overture was plain; for this occasion his overture to *Prometheus* [?] was taken and the announcement that because of obstacles which had presented themselves the new overture would have to be dispensed with today, enabled the numerous audience to guess the sufficient reason."

Schindler says an overture to *Leonore*, Seyfried the overture to *Die Ruinen von Athen* was played on this occasion. The *Sammler* in its contemporary notice confirms Seyfried: "The overture played at the first performance does not belong to the opera and was originally written for the opening of the theatre at Pesth." In 1823, Beethoven in conversation happened to speak of this substitution and remarked: "The people applauded, but I stood ashamed; it did not belong to the rest." In the manuscript book of the text prepared for use in the theatre on this occasion, one is surprised to see the title begun thus:

"LEONORE, FIDELIO
An Opera in Two Acts, etc."

The word "Leonore" is crossed out and "Fidelio" written at the side in red pencil afterwards inked over. There was then on the part of some one—whom?—an intention subsequently abandoned, of thus changing the title. Again, in the list of "properties," stands

A wallet ⎫
2 chains ⎬ Mme. Hönig.

and the same name occurs in the list of the

DRAMATIS PERSONAE

Herr Saal	Don Fernando, minister.
Herr Vogel	Don Pizarro, Governor of a State's prison.
Herr Radichi	Florestan, a prisoner.
M. Hönig	Leonore, his wife, under the name of Fidelio.
Hr. Weinmüller	Rokko, jailer.
Mlle. Bondra	Marzelline, his daughter.
Hr. Frühwald	Jaquino.

Prisoners of State, etc., etc.

Madame Hönig was a new soprano, engaged after the *Hoftheater-Taschen-buch* for 1814 had been printed, whose name appears in that for 1815. Though appointed to the part when this text-book was copied, she gave place before the day of performance to the original Fidelio, Mme. Milder-Hauptmann.

"The opera was capitally prepared," says Treitschke, "Beethoven conducted, his ardor often rushed him out of time, but Kapellmeister Umlauf, behind his back, guided everything to success with eye and hand. The applause was great and increased with every representation."

"Herr van B.," says the *Sammler*, "was stormily called out already after the first act, and enthusiastically greeted." The opera was first repeated on the 26th, when the new overture in E major "was received with tumultuous applause and the composer again called out twice at this repetition." *Fidelio* was repeated not only on May 26, but also on June 2nd and 4th and on Tuesday, June 7th. The theatre was then "closed because of preparations for the spectacle to be presented on the return of the Emperor." After this the theatre closed again for two days and on the 21st was reopened with *Fidelio*.

Meanwhile one of Beethoven's minor productions was now composed for his friend Bertolini. The occasion was an evening festival arranged by the doctor at his own expense on the name-day (St. John's day—June 24) and in honor of Malfatti. It was a little piece for four voices with pianoforte accompaniment to a text written by Abbate Bondi:

> Un lieto brindisi
> Tutti a Giovanni,
> Cantiam così, così,
> Viva longhi anni, etc. etc.

Invitations were extended not only to Malfatti's relatives and personal friends but to a large number of artists of the various professions, resident or temporarily in Vienna—Dragonetti among the musicians. The scene was Malfatti's villa in Weinhaus. There they feasted; the wine flowed; the cantata was sung; Beethoven, "thoroughly unbuttoned," improvised; fun and frolic ruled the hour. "The sport cost me a few hundred florins," laughingly said the good doctor fifty years afterwards.

A letter to Treitschke was written about this time:

Dear worthy Tr! What you say about a quarter of the receipts is understood, of course! And for a moment only I must moreover remain your *debtor*, but I will not *forget that I am*.— As regards a benefit performance for me I should like to have the day set on a week from yesterday, that is next Thursday.—

I called on Hr. Palffy today but did not find him in. Do not let the opera rest too much! It surely would be *injurious*!

I will visit you shortly as I still have a lot to discuss with you. Running out of paper, I must end.

Wholly your Beethoven.

The day here proposed for the benefit was not granted. The *Wiener Zeitung* of July 1st contained a "Musical Notice" which may be quoted as a comment on the first topic of the above note:

The undersigned, at the request of the Herren Artaria and Co., herewith declares that he has given the score of his opera FIDELIO to the aforesaid music establishment for publication under his direction in a complete pianoforte score, quartets, or arrangements for wind band. The present musical version is not to be confounded with an earlier one, since hardly a musical number has been left unchanged, and more than half of the opera was composed anew. Scores in the only authorized copy and also the book in manuscript may be had from me or from the reviser of the book, Hr. Fr. Treitschke, R. I. Court Theatre Poet. Other unauthorized copies will be punished by law.

Ludwig van Beethoven.

Vienna, June 28, 1814.

Moscheles, then just twenty years of age, wrote about this time in his diary: "The offer has been made to me to make the pianoforte score of the masterpiece 'Fidelio.' What could be more desirable?" "We now find entries," says his widow, "of how he carried two, and again two numbers to Beethoven, who looked through them; and then, alternately, 'he changed little' or 'he changed nothing,' or sometimes 'he simplified it' or 'he reinforced it.' One note reads, 'Coming early to Beethoven, he was still in bed; this day he was particularly merry, leaped up at once, and, as he was, went to the window, which opened on the Schottenbastei, to look through the arranged numbers. Naturally the street boys assembled under the window until he cried out: 'Damn the youngsters, what do they want?' I smilingly pointed to his garment. 'Yes, yes, you are right,' said he and hastily threw a dressing-gown over his shoulders.[22] When we reached the last great duet, 'Namenlose Freude,' where I had written down the text 'Ret-terin des Gat-ten,' he crossed it out and wrote 'Rett-erin des Gatt-en'; for it was not possible to sing on 't.' Under the last number I had written '*fine* with God's help.' He was not at home when I carried it to him; and when he sent it back under mine were the words: 'O man, help yourself.'"

Before bidding Moscheles farewell for the next half a dozen years, let us look at a few sentences from the preface to the English translation of Schindler's book, partly for the information they impart and partly to prevent a mistake or two from passing into history on his authority. He thus writes:

"In the year 1809[23] my studies with my master, Weber [Dionysius], closed; and being then also fatherless, I chose Vienna for my residence to work out my future musical career. Above all, I longed to see and become acquainted with *that man*, who had exercised so powerful an influence over my whole being; whom though I scarcely understood, I blindly worshipped. I learnt that Beethoven was most difficult of access and would admit no pupil but Ries; and for a long time my anxiety to see him remained ungratified. In the year 1810, however, the longed-for opportunity presented itself. I happened to be one morning in the music-shop of Domenico Artaria, who had just

[22] Beethoven had forgotten that he no longer lived on the fourth story. (TDR, III, 430, n. 1.) [23] It should be 1808. (TDR, III, 431.)

been publishing some of my early attempts at composition, when a man entered with short and hasty steps, and, gliding through the circle of ladies and professors assembled on business, or talking over musical matters, without looking up, as though he wished to pass unnoticed, made his way direct for Artaria's private office at the bottom of the shop. Presently Artaria called me in and said: '*This is Beethoven!*' and to the composer, 'This is the youth of whom I have just spoken to you.' Beethoven gave me a friendly nod and said he had just heard a favorable account of me. To some modest and humble expressions, which I stammered forth, he made no reply and seemed to wish to break off the conversation. I stole away with a greater longing for that which I had sought than I had felt before this meeting, thinking to myself—'Am I indeed such a musical nobody that he could not put one musical question to me?—nor express one wish to know who had been my master, or whether I had any acquaintance with his work?' My only satisfactory mode of explaining the matter and confronting myself for this omission was in Beethoven's tendency to deafness, for I had seen Artaria speaking close to his ear. . . .

"I never missed the Schuppanzigh Quartets, at which he was often present, or the delightful concerts at the Augarten, where he conducted his own Symphonies. I also heard him play several times, which, however, he did but rarely, either in public or in private. The productions which made the most lasting impression upon me, were his Fantasia with orchestral accompaniments and chorus and his Concerto in C minor. I also used to meet him at the houses of MM. Zmeskall and Zizius, two of his friends, through whose musical meetings Beethoven's works first made their way to public attention [?]: but, in place of better acquaintance with the great man, I had mostly to content myself on his part with a distant salute.

"It was in the year 1814, when Artaria undertook to publish a pianoforte arrangement of Beethoven's *Fidelio*, that he asked the composer whether I might be permitted to make it: Beethoven assented upon condition that he should see my arrangement of each of the pieces, before it was given into the engraver's hands. Nothing could be more welcome to me, since I looked upon this as the long wished-for opportunity to approach nearer to the great man and to profit by his remarks and corrections. During my frequent visits, the number of which I tried to multiply by all possible excuses, he treated me with the kindest indulgence. Although his increasing deafness was a considerable hindrance to our conversation, yet he gave me many instructive hints, and even played to me such parts as he wished to have arranged in a particular manner for the pianoforte. I thought it, however, my duty not to put his kindness to the test by robbing him of his valuable time by any subsequent visits; but I often saw him at Mälzel's, where he used to discuss the different plans and models of a Metronome [the Chronometer], which the latter was going to manufacture, and to talk over the 'Battle of Vittoria,' which he wrote at Mälzel's suggestion. Although I knew Mr. Schindler, and was aware that he was much with Beethoven at that time [?], I did not avail myself of my acquaintance with him for the purpose of intruding myself upon the composer."

As to the *Fidelio*, Moscheles told the writer (February 22, 1856) that he was selected to arrange it because Beethoven was on bad terms with Hummel; and that to hasten the work, Hummel did arrange one of the finales; but when Beethoven received it and looked it through, he tore it to pieces without remark, or explaining why he did so. Two errors in these last sentences will at once strike the reader—that Schindler was then much with Beethoven, and that Beethoven was on bad terms with Hummel. The explanation is easy. Moscheles had translated Schindler's book, and unconsciously had adopted certain ideas from it, which in course of time had taken the form of memories. This is a common experience with us all. The true reason why Beethoven rejected Hummel as the arranger of *Fidelio* is obvious: Hummel was a man of sufficient talent and genius to have a style of his own—and one (as is well known) not much to Beethoven's taste; *Fidelio* arranged by him would necessarily exhibit more or less of this style; moreover, Beethoven could not feel the same freedom in discarding, correcting, making suggestions if the work were done by him, as when performed by a young man like Moscheles.

So the score was not immediately published—a mistake, as the event proved, and as Beethoven himself mentioned in the note to Treitschke below. "In accordance with his wish," says Treitschke, in concluding the account from which so much has been cited, "I offered our work to foreign theatres; several ordered it, others declined because they already had the opera by Paër. Still others preferred to get it in a cheaper way by hiring cunning copyists who, as is still the custom, *stole* the text and music and sacrificed them for a few florins' profit. It was of little use to us that others translated *Fidelio* into several languages and made large sums by it. The composer received scarcely more than a handsome laurel-wreath, and I a little leaf, and the sincere affection of the Immortal."

Meantime the season had far advanced, the summer heats were approaching, the departure of the nobility and the wealthy for their country-seats was near, and Beethoven thought, perhaps justly, that new attractions must be added to *Fidelio* and the public journals moved to say an appropriate word, to secure him a full house at his benefit, so long deferred. Doubtless with this last object in view, he now gave the *Friedensblätter* the song "An die Geliebte" (text by Stoll), which was engraved as a supplement to the number for July 12, and a notice closing with

A WORD TO HIS ADMIRERS

How often in your chagrin, that his depth was not sufficiently appreciated, have you said that van Beethoven composes only for posterity! You have, no doubt, been convinced of your error since if not before the general enthusiasm aroused by his immortal opera "Fidelio"; and also that the present finds kindred souls and sympathetic hearts for that which is great and beautiful without withholding its just privileges from the future.

This was certainly to the purpose. The earliest hint as to what the new attractions of the opera were to be is found in a note to Treitschke:

For heaven's sake, dear friend! It seems that you have no instinct for money-making— See to it that Fidelio is not given *before* my benefit. This was the arrangement with *Schreyvogel*— Since Saturday when you last saw me at the theatre, I have been confined to my bed and room, and not until yesterday did I feel a trace of improvement. I might have visited you today did I know that poets like Phaeacians observe Sunday! We must talk about sending out the opera so that you may receive your quarter share and so it is not sent out in stolen copies all over the world. I know nothing of business but think that if we were to sell the score to a publisher here and it were to be printed, the result would be better for you and me. If I understand you correctly I ought to have the song by this time— Please, dear friend, hurry it up!— Are you angry? Have I offended you? If so, it was done inadvertently, and therefore forgive an ignoramus and musician. Farewell, let me know something soon.

Your grateful debtor and friend Beethoven

Milder has had her aria for a fortnight, I shall learn today or tomorrow whether she knows it. It will not take her long.

Beethoven's benefit performance of *Fidelio* took place on Monday evening, July 18, 1814. The song so impatiently awaited could have been no other than Rocco's "gold aria" which had been sung only in the three perform-ances of 1805. Beethoven, now desiring to give Weinmüller a solo, restored it to the score. Jahn, in his edition of *Leonore*, gives two texts—the original by Sonnleithner and one which he conjectures may have been written by Breuning. From them Treitschke now prepared a text, as we have it, by changing somewhat and improving Sonnleithner's first stanza and joining it to the second stanza of the other, unchanged except by the omission of its close.

As to the new piece for Milder, Treitschke says implicitly it was "a grand aria for Leonore, but as it checked the rapid movement of the rest it was again omitted." In the advertisement of his benefit Beethoven says only: "For this performance . . . two new pieces have been added." The notice in the *Friedensblätter* next day is somewhat more explicit: "*Fidelio* will be given with two entirely new arias to be sung by Mme. Milder and Hr. Weinmüller, for the benefit of the composer"; and from the *Sammler* we learn that at the performance the new aria sung by Madame Milder-Hauptmann "was very effective and the excellent performance seemed to labor under peculiarly great difficulties." What is known from printed sources concerning the aria is this: the text was "Komm' Hoffnung"; it was not the aria already sung by Milder six times this season; it was the one which the composer referred to in the letter above, not certain that she can sing after fourteen days' study. —⋖{The Vienna correspondent for the Leipzig *Allg. Mus. Zeit.* reports; "The second aria with four horns obbligato (E major) which was performed with power and feeling by Mad. Milder-Hauptmann (Fidelio) is beautiful and of great artistic worth. Yet it seems to this critic that now the first act has lost its fast pace and is held up by the performance of these two arias and has become unnecessarily long." As Riemann points out, the critic made the pardonable error of stating that the new aria was accompanied by four horns where actually three horns were supplemented by a bassoon.}⋗—

Now we read in the "Fidelio" sketchbook (p. 107) about the time when Beethoven wrote to Treitschke about "sending out the opera": "Hamburg, 15 ducats in gold; Grätz, 12 fl.; Frankfort, 15 ducats in gold; Stuttgart, 12 ducats in gold; Carlsruhe, 12 ducats in gold; Darmstadt, 12 ducats in gold";— evidently the price of the opera; and on the next page, "Abscheulicher, wo eilst du hin!" i.e., sketches for the recitative; but sketches for the aria are not known. Were the informants not in error and was not the new aria after all the one which Moscheles arranged and which is still sung?[24]

On July 14, 1814, shortly before the performance, Beethoven wrote the following letter to Archduke Rudolph:

Your Imperial Highness! Every time I enquire after your health I hear nothing but good news.— As to my humble existence, up until now I have been bound, unable to leave Vienna in order to be near Y. I. H., and robbed likewise of the pleasure of beautiful nature which is so necessary to me.— The management of the theatre is so honest that in spite of a promise, it has already performed my opera Fidelio without thinking of my benefit. This amiable honesty it would have practised again had I not been on guard like a former French customs officer.— Finally after considerable exertion on my part it has been arranged that my benefit of Fidelio shall take place on Monday, July 18.— This *benefit* is rather an *exception*[25] at this time of the year, but a benefit for the author may become a little festival if the work had at least a modicum of success.— To this festival the master humbly invites his exalted pupil, and hopes—yes I hope that your Imperial Highness will graciously accept and illumine the occasion with your presence.— It would be nice if Y. I. H. would try to persuade the other Imperial Highnesses to attend this representation of my opera.— I myself shall observe here all that respectful homage demands.— Because of *Vogl's* illness I was able to gratify my desire to give the rôle of Pizarro to Forti, for which his voice is better adapted— But because of this there are daily rehearsals, which will benefit the *performance*, but make it impossible to wait upon Y. I. H. in Baden before the benefit.— Please accept my words kindly and Y. I. H. remember me most graciously.— Your Imperial Highness' faithful and most obedient servant,

Ludwig van Beethoven

[24] For further discussion of the problem see *II Beeth.*, pp. 302-06. (TDR, III, 435, n. 1.) See also W. Hess, *Beethovens Oper Fidelio*, pp. 179-80.

[25] Another untranslatable play on words: "Diese *Einnahme* ist wohl mehr eine *Ausnahme*," etc. (TK, II, 286, n. 1.)

Next day, Friday the 15th, appeared, over his own signature, the advertisement of "Beethoven's Benefit" on Monday, the 18th. "Boxes and reserved seats may be ordered Saturday and Sunday in the lodgings of the undersigned on the Mölkerbastei, in the Baron Pasqualati house, No. 94, in the first story." Imagine his comical consternation when the *Wiener Zeitung* came to hand and he read the "Pasqualatischen" instead of the "Bartenstein-'schen" house! But the number was correct and that would save his friends the needless ascent of four flights to his old lodging. The contemporary reports of the performance are numerous and all very eulogistic. Forti, as Pizarro, was "entirely satisfactory"; the "gold aria," although well sung by Weinmüller, "did not make a great effect"; "beautiful and of artistic value was the aria in E major, [etc.]. . . . The house was very full; the applause extraordinary; the enthusiasm for the composer, who has now become a favorite of the public, manifested itself in calls before the curtain after every act." All free tickets were invalid; the pecuniary results must therefore have been in a high degree satisfactory.

Another consequence of Beethoven's sudden popularity, was the publication of a new engraving of him by Artaria, the crayon drawing for which was executed by Latronne, a French artist then in Vienna. Blasius Höfel, a young man of 22 years, was employed to engrave it. He told the writer,[26] how very desirous he was of producing a good likeness—a matter of great importance to the young artist—but that Latronne's drawing was not a good one, probably for want of a sufficient number of sittings. Höfel often saw Beethoven at Artaria's and, when his work was well advanced, asked him for a sitting or two. The request was readily granted. At the time set, the engraver appeared with his plate. Beethoven seated himself in position and for perhaps five minutes remained reasonably quiet; then suddenly springing up went to the pianoforte and began to extemporize, to Höfel's great annoyance. The servant relieved his embarrassment by assuring him that he could now seat himself near the instrument and work at his leisure, for his master had quite forgotten him and no longer knew that anyone was in the room. This Höfel did; wrought so long as he wished, and then departed with not the slightest notice from Beethoven. The result was so satisfactory, that only two sittings of less than one hour each were needed. It is well known that Höfel's is the best of all the engravings made of Beethoven. In 1851, Alois Fuchs showed to the writer his great collection, and when he came to this, exclaimed with strong emphasis: "Thus I learned to know him!"

Höfel in course of the conversation unconsciously corroborated the statements of Madame Streicher, as reported by Schindler, in regard to Beethoven's wretched condition in 1812-13. The effect upon him of his pecuniary embarrassments, his various disappointments, and of a mind ill at ease, was very plainly to be seen in his personal habits and appearance. He was at that

[26] June 23, 1860, in Salzburg. (TDR, III, 437, n. 1.)

time much accustomed to dine at an inn where Höfel often saw him in a distant corner, at a table, which though large was avoided by the other guests owing to the very uninviting habits into which he had fallen; the particulars may be omitted. Not infrequently he departed without paying his bill, or with the remark that his brother would settle it; which Carl Caspar did. He had grown so negligent of his person as to appear there sometimes positively "schmutzig" (dirty). Now, however, under the kind care of the Streichers, cheered and inspirited by the glory and emolument of the past eight months, he became his better self again; and—though now and to the end, so careless and indifferent to mere externals as occasionally to offend the sensitiveness of very nice and fastidious people—he again, as before quoted from Czerny, "paid attention to his appearance."

Meanwhile the controversy with the Kinsky heirs had entered upon a new phase. Dr. Johann Kanka, a lawyer in Prague, in a communication to the author,[27] wrote: "The information [concerning Beethoven] which I am able to give, refers for the greater part to business relations out of which, because of my personal and official position, grew the friendly intercourse with Beethoven which was cultivated for several years." Then, after a rather protracted history of the annuity and the effect produced upon it by the *Finanz-Patent* of 1811, "whereby Beethoven's means of subsistence were materially reduced and his longer residence in Vienna rendered impossible," he continues: "In this fateful crisis, I, as the judicially appointed curator of the estate of Prince Kinsky and later of that of Prince Lobkowitz, was enabled to bring about a more temperate presentation of the case already presented to the authorities charged with testamentary and guardianship affairs, touching the contractual annuities to be paid to Beethoven—a presentation which reconciled a severely literal interpretation of the law with the righteous demands of equity, and by paving the way for mutual concessions to secure a satisfactory judicial decision which Beethoven, actuated throughout his life by the noblest of feelings, bore in faithful remembrance and described to his few trusted friends as the firm cement of the friendly relations which we bore towards each other, and the reason of his continued residence in Vienna."

Dr. Kanka closed with the promise to grant for use in this work, such letters of Beethoven—"precious relics"—as remained in his possession—a promise fulfilled a few days afterwards. Thus, in half a dozen lines—indeed, by the single statement that he was the curator of the Kinsky estate and as such effected a compromise between the parties—the venerable doctor was able to expose the mistakes and destroy the hypotheses of all who treated the topic at length from Schindler onward. Beethoven's lawyer in Vienna was Dr. Adlersburg, and his "legal friend" in Prague, Dr. Wolf, who must

[27] Received July 4, 1859. The venerable man was then eighty-seven years of age. (TDR, III, 441, n. 1.)

have already become heartily weary of his client, for Beethoven himself writes in a letter to the court at Prague: "My continual urging of him to take an interest in the matter, also, I must confess, the reproaches made against him that he had not pursued the matter zealously enough because the steps which he took against the guardians remained without fruit, may have misled him into beginning the litigation." That, as is here insinuated, Wolf instituted the suit against the Kinsky heirs without explicit instructions from his client, is doubtful; but at all events that proceeding brought matters to a crisis, and led to an interview in the course of the summer between Beethoven and the administrator of the estate with the object, on the part of the latter, of effecting a settlement of the affair by compromise. Kanka, a fine musician and composer, and old friend, or rather acquaintance of Beethoven's, and of the same age, was a man also whose legal talents and knowledge must have no less deeply than favorably impressed him. The letters written during the next six months to his new friend, show us how Beethoven first relinquished the notion of a legal claim to the 1800 florins in notes of redemption, then abandoned the claim in equity, and at length came to a rational view of the matter, saw the necessity of compromising, and sought no more than to effect this on the best terms possible.[28]

Sketches for the *Elegischer Gesang*, Op. 118 ("Sanft wie du lebtest") are found among the studies for the new *Fidelio*, and this short work was probably now completed in season to be copied and delivered to his friend Pasqualati on or before the 5th of August, that day being the third anniversary of the death of his "transfigured wife," in honor of whose memory it was composed.

The Sonata in E minor, Op. 90, bears the date August 16, in which connection the following letter to Count Moritz Lichnowsky, dated September 21 from Baden, was written:

Worthy and honored Count and friend!

I did not receive your letter, unfortunately, till yesterday— My cordial thanks for your thought of me and all manner of lovely messages to the worthy Princess Christiane[29]— Yesterday I made a lovely promenade with a friend[30] in the Brühl and the subject of you particularly came up in our friendly conversation, and behold, on arriving here yesterday I find your good letter— I see that you still persist in overwhelming me with kindnesses. As I do not want you to think that *a step* which I have taken was prompted *by a new interest* or anything of that kind, I tell you that a new *sonata* of mine will soon appear *which I have dedicated to you*. I wanted to surprise you, for the dedication was set apart for you a long time ago, but your letter of yesterday leads me to make the disclosure

[28] The letters written by Beethoven to Dr. Kanka, Archduke Rudolph and Baron Pasqualati relative to this subject are printed in full in TDR, III, Appendix III. (TK, II, 290, n. 1.)

[29] Widow of Count Moritz's brother, Prince Karl Lichnowsky.

[30] For whom Beethoven probably wrote the canon "Freundschaft ist die Quelle," WoO 164, according to Kinsky-Halm, since its autograph is dated September 20, 1814. See KHV, p. 672.

now. No new cause was needed for the public expression of my feelings for your friendship and kindness—but you would distress me with anything resembling a gift, since you would totally misapprehend my purpose, and everything of the kind I could only refuse.—

I kiss the hands of the Princess for her thought of me and her kindness, *I have never forgotten how much I owe you all,* even if an unfortunate circumstance brought about conditions under which I could not show it as I should have liked to do—

Concerning what you tell me about Lord Castleregt, the matter is already well introduced. If I were to have an opinion on the subject, it would be that I think it best that Lord Castleregt not write about the work on Wellington until the Lord has heard it here— I am soon coming to the city where we will talk over everything concerning a grand concert— Nothing can be done with the court, I have made an offer—but

Al - lein allein, allein [but, but, but
jedoch silentium !!! however silence]

Farewell, my honored friend, and think of me always as worthy of your kindness—

Your Beethoven

I kiss the hands of the honored Princess C. a thousand times.

Beethoven's "Lord Castleregt" was Viscount Castlereagh, now in Vienna as British plenipotentiary in the coming Congress; and his object was to obtain through him some recognition from the Prince Regent for the dedication of the "Wellington's Victory." Nothing came of it.

There is a letter to Thomson dated September 15, and another in October, the day not specified. Both are in Italian and only signed by Beethoven. In the first, the demand of "4 zecchini" per melody was renewed, and "mille rengraziamente" were sent to the author of a sonnet printed in *The Scots Magazine and Edinburgh Literary Miscellany*[31] which Thomson had enclosed to the composer. The occasion of the poem was the performance of selections of Beethoven's music at a rural festival of artists in England. The hour was advanced to near midnight, when Graham, the Scottish poet, who was present, inspired by the music and by the beauty of the bright moonlit night, improvised the lines:

> Hark! from Germania's shore how wildly floats
> That strain divine upon the dying gale;
> O'er Ocean's bosom swell the liquid notes
> And soar in triumph to yon crescent pale.
> It changes now! and tells of woe and death;
> Of deep romantic horror murmurs low;
> Now rises with majestic, solemn flow,

[31] October, 1813, p. 776, according to Donald W. MacArdle, to whom I am further indebted for the full name of the poet: George Farquhar Graham (1789-1867).

While shadowy silence charms the wind's rude breath.
What magic hand awakes the noon of night
  With such unearthly melody, that bears
  The raptured soul beyond the tuneful spheres
To stray amid high visions of delight?
Enchanter Beethoven! I feel thy power
Thrill every trembling nerve in this lone witching hour.

The letter of October again pressed the demand of "4 zecchini," but was for the most part devoted to urging Thomson to purchase for publication the "Wellington's Victory"—about as preposterous as if Professor Max Müller[32] had solicited the editor of a popular magazine, to which he had contributed articles, to undertake a Sanskrit dictionary.

Beethoven did not get to the country for any lengthy sojourn this summer; he had only a brief stay at Baden. The Congress of Vienna was originally scheduled to meet on August 1st, but was postponed until the early fall. That Beethoven was bearing this Congress and its visiting dignitaries in mind is shown by the next series of "occasional compositions." Next to Op. 90 in the "Fidelio" sketchbook are a few hints for "Ihr weisen Gründer," which, though called a "cantata" in the sketchbook is but a chorus with orchestra—a piece of flattery intended for the royal personages at the coming Congress. It was not finished until September 3rd. This was the only work which Beethoven now had on hand suitable for a grand concert, but he was working on others. Over the title of the manuscript of "Ihr weisen Gründer" is written in pencil by him: "About this time the Overture in C."; this work, what was to be called the "Namensfeier" overture, he now had in hand.

At the same time he was working on a vocal composition of some length. The eventual result would be *Der glorreiche Augenblick*, with text by Alois Weissenbach, but at this point he was attempting to set a text whose author, whoever he was, must have profoundly studied and heartily adopted the principles of composition as set forth by Martinus Scriblerus in his "Treatise of Bathos, or the Art of Sinking in Poetry": for anything more stilted in style, yet more absurdly prosaic, with nowhere a spark of poetic fire to illuminate its dreary pages, is hardly conceivable. A short excerpt from the body of the text will suffice:[33]

Alle Stimmen	All Voices
Hört ihr klirren der Knechtschaft Ketten?	Hear ye the clang of captives' chains?
Hört ihr seufzen des Ebro Fluth?	Hear ye the sighs of the Ebro's flood?
Seht die Donau Ihr roth von Bluth?	See ye the Danube red with blood?
Wer soll helfen? ach, wer soll retten?	Who shall succour? who wipe up the stains?

[32] Philologist (1823-1900), who became Professor at Oxford in 1850.
[33] Text given by Wilhelm Virneisel, "Kleine Beethoveniana," in *Festschrift Joseph Schmidt-Görg zum 60 Geburtstag*, ed. Dagmar Weise (Bonn, 1957), pp. 363-64.

Erste Stimme	First Voice
Und Karl, aus Habsburg altem Haus,	And Karl of Habsburg, ancient line,
Zog, Gott vertrauend, gen ihn aus.	Battled with trust in God divine.
Wo Habsburg schlug am Donaustrand	Where Habsburg struck on the Danube's strands
Da schlug er ihn—und Oestreich stand.	There struck he him and Austria stands.

Zweyte Stimme	Second Voice
Und Wellington, der Spanier Hort,	And Wellington, the Spanish hoard,
Zog, Gott vertrauend, gen ihn fort,	Battled against with trust in the Lord,
Und bey Vittoria schlug er ihn,	And at Vittoria struck them he
Dass schmachvoll heim er musste flieh'n.	Till home with shame they had to flee.

Dritte Stimme	Third Voice
Die heil'ge Moskwa flammet auf,	Holy Moscow burst in flame,
Der Frevler stürzt im Siegeslauf;	The villain plunged ere victory came;
Porussia sieht, die Völker sehn der Freyheit Gluth,	Prussia sees, the people see Freedom's glow,
Und Moskwa gleich flammt Aller Muth.	And Moscow's flames to all courage show.
	[and so forth, *ad nauseam*]]

Neither the Overture nor the choral piece to be set to the above was finished, when the arrival at Vienna of the King of Wurtemburg on the 22nd of September, of the King of Denmark on the 23d and the announcement of the coming of the Russian Emperor with the King of Prussia on Sunday the 25th, brought Beethoven back to the city. Owing to the failure of Lobkowitz, the Court theatres had passed under the management of Palffy. If there be any truth whatever in his alleged hostility to Beethoven, it is not a little remarkable that the first grand opera performed in the presence of the monarchs—Monday the 26th—was *Fidelio*. One of the audience on that evening, in a published account of his "Journey to the Congress," records: "To-day I went to the Court Theatre and was carried to heaven—the opera *Fidelio* by L. v. Beethoven was given." Then follow some fifteen pages of enthusiastic eulogy. That auditor was Alois Weissenbach, R. I. Councillor, Professor of Surgery and Head Surgeon of the St. John's Hospital in Salzburg, where after sixteen years' service in the Austrian armies he had settled, devoting his leisure to poetry and the drama. His tragedy *Der Brautkranz* in iambics, five acts, was produced January 14, 1809, at the Kärnthnerthor-Theater. Whether his *Barmeciden* and *Glaube und Liebe* were also brought out in Vienna we have no means of deciding. At all events, he was a man of high reputation. Of him Franz Graeffer writes:[34] "That Weissenbach was a passionate admirer of Beethoven's is a matter of course; their natures were akin, even physically, for the Tyrolean

---

[34] *Kleine Wiener Memoiren* (1845), pp. 188ff.

was just as hard of hearing. . . . But it was pitiful to hear them shout at each other. It was therefore not possible thoroughly to enjoy them. Strangely enough in a little room, such as in the inn Zur Rose in the Wollzeile, Weissenbach heard much better, and conversed more freely and animatedly. Otherwise the most prolific, amiable, lively of social companions. A blooming man, aging, always neatly and elegantly clad. How learned he was as a physician will not be forgotten."

Weissenbach himself writes:[35] "Completely filled with the gloriousness of the creative genius of this music, I went from the theatre home with the firm resolve not to leave Vienna without having made the personal acquaintance of so admirable a man; and strangely enough! when I reached my lodgings I found Beethoven's visiting card upon my table with a cordial invitation to breakfast with him in the morning. And I drank coffee with him and received his handgrasp and kiss. Yes, mine is the proud privilege of proclaiming publicly, Beethoven honored me with the confidence of his heart. I do not know if these pages will ever fall into his hands: if he learns that they mention his name either in praise or blame he will indeed (I know him and know his strong self-reliance) not read them at all; herein, too, he maintains his independence, he whose cradle and throne the Lord established away from this earth. . . . Beethoven's body has a strength and rudeness which is seldom the blessing of chosen spirits. He is pictured in his countenance. If Gall, the phrenologist, has correctly located the mind, the musical genius of Beethoven is manifest in the formation of his head. The sturdiness of his body, however, is in his flesh and bones only; his nervous system is irritable in the highest degree and even unhealthy. How it has often pained me to observe that in this organism the harmony of the mind was so easily put out of tune. He once went through a terrible typhus and from that time dates the decay of his nervous system and probably also his melancholy loss of hearing. Often and long have I spoken with him on this subject; it is a greater misfortune for him than for the world. It is significant that before that illness his hearing was unsurpassably keen and delicate, and that even now he is painfully sensible to discordant sounds; perhaps because he is himself euphony. . . . His character is in complete agreement with the glory of his talent. Never in my life have I met a more childlike nature paired with so powerful and defiant a will; if heaven had bestowed nothing upon him but his heart, this alone would have made him one of those in whose presence many would be obliged to stand up and do obeisance. Most intimately does that heart cling to everything good and beautiful by a natural impulse which surpasses all education by far. . . . There is nothing in the world, no earthly greatness, nor wealth, nor rank, nor state can bribe it; here I could speak of instances in which I was a witness."

We know no reason to suppose that Beethoven received Weissenbach's

[35] *Meine Reise zum Kongress in Wien* (Vienna, 1816). (TDR, III, 447, n. 1.)

poem before the interview with him; but, on the contrary, think the citations above preclude such a hypothesis. Moreover, the composer's anxiety to have an interview at the earliest possible moment arose far more probably from a hint or the hope, that he might obtain a text better than the one in hand, than from any desire to discuss one already received. What is certain is this: Beethoven did obtain from Weissenbach the poem "Der glorreiche Augenblick," and cast the other aside unfinished—as it remains to this day.

First, Beethoven had to complete his overture, the supposed scope and design of which may occupy us a moment.

Scott said, that when he wrote *Waverly, or 'Tis Sixty Years Since*, it had already become impossible for the people of England and Scotland, in their greatly changed and improved condition, to form any correct conception of the state of public feeling in those kingdoms in 1745, when the Pretender made that last effort against the House of Brunswick which is the subject of *Waverly*, and the defeat of which is commemorated by Handel in *Judas Maccabaeus*. It is equally difficult for us to conceive adequately the sensations caused by the downfall of Napoleon at the time of which we are writing.

When monarchs play chess with armies, "check to the king" means the shock of contending foes and all the horrors of war; but in perusing the history of Bonaparte's campaigns, we become so interested in the "game" as to forget the attendant ruin, devastation and destruction, the blood, carnage and death, that made all central Europe for twenty long years one vast charnel-house. But only in proportion as the imagination is able to form a vivid picture of the horrors of those years, can it conceive that inexpressible sense of relief, the universal joy and jubilee, which outside of France pervaded all classes of society, from prince to peasant, at the fall of the usurper, conqueror and tyrant. And this not more because of that event, than because of the all-prevailing trust, that men's rights, political and religious—now doubly theirs by nature and by purchase at such infinite cost—would be gladly and gratefully accorded to them. For sovereign and subject had shared danger and suffering and every evil fortune together, and been brought into new and kindlier relations by common calamities; thus the sentiment of loyalty—the affectionate veneration of subject for sovereign—had been developed to a degree wholly unprecedented. Nothing presaged or foreboded the near advent and thirty years' sway of Metternichism. No one dreamed, that within six years the "rulers" at this moment "of happy states" would solemnly declare, "all popular and constitutional rights to be holden no otherwise than as grants and indulgences from crowned heads";[36] that they would snuff treason in every effort of the people to hold princes to their pledged words; and that their vigilance would effectually prevent the access of any "Leonore" to the Pellicos, Liebers and Reuters languishing for such treasons in their state prisons. At that time all this was hidden in the future; the very intoxication of joy and extravagant loyalty then ruled the hour.

[36] Laybach Circular of May, 1821. (TDR, III, 450, n. 1.)

It was, as we believe, to give these sentiments musical expression, that Beethoven now took up and wrought out certain themes and motives, noted by him in connection with the memorandum: "Freude schöner Götterfunken Tochter—Work out the overture!"[37] The poetic idea of the work was not essentially changed—the joy of liberated Europe simply taking the place of the joy of Schiller's poem. But the composer's particular purpose was to produce it as the graceful homage of a loyal subject on the Emperor's name-day. How else can the autograph inscription upon the original manuscript be understood: "Overture by L. v. Beethoven, on the first of Wine-month, 1814—Evening to the name-day of our Emperor"? In the arts, as in literature, there is no necessary connection between that which gives rise to the ideas of a work, and the occasion of its composition; the occasion of this overture was clearly the name-day festival of Emperor Franz; hence it has become known as the "Namensfeier" Overture.[38]

From the "first of the Wine-month" (October 1) to the name-day there remained three days for copying and rehearsal. The theatre had been closed on the 29th and 30th of September, to prepare for a grand festival production of Spontini's *La Vestale* on Saturday evening, October 1st; but for the evening of the name-day, Tuesday the 4th, *Fidelio* (its 15th performance) was selected. It was obviously the intention of Beethoven to do homage to Emperor Franz, by producing his new overture as a prelude on this occasion. What, then, prevented? Seyfried answers this question. He writes: "For this year's celebration of the name-day of His Majesty, the Emperor, Kotzebue's allegorical festival play, *Die hundertjährigen Eichen* had been ordered. Now, as generally happens, this decision was reached so late that I, as the composer, was allowed only three days, and two more for studying and rehearsing all the choruses, dances, marches, groupings, etc." This festival play was on the 3rd and rendered the necessary rehearsals of Beethoven's overture impossible. —Nottebohm, however, dates the last sketches for the "Namensfeier" Overture in early 1815 and thus believes that the date on the autograph refers not to the completion of the work, as Thayer had believed, but to the date when Beethoven began to write out his fair copy. Kinsky-Halm concludes from this line of reasoning that the piece was not performed in 1814 because it had not been completed.[39] At any rate, for some reason the overture was not completed until March, 1815.—

Fidelio was sung for the sixteenth time on the 9th. Tomaschek, one of the auditors on that evening, gave to the public in 1846 notes of the impression made upon him, in a criticism which, by its harshness, forms a curious contrast to Weissenbach's eulogy. Having exhausted that topic, however, Tomaschek then describes his meetings with the composer in an account which has a peculiar interest not only because, though general descriptions

---

[37] *Beeth.*, p. 41.

[38] For an account of the various stages of the composition of Op. 115, which according to Nottebohm goes back to 1809, see *II Beeth.*, pp. 14-20.

[39] *II Beeth.*, pp. 20 and 316; KHV, p. 332.

of Beethoven's style of conversation are numerous, attempts to report him in detail are very rare. The description is also valuable because of its vivid display of Beethoven's manner of judging his contemporaries, which was so offensive to them and begat their lasting enmity. One of the contemporaries this time, the "young foreign artist," was Giacomo Meyerbeer (1791-1864). A dramatic poem, *Moses*, words by Klingemann, music (overture, choruses and marches) by von Seyfried, was to be given on the evening of Tomaschek's first call. Tomaschek said he had no desire "to hear music of this kind" and the dialogue proceeded as follows:[40]

B.—My God! There must also be such composers, otherwise what would the vulgar crowd do?

T.—I am told that there is a young foreign artist here who is said to be an extraordinary pianoforte player.

B.—Yes, I, too, have heard of him, but have not heard him. My God! let him stay here only a quarter of a year and we shall hear what the Viennese think of his playing. I know how everything new pleases here.

T.—You have probably never met him?

B.—I got acquainted with him at the performance of my Battle, on which occasion a number of local composers played some instrument. The big drum fell to the lot of that young man. Ha! ha! ha!—I was not at all satisfied with him; he struck the drum badly and was always behindhand, so that I had to give him a good dressing-down. Ha! Ha! Ha!—That may have angered him. There is nothing in him; he hasn't the courage to hit a blow at the right time.

Before Tomaschek visited Beethoven again (November 24th) Meyerbeer's opera *Die beiden Kalifen* had been produced at the Kärnthnerthor Theatre. When Tomaschek came to take his farewell, Beethoven was in the midst of preparations for his concert and insisted upon giving him a ticket. Then the conversation goes on:[41]

T.—Were you at [Meyerbeer]'s opera?

B.—No; it is said to have turned out very badly. I thought of you; you hit it when you said you expected little from his compositions. I talked with the opera singers, and that night after the production of the opera at the wine-house where they generally gather, I said to them frankly: You have distinguished yourselves again!—what piece of folly have you been guilty of again? You ought to be ashamed of yourselves not to know better, nor to be able to judge better, to have made such a noise about this opera! I should like to talk to you about it, but you do not understand me.

T.—I was at the opera; it began with hallelujah and ended with requiem.

B.—Ha, ha, ha, ha, ha! It's the same with his playing. I am often asked if I have heard him—I say no; but from the opinions of my acquaintances who are capable of judging such things I could tell that he has agility indeed, but otherwise is a very superficial person.

[40] *Libussa* (Prague), 1846, pp. 359ff. (TDR, III, 452, n. 2.)   [41] *Ibid.*, 1847, pp. 430ff. (TDR, III, 454, n. 3.)

T.—I heard that before he went away he played at Herr ———'s and pleased much less.

B.—Ha, ha, ha, ha! What did I tell you?—I understand that. Let him settle down here for half a year and then let us hear what will be said of his playing. All this signifies nothing. It has always been known that the greatest pianoforte players were also the greatest composers; but how did they play? Not like the pianists of to-day, who prance up and down the keyboard with passages which they have practised—*putsch, putsch, putsch*;—what does that mean? Nothing! When true pianoforte virtuosi played it was always something homogeneous, an entity; if written down it would appear as a well thought-out work. That is pianoforte playing; the other thing is nothing!

T.—I find it very amusing that . . . [Fuss][42] who himself appears to have a very limited grasp of the instrument, has pronounced him the greatest pianoforte-player.

B.—He has absolutely no grasp of instrumental music. He is a wretched man; I will tell him to his face. Once he praised an instrumental piece excessively which is fit for the ears of goats and donkeys; I can't help laughing over the uncertainty in his heart. He understands vocal music and should stick to it; outside of that he understands wretchedly little about composition.

Beethoven had announced a grand concert for November 20, in the large Redoutensaal but advertisements in the *Wiener Zeitung* of the 18th post-poned it till November 22nd, then till the 27th, and finally till the 29th.[43] On November 30th, the newspaper reports: "At noon yesterday, Hr. Ludwig v. Beethoven gave all music-lovers an ecstatic pleasure. In the R. I. Redouten-saal he gave performances of his beautiful musical representation of Welling-ton's Battle at Vittoria, preceded by the symphony which had been composed as a companion-piece. Between the two works an entirely new . . . cantata, *Der glorrreiche Augenblick*." One would like to know what Beethoven said when he read this; for the symphony supposed by the writer to be composed as a companion-piece (*Begleitung*) to the "Wellington's Victory" was the magnificent Seventh!

The solo singers in the Cantata were Mme. Milder, Dem. Bondra, Hr. Wild and Hr. Forti, all of whom sang well, and Mme. Milder wonderfully. "The two Empresses, the King of Prussia" and other royalties were present and "the great hall was crowded. Seated in the orchestra were to be seen the foremost virtuosi, who were in the habit of showing their respect for him and art by taking part in Beethoven's Akademies." All the contemporary notices agree as to the enthusiastic reception of the Symphony and the Battle, and that the Cantata, notwithstanding the poverty of the text, was, on the whole, worthy of the composer's reputation and contained some very fine

[42] Johann Evangelist Fuss (1777-1819) at that time Vienna correspondent for the *Allge-meine Musikalische Zeitung*. (TDR, III, 457, n. 1.)

[43] The circumstances connected with the last postponement of this concert and the onerous conditions which Count Palffy sought to impose upon Beethoven are interestingly told by Dr. Frimmel in his *Beethoven-Studien*, II, pp. 41ff. (TDR, III, 460, n. 1.)

numbers. The concert, with precisely the same programme, was repeated in the same hall on Friday, December 2d, for Beethoven's benefit—nearly half the seats being empty! And again in the evening of the 25th for the benefit of the St. Mark's Hospital, when, of course, a large audience was present. Thus the Cantata was given three times in four weeks, and probably Spohr, who was still in Vienna, played in the orchestra; yet he gravely asserts in his autobiography that "the work was not performed at that time."

The proposed third concert for Beethoven's benefit was abandoned and there is no clue to the "new things in hand" for it, which Beethoven mentioned in a letter to Archduke Rudolph,[44] unless possibly the "Meeresstille und glückliche Fahrt" may have been begun for the occasion. The most remarkable and gratifying thing in another letter, however, is to find Beethoven once more speaking of "pleasures and joy"[45]—whence arising, we learn from Schindler. True, he does not, nor cannot yet, speak from personal observation; but his well-known relations to the composer began while the memories of these days were still fresh; and what he records is derived from Beethoven himself for the most part, though, as usual, he has inserted a statement or two, honestly made, but not the less incorrect on that account. But first, a paragraph from an article by Schnitzler in Raumer's *Hist. Taschenbuch*, published in 1863: "The role which Razumovsky played in Vienna at this time was one of unparalleled brilliancy. From the first weeks of the Congress his house was full. Thus Gentz notes under date Sept. 18: 'Visited Razumovsky; there innumerable visitors, among others Lord and Lady Castlereagh, Count Münster, Count Westphalen, Mr. Coke, the Marquis de Saint-Marsan, Count Castellafu, all the Prussians, etc.' But as balls soon became the order of the day and Count Stackelberg had given his on October 20, 1814, when the Czar and Czarina of Russia, the King of Prussia and other grandees of all kinds appeared, he also planned one for December 6, and Gentz, who permitted himself the magical vision for only a moment and had to work that night till two o'clock on his dispatches, assures us that this feast was the most beautiful of all that he had attended since the arrival of the French monarch. It was only overshadowed by that which Czar Alexander gave in the same palace, which he borrowed for the occasion from his princely subject."

Turn we to Schindler:[46] "The end of the second period [in Beethoven's life] showed us the composer on a plane of celebrity which may fairly be described as one of the loftiest ever reached by a musician in the course of his artistic strivings. Let us not forget that it was the fruit of twenty years of tireless endeavor. The great moment in the history of the world with which this celebration of his fame was synchronous could not fail to give the incident a brilliancy unparalleled in the history of music. The apparent extravagance of the statement is pardonable when we add that nearly all the rulers of

[44] *A* 509.   [45] *A* 505.   [46] *Biogr.*, I, pp. 233-34.

Europe who met at the Vienna Congress placed their seals on our master's certificate of fame."

As Razumovsky was not elevated to the rank of Prince until June 3, 1815, Schindler, in his next sentences, is all wrong in making that incident "the cause of festivities of a most extraordinary character to which Beethoven was always invited." He continues: "There he was the object of general attention on the part of all the foreigners; for it is the quality of creative genius combined with a certain heroism, to attract the attention of all noble natures. Shall we not call it heroism, when we see the composer fighting against prejudices of all kinds, traditional notions in respect of his art, envy, jealousy and malice on the part of the mass of musicians, and besides this against the sense, his hearing, most necessary to him in the practice of his art, and yet winning the exalted position which he occupies? No wonder that all strove to do him homage. He was presented by Prince [Count] Razumovsky to the assembled monarchs, who made known their respect for him in the most flattering terms. The Empress of Russia tried in particular to be complimentary to him. The introduction took place in the rooms of Archduke Rudolph, in which he was also greeted by other exalted personages. It would seem as if the Archduke was desirous always to take part in the celebration of his great teacher's triumph by inviting the distinguished foreigners to meet Beethoven. It was not without emotion that the great master recalled those days in the Imperial castle and the palace of the Russian Prince; and once he told with a certain pride how he had suffered the crowned heads to pay court to him and had always borne himself with an air of distinction."

There is reason to believe that these receptions in the apartments of the Archduke did not begin until those at Razumovsky's had come to their disastrous end. Huge as the palace was, it lacked space for the crowds invited thither to the Czar's festivities. A large temporary structure of wood was therefore added on the side next the garden, in which, on the evening of December 30th, a table for 700 guests was spread. Between five and six o'clock of the morning of the 31st, this was discovered to be on fire—probably owing to a defective flue—the conflagration extending to the main building and lasting until noon.

"Within the space of a few hours several rooms in this gorgeous establishment, on which for 20 years its creator had expended everything that splendor, artistic knowledge and liberality could offer, were prey of the raging flames. Among them were the precious library and the inestimable Canova room completely filled with sculptures by this master, which were demolished by the falling of the ceiling.

"The loss was incalculable. To rebuild the palace out of his own means was not to be thought of; but Alexander lost no time in offering his assistance and in sending Prince Wolkonski to him to learn how much money would be required to defray the principal cost. The Count estimated it at 400,000 silver rubles, which sum he requested as a loan, and received on January 24, 1815. But the sum was far from enough, and in order to obtain further loans, ownership of the splendid building had to be sacrificed."

And thus Razumovsky also passes out of our history.[47]

Among the visitors to Vienna at the time of the Congress was Varnhagen von Ense, who had gone into the diplomatic service; he came in the company of the Prussian Chancellor von Hardenberg. His attitude toward Beethoven had cooled—probably because of Oliva's complaints touching Beethoven's behavior towards him. His brief report of his meeting with the composer derives some interest from its allusion to Prince Radziwill, to whom Beethoven dedicated the Overture, Op. 115 (which was not published until 1825). The report (printed in Varnhagen's *Denkwürdigkeiten,* Vol. III, pp. 314-15) is as follows: "Musical treats were offered on all hands, concerts, the church, opera, salon, virtuosi and amateurs all gave of their best. Prince Anton Radziwill, who was already far advanced in his composition of Goethe's *Faust* and here gave free rein to his musical inclinations, was the cause of my again looking up my sturdy Beethoven, who, however, since I saw him last had grown more deaf and unsociable, and was not to be persuaded to gratify our wishes. He was particularly averse to our notables and gave expression to his repugnance with angry violence. When reminded that the Prince was the brother-in-law of Prince Louis Ferdinand of Prussia, whose early death he had so deeply deplored and whose compositions he esteemed highly, he yielded a trifle and agreed to the visit. But it is not likely that a more intimate acquaintance followed. I also refrained from taking the uncouth artist to Rahel, for society rendered him obstreperous and nothing could be done with him alone, nothing could be done unless he was disposed to play. Besides, though famous and honored, he was not yet on that pinnacle of recognition which he has since attained."

There is reason to believe that Beethoven also entertained the idea of composing Goethe's *Faust.* As early as October 1808, a writer in Cotta's *Morgenblatt* writes: "The clever Beethoven has a notion to compose Goethe's *Faust* as soon as he has found somebody who will adapt it for the stage for him." Max Unger[48] cites a portion of a letter from Count Heinrich Otto van Leoben (who wrote under the pen name Isidorus Orientalis) to the poet and doctor, Justinus Kerner in Heidelberg on August 29, 1814: "Do you know also that our master [Goethe] is writing a drama for October 18th? I dream of it! And that Beethoven has gotten him to arrange his Faust for music? . . ." Unger believes that at their meetings in 1812 Goethe and Beethoven may have talked over different plots and settled on *Faust.* Beet-

[47] According to Frimmel (*FRBH,* II, p. 52) it is certain that despite the fire, Razumovsky's musicales did not stop abruptly; for example, the quartet players were not pensioned off until 1816.

[48] "Goethes Faust und Beethoven," *Österreiche Musikzeitschrift,* IX, 1950, p. 182.

hoven's setting of "Das Flohlied" (sketched 1790-92, final version 1809) and sketches for "Gretchen am Spinrad" (*ca.* 1799) and "Uns geht es Kannibalisch wohl, als wie Fünfhundert Säuen" (apparently for a canon) remain, however, the only passages from *Faust* with which Beethoven is known to have worked. And after this year there is no further mention of the *Faust* project.

The following letter to the writer Johann Baptist Rupprecht[49] introduces one of Beethoven's new acquaintances:

> With the greatest pleasure, my esteemed R., I shall put your poem to music and I shall shortly deliver it to you in person— Whether it will be heavenly, that I do not know, since I am only earthly. However, I shall do all in my power, to approach as closely as possible your exaggerated prejudice in regard to me.
>
> Your friend and servant Beethoven[50]

The poem was "Merkenstein" which Beethoven set twice. Sketches for both versions are dated by Nottebohm in the fall of 1814.[51] The first version, which is for one voice, was completed on December 22 according to an entry in Beethoven's journal. The second version for two voices (Op. 100) was not written out until the following year. That Beethoven had a high regard for Rupprecht's verse is shown by a later letter to the writer, in which Beethoven states: "—it would give me great pleasure if sometime you would be willing to send me 6 of your poems which are still unknown for me to compose."[52]

Among the sketches to the *Glorreiche Augenblick* appears the theme of the Polonaise for Pianoforte, Op. 89, the story of which is as follows: In a conversation with Beethoven one day, Bertolini suggested to him that, as polonaises were then so much in vogue, he should compose one and dedicate it to the Empress of Russia; for, perhaps, thereby he might also obtain some acknowledgement from Emperor Alexander for the dedication to him of the Violin Sonatas, Op. 30,—for none had ever been made. As usual, Beethoven at first scorned dictation, but at length thought better of the proposal, sat down to the pianoforte, improvised various themes and requested Bertolini to choose one, which he did. When it was completed, they waited upon Prince Wolkonski, to seek through him permission to make the proposed dedication, which was granted. At the appointed time Beethoven was admitted to an audience with the Empress and presented the Polonaise, for which he received a present of 50 ducats. On this occasion he was asked, if he had ever received anything from the Czar? As he had not, a hundred ducats was added for the Sonatas.[53]

---

[49] Rupprecht (1776-1846) was professionally a merchant and manufacturer, but his main interests were writing and botany. Later in life he became a book-censor.

[50] Translation from Sonneck's *Beethoven Letters in America*, p. 132.

[51] *II Beeth.*, pp. 308, 309, 316.

[52] See Sonneck's discussion of this letter, *op.cit.*, pp. 128-36, in which he includes reprints of both versions of "Merkenstein."

[53] In Jahn's notices these sums are doubled. This audience is doubtless the one referred

The compositions of the year were:

—◦◦{"Abschiedsgesang" for Two Tenors and Bass (J. v. Seyfried) WoO 102.[54]

Canon. "Freundschaft ist die Quelle wahrer Glückseligkeit," WoO 164,[55] for Count Lichnowsky on September 20.

Der Glorreiche Augenblick, Cantata for Four Solo Voices, Chorus and Orchestra, Op. 136.

"Ich bin der Herr von zu, Du bist der Herr von von," WoO 199. Written in a sketchbook for the *Glorreiche Augenblick*.[56]

"Des Kriegers Abschied" (Reissig), WoO 143.

Elegischer Gesang for Four Voices and Strings, Op. 118.

Fidelio, Op. 72. Revised and altered with a new Overture in E major.

"Germania" for Bass, Chorus and Orchestra (closing song of Treitschke's *Die gute Nachricht*, WoO 94.

"Ihr wiesen Gründer glückliche Staaten" (Bernard), for Chorus and Orchestra, WoO 95.

"Merkenstein" (Rupprecht), WoO 144 (first version).

Polonaise for Pianoforte, Op. 89.

Sonata for Pianoforte, Op. 90.

"Tremate, empi, tremate" (Bettoni), for Soprano, Tenor and Bass with Orchestra, Op. 116. (Practically composed in 1801-1802, but not known to have been completed and written out for performance and publication until "something for Milder" was needed in the concert of February 27th.)

"Un lieto Brindisi" for Soprano, Two Tenors and Bass and Pianoforte (Bondi), WoO 103.

The publications were:

By Artaria:

Fidelio, Op. 72, Pianoforte arrangement by I. Moscheles.

By *Friedensblätter*, July 12, as a supplement:

"An die Geliebte" (J. L. Stoll), WoO 140 (2nd version).

By Hoftheater Musik-Verlag:

"Germania" (closing song of Treitschke's *Die gute Nachricht*), WoO 94, in pianoforte transcription.

By Ludwig Maisch:

Six Allemandes for Pianoforte and Violin, WoO 42.

---

to by Schindler, as being proposed by the Empress, or perhaps was a consequence of that one. (TDR, III, 487, n. 1.)

[54] Note on the publication in the *Complete Works*: "Beethoven wrote this terzetto at the request of Magistrate Matthias Tuscher for the farewell party of Dr. Leop. Weiss before his removal to the city of Steyer." Beethoven inscribed it: "From Beethoven, so that he may no longer be touched up." [*Um nicht weiter tuschiert zu werden*. The pun on the Magistrate's name is lost in the translation. *Tuschiren* means to touch up with India ink.] (TDR, III, 483; TK, II, 303.)

[55] The autograph, inscribed "Beethoven in the Brühl 1814, September 20th," is in the Joseph Muller Collection in Closter, New Jersey.

[56] Given by Nohl, *Neue Briefe Beethovens*, pp. 83-4.

By Thomson in Edinburgh and Preston in London:

"A Select Collection of Original Irish Airs for the Voice United to Characteristic English Poetry Written for this Work with Symphonies and Accompaniment for the Pianoforte, Violin, and Violoncello. Composed by Beethoven. Vol. 1,"[57] WoO 152 and WoO 153, Nos. 1-4.

[57] See Cecil Hopkinson and C. B. Oldman, *Thomson's Collections of National Song* (Edinburgh, 1940), Plate xi.

From the oil portrait by W. J. Mähler (1804)
Courtesy of the New York Public Library

After the bust by Franz Klein (1812)
Used with permission of the Beethoven-Haus, Bonn

From a lithograph after the silhouette
by Joseph Neesen (*ca.* 1786)
Used with permission of the Beethoven-Haus, Bonn

From the crayon drawing by Stephan Decker (1824)
Used with permission of the Nationalbibliothek, Vienna

PART TWO

CHAPTER XXVIII

THE YEAR 1815

RESOLUTION OF ANNUITY PAYMENTS—
DEATH OF CARL VAN BEETHOVEN—
GUARDIANSHIP OF THE NEPHEW

BEETHOVEN might well have adopted Kotzebue's title: "The Most Remarkable Year of my Life" and written his own history for 1814, in glowing and triumphant language; but now the theme modulates into a soberer key.

In a letter of early December to the Archduke, who was then in Prague attempting to hasten a settlement of the Kinsky payments, Beethoven writes; "—then there is the *matter of a new opera*—the *subject* of which I must decide in the next few days—" The *Sammler* of December 13th explains the allusion to an opera: "It is with great pleasure that we inform the music-loving public that Herr van Beethoven has contracted to compose an opera. The poem is by Herr Treitschke and bears the title: *Romulus und Remus*." The notice was based upon this note to Treitschke: "I will compose Romulus and shall begin in a few days, I will come to you in person! first *once*—then *several times* so that we may discuss the whole matter with each other."

Now here was a promising operatic project; but before six weeks had passed came the *Allg. Mus. Zeitung* bringing Johann Fuss's musical "Review of the month of December," wherein among the items of Vienna news was a notice that "Hr. Fuss had composed an opera in three acts entitled *Romulus und Remus* for the Theater-an-der-Wien"! And this was so; portions of it were afterwards sung by a musical society of which Dr. L. Sonnleithner was a member, and in Pressburg it was put upon the stage in 1818;—but it never came to performance in the theatres of Vienna, perhaps in consequence of measures adopted after the following letter to Treitschke:

I thought I could expedite the matter by sending Herr. v. Schreyvogel a copy of this letter—but no.

You see this Fuss can attack me in all the newspapers, unless I can produce some written evidence *against him*, or [unless] you—or the director of the theatre undertake to make a settlement with him. On the other hand the business of my contract for the opera is not concluded.

I beg of you to write me an answer especially as regards Fuss's letter; the matter would be easily decided in a court of *art*, but much as we should like it to be, this is not the case . . .

The matter was so arranged with Fuss as to leave the text in Beethoven's hands; but how, and on what terms, is not known.

Of the many poets whose names became associated with Beethoven, here might be mentioned the Prussian Imperial Government Councillor Sack from Liegnitz who sent, along with a long letter, the text to his oratorio *Das Weltgericht*.[1] Beethoven does not appear to have even considered the subject.

It was about this time (precisely when the painter could not remember when speaking of it in 1860), that Beethoven sat again for his friend Mähler, who wished to add his portrait to his gallery of musicians. In his *Beethoven Handbuch*, Frimmel writes:[2] "It is a half-length portrait in three, or perhaps four copies, of which one is in Freiburg while others have been preserved by the Karajan family and in the Gesellschaft der Musikfreunde Collection."

On the 25th of January, a grand festival took place in the Burg on the occasion of the Russian Empress's birthday, which in part consisted of a concert in the Rittersaal. The last piece on the program was the canon in *Fidelio*: "Mir ist so wunderbar," and by a whimsical stroke of fortune Beethoven himself appeared, and, to the audience of emperors and empresses, kings and queens, with their ministers and retinues, played once again in public! Wild, who dates the concert a month too soon, gives an account of it in which, after telling of his own success with "Adelaide," he says: "It would be as untruthful as absurd were I to deny that my vanity was flattered by the distinction which the gathered celebrities bestowed upon me; but this performance of 'Adelaide' had one result which was infinitely more gratifying to my artistic nature; it was the cause of my coming into closer contact with the greatest musical genius of all time, Beethoven. The master, rejoiced at my choice of his song, hunted me up and offered to accompany me. Satisfied with my singing he told me that he would orchestrate the song. He did not do this, but wrote for me the cantata 'An die Hoffnung' (words by Tiedge) with pianoforte accompaniment, which, he playing for me, I sang at a matinée before a select audience."[3]

---

[1] For Sack's letter and libretto see W. Virneisel, *op.cit.*, pp. 368-75.

[2] I, p. 44; see also *Beethoven Studien*, i, pp. 59ff.

[3] Although the song was already composed in 1813, Thayer believes that he revised it for

By far the most important event in Beethoven's history during these months, was the final settlement, by compromise, of the annuity affair with the Kinsky heirs, on the 18th of January. So soon as the legal formalities could be ended and communicated to Beethoven, he issued in autograph a power of attorney to Baron Josef von Pasqualati in Prague to collect the money due, and act for him in all things necessary. On March 26th, Pasqualati acknowledged the receipt of 2479 florins V.S. (Vienna Standard) as payment on the annuity in full up to the end of March, 1815. In this instance "W.W." (*Wiener Währung*) meant notes of redemption, since the bank-notes had been retired from circulation in 1812. The compromise decree arrived at through the ministration of Dr. Kanka fixed the original annuity of 1800 florins at 1200 florins, beginning on November 3d, 1812. There was therefore due to Beethoven, for the period from November 3d to the end of March, 1815, 2890 florins, from which was deducted 411 florins, as the equivalent of the 60 ducats paid to Beethoven by Prince Kinsky in October, 1812, leaving 2479 florins as aforesaid. The decision in the case with Lobkowitz also soon followed. According to the judgment of the Court, entered on April 19, 1815, the future annual payments were fixed at 700 florins (the equivalent of 280 fl. conventional coin, silver), and the 2508 fl. arrears were ordered paid in notes of redemption within two months. Payments were made accordingly and (as Dr. v. Köchel reported in a private note to the author), from 1811 up to his death, Beethoven received on the annuity contract the following sums every year:

From Archduke Rudolph	1500 fl.
From Prince Kinsky	1200
From Prince Lobkowitz	700
Total	3400 fl.

This sum, 3400 florins in notes of redemption, was the equivalent of 1360 florins *Conventions Münze*, silver, or 952 Prussian thalers.

Notwithstanding that Prince Lobkowitz's financial affairs had been satisfactorily ordered, his return to Vienna was delayed until the spring of 1815, one reason being that (as he states in a letter to Archduke Rudolph, dated Prague, December 29, 1814) an opinion prevailed in the Austrian capital that his presence would be "unseemly." In this letter he gives expression to his feelings toward Beethoven as follows: "Although I have reason to be anything but satisfied with the behavior of Beethoven toward me, I am nevertheless rejoiced, as a passionate lover of music, that his assuredly great works are beginning to be appreciated. I heard 'Fidelio' here[4] and barring the book, I was extraordinarily pleased with the music, except the two

---

Wild in 1815 before its publication in April, 1816. Wild performed it a month later. (Cf. TDR, III, 550, n. 2.)

[4] *Fidelio* had its first performance in Prague on November 21, 1814. Liebich was the director of the theatre and C. M. von Weber, Kapellmeister. (TDR, III, 492, n. 1.)

finales, which I do not like very much. I think the music extremely effective and worthy of the man who composed it."

Is this not nobly said?

Consider these facts: Lobkowitz was now deprived of the control of his revenues; those revenues, in so far as they were based upon contracts, were subject to the *Finanz-Patent* of 1811; the curators of his estates were also bound by it; and the General Court (*Landrecht*) had no power arbitrarily to set it aside. What that tribunal could and did do was, by its assent and decree, to give binding force to such agreement between the parties in principal, as had obtained the sanction of the curators, with, probably, the consent of the principal creditors of the Prince. It follows then that the concession of Beethoven's full demand of 700 fl. in notes of redemption *could* have been obtained only through the good will and active intervention of Lobkowitz himself, using his personal influence with the other parties concerned. Schindler incidentally confirms this.

Will the reader here pause a moment and think what impression the aspersions on Lobkowitz's character in Beethoven's letters have left upon his mind? Have they not begotten a prejudice so strengthened by "damnable iteration" that it is now hardly possible to overcome it, and believe it unfounded? Lobkowitz, young, generous to prodigality, rendered careless by the very magnitude of his possessions, had, in the lapse of some twenty years, so squandered his enormous resources, as to fall into temporary embarrassments, which threw the responsibility of meeting his pecuniary engagements upon others, who were bound by the nature of their office to pay none but strictly legal claims. Thus Beethoven became a loser in part of what was originally no debt, but a gift—or rather would have been so, but for the interference of Lobkowitz.

We have here another warning of the great caution to be exercised when using private correspondence for purposes of biography. In writing of Beethoven this is especially necessary, because so large a proportion of it consists of confidential notes and communications containing the ebullitions of splenetic moments, and not seldom hasty charges and mistaken accusations, such as he gladly withdrew on learning the truth. To accept all this without question is preposterous; to use it as authentic historic matter without scrupulous examination, is to do great injustice to the dead.

The proof is ample, that Beethoven was already fully convinced of the entire innocence of both Prince Kinsky and Prince Lobkowitz of all desire to escape any really just demands upon them: yet the memory of those noble and generous personages has been made to suffer on the authority of Beethoven's hasty expressions.

A letter written in English, probably by his friend Häring, who had been much in England, and signed by Beethoven, marks the progress of his business with Thomson:

Address.

> Mr. George Thomson, merchant in the musical line.
> Edingbourgh, Scotland.

Sir,

Many concerns have prevented my answers to your favors, to which I reply only in part. All your songs with the exception of a few are ready to be forwarded. I mean those to which I was to write the accompagnements, for with respect to the 6 Canzonettes, which I am to compose I own that the honorary you offered is totally inadequate. Circumstances are here much altered and taxes have been so much raised after the English fashion that my share for 1814 was near 60 £. Besides an original good air,—and what you also wish—an Overture, are perhaps the most difficult undertakings in musical compositions. I therefore beg to state that my honorary for 6 songs or airs must be 35 £ or seventy Impl. Ducats—and for an Overture 20 £ or 50 Impl. Ducats. You will please to assign the payment here as usual, and you may depend that I shall do you justice. No artiste of talent and merit will find my pretentions extravagant.

Concerning the overture you will please to indicate in your reply whether you wish to have it composed for an easy or more difficult execution. I expect your immediate answer having several orders to attend, and I shall in a little time write more copiously in reply to your favors already received. I beg you to thank the author for the very ingenious and flattering verses, which I obtained by your means. Allow me to subscribe myself

> Sir,
> your very obedt. & humble servt.

Vienna, Feb. 7, 1815.   Ludwig van Beethoven.

There is a sketchbook in the Berlin Library, described by Nottebohm, which shows in part what compositions employed Beethoven's thoughts about this time.[5] It contains sketches for marches; an unfinished piano concerto in D;[6] the canon, "Kurz ist der Schmerz"; the last movement of the Violoncello Sonata, Op. 102 No. 1; the last part of the Overture in C, Op. 115 (evidently at the time of preparing the score); a second version of "Merkenstein"; the canon, "Lerne schweigen"; a "Symphony in B minor"; a "Sonata pastorale" for pianoforte and violoncello; a "Sonata in C minor"; the second part of "Meeresstille und glückliche Fahrt"; the last movement of the Violoncello Sonata, Op. 102 No. 2; and various projected fugal movements.— The date of these sketches is fixed by a memorandum of Beethoven on the seventh leaf, referring to Smart's production in London of "Wellington's Victory":[7] "In Drurylane Theatre on February 10th, and repeated by general request on the 13th, *Wiener Zeitung* of March 2nd." This led to inquiry, and Sir George Smart's name, as leader of the Lenten concerts in London, became known to Beethoven, who engaged his friend

---

[5] See *II Beeth.*, pp. 314-20.

[6] For an extended sketch for this work, see *ibid.*, pp. 321-22.

[7] Sir George Smart also introduced to England Beethoven's oratorio (in English and land Beethoven's oratorio (in English and

entitled *The Mount of Olives*) and the Mass in C. The oratorio was first performed on February 25, 1814, the mass in its entirety not until somewhat later. (TK, II, 310, see also n. 1.)

Häring, who knew Smart intimately, to write the following English letter in his behalf:

To Sir George Smart,
     Great Portland St., London.

My Dear Sir George:
     I see by the papers that you have brought forth in the theatre Beethoven's battle and that it was received with considerable applause. I was very happy to find that your partiality to Mr. B.'s compositions is not diminished and therefore I take the liberty in his name to thank you for the assistance you afforded in the performance of that uncommon piece of music. He has arranged it for the pianoforte, but having offered the original to his R. H. the Prince Regent, he durst not sell that arrangement to any Editor, until he knew the Prince's pleasure, not only with respect to the dedication, but in general. Having waited so many months without receiving the least acknowledgment, he begged me to apply to you for advice. His idea is to dispose of this arrangement and of several other original compositions to an Editor in London—or perhaps to several united—if they would make a handsome offer— They would besides engage to let him know *the day of the appearance for sale* of the respective pieces, in order that the Editor *here*, may not publish one copy before the day to be mentioned. At the end of this letter follows the list of such compositions, with the price, which the Author expects. I am persuaded, Sir George, you will exert yourself to benefit this great genius. He talks continually of going to England, but I am afraid that his deafness, seemingly increasing, does not allow him the execution of this favorite idea. You are informed without doubt that his opera: Fidelio, has had the most brilliant success here, but the execution is so difficult, that it would not suit any of the English houses.
     I submit here his list with the prices. None of the following pieces has been published, but No. 2, 4 and 9—have been performed with the greatest applause—

1. Serious Quartetto for 2 violins, tenor and bass............................40 guineas.
2. Battle of Vittoria—Score..70 guineas.
3. Battle of Vittoria arranged for the pianoforte..............................30 guineas.
4. A Grand Symphony—Score...70 guineas.
5. A Grand Symphony arranged for the pianoforte.........................30 guineas.
6. A Symphony—Key F—Score...40 guineas.
7. A Symphony, arranged for the pianoforte................................. 20 guineas.
8. Grand Trio for the pianoforte, violin and violoncello.................40 guineas.
9. Three Overtures for a full Orchestra.............................each 30 guineas.
10. The Three Arrangements for Pianoforte........................each 15 guineas.
11. A Grand Sonata for the pianoforte and violin..............................25 guineas.

The above is the produce of four years labour.
     Our friend Neate has not yet made his appearance here—nor is it at all known where he is roving about. We—I mean mostly amateurs—are now rehearsing Handel's Messiah—I am to be leader of the 2d violins; there will be this time 144 violins—first and second altogether, and the singers and remainder in proportion. I have been so unfortunate, as not to receive a single line or answer from England since my stay in Vienna, which is near three months; this discourages

me very much from writing, for I have dispatched immediately after my arrival several letters and have been continuing to send letters, but all in vain. Amongst those to whom I wrote about two months ago, is our friend Disi—pray if you meet him give him and his very respectable family my best regards. I have passed so many happy hours in his house, it would be highly ungrateful for me to forget such an amiable family.

Beethoven happening to call on me just now, he wishes to address a few lines to you which you will find at the bottom of this. My direction is Monsieur Jean de Häring, No. 298 Kohlmarkt, Vienne.

Poor B. is very anxious to hear something of the English editors, as he hardly can keep those of this city from him, who tease him for his works.

Häring now writes the following for Beethoven to sign:

Give me leave to thank you for the trouble you have taken several times, as I understand, in taking my works under your protection, by which I don't doubt all justice has been done. I hope you will not find it indiscreet if I solicit you to answer Mr. Häring's letter as soon as possible. I should feel myself highly flattered if you would express your wishes, that I may meet them, in which you will always find me ready, as an acknowledgment for the favors you have heaped upon my children.

Yours gratefully,

Vienna 16. March, 1815.   Ludwig van Beethoven.

And now I shall beg, my dear Sir George, not to take this long letter amiss, and to believe that I am always with the greatest regard,

Your most humble and obedient servant,

Vienna 19. March, 1815.   John Häring.

The works enumerated in this letter, taking them in the same order, are Op. 95, 91, 92, 93, 97, 113, 115, 117 and 96. Häring was evidently ignorant that all of Beethoven's new works were even then sold, except for England. Steiner had purchased them, which introduces the consideration of Beethoven's most recent important publisher.

The "K. K. Priv. Chemische Druckerey," the property of Rochus Krasinzky and Sigmund Anton Steiner, passed about 1810 into the hands of Steiner alone. In that year Tobias Haslinger (of Zell in Upper Austria), who had been one of Kapellmeister Glöggl's singing-boys at Linz and assistant in his music-shop, came to Vienna with the design of establishing himself in business, and there soon became acquainted with Steiner. He detailed to Steiner his purposes and plans and induced him to withdraw his prints and other wares from Grund's bookstore in the Singerstrasse, to open a shop of his own in the narrow passage then existing at the northeast corner of the Graben, known as the Paternoster-Gassel, and to employ him (Haslinger) as bookkeeper and manager.[8] From this position he soon rose to be partner

---

[8] Unger dates Haslinger's association with the firm, and thus with Beethoven, as probably in early 1814. See *Ludwig van Beethoven* *und seine Verleger* (Berlin and Vienna, 1921), pp. 5-6.

in the firm, S. A. Steiner and Co. Beethoven conceived an odd and whimsical liking for the young man, and for a few years his relations to the firm became very much the same as those which formerly existed between him and the Kunst- und Industrie-Comptoir. Haslinger had learned divers instruments in Linz, had begun the study of composition there and continued it in Vienna. His Opus 10, "Ideal einer Schlacht," for the pianoforte, had just been published—the subject of Homeric laughter to Jupiter-Beethoven and the other gods. He made his place of business attractive and it became a favorite resort of composers, musicians, singers, writers for the theatre, the public press and the like. In Beethoven's correspondence with the firm the composer was "Generalissimus," Steiner "Lieutenant-General," Haslinger "Adjutant," or rather the diminutive of Adjutant, "Adjutanterl." Their assistants were "Subalterns" and the shop, "Office of the Lieutenant-General."

It will be remembered that in the fall of 1813 Beethoven had arranged for a loan for his brother Carl through Steiner, and that part of the agreement stated that if the repayment of the loan [1814] reverted to Beethoven, he could have an extension in return for granting Steiner certain privileges with a new unpublished sonata. Thus it would seem that this formed the beginning of their relationship in a business way, since beginning with Op. 90, Steiner published a substantial number of Beethoven's works, as is seen in the list below. The actual terms of contract for these works have not been discovered, but the fact that there was a contract, and that Beethoven for some time remained in debt to the publisher, is evident from the correspondence of the next few years.

Our first letter to Steiner is dated February 1, 1815, and shows that Carl van Beethoven was somehow involved.

Most Wellborn Lieutenant General!

I have received today your letter to my brother and am satisfied with it, but must beg of you to pay *the costs of the pianoforte arrangement in addition.* As I am obliged to pay for *everything* in the world and *more dearly than others*, this would be a hardship for me. Besides I don't believe you can complain about the honorarium of 250 ducats— But neither do I want to complain; therefore arrange for the transcriptions yourself. But all must be looked over by me and if necessary improved. I hope that you are satisfied with this.— In addition to this you might *give my brother the collected pianoforte works of Clementi, Mozart and Haydn.* He needs them for *his little son.* Do this, my dearest Steiner, and be not stone,[9] as stony as your name is—Farewell excellent Lieutenant-General, I am always,

Yours truly, General-in-Chief,

Ludwig van Beethoven

The works purchased by Steiner are named in a list, bearing the date of April 29, 1815, which is a copy of an unsigned memorandum,[10] evidently proceeding from Beethoven, which runs thus:

[9] German: *Stein* = English: stone. (TK, II, 313, n. 1.)

[10] Sent by Nottebohm to Thayer along with the letter just cited. (TDR, III, 499.)

NOTE

Concerning the following original musical compositions, composed by the under-signed, and surrendered as property to the licensed art dealer H. S. A. Steiner.

1st. Score of the opera Fidelio.

2d. Score of the cantata Der glorreiche Augenblick.

3d. Score of a quartet for 2 violins, viola and basso.

4th. Score of a grand Trio to be sung with pianoforte arrangement.

5th. Score of the Battle of Vittoria with pianoforte arrangement.

6th. Pianoforte arrangement and score of a Symphony in F.

7th. Pianoforte arrangement and score of a Symphony in A major.

8th. Grand Trio for pianoforte, violin and basso in score.

9th. Grand Sonata for pianoforte and violin in score.

10th. Score of a Grand Overture in E-flat major.

11th. Score of a Grand Overture in C major.

12th. Score of a Grand Overture in G major.

13th. 12 English songs with pianoforte accompaniment and German text.

For all of these works[11] which H. Steiner may use as his property in all places except England, I have been wholly recompensed.

Vienna, April 29, 1815.

The correspondence with Steiner and Co. indicates that the task of arrang-ing the orchestral works for the pianoforte was performed by Haslinger and Anton Diabelli, with occasional assistance from Carl Czerny, under Beet-hoven's superintendence.

Diabelli, born near Salzburg in 1781, had now been for some years one of the more prolific composers of light and pleasing music, and one of the best and most popular teachers in Vienna. He was much employed by Steiner and Co., as copyist and corrector, and in this capacity enjoyed much of Beethoven's confidence, who also heartily liked him as a man. In the composer's comical military staff, he was the "General Profoss," and in the correspondence his name becomes "Diabolus"—for Beethoven could never resist the temptation to a play upon words.

About the first of April Beethoven received a package which proved to be an opera text by Rudolph von Berge, sent to him with a letter by his old friend Amenda from Courland.[12] While this letter was under way Beethoven received a visit from a friend of Amenda's who, on his departure from Vienna, carried with him a letter for Amenda from Beethoven:

Vienna, April 12, 1815.

My dear, good Amenda!

The bearer of this, your friend Count Keyserling, visited me and awoke in me memories of you. You live *happily*, you have *children*, neither of which is true

---

[11] No. 3, Op. 95; No. 4, "Tremate, empi, tremate," Op. 116; No. 8, Op. 97; No. 9, Op. 96; No. 10, *König Stephan*, Op. 117; No. 11, "Namensfeier," Op. 115; No. 12, *Ruinen von Athen*, Op. 113. (TDR, III, 499, nn. 1-7.)

[12] This letter is given in TDR, III, pp. 501-503.

of me. To discuss this would make it too long-winded. More about this another time when you write to me again.— You are one thousand times in my mind with your patriarchal simplicity, and how often I have wanted to have people like you around me.— Unfortunately for my good or that of others, fate denies my wishes in this respect. I can say that I live almost *completely alone* in this greatest city of Germany, since I must live almost in estrangement from all persons whom I love or could love— On what kind of footing is music with you? Have you ever heard any of my great works there? *Great* say I—but compared with the works of the Highest, everything is small— Goodbye, my dear good A, think sometimes of your friend

Ludwig van Beethoven

When you write to me, the only address you need is *my name.*

The opera book sent by Amenda was entitled *Bacchus*, a "Grand Lyric Opera in Three Acts." The libretto was preserved among Schindler's papers in the Berlin Library. It seems likely that Beethoven gave some thought to the opera and experimented with some themes. There are interesting notes on a work with a classical subject, the words apparently the beginning of an invocation to Pan, in a sketchbook of 1815, which Nottebohm[13] describes without deciding whether they belong to Treitschke's *Romulus und Remus* or von Berge's *Bacchus*:

gü - ti - ger Pan
[boun - ti - ful Pan]

not quite so characteristic, it must be evolved out of the B.M.[14] where the dance only intermittently—

Corni

Throughout the opera probably dissonances, unresolved or very differently, as our refined music cannot be thought of in connection with those barbarous times.—Throughout the subject must be treated in a pastoral vein

Folksong

Women: unis.

gütige   heilige
[bountiful   holy]

---

[13] *Il Beeth.*, pp. 329-30. (TDR, III, 503.)

[14] Dr. Riemann suggests that "B.M." stands for "Bachus Motive." (TK, II, 315, n. 1.)

gütiger	schützender	segnender	Pan
[bountiful	protecting	blessed	Pan]

". . . ."

Of some minor compositions belonging to this spring, this is the story: The Prussian King's Secretary, Friedrich Duncker, brought to Vienna, in the hope of producing it there, a tragedy, *Leonore Prohaska,* "which tells the story of a maiden who, disguised as a soldier, fought through the war of liberation." For this Beethoven composed a Soldiers' Chorus for men's voices unaccompanied: "Wir bauen und sterben"; a Romance with harp, 6/8 time, "Es blüht ein Blume"; and a Melodrama with harmonica. Also he orchestrated the March in the Sonata, Op. 26,[15] Duncker preferring this to a new *marcia funebre.*

On the approach of warm weather the Erdödys removed for the summer to Jederslee, never to return to the Schottenbastei; and as Lichnowsky was dead, Beethoven had no inducement to remain in that vicinity and therefore departed from the Mölkerbastei—also never to return. The new lodging was in the third story of a house then belonging to Count Lamberti, in the Sailerstätte, with a double number 1055, 1056, near which he had lived a dozen years before, having the same sunny aspect and the glorious view across the Glacis from the Karlkirche and the Belvidere Gardens, away across the Danube to the blue Carpathian mountains in the distance.

In this house, about the first of June, Häring introduced to Beethoven the very fine English pianist and enthusiastic musician Charles Neate, who after five months' study with Winter in Munich had come to Vienna in the hope of obtaining instruction from the great symphonist. To his application, Beethoven replied in substance: "I cannot teach, but I will give you an introduction to my master, Förster" (which he did by letter), "and you may bring your compositions to me for inspection, and I will examine and remark upon them." In consequence of this permission Neate saw him almost daily. Beethoven spent a part of this summer in Baden, and Neate took a room very near him. There the composer was in the habit of working all the forenoon, dining early at twelve or one o'clock, and, towards evening, walking with Neate—sometimes up the Helenen-Thal, oftener through the

---

[15] The autograph of this version is in the Library of the Paris Conservatory of Music. It is published in the Complete Works Edition, Ser. 25, No. 272. (TDR, III, 482.)

Kinsky-Halm (p. 553) dates the music to *Leonore Prohaska,* fall, 1815—an advance over Thayer's date of spring, 1814.

fields. Neate, in the course of his long life—he was nearly eighty in 1861 when he related these things to the author—had never met a man who so enjoyed nature; he took intense delight in flowers, in the clouds, in everything—"Nature was like food to him, he seemed really to live in it." Walking in the fields, he would sit down on any green bank that offered a good seat, and give his thoughts free course. He was then full of the idea of going to England, but the death of his brother and the adoption of his nephew put an end to the project. Neate remembered the boy as a very beautiful, intelligent lad. Beethoven, at that time, and as Neate knew him, was charmingly good-tempered to those whom he liked—but his dislikes were so strong, that to avoid speaking to persons to whom he was not well affected, he would actually increase his pace in the street to a run. At this time, his dark complexion was very ruddy and extremely animated. His abundant hair was in an admirable disorder. He was always laughing, when in good humor, which he for the most part was, as Neate saw him. In their conversations Neate spoke clearly and found no difficulty in making himself understood if he spoke into his left ear.

One day Neate spoke to him about the popularity of his Sonatas, Trios, etc., in England, and added that his Septet was very much admired:— "That's damned stuff" (or "a damned thing"), said Beethoven, "I wish it were burned!" or words to this effect, to Neate's great discomfiture. Another time, walking in the fields near Baden, Neate spoke of the "Pastoral" Symphony and of Beethoven's power of painting pictures in music. Beethoven said: "I have always a picture in my mind, when I am composing, and work up to it."

Neate brought to Beethoven an order from the Philharmonic Society of London—obtained by the exertions of Ries—for three concert overtures, of which we shall hear more hereafter. It is sufficient to say here, that instead of composing new ones as expected, he gave Neate the overtures to *König Stephan*, the *Ruinen von Ather* and the so-called "Namensfeier," and received for them 75 guineas.

The destruction of Razumovsky's palace suspended the quartets, and Linke, the violoncellist, passed the summer with the Erdödys at Jedlersee. This gave the impulse to Beethoven to write the principal works of this year: the two Sonatas for Pianoforte and Violoncello, Op. 102. The first bears his date: "Towards the end of July"; the second: "Beginning of August." While he was employed upon them, Treitschke called upon him for a closing chorus, "Es ist vollbracht," to a little dramatic piece similar to the *Gute Nachricht* entitled *Die Ehrenpforten*, and prepared to celebrate the second capitulation of Paris. It was performed July 15, 16 and 23; and, on the occasion of the Emperor's name-day, was revived "with appropriate changes" October 3rd and 4th; but (according to the theatre bills) with the chorus "Germania" substituted for "Es ist vollbracht."

This was the last year of Beethoven's personal intercourse with the Erdödys, a very interesting memorial of which, namely, a series of notes and letters, has been preserved and made public by the coolness and decision of Otto Jahn. Being in Munich in 1852, or about that time, he learned that this correspondence was in the hands—if our memory serve—of the widow of Brauchle,[16] and obtained permission to read it in the presence of the possessor. Suddenly starting up, he exclaimed (in effect): "I will copy this at the hotel," and before the lady, in her amazement and perplexity, could refuse or prevent, he was away, and made the only copies then known to be in existence.[17] Several of these papers are only Beethoven's apologies for not coming to Jederslee "today" or "tomorrow"—but all are interesting in the glimpse which they give of the affectionate intimacy which they show as existing between Beethoven and the family. The following undated letter to Countess Erdödy is a sample:

My dear and honored Countess!

You have already given me repeated gifts and that is not right. You deprive me thereby of the credit of having been able to do the least thing for you— It is uncertain whether I can come to see you tomorrow, however much I may want to; but certainly it will be in a few days, but only in the afternoon. My affairs have become very complicated at present; more of this when I see you— Give my regards to your children, who are dear to me and press them all to your heart—for the Magister a slight box on the ears, for the chief bailiff a ceremonious bow. Let the violoncello apply himself; starting on the left bank of the Danube he is to play until everyone has crossed from the right bank of the Danube. In this way the population will soon be increased. What's more I am confident of the route over the Danube that I have already set; with *courage* one may gain any objective if *righteous*. I kiss your hands many times over. Remember with favor your friend

Beethoven

Do not send a carriage, then; I'd rather *risk* it than a *carriage! The music that I promised is coming from the city.*

--⟨The Magister was the tutor, Brauchle, and the chief bailiff, or steward, a man named Sperl.[18] The violoncellist was, of course, Linke, whose name probably inspired the drollery about the left (*linke*) bank of the Danube. The postscript has another play on words: *Wagen* (carriage) as a verb means "to risk."⟩--

A letter to Brauchle is important from a biographical point of view. It reads:

I had scarcely returned home before I found my brother making lamentable inquiries about the horses— Please do me the favor to go to Lang-Enzerdorf

---

[16] Brauchle was the tutor of the Erdödy children.

[17] Jahn related this incident to the writer [Thayer] with much humor, in the autumn of 1860. (TDR, III, 508, n. 1.)

[18] TDR, III, p. 509, cites some verses written by Sperl on July 20, 1815, a poetical invitation to Beethoven, as probably relating to this letter.

about the horses; take horses *at my expense* in Jederslee, I'll gladly reimburse you— His sickness (my brother's) is accompanied by a sort of unrest— Let us be of help where we can, I am *obliged to act thus and not otherwise!*— I await a speedy fulfillment of my wishes and a friendly answer on the subject from you— Do not spare expenses; I'll willingly bear them. It is not worth while to let anyone suffer for the sake of a few dirty florins.

Hastily your friend Beethoven

Best wishes to the dear Countess.

Some time around October 15, Beethoven had returned to Vienna from Mödling where he had been intermittently during the later summer. And now another bitter parting: the Erdödys, accompanied by Brauchle, Sperl and Linke, departed to Croatia.

Turning back to Beethoven's interest in an English market for his compositions, we begin with a letter to an old Bonn acquaintance, Johann Peter Salomon, who since 1781 had been active in London as composer, conductor and violinist:

Vienna, June 1, 1815.

My respected countryman!

I have long hoped for the fulfillment of a wish to see *you* in person in London, and to hear you; but the wish has always been frustrated by manifold hindrances— And for this reason, since it is not to be the case, I hope you will not deny my request, which is that you speak with some publisher there, and offer him the following works for me: a Grand Trio for pianoforte, violin and violoncello (80 ducats); Sonata for pianoforte and violin (60 ducats); Grand Symphony in A (one of my most excellent); smaller Symphony in F—a Quartet for 2 violins, viola and violoncello in F minor—a Grand Opera in score, 30 ducats—a Cantata with choruses and solo voices 30 ducats.—the score of the Battle of Vittoria on Wellington's victory, 80 ducats and also the pianoforte arrangement (if it has not, as I am assured, already been published)— I have set down the honorarium of a few works which I think fair for England, but leave it to you in the case of these as well as the others, to do what you think best as to my fee.

I hear, indeed, that *Cramer* is also a publisher[19] but my pupil Ries wrote me recently that he *had publicly expressed himself against my compositions,* I hope for no other reason than *the good of art,* wherefore I have no objection to offer. However if Cramer wants any of these injurious works of art, he is just as agreeable to me as any other publisher.— I only reserve to myself the privilege of also giving the same works to my local publisher so that the works will appear in *London* and *Vienna* only and simultaneously.—

Perhaps you may be able to point out to me in what manner I may get from the Prince Regent at least the copyist's charges for the *Battle Symphony* on *Wellington's Victory at the Battle of Vittoria,* which I gave him, for I have long

[19] Johann Baptist Cramer (1771-1858), the well-known pianist, had long dabbled in publishing ventures: in 1805 as Cramer and Keys, in 1812 with Samuel Chappell, and in 1824 as Cramer, Addison and Beale.

ago abandoned all hope of ever getting anything more, I was not even vouchsafed an answer as to whether I might dedicate the work to the Prince Regent when I publish it. I hear even that the work has already been published in London in pianoforte arrangement,[20] what a fate for a composer!!! While the English and German newspapers are full of reports concerning the success of this work as performed at the Drury Lane Theatre, and the theatre itself has had some takings from it, the composer does not even have a friendly line to show touching it, not even the expense of copying. Besides all this, he has been denied all profit; for if it is true that the pianoforte arrangement is already published, no German publisher will take it. It is probable that the pianoforte arrangement will soon appear in a reprint by a German publisher and I will lose honor and honorarium.— Your well-known noble character bids me hope that you will take an interest in the matter and show yourself active in my service. The wretched paper money of our country has already been reduced to one-fifth of its value, so I was treated according to the scale. But after much urging I received the full standard though with a considerable loss. But now we have again reached a point where the currency is worth much less than one-fifth of its value, and I am confronted for the second time with the prospect that my salary will be reduced to *nothing* without recourse of any kind.— My only earnings now come from my compositions. If I could count on their sale in England it would be very advantageous to me.— Count on my boundless gratitude. I hope for a speedy, a very speedy answer from you.

Your admirer and friend Ludwig van Beethoven.

The letters to Smart, Salomon and Ries were not in vain; through their efforts, especially Salomon's, Mr. Robert Birchall, Music Publisher of No. 133 New Bond St., was induced to purchase four of the works enumerated by Häring, viz., the pianoforte arrangements of the "Wellington's Victory," Op. 91, and Symphony in A, Op. 92; the Trio in B-flat, Op. 97, and the Sonata for Pianoforte and Violin, Op. 96, for "the sum of one hundred and thirty gold Dutch ducats—value in English currency, sixty-five pounds." The correspondence between the composer and publisher begins with a letter from Beethoven, dated October 28th, in which he informed Birchall that the Battle Symphony in pianoforte arrangement had been sent ahead of the other three works. He urged him to print it speedily for reasons which "Hr. Salomon will have the goodness to explain."

We now reach one of the most important and at the same time most melancholy events in Beethoven's life—an event which exerted the profoundest influence on the rest of his life—the death of his brother Carl Caspar. We introduce it with that brother's last will and testament:

Certain that all men must die and feeling that I am near this goal, but in the full possession of my understanding, I have freely and voluntarily deemed it good to make these, my last dispositions.

[20] According to Kinsky-Halm (KHV, p. 255), the first publication of Op. 91 was not until January, 1816, by Birchall in London, in pianoforte transcription.

1. I commend my soul to the mercy of God, but my body to the earth from which it came and desire that it be buried in the simplest manner in accordance with the rites of Christian Catholicism.

2. Immediately after my death, four holy masses are to be said, to which end I set apart 4 florins.

3. My heirs general are commanded to pay the pious legacies according to law.

4. As my wife at our marriage brought me and paid over 2000 fl. in B. bonds, for which I gave no receipt, I acknowledge receipt of these 2000 fl. in B. bonds and desire that these 2000 fl. in B. bonds as also the deposit be rectified in accordance with the existing marriage contract.

5. I appoint my brother Ludwig van Beethoven guardian. Inasmuch as this, my deeply beloved brother has often aided me with true brotherly love in the most magnanimous and noblest manner, I ask, in full confidence and trust in his noble heart, that he shall bestow the love and friendship which he often showed me, upon my son Karl, and do all that is possible to promote the intellectual training and further welfare of my son. I know that he will not deny me this, my request.

6. Convinced of the uprightness of Hrn. Dr. Schönauer, Appellate and Court Advocate, I appoint him Curator for probate, as also for my son Karl with the understanding that he be consulted in all matters concerning the property of my son.

7. The appointment of heirs being the essential matter in a testament, I appoint my beloved wife Johanna, born Reiss, and my son Karl, heirs general to all my property in equal portions after the deduction of my existing debts and the above bequests.

8. The wagon, horse, goat, peacocks and the plants growing in vessels in the garden are the property of my wife, since these objects were all purchased with money from the legacy received from her grandfather.

In witness whereof, I have not only signed this, my last will with my own hand, but to aid in its execution have also called in three witnesses.

Thus done, Vienna, November 14, 1815.

Carl van Beethoven,

m. p.

Carl Gaber, m. p.

House owner, Breitenfeld No. 9.

Benedikt Gaber, m. p.

House owner, Breitenfeld No. 25.

Johann Naumann, m. p.

House No. 5, Breitenfeld.

("This testament was delivered under seal to the R. I. L. Austrian General Court, by the Karl Scheffer Solicitor Dr. Schönauer, on November 17, 1815, etc.")

The autograph preserved in the City Archives in Vienna shows that the first sentence in Section 5 read originally: "Along with my wife I appoint my brother Ludwig van Beethoven co-guardian." The phrase "Along with my wife" and the "co-" were crossed out. The following fragment in Beethoven's writing, preserved at the Beethoven-Haus in Bonn explains the reason for the change: "I knew nothing about the fact that a testament had been made; however, I came upon it by chance. If what I had seen was really to be the *original text*, then passages had to be stricken out. This I had my brother bring about since I did not wish to be bound up in this with such a bad woman in a matter of such importance as the education of the child."[21]

Codicil to my Will

Having learned that my brother, Hr. Ludwig van Beethoven, desires after my death to take wholly to himself my son Karl, and wholly to withdraw him from the supervision and training of his mother, and inasmuch as the best of harmony does not exist between my brother and my wife, I have found it necessary to add to my will that I by no means desire that my son be taken away from his mother, but that he shall always and so long as his future career permits remain with his mother, to which end the guardianship of him is to be exercised by her as well as my brother. Only by unity can the object which I had in view in appointing my brother guardian of my son, be attained, wherefore, for the welfare of my child, I recommend *compliance* to my wife and more *moderation* to my brother.

God permit them to be harmonious for the sake of my child's welfare. This is the last wish of the dying husband and brother.

Vienna, November 14, 1815.

Carl van Beethoven
m. p.

We, the undersigned, certify in consonance with truth that Carl van Beethoven declared in our presence that he had read the statement on the opposite page and that the same is in accordance with his will, finally we certify that he signed it with his own hand in our presence and requested us to witness the act.

Thus done on November 14, 1815.

Carl Gaber, m. p.
Benedikt Gaber, m. p.
Johann Neumann, m. p.

("This codicil was delivered under seal to the R. I. L. Austrian General Court by the Karl Scheffer Solicitor Dr. Schönauer, on Nov. 17, 1815, etc.")

On November 20, 1815, the *Wiener Zeitung* printed the announcement that Hr. Carl van Beethoven, Cashier in the R. I. Bank and Chief Treasury, aged 38 years,[22] died of consumption on November 16. And so in his own house died the brother Carl whose last moments came with a suddenness which aroused his brother's suspicions that the end had been hastened by poison! Nor would he be satisfied upon the matter until his friend Bertolini had made a post mortem examination "whereby the lack of foundation for the suspicion was proved."

A few weeks before his death, Carl had applied for leave of absence from

---

[21] See Dr. Dagmar Weise, "Beethoven, Entwurf einer Denkschrift," in *Veröffentlichungen des Beethoven-Hauses in Bonn*, III, No. 1 (1953), p. 13.

[22] Actually he was 41½ years old since he was baptized on April 8, 1774. (TDR, III, 519, n. 1.)

his office on the score of his feeble condition; but his petition was refused in a document on which Beethoven afterwards wrote: "This miserable financial product caused the death of my brother, since he was really so sick that he could not carry out his occupation without hastening his death;—a beautiful testimony to this rough high official. L. van Beeth."[23] In fact, however, it made probably little difference; his was evidently one of those common cases of phthisis, where the patient, except to the experienced eye, shows no signs of immediate danger; who at the last moments finds himself free from pain and blessed with a buoyancy of spirit that gives him vain hopes of a prolonged life. It is the last flickering of the flame, as the skillful physician well knows.

As above noted, Carl van Beethoven's will was deposited with the proper authorities on the 17th, and "the R. I. L. Austrian Landrecht [General Court] on November 22, 1815, appointed the widow of the deceased, Johanna van Beethoven, guardian, the brother of the deceased, Ludwig van Beethoven, associate guardian of the minor son Karl." And so, for the present, we will leave the matter.

There is a striking incongruity between Beethoven's pleas of poverty in his letters to correspondents in England at this period and the facts drawn from official and other authentic sources. Let us tarry a moment on this point.

He was now, at the end of 1815, in the regular receipt of his annuity, 3400 florins in notes of redemption; in March and April the arrears, 4987 florins in such notes, had been paid him; the profits of his concerts since January 1, 1814, with presents from crowned heads and others were, if we may trust Schindler, who appears to speak from accurate knowledge, sufficient in amount to purchase somewhat later the seven bank-shares, which at his death, "according to the price current on the day of his death," had a value in convention-coin of 7441 florins; Neate had paid him 75 guineas; for the works sold to Steiner and Co. he had "been wholly compensated"; in March (1816) he received from Mr. Birchall 65 pounds sterling; and there were payments to him from Thomson and others, the aggregate of which cannot be determined.

This incongruity is not essentially diminished either by his taxes—sixty pounds for 1814, he tells Thomson—nor by the 10,000 florins V.S. expended for the benefit of his brother, whether the "Vienna Standard" in the letter to Ries given below be understood as the old five for one, or the new in notes of redemption; for this fraternal charity extended back over a series of years. In this letter to Ries, the reader will observe also a remarkable instance of its writer's occasional great carelessness of statement, where he speaks of

[23] Beethoven's note, given in full (Thayer had quoted only the first phrase) and the answer of October 23rd by Carl's employers to his petition have been published by Schiedermair, "Neue Schriftstücke zu Beet-hovens Vormundschaft über seinen Neffen," NBJ, VIII (1938), pp. 59-60. While the request for leave was refused, his employers considered favorably the idea of lightening his duties.

his "entire loss of salary" for several years; for the Archduke's share had throughout been punctually paid; not to mention again the receipt of what had for a time been withheld of the Kinsky and Lobkowitz subscriptions. The omission of these facts in this and other letters, imparted to Ries an utterly false impression; and on their publication in 1838, to the public also. Hence the general belief that Beethoven was now in very straitened circumstances, and that Carl's widow and child had been left in abject poverty. The truth as to them was this: that the property left them produced an annual income, which with the widow's pension amounted at this time to above 1500 florins. From the day that Beethoven assumed the office of guardian and took possession of the child, he had a valid claim upon the mother for a part of the costs of maintaining him—a claim soon made good by legal process. If he afterward elected to suffer in his own finances rather than press his sister-in-law, this is no justification of the heedless statements in some of his letters now—a truth to be held in mind. And now the letter to Ferdinand Ries:

Wednesday, November 22, Vienna, 1815.

Dear R!

I hasten to write you that today I sent the pianoforte arrangement of the Symphony in A by post to the house of Thomas Coutts and Co. As the Court is not here, couriers go not at all or seldom, and this besides is the safest way.— The Symphony should appear around March; I will fix the day. It has occupied too much time for me to make the term shorter. More time may be taken with the Trio and the Sonata for violin, and both will be in London in a few weeks— I urgently beg of you, dear Ries, to make this matter your concern and to see that I get the money. It will cost a great deal before everything gets there and I need it— I had to lose 600 fl. annually of my salary— At the time of the bank-notes it was nothing,—then came the notes of redemption and because of them I lost the 600 fl. with several years of vexation and entire loss of salary— Now we have reached a point where the notes of redemption are worse than the bank-notes were before. I pay 1000 fl. for house-rent; imagine for yourself the misery caused by paper money— My poor unfortunate brother has just died. He had a bad wife. I may say he had consumption for several years, and to make life easier for him I gave what I may estimate at 10,000 fl. V. S. True that is nothing for an Englishman, but very much for a poor German, or rather Austrian. The poor man had changed greatly in the last few years and I can say that I sincerely lament him, and I am now glad that I can say to myself that I neglected nothing in respect of care for him— Tell H. B[irchall] to repay H. Salomon and you the cost of postage for your letters to me and mine to you. He may deduct it from the sum which he is to pay me. I want those who labor for me to suffer as little as possible—

Wellington's Victory at the Battle of Victoria (this is also the title on the pianoforte arrangement) must have reached Th. Coutts and Co. long ago. Herr Birchall need not pay the honorarium until he has received all the works— Make haste so that I may know the *day* when H. B. will publish the pianoforte arrangement— For today, no more except the warmest commendation of my affairs to

you; I am always at your service in all respects.— Affectionately Farewell, dear R!
Your friend Beethoven

On the same day he wrote to Birchall concerning the shipments—promising "the Trio and the Sonata in a fortnight" and asked that the sum of 130 gold ducats be paid to Thomas Coutts and Co. The Trio and the Sonata, however, were not forwarded until the 3rd of February—a decidedly long "fortnight."

In those days £65 was no small sum for the mere right of republication in England of these pianoforte works and arrangements, and Ries richly merited these words of his old master:[24] "And now my heartiest thanks, dear Ries, for all the kindness you have shown to me, and particularly for the corrections. Heaven bless you and make your progress even greater, in which I take the most heart-felt interest." Ries, writing on September 29th for Salomon, who had broken his right shoulder in a fall from his horse, informed Beethoven that at that date the three overtures purchased by Neate for the Philharmonic Society had not reached London. Beethoven, in December, repeated this to Neate, who was still in Vienna, adding, in substance, his readiness to make any desired written agreement about these things in England. Salomon's misfortune occurred in August; he lingered only until the 28th of November. No higher proof of his reputation in England can be given than the fact that the remains of this Bonn violinist rest near those of Handel in Westminster Abbey.

About the first of December, "a magisterial deputation solemnly delivered" into the hands of Beethoven a certificate conferring upon him the citizenship of Vienna in acknowledgement of his benevolent services on behalf of St. Mark's Hospital.

Schindler somewhere censures the Gesellschaft der Musikfreunde for its long delay in making Beethoven an honorary member. It did what was better. Hardly was it organized, when its directors turned their attention to him; and, in the second year of its legal existence, proposed to him through Zmeskall to compose an oratorio for its use. On the 22d of December, Count Appony reported: "that Hr. L. v. Beethoven, through Hr. v. Zmeskall, had declared his readiness to deliver a large work to the society and that the Board of Management were awaiting his conditions." It was but the course of common propriety—of ordinary delicacy—to leave him free of all obligation to the society until this matter of business should be settled; indeed, that Streicher was one of the principal founders and most influential members of the society is a sufficient pledge, that no disrespect for, nor indifference to, his great merits, had aught to do with the delay, which Schindler blames. We shall find that, so soon as it was certain that Beethoven could not live to fulfill his engagement, the society sent him its honorary diploma. Could it well do this before?

[24] In a letter dated January 20, 1816.

Of noteworthy new friends and acquaintances may be mentioned here Peters, tutor of the young Princes Lobkowitz, and Joseph Karl Bernard, a young literateur and poet—the reviser of Weissenbach's poem—a great admirer of Beethoven's music, soon to be appointed Editor of the official *Wiener Zeitung*. He is the "Bernardus non Sanctus" of the Conversation Books; and the two are the friends whom Beethoven set to music in the text:

Sanct Petrus was ein Fels !	Saint Peter was a rock!
Bernardus war ein Sanct??	Bernardus was a saint??

Another was Anton Halm, "in whose fresh military nature Master Ludwig took delight," says Schindler. He was a native of Styria, and now but twenty-six years of age. After some years' service against Napoleon, he had resigned (1812) his lieutenancy in the 44th Regiment. He was a pianoforte player of very respectable rank, and even before entering the army had appeared in public in Beethoven's C minor Trio, Op. 1, and the C major Pianoforte Concerto, Op. 15. He had now been three years in Hungary, living during the third with his friend, Brunsvik, who gave him a letter to Beethoven upon his departure for Vienna, whither he had come to be tutor in a Greek family named Gyike. "Halm once brought a sonata of his own composition to him," says Czerny, "and when Beethoven pointed out a few errors, Halm retorted that he (B.) had also permitted himself many violations of the rules, Beethoven answered: 'I may do it, but not you.'"

Young Schindler's acquaintance with Beethoven had now advanced a step: He writes:[25]

"Toward the end of February, 1815, I accepted an invitation to become tutor at Brünn. Scarcely arrived there, I was summoned before the police officials. I was questioned as to my relations with some of the tumultuaries of the Vienna University as also certain Italians in whose company I had often been seen in Vienna. As my identification papers, especially the statement concerning the different lectures which I had attended, were not in good order, the latter really faulty—through no fault of mine—I was detained, notwithstanding that a government officer of high standing offered to become my bondsman. After several weeks of correspondence back and forth it was learned that I was not a propagandist and was to be set at liberty. But a whole year of my academic career was lost.

"Again returned to Vienna, I was invited by one of Beethoven's intimate acquaintances to come to an appointed place, as the master wanted to hear the story of the Brünn happening from my own lips. During the relation, Beethoven manifested such sympathetic interest in my disagreeable experiences that I could not refrain from tears. He invited me to come often to the same place and at the same hour, 4 o'clock in the afternoon, where he was to be found nearly every day—reading the newspapers. A handgrasp said still more. The place was a somewhat remote room in the beer-house

[25] I, pp. 230-31.

'Zum Rosenstock' in the Ballgässchen. I was there right often and came to know the place as a quasi-crypt of a number of Josephites of the first water, to whom our master presented no discordant note, for his republican creed had already received a considerable blow through a more intimate acquaintance with the English Constitution. A captain of the Emperor's bodyguard and Herr Pinterics, widely known in musical Vienna, who played an important role in the life of Franz Schubert, were the closest companions of the master and, in the exchange of political views, his seconds actively and passively. From this place I soon began to accompany him on his walks."

But Schindler's intimacy with Beethoven was not yet such as to save him from errors when writing of this time. Thus he gravely assures us that a concert which took place on the 25th of December "provided the impulse which led the Magistracy of Vienna to elect our master to honorary citizenship." And yet the "solemn delivery" of the diploma is already an item of news in the Vienna newspapers of December 15. This concert, in the large Redoutensaal, conducted by Beethoven was for the benefit of the *Bürgerspitalfond* (Citizens' Hospital Fund) and the works performed were "an entirely new overture" (that in C, known as the "Namensfeier"); "a new chorus on Goethe's poem 'Die Meeresstille'"; *Christus am Ölberg*. Between the cantata and the oratorio, Franz Stauffer, "the twelve-year-old son of a citizen of Vienna," played a "Rondo brillant" by Hummel.

The compositions which are known or, on good grounds, are supposed to belong to the year 1815 are:

Canon. "Brauchle, Linke," WoO 167.[26]

Canon. "Glück zum neuen Jahr," for Baron Pasqualati, WoO 165.

Canon. "Kurz ist der Schmerz" (Schiller's *Jungfrau von Orleans*), WoO 166, 2nd version, for Ludwig Spohr's album. At the end is written "Vienna, March 3rd, 1815." The dedication reads: "May you always remember me with affection, dear Spohr, wherever you find true art and true artists, from your Ludwig van Beethoven."[27]

"Das Geheimnis" (Wessenberg), WoO 145.

"Es ist vollbracht" for Bass, Chorus and Orchestra, closing song for Treitschke's *Die Ehrenpforten*, WoO 97.

"Meeresstille und Glückliche Fahrt" for Chorus and Orchestra (Goethe), Op. 112.

"Merkenstein" for Two Voices and Pianoforte (Rupprecht), Op. 100.

Music for Friedrich Duncker's tragedy *Leonore Prohaska*, WoO 96: (1) Krieger-Chor (2) Romanze (3) Melodram (4) Trauermarsch (orchestration in B minor of March from Op. 26).

[26] This canon, written on the names of two of the Erdödy circle, the tutor Brauchle and the cellist Linke, was probably written this summer when Beethoven was seeing a good deal of the Countess and her family at their home in Jederslee. See G. Haupt, "Gräfin Erdödy und J. X. Brauchle" in *Der Bär* (Leipzig, 1927), p. 81.

[27] See Spohr's *Selbstbiographie* (Cassel, 1860), i, pp. 213 and 216 opp.

Overture "zur Namensfeier," Op. 115.

Twelve Folk Songs, WoO 157: 2 English, 5 Irish, 1 Jacobean, 2 Scottish, 1 Sicilian, 1 Venetian. Kinsky-Halm believes that some of these songs were written in 1814 or earlier.[28]

Two Sonatas for Pianoforte and Violoncello, Op. 102.

The ascertained publications of the year are:

By Mechetti:

"Des Kriegers Abschied" (Reissig), WoO 143.

Polonaise for Pianoforte, Op. 89, dedicated to Empress Elisabeth Alexiewna of Russia.

By *Selam*, almanac edited by I. F. Castelli:

"Merkenstein" (Rupprecht), WoO 144.

By Steiner:

"Es ist vollbracht" for Bass, Chorus and Orchestra, closing song for Treitschke's *Die Ehrenpforten*, WoO 97.

Sonata for Pianoforte, Op. 90, dedicated to Count Moritz Lichnowsky.

[28] KHV, p. 657.

CHAPTER XXIX

THE YEAR 1816

THE NEPHEW IN GIANNATASIO DEL RIO'S SCHOOL—NEGOTIATIONS WITH RIES, BIRCHALL AND NEATE

COMPARED with the years immediately preceding, the year 1816 is comparatively barren of large incidents in the life of Beethoven; its recorded history, therefore, is to be found to a still larger extent than before in the composer's extended correspondence together with explanatory annotations. Some of the letters, especially those written to his English friends, are likely to make a somewhat melancholy, and to that extent erroneous, impression. The real record of the writer finds expression in the letters which he wrote to Steiner and Co. and Zmeskall. These are bubbling over with playfulness and jocularity, proving that the writer was generally in a cheerful humor and in this year was anything but the melancholy Beethoven of the romance writers. He seems to have endured the rapid and disquieting increase in his malady, an inevitable consequence of the exertions and excitement attending the rehearsing and conducting of so many large concerts, with surprising patience and resignation. And why not? His pecuniary affairs were in good condition, notwithstanding his lamentations to Ries and others; he had won his lawsuit with his brother's widow, and his artistic ambition must have found complete satisfaction in the great fame which he had won. A letter concerning a new operatic project first invites attention. The eight roles which Madame Milder had played in the past summer in Berlin, had given such keen delight that she had been reengaged for a second and much longer series. Domestic troubles and sorrows, in which her husband, the jeweler Hauptmann, appears to have been entirely the guilty party and which embittered all her future life, rendered her utterly unable for the present to appear upon the stage; and "because of illness and weakness" it was not until several weeks after her return from the baths at Pyrmont that she could begin the new engagement on October 3rd. Meantime, in Berlin *Fidelio* had been put upon the boards and "given for the first time on October 11th with great success." "This opera," said the Berlin *Dramaturgisches Wochenblatt* in its notice of the event, "bears within itself the seeds of a dramatico-musical reformation and will hasten the end of the bastard music." And yet on this evening, the Leonore was Mme. Schultze—Schuppanzigh's sister-in-law. When, three days after, Mme. Milder took the part, its greatness was for the first time fully appreciated; and of the twenty-four evenings to which her engagement extended, this greatest representative then living of Gluck's grandest inspirations devoted eleven to *Fidelio*. This triumph of his opera in Berlin drew from the composer a letter (dated January 6, 1816) full of expressions of gratitude and enthusiastic appreciation of the singer's talents, and giving voice, too, to a rekindled dramatic ambition. He says:

. . . If you were to beg Baron de la Motte Fouqué[1]—in my name—to invent a grand opera subject which would at the same time be adapted to *you*, it would do a great service to me and the German stage.— I should like, moreover, to compose it exclusively for the *Berlin stage* as I shall never bring about another opera for the parsimonious management here. . . .

The letter ends with a musical joke on the name "Hauptmann."[2]

ich küs - se sie   drück - te sie an   mein Herz
[I kiss ____ you   press ___ you to   my heart.]

Ich   der   Haupt - man der   Hauptman
[I'm the   head - man the   headman

(Fort mit allen übrigen falschen Hauptmännern)
[Away with all other false headmen]

The next letter relates to the oratorio for the Gesellschaft der Musikfreunde:

Friday, February 9th, 1816.

My dear Zmeskall!

With dismay I observe for the first time today that I have not yet answered the application of the Gesellschaft der Musikfreunde of the Austrian capital for an oratorio. The death of my brother two months ago, the guardianship of my nephew which thereby devolved upon me, together with many other unpleasant circumstances and occurrences are the cause of my tardy reply.— Meanwhile the poem by Herr von Seyfried is already begun and I shall also soon set the same to music. That the commission is highly honorable, I scarcely need tell you; that is self-evident, and I shall try to execute it as worthily as my small

[1] Friedrich de la Motte-Fouqué (1777-1843), author of "Undine."

[2] The musical reference in the first measure

to the *Fidelio Overture* in E is undoubtedly intentional.

powers will allow— As regards the *artistic means* to be employed in the performance I shall be considerate, but wish to be allowed to depart *from those already
introduced*. I hope that I have made myself understood in this matter. As they
insist upon knowing what honorarium I ask, I inquire in turn whether the
Society thinks 400 ducats in gold agreeable for such a work. I again beg pardon
of the Society for the tardiness of my answer; meanwhile, you, my dear friend
have at least reported by word of mouth my readiness to compose the work,
before now, which sets my mind measurably at ease— My dear Z. I am with
great esteem your friend

Ludwig van Beethoven

The next selections require the preliminary statement of certain facts.
Beethoven's dissatisfaction at the appointment (on November 22, 1815) of
his sister-in-law as the guardian of her son—now nine years old—was expressed in an appeal to the Upper Austrian *Landrecht* on the 28th,[3] to transfer
the guardianship to himself. Next day, the 29th, that tribunal ordered the
petitioner and Dr. Schönauer to appear before it in this matter on December
2nd at 10 o'clock a.m. At that time the subject was deferred to the same
hour on the 13th. Beethoven then appeared and declared that he could
produce "weighty reasons why the widow should be entirely excluded from
the guardianship." Whereupon, on the 15th, it was ordered that he produce
those grounds within three days, "failing which, the preparation of the
guardianship decree to the widow would be proceeded without further
delay." The same day Beethoven signed a petition to the City Magistrates
for an official certificate concerning the "condemnation of his [Karl's]
mother, Johanna van Beethoven, on an investigation for infidelity." The
magistrate answered him on the same day through their secretary that they
could not legally grant him a copy of the judgment against her, but would
communicate the "necessary disclosures" to the tribunal. This was done on
the 21st. ⸱⸱The day before, December 20th, Beethoven wrote a long document to the *Landrecht* presenting his case.[4] In it he emphasized that the
codicil of his brother's will, which divided the guardianship between Johanna
and himself, had been forced behind his back upon the dying man for
signature by his wife. — Then came the Christmas holidays, and no further
action was taken until the 9th of January, when a decision was rendered
in Beethoven's favor, and he was ordered to appear on the 19th to take the
"vows for the performance of his duties." He complied, and on the outside of
this order is written: "Today appeared Ludwig van Beethoven as the legally
appointed guardian of his nephew Karl and vowed with solemn handgrasp
before the assembled council to perform his duties."

This document also empowered the new guardian to take possession of

[3] First published by O. E. Deutsch, "Drei
neue Beethoven-Briefe" in *Österreiche Musikzeitschrift*, VIII (1953), pp. 79ff. In *The
Letters of Beethoven* Miss Anderson gives all
the documents relating to Beethoven's litigation over the guardianship of his nephew from
1815 to 1820, in Vol. III, Appendix C.

[4] First published by Schiedermair, *NBJ*, VIII
(1938), pp. 62ff.

the boy, who of course was still with his mother. But what to do with him? Beethoven could not take him into his own lodging; a child of that age needs a woman's care and tenderness.

A certain Cajetan Giannatasio del Rio was at that time proprietor and manager of a private school in the city for boys, which enjoyed a high and deserved reputation. His family consisted of his wife and two highly accomplished daughters, Fanny and Anna (Nanni), young women of fine talents, of much musical taste and culture, and—especially the elder—enthusiasts for Beethoven's music. The composer, accompanied by his friend Karl Bernard and the boy, visited and inspected the school, and was so much pleased with it and the family, that he determined to withdraw his nephew from the public school, and place him there as pupil and boarder. On February 1st, he wrote to Giannatasio:

With sincere pleasure I inform you that at last on tomorrow I shall bring to you the precious pledge that has been entrusted to me.— Moreover I beg of you again under no circumstances to permit the mother to exercise any influence. How or when she may see him, all this I will talk over with you tomorrow— You may impress this also on your servants, for *mine* in another matter was *bribed by her!*— More about this will follow by word of mouth, though silence would be preferable to me— But for the sake of your future citizen of the world, this melancholy communication is necessary. . . .

[In Karl's hand]: I am very glad to come to you, and am your Karl van Beethoven.

The next day, February 2, the boy was taken from his mother. The intolerable annoyance caused by her appearing in person or sending a messenger daily to take him from the school, drew from Giannatasio on the 11th a written application to the guardian for "a formal authority in a few lines for refusing without further ado to permit her to fetch her son." In his reply, Beethoven writes: "as regards the mother I request that on the plea that he is busy you do not admit her to him at all." He then consulted Joseph Edler von Schmerling, a member of the *Landrecht*, upon the measures proper for him to adopt, and communicated that gentleman's advice to Giannatasio by letter. The same day, taking Bernard with him, he went to the school, and there meeting Giannatasio, the three prepared a formal petition to the *Landrecht*, praying that tribunal to grant the guardian plenary authority to exclude the widow and her agents from all or any direct communication with the boy. This was signed by Beethoven and immediately presented. On the 20th, the *Landrecht* granted, essentially, this petition; but its decree contained this proviso: that the mother might still visit her son "in his leisure hours, without disturbing the course of his education or the domestic arrangements, in the company of a person to be appointed by the guardian or the director of the educational institution." Armed with this authority, Giannatasio on March 8th informed in writing "Madame Jeannette de Beethoven, Vorstadt, Alsergasse, No. 121," that she has in future "to apply solely to the uncle as to whether, how and when" she can see her son. And thus this wretched business again for the present rested. In these days belongs a letter by Beethoven to Giannatasio which begins:

The Queen of Night surprised us yesterday and also delivered a veritable anathema against you; she showed her usual impertinence and malice against me and set me back for a moment and I almost believed that what she said was right; but when I reached home later I received the result of the decision of the *Landrechte* which turns out to be just *what was desired*. I communicate the most necessary points although you will probably *receive a copy of it* towards evening. . . .

Neate was now gone to London. On his departure Beethoven wrote in his album two canons entitled "Das Schweigen" (Silence) and "Das Reden" (Speech), adding, with the date, "January 24, 1816," the words: "My dear English compatriot in *silence* and in *speech* remember your sincere friend Ludwig van Beethoven."

The document concerning the sale of the three overtures to the Philharmonic Society, which Beethoven promised to give Neate, ran as follows:

Hr. Neate has received from me in the month of July, 1816 [*sic*] three overtures in the name of the Philharmonic Society in London and has paid me an honorarium of 75 guineas for the same in consideration of which I bind myself to permit them *nowhere else* to be published in parts[x] although I have the right to perform *the same* wherever I please as well as to publish them in pianoforte arrangement, though not before Hr. Neate shall have written me that they have been performed in London:— Moreover, Hr. Neate has assured me that he will kindly take it upon himself that the Philharmonic Society after a period of one or two years will permit me to engrave and publish these three overtures *in score and in parts*, inasmuch as I can do this only with their consent—with which I present my compliments to the P. S.

Vienna, February 5, 1816.   Ludwig van Beethoven[5]

[x] or in score

The three overtures had already been sold to Steiner, but were not published until many years later.[6] The works entrusted to him, as remembered by Mr. Neate forty-five years afterwards, were: 1) a copy of the Violin Concerto, Op. 61, with a transcription of the solo for Pianoforte on the same pages, which Beethoven said he himself had arranged and was effective; 2) the two Sonatas for Pianoforte and Violoncello, Op. 102, with a dedication to Neate; 3) the Seventh Symphony in score; 4) *Fidelio* in score; and 5) the String Quartet in F minor, Op. 95—all in manuscript.[7] There is some reason to think that besides these works Neate also took a copy of *Der*

[5] In the first sentence Beethoven, of course, meant 1815. For a facsimile of the autograph and the history of this letter see Sonneck, *Beethoven Letters in America*, p. 88.

[6] The Overture to the *Ruinen von Athen* in 1823, the "Namensfeier" Overture in 1825,

and the Overture to *König Stephan* in 1826. (Cf. TDR, III, 544-45.)

[7] Why the concerto was supposed to be in manuscript is not clear since it was published in both forms in 1808. (TDR, III, 543.)

glorreiche Augenblick. On January 20, Beethoven wrote the following letter to Ries in London:

Vienna, January 20, 1816

My dear Riess I see from your letter of January 18[8] that you have safely received both works[9]— As no couriers are going, the *post* is probably the safest, but it costs a great deal. I will send you the bill for what I have paid here for *copying* and *postage* soon. It is very little for an Englishman but much more for a *poor Austrian musician*! See that Hr. B[irchall] recompenses me for this, since *for England* he has the compositions very cheaply—Neate, who has been about to go every moment, but always remains, will bring the overtures with him. Over and over again I have explained to him the injunctions touching them given by you and our deceased S[alomon]—

The symphony will be dedicated to the *Empress of Russia*— The *pianoforte arrangement of the Symphony in A* must not be published before the *month of June*, however, since the *local publisher* cannot do so before this— Tell this at once to Hr. B., my good R.—

The Sonata with violin, which will go from here by the next post, may also *be published* in London *in the month of May*—but the Trio later. (It will also arrive by the next post), I will fix the date myself later.—

And now my heartiest thanks, dear R, for all the kindness you have shown to me and particularly for the corrections.— Heaven bless you and make your progress ever greater in which I take the heartiest interest— Commend me to *your wife.*

As always, your sincere friend,
Ludwig van Beethoven

It is necessary here to state certain facts, both to explain the failure of Mr. Neate to sell any of these works to the London publishers, and to render some of the letters to come intelligible.

The Philharmonic Society was an association of the first musicians of London and its vicinity, and no city on earth could at that time present such an array of great names. Here are a few of them taken alphabetically from its roll: Attwood, Ayrton, Bridgetower, Clementi, Cramer, Carnaby, Dragonetti, Horsley, Lindley, Mazzinghi, Mori, Naldi, Novello, Ries, Shield, Smart, Spagnoletti, Viotti, Watts, S. Webbe, Yaniewicz. Imagine the disappointment of these men, fresh from the performance of the C minor Symphony, when they played through the overtures to *Die Ruinen von Athen* and *König Stephan*, which, however interesting to a Hungarian audience as introductions to a patriotic prologue and epilogue in the theatre, possess none of those great qualities expected from Beethoven and demanded in a concert overture! Nor was the "Namensfeier" thought worthy of its author. Ries speaks thus of the matter: "After I had with much trouble persuaded the Philharmonic Society to permit me to order three overtures from him, which should remain its property, he sent me three, not one of which, in

[8] Miss Anderson notes that Ries's reply was actually on December 18th from his own notation on Beethoven's letter to Birchall on November 22, 1815 (*A,* II, p. 534, n. 2).
[9] Op. 91 and 92.

view of Beethoven's great name and the character of these concerts, could be performed, because expectation was tense and more than the ordinary was asked of Beethoven. A few years later he published all three and the Society did not think it worth while to complain. Amongst them was the overture to *Die Ruinen von Athen*, which I consider unworthy of him." But when it became known that none of the three—Op. 115 possibly excepted—was new, and that not one of them had been composed to meet the Society's order, is it surprising that this act of Beethoven's was deemed unworthy of him, disrespectful, nay, an insult to the Society, and resented accordingly?

Another matter was personal with Mr. Birchall. That publisher, having at last (early in February) received the last of the works published by him,[10] immediately deposited with Coutts and Co. the sum agreed upon, to the composer's credit, and forwarded the following "Declaration" to Vienna for signature, leaving the day of the month blank—as it still remains—to be inserted when signed:

Received . . . . March, 1816, of Mr. Robert Birchall—Music Seller, 133 New Bond Street, London—the sum of One Hundred and thirty Gold Dutch Ducats, value in English Currency Sixty-five Pounds, for all my Copyright and Interest, present and future, vested or contingent, or otherwise within the United King-dom of Great Britain and Ireland in the four following Compositions or Pieces of Music composed or arranged by me, viz.:

1st. A Grand Battle Sinfonia, descriptive of the Battle and Victory at Vittoria, adapted for the Pianoforte and dedicated to his Royal Highness, the Prince Regent—40 Ducats.

2nd. A Grand Symphony in the Key of A, adapted to the Pianoforte and dedicated to

3rd. A Grand Trio for the Pianoforte, Violin and Violoncello in the Key of B-flat.

4th. A Sonata for the Pianoforte with an Accompaniment for the Violin, dedicated to

And, in consideration of such payment I hereby for myself, my Executors and Administrators promise and engage to execute a proper Assignment thereof to him, his Executors and Administrators or Assignees at his or their Request and Costs, as he or they shall direct. And I likewise promise and engage as above, that none of the above shall be published in any foreign Country, before the time and day fixed and agreed on for such Publication between R. Birchall and myself shall arrive.

Instead of *this* document, so indispensable for his security, the publisher received a new demand from Beethoven!—one for five pounds additional, as per memorandum:

Copying	1.10.0
Postage to Amsterdam	1. 0.0
Trio	2.10.0
	£5.0.0

[10] Through Ries. See *A* 609.

---⟨This was transmitted through a letter to Ries dated February 10. On February 28 and April 3 he reiterated his demand for the additional ten ducats, equivalent to five pounds.⟩--- Then he wrote the following letter in May, portions of which were suppressed when printed by Ries:

Vienna, May 8, 1816.

My dear Ries:

My answer to your letter comes somewhat tardily; but I was ill, had much to do and it was impossible for me to answer you sooner.— Now only the most necessary things—not a heller of the 10 ducats in gold has as yet arrived, and I am already beginning to believe, that the Englishmen, too, are only magnanimous in foreign lands; so also with the *Prince Regent* from whom I have not even received the copyists' fees for *my Battle which was sent* to him, nor even written or oral thanks.[11] *Fries deducted* 6 fl. Convention money here from the amount received from Birchall as well as 15 fl. Convention money for postage. Tell B this—and see that you yourself get the draft for the 10 ducats, otherwise it will be like the first time— What you *tell me about Neate's undertaking would be desirable for me.* I need it; my salary amounts to 3400 florins in paper, I pay 1100 house-rent, and my servant and his wife nearly 900 fl., you can figure out what remains. Moreover, I have got to care wholly for my little nephew. Till now he has been in an Institute; this costs me close to 1100 fl. and thus is hard for me, so I must establish myself in decent housekeeping and have him live with me— How much one must earn in order to live here! And yet there is never an end for—for—for—you know it already— As to the dedications, I will wait for another time— A few orders as well as an Akademie would also be welcome from the Philharmonic Society— Besides my dear pupil Ries ought to sit down and dedicate *something good* to me to which the *master would also respond and repay in kind— How shall I send you my portrait?* I hope to have news from *Neate too; urge him on a bit.* Be assured of my sincere interest in your future. *Urge Neate to get to work and to write— My best regards to your wife.* Unfortunately I have none. I found *only one*, whom I shall doubtless *never possess; but I am not a woman-hater* on that account.

Your true friend, Beethoven

The £5 had been deposited with Coutts and Co. on March 15, and the money order was received by Fries and Co. on May 13, as we shall see later, but month after month passed and still the "Declaration" with Beethoven's signature did not arrive. Of the justice, propriety, delicacy of this new demand, nothing need be said; its historical importance is due entirely to the very unfavorable effect which it and the correspondence relating to it produced upon the minds of the London publishers. Mr. Neate was in some degree prepared for the coldness with which those gentlemen received his proposals in Beethoven's behalf, by a letter written to him after the trial of the overtures. One sentence in it he remembered word for

---

[11] The Prince Regent never ordered this work, nor had his permission to present and dedicate it to him been asked before sending it. Beethoven resented the fact that he had not been recompensed until the day of his death. (TK, II, 336, n. 1.)

word: "For God's sake, don't buy anything of Beethoven!" But he was not prepared for the utter refusal in all quarters to listen to him. He besought Mr. Birchall to purchase the overtures. The reply was: "I would not print them, if you would give me them gratis."

As to the score of the Symphony in A (the Seventh), it was folly to expect that the Philharmonic Society would pay a large sum for the manuscript of a work already (March 6) advertised in Vienna for subscription at the price of twenty-five florins.

It is another instance of Beethoven's unlucky tendency to suspect the conduct and motives of others, that seeing in a newspaper a notice of the production of one of his Symphonies by the Philharmonic Society, he at once assumed that it was the Seventh and that Neate had given the use of his manuscript!

Under such circumstances Neate *could* do nothing for Beethoven; nor could he well disclose the true causes of his failure; so the composer characteristically assumed that he *would* do nothing, and, as will be seen, gave vent to his wrath in terms equally bitter and unjust. The letters selected pertaining to these transactions are reserved for their places in chronological order.

Linke's departure with the Erdödys to Croatia was noted in the last chapter; he returned to Vienna in the autumn of 1815 in season to enable Schuppanzigh to begin his winter season of quartets in November. They were given in the hall of the hotel "Zum Römischen Kaiser," and had now ended. So, too, had ended the engagement of Schuppanzigh, Weiss and Linke with Razumovsky. The destruction of his palace, the approach of old age, and failing sight, induced him now to dismiss them with suitable pensions from his service. Schuppanzigh went to Russia; Linke returned to the Erdödys and Weiss remained in Vienna. Before their departure the first two gave each a farewell concert. Schuppanzigh's took place in the palace of Count Deym, the programme being made up entirely of Beethoven's works, viz: Quartet in C major, Op. 59, No. 3; Quintet for Wind-instruments and Pianoforte, Op. 16, Carl Czerny, pianist; and the Septet, Op. 20. Beethoven "entered at the beginning of the quartet" and shared in the deafening applause of the crowded audience.[12]

Concerning this concert Czerny relates the following: "When once, for instance, I played the Quintet with Wind-Instruments with Schuppanzigh, I permitted myself, in a spirit of youthful carelessness, many changes, in the way of adding difficulties to the music, the use of the higher octave, etc.— Beethoven quite rightly took me severely to task in the presence of Schuppanzigh, Linke and the other players. The next day I received the following letter from him, which I copy carefully from the original draft:

[12] See the *Lpz. AMZ*, XVIII (1816), p. 197.

Dear Czerny!

Today I cannot see you, but tomorrow I will call on you myself to have a talk with you.— I burst forth so yesterday that I was sorry after it had happened; but you must pardon that in a composer who would have preferred to hear his work exactly as he wrote it, no matter how beautifully you played in general.— I shall make amends *publicly* at the Violoncello Sonata. Be assured that as an artist I have the greatest wishes for your success and will always try to show myself—

Your true Friend Beethoven

"This letter did more than anything else to cure me of the desire to make changes in the performance of his works, and I wish that it might have the same influence on all pianists."[13]

Linke's concert took place on the 18th of February in the hall of "Zum Römischen Kaiser," the programme, except a Rondoletto for the Violoncello by Romberg, being also entirely Beethoven. Stainer von Felsburg played "a new Pianoforte Sonata,"[14] and Czerny the pianoforte part of the Violoncello Sonata, Op. 69, on which occasion the composer "made amends publicly." And so, except for an occasional visit to Vienna by Linke, two more of our old acquaintances disappear for several years; also Hummel and Wild. Hummel we shall meet again beside Beethoven's deathbed; Wild no more. An album-leaf containing a canon was the farewell to the pianist and composer.

A happy journey, my dear Hummel, think occasionally of your friend, Ludwig van Beethoven, Vienna, April 4, 1816.

On the 20th, Wild gave a little musical festival "in the home of an art-lover," at which he sang the "Adelaide" and "An die Hoffnung," Op. 94. Beethoven was present and played the accompaniments. And this was his farewell to the singer.

On May 15, a letter of condolence to Countess Erdödy was called out by the sudden death of her son in Padua. The lad burst one morning into his

---

[13] *Allgemeine Wiener Musik-Zeitung*, September 20, 1845. Czerny notes that he was to play the Violoncello Sonata, Op. 69, with Linke the next week.

[14] *Lpz. AMZ, op.cit.*; "A new pianoforte sonata by this master, heard here for the first time, surprised all of his numerous admirers." Which sonata was played is unclear; Schindler

(*Biogr.*, I, pp. 240-41) identifies it specifically as Op. 101, but the date on the autograph of this sonata is November, 1816. In his correspondence Beethoven mentioned it for the first time in a letter to Härtel dated July 19, 1816 (*A* 542). Frimmel (*FRBH*, II, pp. 242-43) believes that the sonata played was Op. 90. (Cf. TDR, III, 480 and 586.)

sister's room and, complaining of his head, with a cry of anguish sank dead at her feet. Beethoven labored sadly in his effort to find words of comfort for the stricken mother. On May 13, before he heard the news, he had already written the Countess, so he sent the two letters together. The later letter follows:

Vienna, May 15, 1816.

Dear honored friend!

This letter was already written when today I met Linke and heard of your lamentable fate, the sudden loss of your dear son[15]— How is comfort to be given? Nothing is more painful than the quick unforeseen departure of those who are near us; thus likewise I cannot forget the death of my poor brother. Nothing except—that one can imagine that those who depart quickly suffer less—but I have the deepest sympathy for your irretrievable loss.— Perhaps I have not written you yet that I have not been well for a long time, to this reason for my long silence is to be added the care for my Karl whom I had often contemplated as a companion to your dear son.— I am seized with grief on your account and on my own since I loved your son.— May heaven watch over you, whose state of health may have failed still further, and not increase your suffering which is already so great. Reflect that your son might have been forced to go into battle and might then, like millions of others, have met his death. Besides you are still *mother* to two dear hopeful children.— I hope soon to have word from you. I weep here with you. Do not, however, listen to all the gossip concerning why I have not written you, nor to Linke, who is certainly devoted to you but *very much of a gossip*—and I feel that no go-between is needed between you dear Countess and myself

in haste and respectfully your friend
Beethoven

A few days later the following letter to Neate was written in English, probably by Häring, and only signed by Beethoven:

Vienna, May 18, 1816.

My dear Neate!

By a letter of Mr. Ries, I am acquainted with your happy arrival at London. I am very well pleased with it, and still better I should be pleased if I had learned it by yourself.

Concerning our business, I know well enough that for the performance of the greater works, as: the Symphony, the Cantata, the Chorus, and the Opera, you want the help of the Philharmonic Society, and I hope your endeavour to my advantage will be successful.

[15] There is some confusion about this event. According to Thayer it was Fritzi who died, and in Croatia. However Gunther Haupt in his article "Gräfin Erdödy und J. X. Brauchle" (*Der Bär*, Lpz., 1927, pp. 70ff.) points out (1) that if the death had been in Croatia, it would have had to occur in late 1815 before the trip to Padua, and (2) that of the three children only one was a *son*, August. Marie (Mimi) and Friederike (Fritzi) were the names of the daughters. In another letter to the Countess, Beethoven sends regards to "the daughters" (*A* 722). In a Conversation Book of July-August, 1820, there is the enigmatic entry: "der kleine Gustav in Italien Stad Padua"—["the small Gustav (August) in the Italian city of Padua"]. See Schünemann, II, p. 214.

Mr. Ries gave me notice of your intention to give a concert to my benefit. For this triumph of my art at London I would be indebted to you alone; but an influence still wholesomer on my almost indigent life, would be to have the profit proceeding from this enterprise. You know that in some regard I am now father to the lovely lad you saw with me; hardly I can live alone three months upon my annual salary of 3400 florins in paper, and now the additional burden of maintaining a poor orphan—you conceive how welcome lawful means to improve my circumstances must be to me. As for the Quatuor in F minor, you may sell it without delay to a publisher, and signify me the day of its publication as I should wish it to appear here and abroad on the very day. The same you be pleased to do with the two Sonatas, Op. 102, for pianoforte and violoncello; yet with the latter it needs no haste.

I leave entirely to your judgement to fix terms for both works, to wit, the Quatuor and the Sonatas. The more the better.

Be so kind to write to me immediately for two reasons; 1st, that I may not be obliged to shrink up my shoulders when they ask me if I got letters from you; and 2ndly, that I may know how you do, and if I am in favour with you. Answer me in English if you have to give me happy news (for example, those of giving a concert to my benefit), in French if they are bad ones.

Perhaps you find some lover of music to whom the Trio and the Sonata with the violin, Mr. Ries had sold to Mr. Birchall, or the Symphony arranged for the harpsichord might be dedicated, and from whom there might be expected a present. In expectation of your speedy answer, my dear friend and countryman, I am wholly yours,

Ludwig van Beethoven

We can follow the progress of the business in connection with the compositions to be published in London from the following excerpt from a letter to Ries, which was dated June 11, 1816:

The publisher here has applied to me to have the Trio *published in London on the last day of August,* for which reason I beg of you kindly to speak with Herr B— H. B. can get himself in readiness concerning the pianoforte arrangement of the Symphony in A, since as soon as the publisher here tells me the day I shall immediately let you or B. know—

As I have not heard a syllable from Neate since his arrival in L., I beg you to tell him to give you an answer whether he has sold the Quartet in F minor as I want to publish it here simultaneously, and what I may expect in reference to the Violoncello Sonatas. Of all the other works which I sent by him I am almost ashamed to speak, even to myself for having again been so trustful as to give them to him wholly without conditions trusting that his friendship and care for my interests would find a way— I was given to read a translation of a report in the *Morning Cronigle* about the performance of the Symphony. The same thing will probably happen to this as well as all the other works which I gave to N. as happened to the Battle; I shall probably get nothing for them as I got nothing for that work except to read about the performance in the newspapers. . . .

Here is the place for some excerpts from the diary of Dr. Karl von Bursy, a Courlander, who at this time visited Beethoven with a letter of introduction from his friend Amenda:[16]

"Vienna, June 1.

. . . Beethoven strongly resembled Amenda, especially when he laughed. He enquired most of all about him and expressed feelings of the warmest friendship for him. 'He is a very fine man,' he said. 'I have the misfortune of having all my friends far away from me and I remain alone in hateful Vienna.' He asked me to speak loudly to him because now he was again having particular difficulty in hearing; for that reason he wanted to be in Baden and the country for the summer. He has not been really well for a long time and has composed nothing new. I asked him about Berge's libretto[17] and he said it was very good and with a few changes would probably be suitable for composition. Until now his illness has not permitted this kind of labor and he wishes to write Amenda himself about it. I shouted in his ear that for such work one really has to have leisure and work full time. 'No,' he said, 'Nothing I create is done so continuously without interruption. I always work at several things at a time, first I take up this and then that.' He misunderstood me very often and, when I spoke, had to pay the greatest attention in order to understand me. Naturally this troubled and embarrassed me very much. He also felt the pressure and spoke up himself that much more and indeed very loudly. He told me a great deal about Vienna and his life here. Venom and rancor raged within him. He defies everything and is dissatisfied with everything and blasphemes against Austria and especially against Vienna. He speaks fast and with great animation. Often he beat his fist upon the piano so violently that it made a clear echo in the room. He is not discreet for he quickly confided in me concerning his personal relations and recounted many things about himself and his friends. . . . He had complaints on several counts of the present times. Art no longer stands so high above the ordinary, is no longer so respected and above all is no longer valued in terms of recompense. Beethoven also complained over the bad times in pecuniary matters. . . . 'Why do you remain in Vienna when every foreign ruler would have to make a place for you near his throne?' 'Conditions hold me here,' he said, 'but here things are shabby and niggardly. It could not be worse, from top to bottom everyone is a scoundrel. There is nobody one can trust. What is not down in black and white is not observed by any man, not even by the one with whom you have made an agreement. Moreover one has nothing in Austria, since everything is worthless, that is, paper.' At the time of the Congress Beethoven composed an occasion cantata. The text, he said, was cut and trimmed like a French garden. And yet it never got a definite performance. After many cabals he gave a concert in the Redouten-Saal and received an entrance

[16] The diary was first published, with certain passages censored, in the St. Petersburg *Zeitung* in 1854. (TDR, III, 556.)

[17] It will be remembered that in the previous year Amenda sent Beethoven Rudolph von Berge's libretto entitled *Bacchus*.

fee of 10 ducats from the King of Prussia. Very shabby! Only the Emperor of Russia paid respectably for his ticket with the sum of 200 ducats. The fact that the general manager of the Imperial Theatre, Count Palfi, received a little rebuke for this pleased him very much. He particularly dislikes this man. . . . He is delighted that his Fidelio is given in Berlin so often and with such success. He is saddened by the loss of Milder-Hauptmann. 'Her place is irrecoverable for us,' he said, 'the way she sings cannot be matched by any of the local singers. We could not pay her, therefore she decided to go to Berlin. Music here is very much on the decline. The emperor does nothing for art and the general public puts up with anything. . . .' "

Beethoven had now made up his mind to take his nephew from Giannatasio's care and make a home for him with himself. The removal was to be made at the end of the approaching quarter, and meanwhile Karl was to remain where he was so that he might have proper care during his recovery from the effects of an operation for hernia. Beethoven notified his purpose to Giannatasio on July 28, 1816, and admonished his friend that in the interim the old strictness was to be observed touching the mother's visits. The following passage is from the letter:

As regards the Queen of Night, matters will remain as they have been, and even if the operation should be performed at your place, as he will be ill for a few days and consequently more susceptible and irritable, she is all the less to be admitted to him since all impressions might easily be renewed in K. which we cannot permit. How little we can hope for improvement in her case is shown by the enclosed insipid scrawl which I send you only that you may see how right I am in pursuing the plan against her that was adopted; but this time I did not answer her like a Sarastro but like a sultan.

The surgical operation on the boy was performed by Dr. Smetana; and under the affectionate care which he received at the hands of the Giannatasios he quickly recovered and in September visited his uncle at Baden, going thither with the Giannatasios. Fräulein Fanny tells the story of the visit simply and gracefully:[18]

"While his nephew was still with us, Beethoven once invited us to visit him at Baden where he was spending the summer months, my father and we two daughters with Karl. Although our host had been informed of our coming we soon noticed that no arrangement had been made for our lodging. B. went with us in the evening to a tavern where we were surprised to note that he dickered with the waiter about every roll, but this was because owing to his bad hearing he had frequently been cheated by serving-people. For even then one had to be very close to his ear to make him understand and I recall that I was often greatly embarrassed when I had to pierce through the grayish hairs which concealed his ear. He himself often said:

[18] First published in *Grenzboten* (Leipzig) 1857, Nos. 14 and 15.

'I must have my hair cut!' Looking at him cursorily one thought that his hair was coarse and bristly, but it was very fine and when he put his hand through it, it remained standing in all directions which often looked comical. (Once when he came we noticed a hole in the elbow when he was taking his overcoat off; he must have remembered it for he wanted to put it on again, but said, laughing, taking it completely off: 'You've already seen it!')

"When we came to his lodgings in the afternoon a walk was proposed; but our host would not go along, excusing himself saying he had a great deal to do; but he promised to follow and join us, and did so. But when we came back in the evening there was not a sign of accommodations for our lodging to be seen. B. muttered excuses and accusations against the persons who had been charged with the arrangements and helped us to settle ourselves; O how interesting it was! to move a light sofa with his help. A rather large room in which his pianoforte stood, was cleaned for us girls to use as a bedroom. But sleep remained long absent from us in this musical sanctuary. Yes, and I must confess to my shame that our curiosity and desire to know things led us to examine a large round table which stood in the room. A note-book in particular received our attention. But there was such a confusion of domestic matters, and much of it which to us was illegible that we were amazed; but, behold, one passage I still remember—there it stood: 'My heart runs over at the sight of lovely nature—although she is not here!'—that gave us a great deal to think about. In the morning a very prosaic noise roused us out of our poetical mood! B. also appeared soon with a scratched face, and complained that he had had a quarrel with his servant who was leaving, 'Look,' he said, 'how he has maltreated me!' He complained also that these persons, although they knew that he could not hear, did nothing to make themselves understood. We then took a walk through the beautiful Helenenthal, we girls ahead, then B. and our father. What follows we were able to overhear with strained ears:

"My father thought that B. could rescue himself from his unfortunate domestic conditions only by marriage, did he know anybody, etc. Now our long foreboding was confirmed: he was unhappy in love! Five years ago he had made the acquaintance of a person, a union with whom he would have considered the greatest happiness of his life. It was not to be thought of, almost an impossibility, a chimera—'nevertheless it is now as on the first day.' This harmony, he added, he had not yet discovered! It had never reached a confession, but he could not get it out of his mind! Then there followed a moment which made good for many misunderstandings and grievous conduct on his part; for he acknowledged my father's friendly offer to help him as much as possible in his domestic troubles, and I believe he was convinced of his friendship for him. He spoke again of his unfortunate loss of hearing, of the wretched physical existence which he had endured for a long time. He (B.) was so happy at the noonday meal (in the open air in Helena) that his muse hovered around him! He frequently turned aside and wrote a few measures with the remark: 'My promenade with you cost me some notes but brought in others.' All this happened in September of the year 1816."

That brilliant youth Alois Jeitteles of Brünn, now a student of medicine at Vienna, wrote when hardly twenty-one years of age the beautiful series of songs "An die ferne Geliebte," so exquisitely set to music by Beethoven. Schindler states that the composer thanked the young poet for the happy inspiration; but whether he had found them in a handbook, which is probable, or received them in manuscript, does not appear. But no one can hear them adequately sung without feeling that there is something more in that music than the mere inspiration of the poetry. It was completed not many weeks before the time he wrote in his letter of May 8 to Ries: "I found *only one*, whom I shall doubtless never possess"; and but six months before the above conversation with Giannatasio.

Beethoven's project now was, upon returning to the city, to abandon his tavern life and so arrange his domestic affairs as to have his nephew with him and attend school or study with private tutors—perhaps both. As usual Zmeskall was charged with looking after servants, discovering their qualifications, etc. After Karl should come there would be need of a housekeeper, but meanwhile Beethoven suggested to Zmeskall that he find for him a servant who should be "good, of decent deportment, well recommended, married and not murderous so that my life may be safe." He returned to Vienna near the end of September.

Peter Joseph Simrock[19] of Bonn, then 24 years of age, was now in Vienna. He was often with Beethoven, in Baden, in his lodging in the Sailerstätte and in the inn "Zur goldenen Birn," where Beethoven often dined after the removal of Giannatasio to that quarter. Mr. Simrock also told the writer that he had no difficulty in making Beethoven understand him if he spoke into his left ear; but anything private or confidential must be communicated in writing. On one occasion the composer handed him paper and pencil, remarking that his servant was an eavesdropper, etc. A few days afterwards when Simrock called again, "Now," said Beethoven, "we can talk, for I have given my servant 5 florins, a kick in the rear and sent him to the devil." Everywhere in public, said Simrock, Beethoven railed at Emperor Franz because of the reduction of the paper money. "Such a rascal ought to be hanged to the first tree," said he. But he was known and the police officials let him do what he pleased. He ate extravagantly at the tavern because he ordered haphazard and sent away what was not to his taste.

Another of Beethoven's visitors just now was Alexander Kyd. This gentleman, since July 25, 1810, a Major-General in the East India Company's Engineer Corps, paid the usual tribute to the climate, and, broken down in health, came to Vienna to put himself under the treatment of Malfatti. He

[19] Simrock (1796-1870) was the son of the Bonn publisher, Nikolaus Simrock, and became his successor in the firm. His Bonn accent undoubtedly facilitated his conversations with Beethoven. (Cf. TDR, III, 566.)

thus made the acquaintance of Dr. Bertolini, who gave to Jahn and the present writer the following details:

Kyd was a great lover of music, and, after his long residence in India, enjoyed to the utmost his present opportunities of hearing it. Bertolini took him to Czerny, who during several visits played to him all the pianoforte works of Beethoven then in print. The General was ravished with these compositions, asked for a complete thematic catalogue of the composer's works, and besought Bertolini to introduce him to their author. This took place on the 28th of September "in the house next to the Colorado Palace," said Bertolini. They found him shaving and looking shockingly, his ruddy face browned by the Baden sun variegated by razor cuts, bits of paper, and soap. As Kyd seated himself crash! went the chair. In the course of the interview, the General, showing the common belief of Beethoven's poverty, proposed to him through the Doctor, to compose a symphony for which he would pay him 200 ducats (£100), and secure its performance by the London Philharmonic Society, not doubting that the profits of the work to the composer would thus amount to £1000. He offered also to take him himself to London. To Beethoven's leaving Vienna just now there really seems to have been no serious impediment, other than his nephew; and the boy was certainly in the best of hands so long as he remained with Giannatasio. However, he did not accept the proposition, nor even the order for the Symphony, because Kyd desired to have it rather like the earlier, than the later ones—that is, somewhat shorter, simpler, and more easy of comprehension than these last. The conclusion of the story as told in the Fischoff manuscript corresponds entirely with the Doctor's relation: "When Bertolini related all this to his friend with sympathetic joy the latter received it in an entirely different spirit. He declared that he would receive dictation from no one; he needed no money, despised it and would not submit himself to the whim of another man for half the world, still less compose anything which was not according to his liking, to his individuality. From that time he was also cool toward Bertolini and remained so."

When he afterwards quarrelled with and insulted Malfatti he broke entirely with Bertolini; but both those gentlemen were too honorable ever to disclose the details of this breach. Simrock writes in an autograph notice for this work: "When I visited Beethoven in Vienna on September 29, 1816, he told me that he had had a visit on the day before from an Englishman who on behalf of the London Philharmonic Society had asked him to compose a symphony for that institution in the style of the first and second symphonies, regardless of cost. . . . As an artist he felt himself deeply offended at such an offer and indignantly refused it and thus closed the interview with the intermediary. In his excitement he expressed himself very angrily and with deep displeasure towards a nation which by such an offer had manifested so low an opinion of an artist and art, which he looked upon as a great insult. When we were passing Haslinger's publishing house in the

Graben in the afternoon he stopped suddenly and pointing to a large, power-fully built man who had just entered, cried out: 'There's the man whom I threw down stairs yesterday!' " "Whom I threw down stairs" was, of course, meant metaphorically. It is pretty evident that Beethoven in some degree misunderstood General Kyd's proposition and that this ebullition of spleen was rather directed against Neate and the Philharmonic Society than the General. It is greatly to be regretted that this artistic pride had so little restraining effect upon his correspondence when pecuniary matters form the topic—which remark brings us again to Mr. Birchall. Beethoven had at last discovered the £5 to his credit in the bank of Fries and Co., and signed a receipt for it on August 3d—too late to prevent the following letter being sent to him:

August 14, 1815.

Sir:

Mr. Birchall received yours of the 22d of last month and was surprised to hear you have not yet received the additional £5.0.0 to defray your expenses of copy-ing, etc. He assures the above sum was paid to Messrs. Coutts and Co., March 15th last, to be transmitted to Messrs. Fries and Co., of Vienna for you, which he supposed you would receive as safe as the previous sum. In consequence of your last letter, inquiry has again been made at Messrs. Coutts and Co., respecting it and they have referred to their books and find that Messrs. Fries and Co., were written to on the 13th of May, and in that letter the following extract respecting you was contained.

London, May 13, 1816.

"To Messrs. Fries and Co.:

"We have received from Mr. Birchall a further sum of five pounds [£5] on your account for the use of Mr. Beethoven. You will therefore please to account to that gentleman for the same and include the amount in your next bill upon us.

"Coutts and Co."

If Mr. Beethoven will call on Messrs. Fries and Co., and get them to refer to that letter, no doubt it will be immediately paid, as there is a balance in their favour at Messrs. Coutts and Co., of £5.0.0, which was not included in their last Bill on London.

Mr. Birchall is sorry you have not received it so soon as you ought, but he hopes you will be convinced the fault does not lay [*sic*] with him, as the money was paid the day after Mr. Ries spoke about it.

Mr. Birchall wished particularly to have the Declaration returned to him as soon as possible and likewise wishes you to favour him with the Dedications and opus numbers, which are to be put to the Trio, Sonata and the Grand Symphony in A. The publication of the Sonata has been delayed a long time in consequence of that, but he hopes you will not delay forwarding *all on the receipt of this*. When you write again Mr. Birchall will be glad to know your sentiments respecting writing Variations to the most favourite English, Scotch or Irish airs for the Pianoforte with an accompaniment either for the violin or violoncello—as you find best—about the same length as Mozart's airs "La dove prende" and "Colomba o tortorella" and Handel's "See the Conquering Hero Comes"; with your Variations, be so good, when you oblige him with your terms, as to say whether the airs need be sent you; if you have many perhaps mentioning the name will be sufficient. In fixing the price Mr. Birchall wishes you to mention a sum that will include Copying and Postages.

For R. Birchall.

C. Lonsdale.

Beethoven's reply in English bears all the marks of Häring's pen, being only signed by himself:

Vienna, October 1, 1816.

My dear Sir:

I have duly received the £5, and thought previously you would not increase the number of Englishmen neglecting their word and honour as I had the misfortune of meeting with two of this sort. In reply to the other topics of your favour, I have no objection to write Variations according to your plan and I hope you will not find £30 too much, the accompaniment will be a flute or violin or a violoncello; you'll either decide it when you send me the approbation of the price, or you'll leave it to me. I expect to receive the songs or poetry—the sooner the better, and you'll favour me also with the probable number of works of Variations you are inclined to receive of me.

The Sonata in G with the accompaniment of a violin is dedicated to his Imperial Highness, Archduke Rudolph of Austria—it is Op. 96. The Trio in B-[flat] is dedicated to the same and is Op. 97. The Piano arrangement of the Symphony in A is dedicated to the Empress of the Russians—meaning the wife of the Emp. Alexander—Op. 98.

Concerning the expenses of copying and posting, it is not possible to fix them beforehand, they are at any rate not considerable and you'll please to consider that you have to deal with a man of honour, who will not charge one 6d [sixpence] more than he is charged for himself. Messrs. Fries and Co., will account with Messrs. Coutts and Co. The postage may be lessened as I have been told.

I offer you of my works the following new ones. A grand Sonata for the pianoforte alone £40. A Trio for the Piano with accompt. of Violin and Violoncello for £50. It is possible that somebody will offer you other works of mine to purchase: for ex. the Score of the Grand Symphony in A. With regard to the arrangement of this Symphony for the piano, I beg you not to forget that you are not to publish it until I have appointed the day of its publication here in Vienna. This cannot be otherwise without making myself guilty of a dishonourable act—but the Sonata with the violin and the Trio in B-flat may be published without any delay.

With all the new works which you will have of me or which I offer you, it rests with you to name the day of their publication at your own choice. I entreat you to honour me as soon as possible with an answer having many orders for compositions and that you may not be delayed. My address or direction is:

Monsieur Louis van Beethoven,

No. 1055 and 1056 Sailerstätte, 3te Stock,

Vienna.

You may send your letter if you please direct to your,

Most humble servant,

Ludwig van Beethoven.

Beethoven not only complained of Neate to Ries, but now wrote to Smart of him in such bitter terms that that gentleman suppressed the letter entirely except to show it to Neate himself, whose grief and astonishment at the injustice done him are but partly expressed in this next letter:

London, October 29, 1816.

My dear Beethoven:

Nothing has ever given me more pain than your letter to Sir George Smart. I confess that I deserve your censure, that I am greatly in fault; but must say also that I think you have judged too hastily and too harshly of my conduct. The letter I sent you some time since, was written at a moment when I was in *such* a state of mind and spirits that I am sure, had you seen me or known my sufferings, you would have excused every unsatisfactory passage in it. Thank God! it is now all over, and I was just on the point of writing to you, when Sir George called with your letter. I do not know how to begin to answer it; I have never been called upon to justify myself, because it is the first time that I ever stood accused of dishonor; and what makes it the more painful is "that I stand accused by the man who, of all the world, I most admire and esteem, and one also whom I have never ceased to think of, and wish for his welfare, since I made his acquaintance." But as the appearance of my conduct has been so unfavorable in your eyes, I must tell you again of the situation I was in previous to my marriage.

Until the question upon which my whole happiness depended was decided, whether I should be permitted by the family to marry my wife, which I did on October 2nd, I was not able to appear as an artist. Now I remain a musician. Also I did not want someone else to negotiate for you from the fear that it would not happen as it should. I am notified that I have not kept my word with you, which is untrue; but I have neglected everyone, everything including myself.

I remain in my profession, and with no abatement of my love of Beethoven! During this period I could not myself do anything publicly, consequently all your music remained in my drawer unseen and unheard. I, however, did make a very considerable attempt with the Philharmonic to acquire for you what I thought you fully entitled to. I offered all your music to them upon condition that they made you a very handsome present; this they said they could not afford, but proposed to see and hear your music, and then offer a price for it; I objected and replied "that I should be ashamed that your music should be put up by auction and bid for!—that your name and reputation were too dear to me"; and I quitted the meeting with a determination to give a concert and take all the trouble myself, rather than that your feelings should be wounded by the chance of their disapproval of your works. I was the more apprehensive of this, from the unfortunate circumstances of your Overtures not being well received; they said they had no more to hope for, from your other works. I was not a Director last season, but I am for the next, and then I shall have a voice which I shall take care to exert. I have offered your Sonatas to several publishers, but they thought them too difficult, and said they would not be saleable, and consequently made offers such as I could not accept, but when I shall have played them to a few professors, their reputation will naturally be increased by their merits, and I hope to have better offers. The Symphony you read of in the "Morning Chronicle" I believe to be the one in C minor; it certainly was not the one in A, for it has not been played at a concert. I shall insist upon its being played next season, and most probably the first night. I am exceedingly glad that you have chosen Sir George Smart to make your complaints of me to, as he is a man of honor, and very much your friend; had it been anyone else, your complaint might have been listened to, and I injured all the rest of my life. But I trust I am too respectable to be thought unfavorably of by those who know me. I am, however, quite willing to give up every sheet I have of yours, if you again desire it. Sir George will write by the next post, and will confirm this. I am sorry you say that I did not even *acknowledge* my obligation to you, because I talked of nothing else at Vienna, as every one there who knows me can testify. I even offered my purse, which you generously always declined. Pray, my dear Friend, believe me to remain,

Ever yours, most sincerely,

C. Neate.

Zmeskall, whose patience and forbearance were inexhaustible, had again provided his friend with servants—a man and his wife—and something was done towards making the lodging in the Sailerstätte ready to receive the nephew at the end of the quarter. But this was not yet to be. The circumstances explain the following little letter to Zmeskall of date November 3, 1816:

Dear Z. Your non-recommendation of the servants engaged by me I can also not recommend—I beg of you at once to hand over to me through Hr. Schlemmer the papers, testimonials, etc., which you have from them.—I have reason to suspect them of a theft.—I have been continually ill since the 14th of last month and must keep to my bed and room.—All projects concerning my nephew have foundered because of these miserable persons.—

As ever yours,

L. v. Beethoven

Further information is provided by the following letter to Giannatasio:

Valued friend!

My household greatly resembles a shipwreck, or threatens to. In brief I have been swindled in reference to these people by one who affects to be a connoisseur. Moreover, my recovery seems to be in no hurry. Under such circumstances, to engage a tutor whose inner and outer life is unknown to me and to leave the education of my Karl to chance I can never do, great as are the sacrifices which in many respects I shall again be called upon to make. I therefore beg you, respected G, to keep my Karl again for this quarter. I shall accept your suggestion regarding his cultivation of music to this extent, that two or even three times a week Karl shall leave you at six o'clock and stay with me until the next morning when he shall return to you again by about 8 o'clock. Every day would be too taxing for K. and, since it would always have to be at the same hour, too wearisome and restricting for me— We shall discuss more in detail during this quarter what would be most practicable for K. and considerate also of me, for, in view of the fact that unfortunately my circumstances are continually getting worse, I must refer to this. If your residence in the garden had been better adapted to my health, everything could have been arranged easily— As regards my debt to you for the present quarter I must beg you to bring this to me to be discharged, as the bearer of this has been blessed by God with a certain amount of stupidity which one might not begrudge him if others were not affected by it— Regarding the other expenses for Karl during his illness or matters connected with it, I beg of you to have patience for a few days as I have large expenditures just now on all sides—

I should like also to know how matters stand between me and Smetana in view of his successfully accomplished operation. So far as his compensation is concerned if I were rich or not in the condition of all (except the Austrian usurers) whom fate has bound to this country, I would not ask at all. I mean only an approximate estimate— Farewell, I embrace you with all my heart, and will always look upon you as the friend of myself and of my Karl.

Respectfully, Your L. v. Beethoven

In November, Mr. Lonsdale wrote as follows in behalf of Mr. Birchall:

London, November 8, 1816.

Sir:

In answer to yours of the 1st October, I am desired by Mr. Birchall to inform you, he is glad to find you are now satisfied respecting his promise of paying you £5 in addition to what you before received according to agreement; but he did not think you would have delayed sending the receipt signed after the receipt of the 130 ducats merely because you had not received the £5 . . . , which latter sum was not included in the receipt. Till it comes Mr. Birchall cannot, at any rate, enter into any fresh arrangement, as his first care will be to secure those pieces he has already paid you for, and see how they answer his purpose as a Music Seller and without the receipt he cannot prevent any other Music Seller from publishing them. In regard to the airs with variations, the price of £30, which is supposed you mean for each, is considerably more than he could afford to give, ever to have any hopes of seeing them repay him. If that should be your lowest price—Mr. Birchall will give up his idea of them altogether. The Symphony in A will be quite ready for publication in a week; Mr. Ries (who has kindly undertaken the inspection of your works) has it now looking over— but it will not come out *till the day comes* you may appoint.

Mr. Birchall fears the Sonata in G and the Trio in B-flat have been published in Vienna before his[20]— He will be obliged to you to inform him of the day, when you write, that they were published. I am sorry to say, that Mr. Birchall's health has been very bad for two or three years back, which prevents him from attending to business and as there are, I fear, but little hopes of his being much better, he is less anxious respecting making *any* additions to his catalogue than he otherwise would have been; he is much obliged to you for the offer of the Sonata and the Trio, but he begs to decline it for the reasons before mentioned.

Hoping to hear soon respecting the paper sent for your signature,

I am Sir, for Mr. Birchall, etc.

C. Lonsdale.

P.S. The Sonata in G is published and the Trio will be in a few days. Is Mr. Beethoven's opera of Fidelio published? Where and by whom?

---

[20] According to KHV, pp. 270, 272, both were advertised on July 29th.

To this letter Beethoven sent an answer addressed to Mr. Birchall dated December 14, 1816, as follows:

Vienna, December 14, 1816.—1055 Sailerstätte.

Dear Sir:

I give you my word of honor, that I have signed and delivered the receipt to the house, Fries and Co., some day last August, who, as they say, transmitted it to Messrs. Coutts and Co., where you'll have the goodness to apply. Some error might have taken place that instead of Messrs. C. sending it to you, they have been directed to keep it till fetched. Excuse this irregularity, but it is not my fault, nor had I ever the idea of withholding it from the circumstance of the £5 not being included. Should the receipt not come forth at Messrs. C., I am ready to sign any other and you shall have it directly with return of post—

If you find variations—in my style—too dear at £30, I will abate, for the sake of your friendship, one-third—and you have the offer of such variations as fixed in our former letters for £20 each air—

Please to publish the Symphony in A immediately, as well as the Sonata—and the Trio—they being ready here.

The grand opera Fidelio is my work. The arrangement for the pianoforte has been published here under my care, but the score of the opera itself is not yet published. I have given a copy of the score to Mr. Neate under the seal of friendship and whom I shall direct to treat for my account in case an offer should present—I anxiously hope your health is improving. Give me leave to subscribe myself, Dear Sir,

Your very obedient serv't,

[Postmark, Dec. 31, 1816.]   Ludwig van Beethoven.

This letter closed the correspondence, for upon the death of Mr. Birchall his successor, Mr. Lonsdale, did not deem the connection with the composer to be worth retaining.

In marked contrast to the sombre tone of his letters to England is the playful character of almost all of the numerous notes to Steiner during the year. Here is a sample:[21]

Here is a small piece of field equipment which I am sending over— (as a present)—so that it may march right into your arsenal. As for Herr Diabolus, hold on to him for what abilities he has left; whatever has to be changed can be done as it was in the past with the Symphony in F— Concerning a new sonata for pianoforte, present me with 60 well-armed men and the same could be published at once. I also have some variations in mind which would suit a special holiday, and they also could be made to appear with the help of only 40 well-armed men— Now as regards the state debt of 1300 fl., payment of this cannot yet be considered, moreover the 1300 fl. would look best if they were transformed into the following figure o o o o—

I am astonishingly respectful of the Lt. Gl.

L. v. Beethoven

[21] In Appendix IV of TDR, III are given 34 letters to Steiner and Haslinger of the period 1815-17.

First, it is worth noting the size of Beethoven's debt to Steiner during this period, which was not to be paid off for some years. Second, the humorous reference to a number of "well-armed men" is Beethoven's military paraphrase for the price in ducats.

According to Kinsky-Halm,[22] the "small piece of field equipment" was the song "Der Mann von Wort" on a poem by Kleinschmid. Steiner obliged and the piece did "march into his arsenal" and appeared in print in November. The new sonata was Op. 101, the first of the great set of late pianoforte sonatas for which, as we shall see, Beethoven was to ponder as to the best word for hammer-action when printing the title. Preliminary sketches for the sonata were probably made in the years preceding, but the working out was done in the summer of this year. There are no sketches for the first movement; but sketches for the second appear in a sketchbook formerly belonging to Eugen von Miller of Vienna and now a part of the Koch collection. Before these sketches, come some detailed work on the song-cycle "An die ferne Geliebte," and after, first, work on an incompleted Trio in F minor and then on "Der Mann von Wort."[23] Sketches for the last movement appear in a sketchbook belonging to the Berlin Library. Here also appears, Kinsky-Halm believes, a clue to the variations for "a special holiday" mentioned in the above letter; for after the sonata sketches appears a sketch entitled "Christ ist erstanden Variations" which Beethoven was evidently contemplating as an Easter theme.[24]

The following four letters tell of incidents which make up the history of the latter part of the year 1816. The first is to Zmeskall, dated December 16:

Here dear Z. you will receive my friendly dedication[25] which I hope will be a precious souvenir of our long-continued friendship and be accepted as a proof of my respect and not as the end of a long-spun thread (for you are among my earliest friends in Vienna).

Farewell— Abstain from the decaying fortresses, the attack is more costly than from those well preserved.

As ever, Your friend, Beethoven

N.B. If you have a moment's time please tell me how much a livery will cost now (without cloak) with hat and boot money. The most extraordinary changes have taken place; the man, thank God, has gone to the devil, but on the other hand the wife seems disposed to attach herself here all the more closely.

The next is to Sir George Smart in London, dictated to Häring:

Vienna, December 18, 1816—1055 Sailerstätte, 3rd Floor.
My dear Sir:
You honor me with so many encomiums and compliments that I ought to blush, tho' I confess they are highly flattering to me and I thank you most heartily for the part you take in my affairs. They have rather gone a little back through

22 KHV, p. 277.
23 See *II Beeth.*, pp. 334-46.
24 *Ibid.*, pp. 553-55; KHV, p. 354.

25 To the Quartet in F minor, Op. 95.
(TDR, III, 576, n. 1.)

the strange situation in which our lost—but happily recovered—friend, Mr. Neate, found himself entangled. Your kind letter of 31 Oct. explained a great deal and to some satisfaction and I take the liberty to enclose an answer to Mr. Neate, of whom I also received a letter, with my entreaties to assist him in all his undertakings in my behalf.

You say that the Cantata might serve your purpose for the oratorios and I ask you if you find 50 £ too much to give for it? I have had no benefit for it whatever until now, but I still should not wish to ask of you a price by which you might be a loser. Therefore we shall name 40 £, and if your success should be great, then I hope you will have no objection of adding the 10 £ to make the sum as mentioned. The *Copyright* would be *yours*, and I should only make the condition of my publishing it *here* at a period which *you will be pleased* to appoint and not before.

I have communicated to Mr. Häring your kind intentions and he joins with me in the expression of the highest regard, which he always entertained for you.—

Mr. Neate may keep the different works, except the Cantata if you accept it, and I hope he will have it in his power with your assistance to do something for me, which from my illness and from the state of the Austrian finances would be very welcome.— Give me leave to subscribe myself with the greatest esteem and cordiality—

Ludwig van Beethoven

The following, to Mr. Neate in London, was written in English by Mr. Häring, at Beethoven's dictation:

Vienna, December 18, 1816.

My dear Sir:

Both letters to Mr. Beethoven and to me arrived. I shall first answer his, as he has made out some memorandums, and would have written himself, if he was not prevented by a rheumatic feverish cold. He says: "What can I answer to your warmfelt excuses? Past ills must be forgotten, and I wish you heartily joy that you have safely reached the long wished-for port of love. Not having heard of you, I could not delay any longer the publication of the Symphony in A, which appeared here some few weeks ago.— It certainly may last some weeks longer before a copy of this publication appears in London, but unless it is soon performed at the Phil[harmonic], and something is done for me afterwards by way of benefit, I don't see in what manner I am to reap some good. The loss of your interest last season with the Phil[harmonic], when all my works in your hands were unpublished, has done me great harm—but it could not be helped,—and at this moment I know not what to say. Your intentions are good, and it is to be hoped that my little fame may yet help— With respect to the two Sonatas, Op. 102, for pianoforte and violoncello, I wish to see them sold very soon, as I have several offers for them in Germany, which depend entirely upon me to accept; but I should not wish, by publishing them here, to lose all and every advantage with them in England. I am satisfied with the ten guineas offered for the dedication of the Trio, and I beg you to hand the title immediately to Mr. Birchall, who is anxiously waiting for it; you'll please to use my name with him.— I should be flattered to write some new works for the Philhar[monic]— I mean Symphonies, an Oratorio, or Cantatas, etc. Mr. Birchall wrote as if he wished to purchase my Fidelio. Please to treat with him, unless you have some plan with it for my benefit concert, which in general I leave to you and Sir George Smart, who will have the goodness to deliver this to you. The score of the opera Fidelio is not published in Germany or anywhere else. Try what can be done with Mr. B or as you think best. I was very sorry to hear that the three Overtures were not liked in London. I by no means reckon them amongst my best works, (which, however, I can boldly say of the Symphony in A), but still they were not disliked here and in Pest, where people are not easily satisfied. Was there no fault in the execution? Was there no party spirit?

And now I shall close, with the best wishes for your welfare, and that you enjoy all possible felicity in your new situation of life—

Your true friend,
Louis van Beethoven

On December 28 Beethoven wrote to Dr. Kanka in Prague urging him to accept the appointment, about to be offered by the town of Retz, as curator for a certain Johann Lamatsch in Prague. ⸺According to Frimmel,[26] Johanna Reiss van Beethoven's grandfather on her mother's side was a Lamatsch. Beethoven's interest in the matter was that Karl as Johanna's son could "receive a small fortune, and the Retz affair might enable me to spend a few hundred florins more on the education of my dear nephew." In the spring Beethoven wrote to Kanka that he had received good news from a Retz official named Bayer; and in his draft of a memorandum to the Vienna Court of Appeal, February 18, 1820, concerning his nephew he wrote "in connection with his property I traveled to Retz etc."⸺

The second of the three supporters of Beethoven's annuity disappears at this time from our history. Prince Franz Joseph Lobkowitz, who was born on December 7, 1772, died on December 15, 1816. A reference to the fact occurs in the following letter from Beethoven to Dr. Karl Peters, tutor of the Lobkowitz children:

January 8, 1816
[Should be 1817]

Dear Sir:

Only yesterday did I hear from Herr von Bernard, who met me, that you are here. Therefore I send you these two copies, which unfortunately were not finished until just at the time when the death of our dear Prince Lobkowitz was reported. Do me the favor to hand them to his Serene Highness, the firstborn Prince Lobkowitz, together with this writing. Just today I intended to look up the cashier to ask him to undertake their delivery in Bohemia, not having, in truth, believed any of you to be here. If I may speak of myself, I hope soon to be in a state of tolerably good health and wish you the same— I dare not ask you to come to me for I should be obliged to *tell you why*, which I cannot presume to do just now, any more than why you *do not come* or *do not*

---

[26] See *FRBH*, ii, p. 481.

wish to come— I beg of you to write the inscription to the Prince on the letter as I do not know his given name—the third copy please keep for your wife. Farewell.

Your friend and servant

L. v. Beethoven

--•§{The music that Beethoven refers to was undoubtedly the song-cycle "An die ferne Geliebte," which was dedicated to Prince Lobkowitz.[27] The letter he mentions is one to the young Prince which, according to Miss Anderson,[28] is misdated in the same way as the one to Peters.}§•--

To the few names which this year have appeared in our narrative, there is still to be added one worthy of a paragraph: that of a wealthy young man from Graz, an amateur musician and composer of that class whose idol was Beethoven—Anselm Hüttenbrenner, who came to Vienna in 1815 to study with Salieri, and formed an intimate friendship with Franz Schubert. His enthusiasm for Beethoven was not abated when the present writer, in 1860, had the good fortune to enjoy a period of familiar intercourse with him, to learn his great and noble qualities of mind and heart, and to hear his reminiscences from his own lips. That these, in relation to Beethoven, were numerous, no one will expect; since no young man of twenty-two years, and a stranger, could at the period before us be much with the master except as a pupil—and he took none—or in the position lately occupied by Oliva and soon to be assumed by Schindler: this of course was completely out of the question with Hüttenbrenner. He relates: "I learned to know Beethoven through the kindness of Hr. Dr. Joseph Eppinger, Israelite. The first time Beethoven was not at home; his housekeeper opened to us his living-room and study. There everything lay in confusion—scores, shirts, socks, books. The second time he was at home, locked in with two copyists. At the name 'Eppinger' he opened the door and excused himself, having a great deal to do, and asked us to come at another time. But, seeing in my hand a roll of music—overture to Schiller's 'Robbers' and a vocal quartet with pianoforte accompaniment, text by Schiller—he took it, sat himself down to the pianoforte and turned all the leaves carefully. Thereupon he jumped up, pounded me on the right shoulder with all his might, and spoke to me the following words which humiliated me because I cannot yet explain them: 'I am not worthy that you should visit me!' Was it humility? If so it was divine; if it was irony it was pardonable."

And again: "A few times a week Beethoven came to the publishing house of Steiner and Co. in the forenoon between 11 and 12 o'clock. Nearly every time there was held there a composers' meeting to exchange musical opinions. Schubert frequently took me there. We regaled ourselves with the pithy, often sarcastic remarks of Beethoven particularly when the talk was about Italian music."

---

[27] See Ludwig Nohl, *Neue Briefe Beethovens* (Stuttgart, 1867), p. 122.

[28] See *A* 734a, notes 1 and 3.

Hüttenbrenner remembered as a common remark in Vienna in those days that what first gave Beethoven his reputation on coming there twenty-four years before, was his superb playing of Bach's *Well-Tempered Clavichord*.

Two or three minor notes will close the story of the year. In the concert for the Theatrical Poor Fund, in the Theater-an-der-Wien, September 8th, one of the finales to Beethoven's *Prometheus* music was revived: "A glorious piece worked out in a masterly manner," says a reporter; and the concert for the Hospital of St. Mark was opened with his "Symphony in A, one difficult of execution, which was performed with the greatest precision under the direction of this brilliant composer."[29] More important was a proposition made early in the year by his old friend Hoffmeister in Leipzig for a complete edition of his pianoforte works, which came to nothing and concerning which more in another connection. In July he received another series of songs from Thomson which, according to a letter in French to Thomson, dated January 18, 1817, he had already finished by the end of September.

The works composed in 1816 were:

1815-16. — "Sehnsucht" (Reissig), WoO 146.[30]
Sonata for Pianoforte, Op. 101.
Twenty-five Scottish Songs with accompaniment for piano, violin and violoncello, Op. 108.
Two Canons. "Das Schweigen" and "Das Reden," WoO 168, for Charles Neate on January 24.

1816. Canons.
"Ars longa vita brevis," WoO 170, for Johann Nepomuk Hummel in the beginning of April.
"Ich küsse Sie," WoO 169, for Anna Milder-Hauptmann on January 6.
"Der Mann von Wort" (F. A. Kleinschmid), Op. 99.
March in D for Military Band, WoO 24. The autograph is dated June 3, 1816. In Schindler's papers was found a note from Lieutenant Commander Franz Xaver Embel of the Civil Artillery Corps to Beethoven asking for a "March for Turkish Music"; to which, according to Schindler's notation Beethoven responded with the March in D.[31]
"Ruf vom Berge" (Treitschke), WoO 147.
Song cycle: "An die ferne Geliebte" (Jeitteles), Op. 98. On the autograph: "1816 in the month of April."
Variations for Piano, Violin and Violoncello on the song "Ich bin der Schneider Kakadu" from Wenzel Müller's *Die Schwestern von Prag,* Op. 121a. In a letter to Gottfried Härtel of July 19, 1816, one of the works offered by Beethoven was the "Variations . . . on a Müller theme, composed earlier, but nevertheless not to be rejected."[32]

[29] On December 26, according to Orel, *Ein Wiener Beethoven Buch*, 1921, p. 103.
[30] For sketches see *II Beeth.*, pp. 332-33.
[31] See TDR, IV, p. 476, n. 1.
[32] See *A* 642.

The publications for the year were:

By Artaria:

"Sehnsucht" (Reissig), WoO 146, in a set of three songs from "Blümchen der Einsamkeit" by Beethoven, Gyrowetz and Seyfried.

By Birchall in London:

"Beethoven's Grand Battle Sinfonia. . . . Descriptive of the Battle and Victory at Vittoria," Op. 91, dedicated to Prince Regent George of England, in transcription for pianoforte, in January. See Steiner, below.

By J. Riedl:

Canon. "Glück zum neuen Jahr," WoO 165 as a supplement to "Songs by Goethe and Matthisson Set to Music by L. van Beethoven."

By Steiner:

"An die Hoffnung" (Tiedge), Op. 94.

"Der Man von Wort" (Kleinschmid), Op. 99.

"Merkenstein" (Rupprecht), Op. 100 (2nd version for two voices), dedicated to Count Joseph Karl von Dietrichstein.

Sonata for Pianoforte and Violin, Op. 96, dedicated to Archduke Rudolph.

Song-cycle. "An die ferne Geliebte" (Jeitteles), Op. 98, dedicated to Prince Franz Joseph von Lobkowitz.

String Quartet, Op. 95, dedicated to Nikolaus Zmeskall von Donamovecz.

Symphony No. 7 in A major, Op. 92, dedicated to Count Moritz von Fries.

Trio for Pianoforte, Violin, and Violoncello, Op. 97, dedicated to Archduke Rudolph.

"Wellingtons Sieg oder die Schlacht bey Vittoria in Musik gesetz von Ludwig van Beethoven 91tes Werk," dedicated to Prince Regent George of England, in score and in parts,[33] in February.

By Thomson in Edinburgh and Preston in London:

"A Select Collection of Original Irish Airs," Vol. ii, WoO 153, Nos. 5-20; WoO 154, Nos. 1, 3-6, 8-12; WoO 157, Nos. 2, 6, 8, 11.

By the *Wiener Modenzeitung* (February 29) as a supplement:

"Das Geheimnis" (Wessenberg), WoO 145.

---

[33] According to Kinsky-Halm (KHV, p. 253), this was the first of Beethoven's publica- tions to appear simultaneously in score and in parts.

CHAPTER XXX

THE YEAR 1817

BEETHOVEN AND THE PUBLIC JOURNALS
OF VIENNA—AN OFFER FROM THE
PHILHARMONIC SOCIETY OF LONDON—
BEETHOVEN AND THE METRONOME

BEETHOVEN'S splenetic remarks to strangers in his last years upon the music, musicians and public of Vienna have given rise to widely diffused but utterly false conceptions as to the facts. Thus William Henry Fry, a leading American writer on music in the middle of the nineteenth century,[1] did but express a common opinion in the following: "That composer [Beethoven] worked hard for thirty years. At his death, after the cup of glory had overflowed, his name resounding through Christendom, he left in all a beggarly sum of two or three thousand dollars, having lived as any one acquainted with his career knows, a penurious life, fitted to his poverty and servile position in Vienna."

The popular want of appreciation of his merits "doomed Beethoven to a garret which no Irish emigrant would live in." It is altogether unnecessary to argue against such statements, as the whole tenor of this biography refutes them; but the public press of Vienna deserves a vindication, and the appearance of a new *Allgemeine Musik-Zeitung* on January 2, 1817, affords a suitable opportunity for the little that need be said on the subject. This journal, conducted "with particular reference to the Austrian Empire," and published by Steiner and Co., was, during the first two years, without the name of any responsible editor; the volumes for 1819 and 1820 announce Ignaz von Seyfried as holding that position; the others, up to 1824, bear the name of Friedrich August Kanne. A leading writer in the earlier volumes

---

[1] Mr. Fry was for many years editorial writer and music critic of the *New York* *Tribune*, with which Mr. Thayer was also associated for a time. (TK, II, 358, n. 1.)

was Hofrath Ignaz von Mosel, who already had some local celebrity for his articles on musical topics in the *Vaterländische Blätter* and other periodicals, and who continued a prolific contributor to musical journals to the end of his life in 1844. Beethoven valued him as a writer; but Mosel had the temerity to undertake, like Mozart, the task of revising and modernizing Handel. Of his eight mutilations of that great man's works, two, *Samson* and *Belshazzar*, were printed and, for some fifty years, adopted for performance throughout Austria and Germany—a remarkable proof of the general ignorance which prevailed concerning the works of the greatest oratorio composer; for two such monuments of arrogant presumption, of incompetency to comprehend his author and of a false and perverted taste, probably do not exist unless, perhaps, among the other six works which were not printed. One of Beethoven's sarcasms, remembered by Carl Czerny, indicates his opinion of Mosel's dilettantism. Reading a newspaper once at Artaria's, he saw that Mosel "had been ennobled, particularly because of his services in behalf of music." "The Mosel is muddy where it flows into the Rhine" (*Der Mosel fliesst trüb in den Rhein!*), said Beethoven, laughingly. Kanne ranked with the best musical journalists of the day; and, to use the words of Hanslick, his labors and influence as a critic were considerable, especially because of his enthusiasm for Beethoven.

Taking 1821-1822 as a medium date, the leading political and literary journals in Vienna in those years were the *Wiener Zeitung*, Joseph Karl Bernard, editor; the *Wanderer*, Ignaz von Seyfried, editor; the *Beobachter,* Joseph Pilat, editor; the *Sammler*, Portenschlag and Ledermeyer, editors; the *Wiener Zeitschrift (Modenzeitung)*, Johann Schickh, editor; and the *Theater-Zeitung,* Adolph Bäuerle, editor. Most of these editors were personal friends of Beethoven; and whoever performs the weary task of looking through their myriads of pages sees that all were his admirers and let no opportunity pass unimproved of adding a leaf to his laurels. Still, disappointment at the comparative paucity of matter relating to him follows such an examination. The cause, however, lay in himself; in the small number of his new compositions of high importance, and in the rarity of his appearance before the public. True, there were newspapers, and in divers languages, that took no note of Beethoven and his works because music and musicians were not within their scope; but not one of them was hostile. In short, whether the periodical press be considered as the exponent or the guide of public opinion, in either case its tone at Vienna during the ten years which remained of Beethoven's life is ample refutation of the so oft asserted disregard for and contemptuous neglect of their great composer on the part of the Viennese.

The correspondence of this and the next two or three years is very voluminous. Schindler says most pertinently of it: "During these years our composer, instead of writing many notes, as had been his wont, wrote many letters, referring in part to his domestic affairs, in part to the litigation and in part to the education of his nephew. These letters are, in general, among the least encouraging and most deplorable testimonials to the excitement which attended his passionate prosecution of these objects. Those of his friends and nearer acquaintances who permitted themselves to be drawn into these three matters were so overwhelmed with documents and communications that they blessed the hour in which the lawsuit was brought to a conclusion."[2]

There are few men of whom a most false and exaggerated picture may not be presented by grouping together their utterances, spoken or written at long intervals and in the most diverse moods and states of mind. Thomas Carlyle says: "Half or more of all the thick-plied perversions which distort the image of Cromwell will disappear if we honestly so much as try to represent them in sequence as they were, not in the lump as thrown down before us." Hence, strict chronological order must not lightly be abandoned— never when distortion of the image is thereby produced. But there are series of letters covering comparatively short periods of time, which may be grouped and placed apart with no ill consequence. Such is the series to Steiner and Co.; and such to the Streichers and Zmeskall, which are too unimportant to place in the text. An abstract or analysis of them would serve but a small purpose; but they should be read despite their triviality, for they show, better than any description would, the helplessness of their writer in all affairs of common life; also, by implication, the wretched prospect of any good result to his undertaking the supervision and education of a boy more than usually endowed with personal attractions and mental capacity, but whose character had already received a false bias from the equally indiscreet alternate indulgence and severity of his invalid and passionate father and of his froward and impure mother. Moreover, this undertaking rendered necessary a sudden and very great change in the domestic habits of a man nearly fifty years of age, who, even twenty years before, had not been able, when residing in the family of his Mæcenas, Lichnowsky, to bear the restraints imposed by common courtesy and propriety. It is obvious that there was but one course to be taken for the boy from which a good result might reasonably have been expected; and this was to send him at once to some institution far enough from Vienna to separate him entirely, vacations excepted, from both mother and uncle; to subject him there to rigid discipline and give him the stimulus of emulation with boys of his own age. When it was too late, as will be seen, this idea was entertained, but not sanctioned by the civil authorities. That such a course with the boy would have resulted well, subsequent events leave no doubt; for we know this: that after his uncle's death, although his bad tendencies of character had been strengthened and intensified by the lack of efficient, consistent, firm and resolute restraint from 1815 to 1827, yet a few years of strict military discipline made of him a good and peaceable citizen, a kind and affectionate husband and father. Had Beethoven's wisdom and prudence equalled his boundless affection

---

[2] *Biographie*, I, pp. 263-64. (TDR, IV, 6, n. 1.)

for his nephew, many painful pages in this work would have no place; many which, if the truth and justice to the dead permitted, one would gladly suppress. But it must not be forgotten that Beethoven, on his death-bed, as Schindler relates, expressed "his honest desire that whatever might some day be said of him, should adhere strictly to the truth in every respect, regardless of whether or not it might give pain to this or the other person or affect his own person."

Let us again take up the thread of our narrative. We are still to imagine Beethoven living in the lofty, narrow house, No. 1055-6 Sailerstätte, entered from the street, but its better rooms on the other side looking over the old city wall and moat and out across the Glacis and little river Wien to the suburb Landstrasse, where, fronting on the Glacis, stood the institute of Giannatasio in which his nephew was a pupil, having been placed there in February, 1816.

From the reminiscences of Carl Friedrich Hirsch, as related to Theodor Frimmel, there is reason to believe that Beethoven spent a good deal of time and maybe lived for awhile as well at the hotel "zum Römischen Kaiser" during the winter of 1816-1817. The following is based on Frimmel's account of this conversation.[3] Hirsch was born in 1801, the youngest son of Anna Albrechtsberger. His grandfather was J. G. Albrechtsberger, Beethoven's old teacher in counterpoint. At this time the Hirsch family lived in the Renn-gasse close by the hotel "zum Römischen Kaiser" where the young Hirsch became acquainted with Beethoven. Due to the family relation to Beethoven's former teacher, Hirsch's father mustered up the courage to approach Beet-hoven and arrange that his son take lessons from him two or three times a week in what would now be called harmony. These lessons were given free out of respect for the deceased Albrechtsberger and lasted from Novem-ber, 1816 to the beginning of May, 1817.[4]

According to Hirsch, Beethoven's deafness had advanced to the point where one had to speak to him very loudly. Beethoven watched his student's hands closely and when a mistake was made he would get very angry, become red in the face, and the vein in his temples and forehead would become swollen; he would also give his pupil a severe pinch through indignation or impatience, and once even bit him in the shoulder. He was very strict during the lesson, and burst forth in anger particularly over "false fifths and octaves," at which he would spurt out in a great rage "Well, what are you doing?" After the lesson he was again very "charmant."

Hirsch also described Beethoven's appearance in detail. Of powerful build, his face was a healthy red, his eyebrows very thick and his brow low. His nose was very big and broad, especially the nostrils which were finely "shaped." His bushy thick hair was already partly gray and stood up from

---

[3] *Beethoven Studien*, II, pp. 55-69.

[4] This date is determined by Hirsch's recol-lection that the lessons were broken off at the time when one of Beethoven's friends met a sudden death. This must have been Wenzel Krumpholz, whose sudden death on May 2, 1817, is soon to be mentioned.

his face. His hands were "coarse and stout," his fingers short, the veins on the back of his hands thick, and the nails cut short.

Hirsch gave the following account of Beethoven at his lodgings, which he remembered as at the "zum Römischen Kaiser": "At home Beethoven worked in a flowery dressing-gown, outside the house he wore a dark green or brown coat with gray or dark trousers to match." For his head he had a kind of low top-hat or in warmer weather a brown or dull gold straw hat. In his whole dress Beethoven was very slovenly. "In his rooms there was the greatest disorder, notes, sheets, books lying partly on the desk, partly on the floor. Now and then the master used spectacles for reading but he did not wear them continuously." The pianos upon which Hirsch was taught at Beethoven's were "first an old five-octave, two stringed instrument made of cherry wood then a six-octave mahogany one that was completely out of tune."

Whether Beethoven lived or merely gave lessons at the "zum Römischen Kaiser"—a matter that remains in doubt since the only evidence is from the recollections of one man sixty-three years later—Beethoven's permanent quarters were in the Sailerstätte until April 24th, when once again he changed dwellings.——

There is no record, nor do the sketchbooks show, that in the first half of this year the composer's mind was occupied with any important composition; on the contrary, his time and thoughts were given to the affairs of his nephew, to his purposed housekeeping and to quarrels with his servants, as the frequent letters to the Streichers and Zmeskall show *ad nauseam*.

A curiously interesting picture of the man and his moods is disclosed by the records of Fanny Giannatasio. Of all the members of this family it was the daughter Fanny who recorded the most tender feelings for Beethoven and the most reverence, judging by numerous entries in her diary, of which the following should be quoted here. On March 1 [1817] she writes:

The fact that Beethoven is angry with us is something which has troubled me a lot ever since, although the way he showed it transformed a sad feeling into one more bitter. It is true that Father has not treated him politely, but to people like us who have shown their respect and love for him every time he should not want to retort with biting sarcasm. He probably wrote that letter[5] in one of his man-hating moods and I excuse it willingly. We have not seen him since that evening when Nanni and I lay sick in bed.

On March 6 she writes further:

. . . Moreover, I feel really hurt on account of Beethoven's behavior towards us, my bitterness towards him has gone completely and I have only the anxious wish that the stupid affair be cleared up, and that even were I not to see him often, yet I would know that he was thinking of us with a friendly loving heart. I don't know that now and it disturbs Nanni and me in our dreams! The wicked man! If he knew how many troubled moments he has already given us and could

[5] This letter, which caused such an unhappy reaction, was probably either destroyed, or sent back to the composer, since it does not exist in the letter collections. (TDR, IV, 10.)

understand that in no way have *either of us* deserved this from him and that we have always loved him—he would be compelled in accordance with his affectionate heart—to come here and make everything good between us!

On the 15th of March:

I read over these last lines with an extremely pleasant feeling; for he came—and all is well again. How sorry I am to have to note that Karl is very much to blame for this misunderstanding and sorrier still to see some new signs of his thoughtlessness towards his fine uncle carried out, which were new to him and hurt him all the more.—

When Nanni asked Beethoven if he was still angry, he replied: I think much too little of myself to get angry. Nevertheless he relaxed after an exchange of explanations, whereupon it was found that the cause of this petty coolness was only a misunderstanding. The lack of delicacy in the way Father had fetched Karl, the reminder of the payment which Karl had delivered to him in front of the piano teacher,[6] along with the lie of the latter [Karl] that he had been forbidden to practice the piano; all these things together so affected his already harassed disposition that, forgetting the confidence he had placed in us, he trusted in appearances rather than lovingly turning to his friends. But he came— he even looked embarrassed; he was probably sorry now about his letter and I am living again in the soothing conviction that he cares about us as much as he used to. Altogether my expectations have never been so fully realised as now. If my fulfilled wish—that Beethoven could understand that we cared for him and then love us in return—if this wish could be extended, it would be to live near him and to be able to brighten whenever possible the many gloomy hours of his life.

This wish was partially realised on the 24th of the next month when Beethoven moved to the Landstrasser Glacis No. 268, on the second floor, which was not far from either the Streichers or the Giannatasio family. Among Thayer's papers was found the complete transcript of Fanny's diary which he had received from Nanni Giannatasio's daughter, Frau Pessiak. A warm friendship developed between Thayer and Frau Pessiak, and in two letters to him she imparted further information concerning Beethoven and his relationship with her family.

While at a picnic party in the environs of Vienna, Beethoven stood beside Frau Pessiak's mother on the most beautiful observation point. Suddenly he took out his notebook, tore out a leaf, drew a staff upon it, jotted down the melody of the song "Wenn ich ein Vögelein wär" (Treitschke's "Ruf vom Berge") and handed it to his companion with the words: "Now, Miss Nanni, you write the bass for it." Frau Pessiak continues: "My mother cherished the leaf as a precious souvenir for a long time, then gave it to me because, as she said, I was the most musical one of the family, and would best appreciate the treasure. I have it preserved under a glass and frame." On another day Beethoven brought with him a number of songs, including the one from *Faust* beginning: "Es war einmal ein König der hatt' einen grossen Floh" ("Once upon a time there was a king who had a large flea"). Laughing,

---

[6] Carl Czerny.

Beethoven "took his seat at the pianoforte and played them the conclusion in which he pressed down two adjacent keys with his thumb at the same time and said: 'That's the way to kill him!' Mother and Aunt also had to have a try at this thing which had amused him so." On the occasion of Anna Giannatasio's birthday, Beethoven came and offered a musical congratulation. Approaching her he sang with great solemnity the melody of a canon to the words: "Above all may you lack happiness and health too—." Then he stopped and the lady protested that the wish that she might fail in happiness and health was scarcely a kind one; whereupon Beethoven laughed and finished the sentiment with "at no time!" Here is the canon:

Glück fehl Dir vor al lem, Ge - sund - heit auch— nie - ma - len!

Chiefly from letters written in this year, do we learn a sequence of other happenings. Early in January, as has already been mentioned at the end of the last chapter, Beethoven sent copies of the song-cycle "An die ferne Geliebte," to Court Councillor Peters, tutor in the house of Prince Lobkowitz, for the new prince whose Christian name he did not know.

In December, it will be remembered, he sent Zmeskall the dedication of the String Quartet, Op. 95, for which apparently Zmeskall sent him a gift. On January 30th he wrote the following lines to his friend:

Dear Z;

You want to have me keep company with Schuppanzigh, etc., and thereby you have defaced my pure genuine work. You are not in my debt, but I in yours; and now you have gone and made it still more for me. I cannot write how much this present pains me, and yet I am so honest that I must add that I cannot grant you a friendly glance *in return*. Although you are only a performing musician, you have several times exercised the power of imagination, and it seems to me that it has occasionally put unnecessary whims into your head. At least so it seemed to me from your letter after my dedication. Good as I am and much as I appreciate all the good in you, I am yet angry, angry, angry—

your new debtor
who knows, however, how to avenge himself
Beethoven

But the very next day a note to Zmeskall resumes the habitual vein— jocularity combined with further requests for help in the search for competent servants.

Letters to Steiner at this time refer to the Pianoforte Sonata in A, Op. 101, which was then in the hands of the printers and appeared in February with a dedication to Baroness Ertmann. The suggestion had gone out that German composers substitute German terms in music in place of Italian. With characteristic impetuosity, Beethoven decided to begin the reform at once, although it seems to have involved the reengraving of the title page of the new Sonata. He wrote to Steiner in the military style with which we are already familiar:

To the Wellborn Lieut[enant] Gen[eral] von Steiner for his own hands.

Publicandum

After individual examination and taking the advice of our council we have determined and hereby determine that hereafter on all our works with German titles, in place of pianoforte, *Hammerclavier* be printed; our best Lt. Gen. as well as the Adjutant and all others concerned will govern themselves accordingly at once and put this order into effect.

Instead of Pianoforte, Hammerclavier,—which settles the matter once for all.

Given, etc., etc.   by the

on January 23, 1817.   G[eneralissimu]s

Beethoven was in doubt as to the correctness of "Hammerclavier," thinking that it might better be "Hämmerclavier," and said the matter must be referred to someone versed in languages.[7] In another letter he offered, if necessary, to pay for the engraving of a new title, adding that perhaps the old one might be utilized for another sonata. He based his acceptance of the new word on the belief that the instrument itself was a German invention—a theory long ago disproved as far as the priority of the invention is concerned. He asked that the dedication remain secret as he wanted it to be a surprise.[8]

Baroness Ertmann now lived at St. Pölten, where the command of her husband lay quartered, and thither Beethoven sent a copy of the "Hammerclavier" sonata accompanied by the following letter:

Vienna, February 23, 1816 [*sic*][9]

My dear, valued Dorothea-Cäcilia!

You must often have misunderstood me while I was obliged to appear displeasing to you. This was caused to a great extent by my circumstances, particularly in the days when my muse was less appreciated than it is now. You know the interpretations of the uncalled for apostles who helped themselves along with quite other means than the holy Gospel; I did not want to be counted among them. Receive now what was often intended for you and what may be to you a proof of my affection for your artistic aspirations as well as your person— That I did not hear you play at Cz[erny]'s recently was due to my ill-health which at last seems to be giving way before my strength— I hope soon to hear from you, how it goes at Pölten with the Muses, and whether you care anything for your

admirer and friend
L. van Beethoven, m.p.

All things lovely to your worthy *husband and consort.*

[7] *A* 746.
[8] *A* 742.
[9] Another obvious blunder of the kind to which Beethoven was prone—it should, of course, be 1817. According to Nottebohm (*II Beeth.*, p. 344) the autograph of the Sonata bears the following inscription: "Neue Sonata für Ham. . . . , 1816, im Monath November." Its forthcoming appearance in print was announced by Steiner in Kanne's *Musik-Zeitung* in January, 1817, and it was published a month later. (Cf. TK, II, n. 1.)

Schindler has written of the role that the Baroness played—now so soon to be ended—in the performance of Beethoven's music:[10] "Through the years—until Colonel von Ertmann became a general in 1818 and was transferred to Mailand—she gathered together around her either at her own place or at other places such as Carl Czerny's a circle of true music-lovers and made the greatest contribution generally among the elite of society to the preservation and cultivation of the purest taste. She was a conservatory all by herself. Without Frau von Ertmann Beethoven's piano music would have disappeared much earlier from the repertory in Vienna; this lady, who was beautiful besides with a tall, fine figure, possessed with the loftiest purpose a feeling for the better things, and resisted the pressure of the new direction in the composition and playing of Hummel and his followers. Thus Beethoven had a double reason to honor her as a priestess of music and call her his 'Dorothea-Cäcilia.' "

Beethoven's correspondence of the winter is full of references to his continued ill-health. In several letters he described the "feverish cold" with which he had been afflicted in October, 1816, the effects of which hung on during the winter and spring, limited his activities in the summer, and made his domestic difficulties seem the more intolerable. The picture of his domestic affairs will gain in vividness by imagining the following extracts from the so-called "Tagebuch" of the Fischoff manuscript to be scattered through these preceding pages. Dates are nowhere given; but memoranda of letters to Brentano in April follow which prove these notes to belong to the previous months:

Never again live alone with a servant; there is always danger, suppose, for instance, the master falls ill and the servant, perhaps, also.

He who wishes to reap tears should sow love.

The Compassionate Brothers [the monks] in Tell, form a semi-circle around the dead man and sing in deep tones:

Rasch tritt der Tod den Menschen an	Quick comes the Death of Man
Es ist ihm keine Frist gegeben	For him is granted no delay
Er stürzt ihn mitten in der Bahn	Down he is thrust amidst his span
Es reisst ihn fort vom vollem Leben	From a full life he is torn away
Bereitet oder nicht zu gehn!	To go, prepared or not!
Er muss vor seinen Richter stehen!	Before his judge he must learn his lot![11]

Vidi malum et accepi—(Plinius)

Tametsi quid homini potest dari maius quam gloria et laus et aeternitas.—(Plinius)

What more can be given to man than fame and praise and immortality?

Audi multa loquere pauca.

Something must be done—either a journey and to this end the writing of the necessary works or an opera—if you are again to remain here during the coming

---

[10] I, p. 242.　　　　　[11] End of Act IV.

summer an opera would be preferable in case of circumstances that are only tolerable—if the summer sojourn is to be here, a decision must be made, where, how?

God help me, Thou seest me deserted by all men, for I do not wish to do wrong, hear my supplication, but to be with my Karl in the future, when now no possibility can be found. Oh harsh fate, Oh cruel destiny, no, no, my unhappy condition will never end.

This one thing I feel and clearly comprehend, possessions are not the highest things in life, but guilt is the greatest evil.

There is no salvation for you except to go away, only thus can you swing yourself up to the summits of your art again, while here you are sinking into vulgarity, and a symphony . . . and then away—away—away—meanwhile collect the salary which can be done yet for years.

Work during the summer for the journey, only thus can you carry out the great task for your poor nephew, afterward wander through Italy, Sicily, with a few artists—make plans and be of good cheer for the sake of C.[12]

In my opinion, first the saline baths, like those of Wiesbaden, etc., then the sulphur baths like Aix-la-Chapelle were everlastingly cold. Spend evenings and afternoons in company, it is uplifting and not wearying and live a different life at home.

Sensual enjoyment without a union of souls is bestial and will always remain bestial; after it, one experiences not a trace of noble sentiment but rather regret.

Beethoven's mind was engrossed with the plans of travel indicated in these excerpts throughout the year; he considered a tour of some kind essential to the restoration of his health and the recovery of his creative powers. A remittance from the Kinsky estate falling due in April, he wrote a letter to Kanka asking him to make the collection for him and enclosed a receipt. He complained of still feeling the effects of the inflammatory catarrh with which he had been attacked in the previous October, and ended by asking what would be the consequence if he were to leave the Austrian Empire; would a signature sent from a foreign place be valid?—meaning, probably, would such a signature be looked upon as evidence of a violation of the contract which he was under to his noble patrons not to take up a residence outside the Austrian dominions. His chronic dissatisfaction with the conditions which surrounded him in Vienna, as well as the moody mind in which his illness had left him, also breathes through the following letter (written in German) to Charles Neate in London:

Vienna, April 19, 1817.

My dear Neate!

Since the 15th of October I have had a severe sickness and I am still suffering from the consequences and not quite recovered. You know that I must live from my compositions alone. Since the time of this sickness I have been able to compose but very little, and therefore to earn almost nothing. It would have been all the more welcome had you done something for me—meanwhile I suspect that the result of everything has been—*nothing.*

[12] According to Jahn; others read "L." (TDR, IV, 21, n. 1.)

You have even written *complainingly of me to Häring*, which my straight-forwardness with you does not deserve in the least— Meanwhile I must justify myself in this, namely: the opera Fidelio had been written for several years, but the book and text were very faulty. The book had to be thoroughly remodeled, wherefore several pieces of the music had to be extended, others shortened, others newly composed. Thus, for instance, the overture is entirely new, as well as various other numbers, but it is possible that the opera may be found in London as it was *at first*, in which case it must have been stolen as is scarcely to be avoided at the theatre.— As regards the Symphony in A, as you did not write me a satisfactory reply, I was obliged to publish it. I should as willingly have waited 3 years if you had written me that the Philharmonic Society would accept it—but on all sides nothing—nothing. Now, regarding the *Pianoforte Sonatas* with *Violoncello*, for them I give you *a month's time*; if after that I have no answer from you, I shall publish them in *Germany*, but having heard as little from you about them as about the other works, I have given them to a German publisher who importuned me for them. *But I have bound him in writing (Häring has read the document) not to publish the sonatas until you have sold them in London.* It seems to me that you ought to be able to dispose of these 2 sonatas for 70 or 80 ducats in gold at least. The English publisher may fix the day of *publication* in London and they will appear *on the same day in Germany*. It was in this manner Birchall bought and got the Grand Trio and the Violin Sonata from me. I beg you as a last favor *to give me an answer touching the sonatas as soon as possible.* Frau v. Jenny[13] swears that *you have done everything for me,* I too, that is to say I swear that *you have done nothing* for me, are doing *nothing* and will do *nothing*—summa summarum, *Nothing! Nothing! Nothing!!!*

I assure you of my most perfect respect and hope *as a last favor a speedy reply.*

Your sincere servant and friend

L. v. Beethoven

On May 2nd Beethoven's old friend, the violinist Wenzel Krumpholz died very suddenly of apoplexy while walking on the Glacis. Beethoven commemorated the event by writing his "Gesang der Mönche" (from Schiller's *Tell*) for three male voices with the superscription: "In memory of the sudden and unexpected death of our Krumpholz on May 3rd, 1817." —The twelve-measure composition with its superscription was written out for the musical scholar, Franz Sales Kandler (1792-1831), who, with a letter of introduction from Beethoven[14] was leaving Vienna for Italy. The autograph was later acquired by Alois Fuchs and is now a part of the Koch Collection.[15]—

After the composer's removal to the suburb Landstrasse, his mind was

---

[13] According to Kalischer (*Briefe*, III, p. 170) this was the Countess von Genney mentioned in the Conversation Book of 1823, through whose aid Beethoven rented rooms in a villa in Hetzendorf owned by Baron von Pronay. (TDR, IV, 23, n. 2.) O. E. Deutsch believes rather that this was one of the two

sisters, Therese and Susanna v. Jenny, who were pianists in Vienna and members of the Gesellschaft der Musikfreunde. See *Schubert, a Documentary Biography*, London, 1946, p. 61.

[14] See *A*, III, p. 1415.

[15] See KHV, pp. 566-67.

much occupied with a new matter between himself and the widow van Beethoven, namely, her bearing a share of the expenses of her son's education. This was concluded by a contract signed by both parties on May 10, 1817, binding her to pay at once into court 2,000 florins for the lad's education and support, and in the future to pay to the same tribunal every quarter at least one-half of the pension which the widow was to receive, as well as other contributions. Reference is made to this agreement in the following entries in the Fischoff "Tagebuch" in January or February of the next year:

Karl's mother asked for the contract, the basis of which was that the house should be sold. From the proceeds of the sale it might be counted upon that all debts could be paid out of the one-half and also the half of the widow's income besides the money for Karl's needs and desires, so that she might live not just decently but very well, but inasmuch as the house is not to be sold! which was the chief consideration for the signing of the contract since it was alleged that execution had already been levied against it, my scruples must now cease, and I can well imagine that the widow has cared pretty well for herself, which I most cordially wish her. My duty, O Lord, I have done.— —

It would have been possible without offending the widow, but that was not so, and Thou, Almighty one, seest into my heart, knowest that I have sacrificed the best of my own for the sake of my precious Karl, bless my work, bless the widow, why cannot I wholly follow my heart's inclinations and hereafter for her the widow—

God, God, my refuge, my rock, my all, Thou seest my inmost heart and knowest how it pains me to be obliged to compel another to suffer by my good labors for my precious Karl!!! O hear me always, Thou Ineffable One, hear me—thy unhappy, most unhappy of all mortals.

This was the barren result of negotiations which had cost Beethoven, as to any important work, the first half of the year.

In May, the composer took rooms in Heiligenstadt[16] to try the baths for his illness, of which he speaks in the following letter to Countess Erdödy:

My dear suffering friend,
My most revered Countess!
Too much of the time I have been upset and overloaded with too many cares. Since the 6th of October, 1816, I have been constantly ill, and since October 15 a severe and feverish catarrh has developed because of which I have had to stay a good deal in bed, and it was several months before I could go out even for a bit. *Up until now* I was *still bothered by the effects.* I changed doctors, since mine, a crafty Italian,[17] had strong designs on me and lacked honesty as well as intelligence; this happened in April, 1817. Then every day from April 15 to

---

[16] The building in which Beethoven stayed is still standing today, now Pfarrplatz No. 2 in the 19th district. It is a double house with a courtyard in between; his quarters were in the left wing on the first story. A tablet has been placed under one of the windows from which there is a fine view of the Kahlen—and Leopoldsberg to the north.

[17] More likely Dr. Malfatti than Dr. Bertolini. (Cf. TDR, IV, 27, n. 3.)

May 4 I had to take 6 powders, 6 cups of tea; this lasted until May 4. From this time on I had a kind of powder that had also to be taken 6 times a day, and I had to rub myself three times with a volatile salve, thereupon I traveled here where I am taking the baths. Since yesterday I have been taking a new medicine, namely a tincture of which I must take 12 spoonfuls per day— Each day I hope for the end of this troublesome condition. Although it has improved somewhat, still it seems as though it is going to be a long time before I am completely recovered. How much all of this affects my life you can imagine. My hearing has become worse; and where before I was unable to look after myself and my requirements, now it is even more so. And my cares are still greater because of my brother's child— I have not yet found proper lodgings here; since it is difficult for me to take care of myself, I turn first to this person and then to that, and always I am left as before, and the victim of wretched people. A thousand times I have thought of you dear beloved friend as I do now, but my own misery has depressed me. S[18] has delivered Linke's letter to me; he is staying with Schwab. I have written him briefly to find out what would be the probable cost of journeying to you, but I haven't received any answer. Since my nephew has *vacation time from the last of August* until the end *of October,* it would be *after* that that I *could* visit you if it turns out that I am *cured.* We would of course have rooms for study and would have a comfortable existence, and I would be once again after such a long time among old friends who, unaffected by one or another diabolical human trait, have always sustained *me.* Thus perhaps joy and good health would return to me— Linke must write me in what way I can make the trip with the least cost. For unfortunately my expenses are so great and my income small because of my illness, during which time I have been able to compose but little. And the small capital for the possession of which I am indebted to my deceased brother, I must not lay ahold of. Since my salary grows always smaller and is now almost nothing, I must as a result preserve this capital— Since I write to you, dearest Countess, so candidly, for that reason do not misunderstand me. Regardless of this I need nothing and certainly would not accept anything from you. It is merely a question of the best and most economical way of coming to *you.* Everyone without distinction has to think along *these lines,* so my friend is not to be concerned about this— I hope that your health is in a consistently better state than I was made to believe earlier. May heaven preserve this *most excellent mother* for her children, yes, even if—only for them would you deserve the fullest amount of health— Farewell, best and most beloved Countess, let me hear from you soon—

Your true friend
Beethoven

Heiligenstadt June 19, 1817.

Christoph Kuffner, a poet, afterwards Court Secretary, who, according to Czerny (though Nottebohm questioned it) gave poetical form to the text for the Choral Fantasia,[19] also spent some time in the summer of 1817 in Heiligenstadt, and, as he told Music Director Krenn, often went with Beet-

---

[18] Thayer read this letter "C"; according to Miss Anderson (II, p. 684) this is "S," which, of course, would be the Erdödy steward, Sperl.

[19] Kinsky-Halm support Nottebohm's doubt since the text does not appear in Kuffner's complete works. See KHV, p. 212.

hoven of an evening to Nussdorf for a fish supper in the tavern "zur Rose."
On one of these occasions, when Beethoven was amiably disposed, Kuffner
began:

K.—Tell me frankly, which is your favorite among your symphonies?
B.—[in great good humor] Eh! Eh! The "Eroica."
K.—I should have guessed the C minor.
B.—No; the "Eroica."

Long years afterwards, in 1826, when Kuffner was negotiating with
Beethoven for an oratorio text, he recalled the meetings in Nussdorf and
wrote in Beethoven's Conversation Book: "Do you remember the fisherman's house in Nussdorf, where we sat till midnight in the light of the full
moon on the terrace, before us the rushing brook and the swollen Danube?
I was your guest."

Beethoven soon had his fish with less trouble; he moved to Nussdorf,
where he remained till the beginning of October. —The move was made
probably in late June, for on July 7th Beethoven writes to Nanette Streicher
from Nussdorf: ". . . the bad weather kept me from visiting you the day
before yesterday when I was in the city; yesterday morning I hurried back
here again, but found my servant not at home; he had taken the key to
the house along with him. It was very cool, I had nothing to wear from
the city but a thin pair of trousers; and so I had to wander about for three
hours. This was bad for me and I felt poorly the whole day.— There you
see what housekeeping with servants is like! . . ."

Here, too, he received the following highly important letter from Ferdinand
Ries, written in London on June 9, 1817:

My dearest Beethoven.

For a very long time I have been forgotten by you, although I can think of
no other cause than your too great occupation, and, as I was compelled to hear
from others, your serious illness. Truly, dear Beethoven, the gratitude which I
owe you and always must owe you—and I believe I may honestly say I have
never forgotten it—although enemies have often represented me to you as ungrateful and envious—is unalterable, as I have always ardently desired to prove to you
in more than words. This ardent desire has now (I hope) been fulfilled, and
I hope to find again in my old teacher, my old and affectionate friend. The
Philharmonic Society, of which our friend Neate is now also a director, and
at whose concerts your compositions are preferred to all others, wishes to give
you an evidence of its great respect for you and its appreciation of the many
beautiful moments which your great works have so often provided for us; and
I feel it a most flattering compliment to have been empowered with Neate to
write to you on the subject. In short, my dear Beethoven, we should like to have
you with us in London next winter. Friends will receive you with open arms;
and to give you at least one proof of this I have been commissioned on behalf
of the Philharmonic Society to offer you 300 guineas on the following conditions:

1st. You are to be here in London next winter.

2nd. You are to write two grand symphonies for the Philharmonic Society, which are to be its property.

3rd. You must bind yourself not to deliver any composition for grand orchestra for any concert in London, nor direct any concert before or during our eight concerts, which begin towards the end of February and end in the first half of the month of June (without the consent of the Philharmonic Society), which certainly will not be difficult.

Do not understand by this that we want to tie your hands; it is only in case an opposition which we have once put down should again arise, since the gentlemen might plan to have you for themselves against instead of for us. At the same time it might call up many enemies against you to decline something when the responsibility would rest entirely with us directors, and we should not be obliged to give heed to the matter. We are all cordially disposed in your favor and I believe that every opportunity to be helpful to you in your plans would sooner give us pleasure than any desire to restrict you in the least.

4th. You are not to appear in the orchestra at any concert until our first two concerts are over, unless you want to give a concert yourself, and you can give as many of your own concerts as you please.

5th. You are to be here before the 8th of January, 1818, free from all obligations to the Society except to give us the preference in the future in case we meet the same conditions offered you by others.

6th. In case you accept the engagement and need money for the journey you may have 100 guineas in advance. This is the offer which I am authorized to make to you by the Society.

All negotiations with publishers are left to you as well as those with Sir G. Smart, who has offered you 100 guineas for an oratorio in one act, and who has specially commissioned me to remind you of an answer, inasmuch as he would like to have the work for next winter. The intendant of the grand opera, G. Ayrton, is a particular friend of ours. He does not want to commit himself, but he promised us to commission an opera from you.

Your own concert, or as many concerts as you choose to give, may bring in a handsome sum to you as well as other engagements in the country. Neate and I rejoice like children at the prospect of seeing you here and I need not say that I will do all in my power to make your sojourn profitable and pleasant. I know England, too, and do not doubt your success for a moment.

Moreover, we need somebody here who will put life into things and keep the gentlemen of the orchestra in order.

Yesterday evening our last concert took place and your beautiful Symphony in A-sharp [B-flat] was given with extraordinary applause. It frightens one to think of symphony writers when one sees and hears such a work. Write me very soon an explicit answer and bid me hope to see you yourself here before long.

I remain always

Your thankful sincere friend

Ferd. Ries

My hearty greetings to Herr v. Zmeskall, Zizius, Krumpholz and other friends.

Beethoven was prompt with his answer, but wishing to send a fair copy to Ries and having his own reasons for not wanting Häring's handwriting to appear in the correspondence he sent his letter to Zmeskall for transcription and posting. The letter, which was promptly forwarded to London, was as follows:

Vienna, July 9, 1817.

Dear Friend!

The propositions made in your letter of the 9th of June are very flattering. You will see by this how much I appreciate them; were it not for my unlucky affliction which entails more attendance and cost than ordinary, particularly while travelling and in a strange land, I would accept the Philharmonic Society's offer *unconditionally*. But put yourself in my place; reflect how many more hindrances I have to contend with than any other artist, and judge then if my demands be unfair. Here they are and I beg of you to communicate them to the directors of the said Society.

1) I shall be in London in the first half of the month of January, 1818, at the latest.

2) The two grand symphonies, newly composed, shall then be ready and become and remain the exclusive property of the Society.

3) For them the Society is to give me 300 guineas and 100 guineas for travelling expenses, which will be much more, since I must necessarily take a companion with me.

4) Inasmuch as I shall go to work on the symphonies at once, the Society is to advance me (on the acceptance of this offer) 150 guineas here so that I may provide myself with a carriage and other necessaries for my journey without delay.

5) The conditions respecting my not appearing with another orchestra in public, my not conducting and my preferring the Society under equal conditions are accepted by me and in view of my sense of honor would have been understood as a matter of course.

6) I shall rely upon the support of the Society in the projection and promotion of one, or, if circumstances justify, more benefit concerts. The particular friendship of some of the directors of your esteemed group as well as the kind interest of all artists in my works are a guarantee for this and will increase my zeal to fulfil all their expectations.

7) In conclusion I ask that the consent or agreement to the above be written out in English and sent to me with the signatures of three directors of the Society.

You can imagine that I heartily rejoice at the prospect of becoming acquainted with the estimable Sir George Smart and of meeting you and Mr. Neate again. Would that I might fly to you instead of this letter!

Your sincere admirer and friend,
L. v. Beethoven

To this Beethoven appended an autograph postscript as follows:

I embrace you with all my heart; I purposely employed the hand of another in the above so that you might the more easily read it to the Society. I am convinced of your kind feelings toward me and hope that the Philharmonic Society will approve of my proposition, and you may rest assured that I shall exert all my powers worthily to fulfil the honorable commission of so select a body of artists.—

How numerous is your orchestra? How many violins, etc., etc., *single or double wind-instruments*? Is the hall large, acoustically good?

Your sincere admirer and friend,
L. v. Beethoven

Efforts of the widow van Beethoven to keep in touch with her son, and questions of discipline in his bringing-up and education, were matters which weighed heavily on Beethoven's mind during the summer of 1817, and occasioned more misunderstandings between Giannatasio and the composer, as also much distress in the minds of the former's daughters, especially the solicitous Fanny, as is evidenced by entries in her diary under dates June 25, July 8 and 21, and August 10.[20] In an undated letter which seems to belong to this period, Beethoven explained to Giannatasio that the mother had expressly asked to see Karl at his, the composer's, house and that certain evidences of indecision on his part which his correspondent had observed (and apparently held up to him) had not been due to any want of confidence, but to his antipathy to "inhuman conduct of any kind," and the circumstance that it had been put out of the power of the woman to do the lad harm in any respect. On the subject of discipline he writes:

As regards Karl, I beg of you to hold him to strict obedience and if he does not obey you (or any of those whom he ought to obey) to *punish* him at once, treat him as you would your own child rather than as a pupil, for as I have already told you, during the lifetime of his father he could only be forced to obey by blows; this was very bad but it was unfortunately so and must not be forgotten.

He requested that the letter be read to his nephew. Beethoven's "antipathy to inhuman conduct of any kind" seems to have led him to make concessions to the widow of which he soon repented. In a letter to Zmeskall dated July 30, he says: "After all, it might pain Karl's mother to be obliged to visit her son at the house of a stranger and, besides, there is more harshness in this affair than I like; therefore I shall permit her to come to me tomorrow"; and he urgently begged his friend to be a witness of the meeting. In a note to Giannatasio he informed him of his intentions to take Karl to see his mother at her home, because she was desirous to put herself in a better light before her neighbors, and this might help. But a fortnight after the letter to Zmeskall he changed his mind, as witness a letter to Giannatasio dated August 14, in which he writes:

I wanted this time to try an experiment to see if she might not be bettered by greater forbearance and gentleness and I informed H. v. S[chmerling] of this idea of mine. But it has foundered, for on *Sunday* I had already determined to *adhere to the old necessary strictness*, because in a moment's time she had communicated some of *her venom* to Karl— In short we must stick to the zodiac and permit her to see Karl only twelve times a year, and then so hedge her about

[20] See TDR, IV, pp. 34-7.

that she cannot secretly slip him even a pin. It is all the same to me whether it be at your house, at mine, or at a third place. For once I had believed that by yielding wholly to her wishes she might be encouraged to better her conduct and appreciate my utter unselfishness.

Notwithstanding the jeremiads in Beethoven's letters this year, and the annoyance caused him by his sister-in-law, there are indications in plenty that he was not on the whole in that state of dejection which one might suppose. One of these indications is a work which amused him during the summer, the story of which the careful Dehn admitted into the *Cäcilia*. A musician, whose name is not mentioned, brought to Beethoven the Pianoforte Trio, Op. 1, No. 3, which he had arranged for string quintet (two violins, two violas and violoncello). Though the composer, no doubt, found much to criticize in the transcription it seems to have interested him sufficiently to lead him to undertake a thorough remodelling of the score, on the cover of which he wrote the whimsical title:

> Arrangement of a Terzett as a
> 3 voiced Quintet
> by Mr. Goodwill
> and from the appearance of 5 voices
> brought to the light of day in 5 real voices
> and lifted from the most abject *Miserabilität*
> to moderate respectability
> by Mr. *Wellwisher*
> 1817
> August 14.

N.B. The original 3 voiced Quintet score has been sacrificed as a burnt offering to the gods of the Underworld.

The score of the arrangement is in the handwriting of a copyist with corrections by Beethoven; the title, however, is his autograph. ⸺A humorous letter to Steiner undoubtedly refers to this work and the possible identity of Mr. Goodwill:

Here follows the quintet *for the L—t G—l's office.* I shall know presently what conditions to make pertaining to it. Nothing about this is to be imparted to Hr. Kaufmann for the day after tomorrow I shall write him a letter concerning it, wherewith the whole affair will be finished up. For Hr. K. *has given me nothing other than the opportunity to make this complete revision*—Here is my present to the office of the l—t g—l whereby I insist at this time on some shooting and *advance payment*[21] most especially and therewith punctum—

> The G[eneralissimu]s
> (in thunder and lightning yet somewhat
> feebler than usual.)

[On the outside] To the devil's office of the L—t G—l.

---

[21] Beethoven's pun: *schiessen* (shooting) and *Vorschiessen* (advance payment) is lost in translation.

Steiner, however, did not take the work. — Instead, it was published by Artaria in February, 1819, as Op. 104. Beethoven evidently attached considerable importance to it. He referred to it in letters to Frau von Streicher, Zmeskall and Ries; and it was performed at a musical entertainment of the Gesellschaft der Musikfreunde in Vienna in December, 1818.

Beethoven having obtained possession of his nephew and placed him in Giannatasio's institute, very naturally took measures that he should have systematic instruction in music; to this end he employed Carl Czerny as teacher, and to him we now turn for information on this point.[22] Czerny writes: "In the year 1815 [1816] at his request I began teaching his nephew Karl, whom he had already adopted, and from that time I saw him almost daily, since for the greater part of the time he brought the little fellow to me. From this period I still have many letters written by him, one of which I reproduce here with absolute fidelity because it is musically noteworthy:

My dear Czerny!

I beg of you to have as much patience as possible with Karl even if matters do not go now as well as you and I might wish; otherwise he will accomplish even less; for (but this he must not know) he is already subjected to too great a strain because of the improper division of his studies. Unhappily this cannot be changed at once. Therefore treat him with as much loving consideration as possible, but with seriousness; *then you will have* better success with Karl in spite of the unfavorable conditions.— In regard to his playing for you, I beg that once he has acquired the correct fingering and can play in time and reads the notes with reasonable correctness, you then direct his attention to the matter of interpretation; and when you have gotten *that far* don't stop him *because of trifling mistakes* but point them out after he has finished the piece. Although I have given but few lessons I have always followed this method, it soon makes *musicians* which, at the last, is one of the first purposes of art, and gives the minimum of weariness to master and pupil.— In certain passages like

I wish that he would use all the fingers occasionally as well as in such as these

so that they may be played in a gliding manner. True, such passages sound "pearly" as the phrase goes (played with few fingers) or "like a pearl," but at times other jewels are desirable.— More at another time.— I hope that you may receive all this in the loving spirit in which it is expressed and intended— At any rate I am and will always remain your debtor— May my sincerity be a pledge for future payment so far as possible.—

Your true friend Beethoven

[22] The principal contributions to Beethoven's biography from Czerny's pen are in Schmidt's *Wiener Allg. Mus. Zeitung*, 1845, No. 113; Cocks's *Musical Miscellany* (London, 1852); and manuscript notes in Jahn's papers. (TDR, IV, 46, n. 2.)

Czerny comments:

"Noteworthy in this interesting letter is the very correct view that one ought not to weary the talent of a pupil by too much petty concern (wherein much depends on the qualities of the pupil, it is true) as well as the singular fingering and its influence on interpretation.

"Much more valuable were Beethoven's oral remarks about all kinds of musical topics, other composers, etc., touching whom he always spoke with the greatest positiveness, with striking, often caustic wit and always from the lofty point of view which his genius opened to him and from which he looked out upon his art. His judgment even concerning classic masters was severe, as a rule, and uttered as if he felt his equality. At one lesson which I gave his nephew he said to me: 'You must not think that you will do me a favor by giving him pieces of mine to play. I am not so childish as to desire that. Give him what you think good for him.'

"I mentioned Clementi. 'Yes, yes,' said he; 'Clementi is very good,' adding, laughingly 'For the present give Karl the regular things so that after a while he may reach the irregular.'

"After such conceits, which he was in the habit of weaving into nearly every speech, he used to burst into a peal of laughter. Since irregularities used to be charged against him by the critics in his earlier days he was wont often to allude to the fact with merry humor. At that time (about 1816) I began to have musical entertainments at my home for my very numerous pupils every Sunday before a very select circle. Beethoven was almost always present, he improvised many times with kindly readiness and with that wealth of ideas which always characterized his impromptu playing as much, or often more, than his written works. As his compositions were chiefly played at these meetings and he indicated the tempo, I believe that in this respect I am intimately acquainted with his wishes regarding his works (even his symphonies, which were frequently played in arrangements for two pianofortes)."

No animadversion upon the venerable Carl Czerny is intended in remarking that both in his memoirs and in the language in which he has sometimes recorded them there is occasionally a very disturbing inexactness. "Beethoven was almost always present" at the Sunday music meetings, which can have been true only of the first months, and the words "he improvised many times," must not be understood too literally. Schindler, in whose hands Jahn placed Czerny's notes and other manuscripts for examination and remark, observes touching this improvising: "Only twice; the first time when Frau von Ertmann played one of his sonatas, the other time when Czerny performed Op. 106, which he had repeatedly gone through with him. In the year 1818, and those that followed, Beethoven never improvised outside of his own dwelling." Schindler was certainly mistaken upon this last point, and, very possibly, upon the other.

In August and September the after-effects of the attack of catarrh and the state of Beethoven's health generally were so distressing and so depressing upon his spirits that he seemed to be on the verge of despair. A letter which Zmeskall noted as received by him on August 21 says:

I am sorry to hear of your illness— As for me, I am in despair so often and would like to end my life, for there is never an end to all these afflictions. God have pity on me, I consider myself as good as lost— I must talk with you also about other things. This servant *steals*, I have no doubt about this. So he must go. Because of my health I must *eat at home* and with greater ease. I would like to know your opinion about this— If my condition does not improve I shall not be in London next year but perhaps in my grave— Thank God, the part is nearly played—

In haste
Your L. van Beethoven

On September 11, Beethoven was able to report to Zmeskall that the reply to his letter had been received from the London Philharmonic Society the day before. There was no tone of elation in his note; it merely mentioned the arrival of the letter and a request for the name of someone who could translate it for him, it being in English. As might have been expected the Philharmonic Society rejected the new terms demanded by him, but, as the Society's records show, repeated the old. These were now at once accepted by Beethoven.

And did he now sit himself down zealously and perseveringly to work on a ninth and tenth symphony? Not at all. His thoughts had become engaged upon a new pianoforte sonata—the great one in B-flat, Op. 106. According to Nottebohm, sketches were made for the first movement and the scherzo of the Ninth Symphony during the composing of the sonata between the fall and spring of 1817-1818;[23] and these will be discussed when the history of the symphony is told.

That "indecision in many things," noted by Breuning a dozen years before, was only aggravated by the lapse of time; and this now was his bane. There was really nothing to prevent his departing at once except that the new symphonies were still to be written. If his nephew must remain in or near Vienna, he could nowhere be so well placed as in the school and family of the excellent Giannatasios, who had all the necessary legal power to save the boy from the bad influence of his mother. The effects of such a journey; of a stay of some months in England; of the intercourse of cultivated people; of the enthusiastic admiration which awaited him there, and of the great pecuniary rewards for his labors which were certain, could only have been propitious in the highest degree to both his physical and mental health. There was, too, just now a new and powerful motive for accepting and fulfilling this engagement.

Though the depreciation of the redemption certificates never quite touched the point feared by him in his letter to Ries in 1815, it did once amount to 4

[23] *II Beeth.*, pp. 159-64, and pp. 121-37.

for 1; and the Government was again forced to repudiate its obligations in part. It founded that National Bank (eight shares in which Beethoven soon afterwards purchased), and made a contract with a new institution by which the bank assumed the obligation of redeeming the redemption certificates at the rate of $2\frac{1}{2}$ for 1. It went into full operation July 15, 1817, and thenceforth Beethoven's annuity remained instead of 3,400 florins in that paper, 1,360 florins in silver. But this fatal indecision! Could he have but resolutely taken up any two of the many new symphonies which he had planned, as the sketchbooks show, and once fairly engaged himself upon them, he could not have rested until they were finished; he could, and doubtless would, then have redeemed his promises; and like Handel, Haydn and many other German musicians of far less note, have secured from an admiring and generous London public an ample sufficiency for the future. The standard of excellence was high and catholic in London and musical taste pure and exalted. True, at the first trial of the C minor Symphony by the Philharmonic Society a part of it only was played, for the leader of the violins—really the conductor, as the orchestras were then constituted—declared it "rubbish." But this leader was a German—our old Bonn acquaintance J. P. Salomon. He, however, repented and made amends. At another trial of it, two or three years afterwards, after the first movement, Salomon laid his violin upon the pianoforte, walked to the front and, turning to the orchestra said (through his nose): "Gentlemen, some years ago I called this symphony rubbish; I wish to retract every word I then said, as I now consider it one of the greatest compositions I ever heard!"

We have had occasion heretofore to refer to several young British Beethoven enthusiasts; another is now added to the list—Cipriani Potter[24]—who came just at this time to Vienna, bringing letters to the composer from Neate, Ries, Rode, Dragonetti and others. He heard so much of Beethoven's rudeness of manners and moroseness of disposition, and so often noticed how people shook their heads when he or his music was mentioned, that he hesitated to visit him. Two weeks had thus passed when one day, at Streicher's, he was asked if he had seen Beethoven and if he had letters to him. He therefore explained why he had not seen him. He was told this was all nonsense; Beethoven would receive him kindly. He exclaimed: "I will go out at once!" which he did. He presented a letter or two, one of the first being that of Dragonetti. Upon opening that Beethoven also opened his heart to his visitor and demanded immediately to see some of his compositions. Potter showed him an overture—probably one that had been commissioned and played by the London Philharmonic Society in 1816. Beethoven looked through it so hurriedly that Potter thought he had only glanced at it out of politeness and was greatly astonished when Beethoven pointed to a deep F-sharp in the bassoon part and said it was not practicable. He made

[24] Potter (1792-1871) was Director of the Royal Music Academy in London, esteemed as conductor, pianist and composer. (TDR, IV, 55, n. 1.)

other observations of a similar nature and advised him to go to a teacher; he himself gave no lessons but would look through all his compositions. In answer to Potter's question as to whom he would recommend, Beethoven replied: "I have lost my Albrechtsberger and have no confidence in anybody else"; nevertheless, on Beethoven's recommendation Potter became a pupil of Aloys Förster, with whom he studied a long time until one day the teacher said to him that he had now studied sufficiently and needed only to practise himself in composition. This brought out the remark from Beethoven that no one ought ever to stop studying; he himself had not studied enough: "Tell Förster that he is an old flatterer!" Potter did so, but Förster only laughed. Beethoven never complimented Potter to his face; he would say: "Very good, very good," but never give unequivocal praise. Once Beethoven advised him never to compose sitting in a room in which there was a pianoforte, in order not to be tempted to consult the instrument; after a work was finished he might try it over on the instrument, because an orchestra was not always to be had.

Beethoven used to walk across the fields to Vienna very often and sometimes Potter took the walk with him. Beethoven would stop, look around and give expression to his love for nature. One day Potter asked: "Who is the greatest living composer, yourself excepted?" Beethoven seemed puzzled for a moment, then exclaimed "Cherubini." Potter went on: "And of dead authors?" Beethoven answered that he had always considered Mozart as such, but since he had been made acquainted with Handel he had put him at the head. The first day that Potter was with Beethoven the latter rushed into politics and called the Austrian government all sorts of names. He was full of going to England and said his desire was to see the House of Commons. "You have heads upon your shoulders in England," he remarked. One day Potter asked him his opinion of one of the principal pianists then in Vienna (Moscheles). "Don't ever talk to me again about mere passage players," came the answer. At another time Beethoven declared that John Cramer had given him more satisfaction than anybody else. According to the same informant, Beethoven spoke Italian fluently but French with less ease. It was in Italian that Potter conversed with him, making himself heard by using his hands as a speaking-trumpet; Beethoven did not always hear everything, but was content when he caught the meaning. Potter considered *Fidelio* the greatest of all operas and once remarked to Beethoven that he had heard it in Vienna, which brought out the remark that he had *not* heard it, as the singers then at the opera-house were not able to sing it. He was asked if he did not intend to write another opera. "Yes," replied Beethoven, "I am now composing *Romulus*;[25] but the poets are all such fools; I will not compose silly rubbish." Potter told him of the deep impression made upon him by the Septet when first he heard it; Beethoven replied in effect that

[25] Treitschke had provided the libretto of *Romulus*; it does not appear that Beethoven ever began its composition. (TDR, IV, 57, n. 2.)

when he wrote the piece he did not know how to compose; he knew now, he thought, and, either then or at another time, he said, "I am writing something better now." Soon after, the Pianoforte Sonata in B-flat (Op. 106) was published.

Another visitor now, and probably occasionally during the winter following, was Heinrich Marschner, who had come from Carlsbad to Vienna on the invitation of Count Amadée. He was 21 years old, ambitious and eager to get Beethoven's judgment on some of his compositions, which he carried to the great master in manuscript. Beethoven received him, glanced through the music hurriedly, handed it back with a muttered "Hm," in a tone more of satisfaction than dispraise, and the words: "I haven't much time—do not come too often—bring me something again." The young man was grievously disappointed; he had expected so much more. He did not understand Beethoven's sententious manner, and not until he told the story of his reception to his patron and Prof. Klein of Pressburg, did he recall that Beethoven had looked kindly upon him when he spoke the words and had given him his hand at parting. He had gone to his lodgings in a passion of despondency, torn up the manuscripts, packed his trunk with the resolve to abandon music and return to Leipzig to continue his studies for the profession for which he had been designed. But now, on the advice of his friends, he took a different view of Beethoven's actions, and continued his intercourse with him. The great man was always gracious, and even occasionally let fall a word of encouragement; but an intimacy never sprang up between them.

Beethoven's intercourse with a third new acquaintance was, doubtless, far more delightful than any other. This was Frau Marie Pachler-Koschak, who visited him in August or September, 1817.[26] Beethoven had already heard from Prof. Schneller, whose pupil she had been, of her extraordinary beauty, talents, intellectual culture and refinement, and of her genius for music. He had unconsciously the year before borne testimony to this last in this wise: Her brother-in-law, Anton Pachler, *Dr. jur.* in Vienna, had at her request shown him for an opinion a fantasia composed by her, but without disclosing the author's identity. Beethoven looked at the piece carefully and said that it was a good deal from one who had not studied composition, and if the composer were present he would point out the faults in it; it would take too much time to do this in writing and the composer would find them out for himself if he studied diligently.

Marie Leopold Koschak was born on October 2, 1794, in Graz, the daughter of a respected lawyer, and she attracted attention early in life by her pianoforte playing and talent for composition. In a concert on December 22, 1811, she played Beethoven's *Choral Fantasy* and for a long time intended to devote herself completely to the art; but she gave this up in the interests of her family. In 1816 she married the lawyer, Dr. Carl Pachler in Graz. Her

[26] See *Beethoven und Marie Pachler-Koschak* (Berlin, 1866), by her son, Dr. Faust Pachler, for a discussion of their relationship. (TDR, IV, 59, n. 1.)

house became the center of a cultivated circle, and she continued to keep up her music as much as her domestic duties would allow. Anslem Hütten-brenner wrote of her: "The daughter of the lawyer Koschak was the most beautiful maiden and later for several years the most beautiful woman in Graz and was called 'heaven's daughter.' She glowed with admiration for Jean Paul, Goethe and Schiller, for Beethoven, Mozart and Schubert."

In 1817 her wish to meet Beethoven personally was fulfilled; her brother-in-law Anton brought her to him in August or September (according to her son). She had never been in Vienna, Beethoven never in Graz, so they, of course, had never met previously. But when they did, it could not be as strangers; for his music had been to her like a new divine revelation, and such noble mental and personal qualities as distinguished her always awakened in him feelings akin to worship. Unfortunately absolutely nothing is known of their personal association except that she wrote ten years later that "they were often in each other's company," and that Beethoven wrote her two notes "in pencil"—one utterly illegible, and the other in terms placing her as a player of his pianoforte music even higher than Frau von Ertmann. He wrote:

I am greatly delighted that you will remain another day; we will make a lot more music, you will play the sonata in F major and C minor for me, will you not? I have never yet found anybody who plays my compositions as well as you do, not even excepting the great pianists, for they either have nothing but technique or are affected. You are the true guardian of my intellectual offspring—

Her son has so fully exploded Schindler's assumption that she was the object of Beethoven's "autumnal love" that no words need be wasted upon it. It was, no doubt, upon seeing in Beethoven's papers the letter "M"[27] in this outburst of feeling:

Love alone—yes, only love can possibly give you a happier life— O God, let me—let me finally find the one—who will strengthen me in virtue—who will *lawfully* be mine.
Baden on July 27
when M drove past and seemed to give a glance at me—

A consideration of the dates given in Dr. Pachler's pamphlet proves conclusively, however, that this "M" cannot refer to Marie Pachler, for its writer could never have seen her "drive past" on any 27th of July!

There are few unmarried men of highly sensitive nature who have not had the bitter experience of a hopeless passion, who have not felt how doubly grateful at such times is intercourse with a glorious creature like Madame Pachler, and how beneficial in preventing the thoughts from continually dwelling on the impossible, and thus aiding reason and conscience to gain the victory over the heart and fancy. Now it happens that one of Beethoven's

[27] The letter, which is reproduced in *fac-simile* in Schindler's biography, is a more or less fantastic scrawl or flourish which may be read as an "R" as well as an "M."

transient but intense passions for a married woman, known to have occurred in this period of his life, has its precise date fixed by these passages in the so-called "Tagebuch" from the years 1816 and 1817. "In the case of T. there is nothing to do but to leave it to God, never to go where one might do a wrong through weakness—to Him, to the all-knowing God, be all this committed." And again: "But as kind as possible to T. her attachment deserves never to be forgotten even if the results could never prove advantageous to you." Let the reader recall the passages in his letters showing a strong desire to leave Vienna and read again: "Work during the summer for the journey, only thus can you carry out the great task for your poor nephew, afterwards wander through Italy, Sicily, with a few artists—make plans and be of good cheer for the sake of C. . . ." The last initial is uncertain. Other copies have "L."; what the original was in Beethoven's handwriting is not now to be determined. No instance, however, is known of his writing his nephew's name with a C, and this "C" or "L" was probably T. As the family name of this lady, whose husband was a man of high position and distinction though not noble by birth, is known, it is certain that the T in the above citations is not Therese Malfatti, now Baroness Drosdick; but as her baptismal names have eluded search one can only hint the possibility that the "T" and "M" may indicate the same person, and that this last cry of anguish was written a year or two afterwards when the sight of "M" again, for a moment, tore open a half-healed wound.

In numbers 5 to 8 inclusive of the *Neue Musik-Zeitung* appeared, from the pen of J. S. Kandler, a long article containing historical notices of various attempts to produce a satisfactory instrument for measuring time in music, and closing with an account, taken from the English, of Mälzel's metronome. To No. 25 (June 19) of the same journal, Gottfried Weber contributed a paper "On a chronometric tempo designation which makes Mälzel's metronome, as well as all other chronometric instruments, unnecessary," in which he repeated his idea, already put forth in the Leipzig *Musikzeitung* in 1813, that the simplest and most correct chronometer is a simple pendulum, a bit of thread with a bullet at the end, whose oscillations would mark the duration of measures according to the length of the thread. This article pleased Beethoven, and in one of his variations on the theme of pens he commended it to his "clarissime amice" Zmeskall, as the best invention yet made. Zmeskall took up the subject with interest and in two articles in the same journal called attention to the fact that Neate, in London, had described a time measurer of the same kind which was known in England, but had not remained long in use—"a little ball hanging at the end of a thread and below it a line divided into a scale of inches." Zmeskall approved of Weber's suggestion in principle but improved upon it by proposing that the oscillations of the pendulum indicate the duration of a note instead of a measure, and that the varying lengths of the pendulum be marked by knots in the thread. Beethoven, to whom Zmeskall seems to have sent his contrivance, was interested and lauded its simplicity, playfully wondering whether or not it might be used in measuring from time to eternity.

Music had already come from the press with Mälzel's tempo marks, and Weber, who seems to have had no kindly feeling for him, printed an article, in the number of the journal following Zmeskall's, entitled "Mälzel's Metronome to be had gratis everywhere," and gave a table showing the lengths of a pendulum in Rhenish inches and French centimetres corresponding to all the numbers on the metronome. As the months passed, the metronome had come largely into use in England, France and the United States, but not in Germany and Austria. It was of high importance to the manufacturers of the instruments to obtain the countenance and good will of the composers in those countries also—Salieri, Weigl, Beethoven, etc.— and Mälzel came back to Vienna to try the effect of personal effort, taking the risk of any serious consequences arising from the lawsuit between him and Beethoven. But there were none. The matter was amicably adjusted, each party paying half of the legal expenses which had been incurred. This would be incredible had Beethoven had any substantial grounds for the action; for his sanction of the metronome was of such value that Mälzel would readily have conceded much to obtain it; and the whole tone of the composer's correspondence in this period, so far as relates to his pecuniary affairs, shows how little likely he was to sacrifice any just claim.

Beethoven was at first not well disposed to the instrument, notwithstanding he had joined Salieri and the other composers in strongly recommending the "chronometer" in 1813, which certificate had been used in England *a fortiori* for the new metronome. In a letter[28] Mr. Joseph J. Mickley, of Philadelphia, writes: "Mr. Mälzel, with whom I was well acquainted,[29] told me that he had been particularly anxious Beethoven should mark his music by his metronome, and to get his recommendation; that he (B) refused and became quite indignant, saying: 'It is silly stuff; one must feel the tempos'"; but Beethoven soon yielded to the obvious considerations in favor of the invention. These were presented to the public together with the objections to Weber's and Zmeskall's pendulums, clearly, explicitly and cunningly by Mosel in an article in Steiner's *Musik-Zeitung* on November 27, which put an end to controversy on the topic.

Meanwhile, Beethoven had prepared a table of tempos for his eight symphonies which was printed in the Leipzig *Allgemeine Musik-Zeitung* on December 17 (copied, says Nottebohm, from a little pamphlet published by Steiner and Co. in which also tempos of the Septet were included), and followed this up with a general metronomizing of his works. On the autograph of his song, "Nord oder Süd," he wrote: "100 according to Mälzel; but this must be held applicable to only the first measures, for feeling also

[28] The letter to Thayer is dated May 21, 1873. (TK, II, 385, n. 1; TDR, IV, 65.)

[29] Mälzel lived in Philadelphia for some time before his death at sea on July 21, 1838. (TK, II, 385, n. 1.)

has its tempo and this cannot entirely be expressed in this figure (i.e., 100)."[30]

If the picture of Mälzel drawn by Schindler and his copyists is true, even the most Christian and forgiving spirit could scarcely have demanded more of Beethoven than this public acknowledgement of the value of the metronome by way of heaping coals of fire upon his head; but he did more, by writing to Mosel this very valuable and for us very interesting letter:

I am heartily rejoiced that you agree with me in the opinion touching the time designations which date back to the barbarous period in music. For what, for instance, can be more nonsensical than Allegro, which always means *merry* and how often are we so far from this conception of time that the piece says the very *opposite of the designation.*— As regards these 4 chief movements, which by no means have the correctness or truthfulness of the chief winds, we gladly *put them aside.* It is a different matter with the words used to designate the character of the composition; these we cannot give up, since time is really more the body while *these have reference to the spirit.* So far as I am concerned I have long thought of giving up the nonsensical designations Allegro, Andante, Adagio, Presto; Mälzel's metronome gives us the best opportunity to do this. I give you *my word* that I shall *never use them again* in my new compositions— It is another question whether we shall thereby accomplish the necessary *universal* use of the M[etronome]. I do not think so. But I do not doubt that we shall be decried as *taskmasters.* If the cause might thus be served it would still be better than to be accused of feudalism—I therefore think that it would be best, especially in our countries where music has become a national need and every village schoolmaster ought to use the metronome, that Mälzel try to dispose of a certain number of metronomes by subscription at higher prices, and that as soon as his expenses are thus covered he will be in a position to furnish the needed metronome for the national need so cheaply that the greatest *universality* and *widest distribution* may be expected—It is self-evident that somebody must take the initiative in this matter so that zeal be aroused. As for me you may count on me, and I await with pleasure the post of duty to which you will assign me—

Still more: he joined with Salieri in a public announcement which was printed in the *Wiener Allgemeine Musikalische Zeitung* of February 14, 1818, setting forth that the metronome would attest its utility forever and was indispensable to all students of singing, the pianoforte or other instruments, etc. On one of the last days of December, Beethoven writes to Frau Streicher: "Day before yesterday I was busy with Mälzel, who is in a hurry as he is soon to leave here." What had he so important to do with this "rude fellow, wholly without education or breeding," to cite his own words? Was it in contemplation to make this sudden zeal for the metronome a source of pecuniary profit? No one knows.

On October 2nd, Beethoven wrote a letter to Nanette Streicher from Nussdorf which ends: "Tomorrow I hope to see you for sure, for I am coming in from the country to the Landstrasse just for that reason." One of

[30] Thus copied by Fischoff. (TDR, IV, 66, n. 3.)

the matters to be discussed was a move to the Gärtnergasse which Beethoven had mentioned frequently in his letters to Frau Streicher during the summer. He left Nussdorf for good on October 14. At some point after this date he left the dwelling on the Landstrasse (No. 268) for one in the house "zum grünen Baum," first *étage*, 2nd story, No. 26 in the Gärtnergasse, also in the suburb Landstrasse.✠— He was again near both his nephew and the Streichers (in the Ungargasse), and, with the aid of Frau Streicher, he at last brought his domestic arrangements into such a condition that he might take his nephew to himself. About this time he wrote his friend:

I am occupied in going over my papers to consider what is necessary for the coming move. That your accounts have not been discharged and that I have not visited you can all be ascribed to this. To bring such things as my papers into order demands *dreadful patience*; but we *must cling to it* once it is present because ordinarily there is none. Associated with this is the question of what we need in the way of utensils— Many thanks for your recommendation of the new h[ousekeeper] and for your continuing willingness to give us help, *without which* I would be completely distrustful of everyone. But with three people everything is more easily figured out. I hope to see you tomorrow or the day after tomorrow. In haste

Your friend Beethoven

On one side of a large sheet of paper (it is now preserved in the Berlin Library) he wrote a list of questions which were painstakingly answered on the opposite page by the friend to whom they were addressed (presumably again Frau Streicher). The questions were as follows:

What ought one to give 2 servants to eat at dinner and supper both as to quantity and quality?
How often ought one to give them roast meat?
Ought they to have it at dinner and supper too?
That which is intended for the servants, do they have it in common with the victuals of the master, or do they prepare their own separately, i.e., do they have different food from the master?
How many pounds of meat are to be reckoned for 3 persons?
What allowance per day do the housekeeper and maid receive?
How about the washing?
Do the housekeeper and maid get more?
How much wine and beer?
Does one give it to them and when?
Breakfast?

Beethoven announced his intention to take his nephew to himself at the end of the current quarter in a letter to Giannatasio dated November 1, 1817. The step involved not only an increase in his expenses, but also an abandonment of his engagement with the London Philharmonic Society and of all the profits which might thence arise. Giannatasio, moved by his complaints of poverty, and probably also by a desire to aid him in the proposed visit to London, kindly offered to keep the boy at a much reduced rate of remuneration for board and instruction. Beethoven's reply shows him to be still undecided as to his movements in the coming spring, and it is possible, could he have made ready the required symphonies, that he might have gone to England; but now the new Sonata had got possession of his imagination, and the symphonies must wait.

Brief mention should be made at this point of Beethoven's increasing deafness. Czerny, who saw Beethoven frequently during these particular years, told Jahn that between 1812 and 1816 it gradually became more and more difficult to make oneself understood without shouting. "But it was not until 1817 that the deafness became so extreme that he could no longer hear music either, and this condition persisted for about 8 or 10 years until his death." And further: "Up to 1816, he was still able (with the aid of machines) to hear himself play, but later even this became more and more difficult, and he had to rely on his inner hearing, his imagination, and experience." This may be compared with Schindler's comments in the *Niederrheinische Musikzeitung* 1854, No. 28, where he enlarges somewhat further on Beethoven's hearing ability as regards music and then goes on to say: "During 1818, Beethoven's hearing became too poor for oral conversation, even with the aid of a speaking trumpet, and he was forced to resort to writing."

--✠{There is an interesting passage in a letter dated "Nussdorf, July 7th" from Beethoven to Frau Streicher concerning his hearing at the piano: "Now here is a big request for Streicher. Ask him for my sake to do me the favor of adjusting one of your pianos for my weakened hearing so that it is as loud as possible. I need it. For a long time I have had the intention to buy one for myself, but at the moment it would be very difficult for me. Perhaps somewhat later, though, it will be more easily possible; but until then I want to *have one on loan* from you. I refuse completely to accept it free. I am ready to pay the going price for it within six months in Convention Coin. Perhaps you do not know, that although I have not had one of your pianos all the time, yet I have preferred your make especially ever since 1808— Streicher is the one person who is in the position to send me the kind of piano that I need—"}✠--

On November 15, Anton Halm gave a concert for the benefit of the poor in the Kärnthnerthor-Theater at which the Choral Fantasia was performed. --✠{The composer and pianist Johann Peter Pixis (1788-1874) was at the performance and recorded in his reminiscences that at the point where the chorus enters, the audience's attention was shattered by horrible inappropriate sounds coming from the piano. The efforts of the conductor to avoid the chaos which followed were to no avail and amid grumbles and hisses from the audience the musicians had to come to a halt before continuing the piece. The next day Pixis was stopping in at Steiner's to buy a copy of the Fantasy. "At that point Beethoven entered the store with his usual dark look. I seized the silver horn which was placed here for him, held it to his ear and asked him: 'Were you at the concert yesterday?' His face became darker than before and in a real rage he said, 'The dirty fellow came to me to learn the tempi; I gave them to him and warned him about the passage just before the chorus comes in; I told him that he should pay attention there, otherwise he would get thrown off, and that's exactly what happened to him!' Then I was called by Steiner into his office and when I came back into the store, Beethoven was gone, but several customers who had come in were standing by the table and observed with animated expressions the words which Beethoven had written with a pencil on the white margin of my copy: 'Nicht jeder Halm gibt Ähren!' " (Not every stalk has ears of corn.)[31]

It is probable that to this time is to be assigned a portrait in oils painted by Christoph Heckel, who was a student at the Royal Imperial Academy in Vienna from 1814 to 1818. Beethoven, it is said, made the acquaintance of the painter in Streicher's pianoforte wareroom.

But one public appearance professionally of Beethoven is recorded this year. At the concert for the Hospital Fund on December 25, the first part was devoted to the Eighth Symphony, which was conducted by the composer. In the second part Seyfried produced C. P. E. Bach's oratorio, *The Israelites in the Wilderness*, which he had revised, adding to the accompaniments, curtailing the airs, prefixing it with the well-known fugue on B-A-C-H (orchestrated by himself), and concluding it with the double chorus "Holy, holy, holy." Nottebohm has shown that the sketches for the overture on the name of the great Leipzig cantor which Beethoven once thought of writing, belong to a later period; but it is yet possible, if not likely, that he conceived the idea at this concert.

There is but little to be added to what has been said about the compositions of this almost sterile year. The transcription of the Pianoforte Trio as a quintet (which was the largest work of the year), and the "Song of the Monks," written on the death of Krumpholz, have been mentioned. Besides these we have a few short songs with pianoforte accompaniment. "Nord oder Süd" (also known as "So oder So"), the poem by Karl Lappe, was known and widely liked in a setting by K. Klage. Beethoven's setting seems to have been less well known. "Resignation" ("Lisch aus mein Licht"), words by Count Paul von Haugwitz, was composed in the second half of the year, and the sketches show that Beethoven contemplated a setting for four voices. The year also saw work done on the Pianoforte Sonata in B-flat, Op. 106, and the beginning of the Symphony in D minor.

Lastly there was the composition of a Fugue in D major for five stringed instruments, which was completed on November 28, 1817. This piece was written especially for a manuscript collection of Beethoven's works projected

[31] The pun on the name of the pianist, Halm, is lost in translation. See Willi Reich, "Ein übersehenes Gespräch mit Beethoven," *Schweizerische Musikzeitung*, Vol. 91 (1951), p. 170.

by Haslinger, to be discussed below, and was published by him in the fall of 1827 as Op. 137. Beethoven was particularly interested in fugues at the time. "To *make* a fugue requires no particular skill," he said later to Holz, "in my study days I made dozens of them. But the fancy wishes also to assert its privileges, and today a new and really poetical element must be introduced into the old traditional form." The sketches for the conclusion of the Quintet fugue are mixed with notes from Bach and others showing how zealous were his studies in the form of that time.[32]

In a Conversation Book of January, 1820, one of Beethoven's friends (probably Oliva) writes: "Today I met Haslinger of Steiner's;—he has had your works made into magnificent copies in score."[33] This collection was in the making, according to Unger,[34] from 1817 to 1823 and during this time Haslinger engaged the services of two expert calligraphists, Mathias Schwarz and Friedrich Warsow to make copies of Beethoven's works on beautiful English vellum-paper. The result is a deluxe collection in sixty-two volumes. Originally planned as a preparation for a published edition of the complete works, which was never realised because of difficulty in negotiating with other publishers concerning the rights of particular works, the collection was sold to Archduke Rudolph in 1823 for a sum of 4000 fl. C.M. and after his death was inherited by the Gesellschaft der Musikfreunde, where it may still be seen.[35]

The compositions for the year were:

Canon. "Glück fehl' dir vor allem," WoO 171, for Anna del Rio.
Fugue in D for String Quintet, Op. 137.
"Gesang der Mönche" for Two Tenors and Bass (from Schiller's *Wilhelm Tell*), WoO 104.
"Resignation" (Haugwitz), WoO 149.
"So oder so" (Carl Lappe), WoO 148.
String Quintet, Op. 104, arrangement of the Trio, Op. 1, No. 3.

The publications were:

By Simrock:
"Das Geheimnis" (Wessenberg), WoO 145. Also "An die Geliebte," 2nd version, WoO 140.
Two Sonatas for Pianoforte and Violoncello, Op. 102, without dedication to Countess Marie von Erdödy.
By Steiner:
Sonata for Pianoforte, Op. 101, dedicated to Baroness Dorothea Ertmann.
Symphony No. 8 in F major, Op. 93.
By Thomson in Edinburgh and Preston in London:
"A Select Collection of Original Welsh Airs," Vol. 3, WoO 155 (containing 26 airs by Beethoven and four by Haydn).

[32] See Nottebohm, *II Beeth.*, pp. 349-52. (TDR, IV, 76, n. 4.)
[33] Schünemann, I, p. 200.
[34] *Ludwig van Beethoven und seine Ver-* *leger*, pp. 10-14.
[35] See O. E. Deutsch, "Beethovens gesammelte Werke," in *Zeitschrift für Musikwissenschaft*, XIII (1930), pp. 60-79.

By Wallishauser, as a musical supplement to *Gedichte von Friedrich Treitschke*:
"Ruf vom Berge" (Treitschke), WoO 147, for which it was composed on
December 13, 1816.

By *Wiener Allegemeine Musikalische Zeitung*, March 6th, as a supplement:
Canon. "Das Schweigen," WoO 168. In the issue of June 5th appeared the
solution to this riddle canon by Hieronymous Payer, accompanied by a
humorous canon of his own on the words "Herr Beethoven's Canon is at the
5th below and at the octave."[36]

By *Wiener Modenzeitung*, February 17, as a musical supplement:
"So oder so" (Lappe), WoO 148 (also published singly by Simrock).

[36] See KHV, p. 676, and L. Misch, *Beethoven Studies* (Norman, 1953), pp. 124-26.

CHAPTER XXXI

THE YEAR 1818

A MOTHER'S STRUGGLE FOR HER SON—
THE PIANOFORTE SONATA OP. 106

AN ENTRY in an old "Porter's Book" of John Broadwood and Sons, manufacturers of pianofortes in London, offers an agreeable starting-point for the story of Beethoven's life in 1818. In this book the porter of the firm signs his name, Millet, to the record that on December 27, 1817, he took from the warehouse "A 6 octave Grand Pianoforte, No. 7362 tin and deal case, Thomas Broadwood, Esq., marked ⟨v. b.⟩ care of F. E. J. Bareaux and Co., Trieste (a present to Mr. van Beethoven, Viene), deliv'd to Mr. Farlowes to be shipped." Some time previously Mr. Thomas Broadwood, the then head of the house, with a Mr. Goding (probably the rich brewer), visited the principal cities of the continent and doubtless became acquainted with Beethoven and offered to present to him one of the firm's pianofortes. On January 3, 1818, Mr. Broadwood seems to have informed Beethoven that the instrument had been shipped, and exactly one month later Beethoven sent the following acknowledgment to the generous donor:

Mon très cher Ami Broadwood!

Jamais je n'eprouvais pas un grand Plaisir de ce que me causa votre Annonce de l'arrivée de cette Piano, avec qui vous m'honorès de m'en faire present, je regarderai comme un Autel, ou je deposerai les plus belles offrandes de mon esprit au divine Apollon. Aussitôt comme je recevrai votre Excellent Instrument, je vous enverrai d'en abord les Fruits de l'inspiration des premiers moments, que j'y passerai, pour vous servir d'un Souvenir de moi à vous mon très cher B., et je ne souhaits ce que, qu'ils soient dignes de votre instrument.

Mon cher Monsieur et ami recevés ma plus grande consideration de votre ami et très humble serviteur

Louis van Beethoven.

Vienne le 3me du mois Fevrier, 1818.

This letter was sent to Broadwood by Joseph Anton Bridi of the firm of Bridi, Parisi and Co., in Vienna, who had evidently been commissioned to look after the delivery of the instrument to Beethoven after its arrival in Trieste. At least Bridi, in transmitting the letter to Broadwood under cover and date February 5, informs the latter that he had taken the proper steps to have the pianoforte sent to Vienna by Bareaux (or Barraux) and Co., and asks for instructions how to carry out what he understands to be the donor's desire that the instrument be delivered to Beethoven without his being put to any expense whatever, not even for the import duty. The latter charge must have been in the mind of Beethoven when he wrote a letter, without date, to Count Lichnowsky enclosing a document bearing on the case expressing the hope that he be permitted to receive the instrument and proposing to apply by word of mouth to Count Stadion, the Austrian Minister of Finance. Frau Streicher was also appealed to in the matter, Beethoven begging her in a letter to ask her "Cousin from Cracow" to get from the chief customs official in Vienna an order for the forwarding of the pianoforte, which could be sent to the custom house in Trieste. But neither Broadwood nor Beethoven was called on to pay the duty, the Austrian Exchequer remitting the charge. After some delay the pianoforte was delivered at Streicher's wareroom and later sent to Beethoven at Mödling. While it was still in his possession, Streicher asked Potter to try it, saying that Moscheles and others could do nothing with it—the tone was beautiful but the action too heavy. Potter, who was familiar with the English instruments, found no difficulty in disclosing its admirable qualities. He told Beethoven, however, that it was out of tune, whereupon the latter replied in effect: "That's what they all say; they would like to tune it and spoil it, but they shall not touch it." Beethoven's delight in the pianoforte must have been great. Bridi reports to Broadwood that the composer already rejoiced in it in anticipation and expressed a desire to dedicate the first piece of music composed after its reception to the donor, "convinced that it would inspire something good." His jealousy of it seems to have been so great that he would not permit anybody to tune it except Stumpff, of London, who came with a letter of introduction from Broadwood.

The case of the instrument, simple, plain but tasteful in design, is of mahogany and the structure generally of a solidity and strength paired with grace which caused no little surprise at the time. The compass is six octaves from C, five leger-lines below the bass staff. Above the keys is the inscription: *Hoc Instrumentum est Thomæ Broadwood (Londini) donum, propter Ingenium illustrissimi Beethoven.* On the board, back of the keys, is the name "Beethoven," inlaid in ebony, and below this the makers' mark: "John Broadwood and Sons, Makers of Instruments to His Majesty and the Princesses. Great Pulteney Street. Golden Square. London." To the right of the keyboard are the autograph names Frid. Kalkbrenner, Ferd. Ries, G. G. Ferrari, J. B. Cramer and C. Knyvett; the names of the virtuosi were no doubt scratched upon the instrument as a compliment to Beethoven and an evidence that they had played upon it. Beethoven kept the instrument as long as he lived. At the sale of his effects it was bought by Spina, the music publisher, for 181 florins; Spina gave it to Liszt, in whose house at Weimar it was up to his death. In 1887, Princess Marie Hohenlohe, daughter of Liszt's friend, the Princess Sayn-Wittgenstein, presented it to the National Museum in Buda-Pesth.

Beethoven's London trip had been abandoned without notice or explanation to the Philharmonic Society, apparently; but Ries must have written to him, renewing the offer previously accepted, for on March 5 Beethoven writes to his old pupil as follows:

In spite of my desire, it was impossible for me to come to London this year; I beg of you to say to the Philharmonic Society that my poor state of health hindered me; but I hope that I may be entirely well this spring and then take advantage of the renewed offers of the Society towards the end of the year and fulfil all its conditions. Please ask Neate in my name not to make use, at least not in public, of the many compositions of mine which he has until my arrival in person; no matter what the conditions of his affairs may be I have cause of complaint against him.

Botter [Cipriani Potter] visited me several times, he seems to be a good man and has talent for composition— I hope and wish that your prosperity may grow daily; unfortunately I cannot say that of myself. My unlucky connection with this Archduke has brought me to the verge of beggary. I cannot endure the sight of want. I must give; you can imagine how my present conditions increase my sufferings. I beg of you to write to me soon. If it is at all possible I shall get away from here sooner in order to escape total ruin and will then arrive in London in the winter at the latest.

I know that you will stand by an unfortunate friend; had it only been in my power, and had I not been fettered, as always here, by circumstances, I would surely have done much more for you—A hearty farewell, give my greetings to Neate, Smart, Cramer—although I hear that he is a counter-subject to you and me, yet I already know something of the art of treating such and we shall produce an agreeable harmony in London after all.

I greet and embrace you from my heart.

Your friend Ludwig van Beethoven

All that is lovely to your dear and (as I hear) beautiful wife.

Ries's reverence for royalty, apparently, led him to omit Beethoven's unkind allusion to his august patron and pupil, Archduke Rudolph; Schindler, writing much later, printed it and admitted, very properly, as we know from other instances of the same kind, that Beethoven sometimes used his friends as whipping-boys, and that his words and deeds were not always consistent with each other.

The time had come for Beethoven to take his nephew from the home and institute of the Giannatasios. On January 6 he wrote to inform the director that Karl would leave his "admirable institute" at the expiration of the month and that Giannatasio might rest assured of his and the lad's life-long gratitude: "I have observed in Karl that he already feels grateful, and this is a proof that though he is frivolous he is not malicious, and least of all is he bad at heart. I have hopes of all manner of good from him, all the more because he had been under your excellent care for nearly two years."

After taking Karl to his own home the composer engaged a tutor to prepare him for matriculation at the gymnasium. This tutor, whose name has not been learned, was a professor at the Vienna University and had evidently agreed not only to look after all of the lad's intellectual needs but also to have an eye on some of the domestic affairs and to that end to become a member of the Beethoven household. On this point, Beethoven enjoined secrecy upon Frau Streicher. How long the service of this "steward," as he playfully called him to Frau Streicher, continued is not known, nor how satisfactory it was. He does not become a subject of Beethoven's correspond-ence beyond a single reference to the fact that he once stayed out all night.

Ill-advised and full of evil consequences as was Beethoven's step in taking personal charge of his nephew, it was yet creditable to his heart and bears strong witness to his high sense of duty. His purpose was pure and lofty, and his action prompted by both love and an ideal sense of moral obligation. It was a woeful mistake, however; Beethoven sadly misjudged his fitness to fill the delicate and difficult rôle of guardian and parent. In all his life he had never had occasion to give a thought to the duties which such an office involved. In the conduct of his own affairs he had always permitted himself to be swayed by momentary impulses, emotions and sometimes violent passions, and he could not suddenly develop the habits of calm reflection, unimpassioned judgment and consistent behavior essential to the training of a careless and wayward boy. In his treatment of him he flew from one extreme to the other—from almost cruel severity to almost limitless indulgence, and, for this reason, failed to inspire either respect for his authority or deep affection for his person, to develop the lad's self-control or a desire for virtuous living. Very questionable, too, if not utterly unpar-donable, were the measures which Beethoven took to separate the boy from his mother in spite of the dying wishes of the father. We have seen his protestations at times of his unwillingness to give her pain. When he was cruel in his own confession it was because he imagined himself constrained to be so by a high obligation of duty. There can be no doubt that the woman whom Beethoven called "The Queen of Night" was wicked and vicious, and that his detestation of her was as well founded as his wish to save his nephew from evil communications and influences.

Thayer's opinion of Beethoven's motives in taking charge of his nephew and of the character of his sister-in-law represents the prevailing view on this subject until recent years. But there has come a reexamination of this phase in Beethoven's life by certain writers from the psychological viewpoint. The most thorough of these studies is a book entitled *Beethoven and his Nephew* by E. and R. Sterba,[1] which attempts to analyse the relationship with the psychoanalytic approach of Freud. Beethoven's love for his nephew was an almost all-consuming emotional preoccupation from the time he became Karl's guardian to his death. From all that we know concerning this relationship, Beethoven's possessive instinct and craving for love from this boy was more decisive in guiding his actions than his objective sense of duty. An antipathy to his sister-in-law that had already existed deepened into a hatred when she became the logical person with whom to divide care for the boy, which represented for Beethoven the complete resolution of his life-long craving to love and cherish another. With the existence of this conflict within him it is problematical to what extent many of his opinions concerning her, be they based on suspicion or gossip, can be accepted. Certainly to name Johanna "wicked and vicious" must be accepted as Beethoven's view but not, as Thayer implies, necessarily the truth.

A memorandum in the *Tagebuch* after February 20th reads: "Karl's mother has not seen him since August 10"—a period of more than six months. How often she was allowed to see him during the following months is not of record; we only know from Beethoven himself, in his letters to Frau Streicher, that the mother's instinct drove her to employ the only means by which she could know the condition of her son during the summer in Mödling—i.e., bribing or feeing the servants. That at least is Beethoven's accusation, and exceedingly wroth he was. We have contented ourselves mostly with mere references to Beethoven's letters to Frau Streicher in this period. They are in the main brief notes monotonously asking help in domestic affairs, and though frequently interesting because of their exhibition of characteristic traits and moods, too insignificant to justify the cumbering of these pages with their literal contents. The following letter, however, deserves to be given in full.

Best Frau Streicher!

It was not possible to reply to your last letter sooner. I would have written to you a few days ago when the servants were sent away, but hesitated in my determination until I learned that it was Frau D. in particular who hindered Karl from making full confession. *"He ought to spare his mother,"* she told him; and Peppi cooperated with her.[2] Naturally they did not want to be discovered; they worked together shamefully and permitted themselves to be used by Frau v. Beethoven; both received coffee and sugar from her, Peppi *money* and the *old one* probably also; for there can be no doubt that she was *herself at the house of Karl's mother*; she said to Karl that *if I drove her away* from my service *she would go straight to his mother*. This happened at a time when I had reproved her for her conduct with which I had frequent occasion to be dissatisfied; Peppi who often played the eavesdropper when I spoke with Karl appears to have tried

---

[1] Pantheon, N.Y., 1954.

[2] Frau D. and Peppi were the new housekeeper and cook, engaged some time early in the year. The former is also called "the old woman" by Beethoven in his letters. Beethoven wrote to Frau Streicher in the early winter and referred to Peppi as "a *good* cook." See *A* 894.

to tell the truth; but the old one *accused her of stupidity and scolded her stoutly*—and so she remained silent and tried to throw me off the trail— The story of this abominable deception may have lasted about six weeks—they would not have got off *so easy* with a less magnanimous man. Peppi borrowed 9 or 10 florins for stuff for shirts and I afterwards made her a present of the money and instead of 60 she got 70 florins; she might have denied herself these wretched bribes. In the case of the old woman, who was always the worse, hate may have played a part as she always thought herself slighted (although she got more than she deserved) for the *scornful smile on her face* one day when Karl embraced me, made me suspect *treachery* and how shameless and deceitful such an old woman could be. Just imagine, 2 days before I came here K. went to his mother one afternoon without my knowledge and both the old woman and P. knew it. But now listen to the triumph of a hoary-headed traitress: on the way hither with K. and her, I spoke with K. about the matter in the carriage, although I did not know all; and when I expressed the fear that we should not be safe in Mödling, she exclaimed "*I should only rely upon her.*" O the infamy of it! This was only the 2nd time in the case of a person of such venerable age that *such a thing* happened to me— A few days before when I sent both away I had told them in writing that under no circumstances were they to accept anything for Karl from his mother. Instead of repenting, Peppi tried secretly to take revenge on K., after he had confessed all. This they knew from the fact that in the note mentioned above, I had written that *all had been discovered*— I expected that they would both beg my pardon after this, instead of which they played me one wicked trick after the other. As no betterment was to be expected in such obstinate sinners and I had every moment to fear another piece of treachery, I decided to sacrifice my body, my comfort in order to better my poor misguided Karl; so out of the house they went as a *warning example* to all those servants who may come after—I might have made their certificates of character a little less favorable; but rather I set down the time of service of each at full six months although it was not true. I never practice *vengeance*; in cases where I act *against* the interest of other people, I never do more *against them* than is necessary to protect myself against them or to prevent them from doing further harm.— On account of Peppi's honesty in general I am sorry to have lost her, for which reason I made her certificate more favorable than that of the old woman; also she appears to have been led astray by the old woman. That P.'s conscience was not at ease, however, she showed by saying to Karl that "*she did not dare go back to her parents,*" and, *in fact, I believe she is still here*— I had suspected treachery for a long time until one evening before my departure I received an anonymous letter the contents of which filled me with dread; but they were only suspicions. Karl, whom I took to task in the evening confessed at once but not everything. As I often treat him harshly though not without cause, he was much too afraid to admit everything completely. In the midst of the struggle we reached here. As I often questioned him, the servants noticed it, and the old woman in particular tried to persuade him *not to admit the truth.* But when I gave Karl my sacred assurance that all would be forgiven if he would but confess the truth, while lying would plunge him into a deeper abyss than that in which he already was, everything came to the light of day— Add to this the other data which I gave you before concerning the servants and you will have the shameful story of the two traitresses clearly before you— K. did wrong, but—mother—mother—even a bad one remains a mother— To this extent he is to be excused, particularly by me who knows his intriguing, passionate mother *much too well*.— The priest here knows already that I know about him, for K. had already told me. It is likely that he was not fully informed and that he will be careful; thus we'll guard against K's being mistreated by him, since he appears to be rather a rough man. Enough of that for now. But as K's virtue was put to the test, for there is no virtue without temptation, I will purposely let the matter go by until it happens again (which I do not expect), in which case I will so bethwhack his reverence with such spiritual cudgels, amulets with my sole guardianship and consequent privileges, that the whole parish will shake— My heart has been terribly shaken up by this affair and I can scarcely recover myself— Now to the housekeeping; it needs your help— How necessary this is to us you already know. Do not be frightened away, such a thing might happen anywhere; but if it has once happened and one is in a position to hold it up to one's new servants, it is not likely that it will occur again— You know what we need, perhaps a French woman, and whatever can be found in the way of a chambermaid; good cooking remains the principal thing—also the matter of economy. For the present we have a person who cooks for us, but badly. I cannot write you more today. You will see that *in this matter* I could not act differently; things had gone too far— I cannot yet invite you to visit me here for everything is still in confusion; *nevertheless it will not be necessary to send me to a lunatic asylum*— I can say that I already suffered fearfully from this thing while I was in Vienna, though I kept silence— Farewell; do not let any of this be known as someone might think prejudicially of K. *Only I* who know all the driving wheels here can testify *for him* that he was terribly misled— I beg of you soon to write us something comforting touching the art of cooking, washing and sewing. I am feeling very ill and in need of a stomach restorative.

In haste, your friend

Mödling, June 18, 1818.   Beethoven

"K. did wrong, but—mother—mother—even a bad one remains a mother." Why did he not follow this thought to its ultimate conclusion? Why did he permit, if indeed, he did not encourage the lad to speak disrespectfully of his mother?

Beethoven removed to Mödling on May 19, taking with him his nephew and the two servants referred to in the letter above. He found lodgings in the so-called Hafner House in the Hauptstrasse, now ornamented by a memorial tablet. ⟶It was on the Ungargasse (now Hauptstrasse No. 79). Beethoven had quarters on the first floor, which consisted of a large room with a view on to the court, two small rooms with a view on to both court and garden, and a small dark kitchen where both servants presumably slept.[3] He began taking the baths two days after his arrival and, the

---

[3] The present editor is grateful to the late Dr. Kurt Smolle for these details. The memorial tablet, which is to the right of the front door, bears the incorrect date of 1820, in which year Beethoven visited Mödling but no longer lived in the Hafner House.

desire and capacity for work soon returning, he took up energetically the Pianoforte Sonata in B-flat. Karl was placed in a class of boys taught by the village priest, named Fröhlich,[4] who dismissed him a month later for reasons which became a matter of judicial record before the end of the year. In a document filed as an appendix to Frau van Beethoven's application for the guardianship, Fröhlich set forth that Beethoven had encouraged his nephew to revile his mother, applauding him when he applied vile epithets to her either in writing or by shrieking them into his ear, "thus violating the fourth divine commandment"; that the boy had confessed to him that while he knew that he was doing wrong he yet defamed his mother to curry favor with his uncle, and dared not tell him the truth because he would only believe lies. "This he once told his mother and would have said more had he not feared being found out and maltreated by his uncle." Once, too, Beethoven came to him (the priest) and in a tone of malicious joy told him that his nephew had that day called his mother a "Ravenmother" (*Rabenmutter*—meaning a wicked and unnatural mother). Since Karl's training was thus contrary to all moral principles, since he had also displayed indifference to religious instruction, been guilty of unruly conduct in church and in the streets, so that many of the inhabitants of the village had come to him with complaints, and since admonitions to the boy and appeals to the uncle had borne no fruit, the priest had been constrained to dismiss him for the sake of his other twelve pupils, who had said "they did not want to study with the unruly Karl van Beethoven." These unfortunate first-fruits of Beethoven's error in undertaking personal and sole care of his nephew will call for more attention before the history of the year 1818 is closed, and may be dismissed for the present for more cheerful topics.

Towards the end of the year 1815 the Gesellschaft der Musikfreunde had instituted inquiries through Zmeskall touching Beethoven's willingness to compose a work of magnitude for the Society. Beethoven signified his assent to the project and in turn asked Zmeskall whether or not the Society would allow him 400 ducats as an honorarium. There the matter seems to have rested until May, 1818, on the 17th of which month Vincent Hauschka, a violoncello player and member of the governing committee of the Society, was authorized by his associates to offer Beethoven from 200 to 300 "pieces of gold" for the music to a "heroic oratorio" to be the exclusive property of the Society for one year after the date of its first performance. Hauschka wrote to Beethoven at Mödling and received a droll letter in reply. It bears no date:

First and best member of the Society of Enemies[5] of Music in the Austrian Empire!

---

[4] It was this priest, evidently, against whom Beethoven threatened to launch the thunderbolts of his wrath, as he told Frau Streicher in the letter above. (TK, II, 396, n. 1.)

[5] The play on the words *Freunde* and *Feinde* is impossible in English. (TK, II, 397.)

Ich bin be - rei - - - - t!
[I am a gree - - - - d!]

Ich bin be - rei - - - - t!
[I am a gree - - - - d!] etc.

I have only a *sacred* subject at hand; but you want a heroic one, which is all right by me. But I think to mix in something sacred besides would be suitable for such a crowd.

A - - - - - men!

Herr v. Bernard would suit me very well, but please pay him as well. I will not speak of myself; since you call yourselves music friends, so it is natural that you will settle this account generously——!!! Now farewell, best fellow, I wish you open bowels and the handsomest of close-stools. As for me, I am wandering about here amongst mountains, hollows and valleys, with a piece of music-paper scribbling down many a thing for the sake of bread and money— For to such a pitch have I been brought in this all-powerful *land of the Phaeacians* that in order to gain a little time for a work of magnitude I must always scribble first a great deal for money so that I may hold out during a large work— For the rest, my health is much better and if haste is necessary I can still serve you well—

Ich bin berei   t!   Ich bin be-
A
rei   t!
men!

If you need to talk with me, write me, whereupon I will make all the arrangements about it— My compliments to all of the Society of Enemies of Music—

In haste your friend

Beethoven

The tone and contents of this letter show that it was not designed as an official communication to the Society, but merely as a friendly negotiation. Further correspondence on the matter occurs in the next year.

The same summer saw the beginning of the most widely distributed portrait of Beethoven. At the instance of his uncle, Baron von Skrbensky, a young painter named August von Klöber (born at Breslau in 1793), who was continuing his artistic studies in Vienna, undertook to paint a portrait of the composer. His own account of his acquaintance with Beethoven and the incidents connected with the painting of the portrait (or rather with the original sketch) were published in the *Allgemeine Musikalische Zeitung* of 1864 (p. 324). From it we learn that the artist was introduced to Beethoven by a letter written by Dont.[6] He visited Beethoven at Mödling, after receiving permission to make a drawing of him and found him giving a lesson to his nephew on the Broadwood pianoforte. This fact fixes the date of the picture. Though the artist found it impossible to make himself understood unless he wrote his words or spoke them into an ear-trumpet, Beethoven corrected the errors in the lad's playing, compelled him to repeat passages apparently without difficulty. Klöber's account continues:

"After approximately three-quarters of an hour, he grew uneasy; following Dont's advice I knew that it was time to stop and asked him only for permission to come again tomorrow since I lived in Mödling myself. Beethoven was very understanding and said, 'Then we can meet often because I do not like to sit long. You must take a good look at Mödling for it is very beautiful here, and, as an artist you must be a lover of nature.' On my walks in Mödling I met Beethoven repeatedly, and it was most interesting to see how frequently he stopped, with a sheet of music-paper and a pencil-stump in his hands, as if listening, looked up and down and then scribbled notes on the paper. Dont had told me that if I met him thus I should never address him or notice him because he would then become either embarrassed or disagreeable. Once, just when I was sketching a piece of woods, I saw him climb up a hill from the hollow which separated us, with his broad-brimmed felt hat pressed under his arm; when he got there, he threw himself down at full length under a pine-tree and for a long time stared heavenwards.— Every morning he sat for me awhile. When Beethoven saw my picture he remarked that the treatment of the hair pleased him very much, the other painters hitherto had always made him look so *well-groomed.* . . .

"Beethoven's residence in Mödling was extremely simple as, indeed, was his whole nature; his garments consisted of a light-blue frockcoat with yellow buttons, white waistcoat and necktie, as was the fashion at the time, but everything *negligée.* His complexion was healthy and tough, the skin somewhat pock-marked, his hair was of the color of slightly bluish-gray and very animated—when his hair was tossed by the wind there was something Ossianic-demoniac about him. In friendly converse, however, his expression became good-natured and gentle, particularly when the conversation pleased him. Every mood of his soul found powerful expression instantly in his features."

Klöber's original painting has disappeared. It was a full-length portrait with a bit of Mödling landscape as a background. The nephew Karl was included, reposing under a tree. The composer was depicted with note-book and pencil. —⋙{A drawing of the head, presumably as it was in the painting, has survived and is owned by the publishing house of C. F. Peters in Leipzig.}⋘—

---

[6] Joseph Valentine Dont, a violoncellist, was a member of Beethoven's circle of friends. (Cf. TK, II, 399; TDR, IV, 104, n. 1.)

We now reach an incident in the story of Beethoven's life concerning which much has been written from the biased and frequently erroneous, because uninformed or ill-informed, point of view adopted by Schindler and which it becomes a duty to rectify not only so that the picture of Beethoven as he was may be kept true, but that the better motives and impulses which prompted the woman whom he so cordially detested be placed in their proper light also. The rights of a woman and the honor which a world has always accorded to the strongest, noblest, divinest instinct of woman—maternal love—were at stake. The mother of Karl, though she had been convicted and punished for adultery at an earlier period, and though she might not have proved a safe mentor for her son, was yet a mother, his mother. That fact Beethoven was willing to recognize as palliating the conduct of the boy, but he could not bring himself to recognize that it might also palliate if it did not justify the steps which his harshness compelled a mother to take to gratify the need implanted by nature. Johanna van Beethoven is at least entitled to the same hearing at the bar of posterity that she received in the tribunals of her day, and it is the duty of Beethoven's biographer to strip the story of the quarrel between her and her brother-in-law of the romantic excrescences which many writers have fastened upon it. In this narrative the truth will be told, perhaps for the first time, as it is disclosed by the documents, the evidence and the judicial decrees in the case. To set forth these documents in full in the body of the text would call for the sacrifice of much space and sadly interrupted the story; what is essential in them will be given literally, or in outline, whenever it becomes necessary.[7]

After his dismissal from the class of the parish priest at Mödling, Karl van Beethoven was placed in the hands of a private tutor to be prepared for admission to one of the public schools of Vienna—no doubt that known as the Academic Gymnasium. To enter this school the boy had to pass an examination, and for this purpose Beethoven brought him to Vienna about the middle of August. Frau van Beethoven was now determined to wrest from her brother-in-law the authority, which was his as sole guardian, to keep the boy in his care and to direct his training. She took to her aid Jacob Hotschevar, a *Hofconcipist* (clerk or scrivener in the government service), and petitioned the *Landrecht* of Lower Austria to take from Beethoven the authority to direct the future training of his ward. The *Landrecht* was a tribunal with jurisdiction in litigations and other matters affecting the nobility. Acting on the assumption that the Dutch "van," like the German "von," was a badge of noble birth, it had listened to Beethoven's plea and appointed him sole guardian of his nephew, removing the widow from the joint guardianship directed in the will of the boy's father on the score of her immorality, as we already know.

---

[7] Thayer made or procured transcripts of the tribunals in which the struggle for the possession of Karl van Beethoven were made. Readers whose curiosity is not satisfied by these pages are referred to Appendix III of Vol. IV of TDR. (TK, II, 401, n. 1.) See also *A*, III, Appendix C.

The proceedings were begun in September and were dismissed, as the records show, on the 18th of that month. Three days later, that is, on September 21, she applied to the court again, this time for permission to place her son in the Royal Imperial Convict, where he would have board, lodging and instruction. She and Beethoven as "coguardian" were commanded to appear in court on September 23, and the latter was directed to bring the report of the lad's examination with him. There was a postponement of the hearing till September 30, and on October 3d the widow's application was rejected. Thus far victory had gone to Beethoven.

The postponement of the hearing was made in great likelihood to enable Beethoven to change his residence from Mödling to the city (the house on the Gärtnerstrasse). At any rate, Karl was a public school scholar on November 6th, as Fanny Giannatasio records in her diary on that day, together with the fact that her father had met Beethoven, who had shortly before returned from the country. That the boy was in the third grammar class and remained there during the months of November and December, receiving also instruction in pianoforte playing, French and drawing from a private teacher, is known from the court proceedings which were held later. The lad made good progress in his studies, all seemed well and something of the old cordial relations seemed again to be established between Beethoven and the Giannatasios. Fanny writes: "Yesterday Beethoven was with us once again. We have secured a housekeeper for him. He was here three hours and since his hearing was especially bad this day, we wrote everything down. One cannot be in his company without being impressed with his admirable character, his deep sense of what is good and noble. If Karl would but recompense him for the many sacrifices which he makes for his sake! My hopes are intermingled with serious doubts. He will probably make a journey to London this spring. It might be advantageous to him financially in many ways."

Before long Beethoven was at the Giannatasio house again, according to an entry dated November 20. He became interested in the singing of the sisters, singing with them, which produced a comical effect, as he seldom was in tune; but he helped them to give the correct expression to the music. Fanny now deplored that their childish timidity had so long deprived them of such a pleasure, which would now perhaps be of short duration, since he had received a second invitation from England. Within a fortnight the diary chronicles the severest trial that the boy had yet caused his uncle: he ran away from home and sought a haven with his mother. The sympathetic Fanny wrote later:[8] "One day B. came in great excitement and sought counsel and help from my father, saying that Karl had run away! I recall that on this occasion amid our expressions of sympathy he cried out tearfully: 'He is ashamed of me!'" The incident is recorded in her diary under date of December 5; it occurred, apparently two days before. The diarist's

[8] *Grenzboten*, XVI Jhrg. (1857), p. 31. (TDR, IV, 110, n. 3.)

entry is as follows: "Never in my life shall I forget the moment when he came and told us that Karl was gone, had run away to his mother, and showed us his letter as an evidence of his vileness. To see this man suffering so, to see him *weeping*—it was touching! Father took up the matter with great zeal, and with all my sorrow I feel a pleasurable sensation in the consciousness that now we are *much* to Beethoven, yes, at this moment his only refuge. Now he surely perceives his error if he has wronged us in his opinions. Ah! he can never appreciate how highly we esteem him, how much I should be capable of doing for his happiness! How the uniqueness of his character shows itself once again. The naughty child is again with him with the help of the police—the Ravenmother! Oh! how dreadful it is that this man is compelled to suffer so on account of such outcasts. He must go away from here, or she; that will be the outcome. For the present B. will give him into our care; it will be an act of great kindness on my father's part if he receives him, as he will have to look upon him as one under arrest. . . . It did me good when he went away to note that his thoughts were more diverted. He told me that he had been so wrought up by the matter that it took him some time to gather his thoughts. During the night his heart had beat audibly. Alas! and there remains nothing for me to say except that all that we can do is so little! I would give half my life for the man! He always thinks of himself last. He lamented that he did not know what would become of his housekeeping when Karl was gone."

Beethoven went to the mother immediately in the morning to bring back the boy; she promised to release him in the evening; and since Beethoven feared that she would send him away (to Linz or Hungary), he employed the police to get the boy back and turned him over temporarily to Giannatasio again. He was to remain there apparently for the winter.

At the same time the mother was working for her own interests; and on December 7th made a third application to the court:

Johanna van Beethoven (living at Tiefer Graben No. 238 on the second floor) declares to the R. I. Landrecht of Lower A[ustria] that her son Karl van Beethoven *ran away from his uncle and guardian, Hr. Ludwig van Beethoven, without her knowledge and participation, but the same was again returned to him by her through the R. I. chief of police.* At the same time she requested that, since Ludwig van Beethoven according to report intends to send her son to a school and indeed far away from here, perhaps even abroad, he be denied the permission of chief guardianship and that she *once again* will request the sanction to be permitted to send her son to the R.I. University Convict for education and board.

She repeated this request in a petition of December 10th and added the following points. A letter of Giannatasio's dated March 8, 1816, showed that she had to forgo her desire to visit her son or satisfy it once a month and then "like a thief." After Beethoven took the boy, and especially after his removal to Mödling, she was not permitted to see him at all. She had been assured that her son would be admitted to the Convict, but his testimonials had been withheld from her and so she had been unable to file them with her application for a scholarship. His expenses were 750 florins per year for board, lodging, clothes, books, medicines, etc., to pay which 2,000 florins had been deposited in Court and yielded 100 florins interest per annum. She had pledged herself to give one-half of her pension of 333 florins, 20, that is 116 florins, 40 kreutzers towards his education. This amounted to 380 florins V.S., including the interest on the deposit; and she would gladly pay the difference between this sum and 750 florins until she should get the promised scholarship for her son.

Hotschevar supported these petitions in a document like a modern law brief, explaining his interest in the matter on the grounds that his wife was a stepsister of Frau van Beethoven's deceased mother, that the law permitted such an act in all cases where human rights were concerned and that he, having had experience for several years as instructor in the houses of the aristocracy, could not be blamed if he put the knowledge of pedagogics and psychology thus acquired at the service of a lad to whom he bore a family relationship and brought to the attention of the supreme guardian matters which it (the *Landrecht*) could not possibly know concerning its wards unless proceedings were brought before it. He admitted that Frau van Beethoven had years before been guilty of a moral delinquency for which she had been punished, but asserted her right to a standing in court; he then contended: (1) that the mother had illegally been denied all influence over her son partly with, partly without the knowledge of the court, and (2) that her son could not remain under the sole influence of his uncle and guardian without danger of suffering physical and moral ruin. In support of these contentions he recited that the brothers van Beethoven were eccentric men, so often at odds with each other that they might better be called enemies than friends, Carl van Beethoven being pleasantly disposed toward his brother only when he was in need of money from him, and that the suspicion lay near that the boy had been an object of traffic between them, inasmuch as an agreement touching the payment of 1,500 florins had been made only on condition that Ludwig van Beethoven surrender a document which appointed him guardian. Carl van Beethoven, moreover, knowing the animosity which his brother felt towards his wife, had in a codicil to his will expressly said that he did not want Ludwig van Beethoven to be sole guardian of his son but joint guardian with the mother, and had, for the sake of the boy, admonished more compliancy on the part of the mother and more moderation on that of the brother. Although the Court had deprived the mother of the guardianship over her son, it had granted permission to her to visit him; but this privilege had been withheld from her. The statement of the village priest Fröhlich (which has already been given in these pages) was appended to the widow's application as evidence of the physical and moral degeneration of the boy, and for himself Hotschevar says that he had observed after the boy had run away from his uncle that his hands and feet were frostbitten, that he had no seasonable clothing and that his linen and baths had been neglected. The priest's statement was also appealed to to show that the boy had been led into unfilial conduct, indifference toward religion, hypocrisy, untruthfulness and even theft against his guardian—in short, was in danger of becoming a menace to society. He willingly granted Beethoven's readiness and desire to care for his ward, but maintained that his hatred of the mother, his passionate disposition inflamed by the talebearing of others (once naming Giannatasio), made it difficult for him to employ the proper means. Conceding Beethoven's magnanimity, he yet urged that in view of the danger in which the lad was, he ought to forgo the guardianship or associate with himself either the mother or some other capable person, it appearing from the facts in the case that he was "physically and morally unfit" for the post.

Already on December 9th the court had summoned the petitioner and also Beethoven and his nephew to appear in court on the afternoon of December 11th at 4 o'clock. Beethoven brought Karl Bernard with him, no doubt to protect him in his deafness. On the same day the widow appealed to the court that in case the guardian of her son should make application touching the plans for his future training, it be not granted without giving her a hearing. All three were examined. We quote from the minutes of the *Landrecht*:

The ward Carl v. Bethoven appeared, age 12 years, student in the 3rd Latin class, and was questioned:

Had he received good testimonials?

"Eminent" in Latin, "1st class" in other studies.

Why had he left his uncle?

Because his mother had told him she would send him to a public school and he did not think he would make progress under private instruction.

How did his uncle treat him?

Well.

Where had he been of late?

He had been in hiding at his mother's.

Where would he rather live—at his mother's or his uncle's?

He would like to live at his uncle's if he but had a companion, as his uncle was hard of hearing and he could not talk with him.

Had he been prompted by his mother to leave his uncle?

No.

When did he leave him?

Eight days ago.

How could he say that he could not succeed under private instruction when he had made such good progress?

This had been the case since he had studied in public; before that he had received 2nd class in mathematics and had not made it up.

Had his mother commanded him to return to his uncle?

She had wanted to take him back to him herself, but he had resisted because he feared maltreatment.

Had his uncle maltreated him?

He had punished him often, but only when he deserved it; he had been maltreated only once, and that after his return, when his uncle threatened to throttle him.

How long had he been with his mother?

Two days.

Who had given him instruction in religion?

The same teacher who taught him other subjects, formerly the priest at Mödling, who was not kindly disposed towards him because he did not behave himself in the street and babbled in school.

Had he indulged in disrespectful remarks about his mother?

Yes; and in the presence of his uncle, whom he thought he would please in that way and who had agreed with him.

Was he often alone?

When his uncle was not at home he was left wholly alone.

Had his uncle admonished him to pray?

Yes; he prayed with him every morning and evening.

Ludwig v. Bethoven and Joseph Carl Bernhard appeared. Ludwig v. Bethoven was questioned:

How did his nephew Carl leave him?

He did not know exactly; his nephew had made himself culpable; he had charged him with it and the same day in the evening he had received a note of farewell. He could not tell the cause of his departure; his mother may have asked him to come to her the day before, but it might have been fear of punishment.

What had his nephew done?

He had a housekeeper who had been recommended to him by Gianastasio; two of her letters to Frl. Gianastasio and one of the latter's had fallen into his hands; in them it was stated that his nephew had called the servants abusive names, had withheld money and spent it on sweetmeats.

In whose care was his nephew?

He had provided him with a *Correpetitor* for pianoforte playing, French and drawing who came to the house; these studies occupied all the leisure time of his nephew so completely that he needed no care; moreover, he could not trust any of his servants with the oversight of his nephew, as they had been bribed by the boy's mother; he had placed him in the hands of a priest for the development of his musical talent, but the mother had got into an agreement with him also. He would place his ward in the Convict, but the oversight was not strict enough there among so many pupils.

Did he have any testimonials touching his nephew's studies?

He had appended them to his last examination.

Had his nephew not spoken disrespectfully of his mother in his presence?

No; besides, he had admonished him to speak nothing but the truth; he had asked his nephew if he was fond of his mother and he answered in the negative.

How did he get the boy back?

With the help of the police. He had gone to the mother in the forenoon to demand him of her, but she would promise nothing except that she would deliver him back in the evening; he had feared that she intended to take him to Linz, where his brother lived, or to Hungary; for that reason he had gone to the police; as soon as he got him back he placed him in the care of Gianastasio.

What were his objections to having his nephew sent to the Convict?

It was not advisable at present because, as the professor had said, there were too many pupils there and the supervision over a boy like his ward was not adequate.

What means did he purpose to employ in the education of his ward?

His ward's greatest talent was in study and to this he would be held. His means of subsistence were the half of his mother's pension and the interest on 2,000 florins. Heretofore the difference between this sum and the cost had been paid by him and he was willing to assume it in the future if the matter could but once be put in order. As it was not practicable to place his nephew in the Convict now, he knew only of two courses open to him: to keep a steward for him who should always be with him, or to send him for the winter to Gionastasio. After half a year he would send him to the Mölker Convict, which he had heard highly commended, or if he were but of noble birth, give him to the Theresianum.

Were he and his brother of the nobility and did he have documents to prove it?

"Van" was a Dutch predicate which was not exclusively applied to the nobility; he had neither a diploma nor any other proof of his nobility.

Johanna v. Bethoven appeared.

How did her son come to her from the house of his guardian?

He had come to her in the evening for fear of punishment and because he did not like to live with his uncle.

Had she advised him to return to his uncle?

Yes, but her son did not want to do so because he feared maltreatment.

It looked as if she had concealed her son?

She had written to her brother-in-law that she would send her son back to him, but she had not seen him for a long time and was therefore glad to have him with her for awhile, and for this reason she had not sent him back at once.

Had she been forbidden to see her son?

Her wish to do so had been frustrated by telling her of different places where she might see him, but when she went to the places he was not there.

Had her son been taken from her by the police?

She had herself taken him to the police at 4 o'clock.

How did she learn of the plan to send her son out of the country?

Gionastasio had disclosed the project to the police.

Did she consider that her son had been well treated at his uncle's?

She thought it unsuitable for the reasons given in her former application. She wished to say in particular that v. Bethoven had only one servant and that one could not rely on servants; he was deaf and could not converse with his ward; there was nobody to look after the wants of her son satisfactorily; his cleanliness was neglected and supervision of his clothing and washing; persons who had brought him clean linen had been turned back by his guardian.

What prospects had she for caring for her son?

She had previously had the assurance of Count von Dietrichstein that her son would be accepted at the Convict; she had not been to him since because her application [to the Court] had been rejected.

In whose presence had her son spoken disrespectfully of her?

She had not herself heard him do so, nor could she mention the names of persons who had heard him.

From what source would she meet the deficiency in her income which would have to be applied to the support of her son?

She had no fortune herself but the Hofconcipist Hotschevar would defray the expenses.

Was her husband of noble birth?

So the brothers had said; the documentary proof of nobility was said to be in the possession of the oldest brother, the composer. At the legal hearing on the death of her husband, proofs of nobility had been demanded; she herself had no document bearing on the subject.

Hereupon Ludwig v. Bethoven was called up again to produce those letters of the housekeeper and of Frln. Gionastasio of which there was mention in the record, and to deliver all the school reports of his ward.

It remains a mystery, if Johanna spoke the truth in answering the final question, how the case ever got into the *Landrecht* in the first place. As a matter of fact, it deserves to be mentioned that, as later events showed, the lower court espoused the cause of Frau van Beethoven with something like the zeal of an advocate. Beethoven's last statement that "van" was a Dutch predicate not confined to the nobility and that he had no proof of noble birth, is all that the minutes of the court show bearing on this question. His answer, no doubt, raised a doubt in the mind of the court touching its jurisdiction. While both parties were awaiting the results of their efforts, the *Landrecht* made a decision which cut Beethoven to the quick: on December 18th it sent the proceedings to the Vienna Magistracy.

Schindler's comments on the effect of the reference of the case to the Civic Magistrates demand a moment's attention. Schindler says:[9] "The transfer of the case to the Magistracy was felt as an overwhelming blow by Beethoven. It would be difficult to maintain that Beethoven attached importance to appearing in the public eye as of noble birth, his origin as well as family conditions being well known—especially the latter by reason of the humble social position of his brothers. But it is certain that he laid great weight upon having his lawsuit adjudicated by the exceptional upper court, partly because as a matter of fact there was in that tribunal a better appreciation of his importance (as Dame Giannatasio has noted quite correctly), partly because the lower court had an unfavorable reputation which could not inspire in him a hope for the desired outcome. But nevertheless it may be said as sure that neither his genius nor his works of art would have

[9] *Biogr.*, I, pp. 257-58. (TDR, IV, 114.)

given him the privileged position which he occupied in the circles of the nobility had there not been a presumption that he was an equal. This was variously demonstrated as soon as the occurrence in the aristocratic court became known to the public. Not in the middle classes, but in the upper, the little word 'van' had exercised a palpable charm. It is a settled fact that after the incident in the Lower Austrian *Landrecht* the great city of Vienna became too small for our aggrieved master, and had he not been restrained by his sense of duty which was placed upon him by his brother's will, the projected journey to England would have been undertaken and his sojourn there perhaps become permanent."

In one of the Conversation Books used by Beethoven in 1820, there occurs this remark in Beethoven's handwriting: ". . . when it [*sic*][10] learned that my brother was not of the nobility. It is singular, so far as I know, that there is a hiatus here which ought to be filled, for my nature shows that I do not belong among this plebeian m[ass]"; and, in February, 1820, when Peters had observed his dissatisfaction: "The common citizen should be excluded from higher men, and *I* have *gotten amongst* them."[11]

It is also certain that Schindler was not as well informed as he ought to have been in the premises and that his memory often left him in the lurch, as we have frequently seen already and shall see again. Not exact knowledge but an amiable bias in favor of his hero speaks out of his recital. It is scarcely conceivable that Beethoven should have cherished the thought that possibly he was of noble birth or that he seriously encouraged such a belief among his exalted friends.

The nephew's stay at the Giannatasios was not of long duration and the signs of an imminent disruption of a beautiful and profitable friendship soon showed themselves, though for the nonce amiable relations between Beethoven and the Giannatasio family were continued. Yet Fanny saw her lovely illusions melting away. It had been agreed that Karl should not associate with the other pupils at the institute. Willing, perhaps desirous at first, that such an arrangement should be made, it seems that Beethoven felt his *amour propre* hurt by it as soon as the first fit of resentment against the lad gave way before one of his tender moods; now there ensued one of the old fits of moroseness, dissatisfaction and suspicion. He wrote to Giannatasio that Karl's room should be better heated—that he had never had frostbitten hands and feet when living with him (Hotschevar's accusation was evidently rankling in his breast); moreover, too much importance was being attached to his act, and the consequences to the delinquent were being carried too far. In her diary under date December 14, Fanny recognizes "that his moodiness and his weakness for the lad have taken possession of him again and induced him to believe the *liar* rather than his tried friends"; she concludes with the lamentation "that it will never be possible

[10] Schünemann believes that Beethoven meant "he" for the second word (*er* rather than *es*). See Schünemann, I, p. 215.
[11] *Ibid.*, p. 247.

{ 712 }

to gain Beethoven's entire confidence . . . as to what will happen in the future one can only fear the worst."

Let the rest of the year's history be devoted to Beethoven's creative work. Considering the revival of interest and desire on the part of the composer, the net result, as measured by finished products, was not as large as might have been expected. Two explanations for these circumstances may be offered: the first lies in his domestic miseries and the frame of mind in which they kept him for long stretches at a time—that is obvious; the second may be read in his compositions. He was growing more and more prone to reflection, to moody speculation; his mental processes, if not slower than before, were more protracted, and also more profound, and they were occupied with works of tremendous magnitude. The year produced the Sonata in B-flat, Op. 106 and sketches and partial developments of the Symphony in D minor. The Sonata, so two sketchbooks carefully analysed by Nottebohm[12] show, was begun in 1817, and occupied much of the composer's time during 1818.

In a letter to Archduke Rudolph written in June, 1819, Beethoven shed light on the progress of the sonata the year before: ". . . I enclose two pieces[13] in a fair copy which I wrote already last year [1818] before the name-day of Your Imperial Highness [April 17], but despondency and so many sad circumstances, and my health so bad at the time all made me so *discouraged* that only with the greatest anxiety and embarrassment could I approach Your Imperial Highness. From the time I moved to Mödling until nearly the end of my visit there my health improved, but how many calamities confronted me! Meanwhile many things gathered on my writing desk, from which fact I can assure you that I thought of Your Imperial Highness. . . . To the two pieces which I wrote down in manuscript for the name-day of Y. I. H. two others have been added, the last of which is a large Fugato, so that it constitutes a Grand Sonata which will soon be published and long ago *in my heart* was intended for Y. I. H. . . ."

That work continued on the Sonata during the summer of 1818 at Mödling is also shown by a remark that occurs in the middle of the sketches: "A small house there, so small that one has only a little room— Just a few days in this heavenly Briel— Yearning or longing—fulfillment or deliverance."[14] According to Schindler the work was completed in the autumn of this year. Czerny played it in Beethoven's presence in the spring of 1819, and even earlier in the year a copy had been sent to Ries for sale and publication in England, along with the arrangement for quintet of Op. 1, No. 3. In a letter dated January 30, 1819, he writes Ries:

. . . Do everything *for* me that you can; for I need it. Commissions from the Philharmonic Society would have been very welcome. *The reports which Neate*

[12] *II Beeth.*, pp. 123ff., 352. (TDR, IV, 117, n. 1.)

[13] These were the first two movements.

[14] *II Beeth.*, p. 132. Briel or Brühl is a valley in Mödling. (TDR, IV, 117, n. 3.)

sent me about the near failure of the three overtures were vexing to me; *here each of them not only pleased each in its own way* but those in E-flat and C major made a great impression. The fate of these compositions with the P.S. is incomprehensible to me— You will have by now received the arranged quintet and the sonata. See to it that both works, especially the quintet, are engraved at once. More leisure may be taken with the sonata but I should like to have it published inside of two months, or three at the latest. Your earlier letter referred to I did not receive; wherefore I had no hesitation selling both works here—but that is only for Germany. Moreover it will be three months also before the sonata will appear here; but make haste with the quintet. . . .[15]

The Sonata was sold to Artaria in Vienna for 100 ducats. The publisher sent the proofs to Beethoven on July 24, and announced it in the *Wiener Zeitung* of September 15, 1819 with the following words: "Now we shall put aside all the usual eulogies which would be superfluous anyway for the admirers of Beethoven's high artistic talent, thereby meeting the composer's wishes at the same time; we note only in a few lines that this work, which excels above all other creations of this master not only through its most rich and grand fantasy but also in regard to artistic perfection and sustained style, will mark a new period in Beethoven's pianoforte works." It appeared under both French and German title; the latter follows: "Grosse Sonate für das Hammerklavier Seiner Kais: Königl.: Hoheit und Eminenz, dem Durchlauchtigsten Hochwürdigsten Herrn Herrn Erzherzog Rudolph von Oesterreich Cardinal und Erzbischoff von Olmütz, etc., etc., etc., in tiefster Ehrfurcht gewidmet von Ludwig van Beethoven, Op. 106."

Soon after its publication (on October 1st) Beethoven in a jocose letter asked for six copies of the Sonata and six of the Variations on Scottish songs. Beethoven informed Ries of its publication in a letter dated November 10th and wanted to send him a copy to aid him in correcting the English edition, which was not ready. The Sonata Op. 106 was, therefore, the chief product of the year 1818. Beethoven told Czerny that it was to be his greatest; and so it is, not only in its dimensions but also in its contents. "The Sonata was composed under distressful circumstances," said Beethoven in a letter to Ries (March, 1819), "for it is hard to write almost for the sake of bread alone, and to this pass I have come."

Simultaneously with the Sonata, Beethoven was at work on the Ninth Symphony during a large portion of the year. Not alone the Ninth Symphony, a Tenth also was before his fancy, but with neither of them had Schiller's "Ode to Joy" been brought into association, though the employment of the human voice in one of them was already under consideration. Notes in the *Tagebuch* and sketchbooks which, to judge by their context, were written during the summer sojourn in Mödling show the trend of Beethoven's thoughts on religious subjects which were crystallizing or about to crystallize in the idea of writing a great mass.

[15] The Quintet was published in Vienna by Artaria in February, 1819.

In order to write true church music . . . look through all the monastic church chorals and also the strophes in the most correct translations and perfect prosody in all Christian-Catholic psalms and hymns generally.

Sacrifice again all the pettinesses of social life to your art. O God above all things! For it is an eternal providence which directs omnisciently the good and evil fortunes of human men.

> Short is the life of man, and whoso bears
> A cruel heart, devising cruel things,
> On him men call down evil from the gods
> While living, and pursue him, when he dies,
> With cruel scoffs. But whoso is of generous heart
> And harbors generous aims, his guests proclaim
> His praises far and wide to all mankind,
> And numberless are they who call him good.
>   —*Homer.*

Tranquilly will I submit myself to all vicissitudes and place my sole confidence in Thy unalterable goodness, O God! My soul shall rejoice in Thy immutable servant. Be my rock, my light, forever my trust!

Among the sketches for the Sonata in B-flat are memoranda of vocal pieces which came into his mind during his wanderings in the environs of Mödling. Goethe's "Haidenröslein," to which his mind several times turned, occupied him again. His spiritual exaltation finds expression in fragments which he notes as "written while walking in the evening between and on the mountains," among them this:

Gott al - lein ist un - ser Herr. Er al - lein
[God a - lone is God our Lord. He a - lone]

In his letter to Hauschka Beethoven remarked that he was compelled to do a lot of "scribbling" for the sake of money in order to procure leisure for great works. One such pot-boiler was a pianoforte piece in B-flat which bears the inscription "written upon request on the afternoon of August 14, 1818 by Beethoven." There are sketches for the piece, however, among those for the last movement of the B-flat Sonata.[16] Added to the inscription are the words "written upon the request of a lady unknown to him." According to A. B. Marx,[17] this lady was the Polish pianist, Marie Szymanowska. Published first as a supplement to the Berlin *Allgemeine Musikalische Zeitung* in 1824, it did not receive its strange title of "Dernière pensée musicale" until 1840 when it was published separately by Schlesinger in Berlin.

Further "scribbling" may be explained by the fact that he was still engaged

---

[16] *II Beeth.*, p. 137. (TDR, IV, 131, n. 2.)
[17] *Ludwig van Beethoven, Leben und Schaffen* (Berlin, 1875), I, p. 75.

upon arrangements of folk-songs for Thomson (WoO 156), which were published in Thomson's Vol. vi.[18]

With the folksongs must be associated the Variations for Pianoforte alone, or Pianoforte and Flute (or Violin), which he wrote in this and the preceding year and which were published as Op. 105 and 107. ---C. B. Oldman has established the history of these variations[19] which may be summarized here. On January 1, 1816, Thomson asked the composer to send him specimen airs from Germany, Poland, Russia, the Tyrol, Venice and Spain. From his work on British airs for Thomson, Beethoven's interest in folk-songs had been stimulated and previously he had formed the plan to choose his own songs from different countries and arrange them with accompaniment for trio. Thus Beethoven was willing to fall in with this suggestion and sent eighteen such airs on July 8th, followed by one more air shortly afterwards. Thomson failed to find suitable English verses for these melodies, however; and when he made the naive proposal that Beethoven compose for 36 ducats six potpourri overtures for the pianoforte with these melodies as a basis, Beethoven naturally declined the offer. A request from Birchall for variations to favorite English, Scottish and Irish airs also came to naught. Then on June 25, 1817, Thomson offered 72 ducats for variations (not more than 8) on any twelve of the airs "in an agreeable style, and not too difficult." Beethoven did not answer until February 21, 1818, when he made a counter-proposal: "I am willing to write twelve overtures for you for an honorarium of 140 gold ducats, I am willing to write twelve themes with variations for 100 gold ducats, but if you would like me to write twelve overtures and twelve themes with variations *together* or at the same time, I am ready to ask no more for the twelve overtures and the twelve themes varied than 224 ducats." Thomson replied on June 22nd suggesting that Beethoven could choose the majority of the themes from the Scottish airs that he had already harmonized and add a flute part *ad libitum* to the accompaniment. He added: "And it would be quite desirable if you wrote the variations in a style that is *familiar* and *easy* and a bit brilliant, so that the majority of our ladies may play them and relish them." On November 18, Beethoven acknowledged receipt of 140 ducats in gold for the variations upon the twelve themes and arrangement of eight Scottish airs to be sung or played as trios. Thomson received the twelve sets of variations on December 28th, and he published nine of them in 1819,[20] after Beethoven had made certain revisions in response to Thomson's criticisms. --- Beethoven composed sixteen Themes and Variations on folk-song material in all; six of them were published by Artaria in Vienna (Op. 105) and the other ten by Simrock in Bonn (Op. 107).

---

[18] See KHV, p. 655.
[19] "Beethoven's Variations on National Themes: Their Composition and First Publication," *Music Review*, xii (1951), pp. 45-51.
[20] Entitled "Twelve National Airs with Variations," they were published in three volumes of three each (Op. 105, Nos. 1-6 and Op. 107, Nos. 2, 6, 7). See D. W. MacArdle, "A Checklist of Beethoven's Chamber Music," *Music and Letters*, xxvii (1946), p. 53.

Mention has already been made of Beethoven's plan to select songs of different continental countries to supply with his own accompaniment. Besides the eighteen airs sent to Thomson in 1816, Beethoven sent six more within the next two years and granted the publisher the exclusive right to sell them all in his letter of November 18, 1818. However, of these twenty-four airs[21] only three were used for keyboard variations: WoO 158, Nos. 5, 6 and 16 in Op. 107 as Nos. 1, 5 and 7. Only one is represented in the Collected Works Edition (the Venetian song "La gondoletta," WoO 157, No. 12). The other twenty-three (WoO 158) were published in 1941 by Breitkopf and Härtel.[22]

The compositions for the year were:

1816-18. Twenty-three songs of Different Countries, WoO 158; 1 Danish, 2 German, 1 Hungarian, 1 Italian, 2 Polish, 2 Portuguese, 4 Russian, 3 Spanish, 2 Swedish, 5 Tyrolean.

1817-18. Six Varied Themes for Pianoforte, with optional accompaniment of flute or violin, Op. 105.

Sonata for Pianoforte in B-flat major, Op. 106.

Ten Varied Themes for Pianoforte with optional accompaniment of flute or violin, Op. 107.

Twelve Scottish Airs, WoO 156.

About 1818. Canon. "Ich bitt' dich, schreib' mir die Es-Scala auf," WoO 172, for Vincenz Hauschka.

1818. "Ich bin bereit," WoO 201, in a letter to Hauschka.

"O Hoffnung," WoO 200, 4-measure theme for Archduke Rudolph, who wrote variations on this theme, which were published in December, 1819.

Piece for Pianoforte in B-flat major, WoO 60.

The publications for the year were:

By Thomson in Edinburgh and Preston in London:

"A Select Collection of Original Scottish Airs with Introductory and Concluding Symphonies and Accompaniments for the Piano Forte, Violin and Violoncello by Haydn and Beethoven." Of the thirty songs, twenty-five were by Beethoven (Op. 108) and five by Haydn.

By *Wiener Modenzeitung*, March 31, as a musical supplement:

"Resignation" (Count Paul von Haugwitz), WoO 149.

---

[21] In the letter Beethoven writes "twenty-five melodies" (See *A*, III, p. 1424), but Kinsky-Halm (KHV, p. 663) argue that Beethoven should have written "twenty-four," since on June 17, 1823, Thomson turned the publishing rights of *twenty-four* Beethoven airs over to the publishers Paine and Hopkins.

[22] Ed. by G. Schünemann with the title "Neues Volksliederheft." Previously, two songs, "Bolero a solo" and "Schwedisches Wiegenlied," were published singly. See KHV, p. 664.

CHAPTER XXXII

THE YEAR 1819

KARL'S EDUCATION—THE CONVERSATION BOOKS— COMPOSITION OF THE *MISSA SOLEMNIS* BEGUN

T H E key-note for much that must occupy us in a survey of the year 1819 is sounded by two letters to Archduke Rudolph. The first is a New Year's greeting:

Everything that can be gathered up into one wish and be called salutary; wealth, happiness and a blessing, is included in my wish which is offered to Y. I. H. on this day. May a wish for myself also be graciously entertained by Y. I. H.; namely, that I may continue to enjoy the grace of Y. I. H. in the future.— A terrible event took place recently in my family affairs, which for a time robbed me of all my reasoning powers; and to this must be charged the circumstance that I have not called upon Y. I. H. in person nor made mention of the masterly Variations of my highly honored and exalted pupil, the favorite of the Muses. I do not dare to express either by word of mouth or in writing my thanks for the surprise and favor with which I have been honored, inasmuch as I occupy *much too humble* a position, nor dare I, much as I would like and ardently as I long to do so, *repay like with like*. May the heavens hear and fulfil my wishes especially for the health of Y. I. H. In a few days I hope to hear the masterpiece that was sent to me performed by Y. I. H. himself; and nothing can give me greater joy than to have contributed towards Y. I. H.'s speedy assumption of the position already prepared for Your Highness atop Parnassus.

Beethoven, it will be remembered, had composed a four-measure theme "O Hoffnung" in the preceding year for the benefit of his patron's creative efforts. The Archduke responded to this assignment from his teacher by writing forty variations on this theme and dedicating the work to Beethoven. Of the publishers' interest in this exceptional work we shall hear anon.

The events of the final months of 1818 had indeed been devastating ones for Beethoven, and the "terrible" one was of course Karl's running away to his mother in early December, which to the uncle was not the natural result of a boy of twelve having been forcibly separated from his mother, but a terrible misfortune and personal affront. Unfortunately the struggle between the mother and the uncle over the boy must occupy many pages in the account of the years ahead.

The second letter to the Archduke, however, takes us to a topic of the highest creative endeavor. It was written in early June, and we quote the pertinent passages:

Your Imperial Highness!

On the day when Y. I. H. most graciously sent for me, I was not at home, and immediately thereafter I contracted a violent cold, so that I must write to Y. I. H. reclining near my bed— Despite the mass of congratulations which may have been pouring in to you, my most gracious Sir, I know full well that it will not be without *sacrifice to Y. I. H.* that this new honor is bestowed. But I think of what a widening sphere of action will be opened thereby for you and for your great noble-mindedness. So I can only extend my congratulations about this honor to Y. I. H. along with the others. There is almost nothing that is good—without sacrifice, and this appears to apply directly to the nobler, superior man more than others, thereby his virtue becomes tested.

This I might sing out now from the bottom of my heart, were Y. I. H. completely recovered; but the new sphere of action, the transformation, the subsequent travels will certainly bring back soon the priceless health of Your Imperial Highness to a perfect state; and then I shall elaborate on the above theme with a hearty A—men or Allelujah— . . . .

Beethoven returns to this subject later in the letter:

The day when a High Mass of mine shall be performed at the ceremonies for Y. I. H. will be for me the most beautiful day of my life, and God will inspire me so that my weak powers may contribute to the glorification of this solemn day— . . . .

The new honor "bestowed" upon the Archduke was first his elevation to Cardinal and then to Archbishop of Olmütz. He was officially informed of the first on April 24, 1819, and of the second on June 4, 1819, and the date of his installation was set for March 9, 1820. The following testimony of

---

[1] MacArdle discusses the musical transformation of Beethoven's theme for the Archduke "O Hoffnung" (WoO 200) to the expression "Erfüllung" (WoO 205e) quoted here. See MacArdle and Misch, *New Beethoven Letters* (Norman, 1957), p. 248, n. 4.

Schindler is responsible for the confusion in determining just when Beethoven started composing his great work which was to be known as the *Missa Solemnis*. Schindler writes:[2] "Without invitation of any kind Beethoven resolved to compose a mass for the solemnity, thus turning again after the lapse of many years to that branch of his art towards which, after the symphonies— as he himself often said— he felt himself most drawn. . . . I saw the score begun late in the autumn of 1818, after the gigantic Sonata in B-flat major, Op. 106, had just been finished."

However, in the first edition of his biography (p. 113) Schindler writes: "He began to labor on the new work in the winter of 1818-19." A sketchbook in the Wittgenstein Collection in Vienna has helped to show that Schindler's earlier statement was closer to the mark. This is the first known sketchbook to contain work on the Mass. From pages 4 to 15 there are sketches for variations on a waltz by Diabelli, immediately followed by sketches for the *Kyrie* of the Mass. In discussing the sketchbook, Unger writes:[3] "Until now it had been assumed that the beginning of 1820 was the earliest point of time to date the start of work on the variations—but this sketchbook refers it back to the first months of the year 1819; for the choice of Archduke Rudolph as Archbishop of Olmütz took place on June 4, 1819, and the approaching appointment was certainly known some months earlier, that is, probably in the beginning of 1819. Since the installment was to be solemnized in March, 1820, and the master had decided on this work for that purpose, it may be accepted that the preliminary work fell in the first months of the year 1819."

A pocket sketchbook, filled mostly with sketches for the Mass was acquired by the Beethoven-Haus at Bonn in 1899. It has been transcribed and published by Dr. Joseph Schmidt-Görg, who dates it from December, 1819, to about the middle of April, 1820. The 44 page book (there was originally another sheet) contains a few sketches for the second part of the *Gloria* and all parts of the *Credo*. There are a few ideas for the *Sanctus* and one for the *Agnus Dei*. Thus the *Kyrie* and the *Gloria* were the work of the main part of the year, whereas work on the *Credo* did not begin until well into the fall.

Now to return to the first topic, the family struggle. The long court procedures had been wearing, and the final blow had been the transfer of the case to the City Magistracy because Beethoven was not of the nobility. Doubtless he was also filled with fear as to what the decision of the new tribunal would be.

At this point a few official data are wanting, but the suspension of Beethoven from the guardianship of his nephew can only be stated as having been determined by the magistrates immediately after the beginning of the new year. In consequence of this, the boy was for a few weeks with his

---

[2] *Biogr.*, i, p. 269. (TDR, iv, 326, n. 2.)

[3] "Die Beethoven-Handschriften der Familie W. in Wien" in *NBJ*, vii, pp. 167-68.

mother. On January 10, Fanny Giannatasio writes in her diary: "What Müller tells me about Beethoven pains me deeply. The wicked woman has finally succeeded in triumphing over him. He has been removed from the guardianship,[4] and the wicked son returns to the source of his wickedness. I can imagine Beethoven's grief. It is said that since yesterday he has been entirely alone and eats apart from the others. He ought to know that Karl is glad to be with his mother; it would ease the pain of the separation."

On January 7 the magistrates summoned Beethoven (who still lived in the Gärtnergasse), the boy, the mother, Hotschevar and the curator, Dr. Schönauer, to appear before them on January 11. Of what action was taken that day there is no record, but Hotschevar's attack brought out a vigorous defense in the shape of a letter sent by Beethoven to the Magistracy,[5] in which he maintained the superiority of the educational plan which he was pursuing over that which had been proposed by the mother, proclaimed the magnanimity and virtuousness of all his acts and discharged a broadside of accusation and insinuation against Frau van Beethoven and the priest who had come to her help. We can make room for only a few passages: "His exceptional capacity, and partly also his peculiarities, call for exceptional measures; and I never did a more beneficial or magnanimous act than when I took my nephew to myself and personally assumed charge of his education. Seeing that (according to Plutarch) a Philip did not think it beneath his dignity to direct the education of his son Alexander and give him the great Aristotle for a teacher because he did not consider the ordinary teachers suitable, and a Laudon[6] looked after the education of his son *himself*, why should not such beautiful and sublime example be followed by others? Already during his lifetime his *father* entrusted my nephew to *me* and I confess that I feel myself better fitted than anybody else to *incite my nephew to virtue and industry by my own example.* . . . Had the mother been able to subdue her wicked disposition and permitted my plans to take their quiet development, a very favorable result would have followed; but when a *mother of this sort* seeks to involve her child in the secrets of her own vulgar and evil surroundings, and in his tender years leads him astray to deception (a plague for children!!!), to bribery of my servants, to *untruthfulness*, by *laughing at him* when he tells the truth, yes, even *giving him money* to awaken in him lusts and desires which are harmful, tells *him* that such things are trifles which *by me and others would be accounted* grave faults, the already difficult task becomes more difficult and dangerous. . . . Gifts of fortune may be acquired; *morality* must be *implanted* early (particularly when a child has had the misfortune to suck in *such mother's milk*, was in her care for several years, was put to thoroughly *bad uses, even* had to help

---

[4] He had not been removed, but only temporarily suspended; he retained the supervision of the boy's education. (TK, III, 2, n. 1.)

[5] The letter was dated erroneously February 1, 1818, instead of 1819. (TK, III, 2, n.2.)

[6] Field Marshal, Baron Gideon Ernst von Laudon (1717-90) according to his biographer Wilhelm von Janko, was educated solely by his father, Gerhard Otto von Laudon.

deceive his father). Furthermore, he will inherit from me; and even now I could leave him enough to *keep him from want* while continuing his studies until he should receive an appointment. We need only *quiet and no more interference from the mother,* and *the beautiful goal which I have set* will be attained. . . . Ought I now to reply to the intrigues of a Hr. Court-scrivener Honschova [Hotschevar] *against me,* or to the *priest of Mödling,* who is despised by his congregation, who is suspected of being guilty of *illicit intercourse,* who lays his pupils military fashion on a form to be thrashed and who could not forgive me because I kept watch on *him* and would not permit my nephew to be caned like a brute— Ought I? No, the association of these men with Frau van Beethoven bears *witness* against *them both,* and *only such* could make common cause *with her against me. . . ."*

From the records of the Magistracy and his own words it follows that Beethoven did not send his nephew to a public school, but engaged a private tutor under whose care he continued his studies in an institute conducted by Johann Kudlich.[7] Beethoven held this man in great esteem judging by his letter to the Magistracy (of February 1, 1819) in which he says "That Herr v. Kudlich teaches and practices himself the basic methods of the university which all connoisseurs consider the best as I do myself." Besides the ordinary subjects, Karl received instruction from Kudlich in French, drawing and music; his religious training was entrusted to a priest. This state of affairs lasted till the end of March, when Beethoven announced a desire to resign the guardianship—persuaded to take this step, it is fair to presume, by the magistrates, who, in the end, would have been obliged to remove him. Karl was living with his mother at the time. According to the court records, Beethoven left the matter of education "entirely to Kudlich," but it was given to him to propose the name of a guardian, either in place of himself or as an associate. He consulted earnestly with his friends as to what was to be done with the boy and who would be his guardian, and they were sorely tried by his constitutional indecision.

The friend who was the most helpful and influential in these affairs was the writer and editor, Joseph Karl Bernard. He was born at Horatitz in Bohemia in 1775 and studied in Prague and Heidelberg. In 1800 he became an officer in the Hofkriegsrat at Vienna, from where he worked slowly into the profession of author. He became an editor of the *Modenzeitung* in 1818, and in the fall of the next year assumed the head-editorship of the *Wiener Zeitung.* His acquaintance with Beethoven started at the time of the Vienna Congress, and by 1819 his name was appearing regularly in the Conversation Books. While other members of the circle, such as Oliva, were given the perfunctory jobs of taking dictation and running errands, Bernard was

---

[7] Johann Kudlich's institute was on the Erdbergerstrasse No. 91, in the Landstrasse (TDR, IV, 138, n. 1), the same district in which Beethoven lived at the time. According to Frimmel (*FRBH,* I, p. 308), it was not developed enough to become a school until the following year.

entrusted with a real responsibility: the reworking of the contents of Beethoven's documents until they were legally acceptable. His friendship and advice were invaluable at this time.[8]

In the Conversation Books for March and April, 1819, Bernard writes:[9]

What must be done is to select as guardian a man who has your entire confidence both as respects morality and pedagogical skill, and with whom you may always remain on friendly terms concerning the affair. Since Kudlich has more influence on Karl than . . . Giànatassio [Giannatasio], it is my opinion that you seek no further for someone who would meet every requirement.— It would merely be very troublesome for you.

Beethoven seemed to be in doubt, for he had a preference for his friend the magisterial Councillor Tuscher.[10] In these consultations, the project of sending the boy away from Vienna was discussed, and in that connection the name of Sailer in Landshut[11] was suggested, which appealed to the composer. Bernard says again:

If you want peace of mind I think it wise that you name a guardian as you were willing to do yesterday. But if it is possible to send the boy to Sailer at Landshut, it would, of course, be better still, since then you could feel assured that he was in the best of hands. Even if you have Tuscher as co-guardian, your case will not be bettered, inasmuch as all cares will still rest on you. Perhaps Tuscher and Kudlich might jointly assume the guardianship—this might be very advantageous. All the same, everything will remain as heretofore, even if you send him away he will remain with Kudlich until a change has been made. So long as you are guardian and Karl remains here, you will not only have all the cares as heretofore, but also be compelled to fight the mother and all her intrigues. Have Karl sent for the present again to Kudlich, meanwhile the matter may be straightened out.[12]

Beethoven seems to have expressed a doubt as to Tuscher's willingness to serve as guardian. Bernard continues: "Perhaps he might be more easily persuaded if a co-guardian like Kudlich were appointed.— It is not necessary to settle everything by tomorrow. If we go to Omeyer[13] tomorrow morning, then to Tuscher and Kudlich, we can come to an understanding as to what will be the best thing to do."

Tuscher, if we are correct in recognizing his handwriting, permitted himself to be persuaded, though a bit under protest; he foresaw difficulties. The

---

[8] See Max Unger, "Beethovens Konversationshefte als biographische Quelle," *DM*, Vol. 34 (1942), p. 382.

[9] See Schünemann, I, pp. 30-32.

[10] It was at the request of Matthias von Tuscher that Beethoven wrote the "Abschiedsgesang" in 1814 for the farewell party of Dr. Leop. Weiss.

[11] Professor Johann Michael Sailer at Landshut University in Bavaria. A famous Catholic orator, Sailer later became a bishop at Regensburg. (Cf. TDR, IV, 140, n. 2.)

[12] At the time of this consultation the boy was with his mother. Later, he was with Kudlich and remained there perhaps until Beethoven went to Mödling. Kudlich was instructed not to permit any communication between him and his mother. (TDR, IV, 139, n. 2.)

[13] Joseph von Ohmayer was of noble birth and a doctor of law. He appears in a Conversation Book of 1820 (Schünemann, II, 30).

Magistracy at the suggestion of Beethoven thereupon appointed the Magisterial Councillor Matthias von Tuscher guardian of the boy on March 26. He was commanded to place his ward, then "living with his mother, Johanna van Beethoven," in another place for bringing up and education under proper care, and submit his opinion touching the proposition of the mother and Hotschevar that he be entered in a public institute of learning before the expiration of the second school semester, that Beethoven contribute to the cost and that the share of the mother's pension and the interest on the money deposited for the boy be applied to this end. Tuscher was decidedly of the opinion that the boy must be sent away for a time and was agreed with the plan of placing him with Prof. Sailer in Landshut after it had been broached to him. For this the consent of the Magistracy and the police authorities and a passport were necessary. In the opinion of one of Beethoven's advisers (Bach) Tuscher was to be informed of the plan only after the passport had been obtained, but before the mother, who had already found "a channel," could take steps to communicate with Tuscher. Beethoven applied to the city authorities for a passport for two years for his ward. On April 23, the authorities asked of the Magistracy if there were any objections to the proposed step. The Magistracy objected to the boy's being sent into a foreign country, but asked Tuscher if he were not willing to withdraw his application and name an institute in Austria. Tuscher declined and set forth the great hopes which he placed in the training to be had of a man like Sailer, who, "because of his reverence for the talents of the composer, Beethoven, was especially bound to him," and hence would bestow upon his charge the strictest oversight and care, which was of great importance in the case of a boy who was "extremely cunning and an adept in every sort of craftiness." In replying to the municipal authorities the Magistracy (on May 7) conceded the necessity of withdrawing the boy from his mother's influence, but thought it unnecessary to send him out of the country on this account, against which the mother had protested and the curator of the ward, Dr. Schönauer, had declared himself. The passport was therefore refused. Beethoven had taken a step which seems to have been made to prevent the widow from securing help for her plans from a source higher than any that had yet been invoked and to enlist that higher power in his own behalf. He appealed to Archduke Rudolph to use his influence with Archduke Ludwig, next younger brother of Emperor Franz I, to aid him in his project of sending his nephew far away from the mother's influence. In the letter written to the Archduke[14] he stated that it had been his intention to petition Archduke Ludwig in the premises, but there had thitherto appeared to be no occasion for so doing for the reason that all the authorities who had jurisdiction in the matter were convinced of the advisability of the step, viz.: the Police, the Supervisory Guardianship Court and the guardian.

---

[14] It is undated, but to judge from the contents and the sequence of events it was written in May. (TDR, IV, 142.)

He had heard, however, that the mother intended to seek an audience of Archduke Ludwig to prevent the execution of his plan. Convinced that she would stop at nothing in the way of calumniation, he expressed the hope that his reputation for morality would suffice as a refutation of her slanders, and that Archduke Rudolph would bear testimony in his behalf.

The plan to send the nephew out of the country had been frustrated and had to be abandoned; what further could be done? His mind being filled with artistic projects of the greatest magnitude, Beethoven was desirous to pass the summer months again in Mödling, where he moved on May 12th; but after the experiences of the preceding year nothing could be hoped for his nephew in that quarter. Now he came to a realization of the advantages which Giannatasio's institute had offered and in a letter to Giannatasio asked him again to take the lad till other arrangements had been made. The Giannatasio family were fearful lest such a proceeding might work harm to their institution, and on June 17 visited Beethoven at Mödling to tell him that his wishes could not be complied with. "Grievously as it pained us," Fanny writes in her diary, "to refuse Beethoven anything, I am yet so convinced of the necessity of the step and that it could do us no good, but on the contrary harm, that I prefer to have it so."

Thereupon the lad was sent to the institute of Joseph Blöchlinger.[15] Claudius Artaria, who was one of the teachers there (1821-1824), recalled in later years that Karl was one of the older scholars, "naturally talented, but somewhat conceited because he was the nephew of Beethoven." He also saw the mother there a few times, but remembered nothing in particular in connection with her visits. The lad appears to have prospered during the early part of his stay at the school. In December, 1819 Peters (?) writes in a Conversation Book.[16]

A great deal has been gained in that the boy has again become orderly in his public studies— Plöchlinger [*sic*] moreover, though not exactly brilliant, seems to be good.

The public school system acts as a restraint on him. . . .

Your nephew looks well, handsome eyes—charm, a speaking physiognomy, and excellent bearing. I would continue his education for only two years more. . . .

•~•

He is always present, and thus she can do him no harm. However he is agreed that she spoils the boy—

•~•

When you have acquired the sole guardianship, then do you decide and he will obey.

•~•

Your views are admirable but not always reconcilable with this wretched world.

---

[15] Joseph Blöchlinger (1788-1855) opened his school in 1814 in the Landstrasse suburb on the Kaiserstrasse No. 26 (now Josephstadt- strasse). He had studied with the famed Swiss teacher, Pestalozzi.

[16] Schünemann, I, pp. 128-29.

Tuscher, a member of the Magistracy, was compelled to recognize that his colleagues were wholly under the influence of Frau van Beethoven and Hotschevar, and that he could do no service to his friend or his friend's ward; on July 5, he applied to be relieved of the guardianship which, he said, had become "in every respect burdensome and vexatious," on the ground that "the multiplicity of official duties as well as various other considerations would not permit him longer to administer the office." Beethoven took this action in very bad part, and Tuscher shared the fate of many others of being for a space an object of the composer's critical ill-will. Beethoven now served notice on the Magistracy that he would resume the guardianship under the testamentary appointment and that he had placed his ward in Blöchlinger's institution. On July 15 he wrote to Archduke Rudolph that confusion still reigned in his domestic affairs, no hope or comfort was in sight, all of his structures were blown away, as if by the wind. He adds: "The present proprietor of the institute in which I have placed my nephew, a pupil of Pestalozzi, is of the opinion that it will be difficult for him and my poor nephew to achieve a desirable outcome— But he is also of the opinion that there could be nothing more profitable than removal of my nephew abroad."

Beethoven continued, during the summer and fall, to bombard his friends and those who were helping him with many long letters, containing directives and invectives. Evidently Blöchlinger allowed the boy's mother to visit him at the school, a fact which infuriated Beethoven. Blöchlinger received several violently worded epistles from him on the subject, in which Beethoven refers to himself as "sole guardian" though he had not been legally appointed as such after Tuscher's resignation. Johann apparently entered the controversy in the summer, for in one letter of the summer to Bernard, Beethoven says: "And my worthy brother has become involved (he has just bought an estate worth 20,000 thalers or gulden, and you can be sure that he now helps to corrupt) in that he wants him [Karl] to become an Apothecary, etc." In another letter he says "On no account must my brother be admitted, for he will *only* talk about all that he can have with him. . . ." On Sept. 14 he wrote Blöchlinger: "*Only the following individuals have free access to my nephew, Herr von Bernard, Herr von Oliva, Herr von Piuk, the Referent.*" This last was Franz Xaver Piuk, who was Referent, or Recording Secretary for the court in this affair. Beethoven had written him fully and at the time seemed to have enlisted his support. Further in the letter to Blöchlinger he continues: "*My nephew is not to go out of the house without my written permission*—from which it is plain what course is to be followed towards the mother— I insist that in this respect *strict obedience* be given to what the authorities and I have ordained." Since these letters are highly repetitive in style and content, one should suffice us here, in order to show the composer's distraught state of mind. This is a letter to Bernard in which the recipient, Oliva (who had recently returned to Vienna) and Blöchlinger all come in for chastisement because they took a more moderate view of the boy's mother:

I cannot hide the fact that ever since we have known each other your conduct has often caused me grief. You seem to pay attention to the flattery of poor wretched people and thereupon act the protector; by this means you injure your friends because by this same protection you are hoping to find everything good and for the best. The present affair shows again how false is your stand and how without regard for me you have added new vexations to the old ones— This man is coarse, I might say a very coarse person— You have given your approval to his miserable ideas and betrayed a friend. Only too well did I notice how carelessly everything was arranged with regard to this evil person. Oliva was not smooth enough, and you were not rough enough for this *non-Swiss* lout, for he is, no matter where he may be from, a lout.[17]— *Out of esteem for me he speaks of my unreasonableness*—what logic— On the other hand he solicits *your good will* again— You should not be contagious to this, there *is no honor* from such a creature— But—I must say it occurs to me that you are as much my enemy as a bit my friend— So my nephew should be really hostile to me, and, if so, then he should be allowed to continue so? or attempts could be made to see whether *he loves this raven mother more than me?* You gave your approval to these miserable ideas of this wretched pedagogical creature, without thinking of the complete injustice of it. You yourself a few days ago in the city gave me to understand clearly enough that my nephew hates me—oh, may the whole miserable mob be cursed and damned—

It is not known whether the Magistracy was immediately informed of all of the new steps which Beethoven had taken, though in his draft of the memorandum to the Court of Appeal Beethoven states that he "wrote" to them that he had resumed the guardianship. There is reference in a letter to Bernard dated August 2 that Johanna had forwarded a statement "against me" to the Magistrate.— Be that as it may, as chief guardian the court determined if possible to put an end to the continual friction and undertook an investigation of all the educational experiments which had been made, arriving at the conclusion that the boy had been "subject to the whims of Beethoven and had been tossed back and forth like a ball from one educational institution to another." For this reason it decreed, on September 17, that Tuscher's request for relief be granted, but that the guardianship should not again be entrusted to Beethoven but to the mother, the natural guardian under the law, with a capable and honest man as coguardian. To this office Leopold Nussböck, municipal sequestrator, was appointed.

Beethoven protested against the action in a letter which the Magistracy received on October 31. Having been absent from the city at the time, "on a matter of business," he had made no objection to the appointment of Herr Nussböck as guardian of his nephew, but, returning with the intention of remaining in Vienna, he wished to resume the guardianship, as this was

[17] Blöchlinger was born in Gobelingen, Switzerland (*FRBH*, I, p. 50).

essential to the welfare of the boy, the mother having neither the will nor the strength to look after his training. He was the more insistent on a resumption of this duty since he had learned that owing to lack of money the boy was to be removed from the institution which he had selected for him. He charged that the mother wished to take her son to her home so that she might be able to expend his income, including the half of her pension which she was obliged to devote to his education, upon herself. He asked that the intermediary guardianship be taken from Nussböck and be restored to him without delay.

Acting as a legal advisor to Beethoven at this time was Johann Baptist Bach, who had helped him since 1816 in his dealings with the authorities concerning his nephew. A distinguished Vienna lawyer, Schindler describes him as "a man of many accomplishments including a practising lover of music, who was active on more than a dilettante basis, particularly as violon-cellist in a quartet. The high respect which Dr. Bach enjoyed is demonstrated by the fact that three times he was elected Dean of the Faculty of Law at the University of Vienna."[18] Concerning his petition to the Magistracy, Beethoven wrote to Dr. Bach at great length on October 27:

You will have already received the communication from Frau van Beethoven. That person is too lacking in moral worth for me to refute her attacks against me. His Imperial Highness, Eminence and Cardinal, who treats me as a friend and not as a servant, would unhesitatingly bear witness to my morality, and to all the silly twaddle about Olmütz, not a word of which is true. So far as one knows, His Highness himself will spend at most six weeks of the year there. . . . [Johanna had charged that Beethoven as the Archduke's teacher would now be obliged to spend most of his time at Olmütz.]

The chief points are that I be recognized at once as sole guardian; I will accept no coguardian; that the mother be excluded from intercourse with her son *in the Institute* because in view of her *immorality* there cannot be enough watchmen there and she confuses the master by the false statements and lies which she tells him. Also she has led her son to tell shameful lies and make charges *against me,* and she herself accuses me of having given him too much or too little; I will substantiate all these statements with evidence— But that the claims of humanity may not be overlooked, she may see her son occasionally at my home in the presence of the master and other eminent people. . . . It is my opinion that you should insist stoutly and irrevocably that I be *sole* guardian and that this un-natural mother shall see her son only *at my house.* My well known humanity and culture as well as my accustomed humaneness towards others are a guarantee that my treatment of her will be no less generous than that given her son. Moreover I think that all this should be done quickly and that if possible we ought to get the Appellate Court to assume the superior guardianship. Since I have brought my nephew into a higher category, neither he nor I belong to the M[agistracy] under whose guardianship are only innmakers, shoemakers and tailors—

18 *Biogr.,* I, p. 257.

As regards his present maintenance, it shall be cared for as long as I live, for the future he has 7,000 florins V.S. of which his mother has the usufruct during life—also 2,000 fl. (or a little more since I have reinvested it for him), the interest on which belongs to *him*, and 4,000 florins in silver *of mine* are lying in the bank; as he is to inherit all my property this belongs to his capital. . . .

—◦◦◦⟨The sum of 4,000 florins in silver mentioned in the letter had had an interesting history. The money was presented to Beethoven by the nobility at the Congress of Vienna, but he considered it as savings earmarked for his nephew and therefore untouchable. The money was first deposited with Steiner in July, 1816, at an interest of eight per cent. Three years later Beethoven withdrew it from Steiner and on July 13, 1819, he used it to buy eight shares of bank stock, on the advice of Baron von Eskeles, director of the Viennese bank, Arnstein and Eskeles.[19]⟩◦◦—

The Magistracy disposed of Beethoven's protest and application on November 4, by curtly referring him to the disposition made of his petition in September, when he was removed from the guardianship. Beethoven asked for a reconsideration, but without avail, and the only recourse remaining to him was the appeal to the higher court which had already been suggested to Dr. Bach. The story of that appeal belongs to the year 1820.

Meanwhile the association of Councillor Peters with him in the guardianship had been broached and was the subject of discussion with his friends. In December the following is written in a Conversation Book:

[Bernard] The Magistracy has till now only made a minute of the proceedings and will now hold a session to arrive at a decision. It is already decided that you shall have the guardianship, but a 2nd is to be associated with you. Since no one still has any objection to Peters, there will be no difficulty in this.
[Peters] The matter will be ordered according to your wishes and my humble self will take care of Herr Plechlinger [*sic*]. The mother will not be admitted to the institute unless you are present, 4 times a year is enough.
[Bernard] Nor the guardian either?— The Magistracy has compromised itself nicely.

Further along in the same Conversation Book, Dr. Bach writes: "If we are willing to let the widow be named coguardian, there will be less difficulties in the affair.—As coguardian she will have no authority, only the honor of being associated in the guardianship. She will be a mere figurehead."[20] Whether the conversations noted at the time referred to the case on appeal or to the application still pending before the Magistracy, or some to the one, some to the other, it is impossible to determine. The record of the refusal of the Magistracy has not been procured, but the decree of the Appellate Court gives December 20 as its date.

[19] See the letter from Steiner to Beethoven dated December 29, 1820. See also Max Reinitz, *Beethoven im Kampf mit dem Schicksal* (Vienna, 1924), p. 110; and Max Unger, "Beethoven als Kapitalist," *Schweizerische Musikzeitung*, Vol. 65 (1925), pp. 57ff.
[20] Schünemann, I, pp. 113, 119.

Frequent citations from the so-called "Conversation Books" made in the course of the narrative touching the later phases of the controversy over the guardianship call for some remarks upon this new source of information opened in these years. In the *Niederrheinische Musikzeitung*, No. 28 of 1854, Schindler wrote: "Beethoven's hearing had already become too weak for oral conversation, even now with the help of an ear-trumpet, in 1818, and recourse had now to be had to writing.[21] Only in the case of intercourse with Archduke Rudolph, and here because of his gentle voice, the smallest of the ear-trumpets remained of service for several years more." That he was, partly by the ear and partly by the eye, to judge of the correctness of the performance of his music, Schindler stated in the same article—a fact also known from many other sources; this was the case even to his last year. When after the death of Beethoven, such of his manuscripts and papers as were thought to be salable were set apart, there remained in the hands of von Breuning a lot of letters, documents and Conversation Books. The estimated value in the inventory of the manuscripts and the price obtained for them at the auction sale, indicate how utterly worthless from a pecuniary point of view that other collection was thought to be; as, however, they might be of use to some future biographer, it was well to have them preserved, and doubtless a small gratification to Schindler for his great sacrifices and very valuable services to Beethoven in these last months, the only one which he as guardian to the absent nephew could make; so Breuning gave them to him. The Conversation Books, counting in as such those which were really nothing but a sheet or two of paper loosely folded, were only about 400 in number, or less than fifty per annum for the last nine years of Beethoven's life—that being the period which they cover. There is no source of information for the biographer of Beethoven which at first sight appears so rich and productive and yet, to the conscientious writer, proves so provokingly defective and requires such extreme caution in its use as these Conversation Books. Schindler, who spoke on this as on so many other topics frankly and without reserve, said that he long preserved the books and papers intact, but not finding any person but himself who placed any value upon them, their weight and bulk had led him in the course of his long unsettled life by degrees to destroy those which he deemed to be of little or no importance.

—The earliest surviving Conversation Book, which can be dated late February to early March, 1818, was acquired by the Beethoven Archives at Bonn.[22] Another Conversation Book, written in early September, 1825, a part of the Bodmer Collection, is also at Bonn.[23] The remainder were,

[21] A few conversation sheets may be dated as early as the spring of 1816. See Max Unger, *DM, op.cit.*, p. 377.

[22] *Beethoven-Haus Katalog*, ed. by W. Schmidt-Görg (Bonn, 1935), p. 20. See Ludwig Schiedermair, "Beiträge zum Leben und Schaffen nach Dokumenten des Beethoven-Hauses" in *Veröffentlichungen des Beethoven-Hauses in Bonn*, VI (1930), pp. 12ff.

[23] *Eine Schweizer Beethoven-sammlung*, *Katalog*, ed. by Max Unger, Zurich, p. 80.

in 1845, transferred to the then Royal Library in Berlin, and, in 1855, when they were examined for this work, numbered one hundred thirty-eight.

Thayer's industry in the gathering and collecting of material for this biography, let it be remarked here in grateful tribute, is illustrated in the fact that he made practically a complete transcript of the Conversation Books, laboriously deciphering the frequently hieroglyphic scrawls, and compiled a mass of supplementary material for the purpose of fixing the chronological order of the conversations. The dates of all concerts and other public events alluded to were established by the examination of all newspapers and other contemporary records and the utility of the biographical material greatly enhanced. ⸺This tribute to Thayer was reworded by Krehbiel from one first written by Riemann.[24] The present editor can add that with the disappearance of the Thayer papers, referred to in the preface, the nearest to a basic source for the Conversation Books is the incomplete transcription in three volumes by Schünemann which covers the period from 1818 (February, March) to July, 1823. For the benefit of the reader, references to this source have been given.

To return to the one hundred thirty-eight books used by Thayer, ⸺the oldest of these belongs to the period now before us (1819) and was evidently preserved by Schindler on account of the protracted conversations on the topic of the nephew. We have already made several citations from it and shall have frequent occasion to have recourse to it in the progress of this narrative. The period in which it was used is approximately fixed by a reference to a concert given by the violinist Franz Clement, at which he played an introduction and variations on a theme by Beethoven. This concert took place on April 4, 1819. Apparently in reply to a question put by Beethoven, an unidentified hand writes: "Poor stuff—empty—totally ineffective—your theme was in bad hands; with much monotony he made 15 or 20 variations and put a cadenza [*fermate*] in every one, you may imagine what we had to endure—he has fallen off greatly and looks too old to entertain with his acrobatics on the violin."[25] The last conversations in the book took place about the time of Beethoven's removal to Mödling—shortly before and after.

It was but natural that the Conversation Books preserved are such as place Schindler's relation to the master in the strongest light and those deemed by him essential to the full understanding of the more important events of Beethoven's last years. Most of them bear evidence of the deep interest with which Schindler, while they remained in his possession, lived over the past in them. In many cases he appended the names of the principal writers; so that one soon learns to distinguish their hands without difficulty; and occasionally he enriched them with valuable annotations. The larger of them—

See Th. v. Frimmel, "Ein Konversationsheft Beethovens aus dem Jahre 1825," in *BJ* (Munich, 1909), II, pp. 161ff.

[24] TK, III, p. 12, n. 1; TDR, IV, p. 155, n. 1.

[25] Schünemann, I, pp. 35-6.

ordinary blank note-books—are only of a size and thickness fitted to be carried in the coat pocket. It is obvious, therefore, on a moment's reflection, that at a single sitting with a few friends in an inn or coffee-house, the pages must have filled rapidly as the book passed from hand to hand and one or another wrote question or reply, remark or statement, a bit of news or a piece of advice. A few such conversations, one sees, would fill a book, all the sooner as there is no thought of economizing space and each new sentence is usually also a new paragraph. It strikes one, therefore, that the whole 400 could have contained but a small portion of the conversations of the period they covered. This was so. At home a slate or any loose scraps of paper were commonly used, thus saving a heavy item of expense; moreover, many who conversed with Beethoven would only write upon the slate in order to obliterate it immediately, that nothing should remain exposed to the eyes of others. The books, therefore, were for the most part for use when the composer was away from home, although there were occasions when, it being desirable to preserve what was written, they were also used there. Hence, the collection in Berlin can be viewed as little more than scattered specimens of the conversations of the master's friends and companions, most unequally distributed as to time. For months together there is nothing or hardly anything; and then again a few days will fill many scores of leaves. In a few instances Beethoven has himself written—that is, when in some public place he did not trust his voice; and memoranda of divers kinds, even of musical ideas from his pen, are not infrequent. One is surprised to find so few distinguished names in literature, science and art—Grillparzer's forms an exception and he appears only in the later years; as for the rest, they are for the most part local Vienna celebrities.

This explanatory digression may serve as a modulation to more cheerful themes than that which has occupied us of late.

Though Karl was no longer a member of the Giannatasio household or pupil of the institute, and though there were, in consequence, fewer meetings between Beethoven and his self-sacrificing friends, their relations remained pleasant, and early in 1819 Beethoven found occasion to supplement his verbal protestations of gratitude with a deed. Nanni, the younger daughter of Giannatasio, was married on February 6, 1819, to Leopold Schmerling. When the young couple returned to the house after the ceremony they were greeted by a wedding hymn for tenor solo, men's voices and pianoforte accompaniment. The performers were hidden in a corner of the room. When they had finished they stepped forth from their place of concealment. Beethoven was among them and he handed to the bride the manuscript of the music which he had written to words of Prof. Stein.[26]

[26] Professor Anton Joseph Stein (1759-1844) had been Professor of Classical Literature at the University in Vienna since 1806; he was also tutor in the imperial household. Madame Pessiak-Schmerling, a daughter of Nanni, recounted this incident twice in her letters to Thayer. See TDR, IV, pp. 518 and 521.

--⁣⁣⁣⁣{The version for men's voices in unison and tenor solo is in C major and is probably the second version. The autograph, which was found in the archives of Breitkopf and Härtel and is now in a library at Darmstadt,[27] is inscribed "On January 14th, 1819— For H. v. giannattasio del Rio from l. v. Beethoven." Another version of the song, which is in A major for mixed voices also with piano accompaniment, is owned privately in England. This version has been established as another authentic one by Oldman,[28] who suggests that Beethoven originally intended to include ladies in a harmonized setting for the performance but that this proved impractical. From the description of the event it is clear that the version in C major was the one used.}⁣⁣--

Beethoven made a single appearance as conductor in this year. It was on January 17 at a concert given for the benefit of the Widows and Orphans of the Juridical Faculty of the University. The orchestra was largely composed of amateurs and the programme began with the overture to *Prometheus* and ended with the Seventh Symphony. Among the listeners was P. D. A. Atterbom, the Swedish poet, who wrote a sympathetic account of it.

In the midst of the worries occasioned by the guardianship, Beethoven was elected Honorary Member of the Philharmonic Society of Laibach, an institution which had been founded in 1702 and revived, after repeated interruptions, in 1816. The project of giving him the distinction had been broached in the councils of the society in 1808, but Anton Schmith, a physician in Vienna, whose opinion had been asked, had advised against it, saying: "Beethoven is as freakish as he is unserviceable." Eleven years later the men of Laibach had more knowledge or better counsel, and they sent him a diploma on March 15 through von Tuscher. Acknowledging the honor on May 4, Beethoven stated that as a mark of appreciation he was sending, also through the magistrate, an "unpublished" composition and would hold himself in readiness to serve the society should it ever need him. There is no direct evidence as to what composition he had in mind; but in the archives of the Laibach society there is a manuscript copy of the Sixth Symphony. It is not an autograph except as to its title, Beethoven having written "Sinfonia pastorale" on the cover in red crayon, and corrections in lead pencil in the music.[29]

The time for Beethoven's annual summer flitting had come. Mödling was chosen again for the country sojourn as we already know and Beethoven arrived there on May 12, taking lodgings as before in the Hafner house on the Hauptstrasse. He had, evidently, brought a housekeeper with him and now engaged a housemaid. On the blank leaves of an Almanac for 1819, such as used to be bound in those useful household publications for the reception of memoranda, Beethoven notes: "Came to Mödling, May 12.!!! *Miser*

[27] See KHV, p. 568.

[28] C. B. Oldman, "A Beethoven Friendship," *Music and Letters*, XVII (1936), pp. 328-36.

[29] See F. Keesbacher, *Die philharmonische Gesellschaft in Laibach* (Laibach, 1862), pp. 49-51. (TDR, IV, 158, n. 1.)

sum pauper. . . ." "On May 14 the housemaid in M. came, to receive 6 florins a month. . . . On 29th May Dr. Hasenöhrl made his 3rd visit to K[arl]. Tuesday on the 22nd of June my nephew entered the institute of Hr. Blöchinger with a monthly payment in advance of 75 florins V.S. Began to take the baths here regularly [?] on 28th Monday, for the first [?] time daily." Schindler adds: "On July 20 gave notice to the housekeeper."

In 1810 Adolf Martin Schlesinger had opened his own book store in Berlin. Starting with a music lending library, he soon developed what was to be Berlin's first music publishing house. A few years later his son, Moritz, followed in his father's footsteps and opened a music publishing house in Paris. Father and son worked closely together and often published simultaneously. The Schlesingers were intelligent enough to cultivate Beethoven's friendship and eventually they were to be rewarded with the publication of, among other things, his last three pianoforte sonatas and the string quartets, Op. 132 and Op. 135.[30] In 1819 the father sent Moritz to Vienna to become acquainted with Beethoven. According to young Schlesinger's reminiscences written forty years later,[31] he was first introduced to the composer by Haslinger in the Steiner shop in Vienna, and Beethoven asked him to visit him in Mödling,[32] which happened a few days later.

"After getting out of the wagon I went to the inn and found Beethoven there, who came out the door in a fury and slammed it hard behind him. After I had dusted off a bit I went to the house which was designated as his dwelling. His housekeeper told me that it would be better not to speak to him as he had returned home in a rage. I gave her my visiting card which she brought to him, and after a few minutes to my great astonishment she came out again and bade me enter. Inside I found the great man at his writing desk. Immediately I *wrote* that I was glad to make his acquaintance. This (the fact that I *wrote*) made a favorable impression. He let himself go immediately and told me that he was the most miserable man in the world; a minute ago he came out of the inn where he had asked for a piece of *veal* which he especially desired; but *there was none there*—all this with a very serious and dark expression. I comforted him; we spoke (I always writing) of other things and so he detained me for two hours; then feeling that I would tire or upset him I wanted often to get up but he always held me back. After leaving him I hurried back to Vienna in my wagon and asked my inn boy if there was any roast veal available. Upon finding there was I left it on the platter, well covered up, and, without writing a word, I gave it to the man waiting with the carriage to take to Baden [Mödling] and present to Beethoven in my name. One morning soon afterwards I was still lying in bed when in came Beethoven, who kissed and embraced me and

---

[30] For a description of the Schlesingers see Max Unger, *Beethoven und seine Verleger* (Berlin and Vienna, 1921), pp. 24ff.

[31] For the second edition of A. B. Marx's

Ludwig van Beethoven Leben und Schaffen, 1863. (Unger, *op.cit.,* pp. 25-6.)

[32] Schlesinger writes "Baden" but this is obviously wrong for the year 1819.

said I was the best fellow he had ever met; never had anything made him so happy as this veal for which at that moment he had had such a longing."⟩⟶

Beethoven, as letters to the Archduke dated July 15 and August 31 show, was not in the best of health, but was hard at work on the Mass, with an excursion now and then into the Symphony (Ninth). Schindler presents us with a pathetic, impressive, almost terrifying picture of the state to which his labors lifted him:[33] "Towards the end of August, accompanied by the musician Johann Horzalka still living in Vienna, I arrived at the master's home in Mödling. It was 4 o'clock in the afternoon. As soon as we entered we learned that in the morning both servants had gone away, and that there had been a quarrel after midnight which had disturbed all the neighbors, because as a consequence of a long vigil both had gone to sleep and the food which had been prepared had become unpalatable. In the living-room, behind a locked door, we heard the master singing parts of the fugue in the *Credo*—singing, howling, stamping. After we had been listening a long time to this almost awful scene, and were about to go away, the door opened and Beethoven stood before us with distorted features, calculated to excite fear. He looked as if he had been in mortal combat with the whole host of contrapuntists, his everlasting enemies. His first utterances were confused, as if he had been disagreeably surprised at our having overheard him. Then he reached the day's happenings and with obvious restraint he remarked: 'Pretty doings, these [*Saubere Wirthschaft.*], everybody has run away and I haven't had anything to eat since yesternoon!' I tried to calm him and helped him to make his toilet. My companion hurried on in advance to the restaurant of the bathing establishment to have something made ready for the famished master. Then he complained about the wretched state of his domestic affairs, but here, for reasons already stated, there was nothing to be done. Never, it may be said, did so great an artwork as is the *Missa Solemnis* see its creation under more adverse circumstances!"

The incident doubtless occurred, but Schindler's memory as to his companion was in error. F. Luib brought Horzalka's attention to Schindler's story; the result was recorded by Luib in Thayer's copy of the Schindler biography: "Horzalka knows nothing of this." ⟶⟩Schindler's account must be questioned further, however. In his introduction to the already mentioned "Missa Solemnis" sketchbook at Bonn, Schmidt-Görg sums up that, with a collation of Conversation Books, letters and the notation "still in 1819," on the first page of this sketchbook, the sketches for the *Credo* may be dated for the most part in November-December, 1819.[34] If Schindler is correct in dating his description of the creative struggle late August, 1819, it is much more likely that Beethoven was working on some section of the *Gloria*. It could well have been the final fugue "In Gloria Dei Patris," for in the Bonn

[33] I, pp. 270-71. (TDR, IV, 161.)
[34] Schmidt-Görg, *Ein Skizzenbuch aus den Jahren 1819/20*, p. 16.

sketchbook there are sketches for passages which precede and the *presto* section which ends the fugue, but not for the main fugue subject.

In a conversation of late March or early April, someone, probably Oliva, writes:

— Is the oratorio finished?
I cannot understand how he is so occupied; his professional work amounts to nothing and other than that he does nothing, and yet he talks all the time about so much work and business.[35]

The author in question was Bernard, who had been designated to write the text for the oratorio which Beethoven had been commissioned to write for the Gesellschaft der Musikfreunde. As we shall see, the writing of the libretto remained an obstacle for this project. Meanwhile, on June 15 Beethoven had received an advance payment for the work, for on this date he wrote the following note to the society:

Dear esteemed Sir!
I am lying in bed and from here cannot immediately elaborate on the subject of the oratorio— Meanwhile I shall write to you about it in a few days or speak to you in person. I confirm for you herewith by virtue of my own signature that I have received 400 fl. V.S.

Respectfully and most sincerely
Beethoven[36]

There was a meeting of the Society on November 22 at which Landgraf von Fürstenberg reported that on the written application of Prince von Odescalchi, representing the President, Beethoven had replied that he had long been desirous to compose a work which would reflect honor on the society and that he would do his best to expedite it.[37] That seems to have been the end of the matter for the time being.

There was also during the Mödling sojourn a continuation of the negotiations with Thomson. A Mr. Smith visited Beethoven bearing a letter from the Scottish publisher which called out a playful rejoinder in which Beethoven sought to turn an easy play upon German words into French. Thomson suggested that the introductions and accompaniments to the Scottish songs be made easier ("lighter," in the German idiom); they would be so, Beethoven replied, if the compensation were made more difficult ("heavier" would have been his word had he been permitted to use the German equivalent). As it is, Beethoven's humor becomes rather ponderous, as see the letter which was written in French by Beethoven apparently without assistance:

[35] Schünemann, I, p. 35.
[36] First published by Sonneck (*op.cit.*, p. 92) from the autograph in the Gardner Museum in Boston. See Miss Anderson's comment on the addressee, *A*, p. 816, n. 1.
[37] Karl Ferdinand Pohl, *Die Gesellschaft der Musikfreunde* (Vienna, 1871), pp. 9-10. (TDR, IV, 161, n. 1.)

Vienne le 25me Maj, 1819.

Mon cher Ami!

Vous ecrivés toujours facile très facile—je m'accomode tout mon possible, mais—mais—mais—l'honorare pourroit pourtant être plus difficile, ou plus-tôt pesante!!!! Votre ami Monsieur Smith m'a fait grand plaisir a cause de sa visite chez moi—en hâte, je vous assure, que je serais toujours avec plaisir de votre service—comme j'ai à present votre Adresse par Mr. Smith, je serai bientôt en Etat de vous écrire plus ample—l'honorare pour un Thême avec variations j'ai fixé, dans ma derniere lettre à vous par Messieurs le Fries, a moien dix Ducats en or c'est, je vous jure malgré cela seulement par complaisance pour vous, puisque je n'ai pas besoin, de me mêler avec de telles petites choses, mais il faut toujours pourtant perdre de temps avec de telles bagatelles, et l'honneur ne permet pas, de dire à quelqu'un, ce qu'on en gagne,—je vous souhaite toujours le bon goût pour la vrai Musique et si vous crie facile—je crierai difficile pour facile!!!!!

Thomson endorsed on this letter: "25 May, 1819. Beethoven. Some pleasantry on my repeated requests to make his Symphs and accompgnts. to our National Airs Easy. sent by Mr. John Smith of Glasg."

There are two entries in a Conversation Book which refer to another British commission that was offered him about a month earlier:

[1]

. . . Another commission was brought by the other Englishman, the friend of Smith.— A Mr. Donaldson in Edinburgh wants to know if you will not write a Trio for 3 pianofortes that is difficult and in the style of your Quintet in E-flat.— He wants to announce it as his property.— The remuneration which you demand is to be paid to you in any way you may select.— All three parts of the Trio must be obligato. If perhaps you don't want now to determine the price, you could simply fix a time when it is ready and write to Donaldson in Edinburgh direct.—
These Englishmen speak of nothing else than your coming to England;—they give assurance that if you were to come for a single winter, from September until sometime in May, to England, Scotland and Ireland, you could earn so much that you could live the rest of your life on the interest.

[2]

Today the gentleman is going to write to Donaldson in Edinburgh—the answer can be here in 4 weeks and the gentleman can also be here that long—

◞◦◟

. . . .

Tell him how much you want;—when it might be finished and how you want the payment made.
He is very desirous to have a composition from you and there is no reason to think that it would be returned—
Moreover it is a big work
If you can get 40 ducats for the Sonata he can doubtless pay 100

◞◦◟

By that time the answer may be here from Edinburgh.[38]

Great Britain's monetary reward, had Beethoven accepted all its invitations, would no doubt have been all that the friend of "Mr. Donaldson of Edinburgh" stated and in proportion would have been the appreciation which Beethoven would have found at the hands of the English professional musicians, amateurs and musical laity.

Pathetic and diverting are the incidents which Karl Friedrich Zelter relates in letters to Goethe of his attempts to form a closer acquaintance with Beethoven. On July 29 he writes the following in his letter to Goethe concerning his journey to Austria: "Beethoven, whom I would like to see once during my lifetime, lives in the country and no one can tell me where." On August 16 he writes: ". . . It is said that he is intolerably *maussade*. Some say he is a lunatic. It is easy to talk. God forgive us all our sins! The poor man is reported as being totally deaf. Now I know what it means to see all this digital manipulation around me while my fingers are becoming useless one after the other. Lately Beethoven went to an eating-house; he sat himself down to a table and lost himself in thought. After an hour he calls the waiter: 'What do I owe?' 'The gentleman has not eaten anything yet, what shall I bring?' 'Bring anything you please, but let me alone!'"

Zelter stayed in Vienna from July to September, but saw nothing of Beethoven. Then on September 14 he writes: "The day before yesterday I wanted to pay a visit to Beethoven in Mödling. He wanted to go to Vienna, so we met en route, climbed out and embraced one another affectionately. The poor fellow is practically stone deaf and I could hardly restrain my tears. Then I went on to Mödling and he to Vienna.— — I must tell you about an episode that amused me considerably.— With me on this trip was Steiner, the music publisher, and since it is rather hard to converse with a deaf man on a country road, we arranged a proper meeting with Beethoven at four o'clock in the afternoon in Steiner's music store. After eating we drove back to Vienna at once. Full as a badger and tired as a dog I lay down and slept away the time, slept so soundly that not a thing entered my mind. Then I went to the theatre and when I saw Beethoven there I felt as if I had been struck by lightning. The same thing happened to him at sight of me, and this was not the place for explanations with a deaf man. Now comes the point: In spite of the things of which Beethoven is accused justly or unjustly, he enjoys a popular respect such as is bestowed only upon the most excellent. Steiner had given it out that Beethoven would appear in his little office, which will hold only six or eight persons, for the first time in person at 4 o'clock, and invited guests so generously that in a room crowded to the street, half a hundred brilliant people waited in vain. I did not get an explanation till next day, when I received a letter from Beethoven in

---

[38] Schünemann, *op.cit.*, I, pp. 48-9, 60-61. Schünemann believed that the handwriting was Oliva's; Thayer assumed it was Schindler's.

which he begged my pardon, for he, like me, had passed the time set for the meeting in blissful sleep."

Zelter's letter calls for a slight rectification. It was not the next day but four days later that Beethoven wrote him the letter of explanation, and Zelter's statement that Beethoven had overslept himself was pure presumption—unless he learned it from another source. Beethoven wrote:

Highly respected Sir!

It is not my fault that you were lately besmeared[39] by me, as people say here. Unforeseen circumstances robbed me of the pleasure of passing a few lovely and enjoyable hours with you, which would have been profitable to our art. I hear that you are already leaving Vienna day after tomorrow. On account of my weakened health, my life in the country this year has not been as beneficial to me as usual. It may be that I shall come in again the day after tomorrow, and if you have not already left by afternoon I hope to tell you by word of mouth with really true cordiality how much I esteem you and wish to be with you.

In haste your most faithful friend

Vienna, September 18, 1819.   Beethoven

The autograph of this letter contains what appears to be either a transcript or a draft of a letter which Zelter either sent or planned to send to Beethoven. In view of the fact that it shows a different feeling towards the great composer than that formerly entertained by the teacher of Mendelssohn, it is given here:

To see once more, face to face, in this life the man who brings joy and edification to so many good people, among whom I of course am glad to count myself—this was the purpose, worthy friend, for which I wished to visit you at Mödling. You came to meet us, and my aim was at least not wholly frustrated, for I saw your face. I know of the infirmity which burdens you and you have my sympathty, for I am similarly afflicted. On the day after to-morrow I go from here to resume my labors, but I shall never cease to hold you in high respect and to love you.

Your Zelter

Friedrich Schneider, of Dessau, visited Vienna in the fall of the year and caused a sensation by his organ-playing. He reported that Beethoven had received him graciously and that he, in turn, had heard the master play the pianoforte, his improvisation being the most marvellous thing he had ever listened to.[40]

In August, Johann van Beethoven bought the Wasserhof estate near Gneixendorf. This would bring the brothers closer together in the period to follow. That Beethoven was also interested in acquiring some property at this time is shown by a letter which he wrote to Steiner:

[39] *Angeschmiert*, that is, "deceived" or "cheated."

[40] Nohl, *Beethovens Leben*, III, p. 856. (TDR, IV, 164, n. 3.)

Mödling, October 10, 1819

Dear Steiner!

The day before yesterday I left you a note asking you to come here before the sale of the house; you would really be doing me a great kindness. The sale is on the 13th, thus next Wednesday. It is not possible for me to undertake anything to do with this without your help. The capital cannot be in any way reduced through this since naturally my nephew, who will devote himself to learning, needs support after my death for the continuation of his studies.— If you have had the record of baptism made through a notary, I will gratefully repay you the expense of it.—

To the WORTHY
LITTLE TOBIAS[41]

I have spoken about the Archduke var., I have proposed *you* for them since I do not believe that you will incur a loss from them and it is always honorable to print something from such a Principe Professore.— As to the corporal I beg you to tell him that he is not to sell anything of which I have notified him until I come to the city; also he must not forget to notify those who are moving and the landlady at the Landstrasse that the bell and window shades are mine.— I hope to see you tomorrow or the day after; mornings are the best since we must talk with H. v. Carbon, at which time we could also get a look at the house; and you could examine everything, if necessary also at the registry, and you could act as a judex since my decision will be based completely upon your judgement.— . . . .

--⊷⁂Frimmel[42] has shown that the house in question must have been an old ecclesiastical house called "Christhof" which was in secular possession by 1819 and advertised for sale in August. Beethoven was evidently outbid by Johann Speer, who bought the house and rented the apartment on the first floor to Beethoven the following summer. Carbon can have been no other than Captain Franz Ludwig Carbon who was registered as an owner of property in Mödling.⁂⊷--

The variations composed by the Archduke were, it will be remembered, on a theme composed by Beethoven and given to his imperial pupil as a lesson, and had called forth the obsequious remarks previously quoted in his New Year's letter to the Archduke. His remark to Steiner is explained by the fact that on August 31 he had written to the Archduke as follows:

. . . . As regards the masterly variations of Y. I. H. I think they might be published under the following title, namely:

Theme, or Task
set by L. v. Beeth.
forty times varied
and dedicated to his teacher
by the *Most Serene Author*

---

[41] The letters E[hrenwerthen] T[obiasserl] are large and ornamented. See Max Unger, *Ludwig van Beethoven und seine Verleger*, p. 63.

[42] Theodor von Frimmel, "Beethoven in Mödling," *Beethoven-Forschung*, VIII (1918), pp. 130-39.

There are so many requests for them, and eventually this honorable work will reach the public in garbled copies. Y. I. H. will yourself not be able to avoid presenting copies here and there; therefore, in the name of God, among the many consecrations which Y. I. H. is receiving and of which the world is being informed, let the consecration of Apollo (or in Christian terms Cäcilia) also be made known. True, Y. I. H. may accuse me of *vanity*; but I can assure you that although this dedication is precious to me and I am really proud of it, this is not at all my ultimate aim. Three publishers have appealed for it; Artaria, Steiner and a third whose name does not come to me. Considering but the first two, to which shall the Variations be given? On this point I await the commands of Y. I. H. Both of them have offered to print the variations at *their own cost*. The question now is whether Y. I. H. is *satisfied with the title?* To the question whether or not the variations ought to be published, Y. I. H. ought to close your eyes; if it is done, Y. I. H. *may call it* a misfortune; but *the world will think the contrary . . . .*

Steiner printed the archducal work in the seventh number of his *Musée musical des Clavicinistes* under a slightly changed title, viz.: "Theme [*Aufgabe*] composed by Ludwig van Beethoven, varied forty times and dedicated to the author by his pupil R[udolph], A[rch-] D[uke]." Other evidences of Beethoven's interest in Archduke Rudolph's studies in composition are shown by a letter to his patron dated July 29, 1819. It deserves to be given in full because of passages which, although vaguely worded, give some indication of Beethoven's attitude towards his art.

Your Imperial Highness!

I was indeed sorry to receive the news of a new indisposition of Your Highness; and since I have had no further definite news, I am very much upset— I was in Vienna in order to look in the library of Y. I. H. for some things most useful for me. The central plan is a *quick recognition* of the essential coupled with a *greater artistic unity*[43] in respect of which practical considerations sometimes compel an exception as we may learn in a twofold way from the old composers, where we find stress laid chiefly upon the artistically valuable (among these only the *German Händel* and *Sebastian Bach* had genius). But *freedom, progress*, these are the aims in the world of art as in the whole great universe. Even if we moderns are not so far advanced in *sound technique* [*Festigheit*] as our *forefathers*, yet refinement in manners has opened many new things to us. My exalted pupil in music, already a fellow-contestant for the laurel of fame, must not subject himself to the accusation of one-sidedness—et iterum venturus judicare *vivos*—et *mortuos.*— Here are three poems of which Y. I. H. could perhaps set one to music. The Austrians now know already that the *spirit of Apollo* has newly awakened in the Imperial family. From all quarters I receive requests for something [by you]. The *proprietor of the Modenzeitung* will appeal to Y. I. H. *in writing*, I hope I *shall not be accused of bribery—at court and no courtier, what possibilities??!!!* In my search for music in Vienna I found some resistance from *His Excellency the Chief Steward*. It is not worth the trouble to burden Y. I. H. in writing about it; I only must say this much, that because of this, many talented, good and noble

43 (I.e., text and music.) For a short discussion by Deiters of this letter see TDR, iv, p. 169.

men would be frightened away from Y. I. H., who did not have the good fortune to become acquainted with your excellent qualities of spirit and heart— I wish Y. I. H. a speedy, speedy recovery and some news of it for the sake of *my peace of mind.*—

Your Imper. Highness's most obedient and faithful servant

L. V. Beethoven

That his mind was full of his Mass is indicated by the quotation from the text of the *Credo* and that he was consulting authorities on ecclesiastical music for this purpose is suggested by his reference to Bach and Handel.

It is time to consider further biographical events in chronological order. From the Fischoff manuscript we learn that on October 1 Beethoven was made an honorary member of the Mercantile Association (*Kaufmännischer Verein*) in Vienna.

In the fall of this year was painted probably the best known portrait of Beethoven: the oil painting by Ferdinand Schimon (1797-1852). At a later date it came into the possession of Schindler who deposited it in the Berlin Library; —✥now it is the property of the Beethoven-Haus in Bonn where it can be seen on the third floor.✥— Concerning the origin of this picture Schindler has this explanation.[44] Schimon had permission through Schindler to set up his easel in the chamber adjoining Beethoven's workroom, the composer resolutely having refused a sitting because he was busy on the Mass. From this point of vantage he made his studies and had finished all but the eyes—the most striking feature in the portrait. Out of this dilemma Beethoven unconsciously helped him. He had evidently been impressed with the discretion, or independence, of the young artist who came without a "good morning" and went without a "good evening," and invited him to coffee. Thus Schimon had ample opportunity to supply the one deficiency in his sketches. Schindler adds: "From an artistic point of view Schimon's work is not a distinguished work of art, yet full of characteristic truth. In the rendering of that particular look, the majestic forehead, this dwelling-place of mighty, sublime ideas, of hues, in the drawing of the firmly shut mouth and the chin shaped like a shell, it is truer to nature than any other picture."

—✥According to Schindler it was at the end of October that Beethoven returned to Vienna from Mödling. His new lodging is described by him in a Conversation Book of March, 1820, as "opposite the Auersperg palace in the same house where the coffeehouse is in the Josephstadt Glacis."[45] Since in front of the palace there was nothing but clear expanse all the way to the wall of the inner city, the dwelling would have been more accurately described as to the side of the palace. This move was made so that he could be near the Blöchlinger institute; and Fanny Giannatasio del Rio writes in

[44] *Biogr.*, II, p. 288-89. (TDR, IV, 170, n. 3.)

[45] Schünemann, I, p. 325. The house was owned by a Baron August von Fingerling and had the nickname "Zur goldenen Birne."

Alois Trost has identified the lodging in greater detail. See "Über einige Wohnungen Beethovens" in *Ein Wiener Beethoven-Buch* (Vienna, 1921), pp. 206-208.

her diary on December 1, 1819: "Beethoven, whom we do not hear of now at all lives ... in the Josefstadt naturally because of the boy." But Beethoven may have had a second lodging at the same time since his home is recorded in two court records dated October 30, 1819, and January 7, 1820, as "im Blumenstöckel" near the newspaper office. This house was on the Ballgasse, No. 986 and was known as "Zum alten Blumenstock."[46] Considering Beethoven's constant association with Jos. Karl Bernard in the guardianship matter, which was again occupying his attention, it is not surprising that he should have had quarters here near the editor's office in the Rauhensteingasse. — At the same time he was tormented by spells of indisposition; furthermore, financial distress so threatened him that he attempted to negotiate a loan from the banker Henikstein, and he borrowed 750 florins from Steiner.

It is remarkable that Beethoven, under the circumstances which have been set forth in this chapter, could continue his labors on the Mass which were his principal occupation during the year; it was but another proof of the absorbing possession which the composition of a great work took of him when once fairly begun. So diligently did he apply himself that he had hopes not only of finishing it in time for the installation of the Archduke as Archbishop of Olmütz, but he wrote to Ries on November 10 that he had already nearly completed it and would like to know what could be done with it in London. To Schindler, however, in expressing a doubt that he would have it done in time for the ceremonial, he said that every movement had taken on larger dimensions than had originally been contemplated. Schindler says also that when the day came, not one of the movements was finished in the eyes of the composer.

That the *Gloria* was near its final shape is a fair deduction from a Conversation Book of the same period. Bernard (presumably) writes: "It was decided yesterday that you give a concert either on Christmas or some other day. Count Stadion will give the use of the room, and Schick, Czerny and Janitschek will care for the rest. The programme is to include a symphony, the *Gloria* from your mass, the new Sonata played by you and a grand final chorus. All your works. 4,000 florins are guaranteed. Only one movement of the mass is to be performed."[47] The project is mentioned again by another friend,[48] and Beethoven remarks: "It is too late for Christmas, but it might be possible in Lent."

That he worked occasionally on the Ninth Symphony, especially in the early part of the year, has already been said. — Another work which was not to be completed until a later time was probably conceived in this year. In a letter to Simrock dated February 10, 1820, Beethoven offered his wares which included, characteristically, works that were far from completion. On

---

[46] For this information I am indebted to the late Dr. Kurt Smolle.

[47] Schünemann, 1, p. 123. The Conversation

Book belongs to early December, 1819.

[48] According to Schünemann, 1, p. 126, this was Janitschek.

this list besides the Mass, which he was offering for an honorarium of 125 Louis d'or, Beethoven mentions some "big variations on a well known 'Deutsche,' which, however, I cannot promise you as yet and if you wish them will notify you later of the honorarium." This refers to the variations on a waltz by Diabelli, who conceived the idea of inviting several composers to contribute variations to his theme for a collection to be published as a monument to Austrian talent. Beethoven was not to complete his variations until 1823, but as already mentioned there are sketches for the work alongside those for the *Kyrie* of the Mass, which may be dated 1819.

He also, as Schindler tells us, composed a set of waltzes for a band of seven men who played at an inn in the valley of the Brühl near Mödling, and wrote out the parts for the different instruments. In 1905 Riemann found the parts of these dances in the Archives of the Thomasschule in Leipzig. There are eleven of them in all and they are scored as follows: Nos. 1, 3-8 are for two violins, bass and two clarinets; Nos. 9-11 substitute two flutes for the clarinets; and No. 2 is for flute, clarinet, bassoon and two horns. They were published by Breitkopf and Härtel in 1907.

He wrote a canon for Steiner in the summer, as appears from a conversation recorded in a book of March 20, 1820. An unidentified hand writes:

Last summer you sent a *canon infinitus a due* to Steiner from Mödling

Nobody has solved it, but I have solved it. The second voice enters on the second:

it is infinite.
Go to the devil [Hol Euch der Teufel!]
God protect you [B'hüt Euch Gott!]
was the text.[49]

On September 21 he wrote a canon to the words "Glaube und hoffe" for Moritz Schlesinger, as Beethoven's inscription on the autograph shows.[50] Countess Erdödy was in Vienna at the end of the year, and he sent her a note on December 19, in which he promised to visit her soon, and then scratched down the beginnings of a musical phrase. On December 31 he

[49] According to Schünemann (I, pp. 384-85), this was Czerny. For solutions in four parts to this riddle canon see Ludwig Misch, *Beethoven-Studies* (Norman, 1953), pp. 135-36.

[50] See Misch, *ibid.*, pp. 129-30.

wrote her a New Year canon: "Glück, Glück zum neuen Jahr," which starts approximately with this idea.[51]

--- The completed compositions of the year were few:

Canons: "Glaube und hoffe," WoO 174, for Moritz Schlesinger, on September 21.
"Glück, Glück, zum neuen Jahr," WoO 176, for Countess Erdödy.
"Hol' euch der Teufel!" WoO 173, for Steiner.
"Hochzeitslied" (Stein), WoO 105, for Anna Giannatasio del Rio. Version 1 for Tenor, Men's Voices and Pianoforte; Version 2 for Mixed Chorus and Pianoforte.
Eleven Dances for Seven Instruments, WoO 17.

The publications of the year were:

By Artaria:
Six Themes varied for Pianoforte with optional accompaniment of flute or violin, Op. 105.
Sonata for Pianoforte, Op. 106, dedicated to Archduke Rudolph; in two separate editions, one with French and one with German titles.
String Quintet, Op. 104, arrangement of the Trio, Op. 1, No. 3.
--- By Schlesinger in Berlin:
March No. 1 for Military Band in F, WoO 18.
[By Steiner in *Musée Musical des Clavicinistes* No. 7:
Forty Variations by Archduke Rudolph on a Theme by Beethoven (WoO 200), dedicated to Beethoven.]
By Thomson in Edinburgh and Preston in London:
"12 National Airs with Variations for the Piano and an Accompaniment for the Flute." Of the four projected volumes only three were published with three airs apiece. These consisted of Op. 105, Nos. 1-6 and Op. 107, Nos. 2, 6, 7.

---

[51] The countess also received the dedication of the Violoncello Sonatas, Op. 102, published by Artaria in January, 1819. They had been previously published by Simrock without dedication. (TDR, IV, 177.)

CHAPTER XXXIII

THE YEAR 1820

END OF THE GUARDIANSHIP LITIGATION—
MISSA SOLEMNIS NOT READY
FOR INSTALLATION CEREMONY—PIANOFORTE
SONATA IN E MAJOR, OP. 109

ALMOST involuntarily, in passing in review the incidents of the year whose story has just been told and projecting a view into the near future, the question arises: Where, in these moments of doubt, ill-health, trial, vexation of spirit and torment of body were the old friends of Beethoven who in the earlier years had stood by him faithfully and lovingly? Where was Stephan von Breuning? Alas! he seems to have been an early sacrifice to Beethoven's obstinate course in respect of his nephew. Schindler says that he had advised against the adoption of the boy and thus wounded Beethoven in his most sensitive part. The temporary estrangement began in 1817. Some others of the old friends may have been rebuffed in like manner; some, like the faithful seneschal, Zmeskall, were ill; some were absent from Vienna—Count Brunsvik, Schuppanzigh; some were dead; in some the flames of friendship may have died down because there was so little in Beethoven's public life to challenge their sympathy and support. Count Lichnowsky has dropped out of the narrative and does not appear for some years. What had happened to the ardent friend of the youthful days, Count Waldstein? An entry from a Conversation Book of December, 1819 awakens curiosity and a hope:

Do not speak so loud. Your situation is too well known;—that is the inconvenience of public places, one is completely limited; everybody listens and hears.

Count Waldstein was also sitting nearby.

Does he live here?[1]

[1] Schünemann, I, p. 138.

Beethoven's answer is unrecorded and thus passes the only opportunity which the known material offers from which it might have been learned what caused the death of that beautiful friendship. ⸺Joseph Heer[2] attributes the rift first to Waldstein's absence from Vienna until 1809, during which time he was in military and then the foreign service; second, to the difference in their political views: Waldstein was a zealous Austrian patriot who continued to agitate against the French "usurper" after the war was ended; and third, to Waldstein's carelessness in business matters, which resulted in his going bankrupt soon after his wife's death in 1816, and in his death as a pauper in 1823.⸺

Beethoven was become a lonely man—an enforced seeker of solitude. No doubt many who would have been glad to give him their friendship were deterred by the widespread reports of his suspicious, unapproachable, almost repellent nature. But a miracle happened. Driven in upon himself by the forces which seem to have been arrayed against him, introspection opened wider and wider to him the doors of that imagination which in its creative function, as Ruskin tells us, is "an eminent beholder of things when and where they are not; a seer, that is, in the prophetic sense, calling the things that are not as though they were; and forever delighting to dwell on that which is not tangibly present." Now he proclaimed a new evangel, illustrated a higher union of beauty and truthfulness of expression, exalted art till it entered the realm of religion.

In a Conversation Book of February, 1820, there stands a bold inscription in Beethoven's hand: "The moral law in us, and the starry sky above us—Kant!!!"[3] This and two other citations, the second of which Beethoven surely culled from some book, also deserve to be set down here as mottoes applicable to the creative work which occupied his mind during the year and thereafter:

The world is a king and desires flattery in return for favor; but true art is perverse and will not submit to the mould of flattery. Famous artists always labor under an embarrassment;—therefore their first works are the best, although they may have sprung from dark ground.

'Tis said that art is long and life is fleeting:—
Nay: life is long and brief the span of art!
If e'er her breath vouchsafes with gods a meeting,
A moment's favor 'tis of which we've had a part.[4]

[2] See "Der Graf von Waldstein und sein Verhältnis zu Beethoven," *Veröffentlichungen des Beethoven-Hauses*, ix (Bonn, 1933).

[3] "Two things fill the soul with ever new and increasing wonder and reverence the oftener the mind dwells upon them—the starry sky above me and the moral law within me."—Kant's *Criticism of Practical Reason.* (TK, III, 25, n. 1.)

[4] Schünemann, 1, p. 322. Since the translations are free, no attempt has been made to reproduce Beethoven's illogical punctuation.

Beethoven began the year 1820, as he had begun its immediate predecessor, by sending a New Year's greeting to the august pupil who was now almost continually in his mind—Archduke Rudolph, soon to be Archbishop and Cardinal. The greeting was in the form of a four-part canon beginning with a short homophonic chorus, the words: "Seiner Kaiserlichen Hoheit! Dem Erzherzog Rudolph! Dem geistlichen Fürsten! Alles Gute, alles Schöne!"

Now to take up the story of the incubus which oppressed the composer's mind, the clog which impeded his creative activities much of the year—the legal proceedings concerning the guardianship of nephew Karl. Fortunately for the tinge of these pages the end is not distant.

Two applications made by Beethoven to the Court of Magistrates had been denied and he now asked for a review of these decisions by the Court of Appeals. The action of the Magistracy had grievously pained him, so he informed the superior tribunal, and not only had his rights been set aside, but no regard had been shown for the welfare of his nephew. Against this he now sought relief, and he set forth his grievances: (1) He was testamentary appointee and the *Landrecht* had confirmed him and excluded the mother; circumstances compelling his absence from Vienna, he had arranged that Herr Nussböck should be appointed guardian *ad interim*; back permanently in the city, his nephew's welfare required that he resume the guardianship; (2) The higher education which his nephew's talents demanded neither the mother nor Nussböck could direct—the former because she was a woman and had conducted herself in a manner which had led the *Landrecht* to exclude her, Nussböck because he was too much occupied with his duties as Municipal Sequestrator and, having been no more than a paper-maker, he did not possess the insight and judgment essential to the scientific education of the ward. (3) Having no child of his own, his hopes were set on the boy, who was unusually talented, yet he had been told that he had been held back a year in his studies and that owing to a lack of funds he was to be taken from the institution in which he had been placed and given in the care of his mother; by her mismanagement the boy would be sacrificed, it being the aim of the mother to expend his share of the pension money on herself. He had declared to the Magistracy his willingness to defray the costs at the institute and also to engage other masters for the boy. Being "somewhat hard of hearing" communication with him was difficult and therefore he had asked that a co-guardian be appointed in the person of Herr Peters, councillor to Prince Lobkowitz, whose knowledge and moral character would assure such a training and education as were justified by the boy's capacity. "I know of no more sacred duty than the care and education of a child," he observes. He would offer no objection to the mother's having a "sort of joint-guardianship," but its duties and privileges should be limited to her visiting him and learning what plans were being made for his education; to permit more would be to compass the ruin of the boy.[5]

[5] For the documents concerning Beethoven's litigation about the guardianship of his nephew

This petition was filed on January 7, 1820; three days later the Appellate Court commanded the Magistracy to file a report of the proceedings held before it, together with all minutes and documents. The Magistracy complied on February 5, citing its decision of September 17, 1819, and defending its action on the grounds that (a) Beethoven, owing to his deafness and his hatred of the mother of the ward, was incapable of acting as guardian; (b) the guardianship belonged to the mother by right of law; (c) the commission of an act of infidelity against her husband in 1811, for which she had suffered punishment, was no longer a bar; (d) none of the alleged "injurious disturbances and interferences" had been definitely set forth or proven:

If under injurious disturbances we are to understand that the mother is desirous to see her child once every 14 days or 4 weeks, or to convince herself about the wear and cleanliness of his clothing, or to learn of his conduct toward his teachers, these can appear injurious only in the eyes of the appellant; the rest of the world, however, would find it amiss in a mother if she made inquiry concerning her child only once a fortnight or month.

Answering the second charge, the magistrates showed that the appellant seemed to demand of the mother and other guardian that they themselves should educate the boy in the sciences while at the same time he found them unsuited for the job. For this not even the appellant was fitted, at least he had not demonstrated such a fitness; he had left the preparation for the higher studies to others and this the mother and guardian could also do, having, indeed, a better plan, which was to send the boy to the R. I. Convict, where he could surely make better progress at smaller expense. *Ad tertium,* the failure of the boy to advance in his classes could not be laid to the mother or guardian, but must be charged against the appellant, who had taken the boy away from his studies for the university for two months, kept him at home three months, and sent him to another institution of learning at the end of June; naturally enough he lost a school year.

In a Conversation Book at the beginning of the year, Bernard writes: "The case will soon reach a firm decision since the Appellate Court has intervened."[6] To strengthen his case for this court, Beethoven spent several weeks on a "memorial" which describes the history of the case from his point of view. In turning to Bernard for help in the editing of this document, Beethoven was also confident of its success in the near future. He writes:

Dear Bernard! As I find myself alone again today in these to me confusing circumstances, a true understanding of my memorial has come to me for the first time. Without wishing to be resplendent in another person's feathers, still I believe I should leave it to your discretion to handle everything according to your superior judgement, since you in a few words can say as much or more

---

see TDR, IV, App. 3 (from 1817 to 1820), and *A*, III, App. C (from 1815 to 1820).

[6] Schünemann, I, p. 181.

as I can in sheets. The case would become more forceful and intelligible for the judges as a result. But this must be completed soon. Consider that you are laboring for Karl's happiness and for the only possible state of contentment for me and contributing to it for *the last time*—Once again do as you like with my raw material according to your judgement. In any case you write more clearly than I and the copy would soon be ready.

Your friend and admirer Beethoven

There has survived only Beethoven's sketch[7] of this memorial dated February 18, 1820, and there is no evidence as to whether it was ever presented in court. It is the longest piece of writing in Beethoven's hand, and is divided into seven parts. The first part, entitled "Information concerning Frau B." contains exaggerated charges against Johanna the most serious of which was that her illicit relations with another man in 1811 was the direct cause of her husband's sickness resulting in death.[8] In the second part entitled "Information concerning the supreme guardianship of the Vienna Magistracy" there is a detailed review of the "evil consequences" resulting from the transfer of the case from the *Landrecht* to the Magistracy: and in particular the inconsistencies in Beethoven's eyes of one of their number, Herr Piuk, in his handling of the case. The give and take between Beethoven and Johanna of charges of misconduct with the boy continues. For example, to answer an accusation of violence Beethoven confesses that "once in a passion I dragged my nephew from the chair because he had done something very wicked; and since has had to wear a truss ever since his hernia operation of two years before, the swift pulling consequently caused him some pain in the *most tender place* whenever he turned around quickly. I summoned Herr v. Smetana immediately and he declared that it didn't amount to anything and that not the least damage was done." Beethoven in turn accused Johanna of having fed the child strong drinks when he paid her a visit on her name-day, which resulted in an illness causing his confinement in bed for a period of three weeks. The third part, "Information concerning my nephew and his school-certificates," merely describes the benefits to the child's growth from being removed from the influence of his mother to his uncle's care and to Giannatasio's school. The fourth and fifth part give an account respectively of the educational costs and the nephew's estate. In the "conclusion" Beethoven appeals to the Appellate Court to grant his request; "—*the decision will bring* to my nephew *weal* or *woe*, the latter certainly if it is decided *against me*; for *my nephew needs*

---

[7] This document was found among the letters preserved in Bernard's estate by his daughter. It was first published in the Viennese *Zeit.* in December, 1907. It passed through many hands until it was acquired by H. C. Bodmer, who permitted the manuscript to be facsimiled and transcribed in the Beethoven Archives in Bonn. See Dagmar

Weise, "Beethoven—Entwurf einer Denkschrift an das Appellationsgericht in Wien von 18 Februar 1820" in *Veröffentlichungen des Beethoven-Hauses in Bonn* (1953), Dritte Reihe, 1.

[8] There is no evidence to support the fact that Carl Caspar's health in this year or the next gave way to sickness.

me, not I him." Then follows a supplement in which Beethoven first brings charges of misconduct against Father Fröhlich as an answer to Fröhlich's earlier testimony concerning Beethoven's method of educating his nephew. Then he re-emphasizes charges already stated in the first section: 1) that Johanna conspired with Karl in the spring of 1819 that he do badly in his studies at Kudlich's institute and receive a second or third class so that he would not be removed from Vienna, which aim was realised in the Easter examinations; and 2) that she persuaded the Magistracy to have Beethoven removed from the guardianship. The memorial ends: "Finally I must say that it appears to me that it still has not been clear whether I am to recognize the Magistracy as a competent authority for the guardianship."

The Court of Appeals demanded a more explicit report. The Magistracy complied on February 28, taking advantage of the opportunity to review the proceedings held before the *Landrecht* from the beginning, and to make severe strictures on the conduct of Beethoven in filing an exhibit (F) with his petition in support of which no evidence was offered, though because of it the *Landrecht* was asked to exclude the mother from the guardianship which belonged to her under the law. Again we quote:

This exclusion can have nothing for its foundation except the misdemeanor of which the mother was guilty in 1811, for all the rest contained in appellant's exhibit F is unproven chatter to which the *Landrecht* could give no consideration, but which gives speaking proof of how passionately and inimically the appellant has always acted, and still acts, towards the mother, how little he recks of tearing open wounds that were healed, since after having endured punishment she stood rehabilitated; and yet he reproaches her with a transgression for which she had atoned years before, which had been pardoned by the injured husband himself who petitioned for leniency in her sentence and who had declared her capable and fit for the guardianship of his son in his last will and testament, directing that the son be not taken away from his mother. Regardless of this the appellant last year, certainly not in the interest of the boy's welfare, inasmuch as we have excellent educational institutions here, but only to pain the mother, to tear the heart out of her bosom, attempted to send him out of the country to Landshut. Fortunately the government authorities, acting on information derived from this court, frustrated the plan by refusing a passport.

Let us try now to take a dispassionate view of the case as thus far presented in the pleadings and documents. Not only the law of nature but the laws of the land justified the mother in asserting her right to look after the physical well-being of her child and seeking to enforce it. Dr. Bach seems to have impressed that fact upon Beethoven, wherefore he declared his willingness in the bill of appeal to associate her with himself in the guardianship to that extent. That the Magistrates displayed unusual, not to say unjudicial, zeal in her behalf while defending their own course is indubitable; but we are in no position to judge of the propriety of their course, which seems to have been in harmony with the judicial procedure of the place and period, least of all to condemn them, so long as it was permitted them so to do, for having made a stout resistance when their acts were impugned in the appeal to the higher court.

The "Exhibit F," filed in the proceedings before the *Landrecht*, has not been found and its contents can only be guessed at from the allusions to it in the documents. Obviously it contained aspersions on the moral character of Frau van Beethoven, and it probably was true that they were unsupported by evidence and therefore undeserving of consideration in a court either of law or equity. In a Conversation Book of this year (1820) Beethoven writes of her that she was "born for intrigue, accomplished in deceit, mistress of all the arts of dissimulation." On the other hand, it is singular that the Magistrates in their final effort to justify their course had nothing to say about the present moral standing of the woman whose legal and natural right they claimed to be upholding. Were they in ignorance of what we now know, that her conduct had not only been reprehensible in 1811 (though condoned by her husband) but continued so after her husband's death? Schindler says that she gave birth to a child while the case was pending, and that is confirmed by a statement of nephew Karl's widow to Thayer that in her old age Frau van Beethoven lived in Baden with this illegitimate daughter, who was also a dissolute woman.

But there are many anomalous things to the studious mind in the proceedings which we are reporting, which differ greatly from anything which could happen in a court of chancery or probate in Great Britain or America today. It is certainly repugnant to our present legal ethics that having filed a petition to reverse the action of one court Beethoven should not only have written private letters to a judge of the court of review, pleading his case on personal grounds, but that his counsel should have advised him to visit members of the higher court to present arguments in his behalf. But, no doubt, this was consistent with the customs of contemporary Austria; and it is what happened.

On March 6 Beethoven writes to Karl Winter, a Councillor of Appeal: "I have the honor of informing you that I have written a memorial consisting of information about Fr. van Beethoven, about the Magistracy, about my nephew, about myself, etc. which I will send you within a few days. I *believed* that I owed this to myself to expose the falsity of the many slanders which have been uttered *against me* and to lay bare the intrigues of Frau van Beethoven *against me* to the injury of her own child, as also to place in its proper light the conduct of the Magistrate's Court." He charged that the Magistrates had summoned the widow and her son to a hearing without his knowledge and, as his nephew had told him, the boy had been urged and led on by his mother to make false accusations against him. He had also forwarded a document which proved the wavering and partisan conduct of the Magistrates. He repeated the charge about his nephew's failure to advance in his studies and added that the boy had had a hemorrhage which, had he not been on hand, might almost have cost him his life. These things were not attributable to Herr Tuscher for the reason that the Magistrates had given him too little support and he could not proceed with sufficient energy—this the writer could do in his capacity of uncle, guardian and defrayer of expenses. He asked that the charges against him be re-examined. He cited his expenditures to keep the boy two years in an educational institution, saying that for a period of fourteen months he had received nothing from the widow and after that only a small yearly contribution. Without the guardianship, he would feel relieved of the duty of taking further interest in the boy, but as guardian he would continue to pay all the cost unselfishly in the future. Moreover, he claimed that he had set apart 4,000 florins which was on deposit in bank and was to go to his nephew on his death. Finally, he expressed his hopes and expectations resulting from his relations with the Archbishop of Olmütz.

The case was prepared shrewdly, carefully and most discreetly by Dr. Bach, who seems to have exerted an admirable influence on Beethoven at this crisis. The nature of his advice may be learned from an entry in the Conversation Book by Bernard, who is evidently giving the result of a consultation with Dr. Bach:[9]

He [Dr. Bach] has already discussed the case with the official, Councillor of Appeal Winter, who was already informed by the *Landrecht* where he had been earlier. Now the Magistracy is being asked for a report of its proceedings, and hereupon the case will be decided by the Court of Appeals. He asked if Hr. Nusbeck [*sic*] has already resigned; if not, it would be good if Doct. Bach were to add a statement of resignation in writing from the same as a supplement to the statement already delivered. Doct. Bach has already said that Nusbeck would willingly resign and so the affair runs into no difficulty from this quarter. At this point there is still to be mentioned whether you have given up the guardianship altogether or only in favor of Tusch[er] in order better to effect the removal of the mother thereby. . . .[10] Furthermore it is necessary to proceed as moderately as possible in all things so that it does not appear as if there were malice; also the mother only in the most extreme cases is to be assailed on a point of honor. The whole [question] shall be connected with the reasoning that she cannot now be given any influence over the education because for a boy of this age a woman is not at all suitable. Furthermore it is necessary for you, if you should be asked, to explain that you will continue to bear the education costs,[11] whereupon if worst came to worst you could follow with the threat to withdraw your support altogether. He believes that reproaches might be made over the amount of time that you have had Karl with you[12] because the priests have become involved and the opposition has seized on this to increase the trouble. . . .

---

[9] Schünemann, I, pp. 184-85.

[10] Beethoven adds on the margin: "I appointed Tuscher guardian of the robbed ["des beraubten" is followed by an illegible word]— on the same day that Tuscher resigned I took up the guardianship again." (TDR, IV, 185, n. 2.)

[11] Beethoven adds on the margin: "This is self-evident." (TDR, IV, 185, n. 5.)

[12] Beethoven's comment on the margin is partly illegible: "would not the mother and in part the investments of the boy himself be indebted. . . ." (TDR, IV, 185, n. 6.)

I believe that in order to avoid all subterfuge at this time you should not take Karl into a tavern for a meal, because immediately it means that you lead him into a public place, because you are noticed by everyone and everything will be misrepresented by gossip and false interpretation.

Bach seems to have advised Beethoven to visit two of the judges, Winter and Schmerling, and himself had an interview with the boy, who told his uncle what the advocate had questioned him about.

For the nonce Karl was on his good behavior. Blöchlinger reported favorably on his studies to Bernard, and in a Conversation Book the boy apologized to his uncle for some statements derogatory to him which he had made to the Magistrates. "She promised me so many things," he said, "that I could not resist her; I am sorry that I was so weak at the time and beg your forgiveness; but I will certainly not again permit myself to be led astray—I did not know what results might follow when I told the Magistrates what I did. But if there is another examination I will retract everything that *I said* at the time which was *untrue!*"[13]

The magisterial commission which followed on March 29, had plainly been held at the instance of the Appellate Court. Beethoven was solemnly admonished, and in answer to questions declared: (1) that he still demanded the guardianship of his nephew under the will and would not relinquish his claim; (2) that he requested the appointment of Councillor Peters as associate guardian; (3) that he demanded that Frau van Beethoven be excluded from the guardianship as she had been by the *Landrecht*, and (4) he reiterated his readiness to provide financially for the care of his ward; he would accept an associate guardian, but not a sole guardian, as he was convinced that no guardian would care for his nephew as well as he.

In insisting on a renewed declaration on these points it is likely that the Court of Appeals had some hope that Beethoven might voluntarily renounce or modify his claims or the Magistrates recede from their attitude. Neither contingency occurred, however, and on April 8 the reviewing court issued its decree in Beethoven's favor, he and Peters being appointed joint guardians (*gemeinschaftliche Vormünde*), the mother and Nussböck being deposed. The widow now played her last card:—she appealed to the Emperor, who upheld the Court of Appeals. There was nothing for the Magistracy to do except to notify the result of the appeals to Beethoven, Frau van Beethoven, Peters and Nussböck. This was done on July 24.

Beethoven had won at last. But at what a cost to himself, his art, the world! What time, what labor, what energy had he not taken away from his artistic creations! What had he not expended in the way of peace of mind, of friendship, of physical comfort, of wear of brain and nerve-force, for the privilege of keeping the boy to himself, of watching unmolested over his physical welfare and directing his intellectual and moral training

[13] Schünemann, I, p. 195.

unhindered! At the present moment, however, his joy was unbounded, and he gave it expression in the following letter to Karl Pinterics:[14]

Dear Herr v. Pinterics!

I am reporting to you that the civil senate was authorized by the high Appellate Court to inform me of their decision which gives me complete satisfaction.—Dr. Bach was my representative in this affair, and this *brook* [in German: Bach] was joined by the sea, with lightning, thunder and storm, and the magisterial brigantine suffered complete shipwreck.

Yours faithfully,
Beethoven

Schindler says that "his happiness over the triumph which he had won over wickedness and trickery, but also because of the supposed salvation from physical danger of his talented nephew, was so great that he worked but little or hardly at all all summer—though this was perhaps more apparent than real, the sketchbooks disclosing from now on only empty pages."[15] A wise qualification, for though the sketchbooks may have been empty, there is evidence enough elsewhere of hard work. Yet the Mass was not finished, and for this unfortunate circumstance the guardianship trial was no doubt to blame. To this subject we shall return presently.

Peters, who was appointed joint guardian with Beethoven of the nephew, was a tutor in the house of Prince Lobkowitz and had been on terms of friendship with Beethoven since 1816. His appointment by the court is a confirmation of Beethoven's tribute to him as a man of intellectual parts and of good moral character. His wife had a good voice and was a great admirer of Beethoven, who had presented her with a copy of the song cycle "An die ferne Geliebte."

Bernard and Peters were the subjects for some humor in the Conversation Books and sketchbooks of this time. In the first *Missa Solemnis* sketchbook, now at Bonn, Beethoven wrote out a three-voiced piece on these words:[16]

Sanctus petrus ist ein Fels	Saint Peter is a rock
Auf diesen kann man bauen.	On this one can build.

The next reference is in a Conversation Book of January, 1820.[17] Bernard writes:

Sankt Petrus ist kein Fels	Saint Peter is no rock
Auf ihn kann man nicht bauen.	On him one cannot build.

[14] Pinterics was Count Palffy's private secretary. A friend of Beethoven's during these years, he became a much closer friend of Schubert's. He was widely cultured, and an excellent piano player; and it will be remembered that he sang bass in the "Ta, ta, ta" canon in honor of Mälzel. (Cf. TDR, iv, 188, n. 1.)

[15] *Biogr.*, i, pp. 271-72. (TDR, iv, 188.)
[16] Schmidt-Görg, *op.cit.*, p. 45.
[17] Schünemann, i, p. 183.

Bernardus war ein Sankt   Bernardus was a saint
Der hatte sich gewaschen,[18]   Who washed away the mottles
Er hat der Hölle nicht gewankt,   In front of hell he did not faint
u nicht zehntausend Flaschen   Nor with ten thousand bottles.

Peters answers: "Too bad about your canon which has probably vanished. It would have immortalized me." A month later Peters writes:[19] "The two beautiful canon[s] have certainly been erased" and Bernard answers "Saint Peter is a rock, on this one must . . . [build?]." The first of these canons was probably the one on the name of the poet Wähner, "Wähner es ist kein Wahn,"[20] and an idea of the second is suggested in an undated letter to Peters which follows.

How are you? Are you well or ill? How is your wife?— Permit me to sing something for you:

How are your young princes?

If you are at home this afternoon around 5 o'clock, perhaps I'll visit you together with my *state burden*.

In haste
your Beethoven

Nephew Karl remained at Blöchlinger's institute and continued to cause worry and anxiety to his uncle. Reports to Beethoven concerning his conduct and studies were variable from different persons and at different times. According to Blöchlinger he was unsteady and inclined to be lazy, and it was with great difficulty that he had again been made to work. He writes in March: "Since he has been with us, he had always been treated strictly, otherwise we would not have progressed as far as we now have." In April a cleric declared that he was at heart not a bad child but had been harmed by bad examples. There must have been further bad experiences for again in April someone writes: "Karl has little spirit and NB. despite the knowledge for which he is praised, little intelligence,—that is probably the key to this otherwise unpardonable behavior."[21]

[18] Figuratively: "who was first-rate."
[19] Schünemann, I, p. 240.
[20] See Schmidt-Görg, *op.cit.*, p. 45.
[21] Schünemann, I, p. 380; II, pp. 37, 88. The cleric referred to as "Der Probst von Michaelern," Schünemann (I, p. 152) identifies as Joh. Michael, curate of the Augustinian order at St. Florian who was also Director of the Linz Gymnasium.

Meanwhile, the conversation was frequently about Johanna's immorality and the necessity of Karl's understanding this. Blöchlinger seems to have come around completely to Beethoven's point of view. In June he writes:

She is simply a canaille, I am amply convinced of it, and unfortunately the boy also appears to be becoming one.

•~•

The boy lies every time he opens his mouth. His laziness, for which naturally he must be punished strictly, leads him astray continually. Will you please speak to him? — —

•~•

Perhaps if he could be taken to Salzburg or to some distant place, he could perhaps improve, removed from the influence of his mother. . . .

•~•

. . . It has seemed to me of late that the Beethoven woman was expecting. I would be very glad to know for sure, one would have new evidence for saying to Karl that his mother was immoral, moreover he will have observed it when he was with her. I would like to know it for certain. Karl must get a clear understanding as regards his mother, as you have said yourself; for if he depends on her, he is lost, and to alienate him from her, he must have proof that she is immoral. The other day I also told him that she had been in a house of correction and let him judge whether what his mother had done till now was good for him.[22]

Blöchlinger reports in the same June Conversation Book: "Today we have had a new incident. Karl had his oral examinations today but ran early in the morning again to his mother because yesterday and today he had not learned his lessons." Frau Blöchlinger had to take a coach and servant and bring him back to school; and to get him away from Frau van Beethoven, who was disposed to keep him in concealment, had to promise to see to it that he should not be punished. "I went along to the examination in which he did rather well." Blöchlinger continued with sharp words against the mother saying that her presence in his house brought him shame. He asked for a power of attorney to call in the help of the police every time that Karl should go to his mother.[23] Beethoven went for advice to Bach, who told his client that it was impracticable to get a judicial writ against the mother enjoining her from meeting her son, and impossible to prevent secret meetings and secret correspondence. The practical solution of the problem was to have Blöchlinger refuse to admit the woman to his institute and compel her to see Karl at his uncle's home. This would serve the purpose to some extent, as the mother did not like to meet her brother-in-law.[24]

Meanwhile work on the Mass was continuing, as the sketchbooks show. Exactly what condition it was in at that time we have no means of knowing;

[22] *Ibid.,* II, p. 153.   [23] *Ibid.,* pp. 175-77.   [24] *Ibid.,* p. 202.

it was, however, in a sufficient state of forwardness to enable Beethoven to begin negotiations for its publication. ----⟨In a letter to the firm of Simrock on February 10th Beethoven offered the Mass for 125 Louis d'or. He repeated the offer in a letter of March 9 and suggested on March 14 that perhaps he could ask for a lower figure. What was offered by Simrock as a counter-offer is made clear from Beethoven's answer which follows:⟩--

Vienna, March 18, 1820

Dear Herr Simrock!

I don't know whether I discussed everything completely in my last letter— I am writing you briefly therefore that I can extend the date for the edition of the variations,[25] if you find it necessary.— As regards the mass, I have pondered the matter carefully and might give it to you for the honorarium of 100 Louis d'or which you offered me, provided you agree to a few conditions which I shall propose and which, I think, you will *not* find burdensome. We have gone through the plan for publication here and believe that with a *few modifications* it can be put into effect very soon. This is very necessary, wherefore I shall make haste to inform you of the necessary changes soon— Since I know that dealers like to save post money, I enclose 2 Austrian folktunes here as change with which you can do what you like. The accompaniments are mine— I think a folk-song hunt is better than a man hunt of such exalted heroes— My copyist is not here now; I hope you will be able to read it—in fact you could have many things from me, for which you could show me another favor—

In haste   Yours
Beethoven

Enclosed were the songs "Das liebe Käzchen" and "Der Knabe auf dem Berge."

The enthronement of Beethoven's imperial pupil as Archbishop of Olmütz took place on March 20. The Mass which was to have been the composer's tribute was still unfinished. It may have been for the purpose of offering an explanation to the new dignitary of the church, that Beethoven sought an audience as he states in a letter of April 3:

. . . But now I wish that Y.I.H would kindly tell me how long you have decided to stay in O[lmütz]. Here they say that Y.I.H. would return here at the end of May; yet I heard a few days ago that Your Highness will remain in O *for another year and a half.* Perhaps I have taken the wrong measures, certainly *not as regards Y.I.H.*, but as regards myself. As soon as I have a report about it I will explain everything further. As for the rest I beg Y.I.H. not to give credence to the many reports about me, I have already learned of many which can be called gossip and with which people believe they can please even Y.I.H. If Y.I.H. calls me one of your most treasured objects, I can honestly say that Y.I.H. is to me one of the most treasured objects in the universe. Although I am no *courtier,* I believe that Y.I.H. has learned to know *me well enough* to know that no cold interest, but a sincere affection, has always attached me to yourself and inspired me; and I might well say that Blondel was found

---

[25] Op. 107; underneath Beethoven adds: "i.e., longer than 6 months." (TDR, IV, 193, n. 3.)

long ago, and if no Richard is to be found in the world for me, God will be my Richard— It appears to me that my idea to maintain a quartet will certainly be the best thing to do. Even if there are already productions on a large scale in O[lmütz], something admirable might arise in Moravia through such a quartet—Should Y.I.H. come here again in May as reported above, I advise you to save the children of your muse for me until then, because it is better if I hear them performed first by you. But if there is really to be a longer stay in Olmütz, I will receive them with the greatest pleasure and seek to guide Y.I.H. to the highest peak of Parnassus. . . .

A reference to himself as one who was at court yet not a courtier (*Hofmann*) had been made by Beethoven in an earlier letter. This play on words seems to have been much in his head about this time and it is small wonder that when an opportunity offered for the employment of the pun it should have been embraced. In the Conversation Book used in March, 1820,[26] a strange hand writes: "In the *Phantasie-Stücke* by Hoffmann, you are often spoken of. Hoffmann was musical director in Bamberg; he is now Government Councillor.— Operas of his composition are performed in Berlin." Beethoven remarks, in writing: "Hofmann [*sic*] du bist kein *Hof-mann*."— This may have been what gave Beethoven the impetus to read the essays on his works by E. T. A. Hoffmann and to write the following lines to him. —His love of punning has another outlet here in "unser schwach (weak) starke (strong)." The letter follows:

Vienna, March 23, 1820

I am seizing the opportunity through Herr Neberich[27] to approach a man so full of life and wit as you are— Also you have written about my humble self. Also our *weak Herr Starke* showed me some lines of yours about me in his album. Thus I am given to believe that you take some interest in me. Allow me to say that this from a man with such distinguished gifts as yourself pleases me very much. I wish you everything that is beautiful and good and remain

with high esteem yours faithfully
Beethoven

—Further instances of the play on words occurred in the Conversation Books during March. For instance, Beethoven writes: "nein, nein ich ich heisse Hofmann u. bin kein Hofma[nn] sondern ein Elen[der] schuft" ["No, I am called Hofmann and am no courtier but a wretched fellow"] for which he supplies the sketch of a canon.[28] Beethoven kept the canon in his mind or had a copy of it, and printed it in 1825, when B. Schott's Sons in Mainz asked him for a contribution to their newly formed musical journal *Cäcilia*.

—At this time some new portraits were made of the master. Frimmel has brought to light a half-length drawing in chalk by the artist Hippius

[26] Schünemann, I, p. 314.

[27] Neberich was a wine dealer whom Beethoven had known since at least 1816, when

in a letter to Franz von Brentano he is called "Europe's first wine artist."

[28] Schünemann, I, p. 334. See also p. 384.

which, according to his family, was based on a sitting with the composer. It is almost life-size and is similar to the Schimon in the interpretation of Beethoven's features.[29]

Another of the portraits of Beethoven which have been made familiar by reproductions was begun in 1819. Joseph Stieler, who enjoyed wide reputation as a portrait painter, had come to Vienna from Munich to paint the portrait of Emperor Franz in the latter year. He remained till some time in 1820 and made the acquaintance of Beethoven through a letter of introduction probably given to him by Brentano. Beethoven took a liking to him and gave him three sittings, but because Beethoven refused to sit longer, Stieler had to exercise his imagination or memory in painting the hands. In fact, the painting never received the finishing touches but remained, as those who have seen it testify, "sketchy." In April, 1820, Stieler asks the question: "In what key is your mass? I want to write on the sheet Mass in—." Beethoven writes the answer "D, Missa solemnis in D," and Stieler: "A quarter hour after it has been exhibited I shall send it to Brentano— I thank you thousands and thousands of times for so much patience." Beethoven's friends refer frequently to the picture in their written conversations with Beethoven. Schindler writes that he prefers the portrait by Schimon: "There is more character in it—all agree on that— You were very well two years ago; now you are always ailing." J. Czerny writes: "We were just talking about your portrait.— Oliva thinks it is a very good resemblance." The artist visited Beethoven again at Mödling in July and writes: "Before the exhibition I shall paint your portrait again, but full life-size. Your head makes an excellent effect full face, and it was so appropriate because Haydn was on one side and Mozart on the other."[30] Stieler dated the canvas "1819," but this can only refer to the time when it was begun. Schindler says it reproduces Beethoven's characteristic expression faithfully and that it met with approval, though fault was found with the pose. Beethoven's contemporaries were not used to seeing him with his head bowed down as Stieler represents him; on the contrary, he carried his head high even when suffering physical pain. A lithographic reproduction of the portrait was made by Fr. Dürck and published by Artaria in 1826.

The portrait remained for awhile in the possession of the family of the painter, then passed through several hands by purchase until it reached those of Countess Sauerma in Berlin, in whose possession it was when Frimmel and Kalischer inspected it for purposes of description. —Comparing it to the mask of 1812, Frimmel writes: "The lower third of the face with its broad mouth and irregular cicatrized chin makes a passably good resemblance. But the nose is too broad, the forehead much too high. Only

[29] The drawing of the head is reproduced in Frimmel's *Beethoven im zeitgenössischen Bildnis* (Vienna, 1923), p. 40. According to this source the drawing was last known to be in the possession of the artist's grandson, Ed. Hippius in Moscow.

[30] Schünemann, II, p. 37; I, p. 371; II, pp. 42, 180.

the root of the nose with its small cavities and brows is Beethoven's, but the eyes are placed so high above the cheekbone that their position is uncommon in any face and completely out of the question for Beethoven."[31] Frimmel also criticizes the weakness of the hands but cites the thoughtful expression of the face as perhaps the best thing about the painting. He adds that Stieler, who was an excellent portrait painter, would have undoubtedly corrected many of the errors if he had had the opportunity. According to Frimmel, the portrait is now in the possession of Herr Geheimrat H. Hinrichsen, who acquired it from the music publishing firm of C. F. Peters in Leipzig.

By February Beethoven had returned to live in the house on the Josephstädter Glacis where he stayed until May. In this period the Giannatasio family followed up their intention to visit Beethoven. On April 19, 1820, Fanny writes in her journal: "Tonight we visited Beethoven after not seeing him for almost a year. It seemed to me that he was glad to see us again; on the whole things seem to be going well for him now, at least it is a period in which he is free from the vexations of Karl's mother. I lament exceedingly that every connection with this excellent man has been given up; I was stirred more and more by his genuineness in every regard. His hearing has become a little worse. I wrote everything. He gave me a new beautiful song: 'Abendlied unter dem gestirnten Himmel' which gave me very much pleasure." This setting of a text by Goeble was published in the same year and was dedicated to the distinguished doctor, Anton Braunhofer, with whom Beethoven first became associated in this year.

In the summer of 1820[32] Beethoven went to Mödling again, but he did not take lodgings in the Hafner house for the very sufficient reason that the proprietor had served notice on him in 1819, that he could not have it longer on account of the noisy disturbances which had taken place there. He took a house instead in the Babenbergerstrasse and paid twelve florins extra for the use of a balcony which commanded a view which was essential to his happiness.[33] Here again he took the baths. He worked chiefly on the Mass, which was far from finished. His friends thought that he was further along than he was, and he was frequently asked if it was finished and when it would be performed. Some hurried sketches belonging to the *Credo* are found amongst the remarks of his friends, and also sketches for the *Agnus Dei*. Schindler asks him in August: "Is the *Benedictus* written out in score?— Are those sketches for the *Agnus*?"[34]

In the second *Missa Solemnis* sketchbook at Bonn there is a start to a "Sonate in E moll," which is not further developed. At this same time the

---

[31] *Op.cit.*, p. 45.

[32] The move to Mödling is referred to in a Conversation Book of early May and appears to have taken place at that time.

[33] Babenbergerstrasse No. 116, called

"Christhof," which he had contemplated buying in the fall of 1819. See preceding chapter.

[34] Schünemann, II, p. 201.

last three piano sonatas (Op. 109-111) were projected, to which we can return. Along with sketches to the E major Sonata (Op. 109) there are sketches for the Bagatelles Op. 119, Nos. 7 to 11 inclusive. Their story is known. Friedrich Starke, Kapellmeister of an Austrian regiment of infantry, had undertaken the publication of a pianoforte method which he called the "Wiener Pianoforteschule." Part III of the work, which appeared early in 1821, contained these five Bagatelles under the title "Trifles" (*Kleinigkeiten*).[35] Above them Starke printed: "A contribution from the great composer to the publisher." They must have been asked for in 1820. Somewhere about February of that year an unidentified hand writes in the Conversation Book: "Starke wants a little music-piece by you for the second part of his *Klavierschule*, for which he has contributions from the leading composers besides short notices. . . . We must give him something. Notwithstanding his great deserts in music and literature he is extremely modest, industrious and humble. . . . He understands the art of compiling well. There are now weaklings everywhere even among the strong."[36] To this appeal Beethoven yielded. He wrote the five Bagatelles.

Schindler relates that when Beethoven heard that it was bruited about that he had written himself out, his invention was exhausted, and that he had taken up Scottish melodies like Haydn in his old age, he seemed amused and said: "Wait awhile, you'll soon learn differently." Schindler then adds: "Late in the fall (1820), returned from his summer sojourn in Mödling, where like a bee he had been engaged busily in gathering ideas, he sat himself down to his table and wrote out the three sonatas Op. 109, 110, 111 'in a single breath,' as he expressed it in a letter to Count Brunsvik in order to quiet the apprehension of his friends touching his mental condition." Schindler was dubious about the "single breath" and, indeed, there was considerable lapse of time between the completion of the first of the three sonatas and the last two.[37] ━━━━But Beethoven's correspondence with the Berlin publisher Adolf M. Schlesinger, shows that from the start he considered writing three in a row. On April 30 he writes: ". . . Also I will be willing to hand over to you new sonatas,—but at no other price than 40 ducats per piece, thus a sort of enterprise of three sonatas for 120 ducats." On May 31 he agreed to write them within three months at a fee of 90 ducats. And on September 20 he writes: "The three sonatas are going faster—the first is about ready for proof, and now I am working on the last two without respite."━━━━ The Sonata in E belongs unquestionably to the year 1820. The first theme of the first movement is found in the Conversation Book of April;[38] the work was sketched in part before he began the *Benedictus,* in part while he was at work on this section, the *Credo,* the *Agnus Dei* and the

---

[35] See Frimmel, "Ein unbeachtetes Klavierstück von Beethoven," *Der Merker*, VIII (1917), p. 24, for more on Beethoven's contributions to Starke's publications.

[36] Schünemann, I, pp. 241, 297.

[37] *Biogr.*, II, pp. 2-3. No such letter to Franz Brunsvik has survived.

[38] Schünemann, II, p. 44.

Bagatelles for Starke. It was dedicated to Maximiliane Brentano, and published in November, 1821, by Schlesinger in Berlin.

There was at this time considerable talk in the Conversation Book[39] of publishing a complete edition of Beethoven's works. Bernard told him that Steiner was already counting on it, and Schindler, who was enthusiastic over the project, gave it as his opinion that arrangements must be made with a Vienna publisher so as to avoid voluminous correspondence. Bernard remarks: "Eckstein will so arrange it that you will always get all the profits and will also publish your future works as your property. He thinks that every fourth or fifth piece should be a new one." ⸺Since the beginning of the year, there had also been negotiations with Simrock concerning this idea. A letter written to this firm on August 5 from Vienna shows that Beethoven had just made one of his short visits to the city. He writes: ". . . Regarding the edition of my complete works we believe here that it would be good to add a *new work* to each type of composition; e.g., to the variations a new work of this kind, to the sonatas, each etc. etc. . . . ."⸺ The plan appealed strongly to Beethoven, but nothing came of it at the time, though we shall hear of it later.

It was the discussion of it by his friends which brought out a letter from Beethoven to Haslinger, "best of Adjutants," asking him to decide a bet. Beethoven had wagered 10 florins that it was not true that the Steiners had been obliged to pay Artaria 2000 florins damages for having published Mozart's works, which were reprinted universally.[40]

Archduke Rudolph, now Archbishop of Olmütz, left his residence for some time, having communicated to his teacher his intention to spend a part of the summer in Mödling. Beethoven wrote to him on August 3 making apologies for apparent neglect in not waiting upon him, which he blamed on the lack of a carriage. He wrote again on Saturday, September 2:

Your Imperial Highness!
Ever since Tuesday evening I have not been well but thought that certainly on Friday I would have the pleasure of coming to Y. I. H. But I was mistaken and now today I can inform Y. I. H. that next Monday or Tuesday I definitely hope to be able to pay a visit again to Y. I. H. which will be early in the morning— My indisposition comes from taking an open post carriage in order not to miss Y. I. H. The day was rainy and almost *cold* here in the evening. Nature almost seems to have taken amiss my openness or boldness and punished me for it— The heavens send down to Y. I. H. all that is good, beautiful, and holy, and for me Your good graces!— *But still sanctioned by justice!*—
Your Imperial Highness's ever most obedient and most faithful servant
L v. Beethoven

⸺Misfortune in the Erdödy family is referred to by an unidentified writer at the end of a Conversation Book dated July-early August: "For

---

[39] *Ibid.*, pp. 57, 85-6, 96.　　　　　[40] See *A* 1025.

some time curious things have been reported. Brauchle was imprisoned by the police, and the *Comtesse* Mimi[41] has gone some days ago to the St. Pölten Cloister, on account of the young count[42] that he mistreated so; and he is charged with beating him to death. Sperl[43] and the servant together with the chambermaid have been very often questioned about the murder; generally Sperl has been present all the time at Brauchle's trial in the Waag Gasse 274 on the ground floor and also in the old Wieden; they are telling the police in person everything possible about their lives."[44]

It will be remembered that the death of the boy August (who died at his sister's feet complaining of a pain in his head) brought forth from Beethoven the moving letter of condolence to the Countess Erdödy on May 15, 1816. The Conversation Book entry quoted above shows that four years later in 1820, Brauchle, tutor in the Erdödy household and friend of Beethoven, was implicated in this death. The evidence concerning this case is incomplete, but Gunther Haupt[45] has investigated the family correspondence and the police records that were available and comes to the following conclusions. In April there were already charges against the Countess and Brauchle for mistreatment of Mimi and a recommendation that Mimi "be freed" from them. Investigation showed that the Countess was unusually strict in the supervision of the children's education and that Brauchle was an excellent manager of domestic affairs for the Countess and a very able tutor for the children, especially in music. Letters written by Mimi and the Countess indicated love for each other and penitence for past frictions,[46] and Mimi's references to Brauchle showed friendship and respect. The records showed further that the interference by the police was at the written request of the widow, Countess Sigismund Erdödy, who was not on good terms with her sister-in-law. The attempt to separate mother and daughter appears to have been in order to secure Mimi for her son and Brauchle for herself. That the threat continues in 1821 is shown by letters written by both the Countess and Mimi; neither objective, however, was attained. Whether in 1820 Countess Marie Erdödy was banished from the country, as Thayer was led to understand, or whether she left of her own accord to still the gossip and calumny concerning her and her family is not clear. At any rate, she moved to Munich in 1824 where she died thirteen years later; already in 1830 Brauchle joined her there where he was survived by his wife. Thus ends the incomplete story of a member of the aristocracy, who was Beethoven's particularly close friend and helper.

Karl came to visit his uncle in Mödling, presumably during his school vacation. When the Giannatasio family made a visit to Mödling on October 5, they saw "our good Beethoven" returning Karl to the city.

[41] Nickname of Countess Erdödy's daughter Marie.

[42] To the right is added the word "Gusti"; nickname for the son, August.

[43] Sperl was the steward.

[44] Schünemann, II, pp. 213-14.

[45] "Gräfin Erdödy und J. X. Brauchle," in *Der Bär* (Lpz., 1927), pp. 70-91.

[46] Mimi had attempted suicide, whereupon she was sent to the St. Pölten Convent.

Towards the end of October, Beethoven returned to Vienna and took lodgings at No. 244 Hauptstrasse in the Landstrasse, "the large house of the Augustinians" beside the church.[47] There he was visited by Dr. W. Chr. Müller of Bremen, a philologist and musical amateur who had long admired Beethoven and, with the help of his "Family Concerts," established in 1732, had created such a cult for Beethoven's music as existed in no city in Germany in the second decade of the nineteenth century—according to Schindler. Müller's daughter Elise played the sonatas exceptionally well and was largely instrumental with her father in creating this cult. On his journey to Italy, Müller came to Vienna where he was in October and early November, 1820. He not only visited Beethoven but also saw and observed him from a distance as is shown by an article which he published entitled "Some Things about Beethoven," from which we quote:[48] "This sense of cosmopolitan independence and consideration for others[49] might have been the reason why over and over again he continued a conversation, already started, in restaurants, where he often had his frugal lunch, and expressed opinions freely and candidly about everything, the government, the police, the manners of the aristocracy in a critical and mocking manner. The police knew it but left him in peace either because he was a fantastic or because he was a brilliant artistic genius. Hence his opinion and assertion that nowhere was speech freer than in Vienna. His ideal of a [political] constitution was the English one."

It was through Dr. Müller that we know somewhat of Beethoven's views on the subject of analytical programmes. Among the zealous promoters of the Beethoven cult in Bremen, was a young poet named Dr. Karl Iken, editor of the *Bremer Zeitung*, who, inspired by the *Familien-Concerte*, conceived the idea of helping the public to an understanding of Beethoven's music by writing programmatic expositions of the symphonies for perusal before the concerts. Some of his lucubrations were sent to Beethoven by Dr. Müller, and aroused the composer's ire. Schindler found four of these "programmes" among Beethoven's papers, and he gave the world a specimen. In the Seventh Symphony, Dr. Iken professed to see a political revolution. "The sign of revolt is given; there is a rushing and running about of the multitude; an innocent man, or party, is surrounded, overpowered after a struggle and haled before a legal tribunal. Innocency weeps; the judge pronounces a harsh sentence; sympathetic voices mingle in laments and denunciations—they are those of widows and orphans; in the second part of the first movement the parties have become equal in numbers and the magistrates are now scarcely able to quiet the wild tumult. The uprising

---

[47] According to Frimmel (*FRBH*, II, p. 458), on the basis of a recollection of Karl van Beethoven's daughter, Frau G. Heimler, Beethoven lived for a short time at Alt-Lerchenfeld No. 8 (now Josefstädter Strasse No. 57) in order to be near the Blöchlinger Institute.

[48] *AMZ* (May 23, 1827), No. 21, p. 350.

(TDR, IV, 206, n. 3.)

[49] Müller had just referred to Beethoven's refusal in the last years to accept help, kindnesses, or even an invitation to a meal from friends of his own class, who knew his circumstances, for fear of limiting his freedom and burdening others with his deafness.

is suppressed, but the people are not quieted; hope smiles cheeringly and suddenly the voice of the people pronounces the decision in harmonious agreement. . . . But now, in the last movement, the classes and the masses mix in a variegated picture of unrestrained revelry. The quality still speak aloofly in the wind-instruments,—strange bacchantic madness in related chords—pauses, now here, now there—now on a sunny hill, anon on flowery meadow where in merry May all the jubilating children of nature vie with each other with joyful voices—float past the fancy."

It is scarcely to be wondered at that such balderdash disgusted and even enraged Beethoven. In the fall of 1819, he dictated a letter to Müller—it has, unfortunately been lost—in which he protested energetically against such interpretations of his music. He pointed out, says Schindler, who wrote the letter for him, the errors to which such writings would inevitably give rise. If expositions were necessary, they should be confined to c'. ·acterization of the composition in general terms, which could easily and correctly be done by any educated musician.[50]

Beethoven's complaints concerning his financial condition were chronic and did not cease even in periods where extraordinary receipts make them difficult to understand. That the lamentations in his letters during the two years which we have in review were well-founded, however, is no doubt true. With so engrossing a work as the *Missa Solemnis* on hand there could not have been much time for such potboilers as he mentions and the other sources of revenue were not many. From the records which are at hand, we know something about a few of his monetary transactions. On October 26, 1820, he collected 300 florins on account, apparently, from Artaria and Co., through his old friend Oliva.

On December 17th he again applied to Artaria as follows:

While I thank you most sincerely for the 750 fl. C.M. already lent me for which I handed over to you the receipt from H. Imperial Highness the Cardinal, I am requesting anew, since I am in danger of losing one of my 8 bank shares, the loan of a further 150 fl. C.M. which I promise to pay back to you by 3 months from today at the latest. But in order to show you my gratitude, I am promising in writing to send you presently one of my compositions consisting of one, two or several movements as your property without asking for any kind of honorarium.

ever your obliging
Beethoven

It is not known whether Beethoven delivered any work of this kind. These shares, it will be remembered, had been set apart by him as his nephew's legacy, and he clung to them as a sacred pledge.

Meanwhile a letter from Steiner to the composer shows that he had sent Beethoven a dun, or at least a statement of account, and Beethoven had evidently been unreasonable in his reply. The letter follows:

[50] *Biogr.*, II, pp. 208-11. (TDR, IV, 206.)

Vienna, Dec. 29, 1820

Most highly esteemed Sir and friend Beethoven!

Enclosed are the three overtures in score with the request that you go through them at your convenience as you yourself suggested and correct any errors that may have crept in.— As soon as we have received these corrections we will proceed to engrave and print them in order to bring out the first edition as quickly as possible.

I cannot rest content with your remarks concerning the account sent you; for the cash money loaned you I have charged you only 6% interest, while for the money which you deposited with me I paid you 8% promptly in advance and also repaid the capital promptly. What is sauce for the goose is sauce for the gander (*Was also dem Einen recht ist, muss dem Andern billig sein*). I am not in a position to lend money without interest. As a friend I came to your help in need, I trusted your word of honor and believe that I have not been importunate, nor have I plagued you in any way; wherefore I must solemnly protest against your upbraidings. If you recall that my loan to you was made in part 5 years ago, you will yourself confess that I am not an urgent creditor. I would spare you even now and wait patiently if I were not on my honor in need of cash for my business. If I were less convinced that you are really in a position to give me relief and able to keep your *word of honor* I would, difficult as it would be for me, right gladly remain patient a while longer; but when I remember that I myself returned to you 4,000 florins, conventional coin, or 10,000 florins, Vienna Standard, as capital 17 months ago and at your request did not deduct the amount due me, it is doubly painful to me now to be embarrassed because of my good will and my trust in your word of honor. Every man knows best where the shoe pinches and I am in this case; wherefore I conjure you again not to leave me in the lurch and to find means to liquidate my account as soon as possible.

As for the rest I beg you to accept from me the compliments of the season together with the request that you continue to give me your favor and friendship. It will rejoice me if you keep your word and honor me soon with a visit; it rejoices me more that you have happily withstood your illness and are again restored to health. God preserve you long in health, contentment and enjoyment, this is the wish of your wholly devoted

S. A. Steiner.

The letter contains pencil memoranda by Beethoven. He had evidently added together the various sums which he owed Steiner and they amounted to 2420 florins V.S. He remarks: "The 1300 florins V.S. were probably received in 1816 or 1817— 750 fl. V.S. still later, perhaps in 1819—the 300 fl. are debts which I assumed for Frau van Beethoven and can be chargeable for only a few years—the 70 florins may have been for myself in 1819.— Payment may be made of 1200 florins a year in semi-annual payments."[51] A further memorandum on the cover notes Steiner's willingness to accept payments on April 15 and October 15, 1821. --ᵍᵍIn a letter to Haslinger written on September 5, presumably in 1822, Beethoven writes: "I beg Steiner

[51] For a discussion of the financial transactions between Beethoven and the Steiner firm see Max Unger, *Ludwig van Beethoven und seine Verleger*, pp. 15-17.

to go to Dr. Bach tomorrow afternoon where the 600 fl. C.M. may be received, the other 600 will be available also from Dr. Bach as soon as possible." But the conflict between Steiner and Beethoven was again to come to a head in the year 1823. The three overtures mentioned in Steiner's letter were undoubtedly those to the *Ruinen von Athen* and *König Stephan*, and the "Namensfeier" overture. The increasingly strained relations between Steiner and Beethoven are demonstrated by the fact that after the Symphonies No. 7 and No. 8 and the Pianoforte Sonata in A, Op. 101, no big works were given to Steiner and by the fact that as a result these three overtures were not published right away but in 1823, 1826 and 1825 respectively.}᰽⚬—

The negotiations for the publication of the Mass had already begun; as we know from the letter of March 18 to Simrock, the Bonn publisher was supposed to receive it for 100 Louis d'or along with certain conditions. —⚬᰽{But entries in the Conversation Books show that in Beethoven's circle there was decreasing enthusiasm for the offer, yet increasing need for the money. Already in the latter part of March, soon after the original letter had been mailed, Oliva writes:

100 Louis d'or would be 200 ducats, that would be little. 1 Louis is 2 ducats, one Louis is worth 12 g[ulden] or somewhat more in gold;—Prussian Friedrichs d'or are worth less, I am sure of it. How much have you asked from Simrok? At least 150 Louis d'or? 125 is 250 ducats. I told you that before you came out.[52]

In business transactions with Bonn Franz Brentano in Frankfurt was authorized to act as agent. In April Oliva writes again:}᰽⚬— "Have you written to Simrok that he must not publish the mass *at once* as you want first to send it or hand it to the Archduke?" Again: "If you send the Recepisse on the stage-coach he will certainly send you the money *at once*." And later: "It would be quicker to give the music to the stage-coach and send Brentano the receipt—at the same time informing Simrok that Brentano had been assured of its dispatch; then Brentano can send you the money *at once* without waiting to receive the music." In April again: "But he has not yet replied to your last offer of the mass? I mean Simrock—200 ducats could help you out greatly— Because of your circumstances. You must not delay writing to Simrock or Brentano;— Brentano can send you the money *at once*—or at least very soon.— I am surprised that Simrock has not answered yet."[53]

—⚬᰽{On April 23 Beethoven asked again that the 100 Louis d'or be sent to Brentano and stated that Simrock would receive the Mass "by the end of May or beginning of June." The next letter concerning the Mass is dated July 23 and shows that Simrock had written on July 10 questioning the meaning in monetary terms of the Louis d'or. In his reply, Beethoven held to the value of 2 ducats or the various florin equivalents of one Louis d'or

[52] Schünemann, I, p. 377.   [53] *Ibid.*, II, pp. 11, 32, 33, 79.

and added "—Herewith if everything is settled, I assure you that you will receive the Mass next month."

The contents of Simrock's next letter, which was written undoubtedly in August are suggested by some more of Oliva's entries in the Conversation Books at the end of August.⊱— "Leave Simrok's letter with me, I'll answer it and give you the letter this afternoon;—if you are satisfied with it sign it and I will post it tomorrow. There must be no delay." "He says the Mass can be used only by Catholics, which is not true. He is paying too little rather than too much with 200 ducats."[54] —⊰In his answer of August 30, Beethoven established the florin exchange at 9 per Louis d'or and asked for 900 florins. Beethoven also corrected Simrock as regards the use of the Mass by pointing out that his first mass was supplied in the Breitkopf and Härtel edition with an additional German text and was performed in Protestant cities, and that he would be willing to supply a German text for his new mass.⊱—

The difficulty that had developed is explained in a letter from Simrock to Brentano dated November 12, 1820. It was a misunderstanding concerning the price of the "new grand musical mass" which the composer wished to sell for 100 Louis d'or. The publisher had agreed to the price, understanding Louis d'or to mean what the term meant in Bonn, Leipzig and throughout Germany, namely, the equivalent of Friedrichs d'or, pistoles. In order to avoid unpleasantness after the reception of the Mass he had explained this clearly to Beethoven and in a letter, dated September 23, had repeated that by Louis d'or he meant Friedrich d'or; he was not in a position to give more. He would hold the sum in readiness against the receipt of the Mass, which Beethoven had promised to provide with German as well as Latin words. He was also under the impression that he had asked a speedy decision, as he did not want to keep his money tied up in Frankfurt. Hearing nothing for four weeks he had quit counting on the Mass and made other use of his money. Learning, however, from Brentano's letter of November 8th that Beethoven had agreed to let him have the Mass, he now found himself in the embarrassment of not having the gold Louis d'or on hand; but as Brentano had said nothing on the subject he would in the meantime try to secure the coin, unless Brentano were willing to take the equivalent in florins at the rate of 9.36. He asked to be informed of the arrival of the music so that he might instruct Heinrich Verhuven to receive it on paying the sum mentioned.

Simrock had waited four weeks before abandoning hope that Beethoven would send the Mass; it was ten weeks and more before Beethoven answered Simrock's letter. Then he sent his reply enclosed in a letter to Brentano dated November 28. —⊰The letter follows:

[54] *Ibid.*, pp. 238, 240.

Vienna, November 28, 1820

My dear Simrock!

I received your last letter in the country. After His Imperial Highness the Cardinal returned to his residence and I had to betake myself to him in the city two or three times weekly during the whole summer, my country life which is dear to me was very much disturbed. Not until October was I able to retrieve some of the country life that I'd missed. Your letter arrived at this time, but going back and forth first here then there I did not read it right away. Since I understand nothing about business affairs, I waited for my friend who, nevertheless, has not been here up until now. In the meantime I could not help learning from others that I would lose at least 100 fl. C.M. Being frank, I must confess to you that earlier I could have had 200 ducats in gold, yet your offer was preferable since 100 l[ouis d'or] according to information was supposed to be worth still more. Now it is too late to change since the firm that was supposed to receive the great Mass has commissioned another big work from me, and I would not like to have appeared to have given out on any kind of a proposal—which you will find natural enough. As soon as the Mass is supplied throughout with a German text, I will send it to Hr. F. Brentano in Frankfurt where you can then transfer 100 pistoles instead of Louis d'or according to your interpretation. The translation is costing me at least 50 fl. V.S., I hope at least that you will provide this amount, and so requiescat in pace— I would rather write 10,000 notes than one letter, especially when it's a question of taking *this* and not *that*. Therefore I hope that much more for your favor in the edition of my complete works, which, as you know, means a great deal to me. Since Bonn is regarded as out of the country, the edition there could extend *my leave of absence* out of the country, which is what I want. All good wishes and regards to Wegeler and his whole family. As soon as I find a beautiful Bohemian goblet, I will send him *one again*.

In haste your Beethoven

Thus matters stood with the Mass at the end of 1820, and thus they seem to have remained throughout the next year. Simrock always was to be but never was blest with the score.

Of the performances of Beethoven's music during the year, the following should be mentioned. At the concerts of the Gesellschaft der Musikfreunde the *Eroica* was performed on February 20, the Symphony in C minor and a chorus from *Christus am Ölberg* on April 9, Symphony No. 8 in F major on November 19. On April 17 Fanny Giannatasio records in her diary: "Yesterday I heard once again the harmonies of the two rulers in the realm of tones, a new overture by Beethoven and the overture to *Figaro* by Mozart." The concert was for the benefit of Widows and Orphans; the overture was undoubtedly Op. 115, "Zur Namensfeier."

On October 1, 1819, a new concert series was started, soon to be known as the *Concerts spirituels*. Its founder was Franz Xaver Gebauer (1784-1822), choir director at the Augustinian church. His idea was to enlarge the choir rehearsals into meetings of music-lovers in which was performed not only a choral work in preparation for the next feast day but also a whole symphony. Concerning the founding of these concerts, Mosel writes in the Vienna *Allg. Mus. Zeitung* (April 5, 1820) that "musical jugglery has taken the place of sensitive performance, everywhere the symphonies of Mozart, Haydn, Beethoven have disappeared— Now *Herr Gebauer* makes the proposal to form a special society of a moderate number to bring to performance only symphonies and choruses excluding all virtuoso music (*Concertmusik*) and bravura singing." These concerts were on the one hand more strict in program than those at the Gesellschaft[55] and on the other hand more faulty in performance since the performers were amateurs reading at sight. In the 18 concerts of the first season (1819/20) were performed Beethoven's first four symphonies, the "Pastoral," the Mass in C, and *Meerestille und Glückliche Fahrt,* the last twice. The second season (1820/21) again consisted of ten concerts which included the Symphonies in C minor, A major, and F major (No. 8) and *Christus am Ölberg.*[56]

In Beethoven's circle, Gebauer's choir seems to have been more highly regarded than his new concert series. In a Conversation Book in April Beethoven makes one of his familiar plays on names: Oliva—"Concerning Gebauer"—Beethoven—"Geh! Bauer." [Go! peasant]. Soon Oliva remarks: "Since Gebauer has taken over, the music at the Augustin has improved very much and now the best church music is there." In contrast, Oliva comments on the performance on April 9th: "I forgot to tell you that the dilettantes scraped through your symphony yesterday."[57] And Beethoven wrote the following note in connection with one of these concerts:♪—

To the most famous music store in Europe, Steiner and Company (Pater noster miserere gässel)

I request some tickets (2) from Geh Bauer since some of my friends wish to go to this *musical obscurity* [*Winkelmusik*]—perhaps you have some of these *privy tickets* [*Abtrittskarten*] if so send me one or two—

Your

The score belongs to	Animus
the chorus for which	Beethoven
der *Bauer* has the voice parts.	

This year a furore was created in Vienna by an eight-year-old pianist, Leopoldine Blahetka. She was a pupil of Joseph Czerny,[58] who also taught Beethoven's nephew. He helped her rehearse Beethoven's Concerto in B-flat which she played in public on April 3.

---

[55] The program for the Gesellschaft concert of April 5, for instance, was: Beethoven, Symphony in C minor; Niccolini, Soprano Aria with Chorus from *Il Carlo Magno*; Worzischek, Song for four voices "Gott im Frühling"; Keller, Polonaise for Flute; Beethoven, Chorus from *Christus am Ölberg*.

[56] For further information concerning the *Concerts spirituels* see Eduard Hanslick, *Geschichte des Concertwesens in Wien* (Vienna, 1869), I, pp. 185-90. (TDR, IV, 218, n. 2.)

[57] Schünemann, II, pp. 40, 41.

[58] Joseph Czerny (1785-1842), not a relative of Carl Czerny, was his successor as teacher of Beethoven's nephew Karl. He was a composer, pianist and pianoforte teacher.

An event at the end of the year which could not fail to affect Beethoven was the departure of his friend Oliva, who had been his faithful helper in all kinds of external matters for a number of years. In December, 1820, he took his passport and moved to St. Petersburg, where he settled as a teacher of languages. From now on, Schindler was to become a closer friend and factotum to Beethoven.

The compositions of the year were:

"Abendlied unterm gestirnten Himmel," WoO 150.
Canons:
  "Alles gute, alles schöne" (Goeble), WoO 179, New Year's greeting to Archduke Rudolph.
  "Bester Magistrat, Ihr friert," WoO 177 [around 1820]. Eight measures for four bass voices with accompaniment of violoncello or double bass.
  "Hoffman, sei ja kein Hofmann," WoO 180, probably inspired by the name E. T. A. Hoffmann.
  "Sankt Petrus war ein Fels, Bernardus war ein Sankt," WoO 175, inspired by the names of Karl Peters and Karl Bernard.
  "Wähner es ist kein Wahn," for Friedrich Wähner, Hess Verzeichnis No. 301.
Sonata for Pianoforte, Op. 109.
Around 1820: Three Canons: "Gedenket heute an Baden," "Gehabt euch wohl," and "Tugend ist kein leerer Name," WoO 181, amidst sketches for the *Missa Solemnis*.[59]

The publications of the year were:

By Simrock:
Ten Themes, Russian, Scottish and Tyrolean, Varied for Pianoforte with optional accompaniment for flute or violin, Op. 107.
By the *Wiener Modenzeitung* as a supplement, March 28:
"Abendlied unterm gestirnten Himmel," WoO 150, dedicated to Dr. Anton Braunhofer.

[59] See *II Beeth.*, p. 152.

CHAPTER XXXIV

THE YEAR 1821

ATTACKS OF RHEUMATISM AND JAUNDICE—THE PIANOFORTE SONATAS OP. 110 AND OP. 111

THE information in 1821 concerning Beethoven's life is comparatively meagre. Not only have no Conversation Books of this year survived but also the number of letters existent is very small. Consequently certain portions of the all too rich offerings of the Conversation Books from the past year may be reserved to serve as an introduction to this year. Not all the entries are concerned with the nephew, the price of a commodity, some local news, or a recent musical performance; there are also remarks on topics of general concern—politics, philosophy, literature—which might well be cited as typical for these years. Here are isolated examples drawn from various periods:

[Janitschek][1] If N[apoleon] had come back now, he would have had a better reception in Europe. He understood the spirit of the age and knew how to hold the reins. Our descendants will know better how to estimate him. As a German I was his greatest enemy but as time goes on, I have become reconciled. Dedicated ideals and beliefs are there—his word was worth far more. He had a taste for art and science and hated ignorance. He would have appreciated the Germans more and would have protected their rights. At the end he was surrounded with traitors and the spirit of the generals declined. His best marshals had withdrawn.

The children of the Revolution and the spirit of the age demanded such an iron will. He certainly destroyed the Feudal system everywhere and was the protector of law and justice. His marriage to Princess Louise was the highest culmination point. To give the world peace and good laws was what mattered, and not to want to make more conquests.— Because of pride the greatest fortune became the greatest misfortune. An old torn piece of cloth that can never be

---

[1] Nothing is known of Herr and Frau Janitschek beyond the fact that their names appear frequently along with those of Bernard and Peters during the conversations of 1820. See *FRBH*, I, pp. 238-39.

mended. Instead of being sensible as a result of the experience, they have become still more foolish— That's what happens with privileges. How can one inherit nobleness of the heart? The privileged first of all have established a social contract and then they speak of rights.[2]

[Peters] Kaiser Leopold was a 7 month old child. In order to let him ripen properly he was firmly planted in a freshly slaughtered pig and the meat was subsequently given to the poor which they named Kaiser meat.[3]

[Blöchlinger] Man is living to excess in nature's lap; here he is too much occupied with conceit and with his stomach to realize it. Man should be able to give up everything to preserve himself, otherwise man is lost. There is such a menace, it is a fateful period; we must wait patiently to see what is to be the end of it all and each tend to our own business.

•~•

Meanwhile religion has been pulled into play and the so-called Ligorians[4] have again begun the old Agnosticism and that is respected and called good because there is no alternative.

•~•

It seems to me that we Europeans are going backwards, and America is raising itself in culture. The present relationship at least is not favorable; the just claims of Americans to independence, on the contrary, support this.

•~•

The saddest tendency of this new revolutionary spirit is an egotism poorly demonstrated or rather too clearly shown. What purpose is gained by the murder of Kotzebue? Although he was no moral luminary in the world, yet he was opposed to many a priest's tale (*Bonzengeschichte*) and would have been again probably if he were living.

•~•

What man is in a position to estimate the results of such an act and consequently consider it as good and necessary.[5]

[Kanne] An excellent work, but only the first part concerning Greek history has been published. By Otfried Müller in Göttingen.[6] Buy it. As soon as possible I will send to you a little work by Schleiermacher in Berlin. Fichte!—Schelling! Would you like to read something intelligible by Schelling? about art and academic study?[7] Winckelmann[8] said: one must sketch with fire and work out with sluggishness. . . . You must read Plato in the German translation by Schleiermacher. You must, I will bring it for you. He and Schelling are the greatest! Veneration to their spirits! The matter not the form. The idea is splendid and very original.[9]

---

[2] Schünemann, I, pp. 206-207.

[3] *Ibid.*, p. 243.

[4] Ligurians belonged to the Congregation of the Most Holy Redeemer founded by Alfonso Maria de Liguoris in 1732.

[5] Schünemann, I, pp. 323-24.

[6] Karl Otfried Müller, *Geschichten helle-nicher Stämme und Städte* (Breslau, 1820),

Vol. I.

[7] Fr. Wilh. Jos. von Schelling, *Vorlesungen über die Methode des akademischen Studiums* (Tübingen, 1803).

[8] Johann Joachim Winckelmann, German archaeologist of the 18th century.

[9] Schünemann, I, pp. 344-46.

[Bernard on the subject of inflation]

All Europe is in the same condition. In Spain it was the worst. For 2 years the poor received no wages, the officers had to beg and in the navy they have been dying of hunger. They should go to Armenia to fight in order to gain their back wages. It was the same in France before the Revolution. Because of the bad management of finance, the spending of the court and the excessive demands from the poor, the whole of Europe has become like Spain—no states can any longer save themselves from debts.

It is as with families and single men where no more means of help are at hand. Palfy has instituted a lottery, Stadion also.[10] The whole of Europe is going to the dogs. N[apoleon?] should have been let out for 10 years. Germany must be maintaining 38 courts and perhaps a million princes and princesses, the soldiers who work here on the earthworks receive six groschen V.S. daily even though we have received so many millions in contributions from France. As with the gentleman so with the laborers. They have certainly survived. There still is a pride and an ambition to oppose foreign countries. One simply will not yield, the nobility especially—

Also religion is having to become constitutional; the *Concilien,* common gathering of the bishops, must again be inaugurated to regulate the religious needs of each race according to the degree of its culture, instead of through an absolute judgement of the pope or of the Roman See. All in all we have come down in the world.[11]

Before recounting what is known concerning Beethoven in 1821, a final word should be said concerning his old love, Josephine née Brunsvik, since 1810 Baroness von Stackelberg. After the financial misfortunes which followed his marriage, Stackelberg's situation improved at the end of 1815 when he inherited his brother's property in Russia. Josephine refused to leave Vienna, and he departed with their three daughters who were left with their governess with the Dean of Trautenau in Bohemia. Stackelberg returned with the children to Vienna in 1817 and then left Austria for good. Josephine died on March 31, 1821. Her sister Therese wrote in her journal on July 12, 1817: "If Josephine doesn't suffer punishment on account of Luigi's woe—his wife! What wouldn't she have made out of this hero!" During all of these years did the two meet again? There is no known evidence of any communication after Ludwig's poignant close to their correspondence in 1807; it is known only that Josephine's last years were years of suffering from ill health.[12]

The beginning of the year 1821 found Beethoven still at his home in the suburb Landstrasse, and, it would seem, working as hard as his health permitted. In the *Novellistik* section of the *Allgemeine Musikalische Zeitung*, January 10, 1821, appears: "Herr von Beethofen was sick with a

[10] Prince Palffy and Count Stadion.
[11] Schünemann, II, pp. 58-9.
[12] *Beethoven-Dreizehn unbekannte Briefe an Josephine Gräfin Deym geb. v. Brunzvik,* ed. Joseph Schmidt-Görg (Beethovenhaus: Bonn, 1957), pp. 34-5.

rheumatic fever. All friends of true music and all admirers of his muse feared for him. But now he is on the road to recovery and is working actively."[13] A letter of March 7 to Adolf M. Schlesinger in Berlin starts:

Noble Sir!

Perhaps you are thinking disparagingly of me, but you may soon change when I tell you that for six weeks I have been laid up with a severe rheumatic attack; but now it is much better. You can imagine how many things have come to a standstill. Soon I shall catch up with everything. . . .

Instructions follow concerning the publication of Op. 108 (referred to here as "107. Werk") and Op. 109. Beethoven adds: "Will you add the year number as I have often wished, but no publisher has been willing to do it? Both of the other sonatas will follow soon. . . ."

On February 18 Beethoven wrote a little Allegretto in B minor for the album of his new friend, Ferdinand Piringer. Piringer (1780-1829) was a music-lover who was associated with Gebauer and acted as assistant conductor for the *Concerts spirituels* at the Landhaussaal. The Conversation Books of the next year show that he became one of Beethoven's closer friends.[14]

In April, 1860, the author had a conversation with Horzalka[15] in which the latter spoke very highly of Schindler and his disinterested fidelity to Beethoven. Horzalka also said that in 1820 or 1821, as near as he could recollect, the wife of a Major Baumgarten took boy boarders in her house. Her sister, Baroness Born, lived with her. Frau Baumgarten had a son who studied at Blöchlinger's Institute, and Beethoven's nephew was amongst her boarders. One evening Horzalka called there and found only the Baroness Born at home. Soon another caller came and stayed to tea. It was Beethoven. Among other topics, Mozart came under discussion, and the Baroness asked Beethoven, in writing of course, which of Mozart's operas he thought the most of. "*Die Zauberflöte*," said Beethoven and, suddenly clasping his hands and throwing up his eyes exclaimed, "Oh, Mozart!" As Horzalka had, as was the custom, always considered *Don Giovanni* the greatest of Mozart's operas, this opinion by Beethoven made a very deep impression upon him. Beethoven invited the Baroness to come to his lodgings and have a look at his Broadwood pianoforte.[16]

For the summer he went first to Unterdöbling. He had suffered from rheumatism during the preceding winter and now became a victim of

---

[13] See Frimmel, *Beethoven-Forschung*, VIII, p. 117.

[14] See *FRBH*, II, pp. 21-2.

[15] Johann Friedrich Horzalka (1778-1860), composer and pianist, was born in Triesch in 1778, came to Vienna in 1799, and studied harmony and counterpoint with Emmanuel Förster. He died but a few months after his conversation with Thayer.

[16] In the Conversation Books Baroness Born is mentioned already in the early part of 1820, but it is not until late summer that Horzalka is identified by Oliva: "His name is Horschalka, he is a pupil of Moscheles" (Schünemann, II, p. 234). This suggests that the scene in Vienna described above did not take place until the next winter—1820-21.

jaundice. This attack may have been an *avant-courier* of the disease of the liver which brought him to the grave six years later. He wrote the following letter to the Archduke on July 18:

Your Imperial Highness!

I heard yesterday of the arrival here of Your Highness, which would have given me so much pleasure, but now has become a sad event for me since it may be a rather long time before I can be lucky enough to wait upon Y. I. H. After feeling poorly for a very long time, a *full case of jaundice* finally developed, a disease that is extremely loathsome to me. I hope at least that I will be cured enough to see Y. I. H. before your departure— Also last winter I had a very bad rheumatic fever— Much of this is linked up with the sad situation as regards my economic circumstances. Up until now I had hoped by struggling to the utmost to emerge finally victorious over it. God, who knows my heart and knows how sacredly I as a man fulfill all the duties imposed upon me by humanity, God and nature, will some day free me from this affliction— The Mass will be delivered to Y. I. H. while you are here. Please let me spare Y. I. H. the causes of its delay. The details might prove anything but pleasant to Y. I. H— . . . .

The rest of the letter consists of further expressions of concern about his relationship with his patron.

In order to take a cure prescribed by his physician, Dr. Staudenheim, Beethoven moved to Baden on September 7, where he stayed in the Rathausgasse No. 94.[17]

In 1820 Professor Höfel, who lived at Salzburg in the last years of his life and who engraved the Latronne portrait of Beethoven for Artaria, was appointed to a professorship of drawing in Wiener Neustadt. A year or two afterward, as he said,[18] he was one evening with Eisner and other colleagues in the garden of the tavern "Zum Schleifen," a little way out of town. The Commissioner of Police was a member of the party. It was autumn and already dark when a constable came and said to the Commissioner: "Mr. Commissioner, we have arrested somebody who will give us no peace. He keeps on yelling that he is Beethoven; but he's a ragamuffin, has no hat, an old coat, etc.—nothing by which he can be identified." The Commissioner ordered that the man be kept under arrest until morning, "then we will examine him and learn who he is." Next day the company was very anxious to know how the affair turned out, and the Commissioner said that about 11 o'clock at night he was awakened by a policeman with the information that the prisoner would give them no peace and had demanded that Herzog, Musical Director in Wiener Neustadt, be called to identify him. So the Commissioner got up, dressed, went out and woke up Herzog, and in the middle of the night went with him to the watchhouse. Herzog, as soon as he cast eyes on the man exclaimed, "That *is* Beethoven!" He took him

---

[17] See Th. Frimmel, "Beethoven im Kurort Baden bei Wien" in *NBJ*, IV (1930), p. 73.
[18] This anecdote is recorded in Thayer's notebook as a memorandum of a conversation he had with Höfel on June 23, 1860. (TK, III, 42, n. 2.)

home with him, gave him his best room, etc. Next day came the burgomaster, making all manner of apologies. As it proved, Beethoven had got up early in the morning, and, slipping on a miserable old coat and, without a hat, had gone out to walk a little. He got upon the towpath of the canal and kept on and on; seemed to have lost his direction, for, with nothing to eat, he had continued on until he ended up at the canal-basin at the Ungerthor. Here, not knowing where he was, he was seen looking in at the windows of the houses, and as he looked so like a beggar the people had called a constable who arrested him. Upon his arrest the composer said, "I am Beethoven." "Of course, why not?" (*Warum nicht gar?*) said the policeman; "You're a tramp: Beethoven doesn't look so." (*Ein Lump sind Sie; so sieht der Beethoven nicht aus.*) Herzog gave him some decent clothes and the burgomaster sent him back to Baden in the magisterial state-coach.

A letter written from Baden on September 10, 1821, to Tobias Haslinger accompanying a canon on the words "O Tobias dominus Haslinger, O, O!" deserves to be given here to show that Beethoven's high spirits could at times dominate him in spite of his general misery.

Very best fellow!

Yesterday, in the carriage on the way to Vienna, I was overcome by sleep, naturally enough, since (because of my early rising here) I had never slept well. While thus slumbering I dreamed that I had made a long journey—to no less distant a country than Syria, then to India, back again, even to Arabia; finally I reached Jerusalem. The Holy City aroused in me thoughts of Holy Writ and small wonder that the man Tobias now occurred to me, and how natural that our little Tobias should enter my mind and the pertobiasser, and now during my dream journey the following canon came to me:

But scarcely awakened, away went the canon and nothing of it would come back to my memory. But when, next day, I was on my way hither in the same conveyance (that of a poor Austrian musician) and continued the dream journey of the day before, now awake, behold, according to the laws of association of ideas, the same canon occurred to me again. Now fully awake I held it fast, as once Menelaus held Proteus, only allowing it to change itself into 3 voices.

Farewell. Presently I shall send you something on Steiner to show you that he has no stony [*Steinernes*] heart. Farewell, very best of fellows, we ever wish that you will always belie your name of publisher [*Verleger*] and never become embarrassed [*verlegen*] but remain a publisher [*Verleger*] never at a loss [*verlegen*] either in receiving or paying—Sing the epistles of St. Paul every day,

Alternative[19] with a 3rd voice

go to pater Werner,[20] who will show you the little book by which you may go to heaven in a jiffy. You see my anxiety for your soul's salvation; and I remain with the greatest pleasure from everlasting to everlasting,

Your most faithful debtor Beethoven.

The reference to the Mass in the letter of July 18 to the Archduke could suggest that it was almost ready; but unfortunately that was not the case, for he was working on it constantly during this and the following year. The slow progress is explained partly through his illnesses and partly that he had taken up other composition projects simultaneously. Back in Vienna Beethoven wrote the following letter to Franz Brentano which sheds light on these matters:

Vienna, November 12, 1821

Honored friend!

Don't consider me a shabby or thoughtless genius— For the past year up to the present I have been continually ill; likewise during the summer I had an attack of jaundice, which lasted until the end of August. Following Staudenheim's order I had to go to Baden in September. Since it soon became cold there I was overtaken by a case of diarrhoea that was so violent that I could not keep up the course of treatment and had to flee here. Now thank God things are better and it appears that I am to be cheered up by the return of health and may live again for my art, which for the last two years has certainly not been the case

[19] Beethoven writes "offen" which can mean "alternative" or "open," the latter being the opposite of "verschlossen"—"closed" of the first version.

[20] The dramatic poet Zacharias Werner, who had become a convert to Roman Catholicism and, now an ordained priest, was preaching to great crowds of Viennese. The puns on the German words *Verleger* and *verlegen* are untranslatable. (TK, III, 44, n. 1.)

not only from lack of health but also on account of many other human miseries— The mass might have been sent before this, but had to be *carefully looked through*, for the publishers in other countries do not get along well with my manuscript, as I know from experience. A copy for the engraver must be examined note by note. Moreover, I could not do this because of illness, the more since despite everything I have been compelled to make a considerable number of *potboilers* (as unfortunately I must call them)— I think I am justified in making an attempt to get Simrock to reckon the Louis d'or at a higher rate, inasmuch as several applications have been made from other quarters, concerning which I shall write you soon. As for the rest, do not question my honesty; frequently I think of nothing except that your kind advance may soon be repaid—

with sincere gratitude and respect your friend

and servant Beethoven.

It seems a fair inference from his concluding remark, together with the advice of his friend or friends in the Conversation Book of the previous summer concerning a collection through Brentano as soon as the Mass had been handed over to the stage-coach, that Beethoven had got an advance from Brentano on the money which was awaiting the arrival of the work in Frankfurt. The following letter to Brentano strengthens the inference:

Vienna, December 20, 1821.

Noble man!

I am awaiting another letter respecting the mass, which I shall send you to give you an insight into the whole affair. In any event the honorarium will be paid to you whereupon you will please deduct the amount of my indebtedness to you. My gratitude to you will always be unbounded— I was so presumptuous as not to ask before dedicating a composition of mine to your daughter Maxe. Please accept the deed as a mark of my continual devotion to you and your entire family—do not misinterpret the dedication as prompted by my own interest or as a recompense—this would pain me greatly. There are nobler motives to which such things may be ascribed if reasons must be found—

The new year is about to begin; may it fulfil all your wishes and daily increase your happiness as pater familias in your children. I embrace you cordially and beg you to present my compliments to your excellent, one and only glorious Toni—

Your most respectful faithful Beethoven

I have received from here and elsewhere offers of 200 ducats in gold for the mass. I think I can get 100 florins V.S. more. On this point I am waiting for a letter which I will send you at once. The matter might then be presented to Simrock, who certainly will not expect me to lose so much. Till then please be patient and do not think that you have acted towards an unworthy man.

Brentano informed Simrock of the situation; but the subject is now carried over into the next year and must be left for the nonce, while we return to the history of some other compositions.

Beethoven's dedication of his Pianoforte Sonata in E major, Op. 109, to Maximiliane Brentano was accompanied by the following letter to her:

A dedication!!!—well this is not one that is misused as in many cases— It is the spirit which holds together noble and better men on this earth and which can *never* be destroyed by *time*. This is what is now addressed to you and what recalls you to me as you were in your childhood years, so equally your beloved parents, your admirable and gifted mother, your father filled with truly good and noble qualities, and ever mindful of his children. Thus at this very moment I am on the Landstrasse—and see all of you before me. While I am thinking of the excellent qualities of your parents, there are no doubts in my mind that you have been striving to emulate these noble people and are progressing daily— My memories of a noble family can never fade, may your memories of me be frequent and good—

Affectionately farewell, may heaven always bless you in all your ways—
sincerely and always your friend Beethoven

Vienna
December 6, 1821

Meanwhile Beethoven was writing the two other sonatas concerning which he himself left data. On the autograph of that in A-flat major, Op. 110, he wrote the date "December 25, 1821." Sketches for it follow sketches for the *Agnus Dei* of the Mass, which were begun in 1821. It was published by Schlesinger in Berlin and Paris in 1822 without dedication. There is evidence in a memorandum to Schindler found among the latter's papers that Beethoven intended to dedicate both of the last sonatas to Madame Brentano. "Ries-nichts" ("nothing for Ries"), says the memorandum significantly.[21] Ideas utilized in the C minor Sonata, Op. 111, are found among those for Op. 110 and particularly among some for the *Agnus Dei*. It is noteworthy, as shown by Nottebohm, that in the middle of sketches of Op. 110 there appears the first theme of the first movement of Op. 111, which was designated as a "3tes Stück presto" for the "2te Sonate."[22]

The autograph of the last Sonata, Op. 111, bears the inscription "Ludwig Ludwig am 13ten Jenner [January 13] 1822," and it is plain that most of the work was done in 1821. It was published by Schlesinger at the latest in April, 1823, after Beethoven had offered it to Peters of Leipzig. In a letter of May 1, 1822, Beethoven had left the matter of the dedication up to the elder Schlesinger, but on August 31 of the same year he wrote to the son that it was to be dedicated to Archduke Rudolph. In a letter to the Archduke on July 1,[23] 1823, he writes: "Y. I. H. seemed to find pleasure in the Sonata in C minor, and therefore I feel that it would not be presumptuous if I were to surprise you with its dedication." ⟶ Corrections for these three sonatas occupied a great deal of Beethoven's time. The difficulties with

[21] See *A* 1118.

[22] *II Beeth.*, pp. 467-68. The theme had figured twenty years before in a sketchbook used when the Sonata in A major, Op. 30, No. 1, was in hand. Its key was F-sharp minor, and it may once have been intended for this work. See Nottebohm, *Ein Skizzenbuch von Beethoven* (Leipzig, 1865), p. 19. (TK, III, 49, n. 4.)

[23] Beethoven dated the letter June 1st, but since he refers to an "accompanying receipt of June 27th" he must have meant July 1.

Op. 109 are the subject of letters to Schlesinger throughout the year. The history of the printing of Op. 111 will be told in the chapter for the year 1823. The compositions completed during the year were:

1820-21. Bagatelles for Pianoforte, Op. 119, Nos. 7-11.
1821.   Canon. "O Tobias," WoO 182, in a letter to Tobias Haslinger.
        Piece for Pianoforte in B minor, WoO 61, for Friedrich Piringer.
        Sonata for Pianoforte, Op. 110. According to Kinsky-Halm, the final
        movement was revised early in the next year.[24]

The publications of the year were:

By Schlesinger in Berlin:
  Sonata for Pianoforte in E major, Op. 109, dedicated to Maximiliane Brentano.
By Starke:
  Five Bagatelles for Pianoforte, Op. 119, Nos. 7-11 as Nos. 28-32 in *Wiener Piano-Forte-Schule von Frd. Starke Kapellmeister 3te Abtheilung.*

[24] See KHV, p. 314.

CHAPTER XXXV

THE YEAR 1822

THE *MISSA SOLEMNIS*—BEETHOVEN AND THE PUBLISHERS—THE LAST PIANOFORTE SONATA— MUSIC FOR VARIOUS OCCASIONS

THE events in the year 1822, in which the composition of the great Mass in D comes to an end except for corrections and improvements with which Beethoven never felt that he was done, will be told in a sequence that is as chronological as possible without breaking the individual threads.

At the beginning of 1822, Beethoven still lived at No. 244 Hauptstrasse, Landstrasse, Vienna. The first significant happening to him in the new year was his election as honorary member of the Musik-Verein of Steiermark in Graz, whose diploma, couched in the extravagantly sentimental verbiage of the day and country, bore date January 1.

Beethoven noted the conclusion of the C minor Sonata (Op. 111) on the autograph manuscript on January 13.

Bernard Romberg, Beethoven's old colleague and friend in Bonn, was in Vienna at the beginning of the year, giving concerts with his daughter Bernhardine and his 11-year-old son, Carl, who was also a violoncello virtuoso. Concerning one of the last of these concerts Beethoven wrote to him on February 12:

This last night I have again been *suffering from one of my earaches* which habitually occur in *this season, even your tones* would *today* be merely *painful to me*; this alone is to blame if you do not see me in person— Perhaps I shall be better in a few days in which case I shall still be able to say goodbye to you— Moreover, if you have not received a visit from me, remember the remoteness of my house, my almost ceaseless[1] affairs, all the more since I have been ill for the whole past year, because of which I have been held up on so many works already begun— And, after all, between us there is no need for superficial

[1] I am indebted to Miss Anderson for the reading of these two words which were illegible to Thayer. See *A* 1072.

compliment— I wish for a full tribute of applause to you for your high art and also a *metallic recognition* which nowadays is seldom the case— If I can for a little while, I will see you together with your wife and children whom I greet affectionately herewith.

Farewell   great artist
as always your Beethoven

The "metallic recognition" was made, and according to Hanslick, Romberg's earnings during the Vienna season amounted to 10,000 florins.

And now to resume the story of the Mass. At the beginning of 1822 the work was completed in sketch form, by the end of the year the autograph score was made, and on March 19, 1823, a beautiful copy was sent to the Archduke. Meanwhile negotiations for the publication of the Mass continued not only with Simrock but with a number of other firms as well.

On May 13, 1822, Simrock became impatient and wrote the following letter from Bonn:

To Herr Louis van Beethoven!
      in Vienna!

It is now a year since you promised me for sure that I would receive the mass completely finished at the end of April. Since October 25, 1820, I have had 100 Louis d'or on deposit in Frankfurt from which you should have received your payment immediately. On March 19th you wrote me expressly that you had been bedridden for 6 weeks and had not yet fully recovered. I was supposed to be completely assured; you wrote this only so that I should think nothing differently. Next I asked Brentano [about it] at the autumn fair and again at this Easter fair, but nothing has arrived as usual. So I beg you now to write some words about it once and for all: I write about this so that you will not believe that I have died, which nearly happened this past winter!

Every so often I have taken up the idea of publishing your six symphonies in score, which by now should have been done several times—even publicly advertised; but had not been done because there was no profit in it. I know this very well; but I have wanted to make a worthy monument to my worthy old friend and I hope that you will be satisfied with the edition since I have done all I can with it! I have had the first two appear at the same time and will send you a copy along with the first shipment to Vienna!

We thought that we would see you here during the past summer as you had promised in your letter of March 19, but this has not happened either.

We all greet you sincerely.

                                  N. Simrock

What Beethoven said in reply to this letter is not known, his answer not having been given to the world; it can be surmised, however, from the recital given to Brentano in a letter from Beethoven dated May 19. He had been troubled by "gout in the chest" for four months, he said, and able to do but little work; nevertheless the Mass would be in Frankfurt by the end of the next month, that is, by the end of June, 1822. There was another reason for the delay. Cardinal Rudolph, strongly disposed in favor of his music at all times, did not want the Mass published so early and had returned to the composer the score and parts only three days before. Here we have a very significant statement. What may be called the official copy of the Mass in D was formally presented to Archduke Rudolph on March 19, 1823; here, ten months earlier, he speaks of a score and parts which the Archduke had returned to him three days before. The Mass, therefore, must have had what, for the time being (Beethoven never considered it finished so long as it was in his hands), was looked upon as a definitive shape at the time when Beethoven promised to send it to Brentano for Simrock. The Archduke returned it, as Beethoven says, so that the publication might not be hindered. How long it had been in the hands of the Archduke no one can tell. Now, said Beethoven to Brentano, the score will be copied again, carefully examined, which would take some time owing to his ill health, but it would be in Frankfurt at the end of June "at the latest," by which time Simrock must be ready to make payment. He had received better offers from Vienna and elsewhere, but had rejected all of them because he had given his word to Simrock and would abide by the agreement even if he lost money, trusting to make his losses good by other sales to Simrock who, moreover, might be disposed to make a contract for the Complete Edition. Brentano communicated with Simrock at once and received a letter from the publisher on May 29 expressing regret that sickness had been partly responsible for the delay. He had been expecting the Mass every day for more than a year, during which time the money had lain with Heinrich Verhuven because he did not want Beethoven to wait a single day for it.

Thus on May 19, Beethoven told Brentano that he would keep the faith with Simrock even at a sacrifice. On May 1, however, he had written to Schlesinger in Berlin:

... In regard to my health, things are better again, thank God; as to the Mass I beg of you to get everything in readiness as other publishers have asked for it and many approaches have been made to me, especially from here; but I resolved long ago that it should not be published *here*, as the matter is a very important one for me— For the present I ask of you only that you signify to me whether you accept my last offer of the Mass together with the two songs. As regards the payment of the honorarium, it may wait for no more than four weeks. I must insist upon an early answer, chiefly because two other publishers who want to have it in their catalogues have been waiting for a definite answer from me for a considerable time— Farewell, and write to me at once, it would grieve me very much if *I could not give you just this particular* work.

Respectfully yours   Beethoven

Schlesinger, as we learn from a letter dated July 2, 1822, had received letters from Beethoven under date of April 9, May 1 and May 29.[2] He answered the three at once, excusing his delay on the ground that he had attended the

[2] The letter of May 29 has not survived. For Schlesinger's letter see Unger, *Ludwig van Beethoven und seine Verleger*, No. 121.

fair in Leipzig, where he fell ill, and had remained under the weather for several weeks after his return to Berlin. Meanwhile business had accumulated. He continues:

. . . Everything is in order about the Mass, and I beg you to send it and the two songs as soon as possible and draw on me at fourteen days' sight for 650 R.T., I will honor the draft at once and pay it, for I have no opportunity to make payment to you there [Vienna]; although several music dealers there are extensively in my debt, I cannot count on prompt payment from any of them. These gentlemen have two very ugly traits: 1) they do not respect property rights and 2), it is with difficulty that they are brought to pay their accounts. The book dealers are much sounder. . . .

Schlesinger's son, who had established himself in business in Paris, wrote to Beethoven on July 3rd and in the course of the letter asked him if a third movement of the Pianoforte Sonata in C minor (Op. 111), which he was publishing, had not been forgotten at the copyists. He, like his father a little later (letter of July 13), evidently suspected that they had not received as much music, measured in detached movements, as they had paid for; they missed a rondo finale! The incident may have amused, or (which is more likely) even angered Beethoven; but there must have been a further incursion of Beethoven's displeasure to account for the fact that Beethoven resolved about this time to have nothing more to do with Schlesinger *père*. On June 26 he wrote to Peters of Leipzig, with whom he had now entered into negotiations and to whom he had just offered the Mass, "In no event will Schlesinger ever get *anything more from me*; he has played me a Jewish trick, but aside from that he is not among those who might have received the Mass." When Beethoven was conducting the negotiations with Schott and Sons in Mainz which resulted in the firm's getting the work, he recurred to the Schlesingers in a letter of January 22, 1825, and said: "Neither is Schlesinger to be trusted, for he takes where he can. Both *père et fils* bombarded me for the mass, but I did not deign to answer either of them, since after thinking them over I had cast them out long before." Beethoven's threats were frequently mere *brutum fulmen*; the Schlesingers, *père et fils*, remained his friends to the end and got two of the last Quartets.

On August 22, 1822, Simrock wrote to Beethoven again. Beethoven's answer followed on September 13 and, as it contains more than a mere implication why he refused to abide by his contract, it is given in full here:

Baden, September 13, 1822

My dear and valued Simrock:

You will receive this letter from Baden, where I am taking the baths, as my illness which has lasted two and a half years has not yet ended. Much as I should like to write you about many things I must yet be brief and only reply to your last of August 22nd. As regards the Mass you know that at an earlier date I wrote you that a larger honorarium had been offered me. I would not be so sordid as to haggle with you for a few florins, but my poor health and many other unpleasant circumstances compel me to insist upon it. The minimum that at least four publishers have offered me for the Mass is 1000 florins C.M. at the rate of twenty, or counting the florin at 3 Austrian C.M. at twenty. Much as I shall regret it if we must part just because of this work, I know that your loyalty [*Biederherzigkeit*] will not allow me to lose money on this work, which is perhaps the greatest that I have composed. You know that I am not boastful and that I do not like to show the letters of others or even quote from them; if it were not so I might submit proofs from far and near. But I very much wish to have the matter about the Mass settled as soon as possible, for I have had to endure plots of all sorts on account of it. It would be agreeable if you would let me know as soon as possible if you will pay me this honorarium. If you will, you need only deposit the difference with Brentano, whereupon I will at once send you a well corrected score of the Mass which will suffice you for the engraving. I hope, my dear Simrock, whom I consider the richest of all these publishers, will not permit his old friend to go elsewhere for the sake of a few hundred florins. Concerning all other matters I shall write you soon; I am staying here till the beginning of October. I shall receive all letters which you may write, safely as I did your last, only I beg of you to write soon. Farewell, greet the family cordially for me; as soon as I can I shall write to them myself.

Cordially your old friend, Beethoven

This was evidently answered by Simrock, who, despairing of ever getting the Mass, may have suggested that he would accept other works in lieu of it, for on March 10, 1823, Beethoven wrote again saying (as he had said to Peters in November, 1822) that he should surely receive *a* mass, for he had written two and was only undecided which one to send. He asked Simrock to be patient until Easter, when he would send one of them to Brentano. He intended also to write a mass for the Emperor. As to other works, he offered "a new overture, which I composed for the opening of the new Josephstadt Theatre,"[3] the music to the *Ruinen von Athen*, to *König Stephan*, some songs and "Kleinigkeiten" for the pianoforte. Only for the new overture did he fix a price (50 ducats), but he adds: "You will surely receive one of these two grand masses which are already composed; only be patient until after Easter, by which time I shall have decided which to send." This is the last letter between Beethoven and Simrock which has been found. It leaves the composer promising *a* mass instead of delivering *the* Mass, and that promise unfulfilled;—of a necessity, for the work, though described as "already composed," was never written.

In 1814 C. F. Peters had purchased the Bureau de Musique founded in 1798 by Hoffmeister and Kühnel, publishers of a number of Beethoven's compositions, including the First Symphony, between 1800 and 1805. On May 18, 1822, Peters addressed a letter to Beethoven in which he said that he had long wished to publish some of his compositions but had refrained from applying to him because he did not wish to offend the Viennese publishers; seeing now, however, that he was going outside with his composi-

---

[3] The *Weihe des Hauses* Overture, Op. 124.

tions and giving them "even to the Jew Schlesinger," he would no longer give heed to such considerations. He had spoken to Steiner on the subject at the last fair, who had offered no objections, had, indeed, said that he would be glad if he (Peters) got the works instead of Schlesinger, and had offered his services as intermediary between him and Beethoven, and asked for a list of compositions which he wanted. Thereupon he had given Steiner such a list: symphonies, pianoforte quartets and trios, pianoforte solos "among which there might be small pieces," songs, etc.—anything, in short, which Beethoven should send him would be welcome, for he wanted honor, not profit, from the association. Beethoven replied on June 5:

Sirs!

You have honored me with a letter, and since I am very busy now and have been ill for 5 months, I will answer you concerning only the most necessary matters— Although I met *Steiner* several days ago and asked him jocularly what he had brought for me from Leipzig, he mentioned not a *syllable* about your *commission* or about *you*, but earnestly pleaded with *me to assure him* that *I would give to him alone both my present and future works* and this *in the form of a contract*; I declined— This trait suffices to show you why I often prefer foreign publishers to local; I love straightforwardness and uprightness and am of the opinion that the artist ought not to be belittled; for alas! glittering as is the external aspect of fame, he is not permitted to be Jupiter's guest on Olympus every day; too often and too repulsively vulgar mankind drags him down from the pure ethereal heights.— The *biggest* work that I have written up until now is a great mass with chorus, 4 solos obbligato and large orchestra. Several people have sought to obtain it; I have been offered 100 Louis d'or in hard cash for it; I want however at least 1000 fl. C.M. at the 20 gulden rate—for which I would prepare the pianoforte arrangement myself— Variations on a waltz for pianoforte alone (there are many) for the price of 30 ducats in gold, that is Viennese ducats. Concerning songs I have worked out some longer ones, thus for example a comic aria with full orchestra on a Goethe text, "Mit Mädeln sich vertragen," etc., again another aria of the same genre[4] for each of which I want 16 ducats (pianoforte arrangement upon request)—

For several extended songs with pianoforte, 12 ducats apiece, among which there is also a small Italian cantata with recit.— Also among my German songs there is a song with recitative— A song with pianoforte 8 ducats. For an elegy for four voices with accompaniment of 2 violins, viola and violoncello the price is 24 ducats. For a chorus of Dervishes with full orchestra 20 ducats.[5] Also the following instrumental music would be available: a grand march for full orchestra with pianoforte arrangement written for the tragedy Tarpeja 12 ducats— A romance for violin (solo with full orchestra) for 15 ducats.[6]

A big trio for 2 oboes and one English horn (could be transcribed also for other instruments) for 30 ducats.[7] Four military marches with Turkish music, upon

[4] "Prüfung des Küssens," WoO 89.
[5] Op. 118 and Op. 113, No. 3.
[6] The Romances for Violin, Op. 40 and Op. 50 having been published long before, Beethoven must have had another one in

mind. (TK, III, 59, n. 1.)
[7] The Trio for wind instruments, Op. 87, was already in print. Beethoven had composed variations on "La ci darem" from *Don Giovanni*, WoO 28, for the same instruments and

request I will determine the price— Bagatelles or trifles for pianoforte alone, price upon request— All of the works mentioned above are ready. For a solo sonata for pianoforte 40 ducats, which you could have soon.[8]— A quartet for 2 violins, viola and violoncello 50 ducats, which you could have soon.[9] What I wish for more than all these is an *edition of my complete works* which I could superintend myself. Indeed I have received many propositions, but there were conditions which are hardly ones for me to meet and which I could and would not fulfill. I myself would superintend and edit the whole edition in two, even possibly one or one and a half years with the necessary help, and supply for each composition category a new work. For example, for the variations a new set of variations, for sonatas a new example of a sonata and so on; for each type in which I have, I would supply a new work; and for all this together I would ask for ten thousand florins C.M. at the 20 fl. rate.

I am not a businessman and I would prefer it to be otherwise in this matter, however since it cannot be otherwise my conduct is guided by competition.

I beg you to observe complete silence since otherwise I shall be exposed to many harassments as you already can observe from dealings with these men. Once something is published by you, then I would no longer be bothered by them—

I would welcome a relation developing between us, for from hearing many good things I have been assured about you. Then you would also find that I prefer dealing with someone of this kind rather than with those of the ordinary type of which there are so many— I beg a quick answer from you since just now I must decide about the publication of many works. [I am very sorry that Steiner who has estimable qualities has shown himself again to be but a common tradesman.][10] If you care to, please send me a copy of the catalogue which you gave to Herr Steiner— In expectation of a speedy reply

Yours respectfully   Beethoven

--⋙The pianoforte variations referred to were those on a waltz theme by Anton Diabelli. The full story of this work which dates back to 1819 will be told in the account of 1823, the year in which the variations were completed. During 1822, suffice it to say, the main work on what were to become thirty-three highly original variations was taking place.⋘--

Beethoven was not kept waiting for an answer; Peters' reply is dated June 15. He regretted to hear of Steiner's duplicity and expressed hope that his conduct might have been harmless in intention and caused by his weakness. The works which he wanted and of which he had given a list to Steiner were a quartet for strings, a trio of the same kind, a concert overture for full orchestra, songs, and some small solos for pianoforte "such as

---

the composition was called a Terzetto when performed in 1797. This was probably what he had in mind here and in a similar offer to Peters on November 22. (TK, III, 59, n. 2.)

[8] Since Op. 109-111 were already sold to Schlesinger, Beethoven must have thought himself in readiness to write another if it was desired; there was no lack of material in his sketchbooks. (TK, III, 59, n. 3.)

[9] This suggests that he had already begun work on the Quartet in E-flat, Op. 127. (TDR, IV, 251, n. 6.)

[10] The passage in brackets was in Beethoven's draft of the letter but not in the one that was sent. (TDR, IV, 252, n. 1.)

capriccios, divertissements," etc. Then he took up Beethoven's detailed offer of compositions:

The most admirable among them is your Grand Mass, which you offer me together with the pianoforte arrangement for one thousand florins C.M. which I admit I am ready to accept at this price. . . . Between honest men like us there is no need of a contract, but if you want one send it to me and I will return it *signed*. If not, please state to me in writing that I am to receive the *Mass in question* together with the *pianoforte score* for *1000 florins* at the 20 florin rate and indicate when I am to receive it and that it is to be my *sole* property *for ever*. I want the first so that I may look upon this transaction as *concluded*, and the time I want to know so that I can arrange about the publication. If I were a rich man I would pay you very differently for this Mass, for I suspect that it is something really excellent, especially because it was composed for an occasion; but for me 1000 florins for a Mass is a large expenditure and the entire transaction, *on my word*, is undertaken only in order to show myself to you and to the world as a publisher who does something for art. I must ask another consideration, namely, that *nobody* learn how much I have paid for the Mass— at least not for some time. I am not a man of large means, but must worry and drudge; nevertheless I pay artists as well as I can and in general better than other publishers. . . .

For the present, Peters added, he did not want to publish larger vocal works by Beethoven nor the Mass singly but along with other works, to show the Viennese publishers that there was a contract between him and Beethoven which obliged the latter to send him compositions. To that end he asked for some songs, a few bagatelles for piano solo, the four military marches. He said that he would be glad also to take the new string quartet, but that 50 ducats was beyond his means. Beethoven was at liberty to tell Steiner that he had applied to Beethoven with his knowledge and consent.

Beethoven's answer (incorrectly dated July instead of June 26) may be summarized. He agreed to give him the Mass, which he would receive by the end of July, for the stipulated fee, and enclosed an agreement form which had been prepared by Steiner. Beethoven emphasized that he had never sought commissions from Steiner or any other publisher "because I want to see how extended is the province which my fame has reached." He offered three songs and four marches for 40 ducats and asked for more news on the project of a complete edition of his works.

Peters answered this letter on July 3. He was willing to pay 40 ducats for the songs and marches and to remit part of the honorarium in advance. He was distressed about Beethoven's financial affairs and wanted to help him. "It is wrong that a man like you is obliged to think about money matters. The great ones of the earth should long ago have placed you in a position free from care, so that you would no longer have to live on art but only for art."

Before this letter was received Beethoven had written a second and supplementary reply to the letter of June 15; it is dated July 6. He had reread his letter and discovered that Peters wanted some of the bagatelles and a quartet for strings. For the former he asked 8 ducats each. The quartet was not fully completed, work on it having been interrupted. Here it was difficult to lower the prices, as such works were the most highly paid for—he might almost say, to the shame of the general taste, which in art frequently falls below that of private taste. "I have written you everything concerning the Mass, and that is settled."

On July 12, Peters wrote that he did not know the length of the bagatelles and so could not tell whether they were to be printed separately or together; but he asked that a number be sent him together with word as to how many of such small pieces Beethoven had on hand, as he might take them all. As for songs, he would prefer to have some in the style of "Adelaide" or "Schloss Markenstein." The honorarium for the compositions which were to be sent would now amount to 200 or 300 florins at the 20 florin rate, but as he could not determine the exact amount he asked Beethoven to collect the amount from Meiss (Meisl) Brothers, bankers, on exhibit of receipt and bill of shipment. It was all the same to him whether he collected the money now or later; it was waiting and at Beethoven's disposal. In this manner, so convenient for Beethoven, he would make all his payments for manuscripts purchased. On August 3 Beethoven writes:

. . . I have not made up my mind as to the selection of songs and remaining marches and bagatelles, but everything will be delivered by the 15th of this month. I await your advice in the matter and will make no use at present of your bill of exchange. Of the bagatelles you will receive 4—in conformity with the established price that makes a sum of 360 fl. at the 20 florin rate. Be sure to calculate it exactly— I am not holding you to a higher sum than the others; on the contrary for the songs I have reckoned too little for my time is really too valuable— As soon as I know that the honorarium for *the Mass* and the other works is here all these songs can be delivered by the 15th— . . . .

Peters was prompt in his remittance of the money which was to be subject to Beethoven's order; Beethoven, though less prompt in collecting it, did so prior to his delivery of the manuscripts for which the money was to pay. Singularly enough, the incident which provides for us knowledge of the time when the money was received by Peters' agent served as evidence in Beethoven's excuse for drawing the money without keeping his part of the agreement. On July 25, about a fortnight after the date of Peters' letter of advice, Piringer, associate conductor of the *Concerts spirituels*, who was on terms of intimacy with Beethoven, wrote him as follows:

Domine Generalissime!

Victoria in Döbling—fresh troops are advancing! The wholesalers, Meisl Bros. here in the Rauhensteingasse, their own house, 2nd story, have received advices from Hr. Peters in Leipzig to pay several hundred florins to Herr Ludwig van Beethoven— I hasten on Degen's pinions[11] to convey this glad report to *Illustrissimo* at once.— Today is the first sad day in the Viennese calendar, because yesterday was the last day of the Italian opera.

This letter Beethoven sent to Peters from Baden on September 13 in evidence of his presumption that Piringer, who was a daily caller at the Steiner establishment, had gossiped about the relations between him and Peters. He was sorry that Peters had sent the money so early, but fearing talk he had collected the money. He would send all the little things soon. He had been pressed by the Cardinal, on whom he had to attend several times a week; and work had been forced upon him by the opening of the Josephstadt Theatre; also he wanted to write new trios to some of the marches and revise other works, but illness and too much other employment had prevented. "You see from this at least that I am not a composer for the sake of mere contemptible gain. . . . You will recall that I begged you to keep everything away from this man [Steiner]. Why? That I will reveal to you in time. I hope that God will protect me against the wiles of this wicked man Steiner."

Now there enters a new element into the story of the Mass which is introduced by Beethoven near the end of a letter to Peters dated "Vienna, November 22, 1822":

Dear Sir!

In yours of November 9, in which I believe I was reproached for my *seeming negligence*—the honorarium already sent and yet *nothing received*—how objectionable it seems. Yet I know that if we were together, we could be reconciled in a few minutes— Your order is already assembled except for the *choice* of songs; as a fee for attendance you will receive one more of them than the number agreed upon— I could send you several other bagatelles in addition to the four ordered; there are still nine or ten of them available. If you *would write to me about this right away* I could send them or as many more along with them as you want— Indeed my health has not been fully restored by the baths, yet on the whole I have progressed. Besides I am badly off here since somebody else selected rooms for me that are not suitable, something which is difficult to surmount and has slowed me up not a little in my affairs since things are hardly yet in order— This is the state of affairs with regard to the Mass: already I have finished *one* completely but another is *not yet* finished. There will always be *gossip* about such as us and you have been misled by it. *I do not yet* know which of the two you will receive— Pressed on all sides I must declare the opposite of "the spirit weighs nothing"— I greet you most heartily and hope that a relationship which is profitable and not dishonorable to *me* may exist in the future between us both.

Yours faithfully   Beethoven

The gossip against which Beethoven warned Peters, it is safe to assume, related to the compositions which the latter had purchased but not received;

---

[11] Degen was a popular aeronaut who had not long before excited the interest of Beethoven. (TK, III, 62, n. 1.)

in great likelihood rumors about the Mass had reached Leipzig. Peters was in communication with Steiner and others; and that he knew that the Mass had been planned for the installation of Archduke Rudolph as Archbishop of Olmütz he had indicated when he expressed the belief that it was something "really excellent" because it had been composed for an occasion. The mass which Beethoven had promised to deliver by the end of July, 1822, could therefore have been none other than the Mass in D. It is deserving of mention, however, that there is evidence that Beethoven was thinking of more than one mass at the time—in fact that he had thoughts of three. In a sketchbook of the period is found a memorandum: "The *Kyrie* in the second mass with wind-instruments and organ only";[12] and in another place there are six measures of a theme for a *Dona nobis* with the superscription "Mass in C-sharp minor."[13] To this *Dona* there is still another reference or two of a later date; but that is all. It is likely that the second mass was intended for the Emperor, as we shall see later; Beethoven himself said that he had thoughts of a third.

Peters was getting importunate, and on December 20 Beethoven wrote to him that nothing intended for him was entirely ready; there had been delays in copying and sending, but he had no time to explain. The songs and marches would be sent "next week." There were six bagatelles instead of four, but if he insisted on four a separate arrangement would have to be made. He had so many applications for his works that he could not attend to them all: "Were it not that my income brings in nothing[14] I should compose only operas, grand symphonies, church music or at the outside quartets in addition." Of smaller works Peters might have variations for two oboes and English horn on a theme from *Don Giovanni*—"Da ci la mano" wrote Beethoven, meaning "Là ci darem la mano"—and for full orchestra a "Gratulatory Minuet."[15] He would like Peters' opinion about the complete edition.

During February and March, 1823, Beethoven finally sent on to Peters three songs ("Opferlied," "Bundeslied" and "Der Kuss"),[16] six bagatelles (from Op. 119) and three tattoos (Turkish music) and a march (WoO 18, 19, 20, 24). On March 4, 1823, Peters wrote, in answer to a letter of Beethoven's dated February 15, that he was distressed by the manuscripts that he had received and that he was sending back the three songs since they were not what he had asked for. His objections were that he had wanted extended songs with pianoforte accompaniment and "that I want to have good choice things from you."[17] Just when Beethoven received the songs back is not

---

12 *II Beeth.*, p. 152. (TK, III, 63, n. 1.)

13 *Ibid.*, pp. 541, 543. (TK, III, 63, n. 1.)

14 Beethoven indulges in his propensity for puns: "Wäre mein Gehalt nicht ganz ohne Gehalt." (TK, III, 63, n. 2.)

15 WoO 3. A composition written for a serenade given to Hensler, director of the

Josephstadt Theatre, as will appear later. (TK, III, 64, n. 1.)

16 Op. 121b (first version for 3 solo voices, chorus and small orchestra), Op. 122 and Op. 128. (TDR, IV, 260.)

17 See Kurt Herbst, "Beethovens Opferlied Kompositionen," in *NBJ*, v, p. 142.

clear, since on the one hand, he was offering songs to Simrock in his letter of March 10, 1823, which must have been these three, the only ones yet unpublished; on the other hand, in the next and final letter to Peters of this year, dated March 20, 1823, he was giving instructions for two of these songs, which show that he believed them still to be in Peters' possession.

In this latest letter to Peters, after referring to the marches, bagatelles and Peters's request for a string and a piano quartet, Beethoven writes:—

As regards the Mass I will also send you a document which I beg you to sign, for in any event the time is approaching when you will receive one or the other. Besides yourself there are two other men who also desire each a mass. At present I am resolved to write at least three; the first is entirely finished, the second *not yet*, the third not even begun.— But in view of this I must have an understanding so that I may be secured in any case, you may have the Mass whenever you pay 1000 C.M. . . . .

So far as Peters is concerned the matter must be dropped for a space; he published none of the works sent to him and did not receive the Mass. One of the "two other men" was, in all likelihood, Artaria, Beethoven's old publisher. On August 22, 1822, Artaria received a letter which, as it seems to stand alone so far as the Mass is concerned, may well be printed in full:

Being just now overwhelmed with work, I can only say briefly that I have always returned your favors whenever possible. As regards the Mass I have been offered 1000 florins, C.M. for it. The state of my affairs do not permit me to take a smaller honorarium from you. All that I can do is to *give* you the *preference*. Rest assured that I do not *take a heller more* from you than has been *offered me by others*. I could prove this to you in writing. You may think this over but I beg of you to send me an answer by *tomorrow noon* as tomorrow is post-day and my decision is expected in other places— I will make a proposition to you concerning the 150 florins C.M. which I owe you, but the sum must not be deducted *now*, as I am in urgent need of the 1000 florins— In addition I beg of you to keep everything secret about the Mass. As always
your grateful friend Beethoven

Here *the* Mass (*Missa Solemnis*) is implied and not *a* mass from several. When Beethoven wrote this letter he had offered the Mass to Peters, earlier to Simrock and had indicated the same purpose to Schlesinger. Thus there were not less than four publishers who hoped to receive the Mass. Also he raised their hopes for works which were not ready or even hardly begun.

Because of these striking facts it is appropriate to consider Beethoven's personality and the circumstances under which he lived. The painstaking work that Beethoven put into the works of these late years came from his innermost heart and he never felt that he had done enough. While he was absorbed with this kind of work he was free of his cares and guided only by the demands of his art. In his long letter to Peters of March 20, 1823, already mentioned, Beethoven speaks of the necessity in his position of considering his own interests and adds: "It is another thing during the work itself, since I never think of gain, thank God, but only *how to compose.*" These were his principles.

Then too there was his health and the duress already described which cramped the elasticity of his nature and diminished his delight in creating. "To begin a great work makes me shudder," he is once supposed to have said. So many big plans remained inexecuted and the completion of big works laid considerable claims on his time. So he wrote small pieces and resuscitated old, forgotten ones. Also his income had diminished due to the reduced payments on the pension supplied by his princely admirers and due to his limited productivity of the last few years;—consequently, he was in need of straight cash. His expenses included those for the care of his nephew and the cost of his stays at resorts for the care of his own health, and these compelled him to concern himself with his earnings. Hence came the necessity to get the highest possible fees for his works, for dealings unfortunately with many parties at once, and for acceptance of advance payments. His embarrassments compelled him to borrow money since the bank shares that he owned he no longer considered his own but an inheritance for his nephew and not to be touched. Thus, he owed money, among others, to Steiner and Artaria. To the former he owed nearly 3000 florins, as he wrote to his brother, and this explains not only the painful relations with Steiner but also Beethoven's wish to have his new works published by foreigners. To Artaria he owed 1000 florins; yet it will be remembered he wrote to the firm that the sum of 150 florins which he hoped soon to pay back on his debt must not now be deducted from a possible fee since he needed the whole amount; this sheds light on the extent of his financial cares.

These circumstances invite one's deepest sympathy; the noble impulses of his heart on all other levels and the reasons which necessitated his doing everything to better his affairs are well known; yet the conscientious reporter cannot ignore the actual, public facts and, hard as it is, cannot acquit Beethoven of the reproach that his conduct did not agree with the principles of strict honor and justice. These are dreary episodes in the history of Beethoven which nevertheless cannot be overlooked if he is to be wholly understood as a man; but how withdrawn they are from the heights reached by the works that he composed during these troubled times.

Beethoven finally borrowed money from his brother and asked his help in the sale of his works. This circumstance brings Johann van Beethoven back significantly into this history and invites an inquiry into his character and his conduct with reference to his famous brother. Something of his earlier history has been told in the chapters of this biography which deal with the incidents of the years 1808 and 1812. The brother had grown rich enough in the interim to buy some farm property near Gneixendorf and to make his winter residence in Vienna. There we find him in the spring of 1822 living in the house of his brother-in-law, a baker named Obermayer, at the intersection of Koth- and Pfarrgasse. Thenceforward for a number of years, because of his relationship to his famous brother, and also because of his idiosyncrasies, habits and public behavior (and to a smaller number, the conduct of his wife), he became a conspicuous and rather comical figure in Vienna. Gerhard von Breuning describes him thus:[18] "His hair was blackish-brown; hat well brushed; clothing clean but suggesting that of a man who wishes to be elegantly clad on Sundays; somewhat old-fashioned and uncouth, an effect which was caused by his bone-structure, which was angular and unlovely. His waist was rather small; no sign of embonpoint; shoulders broad; if my memory serves me rightly, his shoulders were a trifle uneven, or it may have been his angular figure which made him look unsymmetrical; his clothing generally consisted of a blue frockcoat with brass buttons, white necktie, light trousers (I think corn color), loose linen-thread gloves, the fingers too long so that they folded at the ends or stuck out loosely. His hands were broad and bony. He was not exactly tall of stature, but much taller than Ludwig. His nose was large and rather long, the position of his eyes, crooked, the effect being as if he squinted a little with one eye. The mouth was crooked, one corner drawn upwards giving him the expression of a mocking smile. In his garb he affected to be a well-to-do elegant, but the rôle did not suit his angular, bony figure. He did not in the least resemble his brother Ludwig."

Breuning also says in his book *Aus dem Schwarzspanierhause*, that he was sometimes seen driving in the Prater with two or four horses in an old-fashioned phaeton, either handling the reins himself or lolling carelessly in the seat with two gallooned servants on the box. Beethoven's friends used to ridicule his brother to his face. In a Conversation Book of early 1823 Count Moritz Lichnowsky writes: "Everybody thinks him a fool; we call him only the Chevalier . . . all the world says of him that his only merit is that he bears your name."[19] No doubt there was something, even a good deal, of the parvenu in Johann's character. He had neither the intellectual nor moral poise to fit him for the place which he thought he was entitled to fill by virtue of his wealth and his relationship to one of the most famous men of his age. Nor could he command respect from a social point of view. Also the indecent behavior of his wife must have been repugnant to Ludwig's circle of friends, and a memorandum found among Schindler's papers discloses that her conduct in Vienna was such that Beethoven again thought of invoking the police.

That Johann van Beethoven was fond of money is indicated in his remarks in the Conversation Books, when his advice to his brother is always dictated by financial considerations. If he lacked appreciation of his brother's real significance in art, he was proud of the world's appreciation of him, and if he could not have high regard for that high moral attitude in the matter which had brought condemnation on his sister-in-law and wife, he at least showed magnanimity in not trying to do his brother injury and being

18 In a note to Thayer. (TK, III, 66, n. 1.)   19 Schünemann, II, p. 396.

always ready to help him when he could. It is very likely that he was not at all musical and that his affectation of appreciation of his brother's works made him a fair subject for ridicule. In a conversation in 1824 the nephew relates that his uncle had been present at a chamber concert. Beethoven wanted to know what he was doing there, and the nephew replies: "He wants to acquire taste; he is continually crying *bravo*." So also Holz relates, in 1826, that Johann had certainly heard the Quartet in E-flat major ten times, yet when it was played in that year he said he was hearing it for the first time.

Exactly when Beethoven went to Oberdöbling in the summer of 1822 is not known, but he was there in July, and an endorsement on the Simrock letter of May 13 would seem to indicate that he was there in that month. His lodgings were in No. 135 Alleegasse. In the spring or early summer he wrote the following letter to Johann:

I was counting on seeing you—but in vain—on Staudenheim's orders I am still having to take medicine, and am not allowed to move about much— I beg you instead of going to the Prater today to come to me with your wife and daughter— I only wish that the benefits which are certain to result from our being together may be achieved without hindrance. I have enquired about lodgings; there are tolerably good ones to be had and you won't have to pay much more than before. From a purely financial point of view, how much can be saved on both sides without our having to sacrifice our pleasure— I have nothing against your wife, I only wish that she would see how much you too might benefit from being with me and that we need not be troubled by all the petty miseries of life.

Now farewell. I hope to see you for sure this afternoon, at which time we could take a drive to Nussdorf, which would do me a lot of good—

Your true brother Ludwig

Peace, peace be with us. God grant that the most natural tie between brothers be not unnaturally broken again. Besides, my life may not be of long duration. I say again that I have nothing against your wife, although her behavior towards me has struck me as strange several times of late. Besides I have been ailing for three and one half months and am very, yes extremely sensitive and irritable. But away with everything which *cannot promote* the object, which is that I and my good Karl maintain a moderate way of life, which is so necessary to me—You have only to look at my house here to see what happens, what it is like when sickly as I am I have to put myself *in the hands of strangers*, not to mention other matters which we have already discussed—

In case you come today, you can pick up *Karl, for this reason*, I am *enclosing* this unsealed letter to H. v. Blöchlinger which you can send off to him at once.—

Here there is no mention of business matters and hence it may be assumed that the letter dates from an early period in the reunion of the brothers. But business considerations prompted two long letters at the end of July which, except for passages concerning those negotiations with publishers about which the reader already knows, should be given in full. The first is dated July 26:

Dear brother!

Because I have been extremely busy and thoroughly uncomfortable with respect to my dwelling and my servants, both of whom are extremely awkward, I have not yet been able to write you. As for my health, it is better. I have been having to drink Johannes spring-water, take powder 4 times a day, and now I am supposed to go to Baden to take 30 baths; I will go there by August 6 or 7 if it is *possible* to do so. If you could only come for a few days to help me, yet the dust and the heat would be too much for you. If it weren't for that you could stay with me in Baden for some 8 days, ad tuum libitum . . . [Negotiations with Peters are summarized.] Also Breitkopf and Härtel have sent the Saxon Chargé d'Affaires to me concerning my works. Also I have received requests from Paris for my works and again from Diabelli in Vienna; in short, people are scrambling for my works; what an *unfortunate fortunate* man I am!!!— That *Berliner* has also turned up— If my health would return I might yet feather my nest.—

The Archduke Cardinal is here, I go to him twice a week. Though there is nothing to be expected from him in the way of magnanimity or money, I am on such a good and confidential footing with him that it would be extremely painful not to show him some agreeable attention. Also I do not think that his apparent niggardliness is his fault— Before I go to Baden, I need some clothes because I am really lacking in them, especially in shirts as you have already seen. Ask your wife what she thinks of this linen, it costs 48 x [kreutzer] V.S. per ell.— If you can come, please do unless this adds trouble for you. I will come to you with Karl in September if I don't go to Olmütz for the sake of the Cardinal, who wishes it very much— As for the house, since it is already taken so be it; now the question is whether it will also suit me![20]— The rooms lead into the garden, but just now garden air is the worst thing for me; then the entrance is through the *kitchen* which is very unpleasant and inconvenient—and now I must pay a quarter year's rent for nothing. Instead of this then, Karl and I, if possible, will arrive at your house in Krems and have a good old time until the money is again retrieved—that is, if I don't go to Moravia— Write me as soon as you receive this; give my greetings to your family. If I did not have to go to Baden, I would certainly have visited you during the coming month, but now things cannot be otherwise. Do come if you can, it would be a great relief for me.— Write at once— Farewell— I embrace you with all my heart

and am as ever your true brother Ludwig

On July 31, Beethoven writes:

Best little brother! Most high and mighty property holder!

Yesterday[21] I wrote to you when I was exhausted by much strain and business, and it may be hard for you to read because of a bad pen. First of all write me how often the post travels from you to me, from me to you. . . . I should be glad if you would write me whether you can spare me something so that I will not be prevented when the time comes from going to Baden, where I must stay for at least a month. You can see that there is no lack of safety here as you will get

[20] The house was in the Kothgasse, and because of Ludwig's indecision, Johann had decided evidently to go ahead on his own.

(TDR, IV, 272, n. 2.)
[21] Evidently Beethoven started this letter on July 27.

the 200 fl. paid back to you with thanks in September.[22] Please send the enclosed note[23] back to me immediately. Moreover, as a trades-man you are always a good counsellor. Likewise the Steiner people are pushing me into a corner. They wish to have in writing that I shall give all my works to them. They are willing to pay for each printed sheet; but I have explained to them that I will not enter into such an arrangement with them until they cancel the debt. For that I have offered them 2 works which I wrote for Hungary[24] and which can be considered as two small operas, from which they have already accepted 4 pieces. The debt amounts to about 3000 fl., but they have outrageously charged me interest, to which I do not agree. I have taken over from Karl's mother a part of her debt since I want to do everything I can for her insofar as it isn't against Karl's interest. If you were here, these things would soon be disposed of; it is only necessity that is forcing me to such transactions. It would be wonderful if you could come and visit Baden with me for 8 days, only you must write immediately what you think about it. Meanwhile get the kitchen and cellar well stocked; for presumably my little son and I will make our headquarters at your house and we have the noble resolve to eat you out of house and home. Naturally this is about our plans for September.

Now farewell, best little brother! Read the Gospel every day; concentrate on the Epistle of Peter and Paul; travel to Rome and kiss the Pope's toe. Sincere greetings to your family. Write soon, I embrace you with all my heart.

Your faithful brother Ludwig

I, secretarius embrace you with all my heart and hope to see you soon again. Karl

N.B. I am not enclosing the order for 300 fl. C.M. because I am afraid that something might happen to it.

The Saxon Chargé d'Affaires sent by Breitkopf and Härtel, mentioned in Beethoven's letter of July 26, was Georg August Griesinger, Haydn's first biographer, who had made Beethoven's acquaintance as a young man. On June 17 he wrote on behalf of the firm to Beethoven expressing Härtel's regret that the business connection which formerly existed had been discontinued and his desire to renew it with an opera. Griesinger gave his address and offered to meet him there or in a place of Beethoven's choosing. —⟐{Beethoven gave the following reply.

It was a pleasure to receive from you a few lines, and as soon as I come to the city I will visit you. Since I have been ailing for 5 months I have to be thrifty with the produce of my art— I was very glad to hear something from you, a man of such merit. (generally—and especially in the writing of Haydn's life)—

With the greatest respect
Yours sincerely Beethoven}⟐—

---

[22] Evidently a loan of 200 florins had already been broached to Johann. (TDR, IV, 273, n. 4.)

[23] A note from Peters informing Beethoven that because he did not yet know how many bagatelles he would want he was assigning him a sum of 300 florins.

[24] *König Stephan* and *Die Ruinen von Athen*. (TK, III, 70, n. 1.)

Mentioned also in Beethoven's letter of July 26 to Johann is his visits twice a week to Archduke Rudolph. The following note to his pupil probably belongs here:

I came home yesterday after I heard that I was not to have the favor of coming to Y. I. H. Yesterday the weather had already had a bad effect on me, hence I am obliged to remain at home today; I will make it good in the following weeks. I regret only that today I must deny myself the favor of seeing and being with Y. I. H.

There must now be recorded some of the facts connected with the visit to Beethoven of Friedrich Rochlitz, distinguished musical *littérateur* and first editor of the Leipzig *Allgemeine Musikalische Zeitung*. Rochlitz arrived in Vienna on May 24 and remained there till August 2. He wrote two letters to Härtel about his experiences in the Austrian capital, one of June 28 from Vienna and the other of July 9 from Baden. The latter contained his account of his meeting with Beethoven and is reprinted in Vol. IV of his *Für Freunde der Tonkunst*.[25] He had never seen Beethoven in the flesh and was eager for a meeting. A friend to whom he went (it is very obvious that it was Haslinger) told him that Beethoven was in the country and had grown so shy of human society that a visit to him might prove unavailing; but it was Beethoven's custom to come to Vienna every week and he was then as a rule affable and approachable. He advised Rochlitz to wait, and he did so until the following Saturday. The meeting was a pleasant one and enabled Rochlitz to study Beethoven's appearance and manner; but the interview was suddenly terminated by Beethoven in the midst of the visitor's confession of his own admiration and the enthusiasm which Beethoven's symphonies created in Leipzig. From the beginning Beethoven had listened, smiled and nodded; but after he had curtly excused himself on the score of an engagement and departed abruptly, Rochlitz learned that his auditor had not heard or understood a word of all that he had said. Rochlitz continues:[26]

"Some two weeks later I was about to go to dinner when I met the young composer Franz Schubert, an enthusiastic admirer of Beethoven. The latter had spoken to Schubert concerning me. 'If you wish to see him in a more natural and jovial mood,' said Schubert, 'then go and eat your dinner this very minute at the inn[27] where he has just gone for the same purpose.' He took me with him. Most of the places were taken. Beethoven sat among several acquaintances who were strangers to me. He really seemed to be in good spirits and acknowledged my greeting, but I purposely did not cross over to him. Yet I found a seat from which I could see him and, since he spoke loud enough, also could hear nearly all that he said. It could not

---

[25] Leipzig, 1832, IV, p. 352.

[26] Following is the translation, with slight modifications, from *Beethoven, Impressions of Contemporaries*, O. G. Sonneck, ed. (Schirmer, 1926), pp. 123ff.

[27] According to Deutsch this may have been the "Blumenstöckl" in the Ballgasse. See O. E. Deutsch, *Memoirs of Schubert* (New York, 1958), p. 304.

actually be called a conversation, for he spoke in monologue, usually at some length, and more as though by hapchance and at random.

"Those about him contributed little, merely laughing or nodding their approval. He philosophized, or one might even say politicized, after his own fashion. He spoke of England and the English, and of how both were associated in his thoughts with a splendor incomparable—which, in part, sounded tolerably fantastic. Then he told all sorts of stories of the French, from the days of the second occupation of Vienna. For them he had no kind words. His remarks all were made with the greatest unconcern and without the least reserve, and whatever he said was spiced with highly original, naïve judgements or comical fancies. He impressed me as being a man with a rich, aggressive intellect, an unlimited, never resting imagination."

After finishing his meal Beethoven approached Rochlitz and beckoned him into a little anteroom, where conversation was carried on with the help of a tablet which Beethoven produced. "He began by praising Leipzig and its music; that is to say the music chosen for performance in the churches, at concerts and in the theatre. Otherwise he knew nothing of Leipzig and had only passed through the city when a youth on his way to Vienna.[28] 'And even though nothing is printed about the performances but the dry records, still I read them with pleasure,' he said. 'One cannot help but notice that they are intelligent and well inclined toward all. Here, on the contrary. . . .' Then he started in, rudely enough, nor would he let himself be stopped. He came to speak of himself: 'You will hear nothing of me here.' 'It is summer now,' I wrote. 'No, nor in winter either!' he cried. 'What should you hear? *Fidelio*? They cannot give it, nor do they want to listen to it. The symphonies? They have no time for them. My concertos? Everyone grinds out only the stuff he himself has made. The solo pieces? They went out of fashion here long ago, and here fashion is everything. At the most Schuppanzigh occasionally digs up a quartet, etc.'[29] And despite all the exaggeration in what he said a modicum of reason and truth remains. At last he had relieved himself and harked back to Leipzig. 'But,' said he, 'you really live in Weimar, do you not?' He probably thought so because of my address. I shook my head. 'Then it is not likely that you know the great Goethe?' I nodded my head vigorously. 'I know him, too,' said Beethoven, throwing out his chest, while an expression of the most radiant pleasure overspread his face.

" 'It was in Karlsbad[30] that I made his acquaintance—God only knows how long ago! At that time I was not yet altogether deaf, as I now am,

[28] This was undoubtedly the Berlin trip of 1796 about which Rochlitz knew nothing. (TDR, IV, 285, n. 1.)

[29] Rochlitz was probably helping out his memory here by drawing a bit on his fancy; Schuppanzigh was at this time still in Russia, having started on a tour through Germany, Poland and Russia in 1815, from which he did not return till 1823. (TK, III, 75.)

[30] They first met in Teplitz in 1812. However, since both went on to Karlsbad it is probable that they saw each other there too. (TDR, IV, 285, n. 5.)

though I heard with great difficulty. And what patience the great man had with me!' He told numerous little anecdotes and gave the most enjoyable details. 'How happy it all made me at the time! I would have died for him ten times over. Then, while I was still brimming with ardor, I thought out my music for his *Egmont*[31] and I did make a success of it, did I not?' ....

'Since that summer in Karlsbad I read Goethe every day, that is, when I read at all. He [Goethe] has killed Klopstock for me. You are surprised? And now you laugh? Ah ha! It is because I have read Klopstock. I carried him about with me for years while walking and also at other times. Well, I did not always understand him, of course. He leaps about so much and he begins at too lofty an elevation. Always *Maestoso*, D-flat major! Isn't it so? But he is great and uplifts the soul nevertheless. When I could not understand him I could sort of guess. If only he did not always want to die! That will come quickly enough. Well, at any rate, what he writes always sounds well. But Goethe—he is alive, and he wants us all to live with him. That is why he can be set to music. There is no one who lends himself to musical setting as well as he. . . .' "

At this point Rochlitz believed that the opportunity had arrived to present Härtel's proposal and wrote it out. According to a note added by Rochlitz, this was to write music for Goethe's *Faust* similar to that for *Egmont*. "He read it. 'Ha!' he cried and flung up his hand. 'That would be a piece of work! That might yield something!' He went on in this fashion for a time, picturing the thought to himself in a manner anything but inept, while, with his head thrown back, he stared at the ceiling. 'But,' he next began, 'for some time past I have been carrying about with me the idea of three other great works. Already I have hatched out much in connection with them, that is to say, in my head. These I must first get rid of: two great symphonies each different from the other, and each also different from all my other ones, and an oratorio. And that will be a long-winded affair; for you see, for some time past I find I no longer settle down to write so easily. I sit and think and think and what I have to say is all there, but it will not get down to paper. I dread beginning works of such magnitude. Once I have begun, then, all goes well. . . .' "

Most of this is in harmony with what we know from other sources. We have seen how laboriously Beethoven developed the works of large dimensions in this period; we know that he had thought of *Faust* as a subject for composition as early as 1808 and that it pursued him in his last years. But Härtel's proposition sent through Griesinger in the same year was for an opera, and it seems likely that the *Faust* idea was independent of it and possibly an original conceit of Rochlitz's. Rochlitz continues his description:

[31] False. *Egmont* was written in 1810, over two years before the time he met Goethe. Rochlitz, it seems, was again indulging his imagination. (TDR, IV, 286, n. 1.)

"Our third meeting was the merriest of all. He came here, to Baden, this time looking quite neat and clean and even elegant. Yet this did not prevent him—it was a warm day—from taking a walk in the Helenental. This means on the road that all travel, even the Emperor and the imperial family, and where everyone crowds past everyone else on the usually narrow path; and there he took off his fine black frockcoat, slung it across his shoulder from a stick, and wandered along in his shirtsleeves. He stayed from about ten in the forenoon to six o'clock in the evening. . . . During the entire visit he was uncommonly gay and at times most amusing, and all that entered his mind had to come out. ('Well, it happens that I am unbuttoned today,' he said and the remark was decidedly in order.) His talk and his actions all formed a chain of eccentricities, in part most peculiar. Yet they all radiated a truly childlike amiability, carelessness, and confidence in every one who approached him. Even his barking tirades—like that against his Viennese contemporaries, which I already have mentioned—are only explosions of his fanciful imagination and his momentary excitement. They are uttered without haughtiness, without any feeling of bitterness and hatefulness—and are simply blustered out lightly, good-humoredly, the offsprings of a mad, humorous mood. In his life he often shows—and for the sake of his own subsistence only too often and too decidedly—that to the very person who has grievously injured him, whom he has most violently denounced one moment, he will give his last thaler the next, should that person need it.

"To this we must add the most cheerful recognition of merit in others, if only it be distinctive and individual. (How he speaks of Handel, Bach, Mozart!) He does not, however, where his greater works are concerned, allow others to find fault (and who would have the right to do so?) yet he never actually overvalues them; and with regard to his lesser things is more inclined, perhaps, to abandon them with a laugh than any other person. He does this the more since once he is in the vein, rough, striking witticisms, droll conceits, surprising and exciting paradoxes suggest themselves to him in a continuous flow. Hence in all seriousness I claim he even appears to be amiable. Or if you shrink from this word, I might say that the dark, unlicked bear seems so ingenious and confiding, growls and shakes his shaggy pelt so harmlessly and grotesquely that it is a pleasure, and one has to be kind to him, even though he were nothing but a bear in fact and had done no more than a bear's best."

Rochlitz concludes by describing his parting with Beethoven, when he had "thrust our good Beethoven into the carriage": "This time my reflections did not turn only, as on the first time I met him, on the grievous complaint with which fate had afflicted Beethoven. After all, I realized that he also had his hours of great gladness and perfect happiness. In other hours, also good ones, he lived in his art or in his plans and dreams regarding it; the evil hours, however, are thrown into the bargain and he takes them, pours out his soul with regard to them and then forgets them. After all, who may claim to be any better off?"

Although little is known of the subsequent relation between Beethoven and Rochlitz, yet an appreciation of this spirited writer remained until the days of Beethoven's last illness when, in answer to a question, he explained that he would choose Rochlitz for his biographer.

Beethoven had a meeting with another man earlier in this year which is of even more interest. This man was Rossini. His operas had been on the current list in Vienna for several years, and with the coming of the composer in person, in the spring of 1822, the enthusiasm for him and his music had grown into a fanatical adoration. Beethoven had seen the score of *Il Barbiere* and heard it sung by the best Italian singers of the period. Moreover, he had a high admiration for the Italian art of song and a very poor opinion of German singers. Rossini was on his wedding trip, having but recently married Colbran, and his elegant manners and brilliant conversation had made him the lion of aristocratic drawing rooms in the Austrian capital. *Zelmira* had been written especially for the Vienna season, though it had been tried at the Teatro San Carlo in Naples in the preceding December. It had its first performance at the Kärnthnerthor Theatre on April 13[32] under the direction of Domenico Barbaja.

Several of Beethoven's utterances concerning the musician, who no doubt did much to divert the taste of the masses away from the German master's compositions, have been preserved. Seyfried recorded that in answer to the question, "What is Rossini?" Beethoven replied, "A good scene painter,"[33] and Seyfried also makes note of this utterance: "The Bohemians are born musicians, the Italians ought to take them as models. What have they to show for their famous conservatories? Behold their idol—Rossini! If Dame Fortune had not given him a pretty talent and pretty melodies by the bushel, what he learned at school would have brought him nothing but potatoes for his big belly!"[34] To Freudenberg at Baden in 1824 he remarked: "Rossini is a talented and a melodious composer; his music suits the frivolous and sensuous spirit of the times, and his productivity is so great that he needs only as many weeks as the Germans need years to write an opera."[35]

The Rossini craze was no doubt largely responsible for some of Beethoven's outbreaks concerning the taste of the Viennese, but on the whole he does not seem seriously to have been disturbed by it. Schindler cites him as remarking on the change in the popular attitude: "Well, they can not rob me of my place in musical history."[36] As for the Italian singers he thought so much of them that he told Karoline Unger that he would write an Italian opera for Barbaja's company.

---

[32] Archduke Rudolph wrote variations on one of the melodies from the opera, which Beethoven corrected. (TK, III, 77, n. 1.)

[33] *Studien*, Appendix, p. 24. (TDR, IV, 291, n. 3.)

[34] *Ibid.*, p. 39.

[35] Karl Gottlieb Freudenberg, *Erinnerungen eines alten Organisten* (Leipzig, 1872), p. 42. (TDR, IV, 291, n. 3.)

[36] *Biogr.*, II, p. 282. (TDR, IV, 291, n. 2.)

As for Rossini, he had heard some of Beethoven's quartets played by Mayseder and his associates, and had enjoyed them enthusiastically. It was therefore natural enough that he should want to visit the composer. Schindler says that he went twice with Artaria to call upon him, after Artaria had each time asked permission, but that on both occasions Beethoven had asked to be excused from receiving him—a circumstance which had given rise to considerable comment in Vienna. The story is not true, but that it was current in Vienna four years afterward appears from an entry in a Conversation Book of August 1826 where somebody asks: "It is true, isn't it, that Rossini wanted to visit you and you refused to see him?" There is no written answer. We repeat: the story is not true. Twice, at least, Rossini publicly denied it. In 1867 Dr. Eduard Hanslick visited him with two friends in Paris. Concerning the interview, Hanslick wrote:[37]

Suddenly, as if he intentionally wanted to call attention to something loftier, he asked if the Mozart monument at Vienna was finished? And Beethoven's? We three Austrians looked rather embarrassed. "I remember Beethoven well," continued Rossini after a pause, "although it is nearly half a century ago. On my visit to Vienna I hastened to look him up."

"And he did not receive you, as Schindler and other biographers assure us."

"On the contrary," said Rossini, correcting me: "I had Carpani, the Italian poet with whom I had already called upon Salieri, introduce me, and he received me at once and very politely. True, the visit did not last very long, for conversation with Beethoven was nothing less than painful. His hearing was particularly bad on that day and in spite of my loudest shoutings he could not understand me; his little practice in Italian may have made conversation more difficult."

This confirms what Rossini told Ferdinand Hiller in 1856:[38] "During my sojourn in Vienna I had myself introduced to him by old Calpani [*sic*]; but between his deafness and my ignorance of German, conversation was impossible. But I am glad that I saw him, at least."

The name of Franz Schubert was introduced in the account by Rochlitz and the impression created is that the younger composer was aware of the master's habits but knew and admired him from afar. In an earlier chapter was given the description by Anselm Hüttenbrenner of the gathering of composers, of whom Schubert was one, between 11 and 12 o'clock a few times a week at Steiner's store in the Paternostergässchen to exchange musical opinions. On April 19, 1822, the firm of Cappi and Diabelli announced their publication of Schubert's variations on a French song for pianoforte, four hands, which was "dedicated to Herr Ludwig van Beethoven by his Worshipper and Admirer Franz Schubert."[39] That this work made

[37] In an article in the *Neue Freie Presse* of July 21, 1867, reprinted in *Aus dem Concertsaal*, 2nd edition (Vienna and Leipzig, 1897), p. 594. (TDR, IV, 292, n. 3.)

[38] Ferdinand Hiller, *Aus dem Tonleben*

unserer Zeit (Leipzig, 1868), II, p. 49. (TDR, IV, 292, n. 4.)

[39] Otto Erich Deutsch, *Schubert, a Documentary Biography*, trans. by Erich Blom (London, 1946), p. 222.

Beethoven more aware of Schubert as a person and an artist is suggested by the following evidence from Kreissle's biography of Schubert: "It should be stated, however, that a gentleman still living at Vienna, an intimate and trusted friend of Schubert's [Herr Josef Hüttenbrenner],[40] shortly after the presentation of his musical work [the four-hand variations to Beethoven], heard from Schubert's own mouth that he certainly visited Beethoven, but that he was not at home, and that Schubert entrusted his variations to the care of the housemaid, or man-servant, and consequently that at that time he neither saw and still less spoke to Beethoven. Hüttenbrenner remarks further that Schubert subsequently heard with great pleasure of Beethoven's enjoying these variations and playing them frequently and gladly with his nephew Karl."[41]

On August 31, Beethoven wrote his brother that he was leaving for Baden the next day or at the most the day after next. In Baden he lived for awhile at the inn "zum goldenen Schwan," which is still standing and has a tablet commemorating his visit.

Here Beethoven began the work which was to call him back into public notice. This was the music for the opening of the Josephstadt Theatre, which the director of the theatre, Carl Friedrich Hensler, director also of the combined theatres of Pressburg and Baden, asked of him immediately after his arrival at the watering-place. Hensler (1761-1825) was a popular dramatist as well as manager and an old acquaintance of Beethoven's, by whom he was greatly respected. He had bought the privilege of the Josephstadt Theatre in Vienna. Carl Meisl, who was a Commissioner of the Royal Imperial Navy, had written two festival pieces for the opening, which had been set down for October 3, 1822, the name-day of the Emperor. The first piece was a paraphrase of Kotzebue's *Ruinen von Athen*, written for the opening of the theatre in Pesth in 1812, for which Beethoven had composed the music. Meisl took Kotzebue's text and made such alterations in it as were necessary to change *Die Ruinen von Athen* into *Die Weihe des Hauses*. Nottebohm's reprint in *Zweite Beethoveniana* (p. 385 *et seq.*) enables a comparison to be made with the piece as it left the hands of Meisl and the original. The new words did not always fit the music and caused Beethoven considerable concern. A choral dance:

> Wo sich die Pulse
> jugendlich jagen,
> Schwebet im Tanze
> das Leben dahin, etc.

[40] Brother of Anselm Hüttenbrenner.

[41] Heinrich Kreissle von Hellborn, *The Life of Franz Schubert*, trans. by Arthur D. Coleridge (London, 1869), II, pp. 263-64. Kreissle, in introducing the testimony, was answering Schindler's improbable story that at this visit the composers met, that hearing a criticism from Beethoven of his variations, Schubert was completely overwhelmed and lost control of himself until he had left Beethoven's house. Josef Hüttenbrenner's remarks (in answer to Ferdinand Luib) are given in O. E. Deutsch's *Memoirs of Schubert*, p. 75. See also Walter Nohl, "Beethoven and Schubert's personal Relations," in *MQ*, XIV (1928), pp. 553-62.

was introduced and to this Beethoven had to write new music, which he did in September. He also revised, altered and extended the march with chorus.[42] Beethoven wrote a new overture also, that known as *Die Weihe des Hauses,* putting aside the overture to the *Ruinen von Athen* because that play had served as a second piece, or epilogue, at Pesth. On a revised copy of the chorus "Wo sich die Pulse" Beethoven wrote: "Written towards the end of September, 1823, performed on October 3 at the Josephstadt Theatre." The 1823 should be 1822, of course, but singularly enough the same blunder was made on a copy of the overture and another composition, the *Gratulationsmenuett,* which was written about the same time. The explanation is probably that offered by Nottebohm,[43] viz.: that Beethoven dated the copies when he sent them to the Archduke. Beethoven's remark in a letter to Johann that he had finished the chorus with dances and would write the overture if his health allowed, also fixes the date of the composition of the overture in September. This Schindler confirms in this anecdote about the origin of the overture:[44] "Meanwhile September was come. It was therefore time to go to work on the new overture, for the master had long ago seen that the one to the *Ruinen von Athen* was for obvious reasons unsuitable. One day, while I was walking with him and his nephew in the lovely Helenenthal near Baden, Beethoven told us to go on in advance and join him at an appointed place. It was not long before he overtook us, remarking that he had written down two motives for an overture. At the same time he expressed himself also as to the manner in which he purposed treating them—one in the free style and one in the strict, and, indeed, in Handel's. As well as his voice permitted he sang the two motives and then asked us which we liked the better. This shows the roseate mood into which for the moment he was thrown by the discovery of two gems for which, perhaps, he had been hunting a long time. The nephew decided in favor of both, while I expressed a desire to see the fugal theme worked out for the purpose mentioned. It is not to be understood that Beethoven wrote the overture to the *Weihe des Hauses* as he did because I wanted it so, but because he had long cherished the plan to write an overture in the strict, expressly in the Handelian, style. . . . The newly organized orchestra of the Josephstadt Theatre did not receive it till the afternoon before the opening, and with innumerable mistakes in every part. The rehearsal which took place in the presence of an almost filled parterre, scarcely sufficed for the correction of the worst of the copyist's errors."

The overture and chorus written for the *Weihe des Hauses* are "occasionals" and were conceived and wrought out in a remarkably short time

[42] Published as Op. 114 and designated as "new" by Beethoven, though not a measure had been added, but only a few lines of text, and the choral music simplified. Steiner published pianoforte arrangements for two and four hands in 1822, and the score in 1826. (TK, III, 80, n. 1; cf. KHV, p. 330.)

[43] *II Beeth.*, p. 396. (TDR, IV, 301, n. 1.)

[44] *Biogr.*, II, pp. 7-8. (TDR, IV, 301.)

for that period in Beethoven's activities. The first was offered for publication to Steiner and, with other pieces, to Diabelli. The negotiations failed and the overture finally appeared from the press of Schott in 1825, with a dedication to Prince Galitzin.

Beethoven's stay in Baden was interrupted by the performance of the *Weihe des Hauses,* which took place, as projected, on October 3, the eve of the Emperor's name-day. All of the 400 reserved seats and boxes had been sold several weeks before. Beethoven had reserved the direction for himself and sat at the pianoforte, the greater part of the orchestra within view, his left ear turned towards the stage. He was still able to hear a little with that ear, as we know from the fact related by Schindler, that he was fond of listening to Cherubini's overture to *Medea* played by a musical clock which stood in a restaurant adjoining the Josephstadt Theatre. Kapellmeister Franz Gläser stood at his right, and Schindler, who had recently abandoned the law, led the first violins. At the dress rehearsal Fanny Heckermann sang timidly and dragged perceptibly in the duet. Beethoven observed this and called the singer to him, pointed out the places in which he wanted more animation, spoke some words of encouragement and advised her to follow the tenor, who was an experienced singer. He then had the number repeated and on its conclusion remarked: "Well done, this time, Fräulein Heckermann!"[45] The tenor was Michael Greiner, with whom Beethoven was acquainted, from Baden, and Fräulein Kaiser sang the part of Pallas. The rehearsal and the performance demonstrated plainly, Schindler says, that under no circumstances was Beethoven able longer to conduct large bodies of performers. The representation, despite the enthusiasm of the performers, stimulated by Beethoven's encouraging speeches, was not a success. Beethoven would take none of the fault to himself, however, though his anxiety led him to hold back the music despite the exertions of his two leaders, whom he admonished against too much precipitancy, of which Schindler protests they were not guilty. There were demonstrations of enthusiasm at the close and Beethoven was led before the curtain by Director Hensler. The work was repeated on October 4, 5 and 6.

Beethoven's return to Baden was on or before October 11, and he stayed in a house in the Magdalenahof, Frauengasse No. 85, belonging to Johann Grundgeyer, who was not only a merchant but also Master of the Baths, Magistrate, and Police Commissioner. This house also still stands and has a memorial tablet. Grundgeyer kept a log of house rentals in which is recorded in 1822 "Hr. v. Beethoven from Oct. 11 2 rooms and 1 kitchen, at 2 fl. 45 k. per day part-payment 20 fl. V.S. 27 finis." It is not known whether the sum of 27 florins was the whole sum or a final payment to be counted with the statement of 20 florins.[46] At any rate, Beethoven could not have been there for more than 2 or 3 weeks because soon he was to contribute

[45] *Ibid.,* p. 9.
[46] See Theodor Frimmel, "Beethoven im

Kurort Baden bei Wien," in *NBJ,* IV (1930), pp. 75-6.

to another musical event in Vienna. At this time Beethoven left his old dwelling on the Landstrasse and moved into quarters next to his brother's house in the Windmühle Vorstadt. Johann's house on the Kothgasse No. 61 was owned by his brother-in-law, the master baker Leopold Obermayer; Beethoven's rooms were in a house on the Oberepfarrgasse No. 60, owned by a certain Johann Ehlers.[47]﹉—

Beethoven's friendly feeling for Hensler gave rise to a new orchestral composition which was part of a tribute paid by the members of the company to their director on November 3, the evening before his name-day. After a performance of Meisl's drama *1722, 1822, 1922*, the audience having departed, the director was called to the festively decorated and illuminated stage, and surrounded by his company in gala dress. A poetical address was read to him by the stage-manager. After he had gone back to his lodgings, the orchestra and chorus serenaded him, the programme consisting of an overture to *The Prodigal Son* by Kapellmeister Drechsel, a concerto for flute by Kapellmeister Gläser, and what Bäuerle's *Theaterzeitung* called "a glorious new symphony" composed for the occasion by Beethoven, the whole ending with the march and chorus from Mozart's *Titus*. The "new symphony" was the *Gratulationsmenuett* of which mention has been made. Nothing is said in the accounts about Beethoven's presence at the serenade, and as *Fidelio* was performed that night at the Kärnthnerthor Theatre, his absence might easily be explained. On the next day Hensler gave a dinner in the property room of the theatre at 3 P.M. Beethoven, Gläser, Bäuerle, Gleich, Meisl, Hopp and others were present.[48] Beethoven had a seat directly under the musical clock. Gläser told Reischl[49] who provided the entertainment to set the clock to the overture to *Fidelio* and then wrote to Beethoven to listen, as he would soon hear it. Beethoven listened and then said: "It plays it better than the orchestra in the Kärnthnerthor."[50]

The *Gratulationsmenuett* was offered to Peters in the letter of December 20. Beethoven was evidently eager to realize quickly on a work which had cost him but little labor—the product of a period in which his fancy seemed to have regained its old-time fecundity and he his old-time delight in work. He offered it elsewhere and gave a copy (the one that he misdated) to

[47] In the *Verzeichniss aller in der Kaiserl. Königl. Haupt-und Residenz-stadt Wien mit ihren Vorstädten befindlichen Häuser*, arr. and ed. by Anton Behsel (Vienna, 1829) is indicated:

Windmühle neue (1823)
Johann Ehlers   60   Polizei Bezirks-
                            direct: Mariahilf
Leop. Obermayer 61 Gassen und Plätze:
                            Oberepfarrgasse

[48] Max Unger, "Vom geselligen Beethoven," *Österreiche Musikzeitschrift*, XII (1957), p. 92, supplies the following identifications: Franz Gläser, son of Beethoven's copyist, Peter Gläser,

and Theatre Kapellmeister; Adolph Bäuerle, author and editor of the *Wiener Allgemeine Theaterzeitung*; Joseph Alois Gleich, productive poet for the Josephstadt stage and scholar in the civil service; Carl Meisl, author of the *Weihe des Hauses*; Friedrich Hopp, author as well as actor. This anecdote was told to Thayer on October 28, 1859 by Hopp. (TK, III, 82, n. 1.)

[49] According to O. E. Deutsch, *Österreiche Musikzeitschrift*, XII (1957), p. 163, Wolfgang Reischl was landlord of the Josephstadt Theatre.

[50] See Schünemann, II, p. 293, for a similar account by implication.

Archduke Rudolph for his collection. Artaria published it in 1832 under the title "Allegretto" with a dedication to Karl Holz. The title on the autograph reads: "Tempo di Minuetto quasi Allegretto" (Allegro non troppo was originally written but then scratched out in favor of): "Gratulations-Menuett."

The revival of *Fidelio* which took place on November 3, after an absence from the stage of three years, was a benefit performance for Wilhelmine Schröder, then seventeen years old. Later as the famous dramatic singer, Madame Schröder-Devrient,[51] she was reputed to be the greatest of all the Fidelios; but she did not reach her full artistic stature until after Beethoven's death. Haitzinger sang Florestan, Zeltner Rocco, Forti Pizarro. Rauscher was Jacquino, Nestroy the Minister, Fräulein Demmer sang Marcelline and Fräulein Schröder, Leonore. Schindler tells a pathetic tale concerning the dress rehearsal. Together with his friends, mindful of the happenings in the Hall of the University in 1819 and in the Josephstadt Theatre only a short time before, Schindler advised Beethoven not to attempt to conduct the performance. He hesitated for a few days, then announced his intention to direct with the help of Umlauf. Schindler escorted him to the rehearsal. The overture went well, the orchestra being well trained in it, but at the first duet it became painfully manifest that Beethoven heard nothing of what was being sung on the stage. He slackened his beat and the orchestra obeyed; the singers urged the movement onward. Umlauf stopped the performance at the rappings on the jailor's lodge-gate but gave no reason to Beethoven. At the same place on the repetition there was the same confusion. Let Schindler continue the narrative: "The impossibility of going ahead with the author of the work was evident. But how, in what manner inform him of the fact? Neither Duport, the director, nor Umlauf was willing to speak the saddening words: 'It will not do; go away, you unhappy man!' Beethoven, already uneasy in his seat, turned now to the right now to the left, scrutinizing the faces to learn the cause of the interruption. Everywhere a heavy silence. Then he summoned me. I had approached near him in the orchestra. He handed me his notebook with an indication that I write what the trouble was. Hastily I wrote in effect: 'Please do not go on; more at home.' With a bound he was in the parterre and said merely: 'Out, quick!' Without stopping he ran towards his lodgings, Pfarrgasse, Vorstadt Leimgrube.[52] Inside he threw himself on the sofa, covered his face with his hands and remained in this attitude till we sat down to eat. During the meal not a word came from his lips; he was a picture of profound melancholy and depression. When I tried to go away after the meal he begged me not to leave him until it was time to go to the theatre. At parting he asked me

---

[51] She met the actor Karl Devrient in 1823 and was his wife for five years after which time the marriage was dissolved.

[52] The confusion in Schindler's address may be explained by the fact that the Oberepfarrgasse was renamed Leimgrubenstrasse. For this information I am indebted to Dr. Kurt Smolle.

to go with him next day to his physician, Dr. Smetana, who had gained some repute as an aurist."[53]

Some details of the representation may be learned from the account in the *Theaterzeitung* of November 9. The day was the name-day of the Empress; the square about the Opera-house was illuminated; the national hymn, "Gott erhalte Franz den Kaiser," was sung; the overture received such applause that it had to be repeated; the great duet and the canon quartet also, and the soprano and tenor were recalled at the end of the opera.

Wilhelmine Schröder-Devrient wrote an account of her debut as Leonore at the request of Gustav Schilling[54] from which we quote in part:

"Under the guidance of my talented mother many of the traits in Leonore's character became clear to me; however I was still too young, too little developed within to have a full understanding of what took place in Leonore's soul, emotions for which Beethoven had conceived his immortal harmonies. At the rehearsals which were led by Umlauf who was then kapellmeister, the limits of my underdeveloped young voice soon became known and many things in my part were changed for me so that the effect did not suffer too much. The last rehearsals were set, when I learned before the dress rehearsal that Beethoven had asked for the honor of conducting the work himself in celebration of the day. On hearing this news a great fear came over me, and I also remember my frightful awkwardness which nearly drove my poor mother, as well as those who were working with me, to despair. But Beethoven sat in the orchestra and waved his baton over everyone's heads, and I had never seen the man before!— At that time the master's physical ear was already closed to all sounds. With a bewildered face and unearthly inspired eyes, waving his baton back and forth with violent motions, he stood in the midst of the performing musicians and didn't hear a note! If he thought it should be *piano* he crouched down almost under the conductor's desk and if he wanted *forte* he jumped up with the strangest gestures, uttering the weirdest sounds. With each piece our courage dwindled further and I felt as though I were watching one of Hoffmann's fantastic figures appear before me. The inevitable happened: the deaf master threw the singers and orchestra completely off the beat and into the greatest confusion, and no one knew any longer where they were. Beethoven, however, knew nothing of all this, and so with difficulty our rehearsal came to an end, with which he seemed to be well satisfied, for he laid down his baton with a cheery smile. But now it was impossible to entrust him with the performance, and Kapellmeister Umlauf had to perform the heart-rending task of pointing out to him that the opera could not be given under his direction. I am told that he resigned himself with a melancholy look upwards, and I found him at the performance on the following night sitting in the orchestra

[53] *Biogr.*, II, p. 11. (TDR, IV, 319, n. 1.)
[54] It was published as a contribution to *Beethoven-Album, ein Gedenkbuch dankbarer*   *Liebe und Verehrung für den grossen Todten* (Stuttgart, 1846).

behind Umlauf lost in profound thought. . . . Beethoven followed the whole performance with eager attention, and he looked as if he were trying to see from each of our gestures whether we had even half understood him.

"Even then they used to call me a little genius; and indeed on that evening a more mature spirit seemed to have come over me, for several touches of sheer genius shone forth from my performance which must not have escaped Beethoven, for the next day he came himself, the great master, to bring me his thanks and his congratulations. With hot tears I moistened the hand that he offered me, and in my joy, I would not have exchanged anything in the world for this praise from Beethoven's lips! He promised at that time to write an opera for me, but unfortunately it remained nothing but a promise."

The two accounts of the rehearsal, while agreeing in general, do not agree in detail. Schindler's direct participation in Beethoven's departure from the scene would seem to make his account the more likely to be correct. Elsewhere, however, Schindler, in declaring that Beethoven never saw Schröder-Devrient as Leonore,[55] shows an obvious lack of memory in recalling these days which lessens the reader's confidence in the exactness of his account. That Beethoven was at a performance is confirmed by a remark of the Darmstadt composer Ludwig Wilhelm Reuling in a Conversation Book of March, 1823: "I saw you in the theatre at the first performance of *Fidelio*.[56]"

Fidelio was repeated on November 4 and also on November 26, December 2 and 17, and March 3 and 18, 1823. According to the *Modenzeitung*, November 12, 1822, "Beethoven attended the second performance, sitting in a box in the front tier." Louis Schlösser, who was at this performance, adds confirmation by telling how he saw Beethoven leaving the theatre in the company of Schindler and von Breuning.[57]

Following Schindler's narrative we learn that Beethoven's woeful experience at the rehearsal led to a resolution on his part to make another effort to be healed of his deafness. He went to Dr. Smetana, who prescribed medicaments to be taken inwardly, thereby indicating, as Schindler asserts, that he had no expectation of effecting a cure, but wanted only to occupy Beethoven's mind, knowing what to expect from so impatient, wilful and absent-minded a patient; for Beethoven was as unready to follow a physician's advice as a musician's, and was more likely to injure himself with overdoses of drugs than to invite the benefit which the practitioner hoped for by obedience to the prescription. The usual thing happened; not only with Dr. Smetana's treatment, but also with that of the priest, Pater Weiss, whom he had consulted some 18 years before and to whom he now returned. For a while he thought that the oil which the priest dropped into his ears was beneficial, and Pater Weiss himself expressed the belief that the left ear, at least, might

[55] *Neue Berliner Musikzeitung*, July 30, 1851.

[56] Schünemann, III, p. 86.

[57] The periodical, *Hallelujah*, IV (1885), p. 232. (TDR, IV, 318, n. 3.)

permanently be helped; but Beethoven grew skeptical, as he always did unless he experienced immediate relief, his work monopolized his attention, and despite the priest's solicitations he abandoned the treatment and yielded himself to his fate. Thenceforward no one heard him lament because of his deafness.

The compositions which were in Beethoven's hands at the close of the year were those which had occupied him in the earlier months. The Mass, several times completed but never complete so long as it was within reach, received what must now be looked upon as its finishing touches. Progress was made on the Ninth Symphony and the Diabelli Variations, and thought given to a quartet, perhaps several quartets.

The Bagatelles for Pianoforte grouped under Op. 119, some of which had been published a year before (Nos. 7-11), were finished; Nos. 1 to 6 were ready for the publisher by the end of 1822—the autograph manuscript bearing the inscription "Kleinigkeiten, 1822 Novemb." Nottebohm thinks that Nos. 2 to 5 were conceived between 1800 and 1804; a sketch for No. 5 (C minor, "Risoluto") is found among sketches made in 1802 for the Sonata in C minor, Op. 30; Lenz says sketches for No. 3 (in D, "a l'Allemande") are among sketches for the last movement of the "Eroica" Symphony; No. 6 (G major) is sketched on a sheet containing experimental studies for a passage in the *Credo* of the Mass; sketches for Nos. 2 and 4 are among suggestions of a melody for Goethe's "Erlkönig," WoO 131,[58] indicating an early period which cannot be determined.[59]

Beethoven offered a number of Bagatelles to Peters on June 5, July 6 and November 22; he sent six to the publisher on February 15, 1823. Peters returned them—Beethoven receiving them on March 19—with the remark that they were not worth the price asked for them and that Beethoven ought to consider it beneath his dignity to waste his time on such trifles; anybody could write them. Schindler says that Peters's action aggrieved Beethoven, which is easily believed.[60] On February 25, 1823, Beethoven sent the eleven Bagatelles to Ries in London with instructions to sell them as best he could. On May 7, 1823, six were offered to Lissner in St. Petersburg. At the end of 1823 they were published by Clementi in London and Schlesinger in Paris, the latter giving them the opus number 112. Sauer and Leidesdorf issued them in Vienna with the same opus number at the end of April, 1824.[61] The number 119 appears to have been assigned to the set after an agreement had been reached with Steiner concerning the works now numbered 112 to 118.

The last known song by Beethoven, "Der Kuss," was finished at this time,

[58] See KHV, pp. 593-94.

[59] The piece added to the set by Diabelli, in his later publication "12 Nouvelles Bagatelles," was an adaption of the pianoforte accompaniment of Beethoven's early song "An Laura" and clearly does not belong to the set.

(Cf. TDR, IV, 321.)

[60] *Biogr.*, II, pp. 44-5. (In his account Schindler confuses them with the set, Op. 126, bagatelles of a higher order and not composed at this time.) (TDR, IV, 322, n. 3.)

[61] KHV, pp. 345-46.

though written down practically as we know it in 1798. Sketches involving the few changes made are found among some for the overture, the *Weihe des Hauses* and the Ninth Symphony. The autograph is dated "December, 1822." In 1825 it was published by Schott and Cappi, numbered 121, and did not receive the number 128 until 1828.[62]

--✷Schindler, in his list of vocal music for Beethoven's last period lists among others: "Op. 121b, 'Opferlied,' Poem by Matthison [*sic*]. For a solo voice with chorus and orchestra, published 1826 by Schott. Op. 122 'Bundes-lied.' Poem by Goethe. For two solo voices and 3-part chorus with accompaniment of 2 clarinets, 2 horns and 2 bassoons, published 1826 by Schott. Both of the preceding songs were written in 1822 for the tenor Ehlers at a concert for his own benefit in Pressburg."[63] Beethoven had known Ehlers since 1814 at which time he sang in Treitschke's Singspiel *Die gute Nach-richt*.[64] Thayer-Deiters dismissed Schindler's composition dates since the last version of "Opferlied," Op. 121b is written for a soprano and not a tenor, and was the work of the summer of 1824. But the discovery of Wilhelm Ehler's Akademie program by Viktor Papp[65] shows that Schindler was more accurate than at first supposed. On December 23, 1822, in Pressburg was given "eine grosse musikalisch deklamatorische Akademie" which included two of Beethoven's newest compositions: the *Gratulationsmenuett* and "Matthisson's Opferlied für drei Solostimmen und Chor, aus Freundschaft für den Concertgeber für diese Akademie komponiert." ("Matthisson's Opferlied for 3 solo voices and chorus composed for this *Akademie* out of friendship for the concert-giver.") This version, which Herbst calls No. 3,[66] is scored for soprano, alto and tenor solo and four-part chorus with accompaniment of 2 clarinets, 2 horns, violas and violoncellos, and was first performed in Vienna in April, 1824. It will be remembered that on February 15 Beethoven wrote Peters that he had sent him three songs, "Bundeslied," "Der Kuss" and "Opferlied." Since this version of "Opferlied" was completed before the end of the year it is fair to assume that "Bundeslied" was also, since Beethoven may well have intended it for Ehler's use, as Schindler records, and for some reason it was not used.}✷--

On September 2, Beethoven received a letter from Charles Neate, which was plainly an answer to an appeal which had been sent by the composer, concerning the publication in London of three quartets. Letters from Ries refer to the same quartets, which as yet existed only in Beethoven's intentions. Neate says that he had found it difficult to obtain subscriptions for the works. He thought, however, that he might still be able to raise 100 pounds, but could not get any money before the arrival of the works in London. There was also apprehension that the compositions would be copied in Vienna. Beethoven had referred to a quartet and possibly some successors

[62] *Ibid.*, p. 389.
[63] *Biogr.*, II, p. 152.
[64] See *A* 472.
[65] *Beethoven és a Magyarok* (Beethoven and the Hungarians) (Budapest, 1927), p. 122.
[66] See "Beethoven's Opferliedkomponisten," *NBJ*, V (1933), pp. 137-53.

in his correspondence with Peters, so that it is more than likely that a determination to return to the quartet field had been formed by Beethoven before the practical and material incentive came to him in the last month of the year from Prince Galitzin—the incentive to which we owe three of the last five quartets.

Prince Nikola[u]s Borissowit[s]ch Galitzin [Golizyn],[67] born in 1794 in Moscow, was an influential force in the musical life of St. Petersburg. He played the violoncello, and his wife (née Princess Helene Saltykow) was an admirable pianist. Prince Galitzin was an ardent admirer of Beethoven's music and had arranged some of his pianoforte works for strings. The first mention of his name was in a Conversation Book in the first half of April, 1820, when Kanne, in answer to some question writes "der Gallizin bor[i]s." This is followed by "wo wir so oft war[e]n" ("where we were so often"); to what this refers and its connection, if any, with the name of the prince is not known. (See Schünemann, II, p. 45.)

Then on November 9, 1822, the prince wrote the following letter to Beethoven:

Monsieur!

I take the liberty of writing you, as one who is as much a passionate amateur in music as a great admirer of your talent, to ask if you will not consent to compose one, two or three new quartets for which labor I will be glad to pay you what you think proper. I will accept the dedication with gratitude. Would you let me know to what banker I should direct the sum that you wish to get. The instrument that I am cultivating is the violoncello. I await your answer with the liveliest impatience. Could you please address your letter to me as follows

To Prince Nicolas de Galitzin at S. Petersburg care of Messrs. Stieglitz and Co. Bankers.

I beg you to accept the assurance of my great admiration and high regard.

Prince Nicolas Galitzin

Beethoven's reply was written in French in Karl's hand and the composer supplied the date and his signature:

Your Highness!   Vienna January 25, 1823

I would not have failed to answer Your letter of Nov. 9 sooner if the multitude of my affairs had not prevented me from writing you. It was with great pleasure that I found that Your Highness is interested in works of my creation. You wish to have some quartets; since I see that you are cultivating the violoncello, I will take care to give you satisfaction in this regard. Inasmuch as I am constrained to live by the products of my mind, I must take the liberty of setting the honorarium for one quartet at 50 ducats. If this is agreeable with your Highness, I beg you to inform me soon and to direct this sum to the banker

[67] For the correct spelling of Galitzin's name and the information concerning his birth I am indebted to Miss Emily Anderson's "Two Letters from Beethoven to Prince Nikolas Galitzin," in *Festschrift Joseph Schmidt-Görg zum 60. Geburtstag*, ed. by Dagmar Weise (Bonn, 1957), pp. 1-9.

Hénikstein in Vienna; I bind myself to finish the 1st quartet by the end of the month of February or at the latest by the middle of March.

In expressing to you my real interest in your musical talent, I thank your Highness for the regards that you have been willing to indicate, in choosing me to increase, if it is possible, your love for music. I have the honor of being

Your Highness's very humble servant
Louis van Beethoven[68]

The smaller compositions completed in this year were:

Bagatelles for Pianoforte, Op. 119, Nos. 1-6. Nos. 2-5 were worked out from early sketches.
"Bundeslied" for Two Solo Voices and Three-part Chorus with accompaniment of 2 clarinets, 2 bassoons and 2 horns (Goethe), Op. 122. Revision of sketches of 1797.[69]
"Der Kuss" (C. F. Weisse), Op. 128. Revision of a sketch of 1798.
Gratulationsmenuett for Orchestra, WoO 3, for a Serenade for Carl Friedrich Hensler.
Music for the *Weihe des Hauses* (Meisl):
Overture in C, Op. 124.
March with Chorus, Op. 114 (revision of Op. 113, No. 6).
Chorus "Wo sich die Pulse," WoO 98.
"Opferlied" for Soprano, Alto, Tenor and Chorus with accompaniment of 2 clarinets, 2 horns, violas and violoncellos, third version (listed with Op. 121b in KHV).
Short Piece for Two Violins for Alexandre Boucher, WoO 34. Boucher (1778-1861) was a French violinist who called on Beethoven with a letter of introduction from Goethe. Beethoven wrote out this musical souvenir of seven measures on April 29.[70]

Progress on large works consisted of:

1821-2. Sonata for Pianoforte in C minor, Op. 111. On the first page of the fair copy Beethoven wrote: "January 13, 1822."
1819-23. Main work on the Thirty-three Variations on a Theme by Diabelli, Op. 120.
1819-22/23. Tentative completion of the *Missa Solemnis* in D major, Op. 123.

The publications of the year were:

By Breitkopf and Härtel:
Overture to *Fidelio* in E major.
By Schlesinger in Berlin and Paris:
Sonata for Pianoforte in A-flat major, Op. 110.
By Steiner:
"Meeresstille und glückliche Fahrt" for Chorus and Orchestra, Op. 112, dedicated to the author, J. W. von Goethe.

---

[68] *Ibid.*, p. 4, for the first printing of this letter. See also *A* 1123.
[69] Hans Boettcher, *Beethoven als Lieder-* *komponist* (Augsburg, 1928), Table IV.
[70] See *FRBH*, I, pp. 57-8.

First continental editions:

By Artaria, Mechetti, Schlesinger, and Steiner:

Twenty-five Scottish Songs with Accompaniment of Pianoforte, Violin and Violoncello, Op. 108, dedicated to Prince Anton Heinrich Radziwill.

By Simrock:

Symphonies Nos. 1-3 *in score.*

CHAPTER XXXVI

THE YEAR 1823

SUBSCRIPTIONS FOR THE *MISSA SOLEMNIS*—MORE NEGOTIATIONS WITH ENGLAND—GRILLPARZER AND OPERA PROJECTS—PROGRESS OF THE NINTH SYMPHONY

THIS period in Beethoven's life was great in inspiration and creation. The great Mass was ready, needing only corrections and a few alterations. Work continued on the new symphony, and the stimulation to write some new string quartets, the big labor of the last years, was already upon him.

The progress of the Mass and the negotiations, still inconclusive, toward its publication have been sketched for the preceding years. Now at last it was possible for the work to reach its destination. It was intended, as we have long known, for Archduke Rudolph; since the plan was first formulated, four years had elapsed. On February 27, 1823, he wrote of his intention to pay him a visit and apologized that he had not written for such a long time:

... but I have been wanting to wait until I had sent the Mass; but then there were really terrible mistakes in it and to such an extent that *every part* had to be read over; it was delayed further by many other affairs that could not be put off, which led to still other circumstances to hinder me, for so much confronts a man when he least expects it. However, that I have had Y.I.H. continually in mind is shown by the copies of some new publications[1] that are being sent which have been ready for Y.I.H. for several months; but I did not want to send them on ahead of the Mass. This *last* is being bound and after that will be respectfully handed over by me to Y.I.H. ...

This took place on March 19, 1823, the evening before the anniversary day of the enthronement of the Archduke as Archbishop of Olmütz, for

[1] The overture and chorus for the *Weihe des Hauses* and the *Gratulationsmenuett*. (TDR, IV, 325, n. 2.)

which solemnization the Mass was supposed to have been ready. In the catalogue of the Rudolphinian Collection, now preserved by the Gesellschaft der Musikfreunde in Vienna, it is entered thus: "*Missa Solemnis*. Partitur. MS. This beautifully written MS. was delivered by the composer himself on March 19, 1823."

The plan to write the Mass for the installation ceremonies seems to have been original with Beethoven; it was not suggested by the Archduke or any of his friends, so far as has ever been learned. He began work upon it at once. —⊷Let us review the chronology here. In the first edition of his *Biographie*,[2] Schindler dates the beginning of the composition of the Mass as the winter of 1818-19. As mentioned earlier, Max Unger[3] has established the time more precisely as the first months of 1819 on the basis of the first sketches for the *Kyrie*, which follow those for the Diabelli Variations, in a sketchbook from the Wittgenstein Collection.⊷— Nottebohm's study[4] of the sketches led him to conclusions which may be summed up as follows: the movements were taken up in the order in which the various portions appear in the Roman missal, but work was prosecuted on several movements simultaneously. The *Kyrie* was begun shortly after the fact of the Archduke's appointment was known; the *Gloria* was completely sketched by the end of 1819, and the *Credo* in 1820. —⊷In the first of the three *Missa Solemnis* sketchbooks at the Beethovenhaus in Bonn, dated by Schmidt-Görg December, 1819-April, 1820,[5] there is evidence to amplify Nottebohm's generalization. Sketches for the *Credo* appear on the very first page of the forty-four page sketchbook, whereas there is still work on the close of the *Gloria* on page 31. There are also a few sketches for the *Sanctus*.⊷— The entire Mass was complete in sketchbook form in the beginning of 1822. But with the elaboration of the sketches the Mass was not really finished, for subsequently Beethoven undertook many changes. The *Allegro* molto which enters in the *Credo* at the words "et ascendit" is shorter in the autograph than in the printed edition. At the entrance of the words "et iterum" and "cujus regni" the autograph is in each case two measures shorter than in the printed score. In the autograph, and also in the copy which Beethoven gave to the Archduke, the trombones do not enter till the words "judicare vivos et mortuous." There are no trombones in the *Gloria*. The trombone passage which now appears just before the entrance of the chorus on "judicare" was formerly set for the horns. After the words "et mortuous" the trombones are silent until the end of the *Credo* in the autograph; they enter again in the beginning of the *Sanctus*, but are silent at the next *Allegro*. They occur in the *Benedictus*, but are wanting in the *Agnus Dei*. He made so many changes in the tympani part of the *Agnus Dei* that he wore a hole in the very thick paper. From

---

[2] [1840], p. 113.

[3] "Die Beethoven Handschriften der Familie W. in Wien," in *NJB*, VII (1937), pp. 167-68.

[4] *II Beeth.*, pp. 148-56. (Cf. TDR, IV, 326, n. 3.)

[5] Joseph Schmidt-Görg, *Ein Skizzenbuch aus den Jahren 1819-20* (Bonn, 1952), pp. 15-16.

the nature of these supplementary alterations it is to be concluded that considerable time must have elapsed before they could all be made. Holding to the date on which the copy was delivered to the Archduke (March 19, 1823), the earliest date at which the Mass can have received its definitive shape as we know it must be set down as the middle of 1823. That he was sincere in his purpose to provide a mass for the installation ceremonies is to be found, outside of Schindler's statement, in a letter to the Archduke in which he says:

The day on which a high mass of my composition is performed at the ceremony for Y.I.H. will be to me the most beautiful in my life and God will enlighten me so that my poor powers may contribute to the glory of this solemn day.

Something was said at the beginning of Chapter XXIII of this biography concerning the views Beethoven entertained on the subject of religion and dogmatic and sectarian Christianity. His attitude towards the Roman Catholic Church becomes an almost necessary subject of contemplation in a study of the *Missa Solemnis*; but it is one into which the personal equation of the student must perforce largely enter. The obedient churchman of a Roman Catholic country will attach both less and more importance, than one brought up in a Protestant land, to the fact that he admonished his nephew when a lad to say his prayers and said them with him (as the boy testified in the guardianship proceedings), that he himself at least once led him to the door of the confessional,[6] that he consented to the summoning of a priest when *in extremis* and that he seemed to derive comfort and edification from the sacred function. It is not necessary, however, to go very deeply into a critical study of the Mass in order to say that while the composition shows respect for traditions in some portions and while it is possible to become eloquent without going beyond the demonstration contained in the music itself, in describing the overwhelming puissance of his proclamation of the fatherhood of God and belief in Him as the Creator of all things visible and invisible, the most obvious fact which confronts the analytical student is that Beethoven approached the missal text chiefly with the imagination and the emotions of an artist, and that its poetical, not to say dramatic elements were those which he was most eager to delineate.

One example of this may be found in the *Agnus Dei*. It was scarcely necessary for Beethoven to do so, but he has nevertheless given us an explanation of his singular treatment of the prayer for peace. Among the sketches for the movement is found the remark: "dona nobis pacem darstellend den *innern* und äussern Frieden" ("delineating internal and external peace"), and in agreement with this he superscribes the first *Allegro vivace*

---

[6] In a Conversation Book of 1820 we read this remark by Beethoven: "What I think of confession may be deduced from the fact that I myself led Karl to the Abbot of St. Michael for confession. But the Abbot declared that as long as he had to visit his mother, confession would be of no avail." (TDR, IV, 335, n. I.) See Schünemann, I, p. 203.

in the autograph with the same words. In the later copy this phrase is changed to "Prayer for internal and external peace,"[7] thus showing an appreciation of the fact that the words alone contain the allusion to peace which in its external aspect is disturbed by the sounds of war suggested by the instruments. The petition for peace is emphasized by the threatening tones of military instruments accompanying the agonizing appeal for mercy sent up by the voices. The device is purely dramatic and it was not an entirely novel conceit of Beethoven's. When the French invaded Styria in 1796, Haydn wrote a mass "In tempore belli" in which a soft drum-roll entered immediately after the words "Agnus Dei" and was gradually reinforced by trumpets and other wind-instruments "as if the enemy were heard approaching in the distance."

By the end of 1822, Beethoven had made the plan of postponing the publication of the Mass in order to sell manuscript copies of it by subscription to the sovereigns of Europe. In the Library of the Paris Conservatory is an unpublished letter from Johann van Beethoven without address but apparently to the Paris publisher Pacini in answer to a request for quartets or quintets by his brother.[8] Johann answered that his brother could not oblige just now since he was working on a symphony, an opera and a big mass, asked the publisher for help in the sale of manuscript copies of this last work at the French court, and offered him a new trio for 2 violins and viola and a big overture.[9]

In the first week of the new year Beethoven sent his brother with a letter to Griesinger of the Saxon Legation asking him to give advice on the subject of subscription to the bearer of the letter, apologizing for not coming in person on the grounds of indisposition. Whether or not Griesinger came to his assistance we do not know, but within a fortnight work on the project had been energetically begun. Schindler was now called upon to write, fetch and carry as steadily and industriously as if he were, in fact, what he described himself to be—a private secretary. Among his papers in Berlin are found many billets and loose memoranda bearing on the subject, without date, but grouped as to periods by Schindler himself and provided with occasional glosses touching their contents. Beethoven took so much of his time in requisition, indeed, that he offered to pay him 50 florins after the collection of one of the subscription fees, but Schindler records that he never received them nor would he have accepted them. He was, as he informed the world

---

[7] *Il Beeth.*, pp. 151-52, 471-72. (TDR, IV, 352, n. 2.)

[8] Max Unger, "Die Beethovenhandschriften der Pariser Konservatorium-Bibliothek" in *NBJ*, VI (1935), p. 122. As Unger points out, Pacini is the likely recipient because there is in the same library the autograph of a letter from Beethoven to Pacini, dated April 5, 1823 which begins: "Monsieur! C'est mon Frère, qui me disait, que vous souhaitiés de

posseder quelquesunes de mes Compositions. . . ." See *ibid.*, p. 117; also *A* 1166.

[9] The symphony was of course the ninth, the opera a reflection of Beethoven's constant search for a good libretto, the big overture that to the *Weihe des Hauses*. But nothing is known of a trio for two violins and viola. This was either a mistake by Johann or an indication that Beethoven intended or was willing to write such a work.

for many years afterward on his visiting card, "L'Ami de Beethoven," and his very considerable and entirely unselfish labors were "works of friendship" for which he wanted no remuneration; but he was very naturally rejoiced when Beethoven presented him with several autograph scores, and we have seen how, after the death of Beethoven, Breuning gave him many papers which seemed valueless then but are looked upon as invaluable now. Moreover, he disposed of his Beethoven memorabilia to the Royal Library of Berlin for an annuity of 400 thalers—all of which, however, does not detract from the disinterestedness of his labors for Beethoven, alive, suffering and so frequently helpless.

The invitations to the courts were issued in part before the end of January. A letter to Schindler, evidently written in that month, asked him to draw out a memorandum of courts from an almanac in which the foreign embassies stationed at Vienna were listed. The invitations were posted on the following dates: to the courts at Baden, Wurtemburg, Bavaria and Saxony on January 23; "to the other ambassadors" (as Beethoven notes) on January 26; to Weimar on February 4; to Mecklenburg and Hesse-Darmstadt on February 5; to Berlin, Copenhagen, Hesse-Cassel and Nassau on February 6; to Tuscany on February 17, and to Paris on March 1. The invitation to the court at Hesse-Cassel had been written on January 23, but it was not sent because, as Schindler says, "it had been found that nothing was to be got from the little courts." The letter came back to Beethoven and its preservation puts in our hands the formula which, no doubt was followed in all the formal addresses. We therefore give it here:

The undersigned cherishes the wish to send his latest work, which he regards as the most successful of his intellectual products, to the Most Exalted Court of Cassel.

It is a grand solemn mass for 4 solo voices with choruses and complete grand orchestra in score, which can also be used as a grand oratorio.

He therefore begs the High Embassy of His Royal Highness, the Elector of Hesse-Cassel, to be pleased to procure for him the necessary permission of your Exalted Court.

Inasmuch, however, as the copying of the score will entail a considerable expense the author does not think it excessive if he fixes an honorarium at 50 ducats in gold. The work in question, moreover, will not be published for the present.

Vienna, 23 January, 1823.   Ludwig van Beethoven.

Only the signature was in Beethoven's handwriting. It is not known how many of these invitations were issued; Schindler's account goes only to the subscriptions received and even here it is not entirely accurate. There were ten acceptances. The first came from the King of Prussia. Prince Hatzfield acted in the matter for Berlin ──▸◦{and Beethoven also invoked the aid of the King's Secretary, Friedrich Duncker.[10]}◦◂── Court Councillor Wernhard, Director of the Chancellery of the Embassy at Vienna, brought the report to

[10] Johann Friedrich Leopold Duncker, died 1842. See FRBH, I, 117.

Beethoven and asked him if he would not prefer a royal order to the 50 ducats. Without hesitation, Beethoven replied "50 ducats," and after Wernhard had gone he indulged in sarcastic comments on the pursuit of decorations by various contemporaries—"which in his opinion were gained at the cost of the sanctity of art."[11] Beethoven received the money, but the score was not delivered, owing, no doubt, to delay in the copying, and in July Prince Hatzfield felt compelled to remind the composer of his remissness. Prince Radziwill in Berlin also subscribed, but he did not receive his copy till more than a year later. On June 28, 1824, a representative of the Prince politely informed Beethoven that he had sent a cheque for 50 ducats to him with a request for a receipt and a copy of the score, but had received neither. Schindler says the fault lay with the copyists; in every copy many pages had to be rewritten.

On July 1, 1823, Beethoven wrote a long letter to the Archduke in which he reported on the progress of his subscription plan and asked for help in obtaining a subscription from the Grand Duke of Tuscany. Because of the light that this letter throws on the role of the Archduke as both patron and student, it is given in full:

Your Imperial Highness!
Since the departure of Y.I.H. I have been ailing for the most part, afflicted especially with severe pain in the eyes, which has improved only to the extent that for the last eight days I have been able with care to use my eyes again. Y.I.H. will learn from the enclosed receipt of June 27 that several pieces of music have been sent you. Since Y.I.H. seems to find pleasure in the Sonata in C minor, I believed that it would not be presuming too much to surprise Your Highness with the dedication. The variations have been copied for five or even six weeks at least, nevertheless it has been too much for my eyes to read through them all; in vain I looked forward to a complete recovery. So finally I let Schlemmer look them over, and although they do not look very elegant, yet they ought to be correct. The Sonata in C minor was printed in Paris and very badly; and since it was reprinted here, I took as much care as possible in correcting it.—

Soon I will send a beautiful printed copy of the variations. In regard to the Mass which Y.I.H. wished to see made more generally useful, the continuously poor state of my health for several years has compelled me to think of means for bettering my situation, more especially because of the heavy debts which I have incurred and also the fact that I had to forego the visit to England which I was invited to make. For this the Mass seemed suitable. I was advised to offer it to several courts. Hard as it was for me to do this I nevertheless did not think that I ought to subject myself to reproach by not doing it. I therefore invited several courts to subscribe for the Mass, fixed the fee at 50 ducats, as it was thought that this was not excessive, nor unprofitable, if a number of subscribers were to be found. Thus far, indeed, the subscription does me honor, their Royal Majesties of France and Prussia having accepted. Also a few days ago I received a letter from my friend Prince Galitzin in St. Petersburg, in which this truly amiable

[11] Schindler, *Biogr.*, II, p. 18. (TDR, IV, 358, n. 1.)

prince informs me that His Imperial Majesty of Russia has accepted and I should soon hear the details from the Imperial Russian embassy here. In spite of all this, however, although others have also become subscribers I have not yet received as much of a fee as I would from a publisher, but I do have the advantage that the work remains *mine*. The costs of copying are large and will be increased by the three new pieces[12] which are to be added, which I shall send to Y.I.H. as soon as I have finished them.—Perhaps Y.I.H. will not find it burdensome graciously to use your influence with H.R.H., the Grand Duke of Tuscany, so that His Highness also might take a copy. The invitation was sent some time ago to the Grand Duke of Tuscany through von Odelgha, his agent here, and O. solemnly assures me that the invitation will surely be accepted; but I am not entirely confident as several months have gone by and no answer has been received. Since the matter is already under way, it is only natural that as much as possible be done to attain the desired result. It was hard for me to undertake this, still harder for me to tell Y.I.H. of it or bring it to your notice, but *"Necessity knows no law"*—But I thank Him above the stars that I am beginning to use my eyes again. I am now writing a new symphony for England, for the Philharmonic Society, and hope to have it completely done in a fortnight. I can not yet strain my eyes for a long period, wherefore I beg Y.I.H. graciously to be patient in regard to Y.I.H.'s variations, which seem to me charming but need a more thorough study by me. Continue especially Y.I.H. to practice, jotting down briefly your ideas at the pianoforte. For this a little table alongside the pianoforte will be necessary. By this means not only is the creative fancy strengthened, but at the same time one learns to get ahold of the most remote ideas. It is also necessary to write without the pianoforte; and sometimes to develop a simple chorale melody with simple and again with varied figurations with counterpoint and again without. This will cause no headache to Y.I.H. but rather give you great pleasure at finding yourself absorbed in the art.—Gradually there comes the capacity to represent just what we wish and feel, an essential need in the case of men of noble mold—My eyes bid me stop.—All that is good and beautiful to Y.I.H. and in saying farewell may I be called the most faithful servant of Your Imperial Highness.

With deepest respect

L. v. Beethoven

This letter was written in Vienna, but from Hetzendorf he sent a postscript asking for help in a different quarter. Much to Beethoven's vexation and impatience the Saxon court was very tardy in its reply, or rather in subscribing, for at first the invitation was declined; but Beethoven was not thus to be put off by a court with which his imperial pupil was closely connected.

Should Your Imperial Highness wish to favor me with a letter, I beg of you to address it "to L.v. Beethoven in Vienna," from whence I receive all letters here safely through the post.—If convenient, will Y.I.H. graciously recommend the Mass to Prince Anton in Dresden, so that His Royal Majesty of Saxony might be induced to subscribe to the Mass, which will surely happen if Y.I.H.

---

[12] These pieces were to be an offertory, a graduale and a "Tantum ergo." (TK, III, 95, n. 1.) See Schünemann, III, p. 90.

were to show the slightest interest in the matter. As soon as I am informed that you have shown me this favor, I shall at once address myself to the Director General of the Theatre and Music there, who is in charge of such matters, and send him the invitation to subscribe for the King of Saxony which, however, I do not wish to do without an introduction from Y.I.H.—*My opera Fidelio* was performe'd with great success in Dresden at the festivities in honor of the visit of the King of Bavaria, all their Majesties being present. I heard all of this from the above-mentioned Director General, who asked me for the score through Weber and afterwards made me a handsome present in return.—Y.I.H. will pardon me for inconveniencing you by this request but Y.I.H. knows how little importunate I am as a rule. However, should there be anything objectionable to you in my request, anything the least unpleasant, you will understand as a matter of course that I would be no less convinced of your magnaminity and graciousness. It is not greed nor the desire for speculation, which I have always avoided, but necessity which compels me to do everything possible to extricate myself from this position. In order not to be too harshly judged, it is perhaps best to be frank. —Because of my constant illness, which prevented me from composing as much as usual, I am burdened with a debt of 2300 florins C.M. which can be liquidated only by extraordinary efforts. If things are improved for me by these subscriptions, for which there is every hope, I shall be able to get a firm foothold again through my compositions.—Meanwhile, may Y.I.H. be pleased to receive my frankness not ungraciously. If I were not apt to be blamed for not being as *active* as formerly, I would have kept silent as I have always done. As regards the recommendations, I am nevertheless convinced that Y.I.H. is always glad to do good *wherever possible* and will make no exception *in my case*—

The Archduke fulfilled Beethoven's wish concerning the Saxon Court, and wrote to the Director General v. Könneritz promising to send the invitation to the King. In a second letter dated July 25th Beethoven enclosed a letter to the King's brother, Prince Anton, which contained an invitation to the King.

These last efforts were successful: King Friedrich August subscribed for the Mass, and on July 31 Archduke Rudolph wrote to his music-master: "My brother-in-law Prince Anton has already written to me that the King of Saxony is expecting your beautiful Mass." On September 12, Prince Anton wrote to Beethoven that he had no doubt his royal brother would grant his wish, especially as he had spoken to him on the subject in the name of his brother-in-law, the Cardinal. The money must have arrived soon afterward, and Beethoven set Schindler's mind at ease by writing to him: "In order that evil report may not longer injure the poor Dresdeners too much, I inform you that the money reached me today, with all marks of respect."

The Grand Duke of Hesse-Darmstadt was appealed to directly under date of February 5; the letter, signed by Beethoven, was forwarded through the Hessian ambassador, Baron von Türckheim, a cultured art connoisseur and subsequently Intendant of the Grand Ducal Theatre in Darmstadt. The composer, Louis Schlösser was in Vienna at the time, and Baron von Türckheim, knowing that he wanted to make Beethoven's acquaintance, gave him the opportunity by asking him to carry the information that the invitation had been accepted to Beethoven, handing him the dispatch with the Grand Ducal seal affixed for that purpose. Schlösser went to Beethoven, "No. 60 Kothgasse, first story, door to the left." Beethoven read the document with great joy and said to Schlösser: "Such words as I have read do me good. Your Grand Duke speaks not only like a princely Maecenas but like a thorough musical connoisseur of comprehensive knowledge; it is not alone the acceptance of my work which rejoices me but the estimation which in general he places upon my works."[13]

No success was met with at the cultivated Court of Weimar, though here Beethoven invoked the assistance of no less a dignitary than Goethe. His letter to the poet is still preserved in the Grand Ducal archives and is worthy of being given in full:

Vienna, February 8th, 1823

Your Excellency!

Still living as I have lived from my youthful years in your immortal, never-aging words, and never forgetting the happy hours spent in your company, it nevertheless happens that I must recall myself to your recollection—I hope that you received the dedication to Your Excellency of "Meeresstille und glückliche Fahrt" composed by me. Because of their contrast, both seemed to me adapted for expression in music; how gladly would I know whether I have fittingly united my harmonies with yours. Advice too, which would be accepted as very truth, would be extremely welcome to me, for I love the latter above all things and it shall never be said of me veritas odium parit.—It is very possible that a number of your poems which must ever remain unique, set to music by me, will soon be published, among them "Rastlose Liebe."[14] How highly would I value some general observations from you on the composition or setting to music of your poems!— Now a request to Y.E. I have composed a Grand Mass which, however, I do not want to publish at present, but which is to be sent to the principal courts; the honorarium for the same is 50 ducats only. I have addressed myself in the matter to the Grand Ducal Weimarian Embassy, which has accepted the appeal to His Serene Highness and promised to deliver it. The Mass can also be used as an oratorio and everyone knows that the benevolent societies are suffering from the lack of such things!—My request consists in this, that Y.E. call the attention of His Serene Highness, the Grand Duke, to this matter so that His Highness may also subscribe. The Grand Ducal Weimarian Embassy gave me to understand that it would be very beneficial if the Grand Duke could be induced to regard the matter favorably in advance.—I have composed [geschrieben] so much but have *gained from it* [erschrieben] scarcely a thing.[15] Now I am no longer alone

---

[13] From Schlösser's *Persönliche Erinnerungen an Beethoven*, published in *Hallelujah*, VI (1885), Nos. 20 and 21. (TDR, IV, 362, n. 3.)

[14] Sketched in 1804 but unfinished. See *II Beeth.*, p. 575 and Hans Boettcher, *Beethoven als Liederkomponist*, p. vi. (Cf. TDR, IV, 364,

n. 2.)

[15] Beethoven is playing on words—"schrieben," to write or to compose, and "erschrieben" —to gain by writing. "Ich habe so vieles geschrieben, aber *erschrieben*—beinahe gar nichts."

but have for six years been father to the son of my deceased brother, a promising youth in his sixteenth year, wholly devoted to learning and already at home in the rich literature of ancient Greece. But in these regions such things cost a great deal and, in the case of young students, not only the present but also the future must be borne in mind; and as much as I formerly kept my thoughts directed aloft I must now also turn my gaze *earthwards*—My income is *worthless*[16]—My poor health has for several years made it impossible for me to make professional journeys or to seize upon the many opportunities which yield *profit*! Could I completely recover my health, I might expect other and better things. —Y.E. must not think that it is because I am asking a favor that I have dedicated "Meeresstille und glückliche Fahrt" to you—this was already done in May, 1822. I had not thought of this method of making the Mass known at that time—not till a few weeks ago.—The respect, love and esteem which I have cherished for the only and immortal Goethe since the days of my youth have remained with me. Feelings like this are not easily put into words, especially by a bungler *like myself*, who has always been bent only on making *tones* his own. But a singular feeling impels me to tell you this, inasmuch as I live in your works—I know that you could not refuse to help an artist who feels only too keenly how far *mere monetary reward* is from *his art*. Yet now he is compelled by *necessity because of others* to work and labor *for others*—The good is always plain to us and therefore I know that Y.E. will not deny my request—

A few words from you would fill me with happiness—

I remain, Your Excellency, with the sincerest and most unbounded respect,

Beethoven.

According to Schindler, who was surely in a position to know, no answer to this letter was ever received; nor did the Grand Duke subscribe. That the invitation reached its destination may safely be assumed from Beethoven's remark about the interest displayed in the plan at the embassy; but the document is not to be found in the archives.

It was an unfortunate time for Goethe, who was now 73 years old. The Swiss student, Frederic Soret records in his conversations with the poet, for February, 1823: "Goethe was very ill in the course of this month." From Goethe's own diaries during the month there is mention of bloodletting, fever and delirium, and at one point the physicians thought they would not be able to save him.[17] A spring of convalescence and a stay at Marienbad during June and July in which Goethe was absorbed by his infatuation for the youthful Ulrike von Levetzow ruled out his penning an answer to the composer.

Bavaria's story is a short one. In a Conversation Book towards the close of May, Schindler writes: "A negative answer has come from Bavaria." To the King of Naples, Beethoven sent a French copy of the letter of invitation practically identical with the formula, and also to the King of France. In

---

[16] "Mein Gehalt (income) ist ohne *Gehalt*" (without worth). The pun cannot be translated into English.

[17] Ludwig Lewisohn, *Goethe: The Story of a Man* (New York, 1949), II, p. 320. See also Romain Rolland, *Goethe et Beethoven* (Paris, 1930), p. 96.

the latter case Cherubini was asked to be the intermediary. The draft of Beethoven's letter to him is still preserved among the Schindler papers in Berlin. Beethoven's interpolations in bad French are given without change:

Highly respected Sir!

It is with great pleasure that I embrace the opportunity to approach you in writing. In spirit I am with you often enough, inasmuch as I value your works more than all others written for the stage. However, the beautiful world of art must deplore the fact that for a considerable period no new theatrical work of yours of large dimensions has appeared, at least not in our Germany. Highly as your other works are esteemed by true connoisseurs, it is a veritable loss to art *not yet* to possess a new product of your great mind for the theatre. True art remains imperishable and the genuine artist feels sincere pleasure in real and great products of genius; and so I too am enraptured whenever I hear a new work of yours and feel as great an interest in it as in my own works.—In brief, I honor and love you—If it were not for my continual ill health I could see you in Paris, and with what extraordinary delight would I discuss artistic matters with you?! —And here I must add that to every artist and art-lover I always speak of you with enthusiasm, otherwise you might perhaps[18] believe, since I am about to ask a favor of you, this this was merely an introduction to the subject. I hope, however, that you will not attribute such low-mindedness to me—

My request is as follows: I have just completed a grand solemn Mass, and I desire to send it to the European courts, because for the present I do not wish to publish it. Through the French Embassy here I have forwarded an invitation to His Majesty the King of France to subscribe to this work. I know that if you would advise His Majesty to take the Mass, he would surely do so. Ma situation critique demande que je ne fixe seulement come ordinaire mes pensées aux ciel au contrairs, il faut les fixer en bas pour les necessites de la vie; whatever may be the fate of my request to you, I shall always love and honor you et vous resteres toujours celui de mes contemporains, que je l'estime le plus si vous me voulez faire une estréme plaisir, c'etoit si m'ecrireres quelques lignes, ce que me soulagera bien—l'art unie touta le monde, how much more then true artists, et peut etres vous me dignes aussi, de me mettre also to be counted amongst this number,

avec la plus haute estime,

votre ami e serviteur

Beeth.

The letter was despatched on March 15. Cherubini did not receive it, and as late as 1841 expressed his great regret at the miscarriage which, however, worked no harm to the enterprise. King Louis XVIII not only subscribed for the Mass but within less than a year sent Beethoven a gold medal weighing twenty-one Louis d'or, showing on the obverse side the bust of the King and on the reverse, within a wreath, the inscription: "Donnée par le Roi à Monsieur Beethoven." Duke d'Achâts, First Chamberlain of the King, accompanied the gift with the following letter:

---

[18] According to TDR, IV, 368, this word is not clear. The present editor is grateful for Miss Anderson's correct reading (*A* 1154).

I hasten to inform you, Monsieur, that the King received with favor the gift of the Score of Your Mass set to Music and charged me to send you a gold medal of him in effigy. I am pleased to be able to transmit to you the evidence of His Majesty's satisfaction and I take this occasion to offer you the assurance of my respectful consideration.

First Chamberlain of the
King's Chamber
Duke d'Achâts

Tuileries, February 20, 1824

"This was a distinction," says Schindler, "than which one more significant never fell to the lot of the artist during his life";[19] but the biographer certainly is in error when he intimates that the medal was given in payment of the subscription price. Beethoven informed Archduke Rudolph that the King had accepted the invitation in his letter of July 1, 1823; the medal was received early in 1824, over eight months later. Beethoven's needs and the reply which he gave the messenger from Prussia when he offered a decoration instead of the 50 ducats, indicate plainly enough how he felt as to the remuneration. Evidently King Louis XVIII paid the money in the regular way and sent the medal as a special mark of distinction.

No subscription was received from the King of Naples. The negotiations with the Grand Duke of Tuscany were more successful, though they dragged on into the next year. They were a subject of discussion in the Conversation Book in which Count Lichnowsky, brother Johann and nephew Karl took part. From remarks there recorded it appears that an appeal was also made to Empress Maria Louisa, Duchess of Parma. Here the agent was again Odelgha and there was a plan to interest Countess Neuberg. Count Lichnowsky seems to have suggested the name of Maria Louisa and offered to write to Count Neuberg, whom he knew, on the subject. It looks also as if the case of the Grand Duke of Tuscany had been exceptional, in that the Mass had been forwarded before the subscription had been received; this at least might be the interpretation of a remark noted by Karl: "I shall go to Odelgha on Sunday. We must get to work, or they will keep the Mass and send nothing."

Schindler says that Beethoven sent a carefully written letter to the King of Sweden to accompany the invitation; but nothing came of it. The King of Denmark subscribed, but as we hear nothing of the particulars, it is most likely that everything went smoothly in his case.

Prince Galitzin was asked to make a plea to the Russian Court and reported in a letter to Beethoven, dated June 2, that the invitation had been accepted and the official notification would follow in due course through the Russian Embassy. The money came soon afterwards. On July 9, Schindler writes in a jocular vein, using a metaphor which had already done service in Beethoven's correspondence:

[19] *Biogr.*, II, p. 20. (TDR, IV, 369.)

I take pleasure in reporting to you herewith, that by command of the Emperor of all the Russias, 50 horsemen in armor are arrived here as a Russian contingent to do battle under you for the Fatherland. The leader of these choice troops is a Russian Court Councillor. Herr Stein, pianoforte maker, has been commissioned by him to quarter them on you. Rien de nouveau chez nos voisins jusqu'ici.

Fidelissimus Papageno.[20]

The director of the business affairs of the Russian Embassy, von Obreskow, appears to have made inquiry as to how the fee was to be paid. Beethoven instructs Schindler as follows:

The letter to H.v.Obreskow follows. Take it along with you and say concerning the money that only a receipt need be sent to me for which, as soon as I return it, the money can be paid to the bearer of the receipt.—As soon as I receive this money you will receive 50 fl. V.S. right away for your trouble. Say nothing more than necessary, for people only find fault with it. Also do not speak of the Mass as not being finished which is not true, for the new pieces are only additions—Don't trouble me with anything else—

Papageno's master wishes you well.

On the back of the page, Beethoven adds a postscript starting on the right hand side in which he employs a device for insertion commonly used in the sketchbooks. At the syllable *vi-* the text proceeds to the answering syllable *de* (on the left hand side) for the words to be inserted.

de if there is occasion,	I have indicated your address.
Always bear in mind	Tell them, but inconspicuously—*vi-*
that these same persons represent	in the appropriate place, how
Majesty itself.	France also simply
	sent you the money—

Impatience at the non-delivery of the Mass at the expected time must have been expressed by the Russian Embassy, for in a note which Schindler dates "in the winter of 1824," Beethoven says:

Mr. v. Schindler:
Here is the Paquett for the Russian Embassy. Please look after it at once—moreover say that I shall soon visit him in person, inasmuch as it hurts me that lack of confidence has been felt in me. I thank God I am in a position to prove that I do not deserve it in any way nor will my honor permit it!—

Prince Galitzin, meanwhile, also became a subscriber, and in a letter of August 3 proposed that the Mass be published by popular subscription at four or five ducats, as there were not many amateurs who could afford to pay 50 ducats for a written copy. "All that I can do," the Prince writes in conclusion, "is to beg you to put me down among your subscribers and to send me a

---

[20] "Papageno" was the name applied to Schindler in his notes when Beethoven wished to enjoin silence on his factotum; the allusion, of course, being to the lip-locked birdcatcher in Mozart's *Zauberflöte*. (TK, III, 102, n. 1.)

copy as soon as possible so that I may produce it at a concert for the benefit of the widows of musicians which takes place annually near Christmas." Plainly, the Prince's subscription was in the existing category; there was no other, and Beethoven, in view of the invitation to the courts, could not at once entertain the subject of a popular subscription for a printed edition. Galitzin also acceded to Beethoven's request that the 50 ducats already deposited in Vienna by him for a quartet be applied to the account of the Mass. He writes of September 23 (October 3): "I have just received your letter of the 17th and hasten to answer that I have instructed the house of Henikstein to pay you immediately the 50 ducats which I fancied had long ago been placed at your disposal." The bankers Henikstein sent the Prince Beethoven's receipt for the 50 ducats "which we paid to him on the order and account of Your Highness as fee for the Mass which we have forwarded through the High State Chancellery." The score was in the hands of Prince Galitzin on November 29, but the performance which he projected did not take place until April 6, 1824. It was the first complete performance of the Mass anywhere.

On June 21, 1823, Beethoven also sent a letter to the St. Petersburg Philharmonic Society announcing the completion of the Mass. He invited the interest of the "illustrious art connoisseurs of the Russian nation" and presented the usual opportunity: a manuscript copy of the Mass for the fee of 50 ducats.[21]

A special invitation to subscribe to the Mass was not extended to the Austrian court for reasons which, no doubt, were understood between Beethoven and Archduke Rudolph and which may have been connected with efforts which were being made at the time to secure a court appointment for the composer. At the request of Artaria, however, an invitation was sent to Prince Nikolaus Esterhazy. Beethoven had little confidence in the successful outcome of the appeal, probably with a recollection in his mind of the Prince's attitude toward him on the occasion of the production of the Mass in C in 1807. His lack of faith in the enterprise was justified; Esterhazy did not subscribe.

No invitation was sent to the English court, probably because Beethoven cherished a grudge in that quarter; but subscriptions were asked of two large singing societies—the Singakademie of Berlin and the Cäcilienverein of Frankfurt. Zelter was director of the Singakademie, and to him Beethoven writes on Feb. 8:[22]

My gallant fellow artist!

Let me make a request to you in writing, since we are so far apart that we cannot speak with one another. Unfortunately too writing can occur only occasionally —I have written a Grand Mass, which might also be performed as an oratorio

---

[21] See MacArdle & Misch, *New Beethoven Letters*, p. 421.

[22] For the corrected German version of this letter, I am indebted to the late Miss Anderson.

(for the benefit of the poor—as is the good custom that has been introduced), but I did not want to publish it in print in the ordinary way, but to give it to the principal courts only. The fee amounts to 50 ducats. Excepting the copies subscribed for, none will be issued, so that the Mass will be practically only in manuscript—However, there must be a passable number if the composer is to gain anything—I have sent a request from here to the Royal Prussian Embassy that His Majesty the King of Prussia might be inclined to take a copy, and have also written Prince Radziwill concerning his taking an interest in it—I ask of you that you do what *you* can in the matter. A work of this kind might also be of service to the Singakademie, for there is little to keep it from being performed by voices alone; but the more doubled and multiplied the latter in combination with the instruments, the more effective it would be—It might also be in place as an oratorio, such as is in demand for the Benevolent Societies—As I have been more or less ill for several years and therefore am not in the most splendid circumstances, I have had recourse to this means. I have written much— but *gained from it*—almost zero!—I am more disposed to send my glances upwards—but a man is compelled for his own and for others' sake to direct them downwards. But this too is part of man's destiny—With sincere regards I embrace you, my dear fellow artist.

Your friend Beethoven

The letter will be seen, on comparison with that written on the same day to Goethe, to be either a draft for the latter in part or an echo of it. There is the same pun on "geschrieben" and "erschrieben," the same lament about having to keep his eyes on the ground while desirous to keep them on higher things, the same reference to the value of the Mass for concert purposes on behalf of charity. As this last point is one which would naturally occur to the writer in addressing a musician and not at all naturally in an appeal to a poet, it is safe to say that the Zelter letter was written first. It is an unpleasant duty to call attention to a very significant difference between this letter and the invitation issued to the courts as well as the letter to Goethe. In the latter he distinctly says that the Mass will not be published in the ordinary way "for the present," thus reserving the privilege of printing it at a future time. To Zelter, and presumably to the Frankfurt society, he plainly intimates that there is to be no publication in the ordinary way at all. It is not a violent presumption that Zelter may have observed this discrepancy, which was of vital moment to his society, and that this may have caused the termination of the negotiations, which began auspiciously enough in a letter written by Zelter on February 22 in reply to Beethoven's. In this letter he said he was ready to purchase the Mass for the Singakademie at his own risk, provided Beethoven would adapt it to the use of the society—that is, arrange it for performance practically without instruments—a proceeding, he explained, which would make it practicable for all similar concert institutions. To this letter Beethoven replied on March 25:

. . . I have carefully considered your suggestion for the Singakademie. If it should ever appear in print I will send you a copy without pay. It is true that it might almost be performed *a la cappella*, but to this end the whole would have to be arranged. Perhaps you have the patience to do this.—Besides, there is already a movement in it which is entirely *a la cappella* and I am inclined to call this style the only true church style. I thank you for your readiness. From *such an honored* artist *as you*, I would never accept anything.—I honor you and desire only an opportunity to prove this to you in deed.

There the matter ended, so far as is known. The negotiations with the Frankfurt society were more successful. On May 19, 1823, J. N. Schelble, director, wrote saying: ". . . The hope of receiving a new composition from you, great master, inspires all the members and reinvigorates their musical zeal; I therefore request you as soon as it is convenient to you to forward a copy of your Mass to me. . . ."

There were, therefore, as appears from this account and the list of names sent in November, 1825, to the publishers of the Mass, ten subscribers, namely: the Czar of Russia, the Kings of Prussia, Saxony, France and Denmark, the Grand Dukes of Tuscany and Hesse-Darmstadt, Princes Galitzin and Radziwill and the Cäcilia Society of Frankfurt. Beethoven's receipts, 500 ducats, were very materially reduced, how much we cannot say, by the costs of copying. In this work his principal helper was a professional copyist named Schlemmer, who could best decipher his manuscript. But Schlemmer was sickly and died before the year was over; his successor was named Rampel, and seems to have caused Beethoven a great deal of annoyance; he probably was made to bear a great deal of the blame for the tardiness of the work, for which, also, the composer's frequent alterations were in part responsible.

The story of Beethoven's plan to get private subscriptions to the Mass has taken the reader well into the year 1823. This story has been related here in order to provide a necessary background for the understanding of Beethoven's other negotiations of the year, especially those concerning the publication of the Mass. It is now time to turn back and take up the other events of the year, presenting them as much as possible in chronological order.

On January 20 Beethoven wrote a little piece for voice and pianoforte in the album of Baroness Cäcilie v. Eskeles,[23] on the words of Goethe: "Der edle Mensch sei hülfreich und gut."[24]

The Symphony in D minor, on which he was working industriously, had been the subject of correspondence between himself and Ries (in London) for some time before the year opened. On July 6, 1822, Beethoven had inquired of his old pupil: "What would the Philharmonic Society be likely to offer me for a symphony?" Ries, evidently, laid the matter before the

---

[23] Wife of the Viennese banker, Baron Bernard v. Eskeles. See KHV, pp. 622-23 for clarification of dedicatee, long thought to be the daughter of v. Eskeles (Baroness Marie, since 1825 Countess Wimpffen).

[24] From the beginning of the last stanza of "Das Göttliche":

"Edel sei der Mensch,
hülfreich und gut!"

directors of the society who, at a meeting on November 10, "resolved to offer Beethoven fifty pounds for a M.S. symphony."[25] Ries conveyed the information to Beethoven in a letter dated November 15. In a reply dated December 20, 1822, Beethoven writes:

My dear Ries!

Overwhelmed with work I could not answer your letter of November 15 until now—I accept with pleasure the offer to write a new symphony for the Philharmonic Society even though the honorarium from Englishmen cannot match that of other nations; for I myself would write gratis for the first artists of Europe, if I were not still poor Beethoven. If I were in London, what would I not write for the Philharmonic Society! For Beethoven can compose, God be thanked —though he can do nothing else in this world. If God gives me back my health, which at least has improved somewhat, I shall yet be able to comply with all the requests which have come from all parts of Europe, even from North America; and I might yet make my way in the world.

The request from North America was for an oratorio from the Handel and Haydn Society in Boston[26] and was made from an unidentified Boston banker to the Viennese banker Geymüller. In a Conversation Book of early April, 1823, Dr. Johann Bihler writes: "The oratorio for Boston?" and Beethoven answers: "I cannot write what I should like best to write, but that which the pressing need of money obliges me to write. This is not to say that I write only for money—when this period is past I hope to write what for me and for art is above all—Faust."[27]

A glimpse into the occupations, cares and perplexities which beset Beethoven at this period is given by the first letter in the series to Ries written in the new year—on February 5, 1823:

My dear good Ries!

I have no further news to give you about the Symphony; but meanwhile you may confidently count on receiving it, since I have made the acquaintance here of a very amiable and cultivated man, who holds an appointment in our Imperial Embassy at London.[28] He will undertake later to forward the Symphony to you in London, so that *it will soon be in London*. Were I not so poor that I am obliged to live by pen I would accept nothing at all from the P.Soc; as it is I must wait until the fee for the Symphony is deposited here.—But to give you an evidence of my affection for and confidence in the society I have already delivered the new Overture referred to in my last letter to the aforementioned gentleman of the Imperial Embassy. As he is to depart from here in a few days, he will deliver it to you in person in London. Goldschmidt will no doubt *know where you live, if not, please tell him*, so that this accommodating gentleman will not be obliged long to hunt for you—I leave to the Society all the arrangements about

[25] George Hogarth, *The Philharmonic Society of London* (London, 1862), p. 31. (TK, III, 110, n. 2.)

[26] See Charles C. Perkins, *History of the Handel and Haydn Society of Boston.* (Boston,

1883), I, p. 87. (TK, III, 87.)

[27] Schünemann, III, p. 149.

[28] A man named Bauer, who is referred to by name in the next letter to Ries to be quoted. (TDR, IV, 382, n. 3.)

the Overture which, like the Symphony, it can keep for eighteen months. Not until after the lapse of that time shall I publish it. And now another request: my brother here, who keeps a horse and carriage, wanted to derive advantage from me and so, without asking me, he offered the Overture in question to a publisher in London named Boosey. Let him be told that at present it is impossible to say whether he can have the Overture or not, I will write to him myself. —It all depends on the Philharmonic Society. Say to him please that my brother made a mistake in the matter of the *Overture*—As to the other works which he wrote to him about, he may have them. He *bought* them of me in order to *profit* from them, as I now see—O frater! I beg of you to write to me as soon as possible after you have received the Overture whether the P. Soc. will take it, for otherwise I shall publish it soon—I have heard *nothing* of your Symphony dedicated to me. If I did not look upon the dedication as a sort of challenge for which I might give you revanche I should long ago have dedicated some work to you. *As it is,* I have always thought that I must first see your *work*; and how willingly would I show you my gratitude in some manner. I am deeply your debtor for so many proofs of your affection and for favors. If my health is improved by a bath-cure which I am to take in the coming summer I shall kiss your wife in London in 1824—

Ever yours

Beethoven

--◆{How Johann became involved with transactions concerning his brother's compositions becomes clear from a letter to Schott in the next year in which Beethoven says "I have given to my brother, to whom I am indebted for many kindnesses, instead of a sum of money which I owe him, the following works"; and he listed an overture (Op. 124), three songs and some bagatelles.[29]}◆-- In his next letter to Ries on February 23, 1823, after referring again to the Symphony and the Overture, he informed him that he had sent two sonatas (Op. 110 and 111) and was sending eleven bagatelles (Op. 119) and asked Ries to traffic with them as shrewdly as possible. Had he received a dedication from Ries, he said, he would have at once inscribed the Overture to him.

--◆{On March 22 Ries was informed that the symphony would be finished in two weeks, and on April 25 that it would be received soon along with thirty-three variations (Op. 120) dedicated to his wife.}◆--

Not long afterward Beethoven wrote another letter to Ries which has been preserved only in part:

—in addition to these hardships I have many debts to pay, for which reason I would be glad to have the honorarium paid to me if you have disposed of the Mass. By then the London copy will have been made. There need be no scruples because of the few souverains who are to get copies of it. If a local publisher made no objections, there ought to be still fewer in London, since I bind myself in writing that not a note of it shall appear in print or otherwise—and, what is

---

[29] See *A* 1321. The bagatelles offered to Johann were his last set, Op. 126, composed at the end of 1823.

more the Revers is a guarantee for everything. Attend to everything soon for your poor friend; I await also your plan of travel. Things have become too awful. I am tormented by the Cardinal worse than before; if I don't go there, it is a crimen legis majestatis. As for payment, I must draw my wretched salary with the aid of a *stamp*— Since you apparently wish a dedication from me, how happy I am to gratify a wish from you, much happier than one from the *finest of fine gentlemen*, entre nous; the devil only knows how one can keep from falling into their hands. The dedication of the new symphony will be *to you*—I hope eventually to receive *yours* to me—

Bauer has herewith a new document for the King which is concerned only with the Battle of Vittoria, of which he has taken along a printed copy. There is no mention of the Mass. Be good enough to tell H. Bauer to open the old one in order to see its contents. H. Bauer does not have the Mass. The thing is for Bauer to open the letter to the King that he took from here, whereupon he will see what was written to the King about the Battle of Vittoria. *The enclosed communication holds to this in the same way*, but there is no longer mention of the Mass. Our amiable friend Bauer shall see only if he can get a butcher's knife or a tortoise for it. It is understood that the printed copy of the score of the Battle will also be given to the King—Bauer *returns here at the end of May*. Please then let him know *right away* that which concerns him—The present letter will cost you a lot of money, so subtract it from what you send me. I am so sorry to have caused you this trouble—God be with you—Best regards to your wife until I myself am there. Watch out, you think I am *old*, but I am a *young old man*—as ever your

Beethoven

Neither Ries received a dedication; the Ninth Symphony was dedicated to the King of Prussia and the Diabelli Variations to Antonie Brentano.

Of the earlier inaction of King George IV upon receiving the score of *The Battle of Vittoria* there has already been mention. Before leaving for England, Bauer visited Beethoven and an entry of his in a Conversation Book of middle February refers again to this matter:

I am of the opinion that the King had it performed, but perhaps nobody reminded him that on that account he ought to answer.

His next entry reads:

I will carry a letter to the King and direct it in a channel which will insure its delivery, since I cannot hand it over in person.[30]

The character of the address to the king can be guessed at from the following draft for an earlier letter which was found amongst Schindler's papers:

In thus presuming, herewith, to submit my most obedient prayer to Your Majesty, I venture at the same time to supplement it with a second.[31]

[30] Schünemann, III, p. 14.
[31] The first request, presumably, was to have been an invitation to subscribe to the Mass in D, and the letter to Ries shows that Beethoven decided subsequently to strike the King of England from his list. (TK, III, 112, n. 1.)

Already in the year 1813, the undersigned took the liberty, at the frequent requests of several Englishmen then living here, to send to Your Majesty his composition entitled "Wellington's Battle and Victory at Vittoria" which no one possessed at that time. The then Imperial Russian Ambassador, Prince Rasoumowsky, undertook to send the work to Your Majesty by a courier.

For many years the undersigned cherished the sweet wish that Your Majesty would graciously make known the receipt of his work to him; but he has not yet been able to boast of this happiness, and had to content himself with a brief notice from Herr Ries, his former worthy pupil, who reported that Your Majesty had been pleased graciously to deliver the work to the then Musical Director, Herr Salomon and Herr Smart for public performance in Drury Lane Theatre. This appears also from the English journals, which added, as did Herr Ries, that the work had been received with extraordinary favor not only in London but elsewhere. Inasmuch as it was extremely humiliating to the undersigned to learn all this from indirect sources, Your Majesty will surely pardon his sensitiveness and graciously permit him to observe that he spared neither time nor cost to lay this before Your Exalted Person in the most proper manner in order to provide a pleasure for Your Majesty.

From this the undersigned concludes, that it may have been improperly submitted to Your Majesty and inasmuch as the most obedient petition which is now submitted, enables him again to approach Your Majesty, he takes the privilege of handing to Your Majesty an accompanying printed copy of the Battle of Vittoria in score, which has been set aside for this highest purpose ever since 1815 and which has been retained so long because of the uncertainty felt by the undersigned concerning the matter.

Convinced of the lofty wisdom and graciousness which Your Majesty has hitherto shown toward art and artists to their appreciation and good fortune, the undersigned flatters himself that Your Majesty will graciously condescend to take all this in consideration and grant his most humble petition.

Convaincu de la haute Sagesse dont Votre Majesté a toujours su apprecier l'art ainsi que de la haute faveur qu'elle accorde a l'artiste le soussigné se flatte que Votre Majesté prendra l'un et l'autre en consideration et vaudra en grace condescendre a sa tres-humble demande.

a Vienne le 24 fevrier.[32]

Among the friends who were offering Beethoven advice in the handling of his affairs was Count Moritz Lichnowsky. According to Schindler, there was a difference of opinion between the count and the composer concerning the signing of an agreement with Steiner, whereupon Beethoven improvised the following canon[33] in the much frequented tavern "zur goldenen Birne":

"Written on Febr. 20 1823 in the coffee house zur Birn on the Landstrasse" [note by Schindler]

[32] According to Miss Anderson, *A*, p. 1005, n. 2, this was added to Beethoven's draft in another hand.

[33] From the Schindler papers (portfolio 1, no. 35) in the Berlin Library. Published in Hermann Hirschbach's *Musik-Krit-Repertorium*, I₁₀ (1844), p. 468. (TDR, IV, 388, n. 5.) See Ludwig Misch, *Beethoven Studies* (Norman, 1953), pp. 121-22. Misch's reading is used here except for his misprint on the final note of measure 4.

Bester Herr Graf Sie sind ein Schaf! Bester Herr Graf Sie sind ein Schaf! Bester Herr Graf
[Best Mister Count You are a fool!]

Sie sind ein Schaf! Bester Herr Graf Sie sind ein Schaf!

Beethoven, however, was not always in such a gay mood; financial difficulties were now crowding in on him. First of all, the debt remained to his friend Franz Brentano in Frankfurt. Meanwhile, Steiner, who may have thought that consideration was no longer incumbent on him, now that Beethoven was offering his works to other publishers, pressed him for the money which he had lent him and threatened to sue him for the balance of the debt. Beethoven presented a counter-claim and demanded that Steiner publish a number of compositions which he had purchased but had not issued. Steiner, now the owner of the works, refused. At this time Beethoven had no ready means at his disposal. He appealed to his brother Johann to go security for him, but he refused. Then he consulted Dr. Bach, who advised him to dispose of one of his shares of bank stock. Beethoven resisted this advice as long as he could, since he considered these shares not his own but his nephew's, so he attempted instead to use them as security for a loan. Schindler was called upon to act as agent in this matter, as is shown by the following notes. The contents of the first part of this first one date Beethoven's trouble with Steiner as being in the early stages of the organization of subscriptions for the Mass:

Very best optimus optime!

I am sending you the calendar. All the local embassies are indicated by where the paper is stuck in. If you would soon make me out a list of the courts from this, then we could hurry things up. By the way, I ask you to *co-operate with him* when my brother interposes; otherwise we might experience *pain* rather than *joy*—

Try to find some philanthropist who will make me a loan on a bank share, so that, first, I need not put too severe a strain on the generosity of my special friends the B[rentanos] and may not myself be subjected to need because of the withholding of this money, due to the beautiful arrangements and precautions made by my *dear* brother!—It would be lovely if you appeared at Mariahilf this afternoon around 3.30 or even in the forenoon—

It must not be apparent to people that the *money* is needed—

In another note he writes:

Dear S,

Do not forget the B.S. [bank share], it is highly necessary. I should not like to be sued for no reason whatsoever. The conduct of my brother is worthy of him—·The tailor is coming today and I hope to hold him off with kind words.

Very hastily yours

Schindler added the following note to the letter: "In 1823 the firm of Steiner and Haslinger had threatened Beethoven with a law suit in connection with his debt of 800 gulden V.S.; this happened before any honorarium had been received for the subscription copies of the Mass. Therefore it was necessary to sell a bank share in order to satisfy the creditors." In 1821 Beethoven was supposed to have begun paying semi-annual installments of 600 florins to Steiner, it will be remembered, and he must have been behind in his payments. However, if, as Schindler says, he sold a bank share, he should have realized about 1250 florins, V.S. on the sale, since, according to Steiner's letter to Beethoven of December 29, 1820, quoted previously, the capital amounted to 10,000 florins V.S. or 4000 florins C.M. Thus he could have liquidated the debt to Steiner with this money, if Schindler's figure of 800 florins is correct. That he did not do so completely, we shall see in the next chapter. Therefore, the inference is that he used it for other creditors as well. He was indebted to other publishers as we know, and even to such a tradesman as the tailor Lind, who had also threatened legal action against him.[34] The figure 800 is at variance with Beethoven's own description of the debt when he wrote on July 31, 1822, that it was about 3000 florins, plus interest. Thus, the picture remains confused, and only this much is certain, that he was deeply indebted,[35] and that this gave impetus to his plans for realizing profit from subscriptions for the Mass.

The Conversation Books of this period show that Schindler, despite his devotion to the master, was stubborn, and unlike the other close friends, dared express criticism or a contrary opinion as the following entries show: The first, in January:[36]

Don't be so undecided, my dear Master!—
now what do you wish me to do in regards to a bank share and how much is one worth?
I would arrange for it right away today in order to have done everything to achieve this purpose.

In April he writes:[37]

Don't think night and day about your debts, when you are well you'll pay them without any pain.

It was while in this distressful state concerning his debts that he took the first step towards making his nephew his legal heir. On March 6, 1823, he wrote to Bach:

[34] See A 1128, 1129.
[35] See Max Unger, "Beethovens Konversationshefte als biographische Quelle," DM, Vol. 34, no. 12, pp. 380ff, for further discussion of Beethoven's debts before he had to sell his eighth bank-share.
[36] Schünemann, II, p. 325.
[37] Ibid., III, p. 126.

Dear honored friend!

Death might come unannounced and give no time to make a legal will, there-fore I hereby attest with my own hand that I declare my beloved nephew Karl van Beethoven to be my universal heir and that after my death everything without exception *which can be called my property shall belong to him*—I appoint you to be his curator, and if there should be no testament after this you are also au-thorized and requested to find a guardian for my beloved nephew K. v. Beet-hoven—to the exclusion of my brother Johann van Beethoven—and secure his appointment according to law. I declare this writing to be valid for all time as being my last will before my death—I embrace you with all my heart—

Your true admirer and friend

Ludwig van Beethoven

The words excluding Johann from the guardianship were written on the third page of the document and on the first there was this later addition: "NB. In the way of capital there are 7 shares of bank stock, whatever else is found in cash is like the bank shares to be his." Shortly before his death he reiterated this bequest with modifications entailed by changed conditions.

In November, 1822, Anton Tayber, Imperial Court Composer, died; and this seemed a favorable opportunity for Beethoven to apply directly for the position. At the urging of Count Lichnowsky, this was done through the "Court Music-Count," Count Moritz Dietrichstein. Both proposed that Beethoven compose a mass for the Emperor. On February 23, 1823 Dietrich-stein wrote the following letter to Lichnowsky:[38]

Dear friend!

It would have been my duty long ago to reply to good Beethoven, since he came to me so trustfully. But after I had spoken with you I decided to break silence only after I had received definite information on the subject in question. I can now tell you positively that the post held by the deceased Tayber—who was not Chamber but Court Composer—is not to be filled again. I do not want to write to Beethoven because I do not like to disappoint a man whom I so sincerely respect, and therefore I beg of you when occasion offers to let him know the fact and then to inform me when and where I may meet him, as I have forgotten where he lives.

I am also sending you herewith the score of a mass by Reutter which Beet-hoven wished to see. It is true that H. M. the Emperor is fond of this style, but Beethoven, if he writes a mass, need not adhere to it. Let him follow the bent of his great genius and have a care only that the mass be not too long or too diffi-cult to perform;—that it be a *tutti* mass and have only short soprano and alto solos in the voices (for which I have two fine singing-boys)—but no tenor, bass or organ solos. . . . If he wishes he may introduce a violin, oboe or clarinet solo.

His Majesty likes to have fugues well worked out but not too long;—the *Sanctus* and *Osanna* as short as possible, in order not to delay the transubstantia-tion, and—if I may add something on my own account—the *Dona nobis pacem* connected with the *Agnus Dei* without marked interruption, and soft. In two

---

[38] See Schindler, *Biogr.*, II, pp. 29-31. (TDR, IV, 393, n. I.)

masses by Handel (arranged from his anthems), two by Naumann and Abbé Stadler, this makes a particularly beautiful effect. These in brief, as results of my experience, are the things which are to be considered and I should congratulate myself, the court and art if our great Beethoven were soon to take the work in hand. . . .

On March 10 Dietrichstein sent Beethoven three texts for graduals and a like number for offertories from which to choose words to be used in the mass to be composed for the emperor. On the count's letter Beethoven wrote the memorandum: "Treat the gradual as a symphony with song—does it follow the Gloria?" Here we have some light on the subject which came up for thought during the account of Beethoven's negotiations with publishers for the Mass in D. It will be remembered that on one occasion he wrote to Peters that he had not made up his mind which mass he should have, and on another that he had three masses, two other publishers having asked for such works. Simrock's hopes, meanwhile, had been diverted from *the* mass to *a* mass. It would seem that Beethoven was much pleased with the interest manifested in his application by Count Dietrichstein, and looked with auspicious eye upon the latter's plan to put him into the Emperor's good books. There can scarcely be a doubt but that he gave considerable thought to the proposed mass while still at work on the Mass in D. He conceived the plan of accompanying the Kyrie with wind instruments and organ only in a "new mass," as he designates it,[39] and sketches for a *Dona nobis pacem* which have been found "for the mass in C-sharp minor"[40] point to a treatment which may be said to be in harmony, so far as can be seen, with Count Dietrichstein's suggestions.

Beethoven spoke of the "second" mass to others besides the publishers. Nothing came of it, however. He decided to postpone work on the mass for the Emperor, pleading the pressure of other obligations in the letter of thanks which he sent to Counts Lichnowsky and Dietrichstein. They and the Archduke Rudolph were greatly disappointed and, if Schindler is to be believed, the Archduke and Lichnowsky reproached him.[41]

In this period, too, the alluring vision of a new opera presented itself, haunted the minds of Beethoven and his friends for a space and then disappeared in the limbo of unexecuted projects. *Fidelio* had been revived on November 3, 1822, at the Kärnthnerthor Theatre. Its success was so great that the management of the theatre offered a commission to Beethoven for a new opera. Beethoven viewed the proposition favorably and his friends hailed it with enthusiasm, especially Count Moritz Lichnowsky. Beethoven's love for classic literature led him to express a desire for a libretto based on some story of the antique world. He was told that such were all worn thread-

[39] *II Beeth.*, p. 152. (TDR, IV, 395, n. 2.)
[40] *Ibid.*, pp. 541, 543. (TDR, IV, 395, n. 3.)
[41] Schindler bases his statements on alleged testimony of the Archduke's secretary Bau- meister, but there is no word of reproval in any of the letters of the two men which have been found. See *Biogr.*, II, p. 33. (TK, III, 117, n. 2.)

bare. In the Conversation Books we see what suggestions were offered by others: a text by Schlegel; Voltaire's tragedies; Schiller's *Fiesco*. Local poets and would-be poets were willing to throw themselves into the breach.

Friedrich August Kanne, editor of the musical journal published by Steiner and Co., wrote a libretto which Beethoven sent to Schindler with the following note:

I am sending you the book by K, which aside from the fact that the first act is lukewarm, has been so admirably written that it really doesn't require one of the first composers—I will not say that it would be just the most suitable things *for me*, but if I can rid myself of obligations to which I am bound, who knows what might happen—or can happen!

In haste your friend
Beethoven

Kindly let me know that you have received it.

Brother Johann writes in a Conversation Book at the end of January: "Spohrschild [*sic!*] visited me today, he sends his regards. And if you tell him to he will write an opera for you."[42] Johann Sporschil (or Sporschill), historian and publicist, was at that time ending his period of study in Vienna and had connections for a brief time with the composer. Beethoven evidently accepted his offer, for Sporschil set to work and composed a libretto in 2 acts, entitled *The Apotheosis in the Temple of Jupiter Ammon*,[43] which was apparently sent to Beethoven act by act. The result was a weak text concocted to serve as a substitute for the text to the *Weihe des Hauses* for which the music, it will be remembered, was drawn principally from the *Ruinen von Athen*. As other plans developed, Sporschil's piece was forgotten.

In the forefront of those urging Beethoven on to a new opera subject was Count Moritz Lichnowsky. In February he writes in a Conversation Book: "Recently I was with a certain Madam Neumann. 2 to 3 years ago she wrote a libretto, *Alfred the Great*, it is said to be very beautiful, I will bring it in 3 or 4 days"; and the count goes on to describe the work which contains, he has heard, a "fabulous spectacle."[44] At the same time he reports that he has been in touch with Grillparzer and writes a few pages later: "I am eager for an answer from Grillparzer. He has a beautiful command of language, a lot of fire and imagination and [is] qualified to write a big poetic work.... This would be something for a second opera.—If he writes something for you, his composition would be the winner."[45]

Franz Grillparzer (born in 1791) by this time was well known to the Viennese as a dramatic poet through his plays *Sappho, The Ancestress* and *The Golden Fleece*; he was now completing his tragedy *Ottokar*. —Since

[42] Schünemann, II, p. 344.

[43] This libretto is among the Schindler papers in the Berlin State Library and has been published by Hans Volkmann, *Neues über Beethoven* (Berlin, 1904), pp. 67-72.

(TDR, IV, 397, n. 1.)

[44] Schünemann, II, pp. 395-96. Schünemann identifies the authoress as Marianna Neumann von Meissenthal (1768-1837).

[45] *Ibid.*, p. 397.

1813 he had had the security of a clerkship in the Lower Austrian revenue administration, and through the influence of his patron, Count Stadion, minister of finance, he was appointed poet to the Court Theatre in 1818. Already he and Beethoven had met several times, and, being musically educated, he admired the composer very highly. Beethoven's renewed interest in the poet, prompted by Lichnowsky, is shown in a note to Schindler: "I am asking you for Grillparzer's address; perhaps I will visit him myself."

Grillparzer has left us an account of his attempt to collaborate with Beethoven on an opera in his *Erinnerungen an Beethoven* (written in 1840).[46] According to this account it was Count Moritz Dietrichstein, director of both court theatres, who informed him that Beethoven was turning to him for a new libretto.[47]

"This request, I must confess, gave me no little embarrassment. Once I had the idea of writing a libretto, still remote enough in itself, I began to doubt if Beethoven who meanwhile had become completely deaf and whose latest compositions without detracting from their high worth possessed a quality of harshness, who to me seemed to be in conflict with the treatment of the singing voice; I doubted, I say, if Beethoven was still capable of composing an opera. The thought, however, of giving to a great man the opportunity for a work which would be at any rate of the first interest overcame all considerations and I agreed.

"From the dramatic material which I had set aside for future adaptation, there were two which, if necessary, would permit of operatic treatment. One was set in the realm of most intense emotion. But aside from the fact that I knew no lady singer who would be able to rise to the main role, I also did not want to give Beethoven the opportunity to step still closer to the extreme limits of music which lay nearby, threatening like precipices, in partnership with material that was semi-diabolical."

This was, as the Conversation Books show, *Drahomira,* a story drawn from Bohemian legendary history.[48] Schindler told Beethoven that the poet would adapt the subject for him, and Lichnowsky reported that the poet wanted to discuss the matter with him.[49] This was in late April. Thus *Drahomira* was considered seriously for a time along with a second subject about which Grillparzer writes: "When I choose the fable of Melusine, so far

[46] Grillparzer wrote his reminiscences as the result of reading Ludwig Rellstab's *Aus meinem Leben.* Grillparzer claimed that reference to his attempt at collaboration with Beethoven on an opera text was misrepresentative. The reference was a remark made by Beethoven to Rellstab in 1825: "It is so difficult to find a good libretto! Grillparzer promised me one, he had already written one, yet we couldn't really come to an understanding. I wanted something entirely different than he!" See Alf. Chr. Kalischer, *Beethoven und seine* *Zeitgenossen* (Berlin, 1908), IV, p. 165.

[47] Alfred Orel in his book *Grillparzer und Beethoven* (Vienna, 1941, p. 16), suggests that Lichnowsky, having sounded out both artists on the idea of collaborating, arranged to have the suggestion from an official source to Grillparzer, in view of Beethoven's pride and artistic conscience.

[48] Only sketches exist. Grillparzer has written "one of my earliest works, around 1809 or 1810." (TDR, IV, 399, n. 1.)

[49] Schünemann, III, pp. 190, 200.

as possible I banished the reflective element and sought, by giving prominence to the chorus, creating powerful finales and treating the third act
almost melodramatically, to adjust myself to the character of Beethoven's last
period. I avoided a preliminary conference with the composer concerning
the subject-matter, because I wanted to preserve the independence of my
views. Moreover, it was possible to make alterations, and in the last instance
it rested with him whether to compose the book or not. In order not to
coerce him in the least I sent him the book by the same channel which had
brought me the call. He was not to be influenced by personal considerations
or embarrassed in any manner whatsoever."

The book appealed to Beethoven, but several conferences between him and
the poet were necessary before it was brought into satisfactory shape. Grillparzer had excluded much of the material in the old legend which was unsuited to dramatic treatment, and strengthened the plot with conceits of his
own invention. As soon as he had sent the text he went to Beethoven at
Schindler's request. At first blush Beethoven was much pleased with the
book, and he wrote Grillparzer a letter which delighted the poet. Grillparzer describes the visit to Beethoven at his lodgings in the Kothgasse
which he made in company with Schindler:[50]

"I found him lying in soiled nightwear on a disordered bed, a book in his
hand. At the head of the bed was a small door which, as I observed later,
opened into the dining-room and which Beethoven seemed in a manner to
be guarding, for when subsequently a maid came through it with butter
and eggs he could not restrain himself, in the middle of an earnest conversation, from throwing a searching glance at the quantity of the provisions
served—which gave me a painful picture of the disorder prevailing in his
domestic economy.

"As we entered Beethoven arose from the bed, gave me his hand, poured
out his feelings of good-will and respect and at once broached the subject
of the opera. 'Your work lives here,' said he, pointing to his heart; 'I am
going to the country in a few days and shall at once begin to compose it.
Only, I don't know what to do with the hunters' chorus which forms the
introduction. Weber used four horns; you see, therefore, that I must have
eight; where will this lead to?' Although I was far from seeing the need of
such a conclusion I explained to him that without injury to the rest of the
book the hunters' chorus could be omitted, with which concession he seemed
to be satisfied, and neither then nor later did he offer any objection to the
text or ask that a change be made. He even insisted on closing a contract with
me at once. The profits of the opera should be divided evenly between us,
etc. I declared to him, and truthfully, that I had not thought of a fee or anything of the kind while at work. . . . Least of all was it to be the subject of
conversation between us. He was to do with the book what he pleased—I

[50] Friedrich Kerst, *Die Erinnerungen an Beethoven* (Stuttgart, 1913), II, pp. 46-8.

would never make a contract with him. After a good deal of talk back and forth or rather of writing, for he could no longer hear speech, I took my leave, promising to visit him in Hetzendorf after he had settled himself there.

"I had hoped that he had given up all thoughts of business in regard to the matter; but a few days later my publisher, Wallishauser, came to me and said that Beethoven insisted upon the execution of a contract. If I could not make up my mind, Wallishauser suggested that I assign the property-right in the book to him and he would arrange with Beethoven, who was already advised of such a step. I was glad to get rid of the business, let Wallishauser pay me a moderate sum, ceded to him all the author's rights, and banished the matter from my thoughts. Whether or not they made a contract I do not know; but I would think so since otherwise Wallishauser would not have neglected to complain to me in his customary way about the money that he had risked."

Otto Jahn's notes of a conversation with Grillparzer state that Beethoven made a contract with Barbaja,[51] who was the *de facto* manager of the Kärnthnerthor Theatre, for 6,000 florins, V.S. (2,500 C.M.). Shortly afterward Barbaja abandoned the contract, saying to Beethoven that he knew that though he was bound by it he could not use the opera. Thereupon Beethoven tore up the document. On April 20, 1824, Duport[52] wrote to Beethoven that Barbaja had sent word from Naples that he would like to have an opera by Beethoven and would give time and terms as soon as he received assurance that his contract from the theatre would be extended from December 1. The extension was not granted. Schindler denied that a contract between manager and composer ever existed.

--❦{Unsatisfied with Meisl's revision of the *Ruinen von Athen*, Beethoven evidently turned to Grillparzer for an improved version of this text, for in early March Grillparzer writes in a Conversation Book:

I am making those changes which you consider necessary.

•∿•

Please give me an approximate idea for the duet; for I am fitting my ideas with yours as regards what is supposed to be sung.

•∿•

Perhaps this duet should have nothing other than Minerva's *joy* in contrast to Mercury's gloomy warnings.

•∿•

I see that the invention of a new treatment is necessary; but it is not created at a moment's notice; the working out of it is much faster than the invention; thus naturally I must ask for time to consider it at home so that I can think it through.

---

[51] Domenico Barbaja was leaseholder of the theatre from 1822 to March, 1825, at which time he took it over.

[52] Louis Antoine Duport, formerly a dancer, was the real owner of the theatre at that time.

If I am to leave the book and my lines here with you, I ask you only to send it back by H. Schindler as soon as you don't need it anymore.—As for the idea of creating the illusion of the Greek epoch nowadays, the censor would give it an emphatic negative vote.

I believe that only that which is *completely sure* should be presented *publicly* even if something *great* is not immediately sent in to the world. This conviction cannot be contradicted. I mean—the power thereto to feel.

The result in relation to the cantata would then be: you have enough intrinsic worth here to hold on to book and material and to provide me with your observations which can be delivered; meanwhile I will be contemplating the material and so perhaps we will come to an understanding. In short the conclusion is: *deliberation*, and I won't do any work without first consulting you directly concerning the plan.[53]

Further conversations about opera plans with reference to both *Drahomira* and *Melusine* continued right up to the time that Beethoven moved to Hetzendorf in the middle of May. With consideration of the summer months the story of Grillparzer will be resumed.

A project which cropped out intermittently during 1823 was the writing of an overture on the musical motive suggested by the letters composing the name of Bach. The thought seems to have become fixed in his mind in 1822, though the device of using

as a motive in composition was at least as old as the Leipzig master's "Art of Fugue," and no doubt familiar to Beethoven. However, he was deeply engrossed in fugal writing at this period, and it is very likely, as Nottebohm suggests, that he conceived an overture on the motive as a tribute to Bach's genius.[54] Several sketches showing different forms of the theme appear in the books of 1823; and a collateral memorandum, "This overture with the new symphony, and we shall have a concert (*Akademie*) in the Kärnthnerthor Theatre," amongst sketches for the last quartets in 1825, shows that he clung to the idea almost to the end. Had Beethoven carried out all the plans for utilizing the theme which presented themselves to him between 1822 and 1825, there would have been several Bach overtures; unfortunately he carried out none.

On April 13, 1823, the boy Franz Liszt, who was studying with Carl Czerny and had made his first public appearance on the first day of the year,

[53] Schünemann, III, pp. 76-7. See also Kalischer, *op.cit.*, pp. 177-80.

[54] *II Beeth.*, pp. 577-80. (TDR, IV, 416, n. 1.)

gave a concert in the small Redoutensaal. A few days earlier he along with his father was presented to Beethoven by Schindler. There is an entry in a Conversation Book which, because of the handwriting and courtly language, was probably written by the father:

I have often expressed the wish to Herr von Schindler to make your high acquaintance and am rejoiced to be able now to do so. As I shall give a concert on Sunday the 13th I most humbly beg you to give me your high presence.[55]

The day before the concert, Schindler writes in a Conversation Book:

Little Liszt has urgently requested me humbly to beg you for a theme on which he wishes to improvise at his concert tomorrow. [Some words crossed out] humilime dominationem Vestram, si placeat scribere unum Thema—

·~·

He will not break the seal till the time comes.

·~·

The little fellow's free improvisations cannot yet, strictly speaking, be interpreted as such. The lad is a true pianist; but as far as *improvisation* is concerned, the day is still far off when one can say that he improvises.

·~·

Czerny Carl is his teacher.
Just eleven years.

·~·

Do come, it will certainly amuse Karl to hear how the little fellow plays.

·~·

It is unfortunate that the lad is in Czerny's hands—

After a brief change of subject Schindler returns to the conversation about Liszt:

Won't you make up for the rather unfriendly reception of the other day by coming tomorrow to little Liszt's concert?

·~·

It will encourage the boy. Will you promise me to come?[56]

According to Nohl who got the story from Liszt himself, Beethoven did attend the concert, went afterwards upon the stage, lifted up the prodigy and kissed him.[57] At the concert, however, the theme upon which he

---

[55] Schünemann, III, p. 170.

[56] *Ibid.*, pp. 135-36.

[57] Ludwig Nohl, *Beethoven, Liszt und Wagner* (Vienna, 1814), p. 199. (TDR, IV, 417, n. 2.) Schindler's references to Liszt in his biography are unreliable since on the question

of Beethoven's attendance at the concert he contradicts himself, claiming in the second edition (1845) that Beethoven was there and in the third edition (1860) that he was not. Schindler's increasing disapproval of Liszt appears to explain the contradiction. Liszt's improvised was not one by Beethoven but a rondo theme of some 20 measures. According to the reviews the improvisation did not please.[58]

Amid the account of the negotiations concerning subscriptions to the Mass there was mentioned the name of Louis Schlösser who at this time was friendly with Beethoven and whose reception by him provides a fine example of the cordiality that Beethoven could offer to young artists. Louis Schlösser (1800-1886) was a violinist in the Darmstadt court orchestra and in the spring of 1822 he received a leave of several years in which to travel and broaden his knowledge through study with foreign artists. He went first to Vienna and then to Paris before returning to Darmstadt where he eventually became kapellmeister. His "Personal Reminiscences of Beethoven," an account written some 50 years later of his stay in Vienna, may be summarized here.[59] For months he was unsuccessful in his attempts to meet Beethoven. Finally on November 4, 1822, at the second performance of *Fidelio* he got his chance to see him at least from a distance. —He was leaving the theatre with his friend Franz Schubert. "Together with us, three gentlemen, to whom I paid no further attention because their backs were turned to me, stepped out of a lower corridor; yet I was not a little surprised to see all those who were streaming by toward the lobby crowding to one side, in order to give the three plenty of room. Then Schubert very softly plucked my sleeve, pointing with his finger to the gentleman in the middle, who turned his head at that moment so that the bright light of the lamps fell on it and—I saw, familiar to me from engravings and paintings, the features of the creator of the opera I had just heard, Beethoven himself. My heart beat twice as loudly at that moment; all the things I may have said to Schubert I now no longer recall; but I well remember that I followed the Desired One and his companions (Schindler and Breuning, as I later discovered) like a shadow through crooked alleys and past high, gable-roofed houses, followed him until the darkness hid him from sight."—

The opportunity to visit Beethoven was finally made by the Hessian Ambassador, Baron von Türkheim, as mentioned earlier, who gave Schlösser the commission of reporting to Beethoven the acceptance of the subscription to the Mass from that court. Climbing up the dark stairs to the first story of the Kothgasse No. 60, Schlösser turned as instructed to the door on the left. —Finding no servant or maid, he opened the door which led into the kitchen "through which one had to pass to gain the living-rooms. . . . After repeatedly knocking in vain at the real living-room door, I entered and

---

own account of the meeting to his pupil, Ilka Horowitz-Barnay, which was made in 1875, the last year of his life, must also be used with caution because of the inaccuracies in detail. Frimmel believed that Nohl's account was essentially correct. See *Beethoven Studien*, II, pp. 93-105. Also Gerth Baruch, "Liszt and

Beethoven" in *Monthly Musical Record*, Vol. 66 (1936), p. 176.

[58] Schünemann, III, p. 135, n. 1.

[59] See footnote 13. For English translation see G. Schirmer's *Impressions of Contemporaries* (1926), pp. 132-48, from which we draw in part.

found myself in a rather commodious but entirely undecorated apartment; a large, four-square oak table with various chairs, which presented a somewhat chaotic aspect, stood in the middle of the room. On it lay writing-books and lead-pencils, music-paper and pens, a chronometer, a metronome, an ear-trumpet made of yellow metal and various other things. On the wall at the left of the door was the bed, completely covered with music, scores and manuscripts. I can recall only a framed oil-painting (it was a portrait of Beethoven's grandfather, for whom, as is known, he had a child-like reverence) which was the sole ornament I noticed. Two deep window-niches, covered with smooth paneling I mention only because in the first a violin and bow hung from a nail, and in the other Beethoven himself, his back to me, stood busily writing down figures and the like on the wood, already covered with scribblings."

Schlösser continues: "The deaf Master had not heard me enter, and it was only by stamping vigorously with my feet that I managed to attract his notice and he at once turned around, surprised to see a young stranger standing before him. Yet before I could address a single word to him, he commenced to excuse himself in the politest manner imaginable because he had sent out his housekeeper, and no one had been in attendance to announce me, the while quickly drawing on his coat; and then first asking me what I wished. Standing so near this artist, crowned with glory, I could realize the impression which his distinguished personality, his characteristic head, with its surrounding mane of heavy hair and the furrowed brow of a thinker, could not help but make on every one. I could look into those profoundly serious eyes, note the amiably smiling expression of his mouth when he spoke, my words always being received with great interest.

"My visit probably occurred shortly after he had eaten breakfast, for he repeatedly passed the napkin lying beside him across his snow-white teeth, a habit, incidentally, in which I noticed he often indulged. Steeped in my contemplation of him I entirely forgot the unfortunate man's total deafness, and was just about to explain my reason for being there to him when, fortunately, I recalled the uselessness of speaking at the last moment, and instead reverentially handed him the letter with its great seal."

Having expressed pleasure over the letter and the visit from him, Beethoven, continues Schlösser, "seized his ear-trumpet, so I explained the unbounded veneration accorded his genial works, with what enthusiasm they were heard, and what an influence the perfection of his intellectual creations had exercised on the cultural level of the day. Though Beethoven was so impervious to flattery of any kind, my words which came stammering from the depths of my soul, nevertheless seemed to touch him, and this induced me to tell him of my nocturnal pursuit of him after the performance of 'Fidelio.' 'But what prevented you from coming to see me in person?' he asked. 'I am sure you have been told any amount of contradictory nonsense; that I have been described as being an uncomfortable, capricious and arrogant person, whose music one might indeed enjoy, but who personally was to be avoided. I know these evil, lying tongues, but if the world considers me heartless, because I seldom meet people who understand my thoughts and feelings, and therefore content myself with a few friends, it wrongs me.'

"He had put down his ear-trumpet, for speaking into it agitated his nerves too greatly; his complaint, so he insisted, did not lie in the weakness of the auditory canals, but was seated in the intestines; his physicians in treating him had made a false diagnosis their point of departure, etc."

From then on, Schlösser wrote his questions on sheets of paper lying at hand. Beethoven spoke of particular passages in his works—would that Schlösser had preserved these remarks!—of the superficial art currents in Vienna, under Italian influence, the "speechlessness" of princely gentlemen. Then he asked Schlösser to show him his compositions, and after inviting him to a meal two days from then (March 3) he dismissed him with the greatest amiability. "Do not hesitate to avail yourself of me whenever I can be useful to you or be of service to you in any way," were his parting words.

On the morning of March 3, Beethoven surprised his admirer by mounting the four flights of steps to pay a return visit. Schlösser writes: "What I did and said in my first confusion I do not know; he, on the other hand, well aware of my embarrassment, at once began to speak: he had called, in order since it was such a pleasant day, to take me along for a little walk before dinner, and to improve the occasion by making the acquaintance of my lodgings, instruments, music and pictures of my parents, which I had mentioned to him. And he actually began to turn the pages of my copy-books of contrapuntal exercises, to look over my little hand-library, in which he found his favorites, Homer and Goethe, and I even had to submit to him a drawing of mine, and all of these things he examined attentively and praised." Beethoven's meal ended with coffee which he himself had prepared with a newly discovered machine, the construction of which he explained. Afterwards there was talk of his abandoned trip to England, his difficulties with the pension payments, *Fidelio* and the attempt to find a good new opera libretto, his new compositions; and as his guest left, he called out "To our next meeting!"

According to Schlösser, Beethoven was living "alternately in the delightful Helenenthal near Baden, where in Nature's open, his creative powers drew their richest nourishment among the hills and the heavily-laded woods, and where ideas, as he expressed himself, flowed to him in quantity. I visited him there, for he felt himself much indisposed: the germ of his future illness was even then present in his body, and yet I could not help but admire the strength of soul with which he fought against it. Nothing about him betrayed his suffering during our excursions in common through the surrounding country; the pictures of the landscapes captured completely his eyes and his feelings. . . ."

He continues: "Only a few weeks later we met in the *Kärthnerstrasse*. His keen eye discovered me first; and coming up to me he at once seized me by the arm with the words: 'If you can spare the time then accompany me to the *Paternostergassel*, to Steiner's (the music shop of Steiner and Haslinger) whom I want to give a good set-down. These publishers always have all sorts of excuses handy. When it comes to bringing out my compositions they would like to put it off until I am dead, because they think they would do a better business with them; but I shall know how to meet them.' (literally). At this encounter I had been so surprised at the very onset to find Beethoven, usually so careless about his attire, dressed with unwonted elegance, wearing a blue frock coat with yellow buttons, impeccable white knee-breeches, a vest to match, and a new beaver hat, as usual on the back of his head. I left him at the entrance to the shop, which was crowded with people while, thanking me for escorting him, he entered Mr. Steiner's office with the latter. I could not resist telling my teacher Mayseder, who lived in the neighborhood, about the striking metamorphosis of Beethoven's elegant appearance, an event which, however, caused Mayseder far less surprise than it had caused me, for he said with a smile: 'This is not the first time that his friends have taken his old clothes during the night and laid down new ones in their place; he has not the least suspicion of what has happened and puts on whatever lies before him with entire unconcern.' . . . I shall only add, to what has gone before, the last conversation I had with this profoundly serious thinker. One day I brought him a new, somewhat complicated composition I had written, and after he had read it he remarked: 'You have given too much, less would have been better; but that lies in the nature of heaven-scaling youth, which never thinks it possible to do enough. It is a fault maturer years will correct, however, and I still prefer a superfluity to a paucity of ideas.' 'What shall I do to find the right way and—how did you yourself attain that lofty goal?' I added, timidly. 'I carry my thoughts about with me for a long time, sometimes a very long time, before I set them down,' he replied. 'At the same time my memory is so faithful to me that I am sure not to forget a theme which I have once conceived, even after years have passed. I make many changes, reject and reattempt until I am satisfied. Then the working-out in breadth, length, height and depth begins in my head, and since I am conscious of what I want, the basic idea never leaves me. It rises, grows upward, and I hear and see the picture as a whole take shape and stand forth before me as though cast in a single piece, so that all that is left is the work of writing it down. This goes quickly, according as I have the time, for sometimes I have several compositions in labor at once, though I am sure never to confuse one with the other. You will ask me whence I take my ideas? That I cannot say with any degree of certainty: they come to me uninvited, directly or indirectly. I could almost grasp them in my hands, out in Nature's open, in the woods, during my promenades, in the silence of the night, at the earliest dawn. They are roused by moods which in the poet's case are transmuted into words, and in mine into tones, that sound, roar and storm until at last they take shape for me as notes.' "

At parting, Beethoven gave Schlösser a sheet containing a canon for six voices on the words, "Edel sei der Mensch, hülfreich und gut," with the inscription: "Words by Goethe, tones by Beethoven. Vienna, May, 1823." On the back he wrote: "A happy journey, my dear Herr Schlösser, may all things which seem desirable come to meet you. Your devoted Beethoven." Beethoven also gave Schlösser, who was going to Paris, a letter of introduction to Cherubini which accomplished his acceptance as a pupil of the Conservatoire.

Another small composition belonging to this time is the birthday cantata for Prince Ferdinand Lobkowitz (born April 13, 1797), son of Beethoven's benefactor, Prince Franz Joseph v. Lobkowitz. The autograph, now lost, was inscribed "Evening of April 12, 1823 before the birthday of his Ser. Prince Ferdinand Lobkowitz."[60] Karl Peters (tutor to the Lobkowitz family) gives this account of its origin: "The copy of a little cantata which he [Beethoven] wrote for me to be performed on the birthday of the Prince ... was in reality written by him and most daintily tied together with blue ribbon. ... The cantata consists only of a few reiterated words, we can hardly say, *composed* by himself, and originated when he heard of the approaching birthday festival of the Prince when visiting us. 'And is there to be no celebration?' he asked, and I answered him, 'No.' 'That will not do,' he replied; 'I'll hurriedly write you a cantata, which you must sing for him.' But the performance was never realized."

Our old friend Schuppanzigh, after an absence of seven years, returned to Vienna in 1823. On April 26 Beethoven sent him a greeting in the form of a five-part canon, "Falstafferel, lass' dich sehen!" ("Falstafferel, let us see you!") In a Conversation Book at the end of April Schuppanzigh reports to Beethoven on many things, including fellow musicians:[61]

Ries is doing very well in London
Ries plagiarized too much from Beethoven
Everything, but with Ries too obviously

Field played beautifully

He should be heard playing Bethoven [*sic*!]
what a unique pleasure

Field is a very good man and his greatest admirer[62]

[60] Ludwig Nohl saw the autograph, which had passed from the family of Karl Peters to Dr. O. Zeithamer of Prague. See *Neue Briefe Beethovens* (Stuttgart, 1867), pp. 221-28.

(TDR, IV, 422, 423, n. 1.)
[61] Schünemann, III, pp. 177-78.
[62] Schuppanzigh heard the composer John Field play the piano in Russia. It will be

I have never heard the instrument handled as well by any other

... This Jewish lad Moscheles is causing a sensation in London, I cannot understand it at all.

Field is earning alot of money from lessons, nevertheless he never has 100 fl. because he uses it all drinking Champagne wine. Beethoven would like Field very much because he is a real Falstaff.

Humel [*sic*] played a *quatre mains* with Field, a most perceptible difference, however was felt by both nonconnoisseurs and connoisseurs. The way Field played reminded me very much of him [Beethoven] Field played his concerto in C minor very beautifully.

On May 4 Schuppanzigh gave a concert at which Piringer conducted the orchestra, and on June 14 the quartet meetings were resumed, with Holz, Weiss and Linke as his associates.

The story of Diabelli and the Mass has been postponed until now because it is intertwined with the last part of the story of the Diabelli Variations. Anton Diabelli, a partner in the firm of Cappi and Diabelli, invited a number of composers to contribute a variation on a waltz theme of his own for a collection to be entitled *Vaterländischer Künstlerverein* ("Native Society of Artists"). The invitations were presumably made in 1819 since the autograph of Carl Czerny's variation (in the Vienna National Library) is dated "March 1821."[63] According to Schindler, Beethoven at first refused the invitation.[64] However, by early 1819 Beethoven had made sketches for four different variations, which come just before the preliminary sketches for the *Kyrie* of the *Missa Solemnis*.[65] Beethoven in his letter to Simrock of February 10, 1820, included mention of some "grand variations on a well known 'Deutsche' which, however, I cannot promise you as yet. . . ." As time progressed, Beethoven's conception of the work grew; according to Schindler, he had in mind first six or seven, then twenty-five variations. On June 5, 1822, he offered Peters "Variations on a waltz for pianoforte alone (there are many) for the price of 30 ducats in gold." The main work, then, was done in this year, and the full thirty-three variations were completed by March or April, 1823.

Meanwhile Beethoven had started negotiations with Diabelli concerning the publication of both the Mass and the Variations. At some point during

---

remembered that Schuppanzigh and Beethoven always addressed each other as "he."

[63] See Heinrich Rietsch, "Fünfundachtzig Variationen über Diabellis Waltzer," in *BJ*, I (1908), p. 31.

[64] See *Biogr.*, II, pp. 34-5. (TDR, IV, 424, n. 3.)

[65] The Wittgenstein sketchbook has 87 pages, of which pages 4-14 contain sketches for what became Variations 11, 18, 19 and 32. See KHV, p. 348.

the growth of the latter, an agreement had been reached to publish the variations separate from the growing collection of variations of the other fifty composers. In the fall of 1822 Beethoven wrote the following letter to the publisher:

Dear D——!

Patience! I am still *not yet* living as a *human, much less* in a way that is suitable and necessary for me—The fee for the Variat. should be 40 ducats at the most if they are worked out on as large a scale as is planned; but if this should *not take place*, it would be set for *less*—Now more about the overture. Along with this I would be glad to give you seven numbers from the *Weihe des Hauses.* I have been offered a fee of 80 ducats for them. I would give you in addition a Gratulationsmenuett for full orchestra, in short, the overture and seven numbers from the Weihe des Hauses and the Gratulationsmenuett, all for 90 ducats—My housekeeper goes to the city today in the forenoon. Please give her for me an answer to my offer—I hope to be able to get to your Var. by the end of next week—Fare well excellent friend

Yours truly
B——n[66]

In March, 1823, Diabelli called Schindler into his shop and had a talk with him which is detailed in a Conversation Book. It is Schindler who is speaking:[67]

Diabelli called me today while I was passing and said to me that he would take the Mass and publish it in two months by subscription. He guarantees you the 1000 florins, as he says he has already told you. You can have as many copies as you want.

•∿•

So often I have wanted to ask you to take better care of your pocketbook. Was there much in it?
Diab. only asks of you that you let him know your decision within a few days, then he will have work begun at once and promises that everything shall be ready by the end of May. You, however, will not have any further care in the matter.

•∿•

I think the proposition a very good one, the more, because the work will be printed at once.

•∿•

Then decide the thing quickly, and settle with him right away.

Beethoven appeared to have doubts or scruples on the score of the invitations sent to the sovereigns.

[66] For a discussion of this letter see Sonneck, *Beethoven Letters in America*, pp. 16ff. [67] Schünemann, III, pp. 87-8.

It will make no difference to the most exalted courts if printed copies are put out.

•◥•

Do you want the 1000 florins in cash at once or later—he assures me that they will be guaranteed to you; the business now is that you come to an understanding.

It appears, now, that Diabelli wanted to publish the three supplementary pieces (Gradual, Offertory and "Tantum Ergo") as well; but Beethoven still hesitated.

It would be best if you were to persuade Diab. to print the work at once, but wait a few months with the publication by subscription. Then you will not be compromised in the matter, nor he either.[68]

Later (there had plainly been another conversation between Schindler and Diabelli):

Diabelli agrees to wait until the tardy answers have been received before opening the subscription. But he is not willing to wait a whole year.[69]

And in April:

As to how you are agreed about it,—the only question is whether you give Diab. the privilege of announcing the subscription a month before he pays.

•◥•

It is his own wish not to take the Mass in hand until he has paid.[70]

And in another Conversation Book in April, Schindler writes:

Diab. told me also that he will pay for the Mass as soon as he receives it, but he would like to have it by July 1 in order to have it ready by the St. Michael Fair.[71]

Subsequently Diabelli asked for it by August 1 and then September 1. Beethoven was firm in his determination to keep faith with his subscribers. He writes to Schindler: "There are only two courses as regards the Mass, namely, that the publisher delay the publication a year and a day; or, if not, we cannot accept a subscription."

Meanwhile from another undated letter to Schindler it is shown that a contract had been made between them: "Nothing is to be changed in the Diabelli contract except that *the time* when he is to receive the Mass from me be left undetermined." Both works were involved and soon difficulties developed. Beethoven writes: "From my little book I see that you have doubts in the matter of the Mass and Diab., wherefore, I beg you to come soon, for in that case we will not give him the Var. either, as my brother knows somebody who wants to take them both. We are therefore in a position to talk to him."

This matter, in which Schindler acted as Beethoven's agent brought out the following:

[68] *Ibid.*, pp. 90-91.   [69] *Ibid.*, p. 97.   [70] *Ibid.*, p. 153.   [71] *Ibid.*, p. 125.

Dear S.! ———

I wish that the business which is so disagreeable to you might be brought to a conclusion soon. Moreover I was not, *unfortunately*, completely *wrong* in not quite trusting Diab.— . . . .

To this letter Schindler provided the following note:

This concerns a contract between Diabelli and us concerning the Mass. Diab. spoke solely of plans for the work which were not only disadvantageous to the work but also damaging for the composer which I completely resisted, whereupon Diab. became very rude and declared that since the contract was as good as closed he would summon me before a court of law if the contract was broken off. This threat, however, did not help him at all; he had to take back the document.

——Thus Diabelli was one more publisher *not* to receive the Mass; but he was to have the consolation of the publication of the thirty-three variations on his own theme. In the Conversation Books of April and May there is repeated reference to the shipment of a copy of the Variations to Ries in England and the dedicating of the work to Ries's wife. During this time, Diabelli had the manuscript, and there are remarks concerning the need of getting him to return it. Brother Johann urged that arrangements for the publication of the Mass and the Variations be made both in London through Ries and in Paris through Schlesinger.[72] Schindler agreed and urged particularly the shipment to London. At the end of April he writes:[73]

Your brother fears that Diab. will not want to give back the manuscript, but of course he must do so.

•~•

If you want to send the Variat. to London, it is high time to do so.

•~•

He is afraid only that they will arrive too late because Diab. will have published them in 3 weeks.

Variat. (with 2 *Schusterfleck*)[74] dedicated to Mada[me] Ries, etc.

•~•

That will please H. Ries very much.

On April 25, 1823, Beethoven wrote a letter to Ries in which he promises: "You will also receive in a few weeks 33 variations on a theme dedicated to your wife." Although the copy for Mme. Ries is dated April 30[75] there was

[72] *Ibid.*, p. 140.
[73] *Ibid.*, pp. 203, 205.
[74] According to Schindler, *op.cit.*, Beethoven made fun of Diabelli's theme and called it a *Schusterfleck*, that is a cobble or a cobbler's patch. Like *Vetter Michel* and *Rosalia* in the

musical terminology of Germany, a *Schusterfleck* is a tune largely made up of repetitions on different degrees of the scale of a single figure or motive. (TK, III, 127, n. 1.)
[75] See KHV, p. 349.

evidently a delay in the shipment as Beethoven says in a letter to Ries dated July 16: "By this time the variations have probably arrived.—I could not write out the dedication to your wife myself since I do not know her name." ᴴᵉ·—

On May 7 Beethoven offered the Variations for publication to Lissner in St. Petersburg. The Variations appeared from the press of Cappi and Diabelli in June[76] with a dedication to Mme. Antonia von Brentano;[77] not, it will be observed, to the wife of Ries. Had there been an English edition there would have been such a dedication, but it is another case in which an English publisher was disappointed in the conduct of the composer. Ries had complied with Beethoven's solicitations and secured a publisher. He closed an agreement with Boosey; but when the manuscript reached London, Boosey was already in possession of a copy of the Vienna edition and the work had also been printed in Paris. The copy made for London bore a dedication written in large letters by Beethoven to Madame Ries; but the printed copies were inscribed to Madame Brentano. Beethoven attempted an explanation and defence in a letter to Ries dated Baden, September 5:

You say that I ought to look about me for somebody to look after my affairs; now this was just what happened with the variat. which were looked after for me by my friends and Schindler. How? The variations were not to appear here until after they had been published in London, but everything went askew. The dedication to Brentano was intended only for Germany, as I was under obligation to her and could publish nothing else at the time. Besides, only Diabelli, the publisher here, got them from me. Everything was done by Schindler, a bigger wretch I never knew on God's earth—an arch-scoundrel whom I have sent about his business—I can dedicate another work to your wife in place of it. . . .

How much blame in this affair really attached to Schindler is not known; it seems pretty apparent that at the same time as Beethoven was fuming against him at home, he was doing duty in London as a whipping-boy. Beethoven, however, went right on calling for the help of the "arch-scoundrel."

After the labors and vexations of town life in the winter, the call of the country in the summer was even more than usually imperative, because the work which had long occupied Beethoven's mind—the Ninth Symphony—was demanding completion. His brother Johann had invited him to visit him on his estate near Gneixendorf, but he had declined. His choice for the summer sojourn fell upon Hetzendorf, a village not far from Vienna,

---

[76] They were advertised as published in the *Wiener Zeitung* on June 16. The Variations were republished in June, 1824, as Part 1 of Diabelli's *Vaterländischer Künstlerverein*, subtitled "Variations for the Pianoforte on a given theme composed by the most select composers and virtuosi of Vienna and the R. I. Austrian States." Part 2 consisted of 50 variations by 50 different composers.

[77] Mme. von Brentano was to have had the dedication of the Pianoforte Sonata in C minor (see letter to Maurice Schlesinger, February 18, 1823, *A* 1140); but then Beethoven changed his mind and decided to dedicate it to Archduke Rudolph (see letter to the Archduke, July 1, 1823, *A* 1203).

where he removed on May 17. After much hesitation, he finally decided upon a villa, surrounded by a beautiful park, which belonged to Baron Müller-Pronay. There was some haggling about the rent and some questioning about the post service—an important matter in view of the many negotiations with publishers, in all of which Schindler was depended on—but eventually all was arranged. Ill health marred the Hetzendorf sojourn. Beethoven's other ailments were augmented by a painful affliction of the eyes which called for medical treatment, retarded his work and caused him no small amount of anxiety. Complaints on this score began in April and were continued through July, on the 15th of which month he writes to the Archduke, "My eyes are better, but improvement is slow. . . . It would be more rapid if I were not obliged to wear glasses. It is an unfortunate circumstance and has delayed me in everything"; and later, when on a short visit to Vienna: "I have just heard that Y. I. H. is coming here tomorrow. If I cannot obey the wishes of my heart, please ascribe it to my eyes. I am much better, but I must not breathe the town air for many more days, for it would have an ill effect on my eyes." In August, very shortly before his departure for Baden: "I am feeling really badly and not only because of my eyes. I propose to drag myself to Baden tomorrow to take lodgings and in a few days will have to go there to stay. The town air has an injurious effect on my entire system and I hurt myself by going twice to my physicians in the city."

At this time Beethoven was continuing to supervise the copying of scores of the Mass, to which was added the unwelcome task of corrections in connection with the publications of the Diabelli Variations and the Pianoforte Sonata, Op. 111. Here is one of the many letters to Schindler from this period:

Samothracian L[umpenker]l![78]

How about the trombone part? It is certain that the fellow still has it—as he did not return it when he brought back the Gloria. There was so much to do in looking over the wretched scribbling that we forgot to take back the trombone part. If necessary I shall come to Vienna to the police—Here, for Rampel, is first the theme of the Var. which is to be copied for me on a separate sheet—then he is to copy the rest to Var. 13 or rather to the end of Var. 12, and so an end of this—

Get from Schlemmer what is lacking of the Kyrie—

Show him my postscript and herewith satis—for such H[auptlumpenkerl]s —there is nothing more to be done—

---

[78] Beethoven had a number of nicknames for Schindler besides *Papageno* with its various qualifications. One of these was *Lumpenkerl*; another *Hauptlumpenkerl*—Ragamuffin and Chief Ragamuffin. In this instance Schindler is a "Samothracian ragamuffin" and Schindler in a gloss tells us that the allusion was to the ancient ceremonies of Samothrace, Schindler being thus designated as one initiated into the mysteries of Beethoven's affairs and purposes. The injunction of silence was understood, of course. Count Brunsvik, Count Lichnowsky and Zmeskall were also initiates. (TK, III, 106, n. 1.)

Farewell—attend to everything—I am obliged to bind up my eyes at night and must be very sparing in my use of them. *Otherwise*, Smetana writes, I shall write but few more notes.

To Wocher, whom I shall visit myself as soon as I come to town, my best compliments, and have the var. been sent yet?

Good wishes

Postscript

Diabelli receives herewith the old and part of the new.

My eyes which are still worse rather than better make everything go slowly. As soon as Diabelli is ready with this, send it out to me whereupon he will get all the rest right away—The idea that one must have the manuscript in order to show ownership is a new one to me which I have never heard before; counter-evidence is already provided by the MSS which I have; several of these were engraved and then I received them back again—

I have been asked sometimes for a document concerning the property right of a work and D. can have this also—

D. could have claimed a copy, but you know what happened, the more since we wanted to hand over the Var. to D. as quickly as possible.

--•❦The unusual story of the publication of the Sonata in C Minor, Op. 111, has waited until now since it involves not only the Berlin and Paris edition published by Schlesinger *père et fils* but also reprints in Vienna by Diabelli and Leidesdorf. There was also an attempt to arrange an English edition which misfired, bringing additional humiliation to Ferdinand Ries. The sonata was first published at approximately the same time by the two Schlesinger firms, probably close to the beginning of the year 1823.[79] In the letter for Schlösser, dated May 6, at the time of his departure from Vienna, Beethoven writes: "Likewise ask Schlesinger . . . what the reason is that I have still received no copies of the Sonata in C minor." Schindler reports ". . . the Paris editions had to be sent twice to Vienna; on account of the extraordinary number of mistakes even in the second proof, the composer demanded that Op. 111 be sent once again to which the management of the firm did not wish to comply. Thereupon it seemed that the sky would collapse over our master."[80]

The *Wiener Zeitung* announced a sonata as "newly arrived" on May 27. Diabelli quickly obtained a printed copy of the sonata and planned a reprint in an attempt, like that of Sauer and Leidesdorf, to capture the business in Vienna. In a letter to Moritz Schlesinger, dated June 3, 1823, Beethoven made a list of errors in the French edition of the sonata and then referred to the two "pirated" editions as follows:

[79] The date is not established. Kinsky-Halm date it in one place as 1822 (p. 319), in another (p. 761) as April, 1823. However, if the reference by Count Lichnowsky to "2 Paris sonatas" in a Conversation Book of early February, 1823 (Schünemann, II, p. 353) is to this sonata (along with Op. 110) then Kinsky-Halm's latter date is too late.

[80] *Biogr.*, II, p. 3.

By a remarkable accident someone sent to me here two copies as a curiosity to show how far one can go in the art of forgery; the one printed in Paris by you and the other here by Leidesdorf are so alike that one cannot tell the difference. Even the price is the same. It appears that you have played into the hands of your friends. Diabelli is now engraving it too, so I hear—therefore—although I have received no copy from you, I believe, nevertheless, that it is my duty to acquaint you with the new mistakes along with the old ones, and ask you please to have them corrected carefully.

As Sonneck points out,[81] Beethoven must have already made a set of *errata* before receiving a printed copy (old mistakes) and then received a copy from someone in Vienna ("I have received no copy from you), from which he listed new mistakes. Notes to Schindler, Diabelli and the Archduke give evidence as to how Beethoven felt about the faulty Schlesinger edition. Here was an opportunity, if he helped with the correcting, for the Diabelli reprint to provide a more accurate printing of the work. This, however, he did not admit to Schlesinger: "Diabelli is now engraving it too, so I hear."

In a letter to Schindler, which Beethoven has humorously divided into "Beginning," "Continuation," and "End," the last part is concerned with this problem:

End.

Inquire from the arch-scoundrel Diabelli if the French copy of the Sonata in C minor has been printed so that I may receive it for corrections. At the same time I have reserved four copies of it for myself, of which one is to be on fine paper for the Cardinal. If now he is his usual scoundrelly self, I will personally sing a bass aria to him in his store, so that it will resound in the store and from there to the Graben.[82]

Further mention of the *errata* was made in a letter from Beethoven to Diabelli[83] in which the composer suggested that Diabelli use the Paris copy as model for his publication, since there were additional mistakes in the other version (Sauer and Leidesdorf). He urged haste in producing the proofs, since he wished to correct them at once. He felt that the other two publishers deserved this treatment, although normally he would not do things in that way. The request for four copies, with one on special paper for the Archduke, was repeated.

The reprint of the sonata followed shortly afterward, as is shown by Beethoven's letter of July 1 to the Archduke previously quoted announcing the dedication of the sonata and the arrival of a reprint copy corrected by him from the French edition. As to the ethics of Beethoven's participation in

---

[81] O. G. Sonneck, *Beethoven Letters in America*, pp. 25-6.

[82] According to Miss Anderson, p. 1037, n. 1, there is a notation by Schindler on the autograph of this letter saying that Diabelli wrote to Beethoven and said that he would take down this bass aria, publish it and even pay him for it, whereupon Beethoven became more patient with him!

[83] First published in English translation by A. H. Fox Strangeways in *Music and Letters*, xv (1934), p. 16. See also *A* 1182.

this reprint of Op. 111, Sonneck makes this significant point: "Neither Schlesinger nor Beethoven could prevent Diabelli from reprinting the work. Once the damage was done to Schlesinger by Diabelli, the composer in Beethoven asserted himself and every instinct of artistic self-protection in him demanded that he undo the damage done to him as the creator of the Sonata by Schlesinger with so very faulty an edition."[84]

As for Beethoven's plan to have Ries arrange the publication in Britain of the last two pianoforte sonatas, Op. 110 and 111 (along with the Diabelli Variations), the situation is more difficult to understand. In 1820, he made an agreement with Schlesinger for the publication of three (Op. 109-111) sonatas, which presumably included rights to sell in England.[85] Already on February 25, 1823, Beethoven writes to Ries ". . . I hope you have already received both sonatas." Again on April 25 ". . . Take care only that the C minor sonata is engraved immediately; I guarantee to the publisher that it will not be published anywhere beforehand, also I will grant him property rights for England if need be, but it must be printed immediately. Since the other one in A flat, if already available in London, has nevertheless been printed with mistakes, he can announce this one then as a correct edition when he prints it." In view of the assurance of a correct version of the A flat Sonata and the guarantee of first printing of the Sonata in C minor, Beethoven must have intended to send Ries manuscript copies of both sonatas. While waiting for them to arrive, Ries had come to an agreement with Clementi as to the fee, just as he had with Boosey in connection with the Variations. Although in a Conversation Book in the beginning of May Schindler writes: "I am surprised that Ries has not mentioned anything about the sonatas. Wocher believes that he must have received them."[86] Ries implies in the *Notizen*[87] that they arrived with the Variations, which, as already mentioned, may have been as late as July. At any rate by the time the sonatas did arrive, Ries had the further humiliation "that the sonata [Op. 111] had already been printed in Paris!"

In his *Erinnerungen an Beethoven*, Grillparzer writes of his promise, after visiting Beethoven, to visit him in Hetzendorf. The poet kept his promise, going thither with Schindler. Part of his account may best be given in his own words: "We took a promenade and entertained each other as well as was possible half in conversation, half in writing, while walking. I still remember with emotion that when we sat down to table Beethoven went into an adjoining room and himself brought forth five bottles. He set down one at Schindler's plate, one at his own and three in front of me, probably to make me understand in his wild and simple way that I was master and should drink as much as I liked. When I drove back to town without Schindler, who remained in Hetzendorf, Beethoven insisted on accompanying me. He sat himself beside me in the open carriage but instead of going only

[84] Sonneck, *op.cit.*, p. 29.
[85] See letter of May 31, 1820. *A* 1024.
[86] Schünemann, III, p. 222.
[87] Page 123.

to the edge of the village, he drove with me to the city, getting out at the gates and, after a cordial handshake, starting back alone on the journey of an hour and a half homeward. As he left the carriage I noticed a bit of paper lying on the seat which he had just vacated. I thought that he had forgotten it and beckoned him to come back; but he shook his head and with a loud laugh, as at the success of a ruse, he ran the faster in the opposite direction. I unrolled the paper and it contained exactly the amount of the carriage-hire which I had agreed upon with the driver. His manner of life had so estranged him from all the habits and customs of the world that it probably never occurred to him that under other circumstances he would have been guilty of a gross offence. I took the matter as it was intended and laughingly paid my coachman with the money which had been given to me."[88]

Following are excerpts from a Conversation Book used during the visit to Hetzendorf. The first permits us to observe the poet's ideas on the music for his own libretto:

Are you still of the opinion that something else ought to be substituted for the first chorus of the opera?

Perhaps a few tones of the hunting-horns might be continued by an invisible chorus of nymphs.

I have been thinking if it might not be possible to mark every appearance of Melusine or of her influence in the action by a recurrent and easily grasped melody. Might not the overture begin with this and after the rushing Allegro the introduction be made out of the same melody.

I have thought of this melody as that to which Melusine sings her first song.

Drahomira

I will send you the plot of this Drahomira in writing.

Grillparzer made many observations concerning music and musicians which must have interested Beethoven even when he did not agree with him. Earlier he had asserted that on the whole the North Germans knew little of music—they would never produce anything higher than *Der Frei-schütz*. Now he writes of Italian opera:

Lablache, and in a degree Fodor, are better actors than the Germans ever had.[89]

---

[88] Thayer saw Grillparzer on July 4, 1860, and got from him a confirmation of both incidents here narrated. (TK, III, 120, n. 1.)

[89] Luigi Lablache was a well-known bass.

Josephine Fodor was first a pianist, then a singer. At this time she was singing at the Kärthnerthor Theatre.

Perhaps Mozart formed himself on Italian opera.

⋅~⋅

It's worse now. You would have trouble to find singers for your opera.[90]

Among the cheering incidents of the summer were the reports which reached him of the production of *Fidelio* under the direction of Weber in Dresden. Weber opened a correspondence on January 28. His diary shows that he continued it with letters dated February 18, April 7 and June 5, and that Beethoven's answers were dated February 16, April 10 and June 9.[91] Most unfortunately all these letters have disappeared, and the only hints we have as to their contents are from the draft for Weber's first communication discovered among the papers of the writer: "*Fidelio*. To Beethoven. The performance in Prague under my direction of this mighty work, which bears testimony to German grandeur and feeling, gave me an intimacy, as inspiring as it was instructive, with the essence through which I hope to present it to the public in its complete effectiveness here, where I have all possible means at my command. Every representation will be a festival day on which I shall be privileged to offer to your exalted mind the homage which lives in my heart, where reverence and love for you struggle with each other."

Weber had received the score of the opera on April 10 from Beethoven, who had to borrow it from the Kärnthnerthor Theatre, whose musical archives were in the care of Count Gallenberg. Through Schindler, Gallenberg sent word to Beethoven that he would send the score, provided two copies were on hand; if not, he would have a copy made. Schindler, reporting the message to Beethoven, adds that Gallenberg had said he thought Beethoven himself had the score: "But when I assured him that you did not have it he said that its loss was a consequence of your irregularity and many changes of lodgings." Nevertheless, Weber got the score and after fourteen rehearsals the representation took place with great success. Von Könneritz, Director-General of the Royal Chapel, reported the triumph to Beethoven and sent him a fee of 40 ducats. Beethoven, in acknowledging receipt on July 17, was emboldened "by the account which my dear friend Maria Weber gives me of the admirable and noble motives of Your Excellency" to ask his intercession with the Saxon court on behalf of the Mass in D, as has already been recorded in this chapter.

Another pleasant experience for Beethoven may be recorded here. In 1822 the Royal Academy of Music of Sweden had elected Beethoven to a foreign membership. The consent of the Austrian government was necessary to his

[90] Schünemann, III, pp. 398-400.

[91] Max Maria von Weber, *Carl Maria von Weber* (Leipzig, 1854), II, p. 466. (TDR, IV, 436, n. 4.) But according to Erwin Kroll, the known dates of Beethoven's answers are April 9 and June 9. See "Carl Maria von Weber and Beethoven," *NBJ*, VI (1935), p. 135.

acceptance of the honor and this seems to have been deferred an uncon-scionably long time; at least Beethoven's letters to the Academy and to King Charles XIV (whom as General Bernadotte, then French Ambassador at Vienna, he had known 25 years before) are dated March 1, 1823. When per-mission came he wrote notes to the editors of the newspapers *Beobachter* and *Wiener Zeitung*,[92] asking them to announce the fact of his election; these letters were to be delivered by Schindler, to whom Beethoven wrote instruc-tions in the following note:

Very best L[umpen]k[er]l from Epirus no less than from Brundusium etc!

Give this letter to the Beobachter. His name must be written on it by you— At the same time ask him whether his daughter has progressed well on the pianof[orte] and whether I might perhaps be of service to her with a copy of my compositions?—I have written down *honorary member*, but I do not know whether this is right or whether just to put *as a foreign member*, *not knowing* about such things and *never* noticing.

You have also something to deliver to Bernardum non Sanctum concerning this story. But also ask Bernard about this rascal Rupprecht. Explain the chit-chat to him and ask how one can apply the leather to such scandalous people.

Ask both philosophical newspaper writers if this is an *appointment to Hon-orary or Dishonorary Membership?*—

I am eating at home, if you want to come, do so—

Beg pardon of Herr Beobachter that the letter looks so confused—There is really too much to be done.

Find out also whether a copy of the Beobachter can be bought.

This letter shows both that Beethoven was not always as indifferent to distinctions of all kinds as he sometimes professed and that in this busy and in many ways troubled period his humor had not left him.

About this time Franz Schoberlechner, a young pianist, appealed to him for letters of recommendation to be used on a concert tour. The letter reached Beethoven through Schindler, to whom he returned it with the curt indorse-ment: "A capable fellow has no need of recommendation other than from one good house to another." Schindler importuned him again and Beethoven answered: "It must be plain to you that I do not want to have anything to do with this matter—as for 'being noble' I think I have shown you sufficiently that I am that on principle; I even think that you must have observed that I have never been otherwise—Sapienti sat—" That ended the matter.

At this time, Beethoven was once again in a position to recommend a colleague, which he did gladly. When Kapellmeister Drechsler of the Joseph-stadt Theatre became a candidate for the post of second court organist, Beethoven recommended him enthusiastically to Archduke Rudolph, whom in a second letter he urged to remain firm notwithstanding the fact that

<hr/>

[92] Joseph Anton von Pilat was editor of the *Beobachter*, and Beethoven's friend J. K. Bernard of the *Wiener Zeitung*. See *A* 1217, 1218.

Abbé Stadler had presented another candidate. Archduke Rudolph spoke to the emperor and Count Dietrichstein in favor of Drechsler, but in vain.

In his letters Beethoven referred to a canon, "Grossen Dank," which he said he had written for the Archduke and which he intended to hand him in person. A sketch for it has been found among those for the Ninth Symphony,[93] but there is no record of its having been received by the Archduke.

Beethoven's domestic affairs continued to plague him. While at Hetzendorf he had the services of a housekeeper whom he described as "the swift-sailing frigate" Frau Schnaps, in letters to Schindler. He had no end of trouble about his town lodging in the Kothgasse where Schindler was living, and was compelled to write long letters to his factotum on the subject. Here is one sent from Hetzendorf on July 2:

The continuous brutality of the landlord from the beginning and for as long as I have been in the house, calls for the help of the R.I. police. Go to them direct. As regards the storm windows, the housekeeper was ordered to look after them and particularly after the recent severe rain-storm to see if they were necessary to prevent rain from entering the room. But she found that it had neither rained in nor could rain in. Believing this, I put on the lock so that the brutal fellow could not open my rooms in my absence as he threatened to do—Tell them further how he behaved towards you and that he posted the bill without notice, which he has no right to do before St. James's day.—

He has also refused to give me a receipt from St. George's to St. James'[94] as this paper shows, because of the demand that I pay a charge for lighting of which I knew nothing. This abominable lodging without a *stove-flue* and with the most wretched sort of *main chimney* has cost me at least 250 florins V.S. for extra expenses above the rent, in order to make it habitable while I was there in the winter.

It was an intentional cheat, inasmuch as I never saw the lodgings in the first story but only in the second, for which reason many objectionable things remained unknown to me. I cannot comprehend how it is possible that *so shameful a chimney, ruinous to human health, can be tolerated by the government.* You remember how the walls of your room looked because of smoke, how much it cost to get rid of some, but not all, of the nuisance—The chief thing now is that he be commanded to take down the notice and to give me the receipt for the rent paid at any rate, since under no circumstances will I pay for that wretched lighting. Furthermore, I had other large expenses in order to make life endurable in that lodging—My sore eyes cannot yet stand the town air, otherwise I would go myself to the imperial police.

Yours faithfully

Lv.Beethoven

Schindler obeyed instructions. In a letter to Beethoven dated July 3rd, he reported that the police director, Ungermann, sent his compliments to Beet-

[93] *II Beeth.*, pp. 177-78.
[94] I.e., for the second quarter-year rental period, April 24-July 25.

hoven, granted all his wishes in advance, but advised him to pay the six
florins for lighting to prevent a scoundrelly landlord from having any kind
of hold upon him. The poster came down, but Beethoven had had enough
and moved to new lodgings in the fall.

Beethoven's nephew Karl pursued his studies at Blöchlinger's Institute till
August and then spent his vacation with his uncle at Baden. He made himself useful as amanuensis and otherwise, and his words are occasionally
found among the notes of conversation. His mother remained in the background for the time being, which is providential, for Beethoven had trouble
enough with his other sister-in-law, the wife of Johann, whose conduct
reached the extreme of reprehensibleness in the summer of 1823, during a
spell of sickness which threw her husband on his back. The woman chose
this time to receive her lover in her house and to make a shameless public
parade of her moral laxness. The step-daughter was not less neglectful of
her filial duties.

Schindler, who in Beethoven's lodgings was living next door to Johann
wrote a letter on July 3 from which we quote: "As I have been visiting
him [Johann] three to four times a day since he took to his bed, and have
entertained him by the hour, I have had an opportunity carefully to observe
these two persons; hence I can assure you on my honor that, despite your
venerable name, they deserve to be shut up, the old one in prison, the young
one in the house of correction. . . . This illness came opportunely for both
of them, to enable them to go their ways without trammel. These beasts
would have let him rot if others had not taken pity on him. He might have
died a hundred times without the one in the Prater or at Nussdorf the other
at the baker's deigning to give him a look. . . . He often wept over the
conduct of his family and once he gave way completely to his grief and
begged me to let you know how he is being treated so that you might come
and give the two the beating they deserve. . . . It is most unnatural and
more than barbarous if that woman, while her husband is lying ill, introduces her lover into his room, prinks herself like a sleigh horse in his presence and then goes driving with him, leaving the sick husband languishing
at home. She did this very often. Your brother himself called my attention
to it, and is a fool for tolerating it so long." Further accounts of his sister-
in-law's misconduct reached Beethoven's ears, and he was frank in his
denunciation of her to his brother. Schindler was asked by Beethoven to lay
the matter before the police, but he managed to postpone that step for the
time being.[95]

Burdened with these difficult relationships, with physical suffering of
different kinds, and with other vexations as well, Beethoven labored at
Hetzendorf on the great work which, already begun, was supposed to be
nearing its end: the *Symphony for England* or, as we are used to naming it,

[95] See *A*, p. 1042, n. 5, for further remarks by Schindler on this subject.

the Ninth Symphony. In his letter to Archduke Rudolph of July 1, already quoted, Beethoven writes: "I am now writing a new symphony for England, for the Philharmonic Society, and hope to have it completely done in a fortnight." The work claimed his attention to such a degree that he strove for solitude and wished if possible to see no one, not even Schindler.

This deep concentration on his big work resulted in much disturbance in his domestic affairs. "Completely preoccupied, he roamed through fields and pastures, sketchbook in hand, without giving a thought to the arranged hour for meals. When he returned he was repeatedly without his hat, which never happened formerly even in the moments of highest inspiration. Up to the middle of August were to be seen big notebooks with notations for his new work." So Schindler writes.[96] The ideas for the symphony had been growing in his mind for a long time before the writing out in this summer; otherwise he would not have been able to write Ries on April 25, 1823: "Right now I am not well because of many vexations that I have had to endure, yes even pain in my eyes! But do not worry; you will have the symphony soon; it is really this miserable situation alone that has been the fault." During the labor on this work there was room for nothing else in his mind; it was so ever-present with him that there was neither paradox nor hyperbole in his words "I am never alone when I am alone."

To the distractions already mentioned there came another which is related by Schindler: "Then the 'raptus' seized him to want to leave the beautiful villa of Baron Pronay and move to beloved Baden; the reason 'because the Baron made deep bows to him every time they met.' " Here Schindler cites the phrase "Humility of man towards man—it pains me" from the second letter to the "Immortal Beloved."

Beethoven may have formed the plan earlier in the year—probably had—but the Baron's excessive politeness helped to turn his departure into something like a bolt. Schindler continues:

"There appeared one morning his swift-sailing frigate, the good old house-keeper, in my room (it must be remembered that since September 1822 Beethoven had shared his room with me in the Pfarrgasse [Kothgasse], Vorstadt Leimgrube) and brought the message: the master feels that he is unable to work any longer in Hetzendorf and must depart from there; he expected me the next day to be with him at 5 o'clock in the morning so that I could help him in the search of a house in Baden. As evidence there were the following lines in his hand: 'Samothracian L—K— Come, the weather is just right. But it is better earlier than later, presto prestissimo, we are leaving from here.'

"This trip from Hetzendorf to Baden and the business there are among my most singular experiences with the great eccentric. Forthwith he began

[96] *Biogr.*, II, p. 51.

to reminisce over the long list of dwellings which he had already occupied there and their inconveniences and unpleasantnesses. There was only one of all that he had occupied which he now wanted; 'but the people have declared in years past that they do not want to take me [Beethoven] in again.' But such declarations had come from other houses there several times already. When we had arrived he requested me to proceed as a go-between to the desired house[97] and in his name to give a promise of better order and respect for other occupants (a chief cause of the complaint). This promise, however, received no attention. I was refused. My persevering friend was deeply troubled by this. Once again the bearer of the flag of truce was sent to the stronghold of the coppersmith with new assurances of good conduct. This time he found a willing ear. One specific stipulation, however, was made, that in order to have the room overlooking the street as in past years, Beethoven must provide it with window shutters. We tried in vain to learn the reason for this strange demand. Meanwhile, since the procurement of this requisite proved necessary for the prevention of bright sunlight for the composer's ailing eyes, this demand was willingly agreed to. A few days later the move took place."[98]

Schindler then gives the reason for the request. Beethoven was in the habit of scrawling all kinds of memoranda on his shutters in lead pencil—accounts, musical themes, etc. A family from North Germany had noticed this in the previous year and had bought one of the shutters as a curiosity. The thrifty smith had an eye for business and disposed of the remaining shutters to other summer visitors. When Beethoven was informed by an apothecary at Baden of this strange transaction, he broke into homeric laughter.

The day of Beethoven's move to Baden was August 13, as we learn from a letter to the Archduke on August 22. Excerpts from two letters to his nephew dated August 16 and 23 show his mood at this time. The first concerns his health and general state of mind:

At first I did not want to tell you anything until my health had improved *here*, which has not yet completely happened. I came here with catarrh and a cold, both severe for me, since the original trouble, moreover, has always been catarrhal, and I fear that this will soon cut through my life's thread or, what is worse, cut it *bit by bit*—Moreover my ruined belly must be restored by medicine and diet, and this I owe to the *faithful servants!* You can imagine how I am racing about, for only today did I again begin my service to the muses *purposefully* (after all *unpurposefully* would be unintentionally)—I *must serve them*, but that is not to be noticed—for the baths invite me at least to the enjoyment of beautiful nature, but nous sommes trop pauvres, et il faut écrire ou de n'avoir pas de quoi. . . .

<hr/>

[97] Rathausgasse No. 94, owned by the coppersmith Johann Bayer, where Beethoven stayed in the late summer of 1821.

[98] *Biogr.*, II, pp. 52-3.

The second reflects the annoyance he felt at Schindler during this period:

... He was with me only a day here to take a lodging, as you know. He slept at Hetzendorf, and as he said, went back to the Josephstadt in the morning. Do not get to gossiping against him, it might work him injury, and is he not already sufficiently punished being *what he is*. It is necessary that I tell him the truth plainly, for his evil character, which is prone to trickery, needs to be handled seriously. ...

At the same time he answered a letter from his brother Johann, now convalescing, in which he felt forced to speak out concerning the latter's family affairs:

Baden, August 19

Dear Brother:

I am rejoiced at your better health. As regards myself, my eyes are not entirely recovered and I came here with a disordered stomach and a frightful catarrh, the first due to the arch-pig of a housekeeper, and the second to a beast of a kitchen-maid whom I had once sent away but whom I took back—You should not have gone *to Steiner*. I will see what can be done. It will be difficult to do anything with the songs *in puris*, as their texts are German, but more likely with the overture.—

I received your letter of the 10th through the hands of the miserable scoundrel *Schindler*. You need only to give your letters directly to the post, from which I am certain to receive them, for I avoid this mean and contemptible fellow as much as possible—Karl cannot come to me before the 29th of this month when he will write you. You cannot be wholly unadvised as to what the two *canailles*, Lout and Bastard,[99] are doing to you, and you will have had letters on the subject from me and Karl, for, little as you deserve it I shall never forget that you are my brother, and a good angel will yet come to rid you of these two *canailles*, this former and present strumpet who slept with her fellow no less than three times while you were ill, and who, in addition to everything else, has your money wholly in her hands. O infamous disgrace, isn't there a spark of manhood in you?!!!—Now concerning another matter. You have my own manuscript of some pieces for the "Ruinen von Athen," which I want urgently because the copies of the score made for the Josephstadt lack several things which are to be found in these manuscript scores of mine. Since I am writing something similar, I want this most urgently, so write where I can get these manuscripts, I particularly ask this of you. About coming to you I will write another time. Ought I so to degrade myself as to associate with such bad company? Mayhap this can be avoided and we might yet pass a few days with you?! About the rest of your letter another time. Farewell. Unseen I hover over you and work through others so that these *canailles* shall not strangle you.—

As always your faithful

Brother.

---

[99] Meaning Johann's wife and step-daughter. (TDR, IV, 452, n. 1.) According to Anderson, *A*, p. 1081, n. 4, this passage and the one beginning "a good angel" through "spark of manhood in you" were deleted by another hand, though still legible. This is true also, at the close of the letter, of the adjective "bad" and the word "canailles."

It is interesting to read that he asked specifically for the original manuscript to the *Ruinen von Athen* "since I am writing something similar." There is no trace of what this composition was. Nohl questioned whether it might have been the opera *Melusine*.[100]

At Baden Beethoven's health improved. In a letter to the Archduke, dated August 22, he complained of a catarrhal trouble, the misery in his bowels and the trouble with his eyes, but adds: "Thank God, the eyes are so much improved that I can again use them considerably in the daytime. Things are going better also with my other ailments; more could not be asked in this short time." He was characteristically optimistic about the completion of his symphony as is shown in a letter to Ries dated September 5 in which he reports: "The score of the symphony has been completed by the copyists during the last few days and consequently Kirchhoffer and I are merely waiting for a good opportunity to send it off." At this time the symphony was not ready, let alone copied; but in his head it was far advanced and in July he was already working out the third movement. Franz Christian Kirchhoffer was a bookkeeper in the Ofenheimer wholesale firm in Vienna. Beethoven wrote several letters to him at this time and both now and later he acted as intermediary between Beethoven and Ries. On September 5 the composer wrote to Kirchhoffer that he would receive the score of the symphony in fourteen days at the most, but that what was really important now was the speedy delivery of the Mass to Ries. The letter ends: "As you can expect, Ries has hardly taken any action at all in this matter so far. Yet I think he will exert himself once the work is in London—Choose a day to come to Baden and you will be received by my Karl and myself with love and friendship."

There were several visitors to Beethoven at Baden in the summer of 1823 who have left accounts of their experiences. One was an Englishman, Edward Schulz, who published his story in the *Harmonicon* in January, 1824. Schulz visited Beethoven on September 28 in the company of Haslinger.[101] He describes it as a *dies faustus* for him and, as Schindler shrewdly observes, it must have also been one for Beethoven, since he managed to hear the conversations of his visitors without the aid of an ear-trumpet. He talked with great animation, as was his wont when in good humor, but says the English visitor, "One unlucky question, one ill-judged piece of advice—for instance, concerning the cure of his deafness—is quite sufficient to estrange him from you forever." He asked Haslinger about the highest possible note on the trombone, but was dissatisfied with the answer which he received; introduced his nephew and showed his pride in the youth's attainments by telling his guest that he might put him to "a riddle in Greek" if he liked. At dinner during a visit to the Helenthal he commented on the profusion of

[100] Ludwig Nohl, *Beethoven's letzte Jahre* (Leipzig, 1877), p. 908. (TDR, IV, 453.)

[101] Schulz had already paid a short visit to Beethoven in 1816. (TDR, IV, 456.)

provisions at dinner, saying: "Why such a variety of dishes? Man is but little above other animals if his chief pleasure is confined to the dinner-table." An excerpt from the letter will serve to advance the present narrative: "In the whole course of our table-talk there was nothing so interesting as what he said about Handel. I sat close by him and heard him assert very distinctly in German, 'Handel is the greatest composer that ever lived.' I cannot describe to you with what pathos, and I am inclined to say, with what sublimity of language, he spoke of the *Messiah* of this immortal genius. Every one of us was moved when he said, 'I would uncover my head, and kneel down at his tomb!' H. and I tried repeatedly to turn the conversation to Mozart, but without effect. I only heard him say, 'In a monarchy we know who is the first'; which might or might not apply to the subject. Mr. C. Czerny—who, by-the-by, knows every note of Beethoven by heart, though he does not play one single composition of his own without the music before him—told me, however, that B. was sometimes inexhaustible in his praise of Mozart. It is worthy of remark that this great musician cannot bear to hear his own earlier works praised; and I was apprized that a sure way to make him very angry is to say something complimentary of his Septetto, Trios, etc. His latest productions, which are so little relished in London, but much admired by the young artists of Vienna, are his favorites. His second Mass he looks upon as his best work, I understood. He is at present engaged in writing a new opera called *Melusine*, the words by the famous but unfortunate poet Grillparzer. He concerns himself but very little about the newest productions of living composers, insomuch, that when I asked about the *Freischütz*, he replied, 'I believe *one* Weber has written it.' You will be pleased to hear that he is a great admirer of the ancients, Homer, particularly his *Odyssey*, and Plutarch he prefers to all the rest; and of the native poets, he studies Schiller and Goethe in preference to any other; this latter is his personal friend. He appears uniformly to entertain the most favorable opinion of the British nation. 'I like,' said he, 'the noble simplicity of the English manners,' and added other praises. It seemed to me as if he had yet some hopes of visiting this country together with his nephew."

A few days after the one just recorded Beethoven received a visit from a man of much greater moment than the English traveller. The new visitor was Carl Maria von Weber. That the composer of *Der Freischütz* was unable in his salad days to appreciate the individuality of Beethoven's genius has already been set forth; and the author of the letter in the *Harmonicon* seems to have learned that Beethoven was disposed to speak lightly of Weber only a month before he received him with most amiable distinction at Baden. He was often unjust in his comments on even his most devoted friends, and we may believe that to Schulz he did speak of the composer as "one Weber," and at the same time accept the account which Max Maria von Weber gives of the reception of his father by Beethoven. From the affectionate biography written by the son, we learn that after the sensational success achieved by *Der Freischütz* Beethoven was led to study its score and that he was so astonished at the originality of the music that he struck the book with his hand and exclaimed: "I never would have thought it of the gentle little man (*sonst weiche Männel*). Now Weber must write operas; nothing but operas—one after the other and without polishing them too much. Casper, the monster, stands out here like a house. Wherever the devil puts in his claws they are felt." He learned to know *Euryanthe* later and was less impressed by it than by its predecessor. After glancing through it hurriedly he remarked: "The man has taken too much pains." Whatever may have been their earlier feelings and convictions, however, the representations of *Fidelio* at Prague and Dresden under the direction of Weber warmed their hearts towards each other. Weber had come to Vienna, bringing with him his pupil Benedict, to conduct the first performance of *Euryanthe*. On his visit in the previous year, when *Der Freischütz* was produced, he had neglected to call on Beethoven, but now some kindly words about *Euryanthe* spoken by Beethoven to Steiner being repeated to him, he made good his dereliction and, announced by Haslinger, drove out to Baden to pay his respects. In his diary Weber noted the visit thus: "The 5th, Sunday (October, 1823), at 8 o'clock, drove with Burger (Piringer), Haslinger and Benedict to Baden; abominable weather; Saw spring and baths; to Duport and *Beethoven*; received by him with great cordiality. Dined with him, his nephew and Eckschlager at the Sauerhof. Very cheerful. Back again at 5 o'clock." On the next day (though the letter is dated "October 5") Weber wrote an account to his wife as follows: "I was right tired but had to get up yesterday at 6 o'clock because the excursion to Baden had been appointed for half-past 7 o'clock. This took place with Hasslinger, Piringer and Benedict; but unfortunately the weather was atrocious. The main purpose was to see Beethoven. He received me with an affection which was touching; he embraced me most heartily at least six or seven times and finally exclaimed enthusiastically: 'Indeed, you're a devil of a fellow!—a good fellow!' We spent the afternoon very merrily and contentedly. This rough, repellant man actually paid court to me, served me at table as if I had been his lady. In short, this day will always remain remarkable in my memory as well as of those present. It was uplifting for me to be overwhelmed with such loving attention by this great genius. How saddening is his deafness! Everything must be written down for him. We inspected the baths, drank the waters, and at 5 o'clock drove back to Vienna."

Max Maria von Weber in his account of the incident says that Beethoven, in the conversation which followed his greeting of the "devil of a fellow," railed at the management of the theatre, the concert impresarios, the public, the Italians, the taste of the people, and particularly at the ingratitude of his nephew. Weber, who was deeply moved, advised him to tear himself away from his discouraging environment and make an artistic tour through

Germany, which would show him what the world thought of him. "Too late!" exclaimed Beethoven, shaking his head and going through the motions of playing the pianoforte. "Then go to England, where you are admired," wrote Weber. "Too late!" cried Beethoven, drew Weber's arm into his and dragged him along to the Sauerhof, where they dined. At parting, Beethoven embraced and kissed him several times and cried: "Good luck to the new opera; if I can I'll come to the first performance."

A generation later Sir Julius Benedict, who had also put his memory of those Vienna days at the service of Weber's son, wrote down his recollections for this work in these words:

"I endeavor, as I promised you, to recall the impressions I received of Beethoven when I first met him in Vienna in October, 1823. He then lived at Baden; but regularly, once a week, he came to the city and he never failed to call on his old friends Steiner and Haslinger, whose music-store was then in the Paternostergässchen, a little street, no longer in existence, between the Graben and the Kohlmarkt.

"If I am not mistaken, on the morning that I saw Beethoven for the first time, Blahetka, the father of the pianist, directed my attention to a stout, short man with a very red face, small, piercing eyes, and bushy eyebrows, dressed in a very long overcoat which reached nearly to his ankles, who entered the shop about 12 o'clock. Blahetka asked me: 'Who do you think that is?' and I at once exclaimed: 'It must be Beethoven!' because, notwithstanding the high color of his cheeks and his general untidiness, there was in those small piercing eyes an expression which no painter could render. It was a feeling of sublimity and melancholy combined. I watched, as you can well imagine, every word that he spoke when he took out his little book and began a conversation which to me, of course, was almost incomprehensible, inasmuch as he only answered questions pencilled to him by Messrs. Steiner and Haslinger. I was not introduced to him on that occasion; but the second time, about a week after, Mr. Steiner presented me to the great man as a pupil of Weber. The other persons present were the old Abbé Stadler and Seyfried. Beethoven said to Steiner: 'I rejoice to hear that you publish once more a German work. I have heard much in praise of Weber's opera and hope it will bring both you and him a great deal of glory.' Upon this Steiner seized the opportunity to say: 'Here is a pupil of Weber's'; when Beethoven most kindly offered me his hand, saying: 'Pray tell M. de Weber how happy I shall be to see him at Baden, as I shall not come to Vienna before next month.' I was so confused at having the great man speak to me that I hadn't the courage to ask any questions or continue the conversation with him.

"A few days afterwards I had the pleasure of accompanying Weber and Haslinger with another friend to Baden, when they allowed me the great privilege of going with them to Beethoven's residence. Nothing could be more cordial than his reception of my master. He wanted to take us to the Helenenthal and to all the neighborhood; but the weather was unfavorable, and we were obliged to renounce this excursion. They all dined together at one table at an inn, and I, seated at another close to them, had the pleasure of listening to their conversation.

"In the month of November, when Beethoven came to town and paid his daily visit to the Paternostergässchen, I seldom missed the opportunity of being one of the circle of young admirers, eager to show their reverence to the greatest musical genius as well as hoping to be honored by his notice. Among those whom I met upon this errand were Carl Maria von Bocklet, his pupil, Worzischek, Léon de St. Louvain, Mayseder, Holz, Böhm, Linke, Schuppanzigh, Franz Schubert and Kanne.

"On the morning after the first performance of *Euryanthe,* when Steiner and Haslinger's shop was filled with the musical and literary authorities, Beethoven made his appearance and asked Haslinger: 'Well, how did the opera go last night?' The reply was: 'A great triumph.' *'Das freut mich, das freut mich,'* he exclaimed, and perceiving me he said: 'I should so much have liked to go to the theatre, but,' pointing to his ears, 'I go no more to those places.' Then he asked Gottdank, the régisseur; 'How did little Sontag get on? I take a great interest in her; and how is the book—good or bad?' Gottdank answered the first question affirmatively, but as to the other he shrugged his shoulders and made a negative sign, to which Beethoven replied: 'Always the same story; the Germans cannot write a good libretto.' Upon which I took his little conversation book and wrote in it: 'And *Fidelio?'* to which he answered: 'That is a French and Italian book.' I asked him afterwards: 'Which do you consider the best librettos?'; he replied *'Wasserträger* and *Vestalin.'* "

Madame Marie Pachler-Koschak, with whom Beethoven had spent many happy moments in 1817, was among those who took the waters at Baden in the summer of 1823, but we are told she searched for him in vain, a fact which shows in what seclusion he must have dwelt some of the time at least. She was more fortunate when she returned in September to complete her cure; and when she left Baden she carried with her an autographic souvenir—a setting of "Das Schöne zum Guten," the concluding words of Matthison's "Opferlied."

Towards the close of October Beethoven returned to Vienna. We know the date approximately from Benedict's account, the first performance of *Euryanthe* having taken place on October 25. He removed to new lodgings —·⊱in the Landstrasse on the corner of the Bockgasse (now Beatrixgasse)[102] and the Ungargasse⊰·—, where his nephew remained with him as long as he continued a student at the University. Here he worked at the Ninth Symphony, more particularly on the last movement.

[102] I am grateful to the late Dr. Kurt Smolle for this information.

The Bagatelles, Op. 126, belong to this period, though their completion fell in the next year. Taking up earlier sketches probably, Beethoven worked on them after the Ninth Symphony was practically complete in his mind and in the sketchbooks. Nottebohm had subjected them to a minute study[103] which leads him to the conclusion that the pieces were conceived as a homogeneous series, the numbers being linked together by key relationship. On the margin of a sketch for the first one Beethoven wrote "Cycle of Trifles" (*Kleinigkeiten*), which fact, their separation from each other (all but the first two) by the uniform distance of a major third, taken in connection with their unity of style, establishes a cyclical bond. When he offered them to Schott in 1824 he remarked that they were probably the best things of the kind which he had ever written. They were among the compositions which had been pledged to his brother, in whose interest he offered them to Schott. They were published by that firm in 1825.

After the conversations with Grillparzer at Hetzendorf on the subject of *Melusine,* there were many others with whom Beethoven discussed the opera and who came to him to tell him of their desire to see it written. Duport was greatly interested, wanted to read the book with care, and asked Beethoven's terms; Lichnowsky was willing to risk the financial outcome; "I will go security," he says in October, "for the money which you want for the opera. After selling the opera to the director you can still reserve the right of disposing of it at home and abroad." And again: "If you do not compose the opera, German opera is finished—everybody says that. After the failure of Weber's opera *Euryanthe* many sent the books back. Freischütz is not a genuine opera. If you can use me in any way, you know me and how sincere I am"; and still again, towards the end of November: "You will get incomparably more without a contract; if you want one, the director will make a contract with pleasure at once.— Talk it over with Grillparzer; it will also be all one to him.— Duport already asked about the opera several days ago." From other quarters Beethoven was urged to write to Duport after the latter had written to him.

In the late fall the composer wrote the following letter to the poet:

Honored Sir!

The management would like very much to know your conditions concerning your Melusine. So far they have spoken out on their own, and this is probably better than our applying pressure concerning the same—My domestic life has been in great disorder for some time, otherwise I would have looked you up already and made another invitation to visit—For the time being write your conditions to the management or to me and I will then forward them myself— Overburdened with work, I could neither pay you a visit earlier nor can I now. I hope this will happen sometime soon; my No. is 323.[104]

[103] *Il Beeth.*, pp. 193ff. (TDR, IV, 477, n. 1.)

[104] Orel (*Grillparzer und Beethoven*, p. 130) notes that the house number was added in pencil after the writing of the letter. This was the house on the corner of the Ungargasse, No. 323, Landstrasse.

In the afternoon you will find me in the coffee-house opposite the Goldene Birne. If you want to come, please come *alone*, this importunate appendix of a Schindler, as you must have noticed in Hetzendorf, has long been extremely objectionable to me—otium est vitium—I embrace you heartily and honor you fully

      Yours with all my heart
      Beethoven

—Grillparzer's visit was evidently at Beethoven's house on the Ungargasse, and the entries in the Conversation Book, which follow, were all written by Grillparzer:

The censor has banned my tragedy Ottokar.

·~·

It is not allowed even in print.

·~·

It applies very much to Austria.

·~·

Who takes the blame for Austria?

·~·

Unfortunately it is really patriotic.

·~·

No one can comprehend the reason for the ban.[105]
You have again taken up Melusine?

·~·

I have already appealed to the management twice but have had no answer.

·~·

I have already said that I was compelled to ask 100 ducats for it. Because as a matter of fact, all the profits of an opera-book remain with the theatre in which it is performed for the first time.

·~·

I could have made a spoken drama out of the same material which would have brought me three times as much.

·~·

I *must* ask so much in order to meet my obligations to Wallishauser.

·~·

For ordinary opera-books they pay up to 300 florins Convention Coin.

·~·

Have you already begun to compose?—Will you please write down for me where you want the changes made?

[105] *Ottokar* was performed for the first time on February 19, 1825.

•◞•

Because then, nevertheless, the piece will have to begin with a *hunt.*

•◞•

Perhaps the last tones of a vanishing hunters' chorus might blend with the introduction without having the hunters enter.

•◞•

To begin with a chorus of nymphs might weaken the effect of the chorus at the close of the first act.

•◞•

I am not quite versed in opera texts.

•◞•

You want to deliver it to the theatre by September.

•◞•

The direction wants to make a creditable showing in the eyes of the public.

•◞•

Doesn't the text of the opera also seem too *long* to you? To whom are you thinking of giving the rôle of Raimund?

•◞•

They are talking of a young tenor who may have made his debut by that time.

•◞•

I believe his name is Cramolini; besides a handsome figure he is said to have a beautiful voice.[106]

•◞•

It is said that the management is having him educated.

•◞•

Forti is a little too gross.

•◞•

Then I am to expect your suggestions as to alterations *in writing. Soon* perhaps? I am not busy at present.

•◞•

I am ready for anything.

For a space there is talk about oratorio texts (*Judith*) and the possibility of musical expression in the case of Christ. Then the text of *Drahomira* is referred to, concerning which Beethoven seems to have asked. Grillparzer says:

[106] Luigi Cramolini (1805-1884) made his debut in *Ioconda* on February 27, 1824.

Drahomira

◦━◦

Great variety, great characters, effects.

◦━◦

The mother of St. Wenzelaus, the Duke of Bohemia.

◦━◦

One of her sons kills the other. She is herself a pagan, the better son is a Christian.

◦━◦

They still show the spot in Prague where she was swallowed up by the earth with horses and equipage.

◦━◦

After I have lost all hope *here* I shall send it to Berlin.[107]

There is much more talk in the Conversation Book about the opera, but neither sequence nor date can always be determined. Lichnowsky told him that the management of the theatre was willing to do anything asked of it and was negotiating with Grillparzer. Brother Johann says: "Grillparzer is coming tomorrow—that is no affair of yours.— You wrote to the management to make arrangements with the poet, and to this it was agreed; hence Grillparzer must make terms." In the same book Schickh, the editor, writes: "Why don't you compose Grillparzer's opera? Write the opera first and then we shall be in a position to wish you also to write a Requiem."

Grillparzer mentions in his *Erinnerungen* that Beethoven told him in Hetzendorf that his opera was ready (whether he meant in his head or in its essential elements in the numerous sketchbooks, the poet could not say), but after the composer's death not a single note was found which could indubitably be assigned to their common work. Why didn't Beethoven compose *Melusine?* Many reasons must be obvious to those who have followed this narrative closely: illness; vexation of spirit; loss of initiative; a waning of the old capacity to assimilate conceptions and ideas which did not originate in his own consciousness and were not in harmony with his own predilections.[108] Moreover, it was the period of his greatest introspection; he was communing more and more with his own soul, and separating himself more and more from all agencies of utterance except the one which spoke most truthfully and directly within him, and to which he entrusted his last revelations—the string quartet. *Melusine* was not composed, but the opera continued to occupy his attention at intervals until deep into the next year, and unless Holz is in error, some of his last labors were devoted to it.

━◦◦ The smaller compositions written in this year were:

---

[107] Orel, *op.cit.*, pp. 74-6.
[108] See Douglas Yates, *Franz Grillparzer* (Oxford, 1946), pp. 139-44, for further reasoning on this question.

Canons:

"Bester Herr Graf, Sie sind ein Schaf!", WoO 183, written of Count Lichnowsky
on February 20.

"Edel sei der Mensch, hülfreich und gut" (Goethe), WoO 185, for Baroness
Eskeles in early May.

"Falstafferl, lass' dich sehen!", WoO 184, for Schuppanzigh on April 26.

"Das Schöne zum Guten" (Matthisson), WoO 202, for Frau Pachler-Koschak
on September 27.

"Der edle Mensch sei hülfreich und gut" (Goethe), WoO 151, for Baroness
Eskeles on January 20.

Lobkowitz Cantata for Soprano, Chorus and Pianoforte, WoO 106, for the
birthday celebration of Prince Ferdinand Lobkowitz (b. April 13, 1797) on
April 12.

Progress on large works consisted of:

1819-22/23. *Missa Solemnis* for Four Solo Voices, Chorus, Orchestra and Organ,
Op. 123, written for Archduke Rudolph of Austria, Cardinal-Archbishop
of Olmütz and presented to him on March 19, 1823.

1822-4. Symphony No. 9 in D minor was the main labor of the year 1823.
Sketches date back to 1817.

1819-23. Thirty-three Variations on a Waltz by Anton Diabelli, Op. 120.

The publications of the year were:

By Cappi and Diabelli:

Variations for Pianoforte on a Waltz by Anton Diabelli, Op. 120, dedication
to Antonie Brentano.

By Schlesinger in Paris and by Clementi in London:

Sonata for Pianoforte in C minor, Op. 111, dedicated to Archduke Rudolph.[109]

By Clementi in London:[110]

Eleven Bagatelles for Pianoforte, Op. 119.[111]

By Steiner:

Overture to the *Ruinen von Athen*, Op. 113.

First printing in score:

By Simrock:

Symphony No. 4 in B-flat major, Op. 60.

---

[109] The question of the chronology of the printings of the last sonata by different publishers is a controversial one. For a summary of this question see KHV, p. 319.

[110] See Alan Tyson, "The First Edition of Beethoven's Op. 119 Bagatelles" in *MQ*, Vol. 49 (1963), pp. 331-38.

[111] According to Kinsky-Halm (KHV, p. 347), opus number 119 was not assigned until the printing of Nottebohm's first *Verzeichniss* for Breitkopf and Härtel in 1851.

CHAPTER XXXVII

THE YEAR 1824

THE HISTORY OF THE NINTH SYMPHONY—ITS FIRST PERFORMANCE—CONTINUED NEGOTIATIONS WITH PUBLISHERS—PRINCE GALITZIN AND OPUS 127

THE year 1823 ended with Beethoven in his new lodging on the corner of the Ungargasse, occupied with work upon the Ninth Symphony, which was approaching completion, oppressed with anxiety concerning his health and worried about his brother's domestic affairs. His eyes continued to trouble him till late in March; Schindler cautioned him not to rub them, as that might increase the inflammation; Karl suggested buying a shade to protect them from the glare of the light; and when Count Brunsvik wanted to take him along with him to Hungary, Schindler advised him to take the trip, as it might be beneficial for his eyes.

About this time Beethoven took an unusually charitable attitude towards Karl's mother. She had been ill for some time as is shown by a remark by Bernard in a Conversation Book of February-March, 1823: "Have you heard nothing concerning your sister-in-law? My housekeeper has told me that she is sick and things are going very badly with her. The doctor has told it to her himself. He said that she could not pay for the medicine. You should have inquired before how the matter stands."[1] That Beethoven seems to have followed up this suggestion is shown by an undated letter to Bernard:

Dear Friend!

I beg of you before the day is over to make inquiries about Frau van Beethoven and if it is possible, to have her assured through her physician that from this month on *so long as I live* she shall have the enjoyment of the whole of her pension, and I will see to it that if I die first, Karl shall not need the half of her

[1] Schünemann, III, pp. 115-16.

pension— It was, moreover, always my intention to permit her to keep the whole of her pension as soon as Karl left the Institute, but as her illness and need are so great she must be helped at once. God has *never* deserted me in this heavy task and I shall continue to trust in Him. If possible I beg you to send me information to-day and I will see to it that my tenacious brother also makes a contribution to her—

Yours sincerely
Beethoven

Beethoven wrote to her on January 8, 1824, possibly in answer to an entreating letter from her:

Many affairs have prevented Karl and myself from sending you our good wishes for the New Year, but I know that, nevertheless, you expect nothing but the best wishes for your welfare from me as well as Karl—

Concerning your need, generally I would have been glad to help you out with a sum, but unfortunately I have too many expenses and debts and am still waiting for a certain amount of money and so am unable right now to prove to you my willingness to give you immediate help— Meanwhile I assure you herewith in writing that you can keep Karl's half of your pension from now on. We will hand over to you each month the receipt whereupon you can collect it yourself since there is indeed no shame (and I know that several of my acquaintances receive their pensions every month) in receiving it monthly. Should I be in a position later on to give you a sum from my bank for the improvement of your circumstances, it will certainly be done—the 280 fl. 25 kr. which you owe Steiner I have likewise taken over already as you have probably been told— Moreover, for some time you have not had to pay any interest on the loan—

You have received two months of pension from me through Schindler— On the 26th of this month or some time after that you will receive the pension payment for this month— Concerning your lawsuit I will soon have a discussion with Dr. Bach—

We wish you all possible good, Karl as well as myself—

Your most willing to help L. v. Beethoven

Beethoven seems to have regretted his magnanimity soon afterwards. In another letter to Bernard he writes:

Dear Bernard!

With so little time it is too much trouble for me to write to the doctor myself, to whom, however, I send best greetings herewith. Now briefly, what she has for sure, pension 406 fl. 30 kr. V.S. and the interest on 6700 fl. V.S. yearly adding to 335 V.S.; she is also to receive 480 fl. V.S. yearly from *Hofbauer*. Since, as I hear, the latter considers her child as his, *he is probably right.* And since she has become such a prostitute I believe that I and Karl even more should be sensitive to the guilt of *her bad behavior.* Hence if this 480 fl. of Hofbauer's is true, I believe she should not be given the whole other half of the pension. Perhaps such an eminent man as the doctor could clarify the thing; at any rate I do *not* want *to come into contact with her*. I am sending her herewith 11 fl. C.M. and ask you to deliver it to her via the *doctor* and further that she does not know from whence it comes.

But I request that she write a statement that she has received this— If all these things could be clarified, one could see what more is to be done for her; and I am ready to help all I can—

Your friend Beethoven⁂—

The nephew was now attending the philological lectures at the university and living in the winter and spring months with his uncle. He had left Blöchlinger's Institute in August, 1823, and matriculated at the university. He was active in the service of Beethoven, doing work as his amanuensis, carrying messages, making purchases, and so on; in fact Beethoven seems to have taken up more of his time than was good for his studies. Karl's involvement with the servants and household affairs is shown by the following excerpts in his hand from the Conversation Books: "Every time that you have trouble with the servants, I have to carry the blame for it; I don't know how I came to that." "If you had made decisions, everything would have been different long since." Beethoven loved his nephew tenderly and was unceasingly thoughtful of his welfare; but the jealousy of his affection led him to exercise a strictness of discipline over him which could not fail to become irksome to a growing stripling. He left him little liberty, and, yielding to a disposition prone to passion, he not seldom treated him with great severity. The youth appears in the Conversation Books as lively, clever and shrewd, and Beethoven, proud of his natural gifts of mind, was indulgent of his comments on others, permitting him apparently to speak lightly and discourteously of the men upon whose help and counsel he was obliged to depend. The result of Beethoven's extremes of harsh rebuke and loving admonition, of violent accusation and tender solicitude, was to encourage him in his innate bent for disingenuousness and deception, and he continued the course which he had begun as a boy of repeating words of disparagement touching those on whom his uncle leveled his criticisms, and of reporting, no doubt with embellishments of his own invention, the speeches which told of the popular admiration in which the great composer was held. By this species of flattery he played upon the weakness of his uncle and actually obtained an influence over him in the course of time which he exploited to his own advantage in various directions. He was naturally inclined to indolence and self-indulgence, and it is not strange that Beethoven's self-sacrifice in his behalf never awakened in him any deep sense of gratitude, while his unreasonable and ill-considered severity aroused a spirit of rebellion in him which grew with his advance towards manhood. Beethoven never seems to have realised that Karl had outgrown the period when he could be treated as a child, and it was a child's submission which he asked of him.

At the beginning of the year the pianist Friedrich Kalkbrenner was in Vienna; on January 25 he gave a recital in the small Redoutensaal. Schindler writes in a Conversation Book: "Did Hr. Kalkbrenner do you the favor of honoring you with a ticket to his concert? Otherwise he has not given out any." At the same time Moscheles had returned from his tour abroad to play in Vienna, but at this particular moment he was taken sick in Prague. Beethoven had heard a great deal about Kalkbrenner; Johann expressed the opinion that he played better than Moscheles; Schindler wrote down that he had scored a triumph. According to Karl, "Moscheles is said to have acknowledged that he did not grasp the meaning of your Variations at all."

Schuppanzigh gave repeated quartet performances at this time; Beethoven's Septet and F minor Quartet especially were received with great enthusiasm. At the performance on February 1 there were present several of Beethoven's friends such as Tuscher, Piringer and Wolfmayer.[2]

Grillparzer's opera-book was a frequent subject of conversation between Beethoven and his friends in the early months of 1824 as already mentioned, but petitions and advice were alike unfruitful. He did not go to work upon it nor yet upon a composition which presented a more urgent obligation. This was the oratorio which he had agreed to write for the Gesellschaft der Musikfreunde and on which he had received an advance of money in 1819. Here the fatal procrastination, though it may have been agreeable to Beethoven, was not altogether his fault. Bernard began the book, but seems to have put it aside after a few weeks.

Reference has already been made to the fact that in 1819 Oliva could not understand Bernard's inaction in the matter.[3] In April, 1820, Bernard himself writes: "I must finish the oratorio completely this month so that you can begin on it at Mödling."[4] His intentions were not carried out, however, for in August, 1820, somebody writes:

I have put it seriously to *Sanctus Bernardus* that it is high time that it be done, that Hauschka himself was urging a completion; he will finish it *this month, id est* in 5 days; and he will talk with you this evening at Cameel's[5]. . . . [two pages later] When I told Bernard that Hauschka had come to you about it he was embarrassed, it seems that he is throwing the blame on you.

He does not want to show his poetical impotency.[6]

At this time Beethoven had a sketch of the first part of the text which Bernard asked to be returned, with the promise that the oratorio text would be finished "in the following weeks."[7] — Finally towards the close of October, 1823, Bernard gave a copy of the complete text of the oratorio, which was entitled *Der Sieg des Kreuzes* ("The Victory of the Cross"), to Beethoven and also one to Sonnleithner for the Society. After waiting nearly three months, the directorate of the society at a meeting held on January 9, 1824, took action, the nature of which was notified to both Beethoven and Bernard.

[2] Johann Nepomuk Wolfmayer, rich Viennese merchant and music-lover to whom Beethoven was to dedicate his last quartet.

[3] Schünemann, I, p. 35.

[4] *Ibid.*, II, p. 55.

[5] *Ibid.*, p. 225. The writer is Oliva, according to Schünemann.

[6] *Ibid.*, p. 227.

[7] *Ibid.*, p. 240.

According to K. F. Pohl,[8] librarian of the society, Leopold v. Sonn-leithner had proposed to the society that there be a performance of the Mass and the Ninth Symphony. Beethoven declared that he wished to give the proceeds of the second performance to the society "in case this would assume the expenses for copying and all other such incidentals." The society estimated the expenses as coming to 1842 florins; this was considered too great and the project was abandoned. Sonneck in his penetrating essay on this subject has rightly emphasized that this gesture on Beethoven's part was made before he received the reminder from the society on January 9 and should be borne in mind when reading the composer's answer to the society. As Sonneck puts it, "Beethoven, embarrassed by his predicament with Bernard's long delayed and unsatisfactory text, proposed a means for squaring his financial account with his creditors which they seriously considered.[9]

The society wrote to Bernard that as it had left the choice of the text which he was to compose to Beethoven, it could not say whether or not the society would make use of the poem which he had sent until Beethoven had set it to music, and the censor had given his sanction. He was also asked to co-operate with the society in stimulating Beethoven to finish the work "so long expected by the musical world."

The letter from the society to Beethoven follows:

Dear Sir!

When the Society of the Friends of Music of the Austrian Empire invited you to write an oratorio four years ago, which proposal you accepted along with its terms; it left to you the choice of a poem and a poet. Soon thereafter it was learned that H. Bernard had undertaken the writing of the poem. As often as we turned to you in this long interim and asked if you were already occupied with this work, we heard that the poem was not yet in your hands. We could not expect that a composer of your stamp should sketch the plan of his musical composition before he had been entrusted with the whole of the poem and had found it worked out and finished according to his wish; therefore we could only turn to H. Bernard and urge him on. Finally he handed in the complete poem to the society near the end of October, 1823, and explained that he had also given a copy over to you. Since on the one hand we could only make use of the text if you, the composer, not only have actually chosen it for composition but also have actually completed the composition; but on the other hand the resolve has been expressed repeatedly by you to deliver such a work to the society, which has been confirmed by the part-payment made on request; we request conse-quently Your Well-born to inform the society categorically whether you will set to music the poem delivered by H. Bernard and at what time we may hope to receive this work to which every friend of music and admirer of your great talent has been looking forward for such a long time with keen expectation.

Receive assurances of the most distinguished respect.

Beethoven wrote the following answer to the society on January 23:

[8] Karl Friedrich Pohl, *Die Gesellschaft der Musikfreunde* (Vienna, 1871), pp. 13-14.
[9] *Beethoven Letters in America*, pp. 95-7.

Dear Sirs!

Since I have been overloaded with business and still plagued continually by an eye trouble, please be good enough to excuse my late answer— Concerning the oratorio I hope that veritas odium *non* parit. *I did not* choose H. v. B[ernard] to write the text; I was assured that the Society had commissioned him— For [since] H. v. B. has been editing the newspaper, it has been difficult to confer with him much. It has become a long story, however, very irksome in fact for me, since H. v. B. had written nothing other than "Libussa" for music, which at that time had not yet been performed. I have known it, however, since 1809 and since that time it has become very much altered; thus I couldn't with full confidence view the undertaking with him as anything but difficult. On account of this I was forced all the more to hold out until I had the whole text; at one point I finally received the first part. But according to B's disposition it had to be changed again, and I had to give it back again, that much I remember. Finally I received the whole at the same time that the Society did, with other obligations having occurred which I could not fulfill because of earlier illness. I have now really had to hurry to keep my word, all the more since you know that I *unfortunately can live only from works that I write. But now a variety of passages have to be altered* in B's oratorio. I have already indicated some and soon will finish and then acquaint B with them. For, though I find the material good and the poem has some value, it cannot remain *as it is*. "Christus am Ölberg" was written by me in collaboration with the *poet* in 14 days, but that poet was musical and had written several things for music and I could consult him at any moment. Let us leave out of consideration *the value* of poems of this sort. We all know that allowances are to be made. The good lies here in the middle; but so far as I am concerned, I would rather set Homer, Klopstock, Schiller to music. If they offer difficulties to be overcome, *these immortal poets* at least are worthy of it— As soon as I am through with making changes in the oratorio with B, I shall have the honor to inform you of the fact and at the same time let the society know when it may with certainty count upon it. That is all I can say about it at present—Respecting the 400 fl. V.S., sent to me *without demand*, I would have sent them back long ago had I been able to foresee that the matter of this oratorio would last much longer than I had imagined. It was grievous to me not to be able to express myself on the subject. In this connection I had the idea of joining with the Society in a concert, in order to provide at least the interest on the sum. But neither Herr Schindler nor my brother was authorized to say anything on the subject, and it was farthest from my thoughts that it should be done *in such a manner*. Please inform H. L. v. Sonnleithner of this too. Also I heartily thank the Society for the offer of the platform and other aid which it proffered me. In due time I shall make use of this offer— I shall be glad to hear whether the Society wishes to make use of my works, among which is a new symphony, later on after my concert. The great Mass is really rather in the oratorio style and particularly adapted to the Society. I shall be especially pleased if my unselfishness and also my zealous desire to serve the Society in whose benevolent deeds in behalf of art I always take the greatest interest, are recognized— Please accept especially my high esteem for you, Sirs, with all respect

Ludwig van Beethoven

Beethoven was frequently urged to set to work on the music of *Der Sieg des Kreuzes*; but he was also advised not to compose it. Archduke Rudolph accepted the dedication of the poem and wrote to Beethoven telling him of the fact and expressing a wish that he would set it to music. But the editor Schikh said to him: "If I were Beethoven I would *never* compose the extremely tiresome text of his oratorio." Beethoven had expressed satisfaction with the subject and the quality of the lines; he discussed changes which he wished to have made with Bernard after he had had time to consider the work as a whole; he promised Hauschka in September that he would compose it as soon as he returned to the city, and asked him to pay Bernard his fee; but he never set seriously to work upon it, though at the end of the letter to Hauschka (which bears date September 23, 1824) he reiterated his promise so that he might, with mock solemnity, attest it by affixing his hand and seal.

The book of the *Sieg des Kreuzes* was based upon the ancient story of the apparition of the cross and the legend *"In hoc signo vinces"* to Constantine the Great, who had crossed the Alps into Italy and lay encamped confronting his enemy Maxentius before Rome. His daughter Julia, who was represented as wife to Maxentius, attempted to avert the battle, but the vision strengthened Constantine's resolve. Julia heard the angelic canticles which accompanied the apparition and was converted to the true faith, persisting in it to martyrdom, to which she was condemned by her husband. Maxentius also heard the voices, but his augurs (allegorical figures representing Hate and Discord) interpreted them to his advantage, whereas similar figures (Faith, Hope and Charity) inspired the Christian army. The battle scene was preceded by pious canticles on the one hand, harsh songs on the other; Constantine promised to raise the Cross on the forum in Rome, victory was celebrated with Christian hymns, "Hosanna!" and "Glory to God!" Beethoven's copy of the libretto has been preserved, and in it are indications that he made some heroic excisions. He permitted Faith, Hope and Charity to remain, but banished Hate and Discord. It is pretty plain that he found nothing inspiring in the work. Holz told Jahn that he said to him, "How could I get up any enthusiasm about it?" Schindler says that Beethoven's failure to set the book caused a rupture of the friendship which existed between him and Bernard. The directors of the Gesellschaft der Musikfreunde dropped the matter, neither importuning Beethoven more nor taking any steps to recover the money paid on account. The society afterwards elected him to honorary membership.

During the account of the oratorio project, we learned that the new symphony was ready or almost ready and that an *Akademie* had already been planned for a performance of the new work. Schindler, who was an eyewitness of events at this time, gives the termination date for the Ninth Symphony as February, 1824, and adds that the conclusion of the work had a cheering effect upon Beethoven's spirits. He no longer grudged himself occasional recreation and was again seen strolling through the streets of Vienna, gazing into the shop-windows through eye-glasses which dangled at the end of a black ribbon, and, after a long interregnum, greeting friends and acquaintances as they passed. The history of the work is far more interesting than that of any other of his compositions, with the possible exception of the Mass in D. Nottebohm has painstakingly extracted from the sketchbooks all the evidence which they afford, touching the origin and development of the work, and presented it in a chapter of his *Zweite Beethoveniana*,[10] and his conclusions have been adopted in the presentation of facts which follow.

Thoughts of a symphony to succeed the Symphonies in A and F major (Nos. 7 and 8) were in the composer's mind while he was making sketches for those two works in 1812; but the memoranda there found tell us only in what key the new symphony was to be; they are mere verbal notes: "2nd Sinfonie, D minor" and "Sinfonie in D minor-3rd Sinfonie."[11] A fugue-theme, identical, so far as the first three measures go, with that of the Scherzo of the Ninth Symphony, presented itself to him and was imprisoned in his notebook in 1815, being recorded among the sketches for the Sonata for Pianoforte and Violoncello in D, Op. 102.[12]

There is another sketch with a note[13] to show that Beethoven was thinking of a new symphony at the time, but the sketch cannot be associated with the Ninth Symphony.

The fugue-theme appeared again in 1817 in an altered form but with the same rhythmic outline.

According to Nottebohm, this was to be the main theme for the Fugue for five stringed instruments. The Fugue, Op. 137, was worked out, however, in D major on a different subject. Both versions of the D-minor theme reappeared in later sketches for the symphony, the composition of which really began when the beginning of the first movement was sketched. Of

[10] Pages 157ff. (TDR, v, 18, n. 2.)

[11] *Ibid.*, p. 111. (TDR, v, 18, n. 1.)

[12] There are several stories touching the origin of the fugue-theme of the Scherzo of the D minor Symphony, two of which may be given for what they are worth. Czerny says that the theme occurred to Beethoven while listening to the twittering of sparrows in a garden. Holz told Jahn that one evening Beethoven was seated in the forest at Schön-brunn and in the gloaming fancied he saw all about him a multitude of gnomes popping in and out of their hiding places; and this stirred his fancy to the invention of the theme. (TK, III, 145, n. 1.)

[13] "Sinfonie at the beginning only 4 voices, 2 viol. viola, basso, amongst them forte with other voices and if possible bring in all the other instruments one by one and gradually." (TK, III, 145, n. 2.)

this fragments are found on loose leaves belonging to the year 1817. By the end of that year and the beginning of 1818 (presumably from September to May) extended sketches of the movement were made. The principal subject was definitely fixed, but the subsidiary material was still missing. The fugue-theme was assigned to the third movement. There was no suggestion of the use of Schiller's "Ode to Joy," but a plain intimation of an instrumental finale.

In 1818 a plan was outlined for the introduction of voices into the slow movement of a symphony which was to follow the Sinfonie in D. It is as follows:

Adagio Cantique.

Pious song in a symphony in the ancient modes—Lord God we praise Thee—alleluia—either alone or as introduction to a fugue. The whole 2nd sinfonie might be characterized in this manner in which case the vocal parts would enter in the last movement or already in the Adagio. The violins, etc., of the orchestra to be increased tenfold in the last movement, in which case the vocal parts would enter gradually—in the text of the Adagio Greek myth, *Cantique Ecclesiastique*—in the Allegro, feast of Bachus [*sic*].

It will be recalled that in 1822 Beethoven told Rochlitz that he had two symphonies in his mind which were to differ from each other. One difference at least is indicated here by the purpose to use voices in a movement to be written in the old modes. His well-known love for classic subjects, no doubt, prompted the thought of the "pious orgies" of a Pagan festival. Schiller's hymn was still absent from his mind. These sketches were all likewise excursions undertaken while Beethoven was chiefly occupied with the composition of the Pianoforte Sonata, Op. 106. What progress, if any, was made with the Symphony during the next four years can not well be determined. The work was interrupted by the composition of other works, notably the Mass in D, the last three Pianoforte Sonatas and the Overture, Op. 124.[14] It was not until the Mass and the Josephstadt music were finished in the sketches that he gave his attention to the Symphony.

In the sketches of 1822, there are evidences of considerable progress on the first movement, little if any on the Scherzo, the fugue-themes of 1815 and 1817 appearing in them almost unchanged. There is no hint as yet of the slow movement, but among the sketches appears the beginning of the melody of the "Ode to Joy" with the underlying words, assigned as a finale. The thought of using the Ode for a concluding movement had presented itself, but only tentatively, not as a fixed determination. Following this sketch, but of another date (to judge by the handwriting and the contents), comes a memorandum indicating that the symphony in mind (perhaps the one to be written for London) was to consist of four movements—the first (no doubt, though it is not mentioned) being the present first, the second in 2/4 time,

[14] Nottebohm might well have added the Diabelli Variations.

the third (presumably) in 6/8, while the fourth was to be built on the fugal theme of 1817 and to be "well-fugued." The next recognizable sketch is for a Presto in 2/4 designated as a second movement and this is followed by the beginning of the first movement preceded by four measures in triple time marked "Alla Autrichien." A third sketch is marked as belonging to a "Sinfonie allemand." It is a new melody to the words beginning Schiller's Ode to be used in a chorus. The accompanying memorandum reads:

Sinfonie allemand after which the chorus

Freude   schöner   Götter = funken   Tochter   aus   E = ly = si = um

enters or also without variations. End of the Sinfonie with Turkish music and vocal chorus.

The last relevant sketch in the book of 1822 is a sort of thematic index to the symphony as it now lay planned in Beethoven's purpose:

The second movement was to be a fugued Scherzo with the theme of 1815, the fourth the Presto in 2/4 time which first appeared in this year, the fifth the "Ode to Joy." In the midst of these sketches appears the significant remark: "Or perhaps instead of a new symphony, a new overture on *Bach*, well fugued with 3——."[15]

The conclusions to be drawn from the sketches thus far are that, as was the case in 1812 when the Seventh and Eighth Symphonies were brought forth as a pair, Beethoven was again contemplating the almost simultaneous production of two symphonies. He did not adhere to the project long, so far as we can know from the written records, and the remark about the substitution of an overture on B-a-c-h probably marks the time when he began seriously to consider the advisability of abandoning what would then have been the Tenth Symphony. With the exception of a portion of the first movement, the Ninth Symphony was still in a chaotic state. Taken in connection with negotiations which had been concluded with the Philharmonic Society of London, it may be assumed, however, that the present Symphony in D minor was associated in Beethoven's mind with the English

---

[15] Nottebohm fills the hiatus with "Trombones? Subjects?" (TK, III, 147, n. 1.)

commission, and that the second, which he had thoughts of abandoning in favor of the overture, was to have been a "Sinfonie allemand." For a time, at least, Beethoven is not likely to have contemplated a choral movement with German words in connection with the symphony for the London Philharmonic Society: this was to have an instrumental finale. The linguistic objection would be invalid in the case of the German symphony, however, and to this was now assigned the contemplated setting of Schiller's poem.

Work now proceeded with little interruption (except that occasioned by the composition of the Variations, Op. 120), and most of the first half of 1823 was devoted to the first movement, which was nearly complete in sketch-form before anything of the other movements appeared beyond the themes which have already been cited. When the foundation of the work is firmly laid we have the familiar phenomenon of work upon two or three movements simultaneously. In a general way it may be asserted that the year 1823 saw the birth of the Symphony, though work was carried over into 1824. The second movement was complete in the sketches before the third—this was about August; the third before the fourth—about the middle of October. The second theme of the slow movement was perfected before the sketches for the first movement were finished. In a Conversation Book used in the fall of the year 1823 the nephew writes: "I am glad that you have brought in the beautiful andante." The principal theme of the movement appears to have been conceived between May and July, 1823, but it had to submit to much alteration before it acquired the lovely contours which we now admire. This was the case, too, with the simple folksong-like tune of the Finale.

Sketches for the Finale show that Beethoven had made considerable progress with the setting of Schiller's Ode before he decided to incorporate it with the Symphony. In June or July, 1823, he wrote down a melody in D minor which he designated "Finale instrumentale":

and which, transposed into another key and slightly altered, was eventually used in the finale of the Quartet in A minor, Op. 132. That it was intended for the Finale of the Symphony is proved by the fact that it is surrounded with sketches for the Symphony in D minor and Beethoven recurred to it twice before the end of the year; there was no thought of the quartet at the time.

When he began work on the Finale, Beethoven took up the choral part with the instrumental variations first and then attacked the instrumental introduction with the recitatives. Once the present "Joy" melody, as noted in the fall of 1822, was adopted, the tune underwent many transformations in the second part before its definitive form was established. Among the musical sketches occur several memoranda containing hints which were carried out in part, for instance: "Turkish music in Wer das nie gekonnt, stehle"; in sketches for the Allegro *all marcia*: "Turkish music—first pianissimo—a few sounds ppmo—a few rests—then the full strength"; a third: "On Welt Sternenzelt forte trombone blasts"; a fourth (in studies for the final chorus: "the height of the voices to be more by instruments" ("die Höhe der Stimmen mehr durch Instrumente") which may be interpreted to mean that Beethoven realized that he was carrying the voices into dangerous altitudes and intended to give them instrumental support.[16]

Other sketches indicate that Beethoven intended for a considerable time to write an instrumental introduction with new themes for the Finale. For this prelude there are a number of sketches of different kinds, some of them conceived while sketches for the first movement were still in hand. Before July, 1823, there are no hints of a combined vocal and instrumental bridge from the Adagio to the setting of the "Ode to Joy." After that month there are evidences that he had conceived the idea of introducing the "Joy" melody played upon wind instruments with a prelude in the recitative style, a reminiscence of the first movement and premonitory suggestions of the fundamental melody. This was the first step towards the eventual shape of the Finale. The lacking element was the verbal link which should connect the instrumental movements with the choral conclusion. This came after his return from Baden to Vienna. The sketches bear out Schindler's remark: "When he reached the development of the fourth movement there began a struggle such as is seldom seen. The object was to find a proper manner of introducing Schiller's Ode. One day entering the room he exclaimed 'I have it! I have it!' With that he showed me the sketchbook bearing the words, 'Let us sing the song of the immortal Schiller Freude,' whereupon a solo voice began directly the hymn, to joy."[17]

By grouping a number of sketches it is now possible to make a graphic representation of the ideas which passed through Beethoven's mind while seeking a way to bridge the chasm between instrumental and vocal utterances by means of a formula of recitative. The sketches are in parts illegible, in parts so obscure that Nottebohm and Deiters differ in their readings. Here

[16] *II Beeth.*, p. 186. [17] *Biogr.*, II, p. 55. (TDR, v, 26.)

is Deiters' version; it may be compared with Nottebohm's in *II Beeth.*, pp. 189ff. Over a portion of an instrumental recitative

occur the words: "No this would remind us too much of our despair"; other sketches follow in the order here indicated:

Heute ist ein feierlicher Tag
[To-day is a solemn day]

mei ne Fru (Freunde?) die - ser sei ge - fei - ert
[my fri (friends?) let it be cele-brat - ed]

durch mit Gesang und [Tanz? Scherz?]
[with song and [Dance? Play?]

O nein dieses nicht etwas
[O no not this something]

ist es was ich fordere
[is this what I ask]

anderes gefällig
[else pleasing]

etc.

There follows:

Then is introduced the Adagio theme and, further, the "Joy" theme:

These are taken up again:

---

[18] Beethoven connected this by a numeral to the above statement of the theme. He crossed out the preceding. (TDR, v, 30, n. 1.)

[19] Under this line Beethoven wrote "was ich. . . ."; then follow two words, "ich selbst," in pencil. (TDR, v, 30, n. 2.)

After stating the "Joy" theme, he takes up the following words:

Later comes the memorandum which Beethoven showed Schindler ("Lasst uns das Lied des unsterblichen Schillers singen, Freude, etc.") and then:

The entire Symphony was finished in sketch-form at the end of 1823 and written out in score in February, 1824. Omitting from consideration the theme of the second movement, noted in 1815 and again in 1817 (probably with an entirely different purpose in mind), the time which elapsed between the beginning of the first movement (1817-1818) and the time of completion was about six and a half years. Within this period, however, there were extended interruptions caused by other works. Serious and continuous labor on the Symphony was not taken up until after the completion of the *Missa Solemnis*; it began in 1822, occupied the greater part of 1823 and ended in the early part of 1824. Beethoven, therefore, worked on the Symphony a little more than a year.

The idea of composing music to the Ode, it will be remembered, already existed in 1793 when Professor Fischenich wrote to Charlotte von Schiller; "He [Beethoven] proposes also to compose Schiller's 'Freude,' and indeed strophe by strophe." ---🎵{It is heard of again in a sketchbook of 1798, where there is a melodic phrase adapted to the words, "Muss ein lieber Vater wohnen."[20]}🎵--- In 1808, Beethoven wrote the Fantasy for Piano, Chorus and Orchestra, Op. 80, in which he first essayed the idea of an orchestral beginning (introduced by a solo piano) leading to a concluding section with chorus; and in letters[21] he compared this work to the choral movement of the Ninth Symphony.[22] Amongst sketches for the Eighth Symphony there crops up a

20 *II Beeth.*, p. 479.

21 For instance, to Probst and to Schott, March 10, 1824.

22 The use of the song "Gegenliebe," composed in 1795, in the Choral Fantasy is striking both by its melodic resemblance to the "Joy" theme and by the similarity of treatment: the theme and variations stated first by the instruments, culminating in the statement by the chorus. (TDR, v, 47.)

melody for the beginning of the hymn amongst material used for the Overture, Op. 115, into which he appears at one time to have thought of introducing portions of it.[23] All these sketches, of course, preceded the melody of 1822, conceived for use in a "Sinfonie allemand." When Beethoven first took up the ode for setting it was to become a "durchkomponierte Lied," i.e., each stanza was to have an illustrative setting; when he planned to incorporate it in an overture he proposed to use only selected portions of the poem, for he accompanies the melodic sketch with the note: "Disjointed fragments like Princes are beggars, etc., not the whole"; and a little later: "disjointed fragments from Schiller's Freude connected into a whole."[24]

The questions which have been raised by the choral finale are many and have occupied the minds of musicians, professional and amateur, ever since the great symphony was first given to the world. In 1852 Carl Czerny told Otto Jahn that Beethoven had thought, after the performance, of composing a new finale without vocal parts for the work. Schindler saw the note in Jahn's papers and wrote in the margin: "That is not true"; but it must be remembered that there was a cessation of the great intimacy between Beethoven and Schindler which began not long after the Symphony had been produced, and lasted almost till Beethoven was on his deathbed. Schindler can not have been present at all of the meetings between Beethoven and his friends at which the Symphony was discussed. Nevertheless he is upheld, in a measure, by the fact (to which Nottebohm directed attention) that Beethoven, if he made the remark, either did not mean it to be taken seriously or afterwards changed his mind; for after keeping the manuscript in his hands six months he sent it to the publisher as we have it. Seyfried, writing in *Cäcilia* (Vol. IX, p. 236), faults Beethoven for not having taken the advice of well-meaning friends and written a new finale as he did for the Quartet in B-flat, Op. 130.[25] Even if one of the well-meaning friends was Seyfried himself, the statement has value as evidence that Beethoven was not as convinced as Czerny's story would have it appear that the choral finale was a mistake. Sonnleithner, in a letter to the editor of the *Allgemeine Musikalische Zeitung* in 1864,[26] confirmed Jahn's statement by saying that Czerny had repeatedly related as an unimpeachable fact that some time after the first performance of the Symphony Beethoven, in a circle of his most intimate friends, had expressed himself positively to the effect that he perceived

[23] Beethoven notes "Freude schöner Götterfunken Tochter Overture ausarbeiten" [*ausarbeiten*—to be worked out]. See *Beeth.*, p. 41. (TDR, v, 49, n. 1.)

[24] "Abgerissene Sätze wie Fürsten sind Bettler u.s.w." The phrase is probably a record of Beethoven's imperfect recollection of the line "*Bettler* werden Fürstenbrüder," which appeared in an early version of Schiller's poem where we now read "Alle Menschen werden Brüder." The thought lies near that

it was the early form of the poem, when it was still an "Ode to Freedom" (not "to Joy"), which first aroused enthusiastic admiration for it in Beethoven's mind. In a Conversation Book of 1824 Bernard says to Beethoven: "Instead of 'Beggars become brothers of princes' it reads in your text 'All men become brothers.'" (TDR, v, 49, n. 2.)

[25] Nottebohm (*II Beeth.*, p. 182) guesses that the advice came from Seyfried himself.

[26] April 6, 1864, pp. 245-46. (TDR, v, 65.)

that he had made a mistake [*Misgriff*] in the last movement and intended to reject it and write an instrumental piece in its stead, for which he already had an idea in his head. What that idea was the reader knows. That Beethoven may have had scruples touching the appropriateness of the choral finale, is comprehensible enough in view of the fact that the original plan of the Symphony contemplated an instrumental close and that Beethoven labored so hard to establish arbitrarily an organic union between the Ode and the first three movements; but it is not likely that he gave long thought to the project of writing a new finale.

For the chief facts in the story of the first performance of the D minor Symphony in Vienna we are largely dependent on Schindler, who was not only a witness of it but also an active agent. Beethoven was thoroughly out of sympathy with the musical taste of Vienna, which had been diverted from German ideals by the superficial charm of Rossini's melodies. He wanted much to produce his symphony, but despaired of receiving adequate support or recognition from his home public. His friends offered him encouragement, but his fear and suspicion that his music was no longer understood by the Viennese and he no longer admired, had grown into a deep-rooted conviction. The project of a concert at which the Mass in D should be performed had been mooted months before.

Since 1822, Beethoven had been acquainted with the young singers, Karoline Unger and Henriette Sontag. On September 8 of that year he wrote to his brother Johann, "Two singers visited us today and since they wanted by all means to kiss my hands and were really pretty, I proposed that they kiss my mouth." Judging from the Conversation Books he saw them a good deal in 1823, and they vied with one another in their expressions of devoted veneration for the master. Near the end of 1823, Schindler writes down: "If they do not come, it is merely the fault of jealousy, for Unger told me that she would come alone; but I replied that she should certainly bring Sontag along with her, it would give you twice as much pleasure: now I am curious [to see] whether it will happen."[27] Unger did come alone in December and again in January from which time springs the involvement of these two artists in the first performance of the new symphony. On January 25, 1824, Unger writes:

When are you going to give your concert? When one is *once* possessed by the devil, one can be content.

•~•

On a regular day in Lent, when 3 or 4 take place, would be best.

•~•

If you give the concert, I will guarantee that the house will be full.

Still a moody suspicion, which the lady thinks it her right to rebuke:

[27] Alfred C. Kalischer, *Beethoven und seine Zeitgenossen* (Leipzig, 1910), III, p. 213.

You have too little confidence in yourself. Has not the homage of the whole world given you a little more pride? Who speaks of opposition? Will you not learn to believe that everybody is longing to worship you again in new works? O obstinacy!

In this mood, Beethoven had turned to Count Brühl in Berlin and inquired whether or not a performance of the new Mass and Symphony might be given in that city, and Brühl had favored the plan. When news of this fact became known in Vienna, a number of Beethoven's friends addressed him in the following memorial:

To Herr Ludwig van Beethoven.

Out of the wide circle of reverent admirers surrounding your genius in this your second native city, there approach you today a small number of the disciples and lovers of art to give expression to long-felt wishes, timidly to prefer a long-suppressed request.

But as the number of spokesmen bears but a small proportion to the many who joyfully acknowledge your worth and what you have grown to be to the present as well as the future, so the wishes and requests are by no means restricted to the number of those who are like-minded with themselves and who, in the name of all to whom art and the realization of their ideals are something more than means and objects of pastime, assert that their wish is also the wish of an un-numbered multitude, their request is echoed loudly or in silence by every one whose bosom is animated by a sense of the divine in music.

It is the wish of those of our countrymen who reverence art to which we desire more especially to give expression; for though Beethoven's name and creations belong to all contemporaneous humanity and every country which opens a suscepti-ble bosom to art, it is Austria which is best entitled to claim him as her own. Among her inhabitants appreciation for the great and immortal works which Mozart and Haydn created for all time within the lap of their homes still lives, and they are conscious with joyous pride that the sacred triad in which these names and yours glow as the symbol of the highest within the spiritual realm of tones, sprang from the soil of their fatherland. All the more painful must it have been for you to feel that a foreign power has invaded this royal citadel of the noblest, that above the mounds of the dead and around the dwelling-place of the only survivor of the band, phantoms are leading the dance who can boast of no kinship with the princely spirits of those royal houses; that shallowness is abusing the name and insignia of art, and unworthy dalliance with sacred things is beclouding and dissipating appreciation for the pure and eternally beautiful.

For this reason they feel a greater and livelier sense than ever before that the great need of the present moment is a new impulse directed by a powerful hand, a new advent of the ruler in his domain. It is this need which leads them to you to-day, and following are the petitions which they lay before you in behalf of all to whom these wishes are dear, and in the name of native art.

Do not withhold longer from the popular enjoyment, do not keep longer from the oppressed sense of that which is great and perfect, a performance of the latest masterworks of your hand. We know that a grand sacred composition has been associated with that first one in which you have immortalized the emotions of a soul, penetrated and transfigured by the power of faith and superterrestrial light.

We know that a new flower glows in the garland of your glorious, still unequalled symphonies. For years, ever since the thunders of the Victory at Vittoria ceased to reverberate, we have waited and hoped to see you distribute new gifts from the fulness of your riches to the circle of your friends. Do not longer disappoint the general expectations! Heighten the effect of your newest creations by the joy of becoming first acquainted with them through you! Do not allow these, your latest offspring, some day to appear, perhaps, as foreigners in their place of birth, introduced, perhaps, by persons to whom you and your mind are strange! Appear soon among your friends, your admirers, your venerators! This is our nearest and first prayer.

Other claims on your genius have been made public. The desires expressed and offers made to you more than a year ago by the management of our Court Opera and the Society of Austrian Friends of Music had too long been the unuttered wish of all admirers of art, and your name stimulated the hopes and expectations of too many not to obtain the quickest and widest publicity, not to awaken the most general interest. Poetry has done her share in giving support to these lovely hopes and wishes. Worthy material from the hand of a valued poet waits to be charmed into life by your fancy. Do not let that intimate call to so noble an aim be made in vain. Do not delay longer to lead us back to those departed days when the song of Polyhymnia moved powerfully and delighted the initiates in art and the hearts of the multitude!

Need we tell you with what regret your retirement from public life has filled us? Need we assure you that at a time when all glances were hopefully turned towards you, all perceived with sorrow that *the one* man whom all of us are compelled to acknowledge as foremost among living men in his domain, looked on in silence as foreign art took possession of German soil, the seat of honor of the German muse, while German works gave pleasure only by echoing the favorite tunes of foreigners and, where the most excellent had lived and labored, a second childhood of taste threatens to follow the Golden Age of Art?

You alone are able to insure a decisive victory to the efforts of the best amongst us. From you the native Art Society and the German Opera expect new blossoms, rejuvenated life and a new sovereignty of the true and beautiful over the dominion to which the prevalent spirit of fashion wishes to subject even the eternal laws of art. Bid us hope that the wishes of all who have listened to the sound of your harmonies will soon be fulfilled! This is our most urgent second prayer.

May the year which we have begun not come to an end without rejoicing us with the fruits of our petition and may the coming Spring when it witnesses the unfolding of one of our longed-for gifts become a twofold blooming-time for us and all the world of art!

Vienna, February, 1824.

Prince C. Lichnowsky	Abbé Stadler	Count Czernin, First
Artaria and Co.	von Felsburg, Court Sec.	Chamberlain
v. Hauschka	Count Ferd. von	Count Moritz v. Fries
M. J. Leidesdorf	Stockhammer	J. F. Castelli
J. E. von Wayna	Anton Diabelli	Prof. Deinhardtstein
Andreas Streicher	Count Ferd. v. Palfy	Ch. Kuffner
Anton Halm	Baron Ed. v. Schweiger	J. N. Nehammer, State
		Secretary

Steiner von Felsburg,	Carl Czerny	Dr. L. Sonnleithner
Bank Sequestrator	Count M. v. Lichnowsky	Steiner and Co.
Count M. v. Dietrichstein	v. Zmeskall	Lederer
Ig. Edler von Mosel,	Court Councillor	J. N. Bihler
R.I. Court Councillor	Kiesewetter	

The most active agent in securing signatures was Count Lichnowsky. It was published in Bäuerle's *Theater-Zeitung* and also in Kanne's journal. This publication and gossip to the effect that he had prompted both writing and printing, annoyed Beethoven greatly. He gave vent to his rage in a remark which he himself wrote in a Conversation Book: "Now that the thing has taken this turn I can no longer find joy in it. The atrocity of attributing such an act to me sickens me with the whole business and I am scarcely able to address even a few words to men of such intellectual prominence. Not a single critic can boast of having received a letter from me. I have never—" there his outburst breaks off; he did not finish the sentence in writing. Schindler tried to ease his mind! "Your fears are groundless," he wrote; "your honor has not been compromised—let that suffice you; nobody will accuse you of having been directly concerned in it." Court Secretary von Felsburg and J. N. Bihler, a tutor in the imperial household, waited upon Beethoven one afternoon to present the address, and talk over its suggestions. Beethoven said he wanted to read it when alone. Later Schindler went to him and found him with the letter in his hand. He was manifestly moved by its expressions and handed it to Schindler to read while he went to the window and gazed out for quite a while. Then he returned to Schindler, said briefly: "It is very beautiful!—it rejoices me greatly!" and when Schindler also had expressed his delight added: "Let us go out for a walk." During the walk he remained sunk in thought.[28]

The object had in view by the designers of the memorial was accomplished;—Beethoven was lifted out of his despondent mood and inspired with new determination. By March Schindler had been informed that the concert would be given in Vienna. He lauded Beethoven's decision and begged him not to distress himself with vain imaginings about the outcome—everything would go gloriously and everybody would esteem it an honor to participate. Expressions of satisfaction poured in on the composer from all quarters, and also offers of help. Beethoven's friends gathered together and discussed the details in the liveliest fashion—the time, the place, the programme, the choir and orchestra, who should sing the solos, the copying of the music in which Beethoven laid great stress on the supervision of the parts, the price of seats, the number of rehearsals. The concert season was drawing to a close and delay was hazardous; but delay there was, for Beethoven was vacillating, full of doubtings and suspicions, and there was a too great multiplicity of counsellors. Schindler was kept extremely busy; Lichnowsky and Schuppanzigh bestirred themselves mightily; brother

[28] *Biogr.*, II, p. 64.

Johann came to the fore with advice and suggestions, especially about the business administration; nephew Karl, much to Schindler's dissatisfaction, not only ran errands but volunteered his opinion on many topics. A page from a Conversation Book will disclose how the consultations with Beethoven were carried on—for Beethoven's consent to every step had to be obtained, which was a pity. In the following excerpt it is Schuppanzigh who is speaking to the composer, whom he, as was his wont, addresses in the third person—as was fitting to the dignity of "Mylord Falstaff."

How about his concert?

It is getting late, Lent will not last much longer.

He ought to give three movements [the Mass is meant, of course].

Under no circumstances a piano piece.

There are no piano players here.

He will need Buringer [Piringer] to provide the best dilettante, Sonnleithner to look after the singers, and Plachetka [Blahetka] for the announcements and bills.

He has offered himself.

Young Sonnleithner has all the amateur singers under his thumb.

Sonnleithner knows them too and understands it.

It would be a good idea *for him* [Beethoven] *to pay a visit to Duport to talk to him once more about me.*

The significance of the concluding remark will appear later. At another time Karl is reporting progress:

Piringer has said that he would undertake the appointment of the instrumentalists. Sonnleithner the chorus. Schuppanzigh the orchestra. Blahetka the announcements, tickets, etc. So everything is looked after. You can give two concerts. . . .

When will you have it announced?

Schuppanzigh is coming tomorrow. . . .

Blahetka offered to stamp the tickets, etc., but I think that all such matters ought to be [entrusted] to your brother. It would be safer. . . .

⁘

Piringer has enough to do with the choruses.

⁘

Piringer is a very capable man but not the man that Schuppanzigh is; in any event it would be unjust to disregard S., as he has taken so much pains and spurred on the others.

At first it was agreed that the place should be the Theater-an-der-Wien. The director, Count Palffy, who had signed the memorial, was willing to provide the theatre and all the forces, vocal as well as instrumental, for 1200 florins, let Beethoven have as many rehearsals as he desired and fix the prices of admission. But a difficulty presented itself at once. At the Theater-an-der-Wien Seyfried was kapellmeister and Clement leader of the orchestra. Beethoven wanted Umlauf to be general conductor of the concert and Schuppanzigh leader of the orchestra. Count Palffy was willing to sacrifice Seyfried, but not Clement—at least, he asked that if Clement was to be displaced it be done with as little injury to his feelings as possible. He therefore suggested that Beethoven write a letter of explanation to Clement, which he felt sure would solve the difficulty. Meanwhile Schindler had begun negotiations with Duport, director of the Kärnthnerthor Theatre. Duport was favorably inclined towards the enterprise and also towards Schuppanzigh; but troublesome questions of another kind were now precipitated— questions about prices of admission, the solo singers and the number of rehearsals. On all these points Beethoven was so irresolute that the project seemed likely to fall by the wayside; in which crisis the leading spirits thought themselves entitled to resort to a stratagem to give stability to the wavering mind of Beethoven. In at least one instance the Conversation Book record was given the appearance of a formal journal of proceedings. It was now planned that Lichnowsky, Schindler and Schuppanzigh should simultaneously call upon Beethoven as if by accident, turn the conversation on the points on which it was necessary for Beethoven to reach a decision and that his utterances should then be put into writing and he be asked, half in jest, half in earnest, to affix his signature to the document. The ruse succeeded for the nonce, but after the conspirators had gone away, Beethoven saw through the trick which had been played on him, and scenting treachery as was his wont, decided off-hand to abandon the concert. He issued his pronunciamento to the three friends in this characteristic fashion:

To Count Moritz Lichnowsky.
I despise treachery—
Do not visit me any more. There will be no concert—

To Herr Schuppanzigh.
Let him not visit me more. I shall give no concert.

To Schindler.
I request you not to come again until I send for you. There will be no concert.

The three friends refused to take umbrage at Beethoven's rudeness; the notes were not accompanied by a silken rope; they gave him time to get over his wrath and suspicion and then went on with the preparations for the concert. In the Conversation Book there appears a record of consultation which was opened formally by Schindler as follows:

Present:
    Mr. L. van Beethoven, a *musikus.*
    Mr. Count v. Lichnowsky, an amateur.
    Mr. Schindler, a fiddler.
Not yet present today:
    Mr. Schuppanzigh, a fiddler representing Mylord Fallstaff.

At this consultation Schindler reported an offer from Palffy to furnish the Theater-an-der-Wien, orchestra, lights, etc., *appertinenta* for 1000 florins, provided a second or third concert be given. At a moderate charge for admission (which would be necessary) he said the receipts would be 4000 florins, which would yield a profit of 2000 florins at the first concert and about 3000 at the second, when there would be no copying charges. The prices would not be so high as at the Redoutensaal. If Duport were to charge only 300 florins, there would still be a further charge of 300 florins for building the platform. Palffy wanted only his expenses. Would Beethoven authorize him [Schindler] and Lichnowsky to complete arrangements with Palffy? He need not be paid, and it would be possible to withdraw from the arrangement at any time. Haste was necessary, for a supervisor must be appointed— Umlauf or somebody else—so that rehearsals might begin. If Schuppanzigh were given too much to do and anything went ill, the conductor would lay the blame on insufficient study. From the record of a subsequent consultation (in March) the following excerpts are made:

> *Lichnowsky*: It is right that the orchestra be doubled, but superfluous to engage more than are necessary; after Schuppanzigh and Umlauf know what is at their service at the Wiedener Theatre we can tell what is needed.
> *Schindler*: Lichnowsky says that a smaller orchestra is more effective at the Theater-an-der-Wien than a large one in the Redoutensaal.
>
> ·~·
>
> You need not take all at the Theater-an-der-Wien, none at all if you do not need them, that is the arrangement with Palffy.
> *Lichnowsky*: Unnecessary expenses must be avoided.
> *Schindler*: You will not have to pay the forces at the Theater-an-der-Wien at all—so that may be deducted.

·~·

The days of performance if agreeable to you would be the 22nd or 23rd or 24th of this month.

Lichnowsky: You will make money, and more if you give a second concert, for which you write a new duet. In the second concert when it will not be necessary that all the pieces be *new*, you will have the same symphony and two other Mass movements.

Schindler: The prices of admission will be considerably modified at 2 florins for the parterre, 2 florins for the gallery and 3 florins for the seats.

•～•

You ought not to seek difficulties where there are none; if the worst comes to the worst, everything will be settled.

•～•

I shall see Schuppanzigh today at noon; but before then Lichnowsky will go to Palffy tentatively to report your decision.

•～•

The conversation continued (probably the next day):

Schindler: Schuppanzigh is greatly pleased that you have come to an understanding with Palffy. He will make use of the entire orchestra of the theatre. He is coming to the Redoutensaal today, as he hopes to find you there.

•～•

The choruses at the theatre are also good; Schupp. says that the women's choir of the society is not of the best because they are all young girls; which is true. . . .

•～•

The Baron[29] took the tempo just once again as fast, therefore your advice was highly important; not until the second time did it go well.

•～•

Besides, the women's choir is thoroughly bad. Falstaff was also convinced and is now glad that nothing but the men's choir will be needed.

•～•

The solo voices are much too weak for the room and too young

•～•

The soprano singer is sixteen years old at the most.

•～•

[29] Baron Eduard von Lannoy, one of the directors of the concerts by the Gesellschaft der Musikfreunde which took place in the Redoutensaal. (TDR, v, 76, n. 2.) On April 4 he conducted a concert with the following program: Haydn, Symphony in D; Paër, So-prano aria from *Griselda*; B. Romberg, First movement of Violoncello Concerto in G; Beethoven, *Opferlied* [3rd version]; Caraffa, Overture to *Le solitaire*; Mozart, Hymn "Preis dir, Gottheit, durch alle Himmel."

Palffy is sending you word through Prince Lichnowsky that he will send you his offer, which you already know, and the promise which he made, to-morrow in writing.

•~•

You are choosing the lesser of two evils.

•~•

Twenty to twenty-four for each part in the chorus are already on hand.

•~•

Of the twelve violins for each part we today selected the six best, who are to be arranged in rank and file.

•~•

The only wish that Palffy has, as he admitted to Lichnowsky today, is that Clement be handled as gently as possible so that his feelings may not be hurt. For this reason we all request you to write a billet to Clement and tell the truth as it is.

•~•

But as there is no question but that he will come to the second concert, I suggest that the direction be then given to him. Schuppanzigh is agreed to this.

•~•

And as Piringer of the Theater-an-der-Wien asserts that as a high R.I. offi-cial he cannot take part, Clement might take first place among the second violins at the first concert and Schuppanzigh at the second.

•~•

Palffy certainly does not want you to take Clement, but only to take the trouble to write him a billet and tell him about the matter. He will certainly be agreeable.

•~•

He [Schuppanzigh] has become much quieter and more *commode* since he was in Russia, for his paunch is already beginning to embarrass him.

•~•

Böhm will play first violin.

•~•

Piringer will not play at the An-der-Wien, which is all one to Schuppanzigh.

But matters were not so easily arranged with Clement as Schindler had imagined. He did not want to be deprived of the honor of playing at the concert, the orchestra of the Theater-an-der-Wien sided with him and declared that it would not play under Schuppanzigh. Schindler appealed to Count Palffy, who knew that though you can lead a horse to water you cannot make him drink. He said that he could command the men to play under Schuppanzigh, but he did not want to be answerable for the mischief which would result. Schindler advised Beethoven that if Palffy stood by Clement the contract for the Kärnthnerthor Theatre be closed with Duport. Up to late in April it was as good as settled that the concert would be given at the Theater-an-der-Wien, though Beethoven's fatal indecision left the point uncertain. With negotiations pending with both theatres, the Redoutensaal came up for consideration, and finally (it would seem as a consequence of advice by the Steiner firm), also a fourth locale. This was the Landständischer Saal, a small room in which the *Concerts Spirituels* took place. Lichnowsky, when he heard that Beethoven was considering such a step, hurried to him with representations that if the hall were taken there would be trouble with Palffy and he himself humiliated and embarrassed, since he had come to an agreement with the manager in his name. He as well as Schindler was sorely tried by the new turn of affairs and represented to Beethoven that the room was too small, holding only 500 persons, and that the court would not go there. But nephew Karl favored the hall because its choice would avoid the difficulties incident to the selection of either of the theatres. Lichnowsky and Schindler did not seek to hide their displeasure from Beethoven because of his willingness to take the advice of others (meaning, no doubt, brother Johann, nephew Karl and Steiner), in preference to theirs, but at length circumstances compelled him to abandon all other plans and agree to take the Kärnthnerthor Theatre. He considered the noon hour as the time for the concert, but Johann told him that an evening concert was worth 1500 florins more than one given in the daytime; he clung to the Landständischer Saal, but Schindler told him that on the day which had been fixed upon there was to be a concert at the Redoutensaal in which Sontag, Unger and the Italian singers would take part. "The girls" would therefore be unavailable for his concert and the court would, of course, go to the fashionable place and affair. As late as April 21, it was publicly announced that the concert would be given in the Theater-an-der-Wien, but at length Beethoven made up his mind, and Schindler was empowered to close with Duport for the Kärnthnerthor Theatre. Palffy yielded to the composer's wishes, but regretfully, saying that he would rather lose 1000 florins than the honor of having the concert in his house. It would seem as if it was the cabal in the orchestra against Schuppanzigh which ended Beethoven's irresolution. Beethoven now decided to take the Court theatre for 400 florins, chorus and orchestra being included as well as the lighting, with the privilege of one or two repetitions on the same terms in eight or ten days. In the letter of April 24 which Schindler sent to Duport, were named Sontag (soprano), Unger (alto), and Preisinger (bass) as solo singers, Umlauf and Schuppanzigh as leaders, the orchestra and chorus were to be augmented from the amateur forces of the Gesellschaft der Musikfreunde. There were to be 24 violins, 10 violas, 12 contrabasses and violoncellos, and the number of wind-instruments was to be doubled, for which reason room would have to be provided for the orchestra on the stage. Duport was requested to fix the date not later than

May 3rd or 4th and was informed that the reason why the agreement with Count Palffy had been cancelled was that the Theater-an-der-Wien was lacking in capable solo singers and that Palffy wanted Clement to lead the orchestra, whereas Beethoven had long before selected Schuppanzigh for the post. With a change of date to May 7 this arrangement was formally confirmed.

But many details remained to be settled, the most vexatious to Beethoven being the prices of admission. Beethoven wanted an advance on the regular tariff. Duport appealed to the Minister of Police, but permission to raise the prices was refused. In the selection of solo singers Therese Grünbaum had been considered, but she was eventually set aside in favor of Henriette Sontag, for whom Beethoven had a personal admiration (he could not know much, if anything, about her voice and art). Jäger had been suggested for the tenor part, but Anton Haitzinger was chosen because, in a spirit of professional courtesy, Jäger refused to take a part away from a Kärnthnerthor singer. Forti and Preisinger were rival candidates for the solo bass parts. The latter was considered the more musical of the two and better fitted for Beethoven's music, and was therefore selected. He took part in the rehearsals, and for him Beethoven made a change in the music of the recitative in the Symphony (Schindler gives it in his biography);[30] but at the last the *tessitura* of the part was found to be too high for him and Preisinger had to withdraw. It was impossible under the circumstances now to appeal to Forti, and the part was entrusted to Seipelt of the company at the Theater-an-der-Wien.

It was originally intended that the programme should consist of the new Overture (Op. 124), the Mass in D and the new Symphony; but realizing that this would make the concert unduly long Beethoven first decided to omit the *Gloria* of the mass, and after the rehearsals had already begun he curtailed the list still more by eliding the *Sanctus*. The large amount of copying involved was done by a staff of men some of whom worked, apparently, under the supervision of the widow of Schlemmer, Beethoven's favorite copyist who had died the year before. The composer angrily rejected Haslinger's suggestion that the chorus parts be engraved, but consented to have them duplicated by lithographic process. The church authorities were opposed to the performance of missal music in a theatre and the censor therefore withheld his approval of the programme. So, in April, at the suggestion of Schindler, Beethoven wrote a letter to the censor, Sartorius, in which he pleaded for his consent to the performance on the ground that he was giving the concert by request, had involved himself in costs by reason of the copying, there was no time in which to produce other novelties, and if consent were refused he would be compelled to abandon the concert and all his expenditures would have been in vain. The three ecclesiastical pieces which were to be performed were to be listed on the programme as hymns.

[30] II, pp. 77-8.

The letter failed of its mission; not until an appeal was made to Count Sedlnitzky, the Police President, through the agency of Count Lichnowsky, was the performance sanctioned.

The rehearsals were now in progress. Dirzka[31] was making good headway with the choruses and was satisfied; Schuppanzigh was holding rehearsals for the strings in the rehearsal-room of the Ridotto; the solo singers were studying under the supervision of Beethoven, sometimes in his lodgings, Umlauf assisting. Accustomed to Rossini's music, the principal singers found it difficult to assimilate the Beethovenian manner, especially as it is exemplified in the concluding movement of the symphony. They pleaded with the composer for changes which would lighten their labors, but he was adamant. Unger called him a "tyrant over all the vocal organs" to his face, but when he still refused to grant her petitions she turned to Sontag and said: "Well, then we must go on torturing ourselves in the name of God!"[32] The choirmaster requested that the passage in the fugue of the *Credo* where the sopranos enter on B-flat *in alt* be altered, because none of the singers could reach the note; but though Umlauf reinforced that argument, a refusal was the only reply. In only one alteration did Beethoven acquiesce;—he changed the concluding passage of the bass recitative, because Preisinger could not sing the high F-sharp; but Preisinger did not sing at all at the concert. The consequences of his obduracy were not realized by Beethoven at the concert, for though he stood among the performers and indicated the tempo at the beginning of each movement he could not hear the music except with his mental ear. The obvious thing happened;—the singers who could not reach the high tones simply omitted them. Duport had allowed two full rehearsals. There was to have been a third, but it was prevented by a rehearsal for a ballet. At the final meeting on May 6, Beethoven was "dissolved in devotion and emotion" at the performance of the *Kyrie*, and after the Symphony stationed himself at the door and embraced all the amateurs who had taken part.[33] The official announcement of the concert read as follows:

GRAND
MUSICAL CONCERT
by
HERR L. v. BEETHOVEN
which will take place
To-morrow, May 7, 1824
in the R. I. Court Theatre beside the Kärnthnerthor.

The musical pieces to be performed are the latest works of Herr Ludwig van Beethoven.

[31] Choral Director of the Kärthnerthor Theatre.

[32] See Schindler, *Biogr.*, ii, p. 76. (TDR, v, 89, n. 1.)

[33] The statement about the *Kyrie* was made by Holz to Jahn; that about the Symphony, by Fuchs. (TK, III, 164, n. 1.)

First: A Grand Overture

Second: Three Grand Hymns with Solo and Chorus Voices.

Third: A Grand Symphony with Solo and Chorus Voices entering in the finale on Schiller's Ode to Joy.

The solos will be performed by the Demoiselles Sontag and Unger and the Herren Haizinger and Seipelt. Herr Schuppanzigh has undertaken the direction of the orchestra, Herr Kapellmeister Umlauf the direction of the whole and the Music Society the augmentation of the chorus and orchestra as a favor.

Herr Ludwig van Beethoven will himself participate in the general direction.

Prices of admission as usual.

Beginning at 7 o'clock in the evening.

The overture was that to the *Weihe des Hauses*; the hymns were the *Kyrie*, *Credo*, and *Agnus Dei* from the Mass in D. Duport had a hand in the drafting of the announcement and wanted to include in it the statement that Beethoven would conduct with Umlauf. In a Conversation Book Schindler reported the fact to Beethoven and added:

I did not know what to reply and so it was omitted this time.

•~•

You *could* surely conduct the overture alone.

•~•

It would put too severe a strain upon your ears and for that reason I would not advise you to conduct the whole.

The theatre was crowded in every part except the imperial box; that was empty. Beethoven had gone in person, accompanied by Schindler, to invite the Imperial Family, and some of its members promised to attend; but the Emperor and Empress had left Vienna a few days before and Archduke Rudolph, who had naturally displayed interest in the affair, was in Olmütz. But we hear of several of Beethoven's present and former friends seated in various parts of the house;—poor, bedridden Zmeskall was carried to his seat in a sedan chair. Some of the foremost musicians of Vienna were in the band—Mayseder, Böhm, Jansa, Linke etc. The performance was far from perfect. There was lack of a homogeneous power, a paucity of nuance, a poor distribution of lights and shades. Nevertheless, strange as the music must have sounded to the audience, the impression which it made was profound and the applause which it elicited enthusiastic to a degree.[34] At one point in the Scherzo, presumably at the startling entry of the tympani at the *ritmo di tre battute*, the listeners could scarcely restrain themselves, and it seemed as if a repetition then and there would be insisted upon. To this

[34] From the review in the Lpz. *AMZ* (July 1, 1824), Vol. 26, p. 438.

Beethoven, no doubt engrossed by the music which he was following in his mind, was oblivious. Either after the Scherzo or at the end of the Symphony, while Beethoven was still gazing at his score, Fräulein Unger, whose happiness can be imagined, plucked him by the sleeve and directed his attention to the clapping hands and waving hats and handkerchiefs. Then he turned to the audience and bowed. The incident is variously related. Schindler and Fräulein Unger (the latter of whom related it to George Grove in London in 1869) say that it took place at the end of the concert. Thalberg, the pianist, who was present, says that it was after the Scherzo. A note among Thayer's papers reads: "November 28, 1860. I saw Thalberg in Paris. He told me as follows: He was present at Beethoven's concert in the Kärthnerthor Theatre 1824. Beethoven was dressed in black dress-coat, white neckerchief, and waistcoat, black satin small-clothes, black silk stockings, shoes with buckles. He saw after the Scherzo of the 9th Symphony how B. stood turning over the leaves of his score utterly deaf to the immense applause, and Unger pulled him by the sleeve, and then pointed to the audience when he turned and bowed. Umlauf told the choir and orchestra to pay no attention whatever to Beethoven's beating of the time but all to watch him. Conradin Kreutzer was at the P.F."

Did Thalberg describe Beethoven's dress correctly? Evidently not. In a conversation just before the concert Schindler writes: "We will take everything with us now; also take your green coat, which you can put on when you conduct. The theatre will be dark and no one will notice it. . . . Oh, great master, you do not own a black frock coat! The green one will have to do; in a few days the black one will be ready."

After the concert Beethoven's friends, as was natural, came together to exchange comments and felicitate him. From Schindler Beethoven received a report which is preserved in the Conversation Book. It gives us a glimpse of his own joy and the composer's happy pride in having been more enthusiastically greeted than the court:

Never in my life did I hear such frenetic and yet cordial applause.

·~·

Once the second movement of the Symphony was completely interrupted by applause.

·~·

and there was a demand for a repetition.

·~·

The reception was more than imperial

·~·

for the people burst out in a storm four times. At the last there were cries of Vivat!

·~·

The wind instruments did very bravely

•〜•

not the slightest disturbance could be heard.

•〜•

When the parterre broke out in applauding cries the 5th time the Police Commissioner yelled Silence!

•〜•

The court only 3 successive times but Beethoven 5 times.

•〜•

My triumph is now attained; for now I can speak from my heart. Yesterday I still feared secretly that the Mass would be prohibited because I heard that the Archbishop had protested against it. After all I was right in at first not saying anything to the Police Commissioner. By God, it would have happened!

•〜•

He surely never has been in the Court Theatre. Well, Pax tecum!

Joseph Hüttenbrenner went with Schindler when he escorted the composer to his lodgings. On the following day Schindler wrote in the Conversation Book:

The whole audience was impressed, crushed by the greatness of your work.

•〜•

In Paris and London the concert would certainly have yielded from 12 to 15 thousand florins; here it may be as many hundreds.

•〜•

After yesterday you must now too plainly see that you are trampling upon your own interests by remaining longer within these walls. In short, I have no words to express my feelings at the wrong which you are doing yourself.[35]

•〜•

When Karl comes home at noon, be so good as to instruct him [to come] after his lectures, this at five o'clock, to the box-office where I will be waiting for him. The box-office will be opened in his presence and he will receive the money.[36]

•〜•

Then I will fetch him at the university at 5 o'clock.

•〜•

Have you recovered from yesterday's exertions?

---

[35] Schindler is referring to a new invitation to Beethoven from Charles Neate to visit London (*Biogr.*, II, p. 89), which is discussed further in the next chapter.

[36] These excerpts prove that in his biography, Schindler's story of showing Beethoven the box-office report the evening of the concert must be false. (TK, III, 168.)

The financial results of the concert fell far short of Beethoven's expectations. The gross receipts were 2200 florins in the depreciated Vienna money, of which only 420 florins remained after paying the cost of administration and copying; and against this pitiful sum some petty expenses were still chargeable. Beethoven was not only disappointed; he was chagrined and thrown into a fuming ill-humor. He invited Schindler, Umlauf and Schuppanzigh to dine with him at the restaurant "Zum wilden Mann" in the Prater. The composer came with his nephew; "his brow was clouded, his words were cold, peevish, captious," says Schindler. He had ordered an "opulent" meal, but no sooner had the party sat down to the table than the "explosion which was imminent" came. In plainest terms he burst out with the charge that the management and Schindler had cheated him. Umlauf and Schuppanzigh tried to convince him that that was impossible, as every penny had passed through the hands of the two theatre cashiers, whose accounts tallied, and that though it was contrary to custom, his nephew had acted in behalf of his brother as comptroller. Beethoven persisted in his accusation, saying that he had his information from an entirely credible source. Thereupon Schindler and Umlauf abruptly left the room. Schuppanzigh remained behind just long enough to get a few stripes on his broad back and then joined his companions in misery. Together they finished their meal at a restaurant in the Leopoldstadt.[37]

It is more than likely that Beethoven's "credible" informant was his brother Johann. He was jealous of Schindler's participation in the composer's business affairs and probably took advantage of a favorable opportunity to strengthen Beethoven's chronic suspicion and growing distrust of what the composer himself looked upon as Schindler's officiousness. In the Conversation Book used at the meeting after the concert, Karl tells his uncle: "Schindler knows from an ear-witness that your brother said in the presence of several persons that he was only waiting for the concert to be over before driving S. out of the house."

Before the second concert Schindler received a letter which on its face shows that he had written Beethoven defending himself against the charges made. Beethoven's letter was as follows:

I do not accuse you of any wrongdoing in connection with the concert, but unwisdom and arbitrary actions have spoiled many things, besides I have a certain fear lest some great misfortune shall some time happen to me through you— Clogged drains often open suddenly, and that day in the Prater I thought you were offensive in several ways—Moreover, there are many times when I would rather try to repay the services which you perform for me with a little gift rather than with a *meal*; for I admit that often you disturb me very much. If you do not see a pleasant face you say at once: "Bad weather again today," for being commonplace yourself how can you help misunderstanding that which is not commonplace? In short I love my independence too much. There will be

[37] Schindler, *Biogr.*, II, p. 88. (TDR, V, 94.)

no lack of opportunities to invite you, but it is impossible to do so continually, inasmuch as thereby all my affairs are disarranged—Duport has consented to next Tuesday for the concert; for the Landständischen Saal, which I might have had for tomorrow evening, he again refuses to let me have the singers; he has also again turned to the police. Therefore please go there with the bill and learn if there is any objection to the second time—I would never have accepted the favors done me gratis and I will not in the future. As for friendship that is a difficult thing in your case; in no event would I like to entrust my welfare to you since you lack judgement and act arbitrarily, and I learned some time ago to know you from a side which is *not to your credit*; and so *did others*—I must confess that the purity of my character does not permit me to recompense mere favors with friendship, although I am ready willingly to serve your welfare—

B

A second concert had been contemplated from the outset, or at least since the opening of negotiations with Palffy. Schindler says[38] that Duport offered to pay all expenses and guarantee 500 florins Convention Money (1200 florins Vienna Standard) with the understanding that the profits should be divided equally between Beethoven and the exchequer of the theatre. But he wanted a change made in the programme. To this change, obviously designed as a concession to the popular taste, Beethoven seems to have given his consent. The concert took place on Sunday, May 23rd, at midday—half-past twelve o'clock, with the following program:

First: A Grand Overture [Op. 124]
Second: A new Terzetto, composed by Herr Ludwig van Beethoven, sung by
  Mad. Dardanelli, Herren Donzelli and Botticelli. ["Tremate, empi, tremate"]
Third: A Grand Hymn, sung by Dlles. Sontag, Unger, Herren Haizinger, Sei-
  pelt and assembled chorus. [Kyrie from the Mass in D]
Fourth: Aria, "Di tanti palpiti," sung by Herr David. [from Rossini's *Tan-
  credi*][39]
Fifth: A Grand Symphony with Solo and Chorus Voices entering in the
  Finale on Schiller's Ode to Joy.

The delightful weather lured the people into the open air, the house was not half full and there was, in consequence, a deficit of 800 florins. Nor was the popular demonstration of enthusiasm over the music as great as at the first concert, and Beethoven, who had not favored the repetition, was so disheartened that he was with difficulty persuaded to accept the 500 florins which Duport had guaranteed to him. He was also vexed to find his old trio, "Tremati, empi tremate," announced as a novelty (it was composed more than twenty years before, and had been performed in 1814), and so was Tobias Haslinger, who had bought but had not published it. Moreover,

---

[38] *Ibid.*, p. 73. (TDR, v, 96.)
[39] According to Schindler (*ibid.*, p. 74), this was transposed a few tones higher and sung almost throughout in a falsetto voice. Schindler says that Sontag also sang her favorite *aria di bravura* by Mercadante, but of this number there is no mention in the *affiche*. Schindler concludes: "This parody of the festive instance (the first concert) our master luckily did not hear." (Cf. TDR, v, 97.)

Haslinger had been overlooked in the distribution of complimentary tickets. Beethoven had to apologize to him for the oversight, which he protested was due to an inadvertence, and also to explain that the announcement of the trio as a new work was of Duport's doing, not his.

Meanwhile a copy of the Symphony was sent to the London Philharmonic Society, through Kirchhoffer; the date may be determined by Beethoven's receipt of £50 from Kirchhoffer "for my symphony delivered to him for the Philharmonic Society in London," dated April 27, 1824.[40]

One outcome of the concerts of May was the appearance of a new portrait of Beethoven. It was a lithographic reproduction of a crayon drawing made by Stephen Decker and was printed as a supplement to the *Wiener Allgemeine Musikalische Zeitung* edited by F. A. Kanne, on June 5, 1824. In this and two subsequent numbers of the journal (June 9 and 16) Kanne reviewed the concerts with discriminating appreciation, ending with an enthusiastic encomium of the composer. In 1827 Steinmüller made a plate of Decker's drawing for Artaria. Schindler and Frimmel agree in saying that the well-known portrait by Kriehuber is an imitation of Decker's drawing, which was made, as Kanne's journal stated, "a few days after his great concert in May, 1824."[41]

During the preparations for the concerts, thought was also given to the usual summer sojourn, and various places—Grinzing, Heiligenstadt, Penzing, Breitensee, Hietzing, Hetzendorf—were canvassed in consultation with Beethoven by his friends. His brother had again offered him a home on his estate and it was expected that Count Brunsvik would come for the concert and take Beethoven back with him to Hungary. In all of the excursions which were made in the vicinity of Schönbrunn in search of a summer home, Schindler accompanied the composer to see, to advise, to negotiate. The choice fell upon Penzing, where an apartment was found in the first story of the house numbered 43 belonging to a tailor in Vienna named Johann Hörr, who was rejoiced to have so distinguished a tenant. Beethoven took it for the summer beginning on May 1, for a rental of 180 florins, C.M. The lodgings were in all things adapted to his needs and Beethoven, entirely satisfied, moved into them soon after the second concert. An old couple lived in the parterre, but otherwise he was the only tenant of the house. But the house lay close to a footbridge over the little stream called the Wien Fluss and people crossing it frequently stopped to gaze into his rooms. He could have saved himself the annoyance by drawing the curtains, but instead he flew into a rage, quarreled with his landlord, against whom he recorded his anger by scrawling the epithet "Schurke" (rogue, wretch, scoundrel, etc.) under his name on the receipt, and removing to Baden (Gutenbrunn).

---

[40] The original is in the British Museum (Add. MS 33965, p. 174); it was first published by D. W. MacArdle, "Four Unfamiliar Beethoven Documents," *Music and Letters,* xxxvi (1955), p. 337.

[41] See Theodor Frimmel, *Beethoven in Zeitgenössischen Bildnis* (Vienna, 1923), pp. 57-8.

—◆◆{The move had taken place by May 27 on which date he wrote from Baden to the Steiner firm requesting some music paper.[42]}◆◆— He stayed there on and off until November; thus he was again paying rent for three lodgings at the same time.

The matter of the subscriptions for the Mass being disposed of (except so far as the deliveries of some of the scores was concerned), and the Symphony completed, Beethoven now had time, while getting ready for their performance, to think also of their publication. On February 5, 1823, Beethoven had assured Ries that the Philharmonic Society could keep the symphony for eighteen months before he would publish it; on January 15, 1825, he wrote Charles Neate assuring him that a year would elapse between the time the society had received the score and its publication. When Beethoven took up the matter of publication again he ignored Simrock, Peters and the Vienna publishers and turned to Schlesinger, Schott and Sons of Mainz and H. A. Probst of Leipzig.

—◆◆{On February 25 Beethoven offered to Moritz Schlesinger in Paris the Mass for 1000 fl. C.M., the Overture (Op. 124) for 50 gold ducats and the Symphony, not to be published until 1825, for 600 fl. C.M., and some new quartets later on.[43]

On the same day, in answer to a letter from Probst, he made an offer of some smaller works to test the publisher's interest with the assurance that if he were prompt he would offer larger works.[44] Probst received the letter on March 1 and answered at once.}◆◆— On March 10 Beethoven offered the Mass and the Symphony for the same prices that he had set for Schlesinger with the added stipulation that in recompense for the necessary delay in the publication of the latter he might have the piano arrangement gratis. Only a portion of this letter has been preserved, but the contents of the lost fragments can be gathered from Probst's answer under date March 22, in which he promised to deposit at once with Joseph Loidl and Co. one hundred imperial ducats to Beethoven's account, to be paid over on delivery of three songs with pianoforte accompaniment (two of them to have parts for other instruments, the third to be an arietta), six bagatelles for pianoforte solo, and a grand overture with pianoforte arrangement for two and four hands. What these works were may easily be guessed. After this business had been arranged to the satisfaction of both parties, Probst said, he would communicate his decision respecting the Mass. Beethoven wrote in July explaining his delay on the score that the compositions "had just been finished" but were now ready for delivery at any moment to Herr Loidl, to whom he requested that the money be sent. On August 10 Beethoven received word that the 100 ducats had already been sent to Loidl and Co. in Vienna. A letter written by Beethoven at this time has been lost, but a portion of its contents can be deduced from Probst's reply a week later—August 16. The Leipzig pub-

[42] See A 1293. [43] See A 1267. de Beethoven," *Revue de Musicologie*, VI
[44] See Charles Bouret, "Une lettre inédite (1922), pp. 13ff. Also A 1266.

{ 914 }

lisher admitted that his action in depositing the money to be delivered in exchange for the manuscript had been due to reports which had reached him concerning difficulties which another publisher had had with the composer. In purchasing manuscripts without examination he was departing from his established rule of action and he trusted to the admiration which he felt for the composer's genius that the latter had set aside works of excellence for him. He would gladly have published the Symphony, but was deterred by the danger of piracy which was peculiarly great in Austria. He promised a speedy and handsome publication of the works purchased.

The other publisher mentioned by Probst was probably Peters, for in a letter dated August 28 Beethoven promised Probst he would write soon to explain his dealings with "Herr Peters." He announced that he had sold the Mass to another publisher and that he had received an advance on the symphony, but that if Probst made up his mind quickly on the latter this other publisher might be persuaded to receive other works for this sum. The last known letter to Probst, which is one of the new letters printed by Miss Anderson,[45] is dated January 26, 1825. The smaller works, for which Probst had deposited the 100 ducats, belonged in reality to his brother, he wrote, as a security against a sum of money advanced to him. Beethoven gave two reasons why negotiations with Probst had come to grief; first, his brother was angry "that you wanted to have all the works tried out before you would pay for them"; and second, his brother had found better offers from other publishers. The only hope that Beethoven could hold out was the possibility of Probst's receiving some string quartets. Once again dealings with a Leipzig publisher had come to nothing.

Beethoven meanwhile had been approached by Schott and Sons or by the editor, Gottfried Weber, of their journal *Cäcilia* to find a Viennese correspondent for their magazine, of which they were going to send a copy. This was before March 10, 1824, for on that date Beethoven answered as follows:—

Dear Sir!

I beg of you most respectfully to give my thanks to the E[ditoria]l S[taf]f of the C[äcili]a[46] for their attention. As for my unimportant self, how gladly would I serve them, were it not that I feel the greater calling compelling me to make myself known to the world through composition. However, I have given instructions to discover a reliable correspondent for you (which is very difficult here because of partisan feeling). If I find something noteworthy about myself (but oh heavens how difficult that is), I will be glad to have it communicated through this person; and, if you specifically require it and my almost incessant affairs allow, I will also make a communication myself—

As for my works for which you have made request, I offer you the following, but your decision must not be long in the making—a new grand solemn mass with solo voices and chorus parts and full orchestra. Difficult as it is to speak

---

[45] *A* 1347.

[46] The German "R—n der C——a" stands

undoubtedly for "Redaktion der Cäcilia" ("editorial staff of the Cäcilia").

of myself, still I consider it my greatest work; the honorarium would be 1000 fl. C.M.: a new grand symphony, which closes with a finale (like my fantasy with chorus but much bigger and more extended) with vocal parts for solos and choruses with words from Schiller's immortal, famous song "An die Freude." The honorarium is 600 fl. C.M. A new quartet for 2 violins, viola and violoncello, the honorarium 50 ducats in gold.—[47]

These matters are presented in accordance with your wishes. As the result of this report, do not judge me as commercially-minded; but as a true artist I cannot disdain competition, through it rather I am in a firm position to work faithfully for my muse and am able to provide in a noble way for many other people— Your answer concerning the works indicated would have to be made very soon.

Yours very truly

Beethoven

In an answer of March 24, the firm accepted the offer of the Quartet at once, but asked either a reduction of the fees for the Symphony and Mass, or permission to pay the money in installments at intervals of six months. Subsequently the firm offered to provide a guaranty for the deferred payments and to consider any proposition which Beethoven had to make. The two letters, dated respectively March 24 and April 10, remaining unanswered, Schott and Sons again wrote on April 19 and still again on April 27, introducing with the former letter Christian Rummel, Kapellmeister of the Duke of Nassau, and asking a contribution to *Cäcilia* in the latter. On May 20, in the midst of his preparations for the second concert, Beethoven replied and repeated his offer of the Mass and Symphony, but held the matter of the Quartet in abeyance. He asked that payment for the other works be made by bills drawn on a Vienna bank payable 600 florins in one month, 500 florins in two months and 500 florins in four months. On July 3 he also conceded the Quartet, which he promised to deliver inside of six weeks. With an answer from Schott on July 19, the business was concluded and, as an undated letter of Beethoven's shows, much to his gratification; the business methods of Schott and Sons were extremely satisfactory to him. But the year came to an end, and the Mainz publishers were still waiting for their manuscripts, while Beethoven was kept busy writing explanations in answer to their questions and requests.

Meanwhile, in a letter to the firm, written in November, he offered for publication the overture which had been performed at his concert [Op. 124], six bagatelles and three songs in behalf of his brother to whom they belonged, the price 130 ducats in gold. These were the works which Probst had agreed to purchase for 100 ducats and the money for which had been sent to Vienna. Schott agreed to buy them for 130 ducats and Beethoven wrote to his brother in Gneixendorf on December 10: "I inform you that Mainz will give 130 ducats in gold for your works; if Herr Probst will not pay as much, give them to Mainz, who will at once send a cheque to you as quickly as to me, these are really honest, not mean, business men. . . ."

[47] Quartet in E-flat, Op. 127, which, however, was not yet completed. (TDR, v, 102, n. 3.)

Johann promptly put himself in communication with Schott and Sons and graciously confirmed the sale of the works at 130 ducats, "Out of respect" for his brother.

Peters, who had been informed of the state of affairs concerning the Mass, evidently sent a complaint, or protest, to Beethoven, for on December 12, 1824, the latter writes:

Dear Sir:

Streicher has written you concerning a certain matter. I told him myself that this affair would run into difficulty, and this is what has happened. I inform you only that the whole affair concerning the Mass is off, since I have now promised it definitely to a publisher, and thus naturally the proposals made by Streicher cannot be carried into effect—You would have received a violin quartet already but for the fact that I had to give it to the publisher who got the Mass, since he expressly asked for this at the same time. But you will receive another one soon for sure, or I will make you an offer of a greater work from which the sum already received would then be subtracted. Only please have patience for a bit since I will certainly satisfy you—You *did wrong to yourself and to me*, and you are still doing the latter, as I hear, in accusing me of having sent you *inferior* works. Did you not yourself ask for songs, marches and bagatelles? Afterwards it occurred to you that the fee was too large and that a larger work might have been had for it. That you showed yourself to be a poor judge of art in this is proved by the fact that several of these works have been and will be published, and that such a thing has never happened to me before—As soon as I can I will liquidate my indebtedness to you, and meanwhile I remain

Yours truly
Beethoven

I am not now *in a position* to do this more quickly.

During the summer of 1824 Karl was continuing his philological studies at the university. On one of his visits to his uncle not long after the concerts the conversation proceeded from the progress of Karl's studies to the question of his choice of a career. Karl writes:[48]

I will not do anything without your consent and will, if you wish, continue to study, or even more begin something new.

You will find my choice rather strange, but I will speak freely, nevertheless, as I prefer to do. The profession which I would like to choose is not a *common* one. On the contrary, it *also* demands study; only of a different kind; and one that is to my liking, I believe.

Soldier

In no company at all[49]

---

[48] This conversation, and others between Karl and Beethoven of a personal nature, are in the appendix to Vol. V of TDR, pp. 506ff.

[49] Presumably Beethoven asked from whence he had gotten the idea.

The regulation is certainly very strict. And mathematics and the science of fortification are certainly not among the lowest.

Later on there is further conversation about Karl's studies which show, even though only Karl's side of the conversation is recorded, that there was conflict between them: Beethoven worried over Karl's effort and use of time; Karl answered that he was exerting himself to the utmost and not seeing anyone but his fellow student Erik with whom he read Greek and Latin.

On August 1 Beethoven wrote to his lawyer friend, Dr. Bach, concerning his nephew and his will:

Most worthy friend!

My heartfelt thanks for your kind recommendation here; I am really well taken care of—I must remind you of the part of my will concerning Karl. I think that I might have a stroke some day, like my worthy grandfather whom I take after. Karl is and remains the sole heir of all that I have and that may be found after my death. However, since one must leave something to one's relatives, even when they are quite uncongenial, my *brother* is to receive my French piano from *Paris*—Karl could bring the will on Saturday if it doesn't inconvenience you in any way—As far as Stein [Steiner] is concerned, he will be satisfied to have his debt completely paid off at the end of this month and at the end of September—For if something comes of the Mainz affair, it will take no longer than that, and the first 600 fl. should at any rate be paid back to two of the most generous human beings[50] who, when I was nearly desperate, kindly advanced me this sum without any interest whatsoever.

With fondest wishes I embrace you.

Respectfully your friend Beethoven

In September of this year the interest of Beethoven's old friend Andreas Streicher, whose wife was a visitor at Baden, seems to have been awakened in a marked degree, and he gave himself to the devising of plans to ameliorate the composer's financial position. In a letter dated September 5 he proposed: first, that six high-class subscription concerts be given in the approaching winter, which, with 600 subscribers, would yield after defraying costs a total of 4,800 florins C.M.; second, that the project for a complete edition of the compositions be revived, which, as he outlined it, he thought might yield a profit of 10,000 florins C.M. From Beethoven's letter of December 12 to Peters, it is clear that Streicher had also acted as intermediary for the composer with this firm.

Streicher tried to make himself useful in still another way. He suggested that manuscript copies of the Mass in D with pianoforte or organ accompaniment be sold to a number of singing societies. This project had already been attempted in the case of the Singakademie of Berlin and achieved in that of the Cäcilienverein of Frankfurt. In a letter from Streicher to the directors of the Gesangverein in Zürich, dated September 17, 1824, is enclosed a note

---

[50] Undoubtedly the Brentanos. (TDR, v, 154, n. 5.)

of authorization from the composer to Steiner, dated the day before, requesting that, owing to the cost of copying, etc., the price be 50 ducats. This was the same that he had asked of his royal subscribers for the full orchestral score. None of the projects came to execution, though the second, which lay close to Beethoven's heart, came up for attention once again at a later date.

Towards the end of September, Johann Andreas Stumpff, a native of Thuringia but a resident of London, was among the visitors at Baden who were admitted to intimate association with Beethoven. This was another Stumpff, not the one who came to Vienna in 1818 with a letter from Thomas Broadwood, and who tuned the new English pianoforte. He was a manufacturer of harps and an enthusiastic admirer of Beethoven's music. Anticipating a meeting with the composer, he had provided himself with a letter of introduction to Haslinger, whose help to that end he asked. He had also gotten a letter from Streicher, whose acquaintance he had made in London. He accomplished his end and wrote a long and enthusiastic account of his intercourse with Beethoven at Baden, whither Haslinger had accompanied him on his first visit.[51] He was received by Beethoven with extraordinary cordiality. The composer accepted an invitation to dinner, entertained his host at dinner in return, played for him on his Broadwood pianoforte (after Stein, at Stumpff's request, had restored its ruins), and at parting gave him a print of one of his portraits and promised to alight at his house if ever he came to London. Much of his conversation, which Stumpff records, is devoted to a condemnation of the frivolity and bad musical taste of the Viennese, and excessive laudation of everything English. "Beethoven," Stumpff remarks, "had an exaggerated opinion of London and its highly cultured inhabitants," and he quotes Beethoven as saying: "England stands high in culture. In London everybody knows something and knows it well; but the man of Vienna can only talk of eating and drinking, and sings and pounds away at music of little significance or of his own making." He spoke a great deal about sending his nephew to London to make a man of him, asked questions about the cost of living there and, in short, gave proof that an English visit was filling a large part of his thoughts. The incidents of the conclusion of the dinner which he gave to Stumpff may be told in the latter's words:

Beethoven now produced the small bottle. It contained the precious wine of Tokay with which he filled the two glasses to the brim. "Now my good German-Englishman, to your good health." We drained the glasses, then, extending his

---

[51] Stumpff's manuscript, which also covered the principal incidents of a trip through Germany, after his death came into the possession of his surviving partner, T. Martin, who permitted Thayer to transcribe all of it relating to Beethoven. Many of his observations parallel those made by Reichardt, Rochlitz, Schultz and other visitors, and their repetition here would add nothing to the story of Beethoven's life and manners; besides, the account is too long to be inserted in full. The reader who wishes to read all of it is referred to TDR, v, pp. 122ff. (TK, III, 181, n. 1.)

hand, "A good journey to you and to a meeting again in London."—I beckoned to him to fill the glasses again and hurriedly wrote in his notebook: "Now for a pledge to the welfare of the greatest living composer, Beethoven."—I arose from my chair, he followed my example, emptied his glass and seizing my hand said: "To-day I am just what I am and what I ought to be,—all unbuttoned." And now he unbosomed himself on the subject of music which had been degraded and made a plaything of vulgar and impudent passions. "True music," he said, "found little recognition in this age of Rossini and his consorts." Thereupon I took up the pencil and wrote in very distinct letters:

"Whom do you consider the greatest composer that ever lived?"

"Handel," was his instantaneous reply; "to him I bow the knee," and he bent one knee to the floor.

"Mozart," I wrote.

"Mozart," he continued, "is good and admirable."

"Yes," wrote I, "who was able to glorify even Handel with his additional accompaniments to *The Messiah*."

"It would have lived without them," was his answer.

I continued writing. "Seb. Bach."

"Why is he dead?"

I answered immediately "He will return to life again."

"Yes, if he is studied, and for that there is now no time."

I took the liberty of writing: "As you yourself, a peerless artist in the art of music, exalt the merits of Handel so highly above all, you must certainly own the scores of his principal works."

"I? How should I, a poor devil, have gotten them? Yes, the scores of *The Messiah* and *Alexander's Feast* went through my hands."

If it is possible for a blind man to help a cripple, and the two attain an end which would be impossible to either one unaided, why might not in the present case a similar result be effected by a similar coöperation? At that moment I made a secret vow: Beethoven, you shall have the works of Handel for which your heart is longing if they are anywhere to be found.

Stumpff relates that Beethoven's brother, who came into the room during his visit, seemed glad to greet him and begged him most amiably to call on him, as he desired to talk with him about a number of things. At parting, Beethoven accompanied Stumpff to the door and said: "That is my brother—have nothing to do with him—he is not an honest man. You will hear me accused of many wrong actions of which he has been guilty. Farewell!" Stumpff returned to London on December 6. He fulfilled his vow touching the gift of Handel's works two years later.

Czerny visited Beethoven in Baden, and a notice from him in Jahn's papers is interesting on account of a remark concerning Napoleon: "In 1824 I went with Beethoven once to a coffee-house in Baden where we found many newspapers on the table. In one I read an announcement of Walter Scott's *Life of Napoleon* and showed it to Beethoven. 'Napoleon,' he said, 'earlier I couldn't have tolerated him. Now I think completely otherwise.' "

In the latter part of the summer Beethoven accepted a commission from Diabelli for "a Sonata in F for Pianoforte, four hands." The project seems to have originated from the publisher, who asked for such a composition and specified the key in a letter dated August 7, 1824. Beethoven, in a letter dated August 24, agreed to compose the work for a fee of 80 ducats in gold, although a sonata for four hands was not in his line. He mentioned the composition and the fee which he was to receive for it in the draft for a letter to Schlesinger next year, but never wrote the work; nor have any certain traces of it been found in the sketchbooks.

Two notes to Haslinger in October show that a new element had entered into Beethoven's worries concerning his nephew. The first is dated "Baden, evening of October 6":

Dear Tobias!

I beg of you most fervently to inquire right away at the house in the Johannisgasse, into which we are going to move, whether Karl slept there yesterday and today, and, if he is at home, to give him this note immediately; if not, to leave it with the caretaker there to give to him—He has been away since yesterday and this evening neither he nor the housekeeper are here. I am alone with a person who can neither speak, read nor write, and I can find scarcely a thing to eat dining out—Once already I have had to go in from here to fetch Karl in Vienna; once he has gone somewhere it is hard to bring him away. I beg of you to notify me right away what you can. I would like to have had a few more peaceful days here; unfortunately I will have to return to the city on account of him. At any rate I beg of you to let no one know of this. God is my witness as to what I have had to endure already because of him. If there is no information from the caretaker in the Johannisgasse, then send someone to the Landstrasse, where I lived before, to ask the caretaker where Frau von Niemetz[52] lives, in order to find out there if he has been to her place or is coming there, so that she will direct him here at once.

Naturally I shall remunerate your servant as well as pay the cost of postage for the letters—Also I beg of you to take care of the letter to my Cain-brother—I beg of you to answer immediately whether or not he has been found.

Most hastily your friend   Beethoven
For God's sake an answer immediately.

The second letter dated "Baden, the day after the 6th Octob. 1824" determines the year date of the first. Touching is the expression of relief expressed in this letter, the first part of which is given here:

Best one!

Our Benjamin arrived here early today, on which account I am firing off 17 and a half cannons—Earlier events through no fault of his et sine mea culpa made me anxious, thank heaven everything goes well and opportunely at times despite my agitatos! With these wretched arrangements it is no wonder one gets anxious about a growing young man, and with it the poisoned breath dragons!—
. . . .

---

[52] The mother of Karl's friend Niemetz, who will be mentioned shortly.

Four years earlier at the Blöchlinger Institute, Karl had made the friendship of a fellow student named Niemetz. By now they were close friends and Karl invited him to join in one of his visits to Baden. The following discussion about Niemetz, in a Conversation Book, marked by Schindler "Fall of 1824 in Baden" has a particular interest in that it includes Beethoven's part in the conversation:

Beethoven: I am very ill pleased with your choice of this friend. Poverty certainly deserves sympathy, but not invariably. I would not want to be unfair to him but to me he is a burdensome guest, lacking completely in decency and manners, which belong in some degree to all well brought up youths and men.—Besides I suspect that his interests are more with the housekeeper than with me—Besides I love quiet; also the space here is too limited for several people since I am constantly busy, and he cannot engage my interest at all.—You still have a very weak character.

Karl: Concerning my choice, I believe that a close acquaintance of four years' duration is really sufficient to get to know a man from *all angles*, especially a boy who cannot possibly remain disguised for such a long time—Thus there cannot be a question of lack of conviction, but merely of the reasons which led me to it, and they are in a word: the very great similarity of character and tastes. If he has been unable to please you, you are free to send him away, but he has not deserved what you have said about him.

Beethoven: I find him rough and common. These are no friends for you.

Karl: If you find him rough, you are mistaken. In any event, I wouldn't have thought that he had given you the opportunity to think it. Also I do not intend to exchange him for another which would be a clear sign of weakness of character, for which you reproach me certainly with injustice; for of all the students at Blöchlinger's I have found *no one* but him who would have cheered up my own, often dreary home, and consequently I feel that I am gratefully indebted to him.

Beethoven: You are not yet in a position to discriminate.

Karl: It is really useless to quarrel over a subject, especially over a [person's] character concerning which I will never abandon my conviction, *so long as I can consider that I myself am not a bad man*, for if there is something good in *me*, he possesses it in at least as high a degree as I, and it would be unfair to be angry with him if you do not judge *me* likewise. For my part I will not stop loving him as I would my brother, if I had one.

Here Beethoven's part in the conversation stops; but this talk shows the boy, just turned eighteen, was in mature command of himself in these inevitable scenes with his uncle, which represented as they did two essentially different points of view.}⬥—

At some point in the first part of November, Beethoven returned again to Vienna, where he took up his new residence—at 969 Johannesgasse, in a house owned by a family named Kletschka. —⬥{From a relative of this family, Dr. Jurié v. Lavandal, Frimmel learned that Beethoven had quarrels with both the housekeeper and his nephew, which led to noisy scenes; further that "at times the deaf master pounded the piano (presumably out of tune) quite unmercifully." As a result of these disturbances, Frau Kletschka finally had to send her young daughter, Nanette, to her boarders to serve notice.[53] But here the story of Beethoven's dwellings is unclear. On the one hand it would appear that he remained at this address throughout the winter, since this address is given as late as April 18, 1825, in a letter from Beethoven to Dr. Braunhofer.[54] Yet from two sources we learn that Beethoven moved to the Krugerstrasse. The writer, Heinrich Friedrich Rellstab, describes his visit in early April, 1825, to see the composer "in the Krugerstrasse No. 767 on the fourth floor."[55] Meanwhile Gerhard von Breuning lists Beethoven's residence for the winter of 1824-25 as "Krugerstrasse 1009 (now 13) . . . second story."[56] Frimmel points out the fallacy of Rellstab's address since at that time there were no numbers under 1000 on the Krugerstrasse. Because of the expense it seems unlikely that Beethoven was once again occupying two dwellings at the same time. But it may well be that, having been ousted temporarily from the Johannesgasse and forced to live elsewhere, he was later allowed to return.

On November 17, 1824, as the autograph attests, Beethoven wrote a four-part canon on the words "Schwenke dich ohne Schwänke," which he sent to Schott and Sons for publication in the *Cäcilia,* where it appeared in April, 1825. There the title is "Canon on one who was called Schwenke." The person whose name has thus been perpetuated was the pianist and composer, Carl Schwencke.[57]

The state of Beethoven's health is suggested by the following letter to Archduke Rudolph, dated November 18, 1824:

Your Imperial Highness

Since I was ill when I returned here from Baden I was prevented from betaking myself, as I wished to do, to Y.I.H. because I was forbidden to go outside. Yesterday was the first day that I could walk in the free air again—Your gracious letter caught me just when I was confined to my bed. As I was in a state of perspiration at that moment, since my poor health resulted from a chill, it was impossible for me to get up, nevertheless I know that Y.I.H. is convinced that I never could neglect the regard due you—Tomorrow at noon I shall have the pleasure of paying my respects; moreover, means will not be lacking to arouse Y.I.H.'s musical spirit which can be nothing but beneficial for art—my refuge—God be praised—

Your Imperial Highness's truly most obedient servant Beethoven

The main composition of the year 1824 was the Quartet in E-flat, Op. 127, the history of which is inevitably wound up with the history of Prince Galitzin's request to Beethoven for three string quartets. The story is now taken up from where it was left off, at the end of the chapter for the year 1822. First, the time schedule of composition. Ideas for the work were

[53] *BJ,* I, p. 75; *FRBH,* II, pp. 462-63.

[54] *BJ,* I, pp. 74-5; see also *A* 1359. Miss Anderson identifies the writer of the address as nephew Karl.

[55] Kerst, II, p. 121.

[56] *Aus dem Schwarzspanierhause,* p. 45.

[57] Born in Hamburg in 1797, son of Christian Friedrich Gottlieb Schwencke, Director of Church Music and Cantor at the Johanneum in Hamburg. (TDR, v, 139.)

probably in the composer's head when he offered a quartet to Peters in June, 1822. The invitation from Galitzin in November, 1822 undoubtedly spurred the work forward, and in January, 1823 Beethoven agreed to write some string quartets. Then the composition and performance of the Ninth Symphony delayed work until the summer of 1824.[58] The main work was done in the second half of 1824 and the beginning of 1825, and the work was first performed on March 6, 1825. By this time there were also preliminary sketches for the first and last movements of the second quartet (Op. 132).[59]

Beethoven's letter to Prince Galitzin of January 25, 1823, has already been given, in which he accepted the invitation to write three string quartets. Galitzin replied on February 23;[60] he expressed his joy over Beethoven's acceptance, notified him that he had made the order to his banker, Stieglitz,[61] to make payment of 50 ducats for the first quartet, stated his eagerness to send 100 more for two more quartets, and instructed him in how to mail the music, urging him to tell no one about it so that he could receive a higher price from his publisher. As already mentioned, Beethoven asked the Prince to subscribe to the Mass and then asked him to permit the 50 ducats for the first quartet to be applied to the subscription for the Mass. Beethoven received this sum from Henikstein, Stieglitz' representative in Vienna, on October 22. A note from Henikstein to the Prince, dated October 25, 1823, shows that the Prince agreed to the redesignation of the money. Meanwhile, during the year, Galitzin was writing to Beethoven frequently concerning the arrival of the first quartet and news of the start of the second. At this time, however, his patience was tempered with understanding of the requirements of artists. In his letter of November 29, 1823, after expressing joy over the arrival of the manuscript of the Mass and enquiring about the pianoforte sonatas that he had been expecting, he says: "I am really impatient to have a new quartet of yours, nevertheless, I beg you not to mind and to be guided in this only by your inspiration and the disposition of your mind, for no one knows better than I that you cannot command genius, rather that it should be left alone, and we know moreover that in your private life you are not the kind of person to sacrifice artistic for personal interest and that music done to order is not your business at all."

On August 3, 1823, Prince Galitzin had first expressed his desire for the score of the Mass so that he could perform the work at St. Petersburg. When the score arrived, however, there was missing a page of the *Gloria*, a precaution that Beethoven had taken against his manuscript being stolen

---

[58] For sketches see *II Beeth.*, pp. 210ff., 534-46.

[59] *Ibid.*, pp. 547ff. See also pp. 180-81.

[60] The letters from Galitzin to Beethoven may be found in the Appendix of TDR, v, pp. 552ff. Of the letters from Beethoven to Galitzin, only three, plus one draft, have been found, out of a total of what must have been at least ten. See *A* 1123, 1244, 1292, 1405.

[61] Baron Ludwig Stieglitz was a banker in St. Petersburg.

while copied. Beethoven wrote a letter of apology and explanation to the Prince on December 13, 1823, with assurances that the missing page would soon arrive, and with further notices concerning the Gloria section.

In his answer of December 30, Galitzin indicated that his performance of the Mass would take place in February or Easter. Since the first fifty ducats from Galitzin had been reapplied to the Mass at Beethoven's request, the Prince now writes: "Let me know whether you need 50 for the 1st quartet, [if so] I will make it immediately available to you." In his next letter, dated March 11, 1824, Galitzin was more impatient and worried as to whether Beethoven was ill and consequently unable to fulfill his promises; he reiterated his wish that if Beethoven should need money, he should feel free to draw it on account with M. M. Stieglitz and Co.; and he announced that the performance of the Mass, which was a benefit for musicians' widows, would take place on April 7. Galitzin's next letter described what was in fact the first full performance in the world of the Mass in D. It deserves to be given in full:

Petersburg, April 8, 1824

Monsieur, I am eager to give you an account of the performance of your sublime masterpiece which we presented here to the public the night before last.[62] For several months I have been extremely impatient to hear this music performed, the beauties of which I foresaw from the score. The effect of this music on the public cannot be described and I doubt if I exaggerate when I say that for my part I have never heard anything so sublime; I don't even except the masterpieces of Mozart which with their eternal beauties have not created for me the same sensations that you have given me, Monsieur, by the Kyrie and Gloria of your Mass. The masterly harmony and the moving melody of the Benedictus transport the heart to a plane that is really blissful. This whole work in fact is a treasure of beauties; it can be said that your genius has anticipated the centuries and that there are not listeners perhaps enlightened enough to experience all the beauty of this music; but it is posterity that will pay homage and will bless your memory much better than your contemporaries can. Prince Radziwill, whom you know is a great amateur of music, arrived just a few days ago from Berlin and was present at the performance of your mass which he had not known before; he was enraptured with it just like myself and all those present.—I hope that your health is restored and that you are going to give us many more products of your sublime genius.—Excuse the nuisance that I often cause by my letters, but it is a sincere tribute from one of your greatest admirers.

P. Nicolas Galitzin

[62] Prince Galitzin was in error either in the dating of his letter or in the phrase "the night before last," for the performance took place on April 7 (April 7—New Style or Gregorian Calendar; March 26—Old Style or Julian Calendar). This date has been established by Boris Schwarz, who has found mention of the concert in two different Russian newspapers as having taken place on March 26th. This evidence supports the March 26 date (Old Style) given by the Lpz. *AMZ* (Vol. 26, May 27, 1824) in reporting the event and the April 7 date (New Style) mentioned by Prince Galitzin himself in his letter to Beethoven on March 11, 1824. See Boris Schwarz, "More Beethoveniana in Soviet Russia," *MQ*, Vol. 49, 1963, pp. 147-49.

Beethoven's next (and last surviving) letter to the Prince is dated "Vienna, May 26, 1824." The letter is in German for the probable reason, as Miss Anderson has pointed out,[63] that Galitzin, in a letter of May 5, 1823, specifically asked Beethoven for "a letter in German and in his own hand so that I may have the pleasure of owning an autograph letter of yours." The letter follows:

My dear and honored Prince!

So many of your charming letters unanswered!—[Please] attribute it only to the overwhelming load of business, and certainly not to neglect on my part— Having been entreated to give a few concerts in which I lost time and money; and to the shame of our present organization in Vienna, I had to be sacrificed to a former dancer Duport, who is lease-holder at the Kärthnerthor. Let me off from repeating a description of the vulgar details, which anyway would revolt and disgust you as it does me. But allow me to tell you that it was a waste for me of much time and money—Here I have learned that the Mass is going to be given in St. Petersburg as a great oratorio. My circumstances force me, since here they do nothing at all *for me*, but rather *against me*, to try a second subscription on this work, and in fact, as Y.E. once wrote me, to offer a printed copy of the score for 5 ducats in gold, which could be printed and delivered in a half year. I cannot send you this invitation until the next post—You will soon receive your quartet, promised so long ago to you, perhaps also the others. If only the inquiries and encouragements from all sides for big works were not so strong. The necessity of the time requires it, *poverty* is helped and aided thereby in every way, what an incentive for such works!—Since I can well imagine that you yourself employ works for this purpose, I will send Y.E. a new overture and a trio which was sung by three local Italians and performed excellently. Should you wish a new big symphony with a finale in which occurs chorus and solo parts, I would have a score of it copied. The cost would be nothing more than a reimbursement for the cost of copying—Perhaps it would be possible through your efforts to be able to have the mass dedicated to His Majesty the Emperor of Russia; perhaps such a generous monarch as the Russian Emperor would even settle on me a yearly pension for which I would first deliver all my big works to His Majesty and would also fulfill speedily His Majesty's commissions and thereby would be able to have helped suffering mankind—

Enclosed is an impression of the medal from His Majesty from France as a sign of his satisfaction with my mass. The medal weighs a half a pound in gold; and [has] Italian verses about me—which . . . the side of genius which outside is radiantly white, only the. . . .[64]

With all the esteem and devotion

from Your Highness's faithful Beetho[ve]n[65]

[63] Emily Anderson, "Two Letters from Beethoven to Prince Galitzin," in *Festschrift Schmidt-Görg* (Bonn, 1957), p. 5. The letter that follows is from her reading of the original autograph; *ibid.*, pp. 6-7.

[64] According to Miss Anderson (*ibid.*, p. 7, nn. 26, 27) there are two incompletions in the last sentence: in the first a word has been erased through smudging, in the second, the rest of the sentence is missing.

[65] It is impossible to match in English the omission of letters in the signature. "Ihre Du[urch]laucht mit aller liebe v. [Ve]rehrung verharre[nder] Beetho[ve]n."

Replying June 16, Galitzin accepted Beethoven's offer of the symphony, the overture and the trio. As regards the Mass, Galitzin answered that to secure permission to dedicate a work to the Emperor one must write to Count Nesselrode, and that he would be glad to distribute as many printed copies of the Mass as possible, but that the difficulty of its performance precluded a large sale. Considering the later history between Beethoven and Galitzin, the postscript is interesting: "If you ever find yourself in the least kind of difficulty, apply quickly to me. I will be only too glad to be able to be of help to you."

In his next letter, dated July 28, he offered the advice already advanced by Schindler, and doubtless by others: "Right now I am convinced that if you wanted to travel in Europe without any treasures other than your compositions, and without any recommendations other than your immortal masterpieces, you would take the world by storm. Your presence alone at Paris, London would eclipse everything else, and the concerts which you would give would not resemble those in Vienna." He was impatient now and mentioned that he had heard that Beethoven was working on a cantata by Bernard and on Grillparzer's *Melusine*. Two more letters were written by Galitzin before the end of 1824. Only the second of the two has survived and is dated December 5. In this letter Galitzin reported that upon his return from a trip he witnessed a flood that completely inundated St. Petersburg. He planned a second performance of the Mass for the benefit of the flood survivors for which he also wanted the scores of the symphony and overture. As regards the quartet, he announced that 50 ducats were being remitted to Count von Lebzeltern, minister of Austria, for remittance to Beethoven, after a delay which was not of his own making, and that Beethoven could expect it soon. This then was the second payment of 50 ducats and was specifically for the first quartet. Beethoven must have written to him in the fall concerning his poor health for Galitzin answers: "I am really very much vexed that you have suffered so from poor health, but suffering is an indispensable part of human life, and it seems that geniuses like yourself ought to impose on nature and force her to respect those like you who are distinguished from the rest of mankind."

By the end of the year the quartet was sent and was acknowledged by Galitzin on April 29, 1825, after having "performed it several times." In the chapter devoted to the year 1826, the story of Prince Galitzin and the Beethoven quartets is continued.

After offering "a new quartet" to Schott on March 10, 1824, Beethoven corresponded with the firm during the year and kept postponing the date of delivery. The Mass and the Symphony were received on January 18, 1825, but still not the quartet. Not until after the first performance on March 6 did the publishers receive the manuscript; on May 7, 1825, Beethoven wrote to them: "You will have received the Quartet by this time, it is the one that was promised to you. I could have an honorarium of 60 ducats from several publishers here, but I have put it off in order to keep my words with you." —∙⚡The compositions completed in this year were:

(1817) 1822-4. Symphony No. 9 in D minor, Op. 125.
1823-4.   Six Bagatelles for Pianoforte, Op. 126.
1824.   Canons:
             "Schwenke dich ohne Schwänke," WoO 187, for Carl Schwencke
                in November.
             "Te solo adoro" (Metastasio), WoO 186, for Carlo Evasio Soliva
                on June 2.[66]
             "Opferlied" for Soprano, Chorus and Orchestra (Matthisson),
                Op. 121b, final version.[67]
             Waltz in E-flat for Pianoforte, WoO 84, for the Viennese actor,
                Carl Friedrich Müller on November 21 (see publications).

The publications of the year were:

In the Berlin *Allgemeine Musikalische Zeitung* supplement, December 8: Piece in B-flat for Pianoforte, WoO 60.
In C. F. Müller's *Musikalisches Angebinde zum neuen Jahre,* a collection of forty waltzes by forty different composers:
Waltz in E-flat for Pianoforte, WoO 84.[68]
By Steiner:
Variations for Pianoforte, Violin and Violoncello on Wenzel Müller's Song, "Ich bin der Schneider Kakadu," Op. 121a.[69]⚡∙—

---

[66] Nothing is known of Beethoven's relation to the musician Carlo Evasio Soliva (*ca.* 1792-1853); see KHV, p. 689.

[67] See Hurt Herbst, "Beethovens Opferliedkompositionen" in *NBJ,* v (1933), pp. 137ff; KHV, p. 354; and *II Beeth.,* pp. 541-42.

[68] See Max Unger, "Zu den Erstdrucken einiger Werke Beethovens" in *Zeitschrift für Musik,* Vol. 105 (1938), pp. 145-48.

[69] Steiner's opus number is simply Op. 121; the "a" had to be added because of Schott's printing in the following year of the final version of the "Opferlied" with the number 121—now designated as Op. 121b. According to Alan Tyson, the work was published about the same time by Chappell and Co. and Goulding and Co. in London. See his *The Authentic English Editions of Beethoven* (London, 1963), p. 121.

CHAPTER XXXVIII

THE YEAR 1825

ANOTHER INVITATION FROM LONDON— INCREASING TROUBLE WITH HIS NEPHEW—THE THREE GALITZIN QUARTETS COMPLETED

IN THE early part of 1824, thoughts of a visit to England had been re-vived by a letter from Charles Neate; it had been determined that the visit should be undertaken in the fall and that Schindler should accompany him. When nothing developed, Neate wrote another letter on December 20, 1824, bringing with it an invitation from the Philharmonic Society of London which kept the thought of an English visit alive in Beethoven's irresolute mind for a considerable space longer. Neate wrote in an extremely cordial vein. He had long wished to see Beethoven in England, he said, where he believed that his genius was appreciated more than in any other country; and now he had received the pleasant charge from the Philharmonic Society to invite him to come. He made no doubt but that in a short time he would earn enough money richly to compensate him for all the inconveniences of the journey. The Philharmonic Society was disposed to give him 300 guineas for conducting at least one of his works at each of the Society's concerts in the coming season, and composing a new symphony and a concerto which was to be produced during his visit but to remain the composer's property. As an additional pecuniary inducement he held out that Beethoven could give a concert of his own at which he would make at least £500, besides which there were many other avenues of profit open to him. If he were to bring along the quartets about which he had written, they would yield him £100 more, and he might therefore be sure of carrying back a large sum of money, enough, indeed, to make all the remainder of his life much pleasanter than the past had been. He told Beethoven that the new Symphony had arrived and the first rehearsal of it was set for January 17. He hoped that

Beethoven would be on hand to direct it at the first concert of the Society and trusted that a report that a copy of it was in Paris was not true.

Beethoven replied on January 15 and again on the 27th. The first letter follows:

Monsieur!

With the greatest pleasure I received your letter of—[December 20] through which you had the kindness to inform me that the Philharmonic Society, with its distinguished artists is inviting me to come to London. I am well satisfied with the conditions made to you by the society, but I wish to propose that besides the 300 guineas that it has promised me I be sent 100 more guineas for traveling expenses; for I need to buy a carriage; also I need to be accompanied by someone. You can see clearly that that is necessary; besides I beg you to let me know the inn at which I may stay in London. I will take a new quartet along with me.

As for the rumor that you wrote about, that there is a copy of the 9th Symphony in Paris, there is no foundation in it at all. It is true that this symphony will be published in Germany, but not before the year has come to an end during which time the Society will be playing it. On this point I must inform you again to have only small rehearsals of this composition, with the four string parts for example; for it is the only way to study well such a work; above all the choruses should be rehearsed. There are still some errors, a list of which I will send you by the next post.—

It seems to me that in the second movement of the Symphony it has been forgotten that at the repetition of the minore after the Presto one must begin again at the sign and continue without repetition right to the ferma, then one goes directly to the Coda.[1]

I beg you to reply as quickly as possible for I am being asked to write a big new composition which I will not begin, however, without hearing from you.[2]— I have to write all the time, not to accumulate wealth—only to provide for my needs.

Now I need to have assurance on this point.—I will be charmed to see you and to know that noble nation, England. I am your sincere friend,

Monsieur,
with the highest regards
Louis van Beethoven

To this letter Neate replied on February 1. He had conveyed the contents of Beethoven's letter to the directors of the Philharmonic Society and had now regretfully to report that they had declined to make any change in their offer. He was personally willing to give the advance asked, but the individual directors were not masters of their conduct in all things; they had to abide by the laws of the Society. He hoped that under the circumstances Beethoven would come; he was sure the trip would pay him, and the directors would impatiently await his presence at the second concert, it being already

[1] He wrote the same thing later to Schott. In the Complete Works Edition, the repetition of the Scherzo is completely written out.

(TDR, v, 161, n. 2.)
[2] This was the oratorio on Bernard's text Der Sieg des Kreuzes. (TDR, v, 161, n. 3.)

too late for the first. There was to be another rehearsal of the Symphony that evening.

Again Beethoven had to struggle with the question as to whether or not he should make the journey to London. He was strongly urged by his desire to earn a large sum of money. His friends pressed him with arguments in favor of the trip. Karl admonished him to make up his own mind without giving heed to the insatiable avarice of his brother, but reminded him that Neate had assured him he would make enough money to be free of care the rest of his life. Johann did not talk of the financial advantage alone but said that he would benefit physically, travel being good for the health. Apparently answering an objection of Beethoven's on the score of his age, Karl reminded him that Haydn also went to London when he was fifty years old—and he was "not so famous." Schuppanzigh burst out with his brusque third person singular: "I wish he would pick up enough courage to make the trip; he would not regret it." Who should accompany him? Schindler had been recommended by Neate, but his name does not occur in these conversations; instead there was talk of Schuppanzigh and young Streicher. But as it turned out, no one was to accompany him, nobody alight with him at either the house of Stumpff or the Hotel de la Sablonière in Leicester Square which Neate had recommended as a French house much visited by foreigners. His doubts, suspicions, fears for his health, anxiety about his nephew, his fatal indecision, prevailed. On March 19 he wrote to Neate that he would make the visit some other time—perhaps in the fall; two days later the Symphony was performed for the first time in London. From that time on there was no further mention of the trip.

In this same letter, however, Beethoven kept alive the idea of selling the quartets in England and wrote that he was satisfied with Neate's offer for them provided that he would be allowed to publish the quartets in a year and a half or two years. On May 25 he reaffirmed his satisfaction with the price already offered of £100 for three quartets but warned that the first quartet was much in demand by different artists and had already been promised them for their benefit; he urged Neate to let him know whether he was satisfied with his conditions, so that he could send the first quartet right away; he stipulated that the honorarium would not be due until he reported the completion of the other two quartets; and he urged haste because of the demands from publishers.

The absence of Ries's name in the negotiations with England is explained by the fact that he was no longer in London. He had purchased an estate in Godesberg, near Bonn, and removed thither in 1824. From there he wrote to Beethoven inviting him to visit him for awhile; he also made various enquiries concerning Beethoven's compositions, for which a word of explanation is needed. In 1817 there had come into being the Lower Rhenish Musical Festival. For the seventh annual meeting, which was to be held at Aix-la-Chapelle, Ries had been invited to be the conductor and he had accepted on

December 24, 1824. During that year reports of the Vienna performance of the Ninth Symphony had spread and it was desired to make the symphony a feature of the festival scheme. In January, 1825, Schott and Sons were asked if the score would be in print by May and replied in the negative on January 25th. Thereupon Ries, who at first was not enthusiastic about performing the symphony, was asked to write Beethoven for a manuscript copy. He also asked for the metronome markings of *Christus am Ölberg*, which was another work slated for performance. Beethoven's answer, which follows, is undated but undoubtedly was written in February:

Dear Ries!

You have pressed so for an answer that I can only tell you the most essential things now. I knew already from Kirchhoffer that you had left London. My very pressing situation has hardly given me the chance to write you anything at all. K[irchhoffer] took the Symphony which certainly won't be able to appear before the end of the summer. These sales at the moment are only preliminaries, the time which the London Philharmonic Society has stipulated will be held to completely.[3] Bremen has *never* received it. Nor did Paris as someone wrote me from London. How much one has to bear if one has the misfortune to become famous!

Now as to what you want. It will be a great pleasure to indicate the tempi of Christus am Ölberge for you by metronome, even though this indication of time is so unstable.—As for the symphony I will make you now a more general offer. My situation forces me to seek resolution of my *needs* [Nöthen] through my *notes* [Noten]. Would it be possible for you to arrange the affair *in this way*? I would send *you* my score of the symphony or a good copy, also a score of the Mass, and the overture which I wrote for the Phil. Society. Also I could give you several small things for orchestra, and for chorus. In this way such a society would be in a position to give two or three concerts instead of one. Perhaps 40 carolins would not be too much for it—I leave the whole matter to you. This concept does not come from *me* but from those who want to rescue me from my *needs* through my *notes*—I take the deepest interest in your property in Godesberg; no one could have a more envious joy over it than I whose deepest desires would be realized by such a property. However, it appears that my destiny is not to be quite the way I want it. Greet your old father heartily for me. I am overjoyed on account of his happiness. I embrace you heartily and hope to be able to write you more soon.

As always your true friend

Beethoven

You write soon too.

Beethoven consented to Ries's request and about March 11 sent the score of the first three movements but only the individual parts of the finale. This was explained in a letter to Ries dated March 19:

[3] In his letter to Neate on January 15, Beethoven promised that the symphony would not be published in Germany until the Society had had the score for a year. Actually it was not published by Schott until August, 1826.

My dear friend!

Just eight days ago, immediately after receiving your letter, the symphony was sent with the next mail-coach to go; three movements copied out in score and the Finale complete in individual parts. I only have *my own* score therefore I could only send you the parts of the Finale. But you will receive the score of the Finale by the mail-coach leaving eight days from now along with other works which I am sending. Along with the symphony there was sent an overture and an Opferlied with chorus, the latter apparently full of mistakes, however. But I will send you from here a list of the mistakes. Also there is still to be sent one contrabassoon part for the Finale of the symphony.[4]

This is all, dear friend, that I can tell you today; I am too pressed. I will thank you in writing myself for your fine proposals, but I cannot today on account of a burnt hand. All good wishes to your father and your wife. You will be satisfied by me in any case.

As ever your true friend   Beethoven

Ries waited in vain for the score of the finale and finally had to have one made from the parts. In a letter dated April 9, Beethoven explained more specifically that it was an approaching concert that prevented him from sending his score of the finale; at the same time he enumerated what was being sent: a revised copy of *Opferlied*, the chorusmaster's score of the symphony finale, and an overture in C, 6/8 time; by the next post the *Kyrie* and the *Gloria*, and an Italian Duet. He was still to send a grand march and chorus and might have added an overture which was yet unknown outside of Vienna, but thought he had sent enough. The overture in C was, of course, Op. 115; the march and chorus were from the *Ruinen von Athen*.

The performance took place on May 23, 1825, the second day of the festival, with the following program: 1. The Ninth Symphony 2. Mozart's *Davidde penitente* 3. Overture to *Die Zauberflöte* 4. *Christus am Ölberg*. The time was too short for the difficult music to be learned thoroughly and at the performance portions of the slow movement and the Scherzo of the Symphony were "regretfully" omitted, a fact that, it is to be hoped, was never known to Beethoven.[5] On June 9 Ries wrote a letter to Beethoven concerning the event. There were 422 performers in chorus and orchestra, and the popular reception of the music was enthusiastic enough to enable him to report to Beethoven that the performance had been a success; and

---

[4] The contrabassoon part is missing from the Aix-la-Chapelle score of the Ninth Symphony, so the part could never have been sent. See Otto Baensch, "Die Aachener Abschrift der neunten Symphonie" in *NBJ*, v (1933), p. 16.

[5] In the *Rheinische Flora* (No. 82, May 26, 1825), J. B. Rousseau writes: "At the performance the Scherzo was omitted, although it had been rehearsed, because lack of time necessitated the abridgement. Other than that the orchestra executed all that was possible after removing countless difficulties in connection with the performance of this symphony." See Eugen Brümmer, *Beethoven im Spiegel der zeitgenössischen rheinischen Presse* (Würzburg, 1932), p. 52.

he sent him 40 Louis d'or as a fee. Ries recognized the symphony as a work without an equal and told Beethoven that had he written nothing else it would have made him immortal. "Whither will you yet lead us?" he asked. Very naturally, Beethoven had reported the negotiations touching a visit to England to Ries, who expressed his satisfaction that he had not accepted the engagement and added: "If you want to go there you must make thorough preparations. Rossini got £2500 from the Opera alone. If Englishmen want to do an extraordinary thing, they must all get together so as to make it worth while. There will be no lack of applause and marks of honor, but you have probably had enough of these all your life."

Mass and symphony had been delivered to Fries, the banker, on January 16, to be forwarded to Schott and Sons. Beethoven informed the firm by letter on January 22 and took occasion to deny the report that the Mass had been printed elsewhere. He was particularly anxious to remove doubt in connection with the Schlesingers: "Schlesinger is not to be trusted, for he takes where he can; both père et fils bombarded me for the Mass and other works, but I did not deign to answer either of them, since after thinking them over I had cast them out long before." The second section of the letter deserves to be given in full:

Schlesinger also wished to publish *all* my quartets and periodically to have from me each time a new one of these and pay me what I wished, but since this could hurt my plan of an edition of my complete works, I also left this unanswered. You might reflect upon this opportunity sometime for it is better to be done *by me* than after my death. I have received offers already about it and also plans, but these firms don't seem to me to be suited for such a big undertaking. I would rather put my trust in you. In general, I would prefer to be paid for it in one lump sum; I would indicate the usual unimportant corrections and supply for every category of works, as for example sonatas, variations, etc. a similar new work—Here are a pair of canons for your journal—three others will follow[6]— as a supplement to a romantic biography of Tobias Haslinger here in three parts. First part, Tobias discovers that he is the apprentice of the famous master Kapellmeister Fux—and holds the ladder for the master's Gradus ad Parnassum. Now since he is inclined towards pranks, he shakes and jogs it causing many who have already climbed up quite a way suddenly to break their necks etc. Now he bids farewell to us mortal men and returns to daylight in the time of Albrechtsberger. 2nd part. The Nota cambiata, which already existed with Fux becomes used regularly by A[lbrechtsberger], the appoggiaturas used to the utmost, the art of creating musical skeletons is worked to extremes etc. Tobias like a caterpillar spins himself anew into a cocoon and then he unfolds himself again and appears in this world for the third time. 3rd part. His wings, hardly grown, waft him to the Paternostergässel: he becomes the Paternostergässel Kapellmeister. A graduate of the appoggiatura school, he retains nothing from it but the *change*,[7]

---

[6] The pair of canons were those on Hoffmann and Schwencke. See KHV, WoO 180 and 187. There is no evidence that the three others were sent. (Cf. TK, III, 190, n. 2.)

[7] A pun on the word *Wechsel*—i.e. *Wechselnote* (appoggiatura) and *Wechsel* (change).

and so he brings forth the friend of his youth and finally becomes a member of several *empty*[8] societies etc. If you ask him about this he will certainly allow this biography to be printed.

Very hurriedly

Yours

Beethoven

The Schotts did not notice that Beethoven had wanted the prior consent of Haslinger, and published the facetious biographical sketch in the April issue of *Cäcilia* with only minor changes, followed it with the two canons entitled "Upon one who is called Schwenke" and "Upon one who is called Hoffmann," and added Beethoven's own signature. In a letter dated February 5 Beethoven had urged Schott as a joke to ask Haslinger for "*my romantic biography of him*" and added: "That is the way to handle this fellow, a *Viennese* without heart. He is the one *who advised me not to deal with you.*" He went on to describe Steiner as a "rascally fellow and skinflint," and Haslinger as a "weakling" whom he made useful to himself in some things.

However, after hearing of the printing in *Cäcilia*, Beethoven dictated the following letter to Schott on August 13:

Dear Sir!

I observed with astonishment in the 7th issue of Cäcilia, p. 205, that, along with the canons, you published a joke, sent in a friendly manner, which can easily be taken for a biting insult, although indeed this was not my purpose at all. To offend anyone has always been inconsistent with my character.

Concerning myself as an artist, I am not known as one to become aroused about anything written about me from the point of view of my art. Concerning myself, however, as a man, I must react entirely differently.

You should have seen at first glance that the whole biographical sketch of my respected friend Herr Tobias Haslinger was only a *joke* and could not be meant otherwise, since I wanted, as my letter said, to heighten the joke even more by a request to him on your part for permission to publish his biography. Well, it appears that it was my flighty and often illegible handwriting which gave rise to the misunderstanding.

The contributions, which you yourself requested to be sent, would have corresponded perfectly to my purpose if you had inserted just the two canons, the titles of which show sufficiently that they couldn't easily be connected with a biography of Haslinger; but I could not have dreamt that you would misuse private correspondence and put such a joke before the public, the absurdities of which, which you chose to insert at the beginning (for example, line 2 "2 canons which as supplements I . . . etc."),[9] cannot be explained at all. The word "empty"

---

[8] The pun is untranslatable: "geleert" literally "emptied," as opposed to "gelehrt" (learned). This is a pun he used several times in his correspondence.

[9] Schott's article is entitled "Canons along with mention of their occasion by Ludwig van Beethoven" and begins: "It gives me pleasure to send from here a few canons to Cäcilia and its readers which I have written as supplements to a humorous romantic biography of the local Herr Tobias Hasslinger. . . ."

["geleert"], which applies to the whole of the humorous outline, could have been permitted in a group which was having an amusing conversation but in public it would never have occurred to me to put it in place of "learned" ["gelehrt"].

That was pushing the jest too far!

In the future I will know enough to guard against new misunderstandings being caused by my writing.

I expect you to print this in the Cäcilia without delay and without additions or deletions. For the affair consists of just what I have explained here, and must not be interpreted in any other way.

Vienna, August 13, 1825   L. van Beethoven

[In Beethoven's own handwriting]

I am counting with complete certainty upon your inserting this statement in the Cäcilia right away.

Yours sincerely

Beethoven

It does not appear that this communication was ever printed, neither does it appear that Beethoven took the matter so greatly to heart as his letter was calculated to make the public believe, had it been printed. On August 10 he wrote to his new friend Karl Holz: "I hear with amazement that the Mainz street-boys really abused my joke! It is contemptible; I assure you it was not at all my intention. What I meant was to have Castelli write a poem along these lines, but just under the name of the musical Tobias, with music by me. Since it has *so happened*, it must be accepted as a dispensation from heaven, it will form a companion-piece to Goethe's Bahrdt *sans comparaison* with all other authors. But I believe Tobias himself has wronged *them* somehow—Voila the revenge! It is better anyhow than to fall into the jaws of some monster[10]—I can't shed tears over it but must laugh like—" To his nephew he wrote: "It was not right for Mainz to do a thing like that, but as it is done it will do no harm. The times demand strong men to castigate these petty, tricky, miserable little fellows—much as my heart rebels against doing a man harm. Besides it was only a joke and I never thought of having it printed." Haslinger may have felt incensed at the publication, but he eventually accepted it in an amiable spirit and it did not lead to any rupture of friendship between the two men.

In a letter to Schott, dated January 26, 1825, which was concerned primarily with corrections of the Mass in D, Beethoven wrote a post-script indicating passages in the *Agnus Dei* where the appoggiaturas had been written incorrectly as eighth notes rather than sixteenth notes. It ends thus: "From this you can observe what copyists I am left with now; the fellow is a stupid Bohemian, a pandour, doesn't understand a thing; at first he writes quarters in the appoggiaturas, then finally eighths. Since I was no longer supervising [the work] I noticed this as it was being hastily wrapped."

---

[10] The remark was made for the sake of a play on words: "Rache" (revenge) and "Rachen" (jaws). (TK, III, 191, n. 1.)

This was probably the copyist Wolanek against whom the composer had railed repeatedly. In delivering some uncompleted manuscripts by messenger some time before Easter, Wolanek ventured a defense of his dignity in a letter which, though couched in polite phrases, was nevertheless decidedly ironical and cutting:[11]

To Herr Ludwig v. Beethoven!

Since I cannot add the finale to the score until Easter and you will no longer need it at this time, I am sending over the complete parts along with what has already been begun for your favorable disposition.

I remain gratefully obliged for the honor rendered by your employment of me; as for more concerning the discordant behavior towards me, I can only regard it smilingly as a good-natured outburst to be accepted. In the ideal world of tones there are so many dissonances, shouldn't they exist also in the real world?

My one comfort is the firm conviction that had Mozart and Haydn, those celebrated artists, been hired as your copyists they would have shared a fate similar to mine.

I request only not to mix with those common copyists who consider themselves happy to be able to maintain their existence by being treated as slaves.

At any rate be assured that I will never have the least bit of cause to blush in front of you on account of my behavior.

Respectfully yours Ferd. Wolanek

Beethoven read the letter, and, in a rage, drew lines across its face from corner to corner. Then in letters two inches long he scrawled over the writing the words: "Dummer, Eingebildeter, Eselhafter Kerl"—("Stupid, Conceited, Asinine Fellow"). That was not enough. There was a wide margin at the bottom of the sheet, just large enough to hold Beethoven's next ebullition: "Compliments for such a good-for-nothing, who pilfers one's money?—better to pull his asinine ears." Then he turned the sheet over. A whole page invited him—and he filled it up the middle with "Dirty Scribbler! Stupid Fellow! Correct the blunders which you have made in your ignorance, insolence, conceit and stupidity, this would be more to the purpose than to try to teach me, which is as if a *Sow* were to try to give lessons to Minerva." The margins were still available: on the right—"*Do you do honor* to Mozart and Haydn by never mentioning *their names*." On the left; "It was decided yesterday and even before then *not to have you* write *any more* for me."[12]

⟩The story of the events leading up to the first performance of the E-flat Quartet has been set forth in detail by Alfred Ebert[13] and may be summarized here. In January, 1825, Schuppanzigh was starting another

---

[11] The letter implies that Beethoven had already treated him to an outburst of temper. (Cf. TDR, v, 175-76.)

[12] According to Unger, these outbursts were never sent in the form of a letter ("Beethovens Handschrift," Heft 4 of *Veröffentlichungen*

des Beethoven-Hauses in Bonn).

[13] "Die ersten Aufführungen von Beethovens Es-dur Quartett (Op. 127) im Frühling 1825" in *DM*, Vol. 9, No. 13 (1910), pp. 42-63, 90-106.

subscription series of quartet concerts and was anxious to have his quartet (Holz, 2nd violin; Weiss, viola; Linke, cello) give the first performance of the work at the opening concert. In a Conversation Book he writes:

If he [Beethoven] has a mind to hand me the quartet for a performance, that is, so I can make it known, there may be a big difference in my present subscription.

In E-flat

He allows me then to be the one to make it known?

Beethoven affirmed the question to the delight of Schuppanzigh, who must have assumed that the quartet was ready, for the following notice appeared on January 20 in Bäuerle *Theaterzeitung*:

The famous musical artist Herr Schuppanzigh will continue his popular quartet performances but in the small *Vereinssaal beim roten Igel*. The first concert is on Sunday, January 23; the most distinguished of the new musical works are: the new renowned double quartet by L. Spohr as introduction, a new quintet [*sic!*] by Ludw. van Beethoven (still in manuscript) and in conclusion by common request the most famous and popular Septet by the same artist.

Schuppanzigh rushed this into print no doubt because he knew how easily Beethoven's decisions could be altered. His fear was justified. At the urging of Johann and Karl, Beethoven had promised the quartet to Linke for a benefit concert. The conflict was discussed and Beethoven was persuaded to let Linke have it first and then let Schuppanzigh perform it as often as he liked. Thereupon Schuppanzigh was invited to lunch to learn the decision. Schuppanzigh writes:

This affair with the quartet is accursed.

That doesn't matter; he can also give it to Linke. His music can be heard more often than once.

I wouldn't say anything if it were not already in the newspaper.

I cannot call it off.

He makes nothing of it.

Linke has said nothing about it to me. If he had spoken to me I would not have asked him for it.

I have said it myself[14] to Linke and he hasn't said a word about it.

---

[14] That Schuppanzigh is performing the music.

But he certainly hasn't promised him because that isn't his habit; he has perhaps given him a half-consent, still that is not yet a solemn promise.

•~•

I recall that Linke spoke to me of a quartet in A Minor which is supposed to be concertante for the cello.[15]

•~•

It is no disadvantage for Linke if he gives it to him now too.

Schuppanzigh succeeded in swinging the decision back in his favor, and Linke was given the hope of getting the A Minor Quartet, which was realized in the fall. In the meantime he was annoyed and held Schuppanzigh responsible for the change. However, by the middle of January the quartet still was not ready so that for his first concert Schuppanzigh had to substitute the Quartet in F Minor, Op. 95.

During January and February there was also much conversation concerning another set of spring concerts of Beethoven's works, in which the name of Schuppanzigh played a prominent part. Karl, who seemed consistently to take sides against Schuppanzigh argued for Ferdinand Piringer, now director of the *Concerts spirituels*: "Piringer demands nothing.—And you must give Schuppanzigh a third of the total of all those concerts." There was similar talk concerning the sale of tickets, the program, and the locale of the concert. Schuppanzigh meanwhile was worried not only about the delay in starting rehearsals for these concerts—which were never to materialize— but also the delay in receiving the new quartet for the second concert on March 6. In the middle of February he asks: "How is the quartet getting on?"

No Conversation Books from this time to the time of the concert have survived[16] to clarify just when Schuppanzigh actually received the parts. However there is a letter[17] from Beethoven to the violinist in which he mentions the fact that the quartet is now his to perform from this moment "until the second Sunday." Since the March 6th concert took place on a Sunday, this could mean that the quartet was sent less than two weeks before performance. In any case, in view of what happened at the performance, and afterwards, it is clear that Schuppanzigh did not have enough time for proper rehearsing of such a difficult work.}~•—

Beethoven was greatly concerned with the outcome, and, as if at once to encourage and admonish the players, he drafted a humorous document and sent it to the quartet for signature. The statement is in another hand[18] and signed by Beethoven. The signatures of the players follow in pencil:

[15] This remarkable statement was made when Beethoven was working on the first and last movements of Op. 132. In the summer of 1825, Holz wrote in a Conversation Book: "The violoncello has very many so-called grateful passages in the new quartet."

[16] In the same Conversation Book referred to above, Johann writes (21 pages later):

"When you have the quartet copied, you will have part of it copied here." Two pages later: "In any case it is safest if you take some pages out and have them copied here or at my house."

[17] See *A* 1350.

[18] According to Thayer (TDR, v, 179, n. 2), this is in Karl's handwriting. However,

Best ones!

Each one is herewith given his part and is bound by oath and indeed pledged on his honor to do his best, to distinguish himself and to vie each with the other in excellence.

Each one who takes part in the affair in question is to sign this sheet.

Schuppanzigh   Beethoven

  Weiss

  Linke   Schindler secretarius

The grand master's accursed violoncello.

  Holz

The last, but only in signing.

The performance took place on March 6, and the result was disappointing. The music was not understood either by the players or the public and was all but ineffective. Schuppanzigh was held responsible and his patience must have been severely taxed by Beethoven's upbraidings and his determination to have an immediate repetition by other players. Schuppanzigh defended himself as vigorously as possible and was particularly vexed because Beethoven cited his brother's opinion of the performance—that of a musical ignoramus. He wanted to play the Quartet a second time, but told Beethoven that he had no objections to the work being handed over to Böhm; yet he protested with no little energy, that the fault of the fiasco was not his individually, as Beethoven had been told. He could easily master the technical difficulties, but it was hard to arrive at the spirit of the work: the ensemble was faulty, because of this fact and too few rehearsals. Beethoven decided that the next hearing should be had from Böhm, and though Schuppanzigh had acquiesced, he harbored a grievance against the composer for some time.

Joseph Böhm[19] had been leader of the quartet concerts in Vienna during Schuppanzigh's long absence. He has left an account of his connection with the work as follows:

> . . . The affair did not come off well. Schuppanzigh, who played first violin, was weary from much rehearsing, there was no finish in the performance, the quartet did not appeal to him, he was not well disposed towards the performance and the quartet did not please. Few were moved, it was a weak *succès d'estime*.
>
> When Beethoven learned of this—for he was not present at the performance— he became furious and let both performers and the public in for some harsh words. Beethoven could have no peace until the disgrace was wiped off. He sent for me first thing in the morning—In his usual curt way, he said to me. "You must play my quartet"—and the thing was settled.—Neither objections nor doubts could prevail; what Beethoven wanted had to take place, so I undertook the difficult task.—It was studied industriously and rehearsed frequently under Beethoven's own eyes: I said Beethoven's *eyes* intentionally, for the unhappy man was so

---

Miss Anderson (III, 1182, n. 5) identifies it as Schindler's hand. This is further borne out by Schindler's signing the document as "secretarius."

[19] Böhm (1795–1876) became a professor of violin playing at the Vienna Conservatory in 1819, a member of the Imperial Orchestra in 1821. He was a teacher of Joseph Joachim.

deaf that he could no longer hear the heavenly sound of his compositions. And yet rehearsing in his presence was not easy. With close attention his eyes followed the bows and therefore he was able to judge the smallest fluctuations in tempo or rhythm and correct them immediately. At the close of the last movement of this quartet there occurred a *meno vivace*,[20] which seemed to me to weaken the general effect. At the rehearsal, therefore, I advised that the original tempo be maintained, which was done, to the betterment of the effect.

Beethoven, crouched in a corner, heard nothing, but watched with strained attention. After the last stroke of the bows he said, laconically, "Let it remain so," went to the desks and crossed out the *meno vivace* in the four parts.

The quartet was performed finally and received with a real storm of applause. Now Beethoven was satisfied. Steiner, who had attended one or more of the rehearsals, was particularly enraptured by it and at once offered to buy it for publication for 60 ducats—a fact which Beethoven did not fail to report to Schott and Sons when he sent the manuscript to them. --◦◦{The work was played three times by Böhm with the other three members of the Schuppanzigh quartet: once for a small audience, twice a few days later for a larger audience in an evening concert on March 23. Then Böhm asked Beethoven's permission to use the quartet in a benefit concert for himself, which he clearly deserved.}◦◦-- On April 28 Bäuerle's *Theaterzeitung* made a report on Schuppanzigh's concert, the details of which are already known, and on Böhm's, which follows: ". . . then a steadfast patron of art and noble connoisseur brought about a new performance of this quartet by the above named man with the substitution for first violin of Herr. Prof. Böhm, since this group in the meantime had played the new quartet for a small group of art lovers with particular success. This professor now performed the wonderful quartet, twice over on the same evening, for the same very numerous company of artists and connoisseurs in a way that left nothing to be desired, the misty veil disappeared and the splendid work of art radiated its dazzling glory. Although Prof. Böhm had a lighter touch, yet this composition was heard from a master; if it was also imperfect yet it was so performed that one had to recognize an artist familiar with Beethoven's spirit; but he has provided a productive growth to his fame through the playing three times of this uncommonly difficult quartet. Such artistic trials of strength are the greatest gain for the art especially if, as here, the loser himself doesn't yield; for every impartial person must confess that Herr Schuppanzigh could not play *this* composition better in so short a time, whether he should not or could not have postponed that performance is another question which may be answered by someone better informed, if he dares to do so."

--◦◦{The quartet had been given one performance by Schuppanzigh, three performances by Böhm already with a fourth one for his benefit in early

---

[20] The mark is *Allegro con moto* in the Complete Works Edition; *Allo. commodo* in others. (TK, III, 193, n. 1.)

April; on April 15 and again in the latter part of April Joseph Mayseder performed the work with his own group at private concerts in the house of Dembscher, an official or agent of the war department of the Austrian Government.}ஃ⸱-- The quartet by now received what Holz described as a "réparation d'honneur."[21] Beethoven was completely satisfied and, no doubt, went to work on its successor with a contented mind.

It has now become necessary to pay attention to the new friend of Beethoven whose name has already been mentioned—the successor of Schindler, as he had been of Oliva, in the office of factotum in ordinary. This was Karl Holz, a young man (he was born in 1798) who occupied a post in the States' Chancellery of Lower Austria. He had studied music with Glöggl in Linz; yet Schuppanzigh also called him his pupil. He was a capable violinist and had already been for some time a member of Böhm's quartet group; then upon Schuppanzigh's return from Russia in 1823, he became a second in the latter's quartet. He seems to have come into closer contact with Beethoven early in the spring of 1825, probably when, having to conduct a performance of the B-flat Symphony at a concert in the Redoutensaal, he asked an audience of the composer in order that he might get the tempi for that work. Though not a professional musician, he gave music lessons, later occasionally conducted the *Concerts spirituels* and eventually became the regular director of these affairs. Emboldened by the kindness with which he was first received he gradually drew nearer to the composer and in August, 1825, an intimate friendship seemed imminent, as is indicated by Beethoven's remark in a letter, dated August 24, to his nephew: "It seems as if Holz might become a friend." He was good at figures, a quality which made him particularly serviceable to Beethoven (who was woefully deficient in arithmetic)[22] at a time when he was dealing with foreign publishers and there was great confusion in money values and rates of exchange. He was also a well-read man, a clever talker, musically cultured, a cheery companion, and altogether an engaging person. All these qualities, no less than the fact that he was strong and independent in his convictions and fearless in his proclamation of them, recommended him to Beethoven, and he does not seem to have hesitated to take advantage of the fact that he entered the inner circle of Beethoven's companions at a time when the composer had begun to feel a growing antipathy to Schindler. He promptly embraced the opportunity which his willing usefulness brought him, to draw close to the great man, to learn of him and also to exhibit himself to the world as his confidential friend. He was not obsequious, and this pleased Beethoven despite the fact that he

[21] In a Conversation Book these comparisons were made: *Karl*: "Mayseder plays more brilliantly, Böhm more expressively." *Holz*: "I believe that Mayseder would play it better.—He conducts the other three while Böhm lets it conduct itself." (TDR, v, 183, n. 2.)

[22] There are pitiful proofs in the Conversation Books that simple sums in addition were more than he could master and that on his deathbed he studied the mysteries of multiplication. (TK, III, 194, n. 1.)

himself was not indisposed to play upon his friends for his own purposes "like instruments," as he himself once confessed.

In a short time Holz made himself indispensable and acquired great influence over the composer. He aided him in the copying of his works, looked into the affairs of nephew Karl and reported upon them, advised him in his correspondence, and directed his finances at a time when he was more than ordinarily desirous to acquire money so that he might leave a competency on his death to his foster-son. In time Beethoven came to entrust weighty matters to his decision, even the choice of publishers and his dealings with them. His prepossessing address, heightened by his independence of speech, made it less easy to contradict him than Schindler. Moreover, the recorded conversations show that he was witty, that he had a wider outlook on affairs than Beethoven's other musical advisors, that his judgements were quickly reached and unhesitatingly pronounced, even concerning composers and art forms. It is astonishing, for example, that he was allowed to express a very bold opinion, contrary to Beethoven's, about Mozart. His speeches were not free from frivolity nor always from flattery, but he lived at a time and among people accustomed to extravagant compliments, and there can be no doubt of his reverence for Beethoven. In April Holz said to him: "I am no flatterer, but I assure you that the mere thought of Beethovenian music makes me glad, first of all, that I am alive."[23] He wanted to be Beethoven's friend, and Beethoven recognized how valuable he was to him, so their friendship gradually became closer.

We owe much of our knowledge of the relations between Beethoven and Holz to Schindler's statements as they appear in his biography,[24] two articles which appeared in the *Kölnische Zeitung* in 1845, and among the glosses on the Conversation Book. But many of his utterances show ill-feeling, which is not unfair to trace back to a jealousy dating back to the time when Holz crowded Beethoven's "Secretary sans Salary" out of Beethoven's service and good graces. There was no open rupture between Beethoven and Schindler, but a feeling of coolness and indifference which grew with the advancement of the younger man in the favor of the composer. The results of Beethoven's fellowship with a cheery companion were certainly not so great as Schindler says, nor so evil and grievous as he intimates. Beethoven was accustomed to drink wine from youth up, and also to the companionship which he found in the inns and coffee-houses of Vienna. It was, moreover, undoubtedly a charitable act to drag him out of his isolation into cheerful company. We know that he was so accustomed to take wine at his meals that his physicians found it difficult to make him obey their prohibition of wine and heating spices when he was ill. Beethoven's table habits were thus described by Holz to Jahn: "He was a stout eater of substantial

[23] J. G. Prodhomme, *Cahiers de Conversation de Beethoven* (Paris, 1946), p. 346.

[24] Vol. II, pp. 107-110; 323-30. (TDR, v, 186.)

food; he drank a great deal of wine at table, but could stand a great deal, and in merry company he sometimes became tipsy (*bekneipte er sich*). In the evening he drank beer or wine, generally the wine of Vöslau or red Hungarian. When he had drunk he never composed. After the meal he took a walk."

Beethoven's letters to Holz bear witness to his fond regard for the man. His name, which in German signifies "wood" and in the literature of the Church also "cross," provided Beethoven with a welcome chance to indulge his extravagant fondness for punning. Thus, in the composer's jovial address book, not distinguished by reverence in anything sacred or profane, Holz becomes "Best Mahogany," "Best Splinter from the Cross of Christ," "Best lignum crucis." --->§{The tone of the letters, unlike those to Schindler, was always respectful and even upon occasion conciliatory, as is shown by the beginning of the following note: "Dear Friend! You can be assured that I am not thinking any more of the recent incident and that this will never change my feelings of gratitude towards you."[25]}§•-- Holz had his entire confidence, and when the great catastrophe of 1826 came, Holz was the strongest prop upon which he leaned.[26]

The E-flat Quartet had been successfully brought forward, a pause had been reached in the correspondence with Schott and Sons and Neate, a summer home for Beethoven was in prospect, and considerable progress had been made in the draft for the second quartet designed for Prince Galitzin, when an illness befell Beethoven which kept him within doors, and for a portion of the time in bed, from about the middle of April to the middle of May, 1825. In the middle of April Schindler writes: "I believe that this is the result of your exertions in recent days and the disorder in your way of living.— —Dear master, think of the future. What will be the result of your working at night? Otherwise it would never have happened."

Beethoven had been told by his physician that he was in danger of an inflammation of the bowels, and as such Beethoven described his ailment in letters to Piringer and to Schott and Sons.[27] Dr. Staudenheim had been in attendance on him before and had insisted upon strict obedience to his prescriptions. Beethoven sent for him again and was apparently unsuccessful in getting him to come to his house where he was confined, for he writes down: "Braunhofer Bauernmarkt No. 588." --->§{The distinguished Viennese doctor, Anton Braunhofer, had been giving medical attention to Beethoven periodically since 1820. On April 18 he received the following letter from the composer:

My honored friend,

I am feeling poorly and hope you will not deny me your help since I am suf-

[25] Letter of April 26, 1826.
[26] For a study of Holz see Walter Nohl, "Karl Holz in seinem Verhältnis zu Ludwig van Beethoven" in *Neue Musik-Zeitung*, Vol. 46 (1925), p. 180.
[27] See *A* 1368 and 1370.

fering great pain. Is it possible for you to visit me as early as today, this I beg of you from the bottom of my heart—

With everlasting gratitude and respect, your

Beethoven[28]

Dr. Braunhofer proved to be even less considerate of the patient's wilfulness than his predecessor, he was so blunt and forceful in his demands for obedience that Beethoven was somewhat awed, and beneficial results followed.[29] Dr. Braunhofer did not want to "trouble" Beethoven for long with medicines, but he gave orders for a strict diet.

No wine, no coffee; no spices of any kind. I'll arrange matters with the cook.

Then I will guarantee you full recovery which means alot to me, understandably, as your admirer and friend.

A sickness does not disappear in a day. I shall not trouble you much longer with medicine, but you must adhere to the diet, you'll not starve on it.

Braunhofer was encouraged that his patient's fever had already lessened, and Karl reminded the composer that the prohibition of spirits had also been ordered under Staudenheim. Braunhofer continues:

You must do some work in the daytime so that you *can sleep at night*. If you want to get entirely well and live a long time, you must live according to nature. You are very liable to inflammatory attacks and were close to a severe attack of inflammation of the bowels; the predisposition is still in your body.

I will give you a powder—

I'll wager that if you take a drink of spirits, you'll be lying weak and exhausted on your back in a few hours. . . .

The doctor inspired him with courage and hope, and admonished him to keep quiet and patient. In dry weather he was to take walks, but even after going to Baden he must take no baths as long as the weather remained damp and symptoms of his illness remained.

When you have been in Baden for awhile, it will be better, and should there be a recurrence, let me know. When are you going?

Do not forget the bit of music, just something unimportant, what matters is that it is your handwriting.

[28] The address "Johannisgasse No. 969 im 4ten Stock, rechts die Tür" is given in another hand, identified by Miss Anderson as that of Karl. See *A* 1359.

[29] For fuller details of the diagnosis and treatment, see Walter Nohl, "Beethoven und sein Arzt Anton Braunhofer," *DM*, Vol. 30, No. 12 (1938), pp. 823ff.

You should be striving to get to the country soon.

•〰•

It will give you fresh air, the walks here are too fatiguing.

•〰•

In the country you can have natural milk.

In the beginning of May Beethoven's condition had improved sufficiently for him to make the long-planned move to Baden, which he did on May 7. On May 13 he wrote to Dr. Braunhofer the following humorous note in the form of a dialogue between doctor and patient:

Esteemed Friend!

D: How is the patient?

Pat: We are in bad health—still very weak, and are belching and so forth. I think that a stronger medicine is going to be necessary, but one which is not binding—By now surely I should be allowed to drink white wine diluted with water, for that mephitic beer is simply revolting to me—my catarrhal condition is as follows: I spit up rather a lot of blood, apparently only from the windpipe. But often it streams out of my nose, as happened frequently last winter as well. There is no doubt that my stomach has become terribly weakened and that my whole system suffers generally from this. I know my nature well enough to know that on its own my strength would hardly be able to be restored.

D: I will help first by being a Brownian then a Stollian.[30]

Pat: I should be glad to have some strength again so that I could be at my desk. Do think this over—*Finis*.

As soon as I come to the city I will see you. Just tell Karl when I can find you. However, it would be helpful to me if you could suggest to Karl what is still to be done. I took the last medicine only once and then lost it—

With respect and gratitude

Your friend Beethoven

Dok-tor sperrt das Tor dem Tod, No-te hilft auch aus der Noth
[Close the door 'gainst Death I plead, Doctor, notes will help in need]

Dok-tor sperrt das Tor dem Tod, No-te hilft auch aus der Noth
[Close the door 'gainst Death I plead, Doctor, notes will help in need]

Written on May 11, 1825 in the Helenthal, Baden on the second Antons Brücke on the way to Siechenfeld.

Beethoven[31]

<hr>

[30] Two schools of medical thought were represented by the Scottish Doctor John Brown (1735-1788) and the Viennese Doctor Maximilian Stoll (1742-1787). Brown attributed sickness to the sensitivity of the organs; Stoll thought in pathological and anatomological terms, which was unusual at that time.

[31] On a Tuesday, May 31, Beethoven wrote to his nephew that he planned to come to the city the next Saturday, June 4. On this trip he wrote out another canon for Braunhofer with the words "I was here, Doctor, I was

Despite the humorous manner of expression, it is clear that Beethoven took his condition seriously and longed to get working again. This happened soon thereafter; on May 17 he wrote to his nephew, "I am beginning to write a bit again." The work taken up was the A Minor Quartet, the progress of which had been interrupted by the illness. In a Conversation Book used in May or June, 1825, Beethoven writes: "Hymn of Thanksgiving to God of an Invalid on his Convalescence. Feeling of new strength and reawakened feeling."[32] As will appear, these words, slightly modified, formed the title of a newly planned second movement to the quartet, the "Song of Thanksgiving in the Lydian mode."

It was while Beethoven was ill in Vienna that Ludwig Rellstab made several visits to him, of which he has left enthusiastic reports.[33] He was 26 years old at the time and had made a mark as essayist and poet; the chief object of his journey to Vienna from Berlin, on which he set out on March 21, was to see the composer. He reached the Austrian capital in the last days of March or the first days of April. His account of the meeting is like many others except that it is written with literary elegance, albeit with that excessive fervor, that *Überschwänglichkeit*, which is characteristic of German hero-worshippers. ⟶Further, Rellstab admitted himself that while he had a clear memory of what had happened in the large he could not remember the words of the conversation literally. The details of his text thus cannot pretend to be accurate.⟵ Zelter had given him a letter of introduction in which he mentioned that Rellstab wanted to write the libretto of an opera to be set by the composer. After Beethoven had warmly greeted his visitor and expressed delight with Zelter's letter, this subject was broached and Beethoven expressed his pleasure at the prospect of getting an opera-book from Rellstab, since it was not easy to get a good poem. He mentioned past difficulties with Grillparzer, since the poet wanted one thing, and he another. Rellstab then quotes Beethoven as saying: "I care little what genre the works belong to, so the material be attractive to me. But it must be something which I can take up with sincerity and love. I could not compose operas like *Don Juan* and *Figaro*. They are repugnant to me. I could not have chosen such subjects; they are too frivolous for me!"

Rellstab had had it in mind to write an opera-book for Weber and had pondered over many subjects, and he now gave a list of these to Beethoven— "Attila," "Antigone," "Belisarius," "Orestes" and others. Beethoven read the names thoughtfully and then apologized for the trouble he was causing his visitor. Rellstab, seeing an expression of weariness in his face, took his departure, after saying that he would send him a specimen of his handiwork.

---

here." On the autograph is written: "On June 4th in the evening when I found that my honored friend Braunhofer was not at home—Beethoven." See KHV, p. 693.

[32] "Dankhimne eines Kranken an Gott bei seiner Genesung Gefühl neuer Kraft und wiederwachtes Gefühl." (TDR, v, 266-67.)

[33] *Aus meinem Leben* (Berlin, 1861), ii, pp. 224ff. (TDR, v, 196, n. 4.)

In a Conversation Book used in the middle of April there is further talk between Rellstab and Beethoven about opera, but the notes, which are fragmentary, give no indications of Beethoven's views.

The most interesting incident of the meetings occurred at a subsequent visit. Rellstab had told that he had been deeply moved (he dared not express a more specific opinion on the subject, being in doubt himself) by the Quartet in E-flat, which he had heard performed twice in succession.[34] He continues: "Beethoven read and remained silent; we looked at each other mutely, but a world of emotions surged in my breast. Beethoven, too, was unmistakably moved. He arose and went to the window, where he remained standing beside the pianoforte. To see him so near the instrument gave me an idea which I had never before dared to harbor. If he—Oh! he needed only to turn half way around and he would be facing the keyboard—if he would but sit down and give expression to his feelings in tones! Filled with a timid, blissful hope, I approached him and laid my hand upon the instrument. It was an English pianoforte by Broadwood. I struck a chord lightly with my right hand in order to induce Beethoven to turn around; but he seemed not to have heard it. A few moments later, however, he turned to me, and, seeing my eyes fixed upon the instrument he said: 'That is a beautiful pianoforte! I got it as a present from London. Look at these names.' He pointed to the crossbeam over the keyboard. There I saw several names which I had not before noticed—Moscheles, Kalkbrenner, Cramer, Clementi, Broadwood himself. . . . 'That is a beautiful gift,' said Beethoven looking at me, 'and it has such a beautiful tone,' he continued and moved his hands towards the keys without taking his eyes off me. He gently struck a chord. Never again will one enter my soul so poignant, so heartbreaking as that one was! He struck C major with the right hand and B as a bass in the left, and continued his gaze uninterruptedly on me, repeated the false chord several times in order to let the sweet tone of the instrument reverberate; and the greatest musician on earth did not hear the dissonance! Whether or not Beethoven noticed his mistake I do not know; but when he turned his head from me to the instrument he played a few chords correctly and then stopped. That was all that I heard from him directly."

Rellstab had planned a short excursion to Hungary and then intended to leave Vienna for his home. Fearful that he might not see Beethoven on his return to the city he went to him to say farewell: "Beethoven spoke very frankly and with feeling. I expressed my regret that in all the time of my sojourn in Vienna I had heard, except one of his symphonies and a quartet, not a single composition of his in concert,[35] why had *Fidelio* not been given? This gave him an opportunity to express himself on the subject of the taste

---

[34] It was probably the performance by Böhm. (TK, III, 201, n. 1.)

[35] As Ebert points out (*DM*, Vol. 9, No. 3, p. 106) this was not Vienna's fault. The B-flat Symphony was played on April 4, and on April 14, the Symphony in A. Schuppanzigh's group performed the quartets, and many concerts started with Beethoven overtures.

of the Vienna people. 'Since the Italians [Barbaja] have gotten such a strong foothold here the best has been crowded out. For the nobility, the chief thing at the theatre is the ballet. Nothing can be said about their appreciation of art; they have sense only for horses and dancers. We have always had this state of things. But this gives me no concern; I want only to write that which gives me joy. If I were well it would be all the same to me!' "

On his departure Beethoven, who had been absent from his lodgings when Rellstab called for his final leavetaking, sent him a letter to Steiner and Co., containing a canon on the words from Matthisson's *Opferlied* of which he had made use on at least one earlier occasion ("Das Schöne zu dem Guten").

During the summer at Baden, there was increasing tension between Beethoven and his nephew. However, before describing this, an account should be given of the composer's relationship to Karl during the early part of the year, in order to give a background for the growing preoccupation of his mind during these months. In the winter of 1824-25 Karl was still pursuing his studies in philology at the University of Vienna. The summer before, he had unsuccessfully tried to persuade his uncle to let him enter the army and abandon the career which had been chosen for him, which was probably that of a professor of languages. In the spring of 1825 Karl again was trying to make a shift in his studies. He wanted to enroll in a training school for a mercantile career, and this time he was successful in persuading his uncle. An early reference to the change occurs in a Conversation Book entry in March:[36]

I wanted to ask you whether perhaps you would not mind if I went to the Italian Opera today because it is the last opera. If I had known yesterday I would have stayed at home in order not to go to the theatre two days in succession. Meanwhile, of course, I am neglecting nothing, and when I once go to the Polytechnic Institute, this will happen very seldom anyhow. But if this is not all right with you, we will drop it. Otherwise I will go in the fourth balcony where it costs 30x.

Beethoven's reluctance in giving his consent to this change is shown by an entry of Karl's in early April:

You know that I will not oppose you if you *wish* me to continue to study; but I really feel that I will progress much better there since in times past I have lost interest. Nevertheless I will never forget my Greek but continue with it consistently and industriously, the more since I am far enough along in it so that reading it is no longer a strain for me but rather a pleasure.

In a letter to Karl Peters[37] Beethoven expressed his opposition to the plan, and took the attitude that Karl dreaded the university examinations because of "false modesty" rather than lack of ability. However, he said that he would agree to the change if Peters thought it best. The decision was finally

[36] All Conversation Book entries concerning Beethoven and Karl's relationship are found in the appendix to TDR, v, 510ff.
[37] See *A* 1360.

made, and Karl's conciliatory attitude towards his uncle at this time is shown by a Conversation Book entry written during the spring:

I am earnestly resolved to continue with zeal on the way that we have chosen; also I see that the subjects are not unpleasant at all. Some of them, for instance history and mathematics, in so far as they affect merchants will be given as well if not better than at the university. Thus it will undoubtedly go well.

Karl entered the Polytechnic Institute about Easter, 1825, and Beethoven arranged to have the vice-director, Dr. Reisser, appointed as co-guardian in place of Peters, with whom he took counsel as he also did, in great likelihood, with Stephan von Breuning. There were two great admirers of Beethoven's music at the Institute, Reisser and Dr. Ignaz von Sonnleithner, one of the teachers. Karl was placed under the supervision of a government official named Schlemmer, who lived in the Alleegasse adjacent to the Karlskirche, and with whom the lad took lodgings. According to reports from Dr. Reisser and Karl himself, he made a good beginning in his studies, although he was hampered by the fact that he had entered late in the term and therefore had a good deal of back work to cover. A special tutor was engaged to help him with this.

After Beethoven's move to the country, Karl was expected to visit his uncle in Baden on Sundays and holidays, but conflict on this point soon developed. Furthermore, now that the two were separated, Beethoven worried about Karl's whole way of life and sought to keep tight control over him, despite the fact that the young man was nearly nineteen. In an undated letter to Schlemmer, Beethoven voiced the suspicion that Karl mingled with bad company in the evenings. He continues: "I request you hereafter to watch out and under no pretext to let him outside of the house at night unless you have received something through Karl in writing from me."

Of Karl's feelings we learn mainly from the Conversation Books; of Beethoven's, from a remarkable series of letters that he wrote to his nephew from Baden, most of which are in the Berlin State Library. In a Conversation Book entry Karl showed the strain he was feeling from the demands on his time made both by his uncle and by his studies. Beethoven had evidently come to Vienna on business. Karl writes:

It is impossible to get everything done today if I also have some things to attend to with you. But I will take some things along because we are very much overloaded and on Sundays have to write out everything that has been presented during the whole of the week.

•~•

I really would like to go out with you today but it is almost impossible to do much out there because it is so much trouble to take along all the books and papers that I need; besides since I must go along with you to see about the lodging, there remains but little time for me.

•~•

Thus I think I will meet you somewhere around 12 o'clock and walk with you to the house and to the other places and eat with you. But then not come out till tomorrow so that I can make the most of having an evening to myself; for you do not realize *how much* there is to write and to study in order to satisfy the wishes of the professors and especially Reisser who watches me, moreover, very attentively.

 ⸺·

The day after tomorrow I could then come back early and be with you all day tomorrow.

 ⸺·

The work doesn't progress as fast as one would think.

And Karl goes on to elaborate in detail the number of subjects and the work for their preparation.

The first series of notes from Beethoven to Karl, written in May, were concerned with the poor weather, his feelings of weakness, household matters about which he asked Karl's help, and mentions of his projected weekend visits. On May 22, however, only fifteen days after his move, there was an abrupt change in the tone of Beethoven's letters upon his hearing that Karl had been seeing his mother. He writes:

Until now [it was] only conjecture although someone assured me that there were secret dealings again between you and your mother—Am I to experience once again the most abominable ingratitude? No, if this bond is to be broken, so be it, but you will be despised by all impartial men who hear of this ingratitude. . . . Shall I get involved again in these vulgarities? No, never again—in God's name if the Pactum weighs upon you—I turn you over to Divine Providence. I have done my job and upon this I can appear before the mightiest of all judges. Do not be afraid to come to me tomorrow, I can still presume, God grant, that *nothing of this* is true, for if it were truly your unhappiness would be unending, lightheartedly as my rascally brother and your—mother would take this matter—

I am expecting you for sure—along with the old woman.[38]

At the end of the next letter, written nine days later, Beethoven was still bitter:

. . . —God is my witness, I dream only of being completely removed from you and from this wretched brother and this abominable family to which I am attached—God grant me my wish, for I *cannot* trust *you* any more—

Unfortunately your Father or better not
your Father

[38] Probably the housekeeper. Throughout the summer correspondence Beethoven complains about the ineptitude of his two servants. The housekeeper is referred to as "the old witch," "the old woman," "the old beast," etc., and her helper as "the wench," "Satanas," etc.

One more letter from the earlier part of the summer deserves to be cited in full, containing as it does one of Beethoven's references to death:

Baden, June 9, 1825

I wish at least that you would come here Saturday, I ask for an answer to no avail—God be with you and with me

as always your faithful Father

I have written to H. v. Reissig[39] to ask you to come here on Saturday. The carriage leaves Vienna around six o'clock and in fact *from the Kugel auf der Wieden.* Consequently you have only to get some work or study done before so that you will not lose anything by this. I am sorry to cause you this trouble— In the afternoon around five o'clock you will return again by the same carriage to Vienna. It is paid for already beforehand. In the morning you can shave here and also get a shirt and necktie in order to arrive there conveniently—Farewell, although I am sulky with you it is not without reason, and I would have liked not to have spent so much in order to have given to the world an *ordinary man*— I hope to see you without fail—Moreover *if the intrigues have already developed,* explain yourself openly and naturally and you will find one who is concerned consistently with what is good.

The lodging was advertised in the newspaper again on Tuesday. If you were unable to do anything, at least someone else could have written if by chance you were unwell—I would rather *not have to think anything else*—You know how I live here, with the cold weather to boot. The continual solitude weakens me even more, for often through my weakness I am really on the verge of feebleness. Oh do not pain me more; the man with the scythe will not be giving me much more time.

If you were to find a good lodging for me in the Alleegasse I would take it.

That Beethoven was becoming increasingly concerned over Karl's life in Vienna is further shown by the fact that he discussed these matters with his friends and asked their aid. On June 10 he wrote to Bernard asking him to see something of Karl since he was worried about his behavior and feared that he was becoming involved again with his mother. He informed Bernard that Reisser was the new co-guardian and said that since he had never met him he was not sure he would be co-operative. Therefore, he asked Bernard to call upon Reisser, to present him with Beethoven's qualifications as guardian, and to inform him that Blöchlinger had never allowed "her" at his house.

In September, at the time of the preparations for the first performance of the Quartet in A Minor, there are some entries by Karl Holz in the Conversation Books which suggest the role he was playing as Beethoven's helper:

On Sunday I was with Karl in order to give him your note; it was evening and I learned from the maid that he had gone out in the early morning and had not come back home to eat—

•~•

[39] Beethoven means Reisser, the co-guardian. During the summer he frequently makes this mistake.

I have a plan to attach him closer to myself, I would like to win him over to my side; perhaps in this way I will learn to know him and his way of life more easily;

•~•

then I will dissuade him in a friendly manner—

•~•

I have lured him into going to a beer house with me because I [wanted] to see if he drinks much; but that does not appear to be the case. Now I will invite [him] at some point to play billiards; then I will see immediately if he has already been practising a long time—

•~•

What harm can come to him if he goes through the city from the Alservorstadt—

•~•

What do other young people do about it?

•~•

I think rather that you should give him something periodically for his efforts and the hardships he endures—

•~•

but no money[40]

•~•

I told him also that he is not supposed to go often into the Josephstadt—

•~•

His reason is because it doesn't cost anything.

•~•

I also told him that his uncle would be more inclined to give him money if [he] listened to some classic pieces at the Burg a few times each month—

•~•

I told him also that I would speak with you about this; he didn't want that.

•~•

He has gotten the love of money from your brother.

The letters continued through the summer alternating between tenderness and reproach. With the young man's sense of money he had no patience whatever, and insisted upon a strict accounting for every florin which he allowed him. In September he was enraged when he heard that Karl had resorted to borrowing from the servants:

... You also borrowed again last Sunday 1 fl. 15 kr. from the housekeeper, that vulgar old kitchen-wench—It was long ago forbidden—Everywhere it is the

[40] Considering the context, Holz may very well have meant "but no money has been given him."

same. I should have gotten along two years with the frock-coat. True, I have the bad habit of wearing an old coat at home, but Herr Karl, oh fie the shame of it, and why? The money-bag Herr L. v. B—n is here only for this purpose—

On the other hand, Beethoven apparently trusted Karl enough to delegate to him not only minor household errands, but important correspondence and negotiations. Throughout this summer's correspondence, along with the scoldings and the reproaches, there are instances of Beethoven's instructing Karl what to do about letters to Galitzin, Peters and Schlesinger, and of his using Karl to represent him in financial transactions.[41]

In early October the letters became even more emotional. On the 5th of the month Beethoven writes from Baden:

Precious, dear son!

I have just received your letter. Filled with anxiety I had today determined to hasten to Vienna—God be thanked, it is not necessary. Do but obey me, and love and happiness of the soul paired with human happiness will be at our side; and you will unite an intensive inner existence with the external, but it were better that the *former* dominate the *latter*—il fait trop froid—I shall see you on Saturday then. Write whether you are coming in the morning or the evening so that I may hasten to meet you—

I embrace you and kiss you a thousand times not as my *prodigal but as my newly born son*—I wrote to Schlemmer. Do not think harshly on that account—I am still so filled with anxiety[42]——My anxiety and my worry over finding you again will show you that your father is full of love.

Ayez la bonté, de m'envoyer a *bottle for lighting* with *matches* from Rospini ou en porte avec vous puisque de celle de Kärtnerthor on ne peut pas faire usage—

Beethoven moved from Baden into the Schwarzspanierhaus, his final residence, on October 15, a Saturday. His letters to Karl during those final ten days in Baden alternate between instructions for moving possessions into the new rooms from the brother's apartments (where they had been stored over the summer) and violent reproaches for his conduct.[43] The following excerpt from a letter dated October 12 shows his state of mind:

I wish that you would stop such *selfishness at my expense. It does as little credit to me as it does towards setting you on the right and proper course.* Continue this way and you will rue the day! Not that I shall die sooner, however much this may be your desire; but while I am alive I shall separate myself completely from you, although I shall not abandon you for this reason or withdraw my support—Look for the fool who has been so sanctified and *so rewarded by you daily.* The worst part is the results that *will come to you* because of your behavior. Who will believe or trust you after hearing what has happened and how you have inflicted mortal wounds upon me and wounded me daily?

[41] See the following letters: *A* 1394, 1400, 1401, 1402, 1413, 1414 and 1437.

[42] According to TDR, v, p. 548, n. 1, a piece of the autograph has been torn off at this place.

[43] See the following: *A* 1440, 1441, 1442, 1444.

The point was made in this and all of these last letters, that he was counting on seeing something of his nephew on Saturday, October 15, when he was coming to Vienna. In another letter, just before he had made the move, he reminded Karl: "It pained me especially that you came out so late on Sunday[44] and hurried off again so early." Then came the move and with it an additional emotional outburst written from Vienna:

My precious son!

Go no further—Come but to my arms, not a harsh word shall you hear. O God, do not rush away in your misery. You will be received as lovingly as ever. What to consider, what to do in the future, these things we will talk over affectionately. On my word of honor no reproaches, since they would in no case do good now. Henceforth you may expect from me only the most loving care and help—Do but come—Come to the faithful heart of

your father Beethoven
Volti sub[ito]

Come home immediately upon receiving this.
Si vous ne viendres pas
vous me tûerès surement
    lisés la lettre et restés
a la maison chez vous, venes
de m'embrasser votre pere
vous vraiment adonné soyes
assurés, que tout cela resterà
entre nous.[45]
Only for God's sake come back home today. It might bring you who knows what danger. Hurry, Hurry.

Karl had clearly absented himself and it can be presumed that he had gone to his mother. At this point the correspondence stops, and the only other letter of the autumn is a matter-of-fact note concerning payment of money to Frau Schlemmer, and a request for some of his nephew's time for some letter-writing.[46] In November the Conversation Books show new points of conflict which are taken up in the next chapter.

During the summer Beethoven received a number of visitors whose meetings with the composer have been recorded either by themselves or in the Conversation Books.

Karl Gottfried Freudenberg, a young musician who afterwards became Head Organist at Breslau and wrote a book of reminiscences entitled *Erinnerungen eines alten Organisten*, visited Beethoven in July of the year and has left a record which is none the less interesting because its lack of literary flourish is offset by succinct reports of the great composer's estimate of some of his contemporaries, and his views on ecclesiastical music. Beethoven, according to Freudenberg, described Rossini as a "talented and a

---

[44] October 9.

[45] According to TDR, v, p. 549, this French part is written on the outside of the letter

under Karl's address, and the final sentences are on the top margin of the letter.

[46] A 1447.

melodious composer; his music suits the frivolous and sensuous spirit of the time, and his productivity is such that he needs only as many weeks as the Germans do years to write an opera." He said of Spontini: "There is much good in him; he understands theatrical effects and the musical noises of warfare thoroughly"; of Spohr: "He is too rich in dissonances, pleasure in his music is marred by his chromatic melody"; of Bach: "His name ought not to be Bach [brook] but Ocean, because of his infinite and inexhaustible wealth of combinations and harmonies. He was the ideal of an organist." This led Beethoven into the subject of music for the church. "I, too, played the organ a great deal in my youth," he said, "but my nerves could not stand the power of the gigantic instrument. I place an organist who is master of his instrument, first among virtuosi." Pure church music, he remarked, ought to be performed only by voices, unless the text be a *Gloria* or something of the kind. For this reason he preferred Palestrina to all other composers of church music, but it was folly to imitate him unless one had his genius and his religious beliefs; moreover, it was practically impossible for singers to-day to sing the long-sustained notes of this music in a cantabile manner.

The visit of Karl August Reichardt, afterwards Court Organist in Altenburg, seems to have been brief, and it is safe to presume that the young man received scant encouragement to remain long, for his talk was chiefly about himself, his desire to get advice as to a good teacher and to have Beethoven look at some of his music.

Otto de Boer was a member of the Academy of Fine Arts in Amsterdam. To gain an audience with Beethoven, he probably had used his predicate as a member of this academy, which had already elected Beethoven as one of its honorary members. This man from Holland must have diverted the composer with his broken German, which looks no more comical in the Conversation Book that it must have sounded; but a canon without words[47] which he carried away with him on August 3rd may be said to bear witness to the fact that he made a good impression on Beethoven, to whom he gave information concerning the state of music in Holland.

Carl Czerny spent some time in Baden. From his written entries it is apparent that he was urged by his erstwhile teacher to get an appointment and to compose in the larger forms. Beethoven was curious to know how much Czerny received for his compositions and Czerny told him that he attached no importance to his pieces, because he scribbled them down so easily, and that he took music from the publishers in exchange.

There is an autograph of a piece for pianoforte of thirteen measures, belonging to Mr. Louis Kramer of Syracuse, N.Y., with the inscription: "Comme un souvenir à Sarah Burney Payne par Louis van Beethoven le 27 Septembre, 1825."[48] This was the daughter of the famous music his-

[47] See KHV, p. 476 (WoO 35).

[48] See O. E. Albrecht, *A Census of Auto-* *graph Music Manuscripts of European Composers in America* (Philadelphia, 1953), p. 30.

torian, Dr. Charles Burney, and she was probably the author of a contribution to the *Harmonicon*, 1825, entitled "A visit to Beethoven."]⟩⟩—

Beethoven's greatest desire now must have been the completion of the order from Prince Galitzin for three quartets. As we already know, the first one, in E-flat, was finished and already performed. The sketches for the second one, in A minor (as established by Nottebohm)[49] date back to 1824. The work was originally to have the customary four movements; labor on it was interrupted by the illness of April and then the plan for the middle movements was changed to include the "Song of Thanksgiving in the Lydian mode," the short march before the last movement, and the minuet. The work was finished by August at the latest. The passage in eighth-notes in the second part of the second movement is practically a quotation from one of the German dances[50] written at least twenty-five years before, with the bar lines shifted so that the change of harmony occurs on the up-beats of the measures. Mentioned already are the references to the Song of Thanksgiving in the Conversation Books; in the original score it is inscribed "Sacred Song of Thanksgiving of a Convalescent to the Divinity, in the Lydian Mode. N.B. This piece has always B instead of B-flat," and in the second section in D major, simply "Feeling new strength." As has already been mentioned in the history of the Ninth Symphony, the principal theme of the last movement was originally conceived for the finale of that work. Immediately after the completion of this quartet, Beethoven set to work on the third quartet for Prince Galitzin. The story of this work comes later, while events must now be told which lead to the first performance of the second Galitzin quartet.

The quartet was to have its first public performance in a benefit concert for the cellist Linke after it had first been given a private hearing. Holz took the responsibility of having the work copied speedily and sent to Beethoven for corrections. The following letter from Beethoven to Karl shows that this arrangement did not result in his always being free of worry:

Baden on Aug. 11

Dear Son!

I am worried to death about the quartet, namely the 3, 4, 5 and 6th movement,[51] Holz has taken them along. The first measures of the 3rd movement have been left here, that is to say 13 in number—*I hear nothing from Holz*—I wrote him yesterday. Usually he writes. What a terrible misfortune if he should have lost it. *Just between us, he is a hard drinker.* Give me reassurance as quickly as possible —you can find out Linke's address at Haslinger's. Haslinger was here today, was very friendly, brought the periodicals and other things and begged for the new quartets. Don't engage in idle talk, it leads to vulgarities—But for God's sake give me some peace of mind concerning the quartet; what a terrible loss. The main ideas have been written on nothing but small scraps of paper, and I shall never be able to write out the whole thing again in the same way.

Your true father.

[49] *II Beeth.*, pp. 547ff.
[50] KHV, p. 448, WoO 13, No. 11.

[51] In its final form the quartet had only five movements.

I also point out to you that the coming *Sunday and Monday* are both holidays, thus you can arrange accordingly. With this opportunity you could perhaps [drive] here with me *Saturday* in the evening if I come in. Thus you gain the whole morning.

The idea of presenting the Quartet in A minor first for a small private gathering appears to have originated in Beethoven's own circle of friends, and apparently Beethoven wanted to have this at his own house. This had to be given up, however, in view of the difficulty for the audience of coming out to Baden for the occasion. Before coming to this, there were some other important visits which Beethoven received at this time, some of which are related in part to this performance.

The visit of the Danish composer, flautist and director, Friedrich Kuhlau, led to a right merry feast, for a description of which Seyfried found a place in the appendix of his *Studien.* The party consisted of Beethoven, the piano-maker Conrad Graf, Haslinger, Holz, Kuhlau, and the oboe teacher, Joseph Sellner. That the boundaries of good taste in conversation and story-telling may have been a bit strained is an inference from the fact that several pages of the Conversation Book containing the recorded relics of the affair are missing. After a promenade through the Helenenthal in which Beethoven amused himself by setting all manner of difficult tasks in hill-climbing, the party sat down to dinner at an inn. Champagne flowed freely, and after the return to Beethoven's lodgings, red Vöslauer, brought from his closet or cellar, did its share still further to elevate the spirits of the feasters. Beethoven seems to have held his own in the van of the revel. He wrote a canon in the Conversation Book with B-A-C-H as an opening motive and the words "Kühl, nicht lau" ("Cool, not lukewarm")—a feeble play on the Danish musician's name, but one which served to carry the music.[52] The next day Kuhlau confessed to Schlesinger that he did not know how he had gotten home and to bed; Beethoven's post-festal reflections may be gathered from the letter which accompanied a copy of the canon, which he sent to Kuhlau by the hands of Holz:

Baden, September 3, 1825

I must admit that the champagne went too much to my head also, yesterday, and that again I was compelled to experience that such things retard rather than promote my capacities. For easy as it usually is for me to meet a challenge of the instant, I do not at all remember what I wrote yesterday.

In handing over letter and canon to Holz for delivery he wrote to him that he had scarcely reached home before it occurred to him that he might have written down a lot of nonsense the day before.

On September 4 Beethoven received a visit from the Paris publisher, Moritz Schlesinger. He had seen Kuhlau in Vienna the day before and learned of their merry meeting and the canon that Beethoven had written on

---

[52] KHV, p. 693, WoO 191. The letters B-A-C-H in German represent the notes B-flat, A, C, B-natural.

Kuhlau's name. Schlesinger reported that Kuhlau was answering with a canon on B-A-C-H, and he asked permission to publish both canons in the journal put out by the Schlesingers in Berlin.

The publisher then came to the point of his visit; he wanted to publish the two new quartets. In mid-July Beethoven had written to Adolf Schlesinger in Berlin,[53] mentioning "two new grand violin quartets" and offering them for 80 ducats each. He could only have meant the A minor, Op. 132, and the B-flat major, Op. 130, not yet composed. Schlesinger was eager to know of the quartets; he asked if he could attend a rehearsal of the A minor quartet. His pertinacity on this matter evidently aroused Beethoven's suspicions, and his pride revolted at the thought that a publisher should ask to hear a work of his which he proposed to buy. Karl assured him that Schlesinger only wanted the privilege of hearing the new works of the master, and suggested that he might also be given a chance to hear the quartet which had already been sold to Schott.[54] Schlesinger also expressed his interest in becoming a sort of dealer *en gros* in Beethoven's products; besides the new quartets, he wanted to publish a Complete Edition, to begin with the chamber pieces, to which end he wanted still another quartet and three quintets. Schlesinger also tried to awaken the composer's literary ambition by offering to republish in the Berlin *Musikzeitung* whatever Beethoven might write to the Mainz journal about the joke on Haslinger. He suggested further that Beethoven ought really to write some essays on what a symphony and an overture ought to be and on the art of the fugue, of which he was the sole repository. He knew how to approach genius on its most susceptible side! He encouraged Beethoven to go to England, where he was so greatly admired. He reported that Cherubini had said to his pupils at the Conservatoire in Paris: "The greatest musical minds that ever lived or ever will live, are Beethoven and Mozart."[55]

At dinner, at Schlesinger's suggestion, the company drank the healths of Goethe and Cherubini. Again Schlesinger urged Beethoven to go to London:[56] "I repeat again that if you will go to England for three months I will engage that, deducting your traveling expenses, you will make 1000 pounds, or 25000 florins V.S. at least, if you give only two concerts and produce some new music. . . . The Englishmen are proud enough to count themselves fortunate if Beethoven would only be satisfied with them." When the toast to Cherubini was drunk, Schlesinger took occasion to satisfy the curiosity of Beethoven touching the status of the composer whom he most admired among living men: "Cherubini has now received the title of Baron from the government as well as the order of the Legion of Honor. It is a proof of the recognition of his talent, for he did not seek it. Napoleon, who

[53] See *A* 1403.

[54] Op. 127, in E-flat.

[55] On the margin Schindler records his doubt that this remark was ever made.

(TDR, v, 238, n. 1.)

[56] The following two quotations were taken by Krehbiel from Thayer's papers and are not included in TDR.

appreciated him highly, once found fault with one of his compositions and Cherubini retorted: 'Your Majesty knows no more about it than I about a battle.' Napoleon's conduct was contemptible. Because of the words that I have quoted he took away all of Cherubini's offices and he had nothing to live on. Nevertheless, he did an infinite amount of good for popular culture. If Napoleon, instead of becoming an insatiable world conqueror, had remained First Consul, he would have become one of the greatest men that ever existed."

It was about this time, also, that Karl told his uncle an anecdote to the effect that Cherubini, when asked why he did not compose a quartet, replied: "If Beethoven had never written a quartet, I would write quartets; as it is, I cannot."

Schlesinger had his way about hearing the new quartet, for it was rehearsed at his rooms at the tavern "zum Wilden Mann" on Wednesday, September 7, preparatory to its performance to a small group (which may have been a sort of dress rehearsal) on the 9th. Beethoven had originally wanted the players to come to his lodging at Baden, but in a letter to Karl dated September 6, he had agreed that this was impractical and suggested they all meet at Schlesinger's. Meanwhile, arrangements for the rehearsals had been made independently of Beethoven, and on the 8th Holz arrived in Baden to report to him the progress of the rehearsal the day before. He mentioned the fact that Karl was present, and also Wolfmayer and Tobias Haslinger, for Wolfmayer "at the Adagio wept like a child" and "Tobias scratched his head when he heard the quartet; he certainly regrets that the Jew Steiner did not take it." He continued about the arrangements for the performance the next day, which was to take place at noon, and stated that the innkeeper had arranged for them to have a larger room. This took place as scheduled, and on September 11 the quartet was performed for a larger group, also at "zum Wilden Mann."

During these days, Beethoven was concerned about making the final arrangements with Schlesinger concerning the purchase of the quartet. In the same letter to Karl referred to above, he urged him to make haste to complete the financial transactions with Schlesinger as he wished to return the money he owed to Peters, and later stated that he could not wait any longer—if Schlesinger wished to hear a rehearsal first, he could not have the quartet. Earlier in the letter he says "Entre nous il est pourtant juif." The negotiations were evidently completed by September 10, as there is a receipt of that date to Schlesinger for 80 ducats received. However, there is mention of two quartets both in this document and in a rough draft of an agreement written by Schlesinger in French, dated September 4th.[57] On the receipt the two quartets are referred to as "Opp. 132 and 134 12th and 17th quartets." Schlesinger had originally been interested in Op. 132,

[57] Unger, *Beethoven und seine Verleger*, p. 91. See also Anderson, III, Appendix G, Nos. 16 and 17.

in A minor, and Op. 130, in B-flat major. What he finally received was Op. 132 and the Quartet in F major, Op. 135, both published after Beethoven's death.⟩⸻

We have an account of both the September 9 and September 11 occasions at "zum Wilden Mann" from the English visitor whom Beethoven received at this time. This was Sir George Smart, who, in the summer of 1825, made a tour of Germany in company with Charles Kemble. He was with Mr. Kemble when that gentleman made the agreement with Weber for *Oberon*, but his "principal reason for the journey," as he himself put it, "was to ascertain from Beethoven himself the exact times of the movements of his characteristic—and some of his other—Sinfonias." By the "characteristic" symphony Smart meant the ninth, which he had directed at its first performance in London on March 21, 1825. Sir George recorded the incidents of his meetings with Beethoven in his journal, from which the following excerpts are taken:[58]

"On the 7th of September, at nine in the morning, I called on Mayseder, who received me most politely. . . . We conversed about Beethoven's Choral Symphony; our opinion agrees about it. When it was performed here Umlauf conducted it and Kletrinski and Schuppanzigh were the leaders. All the basses played in the recitative, but they had the story that it was written for Dragonetti only.

"Friday, September 9th. . . . We then went to Mecchetti's music shop, they, too, are publishers, and bought three pieces for Birchall. . . . Mr. Holz, an amateur in some public office and a good violin player, came in and said Beethoven had come from Baden this morning and would be at his nephew's—Karl Beethoven, a young man aged twenty—No. 72 Alleegasse. . . . At twelve I took Ries[59] to the hotel Wildemann [*sic*] the lodgings of Mr. Schlesinger, the music seller of Paris, as I understood from Mr. Holz that Beethoven would be there, and there I found him. He received me in the most flattering manner. There was a numerous assembly of professors to hear Beethoven's second new manuscript quartette, bought by Mr. Schlesinger. This quartette is three-quarters of an hour long. They played it twice. The four performers were Schuppanzigh, Holz, Weiss, and Lincke. It is most chromatic and there is a slow movement entitled 'Praise for the recovery of an invalid.' Beethoven intended to allude to himself I suppose for he was

[58] Thayer visited Sir George in February, 1861, and received from him permission to make a transcript of all the entries in his journal touching the meetings with Beethoven, also supplementing them with oral information. The journal remained in manuscript for forty years after Sir George's death and then was edited by H. Bertram Cox and C. L. E. Cox. It was published under the title *Leaves from the Journal of Sir George Smart* (Long-mans, Green and Co., London, 1907). The excerpts quoted here are from the published book, and, according to Krehbiel, show signs of having been revised after Thayer made his transcript. See Smart (edition above), pp. 104-105, 108-109, 111, 113-15. (TK, III, 206, n. 1.)

[59] Not the composer but a pianoforte maker of Vienna. (TK, III, 207, n. 1.)

very ill during the early part of this year. He directed the performers, and took off his coat, the room being warm and crowded. A staccato passage not being expressed to the satisfaction of his eye, for alas, he could not hear, he seized Holz's violin and played the passage a quarter of a tone too flat. I looked over the score during the performance. All paid him the greatest attention. About fourteen were present, those I knew were Boehm (violin), Marx ('cello), Carl Czerny, also Beethoven's nephew, who is like Count St. Antonio, so is Boehm, the violin player. The partner of Steiner, the music seller, was also there. I fixed to go to Baden on Sunday and left at twenty-five minutes past two. . . .

"Saturday, September 10th. . . . I called for the music at Artaria's for Birchall, for which I paid, and on our return found a visiting-card from Earl Stanhope and also from Schlesinger of Paris with a message that Beethoven would be at his hotel to-morrow at twelve, therefore of course I gave up going to Baden to visit Beethoven, which he had arranged for me to do. . . . In the morning Mr. Kirchoffer called to say he should invite me to his house. It was he who, through Ries, had the arrangement of procuring the Choral Symphony for our Philharmonic Society.

"Sunday, September 11th. . . . From hence I went alone to Schlesinger's, at the 'Wildemann,' where was a larger party than the previous one. Among them was L'Abbé Stadler, a fine old man and a good composer of the old school, to whom I was introduced. There was also present a pupil of Moscheles, a Mademoiselle Eskeles and a Mademoiselle Cimia,[60] whom I understood to be a professional player. When I entered Messrs. C. Czerny, Schuppanzigh and Lincke had just begun the Trio, Op. 70, of Beethoven, after which the same performers played Beethoven's Trio, Op. 79[61]—both printed singly by Steiner. Then followed Beethoven's quartette, the same that I had heard on September the 9th and it was played by the same performers. Beethoven was seated near the pianoforte beating time during the performance of these pieces. This ended, most of the company departed, but Schlesinger invited me to stop and dine with the following party of ten: Beethoven, his nephew, Holz, Weiss, C. Czerny, who sat at the bottom of the table, Lincke, Jean Sedlatzek—a flute player who is coming to England next year, and has letters to the Duke of Devonshire, Count St. Antonio, etc.—he has been to Italy—Schlesinger, Schuppanzigh, who sat at the top, and myself. Beethoven calls Schuppanzigh Sir John Falstaff, not a bad name considering the figure of this excellent violin player.

"We had a most pleasant dinner, healths were given in the English style. Beethoven was delightfully gay but hurt that, in the letter Moscheles gave me, his name should be mixed up with the other professors. However he soon got over it. He was much pleased and rather surprised at seeing in the

---

[60] Presumably Antonia Cibbini, née Kože-luch, who was among those who attended the performance of the quartet. (Cf. TDR, v, 245.)

[61] Undoubtedly Op. 97 which was published by Steiner. Artaria published the Op. 70 trios in Vienna.

oratorio bill I gave him that the 'Mount of Olives' and his 'Battle Symphony' were both performed the same evening. He believes—I do not—that the high notes Handel wrote for trumpets were played formerly by one particular man. I gave him the oratorio book and bill. He invited me, by his nephew, to Baden next Friday. After dinner he was coaxed to play extempore, observing in French to me, 'Upon what subject shall I play?' Meanwhile he was touching the instrument thus

to which I answered, 'Upon that.' On which theme he played for about twenty minutes in a most extraordinary manner, sometimes very fortissimo, but full of genius. When he arose at the conclusion of his playing he appeared greatly agitated. No one could be more agreeable than he was—plenty of jokes. He was in the highest of spirits. We all wrote to him by turns, but he can hear a little if you halloo quite close to his left ear. He was very severe in his observations about the Prince Regent never having noticed his present of the score of his 'Battle Symphony.' His nephew regretted that his uncle had no one to explain to him the profitable engagement offered by the Philharmonic Society last year."

Smart accepted Beethoven's invitation to visit him at Baden on September 16, and at this meeting accomplished the specific purpose of his visit to Vienna by getting Beethoven to give him the tempo of various movements from his symphonies, by playing portions of them on the pianoforte. He wrote on Beethoven's slate in French, a language which he said Beethoven spoke fluently, in order to get Beethoven's intentions as to the performance of the work. Asked about the recitative for instruments in the last movement, Beethoven's reply was: "The recitative in strict time."[62] Smart objected, that so played, it was not a recitative nor had words to recite. Beethoven replied, "he called it so," and finally closed the discussion with "I wish it to go in strict time." This from a composer was of course decisive.[63]

Though he had been warned not to write in Beethoven's book, Sir George did not, or was not always able to, obey the injunction. A considerable portion of the conversation at the meeting is preserved in a Conversation Book

[62] The exchange between Beethoven and Smart concerning the recitative is based on Thayer's notes from his conversations with Sir George Smart in London in 1861. (TK, III, 208, n. 2.)

[63] The question of how the bass recitatives ought to be played had already been discussed when the rehearsals for the concert of 1824 were in progress, as is shown by Schindler's entries in a Conversation Book in March of that year: "How many contrabasses are to play the recitative?— Will it be possible? All!— There would be no difficulty in strict time, but to give it in a singing style will make careful study necessary.— If old Kraus were still alive we could let the matter go unconcernedly, for he directed 12 contrabasses who had to do what he wanted.— Good; then just as if words were under it?— If necessary I will write words under it so that they may learn to sing." (TK, III, 208, n. 2.) For more concerning the 1824 performance, see Leopold Sonnleithner, *AMZ*, April 6, 1864, pp. 245-46.

which covers three dates, September 16, 19 and 24. From this book some excerpts are made here, since they bear on the subject which filled so large a place in the plans of Beethoven for several years, and were in his mind up to the time of his death—the English tour. Other matters bearing on points of history which have been or may be mentioned, are included. The nephew had translated for Beethoven the announcement of the Ninth Symphony as it appeared on the programme of the Philharmonic's concert of March 21, viz.: "New Grand Characteristic Sinfonia, MS. with vocal finale, the principal parts to be sung by Madame Caradori, Miss Goodall, Mr. Vaughn and Mr. Phillips; composed expressly for this Society." No doubt Beethoven gave expression, as he frequently had done, to his admiration for the English people and possibly also for their national hymn, for Karl translates the stanza:

> Long may he reign!
> May he defend our laws,
> And ever give us cause
> To sing with heart and voice:
> God save the king!

The one-sided conversation proceeds:

Smart: You understand English writing?

Extremement bien

Winter me dit que on l'intention de donner Fidelio a music.

Karl: He would like to know the tempi of the finale of the last symphony. Haven't you it here?
How long have you worked on the symphony?

How long does it last?—1 hour and 3 minutes

¾ hour

We are now going to take a walk.

According to Smart's journal, Beethoven now ordered dinner "with his funny old cook," told his nephew to look after the wine, and the party of five took a walk. "Beethoven was generally in advance humming some passage. . . ." Holz talked to Beethoven now about Schlesinger, telling him that it was the publisher's purpose to print the quartets in succession, which would postpone the appearance of the thirteenth for two years, and advised Beethoven hereafter to make immediate publication a condition of purchase.

He suggested that if he were to threaten not to compose the quintets under the circumstances it might help. The conversations continued:

Karl: He asked why you had not come before now; he said the 300 pounds of the Philhar. Society were not to be looked upon as the principal thing. For that you needed only to appear 2 or 3 times in the orchestra and make money with your own concerts.

He said that in a short time you could make at least 1000 pounds and carry it away with you.

You can do better business with the publishers there than here.

And you'll find 1000 friends, Smarth [*sic*] says, who will do everything to help you.

. . . We'll wait till the year is over before going to England.

. . . You'll not leave London so quickly if we are once there.

Others are living there too, like Cramer, etc.

In two years at least 50,000 florins net. Concerts.

I am convinced that if you were to want to go away from here they would do everything to keep you here.

We shall let Smart conclude the story of the meeting.[64] "On our return [from the walk] we had dinner at two o'clock. It was a most curious one and so plentiful that dishes came in as we came out, for, unfortunately, we were rather in a hurry to get to the stage coach by four, it being the only one going to Vienna that evening. I overheard Beethoven say, 'We will try how much the Englishman can drink.' *He* had the worst of the trial. I gave him my diamond pin as a remembrance of the high gratification I received by the honour of his invitation and kind reception and he wrote me the following droll canon as fast as his pen could write in about two minutes of time as I stood at the door ready to depart.

Ars lon-ga   vi-ta   bre-vis

[64] Smart, *op.cit.*, p. 124. A facsimile of the autograph of the canon is given.

'Written on the 16th of September, 1825, in Baden, when my dear talented musical artist and friend Smart (from England) visited me here.

Ludwig van Beethoven.' "

Smart left Vienna on his return journey to London soon after September 18th. Schlesinger remained a short time longer in which time he saw Beethoven again. In the conversations there is talk of another performance of the quartet at which Holz played first violin[65] since Schuppanzigh was absent, and also a performance that included the quartets both in A minor and E-flat. This last took place probably on September 26 on which day Beethoven writes the following:[66]

Si non per portas   per mu-ros   per mu-ros per muros

I wish for you the most beautiful bride, my worthy one, and I take this opportunity to ask you to remember me to Hr. Marx in Berlin [and see] that he doesn't expect too much of me and leaves me a way out through the back door.[67]

After securing the A minor Quartet and an assurance that he should also have that in B-flat (he had offered to deposit 80 ducats with a Viennese banker against its completion and delivery and Beethoven had accepted his offer), Schlesinger said that he would purchase the first of the three quartets from Schott and Sons so as to have all three for his Complete Edition. Karl, in reporting the fact to Beethoven, expressed his belief that the Schotts would sell for fear that if they did not Schlesinger would reprint the work in Paris without permission. The latter made a strenuous effort to get the autograph score of the A minor, but had perforce to content himself with a copy. Holz represented to Beethoven that the autograph would be an asset for Karl in the future, and Karl was of the same opinion; he supported Holz's assertion with the argument that such "Capitalien" grew more valuable with age and that he was sure Schlesinger would get 30 ducats for the manuscript. Beethoven expressed indifference as to which publisher got the works so long as he was promptly paid. In a letter to Holz of August 24, he writes:

[65] Later Beethoven grew merry at his expense and wrote a canon in the Conversation Book to the words "Holz, Holz geigt die Quartette so, als ob sie Kraut eintreten!" ("Holz fiddles quartets the way they mash vegetables!"), WoO 204. (Cf. TDR, v, 250.)

[66] The canon also appears in a sketchbook in the midst of work on the fugue of the Quartet in B-flat. See *II Beeth.*, p. 11. For solutions to the canon see TDR, v, 249, n. 1; L.

Misch, *Beethoven Studies*, pp. 126-28; and Carl Dahlhaus, "Zwei Rätselkanons von Beethoven" in *Musica*, IX (1955), pp. 500-01.

[67] In 1824, Adolf Berhard Marx (1795-1806) with Moritz's father founded the *Berliner Allegemeine Musikalische Zeitung*, which, during its seven years of existence, championed Beethoven's music. Beethoven is obviously referring to these writings in this letter.

... It is immaterial which hellhound gnaws my brains, since it must needs be so, only see that the answer is not delayed too long. The hellhound in L[eipzig] can wait and meanwhile entertain himself with Mephistopheles (the editor of the L[eipsiger]Musikal[ische] Zeitung) in Auerbach's Cellar. He will soon be plucked by the ears by Beelzebub, the chief of devils. . . .

The Leipzig "hellhound" thus consigned to Beelzebub was, of course, Peters.

The house into which Beethoven moved on October 15 is fully described and pictured in Gerhard von Breuning's book *Aus dem Schwarzspanierhause*. It derived its name from the fact that it had been built by the Benedictines of Spain. In it Beethoven occupied four rooms on the second floor, besides a kitchen and servants' quarters.[68] One of the most important results of Beethoven's removal to these quarters was a reestablishment of the intimate relations which had existed for so many years with the friend of his youth Stephan von Breuning, a Councillor in the War Department of the Austrian Government, who lived hard by. Though there had been no open rupture between him and Beethoven an estrangement had existed from the time when von Breuning had advised against Beethoven's assumption of the guardianship over his nephew. They had met occasionally *ad interim,* but it was not until they became neighbors that the intimate friendship which had existed in earlier years was restored. A beginning in this direction was made when, on a visit to Vienna in August, Beethoven met the Breuning family in the street. It was necessary that changes be made in the lodgings and while waiting for them Beethoven became a frequent visitor at the Breunings, dining with them frequently and sometimes sending them a mess of fish, of which he was very fond. Madame von Breuning meanwhile looked after the fitting out of his kitchen and saw to the engagement of his servants. Concerning the relations which existed between Beethoven and her father's family, Marie, a daughter of Stephan von Breuning, wrote many years after (in a memorandum for Thayer):

"My mother once met Beethoven when on her way to the Kaiserbad on the Danube; he accompanied her for the rather long distance from the Rothes Haus, where she lived. She spent about an hour in the bathhouse (the bath being a warm one) and on coming out was surprised to find Beethoven waiting to accompany her home. She often said that he was always gallant towards women and had paid court to her for a while.

"She related, too, that his animated gestures, his loud voice and his indifference towards others surprised the people in the street, and that she was often ashamed because they stopped and took him for a madman. His laugh was particularly loud and ringing.

"My mother often and repeatedly deplored the fact that she had never heard him play—but my father, in his unbounded tenderness, always replied

[68] In a letter to Dr. Braunhofer, dated February, 1826, Beethoven refers to this address as "Meine Wohnung, Schwarzspanier 2ter Stock, No. 201 Links." See Anderson, p. 1278, n. 3.

when she expressed a desire to hear him: 'He doesn't like to do it, and I do not want to ask him because it might pain him not to hear himself.'

"Beethoven repeatedly invited my mother to coffee, or, as the Viennese say, *zur Jause*; but my mother almost always declined, as his domestic arrangements did not appear altogether appetizing.

"My mother often said to my father that Beethoven's habit of expectorating in the room, his neglected clothing and his extravagant behavior were not particularly attractive. My father always replied: 'And yet he has a great deal of success, especially with women.'

"Beethoven often told my mother that he longed greatly for domestic happiness and much regretted that he had never married."

Beethoven was fond of Stephan von Breuning's son Gerhard, whom, because of his attachment to his father, he dubbed *Hosenknopf* (Trousers-button) and because of his lightness of foot Ariel. He once had the boy play for him, criticized the position of his hands and sent him Clementi's Method as preferable to Pleyel's which the lad was using.

There can be no doubt that the renewed association with von Breuning frequently turned his thoughts to his old home and his boyhood friends in the Rhine country, and his delight must have been keen when at the end of December he received letters from Wegeler, whom he had not seen since he left Vienna twenty-eight years before, and his wife, who had been Eleonore von Breuning. They were tender letters, full of information about their family, each other, friends and relations—real home letters telling of births, marriages, careers and deaths. One would think that they ought to have been answered at once, but Beethoven did not find the time or occasion to write a reply until the next year; thus they will be given in full in a later chapter.

After the private performances in September, the Quartet in A minor received its first public performance in November, advertised on October 27 in the *Sammler* as follows: "L. van Beethoven's newest Quartet in A minor will be performed on Sunday, November 6, 1825 in the Music Society's room at the 'rother Igel' in a benefit concert for Herr Joseph Linke. Also Beethoven's great Trio in B-flat major for pianoforte, violin and 'cello will be presented with Hr. Carl Maria von Bocklet on the piano part."[69] The concert was a great success and reports of it were given to Beethoven by Holz and Nephew Karl. Schuppanzigh received permission to perform the quartet again on November 20.

On November 29, 1825, Beethoven was one of fifteen men elected to honorary membership in the Gesellschaft der Musikfreunde by the directors, Cherubini, Spontini, Spohr, Catel and Weigl being among them. The election was confirmed by the society on January 26, 1826, but the diploma

[69] Concerning the confusion between Bocklet and Würfel in the Conversation Books, see TDR, v, pp. 259-60.

was not issued until October 26, and thus reached Beethoven's hands only a few months before his death.

On November 25, Beethoven wrote to Schott and Sons promising to send them the metronome marks for the Mass in D soon, telling them to print the list of subscribers before the dedication, asking delay in the matter of the dedication of the Ninth Symphony, and requesting that the publication of both works be postponed three months. He gives the title of the Mass as follows:

MISSA

composita, et

Serenissimo ac Eminentissimo Domino Domino

Rudolpho Joanni Caesareo Principi et Archiduci Austriae S.R.E.

tit. S. Petri in monte aureo Cardinali et Archiepiscopo Olomucensi

profundissima cum veneratione dedicata

a

Ludovico van Beethoven

On the same day, he wrote to Peters in Leipzig to the effect that his recent letters had not been definite and certain. He wanted a specific statement that the amount which he (Beethoven) had received as an advance was 360 florins. If Peters was willing to take a quartet for that sum he would send him one soon; if not, and if he preferred to have the money, he would return it to him. "If you had done this at once you might have had two quartets; but you cannot ask me to be the loser. If I wanted to draw the strings together tighter I could ask a larger price. . . . I will send nothing for examination." This, then, was Beethoven's ultimatum: Peters must pay 360 florins for the Quartet or receive back the money advanced three years before. Peters asked for the money and it was paid over to Steiner and Co. on his order on December 7.

Among the musicians who visited the composer at this time may be mentioned Theodore Molt, a man evidently of German birth and now a music teacher in Quebec, who was making a European tour. He gained the privilege of telling Beethoven to his face how greatly he admired him, then asked the favor of a souvenir which he could carry back on a journey of "3,000 hours" as a precious keepsake. For him, on December 16, Beethoven wrote the canon, "Freue dich des Lebens."[70]

Among the performances of Beethoven's works in these last months not already mentioned were the Mass in C in the Karlskirche on September 18 attended by Sir George Smart, the D major Trio in another Schuppanzigh concert on November 13 in which the Bohemian composer, Wilhelm Würfel

---

[70] From Thayer's notebook of 1857: "Circumstance related to me by the son of Mr. Molt. When Mr. Molt called upon Beethoven, December 16, 1825 (B's birthday), Beethoven showed him some verses he had just written complimentary to a young lady and fell into such enthusiasm talking about her that he passed entirely from his musical conversation. Verses poor enough, Mr. Molt said. Mr. Molt also described the meanness of the rooms in which B. lived." (TK, III, 211, n. 1.)

played the pianoforte, the *Eroica* on November 27, the Choral Fantasy, the E-flat Trio on December 11 played by A. Halm, and finally the Septet, which again created great enthusiasm. In this last the players were Schuppanzigh, Weiss, Linke, the double bass player Metzer, the clarinetist Friedlowsky, the horn player Herbst, and the bassoonist Mittag. Mittag related to Thayer the following anecdote. Going home one evening, he stepped into a tavern known as "Zum Dachs" to drink a glass of beer. Smoking was not allowed in the place and there were few guests. In a corner, however, sat Beethoven in an attitude of one lost in thought. After Mittag had watched him a few minutes he jumped up and called to the waiter: "My bill!" "Already paid!" shrieked the waiter in his ear. Mittag, thinking that Beethoven ought not to be left alone, followed him without betraying himself and saw him enter his house safely.

The great contributions which Beethoven made to music in the year 1825 were the quartets in A minor, Op. 132 and in B-flat major, Op. 130, already mentioned above. In March Beethoven had written to Neate that the first of the three quartets which he thought of bringing to London was completed (Op. 127 in E-flat), that he was at work on the second and that it and the third would be finished "soon." As we know, the A minor Quartet was not completed until midsummer because of Beethoven's illness, and upon its completion he set to work immediately on the third of the quartets, that in B-flat. On August 24 he mentioned in letters to Karl Holz and nephew Karl that he expected to finish the quartet by the end of the month, or at most in twelve days. It was not completed until November, however, and during this month Beethoven himself writes in the Conversation Book: "Title for the Quartet," and a strange hand adds: "31ième Quatuor. Pour deux Violons, Viola et Violoncello composé aux désirs de S. A. Monseigneur le Prince Nicolas Galitzin et dédié au même," to which Beethoven adds: "par L. v. B."

Schlesinger had negotiated for this quartet along with that in A minor, it will be remembered, but it was sold to Artaria; in January, 1826, Holz writes: "The Quartet will be printed at once; thus the third Quartet will appear before the first two." This was not the case, as the first of the Quartets, Op. 127, appeared in June, 1826, and the third of the Quartets, Op. 130 in B-flat, did not appear until May, 1827, from the press of Artaria. However, the fact that it did appear before the second Quartet, Op. 132 in A minor, which Schlesinger did not publish until September, 1827, accounts for its having received the earlier opus number. It had its first public performance in March, 1826, and will be further discussed in the next chapter. The Fugue in B-flat, Op. 133, originally formed the finale of the work but was put aside after the first performance; and the present finale, which was composed in Gneixendorf in 1826, was substituted.

Two trifles which kept company wtih the Quartets in this year were a Waltz in D and an Écossaise in E-flat for pianoforte, which were published in a collection of light music by C. F. Müller. There are several allusions to the oratorio commissioned by the Gesellschaft der Musikfreunde in the Conversation Books of 1825, in one of which Grillparzer is mentioned as a likely author for another book; but so far as is known no work was done on *Der Sieg des Kreuzes,* though Bernard did shorten the book.

In a Conversation Book at the very end of the year, in the midst of remarks about New Year's greetings, Beethoven wrote the following:

It is very interesting that the opening idea for the Quartet in C-sharp minor should appear before the close of 1825.[71] Underneath Beethoven writes: "Only the praise of one who has enjoyed praise can give pleasure." —a relic, no doubt, of some of the composer's classic readings.[72]

The compositions of the year may be divided into large works and trifles.

Large works:

Quartet for Strings in E-flat, Op. 127, completed in February.

Quartet for Strings in A minor, Op. 132, completed by August.

Quartet for Strings in B-flat major, Op. 130, first version (with the fugue, later to be separated as Op. 133, as finale) completed in November.

Trifles:

Canons:

"Ars longa, vita brevis," WoO 192, second setting, for Sir George Smart on September 16.

"Ars longa, vita brevis," WoO 193, third setting, date and occasion unknown.

"Doktor sperrt das Tor dem Tod," WoO 189, for Dr. Anton Braunhofer, on May 11.

For two instruments, WoO 35, for Otto de Boer, on August 3.

"Freu' dich des Lebens," WoO 195, for Theodore Molt, on December 16.

"Gott ist eine feste Burg," WoO 188, written perhaps for the album of the Courlander, Colonel von Düsterlohe,[73] on January 12.

"Ich war hier, Doktor," WoO 190, for Dr. Anton Braunhofer, on June 4.

"Kühl, nicht lau," WoO 191 for Friedrich Kuhlau, on September 3 (see *A* 1427).

"Si non per portas," WoO 194, for Moritz Schlesinger, on September 26 (see *A* 1433).

Ecossaise in E-flat for Pianoforte, WoO 86 (see publications).

[71] According to Kinsky-Halm, work began on Op. 131 shortly after the conclusion of the composing of Op. 130, i.e., November, 1825. See KHV, p. 397, also *II Beeth.,* Section I.

[72] Laudari a viro laudate—[Naevius;] Loetus sum laudari me, inquit Hector, opinor apud Naevium, abs te, pater, a laudato viro—

[Cicero ad fam. xv, 6]; Cum tragicus ille apud nos ait magnificum esse laudari a laudato viro, laude digno, ait.—[Seneca, Epist. 102, 16.] (TK, III, 217, n. 1.)

[73] See Hans Volkmann, "Beethoven als Epigrammatiker," in *DM,* Vol. 7, No. 13 (1908), p. 29n.

Piece for Pianoforte, WoO 61a, for Sarah Burney Payne, September 27.
Waltz in D for Pianoforte, WoO 85 (see publications).

The publications for the year were:

By Sauer and Leidesdorf:

For C. F. Müller's collection of dances, *Ernst und Tändeley*: Ecossaise in E-flat
for Pianoforte, WoO 86.

For C. F. Müller's collection of waltzes, *Seyd uns zum zweytenmal will-
kommen!*: Waltz in D for Pianoforte, WoO 85.

By Schott in Mainz:

"Bundeslied" for Two Solo Voices and Chorus and accompaniment of two
clarinets, two bassoons and two horns (Goethe), Op. 122.

"Der Kuss" (Weisse), Op. 128.

"Opferlied" for Soprano, Chorus and Orchestra (Matthisson), Op. 121b.

Overture to *Die Weihe des Hauses*, Op. 124, dedicated to Prince Nikolas
Galitzin.

Six Bagatelles for Pianoforte, Op. 126.

By Schott in *Cäcilia*, No. 7.

Two Canons: "Hoffmann, sei ja kein Hofmann," WoO 180, and "Schwenke
dich ohne Schwänke!", WoO 187.

By Steiner:

Grand Overture in C major ("zur Namensfeier"), Op. 115, dedicated to Prince
Anton Radziwill.

CHAPTER XXXIX

THE YEAR 1826 THROUGH THE AUTUMN

DIFFICULTIES WITH PRINCE GALITZIN— THE NEPHEW'S ATTEMPT AT SUICIDE— GNEIXENDORF—THE LAST COMPOSITIONS

THE year which witnessed the last of Beethoven's completed labors, and saw what by general consent might be set down as the greatest of his string quartets, that in C-sharp minor, Op. 131, beheld also the culmination of the grief and pain caused by the conduct of his nephew. The year 1826 was a year of awful happenings and great achievements; a year of startling contradictions, in which the most grievous blows which an inscrutable Providence dealt the composer as if utterly to crush him to earth, were met by a display of creative energy which was amazing not only in its puissance but also in its exposition of transfigured emotion and imagination.

There was a good deal of talk concerning the performance of Beethoven's works at the beginning of the year, at the Schuppanzigh evening concerts and the *Concerts spirituels,* etc. The new Quartet in B-flat major, Op. 130, was ready to be rehearsed; and at the home of the rich music-lover Dembscher, an agent of the Austrian War Department, there were quartet parties with Mayseder as first violin, at which the A minor Quartet was played. There was talk of new compositions—oratorios on the old text by Bernard and on a new one by Kuffner, the opera on Grillparzer's *Melusine,* a requiem, and a new symphony. Beethoven's thoughts, however, were not with such things but in the congenial region of the string quartet. Having fulfilled his commission for Prince Galitzin by writing the Quartets in E-flat, A minor and B-flat, he had started to work on the Quartet in C-sharp minor, to which we return later in the chapter. That he could continue to write amidst all the disturbing circumstances of this year in the higher and purer regions of chamber music was a source of admiration and wonder to his friends.

The figure which stands out in the highest relief throughout the year beside that of the composer is that of Holz, whose concern for his welfare went into the smallest detail of his unfortunate domestic life and included also a major part of the labors and responsibilities caused by the tragic outcome of the nephew's attempt at self-destruction. Schindler appears at intervals, but with jealous reserve, chary of advice, waiting to be asked for his opinion and pettishly protesting that after it once had been given it would not be acted upon. Stephan von Breuning appears in all the nobility of his nature; and in the attitude and acts of Brother Johann, there is evidence of something as near affectionate sympathy and interest as Beethoven's paradoxical conduct and nature invited of him. Among the other persons whom the Conversation Books disclose as his occasional associates were Schuppanzigh, Kuffner, Grillparzer, Abbé Stadler and Matthias Artaria, whose talk was chiefly about the affairs in which they were concerned.

The year was not far advanced before Beethoven's health was bothering him again; it was the old abdominal complaint of the year before. Near the end of January he was not feeling well; he complained of pains in the bowels and found locomotion difficult. He suffered also from his eyes, and Johann recommended that he use an eye lotion. Dr. Braunhofer was called and made the familiar injunctions. Beethoven was advised to abstain from wine for a few days and also from coffee, which he was told was injurious because of its stimulating effect on the nerves. The patient was advised to eat freely of soups, and small doses of quinine were prescribed. On February 23 the doctor received the following note from his patient:

Honored friend!

How indebted I am to you for your care of me. I have obeyed your orders as much as possible; wine, coffee, everything according to your order. It is difficult to judge right away to what extent there are results in these few days. The pain in my back is not great, but the malady is still there. Therefore I think that I will have reason to use the medicines which you sent me today (the cost of which, however, I don't know)—Do not forget your own interests on account of others. I am very sorry not to be able to prescribe something for you in return and must leave you to your own resources—I hope to see you as soon as possible—

Yours gratefully

Beethoven

In another note to Braunhofer at this time, Beethoven refers to his trouble as "rheumatism or gout." Frequent visits from the doctor and admonitions from his friends to be cautious continued until March, during which month he appeared to improve and, according to the Conversation Books, take an interest again in musical events and other things that were going on in the world.

The event that was personally important to Beethoven at this time was the first performance of his Quartet in B-flat—his "Leibquartett" it is once called in the Conversation Books. Schuppanzigh and his fellows had taken it in hand. They found the concluding fugue extremely troublesome, but the Cavatina entranced them at once; Schuppanzigh entered a record against any change in it. The performance took place on March 21, 1826. The second and fourth movements had to be repeated, but the fugue proved a *crux* as, no doubt, the players had expected it would. Some of Beethoven's friends argued that it had not been understood and that this objection would vanish with repeated hearings; others, plainly a majority, asked that a new movement be written to take its place. Johann van Beethoven told the composer that the "whole city" was delighted with the work. Schindler[1] says that the *Danza alla tedesca*, one of the movements which was demanded a second time, was originally intended for another quartet, presumably that in A minor. Schuppanzigh's high opinion of the Cavatina was shared by many and also by Beethoven himself. Holz said that it cost the composer tears in the writing and brought out the confession that nothing that he had written had so moved him; in fact that merely to revive it afterwards in his thoughts and feelings brought forth renewed tributes of tears.

The doubts about the effectiveness of the fugue felt by Beethoven's friends found an echo in the opinions of the critics. Matthias Artaria, the publisher, who seems in this year to have entered the circle of the composer's intimate associates, presented the matter to him in a practicable light. He had purchased the publishing rights of the Quartet and after the performance he went to Beethoven with the suggestion that he write a new finale and that the fugue be published as an independent piece, for which he would remunerate him separately. Beethoven listened to the protests unwillingly, but, "Vowing he would ne'er consent, consented" and also requested the pianist Anton Halm, who had played in the B-flat Trio at the concert of March 21 to make the four-hand pianoforte arrangement for which there had already been inquiries at Artaria's shop. Halm accepted the commission and made the arrangement, with which Beethoven was not satisfied; "You have divided the parts too much between *prim* and second," he remarked to Halm,[2] referring to a device which the arranger had adopted to avoid crossing of hands—giving passages to the right hand which should logically have been given to the left, the effect being the same to the ear but not to the eye. Nevertheless, Halm presented a claim for 40 florins to Artaria for the work, and was paid. Beethoven then made an arrangement and sent it to Artaria ——via Holz, to whom he sent a note beginning with the salutation "Best Wood of Christ!" in which he asked Holz to give the arrangement to Artaria, hoping that he would take it and give Beethoven 12 ducats for the work. He concludes: "However, Hr. M. knows anyhow that we gladly and often are at his service without payment and shall be —but the present service which I rendered him is too menial not to have to

---

[1] *Biogr.*, Part II, p. 116. See Nottebohm *Beeth.*, p. 53. (TDR, v, 293, n. 1.)   [2] Halm's personal explanation to Mr. Thayer. (TK, III, 224, n. 1.)

insist on compensation—Appointing you now Executor in this matter, I beg of you, honorable Sir, to receive everything."[3]

To this Artaria demurred and asked Beethoven for Halm's manuscript. Beethoven sent it via Holz with instructions to get back his own arrangement in return for it. At the same time he told Artaria that while he did not ask that Artaria publish his work, he was under no obligation to give it to him; he might have it for the twelve ducats.[4] Artaria reconciled himself to the matter and paid Beethoven his fee on September 5. The arrangement which Artaria announced on May 10, 1827, as Op. 134 (the original score being advertised at the same time as Op. 133) was Beethoven's.

There was talk of other performances of the Quartet. Schuppanzigh was indisposed to venture upon a repetition, but Böhm and Mayseder were eager to produce the work at one of their quartet parties at Dembscher's house. But Dembscher had neglected to subscribe for Schuppanzigh's concert and had said that he would have it played at his house, since it was easy for him to get manuscripts from Beethoven for that purpose. He applied to Beethoven for the Quartet, but the latter refused to let him have it, and Holz, as he related to Beethoven, told Dembscher in the presence of other persons that Beethoven would not let him have any more music because he had not attended Schuppanzigh's concert. Dembscher stammered in confusion and begged Holz to find some means to restore him to Beethoven's good graces. Holz said that the first step should be to send Schuppanzigh 50 florins, the price of the subscription. Dembscher laughingly asked, "Must it be?" ("Muss es sein?") When Holz related the incident to Beethoven he too laughed and instantly wrote down the following canon:

Schnell im Eifer
Fast eagerly

[3] See Sonneck, *Beethoven Letters in America*, pp. 77-8.

[4] Beethoven wrote out a canon for Holz, "Da ist das Werk," WoO 197 (KHV, p. 698), with the text: "Here is the work. Bring back the sum—one, two, three, four, five, six, seven, eight, nine, ten, eleven, twelve ducats."

Out of this joke in the late fall of the year grew the finale of the last of the last five quartets, that in F major, Op. 135, to which Beethoven gave the superscription: "Der schwer gefasste Entschluss" ("The difficult resolution"). The story that the phrases: "Muss es sein? Es muss sein," and "Der schwer gefasste Entschluss" had their origin in a scene frequently repeated when Beethoven's housekeeper came to him of a Saturday for the weekly house-money, was spread by Schindler, who was familiar in a way with the Dembscher incident, but assigned it to the Quartet in E-flat. Holz was an actor in the scene and is the better witness, being confirmed, moreover, by the Conversation Book. The joke played a part in the conversations with Beethoven for some time.

Schuppanzigh's attempt to have another benefit concert (*Akademie*) came to nothing. A morning concert in the Augarten, which Schuppanzigh hoped to give on May 1st, finally took place on May 11. Several things by Beethoven were played: an overture, March with chorus from the *Ruinen von Athen,* one of the violin Romances, and perhaps *Adelaide.*[5] The concert went well; the overture and march were particularly liked, and Schuppanzigh played, besides the Romance, a piece by Kreutzer. Among the operas performed during the year was *Fidelio,* with Nanette Schechner in the title role. She made her debut on May 22, 1826, at the Kärthnerthor Theatre in Joseph Weigl's *Schweitzerfamilie.* Both Holz and Schindler reported to Beethoven concerning her singing with high praise and compared her favorably with Milder-Hauptmann. Schechner wanted very much to meet the composer at this time, but her wish was not to be fulfilled until February of the next year.

With the Quartet in B-flat, Beethoven had completed the three works of its kind which he had been commissioned to compose by Prince Nikolas Galitzin. He had taken three years to perform the task, but in the end the patience of his patron had been nobly rewarded. Meanwhile the Prince had been privileged to shine in the musical circles of St. Petersburg as one who stood peculiarly close to the greatest of living composers. During the delay, Prince Galitzin's conduct was in the highest degree honorable. In his letters he was most generous in his offers of assistance, practically giving Beethoven *carte blanche* to draw on his bankers in case of need. After the first performance of the *Missa Solemnis,* for which he had been primarily responsible, he presented his copy of the written score to the Philharmonic Society of St. Petersburg. He was so proud of his collection of Beethoven's music that he applied to the composer himself to help him make it complete. Too eager to wait for the publishers, he commissioned Beethoven to have copies made for him of new works, like the Ninth Symphony and the overture to the *Weihe des Hauses,* at his expense. He entertained the idea of repeating in St. Petersburg the concert which Beethoven had given in Vienna, at which the Symphony had received its first performance. For awhile he contemplated

[5] The Conversation Books mention a performance of the song by Hoffmann, but Thayer believed that this referred to the concert on March 21. (TDR, v, 306, n. 1.)

a repetition of the Mass. His first payment of 50 ducats for the first quartet in October, 1823 had been transferred, at Beethoven's request, to his subscription for the Mass. A second payment of 50 ducats, which was sent on December 5, 1824, was clearly for the first quartet. The work was sent to the Prince at the beginning of 1825, and Beethoven received a letter of grateful acknowledgement, written on April 29.

{After an exchange of letters in June,[6] there is a break in the correspondence until the beginning of 1826. In the summer of 1825 Beethoven had two overtures, *Zur Namensfeier* and the *Weihe des Hauses,* sent to the Prince with a dedication to his patron on the latter. The A minor Quartet, Op. 132, had received its first public performance on November 6, 1825 in Vienna. That the Prince had heard of this performance is shown by his next letter:

St. Petersburg, January 14, 1826

Dear, respected Monsieur van Beethoven,

I am much at fault for not having yet acknowledged the receipt of the overtures which you had the kindness to send me. I was waiting for the shipment of the quartet to express my thoughts all at once. Since that time I have been very ill and then I was obliged to make a trip into the heart of Russia. All these circumstances and unexpected changes here have prevented me from writing to you up until now. I have just read in the musical Gazette of Leipzig that the new Quartet in A minor was performed in Vienna, and I am so impatient to get acquainted with this new masterpiece that I beg you to send it to me by post, like the preceding one, without further delay.

I will remit the amount of 75 ducats to M. Stieglitz to be remitted to you by M. Fries; 50 for the quartet and 25 for the overture which is magnificent and which I thank you very much for dedicating to me. The Leipzig journal referred to your new quartet in such flattering terms that I could not be more impatient to get acquainted with it. Would you forward it as soon as possible, for soon I am leaving for the coronation in Moscow, and then I will send you my address.

I wish you a good and happy new year.

Your devoted friend
Prince Nicolas Galitzin[7]

The A minor Quartet was sent in February, the B-flat Quartet shortly thereafter, as we shall see. But Beethoven waited in vain to be paid for them, and this was a matter of concern to him and those close to him during the months to come.

Holz knew a courier named Lipscher who often went to St. Petersburg, and he volunteered in January to obtain his services if the money did not

---

[6] On June 4 Beethoven had written of ill-health. A letter from the Prince dated June 21 ends: "I will have forwarded immediately the 460 silver florins which are coming to you, very happy to be able to contribute something for the betterment of your circum-stances." There is no record of such a sum having been received.

[7] The Galitzin correspondence covered in this chapter, and the conversations relating to it, are drawn from TDR, v, Appendix ii, pp. 567ff.

arrive soon. In March Johann suggested that his brother write another letter, which he himself would post, for fear that the last quartet had never been received.

In May, Holz writes in the Conversation Books:

The courier Lipscher, who took the third quartet and was supposed to bring back the money, has written from Petersburg: he went to the home of the Prince, who excused himself, he had no time, he could come another day; Lipscher then went 5 or 6 times but was never received; all kinds of excuses were given. A so-called blue note for 5 f.[lorins] given to a servant helped him finally to get through to the Prince again; he was embarrassed again, fumbled through his scores and finally said that Lipscher might come to him before his departure for Vienna and receive the money.

•◠•

The fellow believes it is nothing more than a Russian trick!

•◠•

But he adds that he is not to be put off so easily; he thinks that he will be here in 4 to 5 weeks. And it is certain now that he has received the 2nd Quartet.[8]

At about this time Schindler makes the following entry:

The affair with Galitzin is becoming serious and I wish you a happy outcome.

•◠•

If you had followed my advice, you would have sent at most *one* quartet and then stopped.

•◠•

You have never let yourself be deceived by flattery except by this princely braggart.

In June, Holz writes:

The courier Lipscher has written: "7 times I went to see the scamp, the last time it turned out that he had left for the coronation in Moscow—merely a Russian trick."

•◠•

Several couriers have told me that there has been little action from the embassy; it does not want to have a quarrel with this gentleman.

Lipscher advised Beethoven to turn to the banker Stieglitz in Vienna, who could exert more pressure than the Embassy. Karl urged his uncle to do the same. On August 13 Stieglitz answered a letter of August 2 from Beethoven reporting that the Prince was not at home but probably near Koslow in the Tambow region and that the matter would be attended to upon his return.

Finally in November a letter arrived:

[8] The second of the last two: *i.e.*, B-flat Quartet.

10/22 November, 1826

My dear and respected Monsieur van Beethoven!

You must think I am very inconsistent and fickle to let so much time go by without writing you especially since I have received from you two new masterpieces of your immortal and inexhaustible genius. But the unhappy circumstances that I find myself in, partly from great losses which have brought me several bankruptcies, partly from other considerations that I cannot explain to you, have drawn me away from my usual occupations.

Now I am living in the country in the heart of Russia, and in a few days I will be leaving for Persia to participate in the war there. Before this I will definitely dispatch the sum of 125 ducats to be remitted to you, and I can only offer you my thanks for your masterpieces and my excuses for having taken so long to give you any sign of life. Please let me keep on hearing from you, it means a lot to me. Always write to me at the old address, and tell me, I beg of you, what new things you are composing.

Accept the esteem and regard of one of your greatest admirers.

Pce Nicolas Galitzin

Since this letter was written before his return to St. Petersburg, it shows that he had received both of the last two quartets before his trip and that he recognized his debt to be 50 ducats for each of those quartets and 25 ducats for the dedication of the overture *Weihe des Hauses*. On the outside of this letter there is a notation, probably written by Breuning: "Inquiry sent on January 10, 827 concerning this matter to the banking house, Stieglitz and Company, requesting the delivery of the sum of 125 ducats or a report." Stieglitz answered this inquiry on January 18 reporting that he had sent another reminder to the Prince in Koslow. A final appeal to Stieglitz was written on March 21, 1827, which Beethoven signed on his deathbed. There the matter rested until after his death. The story of later negotiations is told in the Appendix (H).

Now we turn to Beethoven's current relations with his publishers. He was on friendly terms with Matthias Artaria, who had taken the B-flat Quartet and the Fugue and, unlike others, did not delay in preparing them for publication. He visited Beethoven, met him at inns, and wanted him to come to his own quarters. But in the course of a month there was some trouble between the two, possibly in connection with the afore-mentioned piano arrangements of the Fugue. Artaria wanted the "new" Quartet in C sharp minor, but Beethoven decided to give it to Schott.

Serious misunderstandings continued between Beethoven and the firm of Steiner and Haslinger. Perhaps there was still ill-will on Beethoven's part because of Steiner's behavior in the matter of the debt, which had now been settled; the same on Steiner's part was easy to understand since Beethoven was no longer giving him his new works but bringing them out with other publishers, some of whom were foreigners. Steiner had lost out on the bidding for the B-flat Quartet. Also it had been a year ago that the joke on Haslinger had been printed in Schott's magazine, *Cäcilia*. Beethoven frequently needed music from Steiner's firm and was slow in returning it. On the other hand foreign correspondents were using Steiner's as an address with which to get their letters through to Beethoven, and it often happened that they remained there for weeks at a time. Already by the end of January Beethoven requested Schott to communicate with him through Artaria rather than Steiner in order to avoid delay. It is likely that Holz exercised an unfavorable influence here, for he did not care for Steiner and did not miss opportunities to slander him. At the same time, he sought to alienate Steiner from Beethoven and made pronouncements to him concerning Beethoven's way of using people.

The following stern note to Haslinger introduces a new cause for strife.[9]

I report to you that neither the Overture[10] nor the "Elegischer Gesang"[11] need further corrections, also that the titles are correct. But concerning the march with chorus[12] and the vocal terzetto,[13] the faulty notes of before are now indeed correct, but the titles are still not the way I myself indicated. Since this affair has been going on for 6 weeks, and I have many examples in connection with this where I could not overcome your obstinacy, I have handed both titles in their original form to His Honor the Censor, about which I hereby serve you notice.

Vienna, April 9, 826   Ludwig van Beethoven
    I wanted to inform you of the above as a favor so that you may prepare for it. For I will *never* allow these works to appear with the titles which you have set up.

Beethoven's principal worry was in the wording of the title of the piano-vocal score of the Terzett, published in February, which implied that the work was originally scored for piano accompaniment.

At Holz's urging Beethoven sent him with the following note[14] to the Censor's office, the head of which was the Book Censor, Councillor Sartorius:

Highly honored Censor!
    I am threatened by an edition of several of my works, wherein, out of resentment towards me, mistakes indicated by me have not been corrected. The titles are of such a barbaric nature that they would bring disgrace to Vienna. Therefore I request your honor that these works not be allowed to be advertised until I with my own signature have confirmed that these works appear in proper condition.

In the Conversation Books there is much discussion of the affair. In April it is presumably Holz who writes:

He [the censor] cannot recall if Haslinger had already received permission of the censor to publish this.

---

[9] Taken from Unger, *Ludwig van Beethoven und seine Verleger*, No. 94. See also *A* 1480.
[10] To *König Stephen*.
[11] Op. 118.
[12] Op. 114.
[13] Op. 116.
[14] Unger, *op.cit.*, p. 22. See also *A* 1479.

If this has already happened, it would not be easy to remedy; on the contrary, he would have resolved it already.

◦

If it has already happened, we still have the foreign newspapers to whom we can place it in the proper light.

During the summer of 1826 Tobias Haslinger had become the sole owner of the firm when Steiner retired. In the Conversation Book of September, the matter comes up again and Holz writes:

Today Tobias showed [me] the proof-impression of the new title for the Terzett: I discovered a new mistake right away. The printer placed "vor tutti orchestra" well but left out "estratto per il cembalo."

◦

It is to be fixed by the day after tomorrow.

◦

This way one would think one was buying the whole score.

Finally the correction was made according to Beethoven's wishes, and he asked Haslinger to announce this in the newspapers. Beethoven had always maintained a friendly personal relationship with Haslinger, and despite Holz's antagonism this was now resumed, as is shown by letters of this same month, in which Beethoven returns to the old, characteristically mischievous tone.[15]

There was greater confidence in the firm of Schott at Mainz, who continued to bring out Beethoven's new compositions. The E-flat Quartet, Op. 127, appeared in March, 1826, and the Ninth Symphony by the end of August. Schott also received the next work, the C-sharp minor Quartet, Op. 131. Holz said that when he once remarked to Beethoven that the one in B-flat was the greatest of the three quartets (Op. 127, 130, 132) the composer replied: "Each in its way. Art demands of us that we shall not stand still. You will find a new manner of voice treatment (part writing) and thank God there *is less lack of fancy than ever before.*"[16] Afterward he declared the C-sharp minor Quartet to be his greatest. The first form of the fugue-theme in this work, as has been noted, was written down in a Conversation Book in the last days of December, 1825. The quartet was the main work of the next month, and indeed for the first half of 1826 with interruptions only from sickness, preparations for the performance of the B-flat Quartet, and the four-hand arrangement of the Fugue (Op. 133). Before the end of

15 See *A* 1522, 1526, 1530.
16 From Holz's recollections (Wilhelm von   Lenz, *Eine Kunststudie* [Hamburg, 1860], v, p. 217.) (TDR, v, 318, n. 2.)

January the variation theme appears in a Conversation Book in Beethoven's hand:

It is likely that a goodly portion of the work was written within a month and ready for the copyist, for in January Holz suggested that something from the work in hand be tried. Whether or not it was ever played in public in the lifetime of the composer cannot be said with certainty.[17] Schindler says positively that it was not performed by Schuppanzigh. ─•⊰On March 28 Beethoven wrote to Schott and Sons in Mainz and established the price of a quartet *of this kind* at least 80 gold ducats."[18]⊱•─

In another letter to Schott, dated May 20, Beethoven complained of ill health and pressing affairs which prevented him from completing the quartet until now. He restated the fee of 80 ducats, but said that he was willing to be paid in two installments. On July 12 he wrote that the quartet was ready for delivery upon receipt of the draft of the second installment of the fee. The score was turned over to Schott's agent in Vienna on August 12. On the copy Beethoven had written: "Put together from pilferings from one thing and another" ("Zusammengestohlen aus Verschiedenem diesem und jenem"). Because this had alarmed the publishers, Beethoven writes on August 19: "I report to you that the score was delivered to Frank 7 days ago. You wrote me that the quartet must be an original one. I felt rather hurt, so as a joke I wrote on the copy that it was put together from pilferings. Nevertheless, it is *brand new—.*" It was published by Schott and Sons in June, 1827, after Beethoven's death.

The quartet was originally to be dedicated to his friend and admirer, Johann Wolfmayer, as was indicated in a letter to Schott on February 22, 1827. Then on March 10 he wrote again to change the dedication to Baron Joseph von Stutterheim, Lieutenant Field-Marshal, who had made a place for Karl in his regiment.

Now we turn to the projects which the composer's friends tried unsuccessfully to persuade him to undertake. First, there was Bernard's *Der Sieg des Kreuzes* which Beethoven had promised to write for the Gesellschaft der Musikfreunde. At the end of 1825 Kanne's advice had been sought and he recommended an abbreviation of the text. Hauschka gave his approval to the revision. In April Kuffner told Beethoven that he had read Bernard's oratorio book but could not find in it even a semblance of an oratorio, much less half-good execution. These protests could only strengthen Beethoven's distaste for the text. At any rate the plan was definitely laid aside. According to Holz, he never worked earnestly on the subject and yet, at the same time,

---

[17] In a letter to Schott at the end of September, 1826, Beethoven writes of a projected performance "for the benefit of an artist" (Joseph Böhm?) of which there is no record. See *A* 1531. (TDR, v, 318, n. 1.)

[18] See *A* 1472.

showed his intention to write no more "Opern" and piano pieces, but only oratorio. Holz further relates that Beethoven, in reference to his last sonatas, which he called his last but also the best that he had written for piano, said: "It is and remains an inadequate instrument. In the future I shall write in the manner of my grand-master Handel annually only an oratorio or a concerto for some string or wind instrument, provided I have completed my tenth symphony (C minor) and my Requiem."[19]

Perhaps there was something of personal equation in Kuffner's judgement of the Bernard text, for he was ready to write not only one but even two oratorio texts if Beethoven would but undertake their composition. He presented the plan of a work to be called "The Four Elements," in which Man was to be brought into relationship with the imposing phenomena of Nature. Meanwhile, there was discussion of the subject of Saul. Holz relates that "Beethoven had given much study to Handel's *Saul* and read a lot about the music of the ancient Hebrews; he wanted to write choruses in the old modes." In April the conversation was lively on the subject. Kuffner was to revise the text for Beethoven; he was already thinking of a place for the performance. Kuffner intended in his treatment of the story of Saul to make it a representation of the triumph of the nobler impulses of Man over untamed desire. Kuffner set to work; and Holz brought a few sections of the text to the composer. In a Conversation Book he says:

I must take back this one in Kuffner's handwriting by the day after tomorrow. I will take care of your copy.

•~•

I copied this quickly from Kuffner.

•~•

Here there might be a chorus in the Lydian mode as you wanted to bring one in.

Holz urged that it would be a shame if this mode were heard only in a quartet.[20] In May he brought greetings from Kuffner, who was now at work on it body and soul. He also explained that Kuffner intended to treat the chorus as an effective agent in the action, for which purpose it was to be divided into two sections, like the dramatic chorus of the Greek tragedians. Kuffner was sufficiently encouraged to write the book and Holz says that Beethoven finished the music of the first part "in his head." If so, it stayed there, as far as the sketchbooks bear testimony.

His friends also urged him to compose a Requiem mass and such a composition belongs in the category with the oratorio as a work which he had been paid to undertake. Among the ardent admirers of Beethoven and most zealous patrons of the Schuppanzigh Quartets was Johann Nepomuk Wolfmayer, a much respected cloth merchant. One of the methods chosen by Wolfmayer to show his appreciation of the composer was occasionally to

[19] From Holz's recollections to Frau Linzbaur, in Nohl, *Beethoven, Liszt and Wagner*, p. 112. (TDR, v, 326, n. 1.)

[20] Op. 132, third movement.

have a new coat made for him which he would bring to Beethoven's lodgings, place upon a chair and then see to it that an old one disappeared from his wardrobe. We have already heard a similar story from Mayseder. It is said that Wolfmayer sometimes had difficulty in getting the composer's consent to the exchange, but always managed to do it. Early in the second decade of the century Wolfmayer commissioned Beethoven to write a Requiem for him and —⚜offered him 100 ducats as honorarium.[21]⚜— Beethoven promised, but never set to work: though Holz says he was firmly resolved to do so and, in talking about it, said that he was better satisfied with Cherubini's setting of the Mass for the Dead than with Mozart's. A requiem, he said, should be a memorial of the dead and have nothing in it of the noises of the last trumpet and the day of judgement.[22]

There was still talk of an opera, and the matter was constantly being broached by different members of his circle. Brother Johann urged opera as the most remunerative enterprise to which he could now apply himself. The serious von Breuning also advised him to write an opera right away. Duport, director of the Court Opera, sent word through Holz and Johann that conditions were favorable for an opera to be written and that Grillparzer's *Melusine* would be acceptable to him.

Beethoven evidently had expressed the intention or wish to the older Schlesinger to write an opera for Berlin. This information was passed on to the General Intendant of the Berlin Theatre, Count von Brühl, who wrote a letter to Beethoven on April 6.[23] First he expressed the honor it would bring his stage to have a work written for it by such an artist as Beethoven; then he added that Schlesinger had given him Grillparzer's *Die schöne Melusine* which, although full of good things was too close in subject matter to *Undine*, an opera by de la Motte Fouqué and E. T. A. Hoffmann, which had already appeared on his stage.[24] He closed with the hope that Beethoven and Grillparzer would collaborate on another subject. This letter was evidently never answered.

An adaptation to operatic uses of Goethe's *Claudine von Villa Bella* was discussed, apparently with favor, but Kanne, who was designated to take the adaptation in hand, was afraid to meddle with the great poet's drama. So nothing came of the Berlin project or of *Melusine*, though Grillparzer talked it over again with Beethoven and told Holz that though he was not inclined to attach too great importance to it, yet he thought it would be hard to find an opera text better adapted to its purpose than it, from a musical and scenic point of view. To Schindler, Beethoven once held out a prospect that "something would come" of the idea of music for *Faust* which Rochlitz had implanted in Beethoven's mind; but it shared the fate of opera and oratorio.

[21] See *FRBH*, II, p. 466. (Cf. TDR, v, 329, n. 1.)

[22] From O. Jahn's memoranda from Holz. See Nohl, *op.cit.*, p. 111. (TDR, v, 329; also see n. 2.)

[23] See *DM*, Vol. 3, No. 12, p. 437. (TDR, v, 330, n. 1.)

[24] July, 1816.

The sketchbooks bear witness, though not voluminously, to other works of magnitude which were in Beethoven's thoughts in this year but never saw completion. These were a symphony and overture. In a book used towards the end of 1825, containing sketches for the last movement of the Quartet in B-flat, there is a memorandum of a *Presto* in C minor, ¾ time, and of a short movement in A-flat, *Andante*, which Schindler marked as belonging to "the tenth symphony."[25]

There are also much longer sketches for an overture on B-a-c-h, in the midst of which Beethoven had written: "This overture together with the new symphony and we shall have a new Akademie in the Kärnthnerthor."[26] Schindler published the sketches of the symphony in Hirschbach's *Musikalisch-kritisches Repertorium* of January, 1844, and started the story of an uncompleted tenth symphony. Lenz says that Holz wrote to him that Beethoven had played "the whole of the Tenth Symphony" for him on the pianoforte, that it was finished in all of its movements in the sketches, but that nobody but Beethoven could decipher them. Holz, however, made no such broad statement to Otto Jahn, a much more conscientious reporter than Lenz. To Jahn he said that there was an introduction in E-flat major, a soft piece, and then a powerful *Allegro* in C minor, which were complete in Beethoven's head and which he had played to him (Holz) on the pianoforte. This is very different from an entire symphony. In the letter to Moscheles dictated to Schindler on March 18, 1827, bearing a message of thanks to the Philharmonic Society of London for money sent during his illness, the composer says that he will bind himself "to compose for it [the Society] either a new symphony, which lies already sketched in my desk, or a new overture or something else which the Society would like."[27]

[25] *II Beeth.*, pp. 11-12.

[26] Sketches for an overture on B-A-C-H also appear in 1823 and 1824.

[27] From the reading given in *Beethoven als Freund der Familie Wegeler-v. Breuning*, ed. S. Ley (Bonn, 1927), pp. 232-34.

Among Beethoven's intimate friends was Abbé Stadler, an old man and an old-fashioned musician, the horizon of whose aesthetic appreciation was marked by the death-date of his friend Mozart. Castelli says that he used to call Beethoven's music "pure nonsense"; certain it is that he used to leave the concert-room whenever a composition by Beethoven was to be played. Schuppanzigh offered as an excuse for him that he had a long way to go to get home, and it does not appear that Beethoven ever took umbrage at his conduct. Holz, telling Beethoven in February, 1825, that as usual he had left the room when an overture by Beethoven was about to be played, added: "He is too old. He always says when Mozart is reached, 'More I cannot understand.'" But once he stayed and not only listened to a Beethoven piece but praised it. It was the Trio for Strings, Op. 9, which had been composed nearly a generation before! Holz becomes sarcastic: "One might say A.B.C.D. (*Abbé cédait*)." Stadler now had occasion to court Beethoven's favor, or at least to betray the fact that even if he could not appreciate his music he yet had a vast respect for his genius and reputation. In 1825, Gottfried Weber had written an essay, which was published in the *Cäcilia* journal, attacking the authenticity of Mozart's *Requiem*. The article angered Beethoven, as is evidenced by his marginal glosses on the copy of the journal which he read, now in the possession of the Beethoven-Haus in Bonn. The glosses are two in number: "Oh you arch ass!" and "Double ass!" Such a disposition of an attack on the artistic honor of his friend did not suffice Stadler. He published a defense of Mozart, *Vertheidigung der Echtheit des Mozartschen Requiems*, and sent a copy to Beethoven, who acknowledged it thus:

on the 6th of Feby., 1826

Respected and venerable Sir!

You have done a really good deed in securing justice for the manes of Mozart by your truly exemplary and exhaustive essay. Both lay and profane, and all who are musical or who can in any way be accounted such must give you thanks—

Either nothing or a great deal is required to broach such a subject as H[err] W. has done. When it is also considered, as far as I know, that such a one has written a book on composition and yet tries to attribute such passages as

to Mozart, and if one adds to it an example of W[eber]'s own crudities such as we are reminded by H.W.'s amazing knowledge of harmony and melody of the old and dead Imperial composers Sterkel, Haueisen,[28] Kalkbrenner (the father), André (certainly not the other one) and so forth.

Requiescant in pace—But I am particularly grateful to you, my honored friend, for the happiness you have given me in sending me your essay. I have always counted myself among the greatest admirers of Mozart and shall remain so until my last breath—

Reverend Sir, *your blessing very soon*—

With sincere regards, venerable Sir, I remain your faithful

Beethoven

The concluding supplication recalls an anecdote related by Castelli in his memoirs: Beethoven and Abbé Stadler once met at Steiner's. About to depart, Beethoven knelt before the Abbé and said: "Reverend Sir, give me your blessing." Stadler, not at all embarrassed, made the sign of the cross over the kneeling man and, as if mumbling a prayer, said: "Nutzt's nicht, so schadt's nix" ("If it does no good, 'twill do no harm"). Beethoven thereupon kissed his hand amid the laughter of the bystanders. Jahn heard the same story from Fischoff.

Though direct evidence is lacking, it seems obvious to associate the following three-part canon (see WoO 178) with this amusing anecdote:

A remark in a Conversation Book of 1826 indicates that Stadler had urged Beethoven to write a mass. Holz says:

If Stadler tells you to write a mass it is certain that something will be done for it. He knows best of anybody which way the wind blows.

✦

He has Dietrichstein and Eybler in his pocket.

✦

[28] See *A* 1468; I am indebted to Miss Anderson for the reading of this name.

You are well cared for if Stadler favors it.

The conversations of Holz also provide a fleeting glimpse of Schubert in this year. Holz told Beethoven that he had seen the young composer with some one (perhaps Artaria or Mosel) and that the two were reading a Handel score together.

He [Schubert] was very amiable and thanked me for the pleasure which My-lord's [Schuppanzigh's] Quartets gave him; he was always present.

•~•

He has a great gift for songs.

•~•

Do you know the Erlkönig?

•~•

He spoke very mystically, always.

Friedrich Wieck, father of Clara Schumann, spent several hours with Beethoven, having been presented by Andreas Stein, the pianoforte maker. He told about the visit long afterward in a letter to his second wife, which was reprinted in the *Signale* No. 57, in December, 1873, from the *Dresdener Nachrichten*. Beethoven gave his guest wine (to which Wieck was not accustomed), improvised for him for over an hour and talked voluminously about, ". . . musical conditions in Leipzig—Rochlitz—Schicht—Gewandhaus—his housekeeper—his many lodgings, none of which suited him—his promenades—Hietzing—Schönbrunn—his brother—various stupid people in Vienna—aristocracy—democracy—revolution—Napoleon—Mara—Catalani—Malibran—Fodo—the excellent Italian singers Lablache, Donzelli, Rubini and others, the perfections of Italian opera (German opera could never be so perfect because of the language and because the Germans did not learn to sing as beautifully as the Italians)—my views on pianoforte playing—Archduke Rudolph—Fuchs in Vienna, at the time a famous musical personality—my improved method of pianoforte teaching, etc. . . ."

Wieck said that the meeting was in Hietzing in May, and that Beethoven played upon the pianoforte "presented to him by the city of London"—three obvious mistakes, since Beethoven was not in Hietzing in May, but in Vienna, and the Broadwood pianoforte, which was not presented to him by the city of London but by Thomas Broadwood, was in the hands of Graf for repairs in May.

Different proposals for Beethoven's move to the country were already being offered early in the year. In February Johann invited him again to his country house. It is not surprising that Beethoven did not consider it at this time. He was waiting for the money from Prince Galitzin and Karl writes: "If the sums of money should come, you could probably go to the country." Among many possibilities was a move to Ischl.[29] In May Beethoven writes:

[29] In June Karl writes: "I have enquired about Ischl, it is 32 miles from here." (TDR, v, 343, n. 2.)

"It is best to go to Ischl." In June and July there is talk of the baths there which are beneficial to those suffering from gout. Holz offered also to find a house in Baden for him. It had been planned to make a move for the summer, but the place had not yet been decided upon when an event took place which suddenly changed all such thoughts: an attempt by Karl to take his life.

Let us take up the history of Beethoven and his nephew from where we left off. As we have seen, in 1825 Karl had transferred from the University to the Polytechnic Institute. He lived in the Alleegasse with Schlemmer and as a rule came at midday to his uncle's, in whose circle he played an active role. He reported on many things that were happening in the outside world, also on musical and literary developments. He continued to be active in his uncle's affairs (plans, publishers, money), wrote letters for him and ran errands. Holz writes in a Conversation Book, "He has sensible opinions," and again mention is made of his "good talents."

However, since he had enrolled late in the term at the Institute, Karl employed a tutor to help him, and apparently still needed his help a year later. At the time of the change to the Institute, Beethoven made the remark that the expense of the tutor, along with the board at Schlemmer's, would amount to 2000 florins a year.[30] Entries in the Conversation Book of 1825 show that the matter was under discussion and that Beethoven had registered his disapproval of the tutor to Schlemmer, for Karl writes:

I have spoken to Schlemmer about it too. He denied ever having said that; also, since he was not informed about it, he couldn't know to what extent I need him or not.

•~•

My class hours are all distributed. My tutor comes early, from 8.30 to 9.30. Then lectures from 9 to 12. In the afternoon lectures from 3 to 5. I have an hour from 5 to 6.

•~•

In the evenings I do all my assignments.

•~•

Thus after 5. It is always just like today. But it will be a quarter hours later.

Later, there appears in Schlemmer's hand:

I can assure you that as yet he has never stayed away overnight. Also I must tell you that your nephew is at home daily in the evening, and that he goes out early only if it is time for school. But if he were going out to play, then it would have to be instead of school. Otherwise he is at home and he cannot play. In the time that he has been here he has been changing his ways favorably. He said today at lunch that the tutor was not really satisfied, he is negligent in his studies.

[30] See TDR, v, p. 523.

Karl writes:

The lessons are not difficult for me, also I could not have taken up any *earlier* what I am taking with *him* because we take up only those studies which are being given in college.

‿

From my lessons with him I save several hours in which I would have had to work alone for myself.

To another complaint Karl answered: "I would be glad if you would inform yourself; each day the professors are bound to know when I leave since the names are read out. Also H. Reisser sees me daily." Around New Year's Day, 1826, Holz writes: "I have already spoken with Reisser; he says that Karl is behaving himself the way you would expect from a reasonable person.

Karl complains again of his schedule and amount of work: "There is now a great deal to do; and it is frightful to give up Sundays."

At about this time there came up the question of a carnival ball to which Karl wanted to go. Holz spoke approvingly of it and intended to accompany Karl to it, but apparently had to dissuade Beethoven from doing the same:

Nevertheless you would be most embarrassed if you were obliged to let people gape at you.

‿

I will go with him to a regular ball.

‿

I would be afraid, if I were alone with him, he might run away, and I would not know where.

‿

If there is a ball in the Apollo Room, the so-called Ball of the Reformists, you would be noticed there less probably than elsewhere which would certainly be [more] agreeable to you.

The old mistrust of Karl's misuse of free time led to renewed complaints of any long periods of absence. In February Beethoven must have expressed the desire that Karl come to live with him again, for at this time the nephew writes in a Conversation Book:

You go ahead and do what you think is best. I believe simply that the distance[31] would cause a great loss of time, instead of my being, as I am now, a few minutes from home and able to study.

‿

In the summer we will not feel the distance as much.

‿

But it is the *last* year; then we need never be separated any more.

[31] *I.e.*, from the Institute.

Beethoven gave in, but the mistrust remained, and the conflict between them grew. The alternation between strong reproaches, moral sermons and excessive emotional expressions of love served only to diminish bit by bit Beethoven's authority over the boy, and as a result Karl saw less and less of his uncle. Beethoven felt this keenly and asked his brother Johann to find out the reason. At the beginning of March Johann writes in the Conversation Book:

Today I spoke with him earnestly about why he had been to see you so little.

•~•

His answer was approximately as follows. He would very much like to be with you but he fears the frequent rows and reproaches for his mistakes of the past, also the frequent rows with the servants. However, please do not reproach him with this; otherwise he would no longer be candid with me. From here, however, I think that only you can draw him to yourself completely.

•~•

I suppose on account of his frequently poor appearance; I have spoken bluntly to him about it but he consistently denies everything.

Johann then advised his brother to write important letters himself, so that no one else would know their contents. He offered to post them himself. He continues: "In 4 months Karl will be ready with everything, then you must urge him to go immediately into a local or foreign business house, for otherwise he will become a lout [ein Lump] and will let himself live off of you as long as you are living; then he could idle away his time."

Johann advised that in the latter case the guardianship should be placed in the hands of Dr. Bach, because "You are as little able as I to be always running after him." In these conversations we also find Schindler once again, to whom Beethoven had voiced his fears. Schindler replies: "I am sorry to hear it, what all are we to live through with Karl, if it goes on like this." And he advised Beethoven not to depend upon Holz in the management of this affair.

Meanwhile Karl explained again how much work he had to do—for example, "The professors assign so much work over the holidays that one can scarcely get it done. The fair copying is the most disagreeable part because it takes alot of time,"—and its effect on his visits and his participation in outside events. In June he writes: "There is much to be done because the examinations are soon." Holz adds: "Now Karl does not have much longer to study."

Another form of duress came from the uncle's suspicion of the nephew in money matters. Beethoven asked to see the receipts of last month's payment to Schlemmer and expressed misgivings over Karl's demands for funds. Karl writes:

If the receipt is not in my room, Schlemmer can give it to me along with the receipt for this month.

·～·

It will show up all right.

·～·

When I go walking and have a drink and the like. I don't have any other expenses.

This last answer from Karl must have been to a demand from his uncle as to how he used money, and must be weighed against a statement by Schlemmer in the Conversation Books, and later again by Breuning, that the principal reason that circumstances had become intolerable for Karl was that he was heavily in debt.

There were violent scenes, evidently in Karl's rooms which deeply embittered him. Shortly afterwards his uncle visited him again to break down his obstinacy. Here follows Karl's part of the dialogue, which shows what tension had been reached over Beethoven's persistence:

You consider it insolence if, after you have upbraided me for hours undeservedly, this time at least, I cannot turn from my bitter feeling of pain to jocularity. I am not so frivolous as you think. I can assure you that since the scene on Sunday in the presence of this fellow I have been so depressed that the people in the house noticed it. The receipt for the 80 florins which were paid in May I now positively know, after a search at home, that I gave you, as I already said on Sunday; it must and no doubt will be found.

·～·

If I continue to work while you are here it is not in a spirit of insolence, but because I believe that you will not be offended if I do not permit your presence to keep me from my labors, which are now really piling up on me, all the more since we see each other *here,* where there is time, enough to talk over all needful things. You are mistaken, too, when you think that I wait for your coming to *become industrious.* You also seem to accept as *my views* what I repeat to you as the opinions of *others* as, for example, the word of *Haslinger* and the twaddle of Frau Passy.

·～·

I know very well what to think of such gossip, but did consider it my duty to inform you about it.

·～·

I hope that what I have said will serve to convince you of my real views and feelings and put an end to the strain which has existed of late between us, though not on my side by any means.

At one point, judging from a recorded remark by Holz, Karl seems to have raised his hand in physical violence against his uncle. Holz writes:

I came in just as he took you by the breast.

·～·

At the door, as he was coming out.

It is the only allusion to the incident in the book and we know none of the particulars; but it and other scenes of tumult and the utterances which they provoked must have inspired the dreadful conflict of emotions which finds expression in a letter written at this time:

If for no other reason than that you obeyed me, at least, all is forgiven and forgotten; more today by word of mouth, very quietly—Do not think that I am governed by anything but thoughts for your well-being, and from this point of view judge my acts—Do not take a step which might make *you* unhappy and shorten *my* life—I did not get to sleep until 3 o'clock, for I coughed all night long—I embrace you cordially and am convinced that soon you will no longer *misjudge* me; I thus judge your conduct yesterday—I expect you without fail today at one o'clock—Do not give me cause for further worry and apprehension— Meanwhile farewell!

Your real and true Father

We shall be alone, for I shall not permit H.[32] to come—the more so since I do not wish anything about yesterday to be known. Do come—do not permit my poor heart to *bleed any longer*.

The subjects discussed in the Conversation Books continued to be the same: the securing of a position for Karl, the proximity of the examination, the pile of work, done partly with the tutor, the difficulty of coming to see Beethoven as often as the uncle wished. Karl told him specifically that he could not come in the evening. Was it merely work in the evening that detained him? His uncle felt uninformed about how he spent his evenings and in whose company. There was the usual suspicion of the company he kept and of his desire to gamble,[33] to which there was now added talk of his taking flight. Beethoven inquired about him often—too often according to Reisser. He was to be seen in the vestibule of the Polytechnic Institute at noontime waiting to escort his nephew home arm in arm.

At this time Karl was also seeing his mother, which, of course, was directly contrary to Beethoven's wishes. There he saw his friend, Niemetz, with whom his mother had become acquainted. At this time Beethoven wrote a short note to Holz:

Please come as soon as possible, thereupon we can arrange everything. It is no small matter, he wanted to go away again early today.

Most hurriedly
Your Beethoven

The force of circumstances had made Karl sullen and angry. Schindler writes in the Conversation Book that once when he was admonished by his teachers at the Institute and reminded of his duty to his uncle he replied, "My uncle! I can do with him what I want, some flattery and friendly gestures make things all right again right away." According to Holz, Karl said

---

[32] Holz. (TDR, v, 349, n. 2.)
[33] In the Conversation Book, Schindler writes of seeing Karl gambling in coffee-houses with coachmen and mere common people "with whom he often dealt with dishonorably in games." (TDR, v, 351, n. 2.)

that he could wrap his uncle around his finger. A note to Niemetz was subsequently found in which Karl writes: "I had to write you in such a great hurry from fear and worry of being discovered by the old fool."

In the last days of July, Beethoven was notified that Karl had disappeared and was intending to take his life. Evidently Karl had left the house leaving a hint of his purpose. Schlemmer learned of this, and from him Holz, who went to report to Beethoven. They both went to Schlemmer's house where Holz writes out:

I will fetch the police.

⌣

Still he must be moved away from here. He certainly will not take the examination.

⌣

Shall I have Schlemmer fetched?

Then Schlemmer reports:

The story in brief, since you have heard it already from Hr. Holz: I learned today that your nephew intended to shoot himself before next Sunday at the latest. As to the cause I learned only this much, that it was on account of his debts, but not completely, only in part was he admitting that they were the consequences of former sins.

⌣

I looked to see if there were signs of preparations; I found in his chest a loaded pistol all right, together with bullets and powder. I tell you this so that you may act in this case as his father. The pistol is in my keeping.

⌣

Be lenient with him or he will despair.

To the question of possible debts to him, Schlemmer answers: "I have been paid completely—up to the present month, but not yet for August."

Holz questions further, while looking through papers:

This is not his handwriting, yet everything is paid for till the end of July.

⌣

There is still a great deal more to be learned.

Holz then went to the Institute to find Karl and returned to report:

He is not staying here.

⌣

I could not detain him; he said he would come again to Schlemmer's, but he wanted to get his papers from a friend, meanwhile I talked with Reisser.

⌣

I said that I could not wait more than a quarter of an hour.

Beethoven apparently rebuked him for letting his ward out of his sight. He answers:

He would have run away from you just the same.

·～·

I think that if he has made up his mind to injure himself, no one can prevent him.

·～·

He has till September 3 to make up his examinations.

Holz evidently continued his search among Karl's papers: "Here is 30 x more for the rest of Schlemmer's board. He [Karl] said to me, 'What good will it do you to detain me? If I do not escape today, I will at another time.'"

Subsequently Schlemmer writes:

I will unload the gun. My wife has the second pistol.

·～·

Because I was not at home when it was found.

A new suspicion now seized upon the mind of Beethoven. For some reason, though he may also have uttered it orally, he wrote it down in the book: "He will drown himself." Probably he did not want the bystanders to know his thoughts, and the fear was therefore committed to the written page for the instruction of Holz. What else was said at the same time we do not know, for the book here shows a mutilation; some pages are missing. Perhaps Schindler removed them in later years to save the integrity of his account; or they may have been torn out by Beethoven himself when, some weeks later, Holz advised him to look through his books against their possible demand for examination by the police magistrate; they might contain references to affairs which he did not want to bring into public discussion. The missing pages might have helped us in the chronology of the story, but the main facts are before us without them. It was resolved first to go to the house of Niemetz, who it was thought might be privy to Karl's intentions, and then if necessary, to call in the help of the police.

Meanwhile Karl, having given Holz the slip, went straight to a pawnbroker and pledged his watch. From Holz's subsequent account we know that this took place on a Saturday—i.e. July 29th. With the money he bought two new pistols, powder and balls. He did not dare go to his lodgings for the pistols which he had in readiness for the contemplated deed, and the new ones were therefore necessary. For him the circumstance proved fortunate. He drove out to Baden, and spent the night in writing letters. One was to his uncle, and this he enclosed in one to his friend Niemetz. The next morning, it being a Sunday, he climbed up to the ruins of Rauhenstein, in the lovely Helenenthal which his uncle loved so well, and there discharged both pistols toward his left temple. He was a bungler with firearms. The first bullet flew past harmlessly; the second ripped up the flesh and grazed the bone, but did not penetrate the skull. Holz said afterwards that, had he taken with him the pistols which he was obligated to leave at his lodgings, he would have been a dead man; their barrels were charged with powder and ball to above the middle. A teamster came upon him lying among the ruins and, no doubt at his request, carried him to his mother's house in the city.

It was there that Beethoven found him. And to his uncle's questions he answers:

It is done. Now, only a surgeon who can hold his tongue. Smetana, if he is here.

⁘

Do not plague me with reproaches and lamentations; it is past. Later all matters may be adjusted.

⁘

She has sent for a doctor, but he is not at home. Holz will soon bring another one.

Then Beethoven asks: "When did it happen?" and the mother writes the answer:

He has just come. The teamster carried him down from a rock in Baden and has just driven out to you. . . . I beg of you to tell the surgeon not to make a report or they will take him away from here at once, and we fear the worst.

⁘

There is a bullet in his head on the left side.

Smetana was the physician who had treated Karl when he was a boy at Giannatasio's school. Beethoven knew him as a friend. To him he writes:

Most honored Herr von Smetana,
    A great misfortune has happened, which Karl accidentally inflicted upon himself. I hope that he can still be saved, especially by you if you come quickly. Karl has a *bullet* in his head; how, you shall learn—But quick, for God's sake, quick.
                            Yours respectfully,
                                            Beethoven
In order to give help quickly, it was necessary to take him to his mother's, where he now is. The address follows herewith.

Holz took this letter for delivery but, before he left, a surgeon named Dögl had been called in. Returning, Holz had a message from Smetana saying that Dögl was a capable practitioner and that in order not to compromise him he would not come unless Dögl desired to see him in consultation. Karl expressed himself as satisfied and the case was left for the time being in Dögl's hands.

Beethoven went home, but Holz remained some time longer. The matter had to be reported to the police and Holz thought it best to do this himself, as he wanted to be able to inform Beethoven what the consequences of the young man's act were likely to be in case of his recovery. He learned, and so reported, that there would be a severe reprimand and thereafter police surveillance. He also told Beethoven that, after he had left, Karl had said, "If only he would not show himself again," and "If he would only quit his reproaches!" He had also threatened to tear the bandage from the wound if another word were spoken to him about his uncle.

On August 7th,[34] the day being a Monday, the wounded youth, who by his act was in the hands of the law, was removed from his mother's house to the general hospital by the police authorities. If Beethoven was forced to leave the would-be suicide in the hands of his mother for an entire week it was most likely because the police authorities commanded it; he did not yield her a day after her son came out of the hospital.

Meanwhile Holz reported regularly on Karl's condition:

Four of the most skillful doctors come four times daily.

﹒〜﹒

He is getting unfailing care.

﹒〜﹒

As yet there is no fever, but if it should come, then there would be a dangerous crisis.

﹒〜﹒

The Magistrate as a criminal court is now concerned with this.

Under the Austrian code an attempt at suicide was an offence against the Church and guilty persons were remanded to the care of priests who imparted religious instruction until a profession of conversion could be recorded.

The priest will be sent by the Magistrate, you need not concern yourself with this any more.

﹒〜﹒

He will not be released until he has passed a complete examination in religious instruction and has been completely converted, so that there is no longer fear of a relapse.

﹒〜﹒

In such cases the police treat the misguided one with the greatest possible forbearance in order not to arouse stubbornness.

﹒〜﹒

But custody must not be as a punishment but as a means of security for himself.

[34] The date was obtained by Thayer from the records of the hospital on September 22, 1862. F. Helm, then Director of the hospital, certified to the fact of reception, treatment and discharge, but stated that no history of the case could be found in the records. (TK, III, 260, n. 1.)

The instruction was administered to Karl by a Redemptorist, and since the Liguorian penances were proverbially strict, Holz inspired the hope in Beethoven that Karl's secret would be discovered by the priest. "These Liguorians are like leeches," is one of his remarks to the composer while Karl was lying at the hospital.

Strenuous efforts were made by Beethoven through Holz and others to discover what direct cause had led the misguided young man to attempt to end his life. The inquiries made of him at the hospital during the weeks spent there brought scarcely more information from his lips than the first question asked by his mother. Schindler seems to have been persuaded that it was his failure to pass the examinations at the Institute; but this theory is not tenable. Aside from the fact that he had till September 3 to make up his neglected studies, he never himself advanced this as an excuse nor an explanation, but explicitly denied it. In the hospital he told Holz that it would have been easy for him to make himself fit to pass, but that, having made up his mind to do away with himself long before, he had not thought it worthwhile to continue his studies. "He said that he was tired of life," Holz reports to Beethoven, "because he saw in it something different from what you judiciously and righteously could approve." He also phrased it thus: "Weariness of imprisonment." To the examining police magistrate Karl said that his reason for shooting himself was that Beethoven "tormented him too much," and also "I grew worse because my uncle wanted me to be better." To Beethoven's question if Karl had railed against him, Schlemmer replied: "He did not rail, but he complained that he always had trouble." Holz's explanation many years after to Otto Jahn was that "Beethoven was rigorous to excess in his treatment and would not allow him the slightest extravagance." There is a memorandum in the Conversation Books which discloses that Beethoven received specific reports about his conduct, and noted them for reference: "One night in the Prater.—2 nights did not sleep at home." Beethoven stinted him in the matter of pocket-money, and the scores of reckonings in the Conversation Books show how close was the watch kept upon every kreutzer placed in his hands. So he had recourse to borrowing and no doubt, though the fact does not appear in the books, he went into debt at the places he frequented for pleasure. When he shot himself he had paid his lodging bill for the month but owed his tutor. In a Conversation Book there was talk of a sale of books, which did not belong to Karl but to his uncle. Since this constituted a penal offense, a bad conscience along with fear of punishment could have been providing further pressure before the catastrophe. Beethoven, in his efforts to find an explanation that was excusable on moral grounds, wanted to advance a cause of mental disturbance. In his hand appears a note in a Conversation Book: "Mental aberration and insanity; the heat too—afflicted with headaches since childhood."

Stephan von Breuning's son, Gerhard, has described the shattering effect of this attempted suicide upon Beethoven.[35] "The pain which he received from this event was indescribable; he was cast down as a father who has lost his much-loved son. My mother met him on the Glacis completely undone. 'Do you know what has happened? My Karl has shot himself!' 'And—is he dead?' 'No, it was a glancing shot, he is still living, there's hope that he can be saved;—but the disgrace that he has brought upon me; and I loved him so.' " Evidently Gerhard was sent to the master soon after, for he writes in a Conversation Book: "You must come to us for all your meals so that you will not be alone."

The occurrence was soon noised about the city and much sympathy was expressed for Beethoven, as Holz took occasion to inform him. He told him of an invitation from Schuppanzigh, who was delighted when he received Beethoven's acceptance. Holz writes: "He has also invited Wolfmeyer [*sic*] who is overjoyed to be able to see you once again; but My Lord[36] asks that you accept this invitation not for Sunday but for Monday since Wolfmayer is prevented on Sunday from appearing anywhere. Wolfmayer will bring the drinks."

Schindler wrote[37] that the blow bowed the proud figure of the composer, and that he soon looked like a man of seventy. To add to his suffering he was compelled to learn that many persons placed part of the blame for the rash act upon him.

The surgical section in which Karl was placed in the hospital was under the care of a Dr. Gassner, whose assistant, Dr. Seng, had supervision over Karl. He related the following subsequently to Gerhard von Breuning:[38] "In the late summer of 1826 there came to me one day during my inspection a man in a gray coat whom at first glance I took to be a simple peasant. He asked me in a dull voice, 'Are you Assistant Doctor Seng? I was referred to you in the reception office? Is my nephew with you, the dissolute fellow, the scoundrel,' etc. After learning the name of the patient, I answered in the affirmative and told him that he was lying in a room in the three-florin ward, was bandaged for gunshot wound, and asked if I could direct him to him. Whereupon he said, 'I am Beethoven.' And, while I led him to him, he spoke further, 'I did not really want to visit him for he does not deserve it, he has given me too much vexation, but . . .' and then he continued to talk about his nephew's conduct and how he was altogether too spoiled, etc.—But I was astonished to have these things expressed to me by the great Beethoven, and I promised him that I intended to give his nephew the best possible care."

There was no delay in discussing plans for the future of the boy. In fact, prompt decision was necessary, for it was the penal aspects of the case

---

[35] *Aus dem Schwarzspanierhause*, p. 78. (TDR, v, 360.)
[36] Schuppanzigh.

[37] *Biogr.*, II, p. 127. (TDR, v, 360, n. 1.)
[38] *Aus dem Schwarzspanierhause*, p. 79 (TDR, v, 361, n. 1.)

which held the greatest terrors for Beethoven. Shortly after Karl had been put into the hospital, Holz writes:

Here you see ingratitude as clear as the sun; why do you want further to restrain him. Once with the military, he will be under the strictest discipline, and if you want to do anything more for him you need only make him a small allowance monthly. A soldier at once.

Do you still doubt? This is a marvelous document.

It seems likely that this last remark may have been called out by the letter written by the nephew on the eve of his attempt—a letter which has never been found.

Holz also urged him to give up the guardianship. He pointed out that it would be the Magistrate's responsibility to find a replacement and that Beethoven, relieved of his duties, would be free to decide what more, if anything, he would want to do for the boy. He reported: "It is not hatred of you which he feels, but something entirely different." After reminding Beethoven of the sacrifices he had made, Holz writes: "If your good nature had not so often got the better of your firmness you would have driven him away long ago."

As court councillor in the war department, Stephan von Breuning's opinion had especial weight. "A military life will be the best discipline for one who cannot endure freedom; and it will teach him how to live on little," is one of Breuning's first utterances. As we shall see, this opinion, shared by Schindler and Holz, prevailed. As for the guardianship, Dr. Bach joined these three in advising Beethoven to relinquish it, but there was no immediate change as Karl's cure took its course.

To return to other matters, in July, 1826, Schott was ready with the Ninth Symphony, but in a letter of July 26 Beethoven asked him to delay the despatch of the printed score to the King of Prussia, to whom it was dedicated, until he had had the opportunity to send the monarch a manuscript copy, which, he said, would have no value after the publication. The question of who should receive this dedication had been under consideration since April, 1823, when Beethoven had written to Ferdinand Ries promising him the dedication. A year later, in a Conversation Book, Ries was still a candidate along with the Kings of France and Prussia and Emperor Alexander of Russia. The latter died on December 1, 1825; in a letter to Schott, dated January 28, 1826, Beethoven indicated that he was to have received the dedication but that now new arrangements were to be made.

When Beethoven finally decided that the symphony should be dedicated to the King of Prussia, he obtained permission from Prince Hatzfield, the Prussian Ambassador, to do so. On March 28 Beethoven informed Schott that on that very day he had received word from the Ambassador of His

Royal Majesty's acceptance.[39] ♪— At the end of September the presentation copy was ready; Beethoven wrote the title-page, and the score was handsomely bound by Steiner and Co.[40] It was placed in the hands of Dr. Spicker, the King's librarian, with the following letter:

Your Majesty:

It is a piece of great good fortune in my life that Your Majesty has graciously allowed me to dedicate the present work to you.

Your Majesty is not only the father of your subjects but also protector of the arts and sciences; how much more, therefore must I rejoice in your gracious permission since I am also so fortunate as to count myself a citizen of Bonn and therefore one of your subjects.

I beg of Your Majesty graciously to accept this work as a slight token of the high reverence which I give to all your virtues.

Your Majesty's

Most obedient servant

Ludwig van Beethoven

The King's acknowledgement was as follows:

In view of the recognized worth of your compositions it was very agreeable for me to receive the new work which you have sent me. I thank you for sending it and hand you the accompanying diamond ring as a token of my sincere appreciation.

Berlin, November 25, 1826.   Friedrich Wilhelm

To the composer Ludwig van Beethoven

Schindler says that when the case containing the King's gift was opened it was found to contain, not a diamond ring as the letter had described it, but one set with a stone of a "reddish" hue, which the court jeweler to whom it was shown appraised at 300 florins, paper money. Beethoven was very indignant and was with difficulty dissuaded from sending it back to the Prussian Ambassador; eventually he sold it to the jeweler at the value which he had set upon it. Whether or not the ring was the one really sent from Berlin or one which had been substituted for it (as was suspected in some quarters) has never been determined.

After Karl's attempt to end his life, with its crushing effect upon the composer, the friends, Holz in particular, made many efforts to divert Beethoven's mind from his disappointment and grief. They accompanied him on brief excursions into the country which he loved so passionately and which had been closed to him, for the customary happy seasons, by his nephew's act. Again did his brother offer him a haven at Gneixendorf in August, only to receive the curt answer: "I will not come. Your brother?????!!!! Ludwig."

Meanwhile Beethoven was far from idle. He had begun a new quartet, in F major, and Schlesinger, père, who had come from Berlin, negotiated with him for its publication. He had the new finale for the B-flat Quartet on his

[39] See A 1472.
[40] See A 1526 for his humorous instructions to Haslinger regarding this matter.

mind and, as will appear later, several other works occupied him. With Schlesinger he talked about the Complete Edition and some military marches which the King of Prussia was to pay for, as they were to be written for the Royal Band.

Meanwhile a recurring subject of conversation during the summer was the question of Karl's future. As has been mentioned, Breuning, Holz and Schindler favored placing him in the army, while Dr. Bach urged that he be sent off at once to some business house in Trieste, Milan or Hamburg.

In a discussion with his uncle in the hospital Karl writes:

My present condition is still such that I would ask you to make as little mention as possible of what has happened and cannot be altered. If my wish concerning a military career can be fulfilled I will be very happy, in any case I consider it the thing in which I could live and be satisfied. So I ask you to employ the means you think best and above all to see to it after my recovery that I get away from here as soon as possible.

•∿•

With the reminder that I chose this career out of desperation, I am asking you not to be hindered from taking the necessary measures; I am sufficiently composed to be able to reflect calmly and my desire for *this* object will always remain the same.

•∿•

As a cadet in the regiment I could also hope for promotion soon.

•∿•

The same way in which so many have gone.

There was also the immediate question of where Karl would go when he first left the hospital. During the investigation by the court, Holz kept Beethoven informed about all the proceedings and discussions with the counsel in charge. He reported that while Beethoven's management of the affair would be respected fully, the question of where young Beethoven should stay in the future could present difficulties. There was the possibility that he would wish to be with his mother, which the court viewed as a natural response to instinct. At one point Beethoven, after considering the possible measures that might be taken by the court and the police, writes: "My only intent was that he improve; if he is abandoned now, something terrible could still happen."

Beethoven was unalterably opposed to the nephew's being with the mother for even a day. In an interview with Karl he brought the subject up and began to berate her as usual, but the young man interrupted him:

I do not want to hear anything that is derogatory to her; it is not for me to be her judge. If I were to spend the little time I shall be here with her, it would be only a small return for all that she has suffered on my account. Nothing can be said about a harmful influence on me even if it should happen, if for no other reason than the shortness of the time.

•~•

In no event shall I treat her with greater coldness than has been the case heretofore, whatever may be said on the subject.

He repeated his desire for the new career and his wish to leave Vienna as soon as possible. He made clear that his mother would offer no objection to the military career: "All the less, therefore, can I deny her wish to be with me during these days, as I shall in all likelihood not be here again soon. It is self-evident that this will not prevent you and me from seeing each other as often as you wish."

Very reluctantly Beethoven gave his consent that his nephew should become a soldier. But he spilled out his feelings to Holz, who was in Baden, in a letter of September 9, reiterating his dislike of the army as a career. His first thought was to send Karl to a military institute and have him graduated as an officer. This proved impracticable. Meanwhile Breuning, in pursuance of his own plan, consulted Baron von Stutterheim and persuaded him to give the young man a cadetship in his regiment. Having carried the day with his plan, Breuning agreed to accept the guardianship, which had been laid down by Reisser. Beethoven now set down his terms for the cadetship in a pencilled note which, though lacking an address, was undoubtedly for Breuning: "I believe that there are three points to be observed with Karl. First, he is not to be treated as a culprit, which would have exactly the opposite result from what we want; second, in order to become promoted to a higher rank, one cannot live too modestly and meanly; third, too great a limitation on his eating and drinking might have a harsh effect upon him. I am not trying to obstruct you."

Now the plans for this disposition were made. He was to be presented to von Stutterheim as soon as he was discharged from the hospital, take the oath of service the next day, and leave Vienna for Iglau, where von Stutterheim's regiment was stationed, within five or six days. Breuning, as guardian, now found himself confronted by a serious embarrassment. Where should the young man be sent while the preparations for his entry into the military service were being made? Karl did not want to go to his uncle's, nor did von Breuning want to send him there, and he frankly tells Beethoven the reason: "If he were here you would talk to him too much and that would cause new irritation; for he testified in the police court that the reason why he had taken the step was because you harassed him too much."

Beethoven, on the other hand, was still fearful that the magistrate might allow him to go to his mother's, and to guard against this he wrote two letters to that official, a man kindly disposed to him, whose name was Czapka. These letters follow:

1.

Sir!

I earnestly beg of you, since my nephew will be well in a few days, to direct that he be not permitted to leave the hospital with anybody but *myself and Hr. von Holz.* It must not possibly be allowed that he be near his mother, that utterly depraved person. My solicitude and my request are justified by her bad and wickedly malicious character, the belief that she often tempted Karl to lure money from me, the probability that she divided sums with him and was also in the confidence of Karl's dissolute companion, the notice which she attracts with her illegitimate daughter, *the father of whom is still being sought,* and the likelihood that at his m[other]'s home he would make the acquaintance of women who are anything but virtuous. Even the habit of being in the company of such a person cannot possibly lead a young man to virtue—While I recommend this concern to you, I meanwhile send you my best greetings, and only want to point out that, although this has been a very painful affair, I am very glad to have made the acquaintance of a man of such excellent intellect.

 With sincere respect to your honor,

Your obedient servant Beethoven

2.

Sir!

Hofrat von Breuning and I have given mature consideration to what is to be done and have found that at this point it is inevitable that Karl spend a few days with me (while waiting here to leave for the army). His talk is caused by emotions resulting from the impression made on him by my reprimands when he had the idea of making an end to his life. However, after this period he showed himself to be still affectionate towards me. I assure you that for me mankind even in misfortune will always remain sacred. A warning from you would be very effective, also it would not hurt to give him to understand that he will be watched unseen while he is with me—

Please accept my very sincerest regards to you and consider me a warm friend, who wants to do good whenever possible.

Sincerely Beethoven

Late in September Beethoven's brother was again in Vienna. He repeated his offer to give the composer a temporary home and his nephew a harbor of refuge at Gneixendorf. This time Beethoven accepted. Karl was discharged from the hospital on September 25. Johann urged haste both on account of his business affairs and on account of Karl's status. But three days were needed to dispose of the business of finishing the corrections in the manuscript copy of the Ninth Symphony for the King of Prussia, and complete other correspondence. Thus it was on September 28 that Beethoven and his nephew set off for Gneixendorf with Johann for what was supposed to be a visit of a week. A night was passed at a village en route, and Johann's estate was reached in the afternoon of the next day—the 29th—but not too late for the composer to walk through the fields with his brother to take a look at the property. The next day the walk was extended to the vineyards on the hill in the forenoon and to Imbach in the afternoon. There Karl pointed out to his uncle some historical monuments: "This is the cloister where Marga-rethe, Ottokar's wife, died; the scene occurs in Grillparzer's piece." Thus, with other excursions the next day, life at Gneixendorf began.

Gneixendorf was a little village on a high plateau of the Danube valley about an hour's walk from Krems. It was a mean hamlet, with only one street and that narrow, rough and dirty. The houses were low huts. Wasser-hof, the Beethoven estate, lay opposite the village, and was reached by a wagon road which ran a large part of the way along the edge of a ravine, which had been made by torrents cutting into the clay soil. The plateau was almost treeless but covered with fields and vines. There were two houses on the estate, both large and handsome, each with its garden and surround-ing wall, and separated from each other by a road. Beethoven's rooms were on the east side of the house, which was a strongly built two-story stone and mortar structure, and, unless the surrounding trees interfered, had a magnificent view of the Danube valley stretching to the distant Styrian mountains.[41] Johann van Beethoven's possessions compassed nearly 400 acres, most of which he leased to tenants. A lover of hills and forests like Beet-hoven must have found the flat expanses of Wasserhof dreary and monoto-nous in the extreme, yet the distant view of the Danube seems to have com-pensated him in a measure, for in a letter to Schott, dated October 13, he writes: "The scenes among which I am sojourning remind me somewhat of the Rhine country which I so greatly long to see again, having left them in my youth."

Johann had made repeated efforts to persuade his brother to come to Gneixendorf ever since he had acquired the estate in 1819. In 1823 Beethoven wrote: "He always wants me to come to his people—*non possibile per me.*" The obstacle was Johann's wife, about whose behavior, it will be remem-bered, Beethoven had become very concerned in 1823. Urged on by Ludwig, Johann had made himself master of his household, for he wrote in a Con-versation Book of 1824: "My wife has surrendered her marriage contract and entered into an obligation permitting me to drive her away without notice at the first new acquaintance which she makes." Beethoven perhaps suggested that he do this very thing, for Johann continued: "I cannot do that. I cannot know but that some misfortune might befall me." Then Karl: "Your brother proposes that you spend the four months at his place. You would have four or five rooms, very beautiful, high and large. Everything is well arranged; you will find fowl, oxen, cows, hares etc. Moreover, as regards the wife, she is looked upon as a housekeeper only and will not disturb you. . . . You will scarcely see the woman. She looks after the house-keeping and works."

Beethoven was sick when he went to Gneixendorf. He had not recovered from his illness of the early months of the year when Karl attempted to kill himself, and this was not calculated to improve the physical or mental condi-

---

[41] The description is based on that made by Thayer when he visited Gneixendorf in 1860. (TK, III, 239, n. 1.)

tion of so nervous and irritable a being as he. He had never been a comfortable or considerate guest or tenant at the best, and his adaptability to circumstances was certainly not promoted by the repugnance which he felt towards his sister-in-law and his want of honest affection for his brother.

Concerning his life in Gneixendorf, a number of interesting details were told in an article entitled "Beethoven in Gneixendorf," published in the *Deutsche Musikzeitung* in 1862,[42] some of which are worth reciting again. One day Johann went to Langenfeld and Beethoven and other people from Gneixendorf went with him. The purpose was to visit a surgeon named Karrer, a friend of the brother. The surgeon was absent on a sick-call, but his wife, flattered by a visit from the landowner, entertained him lavishly. Noticing a man who held himself aloof from the company, sitting silently on the bench behind the stove, and taking him for one of her guest's servants, she filled a little jug with native wine and handed it to him with the remark: "He shall also have a drink." When the surgeon returned home late at night and heard an account of the incident he exclaimed: "My dear wife, what have you done? The greatest composer of the century was in our house to-day and you treated him with such disrespect!"

Johann had occasion to visit the syndic Sterz in Langenlois on a matter of business. Beethoven accompanied him. The conference lasted a considerable time, during all of which Beethoven stood motionless at the door of the official's office. At the leave-taking Sterz bowed often and low to the stranger, and after he was gone asked his clerk, named Fux, an enthusiastic lover of music, especially of Beethoven's; "Who do you think the man was who stood by the door?" Fux replied: "Considering that you, Mr. Syndic, treated him with such politeness, his may be an exceptional case; otherwise I should take him for an imbecile (*Trottel*)." The consternation of the clerk may be imagined when told the name of the man whom he had taken for an idiot.

Johann's wife had assigned Michael Krenn, son of one of her husband's vinedressers, to look after Beethoven's wants. At first the cook had to make up Beethoven's bed. One day, while the woman was thus occupied, Beethoven sat at a table gesticulating with his hands, beating time with his feet, muttering and singing. The woman burst into a laugh, which Beethoven observed. He drove her out of the room instanter. Krenn tried to follow her, but Beethoven drew him back, gave him three 20-kreutzer pieces, told him not to be afraid, and said that hereafter he should make the bed and clean the floor every day. Krenn said that he was told to come to the room early, but generally had to knock a long time before Beethoven opened the door. It was Beethoven's custom to get up at half-past 5 o'clock, seat himself at a table and write while he beat time with hands and feet and sang. This frequently stirred Krenn's risibles, and when he could no longer restrain his laughter he used to leave the room. Gradually he grew accustomed to it.

[42] Pages 77ff. The article was based largely on information gathered by Mr. Thayer at Gneixendorf in 1860 and had been submitted to him for revision. (TK, III, 241, n. 1.)

The family breakfast was eaten at half-past 7 o'clock, after which Beethoven hurried out into the open air, rambled across the fields shouting and waving his arms, sometimes walking very rapidly, sometimes very slowly and stopping at times to write in a sort of pocketbook. This book he once lost and said: "Michael, run about and hunt my writings; I must have them again at any cost." Michael luckily found them. At half-past 12 Beethoven would come home for dinner, after which he went to his room until about 3 o'clock; then he roamed over the fields until shortly before sunset, after which he never went out of doors. Supper was at half-past 7, and after eating he went to his room, wrote till 10 o'clock and then went to bed. Occasionally Beethoven played the pianoforte, which did not stand in his room but in the salon. Nobody was permitted to enter his rooms except Michael, who had to put them in order while Beethoven was out walking. In doing so he several times found money on the floor, and when he carried it to its owner, Beethoven made him show him where he had picked it up and then gave it to him. This happened three or four times, after which no more money was found. In the evening Michael had to sit with Beethoven and write down answers to questions which he asked. Generally Beethoven wanted to know what had been said about him at dinner and supper.

One day the wife of the landowner sent Michael to Stein with 5 florins to buy wine and a fish; but Michael was careless and lost the money. He came back to Gneixendorf in consternation. As soon as Frau van Beethoven saw him she asked for the fish, and when he told her of the loss she discharged him from her service. When Beethoven came into dinner he asked at once for his servant and the lady told him what had happened. Beethoven grew fearfully excited, gave her 5 florins, and angrily demanded that Michael be called back at once. After that he never went to table any more but had his dinner and supper brought to his rooms, where Michael had to prepare breakfast for him. Even before this occurrence Beethoven scarcely ever spoke to his sister-in-law and seldom to his brother. Beethoven would have liked to have taken Michael with him to Vienna.

Two old peasants told the owner of Wasserhof in 1862 stories which confirm Krenn's account of Beethoven's unusual behavior in the fields. Because of his unaccountable actions they at first took him for a madman and kept out of his way. When they had become accustomed to his singularities and learned that he was a brother of the landlord they used to greet him politely; but he, always lost in thought, seldom if ever returned their greetings. One of these peasants, a young man at the time, had an adventure with Beethoven of a most comical nature. He was driving a pair of young oxen, scarcely broken to the yoke, from the tile-kiln toward the manor-house when he met Beethoven shouting and waving his arms about in wild gesticulations. The peasant called to him: *A bissel stada!* ("A little quieter") but he paid no attention to the request. The oxen took fright, ran down a steep hill and the peasant had great difficulty in bringing them to a stand, turning them and getting them back on the road. Again Beethoven came towards them, still shouting and gesticulating. The yokel called to him a second time, but in vain; and now the oxen rushed towards the house, where they were stopped by one of the men employed there. When the driver came up and asked who the fool was who had scared his oxen the man told him it was the proprietor's brother. "A pretty brother, that he is!" was the answering comment.

The Quartet in F (Op. 135) was completed at Gneixendorf and was to be published by Moritz Schlesinger. —It will be recalled that in September, 1825, Schlesinger was hoping to receive two quartets, Op. 130 and 132, but was given only the latter. This had apparently caused a misunderstanding between them, which is clarified in a letter dated April 22, 1826.[43] Beethoven was hastening to answer a letter that Schlesinger had written him on April 13th, so that the rupture could be healed. He informed Schlesinger that "another new quartet will be finished in two or three weeks at the latest." This refers to Op. 135, about which Beethoven was already thinking. He asked for 80 gold ducats to be paid immediately. Then he explains, "I see from your letter that you misunderstood what I wrote, for I gave the quartet not to my brother but to Matthias Artaria." This of course refers to Op. 130.

When work began on the quartet cannot be determined precisely. In July Beethoven referred to the work to Holz, for the latter writes:

In what key?

But that will be the third in F. There is still none in D minor.

It is singular that there is none among Haydn's in A minor.

It is probable that the first sketches for the quartet and the canon "Muss es sein?" were written about the same time. But it cannot be determined whether or not the motif of the canon was destined from the first for the finale of the quartet. It may have been in Beethoven's mind for that purpose and the sudden inspiration on hearing the story of Dembscher's query "Muss es sein?" may have gone only to the words and the use of them with the music for the canon. That the quartet was to be shorter than the others was known before Beethoven left Vienna. Holz once said to Beethoven before the departure that Schlesinger had asked about the quartet and that he had replied that Beethoven was at work upon it and added "You will not punish him if it is short. Even if it should have only three movements it would still be a quartet by Beethoven, and it would not cost so much to print it."[44]

[43] See *A* 1481.
[44] Holz told Jahn that Schlesinger had bought it for 80 ducats and sent 360 florins in payment; whereupon Beethoven had said: "If a Jew sends circumcised ducats he shall have a circumcised quartet. That's the reason why it is so short." (TK, III, 245, n. 1.)

—❧{In a letter to the Paris publisher at this time Beethoven mentioned the difficulty he had had in completing the quartet, expressed by the motto "Es muss sein" etc., and lamented that for lack of a copyist he had had to write out the parts himself.[45] The date of the autograph is October 30, 1826. On this day his brother took the music to Vienna.}❧—

On October 13 the composer wrote a merry letter to Haslinger, addressed in music as "First of all Tobiasses,"[46] announcing that the quartet was finished. He wanted his help in delivering it to Schlesinger's agent, Tendler and Manstein, and in finding a way to persuade Schlesinger to pay him in gold as the other publishers did. On the same day he also wrote to Schott and Sons enclosing the metronome marks for the Ninth Symphony, which the Conversation Book shows had been dictated to Karl before the departure from Vienna.

The new finale for the Quartet in B-flat was also completed in Gneixendorf, though it, too, had been worked out almost to a conclusion in Vienna. It was delivered by Haslinger on November 25 to Artaria, who gave him 15 ducats for it. Schuppanzigh gave it a private performance in December and told Beethoven that the company thought it exquisite (*köstlich*) and that Artaria was overjoyed when he heard it.

—❧{In September, 1824, Beethoven wrote two different letters to Diabelli concerning the completion of a quintet. In the one he promised the quintet in a little over six weeks for 100 gold ducats; in the other he promised a flute quintet.[47] Nothing more is known of a quintet at the time. But in November, 1826, according to Nottebohm, there were sketches for the first movement of a string quintet in C major on a page originally to be used for the new finale of Op. 130. There were also sketches for other movements.[48] In the catalogue of Beethoven's posthumous effects No. 173 was "Fragment of a new Violin Quintet of November, 1826, last work of the composer."[49] Diabelli's firm bought the 24-measure fragment and published it in pianoforte arrangement, two and four hands, with the title "Ludwig van Beethoven's last Musical Thought, after the original manuscript of November, 1826," and the remark "Sketch of the Quintet which the publishers, A. Diabelli and Co., commissioned Beethoven to write and purchased from his relics with proprietary rights." This last suggests that the fragment was connected with the correspondence of 1824 although there are no signs of a flute.}❧— The published work is a short movement in two divisions, having a broad theme of a festal character, Andante maestoso and a polonaise rhythm.

—❧{The compositions for the year 1826 may be divided into big works and trifles or fragments.

[45] See *A* 1538, 1538ᵃ.
[46] WoO 205ᵏ.
[47] See *A* 1310, 1313.
[48] See *Beeth.*, pp. 79ff., and *II Beeth.*, p. 522. Holz told Jahn that the first movement of a quintet in C for strings, which Diabelli had bought for 100 ducats, was finished in the composer's head and the first page written out. (TDR, v, 407, also n. 1.)
[49] WoO 62, KHV, p. 508.

Big works:

1825-6. Quartet for Strings in C-sharp minor, Op. 131, completed in July.

1826. Arrangement of the Great Fugue (Op. 133) for Pianoforte, four hands, Op. 134.

Quartet for Strings in F major, Op. 135, completed in October.

New Final Movement to the Quartet for Strings in B-flat major, Op. 130.

Trifles and fragments:

Beginning of a Quintet for strings in C major, WoO 62.

Canons:

"Da ist das Werk," WoO 197, to Holz in the beginning of September.

"Es muss sein," WoO 196, for Ignaz Dembscher, in April.

"Signor Abate," WoO 178, probably for Abt. Maximilian Stadler.

"Wir irren allesamt," WoO 198, for Karl Holz in early December.

The works that were published during the year were:

By Schott:

Quartet for Strings in E-flat major, Op. 127, dedicated to Prince Nikolas Galitzin (string parts in March, score in June).

Symphony No. 9 in D minor, Op. 125 ("Sinfonie mit Schluss-Chor über Schillers Ode: 'An die Freude' für grosses Orchester, 4 Solo- und 4 Chor-stimmen"), dedicated to King Friedrich Wilhelm III of Prussia (both in score and in parts in August).

By Steiner:

"Tremate, empi tremate" for Soprano, Tenor, Bass and Orchestra (Bettoni), Op. 116, in February.

March with Chorus from the *Ruinen von Athen*, Op. 114, in April.

Overture to *König Stephan*, Op. 117, in July.

By Haslinger, who took over the Steiner firm:

Elegischer Gesang, for Four Voices and String Quartet, Op. 118, dedicated to Baron Johann von Pasqualati, in July.

CHAPTER XL

DECEMBER, 1826–1827

THE RETURN FROM GNEIXENDORF TO VIENNA—
THE FINAL ILLNESS—DEATH AND BURIAL

THE Conversation Books add nothing to the picturesque side of the account of Beethoven's sojourn in Gneixendorf as it has been drawn from other sources. They indicate that there were some days of peace and tranquility, and that not only Johann, but his wife and nephew also, were concerned with making the composer comfortable and providing him with such diversion as place and opportunity afforded. Several times there was mention of trips in the carriage, such as to nearby Krems where there was some sort of city life; yet travel was not always possible, as was mentioned once, because the carriage was in need of repair. Johann had business which took him occasionally to Vienna. According to Karl he had two years left to pay for his estate. Beethoven was supplied with writing materials from Krems by his nephew, who also found there the opportunity to play billiards. Johann met Holz and Linke in Vienna; the latter was anxious to have the new finale for the B-flat Quartet for an *Akademie*. The money for this movement was in the hands of the baker, Leopold Obermayr, brother of Johann's wife, Therese. Beethoven accepted Therese's offer to go to Vienna and bring the money back to him.

Karl did not neglect his piano-playing; he had brought along four-hand Marches by Lannoy to play with his uncle. "Karl plays very well" writes Therese at one point. But there were also strong scenes between uncle and nephew as could be expected. Karl had to hear frequent reproaches and in conversations was put on the defensive. For example:

You ask me why I do not talk.

Because I have had enough.

Yours is the right to command, and I must endure it all.

.~.

I can only regret that I can give no answer to anything you have said today, since I know of nothing better to do than to listen and to remain silent as is my duty. You must not consider this insolent.

There was little mention of Beethoven's illness. Johann stressed the improvement of his eyes and attributed it to the good air on his estate. According to Gerhard von Breuning,[1] Stephan had been worried, after receiving a letter early in Beethoven's stay at Gneixendorf, that Beethoven was in danger of becoming very ill, possibly dropsical. Referring to an earlier time, Johann writes: "Because of poorly prepared food he would eat nothing at lunch except soft-boiled eggs, but then he would drink more wine so that he often suffered diarrhoea; thereby his belly became bigger and bigger, and he wore a bandage over it for a long time." In the beginning of December he lost his appetite and complained of thirst and abdominal complaints. There had been mention of "edematous" feet. These were clear manifestations of an existing liver disease.

In this condition, it can be imagined how sensitive he became to the increasingly cold weather in Gneixendorf, and how he must have longed for his customary way of living. But the Conversation Books do not make clear Beethoven's attitude on this score beyond occasional complaints about the food. Meanwhile Johann was becoming increasingly concerned about the effect of this life upon his nephew. To avoid an argument with his brother, he wrote him a letter on the subject near the end of November:

My dear Brother:
I can not possibly remain silent concerning the future fate of Karl. He is abandoning all activity and, grown accustomed to this life, the *longer* he lives as at present, the more difficult it will be to bring him back to work. At his departure *Breuning* gave him a fortnight in which to recuperate, and now it is two months.— You see from Breuning's letter that it is his decided wish that Karl *shall hasten* to his calling; the longer he is here the more unfortunate will it be *for him*, for the harder it will be for him to get to work, and it may be that we shall suffer harm.
It is an infinite pity that this talented young man so wastes his time; and on whom if not *us both* will the blame be laid? For he is still too young to direct his own course; for which reason it is your duty, if you do not wish to be reproached by yourself and others hereafter, to put him to work at his profession as soon as possible. Once he is occupied it will be easy to do much for him now and in the future; but under present conditions nothing can be done.
I see from his actions that he would like to remain with us, but if he did so it would be all over with his future, and therefore *this* is *impossible.* The longer we hesitate the more difficult will it be for him to go away; I therefore adjure you— make up your mind, do not permit yourself to be dissuaded by Karl. I think it ought to be *by next Monday,* for in no event can you wait for me, inasmuch as I

[1] *Aus dem Schwarzspanierhause,* p. 84. (TDR, v, 410, n. 2.)

cannot go away from here without *money*, and it will be a long time before I collect enough to enable me to go to Vienna.

On the back is written in pencil, perhaps after some conversation:

Let us leave this until the day you go.

• ∿ •

An old woman.

• ∿ •

She has her share and will get no more.

According to Schindler,[2] Ludwig took his brother's suggestions with bad grace; and before his departure from Gneixendorf there was an exceedingly acrimonious quarrel between the brothers, growing out of Ludwig's demand that Johann make a will in favor of Karl, thus cutting off his wife.[3]

The question of returning to Vienna was now discussed with Karl, whose attitude is shown by the following entry:

I cannot argue against it since we have been here longer than was planned; but *Breuning* himself has said that I cannot go to the Field-Marshal until I am able to appear without any visible sign left of what happened to me, because he wants to overlook the whole affair. This is almost accomplished now except for a little bit which really won't take much more time; therefore I believe that we should stay until next week at least. If I had pomade here then it would be unnecessary. Besides, the longer we remain here, the longer can we remain together, since once we are in Vienna, I naturally will have to leave right away." [The conversation turned to expenses, for Karl writes]: "As regards expenses, wood is so cheap that it is inconceivable that your brother should be at any considerable cost, for you can heat a long time with a cord and he is already overpaid."

Johann's recorded statements vary concerning the financial arrangements with his brother. Once in a Conversation Book he says: "You do not need money here"; and further on: "If you want to live with us you can have everything for 40 florins C.M. a month, which makes 500 f. for a whole year"; and again: "You will need only half of your pension." In another place he writes:

You can be here for 8 months, from March to November, then you will not need such large quarters, and in spring and summer it is much prettier here.

• ∿ •

I will charge nothing for the first fortnight; I would do more if I were not so hard pressed with taxes.

Karl's remarks show that at this time Beethoven was paying for his room. Inasmuch as some of Johann's offers to his brother were made immediately

[2] In a note attached to the letter. (See TDR, v, 412.)

[3] This happened naturally. Therese van Beethoven died on November 20, 1828 at Wasserhof; Johann died in Vienna on January 12, 1848. After costs, over 42,000 florins passed into his nephew's hands.

after this, it shows that Beethoven all along had been tempted by the possibility of a longer and perhaps permanent stay in Gneixendorf.

During this period of decision there was great strain between uncle and nephew. Beethoven asks:

What is the matter? Why are you hanging your head now? Isn't the truest devotion even with its shortcomings enough?

The idea of going from here continues to pain you and I have also taken this into consideration.

Apparently this was followed by further strong reproaches, for Karl writes:

Did you see me speak a word? Hardly—for I was not disposed at all to speak, everything that you say about me needs no refutation. So I beg of you once and for all to leave me alone. If you want to go, good.

If not, good again.

But I beg of you once more not to torment me as you are doing; you might regret it, for I can endure much, but too much I cannot endure. You treated your brother in the same way today without cause. You must remember that other people are also human beings.

These everlastingly unjust reproaches!

Why do you make such a disturbance? Will you let me go out a bit today? I need recreation. I'll come again later.

I only want to go to my room.

I am not going out, I want only to be alone for a little while.

Will you not let me go to my room?

An entry by Therese suggests Beethoven's state of mind when Karl had been gone from the house: "Do not be concerned. He will certainly come home by 1 o'clock. It seems that he has some of your rash blood. I have not found him angry. It is you that he loves, to the point of veneration."

It must be assumed that the Monday referred to in Johann's letter was Monday, November 27; but several days must have elapsed between this date and the time when Beethoven and Karl set out on the fateful journey to Vienna. A determination seems to have been reached when the Conversation Book shows Johann as saying: "If you are to start on Monday the carriage must be ordered on Sunday." There is no recorded conversation touching the use of Johann's carriage, which, shortly before, had carried Johann's wife to Vienna, and which was to carry its owner there as soon as he could make a satisfactory adjustment of his financial affairs. That means of conveyance were discussed is proved by Johann's remark and also by a report made by Karl to the composer: "There is no postchaise to Vienna, but only to St. Pölten. . . . From here there is no opportunity except by a stagecoach."

Exactly how the travelers set out is not clear. In the first edition of his *Biographie*[4] Schindler writes: "This return journey, which that late in the year could not be made in one day, took place in an open carriage since, as Beethoven himself assured me, his brother denied him the use of his closed carriage." In the third edition he states that "his pseudo-brother denied him his closed town-carriage for the trip to nearby Krems, therefore he had to get there in an open calash."[5] Schindler was not at Gneixendorf; and his known antipathy to Johann makes the testimony the harder to evaluate.

Dr. Wawruch, Beethoven's attending physician during the illness which ended in his death, writes:[6] "Oppressed by the sad prospect of a gloomy future, being helpless in the case of sickness in the country, he longed to return to Vienna and used for his trip home the most wretched vehicle of the devil, a milkwagon, as he humorously put it."

Beethoven arrived in Vienna on Saturday, December 2, and as there is a reference to only one night spent in transit (as there had been one on the journey from Vienna to Gneixendorf), it is likely that he left Gneixendorf early in the morning of Friday, December 1. Dr. Wawruch continues: "That December was raw, damp, cold and frosty; Beethoven's clothing anything but adapted to the unfriendly season of the year, and yet he was urged on by an eternal unrest and a gloomy foreboding of misfortune. He was compelled to spend a night in a village tavern where, besides wretched shelter, he found an unwarmed room without winter shutters. Towards midnight he experienced his first fever-chill, a dry hacking cough accompanied by violent thirst and cutting pains in the sides. When seized with the fever he drank a few measures of ice-cold water and longed, helplessly, for the first rays of the morning light. Weak and ill, he permitted himself to be lifted into the *Leiterwagen* and arrived, at last, weak, exhausted and without strength, in Vienna." Wawruch derived his information from Beethoven, possibly in part also from Karl, the only witness from whom a succinct and absolutely correct account was to have been expected; unhappily the tale, which Karl must have been called upon to tell many times, was never reported.

It was Saturday, December 2, then, that Beethoven arrived in Vienna from Gneixendorf and went to his lodgings in the Schwarzspanierhaus. The first thing to be done was to get a doctor. According to Johann, Beethoven

[4] [1840], p. 179. (TDR, v, 415, n. 1.)
[5] [1860], II, p. 131. (TDR, v, 415, n. 1.)
[6] Dr. Wawruch wrote a history of Beethoven's illness entitled "Ärztlicher Rückblick auf Ludwig van Beethovens letzte Lebensepoche" (dated May 20, 1827) which was first published by Aloys Fuchs in the *Wiener Zeitschrift*, April 30, 1842. (TDR, v, 419, n. 2.)

himself wrote to his old doctor, Braunhofer, who gave as his reason for not coming that the distance was too great.[7] Then Dr. Staudenheim was sent for; he promised to come but failed to do so. Then Dr. Wawruch of the General Hospital was called, and came directly. "I was not called until the third day," he writes in his report. It was apparently Holz who sent for him, and he did so on December 5, the day recorded by Karl in a Conversation Book as being the time of Wawruch's first visit. Evidently Holz had hastened to Beethoven upon receiving the following note:

Your official Majesty!

Immediately after my arrival, which occurred a few days ago, I wrote to you, but the letter was mislaid. Thereupon I became unwell so that I decided it would be better to stay in bed—Therefore I shall be very glad if you will come to see me. It will be less inconvenient for you now since everyone has come back from Döbling to the city—

Finally I will just add

Wir ir-ren al-le samt nur je-der ir-ret an-derst.
[We all err only each in a different way.]

As always your friend

Beethoven

The Conversation Book records the following in the handwriting of Holz:

I have had Professor Wawruch called for you; Vivenot[8] is himself sick. I do not know Wawruch personally, but he is known here as one of the most skilful physicians.

He is Bogner's doctor.

He is professor in the hospital.

He will come after dinner.

Wawruch came and introduced himself with the following words in a Conversation Book: "One who greatly reveres your name will do everything possible to give you speedy relief. Prof. Wawruch." Then in his presence the necessary questions to the patient were written out by Karl, including probably the question of the abdominal complaint.[9] Wawruch's report continues: "I found Beethoven afflicted with serious symptoms of inflammation of the lungs. His face glowed, he spat blood, his respiration threatened suffo-

---

[7] Walter Nohl suggests that the reason for Dr. Braunhofer's excuse was that his past experience with Beethoven helped him to diagnose that the patient was in the last stages of his illness and that he did not want to be the doctor in charge at the composer's death. See "Beethoven und sein Arzt Anton Braunhofer,"

DM, Vol. 30, No. 12 (1938), p. 828.

[8] Dominik Vivenot was a medical consultant in Vienna (see *A*, III, p. 1261, n. 2).

[9] According to TDR, v, 419, n. 1, certain pages at this point were removed, presumably by Schindler.

cation and a painful stitch in the side made lying on the back a torment. A severe counter-treatment for inflammation soon brought the desired relief; his constitution triumphed and by a lucky crisis he was freed from apparent mortal danger, so that on the fifth day he was able, in a sitting posture, to tell me, amid profound emotion, of the discomforts which he had suffered. On the seventh day he felt considerably better, so that he was able to get out of bed, walk about, read and write."

Andreas Wawruch was born in 1771 in Nemtschütz in Moravia. At Olmütz he was a student of theology, but before consecration to the priesthood he came to Vienna as tutor and there decided to abandon the church for medicine. In the course of time he became assistant and also son-in-law to Professor Hildebrand, the director of the General Hospital. Thence he went to Prague as professor of general pathology and pharmacology and, returning to Vienna, became professor of special pathology and medical clinics in the surgical department of the hospital. He was an amateur violoncello player and an ardent admirer of Beethoven's music. He died in 1842.

Wawruch's report thus far shows that Beethoven had weathered an attack of pneumonia. Before its continuation, account may be made of one or two letters.

Beethoven's old friends, Franz and Eleonore Wegeler, had written him almost a year ago, and now he finally answered. All three letters deserve to be given.[10] They begin the closing chapter to a friendship which, along with that of Stephan von Breuning, was one of the earliest and one of the most tender.

Coblenz, December 20, 1825

My dear old Louis!

I cannot have one of the 10 Ries children travel to Vienna without recalling memories of you. If you have not received a long letter every 2 months within the 28 years since I left Vienna, you may consider your silence on top of mine as the cause. This is not right at all, and all the less now when we older people want to live so much in the past and delight ourselves to the utmost with scenes of our youth. To me at least my acquaintance and childhood friendship with you, which was limited but blessed because of a good mother, is a very bright point in my life which I contemplate with pleasure and with which I become completely preoccupied when traveling. Now I look up to you as a hero and am proud to be able to say: I was not without influence on his development; he confided in me his wishes and dreams; and when later he was so frequently misunderstood, I knew well what he wanted. Thank God that I have been able to talk with my wife and now more recently with my children about you; yet the house of my mother-in-law was more your house than mine, especially after you lost your own noble mother. Just speak to us once again: yes, I think of you in your gay and in your dark moods! Is it that man is happy, even if he has such a great stature

[10] See Stephan Ley, *Beethoven als Freund der Familie Wegeler—v. Breuning* (Bonn, 1927), pp. 53-9. The editor is grateful to the publishers, H. Bouvier and Co., for granting permission for these translations.

as yours, still but one time in his life, namely in his youth; the rocks of Bonn, Kreuzberg, Godesberg, the Baumschul etc. have been a sounding board for you from which you have been able joyfully to shape many ideas.

Now I will tell you something about myself, about us in order to give you an example of how you must write me in reply.

After my return from Vienna in 1796, things went rather badly for me; for several years I had to live from my practice alone, and this lasted for some years in the poorest environment until I could support myself. Then I became a salaried professor and married in 1802. A year later I received a daughter, who is still living and who has married well. With much genuine intelligence she has the cheerfulness of her father and likes best to play Beethoven sonatas. This gift perhaps is not to her credit but simply hereditary. In the year 1807 a boy was born to me, who is now studying medicine in Berlin. Four years from now I will send him to Vienna, will you receive him? Concerning the family of your friend, my father died on Jan. 1, 1800 in his 70th year. Concerning that of my wife, the school-teacher died four years ago at the age of 72, and Aunt Stockhausen von der Ahr in the same year aged 73. Mama Breuning is 76, and our uncle in Kerpen 85 years old. The latter is still enjoying life and speaks often of you.— Mama and the aunt moved again to Cologne; they lived in the house of their parents, which they occupied again after 66 years, then had it newly built etc. I myself celebrated my 60th birthday in August in the company of some 60 friends and acquaintances, among whom were some of the foremost people of the town.— Since 1807 I have been living here, have a fine house now and a beautiful place. My superiors are satisfied with me and the King gave me decorations and medals. Lore and I are pretty well.

Now I have brought you up to date all at once with our situation; if you want to continue it, please write.—Of our acquaintances Court Councillor Stupp died three weeks ago, Fischenich is Councillor of State in Berlin; Ries and Simrock are two fine old men, but the latter is in much weaker health than the former.

Two years ago I was in Berlin for a month; there I made the acquaintance of the Director of the Singakademie, H. Zelter, a very genial man and extremely frank. The people there consider him uncivil. Hub. Ries in Cassel introduced me to Spohr. You see I am still in communication with artists.

Why haven't you avenged the honor of your mother when, in the Encyclopedia and in France, you were set down as a love-child? The Englishman who wished to vindicate you gave this slander a box in the ears, as we say in Bonn, and [showed that] your mother [would have had to] carry you for 30 years since the King of Prussia, your alleged father, had been dead since 1740.——Won't you ever stop seeing the Stephens steeple? Has traveling no attraction for you? Don't you ever want to see the Rhine again?—All the warmest regards from Frau Lore as well as myself.

Your ancient friend Wglr.

Enclosed was a note from Eleonore Wegeler:

For so long a time dear Beethoven!

It was my wish that Wegeler should write to you once again—now that this wish is fulfilled, I must still add a few words—not only to bring myself more vividly to your memory but to repeat the important question: do you have no

desire to see the Rhine and your birthplace once again?—You will be most welcome as our guest at any time and at any hour—and this would give Weg. and
me the greatest joy—Our Lenchen is grateful to you for so many happy hours—
listens so gladly to our stories about you—knows all the small details of our
happy youth in Bonn—of the quarrels and reconciliations—How happy she
would be were she able to see you! Unfortunately the girl has no musical talent
but through great industry and perseverance she has progressed to the point
where she can play your sonatas, variations and the like; and since music continues to be the greatest relaxation for Weg., she has given him many happy hours
through this. Julius does have musical talent, but until now has neglected it—
and just in the last half year he has been learning the violoncello with pleasure
and delight—Since he has a good teacher in Berlin, I am confident that he will
continue to learn—Both children are big and like their father—also with the gay,
cheerful frame of mind which thank heaven Weg. still hasn't completely lost— —
He gets great pleasure in playing the themes of your variations, the old ones are
his favorites but he has been practising alot and with unbelievable patience on a
new one—your Opferlied stands at the top—He never enters the living room
without going to the piano—still, dear Beethoven! if you could see the way the
lasting memory of you lives on with us—Just tell us once that it means something
to you and that you haven't completely forgotten us—If it were not so difficult to
satisfy our greatest desire, we would already have made a visit to our brother in
Vienna which would certainly have included the pleasure of seeing you—But
such a trip is not possible now since our son is in Berlin—Weg. has told you how
things are with us—We would be wrong to complain—Even the most difficult
period was easier for us than for 100 others—the greatest luck is that we are
healthy and the children are good and well—Neither of them have ever given us
any trouble and we are of good cheer—Lenchen has experienced just one great
grief—that was when our poor little boy died—a loss which none of us will ever
forget. Goodbye, dear Beethoven, and think of us with kind, friendly thoughts—

Eln. Wegeler

Beethoven's reply, a long time in coming, was dictated to Karl:

Vienna, 7th 1obr.[11] 826

My old beloved friend!

I cannot convey the pleasure which the letters from you and your Lorchen
gave me. Truly an answer should have followed with the speed of an arrow;
but I am after all somewhat negligent as a writer because I think that the better
people know me without it. I often form an answer in my head, yet when I want
to write it down in most cases I throw the pen away because I am incapable of
writing the way I feel. I remember all the love that you have constantly given me;
for example how you had my room whitewashed and gave me such a pleasant
surprise;—thus it was with the Breuning family. If we were separated one from
another that was the force of circumstances; each had to follow the object of his
goal and try to reach it; but the eternally firm and unshakeable principles of the

---

[11] Wegeler in his *Notizen* (p. 49) interpreted "1obr." to mean October and subsequent editors agreed until Miss Anderson
pointed out that this was an abbreviation of
"December." See *A*, p. 1321, n. 3. This resolved satisfactorily one of the great puzzles
of the year 1826.

good bind us together ever fast. Unfortunately I cannot write you today as much as I should like since I am bed-ridden and must limit myself to answering some points of your letter. You write that somewhere I am referred to as a natural son of the deceased King of Prussia; this was already mentioned to me a long time ago. But I have made it a principle never to write anything about myself nor to reply to anything written about me. Therefore I gladly leave it to you to make known to the world the honesty of my parents, and my mother in particular.— You write of your son. It goes without saying that if he should come here, he will find in me a friend and father; and whenever I am in a position to serve him or help him in anything, I shall do it with joy.

I still have the silhouette of your Lorchen from which I am reminded how dear to me still is everything good and lovely from my youth.

I will write briefly of my diplomas: I am an honorary member of the Royal Society of Sciences in Sweden, as well as in Amsterdam, and am also an Honorary Freeman of Vienna.— A short time ago a certain Dr. Spiker took my last big symphony with choruses to Berlin; it is dedicated to the King, and I had to write out the dedication in my own hand. Earlier I had sought permission from the Embassy to be allowed to dedicate the work to the King, which he then gave me. At Dr. Spiker's instigation I had to supply a corrected manuscript copy myself with the corrections in my own hand, the same to be delivered to the King since it is supposed to go to the Royal Library. Something has been said to me in this connection about the Order of the Red Eagle, Second Class.[12] What the outcome will be I do not know, for I have never sought for such marks of honor. But at my present age they could not be unwelcome for several reasons—After all I still live by the saying, Nulla dies sine linea; and if I let my muse sleep, it is so that she may reawaken with renewed strength. I hope still to bring some great works into the world and then as an old child end my earthly course somewhere amongst good men—You will soon receive some music through the Brothers Schott in Mainz—The portrait you will find enclosed is indeed an artistic masterpiece, yet it is not the latest one to be done of me.—Of the marks of honor which I know give you joy, I can report also that a medal was sent to me from the deceased King of France with the inscription: Donné par le Roi à Monsieur Beethoven; which was accompanied by a very courteous note from the Premier Gentilhomme du Roi, the Duc de Chartres—

My beloved friend! rest content now, for the memory of the past has taken hold of me; and not without many tears first will you be receiving this letter. The beginning has now been made and soon you will get another letter; and the more often you write me, the more pleasure you will give me. On account of our friendship no kinds of demands are needed, and so goodbye. I beg of you to embrace and kiss for me your dear Lorchen and your children and thereby think of me. God be with you all!

As ever your faithful friend who reveres you

Beethoven

A few days later Beethoven wrote to Schott and asked that the scores of the *Opferlied, Bundeslied,* the song "Bei Chloe war ich ganz allein," Op. 128 and the last bagatelles, Op. 126, be sent at his expense to Wegeler. A

12 Third class is what is talked about in the Conversation Books. (TK, III, 244, n. 1.)

final exchange of letters between these old friends took place in February of the next year. —

Dr. Wawruch visited Beethoven daily from December 5th to 14th and on one day he came twice. His report continues: "But on the eighth day I was alarmed not a little. At the morning visit I found him greatly disturbed and jaundiced all over his body. A frightful choleric attack (*Brechdurchfall*) had threatened his life in the preceding night. A violent rage, a great grief because of sustained ingratitude and undeserved humiliation, was the cause of this mighty explosion. Trembling and shivering he bent double because of the pains which raged in his liver and intestines, and his feet, thitherto moderately inflated, were tremendously swollen. From this time on dropsy developed, the segregation of urine became less, the liver showed plain indication of hard nodules, there was an increase of jaundice. Gentle entreaties from his friends quieted the threatening mental tempest, and the forgiving man forgot all the humiliation which had been put upon him. But the disease moved onward with gigantic strides. Already in the third week there came incidents of nocturnal suffocation; the enormous volume of collected water demanded speedy relief and I found myself compelled to advise tapping in order to guard against the danger of bursting."

At this point we may consider who was in attendance to the sick man. A servant, Thekla, who had apparently come from Gneixendorf (as her name appears in the Conversation Book used there) in the midst of the preparations for the operation was found to be dishonest and was eventually dismissed. There was, however, his reliable housekeeper Sali, who looked after his bodily needs. She is mentioned frequently by Gerhard von Breuning in his *Aus dem Schwarzspanierhause*, and had been found for Beethoven by Gerhard's mother over a year before. The composer's brother had arrived in Vienna about December 10 and thereafter was in regular attendance. As an apothecary he felt he could contribute to the decisions concerning the choice of food for his brother. — The Conversation Books show that Karl was closely involved with Dr. Wawruch's care of the patient. In mid-December there are scattered entries in Karl's hand:[13]

The doctor has allowed rice-soup . . .

You may eat fruit.

Dr. Wawruch's visits: on the 5th of December one time, on the 6th of December 2 times, on the 7th-14th once per day.

[Later] The maid says that you have been drinking water at night, that will not do you any good.

[13] Stephan Ley, *Aus Beethovens Erdentagen* (Bonn, 1948), pp. 207-208.

During the enema you must hold your breath, otherwise it will run out. . . .

•┉•

Take a breath.

•┉•

Do not hold your breath, draw it in.

•┉•

Hold it in hard, but longer.

•┉•

Now hold on, then the enema will work.

Since Holz was now married, his visits were not as numerous, but he still found time to look after the correction and publication of the last compositions and to collect the composer's annuity. Schindler found his way back to the composer's side within a fortnight and seems, at least at first, to have been given more menial labors to carry out. Stephan von Breuning's visits were interrupted by illness and official labors, but his son, the thirteen-year-old Gerhard, frequently lent a gracious touch to the scene by his familiar mode of address, his gossip about his father's domestic affairs and his suggestions of intellectual pabulum for his august friend. He was a daily message-bearer between the two households and brought provisions such as soup from his family's kitchen. Other friends visited too, and from the city began to come expressions of sympathy.

After Dr. Wawruch had reached his decision, Dr. Staudenheim was called in consultation and he confirmed the attending physician's opinion as to the necessity of an operation. Beethoven was told; "after a few moments of serious thought he gave his consent." Wawruch had retained Dr. Seibert, principal surgeon (Primärwundarzt) at the hospital to perform the operation, which took place on December 20. Those present were Johann, Karl and Schindler. Beethoven's sense of humor did not desert him. When, the incision having been made, Dr. Seibert introduced the tube and the water spurted out, Beethoven said: "Professor, you remind me of Moses striking the rock with his staff." Wawruch writes in the Conversation Book:

Thank God it is happily over!

•┉•

If you feel ill you must tell me.

•┉•

Did the incision give you any pain?

•┉•

From today the sun will continue to ascend higher.

•┉•

God save you! [This in English]

•~•

Lukewarm almond milk.

•~•

Do you not now feel pain?

•~•

Continue to lie quietly on your side.

•~•

We shall soon measure off the water.

•~•

Five measures and a half.[14]

•~•

I hope that you will sleep more quietly tonight.

•~•

You bore yourself like a knight.

The operation made necessary renewed care and a close watch on the patient's diet. He was allowed to drink almond milk, but not in too great quantities, and also only a little coffee. During this period he had to remain in a near-lying position while it was being determined whether a second operation would be necessary.

One joyful event brightened the solitary gloom of the sick-chamber in the middle of December. From Johann Andreas Stumpff, of London, Beethoven received the 40 volumes of Dr. Arnold's edition of the works of Handel which the donor had resolved to send Beethoven on his visit in 1824. Gerhard von Breuning pictures the joy of Beethoven at the reception of the gift, which he described as royal compared with that of the King of Prussia.[15] One day the boy was asked to hand the big books from the pianoforte where they rested to the bed. "I have long wanted them," said the composer to his faithful little friend, "for Handel is the greatest, the ablest composer that ever lived. I can still learn from him." He leaned the books against the wall, turned over the pages, and ever and anon paused to break out into new expressions of praise. Von Breuning places all these incidents in the middle of February, 1827, but his memory was plainly at fault. The books arrived in December, for Stumpff preserved the receipt for them, a letter and Reichard's *Taschenbuch für Reisende*, which is dated "December 14, 1826." The gift was sent through the son of Stumpff's friend Streicher.[16]

[14] In his report Dr. Wawruch writes: "The liquid amounted to 25 pounds but the after-flow was certainly five times as much." (TDR, v, 431, n. 1.)

[15] *Aus dem Schwarzspanierhause*, pp. 94-5.

(TDR, v, 424.) The disappointing ring referred to in the preceding chapter had arrived only a few days before.

[16] See *A*, p. 1433 (19).

Just before the first operation (around December 19), Beethoven received a visit from Johann Baptist Jenger, who had been an official in the Chief Command at Graz. He brought two letters from Beethoven's old friend, Marie Pachler-Koschak. The first, written on August 15, 1825, was a letter of recommendation for Jenger who, upon being transferred to Vienna, was anxious to meet Beethoven; it closed with an invitation to come for a summer visit to the Pachler-Koschak country estate outside of Graz. This warm letter had become lost and then was found again; thereupon Frau Pachler wrote a second, dated November 5, 1826, reiterating the invitation for the present year. Too late! By the time he received the letters such an excursion was out of the question. On December 29 Dr. Jenger wrote a letter to Frau Pachler of his visit, from which we quote:

... I was startled as I entered his room, where everything lay pell-mell, as though in a storehouse. He himself lay in bed suffering terribly and since he had not shaved in 3 weeks, you can easily imagine, gracious lady, how he appeared. He greeted me in a very friendly manner and I had to sit on the bed with him. I wrote out the necessary information and delivered both of your letters which he read through attentively and enjoyed thoroughly. Afterwards he asked me to convey his hearty thanks to you, esteemed and gracious lady, and to add that he would write to you himself—as soon as he was able—then he spoke of your especial musical talents with great joy and concluded that it would have been more sensible for him to have gone to you in Graz than to his brother in Upper Austria. Nevertheless he hopes some time soon to see you in Graz, which perhaps will happen next year and about which I shall be advising him frequently, and perhaps I shall be making the trip there with him.

Eight days ago he was tapped for the first time because he was suffering from dropsy in the chest. It has not been successfully stopped and therefore he will have to be tapped soon again. Would to God he were already healthy again!

Stephan von Breuning had called on Beethoven shortly after his arrival, and the work of making a soldier of Karl was begun at once. There were formal calls to be made upon Lieutenant Field Marshal Stutterheim and other officers, a physical examination to be undergone, uniforms to be provided, the oath of service to be taken, and his monthly allowance to be fixed. The Conversation Books show that these preparations were expected to occupy only a few days; instead, they dragged themselves through the month of December. Breuning's illness was no doubt a contributing factor.

In early December, Karl writes:

You are wrong if you think that I have begun to vacillate.

•~•

On the contrary I am glad that the affair has ended the way I wanted it to and will never regret my decision.

A few days later he reports on a visit to Stutterheim:

He was very nice after all and said that before my departure I should come to see him again. The actual entrance into military service will take place the day after tomorrow.

•~•

I will ask about it this afternoon.

•~•

I shall be here for 5 to 6 days more. We cannot go together in any case because the doctor has told me that within the next 6 days you are not allowed to go out.

Around December 19th he writes: "I am already entered. Today I must go to the regiment doctor Von Gulay whose certificate is necessary, and tomorrow again to the Lieutenant Field Marshal." After the first operation, at which Karl was present, as already mentioned, he writes:

A uniform is ready.

•~•

On Saturday [December 23] I will get everything; but tomorrow there is much to be done; your brother must buy the necessary things with me; it is high time; after the holidays I must go to the regiment in Iglau.

•~•

Soon I must ask you for some money because I had to promise a present to the tailor. Today everything will be ready.

Then Johann writes: "Now you need not buy anything more, for he has everything." Later Karl writes:

I must go again to the Lieutenant Field Marshal.

•~•

On the 2nd of January.

•~•

Stage-coach.

•~•

[Johann] The trip takes 2 days with 15 to 20 fl.

After saying his good-byes and New Year greetings, Karl left for Iglau on January 2, 1827. There is no record of the parting, and it is safe to assume that it passed off without emotional demonstration of any kind. But Beethoven's thoughts went swiftly towards his self-assumed duty of providing for the young man's future. The very next day he wrote the following letter to Dr. Bach:

Vienna, Wednesday January 3, 1827

Before my death I declare Karl van Beethoven, my beloved nephew, my sole and universal heir of all the property which I possess in which is included chiefly seven bank shares and whatever money may be on hand.—If the laws prescribe a modification in this I beg of you as far as possible to turn it to his *advantage*.—I appoint you his *curator* and ask you along with his guardian, Hofrat von Breuning, to take the place of a father to him—God preserve you—A thousand thanks for the love and friendship which you have shown me.—

Ludwig van Beethoven

After the close of the letter there is noted the following: "This will of Herr Ludwig van Beethoven, which has *today* been brought to court by Dr. Bach and made known in his presence, (is) to be preserved and copies made—By the Viennese Magistrate, March 27, 827. Schütz"

Thus the will was read immediately after Beethoven's death, and the testamentary disposition, to which we return later. Beethoven had his letter to Bach sent to Breuning to read, who answered as follows:

Dearest friend!

I am still too weak to write much to you, but I think that the following few words from a candid heart should be said to you. Since through Gerhard you have told me that I should read the letter to Hr. Dr. Bach, I have done so and return it to you for the time being with the following observations. That you name Karl as heir in the event, hopefully far distant, that we all leave this life, is appropriate considering your way of thinking and what you have already done for him. But Karl has shown himself up until now to be very reckless, and one doesn't know how his character will shape itself at present; thus I would be of the opinion that for his own good and for the security of his future you limit his power to dispose of capital either during his whole life or at least for a few years more until he has become 24 years old, the age of his majority. In any case he would have enough yearly income at hand and the limitation would protect him from the consequences of reckless actions before he reaches maturity. Speak about this with Hr. Dr. Bach, whom I should think it would be best for you to have visit you. He will arrange everything in the simplest way; I should be glad to be able to talk with you or with Dr. Bach about my observations, for I fear that a mere time limitation will not keep Karl from contracting debts which he will have to pay subsequently from his whole inheritance.

I embrace you warmly.

Beethoven received a letter from his nephew in Iglau on January 13, which begins:

My dear Father,

I have received your letter written by Schindler, I ask only that in the future you include the date so that I can estimate the speed of the post. Concerning your state of health I am glad to know that you are in good hands; I too, had felt some distrust of the treatment of your former (or perhaps present?) physician; I hope improvement will follow.

He reported about his situation in the regiment, asked for money and for the flute part of the Pianoforte Concerto in B-flat (Op. 19), which one of the officers of the regiment wished to play. A postscript reads: "Do not think that the little privations to which I am now subjected have made me dissatisfied with my lot. On the contrary, rest assured that I am living in contentment, and regret only that I am separated so far from you."

Communications from the young man were not many, and Schindler's rebukes and complaints in the Conversation Books about his undutifulness were probably only a reflex of Beethoven's moods and utterances. One cause of dissatisfaction was the fact that a letter to Smart had been sent to him for translation and was not promptly returned. But he acknowledged the receipt of money towards the end of February, and on March 4th he wrote another letter, which has been preserved:

My dear Father,

I have just received the books that you sent me and thank you very much for them.

You will have gotten the translation of the letter to Smart; I don't doubt that it will have favorable results.

Just today a cadet, who had been in Vienna on a furlough, returned to his battalion; and he reports having heard that you had been saved by a frozen punch and are feeling well. I hope that this last is true no matter what the means may have been.

There is little new about myself to tell; the service goes its usual way with the difference only that the weather is much milder, thus the watches also are easier.

Write me very soon about the state of your health; also please give my hearty greetings to H. Hofrat [von Breuning]. I kiss you.

Your loving son Charl.

P.S. Please stamp your letters because I have to pay alot of postage here for which I hardly have enough from my account.

Karl van Beethoven never saw his uncle in life again, nor even in death, for he was not present at the funeral—as indeed in those days of tardy communication and slow conveyance he could not be.[17]

As the year 1826 ended, Beethoven's friends were discussing with Dr. Wawruch the necessity of a second tapping. The surgeon Seibert evidently advised a postponement of the operation. There were now signs of Beethoven's dissatisfaction with his doctor. According to Gerhard von Breuning,[18] Wawruch's visits were ungraciously received; when his name was announced, Beethoven would turn his face to the wall and exclaim, "Oh, the ass!" Schindler tried to sustain the patient's faith in the skill of his physician. In a Conversation Book[19] he writes:

He understands his profession, that is well known, and he is right in following a safe course.

•~•

I have a great deal of confidence in him, but I cannot speak from experience. But he is known as an able man—esteemed and appreciated by his students.

•~•

---

[17] According to Sterba, op.cit., p. 300, Karl did hurry to Vienna, but arrived too late and always regretted it. Concerning Karl's later life, see Appendix I.

[18] Op.cit., p. 90. This sentence does not appear in TDR (see TK, III, 283).

[19] Dated January 5th to 8th by Stephan Ley, whose order of entries is followed. See Aus Beethovens Erdentagen, p. 212.

But as we are here concerned with a *carum caput*, my advice from the beginning has been to take into consultation a physician whose familiarity with your constitution comes from *medical treatment*.

·〜·

Then you always have an appetite?

·〜·

And then Hr. Seibert is really right if he still postpones the second operation, for then it will probably make a 3rd unnecessary. Yet it is better and wiser if you still don't lose faith in your doctor, for after all he has already done a great deal.

—Then Gerhard von Breuning writes:

How are you? . . .

·〜·

Has your belly become smaller?

·〜·

You are supposed to perspire more. . .

·〜·

How was your enema?

·〜·

You should take several

·〜·

Have you read Walter Scott already?

·〜·

Would you perhaps like to read some Schiller. The world history by Schröckh?

·〜·

Descriptions of summer travel?

·〜·

I will bring them to you tomorrow.

The second operation took place on January 8, according to Schindler, who was present. There were no complications; the tapping was accomplished without difficulty, and Dr. Seibert reported that the water was clearer and the outflow greater than the first time. Ten measures were drawn off.

—Before the year's end Schindler was putting in his voice for more medical advice. He writes:[20]

Yesterday I urged your brother earnestly to hold a medical council of men who have known your constitution longer.

·〜·

[20] *Ibid.*, p. 211.

Staudenheim, Braunhofer and Malfatti, three capable men whose judgement is not to be rejected.⟩⟩—

On January 11, according to Jenger in a letter written the next day to Frau Pachler, the desired council of physicians took place and included Dr. Malfatti,[21] who "prescribed for B. nothing hereafter but frozen fruit punch and rubbing of the abdomen with ice-cold water, a remedy with which Malfatti is said to have completely cured a similar patient." It had become an ardent wish of Beethoven's that Malfatti undertake his case, but Malfatti had refused, pleading professional ethics, but no doubt actuated by reasons of a more personal character. Many years before, probably as early as 1813, he had been not only Beethoven's physician but also his friend; indeed he was an uncle of the Therese Malfatti to whom the composer once made an offer of marriage. He had what is easy to imagine to have been the experience of all the medical men who undertook the care of the great man. Beethoven was ever a disobedient and irritable patient. He became dissatisfied with Dr. Malfatti's treatment and commented upon it and him in such a manner as to cause a serious and lasting estrangement. Ten years had elapsed between this incident and the time when Beethoven's longing went out towards his one-time professional friend.[22] Before introducing the following account it should be emphasized that, although Malfatti introduced a new treatment, he did not want to have any discord with Dr. Wawruch, and the latter remained in charge of the case until the end.

Dr. Wawruch, after describing Beethoven's lack of appetite and loss of fluids writes:

"Then Dr. Malfatti, who thenceforth supported me with his advice, and who, as a friend of Beethoven's of long years' standing understood his predominant inclination for spirituous liquors, hit upon the notion of administering frozen punch. I must confess that the treatment produced excellent results for a few days at least. Beethoven felt himself so refreshed by the ice with its alcoholic contents that already in the first night he slept quietly throughout the night and began to perspire profusely. He grew cheerful and was full of witty conceits and even dreamed of being able to complete the oratorio 'Saul and David'[23] which he had begun.

"But this joy, as was to have been foreseen, did not last long. He began to abuse the prescription and applied himself right bravely to the frozen punch. The spirits soon caused a violent pressure of the blood upon the brain; he grew soporous, breathed stertorously like an intoxicated person, began to

[21] According to remarks by Johann in the Conversation Book, either Staudenheim or Braunhofer was also present. See TDR, v, 444.

[22] It was in April, 1817, according to a letter (June 19, 1817) from Beethoven to the Countess Erdödy.

[23] Schindler denies that Beethoven worked on the oratorio of *Saul and David* during his last illness. Thayer in a note directs attention to the fact that Beethoven was confessedly deeply absorbed in Handel's scores, which he had received only a short time before. (TDR, v, 445, n. 3.)

wander in his speech, and a few times inflammatory pains in the throat were paired with hoarseness and even aphony. He became more unruly, and when, because of the cooling of the bowels, colic and diarrhoea resulted, it was high time to deprive him of this precious refreshment."

Schindler now tried to effect a reconciliation between Dr. Malfatti and Beethoven. His account, which was printed in the *Frankfurter Konversationsblatt* of July 14, 1842, is clearly prejudiced against Dr. Wawruch's treatment: "Never shall I forget the harsh words of that man which he [Dr. Malfatti] commissioned me to bear to the friend and teacher who lay mortally ill, when after the second operation (January 8) I repeatedly carried to him the urgent requests of Beethoven that he come to his help or he should die. Dr. Wawruch did not know his constitution, was ruining him with too much medicine.[24] He had already been compelled to empty 75 bottles, without counting various powders, he had no confidence in this physician, etc. To all of these representations Malfatti answered me coldly and drily: 'Say to Beethoven that he, as a master of harmony, must know that I must also live in harmony with my colleagues.' Beethoven wept bitter tears when I brought him this reply, which, hard as it was, I had to do, so that he might no longer look for help to that quarter. . . . Though Malfatti finally took pity on poor Beethoven and abolished Wawruch's medicine bottles at once and prescribed an entirely different course of treatment, despite the pleadings of the patient he refused to remain his *ordinarius* and visit him often. On the contrary, he came only at long intervals, and contented himself with occasional reports from me as to the sick man's condition. He was not willing even to send one of his assistants to Beethoven and consequently Dr. Wawruch remained his daily visitor in spite of Beethoven's protests."

We learn more about Schindler's attempt to bring Beethoven and Malfatti together from his letter to the composer of January 19:

My great master!
    Since I have a rehearsal today at half past eight from which I cannot be absent, I must report the result in writing of my second visit to Malfatti.
    He is coming to you today at half past nine. Knowing perfectly well that the professor has a lecture until ten, I told him [Malfatti] that we are inviting him [Wawruch] to come at half past nine. In order that we don't get into a pickle, you just have to offer the excuse to Malf. that today for the first time you have learned from the Professor that because of his lecture he couldn't come before ten o'clock. Malf. has a meeting in the city at ten o'clock; therefore you have the opportunity that you want to speak with him alone—
    What I am asking you, however, is to make a complete reconciliation with him concerning the past for it still rankles with him to a certain extent; **only** today he again gave me to understand that he could not forget this planned of-

---

[24] What this medicine might have been is known only in part: in the Conversation Books there is mention of almond milk and a salep drink.

fense, as he called it.—Some words of explanation from you will get everything to rights and bring it back on the old, friendly track.

Around two o'clock I shall have the honor of being with you again. Meanwhile summa cum reverentia

Your obliging

Ant. Schindler

A reconciliation took place. Beethoven no doubt, in the warm glow of a recovered friendship, gave the physician a full measure of confidence and hailed in him much more than the ordinary professional leech. It is also safe to assume that Malfatti knew from the beginning that a cure was impossible and strove at once for temporary relief, which in Beethoven's case was the surest of means for cheering him up and reanimating hope within him. By administering frozen punch he stimulated the jaded organs more successfully than Wawruch had succeeded in doing; at the same time he warned against excess in its use and forbade the patient taking it in a liquid form. But this was only at the beginning; when he saw the inevitable end approaching he waived all injunctions as to quantity. Schindler says: "The quantity of frozen punch permitted in the first weeks was not more than one glass a day. Not until after the fourth operation (February 27th), when it was seen that the case was hopeless, were all restrictions removed. The noble patient, feeling the marked effects of a doubled and even trebled allowance meanwhile, thought himself already half saved and wanted to work on his tenth symphony, which he was allowed to do to a small extent."

Schindler then included a note written to him by the composer:

Miracles! Miracles! Miracles! The highly learned gentlemen[25] are both defeated! Only through Malfatti's science shall I be saved! It is necessary that you come to me for a moment this forenoon.

The reiteration of the words "miracles" is indicated by the usual musical sign of repetition ·/·. There is no date in Beethoven's handwriting, but Schindler has endorsed it: "Beethoven's last lines to Schindler on March 17, 1827." The endorsement is of later date and marks another obvious error of memory. Wawruch says that Beethoven abandoned hope after the fourth tapping; Johann van Beethoven records that the physicians declared him lost on March 16. It is hardly possible that Beethoven wrote this note after he himself had abandoned all hope of recovery. More likely the pathetic document is an outburst of jubilation on feeling the exhilaration consequent on Malfatti's prescription, as mentioned in Wawruch's report.

Gerhard von Breuning, prejudiced as he was against Dr. Wawruch, was yet far from unqualified in his praise of Malfatti. He says:[26] "But the usually brilliant physician seems to have been little inspired in the presence of Beethoven. The frozen punch which he prescribed on his first visit to restore

[25] Probably Wawruch and Seibert, according to Schindler. (TDR, v, 449, n. 1.)
[26] *Aus dem Schwarzspanierhause*, p. 92.

the tone of the digestive organs, excessively weakened by Wawruch's overload of medicaments, had, indeed the desired restorative effect; but it was too transient. On the other hand a sort of sweat-bath prescribed a few days after the second [*sic*—should be "third"] operation was so obviously injurious to the patient, filled with longing and hope, that it had to be abandoned after the first application. Jugs filled with hot water were arranged in a bath-tub and covered thickly with birch leaves on which the patient was seated, all of his body but the head being covered with a sheet. Malfatti hoped for a beneficial action upon the skin and to put the organs into a productive perspiration. But the very opposite effect resulted. The body of the patient, which had been emptied of water by the scarcely completed tapping, attracted the moisture developed by the bath like a block of salt; it swelled visibly in the apparatus and in a few days compelled the introduction anew of the tube into the still unhealed puncture."

—Von Breuning's account of the bath is to be compared with an entry from a Conversation Book of January 27-28.[27]

The dry hay-seed bath is supposed to make you perspire, and Malfatti says that this must be tried now since the internal medicine is not having the desired effect. . . .

It is nothing but hayseed in two piles placed on warm jugs; however the first bath is to last no longer than a half an hour.

On January 25 (the date is fixed by a remark of Johann's in the Conversation Book) Schindler had brought word to Beethoven that the mother of the singer Fräulein Schechner had sent for him that morning to tell him about two remedies which had proved efficacious in the case of her father, who had also been afflicted with dropsy. One of these was Juniper berry tea, the other a vapor bath from a decoction, the ingredients of which were a head of cabbage, two handfuls of caraway seeds and three handfuls of hayseed (*Heublumen*). These remedies had been prescribed by the physician of the late King of Bavaria and had worked a cure in the case of Madame Schechner's husband when he was 70 years old. Dr. Malfatti seems to have been told of these remedies and to have prescribed the bath, which, it is said in the Conversation Books, he recognized at once as a cure used by Dr. Harz, the Royal Physician mentioned.

The third tapping took place on February 2nd. Malfatti received the report of the operation from the surgeon. Schindler writes:

I am just wondering whether Malfatti won't want to check up today on the condition of your liver and belly. It would therefore be very good as a matter of caution if Hr. Seybert were sent for at 5 o'clock. He said naturally that he wants to see you again today.

[27] Ley, *op.cit.*, p. 214.

Perhaps to check up. The water is going through the liver.

⋅❧⋅

Then the well-being of the liver is the key to the whole sickness.

⋅❧⋅

You have been able to gain strength again since this.

⋅❧⋅

It would be good in every way if he were here because perhaps he has checked up on everything. So he can give Malfatti the best information about it.

Thus there was talk now of the liver among Beethoven's friends. But it is not possible to determine how long before it had occurred to them that this organ was the seat of the trouble.

Among other friends who visited Beethoven during this period, the Conversation Books show Tobias Haslinger, Piringer, later Schikh, Streicher, Bernard, and the singer, Nanette Schechner. This last arranged through Schindler at the end of February, a short visit to tell the composer of her great admiration for his music. She described her successes in *Fidelio* in Munich, and stated that it was through singing in *Adelaide* that she had won her way to the operatic stage.[28]

On February 1 there came to the composer a cheery letter from his old playmate Wegeler, calling to his mind some of his early flames—Jeanette Honrath and Fräulein Westerholt—and playfully outlining a plan by which the old friends might enjoy a reunion: He would send, he said, one of his patients to Carlsbad and go there with him as soon as Beethoven should arrange also to go there for his convalescence. Then, after a three weeks' trip through South Germany, there should be a final visit to the home of their childhood. And, as before, Eleonore sent a postscript emphasizing the pleasure of the reunion. Beethoven answered the letter on February 17; he told his old friend that he was surprised that he had not received through Stephan von Breuning a letter of December 10 and a portrait bearing the same date, and that he would soon be receiving this portrait and some music through Schott.

Zmeskall, faithful to the old friendship, a bound prisoner to his room through gout, sent greetings and inquiries through Schindler. From his sick-bed Beethoven wrote a short answer, dated by Zmeskall February 18:

A thousand thanks for your sympathy. I do not despair. The most painful feature is the cessation of all activity. No evil without its good side—May heaven

---

[28] Some reminiscences of Schechner's sometime fiancé, the tenor Ludwig Cramolini, were published in the *Frankfurter Zeitung* of September 29, 1907, in which he describes this visit as one made by both himself and his friend during which he sang *Adelaide* and she an aria from *Fidelio* with Schindler at the piano. He dates the visit, however, mid-December, 1826. (Cf. TDR, v, 307, n. 1.) See *BJ*, II, pp. 373-79.

but grant you relief in your painful existence. Perhaps health is coming to both of us and we shall meet again in friendly intimacy.

Warm regards from your old sympathizing friend.

Beethoven

Though Beethoven had received the Handel scores in December, he does not seem to have had an opportunity to enjoy Stumpff's gift thoroughly until he turned to them for intellectual refreshment on his bed of pain. He had signed the receipt for them in December, but it was not until his thoughts turned to his English friends in the hope of pecuniary relief that he wrote a letter to Stumpff under date of February 8.

Most worthy friend!

What great joy was given to me by your sending the works of Handel as a present—for me a royal present!—This my pen cannot describe. An article about it, which I enclose, was even printed by the newspaper.[29] Unfortunately I have been laid up with the dropsy since the 3rd of December. You can imagine in what a situation this places me! Generally I live from the proceeds of my brain only, and thus provide all things for myself and my Karl. Unhappily for a month and a half I have not been able to write a note.

My salary suffices only to pay my semi-annual rent, after which there remains only a few hundred florins. Remember also that it cannot yet be determined when my illness will be over and I again will be able to sail through the air on Pegasus under full sail. Doctor, surgeon, everything must be paid—

I recall right well that several years ago the Philharmonic Society wanted to give a concert for my benefit. It would be fortunate for me if they would come to this decision now. I might still be saved from the poverty which now confronts me. On this account I am writing to Mr. S[mart]. And if you, dear friend, can do anything towards this end I beg of you to cooperate with Mr. S. A letter will also be written about this to Moscheles and if all my friends unite I believe that something can be done for me in this matter.

Concerning the Handel works for H. Imperial Highness, the Archduke Rudolph, I cannot as yet say anything with certainty. But I will write to him in a few days and remind him of it.

I thank you again for your glorious gift, at the same time I beg of you to tell me if I can be of any service to you here; this I would do with all my heart—I present once again to your sympathetic nature my situation here which I have described to you and meanwhile I wish you everything that is good and beautiful. I send you my best regards.

Very respectfully yours,

Beethoven

Stumpff had already been informed of Beethoven's illness by Streicher. It is evident that he went at once to Smart and Moscheles, and knowledge of Beethoven's condition and request was communicated to the directors of the Philharmonic Society forthwith. Beethoven, meanwhile, had written to both Smart and Moscheles, enclosing the letter of the former in the letter to

[29] The newspaper article was printed in the *Modenzeitung*. (TDR, v, 459, n. 3.)

the latter; but the quick and sympathetic action of the Society was no doubt due primarily to the initiative of Stumpff, for the letters could by no means have reached London when the directors held a meeting on February 28. Mr. Dance presided, and those present, as recorded in the Society's minutes, were F. Cramer, Horsley, Moralt, Dragonetti, Neate, Dizi, Beale, T. Cooke, Sir G. Smart, Welsh, Latour, Spagnoletti, Calkin, J. B. Cramer, Cipriani Potter and Watts. The minutes continue:

It was moved by Mr. Neate, and seconded by Mr. Latour:
"That this Society do lend the sum of One Hundred Pounds to its own members to be sent through the hands of Mr. Moscheles to some confidential friend of Beethoven, to be applied to his comforts and necessities during his illness."
Carried unanimously.

Both Stumpff and Moscheles wrote the good news to Beethoven the next day. A portion of Moscheles's letter appears in his translation, or rather paraphrase, of Schindler's biography.[30] In it he said: "The [Philharmonic] Society resolved to express their good will and lively sympathy by requesting your acceptance of 100 pounds sterling (1,000 florins) to provide the necessary comforts and conveniences during your illness. This money will be paid to your order by Mr. Rau, of the house of Eskeles, either in separate sums or all at once as you desire."

He added an expression of the Philharmonic Society's willingness to aid him further whenever he should inform it of his need of assistance. Meanwhile Beethoven's impatience was so great that, having found Smart's address among his papers, he wrote to him a second letter on March 6th, being able now to mention the fact of the fourth tapping on February 27th and to utter the apprehension that the operation might have to be repeated—perhaps more than once. On March 14th he was still without the answer of his English friends and he wrote again to Moscheles telling him of the two letters sent to Smart, urging action and concluding with

Whither is this to lead, and what is to become of me if this goes on for some time?—Truly, a hard lot has befallen me! But I yield to the will of fate and only pray that God in His divine will so order it that as long as I have to endure this death in life I may be protected against want. This will give me strength to endure my lot, hard and terrible though it may be, with submission to the will of the Most High.
So, my dear Moscheles I again bring my affairs to your attention and remain with the greatest respect

Your friend
L. v. Beethoven

Hummel is here and has already made me a few visits.

Scarcely was this letter sent when the letters of March 1st arrived from London. The impression that they made will be recorded later.

---

[30] Moscheles, *Life of Beethoven*, ii, pp. 68-9.

Schindler says that the appeal to London, which had been suggested by Beethoven, had been discussed with the composer by himself and Breuning, who agreed in questioning the advisability of the step which, they said, would make a bad impression if it became known. They reminded Beethoven of his bank-shares, but he protested vigorously against their being touched; he had set them apart as a legacy for his nephew which must not be encroached upon.[31]

There are evidences outside of the importunate letters to London that Beethoven had frequent spells of melancholy during the period between the crises of his disease, which culminated in the third operation on February 2, and the fourth. Some of them were, no doubt, due to forebodings touching the outcome of his illness; some to the anxiety which his financial condition gave him (more imaginary than real in view of the easily convertible bank-shares), and some presumably to disappointment and chagrin at the conduct of his nephew, who had not answered his letter to Iglau. Breuning explained that the negligence might be due to Karl's time and attention being engrossed by the carnival gaieties at the military post, and warned Beethoven that to give way to melancholy was to stand in the way of recovery. We learn this from the Conversation Books which also give glimpses of friendly visits calculated to divert the sick man's mind and keep him in touch with the affairs of the city, theatre and the world at large. Doležalek, Schuppanzigh, and apparently Linke also, came in a group; Beethoven showed them the Handel scores and the conversation ran out into a discussion of international politics. Moritz Lichnowsky made a call and entertained him with the gossip of the theatres. Gleichenstein made several visits, and once brought with him his wife and son. The Countess was a sister of Therese Malfatti, and was disappointed when Beethoven did not recognize her. About the middle of February Diabelli gave Beethoven a print-picture of Haydn's birthplace, which he had published; Beethoven showed it to his little friend Gerhard von Breuning and said: "Look, I got this today. See this little house, and in it so great a man was born!"

Sometime in February—it was probably at the time when Beethoven's mind was so fixedly bent on obtaining help from London—Schindler was either ill or suffering from an accident which kept him for a brief space from Beethoven's bedside. The composer sent him a gift—a repast evidently—and a letter of sympathy which Schindler endorsed as being "in the month of Febr. 1827."

Concerning your accident, since it has already taken place, so soon can we see each other—I can send things to you through someone without any trouble— accept this—Here is something—Moscheles, Cramer—if you have not already received another letter. There is new reason to write on Wednesday, and present him anew with my heartfelt entreaty. If you are still not well by then, one of my [servants] can attend to the posting of it against the receipt—

[31] See *Biogr.*, II, p. 138.

Vale et fave—there is no need for assurance of my sympathy in your accident—
Do take *this meal from me* which has been given from the bottom of my heart—
Heaven be with you.

Your sincere friend

Beethoven

Schindler remarked of this letter that the broken sentences and gaps in his ideas showed that Beethoven was not always thinking connectedly during these days.

More pathetic than even this letter is the picture of the sufferer in his sick-room at the time of the fourth operation on February 27. So wretched were his surroundings that it is scarcely possible to avoid the conviction that not poverty alone but ignorance and carelessness were contributory to the woeful lack of ordinary sick-room conveniences. Gerhard von Breuning wrote[32] that after the operation the fluid which was drained from the patient's body flowed half-way across the floor to the middle of the room; and in the Conversation Books there is mention of saturated bedclothing and a suggestion by the physician that oilcloth be procured and spread over the couch. Beethoven now gave up hope. Dr. Wawruch says: "No words of comfort could brace him up, and when I promised him alleviation of his sufferings with the coming of the vitalizing weather of spring he answered with a smile: 'My day's work is finished. If there were a physician who could help me "his name shall be called Wonderful!" ' This pathetic allusion to Handel's *Messiah* touched me so deeply that I had to confess its correctness to myself with profound emotion." The incident so sympathetically described bears evidence of veracity on its face; Handel's scores were always in Beethoven's mind during the last weeks of his life.

Among Beethoven's visitors in February was Wolfmayer, whose coming must have called up a sense of a long-standing obligation and purpose in the composer's mind.[33] On February 22nd he dictated a letter to the Schotts asking that the Quartet in C-sharp minor be dedicated to "my friend Johann Nepomuk Wolfmayer." The letter then proceeds:

Now, however, I come with a very important request.—My doctor has ordered me to drink very good old Rhine wine. To get a thing of that kind unadulterated is not possible at any price. If, therefore, I were to receive a small number of bottles I would show my gratitude to you in the Cäcilia. I think something might be done for me at the customs so that the transport would not cost too much.—As soon as my strength allows you shall receive the metronome marks for the Mass, for I am now just in the period when the fourth operation is about to be performed.—The sooner, therefore, that I receive the Rhine wine, or Moselle, the more beneficial it will be to me in my present condition; and I beg of

---

[32] *Op.cit.*, p. 104.

[33] It will be remembered that Wolfmayer had commissioned him years before to write a requiem, and had paid him for it. (TK, III, 296, n. 1.)

you most heartily to do me this favor for which I shall be under grateful obligation to you.

With the greatest respect I remain your very devoted

Beethoven

On March 1st he repeated his request:

I am under the necessity of becoming burdensome to you again, inasmuch as I am sending you a packet for the Royal Government Councillor Wegeler at Coblenz, which you will have the kindness to transmit from Mainz to Coblenz. You know without more ado that I am too unselfish to ask you to do all these things gratuitously.

I repeat my former request, namely, concerning *old white Rhine wine or Moselle*. It is infinitely difficult to get any here which is genuine and unadulterated, even at the highest price. A few days ago, on February 27, I had my fourth operation, and yet I am unable to look forward to my complete recovery and restoration. Pity your devoted friend who has the highest esteem for you.

Beethoven

On March 8 the Schotts answered that they had forwarded a case of twelve bottles of Rüdesheimer Berg of the vintage of 1806, via Frankfurt, but in order that he might receive a slight refreshment, they had sent that day four bottles of the same wine, two pure and two mixed with herbs, to be used as a medicine which had been prescribed for his disease. Before the wine reached Vienna, on March 10 Beethoven wrote again to the Schotts:

Gentlemen!

According to my letter the Quartet was to be dedicated to one whose name I have already sent to you. Since then there has been an occurrence which has led me to make a change in this. It must be dedicated to Lieut. Field-Marshal von Stutterheim to whom I am deeply indebted. If you have already engraved the first dedication I beg of you, by everything in this world, to change it, and I will gladly pay the cost. Do not accept this as an empty promise; I attach so much importance to it that I am ready to make any compensation for it. I enclose the title. As regards the shipment to my friend, the Royal Prussian Government Councillor v. Wegeler in Coblenz, I am glad to be able to relieve you wholly. Another opportunity has offered itself. My health, which will not be restored for a long time, pleads for the wines which I have asked for and which will certainly bring me refreshment, strength and health.

I remain with the greatest respect

Your very devoted Ludwig van Beethoven

A few days later Beethoven finally received the great gift from London and dictated the following acknowledgement to Schindler:

Vienna, March 18, 1827

My dear good Moscheles:

I cannot describe to you in words with what feelings I read your letter of March 1. The generosity with which the Philharmonic Society almost anticipated my petition has touched me in the innermost depth of my soul.—I beg you, therefore, my dear Moscheles, to be the agent through which I transmit my sincerest thanks to the Philharmonic Society for the particular sympathy and help.

I found myself constrained to collect at once the entire sum of 1,000 florins C.M., as I was in the unpleasant position of being about to borrow money, which would have brought new embarrassments.

Concerning the concert which the Philharmonic Society has resolved to give for my benefit, I beg the Society not to abandon this noble purpose, and to deduct the 1,000 florins already sent to me from the proceeds of the concert. And if the Society is disposed graciously to send me the balance, I will pledge myself to return my heartiest thanks to the Society by binding myself to compose for it either a new symphony, which lies already sketched in my desk, or a new overture or something else which the Society would like.

May heaven very soon restore me to health, and I shall prove to the generous Englishmen how greatly I appreciate their interest in my sad fate.

Your noble act will never be forgotten and I shall follow this with special thanks to Sir Smart and Mr. Stumpff.

Farewell! With kindest remembrances

From your friend who highly esteems you

Ludwig van Beethoven[34]

My kindest regards to your wife.

I have to thank you and the Philh. Society for a new friend in Mr. Rau. Please deliver to the Philh. Society the metronome marks of the Symphony. Here are the indications.

Metronome indications of tempi for Beethoven's last symphony, Op. 125.[35]

Allegro ma non troppo	88 = ♩
Molto vivace	116 = ♩.
Presto	116 = ♩.
Adagio tempo 1mo	60 = ♩
Andante moderato	63 = ♩
Finale presto[36]	96 = ♩.
Allegro ma non troppo	88 = ♩
Allegro assai	80 = ♩
Alla Marcia	84 = ♩.
Andante maestoso	72 = ♩
Adagio divoto	60 = ♩
Allegro energico	84 = ♩.
Allegro ma non tanto	120 = ♩
Prestissimo	132 = ♩
Maestoso	60 = ♩

Schindler relates[37] that Beethoven on March 24 whispered to him, "write

[34] For the corrected reading of the postscript the present editor is indebted to Ley's version, which is based on the autograph: *Beethoven als Freund der Familie Wegeler— v. Breuning*, p. 234.

[35] To here in Schindler's hand, according to Ley (*loc.cit.*), the rest in another hand. After the first tempo mark there is added, apparently by Moscheles, "e un poco maestoso"; the "1mo" after "Adagio tempo" is crossed out and the words "molto e cantabile" substituted.

[36] In a letter to Schott on October 13, 1826, this section is given the mark "66=♩."

[37] *Biogr.*, II, p. 141.

to Smart and Stumpff," and that he would have done so on the morrow
had Beethoven been able to sign his name.

The history of the Philharmonic Society's benefaction may properly be
completed at this point. The money, as is to be seen from Beethoven's
acknowledgement, was collected by the composer at once. Herr Rau, of
the banking house of Eskeles to whom it had been entrusted, called upon
Beethoven immediately on receiving advices from London. It was on March
15, and two days later he enclosed Beethoven's receipt (dated March 16) in
a letter to Moscheles which the latter transmitted to Mr. W. Watts, Secretary
of the Philharmonic Society. Rau writes:

I have with the greatest surprise heard from you, who reside in London, that
the universally admired Beethoven is so dangerously ill and in want of pecuniary
assistance, while we, here at Vienna, are totally ignorant of it. I went to him immediately after having read your letter to ascertain his state, and to announce to
him the approaching relief. This made a deep impression upon him, and called
forth true expressions of gratitude. What a satisfactory sight would it have been
for those who so generously relieved him to witness such a touching scene! I
found poor Beethoven in a sad way, more like a skeleton than a living being.
He is suffering from dropsy, and has already been tapped four times; he is under
the care of our clever physician Malfatti, who unfortunately gives little hope of his
recovery.

How long he may remain in his present state, or if he can at all be saved, can
not yet be ascertained. The joyous sensation at the sudden relief from London
has, however, had a wonderful effect upon him; it made one of the wounds
(which since the last operation had healed) suddenly burst open during the night,
and all the water which had gathered since a fortnight ran out freely. When I
came to see him on the following day he was in remarkably good spirits and felt
himself much relieved. I hastened to Malfatti to inform him of this alteration and
he considers the event as very consolatory. He will contrive to keep the wound
open for some time and thus leave a channel for the water which gathers continually. Beethoven is fully satisfied with his attendants, who consist of a cook
and housemaid. His friend and ours, Mr. Schindler, dines with him every day
and thus proves his sincere attachment to him. S. also manages his correspondence
and superintends his expenses. You will find enclosed a receipt from Beethoven
for the 1,000 florins (or 100 pounds). When I proposed to him to take half of
the sum at present, and to leave the rest with Baron Eskeles, where he might
have it safely deposited, he acknowledged to me openly that he considered this
money as a relief sent him from heaven; and that 500 florins would not suffice for
his present want. I therefore gave him, according to his wish, the whole sum
at once, Beethoven will soon address a letter to the Philharmonic Society by which
he means to express his gratitude. I hope you will again accept my services whenever they can be of any use to Beethoven. I am, etc.

In a letter, dated March 24, Schindler wrote to Moscheles:[38]

. . . In short, care and anxiety vanished at once when the money arrived, and he
said quite happily, "Now we can again look forward to a comfortable day once

[38] The correct reading of these excerpts is drawn from Ley, op.cit., pp. 236-37.

in awhile"; for there were only 340 fl. V.S. left in the cash-box, and we had economized for some time in the amount of beef and vegetables, which, more than anything else, made him suffer. The other day, it was Friday, his favorite dish of fish was cooked so that he could nibble from it. In short, his delight on receiving this noble gift from the Phil. Society resembled that of a child. Also a large so-called easy-chair had to be procured, which cost 30 f. V.S. in which he could stay at least a half hour per day so that his bed could be properly made up . . . whatever remains of the 1000 f. we want to apply towards a respectable burial, without commotion, in the . . . [churchyard[39]] at Döbling where he ever delighted to roam. . . . Two days after your letter there came one from the worthy H. Stumpf, who also praised yours in the highest terms, all of which affected Beethoven so much. . . . Numerous times during the day he exclaimed, "May God reward them all a thousandfold."

Baron Pasqualati, Beethoven's old friend, in whose house he had lived for a long time, also made an effort to contribute to the composer's physical comfort and well-being. There are several little letters in which Beethoven acknowledges the receipt of contributions from his cellar and larder. One of these has been endorsed by a strange hand as having been sent or received on March 6. It reads:

Most honored old friend!

Hearty thanks for your health-gift; as soon as I have found out which of the wines is the most suitable I will let you know, but I shall abuse your kindness as little as possible. I am rejoicing in the expectation of the compotes and will appeal to you often for them—Even this costs me an exertion—*Sapienta pauca*—Your grateful friend

Beethoven

And a little while afterwards he writes:

Honored friend!

I beg you again today for a cherry compote, but without lemons, entirely simple; also I should be glad to have a light pudding, almost like gruel—my good cook is not yet adept in food for the sick. I am allowed to drink *champagne*, but for the time being please send a champagne glass with it—Now as regards the wine: at first Malfatti wanted it to be only Moselle, but he asserted that there was none genuine to be obtained here. He therefore himself gave me several bottles of Krumpholz-Kirchner† and claims that this is the best for my health since no Moselle is to be had.—Pardon me for being a burden and ascribe it to my helpless condition.

Most respectfully your friend

Beethoven

Others who sent him gifts of wine were Streicher and Breuning, and, as we see from the above letter, Malfatti himself. Why should the doctors any

---

[39] Here there is a hole in the autograph. The English translation of this letter in Moscheles's *The Life of Beethoven* (II, p. 321) supplies the word "churchyard."

† Gumpoldskirchner, a wine made near Vienna. See *A*, III, p. 1343, n. 1.

more deny him what he liked; his days were numbered. Concerning the last few days of his life the Conversation Books provide no clue.

Beethoven's preoccupation with the works of Handel has already been mentioned. He also received great pleasure from the compositions of Schubert with which he became acquainted through Schindler. ⸺{In the first edition of his biography Schindler writes:[40] "And how much Beethoven respected the talent of gifted Franz Schubert, which he really began to know only on his final sick-bed because previously certain people had lacked trust in him and belittled his name! After he had come through me to know the 'Ossian's Gesänge,' 'Die Bürgschaft,' 'Die junge Nonne,' 'Die Grenzen der Menschkeit' etc., he cried out with inner emotion, 'Truly a divine spark dwells in Schubert!' "}⸺

Schindler at one time had expressed the opinion that Schubert was a greater song-composer than Beethoven and excited criticism thereby. As a defense of his opinion he wrote an article which was published in the *Theaterzeitung* (May 3, 1831):

"As the illness to which Beethoven finally succumbed after four months of suffering from the beginning made his ordinary mental activity impossible, a diversion had to be thought of which would fit his mind and inclinations. And so it came about that I placed before him a collection of Schubert's songs, about 60 in number, among them many which were then still in manuscript. This was done not only to provide him with a pleasant entertainment, but also to give him an opportunity to get acquainted with Schubert in his essence in order to get from him a favorable opinion of Schubert's talent, which had been impugned, as had that of others by some of the exalted ones. The great master, who before then had not known five songs of Schubert's, was amazed at their number and refused to believe that up to that time (February, 1827) he had already composed over 500 of them. But if he was astonished at the number he was filled with the highest admiration as soon as he discovered their contents. For several days he could not separate himself from them, and every day he spent hours with Iphigenia's monologue, 'Die Grenzen der Menschheit,' 'Die Allmacht,' 'Die junge Nonne,' 'Viola,' the 'Müllerlieder,' and others. With joyous enthusiasm he cried out repeatedly: 'Truly, a divine spark dwells in Schubert; if I had had this poem I would have set it to music'; this in the case of the majority of poems whose material contents and original treatment by Schubert he could not praise sufficiently. Nor could he understand how Schubert had time to 'take in hand such long poems, many of which contained ten others,' as he expressed it. . . . What would the master have said had he seen, for instance, the Ossianic songs, 'Die Bürgschaft,' Elysium,' 'Der Taucher' and other great ones which have only recently been published? In short, the respect which Beethoven acquired for Schubert's talent was so great that he now wanted to see his operas and pianoforte pieces; but his illness had now become so

[40] Page 256.

severe that he could no longer gratify this wish. But he often spoke of Schubert and predicted of him that he 'would make a great sensation in the world,' and often regretted that he had not learned to know him earlier."

The remark about Schubert recorded in both of Schindler's writings was evidently made more than once. In a letter from Anslem Hüttenbrenner to Ferdinand Luib of February 21, 1858, we find: "Beethoven said of Schubert one day: 'That man has the divine spark!' "[41] In another letter to Luib written two days later, Hüttenbrenner writes:[42] "But this I know positively, that about eight days before Beethoven's death Prof. Schindler, Schubert and I visited the sick man. Schindler announced us two and asked Beethoven whom he would see first. He said: 'Let Schubert come first!' "

Another incident recorded about Beethoven by Gerhard von Breuning deserves to be told here:[43] "One time, as so often happened when I came, I found him sleeping. I sat down on the bed, keeping quiet in order not to awaken him from a sleep that was hopefully giving him strength. I turned the pages of a Conversation Book that was lying on the bed still in use in order to find out who had been here during that time and what had been said. And I found there among other things the entry: 'Your Quartet which Schuppanzigh played yesterday did not please'—When he awoke a short time later, I held this passage before his eyes and asked him what he had to say about it. 'It will please them some day' was the laconic reply which he gave me and to clinch the argument he added knowingly that he wrote only as he thought best and would not permit himself to be deceived by the judgement of the day, ending: 'I know that I am an artist.' "

On March 20, Beethoven signed a document with Schindler and Stephan von Breuning which handed over to Schott the sole copyright and ownership of the C-sharp minor Quartet, Op. 131. It was enclosed in Schindler's letter to Schott of April 12th. On March 21st Beethoven wrote the final appeal to Stieglitz and Co., already mentioned, for the sum of 125 ducats owed him by Prince Galitzin.

In a letter which Schindler wrote to Moscheles, forwarding Beethoven's, he said: "Hummel and his wife are here; he came in haste to see Beethoven once again alive, for it is generally reported in Germany that he is on his deathbed. It was a most touching sight last Thursday to see these two friends meet again."[44] The letter was written on March 14 and the "last Thursday" was March 8th. We have an account of this meeting in Ferdinand Hiller's "Aus dem Ton-Leben unserer Zeit."[45] Hiller was then fifteen years old and had come to the Austrian capital with Hummel, who was his teacher. Hummel had heard in Weimar that Beethoven was hopelessly ill and had

---

[41] See O. E. Deutsch, *Memoirs of Schubert* (New York, 1958), p. 66.

[42] This letter was among Mr. Thayer's papers. (TDR, v, 480.) See Deutsch, *loc.cit.*

[43] *Aus dem Schwarzspanierhause*, p. 95.

[44] See Ley, *op.cit.*, p. 230.

[45] *Neue Folge* (Leipzig, 1871), pp. 169ff. (TDR, v, 481, n. 1.)

(TDR, v, 480, n. 1.)

reached Vienna on March 6; two days later he visited his dying friend. Hiller writes:

"Through a spacious anteroom in which high cabinets were piled with thick, tied-up parcels of music we reached—how my heart beat!—Beethoven's living-room, and were not a little astonished to find the master sitting in apparent comfort at the window. He wore a long, gray sleeping-robe, open at the time, and high boots reaching to his knees.[46] Emaciated by long and severe illness he seemed to me, when he arose, of tall stature; he was unshaven, his thick, half-gray hair fell in disorder over his temples. The expression of his features heightened when he caught sight of Hummel, and he seemed to be extraordinarily glad to meet him. The two men embraced each other most cordially. Hummel introduced me. Beethoven showed himself extremely kind and I was permitted to sit opposite him at the window. It is known that conversation with Beethoven was carried on in part in writing; he spoke, but those with whom he conversed had to write their questions and answers. For this purpose thick sheets of ordinary writing-paper in quarto form and lead-pencils always lay near him. How painful it must have been for the animated, easily impatient man to be obliged to wait for every answer, to make a pause in every moment of conversation, during which, as it were, thought was condemned to come to a standstill! He always followed the hand of the writer with hungry eyes and comprehended what was written at a glance instead of reading it. The liveliness of the conversation naturally interfered with the continual writing of the visitor—I can scarcely blame myself, much as I regret it, for not taking down more extended notes than I did; indeed, I rejoice that a lad of fifteen years who found himself in a great city for the first time, was self-possessed enough to regard any details. I can vouch with the best conscience for the perfect accuracy of all that I am able to repeat.

"The conversation at first turned, as is usual, on domestic affairs,—the journey and sojourn, my relations with Hummel and matters of that kind. Beethoven asked about Goethe's health with extraordinary solicitude and we were able to make the best of reports, since only a few days before the great poet had written in my album. Concerning his own state, poor Beethoven complained much. 'Here I have been lying for four months,' he cried out, 'one must at last lose patience!' Other things in Vienna did not seem to be to his liking and he spoke with the utmost severity of 'the present taste in art,' and 'the dilettantism which is ruining everything.' Nor did he spare the government, up to the most exalted regions. 'Write a volume of penitential hymns and dedicate it to the Empress,' he remarked with a gloomy smile to Hummel, who, however, made no use of the well-meant advice. Hummel, who was a practical man, took advantage of Beethoven's condition

[46] Hüttenbrenner told Thayer that when Hummel came, Beethoven said, "I cannot receive him in bed," immediately got up, put on a sleeping robe, and received him with due respect. (TDR, v, 481, n. 2.)

to ask his attention to a matter which occupied a long time. It was about the theft of one of Hummel's concertos, which had been printed illicitly before it had been brought out by the lawful publisher. Hummel wanted to appeal to the Bundestag against this wretched business, and to this end desired to have Beethoven's signature, which seemed to him of great value. He sat down to explain the matter in writing and meanwhile I was permitted to carry on the conversation with Beethoven. I did my best, and the master continued to give free rein to his moody and passionate utterances in the most confidential manner. In part they referred to his nephew, whom he had loved greatly, who, as is known, caused him much trouble and at that time, because of a few trifles (thus Beethoven at least seemed to consider them), had gotten into trouble with the officials. 'Little thieves are hanged, but big ones are allowed to go free!' he exclaimed ill-humoredly. He asked about my studies and, encouraging me, said: 'Art must be propagated ceaselessly,' and when I spoke of the exclusive interest in Italian opera which then prevailed in Vienna, he gave utterance to the memorable words: 'It is said *vox populi, vox dei*. I never believed it.'

"On March 13 Hummel took me with him a second time to Beethoven. We found his condition to be materially worse. He lay in bed, seemed to suffer great pains, and at intervals groaned deeply despite the fact that he spoke much and animatedly. Now he seemed to take it much to heart that he had not married. Already at our first visit he had joked about it with Hummel, whose wife he had known as a young and beautiful maiden. 'You are a lucky man,' he said to him now smilingly, 'you have a wife who takes care of you, who is in love with you—but poor me!' and he sighed heavily. He also begged of Hummel to bring his wife to see him, she not having been able to persuade herself to see in his present state the man whom she had known at the zenith of his powers. A short time before he had received a present of a picture of the house in which Haydn was born. He kept it close at hand and showed it to us. 'It gave me a childish pleasure,' he said, 'the cradle of so great a man!' Then he appealed to Hummel in behalf of Schindler, of whom so much was spoken afterwards. 'He is a good man,' he said, 'who has taken a great deal of trouble on my account. He is to give a concert soon at which I promised my cooperation. But now nothing is likely to come of that. Now I should like to have you do me the favor of playing. We must always help poor artists.' As a matter of course, Hummel consented. The concert took place—ten days after Beethoven's death—in the Josephstadt-Theater. Hummel improvised in an obviously exalted mood on the Allegretto of the A major Symphony; the public knew why he participated and the performance and its reception formed a truly inspiring incident.

"Shortly after our second visit the report spread throughout Vienna that the Philharmonic Society of London had sent Beethoven £100 in order to ease his sick-bed. It was added that this surprise had made so great an impression on the great poor man that it had also brought physical relief. When we stood again at his bedside, on the 20th, we could deduce from his utterances how greatly he had been rejoiced by this altruism; but he was very weak and spoke only in faint and disconnected phrases. 'I shall, no doubt, soon be going above,' he whispered after our first greeting. Similar remarks recurred frequently. In the intervals, however, he spoke of projects and hopes which were destined not to be realized. Speaking of the noble conduct of the Philharmonic Society and in praise of the English people, he expressed the intention, as soon as matters were better with him, to undertake the journey to London. 'I will compose a grand overture for them and a grand symphony.' Then, too, he would visit Madame Hummel (she had come along with her husband) and go to I do not know how many places. It did not occur to us to write anything for him. His eyes, which were still lively when we saw him last, dropped and closed to-day and it was difficult from time to time for him to raise himself. It was no longer possible to deceive one's self—the worst was to be feared.

"Hopeless was the picture presented by the extraordinary man when we sought him again on March 23rd. It was to be the last time. He lay, weak and miserable, sighing deeply at intervals. Not a word fell from his lips; sweat stood upon his forehead. His handkerchief not being conveniently at hand, Hummel's wife took her fine cambric handkerchief and dried his face several times. Never shall I forget the grateful glance with which his broken eye looked upon her."

The consultations between Beethoven and his legal advisers, Bach, Breuning and others, concerning the proper disposition of his estate by will, which had begun soon after Karl's departure for Iglau, had not been brought to a conclusion when it became apparent to all that it was high time that the document be formally executed. Dr. Bach does not seem to have been consulted at this crisis; haste was necessary, and on March 23 von Breuning made a draft of a will which, free from unnecessary verbiage, set forth the wishes of the testator in three lines of writing. Beethoven had protested against the proposition of his friends that provision be made that Karl should not be able to dissipate the capital or surrender any portion of it to his mother. To this end a trust was to be created and he was to have the income during life, the reversion being to his legitimate heirs. With this Beethoven declared himself at length satisfied; but when Breuning placed the draft before the dying man, who had yielded unwillingly, he copied it laboriously but substituted the words "natural" for "legitimate." Schindler says[47] the copying was a labor, and when Beethoven finished it and appended the signature he said: "There; now I'll write no more." Breuning called his attention to the fact that controversy would ensue from his change in the text, but Beethoven insisted that the words meant the same thing and there should be no change. "This," said Schindler, "was his last contradiction."

[47] *Biogr.*, II, pp. 146-47. (TDR, v, 484, n. 1.)

Hiller's description of the last visit of Hummel pictures the condition of the dying man on this day, and Schindler's statement that it was laborious for Beethoven to copy even the few words of the will is pathetically verified by the orthography of the document which, *verb. et lit.*, is as follows:[48]

Mein Nefffe Karl Soll allein Erbe sein, das Kapital meines Nachlalasses soll jedoch Seinen natürlichen oder Testamentarischschen Erben zufallen—

Wien am März 1827
luwig van Beethoven

According to Gerhard von Breuning,[49] signatures were necessary to several documents—the will, the transfer of the guardianship of the nephew to von Breuning and the letter of January 3, which also made a testamentary disposition of Beethoven's property. These signatures were all obtained with great difficulty. After von Breuning, Schindler and the dying man's brother had indicated to Beethoven, who lay in a half-stupor, that his signature was required, they raised him as much as possible and pushed pillows under him for support. Then the documents, one after the other, were laid before him and von Breuning put the inked pen in his hand. "The dying man, who ordinarily wrote boldly in a lapidary style, repeatedly signed his immortal name, laboriously, with trembling hand, for the last time; still legibly, indeed, but each time forgetting one of the middle letters—once an *h*, another time an *e*."

On the day which saw the signing of the will, Beethoven made an utterance, eminently characteristic of him. The date is fixed as March 23rd by Schindler's letter to Moscheles of March 24th[50] in which he says: "He feels the end coming for yesterday he said to me and H. v. Breuning, 'Plaudite, amici, comoedia finita est.' "[51] ―Gerhard von Breuning writes of this scene:[52] "At the time of my visit to Bockenheim, Schindler told me that Beethoven had called out these words as the doctors were taking their leave after a long consultation, and my memory affirms this reminiscence positively.[53] I recollected most definitely that my father, Schindler and I were present when he spoke the words, and that he expressed these words in his favorite sarcastic-humorous manner as though to imply: nothing can be done. . . ."―

When Beethoven's friends saw the end approaching, they were naturally desirous that he receive the spiritual comfort which the offices of the Roman

---

[48] The editor has followed the reading of Max Unger. See "Beethovens letzte Briefe und Unterschriften" in *DM*, Vol. 34, No. 5 (1942), p. 157.

[49] *Aus dem Schwarzspanierhause*, pp. 105-107.

[50] Ley, *op.cit.*, pp. 235-37.

[51] A common closing line in classical Roman comedy.

[52] *Op.cit.*, pp. 104-105.

[53] Breuning emphasized the date and the occasion to refute a statement in Dr. Wawruch's report and in Schindler's letter to *Cäcilia* (April 12, 1827) that the remark was made after taking the sacrament on March 24. Wawruch was not present; and Schindler, who was there, had already written to Moscheles that it was on March 23rd. In his letter to *Cäcilia* Schindler does not write of the remark on March 24th as one *repeated* from the day before, when it is known to have been made. (Cf. TK, III, 304-305.)

Catholic church offer to the dying, and it was equally natural that Beethoven, brought up as a child of the Church though careless of his duties towards it, should, at the last, be ready to accept them. Johann van Beethoven relates that a few days after the 16th of March, when the physicians gave him up for lost, he had begged his brother to make his peace with God, to which request he had acceded "with the greatest readiness." Confirmation of this is found in Dr. Wawruch's report. Wawruch, it will be remembered, had, at the beginning of his studies, intended to enter the priesthood. At the crisis described by Johann he says he called Beethoven's attention to his impending dissolution "so that he might do his duty as a citizen and to religion." He continues: "With the greatest delicacy I wrote the words of admonition on a sheet of paper (for only so were we able to communicate one to another). Beethoven read the writing with unexampled composure, slowly and thought- fully, his countenance like that of one transfigured; cordially and solemnly he held out his hand to me and said: 'Have the priest called.' Then he lay quietly lost in thought and amiably indicated by a nod his 'I shall soon see you again.'"

Schindler's account, in a letter to the *Cäcilia* dated April 12, 1827, and printed in that journal in May, is as follows: ". . . As the business of the will had been settled, so far as was possible, the previous day, there remained with us only one ardent wish—to reconcile him with heaven and to show the world at the same time that he had ended his life a true Christian. The Professor in Ordinary [Wawruch] therefore wrote and begged him in the name of all his friends to receive the Holy Sacrament; to which he replied quietly and firmly [*gefasst*], 'I wish it.' The physician went away and left us to care for it."

In 1860 Hüttenbrenner wrote:[54] "It is not true, as has been reported, that I begged Beethoven to receive the sacrament for the dying; but I did bring it about at the request of the wife of the music-publisher Tobias Haslinger, now deceased, that Beethoven was asked in the gentlest manner by Herr Johann Baptist Jenger and Frau van Beethoven, wife of the landowner, to strengthen himself by receiving Holy Communion. . . . On the day of her brother-in-law's death Frau v. Beethoven told me that after receiving the viaticum he said to the priest, 'I thank you, ghostly sir! You have brought me comfort!'"

Hüttenbrenner is confirmed by Johann van Beethoven, who wrote in his brief review of his brother's last illness that when the priest was leaving the room Beethoven said to him, "I thank you for this last service." According to Nohl,[55] Beethoven received the viaticum in the presence of Schindler, von Breuning, Jenger and Therese, the wife of his brother Johann.

About one o'clock on March 24th the special shipment of wine and wine

---

[54] In a letter to Thayer which was found among Hüttenbrenner's posthumous papers and printed in the "Gratzer Tagespost" of October 23, 1868. (TDR, v, 488, n. 3.)

[55] *Beethoven*, III, p. 783. Nohl gives no sources. (TDR, v, 489, n. 2.)

mixed with herbs came from Mainz, and Schindler placed the bottles upon the table near the bed. Beethoven looked at them and murmured, "Pity, pity—too late!" He spoke no more. A little of the wine was administered to him in spoonfuls at intervals, as long as he could swallow it. Towards evening he lost consciousness and the death-struggle began. It lasted two days. "From towards the evening of the 24th to his last breath he was almost continually *in delirio*," wrote Schindler to Moscheles.[56] We have a description from Gerhard von Breuning:[57] "During the next day and the day following the strong man lay completely unconscious, in the process of dissolution, breathing so stertorously that the rattle could be heard at a distance. His powerful frame, his unweakened lungs, fought like giants with approaching death. The spectacle was a fearful one. Although it was known that the poor man suffered no more it was yet appalling to observe that the noble being, now irredeemably a prey to the powers of dissolution, was beyond all mental communication. It was expected as early as the 25th that he would pass away in the following night; yet we found him still alive on the 26th—breathing, if that was possible, more stertorously than on the day before."

Anselm Hüttenbrenner, who was a witness of Beethoven's death, writes:[58] "When I entered Beethoven's bedroom on March 26, 1827 at about 3 o'clock in the afternoon, I found there Court Councillor Breuning, his son, Frau van Beethoven, wife of Johann van Beethoven, landowner and apothecary of Lenz, and my friend Joseph Teltscher, portrait painter. I think that Prof. Schindler was also present."

Gerhard von Breuning says that Beethoven's brother was in the room, and also the housekeeper Sali; Schindler adds a nurse from Dr. Wawruch's clinic. No doubt all were present at one moment or another; they came and went as occasion or duty called. Hüttenbrenner says that Teltscher began drawing the face of the dying man, which grated on Breuning's feelings and he made a remonstrance, whereupon the painter left the room. Then Breuning and Schindler went away to choose a spot for the grave. Hüttenbrenner continues: "Frau van Beethoven and I only were in the death-chamber during the last moments of Beethoven's life. After Beethoven had lain unconscious, the death-rattle in his throat from 3 o'clock in the afternoon till after 5, there came a flash of lightning accompanied by a violent clap of thunder, which garishly illuminated the death-chamber. (Snow lay before Beethoven's dwelling.) After this unexpected phenomenon of nature, which startled me greatly, Beethoven opened his eyes, lifted his right hand and looked up for several seconds with his fist clenched and a very serious, threatening expression as if he wanted to say: 'Inimical powers, I defy you! Away with you! God is with me!' It also seemed as if, like a brave commander, he wished to call out to his wavering troops: 'Courage, soldiers!

---

[56] On April 4, 1827. See Ley, *op.cit.*, p. 239.   [58] In a letter to Thayer dated August 20,
[57] *Aus dem Schwarzspanierhause*, p. 108.   1860. (TDR, v, 490, n. 1.)
(TDR, v, 489.)

Forward! Trust in me! Victory is assured!'[59] When he let the raised hand sink to the bed, his eyes closed half-way. My right hand was under his head, my left rested on his breast. Not another breath, not a heartbeat more! The genius of the great master of tones fled from this world of delusion into the realm of truth!—I pressed down the half-open eyelids of the dead man, kissed them, then his forehead, mouth and hands.—At my request Frau van Beethoven cut a lock of hair from his head and handed it to me as a sacred souvenir of Beethoven's last hour. Thereupon I hurried, deeply moved, into the city, carried the intelligence of Beethoven's death to Herr Tobias Haslinger, and after a few hours returned to my home in Styria."

—⚶It is not clear that Hüttenbrenner was accurate in his identification of his companion at the death scene. Two months before writing the above, he had referred to the woman in question as "Karl's mother."[60] But Thayer learned from Karl's wife that his mother "could not have been present at Beethoven's death, as it was a matter of complaint with her that no news of his dying condition reached her until after all was over. Dr. Breuning also thinks that she could not have been there, for he has no recollection of ever having seen either of the sisters-in-law of Beethoven." Stephan Ley[61] suggests logically that the other person was the maid, Sali, whom Hüttenbrenner mistook for "Frau van Beethoven."⚶—

When Breuning and Schindler left the dying man in the care of Hüttenbrenner and "Frau van Beethoven," they went to the cemetery of the little village of Währing, and selected a place for Beethoven's grave in the vicinity of the burial plot of the Vering family, to which Breuning's first wife had belonged. Their return was retarded by the storm. When they reentered the sick-room they were greeted with the words: "It is finished!" The immediate activities of the friends were now directed to preparations for the funeral, the preservation of the physical likeness of the great composer and, so far as necessary, the safeguarding of his possessions. In respect of the latter Gerhard von Breuning tells of a painful incident which happened on the day after Beethoven's death.

Breuning, Schindler, Johann van Beethoven and Holz were met in the lodgings to gather up the dead man's papers, particularly to look for the

[59] Thayer visited Hüttenbrenner in Graz in June, 1860. The transcript in Thayer's notebook of Hüttenbrenner's oral recital is more sententious and dramatic: "At this startling, awful peal of thunder, the dying man suddenly raised his head from Hüttenbrenner's arm, stretched out his own right arm majestically—'like a general giving orders to an army.' This was but for an instant; the arm sunk back; he fell back; Beethoven was dead." (TK, III, 307, n. 2; 308, n. 1.)

[60] See H. E. Krehbiel, *Music and Manners in the Classical Period* (New York, 1898), p. 204. Krehbiel has published in this book

the complete transcript of Hüttenbrenner's remarks to Thayer in June, 1860. (Cf. TK, III, 307, n. 2.)

[61] *Wahrheit, Zweifel und Irrtum in der Kunde von Beethovens Leben* (Wiesbaden, 1955), pp. 41-2. Here Ley also discusses the close of a short piece by Johann on his brother's last sickness and death, now in the Beethovenhaus in Bonn. It is not known for whom Johann wrote, but his claim that Beethoven died in his arms is in direct contradiction to Hüttenbrenner's account. Ley believes it was a fabrication; Johann's vanity from the fame of his brother was well known.

seven bank-shares which the will had given to the nephew. In spite of strenuous search they were not found, and Johann let fall an insinuation that the search was a sham. This angered von Breuning and he left the house in a state of vexation and excitement. He returned to the lodgings in the afternoon and the search was resumed. Then Holz pulled out a protruding nail in a cabinet, whereupon a drawer fell out and in it were the certificates. In later years Holz explained to Otto Jahn: "Beethoven kept his bank-shares in a secret drawer, the existence of which was known only to Holz. While Beethoven lay dying his brother in vain tried to find out where it was." On a copy of this memorandum,[62] Schindler wrote: "First of all after the death, Johann van Beethoven searched for the shares, and not finding them cried out: 'Breuning and Schindler must produce them!' Holz was requested to come by Breuning and asked if he did not know where they were concealed. He knew the secret drawer in an old cabinet[63] in which they were preserved." With the certificates were found the letter to the "Immortal Beloved" and the portrait of the Countess von Brunsvik.[64]

On March 27th, an autopsy[65] was performed by Dr. Johann Wagner in the presence of Dr. Wawruch. In order to facilitate an examination of the organs of hearing, the temporal bones were sawed out and carried away. Joseph Danhauser, a young painter who chanced to be in Vienna, received permission from Breuning to make a plaster cast of the dead man's face. This he did on March 28, but the cast has little value as a portrait, inasmuch as it was made after the autopsy, which had greatly disfigured the features. On the same day, Danhauser made a drawing of the head of Beethoven, which he reproduced by lithographic process. This picture bears the inscription: "Beethoven, March 28, drawn at his death-bed, 1827," and to the left, "Danhauser." This drawing, too, was made after the autopsy. For a bust which he modeled, the artist made use of the cast taken by Klein in 1812. Danhauser never came in contact with Beethoven alive.

The funeral took place at 3 o'clock in the afternoon of March 29th. It was one of the most imposing functions of its kind ever witnessed in Vienna.[66] Breuning and Schindler had made the arrangements. Cards of invitation were given out at Haslinger's music-shop. ⋯⊱{In the Archives of the Vienna Supreme Court there is a document containing a full account of Beethoven's funeral. The material was transcribed by Andreas Zeller, "bürgl. Magistradtischer Konducktansager des bürgl. Grundt Alservorstadt und Breidenfeld" (Director of ceremonies for Alservorstadt und Breitenfeld) and published by Robert Franz Müller:[67]

[62] Preserved among Thayer's papers. (TK, III, 310, n. 1.)

[63] Schindler writes "cash-box" (Biogr., I, p. 97); Breuning "writing-case" (Schwarzsp., p. 112). (TDR, v, 493, n. 1.)

[64] See Appendix C for list of Beethoven's estate.

[65] See Appendix B.

[66] See *Aus dem Schwarzspanierhause*, p. 113; Hiller's *Aus dem Tonleben*, pp. 177ff.; *Der Sammler*, April 14, 1827; Seyfried's *Beethovens Studien*, appendix, pp. 50ff. (TDR, v, 494, n. 2.)

[67] *Beethovens Begräbnis* in *Reichspost*, Vienna, March 26, 1925, p. 2.

"Beethoven died on Monday, March 26, 1827 about 5.45 P.M. Two men kept the death watch. On Tuesday morning Dr. Johann Wagner dissected the corpse. Then it was clothed and laid in a polished oak coffin which rested on ball-shaped gilded supports. On the cover was constructed a gilded cross. The head of the deceased, adorned with a wreath of white roses, rested on a white silk pillow. The face, framed with gray curls, was very lifeless because of the dissection. The folded hands grasped a wax cross and a large lily. And near the body a large lily was placed on the right side and on the left. Over the coffin was spread a coverlet half pulled back. The bier stood in the room in which he died, with his head facing the 'composition room' [music room]. There were eight candles burning on both sides of the coffin. On a table at the foot stood a crucifix and holy water for aspersion together with ears of corn. The good faithful Sali, the Master's maid, tirelessly received the many who wished to pay their last respects to the deceased.

"Thursday was the time of departure. Andreas Zeller, the director of ceremonies, had given out the last gate ticket on the day before. Around noon he stepped into the room and distributed to the invited guests rose bouquets with white silk stitches. They were placed on the left sleeve. Near 3 o'clock poems by Castelli and Seidl were given out as keepsakes.[68] In the morning by order of Breuning Mathias Mann with 5 others had cleaned the roomy court. In this area were gathered Barbaja's singers of the Italian Opera. Before 3 o'clock the house-gate was closed, the court filled to overflowing, and outside the crowd stormily demanded entrance. The military assistance from the Alser Barracks, procured by Breuning, was hardly able to ward off the crowd. Even the schools were closed.

"At 3 o'clock the coffin was closed, carried down and placed in the court. The pall, ordered by Anton Schindler from the 2nd Civil Regiment, was spread over the coffin, the cross was adorned with a 'very beautiful' wreath, and the Evangelical book and the 'very beautiful' civic crown set up. The contour of the coffin was hidden by a group of wreaths. Nine priests from the Schottenstifte blessed the dead. Thereupon Barbaja's court singers sang a funeral song: a chorale by B. Anselm Weber.[69] The singers were Eichenberger, Schuster, Cramolini, Müller, Hofmann, Rupprecht, Borschitzky, and Anton Wranitzky from the orchestra. These singers also carried the coffin into the church.[70] Now the door was opened; the crowd was so jammed that only with the greatest difficulty was the director of ceremonies and his helpers able to organise the procession. Even those standing near the deceased became pressed from their places of honor behind the coffin. From here hung down broad white silk bands. The ends of the pall (not the points) were taken by the eight Kapellmeister—to wit, Eybler, Hummel, Kreutzer, Seyfried on the right; Gänsbacher, Gyrowetz, Weigl, Würfel on the left—the honor escort

[68] See *Aus dem Schwarzspanierhause*, pp. 119-22.

[69] From his opera *Wilhem Tell*.

[70] Trinity Church of the Minorites in the Alserstrasse.

of the sleeping master. They carried candles wrapped in crepe. On both sides of the coffin came the torchbearers: Anschütz, Bernard, Blahetka, Joseph Böhm, Castelli, Karl Czerny, David, Grillparzer, Konrad Graf, Grünbaum, Haslinger, Hildebrandt, Holz, Kaller, Krall, Lannoy, Linke, Mayseder, Meric, Merk, Mechetti, Meier, Paccini, Piringer, Rodicchi, Raimund, Riotte, Schoberlechner, Schubert, Schickh, Schmiedl, Streicher, Schuppanzigh, Steiner, Weidmann, Wolfmayer, and others, with lily bouquets adorning their shoulders. The torches were decorated with flowers.

"Now the procession, which had been formed with so much trouble, started to move, beginning with the carriers of the crosses decorated with flowers. Members of welfare institutions followed. Behind them strode the trombonists: the Blöch brothers, Weidl and Tuschka. Then followed Assmayer's choir with the singers Tiebe, Schnitzer, Gros, Sykora, Frühwald, Geissler, Rathmayer, Kokrement, Nejebse, Ziegler, Perschl, Leidl, Pfeifer, Weinkopf and Seipelt. They sang the *Miserere*, the refrain of which was blown by the trombonists. This *Miserere* was the work specified as music for All-Souls' Day, which Beethoven had written at Linz in 1812 at Glöggl's request. During the evening of March 26th and 27th Seyfried arranged it for voices. *Amplius lava me*[71] was also sung. The parish crucifer was followed by the nine priests from the Schottenstifte, striding slowly before the coffin. The cross-carriers, priests, corporation, and director of ceremonies wore rose bouquets. Behind the coffin in the middle of the boisterous crowd followed Johann and Johanna [? Therese?] van Beethoven, Stephan and Gerhard v. Breuning, Hofrat v. Mosel, the students of Drechsler, Kapellmeister of St. Anna, the pupils of the Conservatory, and numerous friends and admirers of the deceased. At the end of the procession came the 'very lovely ceremonial carriage' pulled by 4 horses which had been ordered from the office of Kirchenmeister of St. Stephan Cathedral. Thus the procession reached the Alsergasse. Gerhard von Breuning (prone to exaggeration) estimated the crowd at 20,000; the *Sammler* at 10,000. When the procession turned into the Alsergasse, a brass band played the 'Marcia funebre' from Op. 26. The church was filled to capacity; the soldiers on duty did not want to admit anyone after the coffin had been carried in. The relatives and friends of the master succeeded only with difficulty to get inside the church. Those who had fainted from the pressure of the crowd were taken across to the hospital.

"The inside of the church shone with candle-light. Zeller's receipt for the cost of lighting the three main altars showed that the town wax dealer had supplied 6 1/2 lbs.[72] But Johann Wolfmayer had candles at all altars, wall brackets, and chandeliers lit at his own expense. The nine priests from the Schottenstifte sang the *Libera* by Seyfried. Then the bier was carried by the bearers, led by the trombonists and priests and followed by the funeral

---

[71] Also written by Beethoven for Glöggl and arranged for voices by Seyfried. The singers and trombonists alternated in the performance. See WoO 30, Nos. 1 and 3.

[72] Cf. with the receipts for wax listed by Ley, *Aus Beethovens Erdentagen*, pp. 239-40.

guests. It was taken through the nave and to the door. The ceremony was over.

"After the religious service the ceremonial carriage took the coffin. A part of the crowd was dispersed but thousands closed in on the procession going slowly along the hospital street. It crossed the Alserbach by the Namentur, passed by the almshouse and the brick-kiln, reached the Währing line, crossed it, reached the right bank of the Währing Brook and went along the brook to the village parish church. The minister, Johann Hayek and a second priest were waiting there. The procession stopped; the coffin was carried into the church and blessed by both of the priests, candles were burning on three altars. After the ceremony the parish singers sang the *Miserere* [motets] and the *Libera*. . . . Now the bearers again took the bier. Many people were still following the procession, the village school-children were there, supervised by the school assistants; then came the local poor people. Before the coffin went the priests, the sacristan, and the acolyte with the censer. The funeral guests followed the coffin accompanied by the prayer leader. The Währing master of ceremonies arranged the procession. With the brook on the right and a slope falling gently on the left, the funeral procession approached the fields of the parish cemetery[73] amid the sound of bells. Before the gates—the present gates were added later—the bearers put their load down. Before the coffin stepped the great tragedian, Heinrich Anschütz, and delivered the gripping obituary by Grillparzer.[74] Thereupon a poem by Schlechta was passed out. And now the great man joined the other dead. The priests consecrated the tomb and blessed the corpse for the last time. By the last light of the spring day the coffin was lowered into the earth. . . . Tobias Haslinger had brought three laurel wreaths which Hummel placed on the grave. According to an old custom, those standing near threw earth on the grave and the torches were extinguished."

In its report *Der Sammler* said: "The crowd was so great that after the roomy court of Beethoven's residence could no longer hold it the gates had to be closed until the procession moved. The coffin containing the corpse of the great composer had been placed on view in the court. After the clergy were come to perform their sacred office, the guests, who had been invited to attend these solemn functions—musicians, singers, poets, actors—all clad in complete mourning, with draped torches and white roses fastened to bands of crape on their sleeves, encircled the bier and the choristers sang the *Miserere* composed by the deceased. Solemnly, sublimely the pious tones of the glorious composition floated upwards through the silent air. The scene was imposing. The coffin, with its richly embroidered pall, the clergy, the distinguished men who were giving the last escort to their colleague, and the multitude round about—all this made a stupendous picture."

[73] Friedhof.   [74] See Appendix A.

On April 3rd Mozart's *Requiem* was sung at the Church of the Augustini-
is,[75] under the direction of Lablache. On April 5th a further observance
was made with a performance of the Cherubini *Requiem* at the Karlskirche.
The grave in the cemetery at Währing was marked by a simple pyramid
bearing the one word

BEETHOVEN

It fell into neglect, and on October 13th, 1863, the Gesellschaft der Musikfreunde of Vienna caused the body to be exhumed and reburied. On June
21st, 1888, the remains of Beethoven and Schubert were removed to the
Central Cemetery in Vienna, where they now repose side by side.

FINIS

[75] According to the report in Landau's *Erste poetische Beethoven-Album* (Prague, 1877), dated March 29, 1827, the *Miserere* and *Libera me* were again performed at the close of the performance by popular request. See Kerst, pp. 239-40.

APPENDIX A

FRANZ GRILLPARZER'S FUNERAL ORATION[1]

STANDING by the grave of him who has passed away we are in a manner the representatives of an entire nation, of the whole German people, mourning the loss of the one highly acclaimed half of that which was left us of the departed splendor of our native art, of the fatherland's full spiritual bloom. There yet lives—and may his life be long!—the hero of verse in German speech and tongue; but the last master of tuneful song, the organ of soulful concord, the heir and amplifier of Handel and Bach's, of Haydn and Mozart's immortal fame is now no more, and we stand weeping over the riven strings of the harp that is hushed.

The harp that is hushed! Let me call him so! For he was an artist, and all that was his, was his through art alone. The thorns of life had wounded him deeply, and as the cast-away clings to the shore, so did he seek refuge in thine arms, O thou glorious sister and peer of the Good and the True, thou balm of wounded hearts, heaven-born Art! To thee he clung fast, and even when the portal was closed wherethrough thou hadst entered in and spoken to him, when his deaf ear had blinded his vision for thy features, still did he ever carry thine image within his heart, and when he died it still reposed on his breast.

He was an artist—and who shall arise to stand beside him?

As the rushing behemoth spurns the waves, so did he rove to the uttermost bounds of his art. From the cooing of doves to the rolling of thunder, from the craftiest interweaving of well-weighed expedients of art up to that awful pitch where planful design disappears in the lawless whirl of contending natural forces, he had traversed and grasped it all. He who comes after him will not continue him; he must begin anew, for he who went before left off only where art leaves off. Adelaide and Leonora! Triumph of the heroes of Vittoria—and the humble sacrificial song of the Mass!—Ye children of the voices divided thrice and four times! heaven-soaring harmony: "Freude, schöner Götterfunken," thou swansong! Muse of song and the seven-stringed lyre! Approach his grave and bestrew it with laurel!

He was an artist, but a man as well. A man in every sense—in the highest. Because he withdrew from the world, they called him a man-hater, and because he held aloof from sentimentality, unfeeling. Ah, one who knows himself hard of heart, does not shrink! The finest points are those most

[1] This translation is drawn from *Beethoven—Impressions of Contemporaries* (G. Schirmer: New York, 1926), pp. 229-31, with a few minor changes to correspond with the version upon which it is based in Grillparzer's Collected Works Edition (see Franz Grillparzer [Gesammelte Werke, Vol. 5] *Autobiographisches Studien*, R. Backmann ed., pp. 420-22, Bergland, Vienna, 1952). A slightly different version of the poem is to be found in Gerhard von Breuning's *Aus dem Schwarzspanierhause*, pp. 116-19, from a copy which his father had received from the poet.

easily blunted and bent or broken. An excess of sensitiveness avoids a show of feeling! He fled the world because, in the whole range of his loving nature, he found no weapon to oppose it. He withdrew from mankind after he had given them his all and received nothing in return. He dwelt alone, because he found no second Self. But to the end his heart beat warm for all men, in fatherly affection for his kindred, for the world his all and his heart's blood.

Thus he was, thus he died, thus he will live to the end of time.

You, however, who have followed after us hitherward, let not your hearts be troubled! You have not lost him, you have won him. No living man enters the halls of the immortals. Not until the body has perished, do their portals unclose. He whom you mourn stands from now onward among the great of all ages, inviolate forever. Return homeward therefore, in sorrow, yet resigned! And should you ever in times to come feel the overpowering might of his creations like an onrushing storm, when your mounting ecstasy overflows in the midst of a generation yet unborn, then remember this hour, and think, We were there, when they buried him, and when he died, we wept.

APPENDIX B

AUTOPSY[1]

March 27, 1827

THE corpse was very emaciated, especially in the limbs, and sown over with black Petechien; the abdomen, which was unusually dropsied, was distended and stretched.

The external ear was large and irregularly formed, the scaphoid fossa but more especially the concha was very spacious and half as large again as usual: the various angles and sinuosities were strongly marked. The external auditory canal was covered with shining scales, particularly in the vicinity of the tympanum, which was concealed by them. The Eustachian tube was much thickened, its mucous lining swollen and somewhat contracted about the osseous portion of the tube. In front of its orifice and towards the tonsils some dimpled scars were observable. The principal cells of the Mastoid process, which was large and not marked by any notch, were lined with a vascular mucous membrane. The whole substance of the Os petrosum showed a similar degree of vascularity, being traversed by vessels of considerable size, more particularly in the region of the cochlea, the membranous part of its spiral lamina appearing slightly reddened.

The facial nerves were of unusual thickness, the auditory nerves, on the contrary, were shrivelled and destitute of neurina; the accompanying arteries were dilated to more than the size of a crow quill and cartilaginous. The left auditory nerve much the thinnest, arose by three very thin greyish striae, the right by one strong clearer white stria from the substance of the fourth ventricle, which was at this point much more consistent and vascular than in other parts. The convolutions of the brain were full of water, and remarkably white; they appeared very much deeper, wider, and more numerous than ordinary.

The Calvarium exhibited throughout great density and a thickness amounting to about half an inch.

The cavity of the Chest, together with the organs within it, was in the normal condition.

In the cavity of the Abdomen four quarts of a greyish-brown turbid fluid were effused.

The liver appeared shrunk up to half its proper volume, of a leathery consistence and greenish-blue color, and was beset with knots, the size of a bean, on its tuberculated surface, as well as in its substance; all its vessels were very much narrowed, and bloodless.

---

[1] See Waldemar Schweisheimer, *Beethovens Leiden* (Munich, 1922), pp. 185-86. See also Seyfried's *Beethoven: Studies*, translated by Henry H. Pierson (Leipzig, 1853), pp. 43-44 from which the major part of the translation was drawn.

The Spleen was found to be more than double its proper size, dark-colored and firm.

The Pancreas was equally hard and firm, its excretory duct being as wide as a goosequill.

The Stomach, together with the Bowels, was greatly distended with air. Both Kidneys were invested by cellular membrane of an inch thick, and infiltrated with a brown turbid fluid; their tissue was pale-red and opened out. Every one of their calices was occupied by a calcareous concretion of a wart-like shape and as large as a split pea. The body was much emaciated.[2]

(Signed) Dr. Joseph Wagner
Assistant in the Pathological Museum

[2] For a recent medical summary of Beethoven's case history, see S. J. London, M.D., "Beethoven, Case Report of a Titan's Last Crisis," *Archives of Internal Medicine*, Vol. 113 (1964), pp. 442-48.

APPENDIX C

BEETHOVEN'S ESTATE

1. LEGAL INVENTORY AND ASSESSMENT[1]
   ON AUGUST 16, 1827
of musical effects and books belonging to the estate of the musician Ludwig van Beethoven, deceased on March 26, 1827, in Vienna at the Schwarzspanier-haus No. 200.

Present:

Brandstätter (Ferdinand), Municipal Secretary
v. Ortowitz (Franz), Commissary ("Sperr-Commissär")
Ohmeyer, substituting for Dr. Bach as Trustee
Hotscherer (Jacob), R.I. "Hof-Concipist" and Guardian (of the nephew)
In addition
   to those especially invited hereto:
Czerny (Carl), composer and petitioned witness
Piringer (Ferdinand), R.I. "Hofkammer-Registr.-Dir.-Adjunct"
Haslinger (Tobias), licensed Art and Music dealer
And both treasurers
Artaria (Dominik), licensed Art and Music dealer
Sauer (Ignaz), former   "   "   "   "

Works Spoken For

For Count Lichnowsky
1 volume of Bach's Inventions and Preludes copied
6 volumes of Handel's works, bound

For H. Schindler
Mass by Beethoven in D written as 3 Hymns

Herr von Zmeskall
Gluck's Iphigenie auf Tauris
Orpheus und Eurydice is salable

Herr v. Kuffner
Text for a Cantata. 1st section. Saul kehrt nach glänzenden Siegen etc.

For the R.I. Court Theatre
Libretto to Fidelio
"   " der edelste Mann

---

[1] Thayer, *Chron. Verzeichniss*, pp. 173-82.

H. v. Piringer
Fux's Gradus ad Parnassum

Steiner and Co.
Complete original score of the 7th Symphony in A
Siegessymphonie von der Schlacht bei Vittoria. Original score
Finale of the 8th Symphony. F major
Der heilige Augenblick. Cantata in score
Parts for a Cantata written out and score for the choral director in 2 packages

---

Artaria and Co.
belonging to same because H. v. Beethoven had borrowed them.
6 volumes of Metastasio's works
Score of the ballet Prometheus
Rondo, primo Amore for voice
Trio for 2 oboes and English horn
Overture to Fidelio
Andante Vivace with song
Sonata for pianoforte

F. Starke, Kapellmeister
No. 175. Trifles for pianoforte for Starke's Klavierschule

No. 204. Reutter. Count Lichnowsky

AUCTION CATALOGUE

I

Beethoven's Own Notes and Notebooks

No.		Appraised Fl. Kr.		Sold Fl. Kr.	
1	Notes and notebooks	1	–	1	15
2	" " "	1	–	1	15
3	" " "	1	–	1	15
4	" " "	1	–	1	16
5	" " "	1	–	1	15
6	Notebook	1	–	1	15
7	"	1	–	1	30
8	Notes	1	–	1	25
9	"	1	–	1	15
10	" and sketches	1	–	1	15
11	Notebook	1	–	2	12

No.		Appraised Fl.	Kr.	Sold Fl.	Kr.
12	Notes and sketches	1	–	1	15
13	Notes	1	–	1	16
14	"	1	–	1	15
15	"	1	–	1	15
16	"	1	–	2	06
17	Notebook	1	–	2	50
18	Notes	1	–	1	22
19	"	1	–	1	30
20	"	1	–	2	10
21	Notebook	1	–	2	02
22	"	1	–	3	–
23	Notes	1	–		
24	Notebook	1	–	3	01
25	Notes	1	–		
26	"	1	–	1	30
27	"	1	–	1	30
28	Notebooks	1	–	2	10
29	Notebook	1	–	2	36
30	Notes	1	–		
				2	03
31	2 Notebooks	1	–		
32	Notebook	1	–	2	03
33	Notes	1	–	2	–
34	"	1	–	1	30
35	Notebook	1	–	2	44
36	Notes	1	–	1	30
37	"	1	–	1	15
38	"	1	–	1	15
39	Notes and Notebook	1	–	1	30
40	Notebook	1	–	2	–
41	Big notebook	1	–	2	–
42	Notes	1	–	1	–
43	Notebook and notes	1	–	1	–
44	"	1	–	1	30
45	2 Notebooks	1	–		
				2	30
46	Notes	1	–		
47	Notebook	1	–	1	10
48	Notes (Notirungen)	1	–	1	10
49	Notebook (Notirbuch)	1	–	1	10
50	Book of Notes (Notirungsbuch)	1	–	1	10
51	Prompter's part from the opera Fidelio, 2 acts, copy with notations in own hand	2	–	2	30

II

Used Sketches, Fragments and Works Unfinished In Part Still Unpublished and Written in Own Hand

No.		Appraised Fl.	Kr.	Sold Fl.	Kr.
52	Quartet sketches	2	–	2	36
53	Sketches	2	–	2	30
54	Quartet sketches	2	–	2	30
55	Completed sketches and pieces	3	–	3	30
56	Completed sketches	3	–	3	01
57	Quartet sketches	2	–	3	–
58	Italian Ariettes	2	–		
59	Sketches for a quintet still unknown	2	–	} 6	30
60	Used sketches	2	–		
61	Copy of the Pianoforte Trio Op. 1, arranged as a quintet anonymously	1	–	1	–
62	Copy of Trio No. 2	2	–	3	–
63	Mass sketches	2	–	3	–
64	Quartet sketches, bagatelles for p.-f.	2	–	2	30
65	Sketches for a Pianoforte Concerto	2	–		
				} 3	–
66	Bagatelles	2	–		
67	Vocal piece with orchestra completed but not wholly orchestrated	3	–	9	30
68	Song	1	–	1	16
69	Sextet	2	–	2	30
70	Original songs	3	–	3	30

III

Autographs of Printed Works

No.		Appraised Fl.	Kr.	Sold Fl.	Kr.
71	Sonate for Pianoforte	–	30	2	33
72	Manuscript printed by Simrock	1	–	1	24
73	2 pianoforte trios together in one copy belonging to Breitkopf	2	–	3	40
74	An die Hoffnung, song		20	1	30
75	Gesang der Nachtigal, song	–	10	1	–
76	Manuscript for pianoforte and other instruments, apparently Scottish songs	1	–	1	30
77	Quartet piece belonging to Schott		30	1	–
78	Quartet piece	1	–	3	03
79	" "	–	30	1	06
80	Finale of the Pastoral Symphony in score	1	30	2	06

No.		Appraised Fl. Kr.		Sold Fl. Kr.	
81	Score of the 4th Symphony 1st piece	1	30	5	–
82	A piece from the opera Fidelio in score	–	40	2	06
83	Abendlied	–	30	1	15
84	Fugue in a quartet	–	30	3	–
85	Fantasy-Sonata	–	45	1	40
86	Sonata for pianoforte and violin	–	45	2	59
87	Kyrie of the 1st Mass in score	1	–	1	24
88	March from Fidelio. Score	–	40	1	40
89	Pianoforte Concerto in E-Flat. Score	2	–	3	45
90	Variations for pianoforte	1	–	1	30
91	Sonata for p.-f. and violoncello	1	–	2	30
92	54th Sonata for pianof., not complete	–	30	–	36
93	Romance for violin. Score	–	30	3	45
94	Quartet piece	–	40	–	52
95	Violin-quartet piece, belonging evidently to Schlesinger	5	–	5	–
96	From Leonore a piece in score	–	20	–	24
97	4th Symphony in score	4	–	5	–
98	Scottish songs	–	40	1	–
99	Songs	–	40	–	48
100	Opferlied. Score	–	40	1	–
101	Sonata for pianoforte	1	–	1	30
102	Violin-quartet piece	4	–	4	–
103	Christus am Oelberg. Score	6	–	7	–
104	Gloria from the First Mass. Score	3	–	5	55
105	5th Symphony. Score	5	–	6	–
106	Andante from the Pastoral Symphony. Score	3	–	1	18
107	Bagatelles for pianoforte	1	–	2	03
108	Finale of the Concerto in E-Flat. Score	2	–	2	20
109	Festival overture in score	2	–	2	30
110	Quintet for violin	2	–	2	30
111	Pieces from Egmont	–	20	–	50
112	Quartet by Haydn in score, copied by Beethoven	–	40	1	–
113	Symphony in score	4	–	5	–
114	Fugue by Sebastian Bach transcribed for quartet by Beethoven	–	30	–	40
115	Concerto for Pianoforte in C major. Score	3	–	4	13
116	Sonata for Pianoforte in A-Flat	1	–	2	–
117	Fragment for a quartet	–	45	1	36
118	Finale of the Quartet in C-sharp minor	1	–	1	20
119	Quartet pieces	2	–	3	–
120	Sketches for a pianoforte sonata	1	–	2	05
121	Variations for pianoforte	1	20	2	–
122	Original score of the Septet	3	–	18	–
123	Quartet piece	–	40	1	–
124	Sonata for pianoforte and flute	1	–	1	30

No.		Appraised Fl. Kr.		Sold Fl. Kr.	
125	2nd Pianoforte Concerto in score	3	–	4	–
126	Last Mass in score	6	–	7	–
127	Quartet piece	–	40	1	–
128	Song to Chloe	–	30	1	06
129	Two Finales to the opera Leonore in score	4	–	5	–
130	Two quartet pieces	1	30	5	10
131	Two vocal pieces	1	–	2	48
132	Agnus Dei in score	1	30	2	–
133	Songs of Gellert	–	30	1	–
134	Songs of Goethe	–	30	1	20
135	Two sonatas for pianoforte	1	30	2	–
136	Piece from a sonata for p.-f. and violin	–	30	–	45
137	Entr'actes to Egmont	2	–	3	–
138	Sonata for pianoforte and violoncello	–	45	1	30
139	Quintet in E-Flat	1	–	2	30
140	Sonatas for pianoforte and violin	1	30	3	12
141	Concerted pieces (or concertos) for pianoforte	5	–	4	–
142	Der Wachtelschlag	–	30	2	–
143	Chorus from Die gute Nachricht	–	40	4	30
144	Copy in another hand of the Eroica Symphony in score with notations in own hand	3	–	3	10
145	Copy in another hand of the Overture to Egmont in score (1810)	1	–	1	09
146	Copy in another hand of the Chorus of Ruinen von Athen	–	40	1	–
147	Copy in another hand of the Triumphal March to Tarpeja in parts written out	1	–	1	45
148	Copy in another hand of the Choral Fantasy in score	1	–	1	20

IV

Remaining Original Manuscripts of Ludwig van Beethoven, Incomplete, Written in Own Hand, Not Yet Printed

No.		Appraised Fl. Kr.		Sold Fl. Kr.	
149	Contrapuntal essays, apparently by other masters, with his own notations. 5 packages.	10	–	74	–
150	Recitative and vocal piece with orchestra in score	5	–	6	03
151	Italian Songs, apparently unknown	3	–	4	–
152	Complete movement of a violin quintet	3	–	4	–
153	Complete vocal piece, Prüfung des Küssens	5	–	6	–
154	Italian Duet in score	5	–	6	12
155	Canon and four-voiced song	2	–	2	30
156	Several songs, appear unknown	1	30	1	45
157	Two complete small pieces for p.-f. from his early period	1	–	1	–

No.		Appraised Fl. Kr.		Sold Fl. Kr.	
158	Song and sacred movement	I	–	} 6	36
159	Two tattoos in score	5	–		
160	Fragment of an unknown trio for pianoforte	I	–	I	20
161	Original cadenza to the 1st Concerto in C major (only the ending is missing)	–	20	–	45
162	March for wind band	2	–	2	20
163	Two songs	I	–	I	12
164	Ruinen von Athen in score, incomplete	10	–	8	–
165	Sketches, apparently for a quartet or voices	2	–	2	20
166	Three original movements of a quartet for pianoforte, 2 violins and violoncello	3	–	4	06
167	Complete vocal work	6	–	9	03
168	Scene and Aria, Italian in a copy of another hand, but the original of 1796	2	–	5	10
169	Some numbers from König Stephen in autograph and some in copy	5	–	3	–
170	Collection of unknown and in part completed movements	3	–	6	36
171	2 complete manuscripts from the 12th year of the composer—a fugue and a concerto for pianoforte	2	–	2	–
172	Pianoforte movements	2	–	3	09
173	Fragment of a new violin quintet of November, 1826, last work of the composer	10	–	30	30
174	Canon in two voices	–	20	I	–
175	(Starke)				
176	Trifles, complete for the p.-f.	3	–	2	–
177	Rondo with orchestra for the p.-f., unknown	10	–	20	–
178	Marches for orchestra, uncertain whether some are known	5	–	10	50
179	Unknown trio for p.-f. and flute and bassoon, earlier work while still in Bonn	8	–	20	–
180	Orchestral piece with chorus, unknown	5	–	6	–
181	Minuets for orchestra, together with a copy	3	–	8	06
182	Movement of an unknown violin concerto	2	–	10	–
183	Song, unknown	I	–	3	50
184	Pianoforte pieces with accompaniment, in part unknown	2	–	6	31
185	Easy caprice for the pianoforte, unknown	I	–	20	30
186	Sehnsucht, song, apparently unknown	I	–	–	48
187	Aria with pianoforte accompaniment, complete	2	–	3	24
188	Song with five-part accompaniment, complete	2	–	8	43
189	Symphony by Haydn in B-Flat, score appears to be by Haydn	3	–	3	30

V

Copied Parts to Beethoven Works

No.		Appraised		Sold	
		Fl.	Kr.	Fl.	Kr.
190	For the last Symphony	3	–	3	30
191	For Christus am Oelberg	2	–	2	30
192	For the Symphony in A major	2	–	3	–
193	Chorus parts to Schiller's Lied an die Freude	1	–	1	12
194	Wellington's Battle	1	30	1	45
195	Overture to Leonore	1	–	3	–
196	Two packages for the overture at the performance in the Josefstadt Theatre (Op. 124)		30	–	40
197	For two symphonies, 2 packages	–	20	–	40
198	For the Mass	–	30	1	–
199	For a Symphony, dances, march music written by different composers	–	30	–	40
200	Madrigals by Lughini, together with 17 different pieces	–	30	1	–
201	18 different pieces	–	20	–	24
202	Leonore by Paër, score	1	–	1	20
203	Copy of a violin quartet in score by Beethoven and sold to H. Schlesinger, along with 19 different pieces	1	30	2	50
204	Reutter, Cantata, Parnassa, Score	1	–	1	–
205	24 different pieces	–	30	–	35
206	13 " "	–	20	–	30
207	Bach's Kunst der Fuge	–	30	1	03
208	17 different pieces	–	20	–	40
209	Beethoven's Symphony in B-Flat and several pieces from Fidelio in score, Copies	1	–	4	30
210	Fanisca by Cherubini. Score "in 4 Livr."	3	–	4	40
211	21 different pieces	–	30	4	50
212	Fidelio in score, complete along with libretto	8	–	15	–
213	Overture in score.—3 and 4 varied songs by Haydn—along with 17 different pieces	1	–	2	10
214	Pianoforte Concerto by Beethoven in score with some corrections in own hand, along with 10 different pieces	1	–	2	–
215	15 different pieces	1	–	3	45
216	Mozart's Zauberflöte in score	3	–	5	36

VI

Printed Music

No.		Appraised Fl. Kr.		Sold Fl. Kr.	
217	Beethoven's Wellington's Victory at Vittoria in score	I	–	4	–
218	The same work	I	–	4	30
219	Beethoven's Mass in score along with 25 different pieces	–	30	3	06
220	18 different pieces	–	30	I	30
221	Messiah by Handel and Mozart Le deux petits Savoyards by Dalairac Idomeneo by Mozart in pianoforte score Mozart's Requiem in score	2	–	7	30
222	Beethoven's Christus am Oelberg in score Fidelio in Pianoforte-score Le Cadi dupé (Gluck). Score	2	–	3	15
223	Beethoven's Symphonies in score Nos. 1,2. Giulio Sabino by Sarti Preindel Gesanglehre	I	–	3	03
224	Haydn's Creation in score	3	–	4	–
225	Haydn Mass No. 3. Score " " " I. " Beethoven's Christus am Oelberg. Score.	I	30	4	–
226	Beethoven's Fidelio in Pianoforte score Select collection of Irish Melodies by Beethoven. 2 volumes. Edinburgh	2	–	15	49
227	Mozart. Don Juan in score along with 15 other pieces	2	–	8	34
228	Mozart. Cosi fan tutte in score, along with 9 different pieces	I	–	6	12
229	Beethoven. Christus am Oelberg in score Fugue by Reicha and Medea by Cherubini in score	2	–	12	–
230	Mozart. Titus in score, along with 10 different pieces	I	–	3	–
231	Haydn. Seasons in score Dalairac. "La Soirée orageuse." Score Salieri. "Les Danaides." Score	2	–	7	12
232	The Mount of Olives by Beethoven Mozart's quartets in score Felix in score Valentine de Milan by Mehul. Score	2	–	8	40
233	Beethoven. Leonore and Christus am Oelberg in pianoforte score along with 6 different pieces	I	–	5	03
234	Symphony by Beethoven, Op. 125, in score, along with 12 different pieces	I	–	7	03

No.		Appraised Fl.	Kr.	Sold Fl.	Kr.
235	Bach's Kunst der Fuge, along with 12 different pieces	1	–	2	32
236	Handel's Keyboard suites, along with 15 different pieces	–	40	2	18
237	Beethoven. Symphony, Op. 125, in score along with 15 different pieces	1	30	7	06
238	Intermezzo, La Serva Padrona by Paisiello 2 Entr'Actes from Egmont by Beethoven along with different music	1	–	1	–
239	Handel's works in 40 calf-bound volumes, London edition	50	–	102	–
240	(crossed out)				
241	Handel's Julius Caesar	1	–	2	10
242 243 244	(crossed out)				
245	Handel's Alexander's Feast. Score. Ms.	1	30	2	–
246	Choruses from Handel's oratorios	–	30	–	40

VII

Books on Music

No.		Appraised Fl.	Kr.	Sold Fl.	Kr.
247	Knecht's Orgelschule and Bach's Art das Klavier zu spielen	1	–	3	40
248	A package of musical newspapers	–	30	3	15
249	Camphuysens Rymens Amsterdam 1647 Collection of Songs Riepel's Tonordnung " Contrapunkt } 5 volumes folio " Setzkunst	1	30	2	–
250	Kirnberger's works, 6 volumes Koch. Harmonie Vogler. Choralsystem Turk. Organist	1	–	2	40
251	Works of Haydn in score. 14 volumes. 8 parts.	2	–	14	03
252	Traite de la Fugue by Marburg and divers other pieces	1	–	1	37

Clavier, bought by Spina   181 fl.
Medals
2 violins   33 fl.

2. Sale of Beethoven's Mss. and Musical Library.[2]

[2] From the *Harmonicon*, April, 1828, as reprinted in Schindler, *The Life of Beethoven*, ed. by Moscheles, II, pp. 373-76.

Vienna, March 16, 1828

The sale of the lamented Beethoven's MSS. and musical library, which lately took place here, excited uncommon interest among the lovers of music, amateurs as well as professional men. The following are the heads under which the articles were arranged in the catalogue:—

1. Fragments from Beethoven's musical portfolio, consisting of noted paper, scraps of various themes, &c. 2. Fragments and sketches in a more complete form. 3. Autographs of scores already published. 4. Autographs of unpublished music. 5. Copies of various Symphonies, Choruses, Overtures, Masses, &c., corrected by the composer's own hand. 6. Printed music and theoretical works. 7. A small collection of works of general literature. 8. A small collection of musical instruments. The contest for several of the articles was warm and spirited, particularly between the well-known music-sellers Artaria, Haslinger, and Steiner. More than forty works, unknown to the public, were brought to the hammer, the greater part of which are productions of Beethoven's earlier years. No doubt the present possessors will, ere long, afford the world an opportunity of enjoying these works of the lamented master. We observed that the greater proportion of them became the property of Artaria, after a severe contest with his brother publishers; several fetched extraordinarily high prices. Besides a great many other articles, Beethoven's last work, an unfinished Quintett, begun in November, 1828, fell to the lot of Diabelli, who triumphantly bore it away, at a very high price, from a host of competitors. The same gentleman also became possessor of a Solo-Capriccio, of a Rondo for pianoforte and orchestra, and of the English pianoforte which Beethoven had received as present from the Messrs. Broadwood. The gold medal which the composer had the honour to receive from Louis XVIII on receiving the copy of one of his grand masses was bought by some anonymous collector. But by far the most interesting article of the whole sale fell to the lot of M. Haslinger—the collection of contrapuntic exercises, essays, and finished pieces, which Beethoven wrote while under the tuition of his master, the celebrated Albrechtsberger, all in his own handwriting, with the interlineal corrections of that master, and his remarks on the margin. It is in five thick volumes, which were evidently preserved with great care. The struggle for the possession of this invaluable relic—the fruit of Beethoven's first studies—was long and spirited; but the stamina of M. Haslinger brought him through; after many a fiercely-contested round, he was at length declared the victor, none of his antagonists coming to time. We are happy to be able to state that this collection of studies, so interesting to the whole musical world, is immediately to be placed in the hands of Kapellmeister Seyfried, who is to prepare it for the press. M. Haslinger also became the fortunate possessor of a pianoforte Trio, consisting of an Allegro, Adagio, Finale, and Variations, composed while Beethoven filled the place of organist in Cologne; of a short Sonata for four hands; of several songs and other vocal pieces; of a small collection, entitled *Zapfenstreiche*

für Türkische Musik; of two violins, with the possessor's seal on each; and lastly, of Beethoven's copy of the works of Handel, Dr. Arnold's edition, in forty volumes folio. The latter, as is well known, was presented to the lamented composer by his friend M. Stumpff, of London, the possession of which tended so much to soothe Beethoven during his last protracted illness. The mind and talents of Handel were kindred to his own, and he was seen for hours hanging over these volumes in rapture and forgetting his sufferings. Two other competitors contended warmly for this prize—M. Gläser of Gotha, and Mr. Schenk, the well-known composer of *Der Dorfbarbier*; but M. Haslinger still retained his honours as champion of the field. We must, however, observe, that, warm as the opposition was between these different opponents, the contest was still conducted with becoming respect—not to say with a certain solemnity due to the relics of the mighty dead. Some of the prices given astonished even the most enthusiastic admirers of the composer, and are the most satisfactory proofs of the deep zeal and love for the art predominant among us.

3. A Record of Beethoven's Estate

According to Fischhoff's notarized copy found in the estate of O. Jahn (taken from Thayer's papers).[3]

The auction was held November 5, 1827, at 1149 Kohlmarkt, rear part of the building, third story, under the direction of Anton Gräfer, the appraiser. Total intake 1140 florins 18 C.M.

[stamp]

Legal [or an account of?] inventory and appraisal of the estate of Ludwig van Beethoven, composer, No. 200 in the suburb of Alser, who died March 26, 1827, a week ago, having left a will.

Cash:

After the death of the departed were found

bills	1215 florins (C.M.)	
coupons	600 (V. S.)	
total	1215 "	600 "

of which 650 florins were entrusted to the guardian of the under-aged nephew, Herr Hofrat von Bräuning [*Sic!*], for funeral and other expenses. 565 florins (C.M.) and 600 florins (V.S.) remained for deposit.

Bank Shares:

One share of the National Bank of Austria, no. 2, page 3099, dated July 13, 1819, with a coupon number 28624, payable to Ludwig van Beethoven, at

[3] See TDR, v, pp. 579-83.

the rate of exchange according to the market report of March 26, 1827, being the date of his death

1063 fl.—

with eight coupons of the first half-year period, 1827.

One share of same, no. 3, page 3099, dated same, with coupon number 28625, payable to same, at same rate of exchange

1063 fl.—

with eight coupons of the first half-year period, 1827.

One share of same, no. 4, page 3099, dated same, with coupon number 28626, payable to same, at same rate of exchange

1063 fl.—

with eight coupons of the first half-year period, 1827.

One share of same, no. 5, page 3099, dated same, with coupon number 28627, payable to same, at same rate of exchange

1063 fl.—

with eight coupons of the first half-year period, 1827.

One share of same, no. 6, page 3099, dated same, with coupon number 28628, payable to same, at same rate of exchange

1063 fl.—

with eight coupons of the first half-year period, 1827.

One share of same, no. 7, page 3099, dated same, with coupon number 28629, payable to same, at same rate of exchange

1063 fl.—

with eight coupons of the first half-year period, 1827.

One share of the National Bank of Austria, no. 8, page 3099, dated July 13, 1819, with coupon number 28630, payable to Ludwig van Beethoven, at same rate of exchange

1063 fl.—

with eight coupons of the first half-year period, 1827

total   7441 fl.—

Outstanding Subsidies:

From the privy office of His Majesty, from the private treasury of His Royal Highness Archduke Rudolf the sum for the period March 1 through March 26, 1827, of an annual grant of 600 fl. C.M.   43 fl. 20

From the electoral Lobkowitz treasury the sum for the same period, of an annual grant of 700 fl. V.S. or 280 fl. C.M.

66 fl. 53

From the royal Kinsky main treasury of Archduke Rudolf at Prag the sum for the period from March 1 through March 26, 1827, of an annual grant of 1200 fl. V.S. or 480 fl.

34 fl. 40

total   144 " 53

Valuables:

1 oval-shaped ring set with emerald, brilliants and rose diamond					90 fl.	—	
1 gold medallion with a picture of Ludwig XVIII 41#					164 "	—	
1 silver watch					8 "	—	
1	"	serving spoon	C. 10½ Loth.[4]	10	"	30	—
1	"	ladle	" 4½ "	4	"	15	—
8	"	tablespoons	" 27½ "	27	"	30	—
5	"	teaspoons	" 4½ "	4	"	30	—
1	"	salt cellar	" 5¾ "	5	"	45	—

total 314 " 30 —

The above listed cash, bank shares and valuables were handed over to the court.

Clothing and Personal Linens: C.M.

2 cloth swallow-tailed coats, 2 spencers, 2 Prince Alberts, 1 blue cloth overcoat   15 fl.

16 assorted knee stockings and 8 pair of trousers   6 "   —

2 hats, 6 pair of boots, 3 pair of suspenders, 6 razors, 2 small pistols, 1 cane, 1 dressing gown   6 "   —

14 shirts, 20 undershirts, 20 ascots and handkerchiefs, 18 pair of socks, 8 night shirts, 14 pair of underpants, 6 night caps   10 "

total 37 "   —

Household Linens and Furnishings:

2 tablecloths, 10 napkins, 10 handtowels, 6 bed sheets, 4 slip covers   4 "   —

2 hardwood bedsteads including a paillasse and 4 mattresses, 7 pillows, 1 light blanket, 3 old quilts, 1 fur cover   12 "   —

In the First Room:

4 small hardwood tables, 8 leather chairs, 3 hardwood chests of drawers, 1 night stand, 2 softwood stools, 1 fire screen, 1 writing desk   6 "   —

2 mirrors in gilded frames, 2 pair of window curtains, 2 money boxes   2 "   —

In the Second Room:

2 old tables, 2 old chairs, 1 hardwood desk, 1 hardwood cupboard, 1 softwood cabinet, 1 night stand, 3 softwood stools, 1 pair of curtains.   6 "   —

[4] Loth=*circa* 1½ oz. in Troy Weight.

In the Third Room:

1 leather easy chair, 1 old sofa, 1 trunk, 2 pair of curtains   4 " —

In the Kitchen:

14 china plates, some earthenware, 1 tin cup, several glasses, bottles, and bowls   4 fl. —

4 brass candleholders, 1 brass mortar, 1 copper tub, 1 rotisserie, assorted iron pots and pans, and the usual kitchen furnishings   6 " —

Maelzel's metronome   8 " —

1 piano by John Broadwood and Son of London in mahogany case   100 " —

      total   152 " —

Instruments:

1 cello	by	Father Zuaneri	40 " —
1 viola	"	Vinc. Reschner	10 " —
1 violin	"	Josef Zuaneri	16 " —
1	"	" Nikolaus Amati	12 " —

      total   78 " —

Printed Music, Manuscripts and Music Books:

According to the record which accompanies the auction papers these were appraised at   480 " 30

Books:

According to the record which accompanies the auction papers these were appraised at 45 fl. 58 kr. V.S., or in C.M.   18 " 20

Accordingly the inventory of the estate is appraised at nine thousand eight hundred eighty-five florins 13 kr. C.M.

9885 fl. 13 kr. C.M.

six hundred florins V.S.

600 fl. V.S.

Cash	1215 fl.	600
Bank Shares	7441 "	
Outstanding Subsidies	144 "	53
Valuables	314 "	30
Clothing and Personal Linens	37 "	
Household Linens and Furnishings	156 [*sic*]	
Instruments	78 "	
Printed Music and Manuscripts	480 "	30
Books	18 "	20

      total   9885 " 13 600

Vienna, October 4. In witness thereof the following:

Dro Bach curator

Jacob Hotschevar (personal signature) as guardian of the under-aged Karl van Beethoven and as witness

Jos. Leop. Krembs (personal signature) as witness

Franz Horny (personal signature) as witness

Fred. Prandstätter (personal signature)

Ignaz Schleicher (personal signature)

Franz Deimal (personal signature) appraiser of jewels

Franz Anton Hausmann (personal signature) appraiser

G. S. Ferdinand Leichtl (personal signature) appraiser of watches

Tobias Sponagl (personal signature) public appraiser

Seb. Zimmermann (personal signature) public appraiser

Martin Stuss (personal signature) appraiser

The town violin makers

APPENDIX D

FIRST PUBLICATION OF WORKS AFTER
BEETHOVEN'S DEATH

THIS list excludes: 1) arrangements by others, unless available in print in no other form; 2) first complete score editions if the work has already been published in parts; and 3) canons.

After 1825.
By Gombart in Augsburg: "An die Geliebte" (Stoll), WoO 140.

1827.
By Matthias Artaria:
Fugue for String Quartet, Op. 133, dedicated to Cardinal Archduke Rudolph of Austria.
The same arranged for Pianoforte Four Hands, Op. 134, dedicated to Cardinal Archduke Rudolph of Austria.
String Quartet in B-Flat major, Op. 130, dedicated to Prince Nikolas von Galitzin.
By Cappi and Czerny: March in D for Military Band, WoO 24, in pianoforte transcription.
By Haslinger: Fugue for String Quintet, Op. 137.
By Schlesinger:
String Quartet in A minor, Op. 132, dedicated to Prince Nikolas von Galitzin.
String Quartet in F major, Op. 135, dedicated to Johann Wolfmayer.
By Schott:
Missa Solemnis for Four Soloists, Chorus and Orchestra, Op. 123, dedicated to Cardinal Archduke Rudolph of Austria.
String Quartet in C-sharp minor, Op. 131, dedicated to Baron Joseph von Stutterheim.

1828.
By Artaria: Three Piano Quartets (1785), WoO 36.
By Diabelli: Rondo a capriccio for Pianoforte, Op. 129.

1829.
By Diabelli: Rondo for Pianoforte and Orchestra, WoO 6, with realisations by Czerny from Beethoven's indications.[1]

1830.
By Artaria: Octet for Wind Instruments, Op. 103.
By Diabelli: Rondino for Eight Wind Instruments, WoO 25.
By Dunst:
Piano Sonata, incomplete, WoO 51, dedicated to Eleonore von Breuning.
Trio for Pianoforte, Violin and Violoncello, WoO 38.
Trio for Pianoforte, Violin and Violoncello, WoO 39, dedicated to Maximiliane Brentano.

[1] See KHV, p. 436.

1832.

By Artaria: Gratulationsmenuett for Orchestra, WoO 3.

In I. v. Seyfried's *Beethovens Studien*, p. 329: "Im Arm der Liebe ruht sich's wohl," WoO 159.

1836.

In *Wiener Zeitschrift für Kunst, Literatur und Mode*, No. 10, supplement: Cadenza to the First Movement of Mozart's *Concerto for Piano-forte and Orchestra in D minor*, K. 466; WoO 58, No. 1.

1837.

By Diabelli: "Seufzer eines Ungeliebten" (Bürger), WoO 118 and "Die laute Klage" (Herder), WoO 135.

By Haslinger: "Der glorreiche Augenblick" for Four Solo Voices, Chorus and Orchestra (Weissenbach), Op. 136.

1838.

By Haslinger: Overture "Leonore No. 1," Op. 138.

1839.

By R. Schumann in the *Neue Zeitschrift für Musik*, VI, supplement: "Gesang der Mönche" for Three Men's Voices from Schiller's "Wilhelm Tell," WoO 104.

1840.

By Haslinger: Triumphant March to Christoph Kuffner's tragedy, *Tarpeja*, WoO 2a.

1843.

In *Allgemeine Wiener Musikzeitung*, Vol. 3 (November 23): "Der edle Mensch sei hülfreich und gut" (Goethe), WoO 151.

1844.

By Haslinger: "Gedenke mein," WoO 130.

1846.

By Artaria: "*Die Ruinen von Athen*, Ein Fest- und Nachspiel, mit Chören und Gesängen, zur Eröffnung des Theaters in Pesth, verfasst von August von Kotzebue, Musik von Ludwig van Beethoven," Op. 113.

1852-53.

By Breitkopf and Härtel. Two earlier versions of Marzelline's Aria, "O wär ich schon mit dir vereint" from *Fidelio* (Op. 72, No. 1) as a supplement to O. Jahn's edition of *Leonore*, Op. 72, version 2 in pianoforte transcription [*see* 1956 and 1960].

1854.

By Breitkopf and Härtel: Leonore Overture No. 2 for Orchestra. (A shortened version had already been published in 1842.)

1858.

By Ewer in London: *Hochzeitslied* for mixed voices, WoO 105, version 2 (with new words by John Oxenford).

1860.

By Peters in Leipzig and Berlin: Twelve Folk Songs arranged for one and several voices, violin, violoncello and pianoforte, WoO 157. (First appearance in print of Nos. 1, 4, 6, 7, 10, 12; of No. 3 in the original arrangement.)

1864.

By Breitkopf and Härtel in the Complete Works Edition:

Series 2

No. 6. March in D for Military Band, WoO 24.

No. 7. Twelve Minuets for Orchestra, WoO 7.

No. 8. Twelve German Dances for Orchestra, WoO 8.

(These pieces had appeared previously only in pianoforte transcription in 1827, 1797 and 1798 respectively.)

Series 9

Cadenza to the Third Movement of Mozart's *Concerto for Pianoforte and Orchestra in D minor*, K. 466; WoO 58, No. 2.

Series 20

No. 4. Music for A. v. Kotzebue's Festspiel, *König Stephan* or *Ungarns erster Wohltäter*, Op. 117. (The overture was published by Steiner in 1826.)

No. 5. "Es ist vollbracht" for Bass, Chorus and Orchestra (Treitschke), WoO 97. (Published in pianoforte transcription in 1815.)

No. 6. "Germania" for Bass, Chorus and Orchestra (Treitschke), WoO 94. (Published in pianoforte transcription in 1814.)

1865.

In *Niederrheinische Musikzeitung* (September 23): "Das liebe Kätzchen" and "Der Knabe auf dem Berge" (KHV, p. 665).

1866.

In Thayer's *Chronologisches Verzeichniss*, No. 98: "Graf, Graf, liebster Graf," WoO 101.

1867.

In *Neue Briefe Beethovens*, ed. by L. Nohl:

No. 33. "Für Elise am 27 April zur Erinnerung von L. v. Bthvn," Piece for Pianoforte in A minor, WoO 59. (The autograph with the above inscription belonged to Therese Malfatti, who presented it to a Fräulein Bredl in Munich. Nohl saw it in the latter's possession.)

No. 255. "Lobkowitz-Cantate" for Soprano, Chorus and Pianoforte Accompaniment, WoO 106.

No. 290. Souvenir for Otto de Boer, WoO 35.

1872.

By Rieter-Biedermann (Lpz. and Winterthur): "Musik zu einem Ritter-Ballet," WoO 1, in pianoforte transcription by F. Dulcken.

1873.

In Gustav Nottebohm's *Beethovens Studien*, pp. 207-21:

Settings of texts by Metastasio:

"Bei labbri che Amore" for Soprano and Tenor, WoO 99, No. 1.

"Fra tutte le pene" for Soprano, Alto, and Tenor, WoO 99, No. 3b.

"Fra tutte le pene" for Soprano, Alto, Tenor and Bass, WoO 99, No. 3c.

"Guira il nocchier" for Soprano, Alto, Tenor and Bass, WoO 99, No. 5a, Version in B-flat.

"Per te d'amico aprile" for Soprano, Alto and Bass, WoO 99, No. 9.

1879.

By Schreiber in Vienna: Fragment of a Concerto in C major for Violin and Orchestra, WoO 5.

1880.

In Grove's *Dictionary of Music and Musicians*, Vol. 2, p. 205: "Sonatina per il Mandolino," WoO 43, No. 1.

1888.

By Breitkopf and Härtel in the Complete Works Edition, Vol. 25:

No. 1. *Cantata on the Death of Emperor Joseph the Second* for Soprano and Bass, Chorus, and Orchestra (Averdonk), WoO 87.

No. 2. *Cantata on the Elevation of Leopold the Second to Imperial Rank* for Soprano, Tenor and Bass, Chorus and Orchestra (Averdonk), WoO 88.

No. 3. Chorus for the Festspiel *Die Weihe des Hauses* for Soprano, Chorus and Orchestra (Meisl), WoO 98.

No. 4. *Chorus for the Allied Princes* with Orchestra (Bernard), WoO 95.

No. 5. "Opferlied" for Soprano, Alto, Tenor, Chorus and Small Orchestra (Matthisson), third version (first version of Op. 121b).

No. 6. Two Arias for Bass and Orchestra: "Prüfung der Küssens," WoO 89, and "Mit Mädeln sich vertragen" (Goethe), WoO 90.

No. 7. Two Arias for Umlauf's Singspiel, *Die Schöne Schusterin* (Stephanie le jeune), WoO 91: (1) for Tenor and Orchestra; (2) for Soprano and Orchestra.

No. 8. "Primo amore" for Soprano and Orchestra, WoO 92.

No. 9. Music for Duncker's drama, *Leonore Prohaska* for Chorus and Orchestra, WoO 96.

No. 10. "Abschiedsgesang" for Three Men's Voices (Seyfried), WoO 102.

No. 12. "Ich, der mit flatterndem Sinn" (Gleim), WoO 114.

No. 14. "Der Gesang der Nachtigall" (Herder), WoO 141.

No. 15. "Man strebt die Flamme zu verhehlen" (for Frau von Weissenthum), WoO 120.

No. 16. "O care selve" (Metastasio), WoO 119.

No. 17. "An Minna," WoO 115.

No. 19. "Trinklied (beim Abschied zu singen)," WoO 109.

No. 20. "Klage" (Hölty), WoO 113.

No. 21. "Elegie auf den Tod eines Pudels," WoO 110.

No. 23. "Musik zu einem Ritterballett" for Orchestra, WoO 1.

No. 24. March No. 2 in F for Military Band, WoO 19.

No. 25. March (Zapfenstreich) in C for Military Band, WoO 20.

No. 26. Polonaise in D for Military Band, WoO 21.

No. 27. Ecossaise in D for Military Band, WoO 22.

No. 29. March for 2 Clarinets, 2 Horns, 2 Bassoons, WoO 29.

No. 30. Three Equale for Four Trombones, WoO 30.

No. 31. Trio for Pianoforte, Flute and Bassoon, WoO 37.

No. 33. Adagio for Mandolin and Cembalo, WoO 43.

No. 34. Two Bagatelles for Pianoforte: No. 1 in C minor, WoO 52; No. 2 in C major, WoO 56.

No. 36. Allegretto for Pianoforte, WoO 53.

No. 37. "Lustig—traurig" for Pianoforte, WoO 54.

No. 39. Six Ecossaises for Pianoforte, WoO 83 (presumably transcriptions from Twelve Ecossaises for Orchestra, WoO 16), *see* 1806-1807.

No. 43. Ecossaise for Pianoforte. (This is a pianoforte transcription of an Ecossaise for Military Band, WoO 23.[2])

No. 44. Allemande for Pianoforte, WoO 81.

No. 46. Fugue for Organ, WoO 31.

1890.

By Breitkopf and Härtel in the Complete Works Edition, Vol. 25, supplement: Concerto for Pianoforte and Orchestra in E-flat, WoO 4.

In *Grove's Dictionary of Music and Musicians*, Vol. 3, p. 424: "Lob auf den Dicken" for Three Solos and Chorus, WoO 100, musical joke on Ignaz Schuppanzigh.

1893.

In *Deutscher Kunst- und Musikzeitung*, No. 6: Piece for Pianoforte (for Ferdinand Piringer), WoO 61.

1901.

In Theodor von Frimmel's *Ludwig van Beethoven* (Berlin), p. 65: Piece for Two Violins (for Alexandre Boucher), WoO 34.

In Alexander W. Thayer's *Ludwig van Beethovens Leben*, Vol. 1, 2nd edition as a supplement: Duo for Two Flutes (for J. M. Degenhart), WoO 26.

1902.

In *Die Musik*, 1/12, pp. 1078-79 and 1081-82:
"Que le temps me dire" (Rousseau), first version, WoO 116.
"Plaisir d'aimer," WoO 128.

In *Die Musik*, 1/12 as a supplement:
Adagio for Mechanical Instrument, WoO 33, No. 1.

1905.

By Breitkopf and Härtel, edited by Erich Prieger: *Leonore* (*Fidelio*) Opera in Three Acts, first version, Op. 73, in pianoforte transcription.

1906.

By Heugel in Paris: Twelve Minuets for Orchestra, WoO 12.[3]

1907.

By Breitkopf and Härtel: Eleven Viennese Dances for String and Wind Instruments, WoO 17.

1909.

In *Beethoven Briefe an N. Simrock* (Berlin), ed. by Leopold Schmidt, Appendix IV: Sonatina for Pianoforte, WoO 50.

1908-10.

By Brandstetter in Leipzig: *Leonore* (*Fidelio*), Opera in Three Acts, Op. 72, in score.

1912.

By C. F. Peters: First Movement of "Duett mit zwei obligaten Augengläsern" for Viola and Violoncello, WoO 32.

In *Der Merker*, III/12 as a supplement: Sonatina for Mandolin and Pianoforte, WoO 44, No. 1.

---

[2] According to KHV, p. 461, this edition was based on a transcription by Czerny first published in his "Musikalischen Pfennig-magazin," Vol. 1, p. 108.

[3] Published in pianoforte transcription in 1903. (*See* 1955.)

1914.

By Breitkopf and Härtel: Variations on "Là ci darem la mano" from Mozart's *Don Giovanni* for Two Oboes and English Horn, WoO 28.

1916.

In the Catalogue of the Heyer Museum in Cologne, ed. by G. Kinsky, IV, music supplement, pp. 3-5: "An Laura" (Matthisson), WoO 112.

1920.

In G. Becking's *Studien zu Beethovens Personalstil* (Leipzig): Scherzo for Mechanical Instrument, WoO 33, No. 2.

1925.

In L. Schiedermair's *Der junge Beethoven* (Leipzig), pp. 425-426: "Punschlied," WoO 111.

1927.

By Breitkopf and Härtel in *Der Bär* (Leipzig), p. 158: "Hochzeitlied für Giannarasio del Rio" (Stein), version 1 in C, WoO 105.

1929.

By Strache: Twelve German Dances for Orchestra, WoO 13, in pianoforte transcription.

1933.

By Schott: Six Minuets for Two Violins and Bass, WoO 9.

1935.

In *Zeitschrift für Musik*, CII/11, pp. 1201-1203: "Que le temps me dure" (Rousseau), WoO 116, versions 1 and 2.

1936.

In *Schweizerische musikpädagogische Blätter*, xxv/15, pp. 226-28: "Quella cetra ah pur tu sei," for Soprano, Alto, Tenor and Bass (Metastasio), WoO 99, No. 10a.

1938.

By Schott: Introduction to Act II (and Triumphant March, *see* 1840) presumably for Christoph Kuffner's Tragedy, *Tarpeja*, WoO 2b.

1939.

By Eulenberg in Leipzig: "Nei giorni tuoi felici," Duet for Soprano and Tenor and Orchestra (Metastasio), WoO 93.

1940.

By Schott: Five Pieces for Mechanical Instrument, WoO 33, in pianoforte transcription. (For No. 1 in original form, *see* 1902; for No. 2, 1920.)

In *Sudetendeutsches Musikarchiv,* No. 1: Andante with Variations for Mandolin and Pianoforte, WoO 44, No. 2.

1941.

By Breitkopf and Härtel: Twenty-three Folk-Songs for Voice and Pianoforte, with accompaniment of Violin and Violoncello, WoO 158. (Inaccurate edition of No. 19 in *DM*, 2/6 [1902], supplement, pp. 2-4. First printing of No. 17 in *Veröffentlichungen des Beethoven-Hauses*, v [Bonn, 1928], plates I-V.)

In *Die Musik,* 33/7, p. 243: "Gia la notte s'avvicina," for Alto, Tenor and Bass (Metastasio), WoO 99, No. 4b.

1945.

In *Jahrbuch der Literarischen Vereinigung Winterthur*, pp. 247-54: "Un lieto brindisi" for Soprano, Two Tenors and Bass with Pianoforte Accompaniment (Bondi), WoO 103.

1949.

By Brucknerverlag in Wiesbaden: "No, non turbati" for Soprano and String Orchestra (Metastasio), WoO 92a.

In *Österreichische Musikzeitschrift* 4/1-2: "Traute Henriette," Hess *Verzeichnis*, No. 151.

1952.

By Breitkopf and Härtel: Romance cantabile for Pianoforte, Flute and Bassoon and small Orchestra (fragment) Hess *Verzeichnis*, No. 13.

By Peters: Second Movement of "Duett mit zwei obligaten Augengläsern" for Viola and Violoncello, WoO 32.

1953.

In *Atlantis* (Vol. 1953), pp. 212-13: "Nei campi e nelle selve" for Soprano, Alto, Tenor and Bass (Metastasio) in two versions, WoO 99, No. 7.

In *Eidgenössisches Sängerblatt*, 17/12, p. 145: "Ma tu tremi" for Soprano, Alto and Tenor (Metastasio), WoO 99, No. 6.

1953-54.

In *Beethoven Jahrbuch*, pp. 251-74: "Zapfenstreich Nr. 1," WoO 18, and "Zapfenstreich Nr. 3," WoO 19, in revised versions.

1955.

By Nagel (Musik-Archiv No. 183): Twelve Minuets for Orchestra, WoO 12, original version.

In *Musik im Unterricht* (November), supplement: "Feuerfarb'" (Mereau), version 1, Op. 52, No. 2.

1956.

In *Rivista Santa Cecilia*, 5/4: "O wär ich schon mit dir vereint," earlier version (in C minor) of Marzelline's Aria from *Fidelio* (Op. 72, version 1, No. 1) in score.

In *Musica* 10/6: "Der freie Mann" (Pfeffel), WoO 117.

1959.

By Breitkopf and Härtel in *Supplement I* to the Complete Works Edition:
Settings of texts by Metastasio:
  "Chi mai di questo core" for Soprano, Tenor and Bass, WoO 99, No. 2.
  "Fra tutte le pene" for Tenor and Bass, WoO 99, No. 3a.
  "Guira il nocchier" for Soprano, Alto and Bass, WoO 99, No. 5b.
  "Guira il nocchier" for Soprano, Alto, Tenor and Bass (version in C), Hess *Verzeichnis*, No. 230.
  "Quella cetra ah pur tu sei" for Soprano, Tenor and Bass, WoO 99, No. 10b.
  "Quella cetra ah pur tu sei" for Soprano, Alto, Tenor and Bass, WoO 99, No. 10c.
  "Scrivo in te" for Soprano and Tenor, WoO 99, No. 4.
  "Sei mio ben" for Soprano and Tenor, Hess *Verzeichnis*, No. 231.

1960.

By Breitkopf and Härtel in *Supplement II* to the Complete Works Edition:
  "O wär ich schon mit dir vereint," earlier version (in C major) of Marzel-

line's Aria from *Fidelio* (Op. 72, version 1, No. 1) in score.

In *Supplement III*: Rondo for Pianoforte and Orchestra, WoO 6, original version (without Czerny's additions; *see* 1829).

1961.

In *Supplement IV*: Part ii ("Seigessymphonie") of the Battle Symphony for Orchestra, Op. 91, original version for Mälzel's "Panharmonikon."

1962.

In *Supplement V*: "Opferlied" (Matthisson) version 1, Hess *Verzeichnis* No. 145.

"La tiranna," WoO 125.

"Hochzeitslied" (Stein), version 2 in A, WoO 105. See 1858.

Earlier versions of "Busslied" (Gellert), Op. 48, No. 6; "Lied aus der Ferne" (Reissig), WoO 138; "Wonne der Wehmut" (Goethe), Op. 83, No. 1.

"Dimmi, ben mio," version 2, Op. 82, No. 1.

Corrected versions of "Der Knabe auf dem Berge" and "Das liebe Kätzchen" (see 1865); "Neue Liebe, neues Leben" (Goethe), WoO 127.

Pianoforte transcriptions by Beethoven of "Freudvoll und leidvoll" (Goethe), simple and elaborated versions,[4] Op. 84, No. 4; "Opferlied" (Matthisson), Op. 121b; "Bundeslied" (Goethe), Op. 122.

---

[4] The simpler version was first published, but with mistakes, by Max Unger in *Zeitschrift für Musik* 102/11 1935 as a supplement.

APPENDIX E

DOCUMENTS PERTAINING TO THE FIRST PROJECTS FOR
A BEETHOVEN BIOGRAPHY
(FROM 1826 TO SCHINDLER'S *BIOGRAPHIE*)

I. In the Beethovenhaus, Bodmer Collection:

"With pleasure I give my friend, Karl Holz, the assurance which has been asked of me, that I consider him competent to write my eventual biography, assuming that such a thing should be desired, and I repose in him the fullest confidence that he will give to the world without distortion all that I have communicated to him for this purpose.

Vienna, August 30, 1826,   Ludwig van Beethoven"

Holz never did write the biography; and after seventeen years he gave over this right to write "an authentic biography of Beethoven with the best documentation" to his friend Dr. Gassner in Carlsruhe in a note dated "Vienna, November 4, 1843."[1] No biography was forthcoming.

II.

The first biography of Beethoven was written by Joh. Aloys Schlosser, a man who hardly knew Beethoven, immediately after his death and rushed into print a few months later. The 93-page book, however, is dated Prague, 1828.

From Thayer's *Ludwig van Beethovens Leben*, 1st edition, ix:

"After Beethoven's death a certain Jacob Hotschevar became the 'legally appointed guardian of Beethoven's nephew and sole heir.' With the publication of Schlosser's wretched little 'biography' of the composer (which begins with the assertion of 1772 as the year of his birth and the naming of his father as Anton v. B.), Hotschevar sent a statement to Bäuerle's Theaterzeitung (Oct. 6, 1827) in which he said that 'we are entitled to expect soon a biography of Beethoven that is worthy of his great artistic talent.'"

In this report he included the remark that "the recently published biography [of Schlosser] . . . was filled with a variety of fundamental inaccuracies."[2]

III. From Schindler's *Biographie*, 1st edition, pp. 1-7:

"When in the course of the illness from which he had been suffering a full four months Ludwig van Beethoven was discussing with Hofrat von Breuning and me the biographies of the Greek Plutarch, Breuning used

---

[1] Schindler, *Biogr.*, II, pp. 326.
[2] See Adolf Sandberger, *Ausgewälte Auf-*   *sätze zur Musikgeschichte* (Munich, 1924), pp. 12-13.

the long awaited opportunity to ask Beethoven—seemingly without any further intentions—whom of his contemporaries he would choose as his biographer. Without hesitation he answered, 'Rochlitz, should he outlive me.' And furthermore he said, quite certainly it can be expected that after his departure, too, many busy pens would be quick to entertain the world with a large number of tales and anecdotes about him; this, indeed, seems to be the lot of all men who have exercised some influence upon their times. And thus it be his sincere wish that whatever be said of and about him in the future *remain unflinchingly true to fact in every respect, even if this or that person feel himself implicated, or even his own person* [Beethoven] *be implicated. . . .*

"Already resigned to his lot, Beethoven read with great attention and anticipation what his older friend Breuning had now written. Then he said very quietly, 'Here and there you see various papers scattered about. Take them and put them to their best use; but in all things remain true to fact. I am making you both responsible for this and therefore write to Rochlitz.'

"Our wishes were fulfilled thus, that he himself supplied us with necessary clues and other information on the papers. What further happened at the bedside of our beloved friend was that in accordance with his wishes I was to gather up all his correspondence, Breuning all other papers, among which was the first score of the opera *Fidelio*. This we quickly did.

"After Beethoven's death we had already decided to express jointly to Herr Hofrat Rochlitz the wish of our late friend. But then Breuning became ill, and two months later he followed his younger friend into the realm beyond. In many respects it was an unexpected death, which placed me—especially with respect to the common efforts centering around Beethoven—in an unpleasant situation. Soon thereafter Breuning's widow entrusted me with the papers which her late husband had kept. And thus it was my duty to turn, alone, to Hofrat Rochlitz, which I did September 12, 1827. On September 18 he replied as follows:

Never have the eccentricities and rather rough edges in Beethoven's nature hid from my eyes the nobility and grandeur of his character. And if I met with him but a few times while I was in Vienna, 1822,—but always in an atmosphere of candor and confidence—this was merely the result of the burdens which lay heavily upon him and made all conversation so difficult. That, together with a recognition of his genius and great merit as an artist, was also the reason for following, to the best of my abilities, the course of his intellectual and private life from an early age to the time of his death, to the extent that it is reflected in his works. And since from time to time I used every opportunity to collect information concerning his public life, I considered myself not entirely incapable of being his biographer when I first learned of his death. Indeed, I had planned to execute the project in this fashion, that Beethoven's life, like that of Maria von Weber, comprise the main section in the third volume of my book, *For Friends of Music*. To this plan are now added your promise of assisting me with materials and the wish, of which you informed me, of Beethoven himself. From all this

I ask you to judge whether or not I be inclined to carry out the request which you, as well as the various other friends of Beethoven, make of me. And thus it saddens me all the more that, in spite of all this, I am unable to do so. My life, which from earliest times has been filled with almost uninterrupted strenuous activity, has begun to take rather harsh revenge upon me. I am now finally forced to accept an almost total change of my previous habits. Most important in this modification of my life is that I spend much less time working at my desk. Lest I should again find such work necessary, or, to be more exact, tempting, I shall not undertake any new and significant assignments. Thus I am necessitated to abandon the thought of fulfilling both your wish and mine. I shall not tell you how deeply it hurts me to have to give you this answer; but one must accept those things which necessity sends.—Do accept my thanks for your trust and confidence, etc. . . . .

"Despite this unambiguous rejection I dared to present my plea to Hofrat Rochlitz once again, this time placing special emphasis upon my assistance in this undertaking; for quite aside from the materials which I was keeping for his use, I was still in possession of many important facts which I had accumulated in the course of my long association with Beethoven,—facts which no other person possessed or ever could possess, for they were my exclusive experiences with that great man.

"As early as October 3, 1827, Herr Hofrat Rochlitz honored me with an answer of which I quote only the following:

Sir, first of all let me thank you for Beethoven's will, which you sent me. I can not describe to you how greatly the unmistakable, tender and childlike goodness delighted me, how deeply the painful suffering of that good soul moved me. Most assuredly this document will have a similar effect upon all who come to know it, outright evil people being an exception. Whenever he will be discussed not as an artist but as a human being, I do not know that anything more favorable and convincing can be said in support of the departed. The request which you repeat for a second time I cannot accept, and it is of no avail for either of us if I add "unfortunately!"

"In view of this explanation, and keeping the former resolve of not handing over to anyone the papers which were in my possession in mind, I made no further moves and now decided to await time and circumstance."

APPENDIX F

BEETHOVEN'S "IMMORTAL BELOVED"

THE name "Immortal Beloved" comes from the second postscript to an undated letter written by Beethoven to an unknown lady.[1] The original, "unsterbliche Geliebte," has been almost consistently translated "immortal beloved," but Miss Anderson in *The Letters of Beethoven* points out that "eternally beloved" is a more accurate translation.[2] The letter was discovered by Holz who, with Stephan von Breuning and Johann van Beethoven, was searching for Beethoven's bank-shares. The letter was first in Schindler's possession and then was transferred to the Berlin State Library. It was first published in the first edition of Schindler's biography of Beethoven in 1840.

Schindler's book was the start of what is now a large and varied literature concerning this famous letter which has been primarily concerned with two unknown facts: the date of the letter and its recipient, if indeed the letter was ever sent at all. To support the various theories the letter and its two postscripts supply, along with the content and tone of the writing as a whole, we have the following clues: 1) The letter was written on July 6th in the morning, the first postscript Monday evening, July 6th, and the second postscript in the morning of July 7th; 2) "My journey was a fearful one; I did not reach here until 4 o'clock yesterday morning. Lacking horses the postcoach chose another route. . . . The coach must needs break down on the wretched road. . . . Esterhazy, traveling the usual road here, had the same fate with eight horses that I had with four"; 3) ". . . not till tomorrow will my lodgings be definitely determined upon"; 4) "Letters must be posted very early in the morning on Mondays—or on Thursdays—the only days on which the mail-coach goes from here to K."; 5) "I have just been told that the mail-coach goes every day—and I must close at once so that you may receive the letter at once."

With no existing envelope to establish the year by postal mark, the evidence must rest on the proposition that Beethoven was not absent-minded when he wrote "Evening, Monday, July 6th"; July 6th fell on a Monday in the years 1795, 1801, 1807, 1812, and 1818. Following is a summary of conclusions reached in the more important writings on the subject of this letter.

Date	Author	Publication	Date Assigned	Recipient
1840	Schindler	*Biographie*, 1st ed.	1806	Giulietta Giucciardi
		Written from an Hungarian bathing-place.		
1860	Schindler	*Biographie*, 3rd ed.	1801-3?	Giulietta Giucciardi

[1] See pp. 533ff. [2] *A*, I, p. 376, n. 1.

		Date	
Date	Author	Publication	Assigned	Recipient

1865   Nohl   *Briefe Beethovens*   1800   Giulietta Giucciardi
    The Countess Giulietta had married Count Gallenberg by 1801.

1879   Thayer-Deiters   *Ludwig van Beethovens Leben*, Vol. 3, 1st ed.
                        1806[8]   Therese von Brunsvik

In the summer of 1806 Beethoven was in Hungary and in Silesia. Thayer believed that Beethoven's correspondence with Gleichenstein concerning plans for marriage were to be dated in 1807 and were, along with the love-letter, connected with Countess von Brunsvik.

1909   La Mara   *Beethovens Unster-*
    (Marie Lipsius)   *bliche Geliebte*   1807   Therese von Brunsvik
    Publication of Therese's Memoirs. Discussion with descendants of Brunsvik and Giucciardi-Gallenberg families. "K" stands for the Brunsvik castle Korompa.

1909   W. A. Thomas-   *Die Unsterbliche*   1812   Amalie Sebald
    San Galli   *Geliebte Beethovens*
    With the elimination of every year but 1812 as the date of the letter, Teplitz is established as the location of the writer and Karlsbad is suggested as the location of its recipient. Beethoven's letter to Breitkopf and Härtel on July 17 establishes Beethoven's time of arrival as July 5. The fact that he is not on the guest lists until July 7 is explained by the passage in the first note: "not till tomorrow will my lodgings be definitely determined upon." In the same letter he instructs the publishers to send some of his works to Amalie Sebald, whose Berlin address he is able to give. Fanny del Rio's diary in 1816 mentions a love of five years ago "a union with whom he [Beethoven] would have considered the greatest happiness of his life"; Beethoven met Amalie Sebald in 1811.

1910   A. de Hevesy   *Petites Amies de*   1801   Unknown
                        Beethoven[4]
    Discussion of Therese's diary. The "Louis" mentioned by Therese ("I have chosen you among millions of men, Louis" etc.) is identified as Count Louis "Guillaume" Migazzi from references in the correspondence of her nephew, Ferdinand Deym.

1910   W. A. Thomas-San Galli   1812   Therese von Brunsvik
    Beethoven und die unsterbliche Geliebte: Amalie Sebald, Goethe, Therese Brunsvik und anderes

---

[8] In Volume 2 (1872), pp. 178-80, Thayer has not yet arrived at the proposition that Beethoven could have misdated the parts of the letter. The implication here is that the year must have been 1807.

[4] Cf. A. de Hevesy, *Beethoven. Vie intime* (Paris, 1927).

In 1812 Therese was staying with her sister Josephine at the Castle Wittschap near Iglau in Moravia. Beethoven may have journeyed to Teplitz by way of either Iglau or Prague, where Therese could have been visiting relatives at the time, for the meeting which preceded the writing of the letter.

1910 M. Unger   1812 Unknown
    Auf Spuren von Beethovens Unsterblicher Geliebten[5]
    Goethe's diary records rain almost daily between July 8 and 18, occasionally till the end of the month, and heavy rain for July 3 and 4. This would account for the wretchedness of road conditions. The details of the postal schedule between Teplitz and Karlsbad are identical to those mentioned in the letter. If Amalie were the recipient, Beethoven would not have missed the chance to give her in person the music that he asked Breitkopf and Härtel on July 17 to send to her in Berlin. The passage in Fanny del Rio's diary cannot refer to the "Immortal Beloved" because of the sentence, "It had never reached a confession, but he could not get it out of his mind!" The letter itself constitutes a full confession. The tone of the notes to Amalie Sebald in September, 1812, is incompatible with that of the letter to the "Immortal Beloved." The similarity in style and use of expression between the letter of July 6-7 and that written on July 17, 1812, to Emilie M. provides a further argument for the year 1812.

1911 Thayer-Deiters Revised by H. Riemann   1812 Unknown
    Ludwig van Beethovens Leben, Vol. 3
    Confirmation of San Galli's and Unger's arguments for the year 1812.

1920 La Mara (Marie Lipsius)   1807 Josephine von Brunsvik Deym
    Beethoven und die Brunsviks
    An attempt to relate the letter to the "Immortal Beloved" with the correspondence of 1804 and 1805 between members of the Brunsvik family which express alarm over the developing relation between Beethoven and Josephine.

1921 Thayer-Deiters   1807 Therese von Brunsvik
    The Life of Ludwig van Beethoven, Revised by H. E. Krehbiel, Vol. 1.
    Krehbiel upholds Thayer's theories despite the existence of modern research on the problem and adds a postscript concerned principally with La Mara's "Beethovens Unsterbliche Geliebte" of 1909.

1927 O. G. Sonneck   1812 Unknown
    The Riddle of the Immortal Beloved
    A confession of love had occurred shortly before the letter was

[5] Cf. M. Unger, "The Immortal Beloved," *MQ*, XIII (1928), pp. 249-59.

written. Since Beethoven was in Prague from July 2 to part of July 4, it is most likely that this confession occurred in Prague and that the lady left for Karlsbad at about the same time that Beethoven left for Teplitz. The passage from the third note, "Oh God, why is it necessary to part from one whom one so loves and yet my life in V [Vienna] is now a wretched life—your love makes me at once the happiest and the unhappiest of men—at my age I need a steady, quiet life,—can that be under our conditions?", suggests that the lady's permanent residence was also Vienna.

1928 R. Rolland   1812 Therese von Brunsvik
Beethoven-les grandes époques créatrices. De l'Héroique
à l'Appasionata

From a study of Therese's diary, made possible by Dr. Marianne de Czeke,[6] Rolland concluded that the years 1809-1813 were a period of crisis in the relation between Beethoven and Therese. If the letter was indeed written to her, her subsequent devotion of her life to philanthropy would dictate that she return the letter to its writer.[7]

1947 K. Smolle   1812 Therese von Brunsvik?
Beethovens Unsterbliche Geliebte

After the publication of the three parts of "Immortal Beloved" letter in Schindler's biography, Therese wrote in her diary (February, 1846): "They must have been addressed to Josephine whom he loved passionately"; was this a cover-up of her own love for Beethoven, which she wished to conceal because of personal pride or wounded love?

1954 S. Kaznelson   1812 Josephine von Brunsvik-Deym-Stackelberg
Beethovens ferne und unsterbliche Geliebte

Josephine married her second husband, Count Stackelberg on February 13, 1810. They bought property in Witschapp, Moravia. A lawsuit developed over the contract for payment, which Stackelberg lost. According to Therese von Brunsvik's Memoirs, this and other business reverses threatened the couple with financial ruin. The state of affairs destroyed their marriage relationship. Stackelberg blamed both sisters, Josephine and Therese, for the financial crisis caused by the legal decision against them, made a scene, and left them at the end of May or early June, 1812. According to Therese, they did not see him again until December 4 when he made an unexpected visit. With the marriage broken, Therese took the four Deym children as well as the two Stackelberg children to Dornbach for the summer; Josephine was left in Vienna alone. There are no entries in Therese's diary between

---

[6] See Dr. Marianne Czeke, *Brunsvik Teréz Gróf nö Naplói és Feljégyzései*; I. Kötet (Budapest, 1938).

[7] Cf. R. Rolland, "La Lettre de Beethoven à l'Immortelle Aimée," *La Revue musicale*, VIII (1927), No. 11, pp. 193-204.

June 9 and August 6, 1812. On April 9, 1813, Josephine gave birth to a daughter, Minona. Since Stackelberg was not with Josephine for over ten months before this date, he could hardly have been the father. Was not this child then the result of a love between Josephine and Beethoven in July, 1812, nine months earlier.[8]

Documentation is given for the identification of the Esterhazy who was "travelling the usual road here." Rolland had already identified him as Prince Paul Esterhazy, son of Nicholas.[9] In 1810 he was appointed Austrian ambassador to Dresden. On June 30, 1812, a message with his signature is sent from Prague. The next message is written from Teplitz on July 8, in which Prince Paul informs his minister, Count Metternich, that he is leaving for Dresden.

From this summary of the more significant discussions of the love letter it emerges that 1812 has now been accepted by all serious students of the problem as the year in which the letter was written, and that the identity of its recipient remains completely in doubt.

In 1927, O. G. Sonneck wrote his "The Riddle of the Immortal Beloved," which has already been listed, as a supplement to the English edition of Thayer's biography. His conclusions, still valid today, form an appropriate ending to the consideration of this problem in Beethoven biography.[10]

"To sum up and conclude: unless Fanny Giannatasio del Rio's ears tricked her, Beethoven in September, 1816, loved as on the first day her whom he had met five years before. But, he said, there had been no confession of love. *It follows that she can not have been the 'Immortal Beloved,'* for the reason that a mutual confession of love fairly shouts at one from out of the letter to the 'Immortal Beloved.' There must have been two women who at about the same time filled Beethoven with love. Who they were, we do not know but, if my argument is correct, then *not one love-riddle* confronts us *but two*.

"The coincidence that approximately five years prior to September, 1816, Beethoven met Amalie Sebald, prevents us from dismissing her peremptorily as one of the two. Psychologically it is quite possible that Amalie from the very first day of their acquaintance struck deep into Beethoven's heart, that this sentiment remained more or less one-sided on his part, that he sought her, without finding her, that delicacy and diffidence forbade him to press his suit and that, while their mutual tender affection drew them closer together during the last few days at Teplitz, time flew by without a mutual confession—and then it was too late. Thus, though Beethoven may have had Amalie Sebald in mind during that reminiscent conversation of September, 1816, *she was not the 'Immortal Beloved.'* Contrariwise, if he then

---

[8] For a vigorous refutation of this argument see J. Schmidt-Görg, *Dreizehn unbekannte Briefe an Josephine Gräfin Deym geb. v. Brunsvik* in *Veröffentlichungen des Beethovenhauses in Bonn*, Neue Folge, III (1957), pp. 38-9, n. 41.

[9] See also M. Unger, *Auf Spuren*, p. 20, n. 1.

[10] Pages 66-7. Copyright, 1927 by G. Schirmer, Inc. Used by permission.

was thinking of the 'Immortal Beloved,' he did not have in mind Amalie Sebald. Furthermore, when he jotted down his despairing confession that 'in this way with A, everything goes to ruin,' he may well have meant Amalie Sebald in the manner suggested by me as conjuring up a conflict between her and the 'Immortal Beloved.' If not, then the *A* stands for the initial of the name of the 'Immortal Beloved' herself and the remark simply expressed the presentiment of disaster for his relations with her. The task then would be to discover a woman other than Amalie Sebald with the initial *A* in her name to whom all circumstantial evidence, whether of a chronological, topographical or psychological nature, would apply. She would have to be a woman who probably lived, as did Beethoven, in Vienna, who was in *K.* during the same week that Beethoven wrote his 'Immortal Beloved' letter at Teplitz on July 6-7, 1812, whom he perhaps met between July 2-4, 1812, at Prague and whom he expected to see again, probably at Teplitz. Until that woman is discovered, the answer to the question 'who was Beethoven's "Immortal Beloved?"' will remain: *Unknown*. And many of us will not regret this at all in these days when privacy is fast becoming obsolete and publicity of private affairs a curse."

To Sonneck's wise conclusion the editor should add the following: as has already been mentioned at the beginning of Chapter 26, the initial from the Fischoff Manuscript, mentioned above, is also in doubt—there is no general agreement that it is to be read as *A*; the hope of a solution following Sonneck's formula is thus no longer to be sustained, and the mystery of the "Immortal Beloved" remains that much further from being solved.

APPENDIX G

DOCUMENTS AND COMMENTS IN THE MÄLZEL CASE

(The documents in the controversy between Beethoven and Mälzel together with Thayer's comments on them appear in TDR, III in Appendix II and in TK, II on pp. 272-76 as footnote 2.)

I

Deposition

OF MY OWN volition I had composed a Battle Symphony for Mälzel for his Panharmonica without pay. After he had had it for a while he brought me the score, the engraving of which he had already begun, and wanted it arranged for full orchestra. I had previously formed the idea of a Battle (Music) which, however, was not applicable to his Panharmonica. We agreed to perform this work and others of mine in a concert for the benefit of the soldiers. Meanwhile I got into the most terrible financial embarrassment. Deserted by the whole world here in Vienna, in expectation of a bill of exchange, etc., Mälzel offered me 50 ducats in gold. I took them and told him that I would give them back to him here, or would let him take the work with him to London in case I did not go with him—in which latter case I would refer him to an English publisher who would pay him these 50 ducats. The *Akademien* were now given. In the meantime Mälzel's plan and character were developed. Without my consent he printed on the placards that it was *his property*. Incensed at this he had to have these torn down. Now he printed: "Out of friendship for his journey to London"; to this I consented, because I thought that I was still at liberty to fix the conditions on which I would let him have the work. I remember that I quarrelled violently with him while the notices were being printed, but the time was too short—I was still writing the work. In the heat of my inspiration, immersed in my work, I scarcely thought of Mälzel. Immediately after the first *Akademie* in the Universitätssaal, I was told on all sides by trustworthy persons that Mälzel was spreading the news far and wide that he had loaned me 400 ducats in gold. I thereupon had the following printed in the newspaper, but the newspaper writers did not print it as Mälzel is on good terms with all of them. Immediately after the first *Akademie* I gave back to Mälzel his 50 ducats, telling him that having learned his character here, I would never travel with him, enraged for good reason because he had printed on the placards, without my consent, that all the arrangements for the *Akademie* were badly made and his bad patriotic character showed itself in the following expressions: I [*unprintable*], if only they will say in London that the public here paid 10 florins: not for the wounded but for this did I do this—and also that I would not let him have the work for London except on conditions concerning which I would let him know. He now asserted that it was a *gift of friendship* and after the second *Akademie* had this expression printed in the newspaper without asking me about it in the least. Inasmuch as Mälzel is a coarse fellow, entirely without education, or culture, it may easily be imagined how he conducted himself toward me during this period and increased my anger more and more. And who would force a gift of friendship on such a fellow? I was now offered an opportunity to send the work to the Prince Regent. It was now impossible to *give him the work unconditionally.* He then came to you and made proposals. He was told on what day to come for his answer; but he did not come, went away and performed the work in Munich. How did he get it? *Theft* was impossible—Herr Mälzel had a few of the parts at home for a few days and from these he had the whole put together by some musical handicrafts-man, and with this he is now trading around in the world. Herr Mälzel promised me hearing machines. To encourage him I composed the Victory Symphony for his Panharmonica. His machines were finally finished, but were useless for me. For this small trouble Herr Mälzel thinks that after I had set the *Victory Symphony* for grand orchestra and *composed the Battle for it,* I ought to have him the *sole owner* of this work. Now, assuming that I really felt under some obligation for the hearing machines, it is cancelled by the fact that he made at least 500 florins convention coin, out of the Battle stolen from me or compiled in a mutilated manner. He has therefore paid himself. He had the audacity to say here that he had the battle; indeed he showed it in writing to several persons—but I did not believe it, and I was right, inasmuch as the whole was *not compiled by me* but by *another.* Moreover, the honor which he credits to himself alone might be a reward. *I was not mentioned at all by the Court War Council,* and yet everything in the two *Akademien* was of my composition. If, as he said, Herr Mälzel delayed his journey to London because of the Battle, it was merely a hoax. Herr Mälzel remained until he had finished his patchwork(?), the first attempts not being successful.

Beethoven m. p.

II

Explanation and Appeal to the Musicians of London by Ludwig van Beethoven

Herr Mälzel, who is at present in London, on his way thither performed *my Victory Symphony and Wellington's Battle at Vittoria* in *Munich* and, according to report, will also give concert performances of it in London as he was also willing to do in Frankfort. This leads me publicly to declare: that I never under any circumstances yielded or gave these works to Herr Mälzel, that nobody possesses a copy of them, and that the only one which I gave out was sent to His Royal Highness, the Prince Regent of England.

The performance of these works on the part of Herr Mälzel, therefore, is a fraud on the public, inasmuch as according to this explanation he is not in possession of them, or if he is in possession of them an infringement on my rights, as he has obtained them in an illegal manner.

But even in the latter case the public will be deceived, for that which Herr Mälzel will give them to hear under the title: *Wellington's Battle at Vittoria and Victory Symphony,* must obviously be a spurious or mutilated work, since he never received anything of these works from me except a single part for a few days.

This suspicion becomes certainty when I add the assurance of musicians of this city whose names I am empowered to mention in case of necessity, that Herr Mälzel said to them on leaving Vienna that he was in possession of the work and showed them parts of it, which, however, as I have already proved, could be nothing else than mutilated or spurious parts.

Whether Herr Mälzel is capable of doing me such an injury?—is answered by the circumstance that he had *himself* announced in the newspapers as the *sole* undertaker of my *Akademien for the benefit of the soldiers wounded in the war* given here in Vienna, at which only works of mine were performed, without an allusion to my name.

I therefore call upon the musical artists of London not to suffer such an injury to me, their colleague, by a performance arranged by Herr Mälzel of the *Battle of Vittoria* and the *Victory Symphony,* and to prevent such an imposition on the London public in the manner set forth.

Vienna, July 25, 1814.

III

Certificate

We, the undersigned, certify in the interest of truth and can vouch under oath if necessary: that there were several conferences between Herr Louis van Beethoven and the Court Mechanician, Herr Mälzel of this city, at the house of the undersigned, Dr. Carl v. Adlersburg, the which had for their subject the musical composition called: "The Battle of Vittoria" and the visit to England; at these, Herr Mälzel made several propositions to Herr van Beethoven to secure the work aforementioned, or at least the right of first performance for himself. But as Herr Mälzel did not appear at the last meeting arranged for, nothing came of the matter, the propositions made to the former not having been accepted by him. In witness thereof.

Vienna, October 20, 1814

Joh. Freiherr v. Pasqualati,

[L.S.]   *K. K. priv. Grosshändler.*

Carl Edler von Adlersburg,

[L.S.]   *Hof- und Gerichts-Advocat*
K. K. Öffentlicher Notar.

The so-called "Deposition" is, in truth, nothing more than an *ex-parte* statement prepared for the use of his lawyer by a very angry man, in whom a tendency to suspicion and jealousy had strengthened with advancing years and with the increase of an incurable infirmity. Mälzel's contra-statement to his lawyer is lost. He had no young disciple planning with zeal to preserve it and give it, with his version of the story, to posterity.

No one who is ignorant of Schindler's honestly meant, but partisan representations, or who, knowing them, can disabuse his mind of any prejudgment thence arising, can read Beethoven's statement without misgivings; all the more, if the facts proved by Moscheles and Stein—tacitly admitted, though utterly suppressed, in the document—are known to him. Nor will he be convinced by all the force of the harsh language of denunciation, that Mälzel did not act honestly and in good faith, when he called the "Victory" his property.

There is nothing in the first part of the statement that requires comment; though in passing it may be observed, that the pathos of "deserted by the whole world here in Vienna" would be increased if one could forget the Archduke, the Brentanos, the Streichers, Breitkopf and Härtel, Zmeskall, and others. It must be borne in mind (in Beethoven's favor) that the paper was written several months after the events of which it speaks; that it was drawn up at a time when its writer was excessively busy; that it bears all the marks of haste and want of reflection; that it was obviously intended for his lawyer's eye alone; that there is evident confusion of memory as to times and events; and that—be it repeated—it is the *ex-parte* statement of an angry man. Take the "400 ducats in gold"; here Beethoven's memory must have played him false, certainly as to the time, probably as to the substance of what he heard from the "trustworthy persons." Mälzel could have had no possible motive to utter so glaring a falsehood; but every motive not to do so. A few weeks later, he might and very probably did assert, that the damages to him arising from the sacrifice of the "Victory" as a piece for his Panharmonicon, from the expense of his prolonged stay in Vienna, from the loss of the holiday season in Munich, from the time, study and labor spent in experiments on Beethoven's ear-trumpets, and from his exclusion from all share in these profitable concerts, which he alone had made possible— that these damages were not less than 400 ducats. Nor does such an estimate appear to be a gross exaggeration. "I therefore had the following printed in the newspaper," continues Beethoven. If the passage which follows be what he desired to have printed, the reasons why the editors refused are sufficiently obvious; if they had cherished no regard for Mälzel and had believed him in the wrong, they must have suppressed such a communication for Beethoven's own sake.

The character of Mälzel—drawn in a few dark lines by his opponent—has no bearing on the real point at issue; it may, however, be observed as remarkable, that Beethoven alone made the discovery, and this not until—after some years of close intimacy and friendship—he had quarrelled with him. There are not many, who having so sagaciously planted and seen the harvest gathered in by another—who, smarting under the disappointment, and irritated by the loss of so much time, pains and labor—would sit down quietly, exhibit Job's patience, and refrain from all expressions of feeling not suited to a lady's boudoir. Nor is it to be supposed that Mälzel acted this Christian part; but then, Beethoven was hardly the man to cast the first stone at the sinner.

The sudden resolution to send the "Wellington's Victory" to the Prince Regent of England, was obviously part and parcel of the proceedings against Mälzel, the object being to defeat there any production of the work by him. Beethoven himself was the only loser by it. The prince never said "thank you" for it.

In the argument against the correctness of Mälzel's copy of the work, Beethoven is, to say the least, unfortunate. His opponent may have had, from *him,* only single parts (in the second paper it stands "a single part"!); but the circumstances were such that Mälzel could have had no difficulty in obtaining temporary use of most, if not all, the parts. Also there were plenty of "musical handicraftsmen" amply capable, after so many rehearsals and public performances, of producing a copy in the main correct.

It is painful to one who loves and reveres the memory of Beethoven, to peruse the closing passages of this document; it is, fortunately, not necessary to comment upon their character. It was not necessary for Beethoven to speak of Mälzel's share in the composition of the work, in the first of these papers; the opposing lawyer would attend to that; but was it just and ingenuous to suppress it entirely in the appeal to the London musicians? Schindler asserts that this appeal prevented Mälzel from producing it. It *could* have had no such effect. The simple truth is, that in those days for a stranger like Mälzel to undertake orchestral concerts in London would have been madness. The new Philharmonic Society, composed of all the best resident musicians, had hardly achieved an assured existence.

The third paper is testimony to a single fact and is so impartially drawn, so skilfully worded, as not to afford a point for or against either of the parties. Schindler closes his history of the affair thus: "The legal proceedings in Vienna were without result, however, the defendant being far away and his representatives knowing how to protract the case unduly, whereby the plaintiff was subjected to considerable expense and ever new annoyances. For this reason our master refrained from prosecuting the case further, since meanwhile the facts had become widely known and had frightened the false friend from making new attempts. The court costs were divided evenly by the litigants. Mälzel never returned to Vienna, but at a later period appealed in a letter to the friend whom he had swindled when he thought that he needed his recommendation for the metronome. This letter, dated Paris, April 19, 1818, is here. In it he represents to Beethoven that he was at work for him upon a hearing machine for use in conducting; he even invited him to accompany him on a journey to England. The master expressed his satisfaction with the metronome to the mechanician; but he never heard more concerning the machines."

Now Schindler's own account of the first two occasions when he spoke with Beethoven, copied into the text, partly with a view to this, shows that he could have no personal knowledge of the Mälzel affair, except its issue; and an examination of his pages proves further that his account of it is but a paraphrase of Beethoven's statement. His own words, written in a Conversation Book, demonstrate that the greater portion of the above citation is nonsense; for those words inform us that Mälzel returned to Vienna in the autumn of 1817; that, then and there, peace was made between the parties, and the old friendship restored; and that thereupon they passed a jovial evening together in the "Kamehl," where Schindler himself sang soprano in the "Ta, ta, ta" canon to the bass of Mälzel! What is the historic value of a narrative so made up and ending with such an astounding lapse of memory?

Mälzel spent his last years mostly in Philadelphia and other American cities. A few men of advanced years are still living there, unless recently passed away—[Thayer is writing in the eighth decade of the nineteenth century]—who retain an affectionate and respectful memory of him as a gentleman and man of culture; they will rejoice in this, at the least, partial vindication of their old friend. Candor and justice compel the painful admission that Beethoven's course with Mälzel is a blot—one of the few—upon his character, which no amount of misrepresentation of the facts can wholly efface; whoever can convince himself that the composer's conduct was legally and technically just and right, must still feel that it was neither noble nor generous.

Mälzel died suddenly on July 21, 1838, on an American brig, while on a voyage between the United States and the West Indies.

APPENDIX H

THE LATER HISTORY OF PRINCE GALITZIN'S PAYMENTS[1]

At the time of Beethoven's death, Prince Galitzin owed Beethoven 100 ducats for two string quartets and 25 ducats for the dedication to the Overture, *Weihe des Hauses*. On March 20, 1829, Hotschevar as guardian of Karl van Beethoven appealed to the Imperial Chancellery to ask the Embassy at St. Petersburg to collect the debt of 125 ducats from the Prince. Galitzin demanded an explanation, but after repeated requests from Karl agreed to pay 50 ducats in two installments of 20 and 30 ducats each. The sums were paid, the latter, as Karl's receipt shows, on November 9, 1832. Karl continued to make representations to the Prince touching a balance of 75 ducats still due and on June 2-14, 1835, Galitzin promised to pay the sum, not as a balance due on his business transactions with Beethoven, but as a memorial *pour honorer sa mémoire, que m'est chère*. Even now the money was not paid, but after a controversy had broken out between Schindler and the Prince over the former's charge that Beethoven had never been paid for the Quartets,[2] Galitzin sent the 75 ducats on October 13-25, 1852,[3] and Karl complaisantly acquiesced in the Prince's request and signed a receipt for the money, not in payment of the debt, but as a voluntary tribute to the dead composer.

The following is Krehbiel's "bit of history derived chiefly from Mr. Thayer's papers."

In the course of time Schindler's partly erroneous statement that the debt which Galitzin owed Beethoven at the time of his death was all on account of the quartets[4] was magnified into the statement made by Heinrich Döring (in his biography) and Brendel (in his *Geschichte der Musik*) that the Prince had "cheated" the composer out of the fee for the Quartets. Prince Nikolas Galitzin had withdrawn to his distant estates in Russia, but at his instigation the cudgels were taken up in his behalf by his son, Prince George, who, stirred into indignation by Döring's biography in particular, sent that writer the following letter: "I can not and do not want to know anything of the past, all the less since it will certainly not be expected of me to contradict the proofs produced by him (his father). But as by the publication of your article you have made the question for me one of the day, I, as a man of honor must do my duty to put an end to these misunderstandings. I have deposited the sum of 125 ducats which you bring in question with Mr. Kaskel, banker in Dresden, for the heirs of Beethoven, and from you, my dear Sir, I expect the necessary information in this matter, since you must have acquainted yourself with the necessary facts while writing your notice. You

---

[1] From TDR, v, pp. 571-78, and TK, III, pp. 229-31.

[2] See *Biogr.* 2nd ed., p. 163. In the third edition the statement was withdrawn.

[3] See the letter from Prince Galitzin to Karl, dated April 16, 1852, in TDR, v, pp. 573-75.

[4] *Biogr.* 1st ed., pp. 162-63.

must admit that hereafter I reserve the right to treat this question as a personal one! In case the family of Beethoven has died out there will be no other disposition of the money deposited with Banker Kaskel than to pay it over to a charity or some other cause which may be directly associated with the name and works of the famous artist. Dresden, July 15-3, 1858."

Karl van Beethoven, sole heir of the composer, had died three months previously, leaving a widow and children, who were his heirs. Prince George's money seemed like a gift of Providence to the widow, who hastened, as soon as she read the letter in a musical journal, to write to Holz as the friend of the dead composer to collect the money for her and express her gratitude to Prince George.[5] Holz complied with part of her request in a letter full of obsequiousness in which he accused Schindler of scandalmongering and offered to provide the Prince with evidence of that gentleman's rascality.[6] But he did not collect the money, which lay still untouched in the vaults of Kaskel in 1861, when Madame van Beethoven, having made a vain application to Prince George, addressed a letter to Kaskel asking whether the money was still deposited with him or had been withdrawn by Prince George. In the latter event she stated that she wanted to contradict a statement circulating by the public press that the heirs of Beethoven had received the gift. Kaskel referred her to Ad. Reichel, a musical director in Dresden and a friend of the Prince, through whom, indeed, the deposit had been made. On April 28, 1861, she wrote to Reichel, reviewing the facts in the case and stating her desire to apply the money, in case it was given to her, to the musical education of her youngest daughter, Hermine van Beethoven, then 8 years of age. Kaskel also wrote to Reichel, sending him Madame van Beethoven's letter and saying that as he had not heard anything from Prince Galitzin for several years he intended to turn the money over to the Municipal Court of Dresden in order to spare himself all further correspondence in the matter. Kaskel wrote to the Prince on May 7, 1861, asking him to prescribe a disposition of the money, for, if Kaskel carried out his determination to send it to the court, it would be frittered away. He urged that the money be given to Madame van Beethoven.

This revival of interest in the subject was evidently due to Mr. Thayer's activity in behalf of the widow and her daughter. Mr. Thayer was in London in 1860 and evidently took up the matter with the Prince. He makes no mention of the subject in his notice written for Grove's "Dictionary" (Art. "Galitzin"); but among his letters the present writer found the following letter, evidently written on the eve of his departure from England in February, 1861.

"Dear Mr. Thayer. Prince Galitzin has asked me to remit to you the enclosed letters, praying you kindly to act for him in the affair, as you will soon be on the spot. He begs you, however, to bear in mind the necessity of proving that the

---

[5] See TDR, v, pp. 576-77.   [6] *Ibid.*, p. 577.

money for these Quartets has not been paid (I fear an impossibility!); but how-ever vexatious this may be to poor Mad. v. B. everyone must defer to the obstacle to her having the money: in the awkward light in which it places the Prince's father. From what I can gather from his conversation he will be most satisfied to have the money appropriated for the purpose you suggested: the M.S.S. At all events Prince G. is quite content to leave the matter in your hands. Wishing you a pleasant journey and a speedy return, believe me, dear Mr. Thayer, Yours sincerely Natalia Macfarren."

The editor's [Krehbiel's] efforts to learn the ultimate disposition of the money deposited with Kaskel have been in vain. Mr. Thayer's papers con-tain no hint of the steps which may have been taken after Mrs. Macfarren's appeal to Prince George; the banking house of Kaskel is gone out of exist-ence; Nephew Karl's daughter, Hermine, is dead. For three years, from 1866 to 1869, she was a student in the pianoforte and harmonium classes of the Conservatory at Vienna, and it seems likely that Mr. Thayer suc-ceeded in having the Dresden deposit applied to her education; but if so he left no memorandum of that fact amongst the papers which have come under the editor's eyes.

APPENDIX I

KARL AND HIS DESCENDANTS

IN HIS article, "The Family van Beethoven," published in the Musical Quarterly,[1] Donald W. MacArdle has presented an admirably complete history of the composer's family and a thorough bibliography on the subject. His collection of material has been a primary source for this appendix.

At the time of his uncle's death, Karl van Beethoven was enrolled in Archduke Ludwig's 8th Infantry Regiment under Baron von Stutterheim at Iglau in Moravia. He hurried to Vienna upon hearing the news but arrived too late for the funeral.

In 1832 he resigned from the army and in August of that year married Caroline Naske. After two years as an administrator of a farm in Niklowitz, he received an appointment as frontier commissioner, which he held for two more years. In 1848 his uncle Johann died. Since Johann's wife, Therese, had already died twenty years before, Karl received the entire estate of his uncle, which amounted to 42,123 florins. He was now the beneficiary of the estates of both his uncles and was able to live the last ten years of his life in comfortable circumstances. He died on April 13, 1858.

Karl's widow was left with five children, one son and four daughters. The youngest daughter was Hermine, who has already been mentioned in connection with the later Galitzin payments in Appendix H. From the marriages of these daughters there were twelve children. The name of Beethoven was continued through Karl's son, Ludwig, who was born on March 8, 1839. In a codicil to his will dated March 23, 1827, Beethoven had indicated that the capital to his estate was to be used by Karl's "natural or testamentary heirs." Thus, from 1858, the year of Karl's death until 1874, the date of her last withdrawal, Caroline received financial support from this source. According to her daughters, she also received help from a pension provided by music-lovers in Vienna as well as from royalties from foreign theaters. She died in 1891.

Karl's son, Ludwig, married Marie Nitche in 1865. He had a varied career which became less and less distinguished as it developed: non-commissioned officer in the army, employee in the Chancellery of the German Order, traveling correspondent or salesman in various cities where, increasingly, he came afoul of the law, and finally, ordinary swindler. According to Sandberger,[2] Richard Wagner gave him introductions in Munich in 1868 and 1869 which led to his wheedling over a thousand florins from King Ludwig. His activities during the next three years, which included his trading in a variety of fictitious Beethoven memorabilia, led to his imprisonment in 1872

[1] *MQ*, xxv, No. 4 (1949), pp. 528-50.
[2] Adolph Sandberger, "Beiträge zur Beet- hoven-Forschung" in *Archiv für Musikwissenschaft*, Vol. 2 (1920), p. 398.

for a term of four years. Nothing definite is known about his life hereafter, but MacArdle has found clues that indicate that he may have come to the United States and been employed as a foreman-inspector on the Pacific Railroad.

Ludwig had a son, Karl Julius Maria, who was born in 1870. He spent most of his childhood in Belgium where he became a journalist. At the beginning of World War I he was living in England with his mother and an adopted brother. Then the family returned to their native Munich, and Karl enrolled in the army. In 1917, he died in an army hospital in Vienna, the last in the composer's branch of the family to bear the name Beethoven.

GENERAL INDEX

Index of Vienna Residences by Year

Beethoven, Ludwig Maria van (brother), 52, 54, 490

Beethoven, Marc van, 43

Beethoven, Maria Magdalena van (mother), 50-52, 54, 55, 63, 71, 79, 89-90

Beethoven, Maria Margaretha Josepha van (sister), 82, 90

Beethoven, Michael van (great-grandfather in Bonn), 41-42, 46

Beethoven Museum, Bonn, 265. *See also* Beethovenhaus

Beethoven, Nikolaus Johann van (brother), biography of, 56, 94, 180-81, 421-22, 540ff., 739, 866, 869; character and appearance, 314-16, 795-96, 1051-52; relationship with B., 303, 420-22, 796-99, 835, 866, 869, 911, 916-17, 974, 1005, 1012-14; relationship with Karl, 726, 835, 840, 931, 989, 1012-14, 1015; letter to B. about Karl, 1013-14; at terminal illness of B., 1022, 1032, 1049, 1051-52 in Conversation Books, 842, 939, 992, 1013-14, 1026. *See also* Beethoven, letters to Johann

Beethoven, Therese van (Obermayer), 542, 866, 869, 1006-07, 1015, 1049

Beethovenhaus, 126, 130, 359, 720, 730, 819. *See also* Schmidt-Görg

Beine, Baron de, 119

Belderbusch, Kaspar Anton von, 15, 17, 33, 35, 37, 46, 56, 108

Belderbusch, Kaspar Anton von, (nephew), 108

Benda, Georg, 29, 30-31, 97

Benedict, Sir Julius, 873-74

Beobachter (Vienna newspaper), 566, 662, 864

Berge, Rudolph von, 617

Berlin, 184-87, 633, 734, 897, 985; B's visit to, 184-87; *Dramaturgisches Wochenblatt*, account of performance of *Fidelio*, 633

Berlin *Allgemeine Musikalische Zeitung*, 928

Berlin, Court of, 194, 822, 833

Bernadotte, Jean Baptiste (later Charles XIV, King of Sweden), 203-04, 386

Bernard, Joseph Karl, 604, 629, 635, 708, 722, 895n, 952, 983, 1054; in Conversation Books, 723, 725, 729, 753-54, 755-56, 775, 880; and oratorio text *Der Sieg des Kreuzes*, 736, 883ff., 971, 983. *See also* Beethoven, letters to Bernard

Bernhard, Frau von, 401

Bertolini, Dr. Andreas, 292, 582, 583, 603, 648

Bettoni (poet), 604, 1011

Bigot de Morogues, 407, 413-15, 444, 465

Bigot, Mme. Marie (pianist), 407, 413-15, 444, 466

Bihler, Dr. Johann, 834

Bildende Künstler, 192

Birchall, Robert (publisher), 623, 638, 649, 653, 660, 961, 962

Birkenstock, Joseph Melchior von, 491

Blahetka, J. L., 873, 900-01, 1054

Blahetka, Leopoldine (pianist), 771

Blaxland, J. H., 215-16

Blöchlinger, Joseph (educator), 725-26, 754; in Conversation Books, 757, 774; his Institute, 734, 866

Blumenstock in Ballgasse, 743

Bocklet, Carl Maria von, 968

Bodmer Collection, 130, 359, 473, 730

Boer, Otto de, 956, 971

Böhm, Joseph (violinist), 940-42, 976, 1054

Böhm, Theatre Company, 80, 81

Bolla, Signora, 182

Bonaparte, Jerome, 442-43, 454-55

Bonaparte, Louis, 556

Bonaparte, Napoleon, 190-91, 204, 348-49, 386-87, 466, 532, 596, 920; B's feelings about, 348-49, 403, 466-67, 920; and Cherubini, 960

Bondi, Clemente, 604

Bonn, history of Electors, 3-10; description of town, court and countryside, 8, 16, 38-40, 75-78; petitions and decrees regarding mu-

INDEX TO COMPOSITIONS

A. INSTRUMENTAL MUSIC

I. WORKS FOR ORCHESTRA ALONE

DUOS

V. CHAMBER MUSIC WITHOUT PIANOFORTE

OCTETS

PIANOFORTE TWO HANDS

B. VOCAL MUSIC

I. MASSES AND ORATORIO

II. WORKS FOR STAGE

VI. WORKS FOR VOICES *A CAPPELLA*

VII. CANONS

VIII. MISCELLANEOUS